τὴν οἰκίαν αὐτῆς · καὶ τῇδε ἦν
ἀδελφὴ καλουμένη Μαρία · ἣ καὶ
παρακαθεσθεῖσα παρὰ τοὺς πόδας τοῦ
ιῦ · ἤκουεν τὸν λόγον αὐτοῦ · ἡ δὲ Μάρθα
περιεσπᾶτο περὶ πολλὴν διακονίαν ·
ἐπιστᾶσα δὲ εἶπεν · κε̅ οὐ μέλει σοι ὅτι
ἡ ἀδελφή μου μόνην με κατέλιπεν δια-
κονεῖν · εἰπὲ οὖν αὐτῇ ἵνα μοι συναντιλά-
βηται · ἀποκριθεὶς δὲ εἶπεν αὐτῇ ὁ κε̅

Μάρθα Μάρθα · μεριμνᾷς καὶ τυρβάζῃ
περὶ πολλά · ἑνὸς δέ ἐστι χρεία · Μαρία δὲ
τὴν ἀγαθὴν μερίδα ἐξελέξατο · ἥτις
οὐκ ἀφαιρεθήσεται ἀπ' αὐτῆς · Καὶ

ἐγένετο ἐν τῷ εἶναι αὐτὸν ἐν τόπῳ τινὶ προσ-
ευχόμενον · ὡς ἐπαύσατο · εἶπέν τις
τῶν μαθητῶν αὐτοῦ πρὸς αὐτόν · κε̅ δί-
δαξον ἡμᾶς προσεύχεσθαι · καθὼς
καὶ Ἰωάννης ἐδίδαξε τοὺς μαθητὰς
αὐτοῦ · εἶπεν δὲ αὐτοῖς · ὁ τὸν προσηνέχθη

**Hermeneia
—A Critical
and Historical
Commentary
on the Bible**

Luke 2

A Commentary
on the Gospel of Luke 9:51—19:27

by
François Bovon

Translation by
Donald S. Deer

Edited by
Helmut Koester

Fortress Press

Minneapolis

Luke 2
A Commentary on the Gospel of Luke 9:51—19:27

Copyright © 2013 Fortress Press, an imprint of Augsburg Fortress

All rights reserved. Except for brief quotations in critical articles or reviews, no part of this book may be reproduced in any manner without prior written permission from the publisher. Write: Permissions, Augsburg Fortress, Box 1209, Minneapolis, MN 55440.

Scripture quotations from the Revised Standard Version of the Bible are copyright © 1946, 1952, 1971 by the Division of Christian Education of the National Council of the Churches of Christ in the USA and are used by permission.

Scripture quotations from the New Revised Standard Version of the Bible are copyright © 1989 by the Division of Christian Education of the National Council of the Churches of Christ in the U.S.A. and are used by permission.

Cover and interior design by Kenneth Hiebert
Typesetting and page composition by
The HK Scriptorium

Library of Congress cataloging-in-publication data is available

The paper used in this publication meets the minimum requirements of American National Standard for Information Sciences—Permanence of Paper for Printed Library Materials, ANSI Z329.48–1984.

Manufactured in the U.S.A.

17   16   15   14   13   1   2   3   4   5   6   7   8   9   10

The Author

François Bovon is Frothingham Professor of the History of Religion at Harvard Divinity School. He received his appointment to Harvard in 1993, where he was chair of the New Testament Department from 1993 to 1998, resuming the chair again in 2001. A native of Switzerland, for twenty-six years he was Professor of New Testament and Christian Origins at the Divinity School of the University of Geneva, where he was also dean from 1976 to 1979, and continues as an honorary professor.

He received his baccalaureate degree and licentiate in theology from the University of Lausanne, and his Th.D. from the University of Basel. He has also received an honorary doctorate from the University of Uppsala, Sweden.

His research has focused on the Gospel of Luke and Acts of the Apostles, as well as noncanonical Acts of the Apostles. His major publications include *De Vocatione Gentium* (1967), *Exegesis: Problems of Method and Exercises in Reading* (editor, 1978), *Les Actes Apocryphes des Apôtres* (editor, 1981), *Luke the Theologian* (1987), *New Testament Traditions and Apocryphal Narratives* (1995), *Écrits apocryphes chrétiens I* (editor with Pierre Geoltrain, 1997), *Acta Philippi* (1999), and *The Apocryphal Acts of the Apostles* (editor, 1999). He is also interested in the history of interpretation and critical editions of new early Christian texts in Greek, traveling regularly to the Vatican Library, the monastery libraries on Mount Athos, Greece, and the monastery of St. Catherine (Sinai) for this research.

Endpapers

Front and back endpapers show an eleventh-century minuscule manuscript of the Gospels on parchment, Egerton 2610, Folios 184 recto and verso. The front endpaper contains Luke 10:38—11:2 and the back endpaper Luke 11:2-8, including a distinctive variant to the Lord's Prayer at 11:2: "Let your Holy Spirit come upon us and cleanse us" (see p. 87). By permission of the British Library; with special thanks to Eldon J. Epp.

Contents

■ **Back Matter**

The name *Hermeneia,* Greek ἑρμηνεία, has been chosen as the title of the commentary series to which this volume belongs. The word *Hermeneia* has a rich background in the history of biblical interpretation as a term used in the ancient Greek-speaking world for the detailed, systematic exposition of a scriptural work. It is hoped that the series, like its name, will carry forward this old and venerable tradition. A second, entirely practical reason for selecting the name lies in the desire to avoid a long descriptive title and its inevitable acronym, or worse, an unpronounceable abbreviation.

The series is designed to be a critical and historical commentary to the Bible without arbitrary limits in size or scope. It will utilize the full range of philological and historical tools, including textual criticism (often slighted in modern commentaries), the methods of the history of tradition (including genre and prosodic analysis), and the history of religion.

Hermeneia is designed for the serious student of the Bible. It will make full use of ancient Semitic and classical languages; at the same time, English translations of all comparative materials—Greek, Latin, Canaanite, or Akkadian—will be supplied alongside the citation of the source in its original language. Insofar as possible, the aim is to provide the student or scholar with full critical discussion of each problem of interpretation and with the primary data upon which the discussion is based.

Hermeneia is designed to be international and interconfessional in the selection of authors; its editorial boards were formed with this end in view. Occasionally the series will offer translations of distinguished commentaries which originally appeared in languages other than English. Published volumes of the series will be revised continually, and eventually, new commentaries will replace older works in order to preserve the currency of the series. Commentaries are also being assigned for important literary works in the categories of apocryphal and pseudepigraphical works relating to the Old and New Testaments, including some of Essene or Gnostic authorship.

The editors of *Hermeneia* impose no systematic-theological perspective upon the series (directly, or indirectly by selection of authors). It is expected that authors will struggle to lay bare the ancient meaning of a biblical work or pericope. In this way the text's human relevance should become transparent, as is always the case in competent historical discourse. However, the series eschews for itself homiletical translation of the Bible.

The editors are heavily indebted to Fortress Press for its energy and courage in taking up an expensive, long-term project, the rewards of which will accrue chiefly to the field of biblical scholarship.

The editor responsible for this volume is Helmut Koester, John H. Morison Research Professor of Divinity and Winn Research Professor of Ecclesiastical History at Harvard Divinity School.

Peter Machinist	*Helmut Koester*
For the Old Testament	For the New Testament
Editorial Board	Editorial Board

Volumes two and three of the French edition (1996 and 2001), and the German (1996 and 2001) and Spanish (2002 and 2004) translations of my commentary on Luke are published here in English in one volume, as they are in the Italian translation published in 2007. The content, however, of these volumes remains the same in all editions and translations. The advantage of merging these two volumes into one is to insist, even typographically, on the unity of Luke 9:51–19:27, the central section of the Third Gospel, the so-called travel narrative.

The very existence of the Lukan travel narrative, that is, the redactional intention to create a long and decisive turn from Galilee to Judea, more precisely to Jerusalem and in Jerusalem to the Temple, has been doubted recently by some scholars, particularly Reinhard von Bendemann (*Zwischen ΔΟΞΑ und ΣΤΑΥΡΟΣ: Eine exegetische Untersuchung der Texte der sogenannten Reiseberichts im Lukasevangelium,* BZNW 101 [Berlin: de Gruyter, 2001]). But while Jesus' teaching is of prime importance in these chapters, the redactional clues underscoring Jesus' movement toward Jerusalem are also evident and meaningful. They bear witness to the ineluctable manifestation of Jesus not only as a generous healer and a powerful messiah, as he appears in the Galilean period (Luke 3:1–9:50), but also as servant messiah ready to suffer and to die (Luke 9:51–19:27). This particular emphasis of the travel narrative goes hand in hand with another Lukan conviction: during the travel from Galilee to Jerusalem, Jesus insists on the formation of his disciples as future leaders of the Church. Luke 9:51–19:27 offers key elements of Luke's Christology and his ecclesiology. That the evangelist was not the only one—nor the first one—to insist on the travel narrative is evident in Mark's gospel. Mark devotes two chapters (Mark 10–11) to the journey from Galilee to Judea (see Mark 10:1, 17, 32, 46 and 11:1, 11-12, 15, 19, 27) and embues it with theological significance as well.

The structure of volume two of this commentary remains the same as volume one. After the bibliography and the translation of the biblical passage, the first part, called "Analysis," examines carefully the way the evangelist rewrites his sources: Mark, Q, and the Special material. The second part, the "Commentary," underscores Luke's literary talent and his theological orientation. The third part, called "History of Interpretation," is expanded in this volume beyond that in volume one. The same will be true of volume three. It is my opinion that interpreters in the period prior to the Renaissance and the Enlightenment, even if they did not have at their disposal the scholarly methods of the modern age, knew how to practice a religious reading of the text that was in harmony with the original intention of the Gospel writers.

Readers are invited to examine carefully indications for the use of this volume that are published at the beginning of the book. I note here an important point: the general bibliography printed at the beginning is not the complete bibliography, but an addition to the general bibliography located in the front matter of volume one. Through their dimensions, these bibliographies bear witness to the extent of research devoted to the Third Gospel in recent years.

While I wrote the first volume in German, I wrote the second and third volumes in my mother tongue, French. To the assistants who helped me in Switzerland,

Denise Jornod, Marcel Durrer, Emi Bätschmann, Frédéric Amsler, Albert Frey, Isabelle Juillard, and Eva Tobler, I add the names of those collaborators who work with me at Harvard: David H. Warren, Laura Beth Bugg, Laura Nasrallah, Ann Graham Brock, Catherine Payoust, Mitzi Jane Smith, Dong-Hee Bae, Laurie A. Sullivan, Peter Vogt, Anna Miller, and Caroline Kelly. I express also my gratitude to the staff of Andover Harvard Library (Harvard Divinity School), particularly Gloria J. Korsman, Renata Z. Kalnins, Michelle A. Gauthier, Laura K. Whitney, Steven M. Beardsley, Donna M. Maguire, and Bernadette C. Perrault.

I am pleased to thank all those who worked on the English translation of this volume: Dr. Donald S. Deer, who furnished in due time an English translation of the text of the commentary; Dr. David H. Warren, who worked on the front matter, particularly the list of short titles, and translation of the footnotes for Luke 9:51–10:42; Dr. Margot Stevenson, who is responsible for the footnotes in chapters 11 and 12; Elisa and John Stern, who provided translation of the footnotes in chapters 13–19; and Daniel Bohac, who has assisted with queries. I appreciate also the collaboration of Professor Helmut Koester's research assistants Chris Hoklotubbe and Daniel Becerra.

I express my deep gratitude to Professor Koester, who insisted on the publication of my commentary in English translation as part of the Hermeneia series. In the academic year 2011–2012, he worked intensively editing this volume of the English translation. I wish also to thank the members of the Hermeneia editorial board, James M. Robinson, Eldon Epp, and Adela Collins, who followed with care and attention the preparation and production of this edition, as well as Neil Elliott, the scholar at Fortress Press responsible for the Hermeneia volumes, and Marissa Wold, Senior Project Manager at Fortress, and Paul Kobelski and Maurya Horgan of HK Scriptorium, who have with meticulous care seen the volumes of this commentary into print.

Cambridge, Massachusetts
April 16, 2012

Reference Codes

1. Sources and Abbreviations

AASFDHL — *Annales Academiae Scientiarum Fennicae: Dissertationes humanarum litterarum*

ABD — David Noel Freedman, ed., *The Anchor Bible Dictionary* (6 vols.; New York: Doubleday, 1992)

ABQ — *American Baptist Quarterly*

ABR — *Australian Biblical Review*

ACEBT — *Amsterdamse Cahiers voor Exegese en bijbelse Theologie*

ACNT — Augsburg Commentary on the New Testament

Acts John — *Acts of John*

Acts Pet. — *Acts of Peter*

Acts Phil. — *Acts of Philip*

Acts Thom. — *Acts of Thomas*

AFTC — Anales de la Facultad de Teologia (de la) Universidad Catolica de Chile

AGJU — Arbeiten zur Geschichte des antiken Judentums und des Urchristentums

AGSU — Arbeiten zur Geschichte des Spätjudentums und Urchristentums

AJBI — *Annual of the Japanese Biblical Institute*

AJP — *American Journal of Philology*

AJT — *American Journal of Theology*

Albertus Magnus [Albert the Great]
   Enarr. in Luc. — *Enarrationes in Evangelium Lucae*

ALBO — Analecta lovaniensia biblica et orientalia

Ambrose, bishop of Milan
   Exp. Luc. — *Expositio evangelii secundum lucam*
   Hymn. — *Hymni*

AmiCl — *L'ami du clergé*

AnBib — Analecta biblica

AnBoll — Analecta Bollandiana

ANF — *The Ante-Nicene Fathers* (ed. Alexander Roberts and James Donaldson, originally under the title *Ante-Nicene Christian Library* in 24 vols.; Edinburgh: Clark, 1867–1972; reprinted in 10 vols.; Peabody, Mass.: Hendrickson, 1994)

AnPh — *Annales de Philosophie*

ANQ — *Andover Newton Quarterly*

ANRW — *Aufstieg und Niedergang der römischen Welt*

ANTC — Abingdon New Testament Commentaries

ANTJ — Arbeiten zum Neuen Testament und Judentum

Anton — *Antonianum*

ANTZ — Arbeiten zur neutestamentlichen Theologie und Zeitgeschichte

APAW.PH — *Abhandlungen der preußischen Akademie der Wissenschaften, Philosophisch-historische Klasse*

Apos. Con. — *Apostolic Constitutions and Canons*

APOT — Robert Henry Charles, ed., *The Apocrypha and Pseudepigrapha of the Old Testament in English* (2 vols.; Oxford: Clarendon, 1913)

Appian
   Bell. civ. — *Bella civilia*

Aristophanes
   Eq. — *Equites*

Aristotle
   Eth. nic. — *Ethica nicomachea*
   Pol. — *Politica*

ArLg — *Archivum linguisticum*

Asc. Isa. — *Ascension of Isaiah*

As. Mos. — *Assumption of Moses*

ASNU — Acta seminarii neotestamentici upsaliensis

AsSeign — *Assemblées du Seigneur*

ASTI — *Annual of the Swedish Theological Institute*

ATh — *L'année théologique*

AThANT — Abhandlungen zur Theologie des Alten und Neuen Testaments

ATJ — *Ashland Theological Journal*

ATLA — American Theological Library Association

ATLA.BS — ATLA Bibliography Series

ATR — *Anglican Theological Review*

Aug — *Augustinianum*

Augustine — Augustine of Hippo
   C. Jul. — *Contra Julianum*
   Conf. — *Confessions*
   Quaest. ev. — *Quaestiones evangeliorum*
   Serm. — *Sermones*
   Serm. Dom. — *De sermone Domini in monte*
   Tract. Joh — *In Evangelium Johannis tractatus*

BAC — Biblioteca de autores cristianos

BAGB — *Bulletin de l'Association G. Budé*

BAGD — Walter Bauer, *A Greek-English Lexicon of the New Testament and Other Early Christian Literature* (trans., ed., and rev. Frederick W. Danker with W. F. Arndt and F. Wilbur Gingrich; 3d ed.; Chicago: University of Chicago Press, 2000)

2 Bar. — *Syriac Apocalypse of Baruch*

Barn.	Epistle of Barnabas	BSRel	Biblioteca di scienze religiose
BBB	Bonner biblische Beiträge	*BT*	*The Bible Translator*
BBET	Beiträge zur biblischen Exegese und Theologie	*BTB*	*Biblical Theology Bulletin*
		BThSt	Biblisch-theologische Studien
BBR	*Bulletin for Biblical Research*	BU	Biblische Untersuchungen
BCPE	*Bulletin du Centre protestant d'études*	*Burg*	*Burgense*
BDF	Friedrich Blass and Albert Debrunner, *A Greek Grammar of the New Testament and Other Early Christian Literature* (trans. and rev. Robert W. Funk; Chicago: University of Chicago Press, 1961)	*BVC*	*Bible et vie chrétienne*
		BWANT	Beiträge zur Wissenschaft vom Alten und Neuen Testament
		BZ	*Biblische Zeitschrift*
		BZNW	Beihefte zur Zeitschrift für die neutestamentliche Wissenschaft
BECNT	Baker Exegetical Commentary of the New Testament	*CB*	*Cultura bíblica*
		CBFV	*Cahiers bibliques de Foi et Vie*
BeO	*Bibbia e oriente*	*CBG*	*Collationes Brugenses et Gandavenses*
BETL	Bibliotheca ephemeridum theologicarum lovaniensium	*CBQ*	*Catholic Biblical Quarterly*
		CBQMS	Catholic Biblical Quarterly Monograph Series
BEvTh	Beiträge zur evangelischen Theologie		
		CCCM	Corpus Christianorum Continuatio Mediaevalis
BFCL	*Bulletin des Facultés catholiques de Lyon*		
		CCSA	Corpus Christianorum Series Apocryphorum
BFCRTh	Beiträge zur Förderung christlicher Theologie		
		CCSL	Corpus Christianorum Series Latina
BFCTL	Bibliothèque de la Faculté Catholique de théologie de Lyon		
		CD	Cairo (Genizah) text of the *Damascus Document*
BGBE	Beiträge zur Geschichte der biblischen Exegese		
		CDios	*Ciudad de Dios*
BHH	Bo Reicke and Leonhard Rost, eds., *Biblisch-Historisches Handwörterbuch: Landeskunde, Geschichte, Religion, Kultur, Literatur* (4 vols.; Göttingen: Vandenhoeck & Ruprecht, 1962–79)	CEA	Collection d'études anciennes
		cf.	(Latin *confer*) compare
		CFr	*Collectanea Franciscana*
		chap(s).	chapter(s)
		Chariton	
		Chaer.	*De Chaerea et Callirhoe*
		ChrCent	*Christian Century*
BHTh	Beiträge zur historischen Theologie	Chromatius	
		In Matth.	*Tractatus in Mattheum*
Bib	*Biblica*	Cicero	
Bib. Ant.	Pseudo-Philo, *Biblical Antiquities* (= *Liber antiquitatum biblicarum* [*LAB*])	*Att.*	*Epistulae ad Atticum*
		Fam.	*Epistulae ad familiares*
		Fin.	*De finibus*
BibOr	Biblica et orientalia	*Tusc.*	*Tusculanae disputationes*
BibS(F)	Biblische Studien (Freiburg im Breisgau, 1985–)	*CleM*	*Clergy Monthly*
		1 Clem.	*1 Clement*
BibS(N)	Biblische Studien (Neukirchen, 1951–)	*2 Clem.*	*2 Clement*
		Clement of Alexandria	
BiLeb	*Bibel und Leben*	*Exc. Theod.*	*Excerpta ex Theodoto*
BJRL	*Bulletin of the John Rylands Library*	*Paed.*	*Paedagogus*
BJS	Brown Judaic Studies	*Strom.*	*Stromateis*
BK	*Bibel und Kirche*	*Quis div.*	*Quis dives salvetur*
BLE	*Bulletin de littérature ecclésiastique*	*CNS*	*Cristianesimo nella storia*
BLit	*Bibel und Liturgie*	CNT	Commentaire du Nouveau Testament
BN	*Biblische Notizen*		
BO	*Bibliotheca orientalis*	col(s).	column(s)
Bonaventure		*Coll Helv*	*Colloquium Helveticum*
Comm. in Luc.	*Commentarius in evangelium S. Lucae*	*Comm*	*Communio*
		Comp	*Compostellanum*
BPAA	Bibliotheca Pontificii Athenaei		
BSac	*Bibliotheca sacra*		

Conc.	*Concilium. Religion in the Seventies/Eighties.*	EFN	Estudios de filología neotestamentaria
ConQ	*Congregational Quarterly*	EHPhR	Etudes d'histoire et de philosophie religieuses
CR	Corpus reformatorum		
CRB	Cahiers de la Revue biblique	EHS	Europäische Hochschulschriften
CRINT	Compendia rerum iudaicarum ad Novum Testamentum	EHS.T	Europäische Hochschulschriften, Reihe 23, Theologie
CRThPh	Cahiers de la Revue de théologie et de philosophie	EKKNT	Evangelisch-katholischer Kommentar zum Neuen Testament
CThAP	Cahiers théologiques de l'actualité Protestante		
CThM	Calwer theologische Monographien	enl.	enlarged
		1 Enoch	Ethiopic *Enoch*
CSCO	Corpus scriptorum christianorum orientalium	*2 Enoch*	Slavonic *Enoch*
		ep.	*epistula* ("epistle")
CSEL	Corpus scriptorum ecclesiasticorum latinorum	*Ep. apost.*	*Epistula apostolorum*
		Epictetus	
CTHP	Collection de théologie heritage et projet	*Diss.*	*Dissertationes*, the *Discourses*
		Ench.	*Enchiridion*
CTM	*Concordia Theological Monthly*	Epiphanius	
CuaBi	*Cuandernos bíblicos*	*Haer.*	*Panarion* (*Adversus haereses*)
CuW	*Christentum und Wissenschaft*	*ErIsr*	*Eretz-Israel*
Cyprian		esp.	especially
Dom. or.	*De dominica oratione*	*EstBib*	*Estudios bíblicos*
Cyril of Alexandria		*EstEcl*	*Estudios eclesiásticos*
Comm. in Luc.	*Commentarii in Lucae evangelium*	ET	English translation
Hom. in Luc.	*Homiliae in Lucam*	*EtB*	*Études bibliques*
Serm.	*Sermones*	*EThL*	*Ephemerides theologicae lovanienses*
Serm. Luc.	*Sermons on Luke*	*EThR*	*Études théologiques et religieuses*
Cyril of Jerusalem		EThSt	Erfurter theologische Studien
Cat. myst.	*Catecheses mystagogicae*	*EuA*	*Erbe und Auftrag*
DAI.A	*Dissertation abstracts international, A: The humanities and social sciences*	Euripides	
		Alc.	*Alcestis*
		Eusebius	
DBSup	L. Pirot and A. Robert, eds., *Dictionnaire de la Bible: Supplément* (Paris: Letouzey et Ané, 1928–)	*Hist. eccl.*	*Historia ecclesiastica*
		Onom.	*Onomasticon*
		EvErz	*Der evangelische Erzieher*
DEB	Centre Informatique et Bible, Abbaye de Maredsous, ed., *Dictionnaire encyclopédique de la Bible* (Turnhout: Brepols, 1987)	*EvK*	*Evangelische Kommentare*
		EvQ	*Evangelical Quarterly*
		EvTh	*Evangelische Theologie*
		Exp	*Expositor*
DECA	Angelo Di Berardino, ed., *Dictionnaire encyclopédique du christianisme ancien* (Paris: Cerf, 1990)	*ExpT*	*Expository Times*
		FB	Forschung zur Bibel
		FBBS	Facet Books, Biblical Series
		FF	Foundations & Facets
Demosthenes		FGLP	Forschungen zur Geschichte und Lehre des Protestantismus
Orat.	*Orations*		
Did.	*Didache*	*FoiTe*	*La Foi et le Temps*
Diogn.	*Epistle to Diognetus*	*FoiVie*	*Foi et vie*
DRev	*Downside Review*	fol.	folio
EcR	*Ecclesiastical Review*	frg(s).	fragment(s)
EDNT	Horst Balz and Gerhard Schneider, eds., *Exegetical Dictionary of the New Testament* (3 vols.; Grand Rapids: Eerdmans, 1990–93)	FRLANT	Forschungen zur Religion und Literatur des Alten und Neuen Testaments
		FThL	*Forum theologiae linguisticae*
		FThSt	Freiburger theologische Studien
ed(s).	edition or edited by	FTS	Frankfurter theologische Studien
EeT	*Église et théologie*		
EeV	*Esprit et vie*		

FZPhTh	Freiburger Zeitschrift für Philosophie und Theologie	Pol.	Letter to Polycarp
GCS	Griechische christliche Schriftsteller der ersten drei Jahrhunderte	Smyrn.	Letter to the Smyrnaeans
		Trall.	Letter to the Trallians
		Imm.	Immanuel
		Int.	Interpretation
GNS	Good New Studies	Irenaeus	
Gos. Mary	Gospel of Mary	Adv. haer.	Adversus haereses
Gos. Naz.	Gospel of the Nazarenes	Epid.	Epideixis tou apostolikou kērygmatos
Gos. Phil.	Gospel of Philip	ITQ	Irish Theological Quarterly
Gos. Thom.	Gospel of Thomas	ITS	Indian Theological Studies
Gos. Truth	Gospel of Truth	JAAR	Journal of the American Academy of Religion
Greg	Gregorianum		
Gregory the Great		JAC	Jahrbuch für Antike und Christentum
Hom. evang.	Homilies on the Gospels		
Moral.	Expositio in beatum Iob, sue Moralium lib. xxxv	JBL	Journal of Biblical Literature
		Jeev	Jeevadhara
GThA	Göttinger theologische Arbeiten	JEH	Journal of Ecclesiastical History
GTL	Göttinger theologische Lehrbücher	Jerome	
		Comm. in Ez.	Commentarii in Ezechielem
GuL	Geist und Leben	Comm. in Is.	Commentarii in Isaiam prophetam
HBT	Horizons in Biblical Theology	Comm. in Jer.	Commentarii in Jeremiam prophetam
Hermas	Shepherd of Hermas	Comm. in Matt.	Commentarii in Matthaeum
Sim.	Similitudes	Epist.	Epistulae
Vis.	Visions	Pelag.	Contra Pelagius
Herodotus		JETS	Journal of the Evangelical Theological Society
Hist.	Historiae		
Hesiod		JITC	Journal of the Interdenominational Theological Center
Op.	Opera et dies		
HeyJ	Heythrop Journal	John Chrysostom	
Hilary of Poitiers		Hom. Col.	Homiliae in epistulam ad Colossenses
Comm. in Matt.	Commentarius in Evangelium Matthaei		
		Hom. in Gen.	Homiliae in Genesim
In Ps.	On the Psalms	Hom. in Joh.	Homiliae in Johannem
Hippocrates		Hom. in Matt.	Homiliae in Matthaeum
Aff.	De affectionibus	Josephus	
Fract.	De fracturis	Ant.	Antiquities of the Jews
Ulcer.	De ulceribus	Ap.	Contra Apionem
Hippolytus		Bell.	Bellum Judaicum
Ref.	Refutatio omnium haeresium	JPTSup	Journal of Pentecostal Theology Supplement Series
HNT	Handbuch zum Neuen Testament		
HNTC	Harper's New Testament Commentaries	JQR	Jewish Quarterly Review
		JSNT	Journal for the Study of the New Testament
hom.	homila(e) ("homily/-lies")		
HThKNT	Herders theologischer Kommentar zum Neuen Testament	JSNTSup	Journal of the Study of the New Testament Supplement Series
		JSOTSup	Journal of the Study of the Old Testament Supplement Series
HTR	Harvard Theological Review		
HTS	Harvard Theological Studies	JTS	Journal of Theological Studies
HUT	Hermeneutische Untersuchungen zur Theologie	JTSA	Journal of Theology for Southern Africa
IBS	Irish Biblical Studies	Jub.	Jubilees
ICC	International Critical Commentary	Justin	Justin Martyr
		1 Apol.	Apologia 1
IDB	G. A. Buttrick, ed., The Interpreter's Dictionary of the Bible (4 vols.; New York: Abington, 1962)	Dial.	Dialogus cum Tryphone
		KatBl	Katechetische Blätter
		KBANT	Kommentare und Beiträge zum Alten und Neuen Testament
Ignatius			
Eph.	Letter to the Ephesians	KD	Kerygma und Dogma
Magn.	Letter to the Magnesians		

KEHNT	Kurzgefasstes exegetisches Handbuch zum Neuen Testament	*NETS*	Albert Pietersma and Benjamin G. Wright, eds., *The New English Translation of the Septuagint and the Other Greek Translations Traditionally Included under That Title* (New York: Oxford University Press, 2007)
KEK	Kritisch-exegetischer Kommentar über das Neue Testament		
KEKSup	KEK, Supplement		
1–4 Kgdms	1–4 Kingdoms (LXX)		
KM	*Die Katholischen Missionen*		
KNT	Kommentar zum Neuen Testament	*NewDocs*	G. H. R. Horsley and S. Llewelyn, eds., *New Documents Illustrating Early Christianity* (North Ryde, N.S.W.: Ancient History Documentary Research Centre, Macquarie University, 1981–)
KT	Kaiser-Traktate		
LAB	See *Bib. Ant.*		
Lat.	*Lateranum*		
LCL	Loeb Classical Library		
LD	Lectio divina	n.F.	neue Folge
Leo the Great		NHC	Nag Hammadi Codex (-ices)
Tract.	*Tractatus*	NHS	Nag Hammadi Studies
lib.	*liber* ("book")	NIBCNT	New International Bible Commentary on the New Testament
Libanus			
Or.	*Orations*		
LiBi	Lire la Bible	NICNT	New International Commentary on the New Testament
LingBibl	*Linguistica biblica*		
LiTh	Lieux théologiques	NIGTC	New International Greek Testament Commentary
LouvSt	*Louvain Studies*		
LQ	*Lutheran Quarterly*	*NJB*	*New Jerusalem Bible*
LSJ	H. G. Liddell, R. Scott, and H. S. Jones, *A Greek-English Lexicon* (9th ed. with revised supplement; Oxford: Clarendon, 1996)	*NKZ*	*Neue kirchliche Zeitschrift*
		no.	number
		NovT	*Novum Testamentum*
		NovTSup	Novum Testamentum Supplement Series
LTJ	*Lutheran Theological Journal*		
LTK	*Lexicon für Theologie und Kirche*	*NPNF¹*	Philip Schaff, ed., *Nicene and Post-Nicene Fathers: First Series* (originally under the title *A Select Library of the Christian Church*; 14 vols.; Buffalo, N.Y. [vols. 1–4]; New York [vols. 5–14]: The Christian Literature Company, 1886–90; reprinted Peabody, Mass.: Hendrickson, 1994)
LTQ	*Lexington Theological Quarterly*		
Lucian			
Luct.	*De luctu*		
Philops.	*Philopseudes*		
LV	*Lumière et vie*		
LXX	Septuagint		
m.	*Mishna. See* Rabbinic writings		
Mart. Pol.	*Martyrdom of Polycarp*		
MB	Le Monde de la Bible	*NRSV*	*New Revised Standard Version*
Menander		*NRTh*	*La nouvelle revue théologique*
Dysk.	*Dyskolos*	n.s.	new series
MHG	*See* Rabbinic writings	*NSNU*	*Nuntius Sodalicii Neotestamentici Upsaliensis*
MPTh	*Monatsschrift für Pastoraltheologie*		
ms(s).	manuscript(s)	NT	New Testament
MT	Masoretic Text	*NTA*	*New Testament Abstracts*
MThS	Münchener theologische Studien	NTAbh	Neutestamentliche Abhandlungen
MThZ	*Münchener theologische Zeitschrift*		
NAB	*New American Bible*	NTD	Das Neue Testament Deutsch
n(n).	note(s)	NTOA	Novum Testamentum et Orbis Antiquus
NEchtBNT	Neue Echter Bibel, New Testament		
		NTL	New Testament Library
NedThT	*Nederlands theologisch tijdschrift*	*NTS*	*New Testament Studies*
Neot	*Neotestamentica*	*NTT*	*Norsk Teologisk Tidsskrift*
Nestle-Aland	Eberhard Nestle and Kurt Aland, *Novum Testamentum Graece* (Stuttgart: Deutsche Bibelgesellschaft, 27th ed., 1993)	NTTS	New Testament Tools and Studies
		NV	*Nova et vetera*
		OBO	Orbis biblicus et orientalis

ÖBSt	*Österreichische biblische Studien*	*PL*	Jacques-Paul Migne, ed.,
OBT	Overtures to Biblical Theology		*Patrologia cursus completus: Series*
OLZ	*Orientalistische Literaturzeitung*		*Latina* (217 vols.; Paris: 1844–64)
Or	*Orientalia*	Plato	
OrChrP	*Orientalia Christiana Periodica*	*Resp.*	*Respublica* (*The Republic*)
Orien	*Orientierung* (Zurich)	*Symp.*	*Symposium*
Origen		Pliny the Elder	
Cels.	*Contra Celsum*	*Nat. hist.*	*Naturalis historia*
Comm. in Matt.	*Commentarii in evangelium Matthaei*	Plutarch	
		Ant.	*Antonius*
Comm. in Rom.	*Commentarii in Romanos*	*Is. Os.*	*De Iside et Osiride*
De princ.	*De principiis*	*Min.*	*Cato Minor*
Hom. in Ex.	*Homiliae in Exodum*	*Mor.*	*Moralie*
Hom. in Lev.	*Homiliae in Leviticum*	*Vit. X orat.*	*Vitae decem oratorum*
Hom. in Luc.	*Homiliae in evangelium secundam Lucam*	Polycarp	
		Phil.	*Epistle to the Philippians*
Hom. in Num.	*Homiliae in Numeros*	Porphyry	
Hom. in Jer.	*Homiliae in Jeremiam*	*Abst.*	*De abstinentia*
Or.	*De oratione*	PoTh	Le Point théologique
ORPB	*Oberrheinisches Pastoralblatt*	*P.Oxy.*	*See* under Papyri
OT	Old Testament	*PrM*	*Protestantische Monatshefte*
OTP	James H. Charlesworth, ed., *The Old Testament Pseudepigrapha* (2 vols.; New York: Doubleday, 1983, 1985)	*Prot. Jas.*	*Protevangelium of James*
		Proy	*Proyección*
		PRSt	*Perspectives in Religious Studies*
		PRStSS	Perspectives in Religious Studies Special Studies Series
p(p).	page(s)		
PalCl	*Palestra del clero*	PSA	Praktische Schriftauslegung für Predigt, Bibelarbeit, Unterricht
Papyri			
P.Oxy.	*Oxyrhynchus Papyri*	*Ps.-Clem.*	Pseudo-Clementine literature
par(r).	parallel(s)	*Hom.*	*Homilies*
ParDi	Parole de Dieu	*Rec.*	*Recognitions*
ParLi	*Paroisse et liturgie*	Pseudo-Macarius	
PaVi	*Parole di vita*	*Hom.*	*Homilies*
PBl	*Pastoralblätter*	*Ps. Sol.*	*Psalms of Solomon*
PCTSA	*Proceedings of the Annual Meeting* (Catholic Theological Society)	*PSV*	*Parola Spirito e Vita*
		PTMS	Pittsburgh/Princeton Theological Monograph Series
PenCath	*Pensée catholique*		
PEQ	*Palestine Exploration Quarterly*	PTS	Patristische Texte und Studien
PerTeol	*Perspectiva teológica*	PW	A. F. Pauly, *Paulys Realencyclopädie der classichen Altertumwissenschaft* (New ed. by G. Wissowa; 49 vols.; Munich: A. Druckenmüller, 1980)
Peter of Alexandria			
Ep. can.	*Canonical Epistle*		
Petronius			
Sat.	*Satyricon*		
PG	Jacques-Paul Migne, ed., *Patrologia cursus completus: Series graeca* (162 vols.; Paris, 1857–86)	Q	The Sayings Gospel
		QD	Quaestiones disputatae
		QR	*Quarterly Review*
		Qumran writings	
Philo		1QapGen	*Genesis Apocryphon* from Qumran Cave 1
Det. pot. ins.	*Quod deterius potiori insidiari solet*		
Deus	*Quod deus sit immutabilis*	4QapocrJoseph[b]	The second copy of *Apocryphon of Joseph* from Qumran Cave 4
Leg. all.	*Legum allegoriae*		
Op. mun.	*De opificio mundi*	1QH	*Hôdayôt* (*Thanksgiving Hymns*) from Qumran Cave 1
Sacr.	*De sacrificiis Abelis et Cani*		
Spec.	*De specialibus legibus*	1QM	*Milḥāmâ* (*War Scroll*) from Qumran Cave 1
Vit. cont.	*De vita contemplativa*		
Vit. Mos.	*De vita Mosis*	1QS	*Serek hayyaḥad* (*Rule of the Community, Manual of Discipline*) from Qumran Cave 1
Philostratus			
Vit. Ap.	*Vita Apollonii*		
Vit. soph.	*Vitae sophistarum*		

11QPs[a]	*Great Psalms Scroll*, the first manuscript found of Psalms in Qumran Cave 11	*RSPhTh*	*Revue des sciences philosophiques et théologiques*
Rabbinic writings		*RSR*	*Recherches de science religieuse*
b.	Babylonian Talmud	*RThL*	*Revue théologique de Louvain*
m.	Mishna	*RThom*	*Revue thomiste*
y.	Jerusalem Talmud	*RThPh*	*Revue de théologie et de philosophie*
Tractates of Talmud and Mishna		*RThQR*	*Revue de théologie et des questions religieuses*
ʾAbot	*ʾAbot*	*RTK*	*Roczniki teologiczo-kanoniczne*
B. Batra	*Baba Batra*	*SacDoc*	*Sacra doctrina*
Bek.	*Bekorot*	*Sal*	*Salesianum* (Torino)
Ber.	*Berakot*	SANT	Studien zum Alten und Neuen Testament
Ḥag.	*Ḥagigah*		
Kil.	*Kilʾayim*	SB	Sources bibliques
Maʿaś.	*Maʿaśerot*	SBAB	Stuttgarter biblische Aufsatzbände
Nid.	*Niddah*		
Pesaḥ.	*Pesaḥim*	*SBFLA*	*Studii biblici franciscani liber annus*
Qidd.	*Qiddušin*	SBibSt	Sources for biblical study
Šabb.	*Šabbat*	SBLDS	Society of Biblical Literature Dissertation Series
Sanh.	*Sanhedrin*		
Šeb.	*Šebiʿit*	SBLMS	Society of Biblical Literature Monograph Series
Soṭ.	*Soṭah*		
Taʿan.	*Taʿanit*	*SBLSP*	*Society of Biblical Literature Seminar Papers*
Yeb.	*Yebamot*		
Yoma	*Yoma*	SBLTT	Society of Biblical Literature Texts and Translations
Zebaḥ.	*Zebaḥim*		
Midrashim		SBS	Stuttgarter Bibelstudien
MHG	*Midraš ha-Gadol*	SBT	Studies in Biblical Theology
Shem.	*Shemot (Exodus)*	*SBTh*	*Studia biblica et theologica*
Midr. Cant.	*Midrash on the Song of Songs*	SC	Sources chrétiennes
Midr. Exod.	*Midrash on Exodus*	*ScC*	*La scuola cattolica*
Midr. Ps.	*Midrash on Psalms*	*ScEcc*	*Sciences ecclésiastiques*
Num. Rab.	*Numbers Rabbah*	*ScEs*	*Science et Esprit*
Other writings		SCHNT	Studia ad corpus hellenisticum Novi Testamenti
ʾAbot R. Nat.	*ʾAbot de Rabbi Nathan*		
PRE	*Pirqe Rabbi Eliezer*	*Scr*	*Scripture*
RAC	*Reallexikon für Antike und Christentum*	*SEÅ*	*Svensk exegetisk årsbok*
		Segond	Louis Segond Bible
RAMi	*Rivista di ascetica e mistica*	*SémBib*	*Sémiotique et bible*
RaR	Religion and reason	Seneca	
RAT	*Revue africaine de théologie*	*Ep.*	*Epistulae morales*
RB	*Revue biblique*	SESJ	Suomen Eksegeettisen Seuran julkaisuja
RBR	*Ricerche bibliche e religiose*		
RDN	*Revue diocésaine de Namur*	SGR	Studien zu den Grundlagen der Reformation
RDT	*Revue diocésaine de Tournai*		
REA	*Revue des études anciennes*	*SJT*	*Scottish Journal of Theology*
REAug	*Revue des études augustiniennes*	*SLJT*	*St. Luke's Journal of Theology*
REB	*Revised English Bible*	SMSR	Studi e materiali di storia delle religioni
RechBib	Recherches bibliques		
Ref	*Reformatio*	SNTSMS	Society for New Testament Studies Monograph Series
RelLi	*Religion in Life*		
ResQ	*Restoration Quarterly*	SNTU	Studien zum Neuen Testament und seiner Umwelt
rev.	revised		
RevistB	*Revista bíblica*	*SO*	*Symbolae Osloenses*
RevSR	*Revue des sciences religieuses*	Sophocles	
RHPhR	*Revue d'histoire et de philosophie religieuses*	*Ant.*	*Antigone*
		SP	Sacra Pagina
RivB	*Rivista biblica*	SPK	Schriften zur Pädagogik und Katechetik
RNT	Regensburger Neues Testament		

SSup	Semeia Supplement Series
StEv	*Studia Evangelica*
STGMA	Studien und Texte zur Geistesgeschichte des Mittelalters
StLeg	*Studium Legionense*
StLi	*Studia Liturgica*
StMiss	*Studia missionalia*
StNT	Studien zum Neuen Testament
StPatr	Studia Patristica
StPB	Studia post-biblica
Str-B	Hermann Strack and Paul Billerbeck, *Kommentar zum Neuen Testament aus Talmud und Midrash,* vols. 1–4 (5th ed.; Munich: Beck, 1969); vols. 5–6 and index (ed. Joachim Jeremias and K. Adolf; 3d ed.; Munich: Beck, 1963)
StTh	*Studia teologica, Scandinavian Journal of Theology*
SUNT	Studien zur Umwelt des Neuen Testaments
s.v.	*sub verbo* ("under the word")
SVF	H. von Arnim, ed., *Stoicorum veterum fragmenta* (4 vols.; Leipzig: Teubner, 1903–24)
SymBU	Symbolae biblicae upsalienses
T. Ab.	*Testament of Abraham*
T. Ash.	*Testament of Asher*
T. Benj.	*Testament of Benjamin*
T. Dan.	*Testament of Dan*
T. Gad	*Testament of Gad*
T. Iss.	*Testament of Issachar*
T. Job	*Testament of Job*
T. Jos.	*Testament of Joseph*
T. Jud.	*Testament of Judah*
T. Levi	*Testament of Levi*
T. Moses	*Testament of Moses*
T. Naph.	*Testament of Naphtali*
T. Sol.	*Testament of Solomon*
T. Zeb.	*Testament of Zebulun*
TBT	*The Bible Today*
TDNT	Gerhard Kittel and Gerhard Friedrich, eds., *Theological Dictionary of the New Testament* (trans. and ed. Geoffrey W. Bromiley; 10 vols.; Grand Rapids: Eerdmans, 1964–76)
TEH	Theologische Existenz heute
TeKo	*Texte und Kontexte*
Tertullian	
Adv. Marc.	*Adversus Marcionem*
An.	*De anima*
Idol.	*De idololatria*
Or.	*De oratione*
Paen.	*De paenitentia*
Praescr.	*De praescriptione haereticorum*
Pud.	*De pudicitia*
TF	Theologische Forschung
TFT.S	Theologische Faculteit Tilburgstudies
Tg. Neof.	*Targum Neofiti*
THAT	Ernst Jenni, ed., *Theologisches Handwörterbuch zum Alten Testament* (2 vols.; Zurich: Theologischer Verlag, 1971–76)
ThBei	*Theologische Beiträge*
ThBl	*Theologische Blätter*
ThBü	Theologische Bücherei
Theodore of Mopsuestia	
Hom. cat.	*Homiliae catecheticae*
Theol	*Theology* (London)
Theol (P)	Théologie (Paris)
Theophrastus	
Char.	*Characteres*
De caus. plant.	*De causis plantarum*
Hist. plant.	*Historia plantarum*
ThG	Theologie der Gegenwart
ThGl	Theologie und Glaube
ThHKNT	Theologischer Handkommentar zum Neuen Testament
ThLZ	*Theologische Literaturzeitung*
Thomas Aquinas	
STh	*Summa Theologiae*
ThQ	*Theologische Quartalschrift*
ThStK	*Theologische Studien and Kritiken*
ThTo	*Theology Today*
ThV	*Theologische Versuche*
ThViat	*Theologia viatorum* (Berlin)
ThWNT	Gerhard Kittel and Gerhard Friedrich, eds., *Theologisches Wörterbuch zum Neuen Testament* (10 vols.; Stuttgart: Kohlhammer, 1932–79)
ThZ	*Theologische Zeitschrift*
ThZ.S	Theologische Zeitschrift Sonderband
TJT	*Toronto Journal of Theology*
TNIV	*Today's New International Version*
TOB	*Traduction œcuménique de la Bible, version intégrale* (2 vols.; Paris: Société biblique française, 1972–75)
trans.	translated by
TRE	*Theologische Realenzyklopädie*
TRG	*Tijdschrift voor rechtsgeschiedenis*
TS	*Theological Studies*
TT	*Teologisk tidskrift*
TThZ	*Trierer theologische Zeitschrift*
TU	Texte und Untersuchungen
TUGAL	Texte und Untersuchungen zur Geschichte der altchristlichen Literatur
TynBul	*Tyndale Bulletin*
TZ(W)	*Theologische Zeitschrift* (Wien)
USQR	*Union Seminary Quarterly Review*

UTSR	*Union (Theological) Seminary Review*
v(v).	verse(s)
VAFLNW.G	*Veröffentlichungen der Arbeitsgemeinschaft für Forschung des Landes Nordrhein-Westfalen. Geisteswissenschaften*
VC	*Vigiliae christianae*
VD	*Verbum domini*
VetChr	*Vetera Christianorum*
VJTR	*Vidyajyoti Journal of Theological Reflection*
v.l.	*varia lectio* (variant reading)
VL	*Vetus Latina: Die Reste der altlateinischen Bibel*
VS	*Verbum salutis*
VSpir	*Vie spirituelle*
VTKG	Vorträge der theologischen Konferenz zu Giessen
VTSup	Supplements to Vetus Testamentum
WA	M. Luther, Kritische Gesamtausgabe (= "Weimar" edition)
WBC	Word Biblical Commentary
WD	*Wort und Deinst*
WdF	Wege der Forschung
WMANT	Wissenschaftliche Monographien zum Alten and Neuen Testament
WSAMA.T	Walberger Studien der Albertus Magnus Akademie: Theologische Reihe
Wst	*Wiener Studien: Zeitschrift für klassische Philologie und Patristik*
WTJ	*Westminster Theological Journal*
WUNT	Wissenschaftliche Untersuchungen zum Neuen Testament
Xenophon	
Cyr.	*Cyropaedia*
Oecon.	*Oeconomicus*
Symp.	*Symposium*
ZBK	Zürcher Bibelkommentare
ZNW	*Zeitschrift für die neutestamentliche Wissenschaft*
ZPE	*Zeitschrift für Papyrologie und Epigraphik*
ZSRR	*Zeitschrift der Savigny-Stiftung für Rechtsgeschichte, Romanische Abteilung*
ZThK	*Zeitschrift für Theologie und Kirche*
ZWTh	*Zeitschrift für wissenschaftliche Theologie*

2. Short Titles

Abel, *Géographie physique*
    Félix-Marie Abel, *Géographie de la Palestine*, vol. 1: *Géographie physique et historique* (3d ed.; EtB; Paris: Gabalda, 1967).

Abel, *Géographie politique*
    Félix-Marie Abel, *Géographie de la Palestine*, vol. 2: *Géographie politique: Les villes* (3d ed.; EtB; Paris: Gabalda, 1967).

Abel, *Grammaire*
    Félix-Marie Abel, *Grammaire du grec biblique suivie d'un choix de papyrus* (2d ed.; EtB; Paris: Gabalda, 1927).

Agricola, *Evangelium Lucae*
    Johann Agricola of Eisleben, *In Evangelium Lucae annotationes . . . , summa scripturarum fide tractatae* (Augsburg: S. Ruff, 1525).

Aland, *Synopsis*
    Kurt Aland, ed., *Synopsis quattuor evangeliorum* (15th ed.; Stuttgart: Deutsche Bibelgesellschaft, 1996).

Albertus Magnus, *Enarr. in Luc.* (ed. Borgnet)
    Albertus Magnus [Albert the Great], *Enarrationes in secundam partem evang[elii] Lucae*, in Auguste Borgnet, ed., *B[eati] Alberti Magni Ratisbonensis episcopi, . . . Opera omnia, ex editione Lugdunensi religiose castigata . . .*, vol. 23: *Enarrationes in secundam partem evang[elii] Lucae (x–xxiv)* (Paris: apud Ludovicum Vivès, 1895).

Aletti, *Art de raconter*
    Jean-Noël Aletti, *L'art de raconter Jésus-Christ: L'écriture narrative de l'Évangile de Luc* (ParDi; Paris: Seuil, 1989).

Aletti, *Quand Luc*
    Jean-Noël Aletti, *Quand Luc raconte: Le récit comme théologie* (LiBi 114; Paris: Cerf, 1998).

Alexander, "Luke-Acts"
    Loveday C. A. Alexander, "Luke-Acts in Its Contemporary Setting with Special Reference to the Prefaces: Luke 1:1-4 and Acts 1:1" (diss., Oxford, 1913).

Alexander, *Preface*
    Loveday C. A. Alexander, *The Preface to Luke's Gospel: Literary Convention and Social Context in Luke 1:1–4 and Acts 1:1* (SNTSMS 78; Cambridge/New York: Cambridge University Press, 1993).

Alexandre, *Dictionnaire*
    Charles Alexandre, *Dictionnaire grec-français composé sur un nouveau plan* (23d ed.; Paris: Hachette, 1888).

Allen, *Herod*
    O. Wesley Allen, Jr., *The Death of Herod: The Narrative and Theological Function of Retribution in Luke-Acts* (SBLDS 158; Atlanta: Scholars Press, 1997).

Ambrose, *Traité*
    Ambrose of Milan, *Traité sur l'Évangile de Luc* (ed. and trans. G. Tissot; 2 vols.; SC 45 [bis], 52 [bis]; Paris: Cerf, 1955–58; 2d ed., 1971–76).

Aquinas, *Catena aurea*
    Thomas Aquinas, *Catena aurea in quatuor evangelia: Nuova editio Taurienensis* (ed. Angelico Guarienti; 2 vols.; Turin: Marietti, 1953) vol. 2.

Arai, "Schaf"
    Sasagu Arai, "Das Gleichnis vom verlorenen Schaf: Eine traditionsgeschichtliche Untersuchung," *AJBI* 2 (1976) 111–37.

Baarlink, *Eschatologie*
Heinrich Baarlink, *Die Eschatologie der synoptischen Evangelien* (BWANT 120; Stuttgart: Kohlhammer, 1986).

Bailey, *Eyes*
Kenneth E. Bailey, *Through Peasant Eyes: More Lukan Parables, Their Culture and Style* (Grand Rapids: Eerdmans, 1980).

Bailey, *Poet*
Kenneth E. Bailey, *Poet and Peasant: A Literary Cultural Approach to the Parables in Luke* (Grand Rapids: Eerdmans, 1976).

Baker, "One Thing"
Aelred Baker, "One Thing Necessary," *CBQ* 27 (1965) 127–37.

Barclay
William Barclay, *The Gospel of Luke: Translation, Introduction, and Interpretation* (Philadelphia: Westminster, 1975).

Barclay, *Handbook*
William Barclay, *And Jesus Said: A Handbook on the Parables of Jesus* (Philadelphia: Westminster, 1970).

Barrett, *Commentary on the Acts*
Charles Kingsley Barrett, *A Critical and Exegetical Commentary on the Acts of the Apostles* (2 vols.; ICC 30–31; Edinburgh: T&T Clark, 1994, 1998).

Barrett, *Holy Spirit*
Charles Kingsley Barrett, *The Holy Spirit and the Gospel Tradition* (London: SPCK, 1954).

Barth, *Interpretation*
Carola Barth, *Die Interpretation des Neuen Testaments in der valentinianischen Gnosis* (TU 37; Leipzig: Hinrichs, 1911).

Bauer, *Leben Jesu*
Walter Bauer, *Das Leben Jesu im Zeitalter der neutestamentlichen Apokryphen* (Tübingen: Mohr Siebeck, 1909; reprinted Darmstadt: Wissenschaftliche Buchgesellschaft, 1967).

Baumbach, *Verständnis*
Günther Baumbach, *Das Verständnis des Bösen in den synoptischen Evangelien* (Theologische Arbeiten 19; Berlin: Evangelische Verlagsanstalt, 1963).

Beck, *Christian Character*
Brian E. Beck, *Christian Character in the Gospel of Luke* (London: Epworth, 1989).

Bede, *In Luc.*
The Venerable Bede, *In Lucae Evangelium expositio* (ed. David Hurst; CCSL 120; Turnhout: Brepols, 1960).

Bendemann, *ΔΟΞΑ und ΣΤΑΥΡΟΣ*
Reinhard von Bendemann, *Zwischen ΔΟΞΑ und ΣΤΑΥΡΟΣ: Eine exegetische Untersuchung der Texte des sogenannten Reiseberichtes im Lukasevangelium* (BZNW 101; Berlin/New York: de Gruyter, 2001).

Bengel, *Gnomon*
Johann Albrecht Bengel, *Gnomon of the New Testament* (trans. Charlton T. Lewis and Marvin R. Vincent; 2 vols.; Philadelphia: Perkinpine & Higgins; New York: Sheldon & Company, 1860, 1862) vol. 1.

Bergholz, *Aufbau*
Thomas Bergholz, *Der Aufbau des lukanischen Doppelwerkes: Untersuchungen zum formalliterarischen Charakter von Lukas-Evangelium und Apostelgeschichte* (EHS 545; Frankfurt am Main/New York: Peter Lang, 1995).

Betz, *Lukian von Samosata*
Hans Dieter Betz, *Lukian von Samosata und das Neue Testament: Religionsgeschichtliche und paränetische Parallelen. Ein Beitrag zum Corpus Hellenisticum Novi Testamenti* (TU 76; Berlin: Akademie-Verlag, 1961).

Betz, *Plutarch's Writings*
Hans Dieter Betz, *Plutarch's Ethical Writings and Early Christian Literature* (SCHNT 4; Leiden: Brill, 1978).

Betz, *Abraham*
Otto Betz et al., eds., *Abraham unser Vater: Juden und Christen im Gespräch über die Bibel. Festschrift Otto Michel* (AGSU 5; Leiden: Brill, 1963).

Beyer, *Syntax*
Klaus Beyer, *Semitische Syntax im Neuen Testament*, vol. 1.1 (SUNT 1; Göttingen: Vandenhoeck & Ruprecht, 1962).

Bieberstein, *Verschwiegene Jüngerinnen*
Sabine Bieberstein, *Verschwiegene Jüngerinnen, vergessene Zeuginnen: Gebrochene Konzepte im Lukasevangelium* (NTOA 38; Göttingen: Vandenhoeck & Ruprecht; Fribourg: Universitätsverlag, 1998).

Black, *Aramaic Approach*
Matthew Black, *An Aramaic Approach to the Gospels and Acts* (2d ed.; Oxford: Clarendon, 1954).

Blinzler, *Prozess Jesu*
Josef Blinzler, *Der Prozess Jesu: Das jüdische und das römische Gerichtsverfahren gegen Jesus Christus auf Grund der ältesten Zeugnisse dargestellt und beurteilt* (3d ed.; Regensburg: Pustet, 1960).

Blumhardt, *Evangelien-Predigten*
Johann Christoph Blumhardt, *Evangelien-Predigten auf alle Sonn- u. Festtage des Kirchenjahres nach dem zweiten Jahrgang der württembergischen Perikopen*, in Christoph Blumhardt, ed., *Gesammelte Werke*, vol. 2 (Karlsruhe: Evangelischen Schriftenverein für Baden, 1887).

Bock
Darrell L. Bock, *Luke* (2 vols.; BECNT 3A–B; Grand Rapids: Baker Books, 1994, 1996).

Bock, *Proclamation*
Darrell L. Bock, *Proclamation from Prophecy and Pattern: Lucan Old Testament Christology* (JSNTSup 12; Sheffield: JSOT Press, 1987).

Bode, *First Easter*
Edward L. Bode, *The First Easter Morning: The Gospel Accounts of the Women's Visit to the Tomb of Jesus* (AnBib 45; Rome: Biblical Institute Press, 1970).

Boers, *Who was Jesus?*
Hendrikus Boers, *Who Was Jesus? The Historical Jesus and the Synoptic Gospels* (San Francisco: Harper & Row, 1989).

Bogaert, *Baruch*
Pierre Bogaert, *Apocalypse de Baruch: Introduction, traduction du syriaque et commentaire* (2 vols.; SC 144–45; Paris: Cerf, 1969).

Bonaventure, *Comm. in Luc.*
Bonaventure, *Commentarius in evangelium S. Lucae,* in R. P. Bernardini, ed., *Bonaventure Opera omnia* (Quaracchi: Collegium S. Bonaventurae, 1882–1902) vol. 7.

Bonnard, *Matthieu*
Pierre Bonnard, *L'Évangile selon saint Matthieu* (2d ed.; CNT 1; Geneva: Labor et Fides, 1982).

Bonz, *Past as Legacy*
Marianne P. Bonz, *The Past as Legacy: Luke-Acts and Ancient Epic* (Minneapolis: Fortress Press, 2000).

Boring, *Continuing Voice*
M. Eugene Boring, *The Continuing Voice of Jesus: Christian Prophecy and the Gospel Tradition* (Louisville: Westminster John Knox, 1991).

Boring, *Sayings*
M. Eugene Boring, *Sayings of the Risen Jesus: Christian Prophecy in the Synoptic Tradition* (SNTSMS 46; Cambridge/New York: Cambridge University Press, 1982).

Bornhäuser, *Sondergut*
Karl Bernhard Bornhäuser, *Studien zum Sondergut des Lukas* (Gütersloh: Bertelsmann, 1934).

Bornkamm, *Geschichte und Glaube*
Günther Bornkamm, *Gesammelte Aufsätze*, vol. 4: *Geschichte und Glaube, Zweiter Teil* (BEvTh 53; Munich: Kaiser, 1971).

Bösen, *Jesusmahl*
Willibald Bösen, *Jesusmahl, Eucharistisches Mahl, Endzeitmahl: Ein Beitrag zur Theologie des Lukas* (Stuttgart: Katholisches Bibelwerk, 1980).

Bossuyt and Radermakers
Philippe Bossuyt and Jean Radermakers, *Jésus, Parole de la grâce: Selon St. Luc* (2 vols.; Brussels: Institut d'études théologiques, 1981).

Bottini, *Introduzione*
Giovanni Claudio Bottini, *Introduzione all'opera di Luca: Aspetti teologici* (Studium Biblicum Franciscanum Analecta 35; Jerusalem: Franciscan Printing, 1992).

Bourgoin, "Préfixe"
Henri Bourgoin, "Ἐπιούσιος explique par la notion de prefixe vide," *Bib* 60 (1979) 91–96.

Bovon, "Évangile de Luc"
François Bovon, "Évangile de Luc et Actes des apôtres," in Étienne Charpentier, ed., *Évangiles synoptiques et Actes des apôtres* (Petite bibliothèque des sciences bibliques, Noveau Testament 4; Paris: Desclée, 1981) 195–294.

Bovon, *L'œuvre.*
François Bovon, *L'œuvre de Luc: Études d'exégèse et de théologie* (LD 130; Paris: Cerf, 1987).

Bovon, "Paschal Privilege"
François Bovon, "Mary Magdalene's Paschal Privilege," in idem, *Traditions,* 147–57.

Bovon, *Révélations*
François Bovon, *Révélations et écritures: Nouveau Testament et littérature apocryphe chrétienne. Recueil d'articles* (MB 26; Geneva: Labor et Fides, 1993).

Bovon, "Studies"
François Bovon, "Studies in Luke-Acts: Retrospect and Prospect," *HTR* 85 (1992) 175–96.

Bovon, *Studies*
François Bovon, *Studies in Early Christianity* (Grand Rapids: Baker, 2005).

Bovon, *Theologian*
François Bovon, *Luke the Theologian: Fifty-Five Years of Research (1950–2005)* (2d rev. ed.; Waco, Tex.: Baylor University Press, 2006).

Bovon, *Traditions*
François Bovon, *New Testament Traditions and Apocryphal Narratives* (trans. Jane Haapiseva-Hunter; PTMS 36; Allison Park, Pa.: Pickwick, 1995).

Bovon and Geoltrain, *Écrits apocryphes*
François Bovon and Pierre Geoltrain, eds., *Écrits apocryphes chrétiens*, vol. 1 (Bibliothèque de la Pléiade 442; Paris: Gallimard, 1997).

Bovon and Rouiller, *Exegesis*
Francois Bovon and Grégoire Rouiller, eds., *Exegesis: Problems of Method and Exegesis in Reading (Genesis 22 and Luke 15)* (trans. Donald G. Miller; PTMS 21; Pittsburgh: Pickwick, 1978).

Brandenburger and Hieke, *Studien*
Stefan H. Brandenburger and Thomas Hieke, eds., *Wenn drei das Gleiche sagen: Studien zu den drei Evangelien: Mit einer Werkstattübersetzung des Q-Textes* (Theologie 14; Münster i. W.: Lit, 1998).

Braun, "Pain"
François-Marie Braun, "Le pain dont nous avons besoin: Mt 6, 11; Lc 11, 3," *NRTh* 100 (1978) 559–68.

Brawley, *Centering on God*
Robert L. Brawley, *Centering on God: Method and Message in Luke-Acts* (Louisville: Westminster John Knox, 1990).

Brawley, *Luke-Acts*
Robert L. Brawley, *Luke-Acts and the Jews: Conflict, Apology, and Conciliation* (SBLMS 33; Atlanta: Scholars Press, 1987).

Brown, "Pater Noster"
Raymond E. Brown, "The Pater Noster as an Eschatological Prayer," *TS* 22 (1961) 175–208; reprinted in idem, *New Testament Essays* (Milwaukee: Bruce, 1965) 217–53 (cited from the latter).

Brown, *Apostasy*
Schuyler Brown, *Apostasy and Perseverance in the Theology of Luke* (AnBib 36; Rome: Pontifical Biblical Institute, 1969).

Bruno di Segni, *Commentaria*
Bruno di Segni, *Commentaria in Lucam* (1791; reprinted *PL* 165; Paris: Migne, [1854]) 333–451.

Brutscheck, *Maria-Marta*
Jutta Brutscheck, *Die Maria-Marta Erzählung: Eine redaktionskritische Untersuchung zu Lk 10, 38-42* (BBB 64; Frankfurt am Main: Hanstein, 1986).

Büchele, *Tod Jesu*
Anton Büchele, *Tod Jesu im Lukasevangelium: Eine redaktionsgeschichtliche Untersuchung zu Lk 23* (FTS 26; Frankfurt am Main: Knecht, 1978).

Bultmann, *Geschichte*
Rudolf Bultmann, *Die Geschichte der synoptischen Tradition: Ergänzungsheft* (ed. Gerd Theissen and Philipp Vielhauer; 4th ed.; Göttingen: Vandenhoeck & Ruprecht, 1971).

Bultmann, *History*
Rudolf Bultmann, *History of the Synoptic Tradition* (trans. John Marsh; rev. ed.; New York/Evanston: Harper & Row, 1968; reprinted New York: Harper & Row, 1976).

Bultmann, *Marburg Sermons*
Rudolf Bultmann, *This World and the Beyond: Marburg Sermons* (New York: Scribner, 1960).

Bultmann, *Theology*
Rudolf Bultmann, *Theology of the New Testament* (trans. Kendrick Grobel; 2 vols.; New York: Scribner, 1951, 1955).

Burchard, "Liebesgebot"
C. Burchard, "Das doppelte Liebesgebot in der frühen christlichen Überlieferung," in Lohse, *Ruf Jesu*, 39–62.

Burridge, *What Are the Gospels?*
Richard Burridge, *What Are the Gospels? A Comparison with Graeco-Roman Biography* (SNTSMS 70; Cambridge/New York: Cambridge University Press, 1992).

Busse, *Wunder*
Ulrich Busse, *Die Wunder des Propheten Jesus: Die Rezeption, Komposition und Interpretation der Wundertradition im Evangelium des Lukas* (FB 24; Stuttgart: Katholisches Bibelwerk, 1977).

Bussmann and Radl, *Treue Gottes*
Claus Bussmann and Walter Radl, eds., *Der Treue Gottes trauen: Beiträge zum Werk des Lukas. Festschrift Gerhard Schneider* (Freiburg im B.: Herder, 1991).

Buzy, *Paraboles*
Denis Buzy, *Les paraboles* (VS 6; Paris: Beauchesne, 1932).

Caba, *Oración de petición*
José Caba, *La oración de petición: Estudio exegético sobre los evangelios sinópticos y los escritos joaneos* (AnBib 62; Rome: Biblical Institute Press, 1974).

Caird
George B. Caird, *Saint Luke* (Westminster Pelican Commentaries; Philadelphia: Westminster, 1978).

Cajetan, *Evangelia*
Tommaso de Vio Cajetan, *Evangelia cum commentariis* (Paris, 1540).

Calvin, *Harmony*
Jean Calvin, *Harmonia ex tribus Evangelistis composita Matthaeo, Marco et Luca; adiuncto seorsum Iohanne, quòd pauca cum aliis communia habeat; cum Ioannis Calvini Commentariis* (Geneva: Robertus Stephanus [= Robert Estienne], 1555), translated as John Calvin, *A Harmony of the Gospels Matthew, Mark and Luke* (trans. A. W. Morrison [vols. 1, 3], T. H. L. Parker [vol. 2]; 3 vols.; Calvin's Commentaries 1–3; Edinburgh: Oliver & Boyd, 1972). Cited from the latter.

Carlston, *Triple Tradition*
Charles E. Carlston, *The Parables of the Triple Tradition* (Philadelphia: Fortress Press, 1975).

Carmignac, *Recherches*
Jean Carmignac, *Recherches sur le «Notre Père»* (Paris: Letouzey & Ané, 1969).

Carrez and Morel, *Dictionnaire*
Maurice Carrez and Francois Morel, *Dictionnaire grec-français du Nouveau Testament* (Neuchâtel: Delachaux & Niestlé; Paris: Cerf, 1971).

Carroll, *Response*
John T. Carroll, *Response to the End of History: Eschatology and Situation in Luke-Acts* (SBLDS 92; Atlanta: Scholars Press, 1988).

Casey, "Jackals"
Maurice Casey, "The Jackals and the Son of Man (Mt 8, 20 ‖ Lk 9, 58)," *JSNT* 23 (1985) 3–22.

Cassidy, *Jesus, Politics, and Society*
Richard J. Cassidy, *Jesus, Politics, and Society: A Study of Luke's Gospel* (Maryknoll, N.Y.: Orbis Books, 1978).

Catchpole, "Friend"
David R. Catchpole, "Q and 'The Friend at Midnight' (Luke xi. 5-8/9)," *JTS* n.s. 34 (1983) 407–24.

Centre d'analyse, *Biblia Patristica*
Centre d'analyse et de documentation patristiques, *Biblia Patristica: Index des citations et allusions bibliques dans la littérature patristique* (7 vols.; Paris: Centre national de la recherche scientifique, 1975–99).

Cerfaux, *Recueil*
Lucien Cerfaux, *Recueil Lucien Cerfaux: Études d'exégèse et d'histoire religieuse de Monseigneur Cerfaux, réunies à l'occasion de son soixante-dixième anniversaire* (3 vols.; BETL 6–7, 18; Gembloux: Duculot, 1954–62).

Chance, *Jerusalem*
J. Bradley Chance, *Jerusalem, the Temple, and the New Age in Luke-Acts* (Macon, Ga.: Mercer University Press, 1988).

Chilton, *God in Strength*
Bruce D. Chilton, *God in Strength: Jesus' Announcement of the Kingdom* (SNTU B 1; Freistadt: Plöchl, 1979).

Chilton, *Profiles*
Bruce D. Chilton, *Profiles of a Rabbi: Synoptic Opportunities in Reading about Jesus* (BJS 177; Atlanta: Scholars Press, 1989).

Christ, *Jesus Sophia*
Felix Christ, *Jesus Sophia: Die Sophia-Christologie bei den Synoptikern* (AThANT 57; Zurich: Zwingli-Verlag, 1970).

Chung, "Word of God"
Chung, Y. L., "The Word of God" in Luke-Acts: A Study of Lukan Theology" (diss., Emory University, 1995).

Clines, *Three Dimensions*
David J. A. Clines et al., eds., *The Bible in Three Dimensions: Essays in Celebration of Forty Years of Biblical Studies in the University of Sheffield* (JSOTSup 87; Sheffield: JSOT Press, 1990).

Coleridge, *Birth*
Mark Coleridge, *The Birth of the Lukan Narrative: Narrative as Christology in Luke 1–2* (JSNTSup 88; Sheffield: JSOT Press, 1993).

Conzelmann, *Theology*
Hans Conzelmann, *The Theology of St. Luke* (trans. Geoffrey Buswell; London: Faber & Faber, 1960; reprinted Philadelphia: Fortress Press, 1982).

Cooper, *Luke's Gospel*
Robin Cooper, *Luke's Gospel: An Interpretation for Today* (London: Hodder & Stoughton, 1989).

Corsato, *Expositio*
Celestino Corsato, *La Expositio euangelii secundum Lucam di sant' Ambrogio: Ermeneutica, simbologia, fonti* (Studia ephemeridis Augustinianum 43; Rome: Institutum Patristicum Augustinianum, 1993).

Coulot, *Jésus et le disciple*
Claude Coulot, *Jésus et le disciple: Études sur l'autorité messianique de Jésus* (EtB 8; Paris: Gabalda, 1987).

Cousin
Hugues Cousin, *Évangile de Luc* (Paris: Centurion, 1993).

Craddock
Fred B. Craddock, *Luke* (Interpretation; Louisville: Westminster John Knox, 1990).

Crane, *Synoptics*
Thomas E. Crane, *The Synoptics: Mark, Matthew, and Luke Interpret the Gospel* (London: Sheed & Ward, 1982).

Crossan, *Four Other Gospels*
John Dominic Crossan, *Four Other Gospels: Shadows on the Contours of Canon* (Minneapolis: Winston, 1985).

Crossan, *Fragments*
John Dominic Crossan, *In Fragments: The Aphorisms of Jesus* (San Francisco: Harper & Row, 1983).

Crossan, *Historical Jesus*
John Dominic Crossan, *The Historical Jesus: The Life of a Mediterranean Jewish Peasant* (San Francisco: HarperSanFrancisco, 1991).

Crossan, "Parable and Example"
John Dominic Crossan, "Parable and Example in the Teaching of Jesus," *NTS* 18 (1971–72) 285–307.

Crossan, *Polyvalent Narration*
John Dominic Crossan, ed., *Polyvalent Narration* (Semeia 9; Missoula, Mont.: Scholars Press, 1977).

Crump, *Intercessor*
David M. Crump, *Jesus the Intercessor: Prayer and Christology in Luke-Acts* (WUNT 2/49; Tübingen: Mohr Siebeck, 1992).

Csányi, "Optima pars"
Daniel A. Csáyni, "Optima pars: Auslegungs-geschichte von Lk 10,38-42 bei den Kirchenvätern der ersten vier Jahrhunderte," *Studia monastica* 2 (1960) 5–78.

Cullmann, *Salvation in History*
Oscar Cullmann, *Salvation in History* (trans. Sidney G. Sowers et al.; NTL; London: SCM, 1967).

Dahl, *Memory*
Nils Alstrup Dahl, *Jesus in the Memory of the Early Church: Essays* (Minneapolis: Augsburg, 1976).

Danker
Frederick W. Danker, *Jesus and the New Age: A Commentary on St. Luke's Gospel* (2d ed.; Philadelphia: Fortress Press, 1988).

Dassmann, *Sündenvergebung*
Ernst Dassmann, *Sündenvergebung durch Taufe, Busse und Märtyrerfürbitte in den Zeugnissen frühchristlicher Frömmigkeit und Kunst* (Münsterische Beiträge zur Theologie 36; Münster: Aschendorff, 1973).

Daube, *Rabbinic Judaism*
David Daube, *The New Testament and Rabbinic Judaism* (Jordan Lectures in Comparative Religion 2; London: Athlone, 1956).

Dauer, *Beobachtungen*
Anton Dauer, *Beobachtungen zur literarischen Arbeitstechnik des Lukas* (BBB 79; Frankfurt am Main: Hain, 1990).

Dauer, *Johannes und Lukas*
Anton Dauer, *Johannes und Lukas: Untersuchungen zu den johanneisch-lukanischen Parallelperikopen Joh 4,46-54/Lk 7,1-10 — Joh 12,1-8/Lk 7,36-50; 10,38-42 — Joh 20,10-29/Lk 24,36-49* (FB 50; Würzburg: Echter, 1984).

Dautzenberg, *Leben*
Gerhard Dautzenberg, *Sein Leben bewahren: ψυχή in den Herrenworten der Evangelien* (SANT 14; Munich: Kösel, 1966).

Dawsey, "Literary Unity"
James M. Dawsey, "The Literary Unity of Luke-Acts: Questions of Style—A Task for Literary Critics," *NTS* 35 (1989) 48–66.

Dawsey, *Lukan Voice*
James M. Dawsey, *The Lukan Voice: Confusion and Irony in the Gospel of Luke* (Macon, Ga.: Mercer University Press, 1986).

Degenhardt, *Lukas*
Hans Joachim Degenhardt, *Lukas, Evangelist der Armen: Besitz und Besitzverzicht in den lukanischen Schriften. Eine traditions– und redaktionsgeschichtliche Untersuchung* (Stuttgart: Katholisches Bibelwerk, 1965).

Delebecque
Édouard Delebecque, *Évangile de Luc: Texte traduit et annoté* (Collection d'études anciennes; Paris: Belles Lettres, 1976).

Delebecque, *Études*
Édouard Delebecque, *Études grecques sur l'Évangile de Luc* (CEA; Paris: Belles Lettres, 1976).

Delobel, *Logia*
Joël Delobel, ed., *Logia — Les paroles de Jésus — The Sayings of Jesus: Mémorial Joseph Coppens* (BETL 59; Leuven: Leuven University Press/Peeters, 1982).

Delobel, "Sayings"

Joël Delobel, "The Sayings of Jesus in the Textual Tradition: Variant Readings in the Greek Manuscripts of the Gospels," in idem, *Logia,* 431–57.

Delorme, *Paraboles évangéliques*

Jean Delorme, ed., *Les Paraboles évangéliques: Perspectives nouvelles, XIIe Congrès de l'ACFEB, Lyon (1987)* (LD 135; Paris: Cerf, 1989).

Delorme and Duplacy, *La parole de grâce*

Jean Delorme and Jean Duplacy, eds., *La parole de grâce: Études lucaniennes à la mémoirs d'Augustin George* (Paris: Recherches de science religieuse, 1981).

Del Verme, *Comunione*

Marcello del Verme, *Comunione e condivisione dei beni: Chiesa primitiva e giudaismo esseno-qumranico a confronto* (Brescia: Morcelliana, 1977).

Denaux, "Old Testament Models"

Adelbert Denaux, "Old Testament Models for the Lukan Travel Narrative: A Critical Survey," in Christopher Mark Tuckett, ed., *The Scriptures in the Gospels* (BETL 131; Leuven: Leuven University Press, 1997).

Denis, *Concordance grecque*

Albert-Marie Denis, *Concordance grecque des Pseudépigraphes d'Ancien Testament: Concordance, corpus des textes, indices* (Louvain: Université catholique de Louvain, 1987).

Denis, *Concordance latine*

Albert-Marie Denis, *Concordance latine des Pseudépigraphes d'Ancien Testament: Concordance, corpus des textes, indices* (Corpus Christianorum Thesaurus Patrum Latinorum, Supplementum; Turnhout: Brepols, 1993).

Denova, *Things Accomplished*

Rebecca I. Denova, *The Things Accomplished among Us: Prophetic Tradition in the Structural Pattern of Luke-Acts* (JSNTSup 141; Sheffield: Sheffield Academic Press, 1997).

Derrett, "Friend"

J. Duncan M. Derrett, "The Friend at Midnight: Asian Ideas in the Gospel of St. Luke," in Ernst Bammel et al., eds., *Donum gentilicium: New Testament Studies in Honour of David Daube* (Oxford: Clarendon, 1978) 78–87; reprinted in idem, *Studies,* 3:31–41.

Derrett, *Law*

J. Duncan M. Derrett, *Law in the New Testament* (London: Darton, Longman & Todd, 1970).

Derrett, *Studies*

J. Duncan M. Derrett, *Studies in the New Testament* (6 vols.; Leiden: Brill, 1977–95).

Descamps and de Halleux, *Mélanges*

Albert Descamps and André de Halleux, eds., *Mélanges bibliques: Festschrift Béda Rigaux* (Gembloux: Duculot, 1970).

Desreumaux, *Codex Sinaiticus*

Alain Desreumaux, *Codex sinaiticus Zosimi rescriptus: Description codicologique des feuillets araméenes melkites des manuscrits Schøyen 35, 36 et 37 (Londres-Oslo) com-prenant l'édition de nouveaux passages des Évangiles et des Évangiles et des Catéchèses de Cyrille* (Histoire du texte biblique 3; Studien zur Geschichte des biblischen Textes 3; Lausanne: Zebre, 1997).

Dewailly, "Pain"

Louis-Marie Dewailly, "'Donne-nous notre pain': quel pain? Notes sur la quatrième demande du Pater," *RSPhTh* 64 (1980) 561–88.

de Wette, *Kurze Erklärung*

Wilhelm Martin Leberecht de Wette, *Kurze Erklärung der Evangelien des Lukas und Markus* (KEHNT 1.2; Leipzig: Weidmannsche Buchhandlung, 1836).

de Wette, *Predigten*

Wilhelm Martin Leberecht de Wette, *Predigten, theils auslegender, theils abhandelnder Art. I–II* (Basel: Neukirch, 1825, 1827).

Dibelius, *Tradition*

Martin Dibelius, *From Tradition to Gospel* (trans. Bertram Lee Woolf; New York: Scribner,1965).

Dillon, *Eye-Witnesses*

Richard J. Dillon, *From Eye-Witnesses to Ministers of the Word: Tradition and Composition in Luke 24* (AnBib 82; Rome: Biblical Institute Press, 1978).

Dodd, *Parables*

C. H. Dodd, *The Parables of the Kingdom* (3d ed.; London: Nisbet, 1956).

Dollar, *Exploration*

Harold E. Dollar, *A Biblical-Missiological Exploration of the Cross-Cultural Dimensions in Luke-Acts* (San Francisco: Mellen Research University Press, 1993).

Dolto, *Psychanalyse*

Françoise Dolto and Gérard Séverin, *L'Évangile au risque de la psychanalyse* (2 vols.; Paris: Delarge, 1980, 1982).

Donahue, *Gospel in Parable*

John R. Donahue, *The Gospel in Parable: Metaphor, Narrative, and Theology in the Synoptic Gospels* (Philadelphia: Fortress Press, 1988).

Dormeyer, "Analyse"

Detlev Dormeyer, "Textpragmatische Analyse und Unterrichtsplanung zum Gleichnis vom verlorenen Schaf: Lk 15,1-7," *EvErz* 27 (1975) 347–57.

Dornisch, *Woman*

Loretta Dornisch, *A Woman Reads the Gospel of Luke* (Collegeville, Minn.: Liturgical Press, 1996).

Dupont, *Béatitudes*

Jacques Dupont, *Les Béatitudes* (3 vols.; Etudes bibliques; Bruges: Abbaye de Saint-Andre, 1958–73).

Dupont, *Christologie*

Jacques Dupont et al., eds., *Jésus aux origines de la christologie* (BETL 40; Leuven/Gembloux: Leuven University Press, 1975; 2d ed., 1989).

Dupont, *Études*

Jacques Dupont, *Études sur les Évangiles synoptiques* (ed. Frans Neirynck; 2 vols.; BETL 70; Leuven: Leuven University Press, 1985).

Dupont et al., *Parabola*
    Jacques Dupont et al., eds., *La Parabola degli invitati al banchetto: dagli evangelisti del Gesù* (Testi e ricerche di scienze religiose 14; Brescia: Paideia, 1978).

Dupont, *Pourquoi des paraboles*
    Jacques Dupont, *Pourquoi des paraboles? La méthode parabolique de Jésus* (LiBi 46; Paris: Cerf, 1977).

Dupont, "Rejouissez-vous"
    Jacques Dupont, "Réjouissez-vous avec moi! Lc 15,1-32," *AsSeign* 55 (1954) 70–79.

Dupont-Sommer and Philonenko, *Écrits intertestamentaires*
    André Dupont-Sommer and Marc Philonenko, eds., *Écrits intertestamentaires* (Bibliothèque de La Pléiade; Paris: Gallimard, 1987).

Easton
    Burton S. Easton, *The Gospel according to Luke* (New York: Scribner; Edinburgh: Clark, 1926).

Ebeling, *Evangelienauslegung*
    Gerhard Ebeling, *Evangelische Evangelienauslegung: Eine Untersuchung zu Luthers Hermeneutik* (3d ed.; Tübingen: Mohr Siebeck, 1991).

Eberle, *Luthers Evangelien-Auslegung*
    Christian Gustav Eberle, ed., *Luthers Evangelien-Auslegung: Ein Kommentar zu den vier Evangelien* (2d ed.; Stuttgart: Liesching 1877).

Eckhart, *Predigten*
    Meister Eckhart, *Predigten*, in Josef Quint, ed. and trans., *Meister Eckhart, Die deutschen und lateinischen Werke: Die deutschen Werke*, vols. 1–3 (Stuttgart: Kohlhammer, 1958–76).

Eckhart, *Sermones*
    Meister Eckhart, *Sermones*, in E. Benz et al., eds. and trans., *Meister Eckhart, Die deutschen und lateinischen Werke: Die lateinischen Werke*, vol. 4 (2d ed.; Stuttgart: Kohlhammer, 1987).

Eckhart, *Traktate*
    Meister Eckhart, *Traktate*, in Josef Quint, ed. and trans., *Meister Eckhart, Die deutschen und lateinischen Werke: Die deutschen Werke*, vol. 5 (Stuttgart: Kohlhammer, 1963).

Edwards, *Theology of Q*
    Richard A. Edwards, *A Theology of Q: Eschatology, Prophecy, and Wisdom* (Philadelphia: Fortress Press, 1976).

Egelkraut, *Mission*
    Helmuth L. Egelkraut, *Jesus' Mission to Jerusalem: A Redaction Critical Study of the Travel Narrative in the Gospel of Luke, Luke 9:51—19:48* (EHS 80; Frankfurt am Main: Peter Lang, 1976).

Eicholz, *Gleichnisse*
    Georg Eicholz, *Gleichnisse der Evangelien: Form, Überlieferung, Auslegung* (Neukirchen-Vluyn: Neukirchener Verlag, 1971).

Elliott, *Essays*
    James K. Elliott, *Essays and Studies in New Testament Textual Criticism* (EFN 3; Cordova: Almendro, 1992).

Ellis
    E. Earle Ellis, *Gospel of Luke* (2d ed.; New Century Bible; London: Oliphants, 1974; reprinted Grand Rapids: Eerdmans, 1981).

Ellis and Grässer, *Jesus und Paulus*
    E. Earle Ellis and Erich Grässer, eds., *Jesus und Paulus: Festschrift für Werner Georg Kümmel zum 70. Geburtstag* (Göttingen: Vandenhoeck & Ruprecht, 1975).

Eltester, *Judentum*
    Walther Eltester, ed., *Judentum, Urchristentum, Kirche: Festschrift Joachim Jeremias* (BZNW 26; Berlin: Töpelmann, 1960).

Ephrem de Nisibie, *Commentaire*
    Ephrem de Nisibie, *Commentaire de l'Évangile concordant ou Diatessaron. trans. from the Syriac and Armenien* (ed. and trans. Louis Leloir; SC 121; Paris: Cerf, 1966).

Ephrem the Syrian of Nisibis, *Commentary*
    Saint Ephrem's Commentary on Tatian's Diatessaron: An English Translation of Chester Beatty Syriac MS 709 with Introduction and Notes (ed. and trans. Carmel McCarthy; Journal of Semitic Studies, Supplement 2; Oxford: Published by Oxford University on behalf of the University of Manchester, 1993).

Epstein, *Babylonian Talmud*
    Isidore Epstein, ed., *The Babylonian Talmud (= The Soncino Talmud)* (18 vols.; London: Soncino, 1978).

Erasmus, *Paraphrasis*
    Desiderius Erasmus of Rotterdam, *Paraphrasis in N. Testamentum*, in P. Vander, ed., *Opera omnia*, vol. 7 (Leyden: Vander, 1706; facsimile reprint London: Gregg, 1962).

Erlemann, *Bild Gottes*
    Kurt Erlemann, *Das Bild Gottes in den synoptischen Gleichnissen* (BWANT; Stuttgart: Kohlhammer, 1988).

Ernst
    Josef Ernst, *Das Evangelium nach Lukas: Übersetzt und erklärt* (RNT 3; Regensburg: Pustet, 1977).

Esler, *Community and Gospel*
    Philip Francis Esler, *Community and Gospel in Luke-Acts: The Social and Political Motivations of Lucan Theology* (SNTSMS 57; New York/Cambridge: Cambridge University Press, 1987).

Euthymius, *Commentarius*
    Euthymius Zigabenus, *Commentarius in quatuor Evangelia: Evangelium secundum Lucam* (ed. Christian Friedrich von Matthäi; Leipzig: Weidmann, 1792; reprinted *PG* 129; Paris: Migne, 1898) 853–1102.

Evans, *Luke*
    Craig A. Evans, *Luke* (NIBCNT 3; Peabody, Mass.: Hendrickson, 1990).

Evans, *Saint Luke*
    Christopher F. Evans, *Saint Luke* (TPI New Testament Commentaries; London/Philadelphia: Trinity Press International, 1990).

Evans and Sanders, *Luke and Scripture*
    Craig A. Evans and James A. Sanders, *Luke and Scripture: The Function of Sacred Tradition in Luke-Acts* (Minneapolis: Fortress Press, 1993).

Evans and Stegner, *Gospels and Scriptures*
Craig A. Evans and W. Richard Stegner, *The Gospels and the Scriptures of Israel* (JSNTSup 104; Sheffield: Sheffield Academic Press, 1994).

Fallon and Cameron, "Gospel of Thomas"
Francis T. Fallon and Ron Cameron, "The Gospel of Thomas: A Forschungsbericht and Analysis," *ANRW* 2.25.6 (1988) 4195–251.

Feiler, "Jesus the Prophet"
P. W. Feiler, "Jesus the Prophet: The Lucan Portrayal of Jesus as the Prophet like Moses" (diss., Princeton Theological Seminary, 1986).

Feld and Nolte, *Wort Gottes*
Helmut Feld and Josef Nolte, eds., *Wort Gottes in der Zeit: Festschrift Karl H. Schelkle* (Düsseldorf: Patmos, 1973).

Fiedler, *Sünder*
Peter Fiedler, *Jesus und die Sünder* (Beiträge zur biblischen Exegese und Theologie 3; Frankfurt am Main: Peter Lang, 1976).

Fieger, *Thomasevangelium*
Michael Fieger, *Das Thomasevangelium: Einleitung, Kommentar und Systematik* (NTAbh 22; Münster: Aschendorff, 1991).

Finkel, *Pharisees*
Asher Finkel, *The Pharisees and the Teacher of Nazareth: A Study of Their Background, Their Halachic and Midrashic Teachings, the Similarities and Differences* (2d ed.; AGSU 4; Leiden: Brill, 1974).

Finnell, "Significance"
B. S. Finnell, "The Significance of the Passion in Luke" (diss., Baylor University, 1983).

Fischer, *Lateinischen Evangelien*
Bonifatius Fischer, *Die lateinischen Evangelien bis zum 10. Jahrhundert,* vol. 3: *Varianten zu Lukas* (Aus der Geschichte der lateinischen Bibel 7; Freiburg im B.: Herder, 1990).

Fitzmyer
Joseph A. Fitzmyer, *The Gospel according to Luke: Introduction, Translation, and Notes* (2 vols.; AB 28–28A; Garden City, N.Y.: Doubleday, 1981, 1985).

Fitzmyer, *"Abba"*
Joseph A. Fitzmyer, "Abba and Jesus' Relation to God," in *À cause de l'Évangile: Études sur les Synoptiques et les Actes offertes au P[ère] Jacques Dupont, O.S.B., à l'occasion de son 70e anniversaire* (LD 123; Paris: Publications de Saint-André/Cerf, 1985) 15–38.

Fitzmyer, *Luke the Theologian*
Joseph A. Fitzmyer, *Luke the Theologian: Aspects of His Teaching* (New York: Paulist, 1989).

Flender, *Heil*
Helmut Flender, *Heil und Geschichte in der Theologie des Lukas* (BEvTh 41; Munich: Kaiser, 1965).

Flusser, *Wesen der Gleichnisse*
David Flusser, *Die rabbinischen Gleichnisse und der Gleichniserzähler Jesus,* vol. 1: *Das Wesen der Gleichnisse* (Judaica et Christiana 4; Bern/Frankfurt/Las Vegas: Lang, 1981).

Föhn, "Essay"
F. Föhn, "Ein exegetischer Essay zu Martha und Mirjam: Herrschaft hat u. hält (auch) die Schwestern getrennt," *Neue Wege* 83, nos. 7–8 (1989) 208–14.

Fonck, *Parabeln*
Leopold Fonck, *Die Parabeln des Herrn im Evangelium: exegetisch und praktisch erläutert* (Innsbruck: Druck und Verlag [Karl Pustet], 1905).

Ford, *My Guest*
Josephine Massyngberde Ford, *My Enemy Is My Guest: Jesus and Violence in Luke* (Maryknoll, N.Y.: Orbis Books, 1984).

France, *Gospel Perspectives*
R. T. France et al., eds. *Gospel Perspectives* (6 vols.; Sheffield: JSOT Press, 1980–86).

Francis, *Subversive Virtue*
James A. Francis, *Subversive Virtue: Asceticism and Authority in the Second-Century Pagan World* (University Park, Pa.: Pennsylvania State University Press, 1995).

Francis of Assisi, *Écrits*
Francis of Assisi, *Écrits* (ed. and trans. Théophile Desbonnets et al.; SC 285; Paris: Cerf, 1981; reprinted with additions and corrections, 2003).

Franklin, *Interpreter*
Eric Franklin, *Luke: Interpreter of Paul, Critic of Matthew* (JSNTSup 92; Sheffield: JSOT Press, 1994).

Freedman and Simon, *Midrash Rabbah*
Harry Freedman and Maurice Simon, eds., *Midrash Rabbah* (3d ed.; 10 vols.; London/New York: Soncino, 1983).

French, "Roman Roads"
David French, "Acts and the Roman Roads of Asia Minor," in Bruce W. Winter, ed., *The Book of Acts in Its First Century Setting,* vol. 2: *The Book of Acts in Its Graeco-Roman Setting* (ed. David W. J. Gill and Conrad Gempf; Grand Rapids: Eerdmans, 1994) 49–58.

Friedrich, *Rechtfertigung*
Johannes Friedrich et al., eds., *Rechtfertigung: Festschrift Ernst Käsemann* (Tübingen: Mohr; Göttingen: Vandenhoeck & Ruprecht, 1976).

Funk, *Five Gospels*
Robert W. Funk, R. W. Hoover, and the Jesus Seminar, eds., *The Five Gospels: The Search for the Authentic Words of Jesus: New Translation and Commentary* (New York: Macmillan, 1993).

Funk, *Language*
Robert W. Funk, *Language, Hermeneutic, and Word of God: The Problem of Language in the New Testament and Contemporary Theology* (New York: Harper & Row, 1966).

Funk, *Precursor*
Robert W. Funk, *Jesus as Precursor* (SSup; Philadelphia: Fortress Press, 1975).

Gander

Georges Gander, *L'Évangile pour les étrangers du monde: Commentaire de l'Évangile selon Luc* (Lausanne: 1986).

Garrett, *Demise*

Susan R. Garrett, *The Demise of the Devil: Magic and the Demonic in Luke's Writings* (Minneapolis: Fortress Press, 1989).

Geerard, *Clavis Patrum*

Maurice Geerard, *Clavis Patrum Graecorum* (5 vols.; CC; Turnhout: Brepols, 1974–87).

Gerhardsson, "Good Samaritan"

B. Gerhardsson, "The Good Samaritan—The Good Shepherd?" *Coniectanea neotestamentica* 16 (1958) 1–31.

Giblin, *Destruction*

Charles H. Giblin, *The Destruction of Jerusalem according to Luke's Gospel: A Historical-Typological Moral* (AnBib l07; Rome: Biblical Institute Press, 1985).

Ginzberg, *Legends*

Louis Ginzberg, *Legends of the Jews* (trans. Henrietta Szold et al.; 7 vols.; Philadelphia: Jewish Publication Society, 1909–69).

Glöckner, *Neutestamentliche Wundergeschichten*

Richard Glöckner, *Neutestamentliche Wundergeschichten und das Lob der Wundertaten Gottes in den Psalmen: Studien zur sprachlichen und theologischen Verwandschaft zwischen neutestamentlichen Wundergeschichten und Psalmen* (WSAMA.T 13; Mainz: Matthias-Grünewald, 1983).

Godet

Frédéric Louis Godet, *A Commentary on the Gospel of St. Luke* (trans. E. W. Shalders and M. D. Cusin from the 2d French ed., 1871; 4th Eng. ed.; 2 vols.; Clark's Foreign Theological Library 45–46; Edinburgh: Clark, 1881, 1890).

Godet, *Commentaire*

Frédéric Louis Godet, *Commentaire sur L'Évangile de Saint Luc* (3d ed.; 2 vols.; Paris: Librairie Fischbacher, 1888, 1889; reprinted as "4th ed." Neuchâtel: Monnier, 1969).

Goergen, *Mission and Ministry*

Donald J. Georgen, *The Mission and Ministry of Jesus* (Theology of Jesus 1; Wilmington, Del.: Glazier, 1986).

Goodenough, *Jewish Symbols*

Erwin R. Goodenough, *Jewish Symbols in the Greco-Roman Period* (13 vols.; New York: Pantheon; Princeton: Princeton University Press, 1953–68).

Gooding

David Willoughby Gooding, *According to Luke: A New Exposition of the Third Gospel* (Grand Rapids: Eerdmans, 1987).

Goppelt, *Theologie*

Leonhard Goppelt, *Theologie des Neuen Testaments* (Göttinger theologischer Lehrbücher; Göttingen: Vandenhoeck & Ruprecht, 1975–).

Gospel according to St. Luke. See New Testament in Greek

Goulder, *New Paradigm*

Michael D. Goulder, *Luke: A New Paradigm* (2 vols.; JSNTSup 20; Sheffield: JSOT Press, 1989).

Gourgues, *Paraboles*

Michel Gourgues, *Les Paraboles de Luc: D'amont en aval* (Sciences bibliques; Montreal: Médias Paul, 1997).

Grangaard, *Conflict*

Blake R. Grangaard, *Conflict and Authority in Luke 19:47 to 21:4* (Studies in Biblical Literature 8; New York: Lang, 1999).

Grässer, *Problem*

Erich Grässer, *Das Problem der Parusieverzögerung in den synoptischen Evangelien und in der Apostelgeschichte* (BZNW 22; Berlin: Töpelmann, 1957).

Graumann, *Christus Interpres*

Thomas Graumann, *Christus Interpres: Die Einheit von Auslegung und Verkündigung in der Lukaserklärung des Ambrosius von Mailand* (Patristische Texte und Studien 41; Berlin/New York: de Gruyter, 1994).

Green

Joel B. Green, *The Gospel of Luke* (NICNT; Grand Rapids: Eerdmans, 1997).

Green, *Theology*

Joel B. Green, *The Theology of the Gospel of Luke* (New Testament Theology; Cambridge/New York: Cambridge University Press, 1995).

Green and McKeever, *Historiography*

Joel B. Green and Michael C. McKeever, *Luke-Acts and New Testament Historiography* (IBR Bibliographies 8; Grand Rapids: Baker, 1994).

Grelot "Quatrième"

Pierre Grelot, "La quatrième demande du 'Pater' et son arrière-plan semitique," *NTS* 25 (1978–79) 299–314.

Grimm, *Jesu Einspruch*

Werner Grimm, *Jesus und das Danielbuch*, vol. 1: *Jesu Einspruch gegen das Offenbarungs-system Daniels: Mt 11,25-27; Lk 17,20-21* (ANTJ 6; Frankfurt am Main/New York: Lang, 1984).

Grimm, "Selige Augenzeugen"

Werner Grimm, "Selige Augenzeugen, Lk 10, 23f: Alttestamentlicher Hintergrund und ursprunglicher Sinn," *ThZ 26* (1970) 172–83.

Grotius, *Annotationes*

Hugo Grotius, *Annotationes in Novum Testamentum, editio nova*, vol. 1: *Quatuor Evangelia et explicationem Decalogi continens* (ed. Christian Ernst von Windheim; Leipzig: Ioannem Carolum Tetzschnerum, 1755).

Groupe d'Entrevernes, *Signs*

Groupe d'Entrevernes, *Signs and Parables: Semiotics and Gospel Texts* (trans. G. Phillips; Pittsburgh: Pickwick, 1978).

Grundmann

Walter Grundmann, *Das Evangelium nach Lukas* (2d ed.; ThHKNT 3; Berlin: Evangelische Verlagsanstalt, 1961).

Grundmann, *Markus*
Walter Grundmann, *Das Evangelium nach Markus* (ThHKNT 2; Berlin: Evangelische Verlagsanstalt, 1965).

Haenchen, *Weg Jesu*
Ernst Haenchen, *Der Weg Jesu: Eine Erklärung des Markus-Evangeliums und der kanonischen Parallelen* (2d ed.; de Gruyter Lehrbuch; Berlin: de Gruyter, 1968).

Hahn, *Hoheitstitel*
Ferdinand Hahn, *Christologische Hoheitstitel: Ihre Geschichte im frühen Christentum* (FRLANT 83; Göttingen: Vandenhoeck & Ruprecht, 1963).

Hahn, *Mission*
Ferdinand Hahn, *Mission in the New Testament* (trans. Frank Clarke; SBT 47; Naperville, Ill.: Allenson, 1965).

Hamann, *Tagebuch*
Johann Georg Hamann, *Sämtliche Werke: Historisch-kritische Ausgabe,* vol. 1: *Tagebuch eines Christen* (ed. Josef Nadler; Vienna: Herder, 1949).

Hamm, *Beatitudes*
Dennis Hamm, *The Beatitudes in Context: What Luke and Matthew Meant* (Wilmington, Del.: Glazier, 1990).

Hamman, "Notre Père"
Adalbert-Gauthier Hamman, "Le Notre Père dans la catéchèse des Pères de l'Église, *La Maison-Dieu* 85 (1966) 41–68.

Hammer, *Interpreting Luke-Acts*
Paul L. Hammer, *Interpreting Luke-Acts for the Local Church: Luke Speaks for Himself* (Lewiston, N.Y.: Mellen, 1994).

Hammond, *Paraphrase and Annotations*
Henry Hammond, *A Paraphrase and Annotations upon All the Books of the New Testament* (2d ed.; London: J. Flesher for R. Davis, 1659).

Hampel, *Menschensohn*
Volker Hampel, *Menschensohn und historischer Jesus: Ein Rätselwort als Schlüssel zum messianischen Selbstverständnis Jesu* (Neukirchen-Vluyn: Neukirchener Verlag, 1990).

Harnack, *Marcion*
Adolf Harnack, *Marcion: The Gospel of the Alien God* (trans. J. E. Steely and L. D. Bierma; Durham, N.C.: Labyrinth, 1990). German: *Marcion: Das Evangelium von fremden Gott. Eine Monographie zur Geschichte der Grundlegung der katholischen Kirche* (TUGAL 45; Leipzig: Hinrichs, 1921).

Harnisch, *Gleichniserzählungen Jesu*
Wolfgang Harnisch, *Gleichniserzählungen Jesu: Eine hermeneutische Einführung* (Göttingen: Vandenhoeck & Ruprecht, 1985).

Hatch and Redpath, *Concordance*
Edwin Hatch and Henry A. Redpath, *A Concordance to the Septuagint and the Other Greek Versions of the Old Testament (Including the Apocryphal Books)* (3 vols.; Oxford: Clarendon, 1897–1906).

Haubeck and Bachmann, *Wort*
Wilfrid Haubeck and Michael Bachmann, eds., *Wort in der Zeit: Neutestamentliche Studien: Festgabe für Karl Heinrich Rengstorf zum 75. Geburtstag* (Leiden: Brill, 1980).

Havener, *Q: The Sayings*
Ivan Havener, *Q: The Sayings of Jesus (With a Reconstruction of Q by Athanasius Polag)* (2d ed.; Good News Studies 19; Wilmington, Del.: Glazier, 1987).

Heininger, *Metaphorik*
Bernhard Heininger, *Metaphorik, Erzählstruktur und szenisch-dramatische Gestaltung in den Sondergleichnissen bei Lukas* (NTAbh n.s. 24; Münster: Aschendorff, 1991).

Heintz, *Simon "le magicien"*
Florent Heintz, *Simon "le magicien": Actes 8,5-25 et l'accusation de magie contre les prophètes thaumaturges dans l'Antiquité* (CRB 39; Paris: Gabalda, 1997).

Hemer, *Hellenistic History*
Colin J. Hemer, *The Book of Acts in the Setting of Hellenistic History* (ed. Conrad Gempf; WUNT 49; Tübingen: Siebeck, 1989).

Hendriks, *Karakteristiek woordgebruik*
W. M. A. Hendriks, *Karakteristiek woordgebruik in de synoptische Evangelies* (3 vols.; Nijmegen, 1986).

Hengel, *Charismatic Leader*
Hengel, Martin, *The Charismatic Leader and His Followers* (trans. James Greig; New York: Crossroad, 1981).

Hengel, *Zealots*
Martin Hengel, *The Zealots: Investigations into the Jewish Freedom Movement in the Period from Herod I until 70 A.D.* (trans. David Smith; Edinburgh: Clark, 1989).

Hermaniuk, *Parabole évangélique*
Maxime Hermaniuk, *La parabole évangélique: Enquête exégétique et critique* (Dissertationes ad gradum magistri in Facultate Theologica consequendum conscriptae 2.38; Paris/Louvain: Desclée, 1947).

Herrenbrück, *Zöllner*
Fritz Herrenbrück, *Jesus und die Zöllner: Historische und neutestamentlich- exegetische Untersuchungen* (WUNT 2/41; Tübingen: Mohr Siebeck, 1990).

Hirsch, *Vorlagen*
Emanuel Hirsch, *Frühgeschichte des Evangeliums,* vol. 2: *Die Vorlagen des Lukas und das Sondergut des Matthäus* (Tübingen: Mohr Siebeck, 1941).

Hoffmann, *Logienquelle*
Paul Hoffmann, *Studien zur Theologie der Logienquelle* (NTAbh n.s. 8; Münster: Aschendorff, 1972).

Hoffmann, *Orientierung*
Paul Hoffmann et al., eds., *Orientierung an Jesus: Zur Theologie der Synoptiker: Festschrift Josef Schmid* (Freiburg im Breisgau: Herder, 1973).

Hoover, "Sayings"
Roy W. Hoover, "Sayings from Q, Parables Round Two," *Forum* 4 (1988) 109–28.

Horn, *Glaube und Handeln*
Friedrich W. Horn, *Glaube und Handeln in der Theologie des Lukas* (1983; 2d ed.; GThA 26; Göttingen: Vandenhoeck & Ruprecht, 1986). Cited after the first edition in 1983.

Houssiau, "L'exégèse"
Albert Houssiau, "L'exégèse de Matthieu 11, 27b selon saint Irénée," *EThL* 29 (1953) 328–54.

Iersel, *Parabelverhalen*
Bastiaan M. F. van Iersel et al., *Parabelverhalen in Lucas: Van semiotiek naar pragmatiek* (Tilburg, Netherlands: Tilburg University Press, 1987).

Iwand, *Gegenwart*
Hans J. Iwand, *Die Gegenwart des Kommenden: Eine Auslegung von Lukas 12* (2d ed.; BibS[N] 50; Neukirchen-Vluyn: Neukirchener Verlag, 1966).

Jacobson, *First Gospel*
Arland D. Jacobson, *The First Gospel: An Introduction to Q* (FF; Sonoma, Calif.: Polebridge, 1992).

Jacques, *Index*
Xavier Jacques, *Index des mots apparentés dans le Nouveau Testament: Complément des concordances et dictionnaires* (Rome: Biblical Institute Press, 1969).

James, "Elijah/Elisha"
D. R. James, "The Elijah/Elisha Motif in Luke" (diss., Southern Baptist Theological Seminary, 1984).

Jeremias, *Lord's Prayer*
Joachim Jeremias, *The Lord's Prayer* (FBBS 8; Philadelphia: Fortress Press, 1964).

Jeremias, *Parables*
Joachim Jeremias, *The Parables of Jesus* (trans. Samuel Henry Hooke; London: SCM, 1954; 2d rev. ed.; London: SCM; New York: Scribner, 1972).

Jeremias, *Proclamation*
Joachim Jeremias, *New Testament Theology*, vol. 1: *The Proclamation of Jesus* (trans. John Bowden; London: SCM, 1971).

Jeremias, *Sprache*
Joachim Jeremias, *Die Sprache des Lukasevangeliums: Redaktion und Tradition im Nicht-Markusstoff des dritten Evangeliums* (KEKSup; Göttingen: Vandenhoeck & Ruprecht, 1980).

Jeremias, "Tradition,"
Joachim Jeremias, "Tradition und Redaktion in Lk 15," *ZNW* 62 (1971) 172–89.

Jeremias, *Unknown Sayings*
Joachim Jeremias, *The Unknown Sayings of Jesus* (trans. Reginald Fuller; London: SPCK, 1957).

Johnson, *Gospel of Luke*
Luke Timothy Johnson, *The Gospel of Luke* (SP 3; Collegeville, Minn.: Liturgical Press, 1991).

Johnson, *Possessions*
Luke T. Johnson, *The Literary Function of Possessions in Luke-Acts* (SBLDS 39; Missoula, Mont.: Scholars Press, 1977).

Jülicher, *Gleichnisreden*
Adolf Julicher, *Die Gleichnisreden Jesu*, vol. 1: *Die Gleichnisreden im Allgemeinen* (2d ed.; Tübingen:

Mohr Siebeck, 1899); vol. 2: *Auslegung der Gleichnisreden der drei ersten Evangelien* (Tübingen: Mohr Siebeck, 1899).

Kaegi, *Grammar*
Adolf Kaegi, *Kaegi's Greek Grammar: With Tables for Repetition* (trans. J. A. Kleist; 21st ed.; Wauconda, Ill.: Bolchazy-Carducci, 1995).

Kaestli, *L'eschatologie*
Jean-Daniel Kaestli, *L'eschatologie dans l'œuvre de Luc: ses caractéristiques et sa place dans le développement du christianisme primitif* (Nouvelle série théologique 22; Geneva: Labor et Fides, 1969).

Kahlefeld, *Parables*
Heinrich Kahlefeld, *Parables and Instructions in the Gospels* (trans. A. Swidler; New York: Herder & Herder, 1966).

Kahlefeld, *Paraboles*
Heinrich Kahlefeld, *Paraboles et leçons dans l'evangile* (2 vols.; LD 55, 56; Paris: Cerf, 1969).

Karris, *Luke*
Robert Karris, *Luke, Artist and Theologian: Luke's Passion Narrative as Literature* (New York: Paulist, 1985).

Käsemann, *Exegetische Versuche*
Ernst Käsemann, *Exegetische Versuche und Besinnungen* (2d ed.; 2 vols.; Göttingen: Vandenhoeck & Ruprecht, 1960, 1964).

Kee, *Models of Community*
Howard C. Kee, *Who Are the People of God? Early Christian Models of Community* (New Haven: Yale University Press, 1997).

Kertelge, *Tod Jesu*
Karl Kertelge, ed., *Der Tod Jesu: Deutungen im Neuen Testament* (QD 74; Freiburg im B.: Herder, 1976).

Kettenbach, *Logbuch*
Günter Kettenbach, *Das Logbuch des Lukas: Das antike Schiff in Fahrt und vor Anker* (2d ed.; EHS 276; Frankfurt am Main: Lang, 1997).

Kilgallen, *Brief Commentary*
John J. Kilgallen, *A Brief Commentary on the Gospel of Luke* (New York: Paulist, 1988).

Kim, *Stewardship*
Kyoung-Jin Kim, *Stewardship and Almsgiving in Luke's Theology* (JSNTSup 155; Sheffield: Sheffield Academic Press, 1998).

Kimball, *Jesus' Exposition*
Charles A. Kimball, *Jesus' Exposition of the Old Testament in Luke's Gospel* (JSNTSup 94; Sheffield: JSOT Press, 1994).

Kingsbury, *Conflict*
Jack Dean Kingsbury, *Conflict in Luke: Jesus, Authorities, Disciples* (Minneapolis: Fortress Press, 1991).

Kirchschläger, *Wirken*
Walter Kirchschläger, *Jesu exorzistisches Wirken aus der Sicht des Lukas: Ein Beitrag zur lukanischen Redaktion* (ÖBSt 3; Klosterneuburg: Österreichisches Katholisches Bibelwerk, 1981).

Kirschbaum, *Lexikon*
Engelbert Kirschbaum et al., eds., *Lexikon der christlichen Ikonographie* (8 vols.; Rome/Freiburg im B.: Herder, 1968–76).

Kissinger, *Parables*
Warren S. Kissinger, *The Parables of Jesus: A History of Interpretation and Bibliography* (ATLA.BS 4; Metuchen, N.J.: Scarecrow Press, 1979).

Klein, *Barmherzigkeit*
Hans Klein, *Barmherzigkeit gegenüber den Elenden und Geächteten: Stüdien zur Botschaft des lukanischen Sondergutes* (BThSt 10; Neukirchen-Vluyn: Neukirchener Verlag, 1987).

Kleine Pauly
Der kleine Pauly: Lexikon der Antike (5 vols.; Munich: Deutsche Taschenbuch Verlag, 1979).

Klemm, *Samariter*
Hans Gunther Klemm, *Das Gleichnis vom barmherzigen Samariter: Grundzüge der Auslegung im 16./17. Jahrhundert* (BWANT 103; Stuttgart: Kohlhammer, 1973).

Klinghardt, *Gesetz*
Matthias Klinghardt, *Gesetz und Volk Gottes: Das lukanische Verständnis des Gesetzes nach Herkunft, Funktion und seinem Ort in der Geschichte des Urchristentums* (WUNT 2/32; Tübingen: Mohr Siebeck, 1988).

Klingsporn, "Law"
Gary W. Klingsporn, "The Law in the Gospel of Luke" (diss., Baylor University, 1985).

Kloppenborg, *Formation*
John S. Kloppenborg, *The Formation of Q: Trajectories in Ancient Wisdom Collections* (Studies in Antiquity and Christianity 2; Philadelphia: Fortress Press, 1987).

Kloppenborg, *Q Parallels*
John S. Kloppenborg, *Q Parallels: Synopsis, Critical Notes and Concordance* (Sonoma, Calif.: Polebridge, 1988).

Klostermann
Erich Klostermann, *Das Lukasevangelium: Erklärt* (2d ed.; HBT 5; Tübingen: Mohr Siebeck, 1929; reprinted 1975).

Klostermann, *Matthäusevangelium*
Erich Klostermann, *Das Matthäusevangelium: Erklärt* (HNT 4; Tübingen: Mohr, 1927).

Knox, *Sources*
Wilfred L. Knox, *The Sources of the Synoptic Gospels* (ed. H. Chadwick; 2 vols.; Cambridge: Cambridge University Press, 1953, 1957).

Koester, *Ancient Christian Gospels*
Helmut Koester, *Ancient Christian Gospels: Their History and Development* (Philadelphia: Trinity Press International, 1990).

Koester, *Synoptische Überlieferung*
Helmut Koester, *Synoptische Überlieferung bei den apostolischen Vätern* (TUGAL 65; Berlin: Akademie-Verlag, 1957).

Koester and Robinson, *Trajectories*
Helmut Koester and James M. Robinson, *Trajectories through Early Christianity* (Philadelphia: Fortress Press, 1971).

Koet, *Five Studies*
B. J. Koet, *Five Studies on Interpretation of Scripture in Luke-Acts* (Studiorum Novi Testamenti auxilia 14; Leuven: Leuven University Press/Peeters, 1989).

Kremer, *Lukasevangelium*
Jacob Kremer, *Lukasevangelium* (NEchtBNT 3; Würzburg: Echter, 1988).

Krüger, *Gott oder Mammon*
René Krüger, *Gott oder Mammon: Das Lukasevangelium und die Ökonomie* (Lucerne: Exodus, 1997).

Kuhn, *Achtzehngebet*
Karl Georg Kuhn, *Achtzehngebet und Vaterunser und der Reim* (WUNT 1; Tübingen: Mohr Siebeck, 1950).

Kühschelm, *Jüngerverfolgung*
R. Kühschelm, *Jüngerverfolgung und Geschick Jesu: Eine exegetisch-bibeltheologische Untersuchung der synoptischen Verfolgungsankündigungen Mk 31,9-13 par und Mt 23,29-36 par.* (Klosterneuburg: Österreichisches Katholisches Bibelwerk, 1983).

Kümmel, *Heilsgeschehen*
Werner Georg Kümmel, *Heilsgeschehen und Geschichte: Gesammelte Aufsätze* (ed. Erich Grässer et al.; 2 vols.; Marburger theologische Studien 3,16; Marburg: Elwert, 1965, 1978).

Kümmel, *Promise*
Werner Georg Kümmel, *Promise and Fulfilment: The Eschatological Message of Jesus* (2d ed.; SBT 23; London: SCM, 1961).

Kurz, *Reading Luke-Acts*
William S. Kurz, *Reading Luke-Acts: Dynamics of Biblical Narrative* (Louisville: Westminster John Knox, 1993).

Kuss, *Auslegung*
Otto Kuss, *Auslegung und Verkündigung: Aufsätze zur Exegese des Neuen Testaments* (3 vols.; Regensburg: Pustet, 1963–71).

Lachs, *Rabbinic Commentary*
Samuel Tobias Lachs, *Rabbinic Commentary of the New Testament: The Gospels of Matthew, Mark, and Luke* (Hoboken, N.J.: Ktav; New York: Anti-Defamation League of B'nai B'rith, 1987).

Lagrange
Marie-Joseph Lagrange, *Évangile selon saint Luc* (4th ed.; EtB; Paris: Gabalda, 1927).

Laland, "Martha-Maria"
E. Laland, "Die Martha-Maria Perikope Lukas 10, 38-42," *StTh* 13 (1959) 70–85.

Lambert, *In divi Lucae*
François Lambert d'Avignon, *In divi Lucae Evangelium commentarii* (Strasbourg: Johann Herwagen l'ancien, 1524).

Lambrecht, *"Eh bien!"*
Jan Lambrecht, *"Eh bien! Moi, je vous dis": Le discours-programme de Jésus (Mt 5–7; Lc 6,20-49)* (LD 125; Paris: Cerf, 1986).

Lambrecht, *Once More Astonished*
Jan Lambrecht, *Once More Astonished: The Parables of Jesus* (New York: Crossroad, 1981).

Lamsa, *Eastern Text*
George M. Lamsa, ed., *The New Testament according to the Eastern Text, Translated from the Original Aramaic Sources* (Philadelphia: Holman, 1940).

Lane, *Gentile Mission*
Thomas J. Lane, *Luke and the Gentile Mission: Gospel Anticipates Acts* (New York: Lang, 1996).

Laufen, *Doppelüberlieferungen*
Rudolf Laufen, *Die Doppelüberlieferungen der Logienquelle und des Markusevangeliums* (BBB 54; Bonn: Hanstein, 1980).

Leaney, *St. Luke*
Albert Robert Clare Leaney, *A Commentary on the Gospel according to St. Luke* (HNTC; New York/London: Harper, 1958).

Lee, *Luke's Stories*
David Lee, *Luke's Stories of Jesus: Theological Readings of Gospel Narrative and the Legacy of Hans Frei* (JSNTSup 185; Sheffield: Sheffield Academic Press, 1999).

Lehmann, *Quellenanalyse*
Martin Lehmann, *Synoptische Quellenanalyse und die Frage nach dem historischen Jesus: Kriterien der Jesusforschung untersucht in Auseinandersetzung mit Emmanuel Hirschs Frühgeschichte des Evangeliums* (BZNW 38; Berlin: de Gruyter, 1970).

Lehnert, *Provokation Israels*
Volker A. Lehnert, *Die Provokation Israels: Die paradoxe Funktion von Jes 6,9-10 bei Markus und Lukas: Ein textpragmatischer Versuch im Kontext gegenwärtiger Rezeptionsästhetik und Lesetheorie* (Neukirchen-Vluyn: Neukirchener Verlag, 1999).

Lémonon, *Pilate*
Jean-Pierre Lémonon, *Pilate et le gouvernement de la Judée: textes et monuments* (Paris: Gabalda, 1981).

Leonardi, "Cercate"
Giovanni Leonardi, "'Cercate e troverete . . . lo Spirito Santo' nell'unità letteraria di Luca 11, 1-13," in Antonio Bonora et al., eds., *Quaerere Deum* (Atti della Settimana Biblica 25; Brescia: Paideia, 1980) 261–88.

Léon-Dufour, *Life and Death*
Xavier Léon-Dufour, *Life and Death in the New Testament: The Teachings of Jesus and Paul* (San Francisco: Harper & Row, 1986).

L'Eplattenier
Charles L'Eplattenier, *Lecture de l'évangile de Luc* (Paris: Desclée, 1982).

Lightfoot, *Commentary*
John Lightfoot, *A Commentary on the New Testament from the Talmud and Hebraica* (4 vols.; Peabody, Mass.: Hendrickson, 1997); a translation of *Horae*

Hebraicae et Talmudicae in quatuor evangelistas cum tractatibus chorographicis, singulis suo evangelistae praemissis (Leipzig: Fridericus Lanckisius, Johannis Colerus, 1675).

Linnemann, *Parables*
Eta Linnemann, *Parables of Jesus: Introduction and Exposition* (trans. John Sturdy; London: SPCK, 1966).

Lipen, *Bibliotheca*
Martin Lipen, *Bibliotheca realis theologica omnium materiarum rerum et titulorum cum indice autorum copiosissimo*, vol. 2 (Frankfurt: Joannis Friderici, 1685) 196–98 (a catalogue of various commentaries on the *Gospel of Luke*).

Lips, *Weisheitliche Traditionen*
Hermann von Lips, *Weisheitliche Traditionen im Neuen Testament* (WMANT 64; Neukirchen-Vluyn: Neukirchener Verlag, 1990).

Loewenich, *Luther*
Walther von Loewenich, *Luther als Ausleger der Synoptiker* (Forschungen zur Geschichte und Lehre des Protestantismus 5; Munich: Kaiser, 1954).

Lohse, *Einheit*
Eduard Lohse, *Die Einheit des Neuen Testaments: Exegetische Studien zur Theologie des Neuen Testaments* (Göttingen: Vandenhoeck & Ruprecht, 1973).

Lohse, *Ruf Jesu*
Eduard Lohse et al., eds., *Der Ruf Jesu und die Antwort der Gemeinde: Exeget. Untersuchungen Joachim Jeremias z. 70. Geburtstag gewidmet von seinen Schülern* (Göttingen: Vandenhoeck & Ruprecht, 1970).

Loisy
Alfred Loisy, *L'Évangile selon Luc* (Paris: Émile Nourry, 1924; reprinted Frankfurt am Main: 1971).

Loos, *Miracles*
Hendrik van der Loos, *The Miracles of Jesus* (trans. T. S. Preston; NovTSup 9; Leiden: Brill, 1965).

Lührmann, *Logienquelle*
Dieter Lührmann, *Die Redaktion der Logienquelle. Anhang: Zur weiteren Überlieferung der Logienquelle* (WMANT 33; Neukirchen-Vluyn: Neukirchener Verlag, 1969).

Luz, *Matthew*
Ulrich Luz, *Matthew: A Commentary* (trans. James E. Crouch; 3 vols.; Hermeneia; Minneapolis: Fortress Press, 2001–7).

Lyon, *Syriac Gospel*
Jeffrey Paul Lyon, *Syriac Gospel Translations: A Comparison of the Language and Translation Method Used in the Old Syriac, the Diatessaron, and the Peshitto* (CSCO 548, Subsidia 88; Leuven: Peeters, 1994).

Mack and Robbins, *Patterns*
Burton L. Mack and Vernon K. Robbins, *Patterns of Persuasion in the Gospels* (Sonoma, Calif.: Polebridge, 1989).

Malbon and McKnight, *New Literary Criticism*
Elizabeth Struthers Malbon and Edgar V. McKnight, eds., *The New Literary Criticism and the New Testament* (JSNTSup 109; Sheffield: Sheffield Academic Press, 1994).

Maldonado, *Comm. in quat.*
  Juan [de] Maldonado, *Commentarii in quatuor evangelistas*, vol. 2: *In Lucam* (Pont-à-Mousson: ex typographia Stephani Mercatoris, 1597; reprinted as vols. 3–4, Paris/Louvain, 1842–43), cited from the 1842–43 edition.

Maloney, *All That God*
  Linda M. Maloney, *All That God Had Done with Them: The Narration of the Works of God in the Early Christian Community as Described in the Acts of the Apostles* (American University Studies Theology and Religion Series 91; New York: Lang, 1991).

Mánek, *Gleichnisse*
  Jindřich Mánek, *. . . und brachte Frucht: die Gleichnisse Jesu* (Stuttgart: Calwer Verlag, 1977).

Manson, *Sayings*
  Thomas W. Manson, *The Sayings of Jesus: As Recorded in the Gospels according to St. Matthew and St. Luke* (London: SCM, 1949).

Manson, *Teaching*
  Thomas W. Manson, *The Teaching of Jesus: Studies of Its Form and Content* (2d ed.; Cambridge: Cambridge University Press, 1935; reprinted 1963).

Marconi and O'Collins, *Luke and Acts*
  Gilberto Marconi and Gerald O'Collins, eds., *Luke and Acts* (trans. Matthew J. O'Connell; New York: Paulist, 1993).

Marguerat, *Jugement*
  Daniel Marguerat, *Le jugement dans l'Évangile de Matthieu* (MB 6; Geneva: Labor et Fides, 1981).

Marshall
  I. Howard Marshall, *The Gospel of Luke: A Commentary of the Greek Text* (NIGTC; Grand Rapids: Eerdmans; Exeter: Paternoster, 1978).

Marshall and Peterson, *Witness to the Gospel*
  I. Howard Marshall and David Peterson, eds., *Witness to the Gospel: The Theology of Acts* (Grand Rapids: Eerdmans, 1998).

Martin, *Syntax Criticism*
  Raymond A. Martin, *Syntax Criticism of the Synoptic Gospels* (Studies in the Bible and Early Christianity 10; Lewiston, N.Y.: Mellen, 1987).

Martini, *Ministers*
  Carlo Maria Martini, *Ministers of the Gospel: Meditations on St. Luke's Gospel* (trans. Susan Leslie; New York: Crossroad, 1989).

Matera, *Passion*
  Frank J. Matera, *Passion Narratives and Gospel Theologies: Interpreting the Synoptics through Their Passion Stories* (Theological Inquiries; New York: Paulist, 1986).

Matson, *Household Conversion*
  David L. Matson, *Household Conversion Narratives in Acts: Pattern and Interpretation* (JSNTSup 123; Sheffield: Sheffield Academic Press, 1996).

Mees, *Parallelstellen*
  Michael Mees, *Ausserkanonische Parallelstellen zu den Herrenworten und ihre Bedeutung* (Quaderni di Vetera christianorum 10; Bari: Istituto di letteratura cristiana antica, 1975).

Melanchthon, *Annotationes*
  Philipp Melanchthon, *Annotationes in evangelia* (Wittemberg, 1544), reprinted in Karl Gottlieb Bretschneider, ed., *Philippi Melanthonis opera quae supersunt omnia: Libri Philippi Melanthonis in quibus enarravit Scripturam sacram, volumen XIV* (CR 12; Halle: C. A. Schwetschke et filium, 1844) 161–1220. Cited from the latter.

Melanchthon, *Postillae*
  Philipp Melanchthon, *Evangelien-Postille* (German ed.: Nuremberg, 1549; Latin ed.: Hanover, 1549), reprinted in Heinrich Ernest Bindseil, ed., *Philippi Melanthonis opera quae supersunt omnia: Libri Philippi Melanthonis in quibus enarravit Scripturam sacram, volumen XXV: Postillae Melanthonianae, partes III et IV atque appendix* (CR 25; Braunschweig: C. A. Schwetschke et filium, 1856).

Menzies, *Empowered for Witness*
  Robert P. Menzies, *Empowered for Witness: The Spirit in Luke-Acts* (JPTSup 6; Sheffield: Sheffield Academic Press, 1994).

Menzies, *Pneumatology*
  Robert P. Menzies, *The Development of Early Christian Pneumatology with Special Reference to Luke-Acts* (JSNTSup 54; Sheffield: JSOT Press, 1991).

Merklein, *Gottesherrschaft*
  Helmut Merklein, *Die Gottesherrschaft als Handlungsprinzip: Untersuchung zur Ethik Jesu* (2d ed.; FB 34; Würzburg: Echter, 1981).

Merx, *Markus und Lukas*
  Adalbert Merx, *Die Evangelien des Markus und Lukas nach der syrischen im Sinaikloster gefundenen Palimpsesthandschrift erläutert* (Die vier kanonischen Evangleien nach ihrem ältesten bekannten Texte 2.2; Berlin: Reimer, 1905).

Metzger, *Textual Commentary*
  Bruce M. Metzger, *A Textual Commentary on the Greek New Testament* (London/New York: United Bible Societies, 1971; 2d ed.; Stuttgart: Deutsche Bibelgesellschaft/United Bible Societies, 1994).

Meurer, *Gleichnisse Jesu*
  Hermann-Josef Meurer, *Die Gleichnisse Jesu als Metaphern: Paul Ricœurs Hermeneutik der Gleichniserzählung Jesu im Horizont des Symbols "Gottesherrschaft/Reich Gottes"* (BBB 111; Bodenheim: Philo, 1997).

Meyer, "Rhetorical Technique"
  Donald Galen Meyer, "The Use of Rhetorical Technique by Luke in the Book of Acts" (2 vols.; diss., University of Minnesota, 1987).

Meyer, *Handbook*
  Heinrich August Wilhelm Meyer, *Critical and Exegetical Handbook to the Gospels of Mark and Luke* (trans. Robert Ernest Wallis; rev. William P. Dickson; 2 vols.; Edinburgh: Clark, 1880, 1883).

Meynet, *Avez-vous lu saint Luc*
  Roland Meynet, *Avez-vous lu saint Luc? Guide pour une rencontre* (LiBi 88; Paris: Cerf, 1990).

Meynet, *Saint Luc*
    Roland Meynet, *L'Évangile selon saint Luc: Analyse rhétorique* (2 vols.; Paris: Cerf, 1988).
Mills, *Luke*
    Watson E. Mills, *The Gospel of Luke* (Bibliographies for Biblical Research New Testament Series 3; Lewiston, N.Y.: Mellen, 1994).
Miyoshi, *Anfang*
    Michi Miyoshi, *Der Anfang des Reiseberichtes Lk 9,51—10,24: Eine redaktionsgeschichtliche Untersuchung* (AnBib 60; Rome: Pontifical Biblical Institute, 1977).
Moessner, *Banquet*
    David P. Moessner, *Lord of the Banquet: The Literary and Theological Significance of the Lukan Travel Narrative* (Minneapolis: Fortress Press, 1989).
Moltmann-Wendel, *Frauen*
    Elisabeth Moltmann-Wendel, *Ein eigener Mensch werden: Frauen um Jesus* (Gütersloh: Mohn, 1980) 22–55.
Monloubou, *Prière*
    Louis Monloubou, *La prière selon Saint Luc: Recherche d'une structure* (LD 89; Paris: Cerf, 1976).
Monselewski, *Samariter*
    Werner Monselewski, *Der barmherzige Samariter: Eine auslegungsgeschichtliche Untersuchung zu Lukas 10, 25-37* (BGBE 5; Tübingen: Mohr Siebeck, 1967).
Moore, *Literary Criticism*
    Stephen D. Moore, *Literary Criticism and the Gospels: The Theoretical Challenge* (New Haven: Yale University Press, 1992).
Moore, *Mark and Luke*
    Stephen D. Moore, *Mark and Luke in Poststructuralist Perspectives: Jesus Begins to Write* (New Haven: Yale University Press, 1992).
Morgenthaler, *Lukas und Quintilian*
    Robert Morgenthaler, *Lukas und Quintilian: Rhetorik als Erzählkunst* (Zurich: Gotthelf, 1993).
Morris
    Leon Morris, *The Gospel according to Luke: An Introduction and Commentary* (Tyndale New Testament Commentaries; London: Inter-Varsity, 1974; reprinted Grand Rapids: Eerdmans, 1988). Citations from the former.
Moulton, *Grammar*
    James Hope Moulton, *A Grammar of New Testament Greek* (4 vols.; Edinburgh: T&T Clark, 1906–63).
Moulton and Milligan, *Vocabulary*
    James Hope Moulton and George Milligan, *The Vocabulary of the Greek New Testament: Illustrated from the Papyri and Other Non-Literary Sources* (1930; reprinted Grand Rapids: Eerdmans, 1963).
Mourlon Beernaert, *Marthe, Marie*
    Pierre Mourlon Beernaert, *Marthe, Marie et les autres: Les visages féminins de l'Évangile* (Écritures 5; Brussels: Lumen vitae, 1992).
Moxnes, *Economy*
    Halvor Moxnes, *The Economy of the Kingdom: Social Conflict and Economic Relations in Luke's Gospel* (Philadelphia: Fortress Press, 1988).

Mülhaupt, *Luthers Evangelien-Auslegung*
    Erwin Mülhaupt, ed., *D. Martin Luthers Evangelien-Auslegung* (2d ed.; 5 vols.; Göttingen: Vandenhoeck & Ruprecht, 1954) (references in this commentary are to volume 3).
Müller, *Zeugnis*
    Paul-Gerhard Müller, ed., *Das Zeugnis des Lukas: Impulse für das Lesejahr C* (Stuttgart: Katholisches Bibelwerk, 1985).
Murdock, *Syriac Peshito Version*
    James Murdock, ed., *The New Testament or the Book of the Holy Gospel of Our Lord and Our God, Jesus the Messiah: A Literal Translation from the Syriac Peshito Version* (New York: Stanford & Swords, 1852).
Mussner, "Begriff"
    Franz Mussner, "Der Begriff des 'Nächsten' in der Verkündigung Jesu: Dargelegt am Gleichnis vom barmherzigen Samariter," in idem, *Praesentia*, 125–32.
Mussner, *Praesentia*
    Franz Mussner, *Praesentia salutis: Gesammelte Studien zu Fragen und Themen des Neuen Testaments* (KBANT; Düsseldorf: Patmos, 1967).
Navone, *Themes*
    John J. Navone, *Themes of St. Luke* (Rome: Gregorian University Press, 1970).
Neale, *Sinners*
    David A. Neale, *"None but the Sinners": Religious Categories in the Gospel of Luke* (JSNTSup 58; Sheffield: JSOT Press, 1991).
Nebe, *Prophetische Züge*
    Gottfried Nebe, *Prophetische Züge im Bilde Jesu bei Lukas* (BWANT 127; Stuttgart: Kohlhammer, 1989).
Neirynck, *Gospel of Luke*
    Frans Neirynck, *The Gospel of Luke: Revised and Enlarged Edition of L'Évangile de Luc. Problèmes littéraires et théologiques* (2d ed.; BETL 32; Leuven: Leuven University Press, 1989).
Neirynck, *Minor Agreements*
    Frans Neirynck et al., eds., *The Minor Agreements of Matthew and Luke against Mark with a Cumulative List* (BETL 37; Leuven: Leuven University Press, 1974).
Nelson, *Leadership*
    Peter K. Nelson, *Leadership and Discipleship: A Study of Luke 22:24-30* (SBLDS 138; Atlanta: Scholars Press, 1994).
Neuhäusler, *Anspruch*
    Engelbert Neuhäusler, *Anspruch und Antwort Gottes: Zur Lehre von den Weisungen innerhalb der synoptischen Jesusverkündigung* (Düsseldorf: Patmos, 1962).
Neuhäusler, *Exigence de Dieu*
    Engelbert Neuhäusler, *Exigence de Dieu et morale chrétienne: Études sur les enseignements moraux de la prédication de Jesus dans les Synoptiques* (trans. F. Schanen; LD 70; Paris: Cerf, 1971).
Neusner, *Talmud*
    Jacob Neusner, ed., *The Talmud of the Land of Israel: A Preliminary Translation and Explanation* (35 vols.; Chicago Studies in the History of Judaism; Chicago: University of Chicago Press, 1982–).

Neusner, *Talmud of Babylonia*
Jacob Neusner, trans., *The Talmud of Babylonia: An American Translation* (BJS; Chico, Calif.: Scholars Press, 1984–).

New Testament Apocrypha. See Schneemelcher, *New Testament Apocrypha*

New Testament in Greek
The Gospel according to St. Luke (eds. American and British Committees of the International Greek New Testament Project; 2 vols.; The New Testament in Greek 3; Oxford: Clarendon, 1984–87).

Neyrey, *Social World*
Jerome H. Neyrey, *The Social World of Luke-Acts: Models for Interpretation* (Peabody, Mass.: Hendrickson, 1991).

Ngayihembako, *Temps de la fin*
Samuel Ngayihembako, *Les temps de la fin: Approche exégétique de l'eschatologie du Nouveau Testament* (MB 29; Geneva: Labor et Fides, 1994).

Nickels, *Targum*
Peter Nickels, *Targum and New Testament: A Bibliography, Together with a New Testament Index* (Scripta Pontificii Instituti biblici 117; Rome: Pontifical Biblical Institute, 1967).

Nineham, *Studies*
Dennis Eric Nineham, ed., *Studies in the Gospels: Essays in Memory of R. H. Lightfoot* (3d ed.; Oxford: Blackwell, 1967).

Nolland
John Nolland, *Luke* (3 vols.; WBC 35A–C; Dallas: Word, 1989–93).

Nolland, "Luke's Readers"
John Nolland, "Luke's Readers—A Study of Luke 4.22-28; Acts 13.46; 18.6; 28.28 and Luke 21.5-36" (diss., University of Cambridge, 1977).

Norden, *Agnostos Theos*
Eduard Norden, *Agnostos Theos: Untersuchungen zur Formengeschichte religiöser Rede* (Leipzig: Teubner, 1913; reprinted Darmstadt: Wissenschaftliche Buchgesellschaft, 1956) 277–308.

Nuttall, *Moment of Recognition*
Geoffrey F. Nuttall, *The Moment of Recognition: Luke as Story-Teller (Ethel M. Wood Lecture)* (London: Athlone, 1978).

Nützel, *Offenbarer Gottes*
Johannes M. Nützel, *Jesus als Offenbarer Gottes nach den lukanischen Schriften* (FB 39; Würzburg: Echter, 1980).

O'Fearghail, *Introduction*
Fearghus O'Fearghail, *The Introduction to Luke-Acts: A Study of the Role of Luke 1:1—4:44 in the Composition of Luke's Two Volume Work* (AnBib 26; Rome: Pontifical Biblical Institute, 1991).

Orbe, *San Ireneo*
Antonio Orbe, *Parábolas evangélicas en san Ireneo* (2 vols.; BAC 331–32; Madrid: Católica, 1972).

Orchard, *Two-Gospel Hypothesis*
John Bernard Orchard, ed., *A Synopsis of the Four Gospels in Greek, Arranged according to the Two-Gospel Hypothesis* (Edinburgh: T&T Clark; Göttingen, 1983). Citations from the latter.

O'Reilly, *Word and Sign*
Leo O'Reilly, *Word and Sign in the Acts of the Apostles: A Study of Lucan Theology* (Analecta Gregoriana 82; Rome: Gregorian University Press, 1987).

Origen, *Comm. in Matt.*
Origen, *Commentarium in evangelium Matthaei*, in Erich Klostermann, ed., *Origenes Werke*, vols. 10–11: *Matthäuserklärung* (GCS 38; 2 vols.; Leipzig: Hinrichs, 1933–35).

Origen, *Hom. in Luc.*
Origen, *Homiliae in evangelium Lucam*, in H. Couzel, F. Fournier, and P. Périchon, eds., *Origène, Homélies sur s. Luc: Texte latin et fragments grecs: Introduction, traduction et notes* (2d ed.; SC 87; Paris: Cerf, 1962).

Origen, *Hom. in Luc.* (ed. Rauer)
Origen, *Homiliae in evangelium Lucam*, in Max Rauer, ed., *Origenes Werke*, vol. 9: *Die Homilien zu Lukas in der Übersetzung des Hieronymus und die griechischen Reste der Homilien und des Lukas-Kommentars* (2d ed.; GCS 49 [35]; Berlin: Akademie-Verlag, 1959).

O'Toole, *Unity*
Robert F. O'Toole, *The Unity of Luke's Theology: An Analysis of Luke-Acts* (GNS 9; Wilmington, Del.: Glazier, 1984).

Ott, *Gebet und Heil*
Wilhelm Ott, *Gebet und Heil: Die Bedeutung der Gebetsparänese in der lukanischen Theologie* (SANT 12; Munich: Kösel, 1965).

Paffenroth, *Story*
Kim Paffenroth, *The Story of Jesus according to L* (JSNTSup 147; Sheffield: Sheffield Academic Press, 1997).

Parker, *Codex Bezae*
David C. Parker, *Codex Bezae: An Early Christian Manuscript and Its Text* (Cambridge/New York: Cambridge University Press, 1992).

Parsons, *Departure*
Mikeal C. Parsons, *The Departure of Jesus in Luke-Acts: The Ascension Narratives in Context* (JSNTSup 21; Sheffield: JSOT Press, 1987).

Parsons and Pervo, *Rethinking*
Mikeal C. Parsons and Richard I. Pervo, *Rethinking the Unity of Luke and Acts* (Minneapolis: Fortress Press, 1993).

Patte, *Semiology and Parables*
Daniel Patte, ed., *Semiology and Parables: Exploration of the Possibilities Offered by Structuralism for Exegesis* (PTMS 9; Pittsburgh: Pickwick, 1976).

Payne Smith, *Cyril*
Robert Payne Smith, *A Commentary upon the Gospel according to S. Luke, by S. Cyril, Patriarch of Alexandria, Now First Translated into English from an Ancient Syriac Version* (2 vols.; Oxford: Oxford University Press, 1859).

Pearson, *Future*
Birger A. Pearson et al., eds., *The Future of Early Christianity: Essays in Honor of Helmut Koester* (Minneapolis: Fortress Press, 1991).

Pearson, *Critici sacri sive doctiss.*
John Pearson, *Critici sacri sive doctiss. virorum in ss. Biblia annotationes et tractatus* (9 vols.; London: Jacobus Flesher, 1660; new augmented ed., Amsterdam: Henricus & Vidua Theodori Boom, Joannes & Ægidius Janssonii à Waesberge, et al., 1698).

Penney, *Missionary*
John M. Penney, *The Missionary Emphasis of Lukan Pneumatology* (JPTSup 12; Sheffield: Sheffield Academic Press, 1997).

Percy, *Botschaft*
Ernst Percy, *Die Botschaft Jesu: Eine traditionskritische und exegetische Untersuchung* (Lund: Gleerup, 1953).

Perrin, *Kingdom*
Norman Perrin, *The Kingdom of God in the Teaching of Jesus* (Philadelphia: Westminster, 1963).

Perrin, *Language*
Norman Perrin, *Jesus and the Language of the Kingdom: Symbol and Metaphor in New Testament Interpretation* (Philadelphia: Fortress Press, 1976).

Perrin, *Rediscovering*
Norman Perrin, *Rediscovering the Teaching of Jesus* (New York/San Francisco: Harper & Row; London: SCM, 1967).

Perrone, "Bibliografia generale"
Lorenzo Perrone, "Bibliografia generale di storia dell'interpretazione biblica. Esegesi, ermeneutica, usi della Bibbia," *Annali di Storia dell'Esegesi* 11 (1994) 325–90, 647–96.

Pervo, *Luke's Story*
Richard I. Pervo, *Luke's Story of Paul* (Minneapolis: Fortress Press, 1990).

Pervo, *Profit*
Richard I. Pervo, *Profit with Delight: The Literary Genre of the Acts of the Apostles* (Philadelphia: Fortress Press, 1987).

Pesch, "Exegese"
Rudolf Pesch, "Zur Exegese Gottes durch Jesus von Nazaret: Eine Auslegung des Gleichnisses vom Vater und den beiden Söhnen (Lk 15,11-32)," in B. Casper, ed., *Jesus: Ort der Erfahrung Gottes* (Freiburg im B.: Herder, 1976) 140–89.

Pesch and Schnackenburg, *Jesus*
Rudolf Pesch and Rudolf Schnackenburg, eds., *Jesus und der Menschensohn: Festschrift Anton Vögtle* (Freiburg im B.: Herder, 1975).

Petzke, *Sondergut*
Gerd Petzke, *Das Sondergut des Evangeliums nach Lukas* (Zürcher Werkkommentare zur Bibel; Zurich: Theologischer Verlag, 1990).

Pherigo, *Great Physician*
Lindsey P. Pherigo, *The Great Physician: Luke, the Healing Stories* (2d ed.; Nashville: Abingdon, 1991).

Phillips, *Paraphrase*
Jane E. Phillips, *Desiderius Erasmus, Paraphrase on Luke* (Toronto: University of Toronto Press, 2003).

Pilgrim, *Wealth and Poverty*
Walter Pilgrim, *Good News to the Poor: Wealth and Poverty in Luke-Acts* (Minneapolis: Augsburg, 1981).

Piper, *Wisdom*
Ronald A. Piper, *Wisdom in the Q-Tradition: The Aphoristic Teaching of Jesus* (SNTSMS 61; Cambridge: Cambridge University Press, 1989).

Pirot, *Paraboles*
Jean Pirot, *Paraboles et allégories évangéliques: la pensée de Jésus, les commentaires patristiques* (Paris: Lethielleux, 1949).

Pittner, *Lukanischen Sondergut*
Bertram Pittner, *Studien zum lukanischen Sondergut: Sprachliche, theologische und form-kritische Untersuchungen zu Sonderguttexten in Lk 5–19* (Erfurter theologische Schriften 18; Leipzig: Benno, 1991).

Plummer
Alfred Plummer, *A Critical and Exegetical Commentary on the Gospel according to St. Luke* (ICC; New York: Scribner, 1896; reprinted 5th ed.; New York: Scribner's Sons; Edinburgh: Clark, 1902). Citations from the former.

Pokorný, *Theologie*
Petr Pokorný, *Theologie der lukanischen Schriften* (FRLANT 174; Göttingen: Vandenhoeck & Ruprecht, 1998).

Polag, *Christologie*
Athanasius Polag, *Die Christologie der Logienquelle* (WMANT 45; Neukirchen-Vluyn: Neukirchener-Verlag, 1977).

Powell, *What Are They Saying*
Mark A. Powell, *What Are They Saying about Luke?* (New York: Paulist, 1989).

Prete, *L'opera*
Benedetto Prete, *L'opera di Luca: Contenuti e prospettive* (Turin: Elle di ci, 1986).

Prete, *Storia*
Benedetto Prete, *Storia e teologia nel vangelo di Luca* (Agnitio Mysterii 3; Bologna: Studio domenicano, 1973).

Price, *Widow Traditions*
Robert W. Price, *The Widow Traditions in Luke-Acts: A Feminist-Critical Scrutiny* (SBLDS 155; Atlanta: Scholars Press, 1997).

Prieur, *Verkündigung*
Alexander Prieur, *Die Verkündigung der Gottesherrschaft: Exegetische Studien zum lukanischen Verständnis von βασιλεία τοῦ θεοῦ* (WUNT 2/89; Tübingen: Mohr Siebeck, 1997).

Prior, *Jesus the Liberator*
Michael Prior, *Jesus the Liberator: Nazareth Liberation Theology (Luke 4:16-30)* (Biblical Seminar 26; Sheffield: Sheffield Academic Press, 1995).

Puech, *Gnose*
Henri-Charles Puech, *En quête de la gnose* (2 vols.; Bibliothèque des sciences humaines; Paris: Gallimard, 1978).

Puig i Tàrrech, "Lc 10, 18"
Armand Puig i Tárrech, "Lc 10, 18: La visió de la caíguda de Satanàs," *Revista catalana de teologia* 3 (1978) 217–43.

Puskas, "Conclusion"
Charles B. Puskas, "The Conclusion of Luke-Acts: An Investigation of the Literary Function and Theological Significance of Acts 28:16-31" (diss., St. Louis University, 1980).

Quasten and di Berardino, *Patrology*
Johannes Quasten and Angelo di Berardino, eds., *Patrology*, vol. 4: *The Golden Age of Latin Patristic Literature: From the Council of Nicea to the Council of Chalcedon* (trans. Placid Solari; Westminster, Md.: Christian Classics, 1986).

Radl
Walter Radl, *Das Lukas-Evangelium* (EdF 261; Darmstadt: Wissenschaftliche Buchgesellschaft, 1988).

Ravens, *Restoration*
David Ravens, *Luke and the Restoration of Israel* (JSNTSup 119; Sheffield: Sheffield Academic Press, 1995).

Ray, *Narrative Irony*
Jerry L. Ray, *Narrative Irony in Luke-Acts: The Paradoxical Interaction of Prophetic Fulfillment and Jewish Rejection* (Mellen Biblical Press Series 28; Lewiston, N.Y.: Mellen, 1996).

Refoulé, *À cause*
François Refoulé, ed., *À cause de l'Évangile: Études sur les Synoptiques et les Actes: Festschrift Jacques Dupont* (LD 123; Paris: Cerf, 1985).

Reid, *Choosing*
Barbara E. Reid, *Choosing the Better Part? Women in the Gospel of Luke* (Collegeville, Minn.: Liturgical Press, 1996).

Reinhardt, *Wachstum*
Wolfgang Reinhardt, *Das Wachstum des Gottesvolkes: Untersuchungen zum Gemeindewachstum im lukanischen Doppelwerk auf dem Hintergrund des Alten Testaments* (Göttingen: Vandenhoeck & Ruprecht, 1995).

Rengstorf
Karl H. Rengstorf, *Das Evangelium nach Lukas: Übersetzt und erklärt* (13th ed.; NTD 3; Göttingen: Vandenhoeck & Ruprecht, 1968).

Rengstorf, *Concordance*
Karl H. Rengstorf, ed., *A Complete Concordance to Flavius Josephus* (4 vols.; Leiden: Brill, 1973–83).

Resch, *Agrapha*
Alfred Resch, *Agrapha: Aussercanonische Schriftfragmente gesammelt und untersucht* (2d ed.; TU 30; Leipzig: Hinrichs, 1906).

Reuss, *Lukas-Kommentare*
Joseph Reuss, *Lukas-Kommentare aus der griechischen Kirche: Aus Katenenhandschriften gesammelt und herausgegeben* (TU 130; Berlin: Akademie-Verlag, 1984).

Richard, *New Views*
Earl Richard, ed., *New Views on Luke and Acts* (Collegeville, Minn.: Liturgical Press, 1990; Wilmington, Del.: M. Glazier, 1991).

Richter Reimer, *Women*
Ivoni Richter Reimer, *Women in the Acts of the Apostles: A Feminist Liberation Perspective* (trans. Linda M. Maloney; Minnepolis: Fortress Press, 1995).

Riesner, *Jesus als Lehrer*
Rainer Riesner, *Jesus als Lehrer: Eine Untersuchung zum Ursprung der Evangelien-Überlieferung* (WUNT 2/7; Tübingen: Mohr Siebeck, 1981).

Robinson, *Nag Hammadi Library*
James M. Robinson, ed., *The Nag Hammadi Library in English* (3d ed.; Leiden: Brill; San Francisco: Harper & Row, 1988).

Robinson, *Structural Analysis*
Neal Robinson, *French Structural Analysis and Its Application to the Narratives of St. Luke's Gospel* (London: n.p., 1976).

Robinson, *Way of the Lord*
William C. Robinson, *The Way of the Lord: A Study of History and Eschatology in the Gospel of Luke* (diss., University of Basel, 1960; Dallas: n.p., 1962).

Roloff, *Kerygma*
Jürgen Roloff, *Das Kerygma und der irdische Jesus: Historische Motive in den Jesus-Erzählungen der Evangelien* (Göttingen: Vandenhoeck & Ruprecht, 1970).

Roosen, "Das einzig Notwendige"
A. Roosen, "Das einzig Notwendige: Erwägungen zu Lk 10, 38-42," *Studia Moralia* 17 (1979) 9–39.

Rossé, *Luca*
Gerard Rossé, *Il Vangelo di Luca: Commento esegetico e teologico* (Rome: Città Nuova, 1992).

Roth, *Character Types*
Samuel John Roth, *The Blind, the Lame, and the Poor: Character Types in Luke-Acts* (JSNTSup 144; Sheffield: Sheffield Academic Press, 1997).

Ruegg, "Marthe et Marie"
Ulrich Ruegg, "Marthe et Marie: Luc 10, 38-42," *Bulletin du Centre protestant d'études* 22, nos. 6–7 (1970) 19–56.

Sabourin
Leopold Sabourin, *L'Évangile de Luc: Introduction et commentaire* (Rome: Editrice Pontificia Universita Gregoriana, 1987).

Sabugal, *Oración*
Santos Sabugal, *Abba! . . . La oración del Señor (Historia y exégesis teológica)* (BAC 467; Madrid: Editorial Catolica Biblioteca de Autores Cristianos, 1985).

Safrai and Stern, *Jewish People*
S. Safrai, M. Stern, et al., eds., *Jewish People in the First Century: Historical Geography, Political History, Social, Cultural and Religious Life and Institutions* (2 vols.; CRINT 1–2; Assen: van Gorcum, 1974–76).

Salo, *Luke's Treatment*
  Kalervo Salo, *Luke's Treatment of the Law: A Redaction-Critical Investigation* (AASFDHL 57; Helsinki: Suomalainen Tiedeakatemia, 1991).

Sanders, *Jews*
  Jack T. Sanders, *The Jews in Luke-Acts* (Philadelphia: Fortress Press, 1987).

Sato, *Q und Prophetie*
  Migaku Sato, *Q und Prophetie: Studien zur Gattungs- und Traditionsgeschichte der Quelle Q* (WUNT 2/29; Tübingen: Mohr Siebeck, 1988).

Sawyer, *Fifth Gospel*
  John F. A. Sawyer, *The Fifth Gospel: Isaiah in the History of Christianity* (Cambridge: Cambridge University Press, 1996).

Scheffler, *Suffering*
  Eben Scheffler, *Suffering in Luke's Gospel* (AThANT 81; Zurich: Theologischer Verlag, 1993).

Schiller, *Ikonographie*
  Gertrud Schiller, *Ikonographie der christlichen Kunst* (5 vols. in 7; Gütersloh: Mohn, 1966–91).

Schlatter
  Adolf Schlatter, *Das Evangelium des Lukas: Aus seinen Quellen erklärt* (Stuttgart: Calwer, 1931).

Schleiermacher, *Schriften des Lukas*
  Friedrich Schleiermacher, *Über die Schriften des Lukas,* vol. 1: *Ein kritischer Versuch* (Berlin: Reimer, 1817).

Schlosser, *Règne de Dieu*
  Jacques Schlosser, *Le Règne de Dieu dans les dits de Jésus* (2 vols.; EtB; Paris: Gabalda, 1980).

Schmid, *Matthäus und Lukas*
  Schmid, Josef, *Matthäus und Lukas: Eine Untersuchung des Verhältnisses ihrer Evangelien* (BibS[F] 23/2–4; Freiburg; Herder, 1930).

Schmidt, *Rahmen*
  Karl L. Schmidt, *Der Rahmen der Geschichte Jesu: Literarkritische Untersuchungen zur ältesten Jesusüberlieferung* (Darmstadt: Wissenschaftliche Buchgesellschaft, 1964).

Schmidt, *Illustration*
  Philipp Schmidt, *Die Illustration der Lutherbibel 1522–1700* (Basel: Reinhardt, 1962).

Schmithals
  Walter Schmithals, *Das Evangelium nach Lukas* (ZBK 3.1; Zurich: Theologischer Verlag, 1980).

Schnackenburg, *Gottes Herrschaft*
  Rudolf Schnackenburg, *Gottes Herrschaft und Reich: Eine biblisch-theologische Studie* (4th ed.; Freiburg: Herder, 1965). ET: *God's Rule and Kingdom* (trans. John Murray; New York: Herder & Herder, 1963).

Schnackenburg, *Kirche*
  Rudolf Schnackenburg et al., eds., *Die Kirche des Anfangs: Festschrift für Heinz Schürmann zum 65. Geburtstag* (EThSt 38; Leipzig: St. Benno, 1977).

Schneemelcher, *New Testament Apocrypha*
  Wilhelm Schneemelcher, ed., *New Testament Apocrypha* (Eng. trans. ed. R. McL. Wilson; 2 vols.; Louisville: Westminster John Knox, 1991, 1992).

Vol. 1: *Gospels and Related Writings;* vol. 2: *Apostles, Apocalypses and Related Subjects.*

Schneider
  Gerhard Schneider, *Das Evangelium nach Lukas* (2d ed.; 2 vols.; Ökumenischer Taschenbuch-Kommentar zum Neuen Testament 3.1–2; Gütersloh/Würzburg: Mohn, 1984).

Schneider, "Antworten"
  Gerhard Schneider, "Jesu überraschende Antworten: Beobachtungen zu den Apophthegmen des dritten Evangeliums," *NTS* 29 (1983) 321–36; reprinted in idem, *Lukas, Theologe der Heilsgeschichte: Aufsätze zum lukanischen Doppelwerk* (BBB 59; Königsstein: Hanstein, 1985) 173–83.

Schneider, *Parusiegleichnisse*
  Gerhard Schneider, *Parusiegleichnisse im Lukas-Evangelium* (SBS 74; Stuttgart: Stuttgarter Bibelstudien, 1975).

Schönbach, *Altdeutsche Predigten*
  Anton Emanuel Schönbach, ed., *Altdeutsche Predigten, Texte* (3 vols.; Graz: Styria, 1886–91; reprinted Darmstadt: Wissenschaftliche Buchgesellschaft, 1964).

Schottroff and Stegemann, *Jesus*
  Luise Schottroff and Wolfgang Stegemann, *Jesus von Nazareth, Hoffnung der Armen* (Stuttgart/Berlin/Cologne/Mainz: Kohlhammer, 1978).

Schrage, *Thomas-Evangelium*
  Wolfgang Schrage, *Das Verhältnis des Thomas-Evangeliums zur synoptischen Tradition und zu den koptischen Evangelienübersetzungen* (BZNW 29; Berlin: Töpelmann, 1964).

Schramm, *Markus-Stoff*
  Tim Schramm, *Der Markus-Stoff bei Lukas: Eine literarkritische und redaktionsgeschichtliche Untersuchung* (SNTSMS 14; Cambridge: Cambridge University Press, 1971).

Schulz, *Nachfolgen*
  Anselm Schulz, *Nachfolgen und Nachahmen: Studien über das Verhältnis der neutestamentlichen Jüngerschaft zur urchristlichen Vorbildethik* (SANT 6; Munich: Kösel, 1962).

Schulz, *Q*
  Siegfried Schulz, *Q: Die Spruchquelle der Evangelisten* (Zurich: Theologischer Verlag, 1972).

Schürer, *History*
  Emil Schürer, *The History of the Jewish People in the Age of Jesus-Christ (175 B. C.–A.D. 135): A New English Version, Revised* (ed. Géza Vèrmes et al.; 4 vols.; Edinburgh: T&T Clark, 1973–87).

Schürmann
  Heinz Schürmann, *Lukas-Evangelium,* vol. 2.1: *Kommentar zu Kapitel 9:51— 11:54* (2d ed.; HThKNT 3.2; Freiburg im B.: Herder, 1994).

Schürmann, "Beobachtungen"
  Heinz Schürmann, "Beobachtungen zum Menschensohn-Titel in der Redequelle," in Pesch and Schnackenburg, *Jesus,* 124–47.

Schürmann, *Gebet*
Heinz Schürmann, *Das Gebet des Herrn als Schlüssel zum Verstehen Jesu* (4th ed.; Botschaft Gottes 2, neutestamentliche Reihe 6; Freiburg im B.: Herder, 1981).

Schürmann, *Gottes Reich*
Heinz Schürmann, *Gottes Reich—Jesu Geschick: Jesu ureigener Tod im Licht seiner Basileia-Verkündigung* (Freiburg im B.: Herder, 1983).

Schürmann, *Untersuchungen*
Heinz Schürmann, *Traditionsgeschichtliche Untersuchungen zu den synoptischen Evangelien: Beiträge* (KBANT; Düsseldorf: Patmos, 1968).

Schüssler Fiorenza, *But She Said*
Elisabeth Schüssler Fiorenza, *But She Said: Feminist Practices of Biblical Interpretation* (Boston: Beacon, 1992).

Schüssler Fiorenza, "Criteria"
Elisabeth Schüssler Fiorenza, "Theological Criteria and Historical Reconstruction: Martha and Mary, Luke 10, 38-42," in *Center for Hermeneutical Studies Protocol Series [Berkeley, Calif.]* 53 (1987) 1–12.

Schwarz, *Jesus "der Menschensohn"*
Günther Schwarz, *Jesus "der Menschensohn": Aramaistische Untersuchungen zu den synoptischen Menschensohnworten Jesu* (BWANT 119; Stuttgart: Kohlhammer, 1986).

Schwarz, *"Und Jesus sprach"*
Günther Schwarz, *"Und Jesus sprach": Untersuchungen zur aramäischen Urgestalt der Worte Jesu* (2d ed.; BWANT 118; Stuttgart: Kohlhammer, 1987).

Schweizer
Eduard Schweizer, *Das Evangelium nach Lukas: Übersetzt und erklärt* (NTD 3; Göttingen: Vandenhoeck & Ruprecht, 1982).

Schweizer, *Parable of God*
Eduard Schweizer, *Jesus, the Parable of God: What Do We Really Know about Jesus?* (PTMS 37; Allison Park, Pa.: Pickwick, 1994).

Scott, *Hear*
Bernard Brandon Scott, *Hear Then the Parable: A Commentary on the Parables of Jesus* (Minneapolis: Fortress Press, 1989).

Seccombe, *Possessions*
David P. Seccombe, *Possessions and the Poor in Luke-Acts* (SNTU B/6; Linz: Studien zum Neuen Testament und seiner Umwelt, 1982).

Segbroeck, *Cumulative Bibliography*
Frans van Segbroeck, *The Gospel of Luke: A Cumulative Bibliography 1973–1988* (BETL 88; Leuven: Leuven University Press, 1989).

Segbroeck, *Four Gospels*
Frans van Segbroeck et al. eds., *The Four Gospels 1992: Festschrift Frans Neirynck* (3 vols.; BETL 100; Leuven: Leuven University Press/Peeters, 1992).

Seim, *Double Message*
Turid Karlsen Seim, *The Double Message: Patterns of Gender in Luke-Acts* (diss., University of Oslo, 1991; revised and reprinted in idem, *Studies of the New Testament and Its World;* Edinburgh: T&T Clark, 1994). Citations for 9:51—14:35 taken from the Oslo diss.; citations from 15:1—19:27 taken from the Edinburgh edition.

Seland, *Establishment Violence*
Torrey Seland, *Establishment Violence in Philo and Luke: A Study of Non-Conformity to the Torah and Jewish Vigilante Reactions* (Biblical Interpretation Series 15; Leiden/New York: Brill, 1995).

Sellin, *Gleichniserzählungen*
Gerhard Sellin, *Studien zu den grossen Gleichniserzählungen des Lukas-Sondergutes: Die ἄνθρωπός τις-Erzählungen des Lukas-Sondergutes, besonders am Beispiel von Lk 10,25-37 und 16,19-31 untersucht* (diss.; Münster, 1973).

Sellin, "Komposition"
Gerhard Sellin, "Komposition, Quellen und Funktion des lukanischen Reiseberichtes (Lk 9,51—19,28)," *NTS* 20 (1978) 100–135.

Sellin, "Lukas"
Gerhard Sellin, "Lukas als Gleichniserzähler: Die Erzählung vom barmherzigen Samariter (Lk 10,25-37)," *ZNW* 65 (1974) 166–89; 66 (1975) 19–60.

Sheeley, *Narrative Asides*
Stephen M. Sheeley, *Narrative Asides in Luke-Acts* (JSNTSup 72; Sheffield: JSOT Press, 1992).

Shelton, *"Filled with the Holy Spirit"*
James B. Shelton, *"Filled with the Holy Spirit": A Redactional Motif in Luke's Gospel* (London: University of Stirling, 1982).

Shepherd, *Narrative Function*
William Henry Shepherd, *The Narrative Function of the Holy Spirit as a Character in Luke-Acts* (SBLDS 147; Atlanta: Scholars Press, 1994).

Shin, *Ausrufung*
Gabriel Kyo-Seon Shin, *Die Ausrufung des endgültigen Jubeljahres durch Jesus in Nazaret: Eine historisch-kritische Studie zu Lk 4,16-30* (EHS 378; Bern/New York: Lang, 1989).

Sieben, *Kirchenväterhomilien*
Hermann Josef Sieben, *Kirchenväterhomilien zum Neuen Testament: Ein Repertorium der Textausgaben und Übersetzungen, mit einem Anhang der Kirchenväterkommentare* (Instrumenta patristica 22; Steenbrugis: Abbatia S. Petri; The Hague: Nijhoff, 1991).

Sloan, *Favorable Year*
Robert Bryan Sloan, Jr., *The Favorable Year of the Lord: A Study of Jubilary Theology in the Gospel of Luke* (Austin: Schola, 1977).

Smitten, *Gottesherrschaft*
Wilhelm T. in der Smitten, *Gottesherrschaft und Gemeinde: Beobachtungen an Frühformen eines jüdischen Nationalismus in der Spätzeit des Alten Testaments* (EHS 42; Bern: Lang; Frankfurt am Main: Lang, 1974).

Smyth, *Greek Grammar*
Herbert Weir Smyth, *Greek Grammar* (1946; rev. Gordon M. Messing; Cambridge, Mass.: Harvard University Press, 1984).

Soards, *Speeches*
Marion L. Soards, *The Speeches in Acts: Their Content, Context, and Concerns* (Louisville: Westminster John Knox, 1994).

Solignac and Donnat, "Marthe et Marie"
A. Solignac and L. Donnat, "Marthe et Marie," *Dictionnaire de spiritualité ascétique et mystique, doctrine et histoire*, vol. 10 (ed. Marcel Viller et al.; Paris: G. Beauchesnes et ses fils, 1980) 664–73.

Sperber, *Bible in Aramaic*
Alexander Sperber, *The Bible in Aramaic Based on Old Manuscripts and Printed Texts* (5 vols.; Leiden/New York: Brill, 1992).

Spicq, *Lexicon*
Ceslas Spicq, *Theological Lexicon of the New Testament* (trans. and ed. James D. Ernest; 3 vols.; Peabody, Mass.: Hendrickson, 1994).

Spicq, *Notes*
Ceslas Spicq, *Notes de lexicographie néo-testamentaire* (3 vols.; OBO 22; Fribourg: Éditions universitaires, 1978–82).

Squires, *Plan of God*
John T. Squires, *The Plan of God in Luke-Acts* (SNTSMS 76; Cambridge/New York: Cambridge University Press, 1993).

Starcky, "Obfirmavit"
Jean Starcky, "Obfirmavit faciem suam ut iret Jerusalem: Sens et portée de Luc 9, 51," *RSR* 39 (1951) 197–202.

Staudinger, *Sabbatkonflikte*
F. Staudinger, *Die Sabbatkonflikte bei Lukas* (diss., Graz, 1994).

Stegemann, *Zwischen Synagoge und Obrigkeit*
Wolfgang Stegemann, *Zwischen Synagoge und Obrigkeit: Zur historischen Situation der lukanischen Christen* (FRLANT 152; Göttingen: Vandenhoeck & Ruprecht, 1991).

Steiner and Weymann, *Paraboles*
Anton Steiner and Volker Weymann, eds., *Paraboles de Jésus* (Lausanne: Évangile et Culture, 1980).

Steinhauser, *Doppelbildworte*
Michael G. Steinhauser, *Doppelbildworte in den synoptischen Evangelien: Eine form- und traditionskritische Studie* (FB 44; Würzburg: Echter, 1981).

Stenger, *Strukturale Beobachtungen*
Werner Stenger, *Strukturale Beobachtungen zum Neuen Testament* (NTTS 12; Leiden/New York: Brill, 1990).

Sterling, *Historiography*
Gregory E. Sterling, *Historiography and Self-Definition: Josephos, Luke-Acts and Apologetic Historiography* (NovTSup 64; Leiden/New York: Brill, 1992).

Strauss, *Davidic Messiah*
Mark L. Strauss, *The Davidic Messiah in Luke-Acts: The Promise and Its Fulfillment in Lukan Christology* (JSNTSup 110; Sheffield: Sheffield Academic Press, 1995).

Strecker, *Jesus Christus*
Georg Strecker, ed., *Jesus Christus in Historie und Theologie: Neutestamentliche Festschrift für Hans Conzelmann zum 60. Geburtstag* (Tübingen: Mohr Siebeck, 1975).

Strecker, *Minor Agreements*
Georg Strecker, ed., *Minor Agreements: Symposium Göttingen, 1991* [1993] (GThA 50; Göttingen: Vandenhoeck & Ruprecht, 1993).

Strobel, *Verzögerungsproblem*
August Strobel, *Untersuchungen zum eschatologischen Verzögerungsproblem auf Grund der spätjüdisch-urchristlichen Geschichte von Habakuk 2,2 ff.* (NovTSup 2; Leiden: Brill, 1961).

Stronstad, *Charismatic Theology*
Roger Stronstad, *The Charismatic Theology of St. Luke* (Peabody, Mass.: Hendrickson, 1984).

Stronstad, *Prophethood*
Roger Stronstad, *The Prophethood of All Believers: A Study in Luke's Charismatic Theology* (JPTSup 16; Sheffield; Sheffield Academic Press, 1999).

Stuhlmacher, *Gospel*
Peter Stuhlmacher, ed., *The Gospel and the Gospels* (Grand Rapids: Eerdmans, 1991).

Suggs, *Wisdom*
M. Jack Suggs, *Wisdom, Christology, and Law in Matthew's Gospel* (Cambridge, Mass.: Harvard University Press, 1970).

Swanson, *Manuscripts*
Reuben J. Swanson, *New Testament Greek Manuscripts: Luke* (Sheffield: Sheffield Academic Press, 1995).

Sweetland, *Journey*
Dennis M. Sweetland, *Our Journey with Jesus: Discipleship according to Luke-Acts* (GNS 23; Collegeville, Minn.: Liturgical Press, 1990).

Sylva, *Reimaging*
Dennis D. Sylva, ed., *Reimaging the Death of the Lukan Jesus* (Athenäums Monografien Theology 73; Frankfurt am Main: Hain, 1990).

Taeger, *Mensch*
Jens-W. Taeger, *Der Mensch und sein Heil: Studien zum Bild des Menschen und zur Sicht der Bekehrung bei Lukas* (StNT 14; Gütersloh: Mohn, 1982).

Talbert
Charles H. Talbert, *Reading Luke: A Literary and Theological Commentary on the Third Gospel* (New York: Crossroad, 1986).

Talbert, *Learning*
Charles H. Talbert, *Learning through Suffering: The Educational Value of Suffering in the New Testament and Its Milieu* (Zacchaeus Studies; Collegeville, Minn.: Liturgical Press, 1991).

Tannehill
Robert C. Tannehill, *Luke* (ANTC; Nashville: Abingdon, 1996).

Tannehill, *Narrative Unity*
Robert C. Tannehill, *The Narrative Unity of Luke-Acts: A Literary Interpretation* (FF; 2 vols.; Philadelphia/Minneapolis: Fortress Press, 1986, 1990).

Tannehill, *Sword*
  Robert C. Tannehill, *The Sword of His Mouth* (SSup
  1; Philadelphia: Fortress Press; Missoula, Mont.:
  Scholars Press, 1975).
Tauler, *Predigten*
  Johannes Tauler, *Die Predigten Taulers: Aus der
  Engelberger und der Freiburger Handschrift sowie
  aus Schmidts Abschriften der ehemaligen Strassburger
  Handschriften* (ed. Ferdinand Vetter; Deutsche
  Texte des Mittelalters 11; Berlin: Weidmann, 1910;
  reprinted Frankfurt am Main: Weidmann, 1968).
  Citations from the latter.
Tertullian, *Adv. Marc.*
  Tertullian, *Adversus Marcionem*, IV (CCSL 1;
  Turnhout: Brepols, 1954) 544–663.
Tertullian, *Against Marcion*
  Tertullian, *Against Marcion,* in Peter Holmes, trans.
  *The Five Books of Quintus Sept. Flor. Tertullianus
  against Marcion Translated* (Edinburgh: T&T Clark,
  1868).
Thayse, *Luc*
  André Thayse, *Luc: L'Évangile revisité* (Lumen Vitae;
  Brussels: Racine, 1997).
Theophylactus, *Enarr. Luc.*
  Theophylactus, Archbishop of Ochrida, *Enarratio
  in evangelium Lucae* (1524; reprinted *PG* 123; Paris:
  Migne, 1864; reprinted 1883) 683–1126.
Thoma and Lauer, *Gleichnisse der Rabbinen*
  Clemens Thoma and Simon Lauer, *Die Gleichnisse
  der Rabbinen* (4 vols.; Judaica et Christiana 10, 13,
  16, 18; Bern: Lang, 1986–2000).
Thompson and Baird, *Critical Concordance*
  J. David Thompson and J. Arthur Baird, *A Critical
  Concordance to the Gospel of Luke* (3 vols.; The
  Computer Bible 41; Wooster, Oh.: Biblical Research
  Associates, 1994).
Thornton, *Zeuge*
  Claus-Jürgen Thornton, *Der Zeuge des Zeugen: Lukas
  als Historiker der Paulusreisen* (WUNT 56; Tübingen:
  Mohr Siebeck, 1991).
Tiede
  David L. Tiede, *Luke* (ACNT; Minneapolis:
  Augsburg, 1988).
Tiede, *Prophecy*
  David L. Tiede, *Prophecy and History in Luke-Acts*
  (Philadelphia: Fortress Press, 1980).
Tödt, *Son of Man*
  Heinz Eduard Tödt, *The Son of Man in the Synoptic
  Tradition* (trans. Dorothea Baiton; London: SCM,
  1965).
Tolbert, *Perspectives*
  Mary Ann Tolbert, *Perspectives on the Parables: An
  Approach to Multiple Interpretations* (Philadelphia:
  Fortress Press, 1979).
Trautmann, *Zeichenhafte Handlungen*
  Maria Trautmann, *Zeichenhafte Handlungen Jesu: Ein
  Beitrag zur Frage nach dem geschichtlichen Jesu* (FB 37;
  Würzburg: Echter, 1980).

Trilling, *Christusverkündigung*
  Wolfgang Trilling, *Christusverkündigung in den synop-
  tischen Evangelien: Beispiele gattungsgemässer Auslegung*
  (Biblische Handbibliothek 4; Munich:Kösel, 1969).
Tucker, *Example Stories*
  Jeffrey T. Tucker, *Example Stories: Perspectives on
  Four Parables in the Gospel of Luke* (JSNTSup 162;
  Sheffield: Sheffield Academic Press, 1998).
Tuckett, *Collected Essays*
  Christopher Mark Tuckett, ed., *Luke's Literary
  Achievement: Collected Essays* (JSNTSup 116;
  Sheffield: Sheffield Academic Press, 1995).
Tuckett, *Luke*
  Christopher Mark Tuckett, *Luke* (New Testament
  Guides; Sheffield: Sheffield Academic Press, 1996).
Tuckett, *Scriptures*
  Christopher Mark Tuckett, ed., *The Scriptures in the
  Gospels* (BETL 131;
  Leuven: Leuven University Press, 1997)
Tuckett, *Synoptic Studies*
  Christopher Mark Tuckett, ed. *Synoptic Studies: The
  Ampleforth Conferences of 1982 and 1983* (JSNTSup 7;
  Sheffield: JSOT, 1984).
Tümpel and Tümpel, *Rembrandt*
  Christian Tümpel and Astrid Tümpel, *Rembrandt
  legt die Bibel aus: Zeichnungen und Radierungen
  aus dem Kupferstichkabinett der Staallichen Museen
  Preussicher Kulturbesitz Berlin* (Berlin: Hessling,
  1970).
Turner, *Power from on High*
  Max M. Turner, *Power from on High: The Spirit in
  Israel's Restoration and Witness in Luke-Acts* (JPTSup
  9; Sheffield: Sheffield Academic Press, 1996).
Tyson, *Images*
  Joseph B. Tyson, *Images of Judaism in Luke-Acts*
  (Columbia: University of South Carolina Press,
  1992).
Tyson, *Luke-Acts*
  Joseph B. Tyson, ed., *Luke-Acts and the Jewish People:
  Eight Critical Perspectives* (Minneapolis: Augsburg,
  1988).
Uro, *Sheep*
  Risto Uro, *Sheep among the Wolves: A Study of the
  Mission Instructions of Q* (AASFDHL 47; Helsinki:
  Suomalainen Tiedeakatemia, 1987).
van der Loos. *See* Loos
Van Linden, *Luke and Acts*
  Philip Van Linden, *The Gospel of Luke and Acts*
  (Message of Biblical Spirituality 10; Wilmington,
  Del.: Glazier, 1986).
Verboomen, *L'imparfait périphrastique*
  Alain Verboomen, *L'imparfait périphrastique dans
  l'Évangile de Luc et dans la Septante: Contribution
  à l'étude du systeme verbal du grec néotestamentaire*
  (Académie Royale de Belgique Classe des Lettres
  10; Louvain: Peeters, 1992).
Vermes, *Jesus the Jew*
  Geza Vermes, *Jesus the Jew: A Historian's Reading of*

the Gospels (London: Collins, 1973).

Via, *Parables*
Dan O. Via, Jr., *The Parables: Their Literary and Existential Dimension* (Philadelphia: Fortress Press, 1967).

Vielhauer, *Aufsätze*
Philipp Vielhauer, *Aufsätze zum Neuen Testament* (ThBü 31; Munich: Kaiser, 1965).

von Bendemann. *See* Bendemann

von Lips. *See* Lips

Waelkens, "L'analyse"
Robert Waelkens, "L'analyse structurale des paraboles: Deux essais: Lc 15,1-32 et Mt 13,44-46," *RThL* 8 (1977) 160–78.

Wagner, *Exegetical Bibliography*
Günter Wagner, ed., *An Exegetical Bibliography of the New Testament: Luke and Acts* (Macon, Ga.: Mercer University Press, 1985) 1–327.

Wailes, *Medieval Allegories*
Stephen L. Wailes, *Medieval Allegories of Jesus' Parables* (Berkeley: University of California Press, 1987).

Wanke, "Bezugs- und Kommentarworte"
Joachim Wanke, "Bezugs- und Kommentarworte" in den synoptischen Evangelien: Beobachtungen zur Interpretationsgeschichte der Herrenwort in der vorevangelischen Überlieferung* (EThSt 44; Leipzig: St. Benno, 1981).

Warren, "Textual Relationships"
W. F. Warren, "The Textual Relationships of $\mathfrak{P}^4$, $\mathfrak{P}^{45}$, and $\mathfrak{P}^{75}$ in the Gospel of Luke" (diss., New Orleans Baptist Theological Seminary, 1986).

Weatherly, *Jewish Responsibility*
Jon A. Weatherly, *Jewish Responsibility for the Death of Jesus in Luke-Acts* (JSNTSup 106; Sheffield: Sheffield Academic Press, 1995).

Weder, *Gleichnisse*
Hans Weder, *Gleichnisse Jesu als Metaphern: Traditions- und redaktionsgeschichtliche Analysen und Interpretationen* (FRLANT 120; Göttingen: Vandenhoeck & Ruprecht, 1978).

Weinrich, *New Testament Age*
William C. Weinrich, ed., *The New Testament Age: Essays in Honor of Bo Reicke* (2 vols.; Macon, Ga.: Mercer University Press, 1984).

Weiser, *Knechtsgleichnisse*
Alfons Weiser, *Die Knechtsgleichnisse der synoptischen Evangelien* (SANT 29; Munich: Kösel, 1971).

Weitling, *Sünder*
Wilhelm Weitling, *Das Evangelium des armen Sünders* (Bern: Jenni, Sohn, 1843).

Wellhausen
Julius Wellhausen, *Das Evangelium Lucae übersetzt und erklärt* (Berlin: Georg Reimer, 1904; reprinted in idem, *Evangelienkommentare* [ed. Martin Hengel; Berlin/New York: de Gruyter, 1987] 459–600).

Wellhausen, *Einleitung*
Julius Wellhausen, *Einleitung in die drei ersten Evangelien* (2d ed.; Berlin: Reimer, 1911; reprinted

in idem, *Evangelienkommentare* [ed. Martin Hengel; Berlin/New York: de Gruyter, 1987] 1–176).

Wengst, *Didache (Apostellehre)*
Klaus Wengst, ed., *Didache (Apostellehre), Barnabasbrief, Zweiter Klemensbrief, Schrift an Diognet, eingeleitet, herausgegeben, übertragen und erläuert* (Schriften des Urchristentums 2: Darmstadt: Wissenschaftliche Buchgesellschaft; Munich: Kösel, 1984).

Wenham, *Pictures*
David Wenham, *The Parables of Jesus: Pictures of Revolution* (London/Sydney: Hodder & Stoughton, 1989).

Wenham, *Rediscovery*
David Wenham, *The Rediscovery of Jesus' Eschatological Discourse* (Gospel Perspectives 4; Sheffield: JSOT Press, 1984).

Wettstein, *Novum Testamentum graecum*
Johann Jakob Wettstein, Ἡ Καινὴ Διαθήκη: *Novum Testamentum graecum, editionis receptae cum lectionibus variantibus . . .* (2 vols.; Amsterdam: Dommeriana, 1751–52).

Wiefel
Wolfgang Wiefel, *Das Evangelium nach Lukas* (HThKNT 3; Berlin: Evangelische Verlagsanstalt, 1988).

Wilder, *Language*
Amos Wilder, *The Language of the Gospel: Early Christian Rhetoric* (New York: Harper & Row, 1964).

Wiles, *Scripture Index*
James W. Wiles, *A Scripture Index to the Works of St. Augustine in English Translation* (Lanham, Md.: University Press of America, 1995).

Wilson, *Luke and the Law*
Stephen G. Wilson, *Luke and the Law* (SNTSMS 50; Cambridge/New York: Cambridge University Press, 1984).

Winter, *Acts*
Bruce W. Winter, ed., *The Book of Acts in Its First Century Setting* (6 vols.; Grand Rapids: Eerdmans, 1993–94).

Winter, "Matthew"
Paul Winter, "Matthew XI 27 and Luke X 22 from the First to the Fifth Century: Reflections on the Development of the Text," *NovT* 1 (1956) 112–48.

Wisse, *Profile Method*
Frederik Wisse, *The Profile Method for the Classification and Evaluation of Manuscript Evidence as Applied to the Greek Text of the Gospel of Luke* (Studies and Documents 44; Grand Rapids: Eerdmans, 1982).

Wisselink, *Assimilation*
Willem Franciscus Wisselink, *Assimilation as a Criterion for the Establishment of the Text: A Comparative Study on the Basis of Passages from Matthew, Mark, and Luke* (Kampen: Kok, 1989).

Wojcik, *Road to Emmaus*
Jan Wojcik, *The Road to Emmaus: Reading Luke's Gospel* (West Lafayette, Ind.: Purdue University Press, 1989).

York, *Last Shall Be First*
    John O. York, *The Last Shall Be First: The Rhetoric of Reversal in Luke* (JSNTSup 46; Sheffield: JSOT Press, 1991).

Zahn
    Theodor Zahn, *Das Evangelium des Lukas: Ausgelegt* (1st–2d ed.; KNT 3; Leipzig/Erlangen: Deichert, 1913).

Zeller, *Kommentar*
    Dieter Zeller, *Kommentar zur Logienquelle* (Stuttgarter kleiner Kommentar Neues Testament 21; Stuttgart: Katholisches Bibelwerk, 1984).

Zeller, *Mahnsprüche*
    Dieter Zeller, *Die weisheitlichen Mahnsprüche bei den Synoptikern* (FB 17; Würzburg: Echter, 1977).

Zimmermann, *Methodenlehre*
    Heinrich Zimmermann, *Neutestamentliche Methodenlehre: Darstellung der historisch-kritischen Methode* (Stuttgart: Katholisches Bibelwerk, 1967).

Zumstein, *Condition du croyant*
    Jean Zumstein, *La condition du croyant dans l'Évangile selon Matthieu* (OBO 16; Göttingen: Vandenhoeck & Ruprecht, 1977).

Zumstein, *Miettes*
    Jean Zumstein, *Miettes exégétiques* (MB 25; Geneva: Labor et Fides, 1991).

Zwiep, *Ascension*
    Arie W. Zwiep, *The Ascension of the Messiah in Lukan Christology* (Leiden/New York: Brill, 1997).

Zwingli, *Annotationes*
    Ulrich Zwingli, *Annotationes in Evangelium Lucae* (Zurich, 1539), reprinted in Melchior Schüler and Ioannes Schulthess, eds., *Ulrich Zwingli Opera* 6.1.6 (Zurich: Schulthess, 1836) 539–681. Cited from the latter.

Commentary

Bibliography

Baumbach, Günther, *Das Verständnis des Bösen in den synoptischen Evangelien* (Theologische Arbeiten 19; Berlin: Evangelische Verlagsanstalt, 1963) 176, 178–79.

Bosch, David, *Die Heidenmission in der Zukunftsschau Jesu: Eine Untersuchung zur Eschatologie der synoptischen Evangelien* (Zurich: Zwingli-Verlag, 1959) 104–8.

Bouwman, Gilbert, "Samaria in Lukas-Handelingen," *Bijdragen: Tijdschrift voor filosofie en theologie* 34 (1973) 40–59.

Bovon, François, *Luke the Theologian: Fifty-Five Years of Research (1950–2005)* (2d rev. ed.; Waco, Tex.: Baylor University Press, 2006) 171–72, 183–84 n. 52, 190–91, 196, 198–201 n. 69, 221, 252.

Burkitt, F. Crawford, "St Luke 9, 54-56 and the Western 'Diatessaron,'" *JTS* 28 (1927) 48–53.

Calmet, Augustin, "Il n'est pas digne de moi! Luc 9, 51-62," *BVC* 77 (1967) 20–25.

Casey, Maurice, "The Jackals and the Son of Man (Matt. 8.29 // Luke 9.58)," *JSNT* 23 (1985) 3–22.

Colomer i Carles, Oriol, "Lc 9, 54-56: Un estudi la critica textual," *Revista catalana de teologia* 1 (1976) 375–91.

Conzelmann, *The Theology of St. Luke* (trans. Geoffrey Buswell; London: Faber & Faber, 1960; reprinted Philadelphia: Fortress Press, 1982) 60–73.

Davies, John G., "The Prefigurement of the Ascension in the Third Gospel," *JTS* n.s. 6 (1955) 229–33.

Dibelius, Martin, *From Tradition to Gospel* (trans. Bertram Lee Woolf; New York: Scribner, 1965) 43, 47–48.

Enslin, Morton S., "Luke and Matthew, Compilers or Authors?" in *ANRW* 2.25.3 (1985) 2368–74.

Evans, Craig A., "'He Set His Face': A Note on Luke 9,51," *Bib* 63 (1982) 545–48.

Idem, "'He Set His Face': Once Again," *Bib* 68 (1987) 80–84.

Feuillet, André, "Deux références évangéliques cachées au Serviteur martyrisé (Is 52, 13—53, 12): Quelques aspects importants du mystère rédempteur," *NRTh* 106 (1984) 549–65.

Flender, Helmut, *Heil und Geschichte in der Theologie des Lukas* (BEvTh 41; Munich: Kaiser, 1965) 35–36.

Flusser, David, "Lukas 9,51-56—ein hebräisches Fragment," in Weinrich, *New Testament Age*, 165–79.

Friedrich, Gerhard, "Lk 9,51 und die Entrückungschristologie des Lukas," in Paul Hoffmann et al, eds., *Orientierung an Jesus: Zur Theologie der Synoptiker: Festschrift Josef Schmid* (Freiburg im Breisgau: Herder, 1973) 48–77.

Heutger, N., "Die lukanischen Samaritanererzählungen in religionspädagogischer Sicht," in Wilfrid Haubeck and Michael Bachmann, eds., *Wort in der Zeit: Neutestamentliche Studien: Festgabe für Karl Heinrich Rengstorf zum 75. Geburtstag* (Leiden: Brill, 1980) 275–87.

Horn, Friedrich W., *Glaube und Handeln in der Theologie des Lukas* (1983; 2d ed.; GThA 26; Göttingen: Vandenhoeck & Ruprecht, 1986) 98, 106, 261–63, 266 (cited after first ed. in 1983).

Lehmann, Martin, *Synoptische Quellenanalyse und die Frage nach dem historischen Jesus: Kriterien der Jesusforschung untersucht in Auseinandersetzung mit Emmanuel Hirschs Frühgeschichte des Evangeliums* (BZNW 38; Berlin: de Gruyter, 1970) 143–45.

Lohfink, Gerhard, *Die Himmelfahrt Jesu: Untersuchungen zu den Himmelfahrts- und Erhöhungstexten bei Lukas* (SANT 26; Munich: Kösel, 1971) 212–17.

Lohse, Eduard, "Missionarisches Handeln Jesu nach dem Evangelium des Lukas," *ThZ* 10 (1954) 1–13.

idem, "Zu den Anfangen der Mission in Samarien," *ThZ* 10 (1954) 158.

Miyoshi, Michi, *Der Anfang des Reiseberichtes Lk 9,51—10,24: Eine redaktionsgeschichtliche Untersuchung* (AnBib 60; Rome: Pontifical Biblical Institute, 1977) 6–32.

Moessner, David P., *Lord of the Banquet: The Literary and Theological Significance of the Lukan Travel Narrative* (Minneapolis: Fortress, 1989) 133.

Nolland, John, *Luke* (3 vols.; WBC 35A–C; Dallas: Word, 1989–93) 2:538 (bibliography).

Radl, Walter, *Paulus und Jesus im lukanischen Doppelwerk: Untersuchungen zu Parallelmotiven im Lukasevangelium und in der Apostelgeschichte* (EHS.T 49; Bern/Frankfurt am Main: Lang, 1975) 103–26.

Robbins, Vernon K., "Foxes, Birds, Burials and Furrows," in Burton L. Mack and Vernon K. Robbins, *Patterns of Persuasion in the Gospels* (Sonoma, Calif.: Polebridge, 1989) 69–84.

Ross, J. M., "The Rejected Words in Luke 9, 54-56," *ExpT* 84 (1972–73) 85–88.

Starcky, Jean, "Obfirmavit faciem suam ut iret Jerusalem: Sens et portée de Luc 9, 51," *RSR* 39 (1951) 197–202.

Tiede, David L., *Prophecy and History in Luke-Acts* (Philadelphia: Fortress Press, 1980) 55–63.

51/ And it happened that the days for him to be taken up[a] were approaching, and he set his face[b] to go to Jerusalem. **52/** And he sent messengers before his face. Having set out on their way, they entered a village of the Samaritans to make ready for him; **53/** but they did not receive him, because his face was set toward Jerusalem. **54/** When his disciples James and John saw it, they said, "Lord, do you want us to command fire to come down from heaven and consume them, even as Elijah did?[c]" **55/** But he turned and rebuked them. **56/** Then they went on to another village.

a   The Greek word ἀνάλημψις (v. 51, "to be taken up") is difficult to translate; it can mean either "taken up" or "ascension" or "death," depending on the context.

b   I have used "face" three times, in vv. 51, 52 and 53, even though it produces a rather cumbersome translation in v. 52.

c   Finally, I follow the longer reading in v. 54 ("even as Elijah did" [ὡς καὶ Ἡλίας ἐποίησεν]), but I prefer the shorter reading in vv. 55-56.

We have now arrived at the beginning of the second part of the Gospel. Up to this point Jesus, Israel's Messiah, has been healing and preaching in Galilee. He has revealed himself as physician, Savior, and king, the Son of God. Now he is en route to Jerusalem. We have learned from the passion predictions (9:22, 44) as well as from the account of the transfiguration (9:28-36) that the outcome of this travel will be the suffering and martyrdom of this Messiah, who is destined to become the suffering Messiah (Acts 26:23). After a solemn introduction (v. 51), the travel narrative (9:51—19:27) opens with an unusual story that is summarized more than it is recounted, and which, in parable-like fashion, signals the new and tragic orientation of this destiny.

This episode may be compared with Matt 10:5b, where Jesus forbids the evangelization of Samaria, literally the entering of a Samaritan town.[1] Luke 9:51-56 and Matt 10:5b are witnesses to the existence of a Samaritan problem. The question could also be asked of the account of Luke, but wrongfully, if its purpose was not to justify or moderate the intransigence of the Matthean Christ. It is better, however, to make a clear distinction between the Matthean and Lukan communities. The Lukan church was unaware of the ban transmitted by Matthew. It was, on the contrary, favorable to a mission in Samaria (cf. Acts 1:8; 8:4-8; 9:31), but it sometimes came up against a certain opposition in that region (cf. Acts 8:9-25). The story reflects the Samaritans' different attitudes in the face of the Christian mission. One village did not welcome Jesus (v. 53), whereas another one, which was probably also in Samaria, seems not to have rejected him (v. 56). So the Samaritan problem does not explain the story, although it does provide a life setting for it. The story we read here has an archaic nucleus; it is not simply a post-Easter projection back into the life of Jesus.

The Traditional Shape of the Story

In the tradition, the story had as its function to render the disciples sensitive to the risks of their profession and to instill in them a proper missionary attitude. It is possible to ascertain the traditional shape of the story that Luke has reworked. Verse 51 did not belong to it; this verse is redactional, as is shown by its syntax, vocabulary, and theology.[2] The story originally began with v. 52.[3] It continued with v. 53a (v. 53b, which is what deals with Jesus' intention, on the other hand, belongs to Luke's redaction) and v. 54, which, except for the vocative "Lord" (κύριε), does not betray any signs of redactional activity (the proper names are certainly anchored in the

1   See Lehmann, *Quellenanalyse,* 143–45; Heinz Schürmann, *Lukas-Evangelium,* vol. 2.1: *Kommentar zu Kapitel 9:51—11:54)* (2d ed.; HThKNT 3.2; Freiburg im B.: Herder, 1994) 31–32.

2   Syntax: ἐγένετο δὲ ἐν τῷ plus the infinitive; καὶ αὐτός, the object before the verb. Vocabulary: συμπληροῦσθαι πορεύεσθαι. Theology: the fulfillment; the journey to Jerusalem; the elevation.

3   The participle πορευθέντες ("having gone") following a conjugated verb as well as the specification of certain locality are non-Lukan elements.

tradition). The content of v. 55 is likewise traditional, even though Luke may have rewritten it in his own way. Verse 56 is redactional in its wording, but tradition could not have ended with Jesus' criticism but must have concluded with their setting off to another destination. In short, if readers were to skip vv. 51 and 53b and not pay too much attention to the Lukan expressions, they would be dealing with the story as found in the tradition.[4]

The Lukan Composition of the Story

Luke was not inimical to the orientation of the story in the tradition. By inserting it into the beginning of the travel narrative, however, he has modified its perspective: although the reader's attention was first directed to the disciples, it is henceforth directed to Jesus. Balancing the rejection of Jesus in Nazareth (4:29-30) is the opposition encountered in Samaria, which in turn anticipates the fatal outcome of the journey to Jerusalem. It is in this way that the Gospel writer has emphasized God's plan and its being carried out in the destiny of the suffering Messiah.

In its redactional form, the unit can be subdivided as follows:

V. 51: *Jesus' **principal plan***
  V. 52a: *Jesus' **command***
    V. 52b: *an **attempt at carrying it out** by the disciples who have been sent*
      V. 53: ***opposition** from anonymous Samaritans*
    V. 54: ***wish expressed** by two named disciples*
  V. 55: *Jesus' **veto***
V. 56: *The beginning of the **carrying out of Jesus' plan***

This unit can thus be understood both in a dynamic way, as a series of reactions, and in a static way, as a chiasmus. To my way of thinking, the two ways of reading the text are complementary and both are required. The story's structure is similar to a balanced photograph; its movement, to the projection of a film.

The State of the Greek Text

In addition to the inevitable differences of detail in the readings of the manuscripts,[5] we have two principal textual variants: (1) Following numerous ancient manuscripts, should we read the indication "even as Elijah did" at the end of v. 54? I would be less inclined to eliminate it as a gloss than modern editors are. Orthodox scribes may have struck it out because of an anti-Marcionite tendency (see Tertullian, *Adv. Marc.* 4.23). (2) Should we include also, between v. 55 and v. 56, the following variant: "and he said, 'You do not know of what spirit you are. The Son of Man has not come to destroy the lives of human beings but to save them.'"[6] This passage is less well attested than the longer text in v. 54. Moreover, the saying about the Son of Man (v. 56a) is a "floating" saying that shows up elsewhere in the Synoptic tradition and is found in different contexts and in various wordings: Luke 19:10; Matt 18:11; cf. Luke 5:32 parr. So this saying could be a gloss here. As for the words "and he said, 'You do not know of what spirit you are'" (v. 55b), they have the advantage of forming a saying by Jesus at the end of an apophthegm. But the very lack of a conclusion for the apophthegm could have occasioned successive extensions that were felt to be necessary: first at the end of v. 55, then at the beginning of v. 56. Furthermore, since the exclamation "You do not know of what spirit you are" (v. 55b) is not Lukan, I opt here for the shorter reading.[7]

---

4 My analysis corresponds roughly to that of Miyoshi, *Anfang*, 6–15. According to Helmut Flender (*Heil und Geschichte*, 35–36), Luke has employed an ancient tradition (vv. 51b, 52b, 53-56) that speaks of Jesus in terms of Elijah *redivivus* and so deprives him of the political component.

5 See *The Gospel according to St. Luke* (ed. American and British Committees of the International Greek New Testament Project; 2 vols; The New Testament in Greek 3; Oxford: Clarendon, 1984–87) 1:212–15.

6 Codex D contains only the first part of this reading; it does not attest the statement about the Son of Man. F. Crawford Burkitt has shown that the Old Latin version of Luke and the Latin version of the *Diatessaron* originally contained the longer text of v. 54 and of vv. 55-56, whereas some important witnesses to the Vulgate have the shorter text (for Burkitt, this shorter text was the primitive Latin text edited by Jerome; see Burkitt, "St Luke 9, 54-56 and the Western 'Diatessaron,'" 48–53). J. M. Ross believes that the longer text of vv. 55-56 corresponds to the primitive text, but he wavers with regard to the text of v. 54 ("The Rejected Words in Luke 9, 54-56," 85–88).

7 The term οἶος is not found elsewhere in Luke-Acts, and the expression "being of such a spirit" is foreign to Luke and can moreover be understood in two ways: (a) "You have the Spirit of God, so

Commentary

■ **51** Jerusalem, which was mentioned in the story of the transfiguration (9:31), appears here as the final destination of Jesus' ministry, literally "travel" or "journey" (the capital could be reached in three days, starting from Galilee and cutting across Samaria). In order to emphasize this perspective, Luke uses solemn, biblical expressions: "days were approaching," "he set his face,"[8] and so on. Moreover, the emphatic "and he," as well as the triple mention of his "face" (vv. 51-53), establish Jesus' identity and his authority as the Messiah. Luke furnished a counterpart to this opening in Acts 19:21,[9] where Paul also announced his intention of going up to Jerusalem before visiting Rome. This means that history repeated itself, albeit with progression. It was inspired by God but carried out by his envoys, who accepted the divine plan.[10] The thread of events and the unfolding of the life of a Christian are pictured as a journey.[11] Luke 13:22, 33; 17:11; and 19:28 remind us that Jesus was on his way to Jerusalem. Jesus' decision was a firm one: the expression "set his face" indicates determination and suggests that Jesus was to face up to his destiny, even to the point of accepting the unjustified suffering that was a part of it (cf. Isa 50:6-7).

Along with the concrete vocabulary concerning the journey, Luke also made parallel use of a term that was rare, abstract,[12] and ambiguous,[13] namely, the word ἀνάλημψις, which referred not only to Jesus' final "being taken up" in the ascension,[14] but also to his passion, and perhaps to his long journey up to Jerusalem as well.[15] This fuzzy and broad semantic field of the word is confirmed by the plural "the days"[16] and by the present infinitive συμπληροῦσθαι ("were approaching"), which carries a durative sense.

---

behave accordingly," or (b) "Your intentions are condemnable; you have the spirit of Satan!" See Frédéric Louis Godet, *A Commentary on the Gospel of St. Luke* (trans. E. W. Shalders and M. D. Cusin; 4th Eng. ed.; 2 vols.; Clark's Foreign Theological Library 45–46; Edinburgh: Clark, 1881, 1890) 2:12. Must one see this as a Marcionite expansion? From a formal point of view, one can compare it with the exclamation of Jesus "You do not know . . ." in Luke 2:49b; 12:56b; 13:27a; 22:60a; 23:34a; as well as in Matt 20:22a; John 8:14c; 11:49b; *2 Clem.* 10.4.

8 The Old Testament uses the expression "to set one's face" in two ways: (a) in the sense of "having the intention to" (in the LXX never translated with στηρίζω), and (b) in the sense of "being opposed to someone" (in the LXX translated with στηρίζω; Jer 21:10; Ezek 6:2; 13:17; etc.). See Starcky, "Obfirmavit," 197–202, who also refers to Isa 50:7. See also Miyoshi, *Anfang*, 9.

9 See Radl, *Paulus und Jesus im lukanischen Doppelwerk*, 103–21.

10 Here and there one finds the idea of fulfillment. Moreover, Acts 19:21 states that Paul was pressed "by the Spirit" and that his visit to Rome was mandatory (theological δεῖ).

11 See the use of περιπατέω ("to walk") in the epistles (e.g., Rom 6:4). On the use of πορεύομαι ("to go") in Luke, see Miyoshi, *Anfang*, 9–10.

12 See the same use of an abstract term for a public office (this time for an inauguration): ἀνάδειξις ("installation") in Luke 1:80. In contrast to

v. 51, v. 31 of this same chapter speaks of ἔξοδος ("departure").

13 See François Bovon, *New Testament Traditions and Apocryphal Narratives* (trans. Jane Haapiseva-Hunter; PTMS 36; Allison Park, Pa.: Pickwick, 1995) 102.

14 Luke uses the verb ἀναλαμβάνω ("to take up") for this purpose in an almost technical sense in Acts 1:2, 11, 22. The noun occurs in *T. Levi* 18:3; *Ps. Sol.* 4:18, and *Kerygma Petrou*, cited by Clement of Alexandria *Strom.* 6.15, 128. See Alfred Plummer, *A Critical and Exegetical Commentary on the Gospel according to St. Luke* (ICC; New York: Scribner, 1896; reprinted 5th ed.; New York: Scribner's Sons; Edinburgh: Clark, 1902) 262. See also BDAG, s.v.; and Gerhard Delling, "λαμβάνω, κτλ.," *TDNT* 4 (1967) 7–9.

15 See Starcky, "Obfirmavit," 197–202; Miyoshi, *Anfang*, 8–9; Gerhard Lohfink, *Die Himmelfahrt Jesu*, 212–17; Gerhard Voss, *Die Christologie der lukanischen Schriften in Grundzügen* (Studia neotestamentica 2; Bruges/Paris: Desclée de Brouwer, 1965) 141; and Bovon, *Theologian*, 196, 183–84 n. 52. On the other hand, Gerhard Friedrich ("Lk 9,51 und die Entrückungschristologie des Lukas," 48–77) sees only an allusion to the death of Jesus.

16 Cf. the similar construction with the singular τὴν ἡμέραν in Acts 2:1 (although a part of the manuscript tradition attests the plural).

■ **52-53** The disciples were sent on ahead to prepare the Lord's way,[17] like new John the Baptists (cf. "prepare" [ἐτοιμάσατε] in 3:4, quoting Isa 40:3). They were to run into opposition just as the forerunner John the Baptist had (cf. 3:19-20). Somewhat clumsily, Luke points out that they were not welcomed, because of what Jesus had in mind to do (v. 53b). The hostility between Samaritans and Jews[18] in this passage is an expression, in a quasi-Johannine manner, of the lack of openness on the part of human beings to God's plan. Luke's repetition of Jesus' firm plan, which corresponded to God's will, goes along with the idea of a Christology of the suffering Messiah.

■ **54-55** At this point James and John, the two sons of Zebedee, reacted inappropriately. Luke did not doubt that God was able to give the apostles the same destructive energy that he had conferred on his prophets in former days. What is more, he put on their lips one of Elijah's expressions (2 Kgs [4 Kgdms] 1:10, 12).[19] James's and John's attitude was due to their zeal for YHWH, a zeal that would resort to the use of any and all means.[20] In the ministries of not only Jesus but also his apostles and the church, however, God's plan is to be carried out not violently but through weakness, that is to say, through the acceptance of defeat, suffering, and finiteness. In the end, this submission turns out to be a strength, since it corresponds to God's will. That is the strength that Jesus drew on to counter his disciples' tempting proposal.[21]

The appearance of proper names is not so surprising in view of the fact that they were important for Luke's special source, L (material peculiar to Luke's Gospel alone). Should we see in their use more than an anecdotal interest? Maybe so, if we consider the fact that another tradition attributed to the same persons visions of grandeur (being seated on the left hand and the right hand of Christ, Mark 10:35-40 par. Matt 20:20-23).

■ **56** Jesus' reproof of his disciples reestablished the unity of the group, as is seen in the fact that Jesus was no longer traveling alone (note the singular in v. 51); now the disciples were accompanying him (note the plural in v. 56). Luke says nothing about what welcome the other village might have given them. Did it open up to the message of the gospel? Luke's silence regarding this matter leaves the question open and draws our attention to Jesus' peregrinations toward his martyrdom in Jerusalem and to the procession of disciples who were soon to be called to a missionary task (10:1-20).

History of Interpretation

These verses got caught up in the controversy that Tertullian carried on against Marcion (*Adv. Marc.* 4.23.8). It appears that Marcion used the present pericope to set the merciful Christ over against the vengeful God of the Hebrew Scriptures. Tertullian replied that a distinction must be made between retribution and revenge. Not just the God of the patriarchs but also Christ is known to punish on some occasions but show tenderness on others. God acted as judge when he caused fire to come down from heaven (2 Kgs [4 Kgdms] 1:9-12). In the present pericope we see Jesus sparing the Samaritans, but at the same time vigorously rebuking his disciples.

Ambrose of Milan cast his interpretation of this passage in the context of a contrast between the potential disciples that Jesus turned away and those that he called (*Exp. Luc.* 7.22–30). As a consequence, he meditated on the virtues of simplicity, fidelity, charity, and the like. In his opinion, what Christ preferred was pedagogical clemency. What he planned to do, then, was not to call the Samaritans to follow the gospel, but to follow through on his destiny by going up to Jerusalem. The Samaritans would come around to the faith in their own time at a later date. Ambrose makes an elegant distinction between the disciples' desire to be welcomed in Samaria, to be recognized—and, one might add, to be loved—and

---

17   On the use of ὡς with an infinitive in a final sense, see BDAG, s.v., 9b, which refers to Acts 20:24. Some manuscripts read ὡστε.

18   See Josephus *Ant.* 20.6 §118: the massacre of the Galileans who passed through Samaria and the vengeance that ensued with the help of the Jews.

19   It does not involve, however, an exact quotation from the LXX (2 Kgs [4 Kgdms] 1:10, 12), where one twice finds the verb "devour" and not "consume."

20   The *Acts of Philip* takes up and develops this motif. During his martyrdom, Philip calls for fire from heaven to fall on his enemies and the earth to engulf them (*Acts Phil.* 132–33).

21   This theme recalls that of the temptation (4:1-13) and especially the refusal of angelic help, Matt 26:51-53; cf. Luke 23:35, 39.

the will of Christ, who aligned himself with God's plan, consequently accepting rejection and suffering. According to Ambrose, the disciples did not sin, since they stuck to the law. But Christ demonstrated perfect virtue in combining charity with the absence of revenge.

Cyril of Alexandria begins his discussion of the passage with an interpretation of Jesus' being "taken away" as an ascension into heaven of which the road of the passion was a part (*Hom. in Luc.* 56).[22] To his way of thinking, the setting of his face stood for the Son's determination as a part of the plan (in the sense of the plan of salvation). He understood the episode concerning the Samaritans as a test that Jesus put his disciples to in order better to train them. It was in the first instance an exercise that was preparatory to the passion. When their Master was martyred, the apostles would have to imitate God and his Son, both of whom knew how to endure injustice, rather than follow the human reflex that would give in to the desire to show anger. It was, moreover, a lesson to be learned in view of the evangelization they were to carry on later. The disciples were indeed to be preachers rather than torturers. As stewards of what was divine, they needed to be ministers whose lives were stamped with tenderness. Cyril subtly reflected in this way on the potential abuses of ecclesiastical power.[23]

Conclusion

The travel narrative begins with a conflict involving different wills. Placed at the beginning of it is, first of all, Jesus' determination, shown in his setting off on the road to Jerusalem, that is, on the road leading to his passion. The Master combined courage with perseverance and clearly demonstrated these traits. Whatever that might cost him, his plan was a willing acceptance of fitting into God's plan, for which God needed this human mediator. Then we have the Samaritans' negative will and finally the vindictive will of the disciples, who were doubtless angry and frustrated. Both the Samaritans and the disciples were clear witnesses of the human tendency to catch on slowly, and so they did not understand either what God intended or how tortuous a route God's plan takes to be carried out. The Samaritans and the disciples operated on the level of violence and revenge; the Father and the Son, on one of persuasion and suffering, dialogue and forgiveness. Confronted by the strategy of God, the king who renounces the option of killing his enemies, human maneuvering counted on drawing on divine power, which is precisely what the Son of God was in the process of renouncing. The divine strategy, for its part, was to prevail with the passage of time, since Jesus' stance was to serve as an example. The disciples would indeed understand it, and eventually adopt it. So the gospel, when it was proclaimed, did produce disciples and give rise to communities of faith. But this very success of love, weakness, and the giving of oneself would also provoke a negative reaction on the part of those who never succeeded in becoming engaged in the process of reconciliation. During the period of the church, persecution was to be the companion of communion. In narrative fashion, vv. 52-56 tell how God's envoy turned his back on the easy way and thereby gave his disciples a lesson. The Christian mission, he told them, must submit to the same requirements. The beginning of the travel narrative thus retells the message of the end of the ministry in Galilee (9:43b-50) and foreshadows the mission that the disciples were entrusted with shortly after (10:1-20). One must be prepared to be rejected. Facing up to it is tantamount to not succumbing to either revenge or discouragement. The gospel's being rejected does not necessarily imply the annihilation of the persons who are witnesses to it. There is a certain distance between the gospel and those who proclaim it.

22   See Robert Payne Smith, *A Commentary upon the Gospel according to S. Luke, by Cyril, Patriarch of Alexandria, Now First Translated into English from an Ancient Syriac Version* (2 vols.; Oxford: Oxford University Press, 1859) 1:253–57. There also exist four Greek fragments of this homily; see Joseph Reuss, *Lukas-Kommentare aus der griechischen Kirche: Aus Katenenhandschriften gesammelt und herausgegeben* (TU 130; Berlin: Akademie-Verlag, 1984) 101–2.

23   In the Middle Ages, the church of the Occident knew of our pericope only in its expanded version with the following variant added to vv. 55-56: "You do not know what kind of spirit you are, for the Son of Man has not come to destroy men's lives but to save them."

Following Jesus in One's Life
(9:57-62)

Bibliography

Black, Matthew, *An Aramaic Approach to the Gospels and Acts* (2d ed.; Oxford: Clarendon, 1954) 207–8.

Blair, H. J., "Putting One's Hand to the Plough: Luke 9, 62 in the Light of 1 Kings 19, 19–21," *ExpT* 79 (1967–68) 342–43.

Casey, "Jackals," 3–22.

Cerfaux, Lucien, *Recuiel Lucien Cerfaux: Études d'exégèse et d'histoire religieuse de Monseifneur Cerfaux, réunies à l'occasion de son soixante-dixième anniversaire* (3 vols.; BETL 6–7, 18; Gembloux: Duculot, 1954–62) 1:488–501.

Coulot, Claude, *Jésus et le disciple: Études sur l'autorité messianique de Jésus* (EtB 8; Paris: Gabalda, 1987) 18–40.

Dupont, Jacques, *Études sur les Évangiles synoptiques* (ed. Frans Neirynck; 2 vols.; BETL 70; Leuven: Leuven University Press, 1985) 1:131–45.

Edwards, Richard A., *A Theology of Q: Eschatology, Prophecy, and Wisdom* (Philadelphia: Fortress, 1976) 100–101.

Glombitza, O., "Die christologische Aussage des Lukas in seiner Gestaltung der drei Nachfolgeworte Lukas 9, 57-62," *NovT* 13 (1971) 14–23.

Grässer, Erich, *Das Problem der Parusieverzögerung in den synoptischen Evangelien und in der Apostelgeschichte* (BZNW 22; Berlin: Töpelmann, 1957) 189.

Hahn, Ferdinand, "Die Nachfolge Jesus in vorösterlicher Zeit," in idem, August Strobel, and Eduard Schweizer, eds., *Die Anfänge der Kirche im Neuen Testament* (Evangelisches Forum 8; Göttingen: Vandenhoeck & Ruprecht, 1967) 7–36.

Hengel, Martin, *The Charismatic Leader and His Followers* (trans. James Greig; New York: Crossroad, 1981) 3–15 and passim.

Hermann, L., "Correction du ν [sic, = k] en α dans une phrase de Jésus," *REA* 83 (1981) 283.

Hoffmann, Paul, *Studien zur Theologie der Logienquelle* (NTAbh n.s. 8; Münster: Aschendorff, 1972) 181–87.

Horn, *Glaube und Handeln*, 193–94.

Javet, J.-S., "Suivre Jésus dans sa marche vers Jérusalem (Lc 9, 51-62)," *ASeign* 44 (1981) 283.

Jüngel, Ernst, *Paulus und Jesus: Eine Untersuchung zur Präzisierung der Frage nach dem Ursprung der Christologie* (4th ed.; HUT 2; Tübingen: Mohr Siebeck, 1972) 181–82.

Klemm, H. G., "Das Wort von der Selbstbestattung der Toten," *NTS* 16 (1969–70) 60–75.

Kloppenborg, John S., *The Formation of Q: Trajectories in Ancient Wisdom Collections* (Studies in Antiquity and Christianity 2; Philadelphia: Fortress Press, 1987) 42, 57 n. 61, 83, 92 n. 5.

Légasse, Simon, "Scribes et disciples de Jésus," *RB* 68 (1961) 321–45 (esp. 340–45), 481–505.

Lührmann, Dieter, *Die Redaktion der Logienquelle: Anhang: Zur weiteren Überlieferung der Logienquelle* (WMANT 33; Neukirchen-Vluyn: Neukirchener Verlag, 1969) 58.

Merklein, Helmut, *Die Gottesherrschaft als Handlungsprinzip: Untersuchung zur Ethik Jesu* (2d ed.; FB 34; Würzburg: Echter, 1981) 56–64.

Miyoshi, *Anfang*, 33–58.

Nolland, 2:538 (bibliography).

Petzke, Gerd, *Das Sondergut des Evangeliums nach Lukas* (Zürcher Werkkommentare zur Bibel; Zurich: Theologischer Verlag, 1990) 104–7.

Piper, Ronald A., *Wisdom in the Q-Tradition: The Aphoristic Teaching of Jesus* (SNTSMS 61; Cambridge: Cambridge University Press, 1989) 165–67 and passim.

Polag, Athanasius, *Die Christologie der Logienquelle* (WMANT 45; Neukirchen-Vluyn: Neukirchener Verlag, 1977) 84–85 and passim.

Prévost, Sylvie, "L'espace significant: Analyse sémiotique de Luc. 9, 57-62" (diss., Université de Montréal, 1990) (unavailable to me).

Sato, Migaku, *Q und Prophetie: Studien zur Gattungs- und Traditionsgeschichte der Quelle Q* (WUNT 2.29; Tübingen: Mohr Siebeck, 1988) 55, 61, 81 and passim.

Schmid, Josef, *Matthäus und Lukas: Eine Untersuchung des Verhältnisses ihrer Evangelien* (BibS[F] 23/2–4; Freiburg: Herder, 1930) 256–57.

Schneider, G., "Nachfolge Jesu' heute?" in idem, *Anfragen an das Neue Testament* (Essen: Ludgerus, 1971) 132–46.

Schrage, Wolfgang, *Das Verhältnis des Thomas-Evangeliums zur synoptischen Tradition und zu den koptischen Evangelienübersetzungen* (BZNW 29; Berlin: Töpelmann, 1964) 168–70.

Schulz, Anselm. *Jünger des Herrn: Nachfolge Christi nach dem Neuen Testament* (Munich: Kösel, 1964) 13–22, 27–29, 40–44, 48–53.

Schulz, Siegfried, *Q: Die Spruchquelle der Evangelisten* (Zurich: Theologischer Verlag, 1972) 434–42.

Schürmann, Heinz, "Sprachliche Reminiszenzen an abgeänderte oder ausgelassene Bestandteile der Spruchsammlungen im Lukas- und Mattäusevangelium," *NTS* 6 (1959–60) 193–210, esp. 204–5.

Schweizer, Eduard, *Lordship and Discipleship* (SBT 28; Naperville, Ill.: Allenson, 1960) 16–17.

Scott, R. B. Y., "The Expectation of Elijah," *Canadian Journal of Religious Thought* 3 (1926) 1–13.

Steinhauser, Michael G., *Doppelbildworte in den synoptischen Evangelien: Eine form- und tradionskritischen Studie* (FB 44; Würzburg: Echter, 1981) 96–121.

Idem, "Putting One's Hand to the Plow: The Authenticity of Q 9, 61-62," *Forum* 5.2 (1989) 151–58.

Strobel, August, "Die Nachfolge Jesu: Theologische Besinnung zu Lk 9, 57-62," *Theologisch-praktische Quartalschrift* 98 (1950) 1–8.

Idem, "Textgeschichtliches zum Thomasevangelium 86," *VC* 17 (1963) 211–24.

Sweetland, Dennis M., *Our Journey with Jesus: Discipleship according to Luke-Acts* (GNS 23; Collegeville, Minn.: Liturgical Press, 1990) 33–35 and passim.

Taeger, Jens-W., *Der Mensch und sein Heil: Studien zum Bild des Menschen und zur Sicht der Bekehrung bei Lukas* (StNT 14; Gütersloh: Mohn, 1982) 170–71.

Tannehill, Robert C., *The Sword of His Mouth* (SSup 1; Philadelphia: Fortress Press; Missoula, Mont.: Scholars Press, 1975) 157–65.

Vaage, Leif E., "Q¹ and the Historical Jesus: Some Peculiar Sayings (7, 33-43; 9, 57-58, 59-60; 14, 26-27)," *Forum* 5.2 (1989) 159–76, esp. 166–76.

Wanke, Joachim, *"Bezugs- und Bekenntnisworte" in den synoptischen Evangelien: Beobachtungen zur Interpretationsgeschichte der Herrenwort in der vorevangelischen Überlieferung* (EThSt 44: Leipzig: St. Benno, 1981) 40–44.

Zimmermann, Heinrich, *Neutestamentliche Methodenlehre: Darstellung der historisch-kritische Methode* (Stuttgart: Katholisches Bibelwerk, 1967) 116–22.

57/ And as they were going along the road, someone said to him, "I will follow you wherever you go." **58/** And Jesus said to him, "Foxes have holes, and birds of the air have nests; but the Son of Man has nowhere to lay his head." **59/** Then to another he said, "Follow me!" He said, "Lord, first let me go and bury my father." **60/** But he said to him, "Let the dead bury their own dead; but as for you, go and spread the news about the kingdom of God." **61/** And still another said, "I will follow you, Lord; but let me first say farewell to those at my home." **62/** But Jesus said to him, "No one who puts a hand to the plow and looks back is fit for the kingdom of God."

The preceding pericope (9:51-56) as well as all of the travel narrative associate Christology with ecclesiology. The present pericope (9:57-62) places the person of Jesus at the heart of the attitude of believers. But whereas the theme of *sending* (the disciples who go on ahead) was dominant in the previous verses, in these verses the center of focus is *following* (the disciples who follow). In short, the Gospel writer has given us three sayings of Jesus on the status of being a Christian in the context of three different encounters with potential disciples.

Although the verb "follow" ($\dot{\alpha}\kappa o\lambda o\upsilon\vartheta\acute{\epsilon}\omega$) suffices to define what it means to be a Christian, since it reduces the definition to what is essential, the readers of the Gospel still have to go into what that means in the scheme of the Gospel, all the while being wary of their preconceived ideas. Following someone can, as a matter of fact, denote adopting a servile attitude, a blind allegiance, a childish dependence, or an imitation that causes one to be estranged. But following also brings to mind the idea of wanting to accompany someone, to be trained, and to foster collaboration. So becoming someone's disciple or student is not necessarily a bad thing. Everything depends on who and what the teacher is, and on the student.

Analysis

In this passage Luke does not seem to be following either the Gospel of Mark or L. He must have picked up again on Q, as suggested by a comparison with the parallel in

Matt 8:18-21.[1] But while the author of the First Gospel places these verses in the context of a series of miracles, Luke puts them at the beginning of the journey, the importance of which he brings out by mentioning "going along" and "the road" in v. 57.

Matthew seems to be acquainted with only the first two of the three dialogues that Luke transmits. Following a rule of the Synoptic tradition, the third one was probably put together by Luke on the model of the first two,[2] with its nucleus being an isolated saying of Jesus (v. 62) that Paul would also appear to have known (see Phil 3:13).[3] The basis for the excuse (v. 61), when compared with the seriousness of the expression of enthusiasm reported in v. 57 or the situation depicted in v. 59, confirms the artificial nature of the third case.

When the Synoptic tradition brought together examples of people being called, it was responding not to a historical requirement but to a catechetical necessity, which Luke also observed by adding a third case. It is instructive to compare these examples with other call narratives, e.g., Mark 1:16-20 or Luke 5:27-28. In these latter texts, the men are called by Jesus and we know their names; moreover, they put up no resistance and immediately follow their new master. Here, by contrast, those would-be disciples mentioned in vv. 57 and 61 remain anonymous and on their own think of committing themselves to serving Christ.[4] All of them leave us guessing as to what their final decision was, while Jesus in turn lays awesome conditions on them. So the Synoptic tradition is acquainted with two types of call narratives,[5] each with its own theological orientation. The triple tradition (Mark 1:16-20 parr.) recounts the irresistible call that the apostles, the known founding figures, received from the Lord; the double tradition (Luke 9:57-62 parr.) stresses the permanent requirements of the Christian life. By leaving in the shadow the disciples' names and what resulted from their being called, this tradition, followed by Luke, confronts readers with a decision to make about their faith.

It is not difficult to determine which parts of the accounts are due to the redactional work of the Gospel writers, especially Luke. As is often the case, the Gospel writer is responsible for the introduction (v. 57a).[6] Then, except for the vocative "Master" found in Matt 8:19, the commitment the first disciple risks making (v. 57b) is identical in Matthew and Luke, because they have both drawn on the same Greek version of Q. Jesus' answer (v. 58), also identical in Matthew and Luke, confirms this analysis.[7]

The respective wordings of the second case in Matthew and Luke differ in their beginning; in this case, Matthew must have the original version, since he follows the rule in this genre and has the disciple speak first (Matt 8:21). Luke, shocked by the "first," which presupposes a call, has corrected the original, thus drawing on Jesus' later answer for "follow me" (Matt 8:22), out of which he makes an initial call (v. 59a), which he has forgone using later (v. 59b). Aside from this one difference, what Jesus says (v. 59b) is the same in the accounts of the two Gospel writers.

Is it possible to go back further than Q? Yes, if we admit that the Synoptic tradition attempted to pour into a single mold two episodes whose development was originally different. What the second disciple says, "Let me first . . . ," presupposes a previous contact with Jesus, probably a call. Luke, who sensed this anomaly, perhaps recovered the original shape of the episode but developed it in a secondary way.

---

1   This opinion is almost unanimous. See, e.g., Schmid, *Matthäus und Lukas,* 256–57; and Miyoshi, *Anfang,* 34.

2   Note that the words "another," "I will follow you," "said," and "first" (v. 61) are borrowed from the first two examples (v. 57 and v. 59).

3   These two motifs in Phil 3:13 (forgetting what is behind and focusing on the goal) are explained by the presence of Jesus' statement (Luke 9:62) in the spirit of the apostle Paul. While I attribute the third case to Luke, Petzke (*Sondergut,* 104, 106–7) attributes it to Luke's sources.

4   The parallel in Matt 8:21 suggests that in that tradition it is the would-be disciple who takes the initiative in the second case, just as in the first.

5   See the commentary on 5:27-28 (1:188–89).

6   Note that Luke is fond of $\pi o \rho \epsilon \acute{v} o \mu \alpha \iota$ ("to go") and $\acute{o} \delta \acute{o} \varsigma$ ("way"), particularly in the account of the journey. Compared with the dative of Matthew, $\pi \rho \grave{o} \varsigma$ $\alpha \grave{v} \tau \acute{o} \nu$ ("to him") must also be Lukan.

7   Compared with the present $\lambda \acute{e} \gamma \epsilon \iota$ ("he says") of Matthew, the historicizing $\epsilon \hat{\iota} \pi \epsilon \nu$ ("he said") of Luke is redactional.

Gospel of Thomas 86 was acquainted with Jesus' first saying, the one about the foxes.[8] On the other hand, sufficient attention has not been paid to the fact that saying 87 of this same Gospel must have been an interpretive rereading of Jesus' second saying, the one about burying the dead: "Jesus said: 'Wretched is the body that is dependent upon a body, and wretched is the soul that is dependent on these two.'"[9] When added to the absence in the *Gospel of Thomas* of any parallel to Jesus' third saying (the one about the plow), this observation confirms the coupling of the first two examples in the tradition. The fact that the *Gospel of Thomas* transmits only Jesus' words and not the entire apophthegms, is certainly due to the literary genre of this document. It is possible, however, that this apocryphal Gospel may have preserved the memory of the secondary character, in Q, of the dialogical structure. Jesus' sayings (on the foxes and the dead) are, in fact, not necessarily answers and do not explicitly suggest following him. In that case Q's catechetical effort would have been all the more remarkable; Q would have made up, from scratch, on the basis of some sayings of Jesus, a dialogical teaching on the radical commitment expected of disciples.

Commentary

■ **57-58** In his introduction, Luke stresses the itinerant existence of the master and his disciples[10] and thus prepares for Jesus' saying about the foxes. The future follower, who makes a statement of lasting commitment,[11] elicits a reply from Jesus that defines such a person as one who is perhaps unaware of the deprivations that his proposed line of action involves.[12] The text, as it develops, does not imply an opposition to following Jesus on a long-term basis. On the contrary, the status of permanent disciple is a Christian innovation (pupils followed their rabbis only for a limited period of time, the time necessary for them to be trained up to the point of getting set up on their own).[13] The stakes in the dialogue are related to another point, namely, the existential repercussions of becoming a follower. Christian readers are reminded of Peter himself, who dared make a similar promise (22:33) without being able in the end to make good on it (22:34, 54-62).[14]

"Along the road": This expression, although seemingly banal, is decisively important for Luke. It refers not only to the Messiah's historical itinerary leading up to the passion (19:36; 24:32) but also to the Way that leads to life (Acts 2:28), the Christian life in its fullness, involving obedience[15] and suffering, the Christian message in its concrete expression of truth (Acts 9:2).[16]

Jesus' warning, expressed as a maxim about the Son of Man,[17] calls our attention to the fact that the Christian life implies a break with emotional ties. The Son of Man is a man on the move (13:33), a homeless person. His fate is less certain than that of agile and mobile ani-

---

8   This text, which in part must be reconstructed, is almost identical to that of Q. The single feature worth noting (unquestionably an interpolation by the author of the *Gospel of Thomas*) is the expression at the end of the sentence: "(and) to rest." See Schrage, *Thomas-Evangelium,* 168–70; August Strobel, "Textgeschichtliches zum Thomas-Logion 86," *VC* 17 (1963) 211–24; Steinhauser, *Doppelbildworte,* 117–21.

9   The play on words "body . . . body" (= corpse) represents an interpretative reiteration of the expression "the dead . . . the dead." One should keep in mind that σῶμα signifies primarily a dead body, a cadaver (e.g., Homer *Il.* 7.79). But it can often refer to a living body, whereas πτῶμα is especially reserved for a cadaver.

10 The words "in the way" can be construed with the verb "traveling" as well as with the verb "said" (see Plummer, 265). Perhaps, as is his custom, Luke deliberately allows the ambiguity to remain.

11 See Anselm Schulz, *Nachfolgen und Nachahmen: Studien über das Verhältnis der neutestamentlichen Jüngerschaft zur urchristlichen Vorbildethik* (SANT 6; Munich: Kösel, 1962) 105. On the verb ἀκολουθέω ("to follow"), see the commentary on 5:27-28 (1:188).

12 See Godet, 2:13; Plummer, 265. Matthew 8:19 specifies that it was a scribe.

13 See Schluz, *Nachfolgen,* 106.

14 On the Hellenistic usage of ἐάν ("if") for ἄν, especially after relative pronouns, see BDF §108.1 n. 3. With ἐάν, the sense is "wherever you go."

15 In the sense of living in accordance with God's will (Deut 26:17; Isa 30:21; Prov 15:10). On ὁδός ("way") in Luke, see Bovon, *Theologian,* 321–23 (a survey of the principal works).

16 Among the variants in v. 57, the most interesting is the presence of the vocative "Lord" at the end of the prospective disciple's promise. On both external and internal evidence, however, I prefer the shorter text.

mals.[18] Even the humblest animals have their shelters and lairs, while the Son of Man, who is nonetheless powerful and lordly, has nowhere to lay his head. He is assuredly not deprived of security, but his security resides not in a material or human protection but in God's love and authority.

Luke implies that Christians share this uncertain destiny, which reminds us of Wisdom's fate among human beings. Following Christ with perseverance is tantamount to losing any sanctuary, the security of a nest, or maternal protection. Becoming a persevering follower of Christ means leaving the reassuring context of one's childhood and moving on as an adult in an inhospitable world such as the one suggested by the previous episode (9:51-56).[19] Following a biblical and Eastern tradition, Jesus expressed himself in a figurative and exaggerated way when he recommended making these breaks with one's emotional ties. He did not expect us to deny the vital importance of either maternal love or a protective bed for a small child. What he had in mind was rather a substitution in which counting on Christ's protection and finding one's shelter in God would replace earthly and human securities. Be that as it may, the Gospel does not say everything at once. What it affirms here is that, for this substitution to work, one must accept making some breaks and sacrifices that touch on the most sensitive parts of one's existence. There will be other passages in which fellowship and protection are promised. For the moment, however, it is advisable to reflect on what is involved in passing from one reality to another, namely, substituting God's interests for one's own advantages. The enthusiastic candidates who promise the whole world have not yet undergone the shock of destabilization that is necessarily involved.

■ **59-60** The second dialogue takes place in three phases. After an invitation, a request is made, which in turn is turned down and replaced by a sending. In this case becoming a follower involves a departure (ἀπελθών) that unfolds as a missionary enterprise.[20] The διά- ("through") in διαγγέλλω ("spread the news") indicates that a diffusion of the message in all directions is required.[21] The content of the proclamation that has been retained by Luke—for v. 60b is entirely redactional—is the kingdom of God. There we have gathered together, in any case, in both specific and general terms, the heart of the gospel: its principal features are a concentration on God, links with Jesus (suffering Messiah and risen Lord), and a perspective that is eschatological in the long term and ecclesial in the short term.[22]

In the midst of the dialogue—the traditional part—there is the apparently legitimate request to "first" go and bury one's father. Already here, as it will again be the case in v. 61, there is perhaps a reference to the prophet Elisha's request to go and say good-bye to his father and mother before following his new master, the prophet Elijah (1 Kgs [3 Kgdms] 19:19-21). The reader, whether Jew or Gentile, is aware of the imperative character of burials and how parents always want their children to accompany them right up to their final resting place.[23]

17 In Q and in Luke, the conversation is about Jesus and not about people in general. On the concept of the Son of Man in Luke, see the commentary on 5:21-24 (1:182–83, esp. n. 31) and Bovon, *Theologian*, 181.

18 On the fox as a symbol of cunning craftiness and its use sometimes to depict humans (as in 13:32), see BDAG, s.v. ἀλώπηξ. One must understand the term in its proper sense, *pace* those few who want to see here a jackal. As for the term φωλεός, it signifies a "hole" or a "den." On the birds and their nests, see I. Howard Marshall, *The Gospel of Luke: A Commentary on the Greek Text* (NIGTC; Grand Rapids: Eerdmans; Exeter: Paternoster, 1978) 410. The term κατασκήνωσις is rare and late. Originally it referred to the action of pitching a tent and then, more generally, to taking up residence. Finally it came to signify the "dwelling" itself, the "home"

as it does here: a "refuge," a "shelter," a "nest." On this verse, see Steinhauser, *Doppelbildworte*, 96–121; Casey, "Jackals." Cf. the similar use of two animals in another saying of Jesus, Matt 10:16 (serpents and doves).

19 It is on the cross that Jesus will rest his head as he returns to the Father (John 19:30).

20 See Miyoshi, *Anfang*, 46–49.

21 See Godet, 2:14–15.

22 On the concept of the kingdom of God in Luke, see the commentary on 13:18 below (p. 297) and Bovon, *Theologian*, 69–71.

23 For attitudes in Judaism, see Sir 7:33; 22:11-12; 38:16-23; *b. Ber.* 1a; see also Hengel, *Charismatic Leader*, 8–9; Str-B 4.1:560–61. As for Greek culture, one should recall that in the tragedy of Sophocles, the main concern for Antigone was to bury her brother, even in the face of the tyrant's prohibition.

The radicalism of the gospel is critical of observing the law and tradition. Jesus' saying is surprising also by virtue of the intentional ambiguity between the figurative meaning and the literal meaning of the expression "the dead."[24] The Gospel of Luke itself (15:24, 32) provides proof of its use in the figurative sense, in both Judaism and later in Christianity, to refer to sinners and pagans.[25]

That being the case, Jesus' order contains a double obligation: (a) that of joining him in an immediate and total way that requires, as a necessary concomitant, (b) a break with one's family ties and with the religion of duty (burying one's father was a religious duty, a gesture of submission to the tradition related to fathers[26]). In Jesus' eyes, it is necessary to leave one's father in order to live, just as it was necessary, according to v. 58, to give up a certain relationship to one's mother. Preferring instead to follow the call of duty, however religious, rather than loving the Lord, is tantamount to keeping company with the dead, to dying. The believer who wishes to live must follow another way, the one put forth by Jesus, namely, going and proclaiming God's reign. By means of a play on words, Jesus' aphorism begins by shutting human reality up inside the phenomenon of death, since here elective mortality is a companion of inescapable mortality. This dramatic situation is not inevitable, however, since there is, in fact, the call and the possibility extended to "go" elsewhere than to the cemetery (the same verb "to go" [$\dot{\alpha}\pi\acute{\epsilon}\rho\chi o\mu\alpha\iota$] is used in both v. 59 and v. 60).[27]

■ **61-62** The world of parents is not the only one that might keep a future disciple from signing on (vv. 57-60). There is also—as Luke was at pains to add, v. 61 being redactional[28]—the world of spouses, other family members, and those with whom one has social relationships, "those[29] at my home." The text stigmatizes here the man who is torn between wanting at the same time to follow Jesus and to keep up contacts with those who are dearest to him, principally his wife and his children (cf. Luke 14:26).[30] If Luke's Jesus does not allow that concession it is because there is a way of taking leave ($\dot{\alpha}\pi o\tau\acute{\alpha}\xi\alpha\sigma\vartheta\alpha\iota$)[31] that, far from signifying a break or a death, maintains the relationship, even if only on a nostalgic plane. The request made by the third speaker[32] (a request worded in terms that are reminiscent of Elisha's request, 1 Kgs [3 Kgdms] 19:19-21)[33] corresponds to that inner inability to tear oneself away.

Jesus' rejoinder is addressed not only to that man but, over his head, to other persons called in the time of Q and Luke. It is a word of wisdom that we meet up with in a related form in Greek literature.[34] The main idea is as follows: those who look back on the work already accom-

---

See also Philostratus *Vit. Ap.* 1.13 (Apollonius buries his father).

24 See Hengel, *Charismatic Leader*, 7–8.

25 See Str-B 1:489 (on Matt 8:21) and 3:652 (on 1 Tim 5:6); Rudolf Bultmann, "$\nu\epsilon\kappa\rho\acute{o}\varsigma, \kappa\tau\lambda.$," *TDNT* 4 (1967) 892–93.

26 See n. 23 above on the obligation to bury one's parents. Hengel (*Charismatic Leader*, 11–12) refers to God's command to Ezekiel not to bury his wife as a sign of God's judgment on Israel (Ezek 24:15-24; cf. Jer 16:1-7).

27 Several exegetes take offense at the unbearable harshness of Jesus' command. Black (*Aramaic Approach*, 207–8) proposes that the original statement was "Follow me and let the undecided (מתנין) bury the dead (מית יהון)." With Marshall (p. 411), I regard this reconstruction as unnecessary.

28 See Zimmermann, *Methodenlehre*, 121.

29 $To\hat{\iota}\varsigma$ here is masculine. If Luke had wanted to speak of one's possessions ($To\hat{\iota}\varsigma$ as a neuter), he would have used $\dot{\epsilon}\nu$ with the dative (involving no motion), not $\epsilon\dot{\iota}\varsigma$ with the accusative (see Godet, 2:15).

30 Certainly, even the disciple of a rabbi would leave his family, but this would not entail a final separation; and the parents in such a case were proud of their son (see Hengel, *Charismatic Leader*, 13–14).

31 $\dot{\alpha}\pi o\tau\acute{\alpha}\sigma\sigma\epsilon\sigma\vartheta\alpha\iota$ (middle voice): "to leave one's rank," then "to separate oneself from," "to bid farewell," "to renounce."

32 According to Miyoshi (*Anfang*, 42–43, 52–55), Luke has constructed vv. 61-62 with the help of an old tradition that he used in connection with 17:31. Miyoshi also underscores the connection between vv. 61-62 and 14:25-35. In both passages, the words $\dot{\alpha}\pi o\tau\acute{\alpha}\sigma\sigma\epsilon\sigma\vartheta\alpha\iota$ and $\epsilon\ddot{\upsilon}\vartheta\epsilon\tau o\varsigma$ are emphasized.

33 Blair ("Putting One's Hand to the Plough," 342–43) supposes that the parallel with Elisha can be stretched from v. 61 to v. 62. In this case, "putting the hand to the plow" means to take it and destroy it, as Elisha broke and then burned the yokes of his oxen. In my judgment, this hypothesis is improbable. I see v. 62 as merely depicting a ploughman focused on his work.

34 For example, in Hesiod, *Op.* 441–45: "Together with these, a strong forty-year-old man should follow

14

plished rather than ahead to what remains to be done, are doing a bad job of plowing. They are not headed straight toward their goal. The saying thus praises those who concentrate on their goal and criticizes those who have any regrets. For a long time already the biblical tradition had been denouncing looking back (Gen 19:17, 26; 1 Kgs [3 Kgdms] 19:20-21), that temptation to believe one can count on what is solid in what one knows (e.g., the "fleshpots" of Egypt), and that lack of confidence and faith in relation to the uncertain goods that are hoped for (Exod 16:3). The only persons fit for and adapted to (εὔθετος)[35] the kingdom are those who are like a laborer who has his mind set on one and only one task, one and only one target.[36]

History of Interpretation

Irenaeus of Lyon's *Adversus haereses* (1.8.3) allows us to go back to one of the oldest interpretations of the Gospel of Luke, that of the Gnostic Ptolemy, who was the leader of western Valentinianism in the middle of the second century. According to the summary Irenaeus gave of Ptolemy's Valentinian interpretation, that interpretation used the three cases in Luke 9:57-62 to mark off the three categories of human beings. The first dialogue (vv. 57-58) allowed us to understand the nature of the person who is "hylic," that is, the material person who is excluded from redemption. The third case (vv. 61-62) symbolized the "psychic" person, an intermediate character, and the second conversation, with its saying about let-

ting the dead bury their dead (vv. 59-60), illustrated the spiritual person, a member of the chosen race. Irenaeus's text is unfortunately too short to allow us to understand the nuances of this Gnostic exegesis and to know if, in the biblical text used by Ptolemy, the conversations followed a different order from the one in our present Gospel of Luke. And, most important of all, at this place in the text, there is no rejoinder from Irenaeus, with the result that his interpretation remains unfortunately unknown to us.

Tertullian has shed light for us on a few exegetical questions (*Adv. Marc.* 4.23.9–11). He forced Marcion, the great proponent of the idea of the Savior's tenderness, to admit that Jesus had been able to occupy the role of a judge by exposing the arrogance and hypocrisy of the person who wanted to be a disciple (vv. 57-58). Next he used the precedent of the priests and nazirites (Num 6:6-7) to explain one's staying away from the funeral rites of one's closest relatives (vv. 59-60). As for the prohibition of turning back (vv. 61-62), he said that we should compare that with the command given to Lot and his family not to look back (Gen 19:17). It will be seen that Hebrew Bible rules must support Jesus' dangerous sayings. Like other ecclesiastical writers, Tertullian presupposed that the three persons who spoke to Jesus never became disciples. Far from being potential Christians, they represent instead hopeless cases.

We find a similar appeal to the Hebrew Bible in the Alexandrian church writer Origen, from whom at least three fragments have come down to us.[37] But it was

---

35 with the plow, after he has breakfasted on a four-piece, eight-part loaf, someone who puts care into his work and will drive a straight furrow, no longer gaping after his age-mates, but keeping his mind on his work" (Loeb 122). See also Pliny the Elder, *Nat. hist.* 18.48–49 §§171–79: "When plowing finish the row and do not halt in the middle while taking breath" (Loeb 5.301). In Epictetus *Ench.* 7, there is an instance with the same statement: Whoever leaves a ship to get water should fix his eyes on the ship. If the captain calls out, he should leave everything and answer the call. In the same way, it happens in real life, Epictetus concludes. If the captain calls out, a man should leave his wife and child and run to the ship.

35 Εὔθετος literally means "well placed," "usable," "practical," "suitable," "convenient," "useful." See Luke 14:35 and Heb 6:7. See also BDAG s.v.

36 In *L'Évangile selon Luc* (Paris: Émile Nourry, 1924; reprinted Frankfurt am Main, 1971) 290, Alfred Loisy sees in the first encounter (vv. 57-58) a call to renounce every comfort; in the second (vv. 59-60) a call to separate oneself from everything that is not connected with the kingdom of God; and in the third (vv. 61-62) a call to view the kingdom of God as the only goal worth striving after.

37 Origen *Hom. in Luc.* frgs. 66 (= Rauer 154), 67 (= Rauer 156), and 68 (= Rauer 157). See H. Couzel, F. Fournier, and P. Périchon, eds., *Origène, Homélies sur s. Luc: Texte latin et fragments grecs: Introduction, traduction et notes* (2d ed.; SC 87; Paris: Cerf, 1962) 514–17; Max Rauer, ed., *Origenes Werke*, vol. 9: *Die Homilien zu Lukas in der Übersetzung des Hieronymus und die griechischen Reste der Lukas- und Lukas-Kommentars* (2d ed.; GCS 49 [35]; Berlin: Akademie-Verlag, 1959) 288–89.

especially the text in the Gospel that Origen sought to understand. In his opinion, v. 58 is a definition not only of the suffering Christ's itinerary but also of the fate of believers who "will have to suffer in the world" (in connection with which he cited John 16:33). An allegorical light was shed on v. 60: coming to the faith corresponds to dying (reference was made to Gal 6:14 and 2 Cor 4:18). The father who died is the devil, and his death was evidently something good in that it allowed the young man no longer to have to take care of him (cf. the prohibition of touching a cadaver in Num 19:16) but instead to be free to listen to the Savior's voice. As for the third case (vv. 61-62), it, too, is to be understood following a spiritual reading: it is one's soul that must be plowed, in order to be rejuvenated and to be allowed to receive the seed of the divine Word (in which connection he quoted Jer 4:3 and Ps 37 [36]:27).

Whereas Ambrose made a striking contrast between the rejected candidate (the first case) and the disciple who was called (the second case) (*Exp. Luc.* 7.22–43), whom he compared directly, Cyril, bishop of Alexandria, focused on the differences in their respective situations (*Hom. in Luc.* 57–59):[38] the first one was wrong in wanting to assert himself; the second had the privilege of being spoken to by the Savior. In his first homily, devoted to vv. 57-58, he used Heb 5:4 and the example of Aaron to support his contention that God chooses his ministers. It is not up to any person to offer their collaboration to the great King. If one is not accepted—a wise observation on his part—it is because of not having severed one's links with the world. Cyril gave in to the tendency to allegorize when he claimed to have tracked down dangerous demons behind the foxes and the birds. He was not the only one to do so. In the second homily, devoted to vv. 59-60, Cyril held that, contrary to normal usage, "bury" does not here mean "inter" but rather "take care of someone up to the point that they draw their last breath." Jesus never forbade anyone to participate in the interment of their father. On the contrary, Scripture commands us to honor our parents. What Jesus initiated

was the establishment of a scale of values. In his eyes, the example of Abraham, who was invited to offer his son (Gen 22:1-19), illustrated the priority that must be given to love of God over love of one's family. The third homily, which was an explanation of vv. 61-62, sought to describe the uncertain fate of divided souls, torn between societal ties and the call of the Gospel.

On two occasions Gregory the Great quoted v. 60 in the *Moralia in Iob*. In book 4.27–51, he criticized the disciple for his hypocrisy. Unlike the three persons in the Gospels who were raised from death (Jairus's daughter, the son of the widow of Nain, and Lazarus), this disciple was not saved from spiritual death since, although he was a sinner, he persisted in swaggering and hid his true intentions. In book 7.30, 41 Gregory saw in the same disciple a man who was making progress in his spiritual journey. Since the Gospel requires us to leave everything behind, Jesus' saying is justified. Although, for the sake of the Lord, he was forbidden to bury his father out of a carnal tendency, in the name of the same Lord he was commanded to perform similar actions out of religious charity toward strangers.

In connection with this same v. 60, Bonaventure referred to Acts 6:2 (*Comm. in Luc.* 9.108).[39] Since the apostles were freed from domestic tasks and from waiting on others so that they could devote themselves to being servants of the Word, it is better to take care of one's soul than one's body and it is understandable that the Lord invites us to proclaim the gospel rather than practice funeral rites; there are plenty of people who can busy themselves with such things.

As for v. 62, it nourishes spirituality, especially the monastic variety; in the light of the use of the metaphor of plowing, Pope Leo the Great reckoned that Christians, as new beings, could not turn back "to the old situation of instability" (*Tract.* 71 §6).[40] The Venerable Bede, Thomas Aquinas, and Francis of Assisi all quoted the same verse; the first of them used it in order to describe the hard preparation of the heart for doing good,[41] the

---

38 Payne Smith, 1:258–71. There also exist several Greek fragments, frgs. 96–99; see Reuss, *Lukas-Kommentare*, 103–5.

39 R. P. Bernardini, ed., *Bonaventure Opera omnia*, vol. 7 (Quaracchi: Collegium S. Bonaventurae, 1882–1902) 250–51.

40 Item alius de passione Domini 6 (CCSL 138A, p. 439).

41 The Venerable Bede, *In Lucae Evangelium expositio* 3.1864–68 (ed. David Hurst; CCSL 120; Turnhout: Brepols, 1960) 213.

second to free monks from appeals from their families,[42] and the third in order to justify the vow of obedience.[43]

Conclusion

As 9:51 and 9:52-56 have amply indicated, Jesus and his disciples have set off on their journey. Verse 57 serves as another reminder of that. As with all journeys, there is the departure, the actual journey itself, and the arrival at the destination. The pericope under study here makes us aware of this triple reality that is also characteristic of every life, especially a Christian one. If the journey itself and the arrival at the destination are referred to only in passing (the journey in v. 57 by the verb πορεύομαι "going along the road," and the arrival at the destination in vv. 60 and 62 by the mention of the kingdom of God), the departure, on the other hand, is at the heart of the pericope, along with all the implied breaking off of ties. By this concentration on separation, the text thus shifts from the teacher (9:51) to the pupils, from Jesus to his disciples. While 9:52-56 showed us the disciples at work, detached from their origin to the point that they went on ahead of their master, the verses involved in our present study, vv. 57-62, bring onto the stage other disciples or, to be more precise, those who are potential disciples, postulants, applicants, candidates.

What Jesus said to them is, at first sight, frightening, intolerable, appalling. Do we not sometimes have an urgent need to "lay our head" somewhere? Do we not also have the right to keep watch over our dead ones, especially those closest to us? Do we not have a direct responsibility with respect to our spouses, children, parents, friends, colleagues, employees, or bosses? In my opinion, this text does not answer these questions, at least not at first. It takes up another theme and asks one, and only one, question: How is our relationship with Christ, and therefore with God, established? That is, how should it be established? The three candidates are reported to have been willing. They wanted to live in Jesus' company, whether that wish was verbalized or not.

That was already something, and yet it was not what fit the bill, for two reasons. First of all, because one's willingness must move this wish from the stage of wishing to that of carrying it out. In the second place, because one must understand in one's mind the meaning of this dream of being in the company of Jesus and what it really entails by way of demands made, and what it really promises.

And in that respect the images speak for themselves. These images that are offered to hesitant and well-intentioned candidates, though harsh, are also indications of love. If you want to "go off" with me, said Jesus to the first candidate, you will have to count on an adult Christian life, devoid of the maternal protection that is so desirable. He made it clear to the second candidate that he would have to count on a life of faith, which requires an intellectual and existential break with one's past, one's ancestors, one's roots, and one's tradition, which is what the father in the story represents. He informed the third candidate that following him would involve saying farewell to all social contacts, ruling out all nostalgia and refusing to have his soul torn in different directions and divided, with one half turned in the direction of the forward thrust of the kingdom, and the other backwards, in the direction of an idealized image of one's origins, a past experienced as one of advantages.

But why give up all these things? There would not even be any advantage, in the short run. On the contrary, the prospect would involve living a life resembling Jesus', and its outcome was known. The prospect held out was an itinerant life without rest (v. 58), a harsh job bearing witness (v. 60), and working without distraction (v. 62).

Still, even after considering the required separation, which involves loss, and the journey, which entails difficulties, the promised destination precludes viewing this decision in favor of Christ as a masochistic or stupidly painful act. I maintain that this text resonates with the same *joie de vivre* and with God's same tenderness as in the Magnificat (1:46-55), or the saying about the little ones (10:21). For the reign of God is not just at the end

---

42   Thomas Aquinas, *Catena aurea in quatuor evangelia ad Luc 9.62* (*Nuova editio Taurienesis*, vol. 2 [ed. Angelico Guarienti; Turin: Marietti, 1953] 140); he specifically cites Bede.

43   Francis of Assisi, *Admonitions* 3.10 and the *Second Rule* (also called *Regula Bullata*; see idem, *Écrits* [ed. and trans. Théophile Desbonnets et al.; SC 285; Paris: Cerf, 1981; reprinted with additions and corrections, 2003] 96–97, 184–85).

of the furrows that one plows (v. 62) but already in the tone of what we say (v. 60b), and even in the wounds associated with our farewells (vv. 58 and 60a).

Even after we become disciples—which is what this text suggests is involved, in the first instance—we still remain in the world. The Christian life is not to be situated outside life in general. Once we become involved as followers of Jesus, we are led to redefine—and here the text provides indirect help with doing it—our relation-ship, which has now become a Christian one, with our relatives, our past, and our social, familial, and professional present. This network of relationships is no longer to be determined by unconscious processes, inherited restrictions, or social necessities. Instead we will be on ethical ground, where we will be given a chance to exhibit our liberty, the expression of our love, and our responsibility.

Sharing the Gospel (10:1-20)

Bibliography

Allison, Dale C., "Paul and the Missionary Discourse," *EThL* 61 (1985) 369–75.

Argyle, Aubrey W., "St. Paul and the Mission of the Seventy," *JTS* n.s. 1 (1950) 63.

Baumbach, *Verständnis*, 178–86.

Beare, Francis Wright, "The Mission of the Disciples and the Mission Charge," *JBL* 89 (1970) 1–13.

Boring, M. Eugene, *Sayings of the Risen Jesus: Christian Prophecy in the Synoptic Tradition* (SNTSMS 46; Cambridge/New York: Cambridge University Press, 1982) 141–49.

Bosold, Iris, *Pazifismus und prophetische Provokation: Das Grussverbot Lk 10, 4b und sein historischer Kontext* (SBS 90; Stuttgart: Katholisches Bibelwerk, 1978).

Bovon, François, *Studies in Early Christianity* (Grand Rapids: Baker, 2005), 195–208.

Bovon, François, *L'œuvre de Luc: Études d'exégèse et de théologie* (LD 130; Paris: Cerf, 1987) 205–20.

Comber, Joseph A., "The Composition and Literary Characteristics of Matt 11:20–24," *CBQ* 39 (1977) 497–504.

Delebecque, E., "Sur un hellenisme de saint Luc," *RB* 87 (1980) 590–93.

Dillon, R. J., "Early Christian Experience in the Gospel Sayings," *TBT* 21 (1983) 83–88.

Dupont, Jacques, *L'ascolto e l'agire: L'antropologia dei vangeli a partire da Luca 10* (La visione dell'uomo nel pensiero cristiano: Antropologia teologica 5; Milan: 1978).

Edwards, Richard A., "Matthew's Use of Q in Chapter Eleven," in Joël Delobel, ed., *Logia – Les paroles de Jésus –The Sayings of Jesus: Mémorial Joseph Coppens* (BETL 59; Leuven: Leuven University Press/Peeters, 1982) 257–75.

Edwards, *Theology of Q*, 28, 38, 101–6.

Esteban J., "Un texto de S. Lucas sobre la obediencia," *Manresa* 34 (1962) 29–34 (on v. 16).

Fitzmyer, Joseph A., *The Gospel according to Luke: Introduction, Translation, and Notes* (2 vols.; AB 28, 28A; Garden City, N.Y.: Doubleday, 1981, 1985) 2:849–64 (with additional bibliography).

Frizzi, Giuseppe, "La 'missione' in Luca-Atti," *RivB* 32 (1984) 395–423.

idem, "Mandare-inviare in Luca-Atti, una chiave importante per la comprensione dell'escatologia di Luca," *RivB* 24 (1976) 359–401.

Gamba, Giuseppe Giovanni, *La portata universalistica dell'invio dei settanta(due) discepoli, (Lc 10:1 e ss.)* (Turin: Scuola grafica salesiana, 1963).

Garrett, Susan R., *The Demise of the Devil: Magic and the Demonic in Luke's Writings* (Minneapolis: Fortress Press, 1989) 46–60.

George, A., "Paroles de Jésus sur ses miracles (Mt 11, 5.21; 12, 27.28 et par.)," in Jacques Dupont et al., eds., *Jésus aux origines de la christologie* (BETL 40; Leuven/Gembloux: Leuven University Press, 1975) 283–302; (2nd ed.; 1989) 429–30 (see additional note).

Gräßer, *Problem*, 189–90 et passim.

Grelot, Pierre, "Étude critique de Luc 10, 9," in Jean Delorme and Jean Duplacy, eds., *La parole de grâce: Études lucaniennes à la mémoirs d'Augustin George* (Paris: Recherches de science religieuse, 1981) 87–100.

Haag, Herbert, *Teufelsglaube* (with contributions by Katharina Elliger, Bernhard Lang, and Meinrad Limbeck; Tübingen: Katzmann, 1974) 282–90.

Hagemeyer, Oda, "'Freut euch, daß Namen im Himmel verzeichnet sind!' (Lk 10, 20)," *Heiliger Dienst* 39 (1985) 160–63.

Hahn, Ferdinand, *Mission in the New Testament* (trans. Frank Clarke; SBT 47; Naperville, Ill.: Allenson, 1965) 41–46, 128–36.

Harvey, Anthony Ernest, "'The Workman Is Worthy of His Hire': Fortunes of a Proverb in the Early Church," *NovT* 24 (1982) 209–21.

Hills, Julian V., "Luke 10.18—Who Saw Satan Fall?" *JSNT* 46 (1992) 25–40.

Hoffmann, Paul, "Lukas 10,5-11 in der Instruktionsrede der Logienquelle," *EKK Vorarbeiten* 3 (1971) 37–53.

idem, *Logienquelle*, 243–54.

Jacobson, Arland D., "The Literary Unity of Q Lc 10,2-16 and Parallels as a Test Case," in Delobel, *Logia*, 419–23.

Jellicoe, Sidney, "St. Luke and the 'Seventy(-Two),'" *NTS* 6 (1959–60) 319–21.

Jeremias, Joachim, *Abba: Studien zur neutestamentlichen Theologie und Zeitgeschichte* (Göttingen: Vandenhoeck & Ruprecht, 1966) 132–39.

Joüon, Paul, "Notes philologiques sur les évangiles," *RSR* 18 (1928) 345–59.

Kirchschläger, Walter, *Jesu exorzistisches Wirken aus der Sicht des Lukas: Ein Beitrag zur lukanischen Redaktion* (ÖBSt 3; Klosterneuburg: Österreichisches Katholisches Bkbelwerk, 1981) 239–42.

Klassen, William, "'A Child of Peace' (Luke 10.6) in First Century Context," *NTS* 27 (1980–81) 488–506.

Kloppenborg, *Formation*, 192–97, 199–203 and passim.

Kümmel, Werner Georg, *Promise and Fulfillment: The Eschatological Message of Jesus* (2d ed.; SBT 23; London: SCM, 1961) passim.

Lang, Bernhard, "Grußverbot oder Besuchverbot? Eine sozialgeschichtliche Deutung von Lukas 10,4b," *BZ* 26 (1982) 75–79.

Laufen, Rudolf, *Die Doppelüberlieferungen der Logien-quelle und des Markusevangeliums* (BBB 54; Bonn: Hanstein, 1980) 201–93.

Lignée, H., "La mission des soixante-douze: Lc 10, 1-12. 17-20," *AsSeign* 45 (1974) 64– 74.

Lührmann, *Logienquelle*, 59–64.

Luz, Ulrich, "Q 10, 2-16; 11, 14-23," *SBLSP* 1985, 101–2.

idem, *Matthew: A Commentary* (3 vols.; Hermeneia; Minneapolis: Fortress Press, 2001-7) 2:151 (bibliography).

Manson, Thomas W., *The Sayings of Jesus: As Recorded in the Gospels according to St. Matthew and St. Luke* (London: SCM, 1949) 73–78, 256–58.

Mees, Michael, "Sinn und Bedeutung literarischer Formen für die Textgestalt des Codex Bezae in Lukas 10–11," *Vetera christianorum* 7 (1970) 59–82.

Mehlmann, Joannes, "Minus quam inter duos caritas haberi non potest," *VD* 45 (1967) 97–103.

Merk, Otto, "Das Reich Gottes in den lukanischen Schriften," in E. Earle Ellis and Erich Grässer, eds., *Jesus und Paulus: Festschrift für Werner Georg Kümmel zum 70. Geburtstag* (Göttingen: Vandenhoeck & Ruprecht, 1975) 201–20.

Merklein, *Gottesherrschaft*, 154–57, 160.

Metzger, Bruce M., "Seventy or Seventy-Two Disciples?" *NTS* 5 (1958–59) 299–306.

Minear, Paul S., *To Heal and to Reveal: The Prophetic Vocation according to Luke* (New York: Seabury, 1976) 8–16, 69–77.

Miyoshi, *Anfang*, 59–82, 90–91, 95–119.

Müller, Ulrich B., "Vision und Botschaft: Erwägungen zur prophetischen Struktur der Verkündigung Jesu," *ZThK* 74 (1977) 416–48.

Neirynck, Franz, "Paul and the Sayings of Jesus," in Albert Vanhoye, ed., *L'apôtre Paul: Personnalité, style et conception du ministère* (BETL 73; Leuven: Leuven University Press/Peeters, 1986) 304–4.

Nielsen, Helge Kjær, *Heilung und Verkündigung: Das Verständnis der Heilung und ihres Verhältnisses zur Verkündigung bei Jesus und in der ältesten Kirche* (Acta theologica Danica 22; Leiden: Brill, 1987) 46–51, 65–71.

Nolland, 2:545–46, 560–61 (bibliography).

O'Hagan, A., "'Greet No One on the Way' Lk 10,4b," *SBFLA* 16 (1965–66) 69–84.

Paul, Shalom M., "Heavenly Tablets and the Book of Life," *Journal of the Ancient Near Eastern Society of Columbia University* 5 (1973) 345–53.

Piper, *Wisdom*, 133–37 and passim.

Polag, *Christologie*, 68–72, 74, 89, 99.

Puig i Tàrrech, Armand, "Lc 10, 18: La visió de la caíguda de Satanàs," *Revista catalana de teología* 3 (1978) 217–43.

Richards, William Larry, "Manuscript Grouping in Luke 10 by Quantitative Analysis," *JBL* 98 (1979) 379–91.

Robinson, James M., "The Mission and Beelzebul: Pap. Q 10, 2-16; 11, 14-23," *SBLSP* 1985, 97–99.

Rosenstiehl, Jean-Marc, "La chute de l'Ange: Origine et développements d'une légende: Ses attestations dans la littérature copte," in *Écritures et traditions dans la littérature copte: Journée d'études coptes, Strasbourg, 28 mai 1982* (ed. Groupe de recherche "Bibliothèque copte"; Cahiers de la Bibliothèque copte 1; Louvain: Peeters, 1983) 37–60.

Sato, *Q und Prophetie*, 309–13 and passim.

Schille, Gottfried, *Die urchristliche Kollegialmission* (AThANT 48; Zurich: Zwingli, 1967).

Schottroff, Luise, and Wolfgang Stegemann, *Jesus von Nazareth, Hoffnung der Armen* (Urban-Taschenbücher 639; Stuttgart: Kohlhammer, 1978) 62–69.

Schrage, *Thomas-Evangelium*, 51–55, 153–55.

Schulz, Siegfried, "'Die Gottesherrschaft ist nahe herbeigekommen' (Mt 10, 7 // Lk 10, 9): Der kerygmatische Entwurf der Q-Gemeinde Syriens," in Horst Balz and Siegfried Schulz, eds., *Das Wort und die Wörter: Festschrift Gerhard Friedrich zum 65. Geburtstag* (Stuttgart: Kohlhammer, 1973) 57–67.

Schulz, *Q*, 360–66, 404–19, 457–59.

Schürmann, Heinz, *Traditionsgeschichtliche Untersuchungen zu den synoptischen Evangelien: Beiträge* (KBANT; Düsseldorf: Patmos, 1968) 137–49.

Spitta, Friedrich, "Der Satan als Blitz," *ZNW* 9 (1908) 160–63.

Sweetland, *Journey*, 35–39 and passim.

Uro, Risto, *Sheep among the Wolves: A Study of the Mission Instructions of Q* (AASFDHL 47; Helsinki: Suomalainen Tiedeakatemia, 1987).

Venetz, Hermann-Josef, "Bittet den Herrn der Ernte: Überlegungen zu Lk 10,2 // Mt 9,37," *Diakonia* 11 (1980) 146–61.

Völkel, Martin, "Zur Deutung des 'Reiches Gottes' bei Lukas," *ZNW* 65 (1974) 57–70.

Vollenweider, Samuel, "'Ich sah den Satan wie einen Blitz vom Himmel fallen' (Lk 10, 18)," *ZNW* 79 (1988) 187–203.

Zeller, Dieter, *Kommentar zur Logienquelle* (Stuttgarter kleiner Kommentar Neues Testament 21; Stuttgart: Katholisches Bibelwerk, 1984) 45–52.

Zerwick, Max, "'Vidi Satanam sicut fulgur de caelo cadentem' (Lc 10, 17-20)," *VD* 26 (1958) 110–14.

1/ **After this the Lord installed seventy-two others of them and sent them on before his face in pairs to every town and place where he himself intended to go. 2/ He said to them, "Even though the harvest is plentiful, the laborers are few; therefore ask the lord of the harvest to send out laborers into his harvest. 3/ Go on your way. See, I am sending you out like lambs into the midst of wolves. 4/ Carry no purse, no bag, no sandals; and greet no one on the road. 5/ Whatever house you enter, first say, 'Peace to this house!' 6/ And if anyone is there who is a child of peace, your peace will rest on that person; but if not, it will return to you. 7/ Remain in the same house, eating and drinking whatever they provide, for the laborer deserves to be paid. Do not move about from house to house. 8/ Whenever you enter a town and its people welcome you, eat what is set before you; 9/ cure the sick who are there, and say to them, 'The kingdom of God has come near to you.' 10/ But whenever you enter a town and they do not welcome you, go out into its streets and say, 11/ 'Even the dust of your town that clings to our feet, we wipe off for you. Yet know this: the kingdom of God has come near.' 12/ I tell you, on that day Sodom will be treated with more clemency than that town. 13/ Woe to you, Chorazin! Woe to you, Bethsaida! For if the miracles performed in you had been performed in Tyre and Sidon, they would have repented long ago, clothed in sackcloth and sitting in ashes. 14/ But at the judgment Tyre and Sidon will be treated with more clemency than you. 15/ And you, Capernaum, will you be exalted to heaven? You will descend to hell. 16/ Whoever listens to you listens to me, and whoever rejects you rejects me, and whoever rejects me rejects the one who sent me." 17/ The seventy-two returned with joy, saying, "Lord, in your name even the demons submit to us!" 18/ He said to them, "I watched Satan fall from heaven like a flash of lightning. 19/ See, I have given you authority to tread on snakes and scorpions, and over all the power of the enemy; and nothing will hurt you. 20/ Nevertheless, do not rejoice that the spirits have submitted to you, but rejoice that your names are written in the heavens."**

This is the so-called sending out of the seventy-two disciples. It is a text from which the church draws its missionary zeal, its art of being present among other people, and its rules of evangelization. The passage does, in fact, brim over with joy (vv. 17, 20); it celebrates the successes that have been possible (v. 13), enlists persons in struggle on behalf of a cause (v. 2), encourages a journeying as a team (v. 1), and promises the backing of God and Christ (vv. 1–2). Yet it is also a text that embarrasses the church and its servants, since certain of the requirements it sets out are not capable of being met and several of its opinions are shocking. The equipment, or rather the lack of it, laid down in v. 4 is a discouragement to even the best-intentioned people; the forbidding of greeting people seems to be a counter-witness (v. 4b); and the condemnation of recalcitrant cities is an expression of a sentiment of revenge (v. 15). This is, in the last analysis, a puzzling text. Just what harvest is in mind (v. 2)? What peace do the disciples have at their disposal without being masters of it (vv. 5-6)? Who are the enemies, the wolves (v. 3), and the Satan (v. 18)—fallen or threatening—that they are going to have to confront?

Analysis

Whatever first reactions readers may have to the above subjects, they cannot fail to notice that a new literary unit begins in 10:1 (cf. "After this"). They will ask themselves where it ends, however. Based on a criterion of themes, it can be said to break off at either v. 12 or v. 16.[1] One structural indication, the temporal complement (v. 21: "At that same hour"), moves me to fix the end of the pericope at v. 20.

A speech by Jesus (vv. 2–16) is the most important part of this pericope; as is often the case (cf. 8:8, 18, 21; 14:35), it ends with a comment on listening. This speech does not develop a line of argumentation; it lays out a series of sayings whose structure and content are heterogeneous: a metaphor, v. 2; a comparison, v. 3; instructions, v. 4; casuistic regulations with brief developments of the themes, vv. 5-13; lamentation, vv. 14-15; and a sapiential oracle, v. 16. A brief description of the setting (v. 1) precedes this string of sayings, which in turn is followed by a dialogue

(vv. 17-20), the heart of which is a new, shorter speech by Jesus, which is introduced by a joyous observation by the disciples upon their return (v. 17). This second speech is composed of three sayings, one with an apocalyptic flavor (v. 18), another with a juridical character (v. 19), and the third with a paraenetic tone (v. 20).

In all of this unit (vv. 1-20), Christology is still present but remains in the background. What Luke places in the foreground is what is involved in the disciples' work: their responsibility, their missionary practice, and their power. So the travel narrative links the training of the messengers with Jesus' destiny, ecclesiology with Christology.

Unlike Matthew, Luke did not combine the two parallel traditions he had inherited (Mark and Q).[2] Instead he used that dual tradition in a creative way to evoke the idea of the two mission fields of the church: Israel and the other nations. The Twelve were to occupy the first field; the seventy-two, the second. This historical and theological perspective gave him the idea of using the Markan text for the account of the sending out of the twelve apostles (9:1-6) and saving the Q text for use in the account of the sending out of the seventy-two evangelists (10:1-20). In Q these messengers had definitely been identified with the Twelve (hence the fusion of Mark and Q in Matt 9:37—10:16). Never mind! In Luke they became "other" disciples, "seventy-two," the number required to correspond to the biblical number of nations (see Genesis 10).[3] All of Luke 10:1 is, moreover, redactional and once more inserts the episode in the context

---

1 Fitzmyer (2:841–64) subdivides vv. 1-20 into four segments (vv. 1-12, 13-15, 16, and 17-20); Gerhard Schneider (*Das Evangelium nach Lukas* [2d ed.; 2 vols.; Ökumenischer Taschenbuch-Kommentar zum Neuen Testament 3.1–2; Gütersloh: Mohn, 1984] 1:234–42) subdivides them into three (vv. 1-12, 13-16, 17-20); and Eduard Schweizer (*Das Evangelium nach Lukas: Übersetzt und erklärt* [NTD 3; Göttingen: Vandenhoeck & Ruprecht, 1982] 113–19) into two (vv. 1-16, 17-20). As for Philippe Bossuyt and Jean Radermakers (*Jésus, Parole de la grâce: Selon St. Luc* [2 vols.; Brussels: Institut d'études théologiques, 1981] 275–88), they regroup all of chap. 10 under the title "The Mission: Revelation of the Father," subdividing it into four segments: vv. 1-16, 17-24, 25-37, 38-42). Charles H. Talbert (*Reading Luke: A Literary and Theological Commentary on the Third Gospel* [New York: Crossroad, 1986] 114–19) sees here a chiasmic structure: A (Luke

9:51-56); B (9:57-62); A′ (10:1-24). Talbert (pp. 111–12) sees this little chiasm as a component of a much larger chiasm, where A (Luke 9:51-56, toward Jerusalem and rejection) and B (9:57—10:24, following Jesus) correspond to B′ (18:35—19:10, following Jesus) and A′(19:11-44 toward Jerusalem and rejection).

2 Matthew 9:35—10:16. On this point and on the origin of the discourse "The Commissioning of the Twelve," see the commentary on Luke 9:1-6 (1:342–43). See also Hahn, *Mission*, 41–46; Hoffmann, *Logienquelle*, 243–54; Lührmann, *Logienquelle*, 59; Schulz, *Q*, 404–19; Schürmann, *Untersuchungen*, 137–49.

3 On seventy or seventy-two, see the commentary below. Luke feels free to vary this number in v. 2 and in v. 17. Elsewhere he does not dare to adapt the discourse of Jesus to this new large number.

of a journey. The speech in vv. 2-16 comes in the main from tradition. In vv. 2-12, Luke kept Q's order[4] better than Matthew did, which is explained all the better by the fact that Matthew combined Q with Mark.

The saying about the harvest (v. 2), aside from one inversion,[5] is identical in Luke and Matthew. We read it also in the *Gospel of Thomas* in another context (*Gos. Thom.* 73).[6] Only small differences distinguish the two versions of the saying about the lambs and the wolves (v. 3 par. Matt 16:16a): the Lukan imperative: "Go on your way," foreign to the saying, is secondary. Luke's word "lamb" ($\dot{\alpha}\rho\dot{\eta}\nu$), a *hapax legomenon* in the New Testament, is original. Matthew replaced it with the more trivial "sheep" ($\pi\rho\dot{o}\beta\alpha\tau o\nu$).[7] Luke was unaware of the call to imitate the serpents and the doves that Matthew added (Matt 10:16b), which could not have come from Q. It is difficult to make a comparison of the gear to take along (v. 4), since Matthew confined himself to Mark's version.[8] Perhaps Luke left his personal mark on this verse by choosing to use $\beta\alpha\sigma\tau\dot{\alpha}\zeta\omega$ ("carry") and by writing $\kappa\alpha\tau\dot{\alpha}$

$\tau\dot{\eta}\nu$ $\dot{o}\delta\dot{o}\nu$ ("on the road") and $\dot{\alpha}\sigma\pi\dot{\alpha}\zeta o\mu\alpha\iota$ ("greet").[9] In the matter of welcome in the houses (vv. 5-6), there are distinct differences between Matthew and Luke as to the language used, even if the content is the same. Here again, Luke seems to have followed Q more closely than did Matthew. At the most one might ask if, for the coming of peace, Q read $\dot{\epsilon}\lambda\vartheta\dot{\alpha}\tau\omega$ ("let . . . come" [Matthew]) or $\dot{\epsilon}\pi\alpha\nu\alpha\pi\alpha\dot{\eta}\sigma\epsilon\tau\alpha\iota$ ("will rest" [Luke]) and, for its disappearance, if it had $\dot{\epsilon}\pi\iota\sigma\tau\rho\alpha\varphi\dot{\eta}\tau\omega$ ("let it return" [Matthew]) or $\dot{\alpha}\nu\alpha\kappa\dot{\alpha}\mu\psi\epsilon\iota$ ("will return" [Luke]). Luke's futures seem in any case to be older and more Semitic than Matthew's imperatives.[10] As for the order to not change houses and the mention of the deserving of pay (v. 7), in their Lukan version they probably correspond to the earliest wording of Q.[11] In the case of the towns (vv. 8-11), welcome and inhospitableness are the two alternatives on the basis of which attitudes are set. The sequence house–town and the two possible reactions were already the reading of Q. Matthew 10:11-14 breaks the parallelism by speaking first of the two cases in which

---

4   Most of the statements follow the same order in Luke and Matthew; vv. 2, 4, 5-6, 10-11, 12 par. Matt 9:37-38; 10:9-10a, 12-13, 14, 15). However, there are some anomalies: Luke places the statement about the lambs and the wolves at the beginning of the discourse (v. 3), whereas Matthew puts it at the end (Matt 10:16a). Luke has the saying about the wages (v. 7c) coming after those about provisions and the house, whereas Matthew places the saying about the wages (Matt 10:10b) between them. In Luke, the remarks about the wages (v. 7c) and the town (vv. 8-11) *follow* those about the house (vv. 5-7a) in contrast to Matt 10:7-14, where remarks about the wages (10:10b) and the town (10:11) *precede* those about the house (10:12-14).

5    $\dot{E}\rho\gamma\dot{\alpha}\tau\alpha\varsigma$ $\dot{\epsilon}\kappa\beta\dot{\alpha}\lambda\eta$ in Luke (who must be correct), but $\dot{\epsilon}\kappa\beta\dot{\alpha}\lambda\eta$ $\dot{\epsilon}\rho\gamma\dot{\alpha}\tau\alpha\varsigma$ in Matthew. Notice, however, that the order of the words in Luke often corresponds to the order in Matthew.

6   See Schrage, *Thomas-Evangelium*, 153–55.

7   *2 Clement* 5.2 cites this saying in a free manner, employing the diminutive $\dot{\alpha}\rho\nu\dot{\iota}\alpha$. Has Matthew added the emphatic $\dot{\epsilon}\gamma\dot{\omega}$ (cf. Matt 12:28), or has Luke omitted it (cf. Luke 12:20)? According to Schulz (*Q*, 405) Luke is the one responsible for deleting it.

8   Matthew must have known, however, the version of Q, as the prohibition about the sandals suggests.

9   Matthew 10:9 chooses the verb $\kappa\tau\dot{\alpha}o\mu\alpha\iota$ perhaps

under the influence of Q (Mark 6:8 and Luke 9:3 have $\alpha\check{\iota}\rho\omega$). The other two expressions are Lukan, $\kappa\alpha\tau\dot{\alpha}$ $\tau\dot{\eta}\nu$ $\dot{o}\delta\dot{o}\nu$ (cf. Acts 8:36; 25:3; 26:13; in a figurative sense, 24:14) and $\dot{\alpha}\sigma\pi\dot{\alpha}\zeta o\mu\alpha\iota$ (cf. Luke 1:40; Acts 18:22; 20:1, 7, 19; 25:13). But Luke did not invent the prohibition against greeting anyone on the road (Luke 10:4b, which Matthew ignores).

10   As for the $\gamma\dot{\epsilon}$ (Luke 10:6b), it must have been added by Luke.

11   The words "eating and drinking whatever is offered to you" (v. 7b) make explicit the meaning of the verb "remain" (v. 7a), but this gloss must have antedated Luke, for it is needed as a justification for the saying about the wages (7c). The word $\mu\iota\sigma\vartheta\dot{o}\varsigma$ in Luke must correspond to Q (Matthew, who more often understands $\mu\iota\sigma\vartheta\dot{o}\varsigma$ in an eschatological sense, replaces it with $\tau\rho o\varphi\dot{\eta}$). As for the prohibition against moving from one house to another (v. 7d), which is missing from Matthew (in order to avoid repetition with Matt 10:11c?), it too makes explicit the meaning of the verb "remain" (v. 7a) and corresponds well to the missionary praxis of Q. According to Hahn (*Mission*, 41–43), the statements about food (vv. 7, 8b) could be secondary. Cf. *Gos. Thom.* 14: "And if you enter any country and travel from place to place, if someone receives you, eat whatever is set before you; tend to the sick among them."

one is welcomed (located in a town or village, and then in a house), and then of a single case (not localized) of rejection. In Luke, who follows Q, the house–town parallelism is more felicitous without, however, being perfect: in the house, the disciples are the first to act; in the welcoming town, it is the inhabitants who make the first move, before the disciples. As a result, there is a cohabitation between them and the disciples (v. 8b) before the disciples heal or preach (v. 9). The final words of v. 8b ("eat what is set before you"), a repetition of the idea in v. 7b, could have been penned by Luke. The disciples' activity in the house was to be limited to a greeting conveying peace, whereas in the town they were to perform healings and to proclaim the kingdom. Matthew seems to have used this material to beef up the sending itself (Matt 10:7-8). The order of miracle–preaching (Luke) must go back to Q, even though Luke himself seems to have been fond of it, too (cf. Acts 1:1). Matthew inverted it, following the same theological requirement that made him place the Sermon on the Mount (chaps. 5–7) before the series of miracles (chaps. 8–9). I do not think that the justification proposed by Matthew alone ("You received without payment; give without payment" [Matt 10:8b]) comes from Q. Was it Luke who added the words "near to you" (v. 9), in connection with God's reign, in order to avoid misunderstanding (since strictly speaking, the reign is still awaited)? The answer to that question is dependent on the connections that exegesis might establish with v. 11b.

The tradition taken over by Mark and the one preserved in Q were in agreement on suggesting to the disciples that they wipe off the dust clinging to their feet when they were not welcomed (in Mark 6:11 and parallels and Luke 10:10-11). Matthew 10:14 was content to adapt Mark's version. Luke, who reproduced the text of Mark in Luke 9:5, has here transmitted Q's version. Was he responsible for adding "into its streets," a phrase of which he was fond?[12] In any case, the direct style comes from the tradition. Verse 11b (the end of what the disciples were to say to the refractory inhabitants) is found only in Luke. Since it is a confirmation and a correction of v. 9b, we must be dealing with a redactional addition with obvious theological importance. In the main, the simplicity of v. 12 in Luke corresponds to Q. As a reader of the Bible, Matthew paraphrased it by adding Gomorrah and by noting that "that day" (Luke 10:12) would be "the day of judgment" (Matt 10:15).[13] As is attested by the whole speech, what Matthew and Luke had in front of them was a *Greek* version of Q, probably in written form. It may be asked if the limitation of the mission to Israel, excluding Gentiles and Samaritans (Matt 10:5b-6), did belong to Q.[14] Luke would have crossed out this statement, which was intolerable to his way of thinking, even when resituated in the pre-Easter period.

The ultimately favorable destiny of a guilty town, Sodom (v. 12), led to the literary attraction of the oracle of doom spoken against the towns of Galilee (vv. 13-15), all the more because one word ($\dot{\alpha}\nu\epsilon\kappa\tau\acute{o}\tau\epsilon\rho o\nu$, "more tolerable," "with more clemency") served as a link and because the names of other sinful towns in Scripture are mentioned, namely, Tyre and Sidon. Even if Matthew placed this oracle later (Matt 11:20-24), it would appear that Luke preserved Q's sequence. The internal differences in the oracle are insignificant, since both Matthew and Luke honored the wording of Jesus' sayings. The oracle in Q itself is a conglomeration of two "woes" whose parallelism Matthew improved on more than Luke did.[15] The first "woe," the one announced on Chorazin and

---

12 Cf. Luke 13:26; 14:21; Acts 5:15 (always plural, as in Matt 6:5 and 12:19, whereas the Apocalypse always has the singular (Rev 11:8; 21:21; 22:2).

13 The $\dot{\alpha}\mu\acute{\eta}\nu$ in Matt 10:15 must also be redactional.

14 So Schürmann (*Untersuchungen*), who places these verses in Q between Luke 10:7 (house) and Luke 10:8 (town). But I am not satisfied with his conclusion since it breaks the parallelism.

15 Luke prefers $\dot{\epsilon}\gamma\epsilon\nu\acute{\eta}\vartheta\eta\sigma\alpha\nu$ over $\dot{\epsilon}\gamma\acute{\epsilon}\nu o\nu\tau o$ (Q no doubt). For clarity he adds "sitting" ($\kappa\alpha\vartheta\acute{\eta}\mu\epsilon\nu o\iota$). It may be that he has deleted $\lambda\acute{\epsilon}\gamma\omega\ \dot{\upsilon}\mu\hat{\iota}\nu$ (Matt 11:22) in order to avoid repetition with v. 12. Did he amend "on the day of judgment" to "at the judgment" for the same reason (cf. v. 12)? There follow in Matthew two sentences unknown to Luke, a secondary syllogism on Sodom (Matt 11:23b, which must serve as a parallel to Matt 11:21) and a doublet to Matt 10:15 par. Luke 10:12. Here again the composition of Matthew appears to be secondary, more developed (cf. the refrain of $\pi\lambda\grave{\eta}\nu\ \lambda\acute{\epsilon}\gamma\omega\ \dot{\upsilon}\mu\hat{\iota}\nu$ in v. 22 with v. 24 in Matthew 11). See Joseph A. Comber, "The Composition and Literary Characteristics of Matt 11:20-24," *CBQ* 39 (1977) 497–504.

Bethsaida, is subdivided into three parts: (a) the woe, (b) justification by means of a comparison, and (c) the apocalyptic perspective. The second part does not have the word "woe" but, with the help of words borrowed from Isa 14:13-15, it does announce with sadness the final humiliation of Jesus' favorite town, Capernaum. The Q tradition makes use of the literary genre of the oracle against the Gentiles,[16] but applies it here to the towns in Israel, thus respecting a habit of turning the oracles back against Israel, a habit that was rooted in the preaching of the historical Jesus.

Even though the idea being defended, which is the solidarity between Jesus and his envoys, is found elsewhere in the Gospel tradition (cf. Matt 10:40; Mark 9:37; and John 13:20), the location—at the end of the discourse—and the wording of the following saying (v. 16) are definitely redactional. Should we see in Matt 10:40 and Luke 10:16 two rereadings of a single saying of Q?[17] That is not certain. In any case, the Lukan version interprets the welcoming (Matt 10:40: "welcomes") in terms of listening (cf. Luke 7:47) and stresses the risk of rejection. Unlike in Matt 10:40, we have here in Luke a pointing out of a succession of rejections ($\dot{\alpha}\vartheta\epsilon\tau\acute{\epsilon}\omega$, "reject," occurs three times), whereas the parallel in Matt 10:40 stresses the welcoming ($\delta\acute{\epsilon}\chi o\mu\alpha\iota$, "welcome," occurs four times).[18]

The following verses—on this everyone is agreed[19]—have been given their structure by Luke. Perhaps under the inspiration of 9:10 par. Mark 6:30, Luke has composed an introduction that includes (a) the joyful return of the disciples and (b) the account of their success, which already announces the theme of victory over the world of demons (v. 17). The Gospel writer next quotes (probably from L) the apocalyptic saying about Satan's fall (v. 18), to which only John 12:31 ("Now is the judgment of this world; now the ruler of this world will be driven out") is close. This is the only place in the New Testament where we read of Jesus having a vision. The following saying (v. 19) has no parallel in the Gospels, aside from the content, but not the wording, of the spurious ending of Mark (Mark 16:17-18). The present structural composition of the saying is very Lukan.[20] The conviction that it expresses, however, was shared by the earliest Christians. We can find an approximate quotation of it, introduced by the words $\kappa\alpha\grave{\iota}\ \pi\acute{\alpha}\lambda\iota\nu\ \dot{\epsilon}\nu\ \dot{\epsilon}\tau\acute{\epsilon}\rho o\iota\varsigma$ $\lambda\acute{o}\gamma o\iota\varsigma\ \ddot{\epsilon}\varphi\eta,$ "and also he said, in other sayings" in Justin Martyr's *Dialogue with Trypho* 76.6.[21] The word $\pi\lambda\acute{\eta}\nu,$ "nevertheless" (v. 20), which occurs here for the third time (cf. vv. 11b and 14), and which expresses a hesitation, is characteristic of the end of passages that Luke has developed. This hesitation involves the nature of the joy expressed in v. 17; it should not be that of domination of the demons but that of being signed up by God. Did Luke himself compose this verse? That can be doubted when we consider the fact that neither the vocabulary of submission nor the theme of having one's name written in the heavens is typical of him. Justin's expression "in other sayings" perhaps alludes to L or another collection of sayings.

Commentary

■ **1** The role Jesus plays here is that of "the Lord" ($\dot{o}$ $\kappa\acute{u}\rho\iota o\varsigma$) who is still alive but already enthroned in Luke's time. He "installed": the verb $\dot{\alpha}\nu\alpha\delta\epsilon\acute{\iota}\kappa\nu\upsilon\mu\iota$ ("install," "commission"),[22] less common than $\dot{\alpha}\pi o\delta\epsilon\acute{\iota}\kappa\nu\upsilon\mu\iota$ ("appoint"), can take on a certain official flavor (Luke 1:80 spoke of the "installation" [$\dot{\alpha}\nu\acute{\alpha}\delta\epsilon\iota\xi\iota\varsigma$] of John the Baptist with respect to Israel). The coordination of the verbs ("installed" and "sent") ought not to mislead us; the purpose of the installation was, in fact, the sending.

16 See Lührmann, *Logienquelle*, 64; Schulz, *Q*, 366.

17 This is the opinion of Schulz (*Q*, 457–59).

18 In v. 17, $\dot{\upsilon}\pi o\sigma\tau\rho\acute{\epsilon}\varphi\omega$ is very Lukan, as are $\lambda\acute{\epsilon}\gamma o\nu\tau\epsilon\varsigma$ (cf. 20:11), $\mu\epsilon\tau\grave{\alpha}\ \kappa\alpha\rho\tilde{\alpha}\varsigma$ (cf. 24:52), and esp. $\delta\alpha\iota\mu\acute{o}$-$\nu\iota\alpha$ (cf. 9:1).

19 For example, Lührmann, *Logienquelle*, 60. According to Miyoshi (*Anfang*, 78–80), Luke could have been influenced here by Mark 9:38-40, a text of Mark that Luke has just taken up (Luke 9:49-50), conspicuous for its use of Num 11:24-30. This parallel with Numbers 11 could explain the number of those sent.

20 Similarities in form with v. 19 can be seen in 4:6; 20:2; 21:15; similarities in theme in 22:29. On the other hand, the notion of treading on serpents and scorpions is not found elsewhere in Luke-Acts; likewise the designation of Satan as the "enemy" (but note its occurrence in Matt 13:25, 39).

21 This text is available in Kurt Aland, ed., *Synopsis quattuor evangeliorum* (15th ed., Stuttgart: Deutsche Bibelgesellschaft, 1996) 262.

22 Retained by D and Old Latin witnesses.

Those whom he chose were "other" disciples[23]—other than the Twelve (9:1), that is—rather than "other than" the messengers sent to Samaria (9:52). Their number had to correspond to the number of nations established in Jewish thought. But the manuscript tradition of Luke 10:1, like the Jewish tradition, fluctuated between seventy and seventy-two. I read "seventy-two," following the text of Genesis 10 in the LXX, rather than "seventy," the reading of the MT of the Hebrew Bible,[24] since Luke customarily follows the text of the LXX rather than that of the Hebrew Bible. Faithful to the missionary rule, which is articulated also in Mark and which was practiced by the earliest Christians (Mark 6:7; cf. Acts 13:2), they went out two by two. They still had a pre-Easter mission that is reminiscent of the sending out of the messengers to Samaria (9:52), which was a preparatory mission, in which they went "before his face"; Luke stresses the implication that they were to go "where he was to go himself." What we are told in the following verses contradicts this perspective, since nothing more is said of Jesus walking in the footsteps of the seventy-two. The contradiction is diminished, however, if we understand, with the help of the redactional reflection in 22:35-38, that Luke thought of the sending out in Luke 10 as a training exercise, a dress rehearsal. The seventy-two were still under the protection of Jesus' proximity.[25]

■ **2** "He said to them"; following Q, what Luke has given us here is an exposition of missionary instructions more than an account of their being put into practice for the first time. The metaphor of the "harvest," which in Scripture is applied especially to the judgment, sometimes takes on—and that is only natural—a positive sense. That is the case here (cf. Isa 9:2; Ps 125[126]:5-6),[26] as it also is in John 4:35.[27] The prayer orients the metaphor[28] in the direction of allegory; the Lord of the harvest makes his dramatic appearance on the scene. But joy is threatened by the lack of laborers, and that fear inevitably gives rise to prayer. That is the meaning of v. 2, taken by itself. But when it is set in its present context, it suggests that Jesus' sending out (vv. 2-3) must correspond to God's intention. It also indicates that the missionary journey was to begin with a prayer, which in turn naturally implied that other disciples would come to join forces with the seventy-two.

■ **3** "Go": Luke adds this imperative in order to be able to insert this verse into the hortatory series.[29] In spite of fear, a lack of preparedness, and limited means, one must go on one's way.[30] The note of confidence, calm, and absence of cares implied in the verb ὑπάγω, "go on your way," used intransitively, contrasts with the following indication: lambs among wolves. This perilous situation calls to mind the way the earliest Christians felt in their Jewish environment,[31] but the memory of Scripture (Isa 11:6: "the wolf shall live with the lamb") also allows hope of an eschatological reconciliation. The *Acts of Philip* (8.15-21 [96–101]) tells how the prophecy was fulfilled in a proleptic way by the conversion to the Gospel of a kid and a leopard (cf. Isa 11:6: "the leopard shall lie down with the kid").[32] *2 Clement* (5.1-4) attests to the fact that Jesus' saying was on Christians' minds and gave rise to

---

23 The large number of witnesses that read a καί before ἑτέρους ("still others") underscores this fact.

24 The Pseudo-Clementine *Recognitions* (1.40) speaks of the "seventy-two" and not of the "seventy," a fact already noted by Godet (2:16–17 n. 1). On the seventy or seventy-two, see Bruce M. Metzger, "Seventy or Seventy-Two Disciples?" *NTS* 5 (1958–59) 299–306; and Sidney Jellicoe, "St. Luke and the 'Seventy(-Two),'" *NTS* 6 (1959–60) 319–21. 𝔓[75] reads "seventy-two."

25 Note the expression οὗ ἤμελλεν αὐτὸς ἔρχεσθαι, which implies (a) the motif of the history of salvation and (b) a christological connotation.

26 In the sense of judgment, the "harvest" appears in Isa 17:5.

27 Is there a literary connection between Luke 10:2 and John 4:35? Probably not.

28 Note the equilibrium in the first sentence: μέν . . . δέ, θερισμός . . . ἐργάται, πολύς . . . ὀλίγος.

29 This development corresponds to that which must have taken place in an earlier stage for v. 2: the sentence (now an affirmation) has been doubled from an exhortation (an imperative).

30 The intransitive ὑπάγω signifies "to retire" or, as here, "to advance calmly." The nuance in this case: with confidence.

31 See the statements about persecution (e.g., Luke 6:22) and the accounts of Jewish hostility in Acts (e.g., 6:8-15; 7:54—8:1; 13:44-48).

32 Ambrose (*Exp. Luc.* 7.48–52 [2.24–26]) is acutely aware of heretical wolves as he preaches on account of the events of 386, during which he saved his church from the Arian bishop Auxentius, when the latter laid claim to it with imperial support.

a legendary development: "Wherefore, brethren, let us forsake our sojourning in this world, and do the will of him who called us, and let us not fear to go forth from this world, for the Lord said, 'Ye shall be as lambs in the midst of wolves,' and Peter answered and said to him, 'If then the wolves tear the lambs?' Jesus said to Peter, 'Let the lambs have no fear of the wolves after their death.'"[33] Then an allusion to Luke 12:4-5 follows.

In vv. 1-3, there is a rich vocabulary connected with sending (ἀποστέλλω, "send"; ἐκβάλλω, "send out"; ὑπάγω, "go on your way," in the imperative).[34] Even though it corresponded to the social practices of the community of Q, it also served Luke's purposes in a missionary situation that was admittedly different but not without analogies.[35] In the thinking of the Gospel writer it recalled the origins of the Christian movement and—especially in Luke 9—those of the apostolic mission. Jesus, God's envoy (10:16b), himself dispatched messengers. If we were to look for an antecedent to this move, we would have to turn to the figure of Wisdom; she also came from God and enlisted humans in collaborating in the mission.

■ 4 Verse 4 is concerned with the way in which the disciples were to accomplish their mission; first of all, as in 9:3, severe limits were placed on the gear to be taken along. No "purse,"[36] no "bag," no "sandals"[37] were Jesus' instructions, which ruled out even the minimum that all travelers need to take for their trip. As we have remarked in connection with 9:3, these instructions, typical of Q's radicalism, had lost their topicality by the time Luke was writing (cf. 22:35-38). Nevertheless, out of deference,

the Gospel writer transmitted them but consigned them to a past time. What he was anxious to emphasize was the missionary's fragility and dependence on the Lord and the inhabitants of the place being visited. There is a possibility that these instructions were intended to distinguish the Christian missionaries from both Jewish pilgrims and itinerant philosophers. Another possibility is that we have here a revival of the Levitical ideal.[38] However—and this is the most important point—for Luke, doing without was no longer a sign of the imminence of God's reign but the memory of an ideal past, of a time when Jesus' presence was a guarantee of peace and security.

Verse 4 next communicates a mystifying ban on greeting anyone on the road (which contrasts with the greeting given in a house, v. 5). Different explanations of this ban have been suggested: eschatological haste, concentration on the basic essentials, fear of making contacts and being lured by them, or training for facing hostility.[39] After much hesitation, I opt for the idea of choosing one's priorities. In other words, it is not until one arrives at one's destination, in a town and then in a given house, that one should greet anyone. Such greetings should be not a simple formality but the expression of the peace that God himself offers.

■ 5-7 Success in a town (vv. 8-11) presupposed access to the houses (vv. 5-7). That is because there was a missionary experience underlying this literary composition. So establishing personal contacts was meant to be a prelude to public proclamation. The house[40] was to be the place where the first exchanges were to take place. The secu-

---

33   The English translation is that of Kirsopp Lake, *The Apostolic Fathers* (2 vols.; LCL; Cambridge, Mass.: Harvard University Press, 1912–13) 1:135.

34   On the use of ἀποστέλλω in Q in the apocalyptic sense of the prophets who encounter hostility as they are sent to reclaim Israel, see Schulz, *Q*, 414.

35   See François Bovon, "Practiques missionaires et communication de l'Évangile dans le christianisme primitif," in idem, *Révélations et Écritures: Nouveau Testament et littérature apocryphe chrétienne: Recueil d'articles* (MB 26; Geneva: Labor et Fides, 1993) 149–62.

36   Βαλλάντιον ("purse") is a rare word, but Luke is fond of it (Luke 12:33; 22:35-36). The prohibition corresponds to μήτε ἀργύριον ("nor money") in Luke 9:3. On πήρα ("satchel"), also found in 9:3, see Wilhelm Michaelis, "πήρα," *TDNT* 6 (1968)

119–21. The reference here is to a leather satchel for carrying food provisions and not to a satchel for begging. Jesus prohibited carrying provisions, not begging.

37   Cf. Luke 22:35, where one finds these same three words: purse, satchel, and sandals. Luke 9:53 would preclude a change of shirt, but the prohibition did not extend to footwear.

38   See the commentary on 9:3-5 (1:345).

39   Cf. the injunction of Elisha to Gehazi in 2 Kgs (LXX 4 Kgdms) 4:29; Luke 9:62. On this prohibition, see Fitzmyer, 2:847; O'Hagan, "'Greet No One on the Way' (Lk 10,4b)," 69–84; Lang, "Grußverbot oder Besuchverbot?" 75–79; and Bosold, *Pazifismus und prophetische Provokation*.

40   Luke alternates between οἶκος and οἰκία. Why? Probably because οἰκία denoted merely the build-

lar acts of eating, drinking, and resting take on value because they serve as vehicles for the communication of the good news. These elements, which are necessary for existence, were to be considered by the missionaries as the limited salary that they nevertheless deserved.[41] The religious "peace" that was to precede the envoys conferred on their mission a sacred dimension. At that time the words were still forceful: "peace" was the fullness of life and relationships, and dynamic and concrete happiness were the signs of the messianic kingdom. That is what a true greeting was meant to be, the opposite of curses that were so commonly uttered, a greeting that could be distinguished from the polite formulas ordinarily exchanged (cf. Matt 5:47). The God who sends his messengers on their way (vv. 3-5) is also the one who accompanies them, for they are talking about his peace. Luke preserved both the Semitic phraseology ("child of peace," literally "son of peace," v. 6) and the biblical imagery (the peace associated with a journey and with communication; cf. 1 Sam [1 Kgdms] 25:5-6; like the "wandering" ark of the covenant that could bring either a benediction or a curse; cf. 1 Sam [1 Kgdms] 4–7 and 2 Sam [2 Kgdms] 2). The missionaries were to stay in the first house that welcomed them; it was this gesture of hospitality that counted, rather than comfort or luxury. It was also the best means to avoid creating rivalry among the members of the community that was coming into being.[42] All it took for communication of the gospel to take place was to have someone there who was a "child of peace." It was not necessary for that person to be a father who could impose belief on each member of his family, as was the case in ancient religion based on the principle of duty. The only presence that counted was that of those

little children who will be mentioned later, in 10:21. Verses 5-7 say, in a more developed way, what Luke had already said in 9:4 about the mission of the Twelve.

■ **8-9** Towns, being larger than houses, could represent the mission field.[43] Proceeding from Galilee to Jerusalem, and from Jerusalem to Rome, Luke's work unfolds thanks to a network of towns and cities. These localities are the nexus of the life, history, power, conversion, implantation, and finally the building up of churches, and the collective acceptance or rejection of the gospel. Luke's focus on these localities matches his interest in mediations and grows out of his effort to historicize.

In other words and in summary, we may say that v. 8 says again in terms of towns what vv. 5-7 said about houses. Once the missionaries get set up in a town they are ready to start work, a *public* work. Verse 9 gives a dazzling summary of the church's mission in wording that certainly corresponds to the pre-Easter period but which was still timely in Luke's day. As is often the case, the Gospel writer places the action ("cure," $\vartheta\epsilon\rho\alpha\pi\epsilon\acute{\upsilon}\omega$) before the spoken word ("say," $\lambda\acute{\epsilon}\gamma\omega$). The charitable action is expressed by a verb ("cure," $\vartheta\epsilon\rho\alpha\pi\epsilon\acute{\upsilon}\omega$) that lays less stress on the healing, which is not in doubt, than on the care that is required.[44] Luke, who sketched out the person of Jesus as physician,[45] has here conferred on his disciples an analogous therapeutic function. The disciples need to pay attention to the care that they must dispense. God will provide the healing, whether it be slow or immediate. The Christian church finds in this command the legitimization of its work of service and hospitality (cf. 10:29-37, where the Samaritan takes charge of the wounded person for as long as necessary).

ing, whereas $o\hat{\iota}\kappa o\varsigma$ denoted not only the building but also its inhabitants.

41   On wages on the servants of God, see Num 18:31; Luke 10:7b par. Matt 10:10b; 1 Cor 9:4-14; Phil 4:18; Gal 6:6; 1 Tim 5:18. Like the sons of Aaron or of Levi, Christian missionaries had no possessions but deserved a part of the offerings in lieu of wages.

42   Ἄν with the subjunctive indicates repetition, a contingency, a condition, or rule (see BDAG, s.v. ἄν; and BDF §380.1b). On ἐπαναπαύομαι ("to rest," "find rest," "support"), see the LXX at Num 11:25-26 and 2 Kgs (4 Kgdms) 2:15, where the Spirit "rests" upon someone. The enclitic particle is often used in composition as it is here: εἰ δὲ μή γε is the

best way to underscore the nuance "but in case of the opposite," "but if not." Ἀνακάμπτω can take three senses: (a) "to bend back" and (b) in the intransitive and figurative sense "to retrace one's steps," "to go and return," "to walk up and down," and (c) "to turn away from." Here it is used in sense (b). See Plutarch *Mor.* 796D; and Diogenes Laertius 5.2; 7.5.

43   The word πόλις ("town") appears five times in vv. 1-16, where it is used to name six different towns.

44   Luke is especially fond of the verb θεραπεύω ("to honor," "to take care of," "to give medical care to," "to care for").

45   See the commentary on 4:40-41 (1:164).

While, according to Luke, John the Baptist did not yet have the right to preach the kingdom (3:3-17), Jesus' disciples, following their master, always have that right. They are even obligated to proclaim the kingdom's imminence, an imminence that the Easter event has modified (the book of Acts maintains the importance of the "kingdom" [βασιλεία] but not that of its imminence). The image conjured up by the Greek verb ἐγγίζω ("draw near," "come near," "approach") is, moreover, more spatial than temporal and is fitting in this chapter, where places play a determining role. Like the peace that can arrive, the kingdom of God has come near. In order to personalize that reality, Luke has added "to you," but he has not lost sight of its objective component, since in v. 11b he recalls, for the sake of the disciples, that the kingdom has come near in an absolute manner, whether the inhabitants of the town accept it or not. This v. 11b is decisive; behind these historical observations[46] there is the divine decision that the believers know ("know," γινώσκετε)[47] by virtue of their faith: independent of human desires and whims, God has come near in order to establish his power of peace and justice.

■ **10-11** The rite involving dust corresponds more or less to the solution advocated for the Twelve in 9:5.[48] The present text stresses the public character of the act ("into its streets"), provides for a word to confirm the act ("say," εἴπατε), and describes the dust in a heavy way (literally, "that which clings to us of your town to our feet"). But the verb used here is less violent than the one in 9:5; there the dust was shaken off (ἀποτινάσσω). Here it is removed by wiping (ἀπομάσσομαι).[49] Finally, in 9:5 the

act served as testimony against the inhabitants, whereas here the use of "for you" (ὑμῖν) suggests that the disciples leave it with them or give it back to them. That means "we're even" and "we haven't taken anything of yours," thereby implying the end of a relationship rather than an act of cursing.

■ **12** The town, as a collective entity, can be held to be just as responsible and culpable as an individual. Here the Synoptic tradition follows the biblical tradition that dared to condemn Babylon, Nineveh, Sidon, Jerusalem, and Sodom. At home with hyperboles, the Jesus of Q, who has become the Lord of Luke, condemns the town, which has refused the preaching of the kingdom, to a fate worse than that of the guiltiest of the towns of the old covenant.[50] Jewish literature, which naturally was acquainted with Sodom's guilt and its stubbornness, encouraged people not to follow its attitude, since a similar fate would meet them all.[51] Here the text goes further and the reader discovers that it is more serious to close one's heart and mind to the proclamation of the kingdom of God in the Gospels than to have that attitude toward the Law or the Prophets.

■ **13-14** Next, two towns in Galilee are criticized. The double "woe" (οὐαί) is more of a lamentation than a curse.[52] The language used here is more than an observation and less than a condemnation. In solidarity with the God of judgment, Jesus prophetically foresees the inexorable fate awaiting these two towns. The names of Chorazin and Bethsaida are anchored in the tradition (Luke himself does not pay them any attention elsewhere).[53] The fatal error of these towns was that, unlike Nineveh

---

46 Note the important usage of πλήν ("but," "only," "nevertheless") in vv. 11b, 14, 20, where it indicates a reservation: in spite of human weakness or refusal, God acts or has acted.

47 On knowing God or God's purpose in Luke, see Luke 1:77; 11:52. On being ignorant of God or of God's purpose, see Acts 3:17; 17:30. See also Bovon, "Le Dieu de Luc," in idem, *L'œuvre,* 235–37.

48 See the commentary on 9:3-5 (1:346).

49 See Paul Joüon, "Notes philologiques sur les évangiles," *RSR* 18 (1928) 353.

50 On Sodom in the OT, see Genesis 19. See also the comparisons with Sodom in Isa 1:9; Jer 23:14; 49:18. In Judaism, Sodom is infamous for its sin (*Jub.* 13:17; *Bib. Ant.* 8:2) and for the just punishment that it received (*Jub.* 20.6; *T. Naph.* 3.4; *T. Ash.* 7.1; *T. Benj.* 9:1; *Bib. Ant.* 45:2). *Jubilees* 20:6 and 22:22

compare idolaters with the people of Sodom. In *Asc. Isa.* 3:10, Isaiah is reproached by a false prophet for having called Jerusalem "Sodom."

51 Accordingly, OT and Jewish tradition adheres to a comparison between them (e.g., Jer 50:40 [LXX 27:40]).

52 See the commentary on 6:24 (1:225).

53 Chorazin is not mentioned either in the OT or in Josephus. It is cited by Eusebius *Onom.* 303 (*Eusebius Werke* 3:147 GCS) and by Jerome *Comm. in Is.* 3 (*PL* 24:127), but they differ as to its precise location. Several modern scholars have identified Chorazin with the ruins of an important city at Kh. Kerazeh, which is just a few kilometers from Capernaum (see Fitzmyer, 2:853). The present-day picture of this town in ruins is perhaps the best commentary on this verse. On Bethsaida, situated on the shoreline

(cf. Jonah 3:6 and Luke 11:32), they did not repent. This is a biblical theme: God offers one last chance through the proclamation by a prophet or through the evidence of a sign: the "deeds of power," "miracles" ($\delta \upsilon \nu \acute{\alpha} \mu \epsilon \iota \varsigma$) done "in you" (we are to understand "by Jesus") have not occasioned any repentance (the verb "to repent" [$\mu \epsilon \tau \alpha \nu o \acute{\epsilon} \omega$] occurs in v. 13). These recalcitrant towns were not able to adopt a penitent attitude, clothe themselves in sackcloth made of goat's wool, or sit on a heap of ashes while scattering them on their head.[54] In the face of such signs, such miracles, those proud foreign cities would have given way before God a long time ago ($\pi \acute{\alpha} \lambda \alpha \iota$) and repented.[55] Their eschatological fate ("at the judgment" [$\epsilon \nu \tau \hat{\eta} \kappa \rho \acute{\iota} \sigma \epsilon \iota$]) will be more tolerable than that of the towns in Galilee.

■ **15** At this point, the voice takes on a more urgent tone ("And you, Capernaum" [$\kappa \alpha \grave{\iota} \sigma \acute{\upsilon}, \ K \alpha \varphi \alpha \rho \nu \alpha o \acute{\upsilon} \mu$]). We can feel emotion, sadness, and betrayed affection breaking in. The ancient oracle against Babylon (Isa 14:14-15) is here turned around and directed against a town in Israel, Capernaum, the town where Jesus' message has rung out the most.[56] Although we do not know what that town's ambitions were, we can readily understand what fate awaited it: being brought down to hell.[57]

■ **16** Luke finishes off this speech to the seventy-two with an assertion of the solidarity between the messengers and the one who gave them their mandate (cf. 9:48a).

We thereby uncover a line of communication that starts from God ("the one who sent me"), passes on to Jesus ("me"), and ends up with the disciples ("you"). Since the one speaking demonstrates an imperturbable prophetic conscience, the envoys cannot fail to sense their worth and feel protected by their ties to him, and through him to God. Not being listened to[58] and being rejected[59] were to be painful experiences for them. On the other hand, although the disciples were to be turned away and not understood, they would be consoled by their communion with the Father and the Son.

■ **17-19** The envoys come back and tell their story. The reader will notice (a) that Luke is not interested here in the installments of the story of their mission, or even in the missionaries themselves; (b) that the success of the messengers is expressed in terms of exorcism and not conversion; (c) that the text is a reflection on the nature and origin of true joy (v. 17, "with joy," $\mu \epsilon \tau \grave{\alpha} \chi \alpha \rho \hat{\alpha} \varsigma$; and v. 20, "do not rejoice . . . rejoice," $\mu \grave{\eta} \chi \alpha \acute{\iota} \rho \epsilon \tau \epsilon \ . . . \chi \alpha \acute{\iota} \rho \epsilon \tau \epsilon$).

Jesus' saying, that Luke was keen to put at the center of the pericope (v. 18), establishes its isotopy: that of exorcisms and not of preaching. The Christian conviction is that, since the coming of Jesus, the demons' strength has waned; the demons submit to the power and to the "name" of Jesus Christ (v. 17b). This conviction ensured the success of Christianity[60] and played out in

---

of the lake northeast of the mouth of the Jordan, see the commentary on 9:10-17 (1:354 n. 7).

54 Most often a dark color, "sackcloth" was a piece of coarse fabric that was worn around the waist (the upper portion of the body being left naked) as a vestment of mourning and of penitence. Other gestures of lamentation or of penitence that accompanied the wearing of "sackcloth" include beating one's breast, cutting one's hair, and sitting in ashes (Jonah 3:6; Job 2:8; Matt 6:16).

55 See the oracles against Tyre and Sidon in Isaiah 23 and Ezekiel 26–28, paired together in Jer 47:4; Joel 4:4 (LXX 3:4); Zech 9:2. In the intertestamental literature, these two cities are less prominent than Sodom.

56 At the beginning of Jesus' ministry, Luke indeed shows less concern for Capernaum (4:23, 31; 7:1) than for Nazareth (4:16-30), but later he makes it a home base for activity.

57 Luke uses the word "Hades," which I translate as

"hell," only twice, here in v. 15 and in 16:23. With the exception of 12:1, Luke avoids the strange word. As for $\overset{\text{``}}{\alpha} \beta \upsilon \sigma \sigma o \varsigma$ (8:31), it does not necessarily refer to the abode of the dead. On the contrast between exaltation and abasement, see Eph 4:8-10.

58 Notice how the text personalizes the communication. It does not say "whoever listens to the word" or "to your word," but "whoever listens to you."

59 In Luke, the verb $\overset{\cdot}{\alpha} \vartheta \epsilon \tau \acute{\epsilon} \omega$ occurs only here in this passage (four times) and in 7:30, and it means "to declare invalid," "to annul," "to break" (a treaty or a promise), "to repulse," "to reject."

60 On the phrase "treading on serpents and scorpions," see Ps 91 (LXX 90):13 (but the names of the animals do not correspond to those in Luke 10:10). See also Mark 16:17-18 and Justin (*Dial.* 76.6), who draws a connection between the text of the psalm and Luke 10:19. Serpents and scorpions are the first dangers to menace Israel in the desert (Deut 8:15). To resist them is to resist temptation and sin (see

narrative fashion in the apocryphal literature and later, the hagiographic literature.[61] The source of Christian joy is to be located elsewhere, however, namely, in the conviction of being known and protected by God.[62] Be that as it may, this relationship to God is lived out here below in superiority in the face of the world of demons. The role of intermediary, which Jesus played between God and God's children, noted in v. 16, turns up again here in v. 19 with a strong emphasis: "See, I have given you authority. . . ." This is an authority that both triumphs and protects.

In order for this authority to be communicable to Christians, Satan had to be defeated. That is the way eschatology was to be fulfilled. The fall of the tyrant, for example, the king of Babylon (Isa 14:12-14), which the biblical prophets perceived and announced ahead of time, was understood in the intertestamental literature as being the fall of Satan himself.[63] Luke placed Jesus in this prophetic and apocalyptic stream. With the speed of lightning, Satan fell from heaven.[64] So the events of the end-time were being played out. As a privileged seer, Jesus was witness to the expulsion and fall of the accuser and tempter, Satan.[65] Luke created the scenario of the victorious return of the seventy-two in order to put the spotlight on this apocalyptic vision. In his thinking, Jesus was not just a spectator of this routing of the Evil One; he was God's principal adjunct. Even though he only

witnessed the fall, he nevertheless participated in the defeat of Satan's militia,[66] in the casting out of demons (cf. Luke 11:20), and in a more general way in the victory over evil.[67] On the other hand, for Luke, as for the Seer John (Rev 12:7-18), Satan's expulsion from heaven did not mean that he was slain once and for all. He still had some last might to throw into the fray. His power *on earth* still had to be blocked step by step by Christ's troops.[68]

The task for our times is to demythologize this doctrinal certitude (or, more exactly, to remythologize it in contemporary idiom): the Gospel, especially this v. 18 in Luke 10, assures us that in Jesus Christ, God decided to overcome evil and that the deity has accomplished the first half of this project. Christians live in the tense situation in which the victory is assured in the middle of the turmoil. They already share in the triumph, the fellowship, and the love, all the while being subject to the last assaults of suffering and dying.

What cheers them up, what must cheer them up, according to v. 20, is not the seductive euphoria of victory but the unshakable assurance of being loved by God. Saying that our names are written in heaven (or in the book of life, Rev 3:5) means that we believe that only God's memory assures the continuity of our life into eternity. This conviction, which is a source of joy, is the ground of our hope against all hope (Rom 4:18).

Miyoshi, *Anfang*, 102). Must one understand this verse in a literal sense? In "Étude critique de Luc 10,9," (in Delorme and Duplacy, *La parole de grâce*, 87–100), Pierre Grelot contends for the figurative sense "victory over evil." But I plead for a literal sense that is open to figurative interpretation.

61 See Rosa Söder, *Die apokryphen Apostelgeschichten und die romanhafte Literatur der Antike* (Würzburger Studien zur Altertumswissenschaft 3; Stuttgart: Kohlhammer, 1932; reprinted 1969) 51–102; and Alain Boureau, *La légende dorée: Le système narratif de Jacques de Voragine (†1298)* (Histoire; Paris: Cerf, 1984) 153–65.

62 On names written in heaven, see Hagemeyer, "'Freut euch, daß eure Namen im Himmel verzeichnet sind!' 160–63; and Fitzmyer, 2:863–64. In the background stands an idea inspired by the royal archives of the ancient Near East, a record of life, a list of those who belong to God. See Exod 32:32-33; Ps 69:28 (LXX 69:29); Mal 3:16-17; *Jub.* 30:19-23; *1 Enoch* 47:3; Rev 3:5, etc.

63 See Puig i Tàrrech, "Lc 10, 18," 217–43.

64 See ibid.; and Rosenstiehl, "La chute de l'Ange," 37–60. When Puig i Tàrrech and Rosenstiehl traced the theme of Satan's fall through Jewish and Christian literature, they found that the devil is hurled down from heaven by God either because he challenged God as a rival or because he refused to respect humankind as God's new creation. Among the numerous texts that they uncovered are *2 Enoch* (long recension) 29:4-5; *Life of Adam and Eve* 14–16; Rev 12:7-18. On Satan and Luke, see "Excursus: The Devil" in the commentary in chap. 4 (1:141–42).

65 Notice how the aspect of the past tense and the duration of this event are indicated by the use of the imperfect: ἐθεώρουν ("I was contemplating").

66 In spite of what others have said, I believe that the power of evil spirits in the Judaism of that time was associated with the power of Satan.

67 See n. 60 above.

68 Among the textual problems posed by vv. 17-20, there is the uncertainty about the order of the

History of Interpretation

At the end of the second century,[69] Irenaeus of Lyons utilized one or another of the verses in this pericope in a doctrinal context or corrected the interpretation being given it by Gnostic adversaries. Thus, the presence of the seventy disciples allowed him to rule out the Gnostic interpretation of the Twelve as figures of the twelve eons emanating from Man and the Church (since there was no group of seventy eons in the system under attack) (*Adv. haer.* 2.21.1). So the knowledge of the gospel depends on the apostolic preaching authorized by the one who said, "Whoever listens to you listens to me . . ." (v. 16) (*Adv. haer.* 3. prologue). Consequently the creed proclaims the true passion and the Easter victory of Christ, who sent the Paraclete on earth, to which the devil had been cast down like a flash of lightning (*Adv. haer.* 3.17.3), and who gave his disciples the authority to tread on snakes and scorpions (v. 19) (*Adv. haer.* 2.20.3).[70] So, as a theologian, Irenaeus restructured the Lukan text, taking as his starting point a confession of faith that was attuned to Christ's passion and resurrection.

For his part, Clement of Alexandria quoted the saying about the plentiful harvest (Matt 9:37 par. Luke 10:2) in the context of the parable of the talents (Matt 25:14-30).

In his opinion, the "laborers" are those who proclaim the Word of God, whether by hand or by word, that is, by written or by oral communication.[71]

It is as difficult to read Tertullian of Africa's *Adversus Marcionem* as it is to understand Racine's *Plaideurs* if we do not understand the historical background. We miss the allusions, and its irony plunges us into uncertainty. It seems clear, however, that Tertullian (*Adv. Marc.* 4.24) was putting up a fight step by step against his enemy, Marcion, and was contradicting, verse by verse, the interpretation that Marcion had developed in his "Antitheses."[72] The constant thrust of Tertullian's argumentation was to show that, by his commands, Jesus was not opposed to the Hebrew Bible but confirmed it or fulfilled it. For example, the order to greet no one on the road is closely akin to the order Elisha gave to Gehazi (2 Kgs [4 Kgdms] 4:29, a recurring parallel drawn throughout the history of Christianity); thus, if the kingdom comes near, that means that it was far away, but if it was far away, then it was already in existence. In spite of Marcion's recriminations, the newness of Christianity was not absolute.[73]

When preaching on Luke 10, Ambrose, bishop of Milan, expounded on it allegorically (*Exp. Luc.* 7.44–65). The framework of contemporary ethological knowledge made it possible for him to identify the wolves with the

---

words in the second half of v. 18, the uncertainty about the tense of the verb "to give" in the first half of v. 19 (present or perfect?), and the uncertainty about the reading in the latter half of that verse (a double negative with the subjunctive or a simple negation with the future?).

69 There are scattered instances as early as the end of the first century where certain statements found in Luke 10:1-20 are quoted in a free manner either directly from Luke's Gospel or from oral traditions: the wages of the worker (v. 7) in 1 Tim 5:8 and in *Did.* 13.1-2; the lambs and the wolves (v. 3) in *2 Clem.* 5.2 (see pp. 25–26 above) and in the apocryphal epistle of Pseudo-Titus on virginity (the citation is in Aland, *Synopsis,* 259); the listening to the witnesses (v. 16) in Justin *1 Apol.* 16.10 and 63.5; the power over the serpents (v. 19) in Mark 16:18 (inauthentic ending) and in Justin *Dial.* 76.6; the harvest (v. 2) in *Gos. Thom.* 73; and the welcoming in the towns and the healing of the sick (vv. 8–9) in *Gos. Thom.* 14.

70 Irenaeus understands here "the power of the enemy" (v. 19b) as "the initiator of apostasy."

71 Clement of Alexandria (*Strom.* 1.7.1) says that the workers are βραχεῖς ("small" in number), where Matthew and Luke have ὀλίγοι ("few" in number). Gregory the Great (*Moral.* 27.30.54) understands v. 2 as an illustration of preaching. Bonaventure (*Comm. in Luc.* 10.4, p. 254) compares good preachers to the harvesters who carry out their work thanks to the sword of God's word.

72 Marcion must have considered the behavior of the Israelites in carrying out the Egyptian vessels during the exodus (Exod 12:34-36) to be robbery and so must have opposed the attitude of the disciples as depriving themselves even of the necessities of life by order of Jesus.

73 Concerning our verses, there is extant a fragment of Origen (*Hom. in Luc.* frg. 69, ed. Rauer 158 [*Origenes Werke* 9:290 GCS]; cf. Origen, *Hom. in Luc.*, p. 519). It bears on the expression "two by two" (v. 1) and stresses the antiquity of the arrangement (cf. Moses and Aaron) that favors a mutual strengthening in the ministry of the word (Origen refers to Prov 18:19 and Eccl 4:9).

heretics and implicitly attack one of them, his enemy Auxentius, the Arian bishop involved in the quarrel over basilicas (in the year 386). As long as the shepherd, that is, the bishop, is there, the flock is not threatened. But he still needs to see the wolf before it sees him. Otherwise, according to ancient zoological concepts, the wolf will take away his voice! What is more—in the eschatological perspective—the sending out of the lambs into the midst of wolves must result in a final reconciliation, as announced in the prophecy in Isa 65:25. Jesus' restrictions on carrying a beggar's bag and sandals (Ambrose adds a staff, with Matthew) allowed Ambrose to create a harmonious composition in which the dominant themes were glorious poverty (no beggar's bag), renunciation of mortal attachments (the leather in the sandals) and giving up of power (the staff).[74] Finally, Ambrose exquisitely juxtaposes the refusal to greet any travelers ("in the presence of divine orders, human considerations must temporarily be set aside" [*Exp. Luc.* 7.64])[75] and the proclamation of peace to those who lived in the house (*Exp. Luc.* 7.63).

In the fifth century, Cyril, patriarch of Alexandria, devoted five sermons to these verses (*Hom. in Luc* 60–64).[76] The most significant one of them, the first (*Hom.* 60), spoke of the mission of the seventy itself.[77] Taking as his starting point a Christology of salvation (the only Son has justified us by faith, purified us, and liberated us from fallen Satan), Cyril declared that this new world inaugurated in Christ needed to be proclaimed: by the Twelve to Israel, then by the seventy to the whole world. Cyril found a prefiguration in Scripture of the path leading from the event to its being preached about: it was announced not only by the choice of the seventy elders installed by Moses (Num 11:16) but also, following a typological exegesis that could already be found in Tertullian's writings (*Adv. Marc.* 4.24), by the

description of the site of Elim with its twelve wells and its seventy palm trees (Exod 15:27).

The Venerable Bede provided an allegorical explanation of v. 4a. Money, that is, wisdom, remains hidden in the purse. But, according to Sir 41:14, hidden wisdom is useless.[78] Concerning v. 4b ("greet no one"), Bonaventure furnished a palette of allegorical interpretations. So one must not greet anyone on the road since salvation is offered not in order to carry on a dialogue with the saints but to imitate them. It is life (*vita*) and not the road (*via*) that must be shared with them.[79]

In connection with the dust to be wiped off (vv. 10-11), Bonaventure brought up preachers, whom he compared to one's feet, while the triple dust that threatened them stands for the world's lack of seriousness, that is, the preachers' vainglory, when they are praised; impatience, when their message is not received; and greed, when they are offered remuneration.[80] In the background of this allegory of the feet, there is probably the text of Isa 52:7 ("How beautiful . . . are the feet of the messenger who . . . brings good news") and the Johannine account of foot washing (John 13). Clement of Alexandria (*Paed.* 2 [8].63.2) had already pointed out that Jesus washed his disciples' feet in order to purify them for preaching.

In commenting on v. 18, the *Glossa ordinaria*[81] gives us Satan as an example not to follow. If the devil himself could be thrown down to earth, how much more do we, who come from the earth, risk the same humiliating fate when we attempt to raise ourselves up by our pride.

When we get to the reformer Calvin, we find once again the relationship between the Twelve ("in order to wake up the Jews to the hope of the salvation that is to come") and the seventy ("in order to spread the news of Christ's coming in all places"). But marked by the humanism of his time, Calvin also gave a historical explanation of the number seventy (it was the number

---

74   In this connection, he writes: "For he has sent them to sow the faith not through coercion but through teaching, not by showing the strength of their power, but by exalting the doctrine of humility."

75   Ed. Tissot, 2:30. As for Chrysostom (*Hom. in Matt.* 46 or 47 [*PG* 58:480]), he cites v. 8 in order to say that mutual love is more important than fasting.

76   Payne Smith, *Cyril*, 1:272–95.

77   Ibid., 1:272–76). The passage summarized here is preserved in Greek (frg. 100 in Reuss, *Lukas-Kom-*

mentare, 106). A dozen Greek fragments of *Hom. in Luc.* 60–64 are extant; see Reuss, *Lukas-Kommentare*, 106–10.

78   Bede, *In Luc.* 3.1928–37 (ed. Hurst, p. 215).

79   Bonaventure, *Comm. in Luc.* 10.10 (ed. Bernardini, p. 255).

80   Ibid., 10.20 (pp. 258–59).

81   *Glossa ordinaria*, Luke 10:17-18 (*PL* 114:285).

of the elders in Exod 18:22 and Num 11:24-30 and of the members of the Sanhedrin that King Herod decided to do away with) before coming to his half-historical, half-theological conclusion: "It appears now that the Lord orders seventy heralds to publicize his coming, in order to promise and give hope of the re-establishment of the state that had fallen."[82]

Further on, Calvin analyzes v. 16, which gives him the occasion to reflect on pastoral ministry, caught up in a chain of accreditations: "And on the contrary, God has decided to govern his Church by means of the ministry of men, and he even often takes from among the common stock those whom he makes into ministers of the Word." The saying in Luke increases the standing of this ministry: "It is, then, a matter for praise and particular commendation of this external ministry, when Jesus Christ says that all the respect and honor accorded to men's preaching, provided it is pure and faithful, God accepts as being accorded to himself." It follows that it is in our interest to (a) "embrace the doctrine of the Gospel" and (b) have confidence in such a human testimony. And it is also in our interest to recognize (before laying into the pope)[83] that "this passage gives magnificent authorization to the status of pastors who faithfully exercise their charge in single-minded love."

Verses 19-20, which speak of names being written in the heavens, could not fail to inspire Calvin. When the disciples returned, Jesus had no reservations about the excellence of the divine gift that they had just applied with success. But, as Calvin wrote, "there is something else that is higher, to which they should give their principal attention." For him, reading v. 20, this higher reality, source of the true joy, could only be "God's free election." Here Christ "wished to touch on the beginning from which all these blessings had proceeded, i.e., God's free election, so that they would not give themselves any of the credit."[84]

Conclusion

Coming back to Luke, here is what I would say by way of conclusion. As there are two types of commissioning stories, one concerning the apostles' names (cf. 5:27-28), the other remaining indeterminate (9:57-62), in Luke there are also two kinds of installation, one of the Twelve, whose names are listed (6:12-16), and another of the anonymous seventy-two (10:1), as well as two sending-off speeches (9:1-6 and 10:1-20). Unlike the Twelve, whose mission was concentrated on Israel, the seventy-two represent the Christian mission among the Gentiles, such as it was practiced in Luke's time. These messengers are sent "before his face," as had been their companions into the Samaritan village (9:52-56). However, it is a question no longer of going on ahead to prepare Jesus' arrival but of going to announce God's reign, as Jesus himself had done. The collaboration is thus one of a different order: it resembles a delegation, as v. 16 suggests. Nevertheless, since the episode occurs before Easter, it has also and foremost the character of a dry run, a dress rehearsal. With time would come Christ's passion and the true mission of the disciples (cf. 22:35-38). As may be seen, Luke tried to paint a historical picture of the life of Jesus and sketch a normative view of the Christian mission at the same time. As a historian, he was aware that contemporary evangelization (cf. his accounts in the Acts of the Apostles) was carried out in a way different from Jesus' and his disciples' attempts at missionary work (cf. Luke 9:1-6 and 10:1-20). Luke was, however, also a theologian and, in addition to the changes, he noted the permanent features of the proclamation of the gospel. Among these abiding features, we should note the following points:

---

82 Jean Calvin, *Harmonia ex tribus Evangelistis composita Matthaeo, Marco, et Luca; adiuncto seorsum Iohanne, quod pauca cum aliis communia habeat; cum Ioannis Calvini Commentariis* (Geneva: Robertus Stephanus [= Robert Estienne], 1555), translated as John Calvin, *A Harmony of the Gospels Matthew, Mark and Luke* (trans. A. W. Morrison [vols. 1, 3] and T. H. L. Parker [vol. 2]; 3 vols.; Calvin's Commentaries 1–3; Edinburgh: Oliver & Boyd, 1972) 2:13 (cited from the English translation).

83 Ibid., 2:17–18.

84 Ibid., 2:19–20.

- The Lord is the one who sends (v. 1).
- The mission is one of the stages in the history of salvation (v. 2).
- The mission and suffering go hand in hand (v. 3).
- In evangelization, it is not just a matter of giving; in the exchange, there is also receiving (v. 7).
- The deed accompanies the word (v. 9).
- The earliest community was centered in homes (vv. 5-7).
- Thought must be given to which means to use or not to use; in other words, the question is raised as to how missionaries are to be trained, as well as how they are to act.
- The Lord God and the Lord Jesus, although they are the senders, do not remain inactive. The reign is ever dawning, whether or not those who receive it accept that fact.

Once the disciples have been sent off, they are of necessity separated from their Lord. That certainly does not mean that all communion with him is cut off, but it is lived in the context of the way faith operates: contact with God is not direct but rather mediated by prayer (v. 2), and henceforth the relationship with Christ partakes of the character of analogy and delegation (v. 16). The disciples, whose anonymity allows us to identify with them, are called to a mature faith. Christ's presence is symbolically summarized by his name (v. 17).

This text takes into account an intense reflection on missionary practice, both the means that are available and the attitudes that are to be adopted. This reflection takes place in a realistic framework, not a utopian one. The kingdom of God, whose lively expansion is announced in vv. 6-10, does not, for the time being, assert itself as being something that is self-evident or a constraint. Nevertheless, it does possess objectivity, and its being near does not depend on either its proclaimers or their listeners. If the life of men, women, and children is to be enriched by this reign, it must be received subjectively. In order to respect this liberty, the God who is coming is mediated through the hands and voices of his human envoys—hence the importance given to mediating agents. In order to avoid the misunderstandings of a theology of glory that would risk puffing up the missionaries, the Lukan Christ strenuously limits the means that may be used, according to the biblical concept of

the holy war. Human intermediaries are necessary, but, in order for the glory of success to redound to God, they will be limited in number and given limited provisions, as Gideon and David were. Since it is a venture of faith, membership will be voluntary. Believing that the kingdom will be drawing near involves accepting the fact that the Christians' God makes himself known, around a table as it were, by means of humans speaking to each other. But it still truly is God and God's kingdom whose presence is to become a reality. Here and there, we read that this human speech will be completed by actions and even by deeds of power, what we call miracles, healings, and exorcisms (vv. 13, 17, and 19), in line with what is found in the rest of the Gospel. These acts will have the force of signs rather than proofs, which will classify them in the category of the word that invites and does not coerce.

Although preachers, their speech, and their actions can be counted among these mediating agents, that is also true of the listeners, the towns in which they live, their houses, and their meal tables. Moreover, the distinction between evangelists and those who are evangelized will tend to fade, since every person spoken to who accepts the transformation represented by repentance and conversion ($\mu\epsilon\tau\acute{\alpha}\nu o\iota\alpha$, v. 13) will in turn become a messenger of the good news.

This strategy on God's part for reaching human beings, through his Son and his envoys, by persuasive rather than coercive means, is not without risks, which are also both objective and subjective. The text pays attention to adversaries, compared to wolves (v. 3). The text speaks of enemies in a mythological mode, in terms of Satan, fallen from heaven, therefore dethroned, and on earth, thus near and threatening (v. 18), and of demons to be exorcised (v. 17). The mention of "wolves" leads us to understand that these objective forces of evil are incarnated in human beings. However, we are not told their names or their categories; this is undoubtedly because no one is of necessity an enemy or lost forever to the cause of the gospel. Any witch hunting is prohibited.

The dominant theme at the end of the pericope is joy, in spite of the fact that God is absent and Christ is distant, and in spite of dangers from the enemy (v. 19) and his henchmen (vv. 3 and 17). This is the joy of the kingdom of God, which has really come near, in spite of war and death (v.11b), which are still active; it is also the joy over the election of believers who know that they are loved for all eternity (the image of our names being written in the book of life; v. 20); and the joy of life in the present, with all the risks and excitement it involves by virtue of the task we have been given, the successes we count on, and the fellowship with our collaborators. Finally, it is the joy inherent in being a part of a circle of believers and having a link to the Father through the Son (v. 16).

The Revelation to the Little Ones
(10:21-24)

Bibliography

Allison, Dale C., Jr., "Two Notes on a Key Text: Matthew 11:25-30," *JTS* 39 (1988) 477–85.

Arvedson, Tomas, *Das Mysterium Christi: Eine Studie zu Mt 11.25-30* (Arbeiten und Mitteilungen aus Neutestamentlichen Seminar zu Uppsala 7; Leipzig: Lorentz; Uppsala: A. B. Lundequistska, 1937.

Bayer, Oswald, "Leichtigkeit: Mt 11, 25-30," *ThBei* 22 (1991) 225–29.

Bieneck, Joachim, *Sohn Gottes: Als Christusbezeichnung der Synoptiker* (AThANT 21; Zurich: Zwingli-Verlag, 1951) 75–87.

Boring, M. Eugene, *Sayings*, passim.

Cerfaux, "L'Évangile de Jean et le 'logion johannique' des Synoptiques," in idem, *Recueil*, 3:161–74.

idem, "Les sources scripturaires de Mt 11, 25-30," in idem, *Recueil*, 3:139–59.

Charlier, Célestin, "L'action de grâces de Jésus (Lc 10, 17-24 et Mt 11, 25-30)," *BVC* 17 (1957) 87–99.

Christ, Felix, *Jesus Sophia: Die Sophia-Christologie bei den Synoptikern* (AThANT 57; Zurich: Zwingli-Verlag, 1970) 81–99.

Cullmann, Oscar, *The Christology of the New Testament* (Philadelphia: Westminster, 1959) 287–89.

Davies, William David, " 'Knowledge' in the Dead Sea Scrolls and Matthew 11:25-30," *HTR* 46 (1953) 113–39.

Deutsch, Celia, *Hidden Wisdom and the Easy Yoke: Wisdom, Torah, and Discipleship in Mt 11, 25-30* (JSNTSup 18; Sheffield: JSOT Press, 1987).

Dupont, *Études*, 2:583–91.

idem, *Les Béatitudes* (3 vols.; EtB; Bruges: Abbaye de Saint-André, 1958–1973) 2:181– 218.

Edwards, *Theology of Q*, 106–7 and passim.

Feldkämper, Ludger, *Der betende Jesus als Heilsmittler nach Lukas* (Veröffentlichungen des Missionspriesterseminars St. Augustin bei Bonn 29; St. Augustin: Steyler, 1978) 151–77.

Feuillet, André, "Jésus et la Sagesse divine d'après les Évangiles synoptiques," *RB* 62 (1955) 161–96.

Garrison, R., "Matthew 11, 25-27 = Luke 10, 21-22: A Bridge between the Synoptic and Johannine Traditions" (Diss., Oxford, 1979).

Giblet, Jean, "La prière d'action de grâce de Jésus dans son contexte lucanien (Lc 10,21-22)," in *Qu'est-ce que Dieu? Philosophie, théologie: Hommage à l'abbé Daniel Coppierters de Gibson* (Publications des Facultés universitaires Saint-Louis 33; Brussels: Facultés universitaires Saint-Louis, 1985) 613–35.

Grimm, Werner, "Der Dank für die empfangene Offenbarung bei Jesus und Josephus," *BZ* n.s. 17 (1973) 249–56.

Idem, *Jesus und das Danielbuch*, vol. 1: *Jesu Einspruch gegen das Offenbarungs-system Daniels: Mt 11, 25-27; Lk 17,20-21* (ANTJ 6; Frankfurt am Main/New York: Lang, 1984), 1–69.

idem, "Selige Augenzeugen, Lk 10, 23f.: Alttestamentlicher Hintergrund und ursprünglicher Sinn," *ThZ* 26 (1970) 172–83.

Grundmann, Walter, "Matth. 11, 27 und die johannischen 'Der Vater–der Sohn'-Stellen," *NTS* 12 (1965–66) 42–49.

idem, "Die *NHIIIOI* in der urchristlichen Paränese," *NTS* 5 (1958–59) 188–205.

idem, "Weisheit im Horizont des Reiches Gottes," in Rudolf Schnackenburg et al., eds., *Die Kirche des Anfangs: Festschrift für Heinz Schürmann zum 65. Geburtstag* (EThSt 38; Leipzig: St. Benno, 1977) 175–99, esp. 183–87.

Hahn, Ferdinand, *The Titles of Jesus in Christology: Their History in Early Christianity* (Lutterworth Library; London: Lutterworth, 1969) 308–15.

Hengel, Martin, "Jesus als messianischer Lehrer der Weisheit und die Anfänge der Christologie," in *Sagesse et religion: Colloque de Strasbourg, octobre 1976* (Bibliothèque des Centres d'études supérieures spécialisés d'histoire des religions de Strasbourg; Paris: Presses universitaires de France, 1979) 144–88.

idem, *The Son of God: The Origin of Christology and the History of Jewish-Hellenistic Religion* (Philadelphia: Fortress Press, 1976).

Hoffmann, Paul, *Logienquelle*, 98–142, 210–12.

Idem, "Die Offenbarung des Sohnes: Die apokalyptischen Voraussetzungen und ihre Verarbeitung im Q-Logion Mt 11, 27 par Lk 10, 22," *Kairos* 12 (1970) 270–88.

Houssiau, Albert, "L'exégèse de Matthieu 11, 27b selon saint Irénée," *EThL* 29 (1953) 328–54.

Hunter, Archibald Macbride, "Crux criticorum— Matt. 11.25-30—A Re-appraisal," *NTS* 8 (1961–62) 241–49.

Iersel, Bastiaan M. F. van, *«Der Sohn» in den synoptischen Jesusworten: Christusbezeichnung der Gemeinde oder Selbstbezeichnung Jesu?* (NovTSup 3; Leiden: Brill, 1961) 146–61.

Jeremias, Joachim, *New Testament Theology*, vol. 1: *The Proclamation of Jesus* (trans. John Bowden; London: SCM, 1971) 56–61.

Klijn, Albertus Frederik Johannes, "Matthew 11, 25 // Luke 10, 21," in Eldon Jay Epp and Gordon D. Fee, eds., *New Testament Textual Criticism: Its Significance for Exegesis: Essays in Honour of Bruce M. Metzger* (Oxford: Clarendon; New York: Oxford University Press, 1981) 1–14.

Kloppenborg, John S., "Wisdom Christology in Q," *Laval théologique et philosophique* 34 (1978) 129–47.

Idem, *Formation*, passim.

Kümmel, *Promise*, 40–42, 111–13.

Légasse, Simon, *Jésus et l'enfant: «Enfants», «petits» et «simples» dans la traditon synoptique* (EtB; Paris: Librarie Lecoffre/Gabalda, 1969) 121–37, 201–4.

Idem, "Le logion sur le Fils révélateur (Mt 11, 27 par. Lc 10, 22): Essai d'analyse prérédactionnelle," in Joseph Coppens et al., eds., *La notion biblique de Dieu: Le Dieu de la Bible et le dieu des philosophes* (BETL 41; Gembloux: Duculot, 1976) 245–74.

Idem, "La revelation aux νήπιοι," *RB* 67 (1960) 321–48.

Luck, Ulrich, "Weisheit und Christologie in Mt 11, 25-30," *WD* n.s. 13 (1975) 35–51.

Lührmann, *Logienquelle*, 64–68, 99–100.

Mertens, Herman-Emiel, *L'hymne de jubilation chez les Synoptiques, Matthieu XI,25-30 —Luc X,21-22* (Gembloux: Pontificia Universitas Gregoriana, 1957).

Miyoshi, *Anfang*, 120–52.

Norden, Eduard, *Agnostos Theos: Untersuchungen zur Formengeschichte religiöser Rede* (Leipzig: Teubner, 1913; reprinted Darmstadt: Wissenschaftliche Buchgesellschaft, 1956) 277–308.

Nützel, Johannes M. *Jesus als Offenbarer Gottes nach den lukanischen Schriften* (FB 39; Würzburg: Echter, 1980) 139–75.

Piper, *Wisdom*, passim.

Polag, *Christologie*, 17, 145, 160–62.

Pryor, John W., "The Great Thanksgiving and the Fourth Gospel," *BZ* n.s. 35 (1991) 157–69.

Quell, Gottfried, and Gottlob Schrenk, "πατήρ, κτλ.," *TDNT* 5 (1967) 945–1022.

Randellini, Lino, "L'inno di giubilo: Mt 11, 25-30; Lc 10, 20-24," *RivB* 22 (1974) 183–235.

Robinson, James M., "Die Hodajot-Formel in Gebet und Hymnus des Frühchristentums," in Walther Eltester and Franz Heinrich Kettler, eds., *Apophoreta: Festschrift für Ernst Haenchen* (BZNW 30; Berlin: Töpelmann, 1964) 194–235.

Sabbe, Maurits, "Can Mt 11, 27 and Lk 10, 22 Be Called a Johannine Logion?" in Delobel, *Logia*, 263–71.

Schumacher, Heinrich, *Die Selbstoffenbarung Jesu bei Mat 11, 27 (Luc 10, 22): Eine kritisch-exegetische Untersuchung* (Frankfurter theologische Studien 6; Freiburg im Breisgau/St. Louis: Herder, 1912).

Schwarz, G., "Ὅτι ἔκρυψας ταῦτα ἀπὸ . . . συνετῶν," *Biblische Notizen [Munich]* 9 (1979) 22–25.

Suggs, M. Jack, *Wisdom, Christology, and Law in Matthew's Gospel* (Cambridge, Mass.: Harvard University Press, 1970).

Winter, Paul, "Matthew XI 27 and Luke X 22 from the First to the Fifth Century: Reflections on the Development of the Text," *NovT* 1 (1956) 112–48.

Wülfing von Martiz, Peter, Georg Fohrer, Eduard Lohse, Eduard Schweizer, and Wilhelm Schneemelcher, "υἱός, κτλ.," *TDNT* 8 (1972) 334–97.

Zerwick, Max, "El júbilo del Señor (Lc 10, 21–24)," *RevistB* 20 (1958) 23–28.

Zumstein, Jean, *La condition du croyant dans l'Évangile selon Matthieu* (OBO 16; Göttingen: Vandenhoeck & Ruprecht, 1977) 130–52.

21/ **At that same hour he rejoiced in the Holy Spirit and said, "I thank you, Father, Lord of heaven and earth, because you have hidden these things from the wise and the intelligent and have revealed them to little ones. Yes, Father, for such was your good pleasure.**
[a]22/ All things have been handed over to me by my Father; and no one knows who the Son is except the Father, or who the Father is except the Son and anyone to whom the Son chooses to reveal him."[a]

23/ **Then turning to the disciples, he said to them privately, "Happy are the eyes that see what you see! 24/ For I tell you that many prophets and kings desired to see what you see, but did not see it, and to hear what you hear, but did not hear it."**

[a] There is a major textual problem in v. 22 that we will take up in the commentary.

We have now arrived, from a theological point of view, at the heart of the Gospel. At this point something new surfaces in a revelation. It is a revelation anchored in time but independent of history; linked to what Jesus said but aimed at each and every generation; full of robustness yet discreet; an object of reflection yet forbidden to the learned. The time of reversals has arrived. The reversal of values and substitution of persons is going to raise the humble to the highest station of those who receive benefits from God. The text makes it clear that this Christian revelation and its concomitant repercussions correspond to God's plan. That is because the Father stands behind the Son and lives in communion with him. Consequently, it is not surprising that what impresses those who read this passage is a sense of fulfillment and eschatological breaking in. Here is the end of the period of long waiting spoken of by the biblical prophets. And here begins the attestation of the Christian paradox, of the hard core of the Gospel.

Analysis

Verses 21-24 of chap. 10 are closely tied to the preceding verses (cf. "At that same hour," v. 21). Although the missionaries' success was chalked up to Satan's defeat (vv. 17-20), now it is explained as the result of the Father's efficacious will (vv. 21-22). By virtue of Luke's manner of composition, the revelation referred to is an integral part of certain historical events, just as the mystery of the Father and the Son is associated with a concrete reality, namely, the small, but proud, Christian community. What it has experienced is the unveiling of God's plan, a decisive step in salvation history, a divine *space* revealed in human *time*. But the text does not communicate that experience directly; rather, at one remove, it transmits, in a metalanguage, on the one hand, a prayer of Jesus that explains what takes place *up above* (see "I thank you," v. 21) and, on the other hand, a diagnosis of what takes place *here below* (vv. 23-24). The solemnity of the hour (see "in the Holy Spirit," v. 21) corresponds to that of Jesus' baptism (3:21-22); the role of children corresponds here to the Son's mission. He and they do not act autonomously; they must make people see and hear what the Father himself does and says.[1]

The parallel in Matthew leads us to believe that, in Q, Jesus' prayer (vv. 21-22) already followed the curse on the towns in Galilee (vv. 13-15).[2] Luke was thus pursuing his rereading of Q, after having composed the episode about the return of the seventy-two disciples (vv. 17-20). At the very outside, we might note that this episode introduces Jesus' prayer more solemnly than do Q and Matt 11:25a. Luke put his stamp on v. 21a: the time has become more precisely "at that same hour" and Jesus' reaction has become a rejoicing caused by "the Holy Spirit."[3]

The text of Jesus' prayer (vv. 21b-22) is virtually identical in Luke and Matthew. Both of them respected Jesus' sayings, being based on the same Greek version of Q. Luke, who was fond of compound verbs, wrote "you have hidden" (ἀπέκρυψας)[4] and thus achieved alliteration with "you have revealed" (ἀπεκάλυψας). Moreover, it seems that it was he, rather than Matthew, who corrected the construction expressing reciprocity: in the place where Q, followed by Matthew, affirmed mutual knowledge (expressed by simple Greek accusatives referring to "the Son" and "the Father") according to a Semitic way of looking at things, Luke, with his sensitivity to the Greek perspective, stressed individual knowledge (with the identities being expressed as "*who* the Son is" and "*who* the Father is"). Where tradition brought out the relational character of such knowledge, the Lukan redaction was attentive to the identity of the persons in question.

The primary manuscript tradition of v. 22 is solid; such is not the case with the secondary tradition.[5] Several patristic citations suggest that a saying was circulating

---

1   See Miyoshi, *Anfang*, 142–50.

2   Note how they are connected in Matt 11:20-24, 25-27.

3   There is uncertainty in the manuscript tradition here in v. 21 between "in the Spirit" (or "in his spirit") and "through the Spirit" (or "through his spirit"). Whichever form of the text is to be retained, one must concede, in my opinion, that Luke wanted to evoke here the participation of the Holy Spirit and not merely the human spirit. More-over, several manuscripts make it explicit that Jesus is the subject of the verbs.

4   Matthew 11:25 has ἔκρυψας. Curiously Luke retains the simple verb γινώσκει ("he knows") in v. 22, where Matthew prefers the compound verb ἐπιγινώσκει ("he knows perfectly," "he recognizes").

5   See Winter, "Matthew," 112–48.

in the second century in which the "my" ($\mu o\upsilon$) after "Father" ($\pi\alpha\tau\rho\acute{o}\varsigma$) was missing (it is also left out of several important manuscripts); in which the words "who the Son is except the Father" are placed after "who the Father is except the Son," or are even omitted;[6] and which opts for the Greek aorist $\check{\epsilon}\gamma\nu\omega$ or the perfect $o\hat{\iota}\delta\epsilon$ and uses the simple expression "reveals him" rather than "chooses to reveal him." There are two possibilities: (a) the primary manuscript tradition is the preferred difficult reading (*lectio difficilior*) (since the unknowability of the Father was, unlike that of the Son, a topos at that time), and the inversion or omission resulted from a Gnostic reworking of the text; or (b) oral transmission was still being freely carried on, and the traditional text resulted from a conscious and polemical stabilization of the wording, which took place at the end of the second century. After due consideration, I read the text found in the primary manuscript tradition, as found in the Nestle-Aland[27] text.

In the preliterary stage, thus anterior to Q, the three sayings concerning thanksgiving had not yet been put together. The first saying (v. 21bc) was at first an isolated one, but must have with time been given an explanatory confirmation from the lips of a prophet, namely, the second saying (v. 21d), before attracting to it the third saying (v. 22), which has similar, but not identical, subject matter. Following this thanksgiving in three stages, Luke was eager to quote a beatitude and its justification (vv. 23b-24). The introduction to it that he composed (v. 23a)[7] did not attempt to distinguish the disciples from

the crowd (since there was no crowd), but to explain that Jesus, after having spoken to God, then turned ($\sigma\tau\rho\alpha$-$\varphi\epsilon\acute{\iota}\varsigma$, "turning") to the disciples. Nor does the expression "privately" put the disciples in a new context; rather, it keeps them in the only one appropriate to the previous thanksgiving (vv. 21-22) and the preceding dialogue (vv. 17-20).[8]

In the text of Luke (v. 23b), which is probably original, the disciples are declared happy to see *what* ($\check{\alpha}$) they see, whereas in Matthew (Matt 13:16) they are happy *because* they see ($\check{o}\tau\iota$).[9] Luke also respected the original text by applying the beatitude to all the persons contemporaneous with the disciples. On the other hand, Matthew, who couples this macarism with a quotation from Isa 6:9-10 on Israel's being made dull, restricts it, in a surge of dualism, to just the disciples (Matt 13:10-17).[10]

A comparison of v. 24 with the Synoptic parallel in Matthew prompts the following three remarks. While Luke has perhaps eliminated the $\mathring{\alpha}\mu\acute{\eta}\nu$ ("truly"), Matthew has certainly substituted the "righteous" for "kings,"[11] thus giving us a picture of past generations that is more ecclesial than political. But which of the two Gospel writers kept the original verb? Probably Matthew, rather than Luke. Matthew used the verb "long to," which is more precise but at the same time more ambiguous, since it often had a negative connotation in the ethical literature of early Christianity. For that verb, Luke probably substituted the less pejorative but more ordinary verb "desire/want to."[12] Lastly, in v. 24a, the presence of an introductory expression suggests that the justification

---

6 Minuscule MSS. 1216 and 1579 and the text of the Old Latin version omit the words "who the Son is except the Father." On the state of the text and for patristic references to it, see Winter, "Matthew," 112–48; see also the apparatus in *New Testament in Greek: The Gospel according to St. Luke*, 1:232. According to Winter ("Matthew," 148), the primitive text is as follows: $\pi\acute{\alpha}\nu\tau\alpha$ $\mu o\iota$ $\pi\alpha\rho\epsilon\delta\acute{o}\vartheta\eta$ $\mathring{\upsilon}\pi\grave{o}$ $\tau o\hat{\upsilon}$ $\pi\alpha\tau\rho\acute{o}\varsigma$. $\kappa\alpha\grave{\iota}$ $o\mathring{\upsilon}\delta\epsilon\grave{\iota}\varsigma$ $\check{\epsilon}\gamma\nu\omega$ $\tau\grave{o}\nu$ $\pi\alpha\tau\acute{\epsilon}\rho\alpha$ $\epsilon\grave{\iota}$ $\mu\grave{\eta}$ $\upsilon\grave{\iota}\grave{o}\varsigma$ $\kappa\alpha\grave{\iota}$ $o\hat{\iota}\varsigma$ $\mathring{\alpha}\nu$ $\mathring{\alpha}\pi o\kappa\alpha\lambda\acute{\upsilon}\psi\eta$ $\alpha\mathring{\upsilon}\tau\grave{o}\nu$ $\upsilon\acute{\iota}\acute{o}\varsigma$. On the interpretation of Irenaeus, see Houssiau, "L'exégèse," 328–54. Against the reconstruction of Winter is the argument that his reading suppresses the formula of reciprocity, which appears to me to be specific and inscribed in the tradition well analyzed by Norden, *Agnostos Theos*, 277–308.

7 According to Schulz (*Q*, 419), in order to do this, Luke has relied on a concise narrative framework

8 that he has taken over from Q. Perhaps Luke did, but I am not so sure of it as Schulz.

8 Short of admitting a change of audience: the seventy-two in the place of the Twelve. In this case, the $\mu\alpha\vartheta\eta\tau\alpha\acute{\iota}$ here would be the Twelve alone. But this is never stated.

9 In the following verse (Matt 13:17), Matthew respects the original $\check{\alpha}$ ("that which").

10 As a result, the $\mathring{\upsilon}\mu\hat{\omega}\nu$ at the beginning of Matt 13:16 must be redactional. It was also Matthew, in my opinion, who added the hearing to the sight. On all of this, see Schulz, *Q*, 419–20.

11 It is well known that the theme of "righteousness" is characteristic of Matthew; see Schulz, *Q*, 420 n. 113.

12 It seems, moreover, that Luke has a tendency to discard personal pronouns rather than add them. In this case, the $\mathring{\upsilon}\mu\epsilon\hat{\iota}\varsigma$ that he transmits must go back to Q.

(v. 24b) is secondary in relation to the beatitude (v. 23b): this justification is the result of an interpretive reflection by a Christian prophet. That development took place at a stage prior to the redaction of Q.

Commentary

■ **21a** There is in Judaism, more particularly in the apocalyptic tradition, an outline for a prayer of thanksgiving.[13] Happy to have received a revelation, the visionary, when inspired, lets his gratitude explode. He stresses the blessed moment he is experiencing, praises as Creator the God who has just revealed himself, thereby linking the origin to the end, and admires the divine plan of salvation. These various elements, present in the book of Daniel (Dan 2:19-23), which served as a literary model for Jewish and Christian apocalypses, appear in Q, and even more in Luke's redaction: "at that same hour," which was originally the hour of a revelation received by Jesus, had, to be sure, become the hour of the mission of the seventy-two, but Luke forgot so little of that apocalyptic origin that he made the disciples' mission coincide with Satan's fall. All of the Christian mission's successes were due to the victory over the devil. Christ was "carried away by happiness," and his rejoicing and praying took place "in the Holy Spirit." His prayer was, in fact, one of thanksgiving, calling on God as creator.[14] While this theme fits the literary genre, the expression "Lord of heaven and earth" is less common.[15] Nor is the use of

the vocative "Father" ($\pi\acute{\alpha}\tau\epsilon\rho$) as an invocation frequent: it has its roots in the historical Jesus' personal use (*abba*) (cf. Mark 14:36; Luke 11:2). By using these two vocatives, "Father" and "Lord of heaven and earth," the Gospel writer sketched out the two complementary characteristics of the only God, namely, divine creative power and redemptive will.

■ **21bc** The rest of v. 21 adheres to the literary genre of thanksgiving and expresses the motif of prayer[16] that it introduces by "because" ($\acute{o}\tau\iota$), which occurs frequently in the Psalms and is present in the Magnificat (1:46-55) and the Benedictus (1:68-79) (see Luke 1:48, 68).[17] As usual, the cause for praise traces back to an action of God[18] expressed by way of an antithetical parallelism with a Semitic flavor and apocalyptic content ("hide" . . . "reveal"). One thing that is new in the text in comparison with its Jewish antecedents reflects Jesus' prophetic identity and gives expression to Christians' pride; it is the change of persons addressed. Those who were in the apocalyptic tradition were faithful to that tradition as they praised God for having revealed his plan to the wise, that is, themselves (Dan 2:21). Jesus and his early Christian followers, who, to be sure, considered themselves to be the recipients of the revelation, knew that they were not part of the intellectual elite in Israel. They neither dared nor wished to call themselves wise. On the contrary, they took over as a self-designation a term that Jesus had drawn from a reservoir other than apocalyptic,[19] namely, "little ones." Inspired by the prophetic

---

13   Cf. Dan 2:19-23; *1 Enoch* 39:9-12 (after a second vision, vv. 3-8); 69:26; 1QH 7.26–27; Josephus, *Bell.* 3.8.3 §354. See Grimm, "Der Dank für die empfangene Offenbarung bei Jesus und Josephus," 249–56. This hymn in the long version of Matt 11:25-30 is often compared to Sirach 51, where one finds the three parts of the Matthean text in a more expanded form (see Norden, *Agnostos Theos*, 280).

14   One also finds $\grave{\epsilon}\xi o\mu o\lambda o\gamma o\tilde{\upsilon}\mu\alpha\iota$ in Dan 2:23 (LXX and Theodotion).

15   Cf. 1QapGen 22.16, 21; Tob 7:17 (B and A); see Fitzmyer, 2:872.

16   Though prayers of thanksgiving are numerous in the OT, Dan 2:19-23 stands alone as an expression of thanksgiving for an apocalyptic revelation.

17   On the literary genre of thanksgiving, see the commentary on 1:57-80 (1:55–57).

18   That God cannot be addressed grammatically in the third person, as one might expect from the lit-

erary genre of the prayer of thanksgiving, but in the second person, is already apparent in the Psalms (e.g., Psalm 145 [LXX 144]).

19   In the OT, the "simple" can either be reproved for their stupidity (this is the advice of Prov 8:5; 9:4-6) or regarded with sympathy (the Psalms picture them as protected by God and call them to aspire to wisdom: Ps 19:7 [LXX 18:8]; 116 [LXX 114]:6). The texts from Qumran follow this second line and expect that they will find understanding and join the ranks of the wise. See 11QPs[a] 154 (18.4–5 = second psalm of the collection of noncanonical Syriac psalms, where one learns that Wisdom is manifested "to make known to the simple her power, to make known her glory to those destitute of judgment"). See Dupont, *Études*, 333; Légasse, "La révélation aux $\nu\acute{\eta}\pi\iota o\iota$," 321–48; idem, *Jésus et l'enfant*, 204. In my opinion, the "simple" are depicted in the Gospel as being in a disadvantaged social situation and as

41

tradition, Jesus cut short the self-congratulation of the visionaries, just as he criticized that of the "scribes" (teachers of the law). There is a clear polemical thrust in this. The early Christians proudly welcomed this attitude. From then on, a new category of believers came into being that was socially less well off and culturally less learned. These "little ones" are to be understood in the proper sense of the word as well as in the figurative sense. They were characterized by their dependence, their ability to listen, and their welcoming attitude. The definition of who they were depended in this case less on contemporary usage than on how Jesus looked on them. Jesus had children in mind, but he also took into consideration the metaphorical category that the term represented. Children and believers, these "little ones," have their own identity and their relational reality. Passages like 9:46-48; 10:25-42; and 12:1-59 make it possible for us to identify who the "little ones" were, and various accounts sketch a picture of them (18:35-43, the blind man; 19:1-10, Zacchaeus; 19:28-44, the crowd). The fact that the Christian community identified with the figure of the "little ones" is a testimony to its understanding of the reversal effected by the divine revelation offered here to Jesus and by Jesus. The Son himself, who said that he had received everything from the Father (v. 22), is himself one of these children. Does he not bear the title of "Son"? Had he not been aware of being a "son" with a small *s*, he would not be the "Son," with a capital *S*.

This verse, which is so theologically tightly packed, is nonetheless eloquent from a sociological point of view. In thus giving theology back to God's people—to use a modern slogan—Jesus, followed by the earliest Christians, did not just create something new; by the attention that he paid to each and every person, an attention that he attributed to God, he placed himself in the sphere of the Psalms, for example Psalm 103 (102); by the reversal that he envisaged, he linked up with a prophetic tradition, that of the tiny remnant of Israel, that of little David defeating Goliath, that of little Daniel who was wiser than all the seers.[20] Jesus also took over the polemical strength of that prophetic tradition, since his saying begins with a negative, thus recalling Isa 29:14 ("so . . .

the wisdom of their wise shall perish, and the discernment of the discerning shall be hidden," *NRSV*) or Isa 44:25 (". . . [I turn] back the wise, and [make] their knowledge foolish," *NRSV*). Although Jesus' prayer was clearly apocalyptic, in the context of the Jewish situation of that time it was also courageous and original. But the newness it expressed was as old as the faith of Israel that it picked up on. According to the earliest Christians, discovering God's solicitude for the "little ones" was tantamount to demonstrating a vigilance that was both social and ethnic. It meant welcoming both those who were economically weak and the Gentiles, whom Israel looked down on. In any case, social and ethnic elements were to be a part of the personal attitude suggested by the term "little ones." Armed to understand the revelation and its thrust, the "little ones" were henceforth also equipped to brave Israel's negative reaction and persecution by a foreign world.

Curiously enough, even if God, who addressed the message, and the "little ones," to whom the message was addressed, are clearly spelled out, the message communicated, about which the prayer gave thanks—"these things" ($\tau\alpha\hat{v}\tau\alpha$) and "them" ($\alpha\dot{v}\tau\acute{\alpha}$)—remains vague, and deliberately so. So the prayer presupposes knowledge of the content of the revelation, but in his redactional process, the author of Q did not see fit to mention what it was. By linking the prayer to the vision of the fall of Satan (v. 18), Luke not only displayed evidence of literary finesse (the two passages both mention a revelation from on high); he may also have found the original content of the revelation, which was imprecise for the reader when detached from its historical roots, namely, Satan's fall as a harbinger and negative counterpart to the inbreaking of God's reign. Nevertheless, it is not certain that Luke wished to make a thematic connection at this point. What he had in mind here was emphasizing the change of persons who receive God's revelation.

■ **21d** The prayer continues with a confirmation (note the "Yes" [$\nu\alpha\acute{\iota}$]). Audaciously, the one praying dared to go back behind God's acts ("you . . . have revealed") to the divine intention ("good pleasure" [$\epsilon\dot{v}\delta o\kappa\acute{\iota}\alpha$]); from the perceptible to what is not known about God.

having a spiritual attitude characterized by open-heartedness, humility, and a willingness to accept others without reservation.

20   Though noting this polemic of Jesus against the wise, Schulz (*Q*, 219) nevertheless overlooks its roots in the OT.

This saying (v. 21d) has a liturgical flavor; it resembles a response or an antiphony. The text may be read, then, in a dialogical manner, as if a second believer was replying to the first, all the while continuing the thanksgiving. Moreover, the saying is chronologically subsequent. We may imagine a Christian prophet who, while praying, used these words to punctuate the hearing of the first saying, namely, the one expressing thanksgiving (v. 21bc). This response is first of all an expression of approval, of a yes, indicating agreement. This convergence of convictions is next made explicit (the Greek conjunction ὅτι is here equivalent to either "that" or "for," rather than "because"). The commentary repeats the first saying, rephrasing it: the revelation to the "little ones," understood here, too, as an event (ἐγένετο), is above all defined as the affirmation of God's salvific plan. Luke enjoys repeating this word εὐδοκία ("good pleasure"), which, in his eyes, summarizes the sparring involved in the gospel, God's plan seen as an argument against evil and as an offer of life to the committed.[21] The "thus" (οὕτως), translated as "such," says to God and to the readers that Jesus' life and the visible beginnings of Christianity incarnate and express God's "good pleasure" (εὐδοκία), more particularly the absolutely good plan and objective state of things such as it is "before you" (ἔμπροσθέν σου, translated as "your"), the Father, but also before us.

■ **22** The origin of the following saying is not the same as that of the prayer. Belonging to another apocalyptic tradition, it gives expression to God's transmission of power or knowledge. The context of Q, and subsequently the context of Luke, directs our attention in the direction of knowledge more than power, which is the opposite of the model in Dan 7:14 and the parallel saying in Matt 28:18. Here in Luke Jesus speaks as the Son of Man: he has received from God a mission of delegated authority. This is the conviction of Christians, in particular Luke. While Jesus pointed in v. 21 to something else, a revelation, here he is speaking about himself. The christological "I" and the christological title "Son" make a sudden and forceful appearance. There may be some doubt as to whether the historical Jesus actually expressed himself in these terms. That being the case, various solutions have been proposed: (a) We may have here a post-Easter saying, a proclamation of the risen One, as in Matt 28:18, which has been transferred back into the pre-Easter period.[22] (b) The saying may have evolved: whereas it indicated reciprocity in its final form, it may originally have been a parable of the historical Jesus using the human image of the relationship between a father and his son.[23] (c) The saying may have been composed by someone in the early church—either a scribe who wrote or a prophet who spoke—who drew on either the Jewish sapiential tradition[24] or an Eastern international outline of religious propaganda.[25] Personally, I recognize the Semitic character of certain terms, as well as the presence in Judaism of similar expressions denoting reciprocity (see Tob 5:2); but the religious nature

21   See Bovon, *L'œuvre*, 228–31.

22   See Rudolf Bultmann, *History of the Synoptic Tradition* (trans. John Marsh; rev. ed.; New York/Evanston: Harper & Row, 1968; reprinted New York: Harper & Row, 1976) 160.

23   See Jeremias, *Proclamation*, 57–58; and more recently Raymond E. Brown, *An Introduction to New Testament Christology* (New York/Mahwah, N.J.: Paulist Press, 1994) 88–89. They have observed that v. 22 corresponds to a Semitic way of speaking that is marked by inversion owing to a lack of specific forms. As an example in everyday life, Jeremias refers to Tob 5:2 (Codex Sinaiticus): "And he himself does not know me, and I myself do not know him." The article ὁ in v. 22 would have originally had a generic sense: "Every father knows his child," and so on. John 5:17-23 builds on a parable of Jesus ("quoted" in 5:19-20a). See further Charles Harold

Dodd, "Une parabole cachée dans le quatrième Évangile," *RHPhR* 42 (1962) 107–15.

24   Zumstein (*Condition du croyant*, 135–40) follows Suggs (*Wisdom*, 83), and Lührmann (*Logienquelle*, 66–68). Our text can be explained from a history-of-religions perspective as a development from wisdom motifs moving in an apocalyptic milieu. On the background of these wisdom motifs, see Christ, *Jesus Sophia*, 83.

25   In *Agnostos Theos* (pp. 277–308), Norden furnishes a series of texts (e.g., Sirach 51; 24; *Poimandres* [= *Corpus Hermeticum* 1] 27–28, 30–31; *Odes of Solomon* 33) and several impressive arguments, even though this exact formula is not found anywhere verbatim. The idea of the transmission of religious secrets is not limited to Judaism. It is sufficient to point out Orpheus and his books or in the same tradition Musaios and his son, who imparted their wisdom

of the saying situates it in the context of a large ancient movement, into which the Gospel of John and the *Corpus Hermeticum* also fit.[26]

Luke, in any case, is quite sure that his readers come to the text with a twofold advance understanding of both the divine Father and an intermediary between this heavenly Father and his terrestrial children. In his eyes, the saying, which has been justly compared with Johannine prose, allows these readers to move on from this feeling to a more exact knowledge. This Son has a name, Jesus, and this Father is the God of Creation and of Israel.[27] The wording, which began by following the category of the Son of Man,[28] continues in the domain of Wisdom, God's daughter, who is a close associate and confidant of her Father.[29] The opening to human beings and the offer made to them to enter into the intimate relationship of the Father with the Son are also specific to this sapiential perspective.[30] We had God's plan in v. 21d. Here we have the Son's will (v. 22). These two wills are in harmony with each other: that is what Christians, following Jesus, trumpet to the Jews in a polemic that the Jews can scarcely endure without reacting violently. Nevertheless, this saying, which is thus in dialogue with not only the Jews but also the Gentiles, is above all the revelation of a totally unprecedented interpersonal relationship: the relationship of the Father with the Son is not an exclusive one but an inclusive one. In spite of appearances, it functions on a ternary, rather than a binary, model. The Father and the Son have a mutual knowledge of each other which, following the Semitic substratum, is characterized by mutual love as well as mutual knowledge, the particular as well as the universal. The more they know each other, the more they are eager to bring others into the circle of their reciprocal love. What is unveiled here is not just God's revelation, or his plan, but God himself. Here the third element is not the Holy Spirit, but God's people, who are that privileged group of "little ones."

Human resistance, individual evil, which is presupposed in the following verses (vv. 23-24), and collective evil, which has been mentioned in a preceding verse (v. 18), had for a long time made that knowledge of God, that recognition, impossible. It was in Jesus that it became possible, hence the following beatitude (v. 23).[31]

■ **23-24** In this respect, Christianity distanced itself from Judaism and prepared itself for a rupture with it. And yet it claimed to be the fulfillment of the hope of all of the people of Israel, represented by its numerous prophets and its successive kings. The representatives of both of these categories were thought of not as chiefs but as antennas pointed toward heaven. Were not the prophets the recipients of oracles and visions,[32] and did not God shower talents, wisdom, and knowledge[33] on the kings

---

to the most noble among humans (see Plato *Resp.* 2.363C, 364E). See Marcel Detienne, *L'écriture d'Orphée* (L'infini; Paris: Gallimard, 1989). Finally, Isis transmits the knowledge of magic to her son Horus. See the tractate of alchemy entitled "Isis the Prophetess to Her Son" in Marcellin Berthelot and Charles-Émile Ruelle, eds., *Collection des anciens alchimistes grecs* (3 vols.; Paris: Steinheil, 1887–88) 1:28–35 (Greek text) and 31–36 (French translation). This tractate exists in two forms, one published after the other. In *Der Poimandres, ein paganisiertes Evangelium: Sprachliche und begriffliche Untersuchungen zum 1. Traktat des Corpus Hermeticum* (WUNT 2.27; Tübingen: Mohr Siebeck, 1987), Jörg Büchli sees *Poimandres* not as arising from a pre-Christian Gnosticism but as a pagan reaction in the third century. It represents a paganized counter-gospel.

26   See preceding note.

27   On υἱός, see the commentary on 1:32-34 (1:51); 3:22 (1:128–30). See also Martin Hengel, *The Son of God: The Origin of Christology and the History of Jewish-*

Hellenistic Religion (Philadelphia: Fortress Press, 1976); van Iersel, "*Der Sohn*"; Wülfing von Martitz et al., "υἱός, κτλ.," *TDNT* 8 (1972) 334–97. On πατήρ, see Gottfried Quell and Gottlob Schrenk, "πατήρ, κτλ.," *TDNT* 5 (1967) 945–1022.

28   On the transfer of all things to the Son of Man, see Dan 7:14.

29   See Christ, *Jesus Sophia*, 81–99.

30   "Come to me, you who are without instruction; take your lodging in my school" (Sir 51:23).

31   On the literary genre of the beatitude, see the commentary on Luke 6:20-22 (1:221–22).

32   On seeing salvation, see the commentary on Luke 2:29-30 (1:102); 3:4-6 (1:121–22). See also *Ps. Sol.* 17:44; 18:6-7. Already Num 12:6-8 singles out Moses as one who has seen God face to face, while the prophets have seen him only in a vision. This distinction is maintained also in the rabbinic period. Here, the fortunate eyes of the disciples have seen the divine realities, as did Moses and the generation of the desert. They are more privileged than the prophets (see *y. Mak.* 19.11 [72a]; 15.2 [44a]).

(David and Solomon come to mind)?[34] What is curious is that the "scribes" are not mentioned here.[35] Had they been given up on, since they had forgotten everything, even hope itself?

History of Interpretation

The saying about the Father and the Son (v. 22) is certainly the one on which the most attention has been focused through the ages. The saying about the "little ones" (v. 21) and the sayings about the happy eyes (vv. 23-24) were the ones that gave Christians the most cause for rejoicing. Attuned to Jesus' criticism of the Pharisees, several authors added a polemical note to their expression of gratitude. For example, Cyril, patriarch of Alexandria, devoted a sermon to v. 21 (Hom. Luc. 65).[36] He noted with grateful satisfaction that the Father revealed to us, who resemble little children, the mysteries that had been hidden for centuries. Then, with the apostle Paul (he quoted 1 Cor 1:17), he maintained that the believers' apparent folly was in fact the only true wisdom. He also mentioned the attacks made by the prophets of old on those who claimed to possess wisdom (Isa 29:14) and applied these philippics to the "scribes" and Pharisees, who rejected the word of the Savior and to whom the mystery of Christ remained hidden.

Cyril turned his attention to vv. 23-24 long enough to preach another sermon on them (*Hom. Luc.* 67).[37] What is original in his interpretation is his exegesis of the verb "to see." On the one hand, there is the historical event. Cyril considered the incarnation to be the central event of history. The Son's coming is what enabled the Father to make it possible to see what had hitherto remained hidden. On the other hand, there is faith, which is the essential element in understanding Christ's intervention in history. Did not Luke have the disciples be the only ones to receive the beatitude? That is the rhetorical question Cyril raised. So the verb "to see" is worth interpreting carefully, and the benediction, linked to the apostolic period, was not showered on all of Christ's contemporaries. What comes under the heading of this event and this faith is the entire content of the Creed to which Christians alone subscribe: the message from the Father that the Son has given us, the good news of the incarnate Word, the presence on earth of the heavenly Lord, the fall of Satan, the shift from blood sacrifices to spiritual sacrifices and especially the soteriological thrust of this plan. For Cyril, salvation corresponds to a turnabout in which the Son made himself man in order to free us from death and shape us in his divine image.

Like the Matthean parallel (Matt 11:27) to this passage, v. 22 was caught up in the two principal doctrinal tempests of early Christianity, the Gnostic controversy and the dispute over the Trinity. First Irenaeus, facing Gnostic dualism, then Tertullian, answering Marcion, attempted to correct the adverse interpretation of Jesus' oracle.[38]

But these people, who pretend to know more about it than the apostles themselves, modify the text as follows: "No one has known the Father except the Son, nor the Son except the Father, and the one to whom the Son will reveal him"; and they explain it in the sense that the true God has not been known by anyone before the coming of our Lord: the God preached

---

In "Selige Augenzeugen, Lk 10, 23f.: Alttestamentlicher Hintergrund und ursprünglicher Sinn," *ThZ* 26 (1970) 172–83, Werner Grimm considers this thought to be present in Luke 10:23–24 but secondary in relation to that indicated in the following note.

33 David, presumed author of the Psalms and regarded as a prophet; Solomon, author of the Proverbs and of Wisdom, and learned and wise (even in the knowledge of magic) before the Eternal One (2 *Bar.* 61:1-4; 77:25).

34 Grimm explains the presence of kings by pointing to a tradition rooted in Isa 52:13-15 ("Selige Augenzeugen, Lk 10, 23f.," 172–83). It would thus concern the kings of the nations and not the kings of Israel. Their misfortune would not be that of having lived before the events of salvation but that of not having known how to recognize and interpret the presence of the Servant. Though Grimm is certain that this thought lies in the foreground of Luke 10:23-24, I am not convinced.

35 They were included, on the other hand, in the negative expression "wise and learned" in v. 21, which refers not only to apocalyptic prophets and the wise but also to the scribes.

36 Payne Smith, *Cyril*, 1:296–301.

37 Ibid., 306–10.

38 See Houssiau, "L'exégèse," 328–54.

by the prophets is not, they say, the Father of Christ. (Irenaeus *Adv. haer.* 4.6.1)

That is how Irenaeus, bishop of Lyon, summarized his adversaries' position, attributing to them the form of the text that we ended up rejecting, but whose antiquity is attested. Then Irenaeus cleverly called attention to the fact that, on the lips of Jesus, this saying attacked "the pretension of the Jews to possess God while at the same time despising his Word" (*Adv. haer.* 4.6.1). As for Irenaeus himself, he felt obliged to maintain the validity of the saying in the face of Gnostic adversaries who, on the contrary, claimed to hold on to the Son while despising the Creator God. Therefore he wrote: "Just like our faith in the Son, our love for the Father must be steady and unshakable" (4.6.2). And he insisted, in beautiful expressions of reciprocity, on the mutual revelation of the Father and the Son: "For no one can know the Father without the Word of God, that is to say if the Son does not 'reveal,' nor know the Son without the 'good pleasure' of the Father" (4.6.3).

Irenaeus, who was a "plan of salvation" theologian, declared that this "double truth" was far from new (4.6.3). The Son, whom he purposely called the Word, had spoken not only in these last times, during his incarnation, but from the very moment of creation and in creation, as he did in the Law and the Prophets. Far from being unknowable, God has been able to be perceived from the beginning. For his part, the Father himself did not limit the manifestation of the Word to the present period, even if this last step was decisive:

Finally, by means of the mediation of the Word in person who became visible and palpable, the Father revealed himself, and, even though all people have not believed in him in a similar way, all have nonetheless seen the Father in the Son: for the invisible reality that was seen in the Son was the Father, and the visible reality in which the Father was seen was the Son. (*Adv. haer.* 4.6.6)

Several years later, the African theologian Tertullian attacked just Marcion's interpretation (*Adv. Marc.* 4.25). Turning around the argument concerning the jealous

God, he attempted to show the inequity of the Father that Marcion claimed was good, with the help of Luke 10:22: since Marcion's God had not given in the past any sign of his existence, can the wise, without injustice, be incriminated for being ignorant? Nor could this God boast of being the revealer, since he has not left any vestigial trace of his presence or any word. We cannot contrast the Lord of heaven and the Father of Jesus Christ. It is the same God who hides and who reveals, who saves and who punishes. That is what Tertullian's God is like, the God who chose the path of enigma and obscurity in order to put the faith of his faithful to the test. Marcion reckoned that the good God had wanted to reveal the good things that the jealous Creator God had hidden. In that case, he ought to have revealed them to the wise, who were innocent of not knowing, and not to the little ones. Furthermore, if the good God entrusts everything to the Son, he also gives him the good things that had been hidden, which, in that case, could not be bad. It would appear that Marcion equated all the "things" given to the Son by the Father with humanity.

Tertullian's line of argument is difficult to understand and I am not sure that I have fully grasped it. I only note that from there on the writer mentions, without naming them, other heretics who based their contrast of the Creator and the Savior on this verse, Luke 10:22. They claimed, said he, that the saying could not be talking about the Creator God, known in Israel through regular contact, and among the Gentiles through nature. Therefore, to their way of thinking, God, known by his only Son, can only be another God. And Tertullian got up his dander once more as he trotted out Scripture.

This same Lukan verse later encouraged a trinitarian interpretation, insofar as it mentions, albeit in the introduction, rather than in the saying itself, the action of the Holy Spirit (see Cyril of Alexandria *Hom. Luc.* 65).[39] As the quarrel between the orthodox and the Arian Christians pertained to the position of the Son, it was the saying itself, and its mention of the Son, that each side was intent on exploiting as supportive of its own standpoint. The orthodox pointed out the dignity of the Son and his equality with the Father; their adversaries, the Arians, concluded from the fact that all things had been entrusted to the Son that there was a period prior to his

---

39   Payne Smith, *Cyril*, 1:296–97.

being begotten, and that the Son was therefore ontologically inferior.[40] As they did with his being anointed as Messiah, the orthodox could interpret the entrusting of all things to the Son two ways: ontologically, by situating it in all eternity; or, in relation to the history of salvation, by locating it at the moment of either the incarnation or the resurrection. In the first case, it is the eternal Son who possesses the entrusting of all things; in the second, the incarnate Son.[41] The sermon that Cyril of Alexandria devoted to this verse (*Hom. Luc.* 66), more than a century after the struggle carried on by his predecessor Athanasius, repeated over and over again the theme of the consubstantiality of the Son and his equality with the Father.[42] For Athanasius, if Christ said that all things had been given to him, it was a manner of speaking, a way of referring to the plan of salvation. Those words are applied to the Son, who has taken on our human condition. Cyril's polemic leads us to conclude that the proponents of the inferiority of the Son in relation to the Father had not yet disappeared from the scene.

Following a theological logic that flies in the face of the literary caesura placed between v. 20 and v. 21, the medieval theologian Bonaventure extracted from this Lukan text a fourfold reason for rejoicing and giving thanks: first, because of the infallible foreknowledge of the one who inscribed our names in the book of life (v. 20); second, because of the irresistible providence of the one who is not only the Creator but also the *gubernator*, that is to say, the one who maintains and governs the universe, who is more particularly the one who did not reveal himself to the wise any more than to the stupid, but to the little ones, that is to say, the humble (v. 21); third, because of the power of the one who handed everything over to the Son (v. 22a), an unfathomable power that only the Son understands and makes understood (v. 22b); fourth and finally, because of the welcome presence of Christ among us (vv. 23-24) (*Comm. Luc.* 10.34–42).[43] Bonaventure quoted several passages of Scripture to confirm each point of his interpretation (e.g., Rev 20:12; 1 Cor 1:19; John 5:19; John 8:56). By means of this chain of convergent quotations, Bonaventure confessed and demonstrated the concordant truth of the revelation.[44]

Conclusion

An important line has been crossed here. After his ministry in Galilee and the double sending out of his witnesses, the Lukan Jesus explains to his disciples that in their microcosm they are experiencing in their lives the turning point of universal history. These men and women have been called to understand this macrocosmic perspective, not a perspective of the objective or elitist knowledge of the wise, but one along the lines of the personal and communal manner of the "little ones." The new God is the God whom humans had believed they were seeing grow old. In fact, this God has not changed. At the outside he is very much alive and being renewed. If he reveals something new or creates something new, he owes it to himself to do it in order to remain himself, he who is both the Creator and the Savior, and in order to share with us his plan for restoration.

We are dealing here with knowledge and communication. Luke has transmitted in writing a prayer, a text therefore addressed to God. The contents of this thanksgiving deal with the knowledge offered by the Father to humans. So this knowledge (in French, *connaissance*) has to do with two different senses of the related French word *reconnaissance*: (a) gratitude and (b) mutual recognition and reunion after a long separation. Moreover, it is a question of a knowledge based on faith, which depends on an attested revelation rather than a confirmed experience. Nevertheless, faith deploys in wisdom—not as erudite knowledge but with religious conviction. It unites within itself the origin (the Creator) and the end (the Redeemer), the Lord and the Father. It takes for granted what is known and discloses the unknown. The God who communicates it reveals himself as the one who is both the same and the "other," that is, the living one. He has a will and plans, a "good pleasure" ($\varepsilon\dot{\upsilon}\delta o\kappa\acute{\iota}\alpha$); he is both

---

40   See Luz, *Matthew*, 2:159.

41   Ibid., 201–2.

42   Payne Smith, *Cyril*, 1:302–5. There exist Greek fragments of three of Cyril's sermons; see Reuss, *Lukas-Kommentare*, 110–15 (= frgs. 112–18).

43   Bernardini, 7:263–66.

44   For further information on the history of exegesis, in particular in the modern period, regarding the parallel text in Matt 11:25-27, see Luz, *Matthew*, 2:159–61, 169–76.

sovereign and charitable. This plan, which is fulfilled in Jesus both in a strong manner and in a weak manner, is at the same time both manifest and secret, in a word, mysterious. This plan turns reality upside down: the forces of evil are rendered powerless, on the one hand, and, on the other hand, the poor, the little ones, the rejected become God's favored friends. This upheaval is both theological and sociological. Sociology does, in fact, confirm it: since early Christianity took note of this turnaround, it gave worth in society to the "little ones" and developed on the margin of official Judaism.

While the text is clear concerning God and his Son, as it is concerning humble and uneducated believers, it remains vague with respect to the message and its content. It probably makes the presuppositions that the ontological and soteriological relationship of the Father to the Son constitutes the center of it; that faith, characterized by knowledge, dialogue, and prayer, is its corollary; and that the gospel fulfills the promise made to the prophets and the kings, all the while thwarting the hostile powers.

The Samaritan or Eternal Life as an Inheritance (10:25-37)

Bibliography

Aus, Roger, *Weihnachtsgeschichte, Barmherziger Samari-taner, verlorener Sohn: Studien zu ihrem jüdischen Hintergrund* (ANTZ 2; Berlin: Institut Kirche und Judentum, 1988).

Beauvery, Robert, "La route romaine de Jérusalem à Jéricho," *RB* 64 (1957) 72–101.

Berger, Klaus, *Die Gesetzesauslegung Jesus, ihr historischer Hintergrund im Judentum und im Alten Testament,* Teil 1: *Markus und Parallelen* (WMANT 40; Neukirchen-Vluyn: Neukirchener Verlag, 1972) 1:136–76, 232–42.

Binder, Hermann, "Das Gleichnis vom barmherzigen Samariter," *ThZ* 15 (1959) 176–94.

Bornhäuser, Karl Bernhard, *Studien zum Sondergut des Lukas* (Gütersloh: Bertelsmann, 1934) 65–80.

Bultmann, *History*, 178, 204.

Burchard, C., "Das doppelte Liebesgebot in der frühen christlichen Überlieferung," in Eduard Lohse et al., eds., *Der Ruf Jesu und die Antwort der Gemeinde: Exegetische Untersuchungen Joachim Jeremias zum 70. Geburtstag gewidmet von seinem Schülern* (Göttingen: Vandenhoeck & Ruprecht, 1970) 39–62.

Crespy, Georges, "La parabole dite 'Le bon Samari-tain': Recherches structurales," *EThR* 48 (1973) 61–79.

Crossan, John Dominic, "Parable and Example in the Teaching of Jesus," *NTS* 18 (1971–72) 285–307.

idem, "The Good Samaritan: Towards a Generic Defi-nition of Parable," *Semeia* 2 (1974) 82–112.

Daniélou, Jean, "Le bon Samaritain," in *Mélanges Bib-liques rédigés en l'honneur de André Robert* (Travaux de l'Institut Catholique de Paris 4; Paris: Bloud & Gay, 1956) 457–65.

Derrett, John Duncan M., "Law in the New Testa-ment: Fresh Light on the Parable of the Good Samaritan," in idem, *Law in the New Testament* (London: Darton, Longman & Todd, 1970) 208–27.

Dolto, Françoise, *L'Évangile au risque de la psychanalyse* (2 vols.; Paris: Delarge, 1980, 1982) 1:153–75.

Ebeling, Gerhard, *Evangelische Evangelienauslegung: Eine Untersuchung zu Luthers Hermeneutik* (3d ed.; Tübingen: J. C. B. Mohr, 1991) 496–506.

Entrevernes, Groupe d', *Signes et paraboles: Sémiotique et texte évangélique* (Paris: Seuil, 1977) 17–52.

Eulenstein R., "'Und wer ist mein Nächster?': Lk 10,25-37 in der Sicht eines klassischen Philolo-gen," *ThGl* 67 (1977) 127–45.

Fitzmyer, 2:881–82, 888–90 (bibliography).

Fritzsche, Hans-Georg, "Die Anfänge christlicher Ethik im Dekalog," *ThLZ* 98 (1973) 161–70.

Fuller, Reginald H., "The Double Commandment of Love: A Test Case for the Criteria of Authenticity," in Luise Schottroff et al., eds., *Essays on the Love Commandment* (trans. R. H. Fuller and Ilse Fuller; Philadelphia: Fortress, 1978) 41–56.

Funk, Robert W., "The Good Samaritan as Metaphor," *Semeia* 2 (1974) 74–81.

Gerhardsson, Birger, "The Good Samaritan—The Good Shepherd?" *Coniectanea neotestamentica* 16 (1958) 1–31.

Gerhardt, Ursula, and W. Gerhardt, "Wer ist mein Nächster?" *Schönberger Hefte* 9 (Frankfurt am Main: Verlag Evangelischer Presseverband in Hessen und Nassau, 1979) 1–9.

Gewalt, D., "Der 'Barmherzige Samariter': Zu Lukas 10, 25-37," *EvTh* 38 (1978) 403–17.

Gourgues, Michel, "L'autre dans le récit exemplaire du Bon Samaritain (Lc 10,29-37)," in Michel Gourgues and Gilles D. Mailhiot, eds., *L'altérité, vivre ensemble différents* (Recherches 7; Montreal: Bellarmin, 1986) 257–68.

Kaiser, H., "Der barmherzige Samariter (Lukas 10, 25-36) . . . ," *Der evangelische Erzieher* 31 (1979) 56–68.

idem, B. Schäfer, and G. Veidt, "Die Geschichte vom helfenden Samaritaner," *Schönberger Hefte* 8, 16–18.

Kieffer, René, "Analyse sémiotique et commentaire: Quelques réflexions à propos d'études de Luc 10,25-37," *NTS* 25 (1978–79) 454–68.

Klemm, Hans Gunther, *Das Gleichnis vom barmherzi-gen Samariter: Grundzüge der Auslegung im 16./17. Jahrhundert* (BWANT 103; Stuttgart: Kohlhammer, 1973).

Klinghardt, Matthias, *Gesetz und Volk Gottes: Das lukanische Verständnis des Gesetzes nach Herkunft, Funktion und seinem Ort in der Geschichte des Urchris-tentums* (WUNT 2.32; Tübingen: Mohr Siebeck, 1988) 136–55.

Lambrecht, Jan, *Once More Astonished: The Parables of Jesus* (New York: Crossroad, 1981) 57–82, 83–84 (bibliography).

Leenhardt, Franz-J., "La parabole du Samaritain (schéma d'une exégèse existentialiste)," in *Aux sources de la tradition chrétienne: Mélanges offerts à M. Maurice Goguel à l'occasion de son soixante-dixième anniversaire* (Bibliothèque théologique; Neuchâ-tel/Paris: Delachaux & Niestlé, 1950) 132–38.

Linnemann, Eta, *Parables of Jesus: Introduction and Exposition* (trans. John Sturdy; London: SPCK, 1966) 51–58, 138–43.

Mâle, Émile, *The Gothic Image: Religious Art in France of the Thirteenth Century* (trans. Dora Nussey; Icon Editions; New York: Harper & Row, 1972) 195–97.

Mazamisa, Llewellyn Welile, *Beatific Comradeship: An Exegetical-Hermeneutical Study on Luke 10, 25-37* (Kampen: Kok, 1987).

Monselewski, Werner, *Der barmherzige Samariter: Eine auslegungsgeschichtliche Untersuchung zu Lukas 10, 25-37* (BGBE 5; Tübingen: Mohr Siebeck, 1967).

Mussner, Franz, "Der Begriff des 'Nächsten' in der Verkündigung Jesu: Dargelegt am Gleichnis vom barmherzigen Samariter," in idem, *Praesentia salutis: Gesammelte Studien zu Fragen und Themen des Neuen Testaments* (KBANT; Düsseldorf: Patmos, 1967).

Neirynck, Frans, "Luke 10, 25-28: A Foreign Body in Luke?" in Stanley E. Porter, Paul Joyce, and David O. Orton, eds., *Crossing the Boundaries: Essays in Biblical Interpretation in Honour of Michael D. Goulder* (Biblical Interpretation Series 8; Leiden: Brill, 1994) 149–65.

idem, "The Minor Agreements and Luke 10,25-28," *EThL* 71 (1995) 151–60.

Perkins, Pheme, *Hearing the Parables of Jesus* (New York: Paulist Press, 1982) 112–32.

Perpich, Sandra Wackman, *A Hermeneutic Critique of Structuralist Exegesis, with Specific Reference to Lk 10.29-37* (Lanham, Md.: University Press of America, 1984).

Pirot, Jean, *Paraboles et allégories évangéliques: la pensée de Jésus, les commentaires patristiques* (Paris: Lethielleux, 1949) 176–77.

Reicke, Bo, "Der barmherzige Samariter," in Otto Böcher and Klaus Haacker, eds., *Verborum veritas: Festschrift für Gustav Stählin zum 70. Geburtstag* (Wuppertal: Brockhaus, 1970) 103–9.

Royse, James R., "A Philonic Use of πανδοχεῖον (Luke X 34)," *NovT* 23 (1981) 193–94.

Sanchis, Pierre, "'Samaritanus ille': L'exégèse augustinienne de la parabole du bon Samaritain," *RSR* 49 (1961) 406–25.

Segbroeck, Frans von, *The Gospel of Luke: A Cumulative Bibliography 1973–1988* (BETL 88; Leuven: Leuven University Press, 1989) 232–33.

Sellin, Gerhard, "Lukas als Gleichniserzähler: Die Erzählung vom barmherzigen Samariter (Lk 10,25-37)," *ZNW* 65 (1974) 166–89; 66 (1975) 19–60.

Sfameni Gasparro, Giulia, "Variazioni esegetiche sulla parabola del Buon Samaritano: Dal 'Presbitero' di Origene ai dualisti medievali," in Enrico Livrea and G. Aurelio Privitera, eds., *Studi in onore di Anthos Ardizzoni* (2 vols.; Filologia e critica 25; Edizioni dell'Ateneo & Bizzarri, 1978–79) 2:949–1012.

Spicq, Ceslas, *Theological Lexicon of the New Testament* (trans. and ed. James D. Ernest; 3 vols.; Peabody, Mass.: Hendrickson, 1994) 3:273–75.

Stegner, W. R., "The Parable of the Good Samaritan and Leviticus 18,5," in Dennis E. Groh and Robert Jewett, *The Living Text: Essays in Honor of Ernest W. Saunders* (Lanham, Md.: University Press of America, 1985) 27–38.

Stein, Robert H., "The Interpretation of the Parable of the Good Samaritan," in W. Ward Gasque and W. Sanford LaSor, eds., *Scripture, Tradition, and Interpretation: Essays Presented to Everett F. Harrison by His Students and Colleagues in Honor of His Seventy-Fifth Birthday* (Grand Rapids: Eerdmans, 1978) 278–95.

Steiner, Anton, "Invitation à la solidarité: Le bon Samaritain (Lc 10, 25-37)," in Anton Steiner and Volker Weymann, eds., *Paraboles de Jésus* (Lausanne: Évangile et Culture, 1980) 101–16.

Str-B 1:353–70, 900–908; 2:176–84.

Suzuki, S., "Verantwortung für den Andern: Lk 10,25-37 bei Bultmann, Barth, Bonhoeffer und K. Tagawa," *Die Zeichen der Zeit* 30 (1976) 331–38.

Tolbert, Mary Ann, *Perspectives on the Parables: An Approach to Multiple Interpretations* (Philadelphia: Fortress Press, 1979) 16–17, 24, 29–30, 57, 59–60, 129 n. 14.

Van Elderen, Bastiaan, "Another Look at the Parable of the Good Samaritan," in James I. Cook, ed., *Saved by Hope: Essays in Honor of Richard C. Oudersluys* (Grand Rapids: Eerdmans, 1978) 109–19.

Venetz, Hermann-Josef, "Theologische Grundstrukturen in der Verkündigung Jesu? Ein Vergleich von Mk 10,17-22; Lk 10,25-37 und Mt 5,21-48," in Pierre Casetti, Othmar Keel, and Adrian Schenker, eds., *Mélanges Dominique Barthélemy: Études bibliques offertes à l'occasion de son 60e anniversaires* (OBO 38; Fribourg, Switzerland: Éditions universitaires; Göttingen: Vandenhoeck & Ruprecht, 1981) 613–50.

Zahn, Theodor, "Ein verkanntes Fragment von Marcions Antithesen," *NKZ* 21 (1910) 371–77.

Zimmermann, Heinrich, "Das Gleichnis vom barmherzigen Samariter: Lk 10, 25-37," in Günter Bornkamm and Karl Rahner, eds., *Die Zeit Jesu: Festschrift für Heinrich Schlier* (Freiburg im Breisgau: Herder, 1970) 58–69.

25/ Just then an expert in the Law stood up to test him, saying, "Teacher, what must I do to inherit eternal life?" 26/ He said to him, "What is written in the Law? What meaning do you read there?" 27/ He answered him, "You shall love the Lord your God with all your heart, and with all your soul, and with all your strength, and with all your mind; and your neighbor as yourself." 28/ He said to him, "You have given the right answer; do this, and you will live."

29/ But he, wanting to justify himself, said to Jesus, "And who is my neighbor?" 30/ Welcoming the question, Jesus said, "A man was going down from Jerusalem to Jericho and fell into the hands of robbers, who stripped him and beat him before going away, leaving him half dead. 31/ By chance a priest was going down that road; and when he saw him, he passed by on the other side. 32/ So likewise a Levite who, as he was passing by the place, saw him, and then passed by on the other side. 33/ But a Samaritan, while traveling, passed by the same place, saw him, and was moved with pity. 34/ He approached him, bandaged his wounds, pouring oil and wine on them. Then he put him on his own animal, brought him to an inn, and took care of him. 35/ The next day he took out two denarii and gave them to the innkeeper, saying, 'Take care of him; and when I come back, I will repay you whatever more you spend.' 36/ Which of these three, do you think, proved to be a neighbor to the man who fell into the hands of the robbers?" 37/ He said, "The one who showed him mercy." Jesus said to him, "Go and do likewise."

This is the parable of the so-called Good Samaritan. The adjective "good" is not in the text. Is it an unwarranted projection? Since the name "Samaritan" brings to mind someone who is marginalized, a member of a disdained community, the traditional title expresses the paradox very well: the bad person is not the person that one would think. On the other hand, the use of the adjective "good" has its down side, in that it is attached to the person, whereas what counts is what the Samaritan does; moreover, this use runs the risk of reducing the parable to a moral lesson.

There is a way to avoid this last result. The study of the history of the interpretation of the parable shows us that in the past the image of the Samaritan was often applied to Christ giving help to humanity, rather than to some charitable Christian. And the Savior's goodness is not a matter of question. But is this christological interpretation legitimate? Commentators will agree that it is, on the condition that such interpretation not be done at the expense of the ethical dimension and that it bring out a structure of compassion and action, rather than allegorizing the story in such a way as to demobilize Christians concerned only with redemption. That kind of christological structure is rooted in God, who is compassionate and active, and acts through the church, whose members carry on their Lord's charitable acts by means of their faith and practice.

Beware, however! This pericope is not limited to the parable. The parable is caught up in a debate the stakes of which are access to eternal life. Jesus and the man with whom he is in dialogue agree on appealing to Scripture and on linking eternal inheritance with practice of the Law. The purpose of the parable is to answer a specific question: Who is my neighbor? Essentially, however, it still has an exegetical and ethical character and is linked to the commandment to love one's neighbor. But that character serves as an intermediary that establishes a link with our love for God and God's love for us.

Since we have here a double commandment, the following two pericopes illustrate it. Luke, who is fond of making his readers see the point, invites them to make an association between the Samaritan and love of one's neighbor, and between Martha and Mary and love of God. I will therefore stress the ethical meaning of the Samaritan episode, without neglecting the christological meaning, and the theological meaning of the story of Martha and Mary, without forgetting the significance of the episode for service. Since he was a theologian of relationships, the Gospel writer could not conceive of an act of love directed toward one's neighbor outside of the framework of divine love, nor of loving allegiance to God outside of a community framework.

Analysis

Analysis of the Structure

The account of the theological and practical debate is along the line of disputes that contemporary rabbis were carrying on.[1] It takes place in two rounds. The first round, in which the important elements are a question (v. 25), a pedagogical counter-question (v. 26), and an answer (v. 27), ends with congratulations and an invitation to action (v. 28). This invitation reopens the debate. By comparison with the first round, the second one progresses in a manner that is both symmetrical and dissymmetrical.[2] Once again we have a question (v. 29), a counter-question (v. 36), and an answer (v. 37a), followed by an invitation to action (v. 37b). But, unlike in the first part, where the normative authority was the scriptural passage quoted by the "scribe" (v. 27), here it is Jesus who tells a story (vv. 30-35), the interior evidence of which is apparent only to the person who hears it and understands it as an authorized commentary on Scripture. The structural similarity between the two stages of the disputation highlights the specificity of the scriptural quotation, on the one hand, and of the parable, on the other. The text does not really have an ending, since the reader does not know if the expert in the Law is going to put into practice what he has understood.[3] If we were to make an outline, we would have the following:

First round	*Second round*
• the expert in the Law's question (v. 25)	• the expert in the Law's question (v. 29)
	• *NORMATIVE STORY* by way of an answer by Jesus (vv. 30-35)
• Jesus' counter-question (v. 26)	• Jesus' counter-question (v. 36)
• *SCRIPTURAL QUOTATION* by way of an answer by the expert in the Law (v. 27)	• the expert in the Law's answer (v. 37a)
• Jesus' congratulations and invitation to action (v. 28)	• Jesus' invitation to action (v. 37b)

---

1 Bornhäuser (*Sondergut,* 65) speaks of "Lehrgespräch." See also Gerhardsson, "Good Samaritan," 24–25.

2 This symmetry has often been noted; see, e.g., Crossan, "Parable and Example, 290; Sellin, "Lukas," 19–20; and Klinghardt, *Gesetz,* 136. With regard to dissymmetry, note the absence of any congratulation in v. 37; all the attention here is directed toward putting love into practice, and without this focus the listener cannot fully appreciate the lesson of the parable.

3 On the structure, see Crossan, "Parable and Example," 287, who distinguishes four parts: vv. 25-28, v. 29; vv. 30-35, and vv. 36-37.

By accepting the second question of the expert in the Law (v. 29),[4] the Lukan Jesus admits that Holy Scripture, however normative it may be, still needs to be explained. He proposes to provide such an explanation himself, by means of a parabolic story. The doctrinal position of Jesus, and subsequently of Christianity, corresponds therefore to a new interpretation of Holy Scripture, just as the differences between the various Jewish sects, then between Judaism and Christianity, and finally among the different Christian communities, can be explained by the variety of these exegetical answers. The very structure of this pericope is a witness to the hermeneutical tensions that characterized the life of the earliest Christian churches and before that, of Jesus' own life. Understanding these verses as the existential option that Luke suggested to rabbis anxious to live in a mixed community is a hypothesis that is incapable of verification.[5] I believe instead that the Gospel writer used the occasion of an episode recounted in honor of his Master[6] to state a universal moral of ethics and perhaps also of Christology.

Analysis of the Origin

In order to be able to move on from the question of the structure of the text to its origin, the commentator compares parallel texts, principally the double commandment of love that Luke read in his copy of the Gospel of Mark (Mark 12:28-34). Everything would lead us to believe that here he is not following that source, given how great the differences with Mark are and how much Luke agrees with Matthew. Among the differences from Mark we can count the content of the question (first commandment, Mark 12:28; inheritance of eternal life, Luke 10:25); the absence (Mark) or the presence (Luke 10:26) of a counter-question from Jesus; the author of

the correct answer (Jesus, Mark 12:29; the expert in the Law, Luke 10:27); and the wording of the biblical quotation (Mark 12:29-31; Luke 10:27). The agreements with Matthew include the description of the person in dialogue with Jesus as an "expert in the Law" ($\nu o\mu\iota\kappa\acute{o}\varsigma$, Matt 22:35; Luke 10:25); the intention to "test" Jesus (Matt 22:35; Luke 10:25); the vocative "Teacher" (Matt 22:36; Luke 10:25); the expression "in the Law" (Matt 22:36; Luke 10:26); and the closeness of the wording of the biblical quotation (Matt 22:37; Luke 10:27). So Luke is perhaps conforming to Q.[7] On the other hand, it is also possible that here Luke is using L,[8] which, unlike Q and Mark, may have joined a parable, that of the Samaritan, to the question about what the most important commandments are. A certain number of indications, namely, the things that Luke does not have in common with Matthew and Mark, lead me to decide in favor of this last hypothesis. Only Luke speaks of the inheritance of eternal life (10:25), inserts a counter-question (10:26), places the decisive answer on the lips of the expert in the Law (10:27), gives a special wording of the biblical quotation and establishes a link with the parable (10:30-35), the aesthetic quality of which reminds us of the major texts of L (cf. Luke 15:11-32 or 24:13-35). Whatever the case may be concerning the origin of the parallel texts, in their present state they vary greatly as to their theme: in Luke, it is a question of the attitude, defined by Scripture and spelled out in the parable, that leads to eternal life; in Matthew and Mark, it is a question of the most important commandments of the Law. The literary quality of the Lukan passage, moreover, confirms the origin I have proposed and the elegant appropriation made of it by the author of the Third Gospel.[9]

---

4   The verb $\acute{\upsilon}\pi o\lambda\alpha\mu\beta\acute{\alpha}\nu\omega$ probably corresponds to the *terminus technicus* found in rabbinic disputes (see Bornhäuser, *Sondergut*, 67).

5   Klinghardt, *Gesetz*, 154–55.

6   One must not overlook those narrative aspects which one could forgo in an actual dispute: the desire to tempt Jesus (v. 25) and the attempt to justify oneself (v. 29).

7   Matthew 22:34-40 combines the Sayings Source with the text of Mark 12:28-34. Christoph Burchard attributes Luke 10:25-28 to a source that was common to both Matthew and Luke, probably Q ("Liebesgebot," 40–43). Wolfgang Wiefel prefers to think that Luke here has before him only Mark

12:28-34 (*Das Evangelium nach Lukas* [HThKNT 3; Berlin: Evangelische Verlagsanstalt, 1988] 207). On this question, see Zimmermann, "Das Gleichnis vom barmherzigen Samariter," in Günter Bornkamm and Karl Rahner, eds., *Die Zeit Jesu: Festschrift für Heinrich Schlier* (Freiburg im Breisgau: Herder, 1970) 58–60.

8   With Fitzmyer, 2:877–78.

9   Notice the elevated style of expression: $\dot{\epsilon}\kappa\pi\epsilon\iota\rho\acute{\alpha}\zeta\omega$ ("to put to the test") in the place of $\pi\epsilon\iota\rho\acute{\alpha}\zeta\omega$ ("to tempt," Matt 22:35); $\dot{o}\rho\vartheta\tilde{\omega}\varsigma$ $\dot{\alpha}\pi\epsilon\kappa\rho\acute{\iota}\vartheta\eta\varsigma$ ("you have answered correctly," v. 28); vv. 29 and 36 are well written.

Commentary

The First Round (vv. 25–28)

■ **25** "Just then" ($K\alpha\grave{\iota}$ $\iota\delta o\acute{v}$) indicates that we are beginning a new episode, but the expression is so vague that it gives us little idea of how much time has elapsed since the preceding pericope. In my opinion, Luke thought of that lapse of time as rather long; he did not place the expert in the Law among the group of disciples (Luke 10:23) but as from another context. Moreover, it was, to his way of thinking, a Jewish expert in the Law, someone with expertise in the field, who recognized Jesus' preeminent erudition. Luke clearly suggests a hierarchy: as a master of theology, Jesus led his student, the expert in the Law, in an exegetical exercise, also indicating what decisive steps he needed to take. The following didactic questions (vv. 26 and 36), the congratulations (v. 28), and the professor's encouragement (vv. 28 and 37) all correspond to the vocative "Teacher" (v. 25).

Was the expert in the Law who stands up here[10] really in search of eternal life?[11] In any case, the direction the text takes would point him in the direction of an authentic search (v. 37). At the outset, he seemed to be more anxious to test Jesus than to guarantee his future. Once he initiated the dialogue, he got totally involved in it and Jesus ended up being the one who tested him. Did he not try to justify himself (v. 29)? Besides, what he was testing

was more Jesus' orthopraxy than his orthodoxy; everything was to hinge on the word "do."[12] What was in question was the orthopraxy of Jesus, the expert in the Law, the priest, the Levite, and the Samaritan, just as it was of Martha and Mary, in the following pericope (10:38-42).

■ **26** Jesus sends him back to Scripture in a rhetorical manner, by means of a double question. The first question introduces the quotation from Scripture; the second, the parable. The interrogative "what?" ($\tau\acute{\iota}$) refers to the text; the question "what meaning?" ($\pi\hat{\omega}\varsigma$), to its interpretation.[13] This linking of the requirement of the Law with eternal life differs greatly from the question as to which commandment is the most important, or first of all (Mark 12:28), or greatest (Matt 22:36). The debate here concerns soteriology. For Jesus, a good Jew, the answer could not be anywhere but in Scripture (v. 26).

■ **27** The answer was to be found (v. 27) in a passage dear to Christians,[14] which was at the same time quite Jewish. It is a question of neither grace nor pardon. Luke does not neglect either of these, any more than he does Christology, but insofar as practical commitment is concerned, he tells us, such commitment must be demonstrated by a double love, expressed in two verses of the Law of Moses, Deut 6:5 (love of God) and Lev 19:18 (love of one's neighbor).[15] The search for a center of the Law and the underscoring of that center corresponded to a perceptible tendency in Judaism of the time, in particu-

---

10   $\mathcal{A}\nu\acute{\epsilon}\sigma\tau\eta$ ("he stood up"). There is something brusque and unexpected in this gesture, like the appearance of the woman with the vase of perfume (Luke 7:37-38, without the verb $\dot{\alpha}\nu\acute{\iota}\sigma\tau\alpha\mu\alpha\iota$, but with $\kappa\alpha\grave{\iota}$ $\dot{\iota}\delta o\acute{v}$ and $\sigma\tau\hat{\alpha}\sigma\alpha$).

11   It may be that the formulation of v. 25 has been influenced by the question of the rich young man (Mark 10:17) in an episode that Luke will take up later (Luke 18:18). But the form of the question has parallels in Jewish literature: Dan 12:2; *4 Macc.* 15:3 (see Fitzmyer, 2:1198–99).

12   $\Pi o\iota\acute{\epsilon}\omega$ ("to do") occurs four times in this pericope (vv. 25, 28, 37a, 37b). See Wiefel, 207.

13   One can also say that the reading corresponds to the scriptural passage.

14   Cf. *Did.* 1.2; *Barn.* 19.2, 5; Polycarp *Phil.* 3.3; Justin *Dial.* 93.2 (see Burchard, "Liebesgebot," 44–45). The two sentences begin with the same verb ("you shall love"), following a rabbinic precedent (Gerhardsson, "Good Samaritan," 6).

15   Luke's text—which is far from being without variants—differs from the text of Deut 6:5 in three points, or so it appears at least in our edition of the LXX: (a) in place of the preposition $\dot{\epsilon}\kappa$ ("out of"), Luke has $\dot{\epsilon}\nu$ ("in," perhaps influenced by Semitic idiom?); the Hebrew text in fact has -$\beth$ ("in"); (b) Luke's text enumerates—as does Mark's, but in a different order—four human faculties where the LXX enumerates only three, following the Hebrew text: Luke has "heart," "soul," "strength," and "mind," while the LXX has "heart," "soul," and "might" (note that the manuscripts of the LXX vary between "heart" and "mind.") Thus, Luke and Mark have what one might call a conflated reading. (c) Luke uses $\dot{\eta}$ $\dot{\iota}\sigma\chi\acute{\upsilon}\varsigma$ ("strength") where the LXX speaks of $\dot{\eta}$ $\delta\acute{\upsilon}\nu\alpha\mu\iota\varsigma$ ("might"). As for Luke 19:18, Luke, in contrast to Matthew and Mark, leaves out the verb "you shall love," perhaps in order to avoid repetition with the first commandment.

lar in the *Testaments of the Twelve Patriarchs*.[16] The wording combines two advantages: that of maintaining a balance between faith and ethics, and that of preferring the ethical level to the ritual level of obedience. The obligatory attachment to a single master (Luke 16:13) does not prevent service to one's neighbor, but on the contrary makes it obligatory.

Although the Sermon on the Plain spelled out the greatest application of love of one's neighbor, namely, love of one's enemies (Luke 6:27), the expert in the Law was satisfied here with a wording (Lev 19:18) that coincides, in its content, with the golden rule (Luke 6:31). On the other hand, he also mentioned the commitment of the whole person implied by the love of God, without saying which responsibility is borne by which of the four anthropological domains he mentioned. Moreover, the listing of these domains serves more as a way of indicating the whole and the global intensity of the commitment than as a way of demarcating the functions of each of them. "Heart" refers to the will and emotions; "soul," to conscious vitality and spiritual sensitivity; "strength," to personal energy; and "mind," to intelligence. Even if Hellenistic Judaism was interested at that time in anthropological and psychological problems, Luke did not lay any more stress on them than did Mark or Matthew. What Luke emphasized most strongly was the putting into practice of what was required, of proper relationships, and of love;[17] in this he followed the earliest Christian theology. The author of Scripture, God, expects from

those whom he loves a living, earnest, and lasting reciprocity, beings with undivided loyalty, with "whole" hearts.

■ **28** The expert's answer satisfies the teacher.[18] Everything that needed to be said has been said, but everything that needed to be done remains to be done. Such stress on doing does not seem to affect the conception in the Gospel of the divine gift and of pardon. Even the apostle Paul links, as is done here, eternal life and action (Gal 3:12; Rom 14:10; and 2 Cor 5:10). In these verses the stress is on the human pole of the relationship rather than the divine one. The following episode, the one about Martha and Mary (10:38-42), will define how they are connected.

The Second Round (vv. 29–37)

■ **29** The first round put the expert in the Law in a difficult position. Although he was on the offensive in v. 25, here in v. 29 he is on the defensive. He wants to justify himself; in other words, for Luke, he does not want to be in the wrong. He wants to be accepted and recognized by both his fellow human beings and by God. He wishes to be given a definition of who his neighbor is that will match his habitual conduct, which is probably restrictive. He wants to avoid the implicit reproach of "you haven't done it" contained in the "do this, and you will live" (v. 28). It is not just his honor that is on the line or his social position in Judaism but also his eternal life. Luke is critical of this self-interested attitude.[19] By means of this

---

16 According to Burchard ("Liebesgebot," 55–56), ancient Judaism did not associate Deut 6:5 with Lev 19:18. In question is whether the Christian conduct of Greek expression originated with Jesus. It all depends on the Jewish or Christian nature of allusions to these commandments contained in the *Testaments of Twelve Patriarchs*: *T. Benj.* 3:3-4; *T. Dan* 5:3; *T. Zeb.* 5:1; *T. Iss.* 5:1; 7:6. Philo (*Spec.* 2.63) distinguishes piety and reverence toward God, on the one hand, from generosity and righteousness toward humans, on the other, and he regards them as the two principal chapters, κεφάλαια, of the Law. Suzanne Daniel refers to *m. Yoma* 8.9 (*Philo of Alexandria, De specialibus legibus, I et II, introduction, traduction et notes* [Les Œuvres de Philon d'Alexandrie 24; Paris: Cerf, 1975] xii). Cf. the Benedictus: "to serve him in holiness and righteousness" (Luke 1:74-75). Even though ancient Judaism did not associate Deut 6:5 with

Lev 19:18, through its exegesis of the Decalogue it did associate one's duty toward God with one's obligation toward a neighbor. This dichotomy owes something to the Greek distinction between piety and righteousness (see Berger, *Die Gesetzesauslegung Jesu*, 143–52). On the Jewish exegesis of Lev 19:18, see J. B. Stern, "Jesus' Citation of Dt 6, 5 and Lev 19, 18 in the Light of Jewish Tradition," *CBQ* 26 (1966) 312–16; and Andreas Nissen, *Gott und der Nächste im antiken Judentum: Untersuchungen zum Doppelgebot des Liebe* (WUNT 15; Tübingen: Mohr Siebeck, 1974) 278–317.

17 On ἀγαπάω ("to love"), see the commentary on 6:27 (1:236–37).

18 On ὀρθῶς ("correctly"), see the commentary on 7:43 (1:296 n. 50).

19 Luke sees in the individual's righteousness that which one believes he or she can obtain on his own, the fundamental trait characteristic of the scribes

parable, he will contrast it with impartial mercy, which is an expression of another kind of justice.

While the text of the quotation clearly speaks of "your neighbor," the expert in the Law's question[20] is ambiguous. It could mean either "And who is my neighbor?" or "And who is near to me?" depending on whether we take $\pi\lambda\eta\sigma\acute{\iota}o\nu$ to be a noun ("neighbor") or an adverb ("near"). What inclines me to take it as a noun and to retain the traditional translation of it as "And who is my neighbor . . . ?" is the proximity to the quotation,[21] the place of $\mu o\nu$ ("my"), and the direction the dialogue takes.

■ **30** Jesus *welcomes* the question insofar as he *understands* it well. These seem to be the two possible meanings of the Greek verb $\acute{\nu}\pi o\lambda\alpha\mu\beta\acute{\alpha}\nu\omega$ here: "welcome" and "understand." We encounter these same two meanings in both Jewish and Greek dialogues.[22]

By way of reply, Jesus recounts the famous parable. Following the traditional system of classification, this parable belongs to the category of "example stories," since it closes with an invitation to imitation and is determined by an objective, nonfigurative vision of reality.[23] These "example stories" all belong to L[24] and serve, in a certain context, as didactic models presented as rhetorical paradigms.[25] This treatment and system of classification have been subjected to criticism.[26] It is indeed possible that the example aspect was overstressed in the course of its transmission by tradition at the expense of its initial metaphorical impact. It also seems possible that the parable may have initially been told for its own sake and that the linking of it with Jesus' debate with the expert in the Law (10:25-28) was an artificial and secondary development. There is certainly tension

between vv. 27 and 29, on the one hand, according to which one's neighbor is the person one is supposed to love, and v. 36, according to which becoming a neighbor of someone else is an ethical objective. There is hesitation in the parable, and the reader is left wondering which one is the neighbor of the other person, the man who was wounded, or the Samaritan. So I will allow the possibility that the parable initially circulated for its own sake. Even if its figurative character was not very distant from the reality that was implied, it was not in the first instance illustrative nor did it serve as an example. Like Jesus' other parables, it had a mobilizing function. It was subsequently joined to the dispute with the expert in the Law, which increased its exegetical and paradigmatic function. This linking took place in a pre-Lukan phase of the tradition. The author of L seems to have received the two units already linked to each other.

Verse 30 lays out the situation and recounts how a man (at the beginning of the verse) came to be half-dead (at the end of the verse). Against this dramatic backdrop two persons file by, led onto the scene by a common ("likewise" [$\acute{o}\mu o\acute{\iota}\omega\varsigma$], v. 32) fate ("by chance" [$\kappa\alpha\tau\grave{\alpha}\ \sigma\upsilon\gamma\kappa\upsilon\rho\acute{\iota}\alpha\nu$], v. 31). They both "pass by on the other side" ($\grave{\alpha}\nu\tau\iota\pi\alpha\rho\tilde{\eta}\lambda\vartheta\epsilon\nu$, vv. 31 and 32). They both belong to the official and respected world of religion. In contrast to these persons, their identity and their attitude, we have a Samaritan, a nondescript individual with a despised background. This man does not pass by but stops and goes into action: a series of definite verbs describe the considered and efficacious steps he takes (vv. 34-35). This man chooses to express his compassion ("was moved by pity" [$\acute{\epsilon}\sigma\pi\lambda\alpha\gamma\chi\nu\acute{\iota}\sigma\vartheta\eta$], v. 33) by means of what he does. The structure of the parable is therefore

---

and Pharisees (Luke 16:15; 18:19). See Walter Grundmann, *Das Evangelium nach Lukas* (2d ed.; ThKNT 3; Berlin: Evangelische Verlagsanstalt, 1961) 223.

20 In Classical Greek, a question can begin with $\kappa\alpha\acute{\iota}$ (BDF §442).

21 Cf. the similar wordings $o\grave{\upsilon}\kappa\ \acute{\epsilon}\sigma\tau\iota\nu\ \sigma o\nu\ \grave{\alpha}\nu\acute{\eta}\rho$ (John 4:18) and $\alpha\grave{\upsilon}\tau\acute{o}\varsigma\ \mu o\nu\ \grave{\alpha}\delta\epsilon\lambda\varphi\grave{o}\varsigma\ \kappa\alpha\grave{\iota}\ \grave{\alpha}\delta\epsilon\lambda\varphi\grave{\eta}\ \kappa\alpha\grave{\iota}\ \mu\acute{\eta}\tau\eta\rho\ \grave{\epsilon}\sigma\tau\acute{\iota}\nu$ (Matt 12:50).

22 See p. 53 n. 4 above, and the commentary on 7:43 (1:296). To the contrary, several commentators (e.g., Marie-Joseph Lagrange, *Évangile selon saint Luc* [4th ed.; EtB; Paris: Gabalda, 1927] 312–13; Marshall, 447) think that the verb has here a

unique meaning found nowhere else in the NT, "to answer."

23 See Adolf Jülicher, *Die Gleichnisreden Jesu*, vol. 1: *Die Gleichnisreden im Allgemeinen* (2d ed.; Tübingen: Mohr Siebeck, 1899) 112–15; Bultmann, *History*, 178; and Sellin, "Lukas," 176–78.

24 Luke 12:16-21 (the rich farmer); 16:19-31 (the rich man and Lazarus); 18:10-14 (the Pharisee and the tax collector); and moreover 14:7-11 and 14:12-14.

25 See Sellin, "Lukas," 179, where he introduces a genre of parables that he calls $\acute{\alpha}\nu\vartheta\rho\omega\pi\acute{o}\varsigma\ \tau\iota\varsigma$.

26 See chiefly Crossan, "Parable and Example"; and Funk, "Good Samaritan as Metaphor," 74–81.

simple: to the given situation (v. 30) correspond two opposite attitudes (an empty look and neglect [vv. 31-32], on the one hand; a watchful eye, compassion, and charitable action [vv. 33-35], on the other). The element of surprise comes from the lack of correspondence between identity and attitude. Good is accomplished by the person usually associated with evil.

One travels about seventeen miles along the road between Jerusalem and Jericho, with a drop in elevation from 2,500 ft. to 820 ft. below sea level (Jericho).[27] "The road goes through the desert right after the Mount of Olives, and has always had the reputation of being overrun with bandits."[28] The term λῃστής ("bandit") could be used in that time, in particular by Josephus,[29] to designate the Zealots, but the identity of these thieves is not important to the story.[30]

There has been a debate concerning the meaning to assign to the Greek particle καί (which can, depending on the context, be translated as "and," "also," etc., following the relative pronoun οἵ ["who"]). In my opinion, it has a double meaning: this first καί slightly reinforces the relative pronoun by giving a greater independence, consequently a certain importance, to the relative clause; with the second καί, it stresses the misfortunes that never come singly.[31] The bandits could have been content with just robbing him, but they also stripped him of his clothes, beat him, and left him in his sad state.[32]

■ **31-32** The priest had probably finished his duties and was going home. Instead of associating love for his neighbor with serving God, he neglected to show compassion, that obligatory complement to piety.[33] The same was true of the Levite, another officiant of the temple, of an inferior rank.[34] Luke considered them to be inexcusable, since, after having seen (ἰδών, vv. 31 and 32), they both shut their eyes. They did not meet with the wounded man; they took leave of the scene and became nonexistent persons, as it were, dead to the present,[35] caught up in their past, driven by ritual regulations[36] and selfish drives. They passed by on the other side, without stopping.[37]

---

27 See Lagrange, 313 (correct his "350" to "250" meters under "le niveau de la mer"); and Beauvery, "La route romaine de Jérusalem à Jéricho," 72–101. On Jerusalem and Jericho, see Fitzmyer, 2:886.

28 Lagrange, 313. Strabo (16.2.41) decries how Pompey annihilated the brigands there. Jerome (*Comm. in Jer.* 3.2) mentions the robbers in this region, while Josephus (*Bell.* 4.8.4 §474) recalls the savage character of the land. See also Marshall, 447.

29 See Karl H. Rengstorf, ed., *A Complete Concordance to Flavius Josephus* (4 vols.; Leiden: Brill, 1973–83) 3:29–30; and idem, "λῃστής," *TDNT* 4 (1967) 257–62. For one example, see Josephus, *Bell.* 2.17.6 §425.

30 Rengstorf believes that Jesus has the Zealots in mind and so implicitly criticizes the brutal manner in which they think they must serve God ("λῃστής," *TDNT* 4 [1967] 261).

31 See BDAG, s.v. καί 2f; BDF §444 and n. 3; Marshall, 447.

32 Περιπίπτω ("to fall upon") is often used of falling upon an obstacle, a danger, an army, or an adversary with the nuance of a chance happening (see Acts 27:41; James 1:2). The adjective ἡμιθανής ("half dead") is a *hapax legomenon* in the NT. See Strabo 2.3.4. In *4 Macc.* 4.11, one reads, "And falling half-dead upon the area enclosed by the Court of the Gentiles in the Temple, Apollonius . . ." (κατα-

πεσών γέ τοι ἡμιθανὴς ὁ Ἀπολλώνιος ἐπὶ τὸν πάμφυλον τοῦ ἱεροῦ περίβολον κτλ.).

33 See p. 55 n. 16 above.

34 On the priests and the Levites, see Joachim Jeremias, *Jerusalem in the Time of Jesus: An Investigation into Economic and Social Conditions during the New Testament Period* (3d ed.; London: SCM, 1969) 198–213. Here Luke follows the practice of mentioning them together and in this order (Lagrange, 313).

35 See Leenhardt, "La parabole du Samaritain (schéma d'une exégèse existentialiste)," 132–38.

36 One must take into consideration that these two servants of God may have desired to avoid any impurity by coming into contact with a dead body (Lev 5:2-3; 21:1-3; Num 5:2; 6:6-8; 19:1-22; Ezek 44:25-27). See Fitzmyer, 2:887.

37 The sense of the rare verb ἀντιπαρέχομαι is not evident, for one of the prepositions (παρά) suggests passage beyond, while the other (ἀντί) suggests a path opposite or against. With some reservation, I opt for the translation "He passed by, crossing over to the other side of the road." Some lines from Strabo of Sardis preserved in the *Anthologia graeca* (*Palatine Anthology*) 12.8 offer an interesting parallel: "While passing by a flower shop on the other side of the street" (ἀντιπαρερχόμενος τὰ στεφανηπλό-κια), the poet notices a young man plaiting a wreath (it is not necessary to emend the text to read ἄρτι

■ 33-35 The Samaritan—the Jews' animosity toward them is well known (see John 4:9)[38]—also passed by there[39] ("the same place" [κατ᾽ αὐτόν], which refers back to "the place," v. 32). He, too, saw the wounded man (the third mention of "saw" [ἰδών], v. 33, after the mentions in vv. 31 and 32), but unlike his two predecessors, he let himself be moved (at the redactional level this mention recalls the emphasis in v. 27 on interiority). He was moved with compassion.[40] A relationship was established between the wounded man and the Samaritan. The vulnerable body of the one awakened the attentive heart of the other. The visible signs of distress (literally) "moved" the Samaritan's "entrails," filling him with solicitude. The Greek verb σπλαγχνίζομαι, literally, "to be moved in one's entrails," in other words "to be moved with compassion," used elsewhere by Luke to speak of God's

and Christ's compassionate love, here designates a type of conduct representing the gospel message (vv. 33-35), which the expert in the Law was going to be called to imitate (v. 36). The Samaritan understood the situation, approached the wounded man, suffered with him, and took steps to relieve his suffering.

Even if certain modern authors rightly insist on the fact that the wounded man must have accepted help, thereby acknowledging his weakness and his dependence,[41] I prefer to call attention to the specific and judicious actions of the Samaritan, who did what needed to be done without overdoing it. The first aid carried out by the Samaritan[42] had three aspects: dressing his wounds, transporting him elsewhere, and arranging for his lodging.[43] Luke next summarizes these actions by a verbal expression, "took care of," that is both abstract

---

παρεχόμενος). He stops and speaks with the young man. Ironically, in the other passage that one can cite, Wis 16:10, the verb signifies "to come over to offer help"! See Lagrange, 313; James Hope Moulton and George Milligan, *The Vocabulary of the Greek New Testament: Illustrated from the Papyri and Other Non-Literary Sources* (1930; reprinted Grand Rapids: Eerdmans, 1963) s.v.; Bauer, s.v.; Johannes Reiling and J. L. Swellengrebel, *A Translator's Handbook on the Gospel of Luke* (Helps for Translators 10; Leiden: Brill, for the United Bible Societies, 1971) 420.

38 In my opinion, with a knowledge of Hebrew, a Greek reader of Luke's Gospel would not have been able to think of the etymological sense of the word "Samaritan," which in Hebrew means the "watchman" or "shepherd." On the other hand, Gerhardsson ("Good Samaritan," 9–22) makes a good case from this etymology that the Samaritan represents the messianic "Shepherd" coming to the aid of Israel (symbolized by the injured man), in contrast to the wicked shepherds (the priest and the Levite).

39 The verb ὁδεύω ("to take to the road") is a *hapax legomenon* in the NT. In Acts 9:7, one finds the verb συνοδεύω ("to take to the road with another"); in Acts 17:1, διοδεύω ("to travel through"); and in Luke 2:44, συνοδία ("a company of travelers"). See further Xavier Jacques, *Index des mots apparentés dans le Nouveau Testament: Complément des concordances et dictionnaires* (Rome: Biblical Institute Press, 1969) s.v. ὁδός.

40 See the analysis of this verb in the commentary on Luke 7:13 (1:272 nn. 43, 44). See also Spicq, *Lexicon*, 3:273–75; and Eulenstein, "'Und wer ist mein Nächster?'" 134–35.

41 For example, Dolto, *Psychanalyse*, 1:149.

42 On the modern social organization of the Samaritan movement, see "Samaritaner," *Brockhaus Enzyklopädie* (17th ed.; Wiesbaden: Brockhaus, 1966–81) 16:403. In organizing first aid from voluntary recruits at the end of the nineteenth century in northern Germany, founder Friedrich von Esmarch made reference to our parable.

43 The order of the oil and the wine is surprising, since wine was customarily used first as a disinfectant, after which oil was then applied to the wound (Bornhäuser, *Sondergut*, 75). Lagrange (p. 314) cites a text from Hippokrates (*Ulcer*. 881), which recommends immersing an arum leaf in wine and oil (in this order) before applying it to a wound. In two other treatises attributed to him, compresses of wine and oil (οἴνῳ καὶ ἐλαίῳ) are prescribed (*Fract.* 29; *Aff.* 42). Fitzmyer (2:888) cites Theophrastus *Hist. plant.* 9.11.1 and *m. Šabb.* 19.2. For other biblical references to the medicinal use of oil, see Isa 1:6; Mark 6:13; Jas 5:14. The expression in v. 34, *pace* Lagrange (p. 314), does not imply that the wound is dressed with a bandage before it is anointed with oil. The statement merely presupposes that both actions are complementary and thus would occur at the same time (ἐπιχέων, "by pouring over," is a present participle). The Samaritan, though wealthy enough to pay for himself a mount, prefers to travel the road on foot—an action as much a renouncement of prestige as it is of comfort (as I know from my own experience on Mt. Athos). The word τὸ κτῆνος at first signified a head of large livestock, a beast of burden, and then eventually came to refer to a mount, in contrast to a

and concrete.[44] When he had done his part, the Samaritan passed the torch on to others, more specifically, the innkeeper (the same verb is used in the command to the innkeeper: "take care of," v. 35). His relief work, which was broken off at this point, was resumed the next day (v. 35) in another manner, when he took a fourth step, turning over two denarii[45] to the innkeeper. Although the priest and the Levite did not take the trouble to even stop for a moment, for his part the Samaritan announced[46] that he would stop by again ("on the way back"; the trip was admittedly related to his own business). This fifth action, because it was only potential, was a way the Samaritan had of limiting the wounded man's dependence on him.

■ **36** The reader will not fail to notice the reversal in the use of the word "neighbor." In the opening dialogue, the expert in the Law was trying to find a neighbor whom he could love. In Jesus' question, which summarizes the parable, it is no longer a question of a neighbor who stood a chance of becoming an object, but rather one of someone who was becoming ($\gamma\epsilon\gamma o\nu\acute{\epsilon}\nu\alpha\iota$) the wounded man's neighbor, as the active subject of a relationship. If there is a tension between vv. 27-29 and v. 36 as to the way this word is used, a tension that can be explained by the reworking of sources, Luke maintains it, probably consciously, and even cultivates it. I would not like to overemphasize this difference, however, since a neighbor, in both Greek and English, is literally a being who is close. Thus, we are dealing with a relational term: if the contact is established, the two persons necessarily

become close to each other, the neighbor to the other person. Everything depends on the conditions that make this proximity possible and on the nature of the link that is made. It is on these conditions that the parable lays emphasis.

■ **37** The expert in the Law's answer joins the interior and exterior aspects of the story, that is to say, the affective one ("mercy," $\tau\grave{o}\ \check{\epsilon}\lambda\epsilon o\varsigma$) and the active one ("the one who showed," $\acute{o}\ \pi o\iota\acute{\eta}\sigma\alpha\varsigma$). It also stresses the relational aspect ("[to] him," $\mu\epsilon\tau'\ \alpha\grave{v}\tauo\hat{v}$). The expert in the Law's evolution continues: at first he is disputatious (v. 25), then reserved (v. 29), and finally he enters into a relationship with Jesus (v. 37a). His verbal response is on the verge of translating into action (v. 37b). The expert in the Law and Jesus finally come to a meeting of minds. The disciple has evolved thanks to the teacher's pedagogical skills. He has understood the new definition of "neighbor" that Jesus wanted to lead him to accept. What had been a question for contemporary rabbis (what extension should be given to the notion of neighbor?) here receives an answer.[47] The answer is not dictated but becomes obvious to the person who has been led to reflection through dialogue and faith.[48] By means of his love and discretion, Jesus was able to become the neighbor of the expert in the Law.[49]

Even if readers often come to a similar understanding of the parable, they do not all emphasize the same aspect of it. Some readers stress Christ's role and even go so far as to assume that Jesus identified himself with the Samaritan and filled the role of the shepherd of Israel.[50]

---

wild beast, $\tau\grave{o}\ \vartheta\eta\rho\acute{\iota}o\nu$, and so is distinct from small livestock (e.g., Rev 18:13, $\kappa\tau\acute{\eta}\nu\eta\ \kappa\alpha\grave{\iota}\ \pi\rho\acute{o}\beta\alpha\tau\alpha$, "cattle and sheep" NRSV). On the inn, see the commentary on Luke 2:7 (1:86 nn. 43, 44).

44 On $\dot{\epsilon}\pi\iota\mu\epsilon\lambda\acute{\epsilon}o\mu\alpha\iota$, see 1 Tim 3:5 (to "care for" the house of God). The adverb $\dot{\epsilon}\pi\iota\mu\epsilon\lambda\hat{\omega}\varsigma$ ("with care") appears in Luke 15:8; the noun $\dot{\epsilon}\pi\iota\mu\acute{\epsilon}\lambda\epsilon\iota\alpha$ ("care") in Acts 27:3. See further Spicq, *Lexicon*, 2:47-53.

45 The silver denarius was a Roman coin that was worth sixteen asses, each as being worth four quadrans. The Roman denarius was the equivalent of the Greek drachma, and these two were each worth one fourth of a Hebrew shekel. The Roman denarius was a day's pay for a common laborer (see Matt 20:2-13). See further B. Kanael, "Münzen, 5," *BHH* 2:1255.

46 So elegantly expressed by Luke!

47 See Str-B 1:353-70; Mussner, "Begriff," 126-27.

48 Bo Reicke emphasizes the maieutics ("Socratic Method") of Jesus ("Der barmherzige Samariter," 104-6).

49 On this understanding of "neighbor," see Mussner, "Begriff," 125-32; Sellin, "Lukas"; as well as nearly all of the other studies cited in the bibliography.

50 Gerhardsson ("Good Samaritan," 1-31) has put forward the hypothesis that Jesus is criticizing the wicked shepherds of Israel and offers himself in the figure of the Good Watchman (see the etymology of the word *Samaritan* on p. 58 n. 38 above), the Good Shepherd (playing upon the words רֹעֶה ["shepherd"] and רֵעַ ["friend," "neighbor," "fellow citizen"]). In the present messianic situation, to fulfill the Law—to love one's neighbor—means to love the Good Shepherd and so choose to follow Jesus.

Others, sensitive to the ethnic thrust of the question about who one's neighbor is, lay emphasis on the ecclesial stakes in the debate: by his study of the Law, Jesus rethought, in terms of the covenant,[51] the makeup of God's people. Still others note the newness of Jesus' message, the way he brings the Law to fulfillment, and the access he provides to eternal life—in short, the eschatological impact of the text.[52] In my opinion, the Christian perspective of imitation (v. 37),[53] in terms of attachment to a person, participation in a common lot, and concrete obedience, places the debate on an ethical level but in a doctrinal and salvific framework, by virtue of God's exemplary mercy and the encouragement afforded by Christ's love.

History of Interpretation

The oldest extant—albeit indirect—interpretation to which we have access would have to be that of the second century Gnostics, perhaps also Marcion's interpretation, and it is allegorical.[54] Adam fell like a traveler into the hands of demons who were downright bandits. Blinded from that point on, he was no longer able to know God, in whom he had his origin. Christ filled the role of the Samaritan for him.

Irenaeus's interpretation was also allegorical, as was Origen's at a later date. Below is a brief extant passage from Irenaeus; there is also an entire homily from Origen. Irenaeus wrote:

For it was to the Holy Spirit that the Lord entrusted man, his own possession, who had fallen into the hands of bandits, that man to whom he showed mercy and whose wounds he himself had bandaged, giving two royal denarii so that, after having received through the Holy Spirit the image and inscription of the Father and of the Son, we might make the denarius given to us bear fruit and so that we might give it back to the Lord multiplied in that way. (*Adv. haer.* 3.17.3)

Irenaeus read the work of Christ in the compassionate action taken by the Samaritan and compared the innkeeper's comforting action to the Holy Spirit.

Origen reported the interpretation of an "elder," hence someone whose interpretation was venerable in his eyes. This was an "elder" who had heard the teaching of the first apostles, rather than a minister of the church:

According to the commentary of an elder who wished to interpret the parable, the man who was going down represents Adam; Jerusalem, Paradise; Jericho, the world; the bandits, the hostile powers; the priest, the Law; the Levite, the prophets; and the Samaritan, Christ. The wounds stand for disobedience; the animal, Christ's body; and the *pandochium*, i.e., the inn that is open to all who wish to stay there, symbolizes the Church. Moreover, the two denarii stand for the Father and the Son; the innkeeper, the head of the Church in charge of administration; and as for the promise made by the Samaritan

---

51 This is the direction taken by Sellin in his interpretation ("Lukas").

52 Hermann-Josef Venetz finds a theological structure in this story that emphasizes the ultimate and new event that Jesus instigated based on the Law ("Theologische Grundstrukturen in der Verkündigung Jesu?" 613–50).

53 The formula "go and do likewise" appears to be deeply rooted in Jewish school practice; see B. Gerhardsson, *Good Samaritan,* 10 n. 1.

54 Monselewski (*Samariter,* 18–28) voices his opposition to Daniélou's attempt to go back to the exegesis of the first Christians of Jerusalem by using the "elder" mentioned in Origen (see below). Jean Daniélou maintains that this first exegesis of our parable corresponds to salvation history ("Le bon Samaritain," 457–65). Apart from the lines of Gnostic exegesis, there exists in a Syriac fragment

(see Theodor Zahn, "Ein verkanntes Fragment von Marcions Antithesen," 371–77) a patristic reference to the interpretation of Marcion: the Savior, who would not be born of a woman and would not have a human body, would appear as the Samaritan between Jerusalem and Jericho. Now admittedly the authenticity of this testimony is disputed. But if it were genuine, then Marcion would have discouraged the figure of the Christ behind that of the Samaritan. In addition, there is another allusion to our parable in the corpus from Nag Hammadi, *Gos. Phil.* 78: spiritual love and knowledge are like a beneficial, fragrant ointment. In pouring on the wine and oil, the Samaritan has anointed the wounded and healed him, for "love covers a multitude of sins" (1 Pet 4:8). See James M. Robinson, ed., *The Nag Hammadi Library in English* (3d ed.; Leiden: Brill, 1988) 155.

to return, that is a figure of the Savior's second coming. (*Hom. in Luc.* 34.3).

Origen himself stressed that christological interpretation by justifying it in terms of the etymology of the word "Samaritan":

> But Providence left that half-dead man to be cared for by the one who was stronger than the Law and the prophets, namely, the Samaritan, whose name means "guardian." (34.4)

The ecclesiological orientation logically follows from the christological meaning:

> This Samaritan "bears our sins" and suffers on our behalf; he carries the dying man and takes him to an inn, i.e., into the Church that welcomes everyone, does not refuse aid to anyone, and to which all are invited by Jesus. (34.7)

Finally, the ethical import of the story, by virtue of a theology of imitation, is not neglected either:

> It is possible for us, therefore, according to what is said: "Imitate me, as I imitate Christ," to imitate Christ and to show mercy to those who "have fallen into the hands of bandits," to go to them, bandage their wounds, pour oil and wine on these wounds, and put these persons on our own animal and carry their burdens, and it is for the purpose of exhorting us that the Son of God does not speak only to the teacher of the Law but also to all of us, saying: "Go and do likewise." If we act that way, we will obtain eternal life in Christ Jesus, "to whom belong glory and power forever and ever. Amen." (34.7)

Even though the allegorical and christological interpretation established itself and remained dominant until the triumph of historical-critical interpretation, it sometimes linked up with ethics, as in the case of Clement of Alexandria (*Quis div.* 28–29), but most often with ecclesiology, as in the case of Ambrose of Milan (*Exp. Luc.* 7.71–84). Here and there, under the influence of the School of Antioch, only the ethical sense was appealed to, as in the case of Isidore of Pelusium (*Letter* 123).[55] Ambrose had a good understanding of the reversal of the question (v. 36 by comparison with v. 29);[56] Cyril of Alexandria unleashed his anger against the Jews (*Hom. in Luc.* 68);[57] and Augustine of Hippo, as he contemplated the wounded man in the parable, reflected on the condition of humans living under a temporal regime, on the origin of sin, and on gratuitousness in the Christian life, even in monastic life (e.g., *Quaest. ev.* 2.19).[58]

Christian art latched onto this parable. The famous Codex Rossanensis (a sixth-century Greek manuscript of the Gospels [= Σ 042]) identified the Samaritan with Christ, since it pictured the benefactor's head adorned with a holy halo.[59] In the Middle Ages, for example in the

---

55 Isidore of Pelusium *Lib.* 4, *Ep.* 123 (*PG* 78:1195–98); see also Monselewski, *Samariter*, 59–60.

56 "Now since no one is more our neighbor than He who has healed our wounds, let us love Him as Lord; let us also love Him as a near relative, for nothing is so near as the head to the members. Let us also love the one who imitates the Christ; let us love the one who sympathizes with the poverty of another out of the unity of the Body. It is not a blood relationship but mercy that makes one a neighbor" (Ambrose *Exp. Luc.* 7.84).

57 Five Greek fragments of *Homily* 68 are extant, frgs. 119–23 in Reuss, *Lukas-Kommentare*, 115–17. The anti-Judaism of Cyril is so pronounced that one might wonder if he has truly understood the parable. As Frédéric Amsler once told me, Cyril of Alexandria does not seem to envision that the expert in the Law in this sermon could be his neighbor! Is Cyril satisfied with explaining just the dialogue of Jesus with the expert in the Law (*Serm. Luc.* 68), or has his exegesis of the parable itself disappeared?

58 See Pirot, *Paraboles*, 176–77, who also provides a translation of this passage into French. Pierre Sanchis lists with annotations the principal passages where Augustine interprets our text ("'Samaritanus ille,'" 406–25). The help so freely offered is shown by the kindness of the Samaritan, who offers to pay the additional expense upon his return.

59 On fol. 7b of this manuscript (Σ or 042), the top of the page is decorated with an illustration of two scenes drawn from our parable. On the left side, the Samaritan discovers the wounded man (nearby an angel offers him assistance). On the right, the Samaritan entrusts the wounded man to the care of the innkeeper. Curiously, the cycle of illustrations relating to the life of Jesus is taken from all of the evangelists, Luke and John included, whereas the manuscript itself contains only the texts of

Sens Cathedral, the doctrinal interpretation of the parable made its appearance in the structure of the stained glass window that represented the parable; divided into three parts, the story is framed, for each of the three episodes, by four scenes where we have successive illustrations of (a) creation and the fall (the traveler who was stripped of his possessions), (b) the gift of the Law (the priest and the Levite passing by), and (c) redemption in Christ (the care given by the good Samaritan). So, for the creators of the iconographic scheme, the parable illustrated the decisive step in the plan of salvation, namely, redemption in Jesus Christ.[60] The decisive influence must have been that of medieval interpretation, particularly the *Glossa ordinaria*.[61] Rembrandt's work, consisting of two oil paintings and several drawings, demonstrates a renewed interest in this story on the part of artists, without a doubt as a result of the Reformation and the affection that Luther had for this parable.[62] Illustrated Bibles pictured criticisms of all those holding a contemporary ecclesiastical office: in Georg Gruppenbach's Bible, Christoph Murrer portrayed the priest or the Levite as a monk in the act of reading his breviary; in Bocksperger-Amman's Bible, the Levite was drawn as an itinerant theologian, while the Samaritan was depicted as a Turk, who was the enemy at that time.[63]

I would like to focus on one of the various medieval interpretations, the prologue to *Gregorius* by Hartmann von Aue (97–143).[64] While the author sticks to traditional interpretation in the first part (the man falling into the hands of bandits, 97–109), in the second part (the care given to the wounded man, 110–43), he provides a more personal interpretation, showing how the soul succeeds in freeing itself from sin. The wounded man stands for the man who looks for *diu saelden strâze*, that is, the way to salvation (63 and 88), navigating between the two opposite sins of *desperatio*, despair, and *praesumptio*, pride—the only way to obtain eternal life. Half-dead, this man symbolizes the sinner, thus every human being. Out of pity for him (110–11), God first sent him two kinds of clothing, in order to protect him: the gift of hope, the hope of being saved; and the gift of fear, the fear of losing eternal life. For that reason he did not stay stretched out on the ground, but, after wobbling, he succeeded in sitting up. At the same time, faith and repentance gave him comfort and purified his wounds by washing them in his blood. They poured oil and wine, that is, grace and the Law, into his wounds. Having done this, grace took him by the hand, put him on its shoulders and led him to the house, where his wounds were given further treatment. The wounds healed without leaving a trace. The presence of the parable in the prologue is to be explained by the correspondences that the author established in the body of his work between the fate of the characters in the story and the theory of spiritual healing that he extracted

Matthew and Mark. For the illustration depicting our parable in this manuscript, see Oskar Leopold von Gebhardt and Adolf von Harnack, *Evangeliorum codex Graecus purpureus rossanensis: Σ litteris argenteis sexto ut videtur saeculo scriptus picturisque ornatus . . .* (Leipzig: Giesecke & Devrient, 1880) plate xiii.

60   Around the image of the traveler that was robbed are scenes of the creation, the fall, the divine punishment, and the expulsion from the garden. Around the images of the two men who pass by on their way to worship are scenes of Moses and Aaron before Pharaoh, Moses receiving the Law, the bronze serpent, and the golden calf. Around the image of the Samaritan are scenes of the trial, the scourging, the crucifixion, and the resurrection of Jesus. Nearly the same presentation can be found in the stained glass windows at Bourges and Chartres (at Rouen, the stained glass that must have reproduced the same composition is badly damaged). See Mâle, *Gothic Image,* 195–97.

61   One finds, for example, the division of the parable into three parts, as in the stained glass in Albertus Magnus ("Albert the Great" of Cologne), *Enarr. in Luc.* 10.30 (in Auguste Borgnet, ed., *Beati Alberti Magni Ratisbonensis episcopi, . . . Opera omnia, ex editione Lugdunensi religiose castigata . . . ,* vol. 23: *Enarrationes in secundam partem evangelli Lucae x–xxiv* [Paris: Ludovicum Vivès, 1895]).

62   See Joachim Poeschke, "Samariter barmherzige," in Engelbert Kirschbaum et al., eds., *Lexikon der christlichen Ikonographie* (8 vols.; Rome: Herder, 1968–76) 4:24–26.

63   See Philip Schmidt, *Die Illustration der Lutherbibel, 1522–1700: Ein Stück abendländische Kultur- und Kirchengeschichte: Mit Verzeichnissen der Bibeln, Bilder und Künstler* (Basel: Reinhardt, 1962) 368, 259.

64   See H.-J. Spitz, "Zwischen Furcht und Hoffnung: Zum Samaritergleichnis in Hartmanns von Aue 'Gregorious'—Prolog," *Münstersche Mittelalter-Schriften* 51 (1984) 171–97. I thank my assistant Eva Tobler for acquainting me with this text.

from the parable. The parable also gives expression to the possibility of being healed of all sin, a possibility offered to those who accept the clothing of hope and do not give way to despair.

This parable played an important role in the thinking of the Reformer Martin Luther, and his interpretation has been subjected to a detailed analysis.[65] In addition to various remarks made in one or another of his treatises, no fewer than ten of Luther's sermons were devoted to this parable. The traditional allegorical interpretation suited his theology of God's compassion so well that he took his time when he returned to it—which was not his usual practice—and oriented it in a polemical way against each and every Roman Catholic theology of works. Luther refused in particular to interpret v. 35b in terms of works of supererogation (i.e., works that go beyond what is required). The surplus is Christ. Moreover, he denied being opposed to good works, and the parable aided him in his denial. Deconstructing an ethic of works based on the righteousness of the Law, he spoke in favor of the practice of love rooted in the refuge found in Christ alone. In that connection he stressed the inn and the innkeeper.[66]

In his commentary on Luke 15:24 François Lambert, the Reformer of Hesse, explained that here allegory is useful but not indispensable, since we are dealing with an "example story" rather than a parable.[67] And Johannes Agricola, in his *Annotationes* on Luke (1525), made it clear that the notion of "neighbor" is a relational concept (*vocabulum reciprocum*).[68] For his part, Ulrich Zwingli stressed how much people prefer to follow their own interests rather than God's absolute requirements. But those who know God and subject themselves to self-examination know what they must do. Action is based on faith.[69] The Reformer Philipp Melanchthon defined the parable of the Samaritan as "an image of all of the Church's doctrine" into which fits love of neighbor.[70] Melanchthon's interest in questions of a philological (the verb $\sigma\pi\lambda\alpha\gamma\chi\nu\acute{\iota}\zeta o\mu\alpha\iota$, "to be moved with pity," v. 35) and historical (topographical indications) order was not just that of an erudite scholar but also that of a man who saw the history of salvation unfolding in a precise time and place. These concrete pieces of information throw a light on the events; this illumination is important.[71] John Calvin joined the two commandments of v. 27 to each other; thought that the "neighbor" is any person;

---

65   See Ebeling, *Evangelienauslegung,* 76–77, 169–70, 496–506; Monselewski, *Samariter,* 85–97, 194–95; Klemm, *Samariter,* 38–57 and passim. Monselewski (*Samariter,* 97), *pace* Ebeling, observes that Luther eventually weakened the christological accent of the parable. And Klemm, *pace* Ebeling, thinks that the fidelity of Luther to the tradition proceeds from two new exegetical connotations. On the pages that follow, I am indebted to all of these studies, esp. to that of Klemm.

66   For references to the numerous passages in Luther, see Monselewski, *Samariter,* 194–99. See also Christian Gustav Eberle, ed., *Luthers Evangelien-Auslegung: Ein Kommentar zu den vier Evangelien* (2d ed.; Stuttgart: Liesching, 1877) 738–49; as well as Erwin Mülhaupt, ed., *D. Martin Luthers Evangelien-Auslegung* (2d ed.; 5 vols.; Göttingen: Vandenhoeck & Ruprecht, 1954) 3:138–56.

67   François Lambert d'Avignon, *In divi Lucae Evangelium commentarii* (Strasbourg: Johann Herwagen l'ancien, 1524) 163; see also Klemm, *Samariter,* 57.

68   Johann Agricola of Eisleben, *In Evangelium Lucae annotations . . . , summa scripturarum fide tractatae* (Augsburg: S. Ruff, 1525) ad loc.; see also Klemm, *Samariter,* 57–58.

69   Ulrich Zwingli, *Annotationes in Evangelium Lucae* (Zurich, 1539); reprinted in Melchior Schüler and Ioannes Schulthess, eds., *Ulrich Zwingli Opera* 6.1.6 (Zurich: Schulthess, 1836) 628–31; see also Klemm, *Samariter,* 63–71.

70   Philipp Melanchthon, *Evangelien-Postille* (German ed., Nuremberg, 1549; Latin ed., Hanover, 1549), reprinted in Heinrich Ernest Bindseil, ed., *Philippi Melanthonis opera quae supersunt omnia: Libri Philippi Melanthonis in quibus enarravit Scripturam sacram, volumen XXV: Postillae Melanthonianae, partes III et IV atque appendix* (Corpus reformatorum 25; Braunschwieg: C. A. Schwetschke et filium, 1856) 388–89.

71   Ibid., 408; see also Klemm, *Samariter,* 79–113. Melanchthon's exegesis is found in his *Postillae,* 373–410, and in his *Annotationes* (*Annotationes in evangelia* [Wittemberg, 1544], reprinted in Karl Gottlieb Bretschneider, ed., *Philippi Melanthonis opera quae supersunt omnia: Libri Philippi Melanthonis in quibus enarravit Scripturam sacram, volumen XIV* (Corpus reformatorum 12; Halle: C. A. Schwetschke et filium, 1844) 355–58.

understood the expert in the Law to be an opinionated, proud, and hypocritical person; refused to see in the adjective "half-dead" an allusion to free will being a part of the half that was alive; and rejected the allegorical interpretation, with its identification of the Samaritan with Christ. Reformed interpretation followed him on this point.[72] As for the Catholic theologian Thomas de Vio, called Cajetan: he gave up on all polemical interpretation, which was unusual for his time, and preferred an anthropological explanation (*omnis homo est proximus*, "every person is a neighbor")[73] to a christological interpretation. The impact of the interpretation of the Jesuit Juan Maldonado was lasting (there were twenty editions of his commentary, which appeared for the first time in 1597, at the end of the sixteenth century, and during the seventeenth century). He did not attempt to skirt any difficulty, limited the contribution of the Church Fathers to what was necessary, and rejected the idea that one's neighbor is the one who spoils us or who needs us. In his opinion, Jesus wished to teach us that every human being, without restriction of race or country, is our neighbor.[74]

Just as the triumph of the historical-critical method coincided with a wave of moralism, the end of christological allegorization of the Samaritan[75] coincided with the emphasis on personal responsibility in the writings of Adolph Jülicher.[76]

Conclusion

Just as the parable of the prodigal son illustrates the love on the part of the Father who forgives, the parable of the Samaritan encourages believers to practice compassion. It thus explains the second commandment, the love of one's neighbor, which has just been quoted (v. 27), and serves as a counterpart to the following passage, the episode of Martha and Mary (vv. 38-42), which is a commentary on the first commandment, the commandment to love God.

A christological interpretation of the parable was often preferred during the course of the history of its interpretation, thus taking the interpretation in another direction. Ought we simply to reject the patristic and medieval equation that made of the Samaritan an image of Jesus Christ? I do not think so, since the parable draws on a model in picturing what the love of one's neighbor is like. For the Samaritan adopts the feelings of Christ himself and repeats Christ's acts. Was not Jesus—he too, he before all others—"moved with pity" in the face of human beings' suffering, solitude, and grief (cf. 7:13)? Did he not come as a physician to care for and save what was lost (cf. 5:31-32)? And behind Jesus' active compassion, there is the symmetrical and programmatic "good pleasure" (the εὐδοκία), the plan of salvation, the active goodness of God (cf. 10:21). Thus, although I maintain the ethical orientation of the passage, I do not underestimate either the christological element, containing an especially exemplary Christology, or the theological rooting in a theology of the plan of salvation.

I am anxious to point out that there is a neighbor at both ends of the communication of love: in the commandment (v. 27), the neighbor is the recipient, the object of compassion; in the parable (v. 36), the neighbor is the origin, the subject of compassion. This observation is not contradictory: it reminds us, on the one hand, that Christian ethics is relational and that when I take care of other people I tie myself to them just as they do to me. It also reminds us, on the other hand, that one's neighbor cannot be objectified in the figure of a certain needy person. The New Testament commentary on

---

72   Calvin, *Harmony*, 3:33–39.

73   Tommaso de Vio Cajetan, *Evangelia cum commentariis* (Paris, 1540) 127; see also Klemm, *Samariter*, 118–19.

74   Juan [de] Maldonado, *Commentarii in quatuor evangelistas*, vol. 2: *In Lucam* (Pont-à-Mousson: ex typographia Stephani Mercatoris, 1597; reprinted as vol. 3–4, Paris/Louvain: 1842–43) ad loc.; see also Klemm, *Samariter*, 158–63.

75   See, at the end of the eighteenth century, the remarks of Johann Georg Hamann, *Tagebuch eines Christen* (London, 1758), reprinted in idem, *Sämt-*

liche Werke: Historisch-kritische Ausgabe, vol. 1: Tagebuch eines Christen (ed. Josef Nadler; Vienna: Herder, 1949) 211–23. According to Hamann, the true neighbor is Jesus, our redeemer, who has become flesh of our flesh: "I am the one half-dead, who has no one else to thank for his life than the Good Sin-bearer" ("Ich bin der Halbtodte, der sein Leben keinen andern als dem barmherzigen Sündenträger zu verdanken hat" [ibid., 212]).

76   Adolf Jülicher, *Die Gleichnisreden Jesu*, vol. 2: *Auslegung der Gleichnisreden der drei ersten Evangelien* (Tübingen: Mohr Siebeck, 1899) 596–97.

the Hebrew Bible commandment encourages us not to "have" neighbors, but to "make ourselves close" to others, in particular those who are unfortunate. By becoming the neighbor of another person, we thereby fulfill the Law, therefore God's will, and adopt Christ's intention and attitude as our own. That is what it is like when it comes to the vitality of reaching out to others and to the realism of a way of acting of which we are capable, a way that proves that the fantasy that we can provide all the help that is needed is invalid.

As a positive figure the parable chose someone who was marginalized and disdained, a negative silhouette of contemporary Jewish society. The choice of a Samari-tan thus surprised self-righteous readers who would not have been expecting such a reaction from such a person. In that way they were led to reflect: they found out that they were less perfect than they thought, that they were more vulnerable; they asked themselves if they were not in need of being helped, if they did not need to change their attitude; they all of a sudden counted on being encouraged by Jesus, the considerate Samaritan; haughty neighbors who had become cared-for neighbors, they resolved that they too would "go" along that famous "road" of encounter and would "do likewise." That is, that they would make themselves be neighbors of the neighbors they would meet.

Martha and Mary (10:38-42)

Bibliography

Augsten, Monika, "Lukanische Miszelle," *NTS* 14 (1967–68) 581–83.

Baker, Aelred, "One Thing Necessary," *CBQ* 27 (1965) 127–37.

Bovon, "Mary Magdalene's Paschal Privilege," in idem, *Traditions*, 147–57.

Brooten, Bernadette J., *Women Leaders in the Ancient Synagogue: Inscriptional Evidence and Background Issues* (BJS 36; Chico, Calif.: Scholars Press, 1982).

Brutscheck, Jutta, *Die Maria–Marta Erzählung: Eine redaktionskritische Untersuchung zu Lk 10, 38-42* (BBB 64; Frankfurt am Main: Hanstein, 1986) 266–85 (bibliography).

Bultmann, Rudolf, "μεριμνάω, κτλ.," *TDNT* 4 (1967) 589–93.

Idem, *History*, 55–56, 60.

Cadbury, Henry J., "Luke's Interest in Lodging," *JBL* 45 (1926) 305–22.

Castel, François, "Luc 10, 38-42," *EThR* 55 (1980) 560–65.

Csányi, Daniel A., "Optima pars: Auslegungsgeschichte von Lk 10,38-42 bei den Kirchenvätern der ersten vier Jahrhunderte," *Studia monastica* 2 (1960) 5–78.

Dauer, Anton, *Johannes und Lukas: Untersuchungen zu den johanneisch-lukanischen Parallelperikopen Joh 4,46-54 / Lk 7,1-10 — Joh 12,1-8 / Lk 7,36-50; 10,38-42 — Joh 20,10-29 / Lk 24,36-49* (FB 50; Würzburg: Echter, 1984) 126–206.

Davidson, J. A., "Things to Be Understood and Things to Be Done," *ExpT* 94 (1982–83) 306–7.

Dibelius, *Tradition*, 118–20.

Dirks, Marianne, "Maria und Marta," *Katechetische Blätter* 105 (1980) 65–67.

Dupont, Jacques, "De quoi est-il besoin (Lc 10, 42)?," in idem, *Études*, 2:1049–54.

Eckart, Maître, "Martha and Mary: Second Discourse [10, 38]," *Parabola* (New York) 5 (1980) 69–73.

Fee, Gordon D., "One Thing Is Needful? Luke 10:42," in idem, *To What End Exegesis? Essays Textual, Exegetical, and Theological* (Grand Rapids: Eerdmans; Vancouver: Regent College Publishing, 2001) 3–42.

Föhn, F., "Ein exegetischer Essay zu Martha und Mirjam: Herrschaft hat u. hält (auch) die Schwestern getrennt," *Neue Wege* 83 (1989), nos. 7–8, pp. 208–14.

Foulkes, J. W. de, "Jesús y una mujer, estudio de una situación," *Pastoralia* 4 (1982) 16–27.

Fritsch-Oppermann, Sybille, "Maria und Marta: Eine Aufforderung zum geschwisterlichen Streit," *Diakonie* 15 (1989) 215–19.

George, Augustin, "L'accueil du Seigneur: Lc 10, 38-42," *AsSeign* n.s. 47 (1970) 75–85.

Hausherr, Irénée, "Utrum Sanctus Ephraem Mariam Marthae plus aequo anteposuerit?" *Orientalia christiana* [Rome] 30 (1933) 153–63.

Kemmer, A., "Maria und Martha: Zur Deutungsgeschichte von Lk 10, 38ff. im alten Mönchtum," *Erbe und Auftrag* 40 (1964) 355–67.

Knockaert, A., "Analyse structurale du texte biblique," *LV* 33 (1978) 331–40.

La Bonnardière, Anne-Marie, "Les deux vies, Marthe et Marie," in eadem, *Saint Augustin et la Bible* (Bible de tous les temps 3; Paris: Beauchesne, 1986) 411–25.

Eadem, "Marthe et Marie, figures de l'église d'après s. Augustin," *VSpir* 86 (1952) 404–27.

La Verdiere, E., "The One Thing Required," *Emmanuel* [New York] 89 (1983) 398–403.

Laland, E., "Die Martha–Maria Perikope Lukas 10, 38-42," *StTh* 13 (1959) 70–85.

Magass, Walter, "Maria und Martha—Kirche und Haus: Thesen zu einer institutionellen Konkurrenz (Lk 10, 38-42)," *LB* 27–28 (1973) 2–5.

Moessner, *Banquet*, 144–45.

Moltmann-Wendel, Elisabeth, *Ein eigener Mensch werden: Frauen um Jesus* (Gütersloh: Mohn, 1980) 23–55.

Prete, Benedetto, "Una sola cosa e necessaria (Lc 10,42)," in idem, *Storia*, 71–103.

Roosen, A., "Das einzig Notwendige: Erwägungen zu Lk 10, 38-42," *Studia Moralia* 17 (1979) 9–39.

Ruegg, Ulrich, "Marthe et Marie: Luc 10 38-42," *BCPE* 22 (1970) nos. 6–7, 19–56.

Ruether, Rosemary Radford, *Sexism and God-Talk: Toward a Feminist Theology* (Boston: Beacon; London: SCM, 1983) 67.

Schmithals, Walter, *Das Eine, das Not tut: Ein biblischer Vortrag zu Lukas 10, 38-42* (Erbauliche Reden 5; Neukirchen-Vluyn: Neukirchener Verlag, 1977).

Schüssler Fiorenza, Elisabeth, "A Feminist Critical Interpretation for Liberation: Martha and Mary. Luke 10, 38-42," *Religion and Intellectual Life* [New Rochelle, N.Y.] 3 (1986) 21–36.

Eadem, "Theological Criteria and Historical Reconstruction: Martha and Mary. Luke 10, 38-42," *Center for Hermeneutical Studies Protocol Series* [Berkeley, Calif.] 53 (1987) 1–12.

Solignac, Aimé, and Lin Donnat, "Marthe et Marie," *Dictionnaire de spiritualité ascétique et mystique, doctrine et histoire* (ed. Marcel Viller et al.; 17 vols.; Paris: Beauchesnes, 1937–95) 10:664–73.

Str-B 2:184–86.

Wall, Robert W., "Martha and Mary (Luke 10.38-42) in the Context of a Christian Deuteronomy," *JSNT* 35 (1989) 19–35.

38/ **Now as they were on their way, he entered a certain village, and a woman named Martha welcomed him into her home. 39/ She had a sister named Mary, who, sitting at the Lord's feet, listened to what he was saying. 40/ Martha was very busy serving him. Coming up to him she said, "Lord, do you not care that my sister has left me to do all the work of serving by myself? Tell her then to come and help me." 41/ The Lord answered her, saying, "Martha, Martha, you are worried and you are busy doing many things. 42/ Only one thing is necessary. For Mary has chosen the good part, which will not be taken away from her."[a]**

a   The text of vv. 41b–42a is uncertain, as the commentary will indicate.

Here two women come in contact with Jesus. With Christians in our day turning to Scripture to hear a voice favorable to the identity and situation of women, we could hardly remain deaf to the chord this text strikes. Nor could we remain deaf to the implications of this text for the current examination of the role of ministry, especially women's role in ministry. Does listening to the Word ("what he [Jesus] was saying," v. 39) not bring to mind the ministry of the Word, and does the verb "serve" (v. 40) not suggest table ministry and other tasks of service?

Unfortunately, in the short story we are about to examine, Luke's manner of telling the story is allusive and the text often remains ambiguous. The "journey" of Jesus and his disciples; Martha's "welcome," "service," and "worries"; Mary's "sitting at the Lord's feet," as well as her "listening to the Word" ("what he was saying")—all these definitely bring to mind certain existential questions of church life. Nevertheless, these elements of the text do not give direct answers to the questions we are asking. Moreover, the more we try to focus in on these suggestive lines of text, the fuzzier they become. Is Martha at fault? Is not Jesus ungrateful and unjust? What is it that is necessary: "few things" or "a single thing"? What is this

"thing"? In the last analysis, what does "the good part" denote? Commentators[1] thus face a formidable task, but when undertaking it they are doubly encouraged—both by valuable recent studies that have prepared the way for them and by the enthusiastic and articulate use of this pericope in the history of the church.

Analysis

What Luke recounts here in a compact fashion is an episode that is both real and ideal, concrete and serving as an example.[2] He starts off by mentioning an ordinary event with unforeseeable consequences: the act of receiving a guest into one's home, which provides the introduction of an outside element into a family situation (v. 38). The use here in the Greek of the aorist tense indicates the specificity of the first part of the story. This is followed by a second part that reflects the particular arrangements the two sisters made on this occasion. The use of the imperfect tense in this part of the story indicates a certain duration (vv. 39-40a). This presentation of the scene soon loses its equilibrium, however, as one of the characters in the story—rather than the author—speaks up and precipitates the following incident. The

---

1   Commentators both male and female. The first draft of these pages received a vehement and passionate reaction from my assistants Isabelle Chappuis-Juillard and Eva Tobler. Since they are women, they have permitted me to modify my interpretation. I was being too hard on Martha. Moreover, since the establishment of the text, which is especially difficult in vv. 41b-42, is inseparable

from its interpretation, I will not separate these two tasks in my exposition.

2   By the terms "real" and "concrete" I do not intend here to defend the historicity of this account. I am referring, rather, to the way that this story is narrated. Luke's skill in writing enables us to visualize the scene. For example, we can see the different attitudes of the two sisters.

episode thus reaches its peak, and at the same time its conclusion, when the Master replies to Martha's complaint (vv. 40b-42). In summary, we have:

1. Jesus, the guest, being welcomed (v. 38)

2. Mary and Martha's arrangements (vv. 39-40a)

3. Martha's complaint and Jesus' reply (vv. 40b-42)

Mary, the central character, has said nothing. The unfolding of the events, which corresponds here to the unfolding of the story line,[3] brings to the fore two different attitudes toward Christ's presence.

Luke is the only Gospel writer who recounts this episode. The analysis of the grammar and style of this passage, moreover, reveals how great the redactor's share was in the shaping of the story. Most of the expressions, such as $\dot{\epsilon}\nu$ $\delta\dot{\epsilon}$ $\tau\hat{\omega}$ ("Now as," v. 38) or $\gamma\upsilon\nu\dot{\eta}$ $\delta\dot{\epsilon}$ $\tau\iota\varsigma$ ("a [certain] woman," v. 38), and words such as "[being] on the way" (v. 38), "listened to" (v. 39), or "the word" ("what he was saying," v. 39), and certain phrases, such as those used in the descriptions of Mary (v. 39) and Martha (v. 40a), reflect the Gospel writer's literary habits.[4] It is most unlikely, however, that Luke himself invented this story. It must have been part of L and have already appeared alongside the story of the (good) Samaritan. The narrative quality of this episode corresponds, moreover, to the acknowledged literary elegance of L. On the one hand, Luke respected the traditional narrative structure of the event as well as the organization of the dialogue; on the other hand, however, he took great liberties in the description of the characters and their attitudes. Commentators are unfortunately not in possession of sufficient material to be able to reconstruct the original, pre-Lukan, shape of the account.[5] The style of this passage reminds us of the episode concerning Zacchaeus (19:1-10), which is also rooted in L. The passage's

theological concerns seem to bring it into proximity with such Pauline affirmations as those found in 1 Cor 7:32-35, where we also find a contrast (is it the same one?) between worrying and focusing on the Lord.[6]

The Gospel of John, which is also acquainted with the two sisters Martha and Mary (John 11:1, 3, 19), also localizes them in a village (John 11:1, 30) and even specifically refers to their home (John 11:20, 31; 12:3).[7] In that connection it talks about Jesus' going ($\pi\text{o}\rho\dot{\epsilon}\text{v}\text{o}\mu\alpha\iota$, John 11:11) to their house, entering the village (John 11:20, 30), conversing with Martha, who started the conversation (John 11:20-27), and Jesus' giving his attention to Mary, who had thrown herself at his feet (John 11:28-33). Further on, it confirms that the two women welcomed Jesus into their home, even going so far as to specify that during the meal Martha "served" ($\delta\iota\eta\kappa\acute{o}\nu\epsilon\iota$, John 12:2). Before that it had talked about Mary being seated ($\dot{\epsilon}\kappa\alpha\vartheta\acute{\epsilon}\zeta\epsilon\tau o$, John 11:20). In spite of these agreements, there are basic differences between the two accounts; in the Fourth Gospel, the attention is focused on the women's brother Lazarus, whose existence is unknown to Luke. Furthermore, in John, the conversations between Jesus and Martha and Mary have to do with Jesus' wonder-working and messianic powers. Later John—unlike Luke—identifies Mary with the woman who anointed Christ (John 11:2; 12:3-9; cf. Luke 7:36-50). For that reason, I would find it difficult to gather into one common tradition the stories found in Luke 10:38-42 and John 11:1-12; 12:1-3. I would also consider it hazardous to picture John reading the Gospel of Luke or Luke drawing on the Gospel of John. My conviction is rather that Luke and John, in line with a practice they sometimes followed, drew on recollections from a common source. They were both acquainted with the tradition according

---

3   Brutscheck (*Maria–Marta*, 30–49) has subdivided the episode a little differently: v. 38, the arrival and welcoming of Jesus; vv. 39-40, two different attitudes before the Lord; vv. 41-42, the Lord approves the attitude of Mary.

4   Ibid., 65–95.

5   Ibid., 133–52. On the relation between this episode and Luke's special source, see Petzke, *Sondergut*, 111–14.

6   Brutscheck, *Maria–Marta*, 145–47, 151, 152. Robert W. Wall believes that Luke 10:38-42 actualizes Deut 8:1-3, while Luke 10:25-28 takes up Deuteronomy 5–6, and Luke 10:29-37 does the same with Deu-

teronomy 7 ("Martha and Mary [Luke 10.38-42]," 19–35). According to Wall, Luke wants to correct a certain reading of Deuteronomy that neglects obedience to God's word. Can one really find such a reading of Deuteronomy? Moreover, could Luke have held such a narrow, controversial view of this biblical book?

7   The connections between our pericope and the Gospel of John (11:1–12:11) have often been investigated, most recently by Dauer, *Johannes and Lukas*, 126–206; and Brutscheck, *Maria–Marta*, 147–50, 251–54 (notes with bibliography, esp. n. 780).

to which there were the two sisters who met Jesus and who took risks by virtue of their commitment to him. These memories were passed on because these same persons, who became Christians after the Easter event, founded a community of believers that met in their village, in their home. It is within the realm of possibility that the name of the village was Bethany, the name used only by John, since the Fourth Gospel is fond of reproducing older pieces of information.[8]

On the redactional level as well as on the level of tradition, the story has both narrative and normative significance. Its having been transmitted owes more to a desire to pass on an opinion of Jesus than to a desire to keep the memory of the two sisters alive. The person of Jesus is what authorizes and even imposes the double reference, that is, to both the episode in the past and its prescriptive character in the present. By the same token, Rudolf Bultmann classes this story among the biographical apophthegms, and Martin Dibelius, among the legends. For his part, Robert C. Tannehill considers it to be "a pronouncement story"; and Jutta Brutscheck, among what she calls stories about Jesus with a normative character.[9] What counts, first, is not so much the label we give to the story as its narrative structure: it is a story told in a compact way in chronological order, with the mention of a limited cast of actors with opposing attitudes and the resolution of the crisis being provided by a decisive declaration by the Master. It is, second, the normative

character of the story that is certain not only to interest,[10] even distract, hearers or readers but also especially to encourage them to opt for a certain stance of faith. The narration, without sacrificing its reference to the past, is also pressed into service as a vehicle of theology (Martha and Mary as two kinds of Christians). It would be hard to say who the transmitters of this story were and what setting they gave it. The theological relationship with 1 Corinthians 7 would suggest a Christian setting among the Hellenists. The themes used—but a demonstration of that will have to wait until we provide a commentary on the passage—situate the story in the setting of Christian catechism, if it turns out that it has more to do with a stance of faith than with ministries.[11]

Commentary

■ **38** The first words of the passage recall Jesus' journey leading to his suffering and death in Jerusalem.[12] The plural "they" ($\alpha \vec{v} \tau o \acute{v} \varsigma$) suggests the communal aspect of this journey,[13] but the itinerant disciples, who are to be understood as being included in the "they," fade away into the shadows, leaving center stage to the local actors in the drama, namely, the two women, and especially the "he" ($\alpha \vec{v} \tau \acute{o} \varsigma$), referring to Jesus.[14]

As Jesus enters the village,[15] Martha welcomes him into her home.[16] It is hard to picture, in the Judaism of that day, a woman managing her own affairs, being the

---

8   See C. H. Dodd, *Historical Tradition in the Fourth Gospel* (Cambridge: Cambridge University Press, 1963) 1–18, 244.

9   Bultmann, *History*, 33, 56, 69; Dibelius, *Tradition*, 51, 104–32, 292–93; Robert C. Tannehill, "Varieties of Synoptic Pronouncement Stories," *Semeia* 20 (1981) 101–19; Brutscheck, *Maria–Marta*, 158–59.

10   See Richard I. Pervo, *Profit with Delight: The Literary Genre of the Acts of the Apostles* (Philadelphia: Fortress Press, 1987).

11   In 1 Cor 7:32-35, Paul employs theological and moral arguments that he has taken from the Hellenistic tradition. Here, it is probably not the thinking of Paul but rather that of the Hellenists that has influenced the pre-Lukan tradition. Laland ("Martha–Maria," 70–85) asks about the *Sitz im Leben*: it concerns instructions about receiving missionaries. The message of this pericope is that this receiving, this ministry, falls within the domain of women. Women have the duty to offer only what is

necessary and the right to hear the word of God. Csányi ("Optima pars," 6) reaches the same conclusion.

12   $\Pi o \rho \epsilon \acute{v} o \mu \alpha \iota$; cf. Luke 9:51, 52, 53, 56, 57; see also Brutscheck, *Maria–Marta*, 53.

13   See Bovon, *Theologian*, 183–84 n. 52.

14   On the christological flavor of the Lukan $\alpha \vec{v} \tau \acute{o} \varsigma$, see Joachim Jeremias, *Die Sprache des Lukasevangeliums: Redaktion und Tradition im Nicht-Markusstoff des dritten Evangeliums* (KEKSup; Göttingen: Vandenhoeck & Ruprecht, 1980) 37–38.

15   The mention of the "village" ($\kappa \acute{\omega} \mu \eta$) must be traditional, since John himself also knows the mention of such a village (John 11:1-30), and since Luke envisions the ministry of Jesus as going "from city to city" rather than "from village to village" (Luke 4:43).

16   Why does the text name only Martha as the owner of the house (note that I have retained here the words "into her house"; see n. 20 below)? In order

head of the household, and especially receiving a man in her home (*4 Macc.* 18:7 furnishes an example of the mother of seven martyrs who, before her marriage, did not receive a single visit from any man, even in the presence of her parents).[17] On the other hand, the liberty of Greek women was much less limited. Grounded in Jesus' openness, Christian preaching encouraged a freer spirit in this Hellenic environment. Luke pictures the situation of his time as having existed in Jesus' day: just as Lydia provided hospitality to Paul (Acts 16:15), Martha welcomed Jesus under her roof. Her house is meant to suggest a house church. Josephus[18] confirms that "welcome" (ὑποδέχομαι) implies hospitality[19] in the fullest sense, involving considerable generosity and following all the rules.[20] In complementarity to the theme of being on a journey, the mention of a stop along the way was not abstract. Welcoming itinerant missionaries was an ongoing concern of the early Christian community.[21]

■ **39** In a single sentence Luke paints the scene. Although related by blood to her sister Martha (v. 39a), Mary[22] is above all related to Jesus by choice and affection (v. 39b). Seated at the feet of the Master, she takes on the role of a disciple;[23] with her whole being, she listens to what is being said by Jesus,[24] who quotes and comments on God's word. The Gospel writer wishes us to conclude that Mary was both attentive to Jesus and devoted to him, and that she zeroed in on the essential. The picture he draws permits us to visualize the action and also prepares us for the expressions "only one thing is necessary" and "choosing the good part" (v. 42), which give us food for thought.

Judaism allowed and even required faith and religious obedience on the part of women. But did it permit them to study with the teachers of the law? This possibility, which is less unlikely than has been believed,[25] must, however, have been the exception rather than the rule. Jesus must have shocked his fellow Jews by the way he

---

to justify all the trouble that she goes to in showing hospitality? The name *Martha* signifies "she who rules," "mistress" in Aramaic (see Fitzmyer, 2:893). Föhn ("Essay," 208–14) understands our pericope as criticizing positions of domination, which are represented by Martha and her attitude.

17 See Ruegg, "Marthe et Marie," 22–23. In order to avoid this difficulty, several expositors have regarded Martha as a widow (so Zahn, 437 n. 15).

18 See Karl H. Rengstorf, ed., *A Complete Concordance to Flavius Josephus* (4 vols.; Leiden: Brill, 1973–83) 4:253. For examples, see Josephus *Bell.* 1.10.2 §180; 6.13.10 §321; 8.7.6 §201; etc.

19 Cf. Luke 19:6 (Zacchaeus receives Jesus); Acts 17:7 (Jason receiving Paul and his companions); Jas 2:25 (Rahab, a woman, though a prostitute, receiving the Hebrew scouts); 1 Macc 16:15 (receiving and feeding, but here with evil intent); Ignatius of Antioch *Smyrn.* 10.1 (two coworkers of Ignatius are received by the Smyrnaeans as "deacons of God"). In contrast, cf. the inhospitality of the Samaritans in Luke 9:52-53; so Bauer, s.v. ὑποδέχομαι. Magass refers to *m. ʾAbot* 1.4 in order to show that Jewish disciples had to receive their master teachers into their houses ("Maria und Martha," 2).

20 Some text-critical problems are encountered in v. 38. Apparently several scribes were disturbed by the awkward proximity of αὐτός and αὐτούς and above all by the reading "into her house," which to them appeared improper. Against both Nestle-Aland and Bruce M. Metzger, *A Textual Commen-*

tary on the Greek New Testament (2d ed., Stuttgart: Deutsche Bibelgesellschaft/United Bible Societies, 1994) 129, I regard the reading "into her house" (εἰς τὴν οἰκίαν αὐτῆς or εἰς τὸν ὄικον αὐτῆς) as being part of the primitive text.

21 On the rules of hospitality with regard to Christian missionaries, see Henry J. Cadbury, "Luke's Interest in Lodging," 305–22; Laland, "Martha–Maria," 77–82; Csányi, "Optima pars," 6; Bovon, *Theologian*, 457 n. 118; and Brutscheck, *Maria–Marta*, 101–2, 228 (esp. n. 555).

22 On the proper name *Mary*, see Bovon, "Paschal Privilege," 147, 228–29 n. 1.

23 Cf. 2 Kgs (LXX 4 Kgdms) 4:38; 6:1 (the disciples of the prophet Elisha sit "before you"); Luke 8:25 (the demoniac cured); and Acts 22:3 (Saul at the feet of Gamaliel). See Brutscheck, *Maria–Marta*, 124–26; Josef Ernst, *Das Evangelium nach Lukas: Übersetz und erklärt* (RNT 3; Regensburg: Pustet, 1977) 355; and Charles L'Eplattenier, *Lecture de l'Évangile de Luc* (Paris: Desclée, 1982) 135–36.

24 "His word"; cf. Luke 4:32; 20:20; Acts 2:41. Listening to the word of God is a theme very dear to Luke: see 5:1; 6:47; 7:29; 8:14, 21; 10:16; 11:28; 14:35; Acts 2:22; 4:4; 10:22; 13:7, 44; 15:7; 19:10; 28:28; see also the excursus "The Word of God" in the commentary on 5:1-11 (1:168).

25 See Brooten, *Women Leaders*, 28, 32, 86, 145, 149–50.

welcomed women into the inner circle of his disciples.[26] In both the Gospel and Acts, Luke notes the presence of female believers. Here he seems to go further, by suggesting that Mary set about studying, without explicitly saying that she did so with a view to carrying on a ministry. But we will have to return to that question after having discussed Martha's "serving" (v. 40).[27]

■ **40** After the harmonious and symmetrical presentation of Martha's welcome and Mary's listening, there comes a potentially critical description that foreshadows Jesus' pronouncement (v. 41). The first element is Martha's hyper-busyness. $Περισπάομαι$ is a very rare verb meaning "be pulled (in all directions at once)," "be absorbed," "be quite busy," "be distracted."[28] It thus has the complementary meanings of withdrawing oneself from one reality and being absorbed by one or more other realities. It usually has a touch of the pejorative associated with it, as in the *Shepherd*, when Hermas criticizes persons worried about their own riches.[29] In Luke's eyes, then, Martha is absorbed by many tasks. Depending on one's sensitivities, one may see a criticism in the mention of her numerous jobs. In that case we would have a scene in which two attitudes are contrasted, one good, the other bad. According to those who subscribe to that view of Martha, she was subject to criticism by letting herself be consumed by her numerous domestic responsibilities. That would, in my view, be forgetting the fact that she is pictured as the mistress of the house (cf. "into her home," v. 38). Her attitude was understandable, all the more because she knew how to entertain an impor-

tant guest. In this latter perspective, we have two contrasting attitudes, the second of which is better than the first. If there is a pejorative shade to $περισπάομαι$, it is to be seen in the perception that this surfeit of activities, understandable but disproportionate, kept Martha from experiencing what was most important at the moment. Furthermore, although this attitude was tied to legitimate concerns, it was nevertheless also related to worries that were misplaced.

The second feature of this scene is $πολλήν$ ("numerous," translated by "many"),[30] which Jesus contrasted with "unique" ($ἑνός$, translated by "only one"). Martha did too much, with the result that her "service" ($διακονία$), which could and should have been positive, was thereby affected negatively. Whatever criticism of Martha there might have been was not directed at either her hospitality or her desire to serve but rather at her excess activity and the worries that occasioned it. At least at the redactional level, there is no opposition in the text between the two ministries of serving food and preaching/teaching. The opposition is to be found instead between two spiritual attitudes.

Martha, who thought of her work as a "service" ($διακονεῖν$), felt left alone ($μόνην$), abandoned by her sister. So she came out of her isolation, came up ($ἐπιστᾶσα$; cf. 2:38), not to engage Mary in conversation but to lodge a complaint about her with the Master. Fatigued and feeling abandoned, Martha laid into Jesus, taking him to task for his indifference ("don't you care . . ."),[31] and into Mary ("that my sister has left me . . .

---

26 See the commentary on 8:1-3 (1:299–302).

27 Regarding v. 39, $ὅδε$ (here $τῇδε$) became rare in Hellenistic Greek (see Marshall, 452). The Semitic expression $τῇδε ἦν ἀδελφή$ (cf. Luke 1:5) either betrays the author's origin or reveals his intention to give a biblical sound to his story. $Παρακαθεσθεῖσα$, a first aorist passive participle from $παρακαθέζομαι$, must be understood here in a reflexive sense on account of $πρός$ with the accusative ("toward"): "having seated herself," "having taken her place" (the variant $παρακαθίσασα$, an aorist participle from $παρακαθίζω$, has practically the same meaning). The same usage occurs in Josephus *Ant.* 6.11.9 §235, and in *Mart. Pol.* 8.2.

28 The simple verb $σπάω$ signifies "to draw," "to pull," "to uproot," "to extirpate." Luke is fond of compound verbs and utilizes them often, as here, with an object modified by the same preposition

serving as a prefix. On $περισπάω$, see Moulton and Milligan, *Vocabulary*, s.v.; BDAG, s.v.; Brutscheck, *Maria–Marta*, 80–81, 211 (with notes); Édouard Delebecque, *Évangile de Luc: Texte traduit et annoté* (Collection d'études anciennes; Paris: Belles Lettres, 1976) 68–69, who stresses the expressive value of this verb and refers to Polybius 3.105.1 and Epictetus *Diss.* 1.8.5.

29 *Hermas* 51.5 (*Sim.* 2.5); cf. ibid. 53.5 (*Sim.* 4.5) (the rich are too distracted with their business).

30 Is this usage of $πολύς$ unusual? $Πολύς$ and $πολύ$ can signify that which is excessive.

31 Mark 4:38 uses this same expression. In the parallel text, Luke 8:24, Luke does not make use of it. See the commentary on 8:22-25 (1:317–21), which alludes to the mutiny of the believers at the apparent indifference of God.

by myself"). Martha made a pitiful sight and called for help.[32] Jesus' retort was more a diagnosis than a criticism. At first look, this retort appears severe, but it was aimed at redirecting Martha to what was essential, to that part that was singular and had priority, the part that Mary had chosen all on her own.

■ **41** It is "the Lord," rather than "Jesus," who answers Martha. His answer, aimed at her on the narrative level,[33] strikes at every reader on the normative level. The "Lord" did not pick up on the language of service, thus situating the exchange elsewhere than in the context of ministry. All of his thinking concerned Martha's worries and unrest. She had been complaining about Jesus' unwillingness to get involved. He invited her to reflect, doing so in an affectionate way, as is indicated by the doubling of the vocative: "Martha, Martha, you are worried and you are busy. . . ." Μεριμνάω ("to worry") is a verb with considerable implications.[34] "Worry" (μέριμνα) pertains to someone or something, looks on the future with anguish, either blocking or precipitating action. A theological meaning was added to this secular one, discreetly in the Septuagint, then more openly in the Gospels:[35] insofar as worries are oppressing, they are certainly not miraculously eliminated by faith, but can be entrusted to God.[36] Human beings must not be worried about achieving self-realization through their works, since God gives them a reason for being by virtue of his love. Once those kinds of worries are overcome, one can be harmoniously occupied with cares of a positive nature.[37] That is because the believer will have given priority to the one thing that is necessary. But we should be on the alert, since the wrong kind of cares or worries can, like demons, make their reappearance.

Martha's many worries brought on an excess of activity (the Greek word θορυβάζω,[38] which is less common than θορυβέω, means, in the active voice, "cause trouble"; the first meaning of θόρυβος is "noise"; but then it also means "commotion," for instance of a crowd).

In short, this passage speaks with precision about a danger in the Christian life: the things one worries about when one isolates oneself from Christ and the Christian community, as well as the thousand and one activities one gets involved in, in an effort to overcome these worries. What constitutes the contrast is the opposition between these worldly worries and faith.[39] The danger is all the greater in that these material concerns come to the mind of the believer as a form of service.

■ **42** The "good part"[40] that Mary chose reminds us of the "good soil" in the parable of the Sower (8:8). It would be tempting to pursue the comparison and estab-

---

32 The verb is not particularly "biblical" since it is attested throughout the Hellenistic world. In the LXX, see Exod 18:22 (the judges will help Moses); Ps 89:21 (LXX 88:22, the hand of God will help the Psalmist); Rom 8:26 (the Holy Spirit comes to the aid of our weakness). See also Moulton and Milligan, *Vocabulary*, s.v.

33 On the doubling of a person's name when questioning him or her, common in Judaism, see Luke 6:46; Acts 9:4; *MHG Shem.* 13.9; and Grundmann, 227. See also the commentary on 6:46 (1:253–54 n. 57).

34 See the remarkable pages of Rudolf Bultmann, "μεριμνάω, κτλ.," *TDNT* 4 (1967) 589–93; see also Moulton and Milligan, *Vocabulary*, s.v.; and Roosen, "Das einzig Notwendige," 14–19.

35 See Ps 55:22 (LXX 54:23): ἐπίρριψον ἐπὶ κύριον τὴν μέριμνάν σου ("Cast your worries upon the Lord"). Walter Schmithals interprets our text as here speaking of God, who, in his grace, supports us (*Das Eine, das Not tut*).

36 See 1 Pet 5:7, which must be referring to Ps 55:22 (LXX 54:23).

37 See 1 Cor 12:25: ἀλλὰ τὸ αὐτὸ ὑπὲρ ἀλλήλων μερινῶσιν τὰ μέλη ("but that the members might have the same concern for each other"). See also 2 Cor 11:28.

38 A *hapax legomenon* in the NT, θορυβάζω is not well attested either in the LXX or in Josephus. Some manuscripts read τυρβάζω, a more common verb meaning "to trouble," and in the middle and passive voice "to be agitated intensely" (see BDAG, s.v.).

39 See again the parallel in 1 Cor 7:32-35 mentioned in n. 11 above.

40 Μερίς indicates the "part" of a whole into which something is divided, e.g., a "district" (Acts 16:12). For a "part" or "portion" in the narrower sense of Luke 10:42, see Acts 8:21 ("Peter says to Simon the Magician, 'There is for you neither a part nor an inheritance in what has happened here, for your heart is not right before God'"). See also 2 Cor 6:15; Col 1:12. In the LXX, see Deut 12:12 and in the Apostolic Fathers, *1 Clem.* 29.2; 35.8. I understand the adjective ἀγαθήν not in a superlative sense ("the best") but in an absolute sense: Everything that God gives and does is good. See further Bovon, *Traditions*, 48–49.

lish a parallel between Martha's activity and one of the other grounds of the parable, for example, the field covered with thorns, which is then commented on in the following way: "As for what fell among the thorns, these are the ones who hear; but as they go on their way, they are choked by the cares and riches and pleasures of life, and their fruit does not mature" (8:14). It is not said at first that Martha's cares or worries were of the same order as those in that parable. Martha was concerned with the Lord's welfare and not with her own riches or pleasures of life. The next thing we need to remember is that it is not certain that Martha was a Christian who was adrift, which was the case of the Christians in mind in the parable. Martha was instead a well-intentioned woman, threatened by her good intentions and her multiplicity of activities, who was in danger of becoming ungrateful toward the one whom she meant to revere, and unjust toward her sister.

We need to get back to Mary. What she was and what she did matched what Jesus wanted and got his approval. In this passage Jesus is called "the Lord" and the story is not only narrative but also normative. It both recounts and proclaims. It says what is and what should be. And what should be is of an order that is both doctrinal and ethical; its exacting normativeness grows out of the proclaimed good news.

The reader, who is located at the crossroads, is called upon to make a choice. The verb "to choose" (ἐκλέγο-μαι)[41] expresses freedom, while the phrase "which will not be taken away from her" signifies the stakes that are involved. A certain anthropological optimism serves as a backdrop to Jesus' observations and implicit imperatives; that same optimism can be found also in the context of the covenant, in Deuteronomy, which issues an invitation to "choose" life, as well as in the *Didache*, where the doctrine of the two ways is developed (see Deut 30:15-20; *Didache* 1–6).

The "part" chosen by Mary was, in that particular situation, being in the presence of the Lord and in a position to listen to what he said. But the Greek term μερίς also suggests the idea of eschatological retribution, expressed in terms of the dividing up of the land, such as it was practiced during the settlement in Canaan. It also recalls the part that God himself represents for those who, like the Levites, do not receive their share in the form of land.[42] It is termed "good," since it corresponds to God's will and derives its nature from him. It will not be taken away from her, that is to say, God, as the eschatological judge, will not insist on having it given back, as he would have a right to do in the case of the wicked. The motif of the last judgment suddenly appears at the end of the passage, as is often the case.

We still have to explain the beginning of the verse and, even before that, to determine the exact wording of the text. The numerous textual variants in the passage have been inventoried and set out in some excellent studies.[43] They can be boiled down to four principal variants: what Jesus said was indispensable, in opposition to Martha's hustle and bustle, was either

- "(only) a few things"
- "(only) one (thing)"
- "few things, or (only) one (thing)"
- or omission of the words about what was necessary as well as those about Martha's noisy concerns.

In the first case, the reading "a few things"[44] encourages Christians to be content with having little here on earth. This being content with having little may be understood either from an ethical point of view (faith takes away excessive preoccupation that I have with

---

41   On ἐκλέγομαι, see the commentary on 6:13 (1:209). There in 6:13, it is Jesus who chooses his disciples; here it is Mary who chooses the good part.

42   Particularly interesting is Ps 73(LXX 72):26, 28: "The God of my heart and my part [μερίς] is God forever. . . . As for me, it is good [ἀγαθόν] to cleave to God, to place my hope in the Lord." Cf. Num 18:20; Deut 10:9; 12:12; 14:27; Josh 18:7; Pss 16(LXX 15):5; 119(LXX 118):57; 142:5 (LXX 141:6); Jer 10:16. See also Brutscheck, *Maria–Marta*, 93, 128–30; 244–46 nn. On the eschatological "part," see Col 1:12; Eph 1:18; Acts 20:32.

43   See Baker, "One Thing Necessary," 127–37; Dupont, *Études*, 2:1049–54 (he opts for the shorter text with ἑνός); Augsten, "Lukanische Miszelle," 581–83 (she retains the shorter text with ὀλίγων); and Csányi, "Optima pars," 6 (he chooses "few things or only one thing is necessary" as the reading).

44   Cf. Sir 11:10: "My child, do not busy yourself with many matters; if you multiply activities, you will not be held blameless" (*NRSV*).

myself) or from an ascetical point of view (I must practice self-denial).

In the second case, the only thing that counts is the practice of one's faith. Caring about the Lord, expressed as fixing one's attention on what is important, puts the cares of this world into their proper perspective and transforms them into expressions of love. This is what it means to talk about the "one thing" that is necessary.[45]

The third textual variant appears to be an awkward conflation, for the "few things" suggests the idea of material possessions, while the "(only) one (thing)" refers to spiritual commitment to God.

The omission of the disputed words, which is the fourth textual variant, may be explained as either an accident or the scruples of scribes refusing to transmit what they did not understand.

So the choice narrows down to one of the first two variants. I do not think that Jesus meant to tell Martha to limit her needs and Jesus' needs to a few things. He was anxious to declare Mary's attitude to be in line with the only thing that counted. To Martha, who isolated herself ("by myself," $\mu \acute{o} \nu \eta \nu$, v. 40) by wanting to do too much ("very busy," $\pi o \lambda \lambda \acute{\eta} \nu$, v. 40), Jesus gave a warning ("doing many things," $\pi \epsilon \rho \grave{i} \ \pi o \lambda \lambda \acute{\alpha}$, v. 41) and told her to take as an example Mary, the one who, by choosing the good part, recognized what was the only thing ("only one thing," $\acute{\epsilon} \nu \acute{o} \varsigma$) that was indispensable. The transformation of "only one thing" into "few things" in the course of the

transmission of the textual tradition may be explained as a misunderstanding. Some scribes believed that Jesus was still talking about Martha's preparations.

It is my opinion that at the redactional level[46] the text is concerned with attentive faith as opposed to human preoccupations. We should not, however, underestimate either the double mention of service in v. 40,[47] or the parallel that we find in Acts 6:2-4. At a pre-Lukan level, the story was told in order to clarify a problem concerning ministries. At that level, it joined two of the community's services by making the proclamation of the word the presupposition of all charitable service.[48]

At the redactional level, Luke did not distinguish between a Mary who preached and a Martha who served, but rather between a Mary who listened and a Martha who wore herself out extending hospitality. In that way, through the image of Mary, he granted a place to women in the community that few ancient religions did, and, through the image of Martha, he declared that serving people at table is not always appropriate. This service is, to be sure, welcome in principle, even indispensable, as witnessed by the help furnished by Peter's mother-in-law (4:39) or by those women who accompanied Jesus (8:1-3). Nevertheless, this ministry must not be separated from faith. It would be without moorings if it no longer drew its nourishment from the word of the Lord but instead from an independent sense of duty or from an individual concern to do good. While Luke did not

---

45 Cf. Ps 27(LXX 26):4: "I have asked one thing from the Lord, and I hold firmly to it: to dwell in the house of the Lord all the days of my life, to gaze on the beauty of the Lord and to take care of his temple" (translation from the Hebrew). Cited by Baker, "One Thing Necessary," 136 n. 90; cf. also Ps 73(LXX 72):26, 28 (cited above in n. 42). According to Roosen ("Das einzig Notwendige," 31–35), the only necessary thing is to love God, not only in words but also in the person of Jesus. It is not wrong to see in our pericope an illustration of the love of God, as in the pericope of the Good Samaritan, an example of the love of neighbor (Luke 10:29-37), the two commandments cited by the scribe (10:25-28). See also Plummer, 290; Grundmann, 225; Marshall, 450, and Wiefel, 212.

46 The Tübingen School, and after it Loisy (p. 310) with some hesitation (he refers to Ezek 23:2-4), saw in Martha the Jewish Christianity of Peter and in Mary the Gentile Christianity of Paul. Against this

view, see Godet, 2:46; and Lagrange, 316. Origen had already advanced this interpretation among others; see n. 55 below.

47 On this vocabulary, see Moessner, *Banquet*, 144: "To the extent that preparations for a meal stifle the life-giving words of Jesus, to the same degree the meal itself can no longer manifest the saving revelation of this life-giving presence."

48 On the literary connections with Acts 6:1-6, see Dupont, *Études*, 2:1051. On the question of ministries, see Ruegg, "Marthe et Marie," 23–26, who believes that at some level of the tradition the account was describing the two sisters in the act of exercising two distinct ministries. In fact, in the Essene literature, the word "part" (v. 42) can designate a responsibility entrusted to someone (CD 1.6; 20.10, 13; 1QH 6.8; 10.28; 14.19; 1QS 4.16, 24; 1QM 10.15; 12.12; 19.4). See Schüssler Fiorenza, "Criteria," 7–8.

seem to be interested in making Mary into a proclaimer of the gospel—in other words, resolving the problem of women in ministry[49]—tradition, on the other hand, was concerned with that problem. Seated at the Master's feet, Mary did count on getting up on her feet. Once trained, was she not going to share her knowledge of the good news with others? Did her "part" not also involve assuming responsibilities, a ministry of the word, just as Martha felt herself to be charged with a ministry of service? It seems certain to me that some of the stakes relative to the ministries of women are in the background of this pericope and that they were clarified at a certain stage of the tradition. As for Luke, without wanting to, his desire to generalize the problem confused the issue somewhat. For what interested him was not finding an answer to the question of ministry but rather giving a reminder of the priority of the word of God and listening to it. In his eyes, only faith could enable us to understand that before engaging in service we must accept being served by Christ. There would be an even great danger in taking the initiative in performing divine service before having welcomed Christ and his word. Luke has perhaps extended prophetic criticism of a religion in which exterior activity would count as being most important. No, the concern to serve, even if it were to serve God himself, can only come in second place. Women and men must

first of all understand that the Lord pays attention to them, that he came to serve (22:27) and not to be served (Mark 10:45). Overwhelmed by her own worries, Martha forgot that the Lord cared for her.[50] She learned from Jesus that she could henceforth unload all her worries on him and on God (1 Pet 5:7).[51]

History of Interpretation

Since Christians have never stopped being interested in Martha and Mary, there are many interpretations dating from the patristic, medieval, and modern periods, and a large number of studies of the passage have also been made.[52] I will focus only on a few significant landmarks in the history of the interpretation of this story.

The first of these is the Alexandrian scholar and commentator Origen.[53] In his *Homiliae in evangelium secundum Lucam*[54] Origen recorded three distinct interpretations of the episode,[55] but provided a special development of one of them, one that was to have a large and lasting success. He compared the episode—and he was the first to do so explicitly—to the distinction between action ($\pi\rho\tilde{\alpha}\xi\iota\varsigma$) and contemplation ($\vartheta\epsilon\omega\rho\acute{\iota}\alpha$), a distinction that he got not from the Bible but from Hellenic culture. Whereas Plotinus accorded unilateral value to contemplation, Origen did not look down on action. He maintained that

49 Several authors stress that this account raises the question of women's rights: the right, like men, to hear the word of God; responsibilities in the deaconate that are entrusted to women, particularly that of showing hospitality; and eventually training for ministerial office. See Ruegg, "Marthe et Marie," 23–30; Moltmann-Wendel, *Frauen*, 23–55 (the Johannine image of Martha is to be preferred over that of Luke); Föhn, "Essay," 208–14 (cf. n. 16 above); Schüssler Fiorenza, "Criteria," 1–12 (placing Jesus at the center of the story keeps the text androcentric); Rosemary Radford Ruether, *Sexism and God-Talk: Toward a Feminist Theology* (Boston: Beacon; London: SCM, 1983) 67 (thanks to Jesus, women are qualified like men to become disciples); Wiefel, 212.

50 Castel, "Luc 10, 38-42," 560–65. Jesus challenges Martha more than he judges her.

51 The two sisters appear also in *Ep. apost.* 9–11 as witnesses of the resurrection and in the *Acts Phil.* 8.2 (94); see Ruegg, "Marthe et Marie," 24–25, 30–31; Bovon, "Paschal Privilege," 147–57.

52 I should mention here particularly the work of Csányi, "Optima pars," 5–78, which covers the patristic period; the article by Solignac and Donnat, "Marthe et Marie," 664–73 (especially helpful for the Middle Ages in the West and the Catholic tradition), and the chapter on Martha by Moltmann-Wendel in eadem, *Frauen*, 23–55.

53 Previously, Clement of Alexandria (*Quis div.* 10) interpreted that, like the rich young man, Martha must also lay aside the law and join Mary at the feet of the Lord. This typology of synagogue–church can be found also in Origen.

54 Origen *Hom. in Luc.* frg. 72 (= Rauer 171; *Origenes Werke*, 9:298 GCS); cf. Origen, *Hom. in Luc.*, pp. 520–23.

55 Origen's second interpretation takes up that of Clement of Alexandria (see n. 53 above), while his third, closely related to it, sees the two women as symbolizing Jewish Christianity and Gentile Christianity.

the two realities are compatible and both indispensable. Drawing on another terminology that did not exactly match up with the pair activity–contemplation, Origen continued with the statement that Martha welcomed the Word of God in her soul in a more bodily way (σωμα-τικώτερον), while Mary received him in a spiritual way (πνευματικῶς). Martha, therefore, corresponds to beginning Christians and Mary, to advanced Christians. If, on the one hand, the former should not look down on contemplation, the latter should not forget to practice the virtues: such is, it would seem, the conclusion that Origen came to in this brief explanation.[56]

Origen's interpretation seems to have gained favor among monastic theologians, all the way from Basil of Caesarea to John Cassian by way of Evagrius Ponticus.[57] These monks considered themselves to be justified in their renunciation of the restless world and their choice of a contemplative life. They were also concerned about the problem of the minimum diet, but it was especially the Messalians who took love of contemplation and scorn of manual labor to the extreme. In their eyes, Mary had received a "great charisma," she was "perfect," while Martha was only "righteous," since she had only received a "minor charisma" (John Chrysostom *Hom. in Joh.* 44.1 [*PG* 59:248–49]). For them Mary was the model of the mystical life.

John Chrysostom probably attacked these same Messalians and insisted on a more literal meaning. In his opinion, Jesus did not criticize Martha for her activity, but for her incapacity to take advantage of the opportunity to listen to the Word of God.[58] Curiously enough, we find the same attachment to the literal meaning in the writings of an Alexandrian, Cyril, who was, moreover, one of Chrysostom's adversaries. For Cyril focused his homily on the links between Christian hospitality and listening to the Word of God (*Hom. in Luc.* 69).[59]

Augustine marks an important step.[60] Although he held to the historicity of the characters in the story, he nevertheless favored the spiritual meaning. His thought was directed to the two lives in God, beyond the iniquitous life in sin. Those two lives are symbolized by Leah and Rachel, Martha and Mary, and Peter and John. One of those lives represents the life of the church in the present time; the other, its life in the age to come. In Augustine's eyes, the two sisters mentioned in the Gospel were acceptable to the Lord, and Jesus did not reprimand Martha for her activity. His interpretation was more ecclesial than anthropological. Martha's ministry was marked by the necessity of the works of compassion that the Lord was willing to carry out through her hands. This ministry will come to an end, whereas the part chosen by Mary will last forever: (a) Martha's numerous tasks distract and distend (*distendere*); (b) Mary's sole concern, in this time, extends and tightens up (*extendere*); (c) she will gather and reap (*colligere*) in the age to come. Contemplation, like Mary's (*extendere*), although it will be perfect in the future (*colligere*), is then, nevertheless, already incipient in the life here below. *Distentio* and *extensio*, Martha and Mary, the two lives, often cohabit in the same person. Although Augustine himself was drawn to the one thing that is necessary, namely, contemplation and retreat far from the world, he nevertheless agreed to become a bishop and to take on numerous tasks. In his own body he lived out the tension between dispersion and concentration, between Martha and Mary, the present time and eternity.

One of the medieval commentators I would like to call attention to is Albert the Great (Albertus Magnus) and his mariological interpretation.[61] He was not, moreover, unacquainted with the distinction between the active life (*vita activa*) and the contemplative life (*vita contemplativa*). Jesus' entry into the house was interpreted as an allegory of the incarnation. The Virgin Mary brought together in her person the best of Martha and Mary (did Albert see some resemblances among these three persons or did he consider the two women who talked with

56   See Csányi, "Optima pars," 10–27.

57   Basil of Caesarea *Regulae fusius tractate*, interrogatio 20 (*PG* 31:974); Evagrius of Pontus *Rerum monachalium rationes* 3 (*PG* 40:1254, authenticity uncertain); John Cassian *Collationes* 1.8; 23.3 (CSEL 13:14–16, 642); see further Csányi, "Optima pars," 28–29, 34–47, 59–64.

58   John Chrysostom, *Hom. Joh.*, 44.1 (*PG* 59:248–49).

59   Payne Smith, *Cyril*, 1:317–20.

60   See Anne-Marie La Bonnardière, "Les deux vies, Marthe et Marie," 411–25, from which I drew inspiration. The principal passages are *Quaest. ev.* 2.20 (CCSL 44b:64); *Sermo* 103 (*PL* 38:613–16; Eng. "Sermon LIII" in *NPNF*[2] 6:427–29); *Sermo* 104 (= *Sermo Guelferbytanus* 29, *PL* 38:616–18; Eng. "Sermon LIV" in *NPNF*[2] 6:429–30).

61   Albertus Magnus, *Enarr. in Luc.* (ed. Borgnet, pp. 71–91).

Jesus to be types of the Virgin?). The link made between this passage and the Virgin was carried so far that the biblical text was to end up serving as the lectionary reading from the Gospel for the feast of the Assumption on August 15.[62] The Mary who was Jesus' friend was so close to Jesus that the Mary who was Jesus' mother must have been taken up to heaven to be with her son. Luther was to protest against making this connection.[63]

What is impressive is the defense that Meister Eckhart made of Martha.[64] Was he influenced in this by his functions as preacher and spiritual counselor in convents for women? According to his interpretation, the Lord loved Martha, as evidenced by his repetition of her name in v. 41. Far from reproaching her for her worries, he congratulated her on the trouble she took. As for Martha's calling for help, that was the expression of a love for others, of a legitimate concern and not of a jealous bitterness. Meister Eckhart recommended to us the two women he called "the beloved Martha" (*die liebe Martha*) and "the beloved Mary" (*die liebe Maria*). They both followed Jesus; Mary was given instruction; Martha was sent out to give instruction and to serve.

It is unfortunate that the Reformation was omitted from the article on Martha and Mary in the French *Dictionnaire de Spiritualité*,[65] as if there were no Protestant spirituality. The Reformation took the following positions: through Luther's voice,[66] it refused to identify Mary with the monastic ideal, stressed listening to the Word as the "one thing [that] is necessary," and disparaged Martha's activity as an effort to be justified by works. Through Calvin's voice,[67] it rehabilitated work and made the secular world into the place where Christians should become involved. Calvin did, however, have three quarrels with Martha: her overdoing her hospitality, her neglecting to profit from Christ's coming to her house, and her contempt for learning.

It would seem as if in the nineteenth century, with the development of charitable organizations, the person of Martha underwent a rehabilitation. In any case, Martha was a popular first name in that century.

Conclusion

Jesus was not anxious to punish Martha. What he said to her certainly reflected his own analysis of what was going on, but it also mirrored the reality of the actions of the mistress of the house. He detected a legitimate, but worried, concern behind Martha's understandable hustle and bustle. Martha's restlessness was due to her having isolated herself; she felt abandoned by her sister and misunderstood by Jesus. Jesus did not doubt for a moment that she wished to serve or that domestic tasks were necessary. All he did was propose a doctrinal hierarchy of values and actions. Priority should be given to listening to the word of God, to taking time out, to the act of sitting down; it consists in not wishing to precede the Lord, in accepting to be served before serving. That is the only thing that is necessary, which corresponds to each person's need; that is the good part, which corresponds to everyone's desire. The silent and immobile Mary incarnates and symbolizes this attention and this faith, which take priority. Here, as everywhere else in the Gospel, anthropology and ethics are secondary, but Christology is primary.

As a man, I first believed that Mary was the opposite of Martha and that seeking the reign of God excluded carrying on any other activity—as if the text were dualistic and set the good of faith against the evil of works, cares, and needs! As if Jesus were punishing Martha! Some wise women who were my teaching assistants made me reflect more on the story and led me to understand, first of all, that Martha's worries were not the worries of the world attacked by the apostle Paul (1 Cor 7:32-35) and the allegorical interpretation of the parable of

---

62 How far back does this usage go?

63 Luther's sermon on August 15, 1523 (Mülhaupt, *Luthers Evangelien-Auslegung*, 3:161).

64 Meister Eckhart, *Predigt* 86: "Intravit Jesus in Quoddam Castellum etc. (Lc 10, 38-42)" (in Josef Quint, ed. and trans., *Meister Eckhart: Die deutschen und lateinischen Werke: Die deutschen Werke*, vols. 1–3 [Stuttgart: Kohlhammer, 1958–76] 3:472–502). Moltmann-Wendel (*Frauen*, 23–55) has followed the

trail of the rehabilitation of Martha in certain feminist movements and works of art from the Middle Ages.

65 Solignac and Donnat, "Marthe et Marie," 664–73.

66 Luther's sermons on August 15, 1522, and on August 15, 1523 (Mülhaupt, *Luthers Evangelien-Auslegung*, 3:156–62; cf. Eberle, *Luthers Evangelien-Auslegung*, 749–53).

67 Calvin, *Harmony*, 2:89–90.

the Sower (8:14). What I understood next was that the Lukan picture of the situation does not consist of a contrast of light and dark, but of a subtle gradation: it is not a question of a "bad part" as opposed to a "good part" chosen by Mary. Martha did not plunge into the world of darkness; she was threatened, which is what caused Jesus to give her affectionate advice ("Martha, Martha . . ."). I am now persuaded that Martha was nowhere encouraged to give up practicing hospitality or serving tables. What Jesus wanted to relieve her of was not her service but what deprived her of her joy and her radiance: fear of being left alone in her work, the impression that all the weight was on her shoulders, and the feeling that God was inactive. Luke thus first of all suggests that we be Mary, then that we become Martha, but a Martha soothed by the Lord and surrounded by her sisters and brothers in the faith. This doctrinal hierarchy can also be visualized spatially: it is incumbent upon Christians first to seek the things that are above (Col 3:1-2; cf. 1:13) and, hanging on to the anchor of hope (Heb 6:19), to serve one another. Picking up on another parameter, one could say: we will be in a position to provide service with our material goods, once we have agreed to be served by Christ, served with spiritual goods (cf. John 4:31-34).

The two kinds of Christian ministry, which go back to Jesus' double activity through word and deed, teaching and charitable action (Acts 1:1), are both indispensable, and this passage confirms their importance. They are, moreover, linked to each other, according to a theological logic that is presupposed and imposed by this pericope. Although the author of the Gospel of Luke paid but scant attention to this problem of ministries, he nevertheless did recognize their importance, which was felt strongly at the level of tradition. He was more attentive to the feminine reality. He was, in fact, happy to announce that Jesus had invited some women to travel along the path of faith and had agreed to welcome them into his school. He certainly did not think that this faith that Mary had welcomed should not be allowed to be expressed. Without his explicitly saying so, he may well have been favorable to the idea of a pastoral ministry carried on by a woman.

The Lord's Prayer (11:1-4)

Bibliography

Baarda, Tjitze, "De korte tekst van het Onze Vader in Lucas 11, 2-4: een Marcionitische corruptie?" *NedThT* 44 (1990) 273–87.

Bahr, Gordon J., "The Use of the Lord's Prayer in the Primitive Church," *JBL* 84 (1965) 153–59.

Barr, James, "'Abba' Isn't 'Daddy,'" *JTS* 39 (1988) 28–47.

Boff, Leonardo, *The Lord's Prayer: The Prayer of Integral Liberation* (trans. T. Morrow; Maryknoll, N.Y.: Orbis Books, 1983).

Bourgoin, Henri, "Ἐπιούσιον expliqué par la notion de prefixe vide," *Bib* 60 (1979) 91–96.

Braun, François-Marie, "Le pain dont nous avons besoin: Mt 6, 11; Lc 11, 3," *NRTh* 100 (1978) 559–68.

Brown, Raymond E., "The Pater Noster as an Eschatological Prayer," *TS* 22 (1961) 175–208, reprinted in idem, *New Testament Essays* (Milwaukee: Bruce, 1965) 217–53 (cited from the latter).

Carmignac, Jean, *Recherches sur le «Notre Père»* (Paris: Letouzey et Ané, 1969).

Chase, Frederic Henry, *The Lord's Prayer in the Early Church* (Piscataway, N.J.: Gorgias Press, 2004).

Cullmann, Oscar, *Prayer in the New Testament* (OBT; Minneapolis: Fortress Press, 1995) 37–69.

D'Angelo, Mary Rose, "*Abba* and 'Father': Imperial Theology and the Jesus Traditions," *JBL* 11 (1992) 611–13.

Eadem, "Theology in Mark and Q: *Abba* and 'Father' in Context," *HTR* 85 (1992) 149–74. Dalman, Gustaf, *The Words of Jesus Considered in the Light of Post-Biblical Jewish Writings and the Aramaic Language* (Edinburgh: T&T Clark, 1902).

Damerau, Rudolf, *Das Herrengebet nach einem Kommentar des Gabriel Biel* (SGR 3; Giessen: Schmitz, 1965).

Idem, *Der Herrengebetskommentar eines Unbekannten und 53 Auslegungen des Herrengebets des Karthäuserpriors Johannes Hagen (gestorben 1475): Textkritische Ausgaben* (SGR 4; Giessen: Schmitz, 1966).

Dewailly, Louis-Marie, "'Donne-nous notre pain': quel pain? Notes sur la quatrième demande du Pater," *RSPhTh* 64 (1980) 561–88.

Dupont, Jacques, and Pierre Bonnard, "Le Notre Père: Commentaire exégétique," in Dupont, *Études*, 2:832–60.

Edmonds, Peter, "The Lucan Our Father: A Summary of Luke's Teaching on Prayer?" *ExpT* 91 (1979) 140–43.

Edwards, *Theology of Q*, 107–8.

Elliott, J. K., "Did the Lord's Prayer Originate with John the Baptist?" *ThZ* 29 (1973) 215.

Fitzmyer, 2:907–9 (bibliography).

Idem, "*Abba* and Jesus' Relation to God," in *À cause de l'Évangile: Études sur les Synoptiques et les Actes offertes au P[ère] Jacques Dupont, O.S.B., à l'occasion de son 70e anniversaire* (LD 123; Paris: Publications de Saint-André/Cerf, 1985) 15–38.

Freudenberger, Rudolf, "Zum Text der zweiten Vaterunserbitte," *NTS* 15 (1968–69) 419–32.

Goulder, M. D., "The Composition of the Lord's Prayer," *JTS* 14 (1963) 32–45.

Grässer, *Problem*, 95–114 and passim.

Grelot, Pierre, "La quatrième demande du 'Pater' et son arrière-plan semitique," *NTS* 25 (1978–79) 299–314.

Guenther, H., "Das Vaterunser: Gebet im Namen Jesu," *Lutherische Theologie und Kirche* 4 (1980) 34–41.

Hadidian, Dikran Y., "The Lord's Prayer and the Sacraments of Baptism and the Lord's Supper in the Early Church," *StLi* 15 (1982–83) 132–44.

Hamman, Adalbert-Gauthier, "Le Notre Père dans la catéchèse des Pères de l'Église," *La Maison-Dieu* 85 (1966) 41–68.

Idem, *Le Pater expliqué par les Pères* (Paris: Éditions franciscaines, 1962).

Harrisville, Roy A., "God's Mercy—Tested, Promised, Done! An Exposition of Genesis 18:20-32; Luke 11:1-13; Colossians 2:6-15," *Int* 31 (1977) 165–78.

Jeremias, Joachim, *The Lord's Prayer* (FBBS 8; Philadelphia: Fortress Press, 1964).

Kuhn, Karl Georg, *Achtzehngebet und Vaterunser und der Reim* (WUNT 1; Tübingen: Mohr Siebedk, 1950).

LaVerdiere, Eugene, "God as Father," *Emmanuel* 88 (1982) 545–50.

Leaney, A. R. C., "The Lukan Text of the Lord's Prayer (Lk 11, 2-4)," *NovT* 1 (1956) 103–11.

Lohmeyer, Ernst, *The Lord's Prayer* (trans. J. Bowden; London: Collins, 1965).

Luz, *Matthew*, 1:307–26 (bibliography 307–8).

Marchel, Witold, *Abba! Père! La prière du Christ et des chrétiens: Étude exégétique sur les origines et la signification de l'invocation à la divinité comme père, avant et dans le Nouveau Testament* (AnBib 19; Rome: Institut Biblique Pontifical, 1963) 191–202.

Marchesi, Giovanni, "La coscienza del Cristo Figlio di Dio: Il Padre 'dimora' stabile del Gesù storico," *Civiltà (La) Cattolica Roma* 132 (1981) 431–47.

Merk, Otto, "Das Reich Gottes in den lukanischen Schriften," in E. Earle Ellis and E. Grässer, eds., *Jesus und Paulus: Festschrift für Werner Georg Kümmel zum 70. Geburtstag* (Göttingen: Vandenhoeck & Ruprecht, 1975) 201–20.

Metzger, Bruce M., "How Many Times Does 'Epiousios' Occur outside the Lord's Prayer?" *ExpT* 69 (1957–58) 52–54.

Miller, Robert J., "The Lord's Prayer and Other Items from the Sermon on the Mount," *Forum* 5 (1989) 177–86.

Niederwimmer, Kurt, *The Didache: A Commentary* (Hermeneia; Minneapolis: Fortress Press, 1998).

Ott, Wilhelm, *Gebet und Heil: Die Bedeutung der Gebetsparänese in der lukanischen Theologie* (SANT 12; Munich: Kösel, 1965).

Petuchowski, Jacob J., and Michael Brocke, *The Lord's Prayer and Jewish Liturgy* (New York: Seabury Press, 1978).

Philonenko, Marc, "'Que ton Esprit-Saint vienne sur nous et qu'il nous purifie' (Lc 11, 2): l'arrière-plan qoumrânien d'une variante lucanienne du 'Notre Père,'" *RHPhR* 75 (1995) 61–66.

Refoulé, François, "La prière des chrétiens" and "La prière du Seigneur et le mouvement oecuménique" in P. Bonnard, J. Dupont, and F. Refoulé, *"Notre Père qui es aux cieux": La prière oecuménique* (Cahiers de la Traduction oecuménique de la Bible 3; Paris: Cerf, 1968) 9–75.

Rordorf, Willy, "The Lord's Prayer in the Light of Its Liturgical Use in the Early Church," *StLi* 14 (1980–81) 1–19.

Idem, and André Tuilier, *La doctrine des douze apôtres (Didachè): Introduction, texte, traduction, notes, appendice et index* (SC 248; Paris: Cerf, 1978) 173–75.

Ruckstuhl, Eugen, "Abba, Vater! Überlegungen zum Stand der Frage," *FZPhTh* 41 (1994) 515–25.

Sabugal, Santos, *Abba! . . . La oración de Señor (Historia y exégesis teológica)* (BAC 467; Madrid: Biblioteca de Autores Cristianos, 1985).

Schelbert, Georg, "Abba, Vater! Stand der Frage," *FZPhTh* 40 (1993) 259–81.

Idem, "Sprachgeschichtliches zu 'Abba,'" in Pierre Casetti, O. Keel, and A. Schenker, eds., *Mélanges Dominique Barthélemy: Études bibliques offertes à l'occasion de son 60e anniversaire* (OBO 38; Göttingen: Vandenhoek & Ruprecht, 1981) 395–447.

Schlosser, Jacques, *Le Règne de Dieu dans les dits de Jésus* (2 vols.; EtB; Paris: Gabalda, 1980) 1:245–322.

Schneider, Gerhard, "Die Bitte um das Kommen des Geistes im lukanischen Vaterunser (Lk 11, 2 v.l.)," in Wolfgang Schrage, ed., *Studien zum Text und Ethik des Neuen Testaments: Festschrift zum 80. Geburtstag von Heinrich Greeven* (BZNW 47; Berlin: Walter de Gruyter, 1986) 344–73.

Idem, et al., "Das Vaterunser," *KatBl* 112 (1987) 580–631 (several articles).

Schnurr, Klaus Bernhard, *Hören und Handeln: Lateinische Auslegungen des Vaterunsers in der Alten Kirche bis zm 5. Jahrhundert* (FThSt 132; Freiburg: Herder, 1985).

Schottroff, Luise, "Das Vater–Mutter–unser: Feministische Theologie und neutestamentliche Wissenschaft," *Evangelische Kommentare* 21.5 (1988) 257–60.

Schulz, *Q*, 84–93.

Schürmann, Heinz, *Das Gebet des Herrn als Schlüssel zum Verstehen Jesu* (4th ed.; Botschaft Gottes 2, neutestamentliche Reihe 6; Freiburg im B.: Herder, 1981).

Schwarz, G., "Matthäus 6, 9-13 / Lukas 11, 2-4: Emendation und Rückübersetzung," *NTS* 15 (1968–69) 233–47.

Segbroeck, *Cumulative Bibliography*, 233.

Sorge, Helga, *Religion und Frau: Weibliche Spiritualität im Christentum* (Stuttgart: Kohlhammer, 1988).

Strotmann, Angelika, *"Mein Vater bist Du!" (Sir 51, 10): Zur Bedeutung der Vaterschaft Gottes in kanonischen und nicht kanonischen frühjüdischen Schriften* (FTS 39; Frankfurt am Main: Knecht, 1991).

Vögtle, Anton, "Der 'eschatologische' Bezug der Wir-Bitten des Vaterunser," in Ellis and Grässer, eds., *Jesus und Paulus*, 344–62.

Völkel, Martin, "Zur Deutung des 'Reiches Gottes' bei Lukas," *ZNW* 65 (1974) 57–70.

1/ And it happened, as he was praying in a certain place, that after he had finished, one of his disciples said to him, "Lord, teach us to pray, as John taught his disciples." **2/** He said to them, "When you pray, say:
Father,
may your name be hallowed,
May your reign come.
3/ Give us each day the bread we need.
4/ And forgive us our sins,
for we ourselves forgive everyone
indebted to us.
And do not lead us into temptation."

The "Lord's Prayer," also known as the "Our Father,"[1] belongs to us and yet escapes us. Although everyone knows it by heart, it nevertheless remains a stranger by virtue of its enigmas, the reinterpretations that have been made of it, the way it has been used, and even the fact that it has been subjected to the wear and tear of time. My commentary on the Lord's Prayer will remind us of the prayer's obscurities; the tracing of the history of its interpretation will explain the shifts in its meaning that have taken place through the centuries; and our own feeling about it will be a reflection of the sentiments this prayer can inspire, sentiments of either confidence or weariness. Moreover, we do not always have the same attitude toward it: Do we want to read it or recite it? Understand it or pray it? We are going to attempt an analysis of the Lukan version, since that is what following the text of Luke prompts us to do, given the fact that pious practice and the liturgy have held on to the Matthean version (Matt 6:9-13). We are aware of the danger of "explaining" a prayer, a danger witnessed to by ancient commentaries, which went off in the direction of meditation and prayer. Be that as it may, a prayer, like any other human expression, is full of explicit meanings. It makes observations and expresses hope, dedicates and implores, by means of invocation and the confession of faith. The Lord's Prayer speaks of God in order to be able to speak more adequately of the human condition.

Analysis

Literary Context

Here the writer of the Gospel of Luke initiates a series of three pericopes about prayer, since following the Lord's Prayer (11:1-4) we have the parable of the insistent friend (11:5-8) and the invitation to ask (11:9-13).[2] As the catechists of the patristic period were to do,[3] the Gospel writer linked this teaching to the quoting of the Law (Luke 10:25-42). Such a linking, at the redactional and literary level, probably matched traditional catechetical practice.[4] Moreover, the two sections fit together harmoniously: Mary, at the Lord's feet, chose to love God; as for the disciples, they learned, from the lips of the same teacher, the invocation that they would address to the same God. This presentation leads one to prayer, to dare to pray. In doing so, it depends on a catechism addressed to Gentile Christians who, in their previous existence, sometimes had no knowledge at all of such an act. Matthew also set the Lord's Prayer in a catechetical context, but he did not think of teaching Christians the rudiments of prayer. Instead, he had to reform the pious practice of his pupils of Jewish origin, by directing them how to pray correctly (Matt 6:5-15), that is, by refusing to follow a routine, by practicing almsgiving (Matt 6:1-4), and by fasting (Matt 6:16-18).[5]

Synoptic Comparison

Looking synoptically at the two versions of the prayer in Matthew and Luke allows us first to note structural differences, and then disagreements as to content. All that the two Gospels have in common is the Lord's Prayer (Luke 11:1-4 par. Matt 6:9-13) and the invitation to prayer (Luke 11:9-13 par. Matt 7:7-11). The First Gospel is unacquainted with the parable we find in Luke 11:5-8; the Third Gospel, of what relates to almsgiving (Matt 6:1-4), the secret place (Matt 6:5-6), brevity (Matt 6:7-8), and fasting (Matt 6:16-18). In the two units that they have in common, the relationship varies widely. Although practically identical in the invitation, they depart from each other with respect to the Lord's Prayer. This departure can be explained as a result of the way the prayer was used—no longer catechetically but liturgically. Each Gospel writer respected as much as he could his own worship customs and the source that was available to him.

These are the principal differences between the two forms of the Lord's Prayer: Luke provides a narrative introduction (v. 1) in place of Matthew's simple impera-

---

1 Luke does not know this address. He says simply: Father.

2 With Loisy, 314; Jeremias (*Lord's Prayer*, 8–10) and Marshall (p. 454) subdivide vv. 9-13 into four parts.

3 Explication of the Decalogue, the Our Father, and the Credo constituted the essentials of this grouping; see, e.g., Cyril of Jerusalem *Mystagogical Catecheses*.

4 The christological character of the travel narra-

tive cannot conceal its catechetical aspects. Roland Meynet (*L'Évangile selon saint Luc: Analyse rhétorique* [2 vols.; Paris: Cerf, 1988] 2:132) makes of 11:1-54 a single section, in five parts, centered on the double benediction in 11:27-28.

5 See Jeremias, *Lord's Prayer*, 8–10.

tive (Matt 6:9a). The matching piece to Luke's vocative, "Father," is Matthew's "Our Father in heaven" (Matt 6:9b). The first two petitions (hallowing of the name and coming of the reign) are identical (Matt 6:9c-10a). Luke was not acquainted with the third petition found in Matthew (on God's will, Matt 6:10b). In the following petition, concerning bread (Matt 6:11), both of the Gospel writers transcribe the enigmatic Greek adjective ἐπιούσιος, but only Luke stresses the durative aspect: he uses the present imperative (which carries the idea of duration), which he reinforces with "each day," whereas Matthew thinks in terms of "this day, today" and uses the aorist imperative (which has a punctiliar aspect). The request for forgiveness begins the same way, but Luke speaks of sins, where Matthew mentions debts (Matt 6:12). What follows in Luke proves that he was acquainted with the idea of debt, but the wording in the two Gospels is different. In Matthew we have "as we also have forgiven [using the aorist in Greek] our debtors [a plural substantive]"; in Luke, "for we ourselves forgive [present] everyone indebted to us [a singular participle]." Finally, the entreaty concerning temptation is a single one in Luke, but double in Matthew (Matt 6:13): "and do not lead us into temptation" is the half that is identical in the two Gospels; "but deliver us from evil" is the half Luke does not have. Luke's version being the shorter one, it goes to the heart of the matter.

Diachronic Perspective

Since I refuse to admit that Luke knew the Gospel of Matthew,[6] I am of the opinion that the two Gospel writers relied here on a common source, the Sayings Source, Q.[7] The divergences between them are due in part to their redactional impulses but also in part to their liturgical and pious practices. As it is for us, the Lord's Prayer was for them both a text and a prayer, a written fragment and

a custom of their worship. Its double relationship complicates any synoptic comparison. As for me, I acknowledge that the Matthean community or Matthew himself furnished a long form of the Lord's Prayer, resulting from a reflective practice in a Jewish environment. The lengthening of the address, the addition of the petition concerning God's will, as well as the doubling of the last petition, are the result of this reflection and these practices.[8] Luke, ever respectful of Jesus' sayings, made the fewest changes possible. Be that as it may, he felt obliged to improve on what was, in the last analysis but a translation in his eyes. Since the word "debt" was not suitable for expressing in Greek a relationship with a religious character, he preferred instead to use the word "sin," which had already entered the Christian sociolect. The "everyone" (παντί) of the same petition is Lukan (cf. 6:30; 7:35; 9:43). His way of stressing the constant need for bread was the result of a requirement that is, this time, theological. As for the moment when the human offer of forgiveness must take place, our commentary will show whether that matter is a question of theology or one of style. In short, Luke respected the general layout and the formal simplicity of the Lord's Prayer more than Matthew did, but he entered into the question of the detailed wording more vigorously than did his partner. The position I take here—I want to point out—agrees with that of Joachim Jeremias and disagrees with that of Jean Carmignac.[9] The *Didache*, which dates from the end of the first century or the beginning of the second, passed on a form of the Lord's Prayer that is very close to Matthew's.[10] The author got it from the First Gospel or from the practice of his church, in this case quite close to the Matthean milieu. A doxology close to the one that has become familiar to us closes the Lord's Prayer in the *Didache*.[11] As is well known, numerous manuscripts of the

---

6   Goulder ("Composition") advances a curious hypothesis: the Our Father was not spoken by Jesus. It was composed by Matthew due to his acquaintance, thanks to Mark, with the teaching of Jesus. According to this author, Luke has no source here besides Matthew, with which he is acquainted and which he corrects.

7   In view of his differences from Matthew as to the arrangement of the pericopes, as well as the wording of the Our Father, one may ask whether Luke follows here his own way.

8   The Matthean additions are precisely adjunct components to each part: at the end of the address, then to each strophe.

9   Jeremias, *Lord's Prayer*, 8–13; Carmignac (*Recherches*, 18–28) regards the long form, which Matthew preserves, as a part of the earliest tradition.

10   The Greek text of *Did.* 8.2-3 in Aland, *Synopsis*, 268. Cf. Niederwimmer, *Didache*, 134–38.

11   "For Thine is the power and the glory for ever." This doxology undoubtedly originates from 1 Chr 29:11–13.

New Testament also add one at the end of the Matthean Lord's Prayer.[12]

An Aramaic origin for the Lord's Prayer is more likely than a Hebrew one. To be sure, pious Jews and particularly those at Qumran prayed in Hebrew, but there is no shortage of Jewish prayers in Aramaic.[13] I would have a hard time picturing Jesus, the companion of the poor and ordinary folk, making his prayer inaccessible by putting it in the priestly form of a language that neither he nor they used on a daily basis. Luke, for his part, did not work from the original; the Lord's Prayer in his source and that he addressed to God was a prayer already worded in Greek.

Formal Structure

In its traditional form, the Lord's Prayer, considered from the point of view of its structure, contains two sequences or strophes of unequal length, preceded by an address.[14] The first contains two lines that end with a rhyme ($\sigma o \upsilon$, "your," twice); the second, three clauses whose symmetrical form and rhythm, at least in Luke, are less evident.[15] Perhaps the translation into Greek and the redactional adaptation broke the rhythm, did away with the parallelism, and caused the rhymes (with "our," $\dot{\eta}\mu\hat{\omega}\nu$) to disappear.[16] The "our" and "us" (in Greek, $\dot{\eta}\mu\hat{\omega}\nu$ and $\dot{\eta}\mu\hat{\iota}\nu$), which reappear throughout the text in an insistent manner, are perhaps the trace of a rhyme that was originally present in this second part. We thus have a pyramidal construction: at the top, the Father alone, then below that, his two possessions, that is, his name and his reign; finally, at the bottom, in the order of decreasing importance, our three realities, good bread, sins that may be forgiven, and final (from every point of view) temptation. Such a construction, in which symmetry and extensions cohabit, was not unknown to Judaism. The Beatitudes (6:20-22) reminded us of these two Jewish literary characteristics.

Jewish Parallels

The Lord's Prayer, in its structure, rhythm, and content, resembles certain Jewish prayers of antiquity more than it does the biblical psalms and their various genres. The *Kaddish* and the *Eighteen Benedictions* can serve as bases for comparison; the first two petitions of the Lord's Prayer are found side by side also in the *Kaddish*, whose structure and brevity make us think of the Lord's Prayer.[17] The *Eighteen Benedictions*, in their earliest part, benedictions 4 to 15, contain some rhymes, some binary rhythms, and some parallelisms. Certain of their themes are also close to the petitions of the Lord's Prayer. Benedictions 4 to 9 mention, one after the other, the benefits of the Torah, the efficacy of conversion, forgiveness of sins, calling for help against the dangers of the outside world, the petition for salvation for body and soul, and the petition for the fertility of the fields and the gift of bread. Benedictions 10 to 15 have an eschatological import; they are concerned with ultimate liberation, the reinstatement of the Diaspora, God's reign and his righteousness, the damnation of renegade Jews, the end of the Gentile empire, the future of righteous proselytes, reward for the children of Israel, Jerusalem's recovery, the coming of the Messiah, and the fulfillment of everything. The Lord's Prayer is a Jewish prayer, insofar as parallels can be found for each petition in Israel's liturgical storehouse. The absence of any explicit Christology is significant in this respect and argues in favor of the authenticity of the Lord's Prayer.

We must point out certain differences, however: unlike the *Eighteen Benedictions*, the Lord's Prayer begins with eschatology (the first two petitions) and continues with the mention of the present time in the last three petitions.[18] The absence of any messianic petition in the Lord's Prayer, moreover, presupposes an eschatology that is in the process of being fulfilled. The earthly existence of Jesus and that of the earliest Christians offering the

---

12 Cf. Matt 6:13, apparatus of Nestle-Aland, 13.

13 See Carmignac, *Recherches*, 30–33.

14 See Schulz, *Q*, 86–87; Schürmann, *Gebet*, 13–16.

15 See Carmignac, *Recherches*, 26.

16 See Jeremias (*Lord's Prayer*, 15), who proposes a retroversion into Aramaic with rhymes in "you" (ʾak) and rhymes in "us" (ʾan). Carmignac, at the end of his life, began to publish numerous retroversions into Hebrew that he had rescued from

oblivion. Their number has increased, since the sixteenth century, to more than sixty. On the question of rhymes, the birth of which one can observe in ancient Judaism, see Kuhn, *Achtzehngebet*.

17 See Carmignac, *Recherches*, 379–82.

18 See Kuhn, *Achtzehngebet*, 40–41; Schürmann, *Gebet*, 106–14.

prayer also seem to have been more uncertain than that of the Jews who recited the *Eighteen Benedictions.* These latter Jews lived a sedentary life that followed the rhythm of the seasons. The address "Father," moreover, is unusual and fits the absence of any vindictive petition.[19]

The Specificity and Function of the Lord's Prayer

Although it has its roots in Judaism,[20] the Lord's Prayer is also a new prayer with respect to its brevity, its being addressed to God as Father, and the eschatological existence that it presupposes. It is not a prayer prepared for a particular occasion but a formulary[21] that the earliest Christians believed—probably rightly—they had inherited from Jesus himself. It fulfilled several important functions: as it was quoted and perhaps explained to new converts in the course of their catechetical training, it was an integral part of personal piety (the *Didache* directed it to be recited thrice daily [8.3]) and of the Sunday liturgy (it was recited, in the patristic period, just before the Eucharist, and still is).[22] Its wayfaring journey began at the outset: it is not possible to speak of a single *Sitz im Leben,* since to the catechism, personal piety, and the Sunday liturgy must be added the mentions of the life of Jesus, in their oral, and later written, form. It is in this last form that the Lord's Prayer has come down to us. Unlike Matthew, Luke did not transmit it in the middle of general instruction but rather at the beginning of a particular teaching. As a means of introducing it, he created an artificial, but plausible, situation. The effort to create a real situation was a success,[23] and one thus has the impression that one is reading an apophthegm: a situation (v. 1a),[24] a disciple's question (v. 1b), and an authoritative answer from the teacher (vv. 2-4).

Commentary

■ **1** There is a convergence of literary indices: v. 1 is Lukan.[25] Without his saying so, the Gospel writer thought of Jesus as being on a later stage of his travel in a certain place ($\dot{\epsilon}\nu$ $\tau\acute{o}\pi\omega$ $\tau\iota\nu\iota$), which must have been a remote area rather than a city or a village. The mention of prayer stresses the Master's spiritual life[26] (he had been praying to the Father not long before—10:21-22) and prepares us for the theme of discussion. After the prayer finished, Jesus was available; after all, had he not interrupted his journey and concluded his meditating? The double mention of "disciples" and of the verb "teach" signals what the pericope will be about: what else could it be about except instruction concerning prayer (the verb "pray" appears three times in vv. 1-2a)? The triteness of this observation derives from the fact that this is a well-worn text, for, as a matter of fact, prayer was not at that time a given: the Jewish Scriptures contain scarcely any instructions on the subject. It was only when personal piety began to develop in conjunction with individual conscience that the rabbis began to pay attention to it. They instructed their disciples,[27] just as did Matthew, in the matter of three works of piety: prayer, almsgiving, and fasting. Luke chose the example of John the Baptist,[28] who, surrounded by his disciples, represented an analogy. The prayer that Jesus was to teach them was to be appropriate to both his disciples and the community: the words "when you pray, say" (v. 2a)[29] serve as an invitation addressed at the same time to each person in particular and to all those joining in the celebration. That was, right from the outset, the twofold way the Lord's Prayer was to be used.

---

19   For this comparison, I owe much to Kuhn, *Achtzehngebet.*

20   See Petuchowski and Brocke, *Lord's Prayer;* Fitzmyer, 2:900–901.

21   See Erich Klostermann, *Das Lukasevangelium: Erklärt* (2d ed.; HNT 5; Tübingen: Mohr Siebeck, 1929; reprinted 1975) 123; Schürmann, *Gebet,* 106–14.

22   See Rordorf, "Lord's Prayer."

23   Such a success that many exegetes regard it as historic; so E. Earle Ellis, *Gospel of Luke* (2d ed.; New Century Bible; London: Oliphants, 1974; reprinted Grand Rapids: Eerdmans, 1981) 164; Marshall, 456.

24   Fitzmyer, 2:898.

25    $\kappa\alpha\grave{\iota}$ $\dot{\epsilon}\gamma\acute{\epsilon}\nu\epsilon\tau o$ $\dot{\epsilon}\nu$ $\tau\hat{\omega}$ $\epsilon\mathring{\iota}\nu\alpha\iota$ $\alpha\mathring{\upsilon}\tau\acute{o}\nu$ (cf. 5:12) and $\epsilon\mathring{\iota}\pi\epsilon\nu$ $\pi\rho\acute{o}\varsigma$ (cf. 11:5) by way of examples.

26   Jesus prays in Luke more often than in Mark or Matthew; see 3:21; 5:16; 6:12; 9:18, 28-29; 22:44-46; Louis Monloubou, *La prière selon Saint Luc: Recherche d'une structure* (LD 89; Paris: Cerf, 1976).

27   See Str-B 2:186.

28   As in 5:33, where he follows Mark.

29   The manuscripts vacillate between the subjunctive (classical) and the indicative (late and inelegant) after $\ddot{o}\tau\alpha\nu$; cf. BDF §382, 4, n. 6.; Nestle-Aland retains the subjunctive. Codex Bezae adds, after the verb "to pray," a phrase inspired by Matt 6:7. This is an example of a discernible tendency in the whole manuscript tradition of the Our Father: the "Mattheanization" of the Lukan text. Matthew, not

■ **2a** "Father": commentators hesitate before interpreting that word. Psychoanalysts have had their say about the image of the father. Feminist theologians have warned about the patriarchal nature of a Father God. Commentators have reconstructed a history of the concept of the paternity of God.[30] The Hebrew Bible sometimes compares God to a father but only rarely refers to him as Father.[31] In such cases, he is the father of the people or of the king and not of just any individual. In this term, the authority of the father is at least as strong a factor as his love. The reserve of the biblical writers in this matter derives perhaps from the need to dissociate themselves from the ambient religions in which the paternity of the gods made certain human realities sacred. We see an evolution in the intertestamental literature: not only is there more and more confessing of God's paternity, but there is also the appearance of calling on God as Father.[32] The Aramaic *'abbā'* should be seen as the equivalent of the Greek vocative πάτερ ("Father"). It was characteristic of Jesus' piety before becoming the common property of Christians. Liturgical use being conservative by nature, the Aramaic word survived alongside its translation, as is shown by Rom 8:15 and Gal 4:6 in Greek (with the nominative ὁ πατήρ serving as a vocative). In order to safeguard the specificity of Jesus as Son, there have been repeated reminders, from Joachim Jeremias[33] on, that there was no evidence of Jewish use of the practice of addressing God as "my Father" or as *'abbā'*. Recent studies by Geza Vermes, Joseph A. Fitzmyer, and James Barr, however, have shattered that hypothesis.[34] What is certain is that Jesus chose the term *'abbā'* as his personal way of addressing God (10:21; Mark 14:36 par. Luke 22:42) and the one he instructed his disciples to use (here, 11:2). Jesus' God loved not only all of his people but also each one of them, male or female. Not only was this personalized love a characteristic of Christ's teaching; it was also to become typical of the New Testament as a whole. By his rejection of long titles[35] and by his choice of this word, Jesus chose a theological option that his disciples, Luke in particular, were anxious to preserve. With the passing of time, Christians attempted to make a distinction between the relationship of the Son to the Father, on the one hand, and that of children to their Father, on the other.[36] As a matter of fact, no passage in the New Testament included Jesus and his disciples together in the invocation "Our Father." For Luke, the disciples—thanks to Jesus' teaching and subsequent suffering and death, as well as to their conversion, faith, and commitment—henceforth dare to call God their Father. They have hope that this tie, now only anticipatory, will achieve full expression in the kingdom of God (6:35), for whose coming they are to ask (11:2). Their ties with the Father are so intense that they proclaim themselves to be his children and declare, in their prayer, that they belong to him.

As for me, I feel that theology as discourse on the Father can shed light on human paternity, provided it avoids the pitfall of projections. I also believe that the reality of God, who is called Father by virtue of historical and cultural imperatives that the Bible has not escaped, also includes all that a mother is for her children and all that a woman can offer. Just as the human being is in the image of God, so also does the feminine specificity reflect a divine reality and express a gift from heaven. What is peculiar to women is their global, holistic way of perceiving the world and loving their opposite numbers,

Luke, used to be the church evangelist whom one knew by heart and by whom one was inspired.

30 See Plummer, 294–95; Lagrange, 321; Grundmann, 229–31 (excursus); Jeremias, *Lord's Prayer*, 17–21; Brown, "Pater Noster," 225–27; Fitzmyer, 2:902–3; Robert Hamerton-Kelly, *God the Father: Theology and Patriarchy in the Teaching of Jesus* (OBT; Philadelphia: Fortress Press, 1979); Geza Vermes, *Jesus the Jew: A Historian's Reading of the Gospels* (London: Collins, 1973) 210–13; Fitzmyer, *"Abba."*

31 See Isa 64:7; Mal 1:6; *3 Macc.* 5:7; 6:3 [4]; Wis 14:3; Sir 23:1. Now *'ābî* ("my Father") is attested at Qumran in a prayer (4Q372). See Raymond E. Brown, *An Introduction to New Testament Christology* (New York: Paulist Press, 1994) 86–87; Cullmann, *Prayer*, 41 nn. 76 and 77.

32 See Carmignac (*Recherches*, 55–60), who furnishes numerous references.

33 Jeremias, *Lord's Prayer*, 18–19.

34 Vermes, *Jesus the Jew*; and Fitzmyer, *"Abba."*

35 Rudolf Bultmann, *Theology of the New Testament* (trans. Kendrick Grobel; 2 vols.; New York: Scribner, 1951, 1955) 1:23–34, cited by Fitzmyer, 2:903. Numerous and valuable manuscripts align Luke's address with that of Matthew; see Nestle-Aland ad. loc.

36 See Conzelmann, *Theology*, 117–20.

their intellectual and affective manner of approaching reality, their peculiar ability simultaneously to pay attention to details and to see the whole picture. And yet these characteristics are due to God. The same may be said of women's perseverance, their courage in the midst of suffering, and their art of mastering birth and death. To paraphrase the Letter to the Ephesians (3:14-15), I would say that all maternity and femininity have their origin in God.

■ **2b** The "name," even if it were to be the name "father," is not a human word but, in a biblical tradition and an Eastern milieu that were not acquainted with nominalism, the very reality of God.[37] There is one qualification: we are talking about God in communication with the outside. The first petition asks to have this manifestation be finally recognized. The use of an imperative is a sign of waiting and hope. The Lord's Prayer begins by calling on God and confessing our allegiance to him, but, unlike certain Psalms,[38] does not continue with praise. The use of the imperative in the passive voice implies a need to have this acknowledgment of God's nature be implemented: first of all by God himself, to whom the petition is addressed; next by means of eschatological intermediaries whom he might choose to enlist. This petition can, in Luke's eyes, be already realized in an anticipatory way in worship, for example; in the very recitation of the Lord's Prayer, God's name is hallowed. The encounter between believers and their Father accomplishes this imperative in a proleptic way. Saying "may your name be hallowed" is tantamount to entering into interaction with God, becoming attached to the image that this name has taken on in history and in life, but also at the end of life and at the end of history. This petition unveils something about God, but it also refers us back to his human opposite numbers.

Ἁγιάζω is "to hallow," "to treat as holy," "to reverence."[39] In the Hebrew Bible, the Israelites had to sanctify God's name (Isa 29:23), that is, respect God's divinity in the face of the profanations of idolatry (Lev 18:21; 20:3) and sin (Lev 21:6; 22:2, 32). They were to praise God and give him glory. God himself sees to it that people give him the respect he is due. In the last analysis God is the only one able truly to "hallow his name." He does so not by condemning his people but by saving them. In so doing, he manifests his will, which explains the Matthean addition "may your will be done." In so doing, he also avoids losing face, since a people routed would be an indication that the One who had brought them into being had been defeated.[40] By speaking of "you" (singular), the first part of the Lord's Prayer is thus also concerned with "us." And for our part, we are to "hallow," "sanctify" God's name not only through prayer but also through the practice of our faith—practice in worship, but especially existential and social practice. Isaiah 5:16 proclaims that the Holy God is made holy by righteousness. Holiness, which is close to sacredness and religion, also proves to be close to what is secular or profane and to the world.

The "reign" of God is a greatness known to the readers. They know that this reality is at the heart of Jesus' preaching (Luke 4:43; 8:1; 9:11) and that of his disciples (9:2). They remember that Jesus' presence has brought that reign near (4:16-20, without that expression being explicit) and that the same is true when God facilitates the disciples' mission (10:9, 11). Imminence is no longer the principal characteristic of this reign for Luke; what does count is accomplishing God's will—this reign has been associated with the coming of Christ (Acts 28:31, which is the christological component); the church owes its eschatological stamp to this reign (which is the ecclesial component); and the poor as well as believers can live by it (6:20, which is the human component). The reign is already partially (8:4-10), proleptically (17:20-21), and mysteriously (8:10) present. It is what is proclaimed, and that constitutes good news (e.g., 8:1) because it is not condemnation but the restitution of the rights of the oppressed and their deliverance. In terms of visibility and power, however, the reign of God is still absent; moreover, it is held back and is something that is awaited (Acts 1:6-8), hoped for (Luke 21:31), and prayed for (here in 11:2). It is this eschatological connotation, rediscovered in the twentieth century, that is

---

37 On biblical realism, see Edmund Jacob, *Theology of the Old Testament* (trans. Arthur W. Heathcote and Philip J. Allcock; New York: Harper, 1958) 84–85, 177–82.

38 Cf., e.g., Psalm 88 (89).

39 See BAGD, s.v.

40 See Lohmeyer, *Our Father*, 84–87.

decisive here: Jesus enlists his disciples in inviting God to come establish in glory his reign that has been so much wished for.[41] He also asks that henceforth daily life, in its ordinariness and with its sorrow, might be put under the power of this paternal king.

Judaism also was waiting for this reign, for which it offered intercessory prayer but did not believe that it was so near, or that it had already penetrated history.[42] Frédéric Godet was typical of many believers in the nineteenth century who attached increased importance to one of those ways that the reign entered history. He believed that as soon as God's image shines in our inner-most heart, God's reign can take hold there.[43]

That is just the tack that one famous and poorly attested textual variant of this second petition takes.[44] In fact, one minuscule manuscript reads the following words here: "may your Holy Spirit come upon us and purify us" (ἐλθέτω τὸ πνεῦμά σου τὸ ἅγιον ἐφ᾽ ἡμᾶς, καὶ καθαρισάτω ἡμᾶς).[45] The same petition, worded slightly differently, was known also to another minus-cule,[46] as well as to Gregory of Nyssa and Maximus the Confessor. A similar petition was known to Marcion, but as a substitute for the first petition (the hallowing of God's name).[47] Although it has weak manuscript attesta-tion, this reading is nevertheless important, for it could be the vestige of a Lukan version that was supplanted by the Matthean text. To this textual reason might be added Luke's interest in the gift of the Holy Spirit (cf. 11:13b; even if he rarely speaks of purification and, once only, Acts 19:6, of the coming of the Spirit).[48] Opinions have been divided on this matter for a century now.[49] Person-ally, I do not think that this petition coheres with our Gospel of Luke.[50] It makes its appearance here and there as a result either of the influence of Marcion's Gospel or of a gloss or an *agraphon* (a saying attributed to Jesus that is not found in one of the canonical Gospels).[51]

---

41   See the summary of numerous modern exegetical positions related to the reign of God according to Luke in Bovon, *Theologian*, 678 (the index indicates on this page, under the rubric "Kingdom," more than twenty references); cf. Merk, "Reich"; Völkel, "Deutung."

42   To speak of the "coming" of the reign of God is not common in the Old Testament. About Juda-ism, see Str-B 1:418–19. In return, the NT evokes it willingly (Mark 9:1; 13:28-30; Matt 10:23), as it signals various "comings": that of the "day of the Lord" (1 Thess 5:2), of the fullness of time (Gal 4:4), of the Son of Man (Luke 21:27), of the "hour" (John 4:21), of judgment (Rev 18:10). On ἔρχομαι, see BAGD, s.v.; Tim Schramm, "ἔρχομαι," *EDNT* 2:55–57.

43   Godet, 2:65.

44   Freudenberger, "Text"; Metzger, *Textual Commen-tary*, 154–56; Schneider ("Bitte," bibliography, 371–73) adds here three titles that I discovered by chance: Alfred Resch, *Agrapha: Aussercanonische Schriftfragmente gesammelt und untersucht* (2d ed.; TU 30; Leipzig: Hinrichs, 1906); idem, *Ausser-canonische Paralleltexte zu den Evangelien III* (TU 10.3; Leipzig: Hinrichs, 1895); P. Samain, "L'Esprit et le royaume de Dieu d'après saint Luc," *RDT* 2 (1947) 481–92.

45   Minuscule 700, that is, British Museum *Egerton* 2610, which dates from the eleventh century.

46   Minuscule 162, that is, Vatican *Barb. gr.* 449, which dates from 1153.

47   Gregory of Nyssa, *De oratione dominica* 3; cf. *Gregorii Nysseni de oratione dominica, de beatitudinibus* (ed. J. F. Callahan; Gregorii Nysseni Opera 7.2; Leiden: Brill, 1992) 39–40; Maximus the Confessor, *Expositio orationis dominicae* 350 (*PG* 90:884)—not Maximus of Turin, as it is too often construed.

48   A request for the coming of the Spirit seems to be rooted in the liturgy; see *Acts Thom.* 27: "Come, holy spirit, and cleanse their reins and their heart, and give them the added seal, in the name of the Father and Son and Holy Ghost" (M. R. James, *The Apoc-ryphal New Testament* [Oxford: Clarendon, 1924); other texts are cited by Schneider, "Bitte," 360. An epiclesis had its place in the liturgies of baptism, the imposition of hands, and the Eucharist.

49   Schneider ("Bitte") draws up a large inventory.

50   Cf. Schneider, "Bitte." This appeal in favor of the Spirit does not necessarily represent a hellenization of the request related to the reign, although from the OT, and then in the NT, one awaits the coming of the purifying Spirit (cf. Ezek 36:25-27; Rom 5:5; Acts 15:8-9). The solution is not, however, to say that the parousia has been delayed. One can resolve this problem more simply, by interpreting the notion of the reign in a way that is not apocalyptic. A similar phrase circulates in Christian literature; see *Did.* 10.6: ἐλθέτω χάρις, "may grace come."

51   A new indication of the "Mattheanization" of the Lukan Our Father is that a great number of manu-scripts transmit the following request: "that your will be done on earth as in heaven."

■ 3 Here we have the first petition using the first person plural, "us." It has to do with "bread," a word that, in the biblical tradition, generically also refers, in a wider sense, to any kind of food. Sharing bread means sharing a meal, eating at the same table.[52] While Matthew, following Q, focuses the petition on the immediacy of today, Luke has in mind the length of one's life and uses an expression[53] that invites God to be faithful on a daily basis ($τὸ καθ᾽ ἡμέραν$[54]). We encountered the same sort of modification with respect to the cross to be carried: Luke added "each day" (9:23) to the traditional saying (Mark 8:34).[55] He thereby testified to his awareness of a durable life for believers and the church, therefore a parousia on the back burner, and expressed his ethical vigilance and thus his hope of being able to persevere (cf. 8:15). Whoever speaks of perseverance presupposes the existence of the means to stick it out. The Gospel wants to spare us the wrong kinds of worries (12:22-32). It does not forbid our giving thought, as believers, to the future; in fact, it even suggests we do so.

The petition is motivated, but in a positive sense. Do not creatures have the right to their life, given the fact that it was granted to them by their Creator? Does the Father not see to his children's well-being? Do believers, regenerated in the covenant relationship (the ecclesial "we/us"),[56] not have the right to invoke the faithfulness of the one who has saved them? Moreover, it is not forbidden to love oneself (cf. the "as yourself" [$ὡς σεαυτόν$] of the second commandment [10:27, quoting Lev 19:18]). So the third petition in Luke is a legitimate one, even though the reader is surprised to read no intercession on behalf of others in this prayer. What is more, bread is here not considered to be the fruit of human labor. It is a gift ("give"; $δίδου$), a miracle that comes from on high. It is a long-standing conviction that the Lord's Prayer presupposes and imposes: the God of Israel has been nourishing his people ever since he created them. In the desert, to those who had abandoned the abundance of Egypt, he offered quails in the evening and manna in the morning. In narrative form, Exodus 16 offers a theology of daily life: believers are on a community trek; the God in whom they place their trust guarantees them what is necessary. This gift is sufficient and is proportionate to each person's needs. Any lack of confidence, any fear for the morrow that might express itself in excessive acquisition of capital, would lead to a disastrous outcome, which would be the consequence of one's doubts and God's punishment. This theology does not concern isolated individuals or the community taken by itself, as a unit, but rather the interactions between the partners to the covenant. The processes of acquisition, distribution, and use of goods do, to be sure, involve "us," but also "you" and "me." The harmonious life of the people is a manner of giving glory to God, of hallowing his name. A passage in the book of Proverbs confirms and spells out this theological comment. The author makes a twofold petition to God, asking the Lord to remove far from him falsehood and lying and give him the food that he needs (לֶחֶם חֻקִּי, Prov 30:7-8). He asks that this portion, a necessary condition for survival as well as the corresponding piece of faith, be sufficient, without being excessive, for abundance could lead the believer to abandon God, and famine could lead to theft (Prov 30:9). The author admirably relates the economic, ethical, and theological considerations, and the solution he advocates agrees with the plan God was to carry out during the exodus. An analogous prayer is to be found in the Lord's Prayer: that believers might have what they need in sufficient quantity, without running the danger of foundering either in riches that would make them forgetful of God or in delinquency that would damage God's very name (see the first petition of the Lord's Prayer). The Hebrew expression for this rightful share is

---

52   See Johannes Behm "$ἄρτος$," *TDNT* 1 (1964) 477–78; Horst Balz "$ἄρτος$," *EDNT* 1:159–60.

53   On the transition to the imperative present, with the result that "today" changes to "each day," see BDF §336.1 and 337.4 n. 4; Klostermann, 124–25. Grelot ("Quatrième") explains the difference here between Matthew and Luke by recourse to the original Aramaic and to Matthew's wavering handwriting.

54   The expression, with the neuter article $τό$ (cf. 19:47 and Acts 17:11 in many manuscripts), has a distributive sense; cf. Aristophanes *Eq.* 1126. "Each day" is an expression dear to Luke; cf. 9:23; 16:19; 19:47; 22:53; Acts 2:46, 47; 3:2; 17:11; 19:9; Fitzmyer, 2:904.

55   See see commentary on 9:23 (1:366).

56   Cf. the creation ($τὰ πάντα$) then the redemption ($ἡμεῖς$) in the confession of faith in 1 Cor 8:6.

literally "the bread of my prescription," that is, the bread whose quantity and duration God has determined for me, according to his plan and in order to provide for my needs. This is the share that is right for me and that is important for me. Is that not quite close to the "daily bread" (ἄρτος ἐπιούσιος) of the Lord's Prayer? Is not the fate of the believer (petitions using "we/us") associated with God's future (petitions using "your")? This tradition of the God who has fed, and feeds, his people and those who believe in him has carried on down through the centuries, as is proved by the story of the multiplication of the loaves (9:10-17).[57] Israel's faith remained very much alive, with its share of confidence and the concrete expression of its needs.

But what kind of bread is talked about? The enigma of the Greek adjective ἐπιούσιος does not make answering that question any easier. This term, used in the three versions of the Lord's Prayer (Matthew, Luke, and the *Didache*), is not found in the Greek language before our Gospels. Origen, who made that observation, supposed that it was a neologism coined by the Gospel writers (*Or.* 27.7). That is not certain, since there is a fifth-century C.E. papyrus, albeit of uncertain attestation, in which the word is used as a neuter substantive, and where it seems to mean the daily portion.[58] Both the ancient versions and the explanations provided by the Church Fathers confirm that the word has a special character. The Old Syriac versions translated it by "continual," "reliable"; the Peshitta, by "for our need," "necessary"; the Old Latin, by "daily." In Luke 11:3, Jerome, the ascetic from Bethlehem, kept the "daily" that he had inherited from the Old Latin, but in Matt 6:11 he translated it by "supersubstantial" (*supersubstantialis*), a translation based on the etymology of ἐπιούσιος (*super* for ἐπί and *substantialis* for the

suffix -ούσιος).[59] Jerome is also the source of a valuable piece of information: he indicated that the *Gospel of the Hebrews* (now usually called the *Gospel of the Nazaraeans*) contained an Aramaic form of the petition in which the bread being asked for was "for the morrow," literally "for tomorrow" (Jerome *Comm. in Matt.* 6.11).[60] The confusion becomes even more pronounced when we read the patristic commentaries. In the East, this bread was thought of as spiritual, "supersubstantial," essential bread, nourishment of faith provided by the Word of God and/or by the Eucharist. Justin stated that it is not ordinary bread that is involved but eucharistic food (*1 Apol.* 65–67). Clement of Alexandria (*Paed.* 1.6.47.2), and later Origen (*Or.* 22–30), the first person to write a commentary on the Lord's Prayer,[61] thought in terms of the spiritual bread of the Logos. There is an obvious link here with John 6. Origen's opinion may well have been a polemical one: there was also an interpretation in the East in which the bread was thought of as a material property.[62]

In the West, Tertullian thought of spiritual goods that we need (*Or.* 9.2); but Cyprian, the first Latin author to write a treatise on the Lord's Prayer, accepted a twofold meaning—spiritual and material, *spiritualiter* and *simpliciter*—all the while emphasizing the identification of the bread with Christ (*Dom. or.* 18). Jerome, as we have just seen,[63] proposed two translations, and he, too, seemed to prefer the spiritual meaning. Augustine discussed three possible meanings, recognized the difficulty involved in the interpretation, and ended up retaining the spiritual meaning of the Word of God. He added that if someone also wanted to think in terms of material bread and eucharistic bread, they would also necessarily have to hold the three meanings together, grouped in a single petition (*Serm. Dom.* 2.7.25–27).[64]

57 See commentary on 9:10-17 (1:352–60).

58 See Friedrich Preisigke, *Sammelbuch griechischer Urkunden aus Ägypten* (5 vols.; Strassburg: Trübner, 1915–55) vol. 1, no. 5224, 20; cf. Metzger, "How Many"; Fitzmyer, 2:904.

59 See BAGD, s.v.

60 Cf. Aland, *Synopsis*, 87.

61 In his works, Origen is acquainted with a form of the Our Father that says, "Give us *your* bread. . . ." That is Marcion's formulation; see Adolf Harnack, *Marcion: The Gospel of the Alien God* (trans. J. E. Steely and L. D. Bierma; Durham: Labyrinth, 1990) 207*–208*.

62 See Dewailly, "Pain," 567–75.

63 See the commentary above on v. 3.

64 In the Middle Ages, Gabriel Biel (*Canonis misse expositio* [3 Lectio 71; Veröff. des Inst. für europ. Geschichte Mainz, 33; ed. H. A. Oberman and W. J. Courtney; Wiesbaden: Steiner, 1966] 183) gave seven different senses to this bread: that of nature, penitence, grace, intelligence, Eucharist, fervent devotion, and glory. See Dewailly, "Pain," 576–77, to which I owe also several patristic references.

These hesitations arise in large part from the meaning that these authors derived from the etymology of the word. Commentators in our day share those hesitations.[65] "There are two different etymologies that are possible for ἐπιούσιος, depending on whether the word is broken down into ἐπ-ιούσιος, with elision of the *iota* of ἐπί, or, without elision, into ἐπι-ούσιος."[66] The first derives from the verb εἶμι (inf. ἰέναι, "to come"); the second from the verb εἰμί (inf. εἶναι, "to be"). "The breakdown into ἐπ-ιούσιος refers to ἐπιέναι, where ἐπί expresses the idea of temporal succession, and more particularly the expression 'the following day' (ἡ ἐπιοῦσα ἡμέρα). The word 'day' (ἡμέρα) is often understood, and the shortened expression ἡ ἐπιοῦσα becomes a substantivized participle from which, by derivation, it is possible to obtain the adjective ἐπιούσιος. Choosing this first etymology leads us to translate ὁ ἐπιούσιος ἄρτος by 'bread for the following day.'"[67] If, on the other hand, the adjective is linked to the verb εἶναι ("to be"), it is taken to be derived from the substantive οὐσία, which has abstract meanings ("essence," "substance," "being") and a concrete meaning ("property," "fortune"). We know of "13 compound adjectives formed with οὔσιος."[68] For example, πολυούσιος, meaning "(very) substantial." Ἐπί would indicate a contact here: "toward essence," not so much of humans' essence ("for our subsistence") as God's ("linked to his essence")—thus a spiritual bread conforming to God's being. Moreover, it is not certain that we should attribute any special meaning to ἐπί (Henri Bourgoin gives a linguist's comment: "To sum it up, ἐπί is a prefix devoid of meaning whose function is to give the impression that οὔσιος is a full form."[69]) Interpretations we give of the word depend on which of the two possible etymologies we appeal to, and so we are justified in classifying them under two main headings:

(a) *bread for the following day,* this day being in a future that is either near or more distant, depending on whether we are looking at it from a historical or an eschatological point of view;[70] in this case, the bread is material but is enriched by biblical connotations.

(b) *necessary bread*, either indispensable for our life or corresponding to the divine, supernatural nature, the perspective thus being christological or sacramental; in this case, the bread is spiritual but is enriched by Christian reflections on the incarnation and the elements.[71]

I am personally hesitant to decide the matter. I have the impression that this petition is in the manna tradition: God's people ask for their food that, although divine in origin, nourishes their stomachs as much as their hearts.[72] The spiritual and the material are linked. In a first phase, on Jesus' lips and before being translated into Greek, the petition had an eschatological significance: give us today (in what form?) the bread of the kingdom (cf. Luke 14:15)! The *Gospel of the Hebrews* seems to have preserved for us this primary meaning.[73] The process of translation into Greek modified the perspective. Without eliminating the chronological component, which was carried over in Matthew's "today" and Luke's "each day," the petition asks for a special kind of bread, a heavenly, divine bread, which theological reflection could not help but compare to Christ, the nourishing Logos and living bread of the Eucharist. In one case, believers express their hunger for the kingdom to come; in the other, for the Word from on high. Time and space enter into the service of faith. Are the categories that are used incompatible?

■ **4** Although the two petitions using "you(r)" were simply juxtaposed, the three petitions using "us/our" are coordinated by "and." They thus form a unit concerning personal and community life. In this life, it is God who

---

65   See BAGD, s.v.; Carmignac, *Recherches*, 118–221; Braun, "Pain"; Bourgoin, "Préfixe"; Grelot, "Quatrième"; Dewailly, "Pain"; Christoph Müller, "ἐπιούσιος," *EDNT* 2:31–32; Fitzmyer, 2:899–900, 904–6, 908–9. The ancient bibliography may be found in Carmignac and recent works in Fitzmyer.

66   Bourgoin, "Préfixe," 91.

67   Ibid.

68   Ibid., 92.

69   Ibid., 96.

70   Jeremias, *Lord's Prayer*, 23–24.

71   On the instability of patristic and medieval exegesis, see, e.g., Braun ("Pain") and Dewailly ("Pain"), who give a material and spiritual sense to the bread of the Our Father.

72   See Grelot, "Quatrième."

73   See the commentary above on v. 3.

is asked to act in his capacity as Creator (for terrestrial food) and Redeemer (for heavenly food). Pardon[74] is also a prerogative of God as Redeemer. The aorist imperative of the Greek ἄφες ("forgive") denotes the punctiliar aspect of this act of pardon as an event, maybe even an eschatological event,[75] rather than as an attitude or something habitual, which is what would be expressed if the present imperative were used. Since Christians are invited by Jesus himself to dare to implore God to grant them ultimate acquittal, they do so in lieu of the last judgment. The Christology we have here is only implicit (it is to be found in the words of the one who teaches the prayer), which is an argument in favor of the historicity of the Lord's Prayer. Christians, including Luke, were to make this Christology explicit and associate pardon with Christ's work.[76]

Following Q, Matthew provided a literal translation; he mentioned "debts."[77] Luke, who was to recall this commercial image one line below ("everyone indebted to us"), preferred first to clarify the situation here. Since a "debt" would not conjure up in Greek a transgression against heaven, he chose the word "sin," literally "failure."[78] To be sure, this word did not spontaneously evoke the transgression of a religious commandment, but in the plural it was already rooted in the language of Christians (cf. the pre-Pauline text of 1 Cor 15:3). With the meaning "failure," it evokes the idea of missed opportunities, failure to achieve one's objectives, lacunae, and mistakes. In the plural, it suggests a guilty existence (cf. 7:47-49) involving a multitude of violations of the two commandments cited in the previous chapter (10:25-28). As a pessimist, Luke contemplated our lives objectively. The fact that he copied out and adapted this petition of the Lord's Prayer proves that he sensed its importance even for those who had already received pardon through Jesus Christ and been converted and baptized. As an optimist, he did not feel, as Paul did, that sin, in the singular, is a sphere that subjugates us.[79] Unlike the rabbis, who reflected on the means that men and women have at their disposal to repay their debts to God, according to Luke, Jesus declares human beings to be insolvent. The only way they can get back on their feet again is by appealing to God's grace.[80]

The second part of the petition provides a comparison between the way God acts and the way we do (this is the only such instance in the Lord's Prayer).[81] Matthew's comparison differs from Luke's. Matthew's text reminds us of the necessity, stated in the Sermon on the Mount (Matt 5:23-24), of being reconciled with one's "brother" (or sister) before appearing before God.[82] There is, as a matter of fact, a biblical tradition that dictates that love of one's neighbor and conversion to God are preconditions for God's condescension: "Forgive your neighbor the wrong he has done, and then your sins will be pardoned when you pray" (Sir 28:2 *NRSV*).[83] But there is another tradition, one on which Jesus' ministry fed, according to which God takes the initiative in the matter of pardoning, since human beings cannot manage on their own and only God's stepping in can break the deadlock in their situation. Thus, Jesus came to save

---

74 Forgiveness has appeared four times already: Luke 1:77; 3:3; 5:20-24; 7:36-50; see the excursus in the commentary on 5:17-26 (1:178–84).

75 Jeremias (*Lord's Prayer*, 29–32) insists on this aspect; so too Grundmann, 233; and also Brown, "Pater Noster," 243–48 (forgiveness as an anticipation of the kingdom).

76 "Christ died for our sins in accordance with the Scriptures" (1 Cor 15:3). Even if it gives way easily to the profit of repentance and conversion, this conception is present in Luke; cf. 22:19-20, 37; Acts 5:31; 20:28. In Acts 26:18, pardon of sins is the fruit of apostolic preaching. See Bovon, *L'oeuvre*, 168–71.

77 See Schulz, *Q*, 91–92; Marshall, 460. In Aramaic, the debt is said to be חוֹבָא and has a figurative meaning to define all that human beings owe to God, for the sake of their faults.

78 On ἁμαρτία in Luke, see Taeger, *Mensch*, 31–44.

79 See ibid., 31–33.

80 See Dupont and Bonnard, "Notre Père," 851–52, a selection.

81 Schwarz ("Emendation," 239) regards this second part as not original: it is, according to him, an addition that provides commentary.

82 See Schürmann (*Gebet*, 84–90), who sees in human action at once the consequence and the condition of forgiveness granted by God.

83 See Carmignac (*Recherches*, 234), who judges that it is not divine forgiveness that must be preceded by our offer of forgiveness to others but the formulation of our request addressed to God.

sinners and not the righteous.[84] But neither Jesus nor the Christians who came after him associated forgiveness with a future laxity. As invested as Jesus was with the eschatological power to forgive, he nonetheless still expected those who were regenerated to give proof of some corresponding acts. Not a *do ut des* ("I give so that you may give something in return") but a radiance. People who are loved let their love overflow. For Luke, the same is true of those who have been forgiven.[85] The "for" ($\gamma\acute{\alpha}\rho$) in Luke's wording brings it close to Matthew's: it evokes a commitment on the part of those who pray the Lord's Prayer. The present ("we . . . forgive") is vague; it says both that we do it as we recite the Lord's Prayer (performative language[86]) and that we will do it on the next occasion (forgiving as freely as we are forgiven). By asking us to forgive seven times, that is, always, Luke indicates that the frequency of forgiveness is qualitative rather than quantitative (cf. Luke 17:3-4). We ourselves forgive the one who repents, just as God does, and God forgives that person, just as we do (cf. the "I repent," $\mu\epsilon\tau\alpha\nu o\acute{\epsilon}\omega$, in 17:4). The petition is addressed to God, but it presupposes an inner attitude on our part that turns to the Father and—in the present ("we . . . forgive," $\alpha\phi\acute{\iota}o\mu\epsilon\nu$)—reestablishes the relationship with others. The parable of the merciless debtor (Matt 18:23-35) illustrates how shocking and unforgivable (Matt 18:32-35) any other attitude would be. The call to be merciful (Luke 6:36-38) says the same thing.[87]

Willy Rordorf has proposed an interesting hypothesis, taking as his starting point the liturgical practice of Christian antiquity and, more particularly, the place of the Lord's Prayer in the eucharistic ceremony.[88] This prayer was recited everywhere before the communion service, in conformity with Matt 5:23-24 (reconciliation with one's brother or sister before offering one's gift at the altar). In the East, moreover, believers gave each other the kiss of peace before reciting this prayer; in the West, afterwards. The conclusion that Rordorf has drawn from this is that the East favored Matthew's wording (forgive us, as we have just done among ourselves by means of the kiss of peace), whereas the West followed Luke's wording (forgive us, as we are going to do among ourselves by means of the kiss of peace). Each custom, like each Gospel, is witness to one aspect of the truth: in one case, may God forgive those who themselves forgive; in the other case, may forgiving enable us to imitate God.

In the LXX, $\epsilon i\sigma\phi\acute{\epsilon}\rho\omega$, when it is followed, as it is here, by $\epsilon i\varsigma$, means "to cause to enter, to bring in."[89] The aorist subjunctive preceded by the particle $\mu\acute{\eta}$ is one of the two ways of expressing the negative imperative, the one that expresses a precise categorical prohibition.[90] A Greek, then, would understand the request to mean "do not lead us into temptation." One question does arise, however, regarding the thrust of the negation. In Semitic languages, this negation before a causative verb can negate either the cause or the effect. The original Aramaic, then, may have meant: "make it so that we do not enter into temptation" rather than "do not lead us into temptation." This suggestion, defended with vigor by Jean Carmignac,[91] preserves the holiness of God, who does not incite to sin and, in a certain sense, does not tempt (cf. Jas 1:13-14). But $\pi\epsilon\iota\rho\alpha\sigma\mu\acute{o}\varsigma$ does not mean sin; it denotes a testing that can lead the believer either to deny God or to reject Satan. While the original Lord's Prayer perhaps had in mind the eschatological testing,[92] the absence of the definite article here leaves the

---

84 Luke loves this tradition; cf. 5:32; 19:9-10. Likewise, it pleases him to recall the obligation imposed by conversion; cf. 15:7. See Bovon, *Theologian*, 273–328.

85 Note the tension between 7:47a (forgiveness by Christ for the love already attested by the woman) and 7:47b (love as a consequence of forgiveness); see the commentary on 7:47 (1:384–85).

86 On this language, see the commentary on 4:21 (1:207 n. 25).

87 One finds another explanation, in e.g., Godet, 2:69; Lagrange, 323. If we, such as we are, know to forgive, how much more strongly will God, if we ask it of him.

88 Rordorf, "Lord's Prayer," 12–14.

89 In return, $\epsilon i\sigma\phi\acute{\epsilon}\rho\omega$, followed by a complement of the dative of person, always signifies, in the LXX, "to bring to," "to make come toward."

90 The other way: $\mu\acute{\eta}$ + indicative present has an iterative or durative sense; see BDF §335–37.

91 Carmignac, *Recherches*, 282–92, 301.

92 This is that of which Rev 3:10 speaks; so Jeremias, *Lord's Prayer*, 29–31; Schulz, *Q*, 92; Brown, "Pater Noster," 248–53.

risks vague. Luke, who knew how to put the word in the plural, was convinced that the disciples, from that time on until the parousia, would not be spared (Luke 22:28; Acts 20:19).[93] Doubt, wear and tear, and lust for money, possessions, or the pleasures of this world would hound them.[94] They would have to have perseverance, faith, detachment, and other virtues.[95] These qualities, whose psychological contours are not delineated by Luke, are human; but prayer, especially the Lord's Prayer, invites us to ask for God's help so that they might take root in us. If there is an entrance into temptation (8:13 speaks of "the moment of temptation"), there is also the possibility of escape, a "way out" ($\check{\epsilon}\kappa\beta\alpha\sigma\iota\varsigma$), as the apostle Paul says (1 Cor 10:13). Testing us is not a bad thing, moreover, but quite the contrary. It is a way, albeit risky, of toughening us up. May the Father spare us too much testing that, like a tempest, would cause us to founder. If we pray in this connection, it is because there is an associated risk: not that God might abuse us but that we might weaken.[96] Knowing our own weakness, are we going to ask to be spared all testing? Reality, which corresponds to our situation, is sure to remind us of the dangers that unfortunately threaten us. So we will pray to the Father that he protect his children and give them the strength they need.

In short, Jesus, who had been tempted and tested, knew what he was speaking about. Where there is no faith, there is no temptation either (note Abraham; Genesis 22). Temptation corresponds to a confusion between good and evil; worse, to a presentation of evil as its opposite, good. Fortunately, we are not conditioned by human reality alone. We are also dependent on God. May he not lead us into too much temptation, since he has the freedom and the power to do so. May he forgive us. If, when we are forgiven, we weather the storms and resist temptation, he will not hand us over to Satan.[97] The believers who recite the Lord's Prayer are situated on the ground between the sins they have committed and the temptation that threatens them. Their existence would hardly be called enviable, were it not for the fact that it has the overarching protection of the God who has chosen forgiveness as the argument to use in dialogue with human beings. But at the same time he has also opted for freedom as a sign of his love. Human beings run the risk of getting lost. The Lord's Prayer invites them to turn to him in order to ask for a way out of their temptation and for the spiritual strength necessary to confront it (1 Cor 10:13).

History of Interpretation

The version of the Lord's Prayer that has become Christians' prayer par excellence is the one in Matthew, not the one in Luke.[98] Through the centuries, there has been scarcely any thought devoted to the differences between the two texts. They have usually been explained in terms of different original situations: Jesus may have entrusted the Lord's Prayer in its Matthean version to the Twelve, but the Lukan version to the larger group known as the disciples.[99] As an instrument of personal piety,[100] the Lord's Prayer has been a part of the baptismal catechism since the third century C.E. New converts had to learn the prayer by heart and recite it at the time of their baptism.[101] It was also made a part of the eucharistic liturgy (from the fourth century C.E. on, at the latest). In the convents, it was recited at each of the liturgical

---

93 Cf. Luke 4:13: "having ended every temptation." Echoing the Our Father, Luke has the following injunction repeated to Jesus: "pray that you may not enter into temptation" (22:40, 46).

94 On this doubt, see 8:12; on the lack of perseverance, 8:13; on the dangers of this world, 8:14.

95 On perseverance, see 8:15; on faith, 18:8; on detachment, 9:23.

96 At the start of his life (4:1-13) and at the end (22:35-46), the Lukan Jesus appears as the true believer who is proved by ordeals.

97 We live during the time of forgiveness. At the parousia, following Heb 9:28, there will be no expiation possible.

98 On the history of reception, see Sabugal, *Oración*; J. A. Robinson, *The Lord's Prayer in the Early Church* (Cambridge, 1891); Hamman, *Pater*; idem, "Notre Père."

99 On this solution and other similar ones that such a solution rejects, see Sabugal, *Oración*, 86, 125, 289–90.

100 *Didache* 8.3 invites the faithful to recite the Our Father three times daily.

101 "Remember well this prayer, you will have to recite it in eight days," says Augustine to his flocks (*Serm.* 58.5).

hours. It even became an object of piety. As a matter of fact, Constantine's mother, Helen, had a church built in its honor on the Mount of Olives. There, following a later tradition, believers could admire an inscription bearing the text of the Lord's Prayer that had supposedly been carved by Jesus himself. This church, which was destroyed and rebuilt several times, is today part of a convent of Carmelites, and the Lord's Prayer is posted there to be read, translated into sixty-six languages.[102]

Most patristic commentaries were written to meet certain practical and catechetical requirements.[103] That may have been the case already with Tertullian's treatise on prayer; it certainly was with Cyprian's, to say nothing of the catechetical homilies of Cyril of Jerusalem, Augustine, and Theodore of Mopsuestia.[104] Only Origen's treatise (*De oratione*) was concerned with something of a different order, in this case a polemic against the Gnostics.

When the preachers explained the prayer to catechumens or believers, they stressed its doctrinal significance; to use Tertullian's expression, it is "the summary of all of the Gospel" (*Or.* 1: "breviarium totius evangelii"). The mention of the title "Father" leads into a reflection on what it means to be in a filial relationship. It is through Christ, the Son, that we become God's children: "The saints, being the image of an image, and that image the Son, take the impression of sonship, not only becoming of the same form as *the body of the glory* of Christ, but also like unto Him who is in the body" (*Or.* 22.4).[105] Commentators were struck by how well the Lord's Prayer was

put together. "The words have an admirable progression to them," wrote John Chrysostom. "The prayer asks us to desire future possessions and to always aim at heaven, but it also desires that, as we wait for that future, we imitate, even here on earth, the life of the angels in heaven" (*Hom. in Matt.* 6 [on Matt 19:5]).[106]

As a prayer, the Lord's Prayer takes its place in the midst of existence: it not only characterizes its nature, but it also orients its destiny. The sharpness of the commentaries on temptation is a witness to that. Origen wrote: "We ask to be delivered from temptation: not to be spared it, which is impossible for human beings here on earth, but rather not to succumb, when we fall into it" (*Or.* 29.9).[107] The believer does not lead this existence, which is undermined by temptation, in isolation; Cyprian stressed the fact that it is a community undertaking: "We do not say: 'My father, who are in the heavens,' nor 'Give me my bread this day.' Nor does anybody request that his debt be pardoned for himself alone, nor ask that he alone be not led into temptation and delivered from the evil one. Our prayer is common and collective, and when we pray we pray not for one but for all people, because we are all one people together" (*Dom. or.* 8).[108]

I would like to recall the following points made in the most erudite of all commentaries, the one by Origen: after a meticulous investigation of the Hebrew Bible, he noted: "But nowhere, in a prayer [in the Hebrew Bible], is God addressed as Father, as he is in the expression full of confidence that the Savior has passed on to us" (*Or.* 22.1).[109] With respect to God's reign, Origen militated

102 See Sabugal (*Oración*, 34–47), who calls attention to the cryptograms of the Our Father and innumerable paraphrases. Among these, see the hymn attributed to Ambrose (*Hymn.* 39); Dante *Purgatorio* 11.1–21. I have a small collection of contemporary paraphrases, one of which is the poem of Kurt Marti, *Abendland: Gedichte* (Darmstadt/Munich: Luchterhand, 1980) 50–52.

103 Hamman, "Notre Père."

104 Tertullian *Or.* 1–9; Cyprian *Dom. or.*; Cyril of Jerusalem *Cat. Myst.* 5; Augustine *Serm.* 56–59; *Serm. Dom.* 2.4.15–11.39; Theodore of Mopsuestia *Hom. cat.* 11, in *Les homélies catéchétiques de Théodore de Mopsueste: Reproduction phototypique du ms. Mingana Syr. 561* (ed. R. Tonneau; Vatican City: Biblioteca apostolica vaticana, 1949) 299–321. A list of other authors can be found in Hamman, "Notre Père," 43 n. 11. Curi-

ously, in his commentary on Luke, Ambrose does not treat the Our Father.

105 Origen, *Prayer/Exhortation to Martyrdom* (trans. and annotated by John J. O'Meara; Ancient Christian Writers 19; Westminster, Md.: Newman Press, 1954) 75.

106 In *Nicene and Post–Nicene Fathers,* First Series, vol. 10: *Homilies on The Gospel of Saint Matthew* (ed. Philip Schaff; 1888; reprinted Peabody, Mass.: Hendrickson, 1994) 134–35. *PG* 57:279.

107 Origen, *Prayer/Exhortation to Martyrdom* (trans. O'Meara) 117.

108 In *On the Lord's Prayer* (trans. Alistair Stewart-Sykes; Crestwood, N.Y.: St. Vladimir's Seminary Press, 2004) 69.

109 Origen, *Prayer/Exhortation to Martyrdom* (trans. O'Meara) 72–73.

against millenarianism and thought of the coming of the reign as taking place from the present on, in believers' inner being. The coming of the reign coincides with Christ's presence: it is in the soul of those who are perfect that the Father reigns with Christ, as in a city (*Or.* 25.1). As both a scholar and a believer, Origen wondered about what the Greek word ἐπιούσιος modifying the word "bread" said about its nature. He did not find the adjective either in the Scriptures or in secular authors. He considered it to have two possible meanings: "supersubstantial," which he preferred, and "for the morrow" (*Or.* 27). In any case, he refused to see in it a reference to material bread. Nor did he adopt the eucharistic meaning, but preferred to identify this bread with Christ, the Word of God, following John 6 (*Or.* 27). As a philologist, Origen deduced from Matthew's text, as well as from Luke's, that our forgiveness must precede God's (*Or.* 28.1). We find this same theology of responsibility in connection with the matter of temptations. The good God puts us to the test but does not lead us astray. He tests our free will (*Or.* 29).

In the fifth century, Cyril of Alexandria devoted eight sermons (*Serm.* 70–77) to the Lukan Lord's Prayer.[110] The most interesting of them, *Serm.* 75, is devoted to the petition for bread. Even though he naturally admitted that we have spiritual needs, Cyril, unlike Origen and many of the Eastern Fathers, refused to allegorize. According to him, what we have here is a petition for material bread of which we have no reason to be ashamed. And if there is a petition, it is because there is poverty and need. Ἐπιούσιος should be translated by "necessary" and "suf-

ficient."[111] There is no coveting of riches associated with this petition. Like soldiers, saints go off to combat with the strict minimum of what is necessary.

We have a short explanation of the Matthean version of the Lord's Prayer by Francis of Assisi, in the form of a prayer[112] that he was accustomed to saying and that he asked his brothers to recite. Throughout this text, what strikes us is the consciousness of God's love and goodness, which must be reflected in our lives. To God in heaven he says, "Enflaming them with love, for you, Lord, you are love." As for the petition for bread, it is a petition requesting the Son: "Give us today our daily bread, your beloved Son, our Lord Jesus Christ." And this is with reference to the love that he demonstrated toward us, and to what he said, did, and endured on our behalf.

The Reformer Martin Luther was at pains—in this matter following tradition—to explain the Lord's Prayer (in its Matthean version) to ordinary folk along with the Ten Commandments and the creed. So he did (in German) on at least four occasions.[113] The invocation "Father" gives expression to the reciprocity of the parental relationship. The word is affectionate, and what is sweeter than hearing a child calling to his or her father?[114] "The daily bread" is Jesus Christ, who nourishes and consoles the soul (Luther leaves no place for a literal explanation).[115] Luther discovered "temptation" in three domains: the flesh, the world, and the devil; he drew up a stimulating list of temptations that necessitate an appeal to God, and a panoply of defensive weapons.[116] Coming as it does from the Lord, the Lord's Prayer is the sublimest and the noblest of all prayers.[117] It is interesting

---

110 The first sermon (70) is general, the second (71) concerns the Father, and the following has diverse requests. Cyril has a long text of Luke 11:2; *Serm.* 74 concerns the will. But he has a short text of Luke 11:4 to which he devotes *Serm.* 76 and 77; see Payne Smith, *Cyril*, 1:321–53.

111 Cyril brings together the word περιούσιος (Titus 2:14), which he understands also in the sense of "sufficient," "next to perfection."

112 See Francis of Assisi, *Écrits* (ed. and trans. Théophile Desbonnets et al.; SC 285; Paris: Cerf, 1981; reprinted with additions and corrections, 2003) 276–77; K. Esser, *Die Opuscula des hl. Franziskus von Assisi: Neue textkritische Edition* (ed. Kajetan Esser; Grottaferrata: Editiones Collegii S. Bonaventurae ad Claras Aquas, 1976) 292–93.

113 These four occasions are as follows: (1) *Auslegung deutsch des Vaterunsers für die einfältigen Laien* (Leipzig, 1519) WA 2:74–130 (an exposition in German on the Lord's Prayer for the simple laity at Leipzig in 1519); (2) *Der grosse Katechismus*, vers 1529, WA 30, 1:123–238 (the large catechism, dated about 1529); (3) *Zwei Predigten, die eine vom 14. Dez., die andere vom 15. Dez. 1528 (in zwei Versionen überliefert)*; (4) *Eine kurze Form der zehn Gebote, eine kurze Form des Glaubens, eine kurze Form des Vaterunsers*, 1520 (the last part, the Our Father, appeared in an independent way already in 1519), WA 7:204–29.

114 Luther, *Auslegung* (n. 113 above), 83.

115 Luther, *Eine kurze Form* (n. 113 above), 225–26.

116 Ibid., 227–29.

117 Luther, *Auslegung* (n. 113 above), 82.

that, in a succession of commentators from Francis of Assisi to Luther,[118] and passing by way of Erasmus (*Paraphrasis* 11.379–80),[119] commentary on the Lord's Prayer was written in the second person singular: in this commentary God was addressed and not explained; under the influence of the text being explained, commentary became prayer.[120]

In 1979, Leonardo Boff published a book devoted to the Lord's Prayer.[121] In his opinion, this prayer regulates relationships between human beings and God, heaven and earth, and religion and politics. God is not concerned solely with his holiness, his reign, and his will, but also with the needs of human beings. They, in turn, make a connection between their daily existence and God's domain. The Lord's Prayer is thus a prayer involving reciprocal relationships. There is no true liberation without an encounter with God, nor any encounter with God outside a social existence.

Moreover, Boff notes the absence of christological and ecclesiological allusions in the Lord's Prayer, which has as its principal subject God in the presence of human beings. He adds that the dialogue takes place not in a relaxed atmosphere but against the somber backdrop of a tragic history. The Lord's Prayer paints a certain picture of God. So Boff traces the evolution of the word "father," starting with the universal anthropological conscience all the way up to Jesus' expression ʾabbāʾ, by way of the religions of antiquity in the Near East and the Hebrew Bible. What follows from this, for the image of God in the Lord's Prayer, is a tension between proximity and distance. Calling God "Father" makes human beings feel close to him (more than it makes them perceive themselves as his descendants). The fact that God is distant, moreover, means that God is not dependent on any race, religion, or place of worship. It is this distance that affords us our only chance to efficaciously transform the world.

Boff next reflects on the meaning that God's paternity can have in a society that turns its back on the patriarchal system and is hard on the father figure. He takes satisfaction in the destruction of paternal images whose only reason for existence is the satisfaction of desires and the calming of fears, in particular the image of God the Father giving legitimacy to a society that is hierarchical and immobilized. Our age is justified in replacing the patriarchate by fraternal/brotherly and sororal/sisterly relationships. Among the criticisms that Freud and Nietzsche leveled at religion, Boff has latched on to a clarification of the faith, to which the paternal image of the Lord's Prayer corresponds. The Lord's Prayer invites us to renounce dreams of omnipotence and proposes the liberation, not the consolation, of those who are oppressed.

At the end of this overview, let me mention a provocative commentary by Elga Sorge, which calls into question the patriarchal face-to-face relationship between the Creator and his creatures and advocates a pantheistic conception of divine energies running through the universe.[122] In her eyes, the Bible combines these two theologies. The Lord's Prayer makes it possible to distinguish them; in particular, it criticizes YHWH, the national God of Israel, the solitary chosen people. It invokes instead ʾabbāʾ, that is, the God who protects love, who is the Father of Jesus, and whose heavenly existence makes it possible to breathe his energies into all things. He is a God of pardon and not of expiation, a God who follows the example of Jesus' disciples' attitude ("for we ourselves forgive . . ."). He is the God whom we implore to act in another way than does Satan, who leads us into temptation, which is the desire to dominate and hatred

---

118 This is the case for *Eine kurze Form* (n. 113 above).

119 Erasmus, *In Evangelium Lucae Paraphrasis*. English: *Paraphrase on Luke* (trans. and annotated J. E. Phillips; Toronto: University of Toronto Press, 2003).

120 Calvin, *Harmony*, 177–85. I retain a conviction that I share here: the requests in "you" concern us also and those in "we" engage God equally. For example, it is salutary for humans that honor be rendered to God (p. 179); humans dare, among other things, to request of God bread (to which Calvin gives here a material sense), if they discover primarily his glory (p. 181).

121 Boff, *Lord's Prayer*.

122 Sorge, *Frau*, 93–97. On pp. 90–91, the author places two prayers face to face, one of which presents God as being dominating ("Herr Vaterunser") (Our Father, as Master) and the other of which celebrates a protective deity ("Mutterunsere") (Our Mother).

of one's enemies. This book levels a feminist critique at a certain image of the father and of power. This critique is penetrating enough to see that the reversal of situations, such as the Magnificat proclaims it, does not mean that all dominations have been brought to an end. It may mean only that the slave has been substituted for the master, without the eradication of the desire for omnipotence. If the opposition between the two divine images is a recollection of the Gnostic systems of the second century C.E., then it seems to me that the critique of patriarchal domination is true to the Gospel, and therefore legitimate.[123]

Conclusion

In order to explain the Lord's Prayer, one has to know how to pray. Aimed at partners in the faith, the commentary must at the same time be a dialogue with God. That kind of doxological commenting, a long-standing procedure, should be the inspiration of any modern commentator. It would put to the test his or her knowledge and intuitions in the context of sharing with the Father. Such interpretation would be illuminated in a new and decisive way. I purposely use the conditional, since I note, in retrospect, that I have not truly carried out that process.

The Lord's Prayer has circulated in writing and orally. Those two ways are similar, however, since they each give expression to the Christian faith, which is rooted in Jesus' religious certainty. And what the Master furnished to be recited in prayer was, in his eyes, nothing other than the essence of the Hebrew faith.

God is tender, near to his people, concerned about the terrestrial destiny of his chosen people, careful to nourish them without stuffing them, and devoted to forgiving them and getting them back on their way to the promised land. He is a God of life, life that combines spiritual experience and material needs.

What this Father is confronted with is not a humanity en masse but a people composed of children, all different and each one having an inestimable worth. They are fragile and confident persons who have been tested and show solidarity. They are flesh-and-blood beings who are thirsty for God.

The Lord's Prayer is one that cements relationships and gives God the highest rank; but in praising his name or his reign, it has as its aim the happiness of the people and the life of each one. In its calling for bread or forgiveness, God's honor is symmetrically shown to be at stake through the matter of human dignity.

The Lord's Prayer is an elementary prayer, focused on what is essential; it does not replace all other prayers. Curiously enough, it does not mention thanksgiving or intercession. So it is a complement to, and not a substitute for, the Psalms.

Spoken by Jesus, the mediator between God and human beings, the one who participates in the life of both heaven and earth, the Lord's Prayer brings material and spiritual possessions together in that concrete unity of salvation that the Hebraic traditions fostered uninterruptedly. God's reign is both tangible and spiritual, like the bread that nourishes our bodies and our hearts.

In this traditional biblical material there is a find, better still a revelation, a revelation of a Father who, in his tenderness and his vigor, protects, nourishes, leads, and saves his children.

---

123 There exist also illustrations of the Our Father and the requests, for example, the engravings of Hans Holbein "the younger" and of Lucas Cranach "the elder"; one finds such illustrations in Gertrud Schiller, *Ikonographie der christlichen Kunst* (5 vols. in 7; Gütersloh: Mohn, 1966–91) 4.1:322–38.

Prayer and Its Granting (11:5-13)

Bibliography

Bailey, Kenneth E., *Poet and Peasant: A Literary-Cultural Approach to the Parables in Luke* (Grand Rapids: Eerdmans, 1976).

Bammel, E., "Rest and Ruhe," *VC* 23 (1969) 88–90.

Bastian, H. D., "Das Gleichnis im Religionsunterricht (Hauptschule – Sekundarstufe I)," *LingBibl* 2 (1970) 12–13.

Berger, Klaus, "Materialien zu Form und Überlieferungsgeschichte neutestamentlicher Gleichnisse," *NovT* 15 (1973) 1–37.

Bovon, *Theologian*, 453–57.

Brox, Norbert, "Suchen und finden: Zur Nachgeschichte von Mt 7, 7b/Lk 11, 9b," in Hoffmann et al., *Orientierung,* 17–36.

Buzy, Denis, *Les paraboles* (VS 6; Paris: Beauchesne, 1932) 579–602.

Caba, José, *La oración de petición: Estudio exegético sobre los evangelios sinópticos y los escritos joaneos* (AnBib 62; Rome: Biblical Institute Press, 1974) 11–23, 63–93.

Catchpole, David R., "Q and 'The Friend at Midnight' (Luke xi.5-8/9)," *JTS* n.s. 34 (1983) 407–24.

Chadwick, Henry, "Prayer at Midnight," in Jacques Fontaine and Charles Kannengiesser, eds., *Epektasis:Mélanges patristiques offerts au cardinal Jean Daniélou* (Paris: Beauchesne, 1972) 47–49.

Delebecque, Edouard, "Sur un hellénisme de saint Luc," *RB* 87 (1980) 590–93.

Derrett, J. Duncan M., "The Friend at Midnight: Asian Ideas in the Gospel of St. Luke," in Ernst Bammel et al., eds., *Donum gentilicium: New Testament Studies in Honour of David Daube* (Oxford: Clarendon, 1978) 78–87. Reprinted in Derrett, *Studies,* 3:31–41.

Dupont, Jacques, "La prière et son efficacité dans l'évangile de Luc," in Dupont, *Études,* 2:1055–65.
Edwards, *Theology of Q*, 108–9.

Fridrichsen, A., "Exegetisches zum Neuen Testament," *SO* 13 (1934) 40–43.

Goldsmith, Dale, "'Ask and It Will Be Given . . .': Toward Writing the History of a Logion," *NTS* 35 (1989) 254–65.

Güttgemanns, Erhardt, "Struktural-generative Analyse der Parabel 'Vom bittenden Freund' (Lk 11, 5-8)," *LingBibl* 2 (1970) 7–11.

Haacker, Klaus, "Mut zum Bitten: Eine Auslegung von Lukas 11, 5-8," *ThBei* 17 (1987) 1–6.

Heininger, Bernhard, *Metaphorik, Erzählstruktur und szenisch-dramatische Gestaltung in den Sondergleichnissen bei Lukas* (NTAbh n.s. 24; Münster: Aschendorff, 1991) 98–107.

Hermaniuk, Maxime, *La parabole évangélique: Enquête exégétique et critique* (Dissertationes ad gradum magistri in Facultate Theologica consequendum conscriptae 2.38; Paris/Louvain: Desclée, 1947) 244, 247–48.

Hjerl-Hansen, Børge, "Le rapprochement poisson-serpent dans la prédication de Jésus (Mt 7, 10 et 11,11)," *RB* 55 (1948) 195–98.

Huffard, Evertt W., "The Parable of the Friend at Midnight: God's Honor or Man's Persistence?" *ResQ* 21 (1978) 154–60.

Jeremias, Joachim, *The Parables of Jesus* (trans. Samuel Henry Hooke; London: SCM, 1954; 2d rev. ed.; London: SCM; New York: Scribner, 1972).

Johnson, Alan F., "Assurance for Man: the Fallacy of Translating *Anaideia* by 'Persistence' in Luke 11, 5-8," *JETS* 22 (1979) 123–31.

Jülicher, *Gleichnisreden*, 2:268–76.

Kloppenborg, *Formation*, 182, 203 n. 132.

Koester, Helmut, "The Extracanonical Sayings of the Lord as Products of the Christian Community," *Semeia* 44 (1988) 57–77.

Kraeling, Carl Hermann, "Seek and You Will Find," in Allen Wikgren, ed., *Early Christian Origins* (Chicago: Quadrangle Books, 1961) 24–34.

Leonardi, Giovanni, "'Cercate e troverete . . . lo Spirito Santo' nell'unità letteraria di Luca 11, 1-13," in Antonio Bonora et al., eds., *Quaerere Deum* (Atti della Settimana Biblica 25; Brescia: Paideia, 1980) 261–88.

Levison, Nahum, "Importunity? A Study of Lk 11, 8 ($\Delta\iota\acute{\alpha}\ \gamma\epsilon\ \tau\grave{\eta}\nu\ \grave{\alpha}\nu\alpha\iota\delta\acute{\iota}\alpha\nu\ \alpha\grave{\upsilon}\tau o\hat{\upsilon}$)," *ExpT* 9.3 (1925) 456–60.

Idem, *The Parables: Their Background and Local Setting* (Edinburgh: T&T Clark, 1926) 80–84.

Magass, Walter, "Zur Semiotik der erzählten Indezenz," *LingBibl* 2 (1970) 3–7.

Metzger, *Textual Commentary*, 157–58.

Ott, *Gebet und Heil*, 23–31, 71–72, 92–112.

Pegg, H., "'A Scorpion for an Egg' (Luke 11:12)," *ExpT* 38 (1926–27) 468–69.

Piper, Ronald A., "Matthew 7:7-11 par. Luke 11:9-13: Evidence of Design and Argument in the Collection of Jesus Sayings," in Delobel, *Logia*, 419–23.

Rickards, Raymond R., "The Translation of Luke 11:5-13," *BT* 27 (1976) 239–43.

Schulz, *Q*, 161–64.

Steinhauser, *Doppelbildworte*, 69–79.

Tolbert, *Perspectives*, 24.

Tuckett, C. M., "Q, Prayer, and the Kingdom," *JTS* 40 (1989) 367–76.

Vara, J., "Una sugerencia: $\kappa\acute{o}\pi\rho\iota o\nu$ lección originaria de $\sigma\kappa o\rho\pi\acute{\iota}o\nu$ en Lucas 11, 11-12," *Salmanticensis* 30 (1983) 225–29.

5/ **And he said to them, "Which one of you having a friend will go to him at midnight and say to him, 'Friend, lend me three loaves of bread; 6/ for a friend of mine on a journey[a] has arrived at my house, and I have nothing to serve him.' 7/ And he says to him from inside, 'Do not bother me! The door has already been locked, and my children are in bed with me; I cannot get up and give you anything.' 8/ I tell you, even though he will not get up and give him anything because he is his friend, at least because of the shamelessness of that man,[b] when he is awakened,[b] he will give him whatever he needs. 9/ And I say to you, Ask, and it will be given to you; search, and you will find; knock, and the door will be opened for you. 10/ For everyone who asks receives, and everyone who searches finds, and to everyone who knocks, the door will be opened. 11/ Which father among you whose son[c] asks him for bread will give him a stone, or if he asks for a fish, will give him a snake instead of a fish? 12/ Or if an egg is asked for, will give him a scorpion[d]? 13/ If you then, who are evil, know how to give good gifts to your children, how much more will the heavenly Father give the Holy Spirit to those who ask him!"**

a   Literally: "from his road."
b   Or: "once he gets up."
c   Literally: "the son."
d   On the text-critical problem in vv. 11-12, see below, pp. 105–6.

We have here a parable whose lesson does not lead to any application; there are imperatives without any direct objects and rhetorical questions that rule out things that should not be done without suggesting what should be done. These lacunae and silences do not signal a weakness in composition. They are rather a formal trick that fills an oratorical function, mobilizing one's intelligence and awakening the conscience of listeners who are thereby intrigued and challenged.

Analysis

Structure

In spite of the disparate origin of its elements and the caesurae represented in the first part of the speech (vv. 5, 8, and 9), vv. 5-13 form a unit.[1] In a first phase (vv. 5-8), Jesus tells a story, which he introduces with a rhetorical question ("Which one of you?" [$\tau\acute{\iota}\varsigma\ \dot{\epsilon}\xi\ \dot{\upsilon}\mu\hat{\omega}\nu\ \ldots$], v. 5) and closes with an interpretative conclusion ("I tell you"

[$\lambda\acute{\epsilon}\gamma\omega\ \dot{\upsilon}\mu\hat{\iota}\nu$], v. 8).[2] In a second phase (vv. 9-10), Jesus speaks up again ("and I say to you," [$\kappa\dot{\alpha}\gamma\dot{\omega}\ \dot{\upsilon}\mu\hat{\iota}\nu\ \lambda\acute{\epsilon}\gamma\omega$], v. 9) in order to invite his listeners to ask questions and to promise them positive answers. The hortatory style of these two verses differs from the didactic style of the preceding parable and the following examples. In a third phase (vv. 11-13), whose structure recalls that of the first phase, a new rhetorical question ("Who among you?" [$\tau\acute{\iota}\nu\alpha\ \delta\dot{\epsilon}\ \dot{\epsilon}\xi\ \dot{\upsilon}\mu\hat{\omega}\nu$], v. 11) introduces three examples (vv. 11-12). These are then commented on authoritatively (v. 13). This conclusion (v. 13) corresponds to the one in the first part (v. 8), but while the parable requires an explanation, which will specify the motive for an action, the examples receive an interpretation that indicates to what reality they are to be related.[3]

The parable such as we read it contains some obscurities that are the result, at least in part, of its having been translated from Aramaic. That is why we are led to ask ourselves where Jesus' question introduced by "which

1   Most often commentators dissociate vv. 5-8 from vv. 9-13; so Marshall, 462–70; Fitzmyer, 2:909–16.
2   Bailey (*Poet*, 119–20) describes vv. 5-8 as a parabolic ballad that has two stanzas of six units each, the sec-

ond resuming the first. The climax is at the center of the second.
3   For an analysis of vv. 9-13, see Schulz, *Q*, 161–64.

one of you" (v. 5) ends.[4] And why do we have the aorist subjunctive in the Greek εἴπη ("say") to describe the first move made by the man petitioning for help,[5] following two future indicatives, "having" (literally, "will have") and "will go" (v. 5) and the same form, a second time, at the beginning of the answer given by the friend who was disturbed in the middle of the night (v. 7)? To whom should we take certain personal pronouns to refer, especially the "his" (αὐτοῦ), which we have translated as "of that man" in conjunction with "shamelessness" (or "impudence," ἀναίδεια, v. 8)? One thing seems sure: vv. 5-7 constitute a unit that, in a Semitic way, combines three elements: (a) an interrogative clause whose subject is "who?" which we have translated as "which one?" (v. 5); (b) a relative clause explaining the situation (v. 6); and (c) an assertion (v. 7), which serves as an apodosis. The implicit answer that is presupposed by the rhetorical question[6] in v. 5 is obviously: "No one."[7]

The harmonious clarity of vv. 9-10 contrasts with the obscurity of the parable. Three times a positive result is promised to the one who follows up on the invitation (v. 9); next the promised result receives a confirmation (at that point the text passes from the second to the third person and generalizes the case by the use of the adjective "every" ("everyone" in our translation, πᾶς, v. 10).[8]

As for the three hypothetical examples (vv. 11-12), they introduce an *a minori ad maius* reasoning, the affirmation that what holds for humans holds all the more for God (v. 13).[9]

The Pre-history of the Text

Examining the origin of the materials, we assign the parable (vv. 5-8) to L and the other sayings (vv. 9-13) to Q. What is surprising, however, is that, contrary to his usual practice, here Luke jumps back and forth from one source to the other. Has he not already just alternated between L (Good Samaritan and Martha and Mary) and

Q (the Lord's Prayer)? Anxious to bring together several teachings about prayer, he is probably inclined to associate the parable with the Lord's Prayer because of the common theme, more particularly of the same need for "bread" (ἄρτος, v. 5, serves as a linking word; cf. 11:3).[10]

Without any parallel in the other Gospels, it is difficult for a commentator to reconstruct the traditional structure of the parable. Nevertheless, what makes the task easier is the examination of another Lukan parable that also comes from L, that is, the one that we have judged to be a doublet of this one, the feminine one that corresponds to this one, namely, the parable of the widow and the unjust judge (Luke 18:1-8).[11] These parables have the following points in common:[12] (1) A person in need appeals to someone else who can help. (2) This request is the occasion for some disturbance (κόπος). (3) In each case, the person to whom the appeal is made talks to himself (that is assumed in the one case but expressed in the other). (4) That person ends up deciding to help for a reason that is far from honorable. (5) Our attention is drawn to the manner in which the solicitation is made. This last point corresponds to a Lukan interest displayed at the beginning of the second parable: "[Jesus] told them a parable to show them that they need to pray always and not lose heart" (Luke 18:1). In my opinion, this is a legitimate concern in chap. 18, since it corresponds to the point of the parable of the widow and the unjust judge. It is much less so in chap. 11, where it appears to have been imported by Luke from chap 18. This observation makes it possible for us to distinguish a traditional orientation, especially noticeable in vv. 5-7, which stresses the granting (the disturbed friend responds positively) and a rereading by the author, principally in v. 8. This rereading underlines the importance of a request that can come no matter when (the host does not hesitate to go knocking on the door at midnight).[13] So the parables in chaps. 11 and 18 are

---

4   Plummer, 298.

5   BDF §366 n. 6; Delebecque, 71.

6   On the question of rhetoric and allegory, see Jeremias, *Parables*, 88–89.

7   See Klaus Beyer, *Semitische Syntax im Neuen Testament*, vol. 1.1 (SUNT 1; Göttingen: Vandenhoeck & Ruprecht, 1962) 287–93; Catchpole, "Friend," 412; Buzy, *Paraboles*, 583.

8   See Fitzmyer, 2:914.

9   Klostermann, 126.

10   See Marshall, 463.

11   Ernst, 365.

12   Catchpole, "Friend," 411.

13   Jeremias, *Parables*, 136–37; Caba, *Oración de petición*, 23–25. On the Old Latin variant that underlines the paraenetic sense, see n. 34 below.

not simple doublets. They fill complementary functions in L (in which it is not certain, moreover, that they were located side by side).[14]

David R. Catchpole suggests that Luke's redaction was even more aggressive.[15] Catchpole in fact attributes the following words to Luke's activity: "even though he will not get up and give him anything because he is his friend, at least [he gets up] because of the shamelessness of that man." For Catchpole, the parable, at the level of tradition, had as Jesus' only lesson: "I tell you, he will get up and give him whatever he needs." Catchpole, who attributes the parable to Q and not to L, believes moreover that he can reconstruct a sequence of pericopes in the tradition: (a) Matt 6:7-8 ("don't pray like the Gentiles"); (b) Matt 6:9-13 par. Luke 11:2-4 (Lord's Prayer); (c) Luke 11:5-9, minus the words that are suspect, with Matt 7:7 as a partial parallel ("ask"); (d) Matt 7:8 par. Luke 11:10 ("everyone who asks"); (e) Matt 7:9-11 par. Luke 11:11-13 ("which father?"); (f) Matt 6:25-33 par. Luke 12:22-31 (worries).[16] Not only do I not follow him in attributing the parable to Q, but neither will I take a position on the sequences he proposes. I feel that the petitions (Luke 11:9-13 and parallel) closely followed the Lord's Prayer (Luke 11:2-4 and parallel) in that source. I will go into the detail of comparisons of these last two items in the course of my commenting on this pericope. For now I will limit myself to noting that Matthew has kept the wording of Q in speaking of "goods" ($\dot{\alpha}\gamma\alpha\vartheta\dot{\alpha}$) that the heavenly Father grants. Luke's wording, the "Holy Spirit" ($\pi\nu\epsilon\hat{v}\mu\alpha$ $\ddot{\alpha}\gamma\iota\sigma\nu$), is therefore a significant redactional interpretation.[17]

Commentary

■ **5-6** Several of Jesus' sayings that come from Luke and L begin as follows: "Which one of you?" ($\tau\dot{\iota}\varsigma$ $\dot{\epsilon}\xi$ $\dot{\nu}\mu\hat{\omega}\nu$).[18] This is a way of engaging listeners,[19] of saying to them: "Put yourselves in that situation!" The shift in the Greek from the future indicative to the aorist subjunctive is understandable, even if someone trained in classical philology finds it shocking.[20] It corresponds to "Imagine yourself saying to him!" The code of friendship[21] is explicitly stated: you go to the house of a friend ($\varphi\dot{\iota}\lambda\sigma\nu$ ... $\varphi\dot{\iota}\lambda\epsilon$, both in v. 5)—and naturally you are also his friend ("because he is his friend" [$\delta\iota\dot{\alpha}$ $\tau\dot{\sigma}$ $\epsilon\hat{\iota}\nu\alpha\iota$ $\varphi\dot{\iota}\lambda\sigma\nu$ $\alpha\dot{\nu}\tau\sigma\hat{\nu}$], v. 8)—who is asleep and you dare disturb him, since another friend of yours ($\varphi\dot{\iota}\lambda\sigma\varsigma$ $\mu\sigma\nu$, v. 6) has come to visit you in the middle of the night. There are rules, duties, and privileges that go with friendship.

Friendship lets you take such a step (just as it allowed you to be disturbed by someone coming to you late in the night!). It also obligates you to welcome your visitor. What a disgrace it would be for you if he had to report later that he was forced to look for a place to stay somewhere else! In this situation, the duties associated with friendship and the laws of hospitality[22] are united. You go asking for bread. It is not known why you do not have any.[23] The word "lend!" ($\chi\rho\hat{\eta}\sigma\sigma\nu$, the imperative of the verb $\kappa\dot{\iota}\chi\rho\eta\mu\iota$, which is a *hapax legomenon* in the New Testament) is aptly chosen. It refers to a friendly loan, without interest.[24] Why ask for three loaves? They were probably small loaves of the kind made in Syria.[25] The

---

14 On the two parables and their links, see Jeremias, *Parables*, 133–38; Ott, *Gebet und Heil*, 23–31; Marshall, 463; Ernst, 365.

15 Catchpole, "Friend," 412–13, 424.

16 Ibid., 423–24.

17 Schulz, *Q*, 161–64.

18 Cf. 11:11; 12:25; 14:28; 15:4; 17:7; Deut 10:6 (LXX); 1 Cor 9:9; Epictetus *Diss.* 1.27.15–21; H. Greeven, "Wer unter euch . . . ," *WD* 5 (1952) 86–101.

19 Loisy (317) and Lagrange (325) insist on this "you."

20 Plummer, 298; Delebecque, 71; Jülicher, *Gleichnisreden*, 2:268–69.

21 On friendship, see Dupont, "La communauté des biens aux premiers jours de l'Église," in Dupont, *Études*, 505–9.

22 On hospitality, see Buzy, *Paraboles*, 581–83; Bailey, *Poet*, 121; Derrett, "Friend"; Bovon, *Theologian*, 456 n. 117.

23 Did the peasant prepare his bread each day or each week? See Bailey (*Poet*, 122), who opts for the weekly meal.

24 *Χρῆσον* is to be distinguished from δανείζω, "to lend some money" to strangers with interest; see Jülicher (*Gleichnisreden*, 2:269), who notes a progressive convergence of these two verbs.

25 See Bailey, *Poet*, 121–24.

laws of hospitality require one to have enough food on hand, even at such an hour of the night.

You tell your neighbor what has happened to you, without either excusing yourself or giving your neighbor a chance to refuse you.[26] In the desert regions of Jordan or Egypt, bedouins move around in the cool hours of the night. In Palestine, where the population is sedentary, that is a more surprising phenomenon. That is just the point here: this is an unexpected situation that creates a problem. In short, the friend who has arrived has been on a journey.[27] When you say "and I have nothing to serve him,"[28] that is a manner of speaking.

■ **7** The indication of the hour is important. That is more a time for thieves to be operating than for the arrival of visitors,[29] more for fear than for joy, which here becomes a time for courage and confidence and for testing the limits of friendship. You now put your sleeping friend to the same test that your friend on a journey has put you to.

Once again, the use of the subjunctive in Greek is important: suppose that this person were to speak as Jesus imagined him speaking! Is such a reaction not understandable? At this hour for sleeping, who wants to be bothered (the Greek word κόπος is here used in the plural)?[30] If this second occurrence of "say" (εἴπῃ) here in v. 7 does indeed have the same force as the first one (in v. 5), it refers to a real possibility. If you happen to awaken someone who is sleeping in order to borrow three loaves from him, he may refuse you, at least in the short term, on the verbal level. But, like the first son in the parable of the two sons in Matt 21:18-31, on the level

of action, he will end up giving you what you want. That is what Jesus says in v. 8. In the meantime, one or two detailed explanations are called for.

The house was a simple one,[31] perhaps consisting of one large room with several corners for the different kinds of activity involved in the life of the family; in any case it would have had a single door (ἡ θύρα; note the article), which would have been closed from the inside by a bolt.[32] Drawing the bolt across to open the door could not have been done without making noise. The little "already" (ἤδη) is another expression of a bad mood and an unwillingness to help. The father was not really going to unlock the door again! The children were sleeping, perhaps between their parents in the only bed in the house, which was a large one.[33] The "I cannot" means "I don't want to." There was thus a triple refusal: to get up out of bed, to unlock the door, and to give anything.

■ **8** The two occurrences of the subjunctive εἴπῃ (vv. 5 and 7) leave a door to the story open, one might say, all the more since the verb "say" is used.[34] Will the grumbling sleeper do what he says? Torn between his needs and his duties, his wish and his friendship, he will, nonetheless, have to make up his mind. But the story breaks off here. And it is the one telling the story who at this point continues by commenting: the sleeper, when awakened, will get up, says the storyteller, and will give him whatever he needs. In the end, hospitality wins out. It is not in the name of friendship but "because of the shamelessness of that man." Some feel that the "shamelessness" in question is that of the sleeper who refuses to be ashamed the following day.[35] He will thus act out of

---

26 See Derrett, "Friend," 36.

27 Codex D makes him arrive opposite to the field, that is, simply outside: πάρεστιν ἀπ᾽ ἀγροῦ. On this reading, see Jülicher, *Gleichnisreden*, 2:270.

28 Παρατίθημί τινι ("to present," "to offer," "to serve [to eat]"); cf. 9:6; 10:8; Jülicher, *Gleichnisreden*, 2:270.

29 "Midnight"; see Chadwick, "Prayer at Midnight." On the thieves in the night, cf. Matt 24:42-44 and par.; 1 Thess 5:2; Rev 3:3.

30 On κόπος, see Jülicher (*Gleichnisreden*, 2:270), who refers to 18:5; Mark 14:6; Gal 6:17; *Hermas Vis.* 3.3.2; Epictetus *Diss.* 2.14.2.

31 On the house, see Jeremias, *Parables*, 136–38, 157–60. On the allegorical interpretation of Augustine, see below under "History of Interpretation."

32 See Jülicher, *Gleichnisreden*, 2:271; Jeremias, *Parables*,

157; Grundmann, 234; Magass ("Semiotik," 3) refers to a scene at the door in Menander's *Dyskalos* 427–86, and for the theme of borrowing and lending, to Theophrastus *Char.* 9.2.7; 10.13; 18.7; 30.20.

33 Cf. Clement of Alexandria, *Exc. Theod.* 86.3 τὰ παιδία τὰ ἤδη ἐν τῇ κοίτῃ συναναπαυόμενα, cited by Jülicher, *Gleichnisreden*, 2:271.

34 The Old Latin and the Clementine edition of the Vulgate read, at the start of this verse: "and if that one [or: that one if] should persist in beating" ("and if that one continued to knock"), glosses that amplify the redactional sense that Luke gives to the parable. Καί ("even if"; cf. BDF §374) implies that the supposition actually happened in fact; Plummer, 299.

35 Levison ("Importunity"; and *Parables*) judges that the neighbor who has awakened will give the bread

fear of the possibility of being made to feel ashamed in case he refuses. In that case, however, we would expect some word other than ἀναίδεια, and we would expect the reflexive ἑαυτοῦ in place of the personal pronoun αὐτοῦ, which is used demonstratively. What in the end causes the sleeper to make up his mind is not the fear of being ashamed but the refusal to have complications.

The meaning, albeit disputed, of the phrase διά γε τὴν ἀναίδειαν αὐτοῦ does, in fact, lead us in that direction.[36] Ἀναίδεια is "lack of modesty" or "of propriety." In the LXX, the verb, the noun, and the adjective refer to "hardness," the "lack of consideration," "the lack of scruples," the "lack of respect," "greed for gain."[37] In Josephus the meaning is "absence of a sense of honor," "irresponsibility," "effrontery," "obtuse persistence."[38] This term makes it impossible to see here an attitude that would, in the last analysis, be positive, that is, courage without timidity, and a legitimate insistence.[39]

The parable does not have an application; it is as if Jesus and later Luke had worn themselves out resolving the two enigmas of the parable itself: (a) What was the final act? and (b) What motivated it? Although v. 13 has an application, v. 8 does not have one, and its absence here has a rhetorical or didactic purpose. Since you have been addressed ("which one of you?" [τίς ἐξ ὑμῶν], v. 5; and "I tell you" [λέγω ὑμῖν], v. 8), what are your thoughts about it? There are therefore two possible answers, each of which presupposes an adaptation to the sphere of faith. The first concerns God: as the central personage of the parable, God "gives," in spite of reserva-

tions he may have. The second concerns believers: follow the example of the person making the request, don't hesitate, go ahead and ask! In both cases—and the context in which the parable is set confirms it—it is prayer that is being talked about. In the first case, the parable has a doctrinal thrust, expressing the goodness of a God who is perhaps asleep, perhaps unhappy, but who nevertheless does not turn away his friends. In the second case, the parable has an ethical thrust, encouraging destitute believers to knock on the right door in spite of everything. The Gospel writer stresses the second interpretation through the immediate context ("And I say to you, Ask, . . . ," v. 9) and the commentary he furnishes on the similar parable in 18:1. On the other hand, the structure of the parable suggests that tradition and L opted for the first one. The two orientations are, moreover, far from mutually incompatible.[40]

■ **9-10** So Luke seems to have inserted the parable into a Q sequence. The "And I say to you," which is Lukan,[41] makes it possible for the Gospel writer to link up again with that source. From a thematic point of view, he continues his teaching on prayer[42] by stressing, just as in v. 8, the responsibility of the person praying.

In v. 9, Luke, like Matthew, carefully preserves the wording of Q: his text is identical to Matthew's. The parallelism, slightly progressive at the level of the meaning, is evident between the three imperatives, which are assured of a reward, in v. 9, and the three actions in v. 10.[43] The style is proverbial and sapiential.[44]

---

in order to *strengthen* his friend (such would be the sense of the Semitic equivalent of ἀναίδεια). Fridrichsen ("Exegetisches") understands it in this way: "because of *his* (his own) shamelessness, which indeed would proceed for days through his refusal." Cf. Jeremias, *Parables* 137–39, 156–59; Eberhard Jüngel, *Paulus und Jesus: Eine Untersuchung zur Präzisierung der Frage nach dem Ursprung der Christologie* (HUT 2; Tübingen: Mohr Siebeck, 1962) 156.

36 On this word, see Caba, *Oración de petición*, 20–22; Catchpole, "Friend," 409–11.

37 Cf., e.g., Deut 28:50; Dan (Theod.) 2:15; Prov 7:13; Sir 23:6; 25:22; 26:11; 40:30.

38 Cf., e.g., Josephus *Bell.* 1.14.1 §276; 6.3.3 §199; *Ant.* 17.5.5 §119; *Vita* 357.

39 Against Derrett ("Friend"), who relies much upon the sense of ἀναίδεια for the one who knocks, but

translates the term here in a positive sense "without hesitation," "with confidence."

40 Verse 8 contains numerous Lukan characteristics: εἰ καί in a concessive sense (cf. 18:4); the enclitic γε, the usage of which is uniquely Lukan in the Gospels (cf. 18:5; Acts 2:18; 8:30; 17:27); διὰ τὸ εἶναι is distinctively Lukan among the evangelists (cf. Luke 2:4; 11:8; 19:11). Redactional in its form, this verse gives the sense of the parable that the evangelist wishes to retain; see Caba, *Oración de petición*, 24.

41 See Schulz, *Q*, 161.

42 See Klostermann, 125.

43 Bailey, *Poet*, 135.

44 Schulz (*Q*, 162–64) regards this style as that of a prophet. These verses belong, in his opinion, to a layer more ancient than Q.

The pair "ask"–"receive" is encountered frequently in the LXX and the New Testament, with both a secular meaning and a religious one.[45] Luke has used it in the Sermon on the Plain: "Give to everyone who asks from you" (6:30). It is found again, in connection with prayer, in v. 13.[46] The passive in this context is a reference to God, and the future refers to the time that follows the prayer (this time does not necessarily correspond to the parousia). Luke shares with Jesus, but also with all of contemporary Judaism, this certitude regarding the granting of what is prayed for.[47]

The pair "search"–"find" is also deeply rooted in the New Testament.[48] Luke made use of it in the episode about Jesus when he was twelve years old (Luke 2:44, 46, 48), and he was to use it in a literary way in Paul's speech in front of the Areopagus: "so that they would search for God and perhaps grope for him and find him—though indeed he is not far from each one of us" (Acts 17:27). Nevertheless, the God of Scripture is first and foremost a God who reveals himself, who takes the initiative. An interpretation that insists on searching for God will not be devoid of danger. It is not stated, moreover, that the Lord is being searched for here. The content of the search may be more banal than that. Nevertheless, the context (v. 13) suggests some things that only God possesses. So the text invites us to ask for bread, in its double form of food and Word (11:3), to be given for our life, without making a separation between what is material and what is spiritual, and for everything that keeps us in contact with God, that is related to his kingdom, and that corresponds to his will and that he intends to grant

us. That way, we do not leave the world but inhabit it in the light of God, under his inspiration (cf. v. 13, where the Holy Spirit is promised). This searching, which is a confirmation of the petition, is assured of success. That is the main point of the text. But that search is to be carried out by those ("you") whom Christ addresses and whom God has already encountered. God's sovereignty can, however, in the case that there is a failure of communication, be addressed to other persons. "I was ready to be sought out by those who did not ask, to be found by those who did not seek me. I said, 'Here I am, here I am,' to a nation that did not call on my name" (Isa 65:1 NRSV).[49]

The third pair "knock"–"open" immediately calls to mind the door of the parable (v. 7).[50] Although Christ, in his parousia, can be the subject of the verb "knock" in 12:36 (cf. Rev 3:20), the situation in 13:25 resembles the one in this pericope. There it is a matter of access to the kingdom, to the narrow door, at which knock those unfortunate folk who will not have struggled the way they should have to gain access to it.[51] The text here in chap. 11 does not indicate any condition for the success of the approach. It is a call to a show of confidence and initiative. But it is the initiative of "you (pl.)," that is, those who have faith and do what is right by God and their neighbor.

Verse 10 confirms that by enlarging the horizon (cf. the "everyone," $\pi \hat{\alpha} \varsigma$). It picks up on the same verbs (except that it has "receive" in place of "be given"), conjugating them this time in the present tense, which is an indication of the certitude (rather than the immediacy) of the prayer's being answered.[52]

---

45 Cf. 1 Sam (1 Kgdms) 1:17; Ps 2:8; 2 Chr 1:7-12; Matt 6:8; 18:19; 20:22; 21:22; Mark 6:22; Leonardi, "Cercate," 276–77.

46 For requests addressed to God, see Matt 6:8; 7:7, 11; 18:19; 21:22; Mark 11:24; John 14:13; 15:7, 16; 16:23-26. For requests addressed to Jesus, see Matt 20:20-22 par.; John 4:10, 14.

47 Sirach 7:10: prayer granted in Judaism; see Str-B 1:450–58; Schulz, Q, 163; Pierre Bonnard, L'Évangile selon saint Matthieu (2d ed.; CNT 1; Geneva: Labor et Fides, 1982) 99 (numerous references).

48 See, e.g., Deut 4:29; Isa 65:1, 10; Jer 29:13-14 (LXX 36:13-14); Prov 8:17; 1 Chr 28:9; Matt 6:33; 12:43; 13:45; Luke 15:8; John 7:34, 36; cf. Leonardi, "Cercate," 277–78.

49 Isaiah 65:1 is cited in part in Rom 10:20.

50 Cf. Acts 12:13-16, the episode where the liberated Peter is knocking on the door of John Mark's house.

51 A neat contrast exists between 11:9 and 13:25, where the unfortunate say, "Lord, open to us!" and where the latter responds to them, "I do not know where you come from."

52 The verbal form varies according to manuscript. One encounters, rarely, the present $\dot{\alpha} \nu o \acute{\iota} \gamma \epsilon \tau \alpha \iota$ and, in its two forms, the future: $\dot{\alpha} \nu o \iota \gamma \acute{\eta} \sigma \epsilon \tau \alpha \iota$ or $\dot{\alpha} \nu o \iota \chi \vartheta \acute{\eta} \sigma \epsilon \tau \alpha \iota$. On the symbolism of the door, cf. Ambrose Exp. Luc. 7.89; Bovon, L'oeuvre, 231–33.

■ **11-12** The text of these verses is uncertain.[53] There is a shorter reading, which is attested by several of the oldest witnesses, Papyrus Chester Beatty I($\mathfrak{P}^{45}$), Bodmer Papyrus XIV-XV ($\mathfrak{P}^{75}$), Codex Vaticanus Greek 1209 (B), the minuscule manuscript Codex Sinaiticus Greek 260 (1241), one or two other Greek manuscripts, several witnesses of the Old Latin version, the Sinaitic Syriac version, and the Sahidic Coptic version. This shorter reading is the one found in the Nestle-Aland[27] and United Bible Societies[4] texts, as well as in the major versions in English: *NRSV, REB, Good News Bible, New Jerusalem Bible,* and *NAB*. It contains only two pairs (fish–snake and egg–scorpion). The longer reading is attested by Marcion (second century), as well as by the overwhelming majority of later witnesses. It has three pairs (bread–stone, fish–snake, egg–scorpion). It is difficult to decide between the two readings, since there may have been an assimilation to Matthew (Matthew has only two pairs: bread–stone and fish–snake), but it is also possible to suppose that an accident of transmission occurred in the beginning of the manuscript tradition (with the eye skipping from one ending to a similar one, omitting the intervening words [parablepsis]). If we conclude that Matthew retained the text of Q,[54] then we have the right to imagine that Luke has also kept the content and the order of it. He then may also have added a third example (egg–scorpion), thus obtaining a triad in harmony with the three petitions of vv. 9-10. As he most certainly would not have eliminated the example of bread that suits his context so well, I end up opting for the longer reading (with the pair bread–stone at the beginning and the Lukan addition of egg–scorpion).[55] That enables me to say that Luke, who amplifies at the end, has the same order as Matthew: bread–stone, then fish–snake. Here is the text of vv. 11-12 in my reading: τίνα δὲ ἐξ ὑμῶν τὸν πατέρα αἰτήσει ὁ υἱὸς ἄρτον, μὴ λίθον ἐπιδώσει αὐτῷ; ἢ καὶ ἰχθύν, μὴ ἀντὶ ἰχθύος ὄφιν αὐτῷ ἐπιδώσει; 12 ἢ καὶ αἰτήσει ᾠόν, μὴ ἐπιδώσει αὐτῷ σκορπίον; "11 Which father among you whose son asks him for bread will give him a stone, or if he asks for a fish, will give him a snake instead of a fish? 12 Or if an egg is asked for, will give him a scorpion?" The addition of the third example underlines the inhumane cruelty of the imagined situations.

The syntax of these verses is confused. Luke adapted a Greek version of Q, which had a strong Semitic flavor, but did so without a great deal of elegance.[56] In putting the Greek for "Which . . . among you" in the accusative, he created a tension, since this person becomes, without transition, the subject of the verb ἐπιδώσει ("will give"). In his effort to be specific,[57] he lamely added τὸν πατέρα ("father"). Finally, in my reading, the double indication of an interrogation (τίνα ["who(se)?" or "which?"], followed by μή [an interrogative particle]),[58] adds to the awkwardness.[59] What he wishes to have Jesus say is, however, simple and striking. There is perhaps a

---

53   Metzger, *Textual Commentary*, 157; 132–33; Fitzmyer, 2:915; Marshall (468–69) presents five hypotheses about the genesis of vv. 11–12.

54   Schulz, *Q*, 162; Bailey (*Poet*, 136) even imagines that Q had three examples; Caba, *Oración de petición*, 71–74; 83–93.

55   Delebecque (72) does the same.

56   Beyer, *Syntax*, 287–97; BDF §469 n. 1; Plummer, 299–300; Lagrange, 327; Delebecque, 72. The phrase recalls, by its construction, 11:5-7; cf. above n.7.

57   The interrogative τίς can be an adjective (BAGD, s.v. τίς, 2) and the substantive that follows can be preceded by the article (BDF §298.2 n. 2). The construction τίνα . . . ἐξ ὑμῶν τὸν πατέρα is not, however, incorrect but it is clumsy. Matthew, who must be following Q, speaks there in more mundane terms of a "man" (ἄνθρωπος), where Luke evokes "the father."

58   The second interrogative particle μή, that is, the one that precedes ἀντὶ ἰχθύος ("instead of a fish") is uncertain. The witnesses to the short text, in the majority, have καί ("and") in place of this word. As for the third μή (v. 12), it is omitted by these witnesses. Μή, like ἆρα, is an interrogative particle that expects a negative response (Latin *num*); see BDF §440; BAGD, s.v μή, C.

59   One encounters such rhetorical questions in 6:32-34; 12:25-26; and Matt 6:25b. They take here (11:11-12) the form of parallel and synonymous examples. The story of the temptations of Jesus is drawn together in this way too, with the bread and the stones (4:3). The Greek proverb is sometimes evoked: ἀντὶ πέρκης σκορπίον ("instead of a rod [fish], a scorpion"); see E. L. A. Leutsch and F. G. Schneidewin, *Corpus paroemiographorum Graecorum*, vol. 1 (Centuria 1.88; Göttingen: Vandenhoeck & Ruprecht, 1839) 29; Caba, *Oración de petición*, 83 n. 71. Ott (*Gebet und Heil*, 102–12), who retains the short text, explains thus the difference in Luke in

rhyming effect (if itacism is admitted): ἄρτον; λίθον; ἰχθύν; ὄφιν; σκορπίον; ᾠόν.[60] There is a common human heritage that is good; an attitude of spontaneity and naturalness, characterized by propriety, decency, and generosity. Here Jesus joyfully notes a display of human wisdom. In the innermost heart of human beings, the order of creation is not normally totally corrupted.

The examples chosen mention the normal daily fare by a lake or a sea in Palestine. We can picture the family table, with the father distributing the courses of food to his children. The Greek verb ἐπιδίδωμι does not mean simply "give," but can also mean "give by holding out to" (because of ἐπί, "to"), "offer," "pass" a plate of food, and so on. There is probably a crescendo in the opposite examples: the stone is harmless, but the snake and especially the scorpion are mortally dangerous. But the son asks for something to live on; he asks for provisions of food. He counts on something ordinary but also essential and vital. The examples add vicious cruelty to simple meanness, since a stone can look like a loaf of bread; a snake, like a fish; and a large, curled-up scorpion, like an egg. Fortunately, humanity is horrified by horror. Reading these examples, attributed to a father, cannot fail to make a reader see red.

Whereas the parable appealed to the code of friendship, the three examples imply the code of kinship. Here again, we sense a crescendo: God is our friend; he is above all our father. To friendship, kinship adds begetting, authority, responsibility, and permanent protection.[61]

■ **13** Here is the conclusion, logically drawn from an *a minori ad maius* reasoning, or in terms of Jewish logic, of the קל וחמר ("light and heavy") principle. If good can rise up from evil, only a much better good can come from good itself. Luke shares the diagnosis that Q, following Jesus, makes of the human race:[62] "who are evil."[63] This pessimistic diagnosis corrects and completes the optimistic diagnosis presupposed by the examples (vv. 11-12). No proof of this malice is offered, for the saying wisely appeals to evidence and experience. The saying does not attribute any demonic origin to this wickedness, which is therefore entirely incumbent on human responsibility. Jesus' realistic wisdom is capable of rejoicing (humans can do good) and lamenting (humans are evil).

The previous examples, v. 13 points out, show that parents know how to "give good gifts" to their children.[64] It is a question of a kind of knowledge, more cultural than natural,[65] that is engendered by paternal and maternal

---

relation to Matthew and Q: Luke replaces the pair "bread–stone" with "egg–scorpion" after denouncing requests for material goods, which are not granted. Serpent and scorpion represent evil and are diabolical animals. "This segment of Luke 11:11-13 is not only excellent for the high estimate that the Holy Spirit enjoys in Luke's writings, but also for the attitude that Luke takes toward earthly gifts and requests for such gifts" (p. 111).

60 There are many species of serpents and many types of scorpions; in every case, for these aforementioned, the small and the large are well known both to inhabitants and to travelers. See Ott, *Gebet und Heil*, 104–6; Feliks and Bo Reicke, "Skorpion," *BHH* 3 (1966) cols. 1815–16. On serpents, see Marie-Louise Henry, "Schlange," *BHH* 3 (1966) cols. 1699–1701.

61 See Grundmann, 235. It is frequent in Judaism to mention the relation between father and son in order to evoke the ties between God and believers; see Bonnard, *Matthieu*, 100.

62 In the Hellenistic era, the verb ὑπάρχω ("to be"), particularly the present participle followed by a nominal predicate, has a tendency to be substituted

for the verb εἶναι ("to be"). Luke is partial to this figure; see Luke 16:24; 23:50; Acts 2:30; 3:2; etc. BAGD, s.v. ὑπάρχω, 2. It would be bold to believe that in modifying Q (which must carry ὄντες; cf. Matt 7:11), Luke wanted to modify the sense by insisting on the ontological character of human malice.

63 Luke uses πονηρός ("evil," "mean") in a way that is both popular and theological, naïve and reflective; cf. 3:19; 6:22, 35, 45; 11:29, 34; 19:22; Acts 17:5; 18:14; 25:18; 28:26.

64 The word δόμα is not very frequent (δωρεά, "gift," "gratification," and δῶρον, "gift," "offering," are the usual words). One finds it again, outside of the parallel (Matt 7:11), only in Eph 4:8, which cites Ps 67 (68):19 (the "gifts" that God does for humans) and in Phil 4:17 οὐχ ὅτι ἐπιζητῶ τὸ δόμα ("not that I seek the gifts"). In the LXX, δόμα is more frequent, translating a dozen different Hebrew words; see Plummer, 300. The pleonasm "good gifts" is explained by the cruel duplicity imagined in vv. 11–12 (evil gifts are there envisioned).

65 Even among animals, the parental instinct is, like

love. The text lays stress on the good issuing from these evil beings: "give good gifts" ($\delta\acute{o}\mu\alpha\tau\alpha$ $\grave{\alpha}\gamma\alpha\vartheta\grave{\alpha}$ $\delta\iota\delta\acute{o}\nu\alpha\iota$).

God, according to the reasoning followed here, must be called "Father."[66] Why did Luke add the enigmatic "heavenly" ($\acute{o}$ $\grave{\epsilon}\xi$ $o\grave{v}\rho\alpha\nu o\hat{v}$)?[67] Perhaps Luke was content here to follow the text of Q, but he did approve of the possible double grammatical association that was involved: it is the God who reveals himself "from heaven" (a link to the word "Father") and the God who offers his presents "from heaven" (a link to the verb "give").

The use of the future "will . . . give"[68] is important for prayer. Since faith consists in waiting for what is still to occur, the future tense corresponds to the petition—it is associated with what will be the final answer.[69] What God is going to give, according to Luke, is the Holy Spirit, an anticipation of the kingdom. It is commonly recognized that the Gospel writer has modified the text of Q, which read "good things" ($\grave{\alpha}\gamma\alpha\vartheta\acute{\alpha}$; Matt 7:11b). He did this for two reasons: for a polemical reason, to combat the naïve desire to have just any kind of petition granted, however material it might be, and in order to spell out the theological implication, since the Holy Spirit is the current form taken by the good things ($\grave{\alpha}\gamma\alpha\vartheta\acute{\alpha}$) with which God enriches us. The Spirit is the means by which God's reign arises in an anticipatory fashion. This is one of the rare mentions of the Holy Spirit in the Gospel, since Luke conceived of its being spread only subsequent to the work accomplished by Jesus Christ. Although Jesus himself lived by the Spirit (from his mother's womb, 1:35; and from the moment of his baptism, 3:22), the disciples were not to receive it until after Pentecost. They had to wait in Jerusalem for the promised Spirit (24:49; Acts 1:4) to be finally shared (Acts 2:1-21).[70] This mention of the Holy Spirit does not imply that God answers prayers only in a spiritual way. The concrete examples of vv. 11-12

are opposed to that point of view. The gift of God's Spirit can make an appearance in the form of daily bread, human love, or a happy event. The New Testament makes no more of a radical dissociation between spiritual goods and material goods than does the Hebrew Bible.

History of Interpretation

The Parable (vv. 5-8)

We will listen to four witnesses to the parable: Origen, Augustine, Albert the Great (Albertus Magnus), and Luther. What they have to say concerns the attitude of both the sleeper who replies favorably and the friend who makes a shameless appeal.

In a Greek fragment of less than a page, the Alexandrian commentator Origen interpreted the parable in a spiritual way. "The words 'who among you' were addressed to the disciples and the phrase 'having a friend' means that God encounters the saints as a friend, as he did with Moses and Abraham."[71] So Origen, who had previously considered God in his role of father, did not neglect to describe him also as a friend. The intertextual network of the Scriptures[72] allowed him then "perhaps" to identify the "midnight" of the parable with the time of this life. He next considered the request for the three loaves of bread as a desire on the part of the disciple to nourish the traveler, to nourish him "with the theology of the Triad [Trinity]" (this explanation was to be dominant for several centuries). Finally, he reflected on the fatigue of the father of the family, whom he identified with God. A weak God, now there's a problem! Origen's solution is not without its beauty: "The question may be raised as to whether we, who 'labor and sag beneath the burden,' don't transmit our sorrows to the Savior."[73] Origen felt that this anthropomorphism was

---

others, a cultural acquisition; see Konrad Lorenz, *On Aggression* (New York: Routledge, 1996).

66 See the commentary above on 11:2a.

67 There are variants in this regard: "the Father in heaven will give" (that is, "the Father of heaven will give") (e.g., $\mathfrak{P}^{75}$ and $\aleph$), "your heavenly Father will give" (e.g., $\mathfrak{P}^{45}$), "your father, the one in heaven, will give" (e.g., C) and "the Father, the one in heaven, will give" (e.g., A, B, D), the text that is very widely attested that I retain. Metzger (*Textual Commentary*, 157–58) is undecided.

68 The verb is in the future also in Matthew.

69 The $\grave{\alpha}\gamma\alpha\vartheta\acute{\alpha}$, the "good things," of Matt 7:11 have an eschatological connotation. It concerns goods associated with the kingdom.

70 See Bovon, *Theologian*, 270–72.

71 Origen *Hom. in Luc.* (Rauer), frg. 76 (Rauer, 182), 9.302–3; *Hom. in Luc.* (Couzel), 526–27.

72 1 Corinthians 7:29 mentions "the appointed time," and Exod 12:29 (in Egypt, which represents this world) signals the arrival at midnight of the destroyer.

73 Origen, *Hom in Luc.* (Couzel), 528–29, with reference to Matt 11:28 and to Isa 53:4.

certainly a manner of speaking, but a manner that was warranted and that allowed a truth about God to be spoken, namely, that "he labors because of the persons who transmit their sorrows to him."[74]

In the summer of 411, in Carthage, Augustine[75] delivered a sermon on this text in which he first examined the parable (vv. 5-8), and then Jesus' sayings (vv. 9-13).[76] His interest oscillated between divine interventions and human activities. On the one hand, there is Christ, who prayed during his incarnation but who, after having been raised to be near the Father, now wants to reply to our requests. This Master exhorts us to make requests and to do so because of his mercy and our weakness. Taking the three loaves as his starting point, Augustine emphasized the unity of the Trinity and then affirmed the following: the best thing that the God who gives has to give is himself. It is that that we must desire and ask for, and not what is visible and transitory. Moreover, the parable does not invite us to pray for ourselves only. It is also concerned with the communication of the faith, therefore evangelization. The disciple does not have a solid enough faith to respond to the traveler's request. So he turns to the Master. Unlike Origen, Augustine refused to make the friend who was sleeping totally equivalent to God, since in his eyes the friend in the parable gives out of weariness, whereas God gives because he wants to. If God is slow in answering prayers, it is because a gift that is too easily acquired loses its value. The bothersome friend ends up receiving the three loaves of the knowledge of the Trinity, which knowledge he will share with his visitor. That way everyone will be satisfied. Augustine continues his homily by going on from the parable to the sayings, thanks to the linking word "bread" (vv. 5 and 11). The three[77] kinds of food that a son can ask for are then understood allegorically: bread is love; the fish, faith; the egg, hope.[78] In our life, the negative forces that threaten us, like the snake and the scorpion, are going to determine the outcome. The sermon closes, as it happens, with a reflection on the earthly and heavenly cities. The very recent fall of Rome suggested to Augustine a development that he tacked on to the parable. The question he asked was a burning one: "By sleeping did he let his house be destroyed?" (Serm. 105.9).[79] In answering that question, Augustine made a distinction between the terrestrial city, which would pass away, and the heavenly city, which God will keep forever. Entering into dialogue with the supporters, both pagan and Christian, of an eternal Rome, he played on the opposition between the poet Virgil's *Georgics* (2.498) and his *Aeneid* (1.278–79). According to Augustine, the true Virgil lucidly announced that empires are destined to perish. When Virgil[80] spoke of an empire that does not end, he did so without conviction and out of a desire to flatter.

The commentator Albert the Great (Albertus Magnus) added the logic of successive distinctions to patristic exegesis, which he presupposed (*Enarr. in Luc* 11.5, 128–29). On the one hand, the passage invites the listener or reader to pray with fervor; on the other, it indicates what should be asked for. The parable itself contains two parts: the similitude (vv. 5-7) and the intention governing the choice of this story (v. 8).[81] The parable in the strict sense of the word (vv. 5-7) contains

---

74 Ibid.

75 After Ambrose (*Exp. Luc.* 7.87–90), I retain the urgent invitation to pray, to pray often and by expressing just requests. Cyril of Alexandria (*Hom. in Luc.* 78) joins the parable (perseverance in prayer) to the Our Father (access to hidden truths) and underlines that the prayer implies access. God knows what is necessary for us. The provisional not-granting is explained as much by our indolence in prayer as by the will of God, who knows the propitious moment. The granting in the end always arrives but not by force, as we hope it to do. Prayer is necessary because of the dangers of this world. Jesus in prayer in Gethsemane must serve as an example for us. Cyril, alas, does not explain the words διά γε τὴν ἀναίδειαν αὐτοῦ in v. 8.

76 Augustine, *Serm.* 105 (*PL* 38:618–25).

77 With the majority of Old Latin witnesses and the Vulgate, Augustine is acquainted with the long text of v. 11; cf. *Serm.* 105.4 (*PL* 38, 620).

78 "There is only hope in the measure that something is not realized; the egg is not yet the chick. Quadrupeds rest their progeny on a wave. Birds, themselves, produce only the hope of progeny" (*Serm.* 105.7; trans. P. Soler in *L'Évangile selon Luc commenté par les Pères* [Paris: Desclée de Brouwer, 1987] 98).

79 Trans. R. G. MacMullen in *NPNF* 6:43.

80 Or rather he makes Jupiter speak of it; in this case, it has to do with a false prophecy by a false divinity.

81 Albert refers to a form of the Vulgate that has a long text at the start of v. 8 (see n. 34 above): "and if this one has continued to knock," which explains the accent that he places on insistence in prayer.

two elements: the necessity of petitionary prayer and the burdensomeness of pertinacious solicitation. Necessity in turn is subdivided into three: dependence on the person to whom one makes a solicitation, the content of the petition, and the reason that makes the petition necessary. After this table of contents, which subdivides the text and its themes, Albert treats each point in turn, mastering the matter that he has subdivided.[82] The intertextual network of Scripture (in other words, a good concordance) comes to his aid in dealing with these different problems. In this way, straining the allegory of the father who had gone to bed with his children, he sees in it, thanks to Isa 8:18, the pure, in heaven, contemplating God, or, by means of Phil 3:20, believers, on earth, in communion with the Father.[83]

Luther used this parable to confirm that, as miserable creatures in the presence of God, we all are but beggars. But these beggars, if we may say so, must practice their occupation, which is to beg, and they must, following the example of the burdensome friend, do so shamelessly. We do so in particular as we advance toward the Table of the Lord of which we are unworthy, but to which we are invited. As we accept what is offered us, we give thanks to Christ at the same time. "Whoever wishes to beg must do so shamelessly. Shame is a useless servant in the home of a poor beggar. Thus Christ, according to Luke 11:5ff., goes so far as to praise a beggar who is shamelessly persistent."[84]

The Saying "Ask . . ." (v. 9)

Verse 9 has had a particularly eventful lot. We find a saying that resembles Luke 11:9 par. attributed to the Savior in the *Gospel of Thomas* and in the *Gospel of the Hebrews* (now usually called the *Gospel of the Nazaraeans*).[85] The *Gospel of Thomas* has: "Let him who seeks continue seeking until he finds. When he finds, he will become troubled. When he becomes troubled, he will be astonished, and he will rule over the All" (*Gos. Thom.* 2). A slightly different form of this saying is found in the *Gospel of the Hebrews*: "He who seeks will not stop until he finds, and when he finds, he will be astounded; and when he is astounded, he will reign; and when he is established in his reign, he will come to rest."[86] In a hymn spoken by Jesus in honor of James, the *Second Apocalypse of James* from Nag Hammadi (NHC V,*4* 55.22–56.5) paraphrases and completes the apocryphal saying.

Taking as his starting point the *Second Apocalypse of James*, Ernst Bammel arrives at the *Gospel of the Hebrews* via the Coptic and Greek versions of the *Gospel of Thomas*: in his opinion, the roots are Jewish and the development, Gnostic.[87] Luke 11:9 is not the source of the development. The canonical saying could have, at the most, influenced ("by way of cross-fertilization") the development of the apocryphal saying. Norbert Brox, on the contrary, considers the apocryphal saying to be a Gnostic amplification of, and commentary on, a canonical saying.[88] I side with him by saying that the appropriation was made at a time when our Gospels were not yet canonical and when the oral form and the independent status of the saying in Luke 11:9 par. were predominant.[89] So the adaptation was made in good conscience: at that time the commentary was not distinguished from the message. From that emerged a context different from that in our Gospels, a lengthening of the structure, and a different meaning: Jesus invited his disciples to seek gnosis.[90] Salvation, rendered possible by the Savior, is involved in

---

82 "De primo dicit . . ." ("He says in the first place") (*Enarr. in Luc.* 11.5, 129).

83 *Enarr. in Luc.* 11.7, 133–34.

84 *Luther's Works,* vol. 38: *Word and Sacrament IV* (ed. Martin E. Lehmann; Philadelphia: Fortress Press, 1971) 133. "Shame is a useless servant in the house of a mendicant" seems to be a proverb that Luther cites.

85 *Gospel of Thomas* 2 (= *P.Oxy.* 654, 1); *Gos. Thom.* frg. 4b (cited by Clement of Alexandria *Strom.* 5.14.96.3; cf. 2.9.45.5); see Aland, *Synopsis,* 269, 517. Cf. *Gos. Thom.* 92, 94. Henri-Charles Puech (*Enquête de la gnose* [2 vols.; Bibliothèque des sciences humaines; Paris: Gallimard, 1978] 2:11) provides a translation

of *Gos. Thom.* 2 and gives other parallels to it (pp. 76–77).

86 See *New Testament Apocrypha* (rev. ed.; ed. Wilhelm Schneemelcher; Eng. trans. edited by R. McL. Wilson; 2 vols.; Louisville: Westminster John Knox, 1991, 1992) 1:177.

87 Bammel, "Rest and Ruhe."

88 Brox, "Suchen."

89 See Koester, "Sayings."

90 Bonnard, *Matthieu,* 431; Helmut Koester, *Ancient Christian Gospels: Their History and Development* (Philadelphia: Trinity Press International, 1990) 60, 81, 186.

that unceasing search, which is combat and asceticism (*Pistis Sophia* 133). We move from "seek and you will find" to "seek *in order to* find." Here it is not a question simply of prayer, as in Luke, but also of the entire spiritual life.

The Church Fathers, who were engaged in dialogue and controversy with the Gnostics, were to attempt to give the "correct" interpretation of Luke 11:9 par. Since they favored a canon of the Scriptures, they were to place their interpretation alongside the text, which in their eyes was sacred. Irenaeus accused the Gnostics of looking for what is already given (*Adv. haer.* 4.6.4; 2.28.2; 2.27.2)[91] and assigned first place to God: "No one can know God without God teaching him. . . . Those to whom the Son will reveal him are the ones who will know him" (*Adv. haer.* 4.6.4). Isaiah 65:1 (God is found by those who are not looking for him) plays a decisive role in this context (Irenaeus *Epid.* 92). Tertullian's view is similar and adds: it is the Jews who must search. Christians, such as the woman in the parable in Luke 15:8, stop looking once they have found what they are looking for (Tertullian *Praescr.* 8.4; 11.1). "Seek," which for the Gnostics is an expression of one's faith, becomes, in the course of controversy, a sign of its absence.

The Alexandrian commentators, for their part, maintained that seeking, the ζήτησις that was dear to Clement's heart,[92] remains an essential element of faith. Faith is not solely passive reception; it is also the quest for a better knowledge of God. Origen was to be more prudent than Clement: while he maintained the necessity of seeking, he resolutely oriented it toward Christ and the Scriptures.[93]

For Augustine, humankind's recognized powerlessness implies the need for a constant seeking that appears in the *cor inquietum*, the "anxious heart," which is always waiting for God (*Conf.* 1.1). While certain commentators, following Thomas Aquinas's line of interpretation (*STh* q. 83, art. 15), saw in the "search" a confirmation of the role entrusted to human beings in the acquisition of salvation, there were more who latched on to the searching for God as a sign of his presence: for example, Blaise Pascal records these words of Jesus to him: "Take comfort; you would not seek me if you had not found me."[94] Paul Tillich adds: "Pure despair—the state without hope—is unable to seek beyond itself. The quest for the New Being presupposes the presence of the New Being, . . ."[95] Karl Barth writes as follows: "human asking and divine giving, human seeking and the divine causing to find, human knocking and the divine opening are mentioned together in Mt. 7:7f. and obviously regarded as standing in a necessary relationship."[96] So why search? Searching is the sign that human beings stay in their place and remain aware of their dependence on God. According to Barth: "A first reason why it is important to understand prayer definitively as petition is because it is thus clearly distinguished from all arbitrary service of God in which man would like to make himself worthy of God and present something worthy to God."[97] In this connection we may quote Dietrich Bonhoeffer: "Judgement and forgiveness are always in the hands of God. He closes and he opens. But the disciples must ask, they must seek and knock, and then God will hear them."[98] Aware of their limits and their dependence on God alone, human beings can thus meditate on this Bible verse with Henri Capieu:

You are the gift and the petition,
    You are joy and torment,
    You are the giver and the gift,
    The beginning and the end.[99]

91 I owe much here to Brox, "Suchen."

92 See Clement of Alexandria *Strom.* 5.1.11.1; 1.16.6; 4.2.5.3; 1.11.51.4; *Quis div.* 10.2.

93 See Origen *Comm. in Matt.* 10.9; *Comm. in Rom.* 7.16; for other references to Luke 11:9 par. Matt 7:7, see Origen, in *Biblica Patristica* 3 (Paris: Centre National de la Recherche Scientifique, 1980) 236–37, 299.

94 Blaise Pascal, "The Mystery of Jesus," from *Pensées* (rev. ed.; New York: Penguin Putnam, 1995).

95 Paul Tillich, *Systematic Theology*, vol. 2: *Existence and the Christ* (Chicago: University of Chicago Press, 1957) 80.

96 Karl Barth, *Church Dogmatics*, vol. 3: *The Doctrine of Creation* (ed. G. W. Bromiley and T. F. Torrance; Edinburgh: T&T Clark, 1961) part 4, p. 106.

97 Ibid., p. 97.

98 Dietrich Bonhoeffer, *The Cost of Discipleship* (2d rev. and unabridged ed.; trans. R. H. Fuller, with some revision by Irmgard Booth; New York: Macmillan, 1959) 167.

99 Henri Capieu, *La source et l'estuaire* (Geneva: Labor et Fides, 1985) 6. This page owes much to Mme Denise Jornod, my assistant for several years.

Conclusion

Luke encourages believers to pray. He is right in doing so, since when believers were pagans they were scarcely used to praying, and as Christians they do not always want to. They have the feeling that prayer also involves learning to give up "gifts" and "goods" that God does not tolerate. They also lack confidence. The corresponding piece to this paraenetic necessity of petition, which purifies the petition and concentrates one's attention on the Father, is the unshakable assurance that the petition will be granted. While the traditions of L and Q stressed the God who answers and who grants what is asked for, the Lukan redaction introduces us to the school of prayer. In it we learn to address God no matter when, but not no matter how; to always ask him anew, but not no matter what. Not that it is necessary to limit our petitions to spiritual goods. Children can ask their father for what they do not have. The poor have a right to ask for the minimum that is necessary to live on. What the Gospel filters is the quality of the petition more than the nature of what is asked for. What we learn above all from Luke is that God, our opposite number, our "other," has the kindness of a father and that he never refuses to answer us.[100] What the text suggests ironically is that God is not an evil being who would engage in giving scorpions or snakes! More than the Pauline epistles, which presuppose the prevenient intervention of the Spirit in prayer (Rom 8:26), it is the Epistle of James that gives the wisest Christian explanation of Jesus' teaching as transmitted by Luke: "If any of you is lacking in wisdom, ask God, who gives to all generously and ungrudgingly, and it will be given you. But ask in faith, never doubting . . ." (Jas 1:5-6a).

---

100 On v. 13, cf. Leonardi ("Cercate," 281), who takes the position in favor of Caba (*Oración de petición*, 78–80), that the gift of the Holy Spirit is the supreme good including all others, and against Ott (*Gebet und Heil*, 108–11), that the gift of the Holy Spirit excludes the goods of this world.

Bibliography

Allison, Dale C., "Who Will Come from East and West? Observations on Matt 8:11-12—Luke 13:28-29," *IBS* 11 (1989) 164.

Baumbach, *Verständnis*, 130–31, 184–85.

Beauvery, R. "Jésus et Béelzéboul (Lc 11, 14-28)," *AsSeign* 30 (1963) 26–36.

Becker, Jürgen, *Das Heil Gottes: Heils- und Sündenbegriffe in den Qumrantexten und im Neuen Testament* (SUNT 3; Göttingen: Vandenhoeck & Ruprecht, 1964) 197–217.

Böcher, Otto, *Das Neue Testament und die dämonischen Mächte* (SBS 58; Stuttgart: Katholisches Bibelwerk, 1972) 9–11.

Cangh, J. M. van, "'Par l'esprit de Dieu – par le doigt de Dieu' Matt 12, 28 par. Lc 11, 20," in Delobel, *Logia*, 337–42.

Couroyer, B., "Le 'doigt de Dieu' (Exode 8, 15)," *RB* 63 (1956) 481–95.

Edwards, *Theology of Q*, 110–12.

Fuchs, Albert, *Die Entwicklung der Beelzebulkontroverse bei den Synoptikern: Traditionsgeschichtliche und redaktionsgeschichtliche Untersuchung von Mk 3,22-27 und Parallelen, verbunden mit der Rückfrage nach Jesus* (SNTU B 5; Linz: Studien zum Neuen Testament und seiner Umwelt, 1980).

Garrett, *Demise*, 43–46.

Gaston, L., "Beelzebul," *ThZ* 18 (1962) 247–55.

George, Augustin, "Note sur quelques traits lucaniens de l'expression 'Par le doigt de Dieu' (Luc 11, 20)," *ScEcc* 18 (1966) 461–66.

Grässer, Erich, "Zum Verständnis der Gottesherrschaft," *ZNW* 65 (1974) 3–26.

Green, H. B., "Matthew 12:22-50 and Parallels: An Alternative to Matthean Conflation," in Christopher Mark Tuckett, ed., *Synoptic Studies: The Ampleforth Conferences of 1982 and 1983* (JSNTSup 7; Sheffield: JSOT Press, 1984) 157–76.

Hamerton-Kelly, Robert G., "A Note on Matthew 12:28 par. Luke 11:20," *NTS* 11 (1964–65) 167–69.

Haufe, G., "Hellenistische Volksfrömmigkeit," in Johannes Leipoldt and Walter Grundmann, eds., *Umwelt des Urchristentums*, vol. 1: *Darstellung des neutestamentlichen Zeitalters* (Berlin: Evangelische Verlagsanstalt, 1965) 77–82.

Hoffmann, *Logienquelle*, 37–38, 70.

Hultgren, Arland J., *Jesus and His Adversaries: The Form and Function of the Conflict Stories in the Synoptic Tradition* (Minneapolis: Augsburg, 1979).

Jeremias, *Sprache*, 199–202.

Jülicher, *Gleichnisreden*, 2:214–40.

Käsemann, Ernst, "Lukas 11, 14-28," in Ernst Käsemann, *Exegetische Versuche und Besinnungen* (2d ed.; 2 vols.; Göttingen: Vandenhoeck & Ruprecht, 1960, 1964) 1:242–48.

Katz, Friedrich, "Lk 9,52–11, 36: Beobachtungen zur Logienquelle und ihrer hellenistisch–judenchristlichen Redaktion" (Dissertation, Mainz, 1973).

Kilgallen, John J., "The Return of the Unclean Spirit (Luke 11:24-26)," *Bib* 74 (1993) 43–59.

Kirschläger, *Wirken*, 229–36.

Kloppenborg, John S., "Q 11.14-26: Work Sheets for Reconstruction," in *SBLSP* (1985) 133–51.

Kruse, H., "Das Reich Satans," *Bib* 58 (1977) 29–61.

Kümmel, *Promise*, 105–40.

Laufen, *Doppelüberlieferungen*, 126–55.

Leclercq, Jacques, "'Scopis mundatum' (Matth. 12, 44; Lc 11.25): Le balai dans la Bible et dans la liturgie d'après la tradition latine," in Jacques Fontaine and Charles Kannengiesser, eds., *Epektasis: Mélanges patristiques offerts au cardinal Jean Danielou* (Paris: Beauchesne, 1972) 129–37.

Légasse, Simon, "L'Homme fort' de Lc 11, 21-22," *NovT* 5 (1962) 5–9.

Limbeck, Meinrad, "Beelzebul – eine ursprüngliche Bezeichnung für Jesus?" in Helmut Held and Josef Nolle, eds., *Wort Gottes in der Zeit: Festschrift Karl Hermann Schelkle zum 65. Geburtstag dargebracht von Kollegen, Freunden, und Schülern* (Düsseldorf: Patmos, 1973) 31–42.

Linton, O., "The Demand for a Sign from Heaven (Mark 8:11-12 and Parallels)," *StTh* 19 (1995) 112–29.

Lorenzmeier, Theodor, "Zum Logion Mt 12, 28; Lk 11, 20," in Hans Dieter Betz und Luise Schottroff, eds., *Neues Testament und christliche Existenz: Festschrift für Herbert Braun zum 70. Geburtstag am 4. Mai 1973* (Tübingen: Mohr Siebeck, 1973) 289–304.

Lövestam, Evald, *Spiritus blasphemia: Eine Studie zu Mk 3,28f par Mt 12,3 If, Lk 12,10* (Scripta minora Regiae Societatis humaniorum litteram Lundensis 1966/1967, 1; Lund: Gleerup, 1968) 44–50.

Lührmann, *Logienquelle*, 32–43.

Luz, Ulrich, "Q, 10, 2-16; 11, 14-23," in *SBLSP* (1985) 101–2.

MacLurin, E. Colin B., "Beelzeboul," *NovT* 20 (1978) 156–60.

Mearns, C., "Realized Eschatology in Q? A Consideration of the Sayings of Luke 7:22; 11:20 and 16:16," *SJT* 40 (1987) 189–210.

Meynet, R., "Qui donc est 'le plus fort'? Analyse rhétorique de Mark 3:22-30; Matt 12:22-37; Luke 11:14-26," *RB* 90 (1983) 334–50.

Neirynck, Frans, "Mt 12, 25a/Lc 11, 17a et la rédaction des évangiles," *EThL* 62 (1986) 122–33.

Oakman, Donald E., "Rulers' Houses, Thieves, and Usurpers: The Beelzebul Pericope," *Forum* 4.3 (1988) 109–23.

Perrin, *Rediscovering the Teaching*, 63–67.

Robbins, Vernon K., "Rhetorical Composition and the Beelzebul Controversy," in Burton L. Mack and Vernon K. Robbins, *Patterns of Persuasion in the Gospels* (Sonoma, Calif.: Polebridge, 1989) 161–93.

Robinson, James M., "The Mission and Beelzebul: Pap. Q 10.2-16; 11.14-23," *SBLSP* (1985) 97–99.

Rodd, C. S., "Spirit or Finger?" *ExpT* 72 (1960–61) 157–58.

Schlosser, *Règne de Dieu*, 1:127–53.

Schulz, *Q*, 203–13, 476–80.

Schürmann, Heinz, "Q Lk 11, 14–36 kompositions-geschichtlich befragt," in F. van Segbroeck et al., eds., *The Four Gospels 1992: Festschrift Frans Neirynck* (3 vols.; Leuven: Leuven University Press, 1992) 1:563–86.

Shirock, R., "Whose Exorcists Are They? The Referents of οἱ υἱοὶ ὑμῶν at Matthew 12:27//Luke 11:19," *JSNT* 46 (1992) 41–51.

Steinhauser, *Doppelbildworte*, 124–47.

Str–B 4:1, 501–35.

Wall, R. W., "'The Finger of God': Deut 9:10 and Luke 11:20," *NTS* 33 (1987) 144–50.

White, L. Michael, "Scaling the Strongman's 'Court' (Luke 11:21)," *Forum* 3.3 (1987) 3–28.

Yates, J. E., "Luke's Pneumatology and Luke 11:20," in Frank L. Cross, ed., *Studia Evangelica 2: Papers Presented to the Second International Congress on New Testament Studies Held at Christ Church, Oxford, 1961* (TUGAL 87; Berlin: Akademie-Verlag, 1964) 295–99.

Zerwick, Max, "In Beelzebub principe Daemoniorum (Luke 11:14-28)," *VD* 29 (1951) 44–48.

14/ He was casting out a demon, and it was mute; when the demon had gone out, the one who had been mute began to speak, and the crowds marveled. **15/** Some of them said, "It is by Beelzebul, the ruler of the demons, that he casts out demons." **16/** Others, who wished to test him, kept demanding from him a sign from heaven. **17/** But he knew what they were thinking and said to them, "Every kingdom divided against itself becomes deserted, and every house falls on another house. **18/** If Satan himself is divided against himself, how will his kingdom stand?—for you say that it is by Beelzebul that I cast out the demons. **19/** Now if it is by Beelzebul that I cast out the demons, by whom do your sons cast them out? That is why they themselves will be your own judges. **20/** But if it is by the finger of God that I cast out the demons, then the kingdom of God has come to you. **21/** When a strong man, fully armed, guards his dwelling place,[a] his possessions are safe.[b] **22/** But when someone stronger than he comes along and overpowers him, he takes away all his arms[c] in which he trusted and divides his plunder. **23/** Whoever is not with me is against me, and whoever does not gather with me scatters. **24/** When the unclean spirit has gone out of the person, it wanders through waterless regions looking for a resting place, without finding any. It then says, 'I will return to my house from which I came.' **25/** When it comes, it finds it swept and put in order. **26/** Then it goes and looks for[d] seven other spirits more evil than itself, and they enter and live there; and the last state of that person is worse than the first."

a   Literally: "his courtyard."
b   Literally: "in peace."
c   Literally: "his panoply," that is, the complete equipment of a soldier.
d   Literally: "leaves, then takes along."

Confronted with this enigmatic text, modern readers are left wondering. Ready to rejoice in the liberating power of Jesus, they remain perplexed in the face of these words full of imagery that the Galilean used to counter the objections and temptations advanced by his adversaries.

This commentary will show that, from the start, Christianity has had to defend its Master, and later its missionaries, against a precise attack, namely, that of practicing magic, and deriving its power from satanic forces rather than from divine power. This is one of the components of this biblical passage.

For people in antiquity, whether authors, readers, or heroes of these stories, the world of demons, like that of angels, was an undeniable reality. So in those days discussions revolved not around the existence of demons but around the right way to overcome them.

Following Jesus, the bearers of the tradition and then the Gospel writers—Luke in particular—were persuaded that in the person of their Lord, who chased out demons and made idols reel, God's reign had truly been set in motion. In fact, it is welcomed only by those persons who opt for faith. Being detached from the Evil One and his troops is one of the two aspects of salvation. Being tied to God and his Son is the other.

As the euphoric end-time is, unfortunately, yet to come, we must—and this is another underlying conviction—increase our vigilance. For a liberation that is not fully worked through runs the danger of ending up resulting in a relapse. To avoid such a short-lived salvation, believers have but one solution, that of remaining attached to Christ, being with him, whatever may come, and over the long haul. The text says it and repeats it to the lukewarm and the undecided.

Analysis

The Literary Unit

Everyone is agreed that a new unit begins in v. 14. But what is less sure is whether it ends in v. 23 or v. 26. Since the comment on the demons continues in vv. 24-26 and no new start is indicated in v. 24, I include these last verses (vv. 24-26) in the unit.

It is likely that Luke thought of this debate in front of the crowd (vv. 14-26) as the first part of a work in two parts, with the second part being vv. 29-36. The turning point is the double benediction in vv. 27-28. All of this is surrounded by a hortatory speech to his closest associates, the disciples (vv. 1-13), and a polemical speech to those farthest from him, the Pharisees (vv. 37-54). The narrative elements (vv. 1-2a, v. 14, v. 29 [cf. v. 16], and vv. 53-54) frame, introduce, and emphasize the dialogues and the sayings.[1]

Jesus' victorious deed (v. 14) brought out a double reaction on the part of the spectators: one, negative (v. 15); the other, doubtful (v. 16). The master responded to them with a general saying (v. 17). At that point, his speech was expanded by three symmetrical sayings (vv. 18-20): three conditional clauses introduced by "if" (ϵi), followed by main clauses, the first two of which are interrogative and the third, affirmative (the first two being, what is more, flanked by a commentary, vv. 18b and 19b). It is to be noted that God's reign (v. 20) corresponds, antithetically, to Satan's reign (v. 18). Furthermore, the reasoning shifts from being a general one ("every kingdom," v. 17) to being a specific one ("I," beginning in v. 18b), to which are opposed other specific ones ("your sons," v. 19).[2]

Jesus' answer continues with a symmetrical set: a parable introduced by "when" ($\H{o}\tau\alpha\nu$, vv. 21-22), which precedes a double gnomic saying (v. 23), followed in turn by an imaginary example[3] that also begins with "when" ($\H{o}\tau\alpha\nu$, vv. 24-26). There is a correspondence between the parable and the example: a harmonious situation (the "strong man," at peace, in v. 21; the "house," in order, v. 25) is suddenly threatened (victory of someone "stronger," v. 22; the sudden emergence of the "seven other spirits more evil," v. 26).

Although vv. 17-26 together constitute Jesus' answer, this answer is subdivided into two parts, the first (vv. 17-20) differing from the second (vv. 21-26) by its style and structure, with an argument in the one part,

---

1   Up to this point, I am in accord with the opinion of Meynet, "Qui donc," 342.

2   Meynet ("Qui donc," 342–47) goes much too far with his formal analysis. I am not so sure about the presence of chiasms. In my opinion, v. 17 is not at the center of a concentric construction but rather is the start of a structural development.

3   Contrary to Meynet ("Qui donc," 343–47), I do not regard the story recounted in vv. 24-26 as a par-

and a narrative in the other. Nevertheless, each part uses a general saying, the first placed at the beginning (v. 17), the second in the middle (v. 23). The second proverbial saying is associated with the speaker, whereas the first remains very general. In this framework, Jesus carries on an argument to justify himself, proceeding from what his hearers can accept to what they ought to recognize: they must reflect, then believe.[4]

Synoptic Comparison

The relationship between Matt 12:22-30, 43-45 and Luke 11:14-26 is such that we must accept the hypothesis of a common dependence on Q.[5] To be sure, if Mark did not know of exorcism, he at least knew of a dispute concerning Beelzebul, but his account (Mark 3:22-27), apart from several details,[6] was not the source of the two other accounts. Matthew, moreover, was acquainted with a second account of the same exorcism (Matt 9:32-34). In that text, the miracle did not lead to any dispute but only to the Pharisees' malicious interpretation: "'By the ruler of the demons he casts out the demons'" (Matt 9:34). Curiously enough, the Lukan exorcism resembles the one in Matthew 9 more than the one in Matthew 12: we are dealing with exorcism rather than a healing (as in Matt 12:22b); the person possessed by a demon is not blind (as in Matt 12:22a) as well as mute; the crowds marvel more than they are amazed (as in Matt 12:23a); and the mention of the resumption of the ability to speak is indicated by a clause using a verb in the aorist tense in Greek and not by a result clause using an infinitive (as in the Greek of Matt 12:22b). While the crowd's admiration is furnished with content in the two texts in Matthew,[7] unlike in Luke 11:14, the adversaries' criticism[8] is virtually identical in Matt 9:34 and Luke 11:15; these two texts must be lined up with Mark 3:22b. The autonomy of the exorcism account in Matt 12:22-24 remains an enigma.

Q

In Q, the brief mention of the exorcism (Luke 11:14 par.) was probably followed by a dispute, which included an account of a reproach (Luke 11:15 par.) and Jesus' reply. In Q, Jesus probed the hearts (Luke 11:17a par.), asserted that every divided kingdom would fall (Luke 11:17b-18), referred to Jewish exorcisms (Luke 11:19 par.), proclaimed himself to be God's instrument (Luke 11:20 par.), played the "strong man" off against "someone stronger than he" (Luke 11:21-22, without parallel),[9] and drew a provisional conclusion (Luke 11:23 par.). On the whole, the parallel texts of Matthew 12 and Luke 11 are quite close and, when they disagree, Luke seems to have been the most respectful of Q. This is the case with respect to the adversaries (they remain anonymous in Luke; Matthew has them be Pharisees); Luke's shorter text in Luke 11:18a (without the unnecessary words "casts out Satan," found in Matthew); the "finger of God" (Luke 11:20, where Matthew avoids anthropomorphism

able. Our text does not really present, therefore, "a couple of parables" (Meynet, "Qui donc," 347).

4 Godet (2:87) subdivides this section in the following way: vv. 14-16, an account of two deeds (healing and a request for a sign), which prompt two discourses, the first (vv. 17-26) with respect to exorcism, and the second (vv. 29-36), with respect to the request for a sign; these two discourses are separated by an episode (vv. 27-28). Lagrange (328), for his part, remarks that the two interventions by Jesus (vv. 17-23 and vv. 29-32) are corresponding responses to two groups of unbelievers (v. 15 and v. 16). As for Marshall (470), he considers 11:14-54 to be a controversy with the Pharisees in four stages: vv. 14-26, vv. 27-28, vv. 29-36, vv. 37-54.

5 See from Jülicher (*Gleichnisreden*, 2:214–15) to Kloppenborg ("Q 11:14–26") and Robinson ("Beelzebul"), by way of Schulz (*Q*, 203–13), Lührmann (*Logienquelle*, 32–34), and Hoffmann (*Logienquelle*, 37–38).

6 Luke contains only slight contact with Mark: the complaint issued by the opponents (v. 15b), which, by reason of the second parallel from Matthew (Matt 9:34b), has, for Luke, a different origin than Mark. It is Matthew, rather, who is inspired by Mark (cf. Matt 12:25c and 29).

7 "Can this be the Son of David?" (Matt 12:23b) and "Never was anything like this seen in Israel" (Matt 9:33b).

8 For Matthew, these are the Pharisees here (Matt 12:24) and there (Matt 9:34); for Luke, "some of them" (v. 15), then "others" (v. 16); for Mark, "the scribes who came down from Jerusalem."

9 In contrast to Lührmann (*Logienquelle*, 33), I make this parable go back to Q; one could also just as well attribute it to Luke himself, if one could forget that our evangelist does not like to make a fusion of his sources from within the same section.

and speaks of the "Spirit of God");[10] and the description of the "strong man" and "someone stronger than he" (Luke 11:21-22; here Matt 12 has contaminated his text of Q with that of Mark 3:27). On the other hand, Luke is wordier: he anticipates the problematics connected with the sign (cf. Luke 11:29-32) by creating a second group of adversaries, more hesitant than hostile (Luke 11:16, without parallel, is redactional);[11] out of a desire for clarity, he has reworded the criticism (Luke 11:18b is without parallel).[12] Curiously enough, the way he worded the reproach the first time (Luke 11:15b) corresponds, as we have seen, to Mark's wording; either he was influenced by Mark, or rather this wording circulated in both Mark and Q (Matt 9:34 uses it). It is Matt 12:24b, in this case, that appears to have given both of them the slip.

Luke has placed the verses on relapse (vv. 24-26) *before* the question about the sign (vv. 29-32); Matthew, who was not acquainted with the double beatitude (Luke 11:27-28), has an inverse sequence. Here again, it is Luke who must have followed the order of Q.[13] As for the contents of these verses on relapse, they are virtually identical in the Gospels of Luke and Matthew, which suggests that their common source, Q,[14] had already been translated into Greek (Matt 12:44 has a "then" [τότε] that Luke does not have, as well as the word "unoccupied" [translating the Greek participle σχολάζοντα]; and in Matt 12:45, the words "with him" [μεθ᾽ ἑαυτοῦ]). The sentence "So will it be also with this evil generation" (Matt 12:45c) is a Matthean redactional addition.[15]

The Tradition prior to Q

Is it possible to go back behind Q? The enigmatic parallel in Matt 9:32-34 suggests that originally the exorcism led only to a hostile remark (Luke 11:14-15 par.). The text of Mark,[16] moreover, presupposes the initial autonomy of the passage about Satan being divided against himself (Luke 11:17-18a par.). The famous saying (Luke 11:20 par.) must have circulated independently.[17] The saying about the sons, which contains, like the reproach, the unusual word Beelzebul (Luke 11:19 par.). seems to have been tacked on to the account of exorcism and could have been the first expansion of it, the first reply to the reproach.[18] The parable about the "strong man" and "someone stronger than he" (Luke 11:21-22) may have circulated independently, as is proved by the parallel in *Gos. Thom.* 35.[19] The same would be true for the double saying (Luke 11:23 par.), the first part of which is found, inverted, in Luke 9:50 par. In all, five or six different elements have been brought together by Q in order to make out of them an apology for Jesus' exorcisms and a violent anti-Jewish polemic.[20]

Literary Genre

The form that this unit has taken is that of a dispute.[21] Jesus' retort became richer with the passage of time, like the reproach, which, in Luke's time, may have split into two (v. 15 and v. 16). The criticism of the exorcisms being initially without an answer (cf. Matt 9:32-34), a first reply (v. 19) was added to it, but that reply was soon to be considered insufficient (a floating saying was to be added to it, v. 20). Then, the comment about Satan was grafted as an opening on to this first set (vv. 17b-18). Finally, the parable about the "strong man" and "someone stronger than he" (vv. 21-22), as well as the double saying (v. 23), were attached to them, soon carrying along in their wake the words about relapse (vv. 24-26).

---

10   Up to this point, I am in accord with Lührmann (*Logienquelle*, 32–33).

11   This was already the opinion of Jülicher (*Gleichnisreden*, 2:216). It is also that of Lührmann (*Logienquelle*, 33).

12   Lührmann, *Logienquelle*, 33.

13   See ibid., 34.

14   See ibid.

15   See Bonnard, *Matthieu*, 185.

16   Mark introduces it almost as a new scene: "And he called them to him, and said to them in parables" (Mark 3:23a).

17   Lührmann, *Logienquelle*, 33.

18   Lührmann (*Logienquelle*, 33) judges, to the contrary, that v. 19 has been created to make a transition just where v. 20 is associated with vv. 17–18.

19   Kruse, "Reich," 42–43. *Gospel of Thomas* 35 is cited below in n. 65.

20   Lührmann (*Logienquelle*, 34) indicates that the opposition to Judaism is more irreconcilable in Q than in Mark.

21   Ibid., 34.

The Social and Ecclesial Setting

All this development took place against a double background, one that was both christological and missionary.[22] Jesus had to be cleared of the tenacious suspicion of magic, and Christian missionaries had to be protected from similar reproaches. The first concern, which was both apologetic and polemical, seems to have been the oldest: the earliest Christians were thereby defending their Master against Jewish attacks. The second concern, of a missionary nature, must have arisen somewhat later, in the Diaspora.

Commentary

■ **14** It is curious that Luke left such an awkward description untouched.[23] Nevertheless, its rough simplicity does have something fascinating about it. The periphrastic imperfect used in the construction lays stress on the duration of the exorcism and perhaps on the effort expended by the exorcist. The text, which had delighted us with its mention of celestial gifts and the Holy Spirit (v. 13), now plunges us into the earthly reality of a world bewitched by the Evil Spirit (v. 14). The demon[24] was one who was "mute" (κωφόν), or "deaf," or "deaf and mute." The matching piece to this reduction to silence, here disastrous, is the sudden gift of speech. In a concrete case, Jesus fulfilled the promise made in v. 13.[25] The wording does not fail to suggest the magnitude of the event: the "one who had been mute" began to speak just as soon as the demon had been cast out. Christians

admitted that Jesus was an exorcist, and they took delight in it, but they still had to justify it.[26] For them, it was a concomitant of the eschatological liberation from a world so much under Satan's control that it had lost its identity. Luke shared the apocalyptic pessimism of his fellow Christians at the same time that he shared their christological optimism. The crowds, for their part, admired what delighted the Christians and irritated certain Jews.

In its brevity—Q did not like narrative[27]—the account contains only two of the five usual elements of an exorcism: skipping the beginning (the encounter and the resistance of the demon), the episode recounts the *apopompe* ("sending away," the work of the exorcist that elicits the expulsion of the demon), then, after having omitted the (optional) mention of the *epipompe* ("sending upon," the new residence of the demon), it points out, by way of conclusion, the impression made on the spectators.[28] By this concentrated way of telling the story, the narrator focuses our attention on the thaumaturge (miracle-worker).

■ **15** Some[29] of the spectators reacted openly. The diagnostic of this first group of adversaries is laid out: Jesus is in the service of God's enemy. These persons accepted the fact of the success of the exorcism,[30] but they categorized it among cases of magic, even though Jesus had not used any formula, had not sought to enrich himself, and had not wished to make the divinity submit to his will.[31] Beelzebul's being categorized as "the ruler of the demons" does not mean *ipso facto* that he must be

---

22　On this double *Sitz im Leben*, see Ernst, 373. Baumbach (*Verständnis*, 184–85) conceives of the pericope as an invitation addressed to the crowds to convert and to have them pass from the world of Satan to the reign of God.

23　Note the lack of transition with v. 13 and the breach of the parataxis. Sensitive to this first mistake, Codex Bezae (D), as well as the Latin manuscripts c and f, revise the verse by establishing a modest transition: "Although he said that, they brought him a mute possessed by a demon, and having cast it out, they marveled."

24　On δαιμόνιον, see the commentary on 4:33-37 (1:216).

25　Even though the traditional account, in conformity with the literary genre of exorcism, does not indicate a request for liberation (such a request would have been only by a gesture, of course!).

26　The Jewish tradition will accuse Jesus of sorcery; see John 7:20; *b. Sanh.* 6.1; Str-B 1:631; Morton Smith, *Jesus the Magician* (San Francisco: Harper & Row, 1978).

27　The only other miracle account in Q: 7:1-10.

28　See the commentary on 8:26-39 (1:427–28).

29　The expression τινὲς δὲ ἐξ αὐτῶν some of them") recalls the τίς ἐξ ὑμῶν ("which one of you") of v. 5 and τίνα δὲ ἐξ ὑμῶν ("which of you") of v. 11.

30　"He casts out the demons." The hostility, by the modern conception, would be expressed by placing this success in doubt. See the critique of miracles in the eighteenth century.

31　On magic in antiquity and in Luke, see Garrett, *Demise*; Florent Heintz, *Trois études préliminaires: Actes 13:6-12; 16:16-19; 19:11-20. Pour servir à l'élucidation des rapports entre pratiques magiques et monde démoniaque dans le christianisme primitif, mémoire de spécialisa-*

identified with Satan. Since there were several "rulers" ($\mathring{\alpha}\rho\chi o\nu\tau\epsilon\varsigma$) in Israel or in the Roman Empire,[32] there may also have been several in the devil's court. Nevertheless, the mention of Satan in v. 18 suggests that we should make that identification.

Oddly enough, there is no mention of Beelzebul in Jewish literature.[33] Long before the Christian era, there was a Philistine divinity at Ekron called Baalzebul, the worship of whom and the name of whom appear to have dropped out of use after some centuries. On the basis of the etymology[34] this name means the "Master of the Abode on high" (this abode being heaven, the high mountain, or the temple). The Hebrew Bible carried this polemic to the point of distorting the enemy's name, ironically calling him Baalzebub, the "God of the flies" (2 Kgs [4 Kgdms] 1:2-16). In my opinion it was this true etymology, "Master of the Abode on high," that those who used this word in Jesus' time were thinking of. Even though God is certainly the "Master of the Abode on high," the God of heaven and the God residing in the temple, did not the enemy, operating with the dualistic concept so widely held in those days, seek to supplant God, to imitate him, to construct a similar and illusory counter-reality? Did Satan not camouflage himself as an angel of light (cf. 2 Cor 11:14)? Did the installation of

the abomination of desolation in the temple of Jerusalem, under Antiochus IV Epiphanes, not become the model of the apocalyptic menace? "For that day will not come unless the rebellion comes first and the lawless one is revealed, the one destined for destruction. He opposes and exalts himself above every so-called god or object of worship, so that he takes his seat in the temple of God, declaring himself to be God" (2 Thess 2:3b-4). The adversaries probably identified Beelzebul with this apocalyptic rival of God, who had to be Satan himself. As pagan gods could be thought of by Jews in those days as demons,[35] God's rival, Master of the heavens and of the Abode on high,[36] dominated all other gods, and thus all other demons of whom he was the "ruler" ($\mathring{\alpha}\rho\chi\omega\nu$). Even if the sense of the word Beelzebul appears to be evident, the choice of such a rare name would seem to be an enigma.[37] The most that could be adduced is a relationship between the theme of the "Abode on high" included in the name Beelzebul and that of the dwelling and the kingdom, which marks a high point of the controversy (v. 17).[38]

■ 16 A second group takes shape in the crowd.[39] Their intention: "to test,"[40] that is, to catch Jesus in some error, religious rather than ethical, to expose his trickery and his lack of divine accreditation. They "kept demanding"[41]

---

tion inédit (Geneva: Faculté autonome de théologie protestante, 1991).

32 For Israel, see Luke 8:41; 12:58; 14:1; 18:18; 23:13, 35; 24:20; Acts 3:17; etc. For the empire, see Acts 16:19; Rom 13:3; 1 Cor 2:6, 8. For superhuman powers, see Eph 2:2. For Christ, see Rev 1:5.

33 The attestations, outside of the Gospels, all seem to depend on them: so *T. Sol.* 3–6 (without doubt a Christian work); Hippolytus *Ref.* 6.34.1; Origen, *Cels.* 8.25-26. The literature about Beelzebul is extensive; see Werner Foerster, "$B\epsilon\epsilon\lambda\zeta\epsilon\beta o\acute{\nu}\lambda$," *TDNT* 1 (1964) 605–6; Gaston, "Beelzebul"; Otto Böcher, "$B\epsilon\epsilon\lambda\zeta\epsilon\beta o\acute{\nu}\lambda$," *EDNT* 1:211–12; Fitzmyer, 2:920.

34 On זְבֻל "elevated residence," see 1 Kgs (3 Kgdms) 8:13; 2 Chr 6:2; Isa 63:15; Hag 3:11; Ps 48 (49):15; the word, however, is rare in the OT. It appears a few times at Qumran: 1QM 12.1, 2; 1QS 10.3; 1QH 3.34. In rabbinic literature, it designates the temple and, once, the fourth of six heavens, *b. Ḥag.* 12b, cf. Str-B 1:632–33.

35 Psalm 95 (96):5, the Hebrew text: "All the gods of the nations are demons."

36 On God as Lord and Master of the heavens, see Dan 5:18-23.

37 Gaston ("Beelzebul," 254–55) issues the hypothesis that Jesus called himself "Master of the house" (Matt 10:25b), which his opponents would have imitated with irony, calling him "Master of the temple," and, by inference, the residence: Beelzeboul.

38 See ibid., 253–55.

39 The word $\mathring{\epsilon}\tau\epsilon\rho o\varsigma$ perhaps retains its sense here of "other of two." Facing Jesus, two groups and two groups only. But that is already one group more than in Matthew and Mark. After the slanderers, then the petitioners, according to Loisy, 322.

40 On this verb, see the commentary on 4:1 (1:191). For Godet (2:90), these people want magic, which answers to no need at all.

41 The verb $\zeta\eta\tau\acute{\omega}$ (twenty-five times in the Gospel, ten times in Acts) expresses for Luke a basic human reality: the desire or the will that is expressed in word and in act. These needs, desire, and will are comprehensible, whether legitimate or culpable, insofar as they correspond to a common anthropological basis, the regenerated or the corrupt will.

from him a sign.[42] They were in agreement with the first adversaries as to the ambiguity of exorcisms, which might be produced by processes that were a product more of magic than of faith. They wished that God, "from heaven," that is, apart from any action on Jesus' part or from any tangible reality, might miraculously express his opinion, that he might approve or disapprove of this Jesus. By this crazy request, this second group exposed the poverty of its own faith. At the beginning of the last pericope on the sign (11:29), Luke was to appear harsh with respect to this group and thereby express his rejection of a theology of glory.

■ **17** There is a formal beginning, indicated by the use in Greek of the emphatic αὐτός ("he"), which has an honorific connotation here.[43] "He," with a capital *H*, can intervene, since he possesses superhuman knowledge.

The man of God shares with his Lord the knowledge of human hearts.[44]

At this point Jesus utters a wisdom saying whose application to the situation is made immediately in the mind of the listener, just as it is next in words supplied by the author (vv. 18-20). Luke first quotes his source without greatly modifying it.[45] Every kingdom that is torn apart and that is prey to civil war ends up being devastated.[46] Then the Gospel writer parts company with his source, which is carefully preserved by Matthew. In place of Semitic parallelism, which repeats the truth, Luke preferred to extend the image:[47] the ruin of houses[48] illustrates the devastation of a kingdom.[49] The book of Revelation and Josephus permit us to picture the cruel end of every war.[50]

---

42   On this word "sign," see the commentary on 11:29-32 below.

43   Αὐτὸς δέ (redactional) and καὶ αὐτός (traditional) can have this christological connotation (Jeremias, *Sprache*, 128).

44   See the commentary on 9:47 (1:507 n. 37); Luke 5:22 and 6:8. As an exception, Luke uses here διανόημα (a *hapax legomenon* in the NT; cf. however, Luke 3:16 D). The parallel in Matthew has ἐνθύμησις (Matt 12:25; as in Matt 9:4, where the word is redactional). By habit, Luke has recourse to διαλογισμός (Luke 5:22; 6:8; 9:47; 24:38); διανόημα could be traditional and derive from Q. See Kloppenborg, "Work Sheets," 142. The sense of the word is "thought," that is, "that which one thinks," in contrast to διανόησις, "thought," that is, the "action of thinking."

45   Q must read μερίζω (cf. Matt 12:25); διαμερίζω must be redactional; see Kloppenborg, "Work Sheets," 142–43. There is, moreover, a slight contamination of Mark 3:24 in the usage and the position of ἐφʼ ἑαυτήν ("against himself").

46   Is there an acquaintance with ancient parallels in this dispute? One thinks, of course, of the well-known political maxim: *divide ut imperes*.

47   One could equally understand that Luke himself offers a parallel. In this case, it would be necessary to translate: "And also family, arisen against family, collapses." (Cf. 21:10: "people will arise against another people and kingdom against kingdom [βασιλεία ἐπὶ βασιλείαν])." On the several ways to understand this second part of the sentence, see Marshall, 474.

48   I translate καί in v. 17 to mean "and so" and not "and also" with Godet (2:91). The houses fall, one upon another, and one against another, with Lagrange (330) and Fitzmyer (2:921), not one after another. The parallel in Matthew implies a kingdom, then a town or a house, although that of Mark has recourse to two examples, kingdom and then house. Deliberately rather than by inadvertence, Luke will have modified the text of Q and the range of comparisons. He understands here "house" in the sense of edifice, although in the source, this word undoubtedly designates a dynasty and a family. One may hesitate about the form of the sentence in Q; on this view, see the several opinions summarized by Kloppenborg ("Work Sheets," 143–44).

49   Luke rarely evokes the disasters of war; cf. the evocation of the destruction of the temple and the fall of Jerusalem in 13:34-35 (the adjective ἔρημος appears there in part of the manuscript tradition); and 21:20-24.

50   Cf. Rev 18:15-19, where the same word ἐρημῶ ("to make desert," "to devastate"; in the passive for a town "to be razed") is used twice. It has to do with the fall of Babylon; cf. Rev 17:16, and Josephus *Bell.* 7.1.1 §§1–4: "The army now having no victims either for slaughter or plunder, through lack of all objects on which to vent their rage—for they would assuredly never have desisted through a desire to spare anything so long as there was work to be done. Caesar ordered the whole city and the temple to be razed to the ground, leaving only the loftiest of towers. . . . All the rest of the wall encompassing the city was so completely levelled to the ground

■ **18** If the devil, the divider, is in turn himself divided, and if the truth set forth in v. 17 applies to his fate, his reign will not last. Neither Luke nor Jesus nor their contemporaries had any doubts about the reality of the devil and the organization of his henchmen. Demonology grew and various names for Satan or his principal collaborators were in circulation. We are dealing with the world of demons, whose final defeat was hoped for, without their final self-destruction daring to be counted on. As we saw in the account of Jesus' temptations (4:1-13), Luke was convinced of the extent of the demonic power and its impact on the empires of this world.[51] He considered the empire of that power still to be alive and well.[52] Only God's forces would be able to put an end to this superpower.[53]

On reflection, I think that the logic of the text is not simple. Let us attempt to spell that out: Jesus' adversaries accused him of being in the service of evil. Luke's Jesus replied in three phases. He began by looking at the presuppositions of the complaint (v. 18): according to his adversaries' diagnosis, a person possessed (Jesus) apparently freed another person possessed (the person possessed by an evil spirit). So a civil war would be taking place right inside Satan's camp (that would be too good to be true!). Alas, the kingdom of evil is far from being divided and, in truth, it is still holding out. Jesus was only too aware of that; he did not act on orders from the prince of demons! Here in v. 18b, Luke repeats the complaint, furnishing still another proof of his exegetical concern.[54] Like us, he sensed the logical difficulty of the text he had inherited. Before turning to the decisive statement that was to constitute the third phase (Jesus works in God's name, v. 20), Jesus is going to refer to the Jewish exorcists. That will be the second phase (v. 19).

■ **19** Luke reproduces the text of Q except for one conjunction, the Greek word καί (usually translated "and").[55] The second argument, the one in this verse, is more directly relevant to the complaint than the first argument and could very well be the earliest answer given by the tradition to the complaint that was made. The Christians who transmitted this saying, being on the defensive, did admit the validity of Jewish exorcisms.[56] All they asked was that Jesus' exorcisms and theirs be recognized as well. Thus, they felt themselves to be an integral part of God's people. Now God's people, from the time of Moses and Aaron on,[57] had been on the winning side of the battle with demons and participated in the triumph of faith over unfruitful magic. If Israel placed Jesus on Satan's side, they were condemning themselves. But in what sense were its exorcists to be its judges? Either, by metonymy, that the last judgment would depend on Israel's attitude toward its own exorcists, or, in the proper sense, that their exorcists, in the sense of 1 Cor 6:2, would become, along with the righteous, assistants to God as judge at the time of the final trial. The first of these hypotheses seems to me to be the more likely one: the people ran the risk of being condemned, if they paid no attention to their own exorcists, just as they had rejected the prophets that God had sent them.

■ **20** While v. 19 looks toward the future, v. 20 has the past and the present in mind. It contains an important saying that must have come from the historical Jesus.[58] It

---

as to leave future visitors to the spot no ground for believing that it had ever been inhabited. Such was the end to which the frenzy of revolutionaries brought Jerusalem, that splendid city of world-wide renown" (trans. H. St. J. Thackeray; LCL).

51 See the commentary on 4:1-13 (1:191–92), excursus on the devil, and (1:194) on Luke 4:6.

52 See Kruse, "Reich."

53 Note the inclusion by the word βασιλεία (v. 17 and v. 18a) and the contrast between ἐρημοῦται ("is deserted") and σταθήσεται ("will stand").

54 See the commentary on 6:27-28 (1:306–13).

55 The καὶ εἰ of Matthew corresponds to Q. The εἰ δὲ of Luke is redactional; see Schulz, Q, 205.

56 On the Jewish believers in demonological matters, see Kruse, "Reich," 31–34; on the Jewish exorcists, see 1 Sam (1 Kgdms) 16:14-23; Luke 9:49-50; Acts

19:13-17; Josephus Ant. 8.2.5 §46; Bell. 7.6.3 §185; 1QapGen 20.29; Fitzmyer 2:921–22; Str-B 4:1:533–35.

57 The expression "finger of God" that is about to follow (v. 20) originates from the account of the first plague (Exod 8:15). Moreover, the plagues of Egypt allow a confrontation between the true exorcists and the charlatans (Exodus 7–12).

58 On this verse component, see Kümmel, Promise, 24, 32–33, 105–7; Couroyer, "Doigt"; Rodd, "Finger"; Hamerton-Kelly, "Note"; Perrin, Rediscovering the Teaching, 63–67; Lorenzmeier, "Logion"; Grässer, "Gottesherrschaft."

reflects his consciousness of his ministry and its relation to the end of time. Since the saying mentions neither Beelzebul nor the complaint lodged against Jesus, and since it is not apologetic in tone, it does not come from the same historical context as the surrounding controversy. It recalls instead the prophetic assurance witnessed to by such sayings as Luke 10:21 (revelation to the little ones), Luke 10:23-24 (to see what you see) or Luke 11:31 (someone greater than Solomon is here). For once, Jesus explicitly involves himself ("I cast out," [ἐγὼ] ἐκβάλλω) in a speech about the kingdom of God. For any non-Christian, this is an immense and shocking claim: Jesus' exorcisms are the signs of the presence of the kingdom. The verb φϑάνω, which has caused a lot of ink to flow, meant, in the Hellenistic period, "reach," "arrive," "be there."[59] Jesus' victory over the evil spirits coincided with the sudden emergence of the kingdom. But we should beware of neglecting the words "to you" (ἐφ᾽ ὑμᾶς). The kingdom truly arrives (it does more than just "come near" [ἐγγίζω]; Mark 1:15), but only to those who welcome it. Christology and eschatology must be thought of in relation to ecclesiology.[60]

Matthew, as we know, speaks of the "Spirit of God," in place of Luke's mention of the "finger of God." It would be hard to conceive of Luke's having avoided a word he loved, "Spirit," in order to substitute for it an anthropomorphism, "finger." So Luke mentions the expression used in Q. The expression "finger of God" appears only a few times in the Hebrew Scriptures: Exod 8:15; 31:18; and Deut 9:10. In the plural (cf. Ps 8:4), it corresponds to the common expression "hand of God" and suggests the idea of power. In the singular, however, it indicates skillfulness. In Exod 8:15, it falls from the lips of the Egyptian magicians, who are stunned by the success of Aaron's rod during the third plague. In Hebrew, the saying is a nominal one and may be rendered by "This is the finger of God."[61] Bernard Couroyer has called our attention to Egyptian parallels (in particular in the *Book of the Dead*).[62] By "this" the magicians must be referring to Aaron's rod, whose divine power they recognized, rather than, in a general sense, to the miraculous event.

A finger is not a hand, and what can be carried out with a finger (e.g., drawing or pointing) does not correspond to what can be done with a hand. The finger then suggests skillfulness or dexterity; the hand, power. By the use of the word "finger" here, Luke, following Q, stresses mediation, instrumentality, efficiency, and skillfulness. With his finger, God has appointed Jesus, given him authority, put his stamp on him, and, probably, invested him with power. Matthew's change of "finger" to "Spirit" is understandable. But current exegesis is wrong in saying that the only idea associated with the "finger" is power.[63]

The Lukan concept of the reign of God[64] is rooted

59 On φϑάνω, see Kümmel, *Promise*, 106–7; Becker, *Heil*, 200–201; Lorenzmeier, "Logion," 296–301.

60 The "to you" is too often neglected by exegetes.

61 All exegesis that does not identify "that" and "finger" must be discarded, according to Couroyer ("Doigt," 483). The miracle would not be the finger of God but much more the effect of his action (ibid., 493).

62 There was great ancient Jewish elaboration on the diverse fingers of God and the diverse activities of each of them; see Couroyer, "Doigt," 492 n. 1. Moreover, Christian exorcists of later centuries, at least in Egypt, made appeal to the finger of God, e.g., in this magical formula (cited by Couroyer, "Doigt," 493): "I call you, Gabriel, by the name Orpha, the complete body of the Father, and Orphamiel, the great finger and law of the Father."

63 E.g., Marshall, 475.

64 On the reign of God here and in Luke in general, see Käsemann, "Lukas 11:14-28," 244 (whoever encounters Jesus is struck by the reign of God, even physically); Becker, *Heil*, 197–216 (the lordship of God and that of Satan stand face to face; contrast the present structure and awaited reality of the kingdom; underscores the "to you"; the kingdom is the realm of salvation; the parables are manifestations of the kingdom; Jesus claims to fight against Satan and to inaugurate the reign of God; the beliefs of the Essenes are clearly different); Kümmel, *Promise*, 107–9 (because of the "already," the "not yet" of Christians differs from the "not yet of Jews"); Lorenzmeier, "Logion" (the reign does not come without the participation of humans; demythologized understanding of satanic forces; the event of the coming of the kingdom is reproduced). Grässer ("Gottesherrschaft") critiques certain positions of Lorenzmeier ("Logion"). Grässer refuses human participation in the coming of the reign. See also Bovon, *Theologian*, 1–10.

in the Christian tradition and, through it, in the Jewish apocalyptic hope and the Hebraic faith in the royalty of YHWH. As Luke 11:20 points out, Christian preaching joins the reign to Christ's ministry. By the preaching of Jesus, considered to be the Son of God and Messiah, by his ministry and his very being, the reign of God has come near to all and has reached those who are anxious to welcome it. An eschatological fulfillment has taken place in the context of a relationship of power on God's part combined with faith on the part of believers. Jesus' word and the mediation of the Spirit make it possible for this event to take place. To be sure, the delay of the parousia modified the earliest hope for an imminent fulfillment but did not transform the fundamental linking of the "already" and the "not yet." Luke warned against belief in an imminent triumphal fulfillment (17:20-21; 21:8; Acts 1:6-8), but he did not consider the time of the church to be an unfortunate parenthesis between the time of Jesus and the time of the kingdom. For him, from the time that God's Word rang out in Jesus of Nazareth (16:16), from the time of the "today" of the fulfillment of prophecies (4:21), from the time of the Pentecost "of the last days" (Acts 2:17), the reign of God has been mysteriously present among believers (Luke 17:20-21), whose salvation has begun (Acts 2:47). Moreover, this reign has been efficaciously clashing with the reign of Satan, who was expelled from heaven (Luke 10:18) but is still powerful on earth. The kingdom belongs to God; it has been made into a present reality by Christ, God's Word, and by God's Spirit, and it is welcomed by believers in the church in a cryptic manner (8:10) that the final mani-

festation will render glorious. The presence of the reign does not eliminate suffering or death in the present, but it does confer on them another meaning. The eschatological renewal has begun. God has come to reestablish his rights and overthrow the powerful (1:51-52). Happy are the poor (6:20). Woe to those who do not get ready to enter the kingdom of God (9:62; 12:31; 18:17, 24-25, 29). The idea of the reign of God summarizes the teaching of Jesus (4:43) and his witnesses (Acts 28:31).

■ **21-22** As is often the case, Matthew temporarily gives the slip to Q and rejoins Mark. Luke, on the other hand, continues to follow Q, while perhaps adapting it to his style.[65] In Luke it is a question of a lord attacked by the enemy, while Mark and Matthew speak of a property owner attacked by a thief. Luke first speaks of a stable and calm situation, then of a brusque and dramatic breaking in of the enemy.[66] The contrast between a strong man and someone stronger than he seems to be inscribed in Scripture. Isaiah 49:24-26 plays on this polemical situation: Israel is oppressed by a powerful enemy but can count on her divine liberator, who is even more powerful.[67] During the time the Gospels were being written, this enemy would have to have been Satan, who occupies the world, the country, and the hearts of the people. He is fully equipped and armed, even to the teeth ($\kappa\alpha\vartheta\omega\pi\lambda\iota\sigma\mu\acute{\epsilon}\nu\circ\varsigma$).[68] He can thus protect and "guard" ($\varphi\upsilon\lambda\acute{\alpha}\sigma\sigma\eta$) his palace (or his farm: $\alpha\mathring{\upsilon}\lambda\acute{\eta}$, literally, "courtyard").[69] His possessions[70] are safe, literally "in peace" ($\mathring{\epsilon}\nu$ $\epsilon\mathring{\iota}\rho\acute{\eta}\nu\eta$).[71]

It is difficult to be sure exactly what the "dwelling place" of our man represents. It may be an anthropologi-

65   On the reconstruction of Q here, see Kloppenborg, "Work Sheets," 147–48. The parallel of *Gos. Thom.* 35 is closer to Matthew/Mark than to Luke: "It is not possible for anyone to enter the house of a strong man and take it by force unless he binds his hands; then he will (be able to) ransack his house" (trans. Thomas O. Lambdin in Robinson, *Nag Hammadi Library*, 130). On the possible Lukanisms of these verses, see Légasse, "Homme fort," 6–7; Kloppenborg, "Work Sheets," 147–48.

66   See Godet (2:95), who notes the difference introduced by $\mathring{o}\tau\alpha\nu$ ("quand," i.e., "when") and $\mathring{\epsilon}\pi\mathring{\alpha}\nu$ $\delta\acute{\epsilon}$ (i.e., "but as soon as").

67   On Isa 49:24-26, see Claus Westermann, *Das Buch Jesaja Kapitel 40–66* (ATD 19; Göttingen: Vandenhoeck & Ruprecht, 1966).

68   On $\kappa\alpha\vartheta\circ\pi\lambda\acute{\iota}\zeta\omega$ ("to equip," "to don arms," "to provide with"), see BAGD, s.v. $\kappa\alpha\vartheta\circ\pi\lambda\acute{\iota}\zeta\omega$: the prefix $\kappa\alpha\tau\acute{\alpha}$ has perhaps an intensive valuation.

69   On $\alpha\mathring{\upsilon}\lambda\acute{\eta}$ ("enclosure," "court"—interior of a house, "outer court" of the temple, "palace," "girders"), see Légasse, "Homme fort," 8; BAGD, s.v. $\alpha\mathring{\upsilon}\lambda\acute{\eta}$, 4.

70   On $\tau\mathring{\alpha}$ $\mathring{\upsilon}\pi\acute{\alpha}\rho\chi\circ\nu\tau\alpha$ ("the goods"), a word dear to Luke (8:3; 12:15, 33, 44; 14:33; 16:1; 19:8; Acts 4:32) and on the goods and their dangers, see Bovon, *Theologian*, 442–48; 470 nn. 33 and 34, 471 n. 42.

71   On "in peace" in the sense of "in security," see Légasse, "Homme fort," 7.

cal perspective,[72] as the context would suggest: Satan occupies the human heart (cf. the person who was mute and possessed by a demon before being liberated [v. 14] and the demon who was expelled but comes back [vv. 24-26]). The model in the Hebrew Bible (Isa 49:24-26) would lead us to think instead of Israel's property. The encounter between God and Satan for its part opens up a cosmic perspective. In the three cases, the strong man represents the believers' enemy.[73] We should reject the hypothesis of a paraenetic text according to which the well-trained believer (cf. 6:40) would be the strong man, threatened by Satan, who is the someone who is stronger than he and who, not being with him, would be against him (v. 23).[74]

Instead, the someone who is stronger,[75] that is, the divine liberator, arrives on the scene[76] and overcomes the strong man, that is, the Evil One. He takes away "all his arms" ($\pi\alpha\nu o\pi\lambda\iota\alpha$, which picks up on $\kappa\alpha\vartheta\omega\pi\lambda\iota\sigma\mu\epsilon\nu o\varsigma$, "fully armed").[77] Placing confidence in arms instead of God is a theme of the Hebrew Bible. Satan's error is precisely that of misplacing his confidence, that is, trusting in himself.[78] "His possessions" ($\tau\grave{\alpha}$ $\dot{\upsilon}\pi\acute{\alpha}\rho\chi o\nu\tau\alpha$ $\alpha\dot{\upsilon}\tau o\hat{\upsilon}$) are now called "his plunder" ($\tau\grave{\alpha}$ $\sigma\kappa\hat{\upsilon}\lambda\alpha$ $\alpha\dot{\upsilon}\tau o\hat{\upsilon}$).[79] What are these possessions? Those who are possessed by demons? The demons themselves? We should think instead in terms of riches and powers (note that the two substantives are in the plural and are neuter). The someone who is stronger takes back these powers and these riches and distributes them.[80] What Luke proposes as an ethical pattern for believers to follow is an analogous pattern: the distribution of the possessions.[81] The enemy's arms and possessions, moreover, should be

---

72 One discovers such a perspective in Jewish apocalyptic literature; see *T. Dan* 6:1-7 (opposition between Satan and the Lord; ultimate victory of the Lord, end of the empire of the enemy); *T. Moses* (also called *Assumption of Moses*) 10 (manifestation of the reign of God, which puts an end to the power of evil; cosmic leaps; Israel avenging the nations; elevation of the saints, which contemplate with joy the defeat of enemies on earth).

73 On ὁ ἰσχυρός, see Walter Grundmann, "ἰσχύω κτλ.," *TDNT* 3 (1966) 397–402; Henning Paulsen, "ἰσχυρός," *EDNT* 2:207–8; Kümmel, *Promise*, 108. Käsemann ("Lukas 11:14-28," 1244–45) refuses to allegorize. It is not necessary to consider here only a metaphor; he concludes: it is only by enfeebling the strong man that one can penetrate his domain. How can Käsemann (p. 245) say that, in accord with our text, the world has already been liberated from the demons?

74 See Meynet, "Qui donc," 334, 342–50. According to Légasse ("Homme fort," 9), Luke respects the traditional "givens," according to which the strong man is a demon figure, but Luke transforms him in the direction of his own preoccupations: evil in one of its most formidable expressions, namely, wealth, is conquered for the benefit of the poor.

75 Literally, "one stronger," "one stronger than he." The article ὁ ("the") is found in many manuscripts, but neither in the most ancient nor in the most important ones. It is, however, necessary to omit it.

76 Note the alliteration, which suggests this irruption: ἐπὰν . . . ἐπελθών, to which corresponds, ἐφ᾽ ᾗ ἐπεποίθει.

77 On πανοπλία, in the literal sense and the figurative, see BAGD, s.v.; 2 Sam (2 Kgdms) 2:21; 2 Macc 3:25; Wis 14:3; Sir 46:6; Eph 6:11, 13; Ignatius *Pol.* 6.2. The expression τὰς παντοπλείας καθωπλίσαντο ("they equipped themselves fully with arms") is found in *4 Macc.* 3.12 (Codex Alexandrinus). According to Légasse ("Homme fort," 7), the LXX, in contrast to Luke, does not understand this word in the sense of the complete equipment of soldiers. Légasse concludes about it that the description in these verse components must be from the Greek milieu of Luke rather than from the LXX. Apart from the usage here of the verb νικῶ ("to vanquish"), the vocabulary of victory, such as is found in the book of Revelation (5:5; 17:14), is absent from the Synoptic Gospels.

78 Cf. Prov 11:28: "He who trusts in his riches will wither, but the righteous will flourish like a green leaf"; Isa 7:9b: "If you will not believe, surely you shall not be established."

79 For τὰ σκῦλα, see BAGD, s.v. Cf. Isa 53:12 LXX, the recompense of the suffering servant: "Therefore he shall inherit many, and he shall divide the spoils of the strong" (καὶ τῶν ἰσχυρῶν μεριεῖ σκῦλα) (*NETS*).

80 On διαδίδωμι, see BAGD, s.v.

81 See nn. 70 and 78 above.

distinguished. We do not know what became of the arms, but we do learn what happened to the possessions. We are still in the realm of the dualistic and dramatic vision of the world: Christ's reign has come along to replace the reign of Satan. The world and the human heart are the places where this struggle takes place. The messianic war has been launched.[82] This is the last chance to choose sides.

■ **23** It is essential to rally to the side of the conquering Christ. Any lukewarmness would be equivalent to hostility; any failure to join, to apostasy. The demanding saying, the opposite of the charitable saying addressed to well-intentioned outsiders that was inserted in another context (9:49-50),[83] has its raison d'être here. It threatens those who are lukewarm and undecided: "Whoever is not with me is against me."

What holds true for the disciple who succeeds in believing (v. 23a) holds even more for the disciple who invites others to believe (v. 23b). Eschatological salvation is often compared to a harvest or to a gathering.[84] The apostles have to collaborate[85] "with me," just as the believers have to be "with me."[86] Being present at Christ's side, in all circumstances, is essential, even vital.

■ **24-26** These verses are witness to the fact that Jesus and the earliest Christians who followed him shared the beliefs of their time: the risk of being possessed by demons, possible exorcism, the necessity of *epipompē* ("sending upon," a new residence for the demon), the

threat of wandering unclean spirits, the comparison of a human being with a house, and the formidable threat of a demonic coalition. All that was a part of their cultural and religious horizon, constituting a common heritage of contemporary Jews and Gentiles.[87]

What exactly does this fragment of Q mean (vv. 24-26)?[88] It states that any liberation is risky and that the emptiness created by the demon's departure, although it allows an initial pleasant improvement, can subsequently be filled by a return in full force of the evil. If that does happen, if a new instance of taking possession does occur, the fate of the person who is possessed then gets worse.

These words, spoken in a neutral way, are at first only a description, a realistic observation of popular wisdom. Yet, already in Q and even more in Luke, they take on a paraenetic coloring. The explicit mention of a threat does, in fact, imply a warning.[89] However manipulative the forces of evil may be, believers have as their duty to resist them. This is the implicit exhortation.[90]

The dualistic perspective of the preceding passage remains in the background of these three verses. Jesus, who must be placed on God's side—in spite of the suspicions (v. 15)—unmasks the enemy's crafty tactics. Like the Law in Rom 3:20, he makes possible a knowledge of sin and thus enables one to become aware and to make a decision: his words, apparently so cold and so neutral, have a paraenetic thrust and constitute a call. Moreover,

---

82   See Grundmann, 239; *T. Levi* 18:2: "And Beliar shall be bound by Him, and He shall give power to His children to tread upon the evil spirits." This passage is followed by an invitation to choose between light and darkness (*T. Levi* 19:1).

83   See the commentary on 9:49-50 (1:511 n. 59).

84   On the eschatological gathering or reassembling of Israel, which is in the present day dispersed, cf. Isa 40:11; Ezek 34:10-16; *T. Naph.* 8:3; *T. Benj.* 10:11; *Ps. Sol.* 8:28; 11:2; *2 Bar.* 78:7 par. Jer 3:8. The theme is taken up in Christian literature: see Matt 25:32; *Did.* 9.4; *2 Clem.* 4.5. On συνάγω, see BAGD, s.v.; see also Hubert Frankemölle ("συνάγω," *EDNT* 3:292–93), who thinks that the verb has neither an ecclesial sense in the NT nor a technical eschatological sense.

85   They can be reassembled or dispersed: goods (15:13); produce of the land (3:17; 12:17-18); sheep (Matt 25:32); an army, a gathering (22:66; Acts

4:31); see Godet, 2:97. I think of the people of God, compared to a flock. Luke utilizes διασκορπίζω for goods (15:13; 16:1) and for people (1:51; Acts 5:37). The pair συνάγω and διασκορπίζω is found in Matt 25:24.

86   The repetition of μετ᾽ ἐμοῦ ("with me") underlines the importance of Christology.

87   Böcher, *Mächte*, 9–12.

88   On the differences between Matthew and Luke and the reconstruction of Q, see the analysis of vv. 14-26 above; Schulz, *Q,* 476–80; and Kloppenborg, "Work Sheets," 148–51.

89   According to Fitzmyer (2:924), "the episode preserves a minatory saying of Jesus."

90   The implicit paraenetic character is reinforced by the immediate context, in particular by v. 23. On the paraenetic character, see Ernst, 376.

Jesus is to be congratulated (v. 27) for having made this diagnosis and uttered this warning (vv. 24-26), as well as for having previously replied so well (vv. 14-23). It is not enough to have been freed from the demon. One must also be inhabited by Christ.

Let us follow the demon's itinerary. It could not have gone out cheerfully. Without it being said in so many words, the demon must have been driven out during an exorcism. Depicted as a living being with a will of its own, the demon looks for[91] a new place to live, a resting place.[92] The desert appears to be the favorite place for this type of demon.[93] It would appear that that is where it looks in vain for a new refuge. Similar to drug addicts deprived of their drugs, it has to have a shelter. Looking on its previous place of residence as "its house,"[94] it goes straight back to it.

The description of the premises is interesting and has symbolic significance. The dwelling that had been vacated was fixed up but not protected. The owner cleaned it, put it in order, and, perhaps, decorated it, as if a celebration were going to take place there—whereas it was actually in danger of being occupied. What is thus compared to a house is a person's inner being. Here then, unlike in vv. 21-22, the perspective is unambiguously anthropological, rather than ecclesiological or cosmic. The Greek word $\sigma\epsilon\sigma\alpha\rho\omega\mu\acute{\epsilon}\nu o\nu$ ("swept," "swept clean"[95]) suggests the idea of sweeping the floor,[96] which thus becomes clean.[97] The Church Fathers were to think of penitence that prepares for the visit of the Holy Spirit.[98] The broom was even to make its symbolic entry into the liturgy. The Greek participle $\kappa\epsilon\kappa o\sigma\mu\eta\mu\acute{\epsilon}\nu o\nu$, which we have translated as "put in order," includes two

---

91 The verb $\zeta\eta\tau\hat{\omega}$ occurs also in vv. 9-10; see the commentary above on 11:9-10.

92 This is the only usage of the term $\dot{\alpha}\nu\acute{\alpha}\pi\alpha\upsilon\sigma\iota\varsigma$ in Luke-Acts; cf. Matt 11:28-29, where the verb and the substantive appear. The verb is found in Luke 12:19 in the famous maxim: "take your ease, eat, drink, be merry!" This vocabulary has not yet received the theological coloring that it will have in the second century, particularly in Gnosticism. The word, which signifies "stop," "pause," "rest" (cf. Gen 8:9 LXX), is used sometimes for the Sabbath: Exod 16:23; 23:12; Lev 23:3. The Letter to the Hebrews provides a meditation on another word $\kappa\alpha\tau\acute{\alpha}\pi\alpha\upsilon\sigma\iota\varsigma$ ("rest" in the promised land; Heb 3:11—4:11).

93 Literally, the "places without water." There were demons of the air, of the earth, of water, of the desert, etc. See Tob 8:3; Bar 4:35; Lev 16:10; Isa 13:21; Rev 18:2; Plummer, 304; Otto Böcher, *Dämonenfurcht und Dämonenabwehr: Ein Beitrag zur Vorgeschichte der christlichen Taufe* (BWANT 90; Stuttgart: Kohlhammer, 1970) 40–73; idem, *Mächte*, 22–25.

94 Two other Lukan passages mention a return to one's own house using the same expression: 1:56 (Mary) and 8:39 (the Gerasene demoniac).

95 $\Sigma\alpha\rho\acute{o}\omega$ is a later form of $\sigma\alpha\acute{\iota}\rho\omega$; Luke uses it in 15:8 for the woman "sweeping" her house in the serach for the lost coin. Cf. *Hermas Sim.* 10.2; cf. BAGD, s.v.

96 There even exists a type of mosaic pavement, called $\dot{\alpha}\sigma\acute{\alpha}\rho\alpha\tau o\omega$ $o\hat{\iota}\kappa o\varsigma$ ("unswept house"), which represents earth strewn with detritus, with shells and pieces of bread, in illusion! Cf. Pliny the Elder, *Nat. hist.* 36.60 §184. These mosaics are brought together with the Pythagorean rule (cf. Diogenes Laertes 8.34) that prohibits collecting the remains of banquets fallen to the ground, because they are reserved for the dead; see M. Renard, "Pline l'Ancien et le motif de l'*asarôtos oikos*," in *Hommages à Max Niedermann* (Latomus 23; Brussels: Latomus, Revue d'études latines, 1956) 307–14.

97 See Leclercq, "Balai." Psalm 76 (77):7 has recourse to the image of "to weed/clean" rather than "to sweep," even if the Vulgate translates it by *scopare*, "to sweep." Isaiah 14:23: "I will sweep Babylon with a broom that makes everything disappear —an oracle of the Lord, the all powerful." Here the usage of *scopare* in the Vulgate is judicious (the LXX has a different text); cf. Rev 12:4 (the tail of the great dragon sweeps [$\sigma\acute{\upsilon}\rho\epsilon\iota$, literally: "pull" or "drag along"] a third of the stars). The Vulgate uses *trahere* ("to pull"), but the *TOB* translates as "to sweep."

98 Leclercq ("Balai," 131) refers to Tertullian *Paen.* 2.6 (CCSL 1:322–23). The whole patristic epoch will follow. Later, in the Middle Ages, the broom would serve ritually to eliminate pride. One would flagellate oneself with a *scopamentum* ("broom"). Thus, brooms came to obtain cultic value in the church.

different connotations of *κόσμος*, namely, order and beauty.[99] The house is clean, nicely fixed up. We might think in terms of flowers, art objects, and lamps;[100] symbolically, in terms of good deeds.[101]

Strength being achieved through unity, the demon preferred sharing the place to staying outside. Its colleagues were numerous and powerful ("seven other spirits more evil than itself"). We are reminded of the man possessed by the demon "Legion" (8:30). The lack of protection explains the ease with which reoccupation took place.[102]

History of Interpretation

For this passage, I will limit myself to a few remarks selected from the writings of the Venerable Bede (*In Luc.* 4.31–116, 231–34). He first noted that Matthew added blindness to the muteness of the Lukan demoniac (v. 14); then he added that the hostility (v. 15) came not from the crowd but from the Pharisees and the scribes; next he concluded that Beelzebub, to be read in preference to Beelzebul or Beelzebud, was god of Accaron (i.e., Ekron, 2 Sam [2 Kgdms] 1:2), *be[e]l* meaning baal and *zebub*, the fly. Beelzebub, the fly man, or the man who has flies, must be interpreted as follows: on account of the filth of the blood involved in sacrifice, because of the rite or even his particularly unclean name, he was called the prince of demons. Next, Bede stated that the kingdom of the Father, the Son, and the Holy Spirit, far from being divided (v. 17), remains stable and eternal, which allowed the author to shoot an arrow at the Arians. In connection with v. 20, he identified the finger of God, which was confessed by the magicians of Egypt (Exod 8:18-19) and used by God for writing the tablets of the Law (Exod 31:18), with the Holy Spirit (the Son being the arm or the hand of God). The image of the finger was well

chosen, in his opinion, which was based on Augustine's, since it suggests the dividing up (*partitio*) of possessions that are offered to both human beings and angels. The reign of God reaches us, when the ungodly are rejected and separated from the believers who have repented of their sins.

The strong man in the parable (v. 21) is the devil; the someone who is stronger (v. 22), the Savior; and the dwelling place (v. 21), the world, which is in bad shape. Then, in connection with v. 23, Bede quotes Jerome (*Comm. in Matt.* 2.12; *PL* 26:83B–C), who, because of the literary context, identified the one who did the scattering with the Evil One rather than with the heretic. It followed that Christ's works could not be compared with Beelzebub's, since Beelzebub wishes to hold the souls captive, while Christ has their deliverance as his goal.

The Venerable Bede next gives a tropological sense to vv. 24-26 (*In Luc.* 4:117–212 [esp. 185–86], 234–36). The house represents the human soul, cleansed by baptism but left empty (the commentator states that here he was influenced by the parallel in Matthew) by neglect of good works, and decorated by the hypocrisy of feigned virtues. The seven demons stand for all sins. Judas's tragic end (cf. Matt 27:3-10 and Acts 1:16-20) and that of Simon the Magician (without saying so, Bede must have been influenced here by Petrine legends, *Acts of Peter* or *Passion of Peter* according to Pseudo-Linus or Pseudo-Marcellus) prove that denying the Lord was counted to be worse than not knowing him.

Conclusion

Throughout this section (vv. 14-26), we are dealing with spaces to be occupied. The theme of control of space lends consistency to a succession of sayings that it would be otherwise difficult to link together. Already

---

99   On *κοσμόω*, see BAGD, s.v.

100   *Acts of John* 27 describes a room decorated in honor of the apostle.

101   The decorations are traditionally the virtues in Greece (see, e.g., Xenophon *Cyr.* 8.1.21) and good works in Christianity (see *Mart. Pol.* 13.2; *Diogn.* 12.1; *2 Clem.* 2.8; 33.7; BAGD, s.v.

102   The interpretation that Ambrose gives of vv. 24-26 concerns the fate of Israel: the Jewish people have cast out the demon by the law. But the latter has

come back, more dangerous than before, not having found rest among the nations touched by Christ. The church is attached to the kingdom of God, which subsists: it prefigures the kingdom united, whereas the synagogue repesents the kingdom divided against itself. Ambrose demonstrates an obviously anti-Semitic theology (*Exp. Luc.* 7.91–95).

in v. 13 we had the affirmation that God's Spirit might break into our human space. It sounded a certain note of pessimism, moreover, by labeling the human race as evil. Then, from v. 14 on, this space appears as the place where metaphysical hostilities take place. The supreme happiness of the arrival of God's reign (v. 20) is unfortunately matched by the tragic return of the demonic power (vv. 24-26).

What makes this reflection on space difficult for the modern reader is that it plays on both the interior and the exterior of the human being. The interior, the heart, similar to a house, is not so small that opposed forces cannot confront each other in it. But these forces themselves come from a field, from another, infinitely vaster, space. Satan's $\beta\alpha\sigma\iota\lambda\epsilon\iota\alpha$ (v.18) is his reign, to which corresponds an estate, a palace (or a farm). Likewise, God's $\beta\alpha\sigma\iota\lambda\epsilon\iota\alpha$ (v. 20), which is also and foremost God's reign, needs space and requires a kingdom. The human heart is a microcosm; its macrocosm corresponds to creation, which in turn is but the microcosm of the divine macrocosm, *divided* between God's legitimate power and the power usurped by Satan. The question, Who is the master of the place? therefore raises other questions about evil. This passage does not address the question of the origin of evil; however, it claims that there is at the same time the present power of negative superhuman forces and the limited, but real, responsibility of human beings. This responsibility increases in proportion to the degree that these human beings are informed, formed, and transformed by Christ, his Word and his Spirit, that is, by the counter-power that these positive superhuman forces represent.

In the face of the operation of these opposing forces, humans can opt for a stance of either mistrust or trust. Mistrust, inspired by fear, will drive them to look for a favorable outcome through magical practices. Trust, inspired by faith, will encourage them to act on the basis of what God has done by way of having the Son come and having the Holy Spirit intervene. This Christian attitude, perhaps slandered, is not limited to choosing God. Happy to welcome him by emptying their house, believers will be keen to decorate their interior by the practice of acts of love and prayer. Their following Christ will be expressed concretely by striving to reproduce Jesus' therapeutic ministry in their own actions, in faith lived out in acts of love. The Christian way will be demonstrated also in its duration. Believers will, at the instigation of their Master, be prudent and therefore will do everything possible in order to persevere and to avoid a fate that would be made more disastrous by the terrible return of a horde of demons.

The Best Beatitude (11:27-28)

Bibliography

Ben-Chorin, S., "Die Mutter Jesu in jüdischer Sicht," *Conc* 19 (1983) 604–7.

Bertram, Georg, "φυλάσσω κτλ.," *TDNT* 9 (1974) 236–41.

Black, Matthew, "The Aramaic Liturgical Poetry of the Jews," *JTS* 50 (1949) 179–82.

Brown, Raymond E., et al., *Mary in the New Testament: A Collaborative Assessment by Protestant and Roman Catholic Scholars* (Philadelphia: Fortress, 1978) 170–72.

Bultmann, *History*, 29–30, 58–59, 63–65.

Corbin, M., "Garder la parole de Dieu: Essai sur Luc 11, 28," in Jacques Audinet et al., *Le déplacement théologique* (PoTh 21; Paris: Année, 1977) 109–18.

Dewailly, L.-M., *Jésus-Christ, Parole de Dieu* (Paris: Cerf, 1969) 141–45.

Dupont, *Béatitudes*, 1:82–87.

Jacquemin, P.-E., "L'accueil de la Parole de Dieu, Lc 11, 27-28," *AsSeign* 66 (1973) 10–19.

McNamara, Martin, *The New Testament and the Palestinian Targum to the Pentateuch* (AnBib 27; Roma: Pontifical Biblical Institute, 1966) 131–33.

Meynet, "Qui donc."

Mulack, Christa, *Maria: Die geheime Göttin im Christentum* (Stuttgart: Kreuz, 1985) 102–3.

Mussner, Franz, "Lk 1, 48f; 11, 27f und die Anfänge der Marienverehrung in der Urkirche," *Catholica(M)* 21 (1967) 287–94.

Riedl, J., "'Selig, die das Wort Gottes hören und befolgen' (Lk 11, 28): Theologisch-biblische Adventsbestimmung," *BiLeb* 4 (1963) 252–60. (In fact, the article applies to both Luke 1:26-38 and Matt 1:18-25).

Schneider, Gerhard, "Jesu überraschende Antworten: Beobachtungen zu den Apophthegmen des dritten Evangeliums," *NTS* 29 (1983) 321–36; reprinted in idem, *Das Evangelium nach Lukas*, 173–83.

Schürmann, Heinz, "Das Thomasevangelium und das lukanische Sondergut," *BZ* 7.2 (1963) 236–60.

Scott, M.P., "A Note on the Meaning and Translation of Luke 11:28," *ITQ* 41 (1974) 235–50.

Str-B 2:187–88.

Wahlberg, Rachel C., "Jesus and the Uterus Image," *ThTo* 31 (1974–75) 228–30.

Zimmermann, H., "'Selig, die das Wort Gottes hören und es bewahren': Eine exegetische Studie zu Lk 11, 27f," *Catholica(M)* 29 (1975) 114–19.

27/ **And it happened, while he was saying this, that a woman in the crowd raised her voice and said to him, "Happy is the womb that bore you and the breasts that nursed you!" 28/ But he said, "Happy rather are those who listen to the Word of God and keep it!"**

These two verses constitute the center of a composition that begins with an instruction to the disciples (11:1-13) and concludes with an attack on the Pharisees (11:37-54). Aimed at the hesitant crowd, these verses promise true happiness to those who warmly welcome the God who speaks to them. Similar to the pericope on the true family (8:19-21), they are not, however, a simple doublet of it.

In spite of its brevity, the present pericope makes use of several parameters. In order to understand it, we must remember the distinctions made in antiquity between feminine and masculine elements, between nature and religion, between activity and receptivity, and between flesh and spirit. By so doing, the reader will see a conception of faith as listening take shape, a conception that contrasts with the disastrous diagnoses (11:15), illegitimate expectations (11:16, 29) and disingenuous applications of the Law (11:39-52).

What association should we make between the faith manifested in v. 28 and the woman's expression of joy in v. 27? The question is a decisive one, since we need to know if we are dealing with a contrast or a difference of degree. Protestant interpretation tends to stress the element of contrast and thus assign more weight to v. 28. Catholic tradition, on the other hand, meditates on v. 27, and speaks of the role of the Virgin Mary.

Analysis

Here we have an example of an apophthegm or a chreia.[1] In a setting that is barely fleshed out, a brief dialogue gives the last word to the Master. Each reply is made up of a nicely turned beatitude that is not followed by any justification. Luke, who was acquainted with isolated beatitudes (1:45; 7:23; 12:37, 43; 23:29; Acts 20:35) and series of beatitudes followed by curses (Luke 6:20-26), here makes use of the formula of two contiguous beatitudes.[2]

The Lukanisms in these few lines are so numerous[3] ("And it happened . . . that" [ἐγένετο δὲ ἐν τῷ followed by an infinitive]; "raised her voice"; "but he" [αὐτὸς δέ]; "listen to the Word of God") that Alfred Loisy considered these verses to be a Lukan creation.[4] I, however, feel that the Gospel writer adapted a traditional apophthegm or at least a traditional beatitude (that of the anonymous woman, v. 27, which might be the only traditional element[5]) to his style.

To whom should we attribute this traditional unit, to Q or to L? In favor of Q we have: the attachment to the Beelzebul episode (11:14-26; Mark 3:22-27), which is found also in the parallel account of the true family, Mark 3:31-35; and the Lukan habit of following the same source for as long as possible.[6] In favor of L: the absence of any parallel in Matthew, and the tone, which recalls

that of the infancy narratives.[7] In the final analysis, I opt for L. Commentators have also wondered if these verses, as well as the pericope on the true family, might not have been two variant versions of a single tradition.[8] Each of these texts, as a matter of fact, makes those who are satisfied with links of kinship listen to the Word. Luke, in any case, did not react to them as doublets since, although attentive to avoiding repetitions, he did not hesitate to transmit the two accounts (in 8:19-21 and here). To tell the truth, the two texts are quite different and part ways not only in their point of departure (Jesus' family breaking in on the scene in the one case, and the woman's beatitude in the other), but also in the final statement of each account (here Jesus states the origin of happiness, and in 8:19-21, true kinship). So we should interpret each unit on its own terms. Finally, I would like to point out what in my opinion is the secondary character of the parallel found in the *Gospel of Thomas*, which astutely links the verses in Luke to a similar but opposite saying in the account of the passion (Luke 23:29): "A woman from the crowd said to him, 'Blessed are the womb which bore you and the breasts which nourished you.' He said to [her], 'Blessed are those who have heard the word of the father and have truly kept it. For there will be days when you [pl.] will say, "Blessed are the womb which has not conceived and the breasts which have not given milk"'" (*Gos. Thom.* 79).[9]

---

1 See Bultmann, *History*, 11, 29–30, 58–59, 63–65; Dibelius, *Tradition*, 162; Mack and Robbins, *Patterns*, 188–89.

2 The formula is found in 14:14-15. In 12:37-43 the situation is different: it is the same person, Jesus, who pronounces two nearly identical beatitudes, separated from one another by narrative developments.

3 Marshall, 481; Jacquemin, "Accueil," 11; Zimmerman, "Selig," 115–17; Jeremias, *Sprache*, 203. Luke is the only one in the NT to use the expression "to raise the voice," which was current in Greek (Acts 2:14; 14:11; 22:22; cf. Luke 17:13 with αἴρω and not ἐπείρω; in the LXX, see Judg 2:4; 9:7).

4 Loisy, 325. I attribute ἐκ τοῦ ὄχλου to the tradition cf. ἐκ τῶν θυγατέρον Ἀαρών, 1:5.

5 According to Bultmann (*History*, 30), the two verse components always circulated together.

6 For Q as source, see Heinz Schürmann, *Traditionsgeschichtliche Untersuchungen zu den synoptischen Evangelien* (Düsseldorf: Patmos, 1968) 231.

7 For S^Lc (Luke) as source, see Fitzmyer, 2:926, for examples. On the style recalling the infancy narratives, see Loisy, 326.

8 See Bultmann (*History*, 30), who refers to David Friedrich Strauss, *Leben Jesu* (Tübingen: Osiander, 1835) 696; Marshall, 481: Jesus could say almost the same thing on two different occasions; Ernst, 378: another tradition.

9 If the first part of the apophthegm (Luke 11:27) remains almost identical, the second (11:28) contains two significant modifications: the Father instead of God and the addition of "in truth." In order to obtain symmetry, next the *Gospel of Thomas* brings back the sentence in Luke 23:29, onto which it latches here by two or three terms, only preserving, as in the preceding passage, the womb and breasts. On this logion 79, see Schrage, *Thomas-Evangelium*, 164–68.

The traditional apophthegm, easily committed to memory,[10] could have been used on various occasions in the earliest Christian communities, in particular in preaching and in catechetical training.[11]

If Luke inserted this episode of L into the sequence of Q, it is because he had a reason to do so. I. Howard Marshall thinks that these verses helped Luke bring the account of the dispute to a conclusion: Jesus' enemies would do better listening to him than attacking him.[12] Heinrich Zimmermann proposes an argument based on structure, namely, the parallel situation in Mark 3:31-35, teaching about the true family, which also follows the Beelzebul episode (Mark 3:22-27). Then Zimmermann gives a reason based on content: by listening to the Word (11:28), the hearers will be able to avoid an unfortunate fate (11:24-26) and will not have any need for a sign (11:29-32).[13] According to our outline of the chapter, which draws on Roland Meynet's article,[14] these verses make up the center of a large composition; they were addressed to the crowds, who were torn between the disciples and their enemies. They show them and offer them the happiness that will match their decision: welcoming or not welcoming the Word of God.

Commentary

■ **27** The vague "this," "these things" ($\tau\alpha\hat{\upsilon}\tau\alpha$), covers the different replies that Jesus has just given, starting with v. 17.[15] While the crowds had admired the exorcism (v. 14), the woman, on the other hand, congratulated Jesus on what he had said. What she expressed was neither a wish nor a complaint,[16] but her enthusiastic approval. This woman lost in the crowd[17] did so in a conventional way, as numerous Jewish parallels show,[18] some of them being influenced by Gen 49:25, a verse that speaks of the benedictions of maternal breasts and womb. To take but one example: "Blessed are the breasts at which you sucked and the womb in which you rested."[19] Martin McNamara supposes that that saying from the *Palestinian Targum* of Gen 49:25 and the one in Luke 11:27 depend on a single tradition. In his thinking, the woman could have heard that paraphrase of Gen 49:25 during a synagogue service. The expression appears, moreover, to have become proverbial at that time. Whether she was thinking of the proverb or the text of Genesis, either on her own or under the influence of the liturgy, the woman who spoke to Jesus was congratulating the son as much as, if not more than, the mother.

There are also many Jewish witnesses that designate maternity as the source of a woman's dignity and her raison d'être.[20] This anonymous woman who was listening to Jesus was not of another mind. The happiness to which she gave expression was therefore not that of the beatitudes but that of a privilege, which we can admit with this woman: being able to gestate, and then nurse, a

---

10   Jacquemin, "Accueil," 15.

11   Bultmann (*History*, 58–64) speaks of a biographical apophthegm. In his wake, I consider that it is this precise apophthegm that should be the true biographical interest conveyed by Jesus. Bultmann (p. 64) agrees here with Dibelius (*Tradition*, 164) by retaining preaching as the *Sitz im Leben*.

12   Marshall, 480.

13   Zimmermann, "Selig," 118–19.

14   Meynet, "Qui donc," 342.

15   And not only the topic about relapsing, vv. 24-26.

16   One can imagine that she would have well loved to have a similar son and that she was disappointed with her own children or that she envied Mary! See Plummer, 305; Marshall, 481.

17   A woman in the crowd recalls the woman with the flow of blood (8:40, 43-44).

18   See Str-B 2:187–88 and 1:161; Bultmann, *History*, 29–30; Plummer, 306; Grundmann, 240; especially,

McNamara, *Targum*, 131–33; and Fitzmyer, 2:928. In his benedictions and his oaths, the Semite often avoids direct disourse; see Ernst, 377.

19   The *Palestinian Targum* of Gen 49:25, translated here according to *Tg. Neof.* 1. This exclamation is found, in the third person, in *Gen. Rab.* 98; 120 to Gen 49:25; see McNamara, *Targum*. Note that, by contrast to the many recensions of the Targum, Luke places the womb before the breasts. *'Abod. Zar.* 2.8 (10) may also be cited: "Blessed is the one who has given birth to you" (a sentence attributed to Johanan ben Zakkai, around 80 of our era, in relation to R. Joshua ben Hananiah). And *2 Bar.* 54:10 "Happy my mother among those who give birth! May she be blessed among women, she who put me on earth!"

20   Ben-Chorin (*Mutter Jesu*) recalls that familial relationships do not uniquely represent, in ancient Judaism, a natural reality. They constitute the

child.[21] And when the child succeeds in life, is that not a legitimate cause for rejoicing? The opposite sayings send a chill up and down one's spine and can only apply to the worst calamities, Jesus' death and the end of Jerusalem: "Daughters of Jerusalem, do not weep for me, but weep for yourselves and for your children. For the days are surely coming when they will say, 'Blessed are the barren, and the wombs that never bore, and the breasts that never nursed'" (23:28b-29 *NRSV*). And "Woe to those who are pregnant and to those who are nursing infants in those days! For there will be great distress on the earth and wrath against this people" (21:23 *NRSV*).

■ **28** "But he": the "he" ($αὐτός$) has a formal connotation[22] and the "but" ($δέ$), an adversative force. As for the word $μενοῦν$, it has caused a lot of ink to flow.[23] First of all, in classical Greek it was a postpositive word, that is, it could not be used at the beginning of a clause; next, as a compound particle, it contains two elements: $μέν$,

marking correlation, and $οὖν$, "therefore," a logical element. In any case, $μενοῦν$ expresses a reservation, either because the speaker wishes to contrast another truth with the one just heard, or because he or she is anxious to correct what has been said previously. Some possible translations are: "rather" (BAGD, Twentieth Century New Testament, Moffatt, Good News Bible, *NAB*, *NRSV*), "nay rather" (Weymouth), "on the contrary" (BAGD), "more truly" (Zerwick-Grosvenor), "better" (Goodspeed), "no, rather" (Montgomery), "Yes, but better still" (C. B. Williams), "yes, but" (Phillips, Beck), "no" (Schonfield's Original New Testament, *NEB*/ *REB*), "it is better to say" (Translator's New Testament), "true, but rather" (Barclay), "that's true, but" (Contemporary English Version), and "by no means" (Cassirer).[24] The restrictive nature of $μενοῦν$ has been emphasized by the addition of the enclitic particle $γε$ in countless manuscripts. Scribes definitely sensed the contrast and

---

nucleus of cultic and sacral alliance. This explains the importance of maternity in Israel. Against this background, we must understand the attitude of Jesus, which is so hostile to his family and so distant with respect to his own mother.

21 The word $κοίλια$ designates the "cavity of the womb" and the "lower womb"; the "organs of digestion" (cf. Matt 12:40; Mark 7:19; Rom 16:18; 1 Cor 6:13; Phil 3:19; Rev 6:9-10), then the "maternal breast," which carries a child (cf. 1:15, 41, 42-43; 2:21; 23:29; Acts 3:2; 14:8; John 3:4; Gal 1:15); cf. BAGD, s.v. The verb $βαστάζω$ is not used otherwise in the NT for pregnancy, but cf. John 19:17 (Jesus himself carries his cross); Rom 11:18 (to carry a root); Gal 6:17 (to carry the stigmata of Jesus in one's body); *Barn.* 7.8 (to carry the goat in the desert); ὁ $μαστός$ means "udder" "breast" "chest" (also of a man; cf. Rev 1:13), "bosom" "small hill" "nipple." Josephus (*Bell.* 7.6.3 §118) mentions a grotto near to the royal citadel Macheron, protected by a rock, "above which protrude, as it were, two breasts, a little distance apart, one yielding extremely cold water, and the other extremely hot. These when mixed provide a most delightful bath, possessing general medicinal properties" (trans. H. St. J. Thackeray; LCL); cf. BAGD, s.v. The verb $θηλάζω$ signifies at once "to suckle" and "to suck." Luke 21:23 uses it in the first sense, but Luke 11:27 in the second. In Christian iconography, the representation of Mary suckling Jesus (the Virgin *galaktotrophousa*) is rare, and the first representations (e.g.,

the crater of marble, conserved in the National Museum of Rome) are oriental, more appreciated in Egypt (where the type of Isis *lactans* is familiar) than in Byzantium. See Schiller, *Ikonographie*, 4.2:22 and illustrations nos. 418–20. In the Middle Ages, one speaks of young girls or pious women, such as Ludwigia of Holland or Gertrude of Belgium who, around Christmas, seem to be supplied with milk even though they are virgins and are not pregnant. That the quasi-maternal affection of this piety is of concern to Luke is not stated (11:27-28).

22 See Jeremias, *Sprache*, 108, 203.

23 See Godet, 2:101: The particle "gives a certain truth to what has just been said ($μέν$) as a consequence of the facts mentioned ($οὖν$), which is completely oppose the complete and real truth." Plummer, 306: the word shows the inadequate character of the woman's speech. Lagrange, 336: it sometimes confirms, sometimes corrects. Sophie Antoniadis, *L'Évangile de Luc: esquisse de grammaire et de style* (Paris: Société Les Belles Lettres, 1930) 317: "He expresses a strong assurance which denies, in some way, the preceding idea." Jacquemin ("Accueil," 13) marks here a gradation, not an opposition; See BAGD, s.v.; cf. Rom 10:20.

24 "Heureux plutôt" ("Blessed rather"), translates Loisy, 326. Scott ("Note," 235) prefers "Yes, blessed indeed," to "No, blessed rather."

were anxious to bring it out; this is a valuable piece of information for us.

What reservation was involved? There are several possible interpretations. Influenced by the uncertain parallel in Mark 3:31-35, some have seen in it the initial indication of a criticism of kinship ties on Jesus' lips.[25] Others, sensitive to the crescendo that, unlike the contrast, makes it possible for Mary's honor to be safeguarded, see Jesus' reaction in a different light: it is all well and good to congratulate my mother, he meant to say, but the important thing is to be found elsewhere.[26] M. P. Scott has even gone further: Mary, the type of God's people, must not be blessed for simply having given birth to the Messiah.[27] What saves the people is faith, that is, listening to a Word of God that renews the covenant and extends to the Gentiles.

Personally, I would combine the parameters: flesh/spirit, singular/plural, man/woman, and activity/receptivity. The reservation is, first of all, an act of modesty: You honor me; well and good! But let us speak of something else. That something else is a happiness of a different order: that of listening to a word that opens onto a life other than familial success. From Luke's perspective this other reality concerns the woman rather than Jesus: she is not far from becoming one of those happy ones. Was she not the first to have listened to Jesus and to have admired what he said? Perhaps her faith was not yet perfect, but, in any case, she was opposed to the hardening of the position of the enemies (v. 15) and of the skeptics (v. 16). You have congratulated me, Jesus replies to her; it is rather up to me to honor you, you and all those who will listen. The plural and what goes with it, the ecclesial component, are not without their significance. The people of God is and always has been constituted by its relationship to the Word of God,[28] and not by procreation from generation to generation. That is what is implied by the plural "those who listen" (οἱ ἀκούοντες). What is valid for the people is valid also for each person, as well as for Jesus himself and for Mary, and for this anonymous woman. The supreme honor of a woman—Rachel C. Wahlberg's article helps us recognize this fact[29]—is therefore no longer a matter of maternity, but rather of living as a believer in the presence of God.[30]

Luke's Jesus gave a reminder of the fundamental necessity of listening,[31] the priority of the Word of God (v. 28) over the benefits of creation (v. 27). This receptivity, which contrasts with the most beautiful deed, does not, however, subsist by itself. For Luke, listening to the Word precedes and implies a Christian "doing" of a new kind.[32] The text here calls it "keeping."[33] Keeping the

---

25   Calvin (*Harmony*, on 11:27-28 and par.) sees in the phrase of Jesus an indirect correction of the woman's exclamation. Mary, regenerated by the Spirit, is more honorable than Mary, mother of Jesus. See Plummer, 306; Marshall, 482; Ernst, 377. Verse 27 recalls the benediction in 1:42 and the beatitude announced in 1:48, although v. 28 refers to the beatitude in 1:45.

26   The speech of the woman, while certainly insufficient, is important. Godet, 2:100: earthly relationships are only of value when sanctified by God's love; Lagrange, 335: nobody says anything; she allows her mother's heart to speak. See also Zimmermann, "Selig," 117; Jacquemin, "Accueil," 11–13.

27   See Scott, "Note," 247. In an interesting way, he insists on the notion of the people of God (which is refused otherwise by Godet, 2:100) and on the division that threatens this latter concept (which is announced by Simeon, 2:34–35, and realized; cf. Acts 28:24-25).

28   Grundmann, 240: by listening to this word, one avoids lapsing back into the power of the devil (vv. 24–26); Marshall, 480: this word of God is understood in the word of Jesus. See also Ernst, 377–78.

29   Wahlberg, "Uterus": Jesus is opposed to a conception of women defined on the basis of motherhood. Mulack (*Maria*, 102–3) considers that there were, in primitive Christianity, discernible forces that were interested in turning the son of Mary into the son of the heavenly Father.

30   This macarism recalls 10:23: "Blessed are the eyes that see what you see."

31   Cf. the almost identical terms in 8:21, where one has to "do" instead of to "keep."

32   Cf. the presence of the verb "to make" in 8:21; Mark 3:34; Rom 2:13.

33   This is what Mary, the believer, does: συνετήρει ("treasure"; 2:19) and διετήρει ("treasure with care"; 2:51). On φυλάσσω ("to keep"; 18:21; Acts 7:53), see Georg Bertram, "φυλάσσω κτλ.," *TDNT* 9 (1974) 236–41; Jacquemin ("Accueil," 15) refers to 6:47-49 and 8:11-15. Corbin ("Garder," 116–18) refuses to translate φυλάσσω as "to put into practice." He retains the sense of "to keep" and comments: "We must keep that which holds us in

Word means causing it to grow, making it produce, and keeping it alive. Here is the ethical field of perseverance, the necessary complement of faith, the incarnation of a Word, as concrete as a pregnancy and a birth.

History of Interpretation

Maximinus, bishop of the Goths, who died in 428, delivered a sermon on these verses (11:27-28), as well as on the sign of Jonah (11:29-32).[34] Although he scarcely connected vv. 27 and 28 to each other in his commentary, in his sermon, he did provide a lively commentary on each of these verses. The heartfelt cry of the anonymous woman who was listening to Jesus was, in his opinion, inspired by the Holy Spirit. That woman was right in reflecting onto the mother the praise of the son. Mary deserved to be blessed and to become not only a servant but also the mother of the Lord. Jesus' reply praising believers represents the fulfilled beatitude (more perfect, implied Maximinus, than the woman's). For Maximinus, who was at least as sensitive, if not more sensitive, to the ethical content than to the doctrinal content, listening to the Word was the remembrance of "God's words" and the observance of the Decalogue and the golden rule.

The commentary by Albert the Great (Albertus Magnus) spreads over some twenty pages (*Enarr. in Luc.* 9.27–28). Writing from a mariological perspective, he gave special worth to the beatitude of the listening woman, whose name, according to him, was Stella, and he devoted lengthy praise to the womb of the Virgin Mary. Stella was Martha's servant, and she traveled in the company of the two sisters in their odyssey as far as Marseille. Weak woman that she was, she still had the courage to raise her voice. To that "servant," who had remarkable dignity, in contrast to the scribes' hostility, Jesus replied,

without directly contradicting her, that Mary would never have become the blessed mother that she was, if she had not first been an attentive listener to the Word of God. Whereas modern commentators juxtapose Mary's faith and her maternity, Albert connected them—and he was not alone in doing so in the Middle Ages—in an impressive way by stressing the temporal precedence of faith with respect to maternity. Mary was able to shelter Christ in her flesh only because she had first welcomed him in her spirit.

The preacher Meister Eckhart delivered a long sermon on this text.[35] From our point of view, the most interesting part is the contrast he made between the mother, who expected a flesh-and-blood child, and God the Father, who transmitted his life to the Son. There was more happiness for Mary in being a believer than in being a mother. Listening to the Word of God was what counted for her, as for us. Eckhart noted that it was Jesus, and not the preacher, who set that drastic priority for Christ's mother. He then reflected, in a speculative way, on this God who speaks and gives life. What the attentive ear can hear is that Christ was born of the Father and remained and remains in perfect identity with him, even in the period during which he assumed human nature. True God and true man, Christ is the Word to hear and to preserve. It is the soul that keeps this word and keeps the Father, the believer, and all things together. Following the lead of Gregory the Great, Eckhart also enumerated the four necessary conditions for hearing the Word well: dying to oneself, giving up the world, reaching up completely to God, and practicing the golden rule (cf. Luke 6:31).[36]

For Zwingli, as for Calvin, the woman's beatitude concerned Christ more than Mary.[37] Mary's holiness was born of Christ's and not the other way around.[38] It

---

its keeping, we are a child who takes the hand of his big brother on the road and keeps watch upon this hand, which has already kept watch over him" (p. 17). The word has put us on the path and we must keep watch to remain cleaved there, in walking with Christ.

34 Maximin, *Sermo de sancto Evangelio Luke* 11:27 (*PL* 57:814–15).

35 Meister Eckhart *Predigten* 49, in Josef Quint, ed. and trans. *Meister Eckhart: Die deutschen und lateinischen Werke* (3 vols.; Stuttgart: Kohlhammer, 1958–76).

36 In a Latin sermon, perhaps of December 8, 1517 (WA 4:625), Luther opposes to the carnal reaction of the women the spiritual listening of the Word of God. In 1925, in his "Fastenpostillen" (WA 17.2:214–22), the reformer considers v. 28 of Luke 11 as the heart of the Gospel. He had read the assurance of salvation by listening to the Word and not by works.

37 Zwingli, *Annotationes*, 639; Calvin, *Harmony,* on 11:27-28 and par.

38 Zwingli, *Annotationes*, 639.

is better to be regenerated than to give birth to Jesus.[39] The anonymous woman who was listening to Jesus forgot the most important thing: that Jesus Christ brings salvation through his word. Spiritual life consists in listening and keeping that word. According to Calvin, the papists only honor v. 27, which speaks of the honor attributed to the Virgin Mary, and neglect v. 28, the correction that provides a reminder of the Word of God.[40] This judgment is manifestly incorrect. We should rather say that contemporary Catholic interpretation found a crescendo between vv. 27 and 28, whereas Protestant interpretation saw a contrast between them. Erasmus's interpretation confirms this diagnosis: he likened the anonymous woman to the church, a positive figure opposed to the hostile scribes, who were a symbol of the synagogue.[41] This woman believer needed to be led by Christ to a more solid faith. In view of the eternal beatitude, Erasmus insisted less on listening than on the fruits one needs to produce.

Conclusion

We should first point out the likable profile of this anonymous woman, whose enthusiasm was in contrast to the skepticism of those who were looking for signs (11:16, 29) and the opposition of the legalistic theologians (11:15, 39-52). She substituted an atmosphere of joy and well-being for a climate of reproaches. Even if what she said was going to be corrected, she detected in Jesus an essential reality. Her heart was able to see something invisible.

Jesus, however, turned her attention away almost brusquely to something else, in two different directions. Away, first of all, from his mother and from himself. Next, away from natural ties. In his eyes, happiness depends not on physical contact or on belonging to a family but rather on an attitude of faith that pays attention to the Word of God. "Blessed are those who have not seen and yet have come to believe" (John 20:29)

was the reply Jesus gave to the unbelieving Thomas, and that reply is in theological harmony with this text. What counts is not belonging to Jesus' family, nor having been one of his direct companions, nor having witnessed his miracles or his signs. What counts, in any period of history, is being open to Jesus' witness to God, a witness coming from God.

Welcoming the Word of God is an extraordinary opportunity offered everywhere to those who were perhaps not born in proximity to Jesus, nor in Judaism, nor in Christianity. Although this text says nothing about the way in which the Word is communicated, it does nonetheless presuppose its existence and its accessibility. By the happiness it displays of this contact with God, this pericope contrasts strongly with the demonic possessions, the internecine divisions, and the scrupulous observances of the surrounding pericopes.

As is often the case, Luke reminds us here that believers could not be satisfied with listening to God passively or absentmindedly (cf. 8:4-15). Their faith must be expressed outwardly in acts of love (8:21) and lived out over a period of time, that is, carried out with perseverance (8:15). Here in v. 28, the verb "keep" ($\phi\upsilon\lambda\acute{\alpha}\sigma\sigma\omega$) has that double connotation of keeping and continuing to keep. At Jesus' invitation, believers put into practice the command to love, and they withstood the vicissitudes of time as well as the risks of being discouraged.

Jesus' mother had the good fortune to bear her son and then to nurse him. Those who listen to the Word of God and obey it resemble her, for they in turn become bearers of Christ. In both cases they thus achieve happiness, the state of beatitude wished for by God and that he offers to his children. Mary herself, according to the infancy narrative (1:38, 45; 2:19, 51) and the beginning of the book of Acts (Acts 1:14), was not just Jesus' mother. She was also a believer, and thereby one of those happy persons of whom v. 28 speaks.

---

39 Calvin, *Harmony*, on 11:27-28. In the same context, the reformer adds a second reason for the correction that Jesus gives to the anonymous listeners: he reproves them, because human beings have a

tendency to neglect the facts and gifts of God that they recognize ""with a full mouth."
40 Ibid., 319.
41 Erasmus, *Paraphrasis*, 383–84.

Jesus Has Given No Sign Other Than Himself (11:29-32)

Bibliography

Adam, A.K.M., "The Sign of Jonah: A Fish-Eye View," *Semeia* 51 (1990) 177–91.

Bonsirven, Joseph, "Hora Talmudica: A propos du logion sur le signe de Jonas," *RSR* 24 (1934) 450–55.

Bowman, John, "Jonah and Jesus," *ABR* 25 (1987) 1–12.

Catchpole, David R., "The Law and the Prophets in Q," in E. Earle Ellis, Gerald F. Hawthorne and O. Betz, eds., *Tradition and Interpretation in the New Testament* (Grand Rapids: Eerdmans, 1987) 95–109.

Colpe, Carsten, "ὁ υἱὸς τοῦ ἀνθρώπου," *TDNT* 8 (1972) 400–477.

Correns, D., "Jona und Salomo," in Haubeck and Bachmann, *Wort*, 86–94.

Dassmann, Ernst, *Sündenvergebung durch Taufe, Busse und Märtyrerfürbitte in den Zeugnissen frühchristlicher Frömmigkeit und Kunst* (Münsterische Beiträge zur Theologie 36; Münster: Aschendorff, 1973) 386.

Draper, J. A., "The Development of 'the Sign of the Son of Man' in the Jesus Tradition," *NTS* 39 (1993) 1–21.

Duval, Yves Marie, *Le livre de Jonas dans la littérature chrétienne grecque et latine: Sources et influence du Commentaire sur Jonas de saint Jérome* (2 vols.; Paris: Études augustiniennes, 1973).

Edwards, Richard Allen, *The Sign of Jonah in the Theology of the Evangelists and Q* (London: SCM, 1971).

Idem, *Theology of Q*, 113–15.

Gibson, J., "Jesus' Refusal to Produce a 'Sign,'" *JSNT* 38 (1990) 37–66.

Ginzberg, Louis, *Legends of the Jews* (trans. Henrietta Szold et al.; 7 vols.; Philadelphia: Jewish Publication Society, 1909–69) 4:246–53; 6:348–52.

Goodenough, Erwin R., *Jewish Symbols in the Greco-Roman Period* (13 vols.; New York: Pantheon; Princeton: Princeton University Press, 1953–68) 12:100.

Green, H. B., "The Credibility of Luke's Transformation of Matthew," in Tuckett, *Synoptic Studies*, 157–76.

Hampel, Volker, *Menschensohn und historischer Jesus: Ein Rätselwort als Schlüssel zum messianischen Selbstverständnis Jesu* (Neukirchen-Vluyn: Neukirchener Verlag, 1990).

Hoffmann, *Logienquelle*, 37.

Howton, "The Sign of Jonah," *SJT* 15 (1962) 288–304.

Jeremias, Joachim, "Ἰωνᾶς," *TDNT* 3 (1966) 406–10.

Linton, Olof, "The Demand for a Sign from Heaven (Mk 8:11-12 and Parallels)," *StTh* 19 (1965) 112–29.

Lührmann, *Logienquelle*, 36–43.

Merrill, Eugene H., "The Sign of Jonah," *JETS* 23 (1980) 23–30.

Mora, Vincent, *Le signe de Jonas* (Paris: Cerf, 1983).

Mussner, Franz, "Wege zum Selbstbewusstsein Jesu: Ein Versuch," *BZ* n.F. 12 (1968) 161–72, esp. 169–71.

Rengstorf, Karl Heinrich, "σημεῖον κτλ.," *TDNT* 7 (1971) 200–261.

Schmitt, G., "Das Zeichen des Jona," *ZNW* 69 (1978) 123–29.

Schulz, *Q*, 250–57.

Schwartz, Daniel R., "The End of the ΓΗ (Acts 1:8): Beginning or End of the Christian Vision," *JBL* 105 (1986) 669–76.

Seidelin, Paul, "Das Jonaszeichen," *StTh* 5 (1951–52) 119–31.

Stommel, Eduard, "Zum Problem der frühchristlichen Jonadarstellungen," *JAC* 1 (1958) 112–15.

Tödt, Heinz Eduard, *The Son of Man in the Synoptic Tradition* (NTL; London: SCM, 1965).

Vögtle, Anton, "Die Spruch von Jonas Zeichen," in idem, *Das Evangelium und die Evangelien: Beiträge zur Evangelienforschung* (Düsseldorf: Patmos, 1971) 103–36.

Zeller, D., "Entrückung zur Ankunft als Menschensohn (Lk 13, 34f; 11, 29f)," in *A cause de l'Évangile: Études sur les Synoptiques et les Actes. Offertes au P. Jacques Dupont, O.S.B. à l'occasion de son 70e anniversaire* (LD 123; Paris: Cerf, 1985) 513–30.

29/ When the crowds were increasing, he began to say, "This generation is an evil generation. It asks for a sign, and no sign will be given to it except the sign of Jonah. 30/ For just as Jonah became a sign to the people of Nineveh, so the Son of Man will be to this generation. 31/ A queen of the south will rise at the judgment with the people of this generation and condemn them, because she came from the ends of the earth to listen to the wisdom of

Solomon, and see, something greater than Solomon is here! 32/ The people of Nineveh will rise up at the judgment with this generation and condemn it, because they repented at the proclamation of Jonah, and see, something greater than Jonah is here!

In these verses Luke introduces a threatening Christ who upbraids those to whom he speaks for their lack of spiritual lucidity. The criticism is made, however, against a background of generosity and happiness: Is there not here something greater than King Solomon and the prophet Jonah? Unlike the writer of the Gospel of Matthew, the writer of the Gospel of Luke gives a coloration to the pericope that is more ethical than christological. Eager to witness a sign, that generation remained blinded to the one who was shown to them, the Son of Man. This surprising and distressing observation leads us to ask, What stance and what involvement are required of faith? How do signs operate at the two opposite ends of the communication circuit? What is the divine art of persuasion?

Unfortunately, commenting on these verses produces an accumulation of difficulties. To the complex history of the traditions we must add Lukan redaction, which did not eliminate all the ambiguities. Given the wide spectrum of interpretations,[1] our approach remains hesitant, whether we make our approach to the text through its origin or through its structure.

Analysis

Luke explicitly locates this speech by Jesus in a public setting (v. 29a), between instruction of his disciples (vv. 1-13) and the attack on his enemies (vv. 37-54), and after the double beatitude (vv. 27-28), which serves as a transition between the Beelzebul episode (vv. 14-26) and this passage (vv. 29-32). The crowds are invited to side with the disciples, that is, the believers, and to part company with the enemies.[2] Like the double beatitude, these verses have a metalinguistic character: they are a speech, a reflection on a dialogical situation.[3] This reflection is aimed at Luke's readers, who are invited to not succumb to the same blindness as Jesus' generation.

For a reason difficult to grasp (a desire to make a better link between the pericopes?),[4] Luke prepared the ground by already inserting the request for a sign in the dispute about Beelzebul (v. 16). The apophthegm is thus split up. Following a brief reminder of the situation (v. 29a), the account begins not with the question (cf. v. 16) but with the answer, that is, with Jesus' speech. The Lukan Christ offers a harsh diagnosis (v. 29b), from which he draws the conclusion (v. 29c). Then, in a comparison with Jonah, whose name serves as a linking word (v. 30), he justifies not so much his diagnosis (v. 29b) as the follow-up he gave it, the promise of the sign of Jonah (v. 29c). Then he adds to this comparison two parallel sayings, one on the queen of Sheba (v. 31) and the other on the people of Nineveh (v. 32, whose name, here once again, serves as a linking word with v. 30). These two mentions make it possible to understand the sign of

---

1   For examples of various interpretations, see Seidelin ("Jonaszeichen"): an enigma desired by Jesus; Vögtle ("Spruch"): v. 30 = the correct Christian interpretation of v. 29, which goes back itself to Jesus; Linton ("Sign"): on the notion of sign through the OT and Judaism; Howton ("Jonah"): Jonah = dove; Edwards (*Sign*): monograph covering the subject, state of the question; in Luke link with disciples, universalism, repentance and forgiveness, new age of the Spirit and ethics, vision of a historian, the evangelist, critical heir of Q; Schmitt ("Zeichen"): thanks to a text of *Vitae Prophetarum* (Theodor Schermann, ed., *Prophetarum vitae fabu-*

losae indices apostolorumque domin and *Propheten- und Apostellegenden* [Leipzig: Teubner, 1907] 56–57), who refers to a τέρας ("miracle") of Jonah, the sign of Jonah (Luke 11:29), aimed at the end of Jerusalem; Bowman ("Jonah"): Jewish interpretation of Jonah. See also Luz, *Matthew*, 2:271–85, 443–45.

2   See the commentary on 11:14-26 above.

3   On the metalanguage, see Oswald Ducrot and Tzvetan Todorov, *Dictionnaire encyclopédique des sciences du langage* (Paris: Seuil, 1972) 40–41.

4   See the commentary on 11:16 above.

Jonah better and the danger there is in neglecting it. The expression "this generation," which is found in the four parts of the speech, provides the whole with a structural and thematic unity. Jesus' speech is to be continued, without a break, by the sayings about the lamp and the eye (vv. 33-36). While the double beatitude stressed the importance of hearing, vv. 29-32 and later vv. 33-36 point out the dangers of deficient sight and the responsibility of the eye.

The earliest Christians were very much concerned with the request for a sign, to the point that the request is found both in the Gospels and in the Epistles. The apostle Paul declares it to be the quintessence of Judaism (1 Cor 1:22);[5] the writer of the Gospel of John associates it with the saying about the destruction of the temple (John 2:18-22), while the double tradition (Q) and the triple tradition (Mark 8:11-12) pay special attention to Jesus' negative reaction to it. As is often the case, Matthew, who was not afraid of doublets, preserved the two versions of it (Matt 12:38-42 [= Q] and Matt 16:1-4 [= Mark]), while Luke preferred to keep only one mention of the episode, the one from Q (here, Luke 11:29-32). We should point out, however, that in the previous request (v. 16), for some curious reason, Luke drew on the triple tradition: some people wanted to "test" Jesus and asked for a sign "from heaven," details absent from Q (Matt 12:38). When we come to Jesus' answer, we note the redactional character of the introduction, which is not surprising (v. 29a). In what follows, Luke made few changes in Jesus' sayings. Nevertheless, he subdivided the first sentence (cf. Matt 12:39) and standardized the formula "this generation" (Matt 12:39: "a generation") once and for all. On the other hand, Matthew, following the Deuteronomistic topos,[6] added "and adultery" to the "evil generation," and then added "the prophet" to "Jonah" before opting for the Greek compound verb ἐπιζητεῖ ("seek for," "search for") in place of the simple verb ζητεῖ ("seek," "ask for"), which Luke has retained here in spite of his preference for compound verbs.[7] There are considerable differences between Luke and Matthew in v. 30: Luke seems to have kept the text of Q, which implied Jonah's preaching to the people of Nineveh, while Matthew, taking the prophet's fate as his starting point, speaks of the death and resurrection of the Son of Man (Matt 12:40).[8] The two parallel sayings about the queen of Sheba (v. 31) and the people of Nineveh (v. 32) are virtually identical in Luke and Matthew, aside from the difference that their order is inverted. We cannot know what the sequence was in Q. Luke may have reestablished the order found in the Hebrew Bible (queen of the south, then the people of Nineveh), unless Matthew deferred to a Jewish liturgical tradition mentioning Jonah before Solomon.[9]

If one wished to attempt to make a breakthrough in establishing the origin of this pericope,[10] one would have to say the following. Behind the double and triple traditions lay a brief apophthegm: Jesus firmly refused to grant a sign when asked to do so (Mark has preserved this initial reply).[11] This account was rapidly expanded, as is shown by the tradition hiding behind Q: in place of Jesus' firm refusal was substituted a refusal qualified by an exception (the addition, manifestly Christian, of "except the sign of Jonah"). As was often the case, an expansion of the tradition then appeared to be necessary, and it took the form of a commentary. Thus, a commentary in the form of a saying was written; it is to be traced back to the earliest Christians rather than to Jesus (v. 30). The authors of this saying wanted to explain the

---

5   Note the plural σημεῖα. Paul implies that Israel has always requested signs.

6   See Deut 32:5; and the commentary on 9:41 (1:387).

7   Sophie Antoniadis, *L'Évangile de Luc: esquisse de grammaire et de style* (Paris: Société Les Belles Lettres, 1930) 99.

8   Schulz, *Q*, 251–52.

9   Bonsirven ("Hora") and Correns ("Jona") refer to *m. Taʿan* 2.4 and 2.1; Schulz, *Q*, 252.

10   See the works mentioned in n. 1 above, especially those of Seidelin, Vögtle, and Edwards; see also Schulz, *Q*, 251–54, and the commentaries.

11   Note the Semitisms of Mark 8:12bc, e.g., τί ἡ γενεὰ αὕτη ("why does this generation?"), ἀμὴν λέγω ὑμῖν ("truly I say to you") and εἰ δοθήσεται ("it will not be given"); see Edwards, *Sign*, 75–77. I believe that Matt 16:1-14 inserts the clause of exception, "except the sign of Jonah," in parallel to Mark 8:11-12 under the influence of another version, that of Q.

reason for the exception and to indicate that the Son of Man would be for that generation what Jonah had been for the people of Nineveh—for Q, and later for Luke, the preacher of repentance; for Matthew, the suffering hero (Matthew, as I have said, did not hesitate to profoundly modify this saying and, consequently, the commentary on it). The history of the tradition is a history of interpretation. In the case of Q, and later of Luke, the commentary took on an anthropological meaning (acceptance or refusal of the sign); in the case of Matthew, a christological meaning (the sign indicates Jesus' own destiny). Moreover, two parallel, perhaps authentic, sayings were in circulation. Since thematic and structural points of connection were not lacking, these two sayings of Jesus were added to the apophthegm during its evolution. Q reveals to us that state of the text, which had already undergone considerable evolution. Those who transmitted Q were right in the middle of a controversy with Israel; they stressed the importance of the presence of Jesus, a prophet ("proclamation," $\kappa\dot{\eta}\rho\nu\gamma\mu\alpha$, v. 32) and teacher of "wisdom" ($\sigma o\phi\dot{\iota}\alpha$, v. 31); the decisive nature of the attitude that each person takes with respect to Jesus; and the disappointing results of the Christian mission, which will be compensated for only by the condemnations on the day of judgment ($\dot{\epsilon}\nu\ \tau\hat{\eta}\ \kappa\rho\dot{\iota}\sigma\epsilon\iota$, vv. 31 and 32).[12] In Q, this text followed the Beelzebul episode (vv. 14-26). When Luke, who had inherited this text, transmitted it he respected both its position and its wording. By having v. 16 precede this pericope, he tightened the links between the sign of Jonah and Christ's miracle-working activity, just as he was to compare the prophet Jonah with the preacher Jesus in vv. 33-36.[13]

Commentary

■ **16** In order to justify Christ's critical speech, Luke had already taken the precaution of mentioning the seeking of a sign beginning in the previous episode (v. 16). The "others" mentioned in that verse wanted to "test" Jesus in the pejorative sense.[14] They believed that they could achieve that by asking[15] him for a sign from heaven, that is, a divine accreditation that would have removed, not only from their sight but also from their faith, the ambiguity inherent in every human activity, including exorcisms.[16]

■ **29** Jesus was to make a reply. But before having him do so, Luke is anxious to remind us of the crowd's presence. He accomplishes this by using the plural "crowds," of which he was fond (cf. v. 14) and, above all, by resorting to a rare and well-chosen verb, $\dot{\epsilon}\pi\alpha\vartheta\rho o\dot{\iota}\zeta o\mu\alpha\iota$. This New Testament *hapax legomenon*[17] means "to gather together," "to crowd together"; by the use of this verb, Luke helps us visualize the crowds: they have become more numerous and thicker.[18]

By saying that Jesus "began" ($\ddot{\eta}\rho\xi\alpha\tau o$) to speak, Luke indicates that a new literary unit has begun. He gives in to his tendency to use that verb, and he lets us know that he will henceforth be concentrating his attention on a new part of the speech.[19]

The Gospel writer strengthens Q's wording by making an independent clause out of it: "this generation is an evil generation."[20] The biblical expression "this generation" refers above all to God's people in their present state.[21] This generation is "evil"[22] less by moral negligence than by doctrinal deficiency. It is unable to recognize

---

12 On Q, see Schulz, *Q*, 254–57. On $\ddot{\epsilon}\sigma\tau\alpha\iota$, which aims at the parousia, see Vögtle, "Spruch," 129.

13 See the commentary on 11:33-36 below.

14 On the verb $\pi\epsilon\iota\rho\dot{\alpha}\zeta\omega$, see the commentary on 4:1-13 (1:141).

15 The verb $\zeta\eta\tau\dot{\epsilon}\omega$ ("to seek") in a number of manuscripts is rendered $\dot{\epsilon}\pi\iota\zeta\eta\tau\dot{\epsilon}\omega$ ("to research") and in 1 Cor 1:22 by $\alpha\dot{\iota}\tau\dot{\epsilon}\omega$ ("to request"). Here the request is illegitimate, because it does not spring from faith. The lapidary formula: "seek [$\zeta\eta\tau\epsilon\hat{\iota}\tau\epsilon$ same verb] and you will find" (11:9) concerns legitimate requests that emanate from believers.

16 See Linton ("Sign"), who insists that the sign should not necessarily be a miracle, but an event that confirms the divine promise; see too the commentary on 11:14-26 above.

17 The verb is also absent from the work of Josephus; cf. Plutarch, *Vit. X. orat.*; *Ant.* 44.2.

18 Luke has signaled repeatedly the attraction of the crowds to Jesus (4:42; 5:1; 6:17) and the success with which his preaching meets, at least at the start (4:14-15, 22, 32, 37).

19 See Plummer, 305.

20 The repetition of the word is not essential. One part of the manuscript tradition omits it.

21 The expression or a similar expression is found in the following passages: 7:31; 9:41; 11:50-51; 17:25; Acts 2:40; see n. 6 above.

22 On $\pi o\nu\eta\rho\dot{o}\varsigma$ in Luke, see Baumbach (*Verständnis*, 123–38, esp. 125 and 131–32), who speaks of ethical dualism, which opposes not the good believer to the bad among the people of God, but the believers to

God's hand at work. It even reverses the sense of reality, since it hesitates to recognize Jesus and connects his power with the world of Satan. It disqualifies itself less by ethical defect than by having a faith that is unwilling to accept either the facts or revelation.

By making a distinction between Zechariah, who asked for a sign out of lack of trust (1:18), and Mary, who received one in order to strengthen her faith (1:34-35), Luke has already reflected on the concept of signs. His perception of this reality is in the tradition of Scripture.[23] God is the master of signs: he can take the initiative of giving them (Isa 7:14), just as he can respond either positively or negatively to those who ask him for them. On the human side, what is important is the attitude with which one solicits a divine recognition or sign. There is a long list of those who, trembling with fear when presented with a prophecy, have wished to receive confirmation of it by means of some exterior sign, for example, Gideon (Judg 6:36-40) or Hezekiah (2 Kgs [4 Kgdms] 20:8-11). Each of these beggars realized that his attitude, however understandable it may have been, was nonetheless rooted in doubt. That is why Ahaz preferred not to ask for a sign, so as not to test the Lord (Isa 7:12). If the relation between God and the person with whom he is speaking is based on trust, however, it is possible for a sign to occur: it becomes a tangible proof of grace from on high, an anticipation at a point in time of total fulfillment.[24] So there are three phases: in the first phase, God's prophetic word sounds out against a background of crisis. In the second phase, a sign occurs. In the third phase, the divine oracle is fulfilled. The Scriptures, to get to the point of our text, announced the kingdom of God. The coming of the Son of Man was the sign of it. Its fulfillment was still awaited. The reaction to the Word and to the sign was situated in the "today" of that

era. That generation, unfortunately, although asking for divine signs, remained deaf to the Word and blind to the sign. It was radically set off from those fortunate persons "who listen to the Word of God and obey it" (11:28), even in the absence of accompanying visible signs (cf. John 20:29).

The biblical structure of the sign is therefore complex; its complexity is due to the nature of its underlying relationship. In the system related to faith, the sign occurs as part of the support system; in the system related to doubt or hostility, it is rejected.

"Except the sign of Jonah." These enigmatic words have given rise to numerous, often divergent, commentaries. The genitive of the Greek word translated "of Jonah"(Ἰωνᾶ) is itself already ambiguous: Was Jonah himself the sign, or was it the sign that Jonah received, or the sign that Jonah gave?[25] The name "Jonah," a very rare one, rightfully causes us to think of the hero of the biblical book, but some subtle minds have thought in terms of either John the Baptist[26] (Jonah in that case being an abbreviation of Johanan), or a dove, which is the meaning of the Hebrew word translated Jonah (in that case, then, it would be less the dove of the Holy Spirit than the one symbolizing the people of Israel or its suffering representative).[27] Among these suggestions I would favor (a) Jonah himself as the sign and (b) the allusion to the *prophet of Israel*. But we should not only reread the book of Jonah but also realize what thoughts this prophet brought to mind at that time. That can be discovered in the midrashic writings,[28] the patristic literature, and the earliest Christian art.[29] What struck people in no uncertain way was Jonah's fate. Jewish Haggadah had him traveling in his sea monster, looking through the monster's eyes as one would through portholes. At that point the unfortunate man encountered the monster of

the nonbelievers in the world. The "bad" are characterized by the absence of conversion and the Holy Spirit.

23 See Linton, "Sign."
24 I am inspired by the article of Linton ("Sign"); see also Rengstorf, "$\sigma\eta\mu\epsilon\hat{\iota}o\nu$ $\kappa\tau\lambda$."
25 See Jeremias, "Ἰωνᾶς." It is suggested that the formula "except the sign of Jonah" has the following sense: the sign of Jonah will certainly be given for them. Cf. Colpe, "ὁ υἱὸς τοῦ ἀνθρώπου."
26 Against this opinion, see Jeremias, "Ἰωνᾶς," 408–9.
27 See Howton, "Jonah."

28 Str-B 1:645–49; Jeremias, "Ἰωνᾶς," 408–9; Correns, "Jona"; and esp. Bowman, "Jonah."
29 See Stommel, "Jonadarstellungen"; Dassmann, *Sündenvergebung*, 386; Duval, *Le livre de Jonas*; W. Wischmeyer, "Die vorkonstantinische christliche Kunst im neuen Licht: Die Cleveland-Statuetten," *VC* 35 (1981) 235–87, esp. 263 n.78.

all monsters, Leviathan, who was fated to be devoured by the elect during the banquet of the kingdom. Next he discovered the undersea mysteries. Finally, he prayed to God, who brought him back living from death.[30] Jonah was a model of the believer who was saved. That is also the way that the earliest Christian artists interpreted him. By drawing him so often in their catacombs,[31] they recalled the resurrection that was promised to those who believe in Jesus Christ, whose fate so closely called to mind that of the prophet of old. To my way of thinking, these data confirm the hypothesis proposed in the "Analysis": the words "except the sign of Jonah" are a correct Christian interpretation of Jesus' categorical refusal to provide a sign. They indicate that Jesus did not give any sign except himself. His word and his life were God's only ultimate sign. Since Jesus' fate included a stay among the dead and a return to life, he was compared to Jonah. But that was not all there was to Jonah; he had also been the preacher, at first recalcitrant but later willing, who was sent to the Gentiles, who had a sharper spiritual hunger than did the people of Israel (Jonah 3:4-10). The double saying about the queen of Sheba and the people of Nineveh, which circulated in the early church, brings to mind Israel's resistance to the gospel and the obvious Christian universalism. That, too, was what Jonah embodied. Luke was sensitive to that relationship and, unlike Matthew, did not stress Jonah's death and deliverance here. The picture he drew of Christ was more of a Jonah[32] who invited people to conversion[33] than one who symbolized salvation.

■ **30** The interpretation of the sign of Jonah found in this verse goes back to Q, and Luke took it over literally, even if he understood it his own way. In his eyes, it was more anthropological than christological, and more ethical than soteriological.[34] It would be difficult to overstate the distinctions among the different Gospel writers with regard to their rereadings. Luke, in fact, was unacquainted with the Matthean allegory of Jonah's stay in the belly of the sea monster. For him, the Son of Man—that is, God's lieutenant—was set as a sign before human beings during his ministry and not through his death.[35] Just as Jonah's message had an effect, likewise Jesus' ministry made possible the salvation or the judgment of his generation. Simeon's prophecy had already stated it: he is destined ($\kappa\epsilon\hat{\iota}\tau\alpha\iota$, 2:34) as a sign that will be opposed, as a riddle and a witness.[36] His presence alone compels one to make a decision; if the decision is in favor of him, a recovery will follow (the "rising" or "resurrection," $\dot{\alpha}\nu\dot{\alpha}\sigma\tau\alpha\sigma\iota\varsigma$); if the decision is to oppose him, what will happen is the fall (the $\pi\tau\hat{\omega}\sigma\iota\varsigma$). Human responsibility is thus formidable: there is no cheap grace. According to 11:30, God "gives" his Son, but it is an offer that still must be accepted. The incarnate Son of Man, moreover, is only a sign; that is, he is not the eschatological plenitude. He who is its anticipation comes to the aid of faith. Such was Luke's characteristic interpretation. Matthew's christological interpretation, more traditional, opted for a mention of the cross and the resurrection. Luke's anthropological interpretation, more mobilizing, addressed itself to those who hesitate and placed the

---

30 See esp. *PRE* 10; *m. Taʿan.* 2.1 and 2.4; *b. Sanh.* 89ab; *3 Macc.* 6:8; Josephus *Ant.* 9.10.2 §213.

31 For example, in the Roman catacombs of Saint Calliste and Saints Peter and Marcellin.

32 As a result of contamination by Matt 12:39, a great number of manuscripts add "the prophet" after "Jonah."

33 One could also think of the sign that Jonah received from God: God made a plant grow and then die, a plant that offered shade and protection to Jonah. If Jonah had pitied his plant, should God not have taken pity on Nineveh? This generation—that is to say, Israel—should admit the mercy of God with regard to the nations. The symbolic correspondence falters, however; it would be necessary to bring together the crowds not with the Ninevites but with an ungrateful Jonah, and with Jesus as the plant and not Jonah. Verse 30 is opposed to this interpretation, although it considers that Jonah himself is the sign given by God.

34 Codex Bezae (D), as well as some ancient Latin manuscripts, insert, at the end of v. 30, a text close to Matt 12:40. They thus add a christological and soteriological interpretation to the Lukan text. See the apparatus of Nestle-Aland[27].

35 On this verse, see Vögtle ("Spruch," 127–33), who sees here a correct Christian interpretation of the authentic sentence in v. 29. At the parousia, the Son of Man will be resuscitated, as a sign for the Jews of confirmation. See Colpe, "ὁ υἱὸς τοῦ ἀνθρώπου," on the Son of Man in Luke. see also the commentary on 5:21-24 (1:183 n. 31).

36 See the commentary on 2:34 (1:104).

choice at the intersection of death and life. The Son of Man, a unique sign, is a source of contemplation in Matthew, but of commitment in Luke. For Luke, that is the function of Jesus' message; it is a message and not a destiny, but a message communicated through acts, speech, and suffering. In that way, an analogy is drawn between the fate of the Son of Man and that of his followers. For Luke, the future ("will be," ἔσται) corresponds to the time of Christ and of the church. It makes it possible to include not only Jesus' earthly ministry but also his resurrection, but in no case in the exclusive sense given it in Matt 12:40.[37]

We have Jonah as a foreigner among Gentiles; Jesus, as the foreigner among us. Our natural xenophobia runs the risk of costing us dearly. And yet it is for our sake that God has placed this sign among us. He will place no other one than that one; he "gave" it. It is probably not the one we were asking for. Perhaps we were not asking for any sign. Luke's summons to "conversion" (μετάνοια), to a return to God, has never been as urgent as in this saying. As a matter of fact, the Gospel writer gave all his attention to this saying. Convinced of the goodness of God, the one who placed this unique sign among us, he fervently hoped that his generation, more than Jesus' generation, would recognize and welcome the Son of Man. Verses 31-32 will take away from this urgency any appearance of forced penitence, since

they will say that something greater than Jonah is here, something more than a coercive proclamation. What we have is an inviting and generous proclamation.

■ **31** This verse is polemic, insofar as Israel counted on judging the Gentile nations at the end of time.[38] Jesus reversed the perspective and affirmed that Israel would be condemned by the Gentile nations and that men would be condemned by a woman. He also supposed that "this generation," that is, the recalcitrant people of God, would be judged by the true people of God, since the queen of the south (see 2 Kgs [3 Kgdms] 10:1-3; 2 Chr 9:1-12)[39] or the people of Nineveh did not represent just any nations so much as they did the Gentiles who were newly converted to God and who were true believers. The text stresses their faith: she "listened" (cf. v. 28) to the wisdom of Solomon, and the Ninevites "repented" after listening to Jonah's proclamation. The queen came from the ends of the earth,[40] that is, she paid the price necessary to get there. The people of Nineveh, who were powerful lords, did not hesitate to repent. All of them paid their respects; she paid hers to knowledge, "wisdom" (σοφία);[41] they paid theirs to the prophetic revelation, the "proclamation" (κήρυγμα).[42] We know the story of the queen of the south from the First Book of Kings (1 Kgs [3 Kgdms] 10:1-12) and the Second Book of Chronicles (2 Chr 9:1-12). There is no other mention of her in the New Testament. The great lady had come

---

37 The future ἔσται has incited many scholars to invoke the resurrection of Jesus or the parousia of the Son of Man; for the resurrection, see Theodor Zahn, *Das Evangelium des Lukas: Ausgelegt* (KNT 3; Leipzig: Deichert, 1913) 476–77, and already Cyril of Alexandria *Hom. in Luc.* 82; Reuss, *Lukas-Kommentare*, 128–29; Payne-Smith, *Cyril*, 2:375–76; for the parousia, see Erich Klostermann, *Das Matthäusevangelium: Erklärt* (HNT 4; Tübingen: Mohr, 1927) 112; Bultmann, *History*, 124; Vögtle, "Spruch," 128–30. In my interpretation, this does not refer only to the preaching of Jesus; rather, his entire person is the sign. In this sense, see Grundmann, 242; and Manson, *Sayings*, 91; for the preaching, see Kümmel, *Promise*, 104; Tödt, *Son of Man*, 52–54; 210–14; cf. Vögtle, "Spruch," 127 n.105.

38 Cf. Dan 7:22; Wis 3:8. Christians recapture this hope for their benefit (1 Cor 6:2; Rev 3:21; 20:4). According to Matt 19:28 and Luke 22:30, the Twelve will judge the twelve tribes of Israel. Luke has a reference to "men" (μετὰ τῶν ἀνδρῶν) that Mat-

thew ignores. He underlines this paradox: a woman will judge men; a pagan, some Jews (with Lagrange, 338).

39 Ambrose (*Exp. Luc.* 7.96) identifies Solomon with Jesus and the queen of Sheba with the church.

40 The expression τὰ πέρατα τῆς τῆς (cf. Rom 10:18) differs from that of Acts 1:8 ἔσχατον τῆς τῆς; see W. C. van Unnik, "Der Ausdruck ἕως ἐσχάτου τῆς γῆς (Apg 1:8) und sein alttestamentlicher Hintergrund," in idem, *The Collected Essays of W.C. van Unnik* (Leiden: Brill, 1973) 385–401.

41 For σοφία, see 2:40, 52; 7:35; 11:49; Acts 6:3, 10; 7:10, 22; see also the commentary on 7:35 (1:277–78). For Ambrose (*Exp. Luc.* 7.96), wisdom (v. 31) allows one to avoid sin; and penitence (v. 32), to destroy it.

42 On κήρυγμα, of which this is the only usage in Luke-Acts, see Otto Merk ("κῆρυξ, etc.," *EDNT* 2:288–92, esp. bibliography, 288), which, according to Luke 11:32, recalls Luke 12:3, where the verb κηρύσσω ("to proclaim") appears.

to test Solomon's wisdom by means of riddles. Having looked with her own eyes and heard with her own ears, she was profoundly moved, and she admitted that there really was more to it than the testimonies she had heard, even though they were extravagant. Solomon turned out to be wiser and wealthier than the queen had been told. What is there to say about this woman who had a great intellectual curiosity, had an iron will, and was unwaveringly straightforward? Only that at the end of her visit she praised the Lord, the God of Solomon, who loved the people of Israel and had given them a good king. The queen of the south will prevail on the day of judgment, since she took the trouble to go and see for herself, let herself be persuaded, and ended up joyfully admitting the truth.

The words "and see, something greater than Solomon is here!"[43] are an amplified echo of the queen of the south's interjection of praise. She had discovered more than she had been told. Christians place more trust in Jesus, who is nevertheless still deprived of the glory of his parousia, than in King Solomon. At that time, Solomon was not only the "Son of David," but he was also the inheritor of the promises, a master of wisdom, author of proverbs, and custodian of arts and sciences.[44] To claim that there is here and now something greater[45] than Solomon is to dare to say a great deal in few words.

■ **32** As for Jonah,[46] he represents not only what it is to be a prophet but also, and especially, a prophet in exile, in the Diaspora. The Christian situation is to be read the same way: in the eyes of Christians. Jesus was an eschatological prophet who welcomed converts from among the Gentiles. Jonah's hesitations about preaching to foreigners reminds us of Jesus' misgivings, as well as those of the earliest Christians,[47] about welcoming Gentiles into the Christian community.[48] But there is also something greater than Jonah, namely, the Son of Man, who is able to pardon and to save.

History of Interpretation

The Venerable Bede made a connection between these verses and the account of the transfiguration (*In Luc.* 4.273–77). Here, when the people demanded a sign from above, they received one only from below: the sign of the incarnation, and not one of divinity; the sign of the passion, and not one of glorification. In the case of

---

43 Luke deliberately uses the adverb ὧδε (seventeen usages in Luke-Acts our of sixty-one in the NT). He gives it often, as here, a theological valuation; see, e.g., 4:23; 9:33; 14:21; 17:21, 23; 24:6.

44 On Solomon, see Corren, "Jona"; Gerhard Schneider, "Σολομών," *EDNT* 3:257; André Dupont-Sommer and Marc Philonenko, *Écrits intertestamentaires* (Bibliothèque de La Pléiade; Paris: Gallimard, 1987) 1844: index by J.-M. Rosenstiehl, which permits one to reconstruct many intertestamental texts.

45 On πλεῖον, cf. 7:43 and 21:3; BAGD, s.v. πολύς, 2.2c; see also Mussner ("Selbstbewusstsein," 170), who refers to the enigmatic and christologically vague character of this neuter.

46 One finds the example of Jonah again in *1. Clem.* 7.7, who judges that repentance is preached to each generation: "Jonah proclaimed destruction to the Ninevites; but they, repenting of their sins, propitiated God by prayer, and obtained salvation, although they were aliens [to the covenant] of God" (trans. Roberts and Donaldson, *ANF*). Justin *Dial.* 107.1 is without doubt the first Christian author to refer to our passage. In fact, he cites the Matthean parallel, Matt 12:39.

47 Christianity was inclined to offer the gospel to the nations; see Matt 10:5-6; Mark 7:27; Acts 10:1-11, 18; 11:19-24; Col 1:26-27; Eph 3:8-12; Rom 16:25-27.

48 Note that vv. 31 and 32 use two verbs related to the resurrection: ἐγείρω and ἀνίστημι. Here they perhaps have the sense of "raise oneself." The expression is found again outside of the context of "judgment" in 10:14; the word "judgment" is in 11:42. Here are the only usages in Luke of the verb κατακρίνω, which can signify either "to put forth an accusation" or "to condemn." One finds the formula, which is already stereotyped, "judge the living and the dead," in Acts 10:42 (cf. Luke 11:19), and the verb "to judge" for the last judgment in Luke 6:37; 22:30; Acts 17:31. There is lacking, to my knowledge, a study of the last judgment in the work of Luke; see Daniel Marguerat, *Le jugement dans l'Évangile de Matthieu* (MB 6; Geneva: Labor et Fedes, 1981); Wolfgang Schenk, "κατακρίνω, etc.," *EDNT* 2:259–60; Mathias Rissi, "κρίνω, etc.," *EDNT* 2:318–21; Wolfgang Schenk, "κριτής, etc.," *EDNT* 2:322.

the transfiguration on the mountain the Son gave his disciples a sign from heaven; he showed them the glory of eternal beatitude.

The queen of the south, on the other hand, might represent, in the allegorical sense, the church, for example, for Ambrose (*Exp. Luc.* 7.96),[49] or, in the tropological (moral) sense, the soul in dialogue with its Lord, for example, for Theophylact.[50]

"And see, something greater than Jonah is here!" Bonaventure laid stress on the length of Jesus' ministry and the power of his miracles (*Comm. in Luc.* 11.68). Three years were not enough to convince the Jews, whereas three days turned the people of Nineveh around. No one will be surprised, then, at the anti-Semitic tone that the medieval commentary takes on at this point.

At the end of his explanation, Bonaventure linked this passage, in an original way, with Gal 3:1 (Christ pictured as crucified while the Galatians looked on) (*Comm. in Luc.* 11.68). He thought that what Jesus was while living in the presence of his contemporaries is what the cross has become for us. Thus, believers have the conviction that if they do not doubt and do not become lukewarm in the matter of listening to the Word, nor cold in that of penitence, Christ will not condemn them.

Conclusion

Christians are not yet in the immediate presence of their Lord. In the interim, there is room for doubt or faith, in any case for responsibility and making decisions. However, God has not simply imposed on us the weight of separation and distance. In addition to the word of prophecy that gives cause for hope, he has also offered us the sighting of signs.

Through a paradox whose consequences, unfortunately, can become tragic, those who receive this gift both wish for a sign and do not know how to see it. The Gospel writer invites his readers to change their way of looking at things, and then to discover the sign of the Son of Man, offered to human beings in order to help them believe. He knew that the first generation had remained insensitive to the sign and had even become hostile to the Son of man. He hoped, however, that the memory of the Son of Man, and of what he had said and done, would serve as a welcome mediation for the faithful. Thus it is that, in the alternation between confidence and reflection and between faith and sight, Christians repent, in the steps of the people of Nineveh, and, following the queen of the south, they learn some unheard-of news. They discover that there is something there greater than a wise man or a prophet. There is the Son of man. History has swung over into eschatology.

---

49 See n. 39 above.
50 Cited by Aquinas, *Catena aurea* 11.9.

The Lamp and the Eye (11:33-36)

Bibliography

Alliata, E., "La κρύπτη di Lc 11, 33 e le grotte ripostiglio delle antiche case palestinesi," *SBFLA* 34 (1984) 53–66.

Allison, Dale C., Jr., "The Eye Is the Lamp of the Body (Mt 6, 22-23; Lk 11, 34-36)," *NTS* 33 (1987) 61–83.

Betz, Hans Dieter, "Matthew 6, 22f. and Ancient Greek Theories of Vision," in Ernest Best and R. McL. Wilson, eds., *Text and Interpretation: Studies in the New Testament Presented to Matthew Black* (Cambridge: Cambridge University Press, 1979) 43–56.

Brandt, W., "Der Spruch vom lumen internum: Exegetische Studie," *ZNW* 14 (1913) 97–116; 177–201.

Cadbury, Henry J., "The Single Eye," *HTR* 45 (1954) 69–74.

Delebecque, Édouard, "La lampe et l'oeil (11, 33-36)," in Édouard Delebecque, *Études sur le grec du Nouveau Testament* (Aix-en-Provence: Université de Provence, 1995) 85–88

Derrett, J. Duncan M., "The Lamp Which Must Not be Hidden (Mark 4:21)," in Derrett, *Law*, 189–207.

Dupont, Jacques, *Béatitudes*, 1:82–87.

Idem, "La lampe sur le lampadiare dans l'évangile de saint Luc (Luc 8, 16; 11, 33)," in Dupont, *Études*, 2:1032–48.

Idem, "La transmission des paroles de Jésus sur la lampe et la mesure dans Marc 4, 21-25 et dans la tradition Q," in Dupont, *Études*, 1:259–94.

Dupont–Sommer, André, "Note archéologique sur le proverbe évangélique: Mettre la lampe sous le boisseau," in *Mélanges syriens offerts à monsieur René Dussaud: Secrétaire perpétuel de l'Académie des inscriptions et belles-lettres* (2 vols.; Paris: Geuthner, 1939) 2:789–94.

Edlund, Conny, *Das Auge der Einfalt: Eine Untersuchung zu Mt 6, 22-23 und Lk 11, 34-35* (ASNU 19; Copenhagen: Munksgaard; Lund: Gleerup, 1952).

Edwards, *Theology of Q*, 115.

Fiebig, P., "Das Wort Jesu vom Auge," *ThStK* 89 (1916) 499–507.

Garrett, Susan R., "'Lest the Light in You Be Darkness': Lk 11:33-36 and the Question of Commitment," *JBL* 110 (1991) 93–105.

Hahn, F., "Die Worte vom Licht Lk 11, 33-36," in Hoffmann, *Orientierung*, 107–39.

Jeremias, Joachim, "Die Lampe unter dem Scheffel" (1940), in idem, *Abba: Studien zur neutestamentlichen Theologie und Zeitgeschichte* (Göttingen: Vandenhoeck & Ruprecht, 1966) 99–102.

Jülicher, *Gleichnisreden*, 2:79–88, 98–108.

Kasteren, J. P. van, "Analecta exegetica, V," *RB* 3 (1894) 61–63.

Koester, Helmut, and James M. Robinson, *Trajectories through Early Christianity* (Philadelphia: Fortress, 1971) 180–82.

Nebe, G., "Das ἔσται in Lk 11, 36 – ein neuer Deutungsvorschlag," *ZNW* 83 (1992) 108–14.

O'Toole, Robert F., *The Unity of Luke's Theology: An Analysis of Luke-Acts* (GNS 9; Wilmington, Del.: Glazier, 1984) 172, 198, 200–203.

Philonenko, M., "La parabole sur la lampe (Luc 11, 33-36) et les horoscopes qoumrâniens," *ZNW* 79 (1988) 145–51.

Prete, Benedetto, "Il logion sulla lampada nelle duplice attestazione di Luca 8, 16 e 11, 33," in idem, *L'opera di Luca: Contenuti e prospettive* (Turin: Elle di ci, 1986) 183–203.

Puech, *Gnose*, 2:182–200.

Schneider, Günther, "Das Bildwort von der Lampe: Zur Traditionsgeschichte eines Jesus-Wortes," *ZNW* 61 (1970) 183–209.

Schulz, *Q*, 468–70, 474–76.

Schwencke, F., "Das Auge ist des Leibes Licht (Mt 6, 22f, Lk 11, 33-36)," *ZWTh* 55 (1913) 251–60.

Sjöberg, E., "Das Licht in dir: Zur Deutung von Mt 6, 22f. par.," *StTh* 5 (1951) 89–105.

Vaganay, Léon, "L'étude d'un doublet dans la parabole de la lampe," in idem, *Le problème synoptique: Une hypothèse de travail* (Tournai: Desclée, 1954) 426–42.

Zimmermann, *Methodenlehre*, 181–91.

33/ **"No one after lighting a lamp puts it in a hidden place,[a] but on the lampstand, so that those who enter may see the radiance.[b] 34/ Your eye is the lamp of your body. If your eye is sincere, your whole body is also full of light; but if it is evil, your body is also full of darkness. 35/ Therefore take care so that the light in you is not darkness. 36/ If then your whole body is full of light, with no part of it in darkness, it will be as full of light as when a lamp gives you light with its brightness."**

a I omit the words "nor under a bushel" that appear in certain translations; see below, p. 145 n. 5.

b I follow, with Nestle[25], the reading "radiance" (φέγγος), but the reading "light" (φῶς), which corresponds to 8:16, has equally good attestation. It is the reading of the text of Nestle-Aland[27].

Throughout the section in which Jesus is surrounded by the crowd (vv. 14-36), the discussions take place against a dualistis background. Those who are happy to listen to the Word of God are opposed to those who, being blind to Jesus, ask for a sign. This is the context in which the proverbial saying about the lamp (v. 33) and the little development about the eye (vv. 34-36) must be interpreted.

Analysis

These four verses are still a part of the speech that Jesus has been giving to the crowds (from v. 29 on), since there is no structural indication of an interruption. The transition is abrupt, however, since the proverbial mention of the lamp (v. 33) follows a drawing of a parallel between two concrete situations, Jesus' and Jonah's (v. 32). In spite of the linking word "lamp," the transition to vv. 34-36 is not any easier, since those verses form a unit of their own. Luke is to indicate a break between vv. 36 and 37. Jesus' speech will be interrupted there by the Pharisee's invitation (v. 37); from there on the Lukan text will take another tack.[1] So Luke did not want to, or did not dare to, improve the arrangement of the sayings he had taken over. Everything leads us to believe that here he was continuing to quote Q, which he had been following up to here and whose sequence he respected. Matthew, on the other hand, dismantled it (cf. Matt 5:15; 6:22-23).

For once, it is Luke who transmits a doublet, while Matthew retains only one occurrence, the one derived from Q (Matt 5:15). After having used the saying about the lamp derived from Mark in the chapter on the Word of God (8:16), Luke does not hesitate to reproduce it here using Q (v. 33). In his writing, there is considerable resemblance between the two sayings, as is to be seen from the following comparison of two literal translations of the two occurrences:

Luke 8:16	Luke 11:33
"Now no one,	"No one,
after having lit a lamp,	after having lit a lamp,
covers it with a jar	puts it in a hidden place,
or puts it under a bed,	
but he puts it on a lampstand,	but on the lampstand,
so that those who enter	so that those who enter
may see the light."	may see the radiance."[2]

In both cases, Luke prefers the affirmative wording of Q to the interrogative wording of Mark. He provides a subject for the verb, thus substituting the expression "no one" for the impersonal and Semitizing plural of Q. "To light" ($ἅπτω$) is more precise than "to keep burning" ($καίω$) (Q, as in Matt 5:15).[3] With Q, he speaks of "a [one] lamp" among others and not of "the lamp" (Mark 4:21).[4] In place of parataxis (Q; Matt 5:15), he opts for the hypotaxis of a participle, "having lit" ($ἅψας$). Mark and Q felt it necessary to mention "the bushel." Both times (8:16; 11:33) Luke avoids this Latinism, which would have been shocking to a Greek ear. In its place he substitutes an expression that, in his eyes, is equivalent: "covers it with a jar," in 8:16; and here, in 11:33, a less precise counterpart, "in a hidden place" ($εἰς κρύπτην$).[5] By adding, in 8:16, "or puts it under a bed,"[6] Luke follows Mark. Here in 11:33, in line with Matthew, he settles for a single example. In 8:16, Luke repeats the verb "put" and eliminates the definite article: "a lampstand." But here, he keeps it, since it is a particular lampstand on which the lamp is to be put. By choosing to use the indefinite article in referring to the lamp, to the bed, or, in 8:16,

---

1   Nestle-Aland signals these brusque transitions by creating an identation after v. 32 and another, a bit more liberal, after v. 33.

2   Dupont, "Lampe," 1033.

3   In popular terms, the text of Mark conceives of the lamp as though a person: "it arises"!

4   The latter being a popular expression or evocation of a poor household.

5   He thinks perhaps of the place where one arranges the bushel; see Dupont, "Lampe," 1035. As my explanation implies, I follow here the short text. I estimate, with Dupont ("Lampe," 1034–35), that the words "nor under a bushel," absent from the more ancient witnesses ($\mathfrak{P}^{45}$ and $\mathfrak{P}^{75}$) and of many others (see the apparatus of Nestle-Aland[27]), have been inserted in Luke 11:33 by contamination of Matt 5:15; Hahn ("Licht," 110 n. 8) does not exclude this hypothesis. In the commentary on 8:4-21 (1:313 nn. 66, 67), I was again partial to the long text.

6   A bed among others in the grand lodgings that he imagines (Mark thinks only of a bed of a modest house); see n. 4 above.

to the lampstand, Luke avoids popular expressions and gives the impression of a well-furnished and well-equipped house, whereas Mark and Q spoke in simple language of a humble Palestinian house. Finally, unlike Mark, but following Q, he gives a reason for lighting the lamp, once again seeing the scene in his way. While Matthew, faithful to Q, thought in terms of the people who lived in the house, Luke conceives of visitors who entered through a vestibule that naturally had to be illuminated. These visitors see "the light" ($\tau\grave{o}\ \varphi\tilde{\omega}\varsigma$) in 8:16 and "the radiance" ($\tau\grave{o}\ \varphi\acute{\epsilon}\gamma\gamma o\varsigma$) in 11:33.

This is the way commentators succeed in reconstructing two ancient wordings of the saying in question with the principal help of Matt 5:15, on the one hand, and Mark 4:21, on the other. It is not possible, however, for them to reconstruct the original saying itself. One of the wordings, that of Q, which is not interrogative, provides only a negative example, the bushel, but adds the beneficial effect of the action. The other, that of Mark, which is interrogative, indicates two wrong destinations, the bushel and the bed, but does not mention the favorable outcome.[7]

The next three verses have only one parallel, Matt 6:22-23. This unit opens with an affirmation: "Your eye is the lamp of your body."[8] It continues, in a parallel and antithetic fashion, with two possibilities, one positive, the other negative.[9] It ends with a conclusion. It is at this point that the differences appear. Whereas this is an exclamation in Matthew—"If then[10] the light in you is darkness, how great is the darkness!"—Luke gives a warning and provides encouragement: "Therefore take care so that the light in you is not darkness." There is no doubt that Luke, the moralist, was the one who transformed the exclamation of shock or irony into an invitation to lucidity and action.[11]

The material in v. 36 is found only in Luke, but it does not seem to be Lukan in either its structure or its content.[12] It must have been a traditional floating saying, probably absent from Q,[13] that Luke used here to complete the consequences drawn from the two cases in mind (the sincere eye and the evil eye). He can thus add a favorable outcome (v. 36) to the encouragement that was given (v. 35). The words that make up the end of v. 36, "as when a lamp gives you light with its brightness," upset the balance of the saying. Even though they are not typically Lukan,[14] they must be considered to be an addition made by the Gospel writer, who was anxious to reinsert the image of the lamp, in order to make a connection with v. 33 and thus create an effect of inclusion.

I would say the following as a summary of the origin of vv. 34-36: in the beginning, there was an affirmation (the eye = the lamp of the body), followed by two possible outcomes (a good situation and a bad situation, Matt 6:22-23a and v. 34 here in Luke 11). Next, the tradition was to draw a first conclusion (Matt 6:23b, cf. v. 35 here in Luke 11). Finally, Luke took over the whole, transformed the first conclusion into an exhortation (v. 35) and added to all of that a floating saying, with a similar theme and related terminology (v. 36ab), which he added to v. 36c in order to adapt it to its new setting.[15]

---

7 See Dupont ("Lampe," 1032–33); Schneider, "Lampe," 186, 190; Hahn, "Licht," 109–14; Zimmermann, *Methodenlehre*, 183–84, 189–90. *Gospel of Thomas* 33 contains the sentence about the lamp in a formulation that has a rapport with Luke 11:33. This reference indicates the "hidden place," that which is situated after and not before the mention of the "bushel" (in contrast to the long text of Luke 11:33) and evokes, in the singular (Luke 11:33 in the plural) the one who enters, adding, beyond Luke 11:33, the one who leaves. I hesitate to consider this version of *Thomas* as independent of the Gospel of Luke; see Schrage, *Thomas-Evangelium*, 81–85; Hahn, "Licht," 113. In another sense, see Koester and Robinson, *Trajectories*, 180–82.

8 The texts in Matthew and Luke are identical, with a small difference: "your eye" (Luke); "the eye" (Matthew).

9 The differences between the two evangelists are minimal; see Schulz, *Q*, 468–69.

10 Curiously, this "if then," absent from v. 35 of Luke, figures at the head of v. 36, without parallel in Matthew.

11 Schulz, *Q*, 469.

12 On the archaic and Semitic character of this verse from the point of view of Qumran, see Philonenko, "Horoscopes."

13 On this question, see Hahn, "Licht," 108.

14 Neither $\dot{\omega}\varsigma\ \ddot{o}\tau\alpha\nu$ nor $\dot{\eta}\ \dot{\alpha}\sigma\tau\rho\alpha\pi\dot{\eta}$ nor $\varphi\omega\tau\acute{\iota}\zeta\omega$ is characteristic of Luke; see F. Hahn, "Licht," 132–33.

15 On the redactional work of Matthew, see Luz, *Matthew*, 1:330–34.

Commentary

■ **33** Formerly isolated,[16] the proverbial saying about the lamp serves here as a polemical confirmation.[17] The reign of God has reached the people in the ministry of Jesus, who was an exorcist (v. 20) and a preacher (v. 28). Something decisive has begun, has been "ignited."[18] In the darkness—Satan has just been mentioned (vv. 18, 21-22)—shines a lamp.[19] In spite of the requests for a sign, Jesus is not going to act otherwise than expected (v. 33). "When a lamp is lit," notes one commentator, "it is not in order to hide it."[20] What it causes to shine is visible (cf. v. 36).[21] Those who enter can see clearly. Luke is only slightly allegorizing. Nevertheless, we should recall his rereading of the parable of the two houses and his commentary on it: "Every one who comes to me and hears my words and does them . . ." (6:47). These words should be compared with the expression "those who enter" here in v. 33. "Those who enter" are the crowds who have come toward him in close ranks: they can "see" (βλέπωσιν) Jesus, who is God's sign, and observe his "radiance"

(φέγγος).[22] They still must look carefully and must have the ability to see. That is what vv. 34-36 are going to explain.[23]

Excursus: The Eye, Lamp of the Body

The Greeks had various theories about vision, in particular one about intromission (particles enter the eye) and another about extramission (light rays come out of the eye).[24] This latter theory, defended by Parmenides, the Pythagoreans, and the Stoics, is similar to a belief widely held in most civilizations, in particular that of Israel. To see is to project rays of light. The sun was, moreover, often considered to be an eye, and eyes were compared to stars.

Pythagoras, according to some of his disciples, called the eyes "doors of the sun." Heraclitus, on the other hand, said that "the eyes are, as a matter of fact, more precise witnesses than the ears." In his poem on nature, Empedocles was the first to compare the eye to a lamp: the process of vision may be compared to a man who goes out in the middle of a winter's night and, because of the darkness outdoors, takes along a hurricane lantern.[25] Lastly, Plato developed a theory of vision that incorporated the elements of

---

16 On the sense of the sentence in the mouth of Jesus, see Jeremias, "Lampe," 99–102; Jesus applied the sentence to his person; on the sense in the sayings source, see Schulz, *Q*, 475–76 (the community had the consciousness of having been mandated by God).

17 Dupont ("Lampe," 1044–47) is wrong to envisage only an ill-disposed audience. The crowds who surround Jesus are in a bad plight, but they are not unreachable.

18 Luke 12:49: "It is a fire that I have come to bring upon the earth." Ἅπτω from v. 33 is found in Acts 28:2 "to light or kindle a fire."

19 On the lamp and the lampstand, see the commentary on 8:16 (1:404–5).

20 Dupont, "Lampe," 1045. Wiefel (225) writes in this regard: "The originally independent word picture has received a new meaning in a christological context, while preserving its meaning as an everyday experience."

21 The activity of igniting corresponds, by analogy, to that of Jesus. But to hide the light causes one to think of the attitude of Jesus' opponents. Εἰς κρύπτην suggests less the secret than what is hidden and somber. Luke imagines, without doubt, a cave, a cellar, or a somber shelter. Alliata ("Grotte"), whose work I know only by summary (*NTA* 30 [1986] no. 155), is thinking of grottoes that one finds beside or

in the ancient houses of Palestine. In my opinion, these words go back to Luke and must be understood not in a Palestinian framework but rather in a Greek one. Κρύπτη is here a substantive: the "somber corridor," the "hidden coin," the "mouth of the cave," the "hidden place"; see BAGD, s.v.; and Dupont, "Lampe," 1035.

22 Τὸ φέγγος, the "glimmer," the "brightness," the "light," in particular that of the moon (τὸ φεγγάρι in modern Greek); τὸ φῶς, that is, the "light," in particular, that of the sun.

23 Dupont ("Lampe," 1048) observes: "Rather than complain of a lack of light, they should realize that evil is in them, and seek to correct themselves."

24 See Betz, "Greek Theories"; Allison, "Eye"; Delebecque, "L'oeil"; Charles Mugler, *Dictionnaire historique de la terminologie optique des Grecs* (Paris: French & European Publications, 1964) 7–13 passim.

25 The reader will find the fragments of Pythagoras, Heraclitus, and Empedocles in Hermann Diels and Walter Kranz, *Die Fragmente der Vorsokratiker: Griechisch und Deutsch* (3 vols.; 11th ed.; Berlin: Weidmann, 1964) 58B 1a (1:450; 13); 22B 101a (1:173; 15–16); 31B 84 (1:342; 4–9); Hermann Diels and Rosamond Kent Sprague, *The Older Sophists: A Complete Translation by Several Hands of the Fragments in Die Fragmente der Vorsokratiker, Edited by Diels-Kranz.*

the doctrines of intromission and extramission. In his view, the light of the eye must fuse with the light of the sun in order for one to see. His reflections on this subject are found in books 6–7 of the *Republic* and in *Timaeus*. To explain things, he used the parable of the sun (*Resp.* 6.507B–509C), the parable of the parallel lines (*Resp.* 5.509C–511B), and the parable of the cavern (*Resp.* 7.514A–518B). He declared that the eye is the sense organ that most closely resembles the sun (*Resp.* 6.508B).

In this domain there may have been an influence of Greek philosophy on Jewish and early Christian literature, but it is unlikely that the saying "your eye is the lamp of your body" is a quotation of a Greek proverb.[26] There are too many parallel texts in the Hebraic tradition.[27] We may quote the vision of the man clothed in linen in Dan 10:6: "his eyes [were] like flaming torches" (*NRSV*) (οἱ οφθαλμοὶ αὐτοῦ ὡσεὶ λαμπάδες πυρός); the vison of the chandelier in Zech 4:10: "These seven [= the lamps, λύχνοι, from v. 2] are the eyes of the LORD" (*NRSV*); and especially the *T. Job* 43:5-6a: "Elihu, Elihu—the only evil one—will have no memorial among the living. *His quenched lamp* (λύχνος) lost its luster, and the splendor of his lantern *will flee* from him into condemnation. For this one is the one of darkness and not of light."[28]

■ **34** According to the saying, the eye makes it possible for the body, that is, the entire being, to see in the darkness and therefore to live. It does so by shining, like a lamp, that is, by letting the light radiate out from itself.

So, does the "body" resemble the men and women of the preceding passage (v. 33), who, thanks to the lamp on the lampstand, can get their bearings when they enter the house? Probably not, since what follows in the text does not speak of the exterior but rather the interior of the body. The "body" must be compared to a house that gets the illumination it needs from its lamp, rather than to these human visitors. The "eye" is indeed the "lamp" of the "body." So it seems preferable to me to depend on the following passage (vv. 35-36), which forms a unit with the initial proverb, rather than on elements borrowed from the other parable, namely, the one in v. 33.

From v. 34b on, the text links the quality of the body with that of the eye. But in which direction does the interaction work? Two meanings come to mind: either the eye is good, because the body already is,[29] or, in the opposite direction, the body becomes good, because the eye, which is already good, transforms it. In the figurative sense of the words, the first translation leads to a theological meaning and the second, to an ethical meaning. But the following verse (v. 35) appeals to a sense of personal responsibility, and the adjectives here in v. 34, "sincere," "without guile" (ἁπλοῦς), and "evil," "wicked" (πονηρός), also favor an ethical orientation. In particular ἁπλοῦς is not used in Greek to describe a healthy organ.[30] These observations lead me to opt for the second interpretation: "When your eye is without guile, your

---

With a New Edition of Antiphon and of Euthydemus (Indianapolis: Hackett, 2001).

26 That is the opinion of Betz ("Greek Theories"), who judges that the progress of the text corrects the proverb from an ethical point of view. Personally, I have not found such a proverb in the collections of Greek proverbs, e.g., in Ernst von Leutsch and Friedrich Wilhelm Schneidewin, *Corpus paroemiographorum Graecorum* (2 vols.; Göttingen: Vandenhoeck and Ruprecht, 1839–51) (English: Cambridge: Cambridge University Press, 2010). The closest is: ὀφθαλμοὶ ἀλλήλων ἀνταωακώμενοι ἀπομάττουσιν ὡς ἐν κατόπτρῳ τῶν σωμάτων εἴδωλα, "the eyes, reflecting one in the other, grasp the images of the body as in a mirror" (79c). Betz thinks that he has discovered a similar composition, but relying on a physiological plan, according to Theophrastus, *De sensibus*; see G. M. Stratton, ed., *Theophrastus and the Greek Physiological Psychology before Aristotle* (New York: Macmillan, 1917).

27 With Allison, "Eye"; and Philonenko, "Horoscopes."

28 Trans. R. P. Spittler, in *OTP* 1:862. Cf. Ps 37 (38:10): "light of my eyes"; Prov 15:30: "light of the eyes" (i.e., a luminous look); Prov 20:27: "the human spirit is the lamp of the Lord"; Tob 10:5 "my son . . . light of my eyes"; cf. Tob 11:13 (Codex Sinaiticus); *4 Bar.* 7:3; *1 Enoch* 106:2: "at his birth, the eyes of Noah enlighten the whole house"; John 11:10: "because the light is not in him"; Eph 1:18: "the eyes of the heart enlightened." For other texts, see Allison, "Eye," 66–71.

29 This is the interpretation of Allison ("Eye," 74–76), who indicates that certain conditional phrases must be understood in such a way, e.g., Luke 11:20 ("it is because the kingdom of God has come among you that I can cast out demons").

30 Sjöberg, "Licht," 191.

whole body is also full of light; but if it is evil, your body is also full of darkness."[31]

What is involved here? What makes the interpretation difficult is the fact that we are dealing with two levels of meaning, the literal and the figurative, and the possible shift from one to the other. In connection with these verses, Marc Philonenko has reminded us of the Essene anthropology with its concept of the inner parts of human beings, which are made up of darkness or light.[32] Luke 11:34-36 presupposes an anthropology of this kind, perhaps simpler, which pictures in each human being a zone of light and a zone of darkness. Verse 36, with its mention of "[a] part" ($\mu\acute{\epsilon}\rho o\varsigma\ \tau\iota$) would lead us to think that the light/dark contrast can exist, even if it does not represent the ideal condition. To such a way of thinking, inner light or darkness is not to be taken literally. These two conditions do not correspond to the physiological result of the fluttering of the eye but rather to a good or a bad relationship with God. That is the tack that the Gnostic rereading of this saying took in the *Gospel of Thomas*[33] and in Origen's commentary.[34] Consequently, "the eye" must not be understood in the primary sense, any more than should "the body," for that matter. "The lamp" is thus an image that makes it possible to interpret a word, "the eye," that should not be taken literally. In our religious life, what fulfills the role of the eye in our daily existence? The inner gaze, the eye of faith, the soul? It does not matter much which words are used. The saying declares that the human being has a spiritual organ that puts it in contact with God and determines the whole of its life of faith. This "eye," which

functions in a decisive way as a watchman, an opening, and a canal, is involved in exterior relations on behalf of the inner being and is the bearer of a light that it receives and transmits. The text does not suppose that we have an inner "light" in ourselves. We have a "lamp." Nor does the text say that we are able on our own to light or to put out that "lamp." But we have to maintain it and not neglect it. The light of the "body" will depend on the "lamp," but that "lamp" is nothing unless it receives its "light" from elsewhere.

That "eye," then, can be either "sincere" ($\dot{\alpha}\pi\lambda o\hat{\upsilon}\varsigma$) or "evil" ($\pi o\nu\eta\rho\acute{o}\varsigma$). The condition of being sincere ($\dot{\alpha}\pi\lambda\acute{o}\tau\eta\varsigma$)[35] is literally that of not being folded in two and, figuratively, that of simplicity, uprightness, integrity, sincerity, absence of malice, and sometimes generosity. Conny Edlund interprets $\dot{\alpha}\pi\lambda o\hat{\upsilon}\varsigma$ in the sense of simplicity, totality, of the total gift of one's being to God.[36] $\text{'}A\pi\lambda\acute{o}\tau\eta\varsigma$ is the most important virtue, according to *T. Iss.* 3-6, and it was a part of the ethical vocabulary of the earliest Christians.[37] $\Pi o\nu\eta\rho\acute{\iota}\alpha$ is less difficult to define: it is wickedness, maliciousness, and sometimes greed.[38]

Just because a figurative sense has been proposed here, one should not conclude either that the immediate reality is secondary or that existence is dualistic. On the contrary, the voice that finds expression in this verse is convinced that this inner "eye," which is our most prized possession, is what determines our whole life, including the physical world. That voice is even so convinced of the interdependence of the spiritual and the material, of the ethical and the physical, that it allows the ambiguity sur-

---

31   I am inspired by the study and translation of Delebecque, "L'oeil."

32   See Philonenko, "Horoscopes"; also Brandt, "Lumen," 181, on preparing the interior organ of spiritual cognizance.

33   See *Gos. Thom.* 24: "There is light within a man of light, and he lights up the whole world. If he does not shine, he is darkness" (trans. Thomas O. Lambdin, in Robinson, *Nag Hammadi Library*).

34   Origen, *Hom. in Luc.* (Rauer), frgs. 78 and 79 (Rauer 186, 187); 9.305–7; cf. *Hom. in Luc.* (Couzel), 530–37. The "lamp" is the intelligence, the faculty of vision. The "body" is the soul, in an allegorical sense, since the intelligence, this lamp, enlightens the entire soul. "Your luminous body" is you who no longer sin.

35   See Brandt, "Lumen," 189–201; Edlund, "Einfalt"; Sjöberg, "Licht"; Allison, "Eye," 76–77; Philonenko, "Horoscopes," 148–49; in the LXX: 1 Macc 2:37; Wis 1:1.

36   See Edlund, "Einfalt." He chooses as the Hebraic equivalent תָּמִים ("immaculate," "entire," "perfect"). Sjöberg ("Licht") and Allison ("Eye") prefer the Aramaic שְׁלִים ("immaculate," "perfect").

37   For $\dot{\alpha}\pi\lambda\acute{o}\tau\eta\varsigma$, see Rom 12:8; 2 Cor 8:2; 9:11, 13; Eph 6:5; Col 3:22; for $\dot{\alpha}\pi\lambda\hat{\omega}\varsigma$, see Jas 1:5. With its parallel (Matt 6:22), our passage represents, in any case, the only NT attestation of the adjective $\dot{\alpha}\pi\lambda o\hat{\upsilon}\varsigma$; for this vocabulary, cf. *Barn.* 19.2; *Hermas Vis.* 1.2.4; *Sim.* 9.24.2–3 and passim.

38   See BAGD, s.v.

rounding the words "eye" and "body" to remain. Verse 34 is both a parable and a description.[39]

■ **35** The verb σκοπέω ("take care," "examine"), which Luke introduces on purpose, also belongs to the ethical vocabulary of the early church.[40] It is surprising to read σκόπει οὖν μή . . . ("therefore take care . . . not) followed by the indicative rather than the subjunctive (unless we are dealing with an interrogative, rather than a purpose, clause).[41] A light that is darkness is a paradoxical and suggestive expression. It rules out any assured possession of the light. Light can get lost, go out. All the more reason to watch out, to "take care" that things do not turn out that way. Giving an ethical sense to this verse, as Luke has done, does not, however, rule out a theological perspective; the interior light comes from God. It is not necessarily a question of the Holy Spirit, or of an innate spiritual essence, but rather of the share that God has distributed to us, of the participation in his reign, of the word that he has caused to be spoken, of the grace he has given, of the light that he has caused to shine in our hearts (2 Cor 4:6), and of the oil that makes it possible for the wise young women's lamps to burn (Matt 25:4, 7, 10).[42]

Thus, Luke, who adapted this saying, spoke of a warning and an exhortation addressed by Jesus to those critical or skeptical persons to whom he was speaking: the only sign that God offers is the light shown by Jesus. But everyone must still prepare in their inner self to see this light.

■ **36** Verse 36 has given rise to many interpretations.[43] Is it not tautological? If it is, does that not mean that the text has been corrupted? There are two ways out of that impasse: looking at the word order (ὅλον φωτεινόν, or φωτεινὸν ὅλον) and then paying attention to the future ἔσται.[44] That allows us to paraphrase: so if your whole body is full of light, then everything will be full of light. The impact of the light increases as it goes: starting from you and radiating around you.[45] Moreover, there is a passage of time: from the present to the future. Is it a promise of missionary success (cf. Matt 5:14-16 and Phil 2:15) or of eschatological glorification (cf. Phil 3:21; 2 Cor 3:18)? The one does not rule out the other.

Verse 36c is reminiscent of the image of the lamp as it was used in v. 33. Ἀστραπή is, in the first instance, "lightning," then "brightness," the meaning that is appropriate here.[46] The use of the second person singular ("you") is to be explained by the previous context, where the reader is addressed (from v. 34 on). According to the end of this verse, believers will become full of light, as they did on the occasion of their first encounter with Christ.

History of Interpretation

For Ambrose, bishop of Milan, who stressed God's precedence, the lamp of v. 33 is faith, and the light that causes it to shine is the Word of God: "But the lamp cannot shine, unless it has received light from elsewhere" (*Exp.*

---

39 Let us note that the adjective φωτεινός signifies at once "enlightened" and "enlightening," "illumined" and "luminous"; see van Kasteren, "Analecta." The stars, created on the fourth day, have this double characteristic: Gen 1:14-19 LXX.

40 See Rom 16:17; 2 Cor 4:18; Gal 6:1 (with μή as here); Phil 2:4; 3:17.

41 See BDF §§369.2; 370; Brandt, "Lumen," 97–99.

42 Sjöberg ("Licht") analyzes the expression "the light which is in you," explaining it with the aid of the biblical symbol of light, proposing Prov 20:27 ("The human spirit is the lamp of the Lord, searching every inmost part") and rabbinic exegesis, before arriving at a conclusion that is close to mine: "the light which is in you" is not an organ of spiritual perception but the portion of divine light offered by revelation. Brandt ("Lumen," 103–7, 177–201) refers to Hos 4:6-7: because Israel has rejected knowledge, God will reject Israel.

43 See Hahn, "Licht," 129. Allison ("Eye," 79) believes, following C. C. Torrey (*The Four Gospels* [New York: Harper, 1947] 309) that we have here a bad translation of the Aramaic. The Aramaic, according to Torrey, means, "If however your whole body is lighted up with no part dark, then all about you will be light, just as the lamp lights you with its brightness."

44 Delebecque, "L'oeil," 87; Hahn, "Licht," 129–32.

45 See van Kasteren, "Analecta."

46 On this word, see Hahn ("Licht," 131–32), who considers it through the eschatological optic (cf. Luke 17:24).

Luc. 7.98).[47] This lamp of our faith is no longer dependent on the Law, which extinguished the lamp of the early Jewish rituals, but rather on the grace received in the church. Psalm 119 (118):105; John 1:9; and Luke 15:8 serve as scriptural orchestration.

The eye, the lamp of the body, on the other hand, has been assigned various metaphorical meanings.[48] It can refer to faith, a faith that runs the risk of being blinded by the darkness of sin, which was the interpretation of Chromatius, bishop of Aquileia.[49] Moreover, the eye can stand for apostles or bishops (in this case, the "body" represents the church). Hilary, bishop of Poitiers, in particular, reckoned that the Word of God serves as a lamp or a lantern, before every "apostolic person" becomes a lamp or a lantern for other members of the ecclesial body.[50] Chromatius, in turn, said that just like an eye, the most beautiful and most precious of the organs of the body, the bishop sheds light on the church by pure preaching of the faith and doctrine.[51] If the bishop also puts the gospel into practice in his life, he will remain a luminous model for his faithful members.

Another interpretation, of Augustinian origin, was to have lasting success:[52] the eye stands for the intention. The eye is to the body what intention is to action. In its function of intention of the heart, the eye wishes to do good. For that to happen, the intention must be free of all hypocrisy and all pride. Alas, although the eye can be sincere and single, it can on occasion also be dark and evil.[53]

Finally, we should call attention to an allegorical and poetical explanation produced by Ephraem Syrus (fourth century).[54] Since human beings possess two eyes and since the biblical text speaks of an evil eye and a sincere eye, this Church Father thought of Eve and Mary. The former was a left and blind eye, whereas the latter was, and remains, a right and luminous eye. Through one of them, humanity sank into darkness and exchanged truth for error. Through the other, it discovered its error and understood that what it had believed to be a gain was in reality the loss of its life.

Conclusion

Christ is the light of the world (cf. John 8:12). He is the lamp that has its place on the lampstand (v. 33). In turn, Christians are the light of the world (cf. Matt 5:14), those whose "eye," "the light of the body," provides light to both the inner being and the outer being (vv. 34-36). God's gift is great; our responsibility is likewise great. Both sincerity and evil depend on the good use to which we put the gifts we have received from the Lord. Although the warning (v. 35) is directed at the danger, the hope expressed in v. 36 concerns success: thanks to its "eye," the "body" is God's receptacle and vehicle, luminous in both meanings of the word φωτεινός. It receives light and sheds it; it welcomes it and reflects it. God does not hoard what he is and has for himself; what he is and has is received and expended in and through us.

47   Trans. Theodosia Tomkinson in Saint Ambrose of Milan, *Exposition of the Holy Gospel according to Saint Luke* (Etna, Calif.: Center for Traditionalist Orthodox Studies, 1998) 272.

48   My assistant, Mme. Eva Tobler, discovered for me a mine of information about the Middle Ages and antiquity: Gudrun Schleusener-Eichholz, *Das Auge im Mittelalter* (Münstersche Mittelalter-Schriften 35.1–2; Munich: Fink, 1985) 132–38, 175–79, 691–93. I owe the following references to this work.

49   Chromace d'Aquilee, *In Matth.* 17.1.1–2.2 (CCSL 9:439–40).

50   Hilary of Poitiers, *In Ps.* 118 (CSEL 22:476).

51   See n. 49 above.

52   See Schleusener-Eichholz, *Das Auge im Mittelalter*, 177–78 (n. 48 above).

53   Augustine, *C. Jul.* 4.3.33 (*PL* 44:755); Gregory the Great, *Moral.* 10.23, 41; 28.11.30 (CCSL 143:566; 143B:1418–19).

54   Ephrem of Syria *Hymn on the Church* 37; see Schleusener-Eichholz, *Das Auge im Mittelalter*, 178–79 (n. 48 above); and Sebastian Brock, *L'oeil de lumière: La vision spirituelle de saint Éphrem. Suivi de la Harpe de l'Esprit, florilège de poèmes de saint Éphrem* (Les Mauges: Editions de l'Abbaye de Bellefontaine, 1991) 81–90.

A Meal That Went Wrong (11:37-54)

Bibliography

Becker, Hans-Jürgen, *Auf der Kathedra des Mose: Rabbinisch-theologisches Denken und antirabbinische Polemik in Matthäus 23, 1-12?* (ANTZ 4; Berlin: Institut Kirche und Judentum, 1990).

Beilner, Wolfgang, *Christus und die Pharisäer: Exegetische Untersuchung über Grund und Verlauf der Auseinandersetzungen* (Vienna: Herder, 1959) 220–35.

Brawley, Robert L., *Luke-Acts and the Jews: Conflict, Apology, and Conciliation* (SBLMS 33; Atlanta: Scholars Press, 1987) 84–106.

Bultmann, *History*, 118–19, 135.

Christ, *Jesus Sophia*, 120–35.

Correns, D., "Die Verzehntung der Raute, Lk 11, 42 und M Schebi ix 1," *NovT* 6 (1963) 110–12.

Cousin, H., "Sépulture criminelle et sépulture prophétique," *RB* 81 (1974) 375–93.

Del Verme, Marcello, "I 'guai' di Matteo e Luca e le decime dei Farisei (Mt 23, 23; Lc 11, 42)," *RivB* 32 (1984) 273–314.

Derrett, J. Duncan M., "'You Build the Tomb of the Prophets' (Lk 11, 47-51; Mt 23, 29-31)," in idem, *Studies in the New Testament* (6 vols.; Leiden: Brill, 1977–95) 2:68–75.

Edwards, *Theology of Q*, 115–19.

Ellis, Edward Earle, "Luke 11:49-51: An Oracle of a Christian Prophet?" *ExpT* 74 (1962–63) 157–58.

Farris, R., "La chiave della conoscenza (Lc 11, 52 par)," *PSV* 18 (1988) 113–26.

Freudenberg, Jürgen, "Die synoptische Weherede: Tradition und Redaktion in Mt 23 par" (Dissertation, Münster, 1972).

Frizzi, Giuseppe, "L'ἀπόστολος delle tradizioni sinottiche (Mc, Q, Mt, Lc, e Atti)," *RevistB* 22 (1974) 3–37.

Idem, "Carattere originale e rilevanza degli 'apostoli inviati' in Q/Lc 11, 49-51; 13, 34-35/ Mt 23, 34-36. 37-39)," *RivB* 21 (1973) 401–12.

Garland, David E., *The Intention of Matthew 23* (NovTSup 52; Leiden: Brill, 1979). Haenchen, Ernst, "Matthäus 23," in idem, *Gott und Mensch: Gesammelte Aufsätze* (Tübingen: Mohr Siebeck, 1965) 29–54.

Hoffmann, *Logienquelle*, 158–71.

Jacobson, Arland Dean, "Wisdom Christology in Q" (Dissertation, Claremont University, 1978).

Jeremias, Joachim, *Heiligengräber in Jesu Umwelt (Mt 23, 29; Lk 11, 47): Eine Untersuchung zur Volksreligion der Zeit Jesu* (Göttingen: Vandenhoeck & Ruprecht, 1958).

Klein, G., "Die Verfolgung der Apostel, Luk 11, 49," in Heinrich Baltensweiler and Bo Reicke, eds., *Neues Testament und Geschichte: Oscar Cullmann zum 70. Geburtstag* (Tübingen: Mohr Siebeck, 1972) 113–24.

Kloppenborg, *Formation*, 139–47.

Kosch, Daniel, *Die eschatologische Tora des Menschensohnes: Untersuchungen zur Rezeption der Stellung Jesu zur Tora in Q* (Göttingen: Vandenhoeck & Ruprecht, 1989) 61–212.

Kühschelm, Roman, *Jüngerverfolgung und Geschick Jesu: Eine exegetisch-bibeltheologische Untersuchung der synoptischen Verfolgungsankündigung Mk 13, 9-13 par und Mt 23, 29-36 par* (ÖBSt 5; Klosterneuburg: Österreichisches Katholisches Bibelwerk, 1983) 31-33, 39-40, 147-62, 299 n. 2.

Kümmel, Werner Georg, "Die Weherufe über die Schriftgelehrten und Pharisäer (Matthäus 23, 13-36)," in idem, *Heilsgeschehen und Geschichte: Gesammelte Aufsätze* (ed. Erich Grässer et al.; 2 vols.; Marburger theologische Studien 3.16; Marburg: Elwert, 1965–78) 2:29–38.

Lachs, Samuel Tobias, "On Matthew 23:27-28," *HTR* 63 (1975) 385–88.

Légasse, Simon, "L'oracle contre 'cette génération' (Mt 23, 34-36 par. Lc 11, 49-51) et la polémique judéo-chrétienne dans la Source des Logia," in Delobel, *Logia*, 237–56.

Linton, O., "Le *parallelismus membrorum* dans le Nouveau Testament: Simples remarques," in Albert Descamps and André de Halleux, eds., *Mélanges bibliques: Festschrift Beda Rigaux* (Gembloux: Duculot, 1970) 498.

Lührmann, *Logienquelle*, 43–48.

Manson, *Sayings*, 94–116.

Marguerat, *Jugement*, 34–35, 345–66.

Marshall, I. Howard, "How to Solve the Synoptic Problem: Luke 11:43 and Parallels," in William C. Weinrich, ed., *The New Testament Age: Essays in Honor of Bo Reicke* (2 vols; Macon, Ga.: Mercer University Press, 1984) 2:313–25.

Matura, Thaddee, *Le radicalisme évangélique: Aux sources de la vie chrétienne* (LD 97; Paris: Cerf, 1978) 101–2.

Miller, Robert J., "The Rejection of the Prophets in Q," *JBL* 107 (1988) 225–40.

Moxnes, Halvor, *The Economy of the Kingdom: Social Conflict and Economic Relations in Luke's Gospel* (Philadelphia: Fortress, 1988) 109–26.

Neusner, Jacob, "'First Cleanse the Inside': The 'Halakhic' Background of a Controversy-Saying," *NTS* 22 (1976) 486–95.

Pesch, Wilhelm, *Der Lohngedanke in der Lehre Jesu verglichen mit der religiösen Lohnlehre des Spätjudentums* (MThS 1.7; Munich: Zink, 1965) 40–43.

Quispel, Gilles, "An Apocryphal Variant in Macarius," *Orientalia lovaniensia periodica* 6–7 (1975–76) 487–92.

Safrai, S., and M. Stern, eds., *Jewish People in the First Century: Historical Geography, Political History, Social, Cultural and Religious Life and Institutions* (2 vols.; CRINT 1–2; Assen: Van Gorcum; Philadelphia: Fortress Press, 1974, 1976) 2:610–11, 801–4, 828–33. Sand, Alexander, *Das Gesetz und die Propheten: Untersuchungen zur Theologie des Evangeliums nach Matthäus* (BU 11; Regensburg: Pustet, 1974) 84–95.

Sanders, Jack T., *The Jews in Luke-Acts* (Philadelphia: Fortress Press, 1987) 101–5 and passim.

Schmid, *Matthäus und Lukas*, 319–32.

Schulz, *Q*, 94–114, 336–45.

Schürmann, Heinz, "Die Redekomposition wider 'dieses Geschlecht' und seine Führung in der Redequelle (vgl. Mt 23, 1-39 par Lk 11, 37-54)," *SNTU* 11 (1986) 33–81.

Schwarz, G., "'Unkenntliche Gräber' (Lukas 11, 44)," *NTS* 23 (1976–77) 345–46.

Seitz, Oscar J. F., "The Commission of Prophets and 'Apostles': A Re-Examination of Matthew 23:34 with Luke 11:49," in *StEv* 4 [TU 102] (1968) 236–40.

Smith, Dennis E., "Table Fellowship as a Literary Motif in the Gospel of Luke," *JBL* 106 (1987) 613–38.

Steck, Odil Hannes, *Israel und das gewaltsame Geschick der Propheten: Untersuchungen zur Überlieferung des deuteronomistischen Geschichtsbildes im Alten Testament, Spätjudentum und Urchristentum* (WMANT 23; Neukirchen-Vluyn: Neukirchener Verlag, 1967) 50–52.

Steele, E. Springs, "Jesus' Table-Fellowship with Pharisees: An Editorial Analysis of Luke 7:36-50; 11:37-54 and 14:1-24" (Dissertation, University of Notre Dame, 1981).

Idem, "Luke 11:37-54: A Modified Hellenistic Symposium?" *JBL* 103 (1984) 379–94.

Wild, Robert A., "The Encounter between Pharisaic and Christian Judaism: Some Early Gospel Evidence," *NovT* 27 (1985) 105–24.

Zeller, *Kommentar*, 65–72.

37/ While he was speaking, a Pharisee invited him to dine with him. He went in and took his place at the table. **38/** The Pharisee was amazed to see that he had not first washed before dinner. **39/** The Lord said to him, "Now you Pharisees purify the outside of the cup and of the dish, but inside you are full of greed and wickedness. **40/** You fools! Did not the one who made the outside make the inside also? **41/** So give instead for alms those things that are within; and see, everything will be pure for you. **42/** But woe to you Pharisees! For you tithe mint and rue[a] and every kind of garden herb, and neglect judgment and the love of God; it is these you ought to have practiced, without neglecting the others. **43/** Woe to you Pharisees! For you love to have the seat of honor in the synagogues and to be greeted with respect in the marketplaces. **44/** Woe to you! For you are like graves that are unmarked, and over which people walk without realizing it."

45/ Then one of the experts in the Law said to him, "Teacher, when you say these things, you insult us too." **46/** He answered, "Woe also to you experts in the Law, for you load people with burdens hard to bear, and you yourselves do not lift a finger to ease them. **47/** Woe to you, for you build the tombs of the prophets, while your ancestors are the ones who killed them. **48/** So you are witnesses and approve of the deeds of your ancestors; for they killed

a   Garden herb.

the prophets, and you build [their tombs].
49/ Therefore the Wisdom of God also said, 'I
will send them prophets and apostles, some
of whom they will kill and others of whom
they will persecute,' 50/ so that this generation may be charged with the blood of all the
prophets shed since the foundation of the
world, 51/ from the blood of Abel to the blood
of Zechariah, the one who perished between
the altar and the temple. Yes, I tell you, it
will be charged against this generation. 52/
Woe to you experts in the Law! For you have
taken away the key of knowledge; you did not
enter yourselves, and you hindered those who
wanted to enter." 53/ After he went outside,
the scribes and the Pharisees began to be
very hostile and to have him talk about many
things, 54/ laying traps for him, to catch him
in something he might say.

As good Christians, we have a hard time admitting it, but here Jesus did not behave very well. He was lacking in the basic elements of courtesy, and, not satisfied with that lack of civility, he inveighed against those with whom he was dealing. Jesus was really unbearable, and some people did not put up with him (vv. 53-54). This wise man who took the risks of being wildly imprudent reminds us of certain Greek philosophers or Hebrew prophets. Like them, he intended to shake up people's consciences and make them accept a new doctrinal or ethical position. This is the picture Luke presents here of Jesus, and it is also the theological function of this episode.[1]

Analysis

Jesus' polemic against the Pharisees and the scribes (11:37-54) corresponds to Jesus' teaching of the disciples (11:1-13), skipping over the two dialogues in the presence of the crowds (11:14-26 and 11:29-36) and the double beatitude (11:27-28). What corresponds here to the group's rest (11:1) is a meal (11:37) that turns into an occasion for discussion, as is customary in such an account. In fact, the dialogue serves as a foil for an all-out attack by Jesus, which provokes general hostility (vv. 53-54).[2]

The Scenario

The story begins with a gracious invitation. Instead of behaving properly, Jesus, who had accepted the invitation, shocks his host. Although the Pharisee says nothing, he is unable to hide his surprise and disapproval. Jesus counterattacks with a salvo of three woes. Coming to the support of the host, another guest plunges into the fray. That is a grave mistake on his part, since he in turn receives a triple volley of tongue-lashing. Jesus, who sticks to his guns, cannot help but harvest the fruit of his excesses. The initial graciousness is matched by final hostility. Having become his enemies, those with whom he was talking do, in fact, organize a reaction to express their offense. This inexorable scenario represents the whole Gospel in miniature and, for that reason, prepares the reader for the dramatic death of Jesus, prophet of the kingdom.

---

1   Luke's intentions rest sometimes on traditional pre-
     scriptions that he transmits with fidelity but without
     conviction, for example, the last phrase of v. 42, and
     that he will ignore in the book of Acts, whose ethic
     is less Jewish even than the sayings attributed here
     to Jesus.

2   The hostility against Jesus is manifest, beginning
     with the episode at Nazareth (4:28); see n. 7 below.

Here is a schema of what that scene looks like:

v. 37 invitation to the meal, acceptance, and neglect of customs
   v. 38 the Pharisee's shocked astonishment
      vv. 39-41 principal reproach expressed by Jesus
         v. 42 first woe (tithe)
         v. 43 second woe (seats of honor)
         v. 44 third woe (graves)
      v. 45 outraged reaction of an expert in the Law
         v. 46 first woe of the second series (burdens)
           vv. 47-48 second woe (tombs of the prophets)
              vv. 49-51 "scriptural" argument
         v. 52 third woe (key of knowledge)
vv. 53-54 outcome and verbal aggressiveness.[3]

Synoptic Comparison and Origin of Materials

The introduction and the conclusion are without any exact Synoptic parallel. They are the work of Luke,[4] who, as in 7:36 and 14:1, has constructed a symposium. The saying about the cup and the dish (v. 39) may have given him the idea. The style of these verses confirms their redactional character.[5] Nevertheless, Luke's source probably mentioned the presence of the scribes and the Pharisees (cf. v. 53). Moreover, in writing the introduction and the conclusion of this pericope, Luke may have been influenced by two passages in the Gospel of Mark. At the beginning (v. 38), he makes reference to the dispute in Mark 7 that he omitted where it would have been located had he followed Mark (it is a part of the big omission and would have been located between 9:17 and 9:18). Mark 7:1-9 does in fact mention the theme of unwashed hands, in relation to Jesus' disciples, and refers in that connection to several different Jewish customs, such as the washing of cups.[6] At the end (vv. 53-54), Luke was perhaps influenced by Mark 12:13, which mentions traps set for Jesus, a verse that Luke knew and used later (20:20).[7]

Jesus' polemical sayings (vv. 39-44 and vv. 46-52) do not come from the triple tradition. Of all this fund of material, Mark knows only a saying parallel to Luke's v. 43 (on the places of honor, Mark 12:38b-39) that Luke, moreover, was to use later on without shying away from the use of a doublet (20:46). Matthew, on the other hand, used each of these sayings in chap. 23, in the long speech against the Pharisees,[8] and the *Gospel of Thomas* worked in two of them in different contexts.[9] A commentator would nevertheless hesitate to conclude from this that Luke and Matthew were here directly dependent on Q, since not only does the order of the sayings vary completely, but more importantly their wording does not betray that air of relationship that is found in the other passages of Q. Here is a table of the correspondences:[10]

Luke 11:39-41	inside–outside	Matt 23:25-26
Luke 11:42	tithe	Matt 23:23
Luke 11:43	places of honor	Matt 23:6-7
Luke 11:44	tombs	Matt 23:27-28
Luke 11:46	burdens	Matt 23:4
Luke 11:47-48	tombs of the prophets	Matt 23:29-31
Luke 11:49-51	sending of the prophets	Matt 23:34-36
Luke 11:52	key	Matt 23:13

---

3   Godet (2:109–10) divides the material in this way (a) 11:37-44; (b) 11:45-54; (c) 12:1-12; Lagrange (341) otherwise: (a) 11:37-41; (b) 11:42-52; (c) 11:53-54. On these formal aspects, see Marshall, 490; and Fitzmyer, 2:942–44.

4   This is generally admitted; see Fitzmyer, 2:943–44; Lührmann, *Logienquelle*, 44.

5   Schürmann, "Redekomposition," 37 nn.13, 14: Evident in v. 37, the Lukanisms are less in v. 38; certainly redactional, vv. 53-54 are inspired by Mark 12:13 and take up again from the sayings source the expression "the scribes and the Pharisees."

6   Loisy, 331; Ernst, 383; Lührmann, *Logienquelle*, 44. Marshall (491) doubts such support from Mark.

7   The evangelist refers several times to the reactions of Jesus' opponents: at the end of the healing of the man with the withered hand (6:11); as an overture to three parables of grace (15:1); at the time of the sojourn in Jerusalem, on the part of the Pharisees (19:39), then some high priests and scribes (19:47-48; 20:19-20; 22:2).

8   For bibliography, see Schürmann, "Redekomposition," 33–34 n. 2.

9   See *Gos. Thom.* 39, the Greek form of which is known from *P.Oxy.* 655 (2b), which, reconstituted with the help of the Coptic, is cited by Aland, *Synopsis*, 280: "Jesus said, the Pharisees and the scribes have received the keys of knowledge (and) they have hidden them. They have not entered and, those who would enter, they have not let them (enter). But you, be prudent as serpents and guileless as doves." See also *Gos. Thom.* 89: "Jesus said, 'Why do you wash the outside of the cup? Do you not realize that he who made the inside is the same one who made the outside?'" (trans. Thomas O. Lambdin, in Robinson, *Nag Hammadi Library*).

10   Marshall, 491–93; Haenchen, "Matthäus 23," 36.

While Matthew seems to have enlarged on his source with the help of other traditions,[11] it is possible that Luke has pruned his. The German commentator Heinz Schürmann thinks that if Luke omitted the attack on the Pharisees who were sitting on Moses' seat (Matt 23:2-3), he did so for a doctrinal reason; he may also have omitted the saying about the exaltation of those who humble themselves (Matt 23:12) and the one about the Pharisees' proselytism (Matt 23:15). At the conclusion of his study, Schürmann came up with the following surprising result: it is probably Matthew who best kept to the order of Q, which Schürmann has reconstructed as follows: "Matt 23:(2-3), 4, 6b-7a (12), 13 (15), 23, 25-26, 27, 29-31, 34-36, 37-39 = Luke 11:46, 43, 52, 42, 39-41, 44, 47-48, 49-51."[12] Other commentators, such as Pierre Bonnard and I. Howard Marshall, think instead that Luke relied on a form of Q different from the one used by Matthew.[13] Most commentators believe that Luke respected Q's order better than did Matthew; this is the opinion of Josef Schmid, Wilhelm Pesch, Werner Georg Kümmel, and Siegfried Schulz.[14] Some other commentators, struck by the differences, attribute the tradition that Luke used to L rather than to Q.[15] Finally, still others, such as Dieter Lührmann and Dieter Zeller, state their uncertainty and do not express their opinion on the subject.[16]

The Woes in Q

I personally opt for the following solution: (1) the setting is redactional (vv. 37-38 and vv. 53-54). (2) The subdivision between Pharisees and scribes is also redactional.[17] So Luke created the transition by writing v. 45 and sought an equilibrium between the two attacks (vv. 39-44 and vv. 46-52). (3) Each of the two Gospel writers put together the whole of his group of woes: Matthew's add up to seven (a figure representing totality), while Luke has two series of three. They have only four woes in common (tithe, tombs, tombs of the prophets, and key). Moreover, Matt 23:6-7 and 23:4 betray a knowledge of the content but not the wording of two other Lukan woes (places of honor and burdens). In vv. 39-41 (inside/outside), Luke has given us the contents of what is a woe in Matt 23:25-26. He betrays no knowledge at all of two other Matthean woes (proselytizing and the blind, Matt 23:15 and 23:16-21). Finally, numerous manuscripts read and eighth woe in the Gospel of Matthew (23:14).[18] So the Synoptic, and later the manuscript, tradition, had a tendency to multiply the woes, to confer that wording on traditional materials, and purely and simply to create new invectives.[19] If we should accept the tracing of the four common woes back to Q, we might conclude that that source already contained a collection of seven woes,[20] the three other ones in Q to be taken to be among (a) the two in Luke with whose content Matthew was acquainted without following the wording (the places of honor and the burdens), (b) the one in Matthew with whose content Luke was acquainted without following the wording (inside/outside), and (c) those of which Luke betrays no knowledge (proselytizing and the blind). (4) It is impossible to reconstruct the traditional order of the woes with certainty. Perhaps the tithe came before outside/inside (cf. Matt 23:23-26). Owing to the importance of the theme and because of the meal he had in mind, Luke put the sayings on outside/inside first.[21] Did the woe concerning access to the kingdom (key) that Matthew placed at the beginning also come first in the source? It is possible, since Luke kept it until the end.[22]

---

11 Cf. Matt 23:2-3, 5, 8-10, 11, 12, 15, 16-22, 24; cf. Bultmann (*History*, 118), who hesitates over vv. 8-10.

12 Schürmann, "Redekomposition," 37–40; quotation from 58.

13 Bonnard, *Matthieu*, 333; Marshall, 493.

14 Schmid, *Matthäus und Lukas*, 325–26; Pesch, *Lohngedanke*, 41–42; Kümmel, "Weherufe," 31; Schulz (*Q*, 94 n. 5, 95).

15 E.g., Adolf Schlatter, *Das Evangelium des Lukas: Aus seinen Quellen erklärt* (Stuttgart: Calwer, 1931) 303.

16 Lührmann, *Logienquelle*, 45; Zeller, *Kommentar*, 65–66.

17 This point is controverted. Schmid (*Matthäus und Lukas*, 323–26) and Kümmel ("Weherufe," 31) hold that the division of the discourse into two parts is anterior to Luke. Lührmann (*Logienquelle*, 45) is of the opposite opinion.

18 Bonnard (*Matthieu*, 338) refuses the Matthean origin of v. 14, which "has nothing to do here."

19 About this propensity, which is apparent also with regard to the beatitudes, see commentary on 6:20-26 (1:220–29).

20 Bultmann, *History*, 118; Lührmann, *Logienquelle*, 45.

21 See Loisy, 330–31; Zeller, *Kommentar*, 66.

22 See Marshall, 493.

In order to make it possible to end up with this result, he also shifted the position of the "scriptural proof" (vv. 49-51), which comes almost at the end of Matthew's composition (Matt 23:34-35).[23] Tied to each other by the linking word "tombs," the two woes on whitewashed tombs and the tombs of the prophets follow in the same order in both Matthew and Luke; from that we may conclude that that order was traditional. As was his custom, Luke probably did not modify the order except at the beginning and the end of the text. (5) Matthew worked into Jesus' speech the lament over Jerusalem (Matt 23:37-39), which Luke reproduced later in his text (Luke 13:34-35). Although there is no doubt about these verses belonging to Q, we are not sure what their original location was.[24] (6) There are two parts to Matthew 23, one containing observations (vv. 1-12), the other invectives (vv. 13-36). In the much shorter speech in Luke, we also find such a division: vv. 39-41 (observation) and vv. 42-52 (woes). This structure probably corresponds to that in Q.

The Lukan Reinterpretation

Luke, then, included a series of invectives in the account of the meal. He thus combined the literary genres of the Greek symposium and the Hebraic woe. From the former[25] he took especially the discussion taking place during the meal (more exactly, during the second phase of the meal, the one where people conversed while drinking after having eaten); the highlighting of the guest of honor, Jesus, whom he calls the Lord (v. 39); the mention of the welcoming host, a Pharisee (v. 37); and the statement by the scribe that allows the discussion to start up again (v. 45).[26] The discussion thus takes on the nature of a violent critique that, in its own way, serves as an instruction.

The author made traditional use of the second literary genre, the woe, which, rooted as it was in the prophetic tradition, belongs to the category of judgment oracles. In the book of Isaiah (Isa 5:8-25; cf. 10:1-11; etc.),[27] we meet a series of woes: following on the "woe" ($o\mathring{v}\alpha\acute{\iota}$ in the LXX) we have grievances, which can be more or less developed, and the contents of the resulting condemnation (introduced by "for this reason," $\delta\iota\grave{\alpha}$ $\tauo\hat{v}\tauo$ in the LXX; see Isa 5:24). All these elements, which are found also in the Q tradition, are reproduced in Luke. The $\delta\iota\grave{\alpha}$ $\tauo\hat{v}\tauo$ introduces a scriptural justification that includes the wording of a punishment. The introduction of this quotation, "Therefore the Wisdom of God also said . . ." (Luke 11:49) resembles the expression used by God's envoy, the prophet, when he announces God's judgment ("Thus says the Lord . . ."). The confirmation in Luke 11:51b, "Yes, I tell you . . ." ($\nu\alpha\grave{\iota}$ $\lambda\acute{\epsilon}\gamma\omega$ $\mathring{v}\mu\hat{\iota}\nu$ . . .), makes the judgment relevant to that generation. This judgment had an apocalyptic quality (since "this generation" was considered to be the last one),[28] which was probably lost in the Lukan redaction.

At the level of the Q tradition, the series of woes had a double function: it served the preachers in their direct polemical discussions with Israel and, in an indirect way, it served the catechists who had the task of pointing out to the catechumens the difference between the synagogue and the church.[29] It was probably this second use that became decisive at the redactional level when Luke inserted the series of invectives in the literary genre of the banquet. We should not forget that these woes come soon after a beatitude (11:28) and that they are not the first ones in the Gospel. Luke had already let loose a series of four of them (6:24-26), as an appendix to the beatitudes.

---

23 See Lührmann, *Logienquelle*, 45.

24 Schürmann ("Redekomposition," 41, 56–58) is of the opinion that these verses constitute part of the traditional discourse. It is Luke who would have displaced them.

25 See the commentary on 7:36 (1:293); Josef Martin, *Symposium: Die Geschichte einer literarischen Form* (Paderborn: Ferdinand Schöningh, 1931); Xavier de Meeûs, "Composition de Lc 14 et genre symposiaque," *EThL* 37 (1961) 847–70; Steele, "Table-Fellowship"; idem, "Symposium"; Smith, "Table Fellowship."

26 Beyond the interest in a privileged guest, the literary genre seems to impose a progressive disclosure of the identity of the invited guests. Thus, one can learn in v. 45 only that there are scribes present and in v. 54 that some other Pharisees participate in the meal; see Steele, "Symposium," 389.

27 See Claus Westermann, *Grundformen prophetischer Rede* (BEvTh 31; Munich: Kaiser, 1964) 137–42; Lührmann, *Logienquelle*, 46; Haenchen, "Matthäus 23," 37.

28 Hoffmann, *Logienquelle*, 168.

29 Ibid., 169–71.

Luke did not hesitate to introduce us here to an aggressive Jesus. That polemical initiative was probably due to a theological requirement, that of effecting an ethical reversal, which corresponded in reality to a return to the original meaning. That meant achieving an inner and authentic ethic, rejecting vain ritualism, and promoting the Christian virtues that are in fact essentially biblical virtues.

Why, moreover, did he divide up the salvos between the ones against the Pharisee and the ones against the expert in the Law? What contemporary opponents did they represent? Judaism, with its variety? Judaism and a harmful form of Christianity? Two movements within the church that deserved criticism? We will attempt to answer those questions in our detailed commentary. At this point, we can say that Luke was focusing on two groups of opponents and at the same time attempting to address each Christian personally.

Commentary

■ **37-38** The Pharisee was so anxious to invite Jesus that he addressed him an invitation while Jesus was still speaking. Are we to understand that he interrupted Jesus? Probably not, since he demonstrated politeness. Jesus—whose name never appears in the Greek of this pericope, only the title "Lord" in v. 39—had scarcely been invited than he accepted the invitation, and he immediately took his place at the table.[30] Well-intentioned and very happy, the Pharisee was delighted to welcome Jesus to his table. The Greek verb ἐρωτάω ("to question") can also mean "request," "ask," "invite someone."[31] Luke uses the same verb for an invitation in 7:36. The host "requests" Jesus to[32] come eat a meal with him

at his house; that is, he "invites" him. Ἀριστάω means "to eat a meal," a lighter one, either in the morning or at noon (τὸ ἄριστον, v. 38; the main evening meal is called τὸ δεῖπνον; cf. 14:12).[33]

Βαπτίζω is the intensive form of βάπτω, which means "plunge," "wash," and "dye." Βαπτίζω,[34] which has practically the same meaning as βάπτω (except it, unlike βάπτω, does not mean "dye"), refers, in a Jewish context, to ritual ablutions (cf. Heb 6:2; 9:10), then to John the Baptist's baptism (cf. Luke 3:7), and finally to Christian baptism. John 13 uses two other verbs, λούω ("to bathe," "wash," by plunging into water) and νίπτω ("to wash," in running water). In Modern Greek τὸ λουτρό refers to the bathroom, τὰ λουτρά to the public bathhouse, and ὁ νιπτήρας to the washbasin, or bathroom sink. In Classical Greek βάπτω and βαπτίζω were scarcely ever used for bodily washing, but rather for the cleaning of objects that were plunged into water (ῥαντίζω means "spray," "sprinkle," "splash"). While the Essenes practiced an ablution of the whole body plunged into water before their meal, which they considered to be holy (see Josephus *Bell.* 2.8.5 §129), other Jews were content to wash their hands (Mark 7:2-3 uses in this instance the verb νίπτω), or even their feet.[35] Ritual ablutions, which in the Hebrew Bible were required only of priests, had been extended to all of the people, according to rules that varied depending on which religious movement was involved. The symbolic meaning of water had become more important, as is indicated by the different Baptist movements within Judaism.[36]

Jesus was invited by a Pharisee, one of those influential persons with whom he carried on disputes about the Law and with whom Christians were in agreement about the resurrection.[37] The Pharisee was astonished and

---

30 Ἀναπίπτω, "to lay oneself down," "to sit down at table"; cf. 14:10; 17:7; 22:14; Mark 6:40 par. Luke utilizes ἀνάκειμαι and κατάκειμαι for "to be at table"; see Marshall, 494.

31 BAGD, s.v. Note the historical present, rare in Luke.

32 The ὅπως after ἐρωτάω is correct, in contrast to ἵνα of 7:36.

33 See Marshall, 493; Grundmann (247) recalls that ἄριστον finally signifies "meal," of any kind whatsoever.

34 See 2 Kgs (4 Kgdms) 5:14; Sir 34:25; Jdt 12:7-9; Mark 7:4; John 4:1-2; Werner Bieder, "βαπτίζω κτλ.," *EDNT* 1:192–96; BAGD, s.v.; Plummer, 309;

Lagrange, 342; Loisy, 331; see also the commentary on 12:50 below.

35 On John 13, see C. K. Barrett, *The Gospel according to St. John* (London: SPCK, 1978) 440–42.

36 Joseph Thomas, *Le mouvement baptiste en Palestine et en Syrie 150 av. J.-C.–300 ap. J.-C.* (Gembloux: Duculot, 1935); Phillipe Reymond, *L'eau, sa vie, et sa signification dans l'Ancien Testament* (VTSup 6; Leiden: Brill, 1958); for bibliography on the Jewish rules of purity, see BAGD, s.v. βαπτίζω 1.

37 Cf. 5:17-26; 6:2-5; 7:30, 36-50; see the commentary on 5:17 (1:181); Mark Allen Powell, "The Religious

amazed by Jesus' unexpected attitude and disapproved of it.[38] He had not foreseen what was going to happen, nor had he intended to put Jesus to the test. In Luke's eyes, Jesus and the Pharisees did not differ in the way they approached questions of hygiene or good manners; their different ways of doing things arose out of differing concepts of religion.

■ **39** The Lord replied with all of his authority; he could read hearts and knew the Pharisee's reaction before the latter even opened his mouth. Jesus advocated an interior concept of religion as opposed to an exterior one. Luke was delighted at the triumph of ethical truth over ritual obligation. What counts is not the outside of objects, which are themselves exterior (the place settings), but the inside of the inner being (the human heart). Note the shift from "the outside of the cup and of the dish" (τὸ ἔξωθεν τοῦ ποτηρίου καὶ τοῦ πίνακος) to "inside you" (τὸ . . . ἔσωθεν ὑμῶν).[39] The decisive verb here is "to purify" (καθαρίζω).[40] What mattered

for Jesus, for the Christian tradition, and for Luke was a purification that eliminated the whole lot (γέμει) of greed (ἁρπαγή)[41] and wickedness (πονηρία).[42] The name of this purification is "repentance" and "conversion" (μετάνοια), and it is to show up in the contrast to greed and wickedness, namely, generosity ("give . . . alms," v. 41). Whereas Matthew called the Pharisee's attitude hypocrisy (Matt 23:25), Luke does not take over that reproach. For him it is a question of egocentric wickedness rather than hypocrisy.[43]

The biblical tradition, on which the sacerdotal ideal had left its mark, had imposed on the people a daily routine and a social organization dominated by the distinction between purity and impurity. In the time of Christ, various interpretations of that ritual heritage circulated concurrently in Israel. The Pharisees did not share the views and practices of the Essenes, who had transferred the temple purity rules to their community. Jesus, followed by the earliest Christians, took part in

---

Leaders in Luke: A Literary-Critical Study," *JBL* 109 (1990) 93–110.

38 If the verb θαυμάζω ("to be astonished," "to admire") contains a negative nuance, it suggests flattery more than irritation. See Plummer, 309. Godet (2:110) declares it malevolent, but Lagrange (342) does not find it so hostile.

39 This is an example of antithetical parallelism; see Jeremias, *Proclamation*, 13–20. The ὑμῶν adheres to the following, to the greed and wickedness. The text would oppose the exterior and the interior of the dishes. This is not likely; see Godet, 2:112; and Marshall, 495. On the exterior and interior, see Godet, 2:112; Lagrange, 342; Marshall, 494; Ernst, 385. Τὸ ποτήριον means "goblet," "chalice," "glass"; ὁ πίναξ is "dish" or "plate." Following a genetic analysis of *m. Kelim* 25.1 and 7–8, Neusner ("Inside") is of the opinion that at the time of Jesus the dominant opinion was that of the house of Shammai: the purity of the interior of the dish is independent of that of the exterior and reciprocally. The opinion attributed to the house of Hillel, according to which the purity of the interior of the dish is determinant, must date after 70. The sentence of Jesus attacks, in this case, the opinion of the school of Shammaï and conveys to humans the distinction between the interior and exterior of the culinary utensils. Quispel ("Apocryphal") examines the canonical formulations of our sentence in Macarius, 'Abd al–Jabbar, the Diatessaron, the Pseudo-Clementines and *Gos. Thom.* 39.

40 Judith, who makes ablutions in a bath, returns to the tent pure (καθαρά) (Jdt 12:5-9). The heroine must be purified from contact with the pagans. She respects also alimentary rules (Jdt 12:1-4). Christianity introduces another concept of purity, to know purification offered by God in his Son: cf. Acts 10:15; 11:9; 15:9; 2 Cor 7:1; Eph 5:26; Titus 2:14; Heb 9:14; 1 John 1:7, 9. The Epistle to the Hebrews treats this passage by conceiving another; see Heb 9:23 (*NRSV*) "Thus it was necessary for the sketches of the heavenly things to be purified with these rites, but the heavenly things themselves need better sacrifices than these."

41 Cf. Heb 10:32; ἡ ἁπαγή means "rapine," "booty," "rapacity"; ἅρπαξ means "rapacious," "greedy" (Luke 18:11; Matt 7:15; 1 Cor 5:10-11; 6:10). The verb ἁρπάζω ("to ravish") can have a neutral sense or positive; for the negative sense, see Matt 12:29. For ὁ ἁρπαγμός ("object of rapine," "prey") see Phil 2:6. See Werner Foerster, "ἁρπάζω κτλ.," *TDNT* 1 (1964) 472–73.

42 On πονηρός and πονηρία, see the commentary on 11:34 above.

43 Against Godet, 2:111. The νῦν is remarkable: it concerns less "here are where things have come now" (see Lagrange, 342) than "you here then, I catch you in the act" (see Godet, 2:112). The text must be a curse in Q; see Klostermann, 130. Luke has made an initial contestation of it.

that quarrel of interpretations, which turned into a battle over differing practices. The fall of the temple forced the Pharisees to rethink their practices, just as the distance from Jerusalem and contact with Gentiles made the Jews of the Diaspora (e.g., Philo of Alexandria) rethink their practices.[44] Jesus' eschatological freedom (v. 38) was accompanied by an ethical way of looking at purity (v. 39). Greek-speaking Christians could not help but be delighted by it.[45] Under the influence of Paul, Luke declared in Acts that only God, through his Holy Spirit, purifies human hearts, and that in our day it is by faith, rather than by obedience, that true ethics is lived out, the ethics of compassion and love, and no longer the ethics of ritual and the Law (Acts 10:9-16, 34-35; 15:8-11).

■ **40-41** Jesus let his anger explode, since he observed that the Pharisees perverted the order of what was pure and what was impure. Luke considered such surprising violence to be necessary for communication (cf. the *Verfremdung* of Bertolt Brecht) and that it was theologically legitimate. Polemic and edification are not incompatible. As a result, he was also aware that an indirect consequence of this fit of anger would be the violence of the crucifixion.

Outside and inside are subsumed under the category of creation. "The one who made" (ὁ ποιήσας) refers to

God as creator.[46] What is the implication of this rhetorical question?[47] That one's attitude toward God consists in sanctifying both the inside and the outside. It would be ridiculous to believe or live the opposite.[48] The expressed requirement does not eliminate concern for the outside. But, as v. 41 indicates, one must begin with the inside, and the result will be that a pure inside will purify everything, that is, the outside as well (cf. 1 Sam [1 Kgdms] 15:22; Hos 6:6; Isa 58:1-14; Titus 1:15). Jesus—the text understands—is pure inside, so his hands were, too, as he entered the Pharisee's house.

The Matthean parallel required only inner purity (Matt 23:26) without expressly stating how it was to be obtained. Luke—and on this point he added to Matthew—indicated a step to take that would reverse a person's natural tendency. He contrasted greed and wickedness with generosity. The Greek word πλήν, which can mean "only," "nevertheless," translated here as "instead," poses a problem, since it is not immediately obvious what it is contrasted with.[49] This conjunction probably distinguishes a bad attitude from a good one. "Those things that are within" (τὰ ἐνόντα) is ambiguous; since it cannot be a question of what is inside dishes of food, it must refer to what is inside human hearts,[50] which is greed and wickedness.[51] By metonymy, it is also a ques-

---

44　See Friedrich Hauck, "καθαρός, κτλ.," *TDNT* 3 (1966) 413–26, especially the rich bibliography.

45　It is ironic that *Ps. Sol.* 4:3, a text that, in my opinion, has a Pharisaic tendency, gives a vivid description of the attitude stigmatized in Luke 11:39: "And his hand is first upon him as though he acted in zeal, And yet he is himself guilty in respect of manifold sins and of wantonness" (trans. G. Buchanan Gray in *APOT*). *Testament of Moses* 7:9 critiques those who say great things while having impure things in their hand and in spirit.

46　One imagines the potter who takes care of the exterior and the interior; see Marshall (495), who indicates another interpretation: the one who is occupied by the exterior is not occupied by the interior; cf. 2 Sam [2 Kgdms] 19:25.

47　Οὐχ can introduce a rhetorical question to which the response is yes; see BDF §§427, 2a; 440.

48　Cf. ἄφρονες ("fools"), v. 40; cf. 12:20; 1 Cor 15:36; 2 Cor 11:16, 19; Eph 5:17; 1 Pet 2:15. This is a word familiar to Paul; see Plummer, 310; Lagrange, 342; Dieter Zeller, "ἀφροσύνη, etc.," *EDNT* 1:184–85; Str-B 1:278–80; 2:102. This intellectual deficiency is,

in fact, a spiritual deficit (see Mark 7:21-22). Rooted in the biblical tradition (Ps 48 [49]:11-21; Wis 12:23-24), the ἀφροσύνη of the NT can be understood, at least in part, by the Greeks; ἀφροσύνη was one of the four cardinal vices of the Stoics.

49　For πλήν, cf. 6:24; Ps 48 (49):16 LXX; see BDF §449 and BAGD, s.v.

50　On τὰ ἐνόντα, see Loisy, 333; Grundmann, 247–48; Marshall, 495. On the double accusative, see BDF §158: the second accusative indicates the result, while the first designates the object. See 9:14; 12:33 (δότε ἐλεημοσύνην—the word ἐλεημοσύνη is found eight times in Acts, e.g., 3:2–3). On the hypothesis of Julius Wellhausen (*Einleitung in die drei ersten Evangelien* [Berlin: Reimer, 1905] 36–37), which supposes a confusion between two Aramaic words דכי ("to clean") and זכי ("to give alms"), see Loisy, 333; Marshall, 496; and especially Fitzmyer, 2:947.

51　See the self-assessments of the Pharisees and tax collectors (18:11-13); Grundmann, 248.

tion of the inside of the chamber of the heart that this greed has filled up. They are the ill-earned gains that the believer, anxious to be pure, must offer as alms. In Luke, one's attitude toward money is the test and the symbol of one's attitude toward God.[52] As expressions of one's faith and ethics Luke prefers generosity and sharing.[53] Compared to the ethics of Acts, to which we called attention above, this passage in the Gospel remains at the anthropological level. It does not yet express the idea according to which one must have already received something from God in order to be able to give oneself. The reason that Luke does not yet state this ethical theocentrism is that he respected his sources, where what is at stake is the type of observance, and because he was waiting for Pentecost to defend the idea of God—Father, Son, and Spirit—acting efficaciously to purify human hearts.

■ **42** Luke here begins his first series of woes.[54] It has to do with the meticulous practice of the tithe[55] at the expense of more basic requirements. We have here come to the heart of the subject, but we must first explain certain details.

Although both Matthew and Luke mention mint, they differ with respect to the two other plants: Luke speaks of "rue." This garden herb, a medicinal plant, figured in the calculation of the tithe, if it was cultivated but not if it was picked from a wild plant.[56] Matthew 23:23 mentions "dill" here. Luke then generalizes: "and every kind of garden herb," where Matt 23:23, more exact, speaks of "cumin."

As for the major requirements, each of the Gospel writers puts in his two cents by way of choices and commentaries ("the weightier matters of the law" [Matt 23:23] seems to be a redactional gloss). Luke and Matthew both have "judgment" ($\tau\grave{\eta}\nu$ $\kappa\rho\acute{\iota}\sigma\iota\nu$) before going their separate ways. To that Luke adds "the love of God"; Matthew, "mercy and faith." Luke understood the word $\kappa\rho\acute{\iota}\sigma\iota\varsigma$, which must have referred to the "Law" or to "justice," in the sense of God's "judgment." What the Pharisees neglected[57] was the relationship with the God who makes demands ("judgment," $\kappa\rho\acute{\iota}\sigma\iota\varsigma$) and who loves ("love," $\dot{\alpha}\gamma\acute{\alpha}\pi\eta$).[58] For Luke, what comes first is faith, rather than ethics. Only an authentic relationship with God leads to a truly ethical existence. By pronouncing this woe, the Lukan Jesus dismantled pseudo-knowledge and false values. When a tithe of modest consumer goods becomes a priority observance, then the result is a travesty of ethics and even theology. And what is most important is that justice that goes beyond equity and love

---

52   See the commentary on 6:20, 24 (1:224–25)

53   There are remarkable variants in Codex Bezae (D): in v. 37, another manner of formulating the invitation; in v. 38, in place of "having seen, he was surprised that . . .": "scarcely sure of his judgment, he began to say within himself, why. . . ."

54   On $\dot{\alpha}\lambda\lambda\acute{\alpha}$, see Godet, 2:114: the real conduct of the Pharisees is opposed to that known by foreknowledge by Jesus in the preceding verse; it is redactional. See Loisy, 333; Marshall, 496. On $o\dot{\upsilon}\alpha\acute{\iota}$, see discussion in this section above. There is more indignation than mildness in this exclamation. Lagrange (343) believes that this word expresses not a curse but a warning.

55   The verb $\dot{\alpha}\pi o\delta\epsilon\kappa\alpha\tau\acute{o}\omega$ means "to set apart the tithe," and "to give tithes." Elsewhere one finds also $\dot{\alpha}\pi o\delta\epsilon\kappa\alpha\tau\epsilon\acute{\upsilon}\omega$ (cf. 18:12 v.l.). The tithe, distinct from the annual tax for the temple, was a religious tax that recalled the rights belonging to God. It applied originally to the products of earth and livestock (Lev 27:30-32; Deut 14:22-29; cf. Gen 14:20; Num 28:21). The Pharisees, as our passage attests, had considerably expanded the application of it, in particular to the products of the garden.

See X. Léon-Dufour (*Dictionnaire du Nouveau Testament* [Paris: Seuil, 1975], s.v.). On this verse, see Del Verme, "Guai."

56   According to *m. Maʿaś.* 1.1, all the plants that one can plant and eat must be entered into the calculation of the tithe. According to *m. Šeb.* 9.1, rue, an herbal plant, did not enter into this category, as much as it was the gathering of wild things. If care was put into planting it, it must be factored into the tithe. Cf. Correns, "Raute"; Del Verme, "Guai," 311–13.

57   Luke utilizes $\pi\alpha\rho\acute{\epsilon}\chi o\mu\alpha\iota$ (Deut 17:2; Luke 15:29), then $\pi\alpha\rho\acute{\iota}\eta\mu\iota$, where Matthew returns twice to $\dot{\alpha}\phi\acute{\iota}\eta\mu\iota$; Lagrange, 344.

58   On $\kappa\rho\acute{\iota}\sigma\iota\varsigma$, cf. Gen 18:19, 25 LXX; Deut 10:18 LXX; Plummer, 311; Mathias Rissi, "$\kappa\rho\acute{\iota}\nu\omega$, etc.," *EDNT* 2:318–21. On $\dot{\alpha}\gamma\acute{\alpha}\pi\eta$, cf. Matt 24:12; and see the commentary on 6:27 (1:234). This is the only usage of the substantive in Luke-Acts. Verse 42 is a novel example of antithetical parallelism; see n. 39 above. Loisy (333) thinks that by these words that Luke wishes to accentuate the double precept of charity (10:25-28).

that exceeds kindness sink dramatically into oblivion. And then God, who is righteous and good, is no longer the person with whom believers deal directly.

The end of the verse,[59] which Matthew also knew, is a gloss attributable to Q, which in my opinion betrays Luke's, even more than Q's, conception of Jesus' intention. This gloss piles on requirements, whereas Jesus advocated what was essential, thereby taking care of what was secondary at the same time.[60]

■ **43** The second woe reproaches the Pharisees for their vanity. They loved[61] to swagger in the synagogues and to be greeted with respect in the marketplaces.[62] Mark also reproduced this complaint, derived here from Q (Mark 12:38b-39 par. Luke 20:46). While Matthew added to Q the mention of the banquets, Luke was satisfied with the marketplaces in Q, thus lending a manifest ostentation to the Pharisees' ambitions. In order to unmask the disastrous way the Pharisees carried on, moreover, Luke used the fine verb "to love" ($\dot{\alpha}\gamma\alpha\pi\dot{\alpha}\omega$), here with the meaning "appreciate," "look for," in the same place that Matthew settled on another verb for love, $\varphi\iota\lambda\dot{\epsilon}\omega$ "love," "accept." What the Gospel writer has Jesus denounce

is a warped ethics of "love" ($\dot{\alpha}\gamma\dot{\alpha}\pi\eta$), since "loving" to show off means pushing others into the background. While the command to love one's neighbor counts on an equal respect for both the other person and oneself, the betrayal that the Gospels attribute to the contemporary Jewish leaders created an imbalance in this two-party equation in favor of personal interest.

■ **44** The parallel in the First Gospel, Matt 23:27-28, shows how a single saying, now lost, could have given rise to two quite different statements.[63] The author of Matthew kept the previous distinction (Matt 23:25-26) between outside and inside. Jesus' opponents, seen from the outside, appeared to be as beautiful as newly white-washed tombs,[64] but on the inside, they were full of the impurity that is brought about by death (Matt 23:27). As if we had not gotten the point, the good catechist clearly spells that out for us (Matt 23:28). Luke also compares the Pharisees to graves and preserves the link between death and impurity (while life, a gift from God, is associated with purity, death in Israel belonged to the order of impurity—our hesitation about touching a cadaver is inherited from this ancient belief). But the

---

59 See Marshall, 498; Jakob Jervell (*Luke and the People of God: A New Look at Luke-Acts* [Minneapolis: Augsburg, 1972] 139) believes that Luke adheres to this clause favorable to ritualism. See also Polag, *Christologie*, 80.

60 See the commentary above on 11:40-41.

61 The verb $\dot{\alpha}\gamma\alpha\pi\dot{\alpha}\omega$ has undoubtedly prompted Luke to modify the text of Q in the verse preceding and to have recourse to the term $\dot{\alpha}\gamma\dot{\alpha}\pi\eta$.

62 Matthew's enlarging of this section to encompass the meal (Matt 23:6), placed at the head, must be redactional. If Luke had found this mention in Q, he would have certainly retained it (cf. 14:7-11). One series of Lukan manuscripts adds the meal at the end of the enumeration. Distinct from the chair of Moses (Matt 23:2), the first places were reserved for the doctors of the Law, not for the Pharisees; see Str-B 1:914–16; Jeremias, *Proclamation*, 142–46. Luke 20:46 mentions the scribes who appreciate this privilege. About the agency of the synagogues and their furniture, see Fitzmyer, 2:949; Marilyn Joyce Segal Chiat, *Handbook of Synagogue Architecture* (BJS 29; Chico, Calif.: Scholars Press, 1982). On this theme, cf. *T. Mos.*7:4 and John 12:43. In every case, in the eyes of Luke, the responsible ones are more culpable than the people.

63 See Polag, *Christologie*, 82 n. 261. Ernst (387) thinks that the pre-Lukan tradition has transformed the logion into a warning against dangerous seduction; on the contrary, for Schmid (*Matthäus und Lukas*, 327), the Lukan form must be primitive; Schulz (*Q*, 105–6) and Zeller (*Kommentar*, 67–68) are of the same opinion.

64 According to Num 19:16, the one who touches the dead, the bones or the sepulchre is impure for the week. Whence this usage? On the fifteenth of the month Adar, whitewashing the tombs for the people, in particular for the pilgrims for the feast of Passover, does not render one impure involuntarily (Str-B 1:936–37; Godet, 2:114; Plummer, 312). Schwarz ("Gräber") thinks that $\kappa\epsilon\kappa o\nu\iota\alpha$-$\mu\dot{\epsilon}\nu o\iota$ and $\ddot{\alpha}\delta\eta\lambda\alpha$ are two correct translations of יֻשַּׁד, of the verb שׁוד, which, in the *piel* passive participle signifies being "hidden," "misjudgment," "repainted," "rough-cast." Matthew has understood the subject on the basis of his knowledge of Jewish customs. $M\nu\eta\mu\epsilon\hat{\iota}o\nu$ ("tomb") in Luke evokes the memory that one must keep of the dead; $\tau\dot{\alpha}\varphi o\varsigma$ ("sepulchre") in Matthew suggests the fact that one has been buried. For $\ddot{\alpha}\delta\eta\lambda o\varsigma$ ("which lacks evidence," "that one cannot recognize," "imprecise," "invisible") see BAGD, s.v.

saying in Luke has in mind the relationship with others and not oneself and the propagation of evil rather than hypocrisy. You look healthy and pure, but death and impurity have left their stamp on you. So you are graves without being conscious of it, and other people are even less aware of it. The result of this is that when people enter into contact with you (by walking over you without realizing it, to keep the imagery), they make themselves impure (a consequence that is very real, although only implicit). Your fault, then, is that of causing evil, whereas your mission is to protect what is good. You lead people to sin, whereas you ought to lead them to holiness. That is a terrible accusation to have to make of spiritual guides.[65] That indictment corresponds to the last woe in the second series, the one about having stolen the key of knowledge (v. 52). The saying also suggests forgetting as a result of lack of knowledge. This forgetting, a symbol of time that passes, can, however, have a positive quality about it. It invites us to move on from ancient times to the new age of the Gospel and of the kingdom.

■ **45** This Lukan verse[66] is enough to justify a scribe's claiming to have ulcers. Luke had at his disposal no fewer than three different terms with which to refer to teachers of the Law: νομικός as here and in 7:30; 10:25; and 14:3; νομοδιδάσκαλος in 5:17 and Acts 5:34; and γραμματεύς, e.g., in 11:53, the word that occurs most frequently in both Luke and the other Synoptic Gospels (eighteen times in Luke-Acts, one of which refers to a Gentile, the town clerk for the citizens of Ephesus [Acts 19:35]). A Greek reader would have understood the word γραμματεύς, which Luke had inherited from the Synoptic tradition, as a "secretary"; νομικός as an "expert in the Law"; and νομοδιδάσκαλος as a "teacher of the Law." But for Luke, these three terms were synonyms that referred to members of the official cast of experts, wise men, teachers, trained and consecrated rabbis. Some of

them belonged to the party of the Pharisees, and they functioned as leaders in this lay movement.[67]

The teacher in this pericope felt that Jesus' words, to his way of thinking insulting, hit him "also," as well as his colleagues (καὶ ἡμᾶς). Were not the scribes responsible for the detailed codification of the legal instructions? Ὑβρίζω has the strong meaning of "insult."[68]

The redactional insertion of this verse allows Luke to have the dispute come up again and to open a second front. Jesus first attacked the Pharisees, but from this point on he lays into the legal experts. Often mentioned side by side (e.g., Luke 5:17, 21; 7:30), they should be distinguished. While the Pharisees who are depicted in the Gospel seem to have been in leadership roles in a religious movement, the scribes are legal experts with standing. So the difference did not consist in their respective hierarchical positions but rather in their places in society: Luke had in mind two social groups or movements within Judaism and, for his time, two rival trends within the church, on whose leaders he pours out Jesus' tirades.

■ **46** Jesus gave tit for tat, replying to one καί ("too," v. 45) with another καί ("also," v. 46): "Woe also to you experts in the Law." What a reversal and what a violent reaction for the unfortunate scribe who believed he was on the right side!

Like the other woes, this fourth one has a binary structure.[69] The first affirmation runs: "you load . . . (with)," that is, "you say." The second one: you yourselves lift nothing, that is, you do nothing. We find here once again the contrast between speaking and doing against which Jewish piety reacted, followed by Christian piety, e.g., the Epistle of James (Jas 2:12-17).[70] The evil is all the more serious for being the words of the leaders, which consist not in beautiful promises but in requirements imposed on others. On the one hand, we have heavy

65 See Marshall, 499.
66 The style (usage of δέ, of the indefinite τις followed by the genitive) and the vocabulary (νομικός, διδάσκαλος, ὑβρίζω) are Lukan; see Ernst, 387; Wiefel, 229.
67 See Godet, 2:116; Plummer, 312; BAGD, s.vv. νομικός, νομοδιδάσκαλος, and γραμματεύς.
68 For ὑβρίζω, see 18:32; Acts 14:5; Matt 22:6; 1 Thess 2:2. Plummer (312) indicates that in classical Greek the verb is not transitive, but is followed by εἰς + accusative. Grundmann (248) underlines

that, despite his humiliation, the scribe calls Jesus "Teacher."
69 See Jeremias, *Proclamation,* 15 n. 3.
70 Cf. *Sifre* 26.3 (110): "The one who learns in order not to practice, it would be better for him that he was not created"; cited by Bonnard (*Matthieu,* 334), who mentions other rabbinic texts.

burdens;[71] on the other, do-nothing kings. The saying is well crafted, ironic, and biting.[72] We detect here the Lukan idea that obedience to the Law is onerous rather than cheerful (cf. Acts 15:10).[73] Since the opponents here are leaders, the critique, in the Christian context, is aimed at the evil leaders of the communities.[74] What comes immediately to mind is the ritual obligations and practices that oral tradition, of which the Pharisees were so fond, had added to the requirements of the Law. There were, for instance, thirty-nine categories of work that were forbidden on the day of the Sabbath and 613 commandments.[75]

■ **47-48** The fifth invective stigmatizes an existential inconsistency and a religious abuse. In the background is the conviction, inherited from Deuteronomy, that the people of Israel were cantankerous and that they repulsed God's envoys.[76] This self-criticism, rare among the Near Eastern civilizations, took on an extreme form in Israel, beginning with the Persian period: the price that the prophets, the true ones, had to pay for their commitment was their lives. They were martyred by persons who shared their nationality and religion.[77] Added

to that was the relatively recent custom of the veneration of tombs.[78] We know of the grotto of Machpelah, near Hebron, where the tomb of the patriarchs is located.[79] The book of Acts speaks of David's tomb (2:29), and this verse in Luke, of the tombs of the prophets. The saying is not an attack on religious constructions, although it hardly seems to be favorable to them. It vehemently criticizes the contradiction between venerating the martyrs of long ago and at the same time adopting the attitudes and actions of the ancestors that were the very ones that led to those executions. The text subtly juxtaposes the memory of the martyrs ("the tombs of the prophets," τὰ μνημεῖα τῶν προφητῶν) and joining the executioners ("So you are witnesses and approve of . . . ," ἄρα μάρτυρές ἐστε καὶ συνευδοκεῖτε).[80] The scribes are not yet accused of murder, but they are already accused of complicity. Hence, the final irony: you build, to be sure, but in the process of wishing to honor the memory of the prophets who were persecuted, you take the side, like witnesses to a capital execution, of your persecuting ancestors.[81] We should understand that Christians, as

---

71 For the motif of "burdens" (φορτία) the term "oppressive" (δυσβάστακτα) was a common theme (Gottlob Schrenk, "Βάρος κτλ.," *TDNT* 1 [1964] 553–61, esp. 560–61) that applies, figuratively, to all sorts of calamaties and obligations. See also Konrad Weiss, "φέρω κτλ.," *TDNT* 9 (1074) 56–87. By contrast, the yoke of Jesus is easy and his burden light (Matt 11:30), a sentence curiously absent from Luke.

72 Note the detail of the finger, as in our expression "not lift a finger"; προσψαύω signifies "to touch lightly," "to touch," "to touch upon"; it is a somewhat refined verb. See Marshall (500), who pursues, rightly, another interpretation.

73 Jervell (*Luke and the People of God*, 133–51 [n. 59 above]), in my opinion wrongly, conceives of Luke as a partisan of the Law under all its aspects; he sees here an ecclesiological preoccupation.

74 Matthew 23:4 has concrete aspects: one joins; one lays upon the shoulders; one does not "lift a finger" to displace the charges of the Law. In the ensemble, the Matthean formulation has the same sense as in Luke, but it is less rhetorical.

75 On these thirty nine categories, see *m. Šabb.* 7.2.

76 See the commentary on 6:20-26 (1:224–28); cf. Acts 7:51-53.

77 Cf. Heb 11:32-40; *Asc. Isa.* 1:5; Steck, *Israel*; Schulz, *Q*, 109; Miller, "Rejection."

78 Jeremias, *Heiligengräber*. The form οἰκοδομεῖτε at the end of v. 48, without the direct object complement, creates a difficulty, which is why the majority of manuscripts add a complement; see Marshall, 500–501. The same usage, without the complement, is found in 17:28. Luke likes this verb.

79 A. Lemaire, "Tombe," *DEB*, 1272–73.

80 On the word "witness," see Godet, 2:118–19 (you fill the office of witness as it is required for execution by stonings); Deut 17:7; Acts 7:58. One finds συνευδοκέω ("to approve") in Acts 8:1: the young Saul, witness to the martyr Stephen, gave his approval, along with others. Luke blames religious fanaticism, the persecuting orthodoxy; see Godet, 2:117–18.

81 See Lagrange, 346; Haenchen, "Matthäus 23," 41–42. On these verses (vv. 47-48), see Derrett, "Tombs." The Hebrew word בּוֹנִים could be understood in the sense of either builders or interpreters, so that there is a wordplay between this participle and the plural substantive of "son" (בָּנִים). Since constructing tombs signified neglecting the memorial, although they know this is wrong, Jesus' interlocutors are therefore. They understand the good actions of the prophets without making amends;

they transmitted this saying,[82] could not help but think of Jesus' martyrdom. He was the victim of the Jewish authorities, the scribes in particular. Just how much the bearers of the Synoptic tradition were affected by this saying can be seen by the fact that it is confirmed by the oracle of Wisdom (vv. 49-51). These verses constitute one of the most violent passages in the Gospels because of the accusation in them of collaboration with the enemy and homicide committed against God's envoys.[83]

■ **49-51** These words[84] from the Wisdom of God[85] serve both as a quasi-scriptural confirmation of Jesus' woe (vv. 47-48) and as a saying from a judgment oracle (cf. the "therefore," $\delta\iota\grave{\alpha}$ $\tauo\hat{\upsilon}\tauo$ = לְכֵן). Jesus' analysis of the situation put the sons on the side of their fathers[86] rather than on the side of the children of Wisdom (7:35), that is, God's envoys.[87] The Wisdom of God is not to be identified with Jesus. It is rather the equivalent of the Word

of YHWH that finds expression in the mouth of the prophet. But some time has passed: the Word of God has become Scripture, a reference more than an occurrence. That can be seen in the analogous relationship that, at the end of the book of Acts, is established between the Holy Spirit and the apostle Paul through the prophet Isaiah (see Acts 28:25-27). The Wisdom of God, that direct collaborator in the work of creation and redemption, that little girl now grown up, speaks. She promises an uninterrupted flow of prophets and apostles. The prophets were the sentries of the old order;[88] the apostles, witnesses of the new.[89] That is how Luke understood these figures, but there were also prophets in the early church and, by virtue of the etymology of the word "apostle," the apostle is an envoy like the messengers that God sent in former times.[90] That faithfulness corresponds to a continuity of rejection: the matching piece of the history

---

they contemplate the death of these prophets without turning aside from the opinion of their persecuting fathers. Such is the opinion of Derrett.

82 Verse 47 seems to distinguish the son from the fathers; v. 48 brings them together and draws the conclusion ($\check{\alpha}\rho\alpha$ ["thus," "then," "consequently"] in classical Greek never occurs at the start of a phrase); see Marshall, 500.

83 The text of Matthew is not so lapidary and is more explicative. It corresponds, undoubtedly, to an effort to make explicit the allusive character of the sentence of Q, of which Luke, due to certain stylistic improvements, is a good witness, at least in v. 47. In v. 48, it is advisable perhaps to follow Matt 23:31 in order to find Q, which could throw this invective upon the Pharisees. Luke omits the name of the adversary; Matthew standardizes it. The reconstructions of Q vary; see Hoffmann, *Logienquelle*, 164–71; Schulz, *Q*, 108–10; Zeller, *Kommentar*, 70–72; Miller, "Rejection." Ἀποκτείνω (Acts 3:15), $\check{\alpha}\rho\alpha$, $\mu\acute{\alpha}\rho$-$\tau\upsilon\rho\epsilon\varsigma$, $\sigma\upsilon\nu\epsilon\upsilon\delta o\kappa\acute{\epsilon}\omega$, and $\check{\epsilon}\rho\gamma o\nu$—all this vocabulary is common to Luke. In return, the mention of the just (Matt 23:29) and the fulfillment of the measure of the fathers (Matt 23:32) are Matthean.

84 On vv. 49-51, see Steck, *Israel*, 50–52, 223–26; Lührmann, *Logienquelle*, 43–48; Christ, *Sophia*, 164–71; Schulz, *Q*, 108–10; Jacobson, "Wisdom"; Légasse, "Oracle"; Kühschelm, *Jüngerverfolgung*, 32–33, 39–40, 147–62; Zeller, *Kommentar*, 70–72; Miller, "Rejection." Verses 47-51 do not go back to Jesus but to some Christian prophets, some "Q prophets," who were believed to be inspired by the resurrected Jesus.

85 Matthew has kept "that is why" but eliminated the reference to "the Wisdom of God." It is then the Matthean Christ who speaks.

86 To the death and persecution of the prophets of Luke 11:49 Matt 23:34 adds crucifixion and flagellation. Matthew distinguishes what happens in the synagogues and in the cities.

87 Cf. Seitz ("Commission"), who associates Matt 23:34 with the sending of the Twelve and Luke 11:49 with that of the seventy-two. He examines a series of verses of the OT related to the departure of the envoys of God: Exod 23:30; 1 Kgs (3 Kgdms) 19:10, 14; Jer 7:25-26; 25:4-14; 26:5-6; 29:19; 35:15; 44:4-5; Mal 3:1, 23.

88 See Ellis ("Oracle"), who imagines Christian prophets. Matthew has a triad: prophets, sages, and scribes.

89 See Klein ("Apostel"), who inclines toward the Christian apostles. Frizzi ("Carattere") thinks that Luke has a retrospective vision, toward what happened in the history of salvation, and Matthew has a prospective vision, toward the future of the church. See also Frizzi, "L' $\dot{\alpha}\pi\acute{o}\sigma\tauo\lambda o\varsigma$." The only usage of $\dot{\alpha}\pi\acute{o}\sigma\tauo\lambda o\varsigma$ in the LXX is 1 Kgs (3 Kgdms) 14:6. In the Greek translation transmitted by Origen, the prophet Ahija says to the wife of Jeroboam, who has been sent to him, $\dot{\epsilon}\gamma\acute{\omega}$ $\epsilon\dot{\iota}\mu\iota$ $\dot{\alpha}\pi\acute{o}\sigma\tauo\lambda o\varsigma$ $\pi\rho\acute{o}\varsigma$ $\sigma\epsilon$ $\sigma\kappa\lambda\eta\rho\acute{o}\varsigma$, "I am, myself, sent near to you, hard [i.e., in order to speak to you in a hard way]."

90 It is curious that Matthew speaks of blood spilled out "upon the earth," and Luke of blood spilled out "since the foundation of the world" (the only usage in Luke-Acts). On this last expression, which does

of salvation is the history of refusal; of the offer of life, the withdrawal of life, murder, and persecution (why that order?); of the blood offered, the blood shed. That situation (v. 49) cannot last. A consequence ("so that," ἵνα) that is called for is that all this blood that is shed—from that of the first righteous person who was assassinated, Abel, to the last, Zechariah, whether we are dealing with the prophet at the end of Scripture or the person by the same name at the end of time (who died during the siege of Jerusalem),[91]—must be answered for.[92] Those who must answer for it are those who shed it: "this generation," either insofar as it inherits the sin of its ancestors, or insofar as it refers to the obdurate race of Israel. What God is it who speaks out here? Is it the vengeful God who is going to exact punishment by calling for blood to be paid? What Wisdom, the one that strikes a wise balance between the sin and the punishment, or the one that coincides with the folly of the cross, which pardons?

In v. 51b,[93] Jesus speaks again and makes Wisdom's judgment his own. It is not stated that we are talking about vengeance. It must be a question of what is right, of order and, in the last analysis, of harmony. It is not right for victims to continue to be sacrificed. It is not right for the torturers to have the last word, or for the strongest persons to triumph. Early Christians, followed in turn by Luke, made Jesus' criticism of Israel their own with a violence that can be explained, without being excused, by the persecutions to which the early church was subjected. In our day, we must direct it against all those who commit aggression and oppression.

■ 52 What Luke used as an ending was used as a beginning in Matthew. The opponents—in Luke the experts in the Law, in Matthew the scribes and the Pharisees—prevent the faithful from entering into the kingdom of God. This reign is thought of in terms of a palace, a temple, or a city. In order to get into it, one must go through a door. According to Matthew, the religious leaders blocked access ("you shut out," κλείετε); according to Luke, they have stolen the key to it ("you have taken away the key," ἤρατε τὴν κλεῖδα). The result is the same in both Gospels: they cannot enter (we must imagine that they have lost the stolen key),[94] and those who are in their charge have even less of a chance of getting in there. They have hindered them from doing so ("you hindered," ἐκωλύσατε).[95] In Matthew it is a question of the kingdom; in Luke, of "knowledge" (γνῶσις). This is not a Lukan term and must go back to a sapiential wording in Q. Luke did not think of this wisdom as gnosis; for him, it was a question of faith's intelligence (as in v. 40 in relation to the "fools"), of the wisdom of conversion, of the knowledge of God's plan in history, and of God's will in the destiny and the message of Christ.[96]

History resembles a battlefield (vv. 47–51); eschatology, a palace to which entry is blocked and forbidden (v. 52). What hope is there left?

■ 53-54 Although these two verses are terrifying in their content, they are well written. They contain redactional turns of phrase, but the vocabulary is not typically Lukan.

The meal ended as abruptly as it had begun. Jesus went "outside,"[97] the scribes and the Pharisees began to

---

not appear in the LXX but appears about ten times in the NT, see Plummer, 314; Fitzmyer, 2:950.

91 The reference to Zechariah may be to the priest of this name who was stoned in the court of the temple in the reign of King Joash (2 Chr 24:20-22). On the model of Abel, drawn from the first book of Scripture, one may find here, with this Zechariah, an example extracted from what was then held to be the last book of Scripture. Matthew names him "son of Barachiah" (Matt 23:35) and identifies him, this doer, as the biblical prophet and author of the prophetic book (Zech 1:1). One may think also of the father of John the Baptist (Prot. Jas. 23–24), or of Zechariah "son of Baris," assassinated by the Zealots in the middle of the temple during the first Jewish revolt (Josephus Bell. 4.5.4 §§335–43); see the commentary on 1:5-25 (1:33 n. 14); Fitzmyer, 2:951.

92 According to Matthew, the blood must "come upon you" (Matt 23:35). On ἐκζητέω, Gen 9:5 LXX, see Horst Balz and Gerhard Schneider, "ἐκζητέω," EDNT, 1:410; Plummer, 314; Fitzmyer, 2:950.

93 Matthew 23:26: "Truly, I say to you, all this will happen within this generation."

94 Codex Bezae (D) and some other manuscripts have: "you have hidden the key."

95 On κωλύω, see Oscar Cullmann, "Les traces d'une vieille formule baptismale dans le Nouveau Testament," RHPhR 18 (1938) 174–86.

96 On Gos. Thom. 39, see Schrage, Thomas-Evangelium, 91–94; Quispel, "Apocryphal."

97 The text of vv. 53–54 is uncertain: in place of a departure by Jesus, a good number of witnesses mention "while he was saying to them these things"; in place of vv. 53–54, such as Nestle-Aland[27] edits them, Codex Bezae (D) and some others have:

be terribly ("very," δεινῶς) hostile,[98] literally, "to have"[99] with "gall" as the understood object. These emotions are demonstrated here by incessant questions ("have him talk about many things")[100] and traps ("laying traps for him")[101] in order to make him talk ("to catch[102] him in something he might say"). Although his opponents started out by attacking Jesus verbally, they were to end up, at the time of his passion, by acting violently. Then followed Jesus' arrest, condemnation, and execution. This pericope, which is a Gospel in miniature, is also an announcement of the subject, or better still, a start on it, one of those symbolic actions that the prophets of Israel performed as an oracle of misfortune or happiness.

History of Interpretation

In his effort to counter the Marcionites, the African theologian Tertullian took a two-pronged approach, both doctrinal and exegetical (*Adv. Marc.* 4.27). Taking his confession of faith as his starting point, he attacked his adversaries' hostility to God as Creator. He examined the Lukan text and was happy to find in it confirmation of, and even a basis for, his doctrinal conviction. He rejected the Marcionite interpretation of the text and expressed his own reading of it. The polemics in which he was involved precluded any calm, meditative interpretation but did lend fullness of insight to his understanding as a reader.

Tertullian—and this is what is original in his inter-

pretation—was delighted with this angry Christ who has bothered so many believers. Why? Because the faults that the Marcionites found with God as judge in the Hebrew Bible are to be found again here applied to Christ himself. In the preceding pericopes, as well as in this one, Christ does indeed come off as changeable, fickle, and capricious. Who resembles my God more, Tertullian exclaimed at this point, than Christ himself? By that we are to understand: if the Marcionites succeed in reconciling this aggressive Christ with their God of love, do I not also have the right to believe in one and only one God, the God of Abraham, Isaac, and Jacob, and the God of Jesus Christ, one and the same God, who is righteous and good?

Tertullian thus demonstrated that Jesus' anger corresponded to his righteousness and that that righteousness represented the vigorous face of his love. While the Marcionites considered Christ here to be the honorable adversary of a cruel creator God, Tertullian had no trouble in demonstrating, with vv. 39-41 as support for his position, that Jesus' remarks were here aimed not at the one who established the Law but rather at those who interpreted the Law poorly.

What the Law requires, in the first place, is the practice of the great commandments[103] (he quoted the first commandment at this point). On the subject of burdens (Luke 11:46), Tertullian said that these supplemental burdens were the human regulations that were added by the teachers of the Law. They were also the abuses

---

"While saying these things to them, in the presence of all the people, the Pharisees and the lawyers began fiercely to strive and to dispute with him about a large number of subjects, seeking to seize an occasion by his subjects, so that they might find something with which to accuse him."

98 For ἐνέχω (with χόλον to be supplied), "to have gall against," "to have anger against," see Gen 49:23 LXX; Mark 6:19; BAGD, s.v.

99 For δεινῶς ("terribly"), cf. Matt 8:6; and see BAGD, s.v.

100 The verb ἀποστοματίζω signifies by custom "to say" that which must be understood by the heart, then "to recite aloud," "to utter by heart," "to respond." These meanings are not fitting here. If v. 54 is taken as the inspiration, one will translate, "to wrest responses" or to "press with questions"; see LSJ, s.v.; Moulton and Milligan, *Vocabulary*, s.v.; BAGD, s.v.; Plummer, 315–16.

101 For ἐνεδρεύω ("to lay an ambush," "to lie in wait for someone"), cf. Acts 23:21; Deut 19:11; Prov 26:19; see also BAGD, s.v.; Plummer, 315–16.

102 For θηρεύω ("to chase," "to hunt down," "to seek to capture," "to catch insidiously"), see Moulton and Milligan, *Vocabulary*, s.v.; Plummer, 316; Marshall, 508.

103 The text of Luke 11:42 has: "the judgment (κρίσις) and love of God." As Marcion's God was not rightly a judge, he modified this text into: "the calling (κλῆσις) and love of God," whence the expressions of Tertullian: "neglecting the calling and the love" and "from which God, the calling and the love" (*Adv. Marc.* 4.27.4; cf. Epiphanius, *Haer.* 42.11.6, schol. 26). See also Harnack, *Marcion*, 210; P. Holmes, *The Writings of Quintus Septimus Florens Tertullianus* (3 vols.; Edinburgh: T&T Clark, 1869–70) 1:294 n. 7.

committed by the leaders in exploiting the people.[104] To this restoration of the proper priorities with respect to understanding what was in God's will Tertullian added an indispensable corollary: obedience is more spiritual than physical. We must be about what our souls desire (the inside) before deciding what our bodies should do (the outside). That was the anthropological significance of the metaphors "cup" and "plate" (v. 39) as seen by him and as seen by the Marcionites. The image of the key (v. 52) confirms that we are dealing with a conflict of interpretations. The reason the Pharisees had "taken away the key," in Tertullian's opinion, was that they had obscured the true meaning of the Law. God prefers mercy to sacrifices (an allusion to Hos 6:6).

The various woes support Tertullian's position;[105] like Jesus, the God of the old regime detested those arrogant persons who take the seats of honor (v. 43). Tertullian then alluded to two passages in the Hebrew Bible pointing in the same direction: God called those persons "rulers of Sodom" (Isa 1:10) and forbade "[putting] confidence in princes" (Ps 118 [117]:9).

The Pharisee's very attitude confirms Tertullian's exegesis. The reason the Pharisee was surprised by his guest's reaction was that he knew that Jesus worshiped the same God he did and was not a priest of a new divinity.

In short, Tertullian was far from complaining about Jesus' invectives. On the contrary, they allowed him to show that Christ has brought not knowledge of a new God but confirmation of the old God. Moreover, he corrected the interpretation that the Jewish teachers had given of God's will.[106]

Conclusion

One might hesitate, in reading this part of the Gospel, between admiration and revulsion. Should we, like Tertullian, take pleasure in Christ's victorious sparring here, or complain about a vehemence that is so uncharacteristic of the Gospels?

Added to this theological problem over holy displays of anger is an uncertainty on the scholarly level. Was

---

104 Tertullian alludes to Isa 5:8, 23; 3:15; and 10:2 and then attributes two independent citations to Isaiah (cf. Amos 6:1 and Isa 3:4, 12).

105 Tertullian asks why Jesus condemns the builders of tombs destined for the persecuted prophets. I have difficulty grasping the explanation that he finally gives. I ask: Is the prophet, or rather God, this "fanatical" man that the Marcionites accuse of requiring reparation for the fathers, on the part of his descendants up until the fortieth generation (*Adv. Marc.* 4.27.8)?

106 Having opted to review only the exegesis of Tertullian, I refer here to some other notable commentaries. Ambrose (*Exp. Luc.* 7.101) juxtaposes, without articulating them theologically, two sources of purification: alms, which come from the human, and the Word of God. Elsewhere, twice he rejoices in the beauty of the biblical passage (*Exp. Luc.* 7.102 and 106) and succumbs, alas, often to anti-Semitic sentiments. Augustine (*Serm.* 106.2.2–4.4 [*PL* 38:626–27]), cited by Aquinas (*Catena aurea* 11.11), interprets vv. 41-42 in a tropological way: to give alms is not to pay tithes but to give mercy. One must begin with oneself (one cannot be generous with others if one is cruel with oneself). Return to your own conscience and you will find there your soul, in the process of imploring. Then give alms. "The judgment" (v. 42) is not to give pleasure to oneself, and the "love" is to please God and neighbor. You

may love however much, but if you do not give alms to your soul, you will have done nothing. Cyril of Alexandria (*Hom. Luc.* 86; see Payne Smith, *Cyril*, 2:394–95), cited by Aquinas (*Catena aurea* 11.12), gives two convergent interpretations of the "key" (v. 52). First, if the Jewish leaders had understood the OT in a typological way, access to Christ would have opened to them. Second, it refers to faith, according to Isa 7:9. Bede (*In Luc.* 4.410–12) judges that v. 40 permits one to contradict the Manichean ethic, which declares the soul created by God and the body created by the devil. Francis of Assisi (*Letter to All the Faithful* 2.32–36), in controversy undoubtedly with the Cathars, believes that works, such as fasting, must be performed in the Catholic Church. It is necessary to respect the clergy, because it is through their ministry that one obtains the purity of which vv. 41–42 speak: grace for the proclamation of the Word and dispensation of the sacraments. The obligation of v. 42 holds first for the minority, who must accomplish great works and not neglect the small (Francis of Assisi, *Écrits*, 232–35). For Zwingli (*Annotationes*, 645) the "key" of v. 52 represents the knowledge of God and his will, which opens for us a heavenly treasure. By having preferred earthly treasures, the powerful, at the threshold of death, attest and invoke one great power, the justice of God, which, during their lifetime, they have not wished to recognize.

Luke in agreement with what he wrote? As commentators analyze these lines in the Gospel, they must answer in the affirmative, since the author does not express any disapproval of Jesus. Leafing through the summaries in Acts—in other words, those rare passages where an ethical position is expressed—commentators are surprised to find so few verbal affinities with this chapter in Luke. Should the conclusion be drawn that the author was illogical, being a better narrator than thinker in this case?

Here is my answer. Luke was faithful to his sources and adhered, in the main, to what he had received from tradition. But he was not, for all that, a mediocre theologian, since he succeeded in endowing the ancient sayings of Jesus as well as the more recent wordings of the church with doctrinal consistency. Out of those old conflicts with the Pharisees, he extracted a lively view of ethics. Every believer and every person entrusted with a ministry runs a risk. Adherence to the faith, far from stabilizing one's ethical energies, on the contrary awakens them and arouses them. Consequently, in order to live out one's faith, the only choice one has is between "beatitude," that is, happy obedience, and "woe," that is, unhappy obedience and relapse. Jesus' irreproachable attitude expressed in the "woes" in this pericope provides us with a negative that we can develop into a picture of what is involved in full-fledged true obedience.

As is always the case, sin is lying in ambush not in one's conduct but in one's intimate intentions. Everything depends on one's inner being, one's priorities, regardless of whether these priorities are assigned to the basic commandments, to seeking not one's own righteousness but the welfare of the other and, thereby, God's glory. As a witness to the Christianity of the Hellenists, as a disciple of Paul, and, to be sure, in his own way, of Jesus, Luke connected with the prophetic requirement of the Hebrew Bible, in its basic expectation. What is important is mercy and not sacrifices, moral purity and not ritual cleanliness. What counts is a humility that is aware of being in God's hands and not the self-sufficiency of powerful persons in high places. What God expects from those to whom he gives life time and again is that they break the murderous vicious circle of violence—and he is ready to give them the means to do so. But they have to be willing to receive it. If they give themselves over to it, they will succeed in achieving "beatitude," but not without having rubbed shoulders with, even having confronted, this very violence that, like a hydra, constantly raises its ugly head in order to persecute those who are in favor of love.

Jesus himself, who was pure on the inside, dared to give expression to the requirement and to denounce the abuse. His incitement, he knew full well, could not but arouse opposition, at first latent but later vehement. He did not hesitate to put up a fight and to risk his life.

169

Confessing One's Faith (12:1-12)

Bibliography

Allison, Dale C., "The Hairs of Your Head Are All Numbered," *ExpT* 101 (1990) 334–36.

Baer, Heinrich von, *Der Heilige Geist in den Lukasschriften* (BWANT 3.3; Stuttgart: Kohlhammer, 1926) 136–45.

Barrett, C.K., *The Holy Spirit and the Gospel Tradition* (London: SPCK, 1954) 103–7.

Bertrand, D. A., "Hypocrites selon Luc 12, 1-59," *Christus* 21 83 (1974) 323–33.

Boring, M. Eugene, "The Unforgivable Sin Logion Mark 3:28-29/Matt 12:31-32/Luke 12:10: Formal Analysis and History of the Tradition," *NovT* 18 (1976) 258–79.

Bornkamm, Günther, "Homologia: Zur Geschichte eines politischen Begriffs," *Hermes* 71 (1936) 377–93.

Idem, "Das Wort Jesu vom, Bekennen," *MPTh* 34 (1938) 108–18.

Bovon, *L'oeuvre*, 205–20.

Brown, Schuyler, *Apostasy and Perseverance in the Theology of Luke* (AnBib 36; Rome: Pontifical Biblical Institute, 1969) 45–56.

Bultmann, Rudolf, *Das Evangelium des Johannes: Ergänzungsheft* (Göttingen: Vandenhoeck & Ruprecht, 1950) 52–53.

Casey, Maurice, "The Son of Man Problem," *ZNW* 67 (1976) 147–54.

Catchpole, David R., "The Angelic Son of Man in Luke 12:8," *NovT* 24 (1982) 255–65.

Colpe, Carsten, "Der Spruch von der Lästerung des Geistes," in Lohse, *Ruf Jesu*, 63–79.

Congar, Yves M. J., "Le blasphème contre le Saint-Esprit (Matt 6, 32.34; 12, 22-32; Mc 3, 20-30; Lc 11, 14-23; 12, 8-10," in *L'expérience de l'Esprit: Mélanges E. Schillebeeckx* (PoTh 18; Paris: Beauchesne, 1976) 17–29.

Coppens, J., *La relève apocalyptique du messianisme royal: Le Fils de l'homme néotestamentaire* (BETL 55; Leuven: Leuven University Press, 1981) 13–16, 105–7, 157–86.

Dautzenberg, Gerhard, *Sein Leben bewahren: ψυχή in den Herrenworten der Evangelien* (SANT 14; Munich: Kösel, 1966) 135–63.

Dupont, Jacques, "La transmission des paroles de Jésus sur la lampe et la mesure dans Marc 4, 21-25 et dans la tradition Q," in Dupont, *Études*, 1:259–94.

Edwards, *Theology of Q*, 120–23.

Fitzer, Gottfried, "Die Sünde wider der Heiligen Geist," *ThZ* 13 (1957) 161–82.

Fleddermann, Harry, "The Cross and Discipleship in Q," in *SBLSP* (1988) 472–82.

Idem, "The Q Sayings on Confessing and Denying," in *SBLSP* (1987) 606–16.

Friedrichsen, A., "Le péché contre le Saint-Esprit," *RHPhR* 3 (1923) 367–72.

Goppelt, *Theologie*, 1:231–33.

Hahn, *Hoheitstitel*, 32–36, 40–42.

Hampel, *Menschensohn*, 152–58.

Higgins, A. J. B., "'Menschensohn' oder 'ich' in Q: Lk 12, 8-9/Mt 10, 32-33?" in Rudolf Pesch and Rudolf Schnackenburg, eds., *Jesus und der Menschensohn: Festschrift Anton Vögtle* (Freiburg im B.: Herder, 1975) 11–36.

Holst, R., "Reexamining Mk 3:28f and Its Parallels," *ZNW* 63 (1972) 122–24.

Iwand, Hans J., *Die Gegenwart des Kommenden: Eine Auslegung von Lukas 12* (2d ed.; Biblsche Studien 50; Neukirchen-Vluyn: Neukirchener Verlag, 1966) 7–18.

Kloppenborg, John S., "The Q Sayings on Anxiety (Q 12.2-7)," *Forum* 5.2 (1989) 83–98.

Koester and Robinson, *Trajectories*, 132–33, 166–71.

Köhler, K., "Zu Lc 12, 4.5," *ZNW* 18 (1917–18) 140–41.

Kümmel, Werner Georg, "Das Verhalten Jesus gegenüber und das Verhalten des Menschensohns," in Pesch and Schnackenburg, *Jesus*, 210–24.

Lambrecht, J., "Are You the One Who Is to Come, or Shall We Look for Another?" *LouvSt* 8 (1980) 115–28.

Laufen, *Doppelüberlieferungen*, 156–73.

Leisegang, H., *Pneuma Hagion: Der Ursprung des Geistbegriffs der synoptischen Evangelien aus der griechischen Mystik* (Veröffentlichungen des Forschungsinstituts für vergleichende Religionsgeschichte an der Universität Leipzig 4; Leipzig: Hinrichs, 1922) 96–134.

Lindars, Barnabas, "Jesus as Advocate: A Contribution to the Christology Debate," *BJRL* 62 (1980) 476–97.

Lövestam, Evald, *Spiritus blasphemia: Eine Studie zu Mk 3, 28f par Mt 12, 31f. Lk 12, 10* (Scripta minora Regiae Societatis humaniorum litterarum Lundensis; Lund: Gleerup, 1968).

Lührmann, *Logienquelle*, 49–52.

Marguerat, *Jugement*, 72–73.

Marshall, I. Howard, "'Fear Him Who Can Destroy Both Soul and Body in Hell' (Mt 10:28 R.S.V.)," *ExpT* 81 (1969–70) 276–80.

McDermott, J. M., "Luke 12:8-9: Stone of Scandal," *RB* 84 (1977) 523–37.

Mitton, Charles Leslie, "Leaven," *ExpT* 84 (1972–73) 339–43.

Moulton, H. K., "Luke 12:5," *BT* 25 (1974) 246–47.

Negota, Athanase, and Constantin Daniel, "L'enigme du levain: ad Mc 8, 15, Mt 16, 6 et Lc 12, 1," *NovT* (1967) 306–14.

Niven, W.D., "Luke 12:4," *ExpT* 26 (1914–15) 44–45.

Pesch, Rudolf, "Jésus, homme libre," *Conc (French)* 93 (1974) 246–47.

Idem, "Über die Autorität Jesu: Eine Rückfrage anhand des Bekenner- und Verleugnerspruchs Lk 12, 8f par.," in Schnackenburg, *Kirche*, 25–55.

Puech, *Gnose*, 2:59–62.

Reicke, Bo, "A Test of Synoptic Relationships: Matthew 10:17-23 and 24:9-14 with Parallels," in William R. Farmer, ed., *New Synoptic Studies* (Macon, Ga.: Mercer University Press, 1983) 200–209.

Robinson, James M., "Worksheets for Q 12," in *SBLSP* (1987) 586–605.

Sato, *Q und Prophetie*, 212–14.

Schippers, R., "The Son of Man in Mt 12:32 = Lk 12:10, Compared with Mk 3:28," in *StEv* 4 [TU 102] (1968) 231–35.

Schmid, *Matthäus und Lukas*, 268–75.

Schneider, Gerhard, "'Der Menschensohn' in der lukanischen Christologie," in Pesch and Schnackenburg, *Jesus*, 267.

Schrage, *Thomas-Evangelium*, 34–37.

Schulz, *Q*, 66–76, 157–61, 246–50, 442–44, 461–65.

Schürmann, Heinz, "Beobachtungen zum Menschensohn-Titel in der Redequelle," in Pesch and Schnackenburg, *Jesus*, 127–47.

Scroggs, Robin, "The Exaltation of the Spirit by Some Early Christians," *JBL* 84 (1965) 358–73.

Spicq, *Notes de lexicographie*, 2:621–22, 936–43.

Stegemann, Wolfgang, *Zwischen Synagoge und Obrigkeit: Zur historischen Situation der lukanischen Christen* (FRLANT 152; Göttingen: Vandenhoeck & Ruprecht, 1991) 40–84.

Sweetland, Dennis M., "Discipleship and Persecution: A Study of Luke 12: 1-12," *Bib* 65 (1984) 61–80.

Idem, *Journey*, 97–99 and passim.

Idem, "The Understanding of Discipleship in Lk 12, 1–13, 9 (Dissertation, University of Notre Dame, 1978).

Talbert, 140–41.

Tannehill, Robert C., *The Narrative Unity of Luke-Acts: A Literary Interpretation* (2 vols.; FF; Philadelphia/Minneapolis: Fortress Press, 1986, 1990) 240–46.

Tödt, *Son of Man*, 118–20, 312–18.

Vielhauer, Philipp, "Gottesreich und Menschensohn in der Verkündigung Jesu," in idem, *Aufsätze zum Neuen Testament* (ThBü 31; Munich: Kaiser, 1965) 55–91, esp. 76–79.

Idem, "Jesus und der Menschensohn," in Vielhauser, *Aufsätze*, 92–140.

Wellhausen, Julius, *Einleitung in die drei ersten Evangelien* (2d ed.; Berlin: Reimer, 1911; reprinted as idem, *Evangelienkommentare* [ed. Martin Hengel; Berlin/New York: de Gruyter, 1987]) 123–30.

Williams, J. G., "A Note on the 'Unforgivable Sin' Logion," *NTS* 12 (1965–66) 75–77.

Wrege, Hans-Theo, *Die Überlieferungsgeschichte der Bergpredigt* (Tübingen: Mohr Siebeck, 1968) 156–80.

Idem, "Zur Rolle des Geisteswortes in frühchristlichen Traditionen (Lc 12, 10 par.), in Delobel, *Logia*, 373–77.

Wuellner, Wilhelm, "The Rhetorical Genre of Jesus' Sermon in Luke 12:1—13:9," in Duane F. Watson, ed., *Persuasive Artistry: Studies in New Testament Rhetoric in Honor of George A. Kennedy* (JSNTSup 50; Sheffield: Sheffield Academic Press, 1991) 93–118.

Idem, "The Rhetorical Structure of Luke 12 in Its Wider Context," *Neot* 22 (1988) 283–310.

1/ Meanwhile, when the crowd gathered by the thousands, so that they trampled on one another, he began to say to his disciples, "In the first place, beware of the leaven of the Pharisees, which is hypocrisy. 2/ Nothing is covered up that will not be uncovered, nor anything secret that will not become known. 3/ In consideration of that, whatever you have said in the dark will be heard in the light, and what you have whispered in the storerooms will be proclaimed from the housetops.

4/ "I tell you, my friends, do not fear those who kill the body, and after that can do nothing more. 5/ But I will show you whom to fear: fear him who, after he has killed, has authority to cast into Gehenna. Yes, I tell you, that is the person to fear! 6/ Are not five sparrows sold for two assaria? Yet not one of them is forgotten in God's sight. 7/ But even the hairs of your head are all counted. Do not be afraid; you are of more value than many[a] sparrows.

8/ "I tell you, everyone who acknowledges me before [other] human beings, the Son of Man also will acknowledge him before God's angels; 9/ but whoever denies me before [other] human beings will be denied before God's angels.

10/ "And everyone who speaks a word against the Son of Man will be forgiven; but whoever blasphemes against the Holy Spirit will not be forgiven.

11/ "When they bring you before the synagogues, the rulers, and the authorities, do not worry about how you are to defend yourselves or what you are to say, 12/ for the Holy Spirit will teach you at that very hour what you ought to say."

a   Under the influence of Hebrew, "many" could have the meaning "all the."

Only a long commentary will make it possible to discover the thematic unity of these twelve disparate verses. The vital clue that Luke left is, as we will see, the attitude of faith that Christians must adopt in the face of invitations from a God who is Father, Son, and Holy Spirit. This is what explains the presence, side by side, of such diverse sayings as those about the leaven of the Pharisees, the truth that is in the end striking, the Father who is both formidable and protector, the Son who is both confessed and confessing, and the Spirit who is an advocate who is not to be disowned. In order to be able to understand these verses, a commentator must analyze their origin in Q and find parallels to them in the early noncanonical Christian literature.

Analysis

Luke has put an end to the polemic against the Pharisees that was begun during a meal (11:53-54). While he mentions these enemies once more (12:1b), from here on he no longer considers them to be the ones whom Jesus is addressing. Luke first notes the enormous crowd (12:1a), mentioned or presupposed on several occasions in preceding verses (11:14, 15, 16, 27, 29). The people in that crowd, who could be attentive or critical, anxious to see signs or to hear speeches, were those to whom the Word was to be addressed, the Word that is going to be the topic in what follows. Up to that point having been given the wrong orientation by the Pharisees, the people were in need of the disciples' attention. Nevertheless, in this new speech—for that was still the way Jesus was intervening—Jesus spoke to the disciples (12:1a). God's presence in the sayings added, one might say, a final protagonist to the scene.

The writer of the Gospel of Luke quoted a collection of sayings taken from Q (12:2-12) before connecting with L (12:13-21). Before this unit he placed a warning against the leaven of the Pharisees (12:1b), to which there is a corresponding warning in the triple tradition (Mark 8:15//Matt 16:6). The Gospel writer may have found this saying in this position in Q, or may have wished to place it here in order to create a harmonious transition between the preceding woes and the following speech.[1] Since Matthew and Luke used the first sayings, which are nevertheless quite diverse, in the same order (Matt 10:26-33 par. Luke 12:2-9), it is evident that these sayings were found together, and in that order, in Q.[2] The following verses also come from Q, since they are also encoun-

1   On the origin of v. 1, see Fitzmyer, 2:953–54: v. 1a is Lukan; v. 1b derives from L rather than from Q or, despite the parallel with Mark 8:15, from Mark.

2   The sentence about what is hidden and what is revealed (Luke 12:2) is known also from Mark (Mark 4:22). The same is the case of the sentence of confession and disavowal (Luke 12:8-9; cf. Mark 8:38).

tered in Matthew. Mark was acquainted with more than one of them, but with different wording and in various contexts: Mark 4:22 par. Luke 8:17 (hidden–revealed; cf. Luke 12:2); Mark 8:38 (confession, cf. Luke 12:8-9); Mark 3:28-29 (sin against the Holy Spirit; cf. Luke 12:10) and Mark 13:9, 11 (help from the Holy Spirit; cf. Luke 12:11-12). I personally think that Luke kept Q's sequence. Matthew, on the other hand, disturbed it by inserting the saying about the sin against the Holy Spirit (Matt 12:31b-32a par. Luke 12:10) into Mark's version of this saying of Jesus (Matt 12:31a, 32b par. Mark 3:28-29). As for the double saying about the help from the Holy Spirit (Luke 12:11-12), Matthew used it in the same missionary speech, but before (Matt 10:17-20) and not after the first sayings (Matt 10:26-33 par. Luke 12:2-9). Once again he drew on the Markan version (Mark 13:9, 11), with his text having been but slightly contaminated by Q.[3] Luke left aside the Markan version of the saying about the sin against the Holy Spirit (Mark 3:28-30), which Mark placed at the end of the episode about Beelzebul (Mark 3:22-27), while elsewhere (Luke 21:12-15) Luke used the word about the help offered by the Holy Spirit (Mark 13:9, 11), thus allowing a doublet to occur. In short, in 12:1-12 Luke maintained the order and all of Q, while Matthew, more respectful of Mark, modified this order (Matt 10:26-27 and 12:32) and eliminated Q's version of one of these doublets (cf. Matt 10:17-20).

Q is both a tradition that Luke drew on and itself a redaction in which scattered sayings of Jesus have been collected. The subjective and secondary character of this collection drawn up by the redactional activity of Q is to be seen both at the level of intratextuality and at that of intertextuality. An attentive reader of Luke 12:1-12 will notice such striking differences in wording and context between one or the other group of sayings that he or she will conclude that they have a composite origin:[4] v. 1 is a warning (with an imperative); v. 2, a sort of proverb of which v. 3 offers the application to preachers (who are addressed in the second person plural); v. 4, distinguished by a new point of departure ("I tell you," $\lambda\acute{\epsilon}\gamma\omega$ $\delta\grave{\epsilon}$ $\acute{\nu}\mu\hat{\iota}\nu$), goes hand in hand with v. 5: both of these verses express certitude and indicate a way to be followed; vv. 6-7 form an exhortation based on examples drawn from daily life; vv. 8-9, marked off by the same introduction as in v. 4 ("I tell you," $\lambda\acute{\epsilon}\gamma\omega$ $\delta\grave{\epsilon}$ $\acute{\nu}\mu\hat{\iota}\nu$), make up an antithetical parallelism; v. 10, on another theme, is another parallel of the same type (the "you" [plural] is absent from vv. 8-9 and v. 10); as for vv. 11-12, they give voice, with the reappearance of the "you (plural)," to a new encouragement.

These sayings or groups of sayings make sense in themselves, and their varied content confirms what their wording presupposes. Verse 1 warns against the adversaries' hypocrisy. Verses 2 and 3 deal with the dimensions taken on by Christian proclamation; vv. 4-5, the minor and major risks one might encounter; vv. 6-7, the protection one can count on; vv. 8-9, the confession of faith; v. 10, an unpardonable sin; vv. 11-12, the help that the Holy Spirit will offer when it is needed. These verses, focused as they are on the communication of the Word, complete the missionary speeches (9:1-6 and 10:1-20).

It was also for structural and thematic reasons that the authors of Q grouped certain sayings together: the contrast between the Pharisees' hypocrisy (v. 1) and the integrity of the Christians (vv. 2-3); the unfortunately logical linkage between preaching (vv. 2-3) and persecution (vv. 4-5); the same confidence in the omnipotence of God (vv. 4-5) as in God's providential protection (vv. 6-7), a confidence that finds expression in respect rather than fear; the correspondence between the preaching of the gospel (vv. 2-3) and the confession of faith (vv. 8-9); between faith (vv. 8-9) and life with its risks of relapse (v. 10); between the rejection of the Spirit (v. 10) and the conviction of its help (vv. 11-12). Although what is visible (v. 2) differs from what is audible (v. 3), the pair "dark–light" (v. 3) guarantees a formal link with the preceding words (v. 2). The vocabulary of fear ($\varphi o\beta\acute{\epsilon}o\mu\alpha\iota$) lends a structural unity to vv. 4-7; the isotopy of death and life, a thematic unity. The title "Son of Man" favored the bringing together of the words about confession (vv. 8-9) and sin (v. 10), just as the term "Holy Spirit" made possible

---

3   There is a slight influence of Q upon Matt 10:17-20: $\mu\grave{\eta}$ $\mu\epsilon\rho\iota\mu\nu\acute{\eta}\sigma\eta\tau\epsilon$ $\pi\hat{\omega}\varsigma$ $\grave{\eta}$ $\tau\acute{\iota}$ $\lambda\alpha\lambda\acute{\eta}\sigma\eta\tau\epsilon$ (Matt 10:19b par. Luke 11b).

4   See Kloppenborg, *Formation*, 208–16.

the linking of vv. 11-12 (the help from the Holy Spirit) with v. 10 (sin against the Holy Spirit).[5]

Moving on from intratextuality to intertextuality, we discover parallels to these verses dispersed among numerous noncanonical texts. This very scattering confirms their distinct origins and their respective independence.[6] As we have seen, various sayings are also found in Mark, isolated from each other, and in other contexts (Mark 4:22; 8:38; 3:28-29; 13:9, 11). *Gospel of Thomas* 5–6 is also acquainted with the saying about what is hidden and what is revealed but does not connect it to the proclamation; on the contrary, it links this preaching, with which it is not unacquainted, with another saying, the one about the lamp (*Gos. Thom.* 33; Luke 11:33). And as for the saying about the sin against the Holy Spirit, a parallel is to be found in *Gos. Thom.* 44. Unlike the order of Luke, the *Second Epistle of Clement* quotes Jesus' saying about the real fear (Luke 12:4-5) in connection with the sending out of the disciples like lambs into the midst of wolves (*2 Clem.* 5.2-4), while Matthew yokes that saying about the lambs and the wolves (Matt 10:16) to help from the Holy Spirit in the time of persecutions (Matt 10:17-20; cf. vv. 11-12 in this pericope in Luke). Justin Martyr makes mention, side by side, of human powerlessness (Luke 18:27) and the fear of God (vv. 4-5 in this pericope). We need to stress the fact that here both of these authors seem to be quoting oral traditions rather than our written Gospels. They are, then, valuable witnesses to the isolated transmission of these sayings and to their ini-

tial autonomy. The quotations in 2 Tim 2:12 (on confession and denial; vv. 8-9 in this pericope) and Rev 3:5 (on the ultimate confession of Christ; v. 8 in this pericope) point in the same direction, namely, an oral tradition.

The verse-by-verse exegesis here will make it possible for us to examine the individual origin and particular development of each of the sayings in this pericope.[7] Grasping the meaning that Q gave to this sequence is important for an understanding of Luke, namely, the proclamation of the good news by Jesus' disciples.[8] They were invited to preach without hesitation (vv. 2-3) and to not be afraid of persecutions (vv. 4-5). Their confidence in the Savior and Creator God (vv. 6-7) obliged them to commit themselves to confessing their faith in court (vv. 8-9). That invitation, which also held good for those who listened to them, was accompanied by a warning (against disowning, v. 10) and a promise (help from the Holy Spirit, vv. 11-12).[9] While this teaching may be thought of in a prophetic and apocalyptic perspective, the sapiential nature of several of these sayings must also be recognized.[10] Taken together, they suit itinerant preachers who were in a hurry to announce the promise and requirement of the gospel and the present authority and imminent coming of the Son of Man.

Before embarking on detailed exegesis, I would like to point out the redactional perspective in which Luke conceived the sequence according to certain modern and contemporary commentators. Frédéric Godet, followed on this point by Alfred Plummer, understood these

---

5   On the formal and thematic correspondences, see Schweizer, 134; and Zeller, *Kommentar*, 72–74.

6   These parallels are furnished at the end of the pericopes in Aland, *Synopsis*, 282–83; they are utilized by Kloppenborg, *Formation*, 208–16. The parallels of Mark are not to be forgotten: Mark 4:22; 3:38; 3:28-29; 13:9, 11. On parallels in the *Gospel of Thomas*, see Koester and Robinson, *Trajectories*, 129–32, 166–70; see also Koester, *Ancient Christian Gospels*, 91, 93.

7   On the significance of the composition of Q, see Schmid, *Matthäus und Lukas*, 268–75; Lührmann, *Logienquelle*, 49–52; Edwards, *Theology of Q*, 120–22; Zeller, *Kommentar*, 72–78; Kloppenborg, *Formation*, 208–16; Robinson, "Worksheets."

8   See Lührmann, *Logienquelle*, 49.

9   Ibid., 49–52.

10   See Lührmann, *Logienquelle;* Schulz, *Q*, 66–76, 157–61, 246–50, 442–44, 461–65. Zeller (*Kommentar*,

72–78) insists on the prophetic and eschatological character of these verses. Schulz distinguishes two layers: an ancient layer of Q where a sentence expressing inspirational enthusiasm is confirmed by one or several sayings of experience from popular wisdom (e.g., Luke 12:4-7); and a more recent layer where a sentence from popular wisdom is followed by a saying from prophetic enthusiasm (e.g., Luke 12:2-3). Several recent American works situate the verses, on the contrary, in a sapiential milieu; see esp. Kloppenborg (*Formation*, 208–16), who concludes that two prophetic sentences (Q 12:8-9 and 12:10) have been introduced within a sapiential passage: Q 12:2, 3, 4-5, 6-7, 11-12. Edwards (*Theology of Q*, 120–23) believes that Q combines wisdom and eschatology.

verses as an encouragement offered to the disciples, who were threatened by persecutions.[11] He found four different reasons for hope: the certitude that their cause would be successful (vv. 1-3); the assurance given with respect to themselves (vv. 4-7); the promise of compensation (vv. 8-10); and the certitude of powerful help (vv. 11-12). Marie-Joseph Lagrange found a double warning here: in a hostile environment, the disciples must preach the truth and prepare themselves for persecutions.[12] Walter Grundmann thinks that 12:1-53 places the Christian community in the world and that this composition begins by an appeal to have confident and confessing faith.[13] He divides the section into three parts (vv. 1-3, 4-7, and 8-12). Dennis M. Sweetland stresses the context of persecution and understands the exhortation in Luke as a struggle against hypocrisy and fear of death and of the courts.[14] I. Howard Marshall sees 12:1-13, 21 as a unit pertaining to the imminent crisis.[15] At the beginning of this unit, the present pericope issues an invitation to give courageous witness in a context of persecution and in the perspective of the last judgment. Wolfgang Wiefel declares that Luke, in these verses, warns against hypocrisy (vv. 1-3), then issues an invitation to fearless confidence (vv. 4-7) and to free confession (vv. 8-12).[16] D. Bertrand thinks that, for the author of Luke, chap. 12 came under the heading of hypocrisy.[17] In the first section (vv. 1-12), the Gospel writer announced the subject (vv. 1-3) and then pointed out two possible consequences of hypocrisy for those who are not firmly opposed to the Master. Among Jesus' friends, hypocrisy can indeed take on a passive aspect, namely, fear (vv. 4-7), and among people in general, an active aspect, namely, haughty ostentation (vv. 8-12).[18]

Commentary

■ **1** The crowd was present when the exorcism took place (11:14). It had grown by the time a sign was requested (11:29). Here[19] in 12:1 there were so many[20] people[21] that they trampled on one another.[22] The crowd here reminds us of the eschatological gathering. Luke was fond of pointing out Jesus' quantitative success.[23] The text pictures the people, who were increasingly numerous, at the mercy of the Pharisees or the disciples.

Jesus begins a new speech, as in 11:29. The "in the first place" ($\pi\rho\hat{\omega}\tau\text{o}\nu$) causes a problem: it can be taken either with what follows ("beware," $\pi\rho\text{o}\sigma\acute{\epsilon}\chi\epsilon\tau\epsilon$), or with what precedes ("to his disciples," $\pi\rho\grave{\text{o}}\varsigma$ $\tau\text{o}\grave{\upsilon}\varsigma$ $\mu\alpha\vartheta\eta\tau\grave{\alpha}\varsigma$ $\alpha\grave{\upsilon}\tau\text{o}\hat{\upsilon}$). In other instances, Luke sometimes placed this adverb before, sometimes after, the verb, which makes

---

11   See Godet, 2:125–26; Plummer, 317.
12   See Lagrange, 351.
13   See Grundmann, 251.
14   See Sweetland, *Discipleship*, passim.
15   See Marshall, 508–9.
16   See Wiefel, 232.
17   See Bertrand, "Hypocrites."
18   Tannehill (*Narrative Unity*, 240–46) thinks that Luke 12:1-13 constitutes a single discourse, whose theme of hypocrisy is important in Luke 12:1-3, and which, in Luke 12:4-34, forms a unity aimed at relieving the disciples of fear and cares.
19   Ἐν οἷς ("while"); cf. Acts 24:18 (*v.l.*); 26:12; Phil 4:11; 2 Pet 2:12 is attached again to what precedes; cf. ἐν ᾧ Luke 5:34; 24:44 (D). The subordination is indicated in a pleonastic fashion by ἐν οἷς and by the genitive absolute.
20   Ἐπισυνάγω ("to assemble together") evokes a movement (ἄγω) of assembling together (σύν) to a place (ἐπί). Cf. Luke 13:34; 1 Kgs (3 Kgdms) 18:20; Ps 105 (106):47; in Matt 24:31 for the eschatological reassembly; *T. Naph.* 8:3. For the reassembly at the time of the parousia, 2 Thess 2:1 uses the substan-

tive ἐπισυναγωγή, which Heb 10:25 employs to designate the Christians who are assembled. The verb συνάγεσθαι is utilized frequently in Acts in order to designate cultic reunions, e.g., Acts 20:7. Cf. Dupont-Sommer and Philonenko, *Écrits intertestamentaires*, index, s.v.
21   For the "myriads" or the "dozens of thousands," that is to say, "very numerous" persons, cf. Acts 21:20; Acts 19:19 (for money); Heb 12:22; Jude 14; Rev 5:11; 9:16 (for the angelic armies).
22   The verb καταπατέω ("to trample under foot," "to tread down") is utilized with respect to grain treaded down along the path (Luke 8:5); of pearls before swine (Mark 7:6); of salt that has lost its savor (Matt 5:13); and of Christ denied (Heb 10:29). Codex Bezae (D), as well as Latin and Syriac witnesses, expresses the verse in another manner: "while large crowds surrounded him in a circle to the point of choking one another."
23   See 4:14, 22, 37, 40, 42; 5:15; 6:17-19; 8:4, 40; 9:14, 37; 11:29; Fitzmyer, 2:954.

it difficult to decide (cf. Luke 14:28, 31). I opt for the link with the imperative "beware." The saying is both a warning and a threat; however, it adds no mention of the eventual consequences or punishments.[24]

"Leaven" is an important biblical term.[25] The lump of old fermented dough, which, when incorporated into the new dough, causes the loaf of bread to rise, was considered to be an impure element; the loaves of unleavened bread that alone were fit to be offered to God in sacrifice recalled the exodus from Egypt, the Israelites' haste, and the power of God as liberator. That is why every Jewish family gets rid of every trace of leaven when the Passover feast is approaching, in order to facilitate a new departure in harmony with God's will. In the parable of the leaven (13:20-21), Jesus, wishing to surprise his listeners, uses this negative image to express the positive reality of the kingdom of God. Under the influence of this unexpected use, Christian piety through the centuries has spread this positive connotation of the leaven, with the result that modern readers have trouble taking in the negative baggage associated with the term here or in Paul's writing (1 Cor 5:6-8). Just as the Essenes criticized the Pharisaic interpretation of the Law, so, too, did Jesus attack the same adversaries (cf. 7:30, 39; 11:37-54).

The disciples were invited to be on their guard,[26] that is, to beware of the "leaven," in order not to be contaminated. By "leaven," we should understand the leaven that the Pharisees had (subjective genitive), rather than the leaven the Pharisees were (epexegetical genitive). By this command Jesus trained his disciples in matters of faith and its communication. From that moment on, the crowd could gather and grow, thanks to the positive power of the gospel, and no longer be under the influence of the "leaven" of the Pharisees.

While Luke, unlike Matthew,[27] never calls the Pharisees hypocrites, curiously enough, he is the only Gospel writer to interpret this leaven in terms of hypocrisy.[28] The term "hypocrisy," "the act or practice of pretending to be what one is not or to have principles or beliefs that one does not have . . . *esp.*: the false assumption of an appearance of virtue or religion"[29] is a term that in our day has been secularized and applies to a moral defect. In the seventeenth century—we only have to think of Molière's *Tartuffe*—it was still a religious term that was applied to a falsely sanctimonious person posing as a saint. In the Gospel, the term has a more radical thrust: it is a malady of judgment that is more serious than a doctrinal error or a moral deviation. Hypocrisy consists in making unworthy judgments all the while knowing full well, or having a vague notion, that they are unworthy.[30] If we think of the woes in chap. 11 that this term summarizes, we will grasp the inconsistency between what is said and what is done, and the confusion between what is essential and what is secondary.[31]

---

24   See Fitzmyer, 2:954. On πρῶτον, see Klostermann (113), who attaches it again to what follows, and Fitzmyer (2:954), who links it to what precedes. Ἀπό is normal after a verb of warning; see Plummer, 318.

25   On leaven, see Bernard Gillieron, *Dictionnaire biblique* (Eaubonne: Moulin, 1985), s.v.; Mitton, "Leaven." Fitzmyer, 2:954–55.

26   Προσέχετε ἑαυτοῖς ("pay attention to yourselves"); cf. 17:3; 20:46 without ἑαυτοῖς; 21:34; Acts 5:35; Acts 20:28; in the LXX, cf. Gen 24:6; Exod 34:12; Deut 4:9. See Plummer, 317; Marshall, 511; Fitzmyer, 2:954.

27   See Matt 23:13, 15, 23, 25, 27, 29.

28   Implicitly perhaps Mark 8:15 par. Matt 16:6. It could be that this interpretation, which recalls the Jewish technique of the pesher, may be anterior to Luke. Sweetland (*Discipleship*, 66), on the contrary, considers this explication to be redactional. The order of words varies according to the manuscripts, many of which say, "of the leaven of the Pharisees which is hypocrisy."

29   This is the definition of the Petit-Larousse dictionary.

30   I summarize here the article of Bertrand, "Hypocrites."

31   This link with the curses of chap. 11 is certain. Having its origin in the theater, where one speaks under a mask or persona (ὑπό), the term ὑπόκρισις designates the deceitful character of a person whose plans carry neither judgment nor conviction. In the Septuagint (2 Macc 6:25; cf. Isa 32:6 in the versions of Aquila and Theodotion) and in the Jewish Hellenistic literature, the term designates less the comedian or the trickster than the one who does not conform to the will of God, that is, less the culpable believer who knows hypocrisy than the one unveiled as such by the prophet or God himself. See Bonnard, *Matthieu*, 79, 97, 322, 338, and 431, which refers to the *Apocryphon of John* (NHC I,2), 7, 17-22, and 9, 24-33; Ulrich Wilckens, "ὑποκρίνομαι κτλ.," *TDNT* 8:559–71; Heinz Giesen, "ὑπόκρισις, etc." and "ὑποκριτής, etc.," *EDNT* 3:403–4.

■ **2** The saying is read by the double tradition (here and Matt 10:26), the triple tradition (Mark 4:22 par. Luke 8:17), the *Oxyrhynchus Papyrus* 654 (Logion 4), the *Gospel of Thomas* (Logia 5–6), and, with various wordings, the *Kephalaia*, "the major doctrinal commentary of the later Manichean tradition."[32] Logia 5–6 of the *Gospel of Thomas* twice give a short form of the saying that is close to Luke 8:17, which it uses in support of a criticism of rituals and as an invitation to genuine knowledge. The first time it appears it is preceded by the following significant words: "Know what [or: who] is before your face." The *Oxyrhynchus Papyrus*, which also contains that introduction, also has a prolongation: "Jesus said: 'k[now what is before] your sight and [what is veiled] of you will be unveiled [to you]; [for there is nothing that is] hidden which will not [become] evident nor buried which w[ill not be raised]." The last part of the saying is found also independently on a funerary wrapping: "Jesus said: 'There is nothing that is buried that will not be raised.'"[33] Finally, in the *Kephalaia*, we also find the introduction and the saying: "Know what [or: who] is before your face, and what is hidden from you will in fact be revealed to you.'" This variety in the transmission suggests that Jesus' sayings circulated orally and were reworked according to the respective convictions of those responsible for their circulation or in line with the requirements of the moment. The *Gospel of Thomas* in particular is not exclusively dependent on our canonical written Gospels.

It is not difficult to recover the wording of this saying in Q. All we have to do is set aside Matthew's introduction ("So have no fear of them"; Matt 10:26), ignore the occurrences of the particles γάρ (Matthew) or δέ (Luke) and attribute to Luke the compound verb (συγκα-λύπτω). Following others, Rudolf Laufen and Jacques Dupont have reconstructed the same text of Q: οὐδέν ἐστιν κεκαλυμμένον ὃ οὐκ ἀποκαλυφθήσεται, καὶ κρυπτὸν ὃ οὐ γνωσθήσεται, "nothing is covered up that will not be uncovered, nor anything secret that will not be known."[34] This saying, which has the secular wording of a proverb,[35] expresses a pastoral concern in Q: there is no reason for preachers to lose their confidence. As life's experiences demonstrate, everything ends up being known. Such are God's will and God's promise. Even though their message may be vilified, in the end, light will bring out its truth. This is the way Q introduced a set of recommendations.[36]

In Luke, the saying invites the disciples, faced with a crowd representing both a threat and a promise, not to act like the Pharisees, whose hypocrisy will be exposed.[37] The disciples have nothing to hide. The openness of the gospel is their best weapon. They must not let themselves be intimidated by threats, nor discouraged because they feel that they themselves are insignificant. They must not hesitate to proclaim what they believe. That is the meaning of v. 2.

We should note that the parallel clauses end with the mention of two complementary aspects: the subjective aspect, which is not only faith but knowledge (γνωσθή-σεται), which matches the objective aspect of the revelation (ἀποκαλυφθήσεται). It is not surprising to learn that a Gnostic interpretation was given to this saying. It appears, as a matter of fact, that Clement of Alexandria (*Strom.* 1.12.3) understood it in a Gnostic perspective rather than in an eschatological sense. In his opinion, the Lord meant to say that what is hidden is revealed only to the person who listens in secret and also that commu-

---

32   *Gospel of Thomas* 5–6: "Jesus said, 'Recognize what is in your sight, and that which is hidden from you will become plain to you. For there is nothing hidden which will not become manifest . . . because all is plain in the sight of heaven. For nothing hidden will not become manifest, and nothing covered will remain without being uncovered'" (trans. Thomas O. Lambdin, in Robinson, *Nag Hammadi Library*. Cf. Schrage (*Thomas-Evangelium*, 34–37), who reverts to *Kephalaia* 163, 28–29; and Puech, *Gnose*, 2:59–62. The definition of *Kephalaia* is derived from Michel Tardieu, *Le Manichéisme (Que sais-je?)* (Paris: Presses universitaires de France, 1981).

33   Fragment of a shroud from the provenance of Behnesa, the ancient Oxyrhynchos, acquired in 1953 by M. Roger Rémondon; see Puech, *Gnose*, vol. 2, frontpiece photo and analysis 2:59–62.

34   Laufen, *Doppelüberlieferungen*, 156; Dupont, "Transmission," 214.

35   Bultmann (*History*, 101, 107) considers that the tradition has borrowed this proverb from everyday wisdom.

36   See especially Dupont, "Transmission," 214–19; and Schulz, *Q*, 461–65. According to Laufen (*Doppelüberlieferungen*, 156–57), if the Q form of the logion is a wisdom saying, Mark's form expresses a paradox: the secret in view of the manifestation.

37   See Plummer, 318; and Lagrange, 352.

nication is possible only to the degree that the believer is able to grasp the meaning presented in a veiled manner. So God's plans are not intended for everyone. On the contrary, the Reformer Calvin understood what Jesus said in a missionary sense: "For never was so great a clap of thunder heard in any corner of the globe, than the sound of the voice of the Gospel over the whole world."[38] Although I share Calvin's position as to the saying's missionary orientation, I hesitate to see its fulfillment in the history of the church. Instead, the saying announces its eschatological unveiling.

■ **3** Q had already attached this saying, unknown to Mark, to the preceding verse. While Luke left the stamp of his style on the saying (ἀνθ' ὧν, "in consideration of that"; ὅσα, "whatever"; and πρός, "[said] in [the ears]" [= "whispered"], with a verb expressing speech), Matthew did not hesitate to abbreviate it and modify its contents:[39] in Matthew, "whatever you have said" becomes "what I say to you" and "will be proclaimed" becomes "proclaim it." Note also, in the two segments of the parallel, the shift from the indicative to the imperative.

Since I am not sure whether Q had a wording of the saying with the indicative or the imperative, I will focus on the meaning that this beautiful example of *parallelismus membrorum* took on in Luke. Although the previous

saying included the disciples only implicitly, here they are addressed explicitly ("you have said" [εἴπατε]; "what you have whispered" [ἐλαλήσατε]). We are dealing with their word, without a doubt of their proclamation of the gospel. In the first instance, Luke has in mind the discrete character of the witnessing ("in the dark," ἐν τῇ σκοτίᾳ/[40]); the almost intimate communication of the gospel (in the storerooms). Τὸ ταμεῖον or τὸ ταμιεῖον is a windowless room that can be locked: the "storeroom," the "pantry," the innermost place in an apartment, the "bedroom," the "alcove," the "cell," sometimes simply the "chamber"; sometimes the word takes on a theological dimension in Gnosticism and in Christian monasticism.[41] Here it refers to the interior and suggests a witnessing that is almost secret.[42] Luke continues by saying, well then, this message, in the end, "will be heard" (in the strongest sense, ἀκούω can mean not only "listen (to)," "hear," but especially "understand," "welcome," "accept," and "obey").[43] Was Luke thinking of the time of the church or of the end-time?[44] Or do we need to make a choice? Just as we shifted in v. 2 from the objective ("will be uncovered") to the subjective ("will become known"), here we shift from the subjective ("will be heard") to the objective ("will be proclaimed"[45]). It is therefore impossible to think exclusively in terms of an

---

38   Calvin, *Harmony*, 1:305.

39   Cf. the doublet of the triple tradition, Luke 8:17; Schulz, *Q*, 462. Cf. *P.Oxy*. 1.8: "Jesus says: what you understand in your ear alone, that [proclaim upon the rooftops]." See Aland, *Synopsis*, 282; for ἀνθ' ὧν, cf. 1:20; 19:44; Acts 12:23; "in exchange for what," "in return for what," "while" (the "because" of the *TOB* is not completely exact); cf. Godet, 2:128; Plummer, 318; Lagrange, 352.

40   The contrast obscurity–light, which makes appeal to the eye, is surprising, because it is not well suited as an integral part of the ear. The appearance of this contrast can be explained either by concern to pursue the image of v. 2 or by an allegorical embryo.

41   Cf. Gen 43:30 LXX; Deut 28:8; 1 Kgs (3 Kgdms) 22:25; 2 Kgs (4 Kgdms) 4:33; Isa 26:20 LXX; Sir 29:12; *T. Jos*. 3:3. In Luke 12:24, the word designates, in the context of ἀποθήκη ("store"), a "reserve" or a "cellar." In Matt 6:6, it is the personal chamber, which is private. The NT knows rather the contracted Hellenistic form (ταμεῖον). The classical form is ταμιεῖον. In the *Acts of Philip*, Christ

is named: "the chamber (ταμεῖον) of those who pray" (*Acts Phil*. 13.5); cf. Horst Balz and Gerhard Schneider, "ταμεῖον (ταμιεῖον), etc.," *EDNT* 3:333.

42   On the first Christian witnesses and the diverse forms that they could take, see Henri-Pierre de Lagneau, *Apostolat des premiers chrétiens* (Paris: Ouvriéres, 1957) 11–41, 91–117.

43   Cf. Acts 26:29: of hearing the faith; BAGD, s.v. ἀκούω, 4–5.

44   See Schulz, *Q*, 464–65; Dupont, "Transmission," 230 n. 115; Lagrange, 353: "Indeed, Christian preaching passed from the catacombs to the balcony of Saint Peter."

45   On κηρύσσω in Luke, see the commentary on 3:3 (1:120–21 n. 16). On the importance of testimony, one must reread the whole book of Acts and also the passages where the apostolic ambition of Paul is expressed (e.g., 1 Cor 9). There is a parallel sentence attributed to Hillel; see Plummer, 318.

eschatological proclamation at the time of the parousia. We are already also dealing with the public proclamation of the gospel. Luke is proud of the fact that the good news had left Palestine (Acts 26:26) and reached the whole world.

The terraced roofs[46] were places where conversation took place and therefore, why not also proclamation (the listeners themselves being on the roof or down below in front of the house)? This verse is for the ear what the saying about the lamp was for the eye (11:33):[47] the gospel must be proclaimed at full strength, declared at full voice. Visible and audible: God, hidden and revealed in the verbs in the passive voice, is anxious for this enterprise to succeed, since he loves human beings. But he needs the cooperation of men and women, since the sending of the Son would amount to nothing without the apostolic proclamation; reconciliation, without the word of reconciliation (2 Cor 5:18-19); the gospel ("whatever," ὅσα),[48] without the apostle ("proclaim," κηρύσσω).[49] There is an inherent strength in the proclamation of the gospel that renders it invincible and ultimately triumphant.[50] And that is true in spite of the weakness of human beings trying to be faithful to it and to communicate it the best way they can.

One more point: the arcane discipline that was called for in ancient times[51] will come to the mind of whoever likes secrets and confidences: pearls were not to be thrown to pigs (Matt 7:6). If the disciples are called on here to beware of the contagious leaven of the Pharisees, it is because they must keep out of things. Likewise, their message must not be hackneyed: it is protected, and so it also takes its place in secret. There is therefore a time for confession, promise, confidence, and secret: the gospel is also that. There will be a time for publicity, affirmation, and proclamation.

■ **4-5** In this case it is Matthew who has preserved the text of Q better than Luke.[52] Luke is responsible for at least two of the three metalinguistic clauses that are absent from Matthew ("I tell you, my friends"; "I will show you whom to fear"; "yes, I tell you, that is the person to fear"). We may hesitate with respect to the first one, since "I tell you" could have been a literary structuring device as far back as Q, one that would recall the constant "Jesus said" introducing nearly every saying in the *Gospel of Thomas*.[53] Moreover, although Luke was fond of the word "friend," nowhere else did he ever place it on the lips of Jesus when he was addressing his disciples.[54] The second and third instances, however, which express one of the didactic concerns dear to Luke, are certainly redactional. At the semantic level, the first wording expresses the Lord's affection; the second, the Master's authority; the third, the Savior's solidarity. Moreover, Luke clearly avoided the expression "kill the soul," which occurs twice in Matthew, and preferred instead weighty

---

46 On τὸ δῶρα, cf. 5:19; 17:31; Acts 10:9; Loisy, 340; Rolf Knierim, "Dach," BHH 1:311.

47 Marshall, 512; cf. Matt 5:14-16: the evangelist refers to a village situated upon a height that could not be hidden, before citing the logion about the lamp, which he applies to Christians.

48 I understand ὅσα ("all that," "that which") as referring in content to the apostolic witness. Moreover, one can see here simply a mention of all that one can recount. In this case, it can be forgotten that the "you" of "you will have said" concerns the disciples; on this point, see Marshall, 512.

49 On this fundamental structure, see François Bovon, *L'Évangile et l'Apôtre: Le Christ inséparable de ses témoins* (Aubonne: Moulin, 1993) 7–32.

50 See Grundmann, 253; Dupont, "Transmission," 230.

51 The ancient liturgy contained a liturgy of the word accessible to each and a liturgy of the sacrament reserved for those baptized.

52 See Schulz, Q, 157–61. Lührmann (*Logienquelle*, 50 n. 5) thinks, on the contrary, that it is Matthew who

has condensed the text in order better to make the parallelism work out. I am preparing preliminary papers for an American group of the Society of Biblical Literature, directed by James M. Robinson: they indicate the opinions of modern exegetes, which are strongly divided. On the citations of these verses in *2 Clem.* 5.2–4 and Justin, *1 Apol.* 19.6–7, see Helmut Koester, *Synoptische Überlieferung bei den Apostolischen Vätern* (TU 65; Berlin: Akademie-Verlag, 1957) 94–99.

53 For the Lukan character of these first words of v. 4, see Grundmann, 253; Laufen, *Doppelüberlieferungen*, 161; for one origin in Q, see Schmid, *Matthäus und Lukas*, 274–75; on this formula, see Kloppenborg, *Formation*, 210 n. 164.

54 Luke utilizes the word φίλος eighteen times (fifteen times in the Gospel and three times in Acts). Matthew has it only once (Matt 11:19) and Mark never.

circumlocutions ("and after that can do nothing more" and "who, after he has killed, has authority to cast into Gehenna").[55]

The formal and cordial introduction brings Jesus close to his disciples in an almost Johannine key.[56] This affection inside the community is all the more important because of the threat from external aggression. Jesus, full of kindness and authority, does not abandon his disciples at the moment of the crucial decision. He issues them an audacious exhortation that is rooted in a double conviction: our life does not stop after this present life, and God is stronger than our death. In a time when torture was more prevalent than ever, if Christians, following their Master, were not to remember that saying, where might hope spring from? Luke's God, stronger than death, is also more dangerous than death. His love, which muzzles the Grim Reaper, is accompanied by his righteousness. Expressed in terms full of imagery that Luke, or the oral tradition on which he drew, borrowed from the Hebraic religious world, God can cast into Gehenna.[57] As a way to follow the path that does not lead either to physical death or to eternal death (the "sec-

ond death" of Rev 2:11; 20:6, 14; 21:8), the Lukan Jesus proposes a third way: the fear of the Lord, which, in the biblical sense, means respect, veneration, and confident submission.[58] The Christian catechism instructs us to keep that fear for God alone and to pay only honor or homage to human authorities (cf. 1 Pet 2:17). The disturbing affirmation in these verses implies the hope of a personal resurrection.

Luke avoided the expression "kill the soul,"[59] since he thought of $\psi\upsilon\chi\acute{\eta}$ not in the Semitic sense of "life" but in the Christian sense of "soul," that is, creaturely existence that goes beyond our corporeal life. By eliminating the expression, he also avoided being the object of ridicule on the part of his Greek readers, who, for the most part, would have given to the word $\psi\upsilon\chi\acute{\eta}$ the idea of immortality. Luke declared his belief that the same God who laughs at persecutors does not necessarily go easy on those who are persecuted either. One more reason to respect him and to make his will our own.[60]

Finally, we should point out that there are Jewish parallels to these two verses, in particular *4 Macc.* 13:14-15 and *1 Enoch* 101. The *NRSV* translates the first of those

---

55   It concerns God and not the devil (cf. Jas 4:7; 1 Pet 5:9). He is the one who has the power over death and over Gehenna (with Marshall, "Fear," 278; Godet, 2:129; Lagrange, 353; Plummer, 319) is uncertain.

56   Cf. John 15:14-15; note as here (Luke 12:4-5) the context of persecution (John 15:18-19). See Spicq, *Notes de lexicographie,* 2:936–43; K. Treu, "Freundschaft," *RAC* 8 (1972) cols. 418–34; Hans-Joseph Klauck, "Kirche als Freundesgemeinschaft? Auf Spurensuche im Neuen Testament," *MThZ* 42 (1991) 1–14.

57   This is the only usage of the word "Gehenna" in Luke: the word, present also in the Matthean parallel, certainly derives from Q. On Gehenna as the place of eternal pain, see Fitzmyer, 2:959–60; and O. Böcher, "$\gamma\acute{\epsilon}\epsilon\nu\nu\alpha$," *TDNT* 1 (1964) 657–58; even though the word $\gamma\acute{\epsilon}\epsilon\nu\nu\alpha$ is again absent from the LXX, he points to 2 Kgs (4 Kgdms) 16:3; 21:6; 23:10; Jer 7:31-32; 19:6; Isa 31:9; 66:24; *1 En.* 10:13; 18:11-16; 27:1-4; 54:1-6; *2 Bar.* 59:10; 85:13; *4 Esdr.* 7:36; *Jub.* 9:15; 1QH 3.28–36. Moulton ("Luke, 12:5") believes that the text does not say that God himself kills: the words $\mu\epsilon\tau\grave{\alpha}$ $\tau\grave{o}$ $\mathring{\alpha}\pi o\kappa\tau\epsilon\widehat{\iota}\nu\alpha\iota$ (literally, "after killing him") do not necessarily have God as the implicit subject. They can refer to the putting to death by the men of v. 4, which seems to

me difficult to accept on grammatical grounds. In my opinion, the NT never says that God kills, and the link with v. 4 imposes a human subject.

58   Four times Luke utilizes the aorist of $\varphi o\beta o\widehat{\upsilon}\mu\alpha\iota$ in vv. 4–5: twice in the subjunctive and twice in the imperative, insisting thus upon the punctual aspect of the verb, where Matthew has the present imperative, which is durative and iterative. Matthew must follow Q (cf. Luke, who utilizes also the imperative present in v. 7). On the fear of God, see Horst Balz and Günther Wanke, "$\varphi o\beta\acute{\epsilon}\omega$ $\kappa\tau\lambda$.," *TDNT* 9 (1974) 197–205; A. Dihle, J. H. Waszink, and W. Mundle, "Furcht (Gottes)," *RAC* 8 (1972) cols. 661–99; K. Romaniuk, "La crainte de Dieu à Qumrân et dans le Nouveau Testament," *RevQ* 4 (1963) 29–38; Horst Balz, "$\varphi o\beta\acute{\epsilon}o\mu\alpha\iota$" and "$\varphi\acute{o}\beta o\varsigma$," *EDNT* 3:429–34; Louis Derousseaux, *La crainte de Dieu dans l'Ancien Testament* (LD 63; Paris: Cerf, 1970); Marshall, "Fear"; Schulz, *Q,* 160 n. 170.

59   All the commentaries and all the studies about Q ask about this subject, e.g., Marshall, 513; Schulz, *Q,* 158. Note the usage of $\mathring{\alpha}\pi o\kappa\tau\epsilon\acute{\iota}\nu\omega$ in Luke and $\mathring{\alpha}\pi o\kappa\tau\acute{\epsilon}\nu\nu\omega$ in Matthew (the two forms have the same sense).

60   On these verses, see Köhler ("Zu Lc 12, 4-5"), who thinks that the words "after that, there is nothing more" had their origin in a gloss of a copyist, who

texts thus: "Let us not fear him who thinks he is killing us, for great is the struggle of the soul and the danger of eternal torment lying before those who transgress the commandment of God."[61] I would not personally set an apocalyptic interpretation over against a sapiential reading of this passage. Wisdom provides some examples, and the time was decisive for both the bearers of the Q tradition and Luke himself.[62]

■ **6-7** This small unit contains a double saying (a rhetorical question followed by an affirmation of faith), a second example (condensing into a single clause what the preceding saying fragmented) and an invitation justified by a sapiential comparison. As the end refers to the initial example, that is, to the sparrows, we may conclude that the second example, the one about hair, was added here in a way that is at the same time both eloquent and awkward.[63]

Among the differences between Matthew and Luke, let me point out the number and the price of the sparrows (Matthew has two sparrows for one assarion, whereas Luke has five sparrows for two assaria!—the assarion was a small unit of currency); and Matthew's more concrete style ("not one of them will fall to the ground apart from your Father") compared with Luke's more abstract style ("not one of them is forgotten in God's sight").[64] To reconstruct Q, we should trust Luke's figures and follow Matthew's wording (with hesitation concerning the word "Father," which is so Matthean).

The first example presupposes a trade in birds such as is still carried on in Italy.[65] The $\sigma\tau\rho\upsilon\vartheta\iota\upsilon$ is the "sparrow" and the $\dot{\alpha}\sigma\sigma\dot{\alpha}\rho\iota\upsilon$, the assarion, a Roman bronze coin (the denarius, which represented roughly a day's wages, was divided into sixteen assaria: the assarion, in turn, was divided into four quadrantes).[66] The idea is that many sparrows could be bought with not too much money. Although the sparrow is cheap, "you," by contrast, are worth a great[67] deal.

Well—and this is a certitude of the Jewish faith that the author shares with his reader—God, whose greatness and power are boasted about, does not overlook[68] the sparrow, which is infinitely small in his eyes. The consequence of this argument *a minori ad maius* is that, since you are worth much more, you have nothing to fear: God does not forget you, especially during times of persecution. It is better to say it because, since Golgotha, there could have been doubts about it.

was surprised to find nothing more in the Gospel of Luke that resembled the text of Matthew. See also Marshall, "Fear"; Kloppenborg, *Formation*, 208–10.

61 For the rabbinic texts, see Str-B 4.2:1029–43; and Manson, *Sayings*, 107.

62 Schulz (*Q*, 160) insists on prophetism, and Kloppenborg (*Formation*, 209–11) on wisdom.

63 Bultmann (*History*, 94) thinks that Matt 10:31 par. Luke 12:7b is secondary; Schulz (*Q*, 160), on the contrary, is not convinced that Matt 10:30-31 par. Luke 12:7 can be an addition.

64 A more detailed comparison is in Schulz, *Q*, 158–59.

65 On the birds according to the witnesses in antiquity, see Friedrich Simon Bodenheimer, *Animal and Man in Bible Lands* (Collection des travaux de l'Académie internationale d'histoire des sciences 10; Leiden: Brill Archive, 1960) 53–64. Note that the form $\tau\dot{o}$ $\sigma\tau\rho\upsilon\dot{\upsilon}\vartheta\iota\upsilon$ (with a different accent) designates a plant, the saponaria, or a fruit (quince?). Since the fruits, different from plants, can also fall to the ground, did the evangelist want to make allusion to fruits rather than to birds? That is unlikely, because there did not seem to be any uncertainty among the Byzantine scribes on the subject of the accentuation of this word.

66 See Xavier Léon-Dufour, ed., *Dictionary of Biblical Theology* (2d ed.; London: Chapman, 1973) s.v. *monnaies*; Marshall, 519.

67 The word $\pi\upsilon\lambda\lambda\tilde{\omega}\nu$ creates difficulty. One must attach it to $\sigma\tau\rho\upsilon\vartheta\iota\omega\nu$ ("sparrows"): "you are worth more than many sparrows." But why "numerous," "a good many of them"? Two minuscule manuscripts (239 and 241) have $\pi\upsilon\lambda\lambda\tilde{\omega}$ ("much") as adverbial, which is conducive to the translation "you differ much from sparrows." This reading is supported by the manuscript of the Old Latin (Codex Vercellensis, fourth century). The parallel in 12:24 should not be forgotten.

68 Among the anthropomorphisms, the Bible refers to sleep and forgetting: God does not sleep and he does not forget ($\dot{\epsilon}\pi\iota\lambda\alpha\nu\vartheta\dot{\alpha}\nu\omega\mu\alpha\iota$); cf. Pss 9:13; 73 (74):19, 23; Heb 6:10; cf. BAGD, s.v. Fitzmyer (2:960) refers to Isa 49:15 for a comparison similar also to Acts 10:31. It is possible that Matthew may be more aware here of the omnipotence of God and Luke of God's omniscience; see Grundmann, 254.

The well-known example of hair (cf. Luke 21:18; Acts 27:34)[69] confirms God's omniscience and providence.[70] To pick up on Frédéric Godet's words, God is attentive to all the details of life, and if a Christian dies, it is with God's assent, so—in the end—it is for his or her good.[71]

■ **8-9** The speech, which moves along to the rhythms of the rhetorical introductions and the situations addressed, offers encouragement to the disciples frightened by the consequences of their commitment. Verses 8-9 are part of that logic of commitment.[72]

Here in vv. 8-9 we have two parallel sayings that contrast two situations like the two ways in Deut 30:15-20. The active way of confession leads to approval. The way of denial, which is no less a matter of decision, leads to the "I do not know where you come from" (13:25). Luke never stops coming back to this existential dualism. He has already spoken of it using the images of the two trees (6:43-44), of two human beings (6:45), and of two houses (6:47-49). He will bring it up again in the parables of the good and evil servants (12:36-40 and 13:23-28). The Lukan Christ does not use these teachings to lay out a varied choice of attitudes and options. He only proposes one way, whose worth he shows by affirmation (v. 8) and contrast (v. 9).

Some slight lameness has crept into the symmetry of the two sayings (vv. 8 and 9): the "everyone" ($\pi\hat{\alpha}\varsigma$) of the confession has no equivalent in the denial. Luke counted on the confession being the rule, and the denial, the exception. Moreover, although the Son of Man himself ($\kappa\alpha\grave{\iota}\ \acute{o}\ \upsilon\acute{\iota}\grave{o}\varsigma\ \tau o\hat{\upsilon}\ \dot{\alpha}\nu\theta\rho\acute{\omega}\pi o\upsilon$) comes forward to defend the cause of the believer, he is not mentioned in connection with the condemnation: the passive "will be denied" ($\dot{\alpha}\pi\alpha\rho\nu\eta\vartheta\acute{\eta}\sigma\varepsilon\tau\alpha\iota$) suggests either a self-denial or a rejection by God (the so-called divine passive).

These two verses, particularly v. 8, have probably been the ones most studied of all passages in the New Testament in the past few years,[73] since they have been involved in three interrelated debates: the questions of Q, the Son of Man, and—last but not least—Jesus' self-consciousness. In all three cases, what has been examined from all angles has been the saying at the level of tradition. There have been few studies highlighting Luke's perspective.

The saying about denial circulated in the tradition first attested in Mark (Mark 8:38 par. Luke 9:26) and the double tradition (here in Luke 12:9 par. Matt 10:33).[74] In three of four cases in these texts (all but Luke 12:9) there is mention of the Son of Man (or "I") in connection with the settlement of accounts. We are obliged to conclude that it was Luke who preferred the passive "will be denied" ($\dot{\alpha}\pi\alpha\rho\nu\eta\vartheta\acute{\eta}\sigma\varepsilon\tau\alpha\iota$). The tradition first attested in Mark speaks of "shame" ($\dot{\varepsilon}\pi\alpha\iota\sigma\chi\acute{\upsilon}\nu o\mu\alpha\iota$); the double tradition, of denial ($\dot{\alpha}\rho\nu o\hat{\upsilon}\mu\alpha\iota,\ \dot{\alpha}\pi\alpha\rho\nu o\hat{\upsilon}\mu\alpha\iota$), which balances better with "confession" ($\dot{o}\mu o\lambda o\gamma\acute{\varepsilon}\omega$) and must be original. The presence of "my words" alongside "me" in the tradition first attested in Mark is secondary by comparison with the simple "me" in the double tradition.

Curiously enough, the triple tradition is unacquainted with the saying about confession. Since Q transmits the oldest version of the saying about denial, it is likely that it has also rescued the saying about confession from the oblivion into which Mark had sunk it.

As for me, I think that the opening "I tell you" (v. 8), which Matthew omitted, comes from tradition; I also suppose that Q read $\dot{o}\varsigma\ \dot{\alpha}\nu$ followed by the subjunctive twice (cf. Luke's v. 8 and Matt 10:33); that it also read "before the angels of God" twice (Matthew has "before my Father in heaven" both times); and the Son of Man twice (cf. Luke v. 8 for the first saying and Mark 8:38 par. Luke 9:26 for the second one). So it was Luke who consciously modified "the Son of Man will deny him"

69 Fitzmyer (2:960) refers to 1 Sam (1 Kgdms) 14:45; 2 Sam (2 Kgdms) 14:11; 1 Kgs (3 Kgdms) 1:52.

70 The expression "before God" is a frequent Hebraism in Luke; see Godet, 2:130; Plummer, 320.

71 Godet, 2:130–31.

72 Comprehensive studies of the redactional aspects are found in Bertrand, "Hypocrites"; Sweetland, *Discipleship*.

73 In addition to the bibliography given at the head of this section, see, on the parallel in 9:26, the commentary on 9:23-27 (1:363–68). See also Fitzmyer, 1:79 and 2:958, 961; Wiefel, 231; van Segbroeck, bibliography, 233 (which refers to eleven titles).

74 On the Q form of vv. 8-9, see Schulz, *Q*, 66–76; Polag, *Christologie*, 98–99, 102–17, 133–34; Kloppenborg, *Formation*, 211; Fleddermann, "Confessing."

into "will be denied" (preferring ἀπαρνέομαι, which stresses the act of reaction, to ἀρνέομαι, which might suggest an initiative). Finally, it was Luke who alternated between one Greek word for "before" (ἔμπροσθεν, twice in v. 8) and another, literally "in the sight of" (ἐνώπιον, twice in v. 9). Matthew, on the other hand, reproduced Q's monotonous ἔμπροσθεν four times.

For Luke, the transition from "I" to "the Son of Man"[75] did not imply a change of person, but rather one of period and status. It was the transition from the passion to the elevation. The same was true for the tradition, which doubtless lent an accent of imminence to this final trial, for which the angels constituted the court. As for the historical Jesus,[76] he distinguished himself from the Son of Man, whom he perhaps thought of in an apocalyptic perspective, like the presence of God himself. So I refuse to see in this figure a sacramental or angelic corporate personality. In opposition to many scholars, I accept the authenticity of the original saying and the initial distinction of the persons.

The fact that the second half of v. 8b refers to the last judgment has too often prompted the suggestion that the confession was limited to a judicial questioning. An examination of the verb ὁμολογέω ("to confess") in the LXX leads to another conclusion.[77] This verb presupposes in the first instance a strong attachment, a relationship of obedience and faithfulness (thus Job 40:9; 1 Esdr LXX 4:60; 9:8). Moreover, it implies an inner availability and a willingness to affirm one's allegiance to the God of the ancestors in all circumstances and not just in the narrow (unfortunately likely but not exclusive) framework of a persecution and a penal proceeding.[78] This witnessing can then be given in the presence of listeners who are either neutral, favorable, or hostile. The word is used in the New Testament in the same way: Luke 10:21 par. Matt 11:25 uses ἐξομολογέομαι to refer to thanksgiving in response to a revelation; Acts 23:8 says that the Pharisees "confess" (ὁμολογοῦσιν), that is, acknowledge with faith, that there is a resurrection and that there are angels, doing so naturally at all times and not just during a trial. John (1:20; 9:22) and Paul (Rom 10:9-10) use the word in the same way: they tie the verbal confession more closely to the inner conviction and the latter to its object, without speculating as to the exterior occasions of its expression. The Greek words for "before" (ἔμπροσθεν) and "in the sight of" (ἐνώπιον) must not be limited to the context of a trial in court.[79] When Peter denied his Master (ἀρνέομαι; Luke 22:57), he was in public but not involved in a trial. When Paul associated confession with salvation, he was thinking of all of life and not just of the moment of persecution (Rom 10:9-10). There are nevertheless times when one must choose sides and publicly declare one's conviction. These critical moments are determining ones: they categorize a person.

In v. 8 the Greek preposition ἐν ("in") is used twice after the verb ὁμολογέω ("to acknowledge"), once before the pronoun translated "me" (ἐν ἐμοί), and once before the one translated "him" (ἐν αὐτῷ), while the following verse (v. 9) uses the Greek verb for "to deny" (ἀρνήεομαι) without a preposition before the pronoun "me" (με). The use of the verb ἀρνέομαι in v. 9 with a direct object (without a preceding preposition) is normal in Greek; the use of the verb ὁμολογέω in v. 8 with the preposition ἐν ("in") is curious, even incorrect. A Semitic influence has been suggested.[80] One could also speak of the Christian faith, which, like the Jewish faith,

75   On the Son of Man here, see Tödt, *Son of Man*; Vielhauer, "Gottesreich"; idem, "Jesus und der Menschensohn"; Carsten Colpe, "υἱὸς τοῦ ἀνθρώπου," *TDNT* 8 (1972) 400–477; Higgins, "Menschensohn"; Kümmel, "Verhalten"; Casey, "Son of Man"; Schneider, "Menschensohn"; McDermott, "Stone"; Catchpole, "Angelic Son of Man."

76   On the authenticity of the two logia, see McDermott, "Stone"; Pesch, "Autorität."

77   See Catchpole, "Angelic Son of Man," 257–58. On ὁμολογέω, see Otto Michel, "ὁμολογέω κτλ.," *TDNT* 5 (1967) 199–220; Spicq, *Notes de lexicographie*, 2:621–22; Otfried Hofius, "ὁμολογέω etc.," *EDNT* 2:514–17.

78   Cf. 2 Macc 6:6: "It was not permitted to celebrate the sabbath nor to observe the feasts of their fathers, nor simply to confess (ὁμολογεῖν) that one was Jewish."

79   With Catchpole, "Angelic Son of Man," 259.

80   See Plummer, 320; Lagrange, 355; Fitzmyer, 2:960; BDF §220.3; O. Hofius, "ὁμολογέω," 514–17 (n. 77 above).

is trust put "in" someone, leaning "on" someone for support.[81]

The pair "acknowledge"–"deny," made up of opposites, is logical and traditional. The Fourth Gospel uses the two verbs side by side (see John 1:20). So an ethical dualism, which was omnipresent at that time, as well as a Jewish identity, which has often been contested, favored this use.

Early Christianity encountered the tragic element in its conflict with Judaism, its closest relative: they shared a common membership in the chosen people; faith in the God of the ancestors as Creator and Savior; the common requirement of commitment and confession of one's faith; the same organization of trust and obedience; and a single faith threatened by the society of antiquity. But they differed fundamentally concerning the role attributed to Jesus, who for some was a false prophet and a magician but for others was the supreme revealer of God, Master and prophet, Messiah and Lord, Son of God and Son of Man. The cohabitation of the Son with the Father in Christian faith modified the Jewish faith to such a point that the only possible result could be rejection and persecution. From Jesus to Luke, Christians were on the side of the weak and the persecuted. The church, alas, was to take its revenge.

The two sayings, which are phrases of sacred, prophetic, and eschatological law,[82] speak less of Jesus or the Son of Man than of believers' decisive responsibility. Everything plays out here and now. Neutrality is forbidden. But it will also be absent at the time of judgment: at that moment—such is the soteriological thrust of the two sayings—active adherence to Jesus will be decisive for obtaining salvation. We must in this matter compare Jesus' promise to the disciples who persevere with him in his trials (22:28-32) with the attitude of the same disciples during his passion (22:21-23, 33-34, 54-62; 23:49).

■ **10** It is evident that this saying circulated in two forms: in the tradition first attested in Mark (see Mark 3:28-29) and in the double tradition (here, Luke 12:10).[83] Matthew, the collector, juxtaposed the two recensions (Matt 12:31-32). There are numerous structural differences: with an introduction (Mark) or without one (Q); what will be forgiven is sins and blasphemies (Mark) or a spoken word (Q); forgiveness will be simply refused (Q) or refused "forever" (Mark). But there is one fundamental difference: on the one hand, forgiveness will be granted "to human beings" for every sin or blasphemy (Mark); on the other, with the preposition "against," every "word against the Son of Man" will be forgiven (Q). The difference must be explained on the basis of divergent translations of an ambiguous Aramaic original. Julius Wellhausen's hypothesis will be recalled here as applicable: the expression "son of man" in Aramaic can mean "man" in the generic sense, like our "one," that is, also "me," or "Son of Man."[84] Since both of the versions mention only one guilty person in their second half, the plural "to human beings" in the first half is suspect. It must correspond to a tendentious translation (a phenomenon also found in Matt 9:8). To my way of thinking, the oldest wording of the saying already mentioned the Son of Man, and it distinguished him from the Holy Spirit. If Jesus himself was the one who uttered this saying, he must not have taken the words "Son of Man" in the glorious sense of the term but rather in the personal sense of "me." It follows that the two different translations were interpretations that appealed to this text. By virtue of its conciseness and symmetry, Q's wording must be closer to the original than Mark's. Luke, in turn, must be closer to Q than is Matthew: Matthew's ὃς ἐάν or ὃς ἄν followed by the subjunctive would appear to be secondary by comparison with Luke's indicative (but the πᾶς in Luke's πᾶς ὅς ["whoever"] is redactional). Moreover, Matthew's chronological indication ("either in this age or in the age to come"), which is absent from Luke, was inspired by Mark ("never"). It was obviously added to Q's version.

We know of two other wordings of this saying that are not necessarily based on our written Gospels. At the same time that they confirm an original short version, they are also witnesses to the liveliness of oral transmission in the second century and the partisan application of the sayings to diverse existential and ecclesial circumstances. The *Didache* uses the saying in order to impose

---

81   See Godet, 2:131.

82   See Ernst Käsemann, "Sätze heiligen Rechtes im Neuen Testament," in idem, *Exegetische Versuche*, 2:69–82; Kloppenborg, *Formation*, 211 n. 167.

83   On the genesis of this sentence, see Schulz, *Q*, 250–55; Kloppenborg, *Formation*, 211–14.

84   See Wellhausen, *Einleitung*, 75–76; this position is discussed by Tödt, *Son of Man*, Excursus 4, 312–18.

Christian prophetism: "Do not test or examine any prophet who is speaking in a spirit, 'for every sin shall be forgiven, but this sin shall not be forgiven'" (11.7).[85] The *Gospel of Thomas*, for its part, enlarges on the saying in a trinitarian way and, in the place of a temporal marker, uses a double locative marker: "Jesus said, 'Whoever blasphemes against the Father will be forgiven, and whoever blasphemes against the Son will be forgiven, but whoever blasphemes against the Holy Spirit will not be forgiven either on earth or in heaven'" (44).[86] If we eliminate these developments, we discover a basic form of the saying that could be older than Mark and Q, and that confirms our analysis of how it developed.

On Jesus' lips,[87] the saying tolerated someone's making a mistake as to Jesus' identity, but condemned any error with respect to God's plan. In the post-paschal period, for those who carried on the tradition, the saying absolved those who were mistaken as to the identity of the earthly Jesus but did not tolerate any failure with respect to the gospel message, which was inspired by the Holy Spirit. By virtue of its double structure, the saying thus corresponded to the apostolic witness: the "ignorance" (ἄγνοια) of the Jews (Acts 3:17), which had led to Jesus' death, was forgivable; but once Christians had committed themselves to following the way of conversion, faith, and inspiration, they could no longer allow themselves any relapse. Any questioning, at that time, of God's salvific plan could result only in condemnation. Is it possible to forgive someone who refuses to be forgiven? The Acts of the Apostles, in a narrative fashion, witnesses to the final offer of salvation and the gift of the Holy Spirit to those who spoke "against the Son of Man." That is how it sees the saying, and this is confirmed in a theological mode by the apostle Paul and the author of the Epistle to the Hebrews.[88] Such a severe attitude could not be maintained throughout the history of the church. Moreover, it has been oriented more toward ethics than toward theology. It has been perhaps more theatrical than juridical. The apostle Paul himself hoped for a new birth for the guilty Galatians (Gal 4:19) and, in Revelation, John called sinful Christians to conversion (Rev 2:5).

This interpretation of the saying becomes even more evident if a pattern of the Hebrew Bible, visible in Moses' ministry, is recalled.[89] God offered his salvation to a generation that refused it, became stubborn, and condemned itself for good by asking for other signs or dodging those that were offered to it. What is allowed is being mistaken about God's envoy; what is not is turning down God's gift. If we take our cue from this outline, we will attribute to the Holy Spirit a dynamic and soteriological element: it is an equivalent of God's hand (of "God's finger" [Luke 11:20], identified, moreover, with God's Spirit in the parallel in Matt 12:28). Blaspheming against the Holy Spirit means resisting God's Spirit, that is, the active will of the God who saves: Deut 18:14-20 announces this type of act of God and the kind of prophet, like Moses, whom he invests with this mission. Alas, as Acts tells it: "You stiff-necked people, uncircumcised in heart and ears, you are forever opposing the Holy Spirit, just as your ancestors used to do. Which of the prophets did your ancestors not persecute?" (Acts 7:51-52a). In the language of the Psalms: "They angered the LORD at the waters of Meribah, and it went ill with Moses on their account; for they made his spirit[90] bitter . . ." (Ps 106 [105]:32-33a).

---

85. The *Second Letter of Clement* cites two sentences connected to ours: *2 Clem.* 13.2: "For the Lord saith, My name is continually blasphemed among all the Gentiles"; and again, "Wherefore is my name blasphemed, whereby is it blasphemed? in that ye do not the things that I will" (trans. C. H. Hoole, in *The Apostolic Fathers* (2d. ed.; London: Rivingtons, 1885).

86   See Schrage (*Thomas-Evangelium*, 98–100), who refers to the *Apocryphon of John* (NHC II,*1*, 27, 21–31; III,*1*, 36, 4–15; Codex Berlin 8502, 70.8–71.2) and doubts that the logion of the *Gospel of Thomas* reflects here anything other than the sentence of Matthew and Luke. The resumption of the Synoptic saying by the author of the *Apocryphon of John* merits attention. See Rodolphe Kasser, "Le livre secret de Jean," *RThPh* 3 series 17 (1967) 21–22; Michel Tardieu, *Écrits gnostiques: Codex de Berlin* (Sources gnostiques et manichéennes 1; Paris: Cerf, 1984) 155, 334.

87   Williams, "Note": Jesus attacked those who refused to see in him the Holy Spirit at work.

88   Cf. Acts 2:22-41; 3:13-26; Rom 8:1-17; Heb 6:4-6; 1 John 5:16-18.

89   See Lövestam, *Blasphemia*.

90   It could be a matter of the spirit of Moses. In the LXX, of which the text is a little bit different but the idea similar, there is the same ambiguity. There it concerns vv. 32-33.

If, at first, it was the Jews who had their reservations about the gospel and who were the target of this attack,[91] the front lines changed over a period of time. The text was later applied to certain Christians: in the first instance to apostates, in the second to heretics. On the basis of patristic exegesis, a distinction can be made between a Gentile or Jewish existence previous to baptism, which is exonerated, and Christian living when it results in the rejection of what constitutes the center of the faith and the essence of salvation. The latter attitude, called sin against the Holy Spirit, received at the moment of baptism, is not forgivable.[92]

The *Didache*'s appropriation of the saying marks still another usage, the one of Christian prophets,[93] who, on the defensive, had to deal with legalistic fellow Christians or ministers bent on clerical domination.

Luke, on the other hand,[94] received this saying linked by the term "Son of Man" to the twin clauses about confession. At first blush, this proximity would appear to be enigmatic, since v. 9 makes a denial of the Son of Man unforgivable, whereas v. 10 offers forgiveness to the person who offends this same Son of Man. It is only an apparent contradiction.[95] Attentive readers will note that the two syntagms of v. 10 correspond to the two sayings of vv. 8 and 9. Luke even took care to bring out the correspondence: vv. 8 and 10a begin with a euphoric general expression ("everyone," $\pi\hat{\alpha}\varsigma$ $\delta\varsigma$), while vv. 9 and 10b begin with a dysphoric particular indication ("whoever"). These similarities provide food for thought: we have, on the one hand, the Christian faith that is confessed, which does not rule out inevitable but forgivable

sins; on the other, the unforgivable rejection of the Son of Man who represents God's plan made tangible by the Word and the Holy Spirit. Luke calls the sins that are forgivable "word," "speech" ($\lambda\acute{o}\gamma o\varsigma$);[96] the unforgivable attitude, "blasphemy";[97] blasphemy is, in fact, an attack not only on God's holiness, but above all on his salvific activity. As one British commentator has put it somewhat trivially: "Grace, like bodily food, may be rejected until the power to receive it perishes."[98] In more theological language: no one who rejects salvation can live.

■ **11-12** While the title "Son of Man" served as a phrase linking vv. 8-9 and v. 10, it is the mention of the "Holy Spirit" that fills the same function between v. 10 and vv. 11-12. All the sayings are uttered against a background of persecutions. The one in v. 10 has in mind a blasphemous denial; the ones in vv. 11-12, the preceding moment of interrogation. The one is disturbing; the other, comforting. This latter saying (vv. 11-12) links up with vv. 4-7; the "do not worry" ($\mu\grave{\eta}$ $\mu\epsilon\rho\iota\mu\nu\acute{\eta}\sigma\eta\tau\epsilon$) of v. 11 corresponds to the "do not fear" ($\mu\grave{\eta}$ $\varphi o\beta\eta\vartheta\hat{\eta}\tau\epsilon$) of v. 4. The question has been raised as to whether vv. 8-9 and 10, which are more threatening, have been inserted secondarily into an earlier sequence that included vv. 2, 3, 4-5, 6-7, and 11-12, where the language is more encouraging.[99] All that must have taken place during the progressive formation of Q, since the whole of vv. 2-12 constitutes a unit at the level of Q. The mention of worries must have linked this sequence in Q to the following one, 12:22-32, dominated in fact by the theme of worries.

The Jesus of the four Gospels promises the support of the Holy Spirit. The Fourth Gospel contains the famous

---

91   See Fridrichsen, "Péché"; Günther Bornkamm, "Enderwartung und Kirche im Matthäusevangelium," in W. D. Davies and D. Daube, eds., *Studies in Honour of C. H. Dodd* (Cambridge: Cambridge University Press, 1954) 222–60, who argues that Q has separated the time of Jesus from the postpaschal time of the Holy Spirit; Wrege, *Bergpredigt*, 156–80 (the logion is addressed to disciples who have failed before Easter).

92   Barrett, *Holy Spirit,* 103–7; Lagrange, 355–56; Marshall, 517–19.

93   See Boring, "Unforgivable": Luke 12:10 is an oracle pronounced by a Christian prophet; Scroggs, "Exaltation": the sentence gives rise to an enthusiastic current, near to that which Paul attacks in 1 Cor 12:3.

94   See Sweetland, *Discipleship*, 72–74; Congar, "Blasphème."

95   The diverse solutions are summarized by Kloppenborg, *Formation*, 212–13.

96   See Godet, 2:132–33.

97   On the Lukan usage of the verb $\beta\lambda\alpha\sigma\varphi\eta\mu\acute{\epsilon}\omega$, partly meaning "to offend," partly meaning "to blaspheme (God)," cf. Luke 20:65; 23:39; Acts 13:45; 18:6; 15:30; 26:1. See also $\beta\lambda\alpha\sigma\varphi\eta\mu\acute{\iota}\alpha$ in Luke 5:21 (the only occurrence in Luke); and $\beta\lambda\acute{\alpha}\sigma\varphi\eta\mu o\varsigma$ in Acts 6:11 (the only usage in Luke).

98   Plummer, 321; Godet (2:132) judges that the episode of Beelzebul illustrates what could be the sin against the Holy Spirit. Loisy (342–43) refers to the incredulity which knows what must not be forgiven.

99   See Kloppenborg, *Formation*, 214–16.

sections on the Paraclete, to say nothing of the Johannine Pentecost. John 14:26 is often quoted as a parallel to this passage in Luke: "But the Paraclete [*NRSV*: Advocate], the Holy Spirit, whom the Father will send in my name, will teach you [διδάξει, as in Luke 12:12] everything, and will remind you of all that I have said to you." The Johannine passage appears against a backdrop of the absence of the Son more than of persecutions, and in that it is closer to the promises of the risen Christ in Luke 24:49 and Acts 1:4-5 than to the present passage in Luke.[100]

The help of the Spirit during a trial is guaranteed in the double tradition, in the triple tradition, and perhaps in L. Luke does not avoid the doublet. Here he is following Q; and in 21:14-15, Mark, or perhaps L. Matt 10:17-20 follows Mark in the main: Mark 13:9 is found also in Matt 10:17-18, and Mark 13:11 in Matt 10:19-20.[101] Matthew seems not to have used Q's version, aside from one or two details.

In 12:11-12, however, Luke follows Q.[102] He begins with an enumeration of the threatening authorities. Even if this list recalls Mark 13:9 par. Luke 21:12 par. Matt 10:17-18, it must come from Q, but with a few stylistic ameliorations that, in the absence of a Matthean parallel, can only be conjectured. The verbal expression "to defend oneself" (ἀπολογέομαι), wisely chosen, must be explained in terms of a Lukan intervention, since it is also found redactionally in 21:14. "Bring (before)" (εἰσφέρω), "do not worry" (μὴ μεριμνήσητε), and "what you are to say" (τί εἴπητε) are expressions from Q. In v. 12, "the Holy Spirit" comes from Q (Luke 21:15

has "I" as the advocate in the place of the Spirit), as well as the verb "teach" and the mention of the hour. On the other hand, "what you ought to say" (ἃ δεῖ εἰπεῖν) has a Lukan ring to it.[103]

Structurally, the saying subdivides into three parts. First, a temporal subordinate clause indicates the objective possibility of legal proceedings. Then the main clause issues an invitation, in the imperative mood, to not in that case fall into the subjective attitude of worrying. Finally, this exhortation is provided with a justification (cf. the "for," γάρ) in an affirmation that is at the same time a promise (cf. the future "will teach you," διδάξει). The persons to whom the saying is addressed are designated by the same "you" as in the entire sequence (12:2-12), that is, Jesus' disciples.[104]

The situation pictured here can happen, even be repeated (v. 11a; "when," ὅταν, usually followed by the subjunctive has this double shade of meaning of possibility and iteration).[105] It is still a Jewish context: Christians are being pursued by Jewish authorities (cf. the word "synagogue"). That matches the situation of Christianity between the years 40 and 100.[106] The mention of synagogues alerts us to the fact that the threat is local and not just centered in Jerusalem. So the Christians' fate depends on synagogal authorities under the influence, at that time, of the Pharisees. We know that, following the defeat of 70 and the fall of the temple, Judaism was reorganized around synagogues and aspired to a greater disciplinary cohesion. The twelfth of the Eighteen Benedictions, an old Jewish prayer, asks for the extermination of the Nazareans and of the mysterious *minim*.

---

100 On John 14:26, see George Johnston, *The Spirit-Paraclete in the Gospel of John* (SNTSMS 12; Cambridge: Cambridge University Press, 1970) passim.

101 Luz, *Matthew*, 2:85–86.

102 My analysis approaches that of Schulz (*Q*, 442–43) and rules out that of Sweetland (*Discipleship*, 74–76), who considers, wrongly, that Luke combines Q and Mark in v. 11 and that v. 12 is a Lukan adaptation of Mark 13:11.

103 My text of Q approaches that established by Sato, *Q und Prophetie*, 212.

104 One finds such a structure in the phrase; cf. Matt 6:2, 6, 16.

105 BDF §382.3. The iterative nuance is accentuated by the employment of the present subjunctive: εἰσφέρωσιν and not the aorist εἰσενέγκωσιν.

106 About the first religious complaints, administrative worries and penal pursuits, cf. 6:22-23; 21:12-19; Acts 4:1-22; 5:17-42; 6:8—8:4; 9:1-2; 12:1-3; 13:50-52; 14:2-6; 17:5-8, 13; 18:6, 12-17. For chap. 21 to the whole end of Acts, see Jean Zumstein, "L'apôtre comme martyr dans les Actes de Luc: Essai de lecture globale," *RThPh* 112 (1980) 371–90; for 1 Thess 2:14-16, see Traugott Holz, *Der erster Brief an die Thessalonicher* (Neukirchen-Vluyn: Neukirchener Verlag, 1986) 99–113; for 1 Pet 3:14-17; 4:12-19, see N. Brox, *Der erste Petrusbrief* (Zurich: Benziger, 1979) 155–63, 210–225; see also Jacques Moreau, *La persecution du Christianisme dans l'Empire Romain* (Paris: Presses universitaires de France, 1956).

This request was directed particularly at Christians and resulted in their excommunication from synagogue worship. These verses in Luke perhaps reflect a previous situation, although we do not know exactly what the power of Jewish authorities was, or what sentences they could impose.[107] The Talmudic tradition mentions three punishments: warning, minor banishment,[108] and major banishment. The term "synagogue" is, moreover, vague, and it is not certain that a true legal proceeding is involved. If it was, we may think in terms of local sanhedrins.[109] If it was not, we might picture some synagogue leaders summoning some Christians to interrogate them. These interrogations alone would have been enough to intimidate them greatly.

The list of authorities continues with the mention of "rulers" (ἀρχαί) and "authorities" (ἐξουσίαι).[110] These are vague expressions. Since Luke sometimes speaks of Jewish "leaders" (ἄρχοντες),[111] he must have understood the ἀρχαί to have been Jewish authorities. Since the text seems to follow the hierarchy in ascending order, we should probably think of the Sanhedrin of Jerusalem.[112] As for the "authorities," Luke may have seen in them the Roman power. To be sure, the Roman rulers[113] did not pursue Christians until the time of Pliny and Trajan. Nevertheless, when accusations were made and complaints lodged, they had to deal with them.[114] The book of Acts gives Luke's readers a chance to get a picture of what these dangers could be like.[115]

The second clause (v. 11b) is an invitation to leave an empty place in us, in other words not to worry but to turn our worries over to God (cf. 1 Pet 5:7); not to exaggerate the danger; not to be obsessed by secondary considerations; not to be carried away, as it were, by a tidal wave. This attitude, which will be set forth and explained in vv. 22-32, implies another way of looking at reality, and some soul-searching. It is accompanied by serenity, a sense of victory, and a feeling of inner well-being.[116]

The third clause (v. 12) is the positive pole corresponding to the negative pole that the second clause represents. The presence matches the empty place, knowledge, and ignorance. The text does not suggest that we do not have to reflect on the content of our faith or on how we will word our defense. It does promise emotional support and cognitive instruction. The Holy Spirit does not speak on his own[117] but teaches us to speak. We will say what we need to say, with the how (πῶς) and what (τί) automatically coming to us on their own "at the moment," "at that very hour" (ἐν αὐτῇ τῇ ὥρᾳ).[118]

This is one of those rare occasions when the Gospel of Luke speaks of the Holy Spirit and relates it not to Christ but to Christians (cf. 3:16; 11:13; 24:49). For Luke, the Spirit offered to believers represents the companionship of Christ during the time of the church.[119]

107 On the "synagogues" and the extent of the judicial power of their authorities, see 2 Cor 11:24; Stegemann, *Zwischen*, 91–112 (the judgment of this author differs from mine). According to Plummer (321), the synagogue, responsible for the discipline, pronounces the sentence of excommunication (Luke 6:22), which is executed by the ὑπηρέτης, the "guard." (Luke 4:20).

108 See G. Lindeskog, "Ausschliessung," *BHH* 1:168.

109 On the local sanhedrins, see Emil Schürer, *The History of the Jewish People in the Age of Jesus-Christ (175 B.C.–A.D. 135): A New English Version, Revised* (ed. Geza Vermes et al.; 4 vols.; Edinburgh: T&T Clark, 1973–87) 2:225–26.

110 The pair ἀρχή and ἐχουσία is found in the singular in 20:20 with respect to the governor; cf. 1 Cor 15:24; Eph 1:21; and Col 2:10; in the plural, as here, cf. Eph 3:10; Col 1:16; 2:15; and Titus 3:1. See Oscar Cullmann, *The State in the New Testament* (New York:

Scribner, 1956) 95–114; Ingo Broer, "ἐχουσία, etc.," *EDNT* 2:9–12.

111 Cf. Luke 8:41; 12:58; 14:1; 18:18; 23:13, 35; 24:30.

112 See Joachim Jeremias, *Jerusalem in the Time of Jesus: An Investigation into Economic and Social Conditions during the New Testament Period* (Philadelphia: Fortress Press, 1975) 252–57.

113 On the role of Roman power facing the first Christians, cf. Stegemann, *Zwischen*, 187–267.

114 Cf. Moreau, *La persecution*, 21–64 (n. 106 above).

115 Harry W. Tajra, *The Trial of St. Paul: A Juridical Exegesis of the Second Half of the Acts of the Apostles* (WUNT 2.35; Tübingen: Mohr Siebeck, 1989).

116 See Rudolf Bultmann, "μεριμνάω κτλ.," *TDNT* 4 (1967) 589–93; Dieter Zeller, "μεριμνάω, etc.," *EDNT* 2:408.

117 See Lagrange, 357.

118 Cf. Exod 4:12; John 14:26; 15:26; 2 Tim 4:17.

119 Bovon, *Theologian*, 225–72; Grundmann, 255: the

History of Interpretation

With some trepidation, Athanasius of Alexandria laid out the sense he gave to the disturbing sin against the Holy Spirit (Matt 12:31-32, par. Luke 12:10) (*Epistula ad Serapionem* 4.8–23).[120] By way of preparing an answer to the person who sought his advice on this subject, he reread Origen and Theognostus. These two Alexandrian teachers "both say that the blasphemy against the Holy Spirit takes place when those who have been honored by the gift of the Holy Spirit, in baptism, lapse into sin" (4.9).[121] Hebrews 6:4-6 served as the scriptural basis for their argument. Athanasius pointed out that, starting from this common basis, these two authors added some personal opinions. In quoting them, he thus preserved a passage from Theognostus, who, as he defended his position, refused to grant any superiority to the Spirit over the Son: "That is because the Son demonstrates condescension toward those who are imperfect, while the Spirit is the seal of the perfect" (4.11). Athanasius, on the other hand, looked for a more profound meaning, in fact, a different meaning. For him it was not the state of the sinner—whether not yet a Christian or already a Christian—that counted. The important thing was the content of the sin: what is unforgivable is the blasphemy that attacks the Son's divinity, called "Spirit" by Jesus, in contrast to his humanity, designated by the title "Son of Man." Attacking Christ the man as a man or Christ as God, while hesitating as to the nature of his body, is a serious matter, but it is forgivable. "But when, surpassing the ignorance and blindness of every one else, those who seem to know the Law—such as the Pharisees in that time—fall for folly and deny outright the existence of the Word in the body, or else when they go so far as to attribute the works of the divinity to the Devil and his demons, they justly receive punishment because of their unforgivable ungodliness (4.12). If I have correctly understood the argument, there is a sin against the Holy Spirit when Christ's divinity is denied, when God is confused with the devil, and when Jesus Christ's good deeds are attributed to Beelzebul. That is the sin of which the Pharisees of that time and Arians of our day have made themselves guilty. The unforgivable sin is, then, a denial of the Trinity and a refusal of its work of compassion.

Cyril, patriarch of Alexandria, brought together in one pericope the end of chap. 11 and the beginning of chap. 12 of Luke, uniting in that way in a single expression of disapproval the confiscation of knowledge and Pharisaic hypocrisy (*Serm. Luc.* 86).[122] These two faults are complementary, since one of them impedes understanding of the christological significance of the Law (11:52) and the other (12:1) silences Jesus (an allusion to the intervening verses, 11:53-54). Dividing up the text that way also prompted Cyril to identify the hidden truth (12:2-3) as that which the so-called spiritual guides maliciously steal (11:52) and mask with their hypocrisy (12:1).

As a responsible teacher of his flock, Cyril interpreted, in the two following sermons (*Serm. Luc.* 87–88),[123] true fear (vv. 4-7) and confession of faith (vv. 8-10). To his way of thinking, these verses are to be placed in a context of persecution, and a good comprehension of them requires clarifying them in the light of the Pauline epistles. In Rom 8:35, Christ, who is stronger than tribulations, gives meaning to "my friends" and to "those who kill the body" (v. 4). 1 Corinthians 1:20, which talks about the one who is wise and the one who is foolish, allows us to understand divine Providence (vv. 6-7). Philippians 1:21 ("For to me, living is Christ and dying is gain") and Rom 10:6-10 (the Word is in my heart) serve as commentary on v. 8. Finally, 2 Cor 3:17-18 (the Lord is the Spirit and transformation from one degree of glory to another), allows us to understand the Christ whom we must confess and the ultimate happiness of those who make that confession (v. 8). These overtones led Cyril to speak of the sin against the Holy Spirit: it consists not in

---

Holy Spirit is to preaching what the resurrection is to the passion.

120   *PG* 26:648–76. In fact, it undoubtedly concerns a text, of independent origin, of Athanasius which has been hooked to the fourth epistle of this author addressed to Serapion. See M. Geerard, ed., *Clavis Patrum Graecorum* (7 vols.; Leuven: Instituut voor Vroegchristelijke en Byzantijnse Studies 1974–2010) 2:2096.

121   Athanasius, *The Letters of Saint Athanasius Concerning the Holy Spirit* (trans. C. R. B. Shapland; New York: Philosophical Library, 1951).

122   See Payne-Smith, *Cyril*, 2:393–97.

123   See Ibid., 398–408. Cyril does not comment on vv. 11-12. There exist some Greek fragments of these homilies; see Reuss, *Lukas-Kommentare*, 133–38, frgs. 156–64.

uttering blasphemies against the Holy Spirit only, but in condemning the entire divine nature, Father, Son, and Spirit. By contrast, the forgivable sin against the Son of Man refers to a misunderstanding, also pagan, of the mystery of Jesus Christ. Concerning the sin against the Holy Spirit, here Cyril seems to have combined Athanasius's interpretation (negation of the divine nature of the Trinity) and that of Origen (denial by believers of the Holy Spirit that dwells in them).[124]

That is roughly the same interpretation that is found in the writings of Ambrose of Milan (*Exp. Luc.* 7.119–21). He pointed out, however, that to the danger of forgetting Christ's divine nature we must add the risk of forgetting his human nature. In the writings of the Venerable Bede what stands out is the ecclesial orientation: the one who sins against the Spirit is the one who denies Christ and refuses the repentance leading to the absolution offered by the church. Bede[125] invited his readers to refer to the writings of Augustine, where he had already found the interpretation he had in mind. He further pointed out that, understood in this way, the sin against the Holy Spirit does not concern the Jews (Augustine *Serm. Dom.* 22.75).[126]

Some Eastern commentaries reappeared in the West thanks to the *Catena aurea* of Thomas Aquinas (12.3), who made extensive use of Athanasius, who, as we have seen, had passed on the interpretations of Origen and Theognostus. It is possible for both catechumens and pagans to attack Christ. They will be forgiven if they reach the stage of baptism, which confers regeneration. On the other hand, if believers reject the Spirit they have received, they are not able to receive the forgiveness associated with baptism. The sin against the Holy Spirit is thus a risk for those who have attained perfection and not for beginners.

Bonaventure,[127] on the other hand, indicated in three points what constituted the sin against the Holy Spirit: (1) those persons who maliciously fight against the truth cannot be forgiven, not because they would not be promised forgiveness but because they are incapable of accepting it; (2) the offer of forgiveness could not be granted to those persons who fight against the grace by which human beings are prepared for penitence; (3) by receiving the Spirit—to be understood as being received at baptism—a believer has accepted the entire Trinity. Thus, whoever is opposed to the Spirit is the one who is in greatest contempt of the divine power, who is the greatest slanderer of truth, and who is the greatest persecutor of supreme goodness.[128]

Conclusion

The entire pericope deals with a Christian's word and its consequences: the word of truth opposed to the hypocritical word (v. 1); the word spoken in opposition to cowardly, deceitful, or mortal silence; the word that can be checked against reality (vv. 2-3); the word that proclaims the objective gospel, which witnesses to an unshakable subjective conviction (vv. 8-10), and which defends both of them (vv. 11-12); and the word that takes risks (vv. 4-7, 11-12).

The sequence reiterates Christ's unfailing friendship (v. 4), which is given to us by Christ's words ("I tell you," vv. 4, 8) and by his Spirit (v. 12).

Out of this dialogue, from word to word, in diverse circumstances that are sometimes determined by the decisive moment, new words must well up. What follows the kerygma (vv. 2-3) is the confession of faith (vv. 8-9), and what follows this pair is the defense (vv. 11-12).[129] While the keryma and the confession are focused on Christ and directed by him, the defense is more a matter for the Holy Spirit. If we do not forget the presence of the Father, God of providence (vv. 6-7), forgiveness (v. 10) and final judgment (vv. 8-9), we will notice the trinitarian unity of a passage that at first reading would appear to be illogical.

124 For Athanasius, see above n. 120; Origen *De Princ.* 1.3.7; cf. Luz, *Matthew,* 2:206–7.
125 *In. Luc.* 4.707–66.
126 *PL* 34:1267.
127 *Comm. in Luc.* 12.15–16, on Luke 12:10.

128 On the history of interpretation, especially among the Reformers, see Luz, *Matthew,* 2:206–9.
129 For ἀπολογέομαι, cf. 21:14; Acts 19:33; 24:10; 25:8; 26:1-2, 24; see Ulrich Kellermann, "ἀπολογέομαι etc.," *EDNT* 1:147.

The Fatal Forgetting in the Dialogue (12:13-21)

Bibliography

Ameling, W., "*ΦΑΓΩΜΕΝ ΚΑΙ ΠΙΝΩΜΕΝ*: Griechische Parallelen zu zwei Stellen aus dem Neuen Testament," *ZPE* 60 (1985) 35–43.

Baarda, Tjitze, "Lk 12,13-14: Text and Transmission from Marcion to Augustine," in Jacob Neusner, ed., *Christianity, Judaism and Other Greco-Roman Cults: Studies for Morton Smith at Sixty* (4 vols.; Studies in Judaism in Late Antiquity 12; Leiden: Brill, 1975) 1:107–62.

Bailey, Kenneth, *Through Peasant Eyes: More Lukan Parables, Their Culture and Style* (Grand Rapids: Eerdmans, 1980) 57–73.

Baur, Wilhelm, "Der 'Endverbraucher': Betrachtung zum Gleichnis vom reichen Kornbauern (Lk 12, 16-21)," in idem, *Von der Liebe: Ein Zeugnis für lebendiges Christenthum* (Frankfurt a. M.: Schriftenniederlage des Evang. Vereins, 1883) 70–74.

Beydon, France, *En danger de richesse: Le chrétien et les biens de ce monde selon Luc* (Aubonne: Moulin, 1989) 40–46.

Birdsall, J. N., "Luke 12:16ff. and the Gospel of Thomas," *JTS* 13 (1962) 332–36.

Bornhäuser, *Sondergut*, 81–93.

Ciordia, J. A., "'Maestro, di a mi hermano . . .' (Lc 12,13-21)," *Mayéutica* 10 (1984) 168–73.

Crossan, John Dominic, "Parable and Example in the Teaching of Jesus," *NTS* 18 (1971–72) 285–307, esp. 296–97.

Daube, David, "Inheritance in two Lukan Pericopes," *ZSRR* 72 (1955) 326–34.

Degenhardt, Hans Joachim, *Lukas, Evangelist der Armen: Besitz und Besitzverzicht in den lukanischen Schriften. Eine traditions- und redaktionsgeschichtliche Untersuchung* (Stuttgart: Katholisches Bibelwerk, 1965) 69–80.

Del Verme, Marcello, *Comunione e condivisione dei beni: Chiesa primitiva e giudaismo esseno-qumranico a confronto* (Brescia: Morcelliana, 1977).

Derrett, J. Duncan M., "The Rich Fool: A Parable of Jesus Concerning Inheritance," in Derrett, *Studies*, 2:90–120.

Dupont, Jacques, "L'apres-mort dans l'oevre de Luc," *RThL* 3 (1972) 3–21.

Idem, *Beatitudes*, 3:113–18.

Idem, "Die individuelle Eschatologie im Lukasevangelium und in der Apostelgeschichte," in Hoffmann, *Orientierung*, 37–47.

Eichholz, Georg, *Gleichnisse der Evangelien: Form, Überlieferung, Auslegung* (Neukirchen-Vluyn: Neukirchener Verlag, 1971) 179–91.

Gaide, G., "Le riche insensé, Lc 12, 13-14," *ExpT* 98 (1987) 267–70.

Gorringe, T., "A Zealot Opinion Rejected? Luke 12:13-14," *Expository Times* 98 (1987) 267–70.

Harnisch, Wolfgang, *Gleichniserzählungen Jesu: Eine hermeneutische Einführung* (Göttingen: Vandenhoeck & Ruprecht, 1985) 82–85 and passim.

Heininger, *Metaphorik*, 107–21 and passim.

Herin, T. J., "Luke 12:13—14:35 as an Introduction to Luke as Preacher" (Dissertation, Union Theological Seminary, New York, 1974).

Horn, *Glaube und Handeln*, 58–66.

Iwand, *Gegenwart*, 18–26.

Jeremias, *Parables*, passim.

Johnson, Luke T., *The Literary Function of Possessions in Luke-Acts* (SBLDS 39; Missoula, Mont.: Scholars Press, 1977) 127–71.

Joüon, Paul, "Notes philologiques sur les Évangiles—Luc 12, 21," *RSR* 18 (1928) 353– 54.

Idem, "La parabole du riche insensé (Luc 12, 13-21)," *RSR* 29 (1939) 486–89.

Jülicher, *Gleichnisreden*, 2:608–17.

Klaiber, Walter, "Eine lukanische Fassung des Sola Gratia: Beobachtungen zu Lk 1, 5-56," in Johannes Friedrich et al., eds., *Rechtfertigung: Festschrift Ernst Käsemann zum 70. Geburtstag* (Tübingen: Mohr; Göttingen: Vandenhoeck & Ruprecht, 1976) 211–28.

Laconi, M., "Ricchi davanti a Dio," *SacDoc* 34 (1989) 5–41.

Linnemann, *Parables*, 4–5, 14–16, 23–47.

Magass, W., "Zur Semiotik der Hausfrömmigkeit (Lk 12, 16-21): Die Beispielerzählung 'Vom reichen Kornbauer,'" *LingBibl 4* (1971) 2–5, no. 4–5.

Mara, Maria Grazia, *Ricchezza e povertà nel cristianesimo antico* (Studi Patristici 1; Rome: Città Nuova, 1980) 7–32, esp. 30–32.

Massaux, Edouard, et al., *The Influence of the Gospel of Saint Matthew on Christian Literature before Saint Irenaeus* (New Gospel Studies; Macon, Ga.: Mercer University Press, 1993) 479–81.

Moule, C. F. D., "H.W. Moule on Acts 4:25," *ExpT* 65 (1953–54) 220–21.

Neuhäusler, Engelbert, *Exigence de Dieu et morale chrétienne: Études sur les enseignements moraux de la prédication de Jésus dans les Synoptiques* (trans. F. Schanen; LD 70; Paris: Cerf, 1971) 247–69.

Orbe, Antonio, *Parábolas evangélicas en san Ireneo* (2 vols.; BAC 331–32; Madrid: Católica, 1972) 2:105–16, 196–97, 428–29.

Reid, John, "The Poor Rich Fool: Luke 12:21," *ExpT* 13 (1901–2) 567–68.

Schrage, *Thomas-Evangelium*, 151–53, 131–33.

Schürmann, Heinz, "Sprachliche Reminiszenzen an abgeänderte oder ausgelassene Bestandteile der Spruchsammlung im Lukas- und Mattäusevangelium," in Schürmann, *Traditionsgeschichtliche Untersuchungen,* 111–25.

Idem, "Das Thomasevangelium und das lukanische Sondergut," in Schürmann, *Traditionsgeschichtliche Untersuchungen,* 228–47.

Schwarz, G., "Ταυτῇ τῇ νυκτὶ τὴν ψυχὴν σου ἀπαιτοῦσιν ἀπὸ σοῦ?" *BN* (1984) 36–41, no. 25.

Seccombe, David P., *Possessions and the Poor in Luke-Acts* (SNTU B/6; Linz: Studien zum Neuen Testament und seiner Umwelt, 1982) 137–45, 158–59.

Sellin, Gerhard, "Lukas als Gleichniserzähler: Die Erzählung vom barmherzigen Samariter (Lk 10, 25-37)," *ZNW* 65 (1974) 166–89; 66 (1975) 19–60.

Seng, E. W., "Der reiche Tor: Eine Untersuchung von Lk 12:16-21 unter besonderer Berucksichtigung form- und motivgeschichtlicher Aspekte," *NovT* 20 (1978) 136–55.

Spicq, *Notes de lexicographie,* 2:704–6.

Tarelli, C. C., "A Note on Luke 12:15," *JTS* 41 (1940) 260–62.

Welzen, H., "De parabel van de rijke boer (Lc 12, 13-21)," in Bastiaan Martinus Franciscus van Iersel et al., *Parabelverhalen in Lucas: Van semiotiek naar pragmatiek* (TFT-Studies 8; Tilburg: Tilburg University Press, 1987).

13/ Someone in the crowd said to him, "Teacher, tell my brother to divide the family inheritance with me." 14/ But he said to him, "Hey you[a], who set me to be a judge or arbitrator between you?" 15/ Then he said to them, "Take care and be on your guard against all kinds of greed; because, for those who are affluent, life does not depend on what they themselves possess." 16/ He told them a parable, as follows: "The land of a rich man produced abundantly. 17/ He thought and said to himself, 'What should I do, for I have no place to store my crops?' 18/ Then he said, 'I will do this: I will pull down my barns and build larger ones, and there I will store all my grain and my goods. 19/ And I will say to my soul, "My soul, you have ample goods laid up for many years; relax, eat, drink, be merry."' 20/ But God said to him, 'You fool! This very night your life is being demanded of you. So the things you have prepared, whose will they be?' 21/ So it is with those who store up treasures for themselves but are not rich in God."

a   Literally: "man" (in the sense of human being).

The verses we are going to analyze express a paradox. On the one hand, they stress the importance of speech and communication (the verb "say" is omnipresent in this passage). On the other, they illustrate the difficulty there is in understanding someone else's point of view and the dangers, sometimes mortal, of withdrawal. Since this paradox is common to both of the episodes, I have brought vv. 13-15 and 16-21 together as a single pericope. Moreover, the reader is struck by the allusive, subtle, and figurative nature of Jesus' words.

Analysis

A question (v. 13) shifts our attention away[1] from the theme of confession (vv. 1-12) toward that of money (vv. 13-21). The audience, made up of disciples surrounded by the crowd, stays the same. Jesus first answers (v. 14) the anonymous person in the crowd (v. 13), then speaks to "them" (v. 15, then v. 16), and finally, in the following pericope, to "his disciples" (v. 22). This vague "them" refers to a circle larger than the disciples, that is, the crowd. The numerous occurrences of "he said"[2] allow the Gospel writer to line up sayings that are structurally distinct but fundamentally related.

Verses 13-14 constitute a brief apophthegm.[3] Verse 15 is a transitional saying that extracts a general recommendation from the episode and prepares for the following speech. As the term "parable" ($\pi\alpha\rho\alpha\beta o\lambda\acute{\eta}$)[4] suggests, Jesus then tells a story, one that serves to teach a lesson.[5] In this parable with the mention of "a man" ($\check{\alpha}\nu\vartheta\rho\omega\pi\acute{o}\varsigma$ $\tau\iota\varsigma$)[6] there is only one character up to the end of the story, where a second character, God, speaks up.[7] The flourishing situation of this man (v. 16) prompts him to reflect and leads him into a monologue, a literary device used by Luke in his work.[8] This interior monologue contains a question (v. 17), an initial answer (v. 18), followed by a second answer (v. 19). Then we hear the voice of the one to whom the man, wrapped up in himself, had forgotten to pay attention: God (v. 20). This speech by God is made up of a judgment (v. 20a)[9] and a rhetorical question (v. 20b). The future tense indicating what the human being is projecting ("I will say," $\dot{\epsilon}\rho\hat{\omega}$, v. 19) is matched by the future tense indicating what God is projecting ("will . . . be," $\check{\epsilon}\sigma\tau\alpha\iota$, v. 20).[10] Verse 21, which is located outside the parable, draws the lesson from this story, the narrative outcome of which the Lukan Jesus did not see fit to tell us.[11] The following pericope makes a connection via a recommendation that fits the context: do not worry about what you will eat, etc. (v. 22). This latter pericope deals with worries, a theme to which the pericope preceding the one we are studying had already alluded (v. 11).

It is likely that the apophthegm (vv. 13-14) and the parable (vv. 16-20) had different origins. The *Gospel of Thomas*, which quotes both of them, does not place them one after the other. Verses 15 and 21 each have a hermeneutical function, which prompts us to declare them secondary. If v. 15 had an autonomous existence before being attached here, v. 21 can only have arisen as a commentary on the parable.

Even though the verses that preceded (12:1-12) and those that follow (12:22-32) come from Q, it would be difficult to maintain that these verses (12:13-21) had the same origin. Matthew[12] is unacquainted with them, and their style as well as their genre and content are related to the other units of L.[13] Making these verses out to be a creation of Luke himself[14] runs into the difficulty that they came into being progressively. I personally would say that Luke has inserted here, with adaptations, a

---

1   For the questions and remarks of an interlocutor in a collection of sentences or a discourse, cf., e.g., 11:27, 37-38, 45; 17:5.

2   Nine phrases of this brief pericope begin by the verb "say"!

3   See Schneider, "Antworten," 325.

4   On $\pi\alpha\rho\alpha\beta o\lambda\acute{\eta}$ in Luke, see the commentary on 8:4 (1:407 n.17).

5   See Jülicher, *Gleichnisreden*, 2:608–17.

6   See Sellin, "Gleichniszähler," 184–85.

7   The rich man (v. 16), then God (v.20).

8   See Heininger, *Metaphorik*, 107–21.

9   In the style of the oracles of punishment of an individual in the OT, which never attack a general culpability but always precise transgression, this parable begins with the mention of the mistake (here the simple "fool" recapitulates his plan) and finishes with the mention of pain. See Seng, "Tor," 139–40.

10   The moral of the story for Loisy (446) is that man proposes, God disposes.

11   It suffices that God speaks in order that it may be so, just as in the story of the creation (Genesis 1; cf. Ps 32 [33]:9).

12   See Fitzmyer, 2:968.

13   Luke's special source (L) is the only document to recount parables in the genre of *Beispielerzählung*, the "exemplary story"; see Wiefel, 236. Monologues are also characteristic of this source, as too the narrative quality and the psychological finesse of the story. That our verses belong to his special source is generally admitted today; see Fitzmyer, 2:971; Wiefel, 236.

14   This is the opinion of Michael D. Goulder, *Luke: A New Paradigm* (2 vols.; JSNTSup 20; Sheffield: JSOT Press, 1989) 2:534–38: Luke is inspired by Matt 6:19-26 and also by Ecclesiastes according to the LXX.

composite unit of L, which had behind it a long history. The apophthegm and the parable had, in fact, circulated independently, before being brought together in L. This operation was accompanied by an effort at interpretation of which vv. 15 and 21 are the fruit.[15] Luke himself may have touched up the received text here and there, clarifying it or reorienting it, as our verse-by-verse commentary will demonstrate.[16]

Here are the corresponding passages of the *Gospel of Thomas*, in which the apophthegm comes after the parable and various sayings: "[A man said] to Him, 'Tell my brothers to divide my father's possessions with me.' He said to him, 'O man, who has made Me a divider?' He turned to His disciples and said to them, 'I am not a divider, am I?'" (*Gos. Thom* 72). "Jesus said, 'There was a rich man who had much money. He said, "I shall put my money to use so that I may sow, reap, plant, and fill my storehouse with produce, with the result that I shall lack nothing." Such were his intentions, but that same night he died. Let him who has ears hear'" (*Gos. Thom.* 63).

In the apophthegm, the parallel texts are very similar, except, however, for the fact that in the *Gospel of Thomas* there are several "brothers" instead of just one, "my father's possessions" instead of the "family inheritance," and especially just an "arbitrator" or "divider," instead of Luke's "judge" and "arbitrator." The apocryphal Gospel is unacquainted with the canonical moral (Luke 12:15) and stresses the theme of the "divider." This comparison shows, on the one hand, that v. 15 in Luke is secondary, but, on the other hand, that there is, here and there, a tendency to draw a lesson. The author of the *Gospel of Thomas* thought of Jesus as one who unites. Any thought of division was to him unbearable. That was what stuck in his mind in his conclusion, in the rhetorical question.[17] I do not exclude the possibility that besides our written Gospel of Luke he may have known some oral traditions. So the presence of just the word "divider" or "arbitrator" corresponds to a part of the Lukan manuscript tradition.[18]

The parable is recounted in such a different manner that in the *Gospel of Thomas* it must depend more on oral tradition than on the written text of Luke. Indeed, although the narrative structure is similar, the rich man's plan is different and, instead of the judgment pronounced by God, what is mentioned is the fatal outcome. The man speaks to himself only once; he does not think of demolishing then reconstructing, but of investing and then profiting from his supplemental revenues. The man in the *Gospel of Thomas* is afraid of having to do without, whereas the one in Luke speaks in terms of the Greek watchword of enjoyment. And what is most important, the lesson in Luke 12:21 is absent from the apocryphal Gospel. Here again, the *Gospel of Thomas* felt the need to conclude with an exhortation. It did so by using a saying about hearing that is found also in certain manuscripts of Luke.[19] By virtue of its narrative and literary quality, the Lukan version must come from L, whose aesthetic concern is well known. By comparison with the version of the *Gospel of Thomas*, the Lukan one must be secondary. By saying that, I am aware that I am going against the consensus[20] and that I am allowing that, in certain passages, the apocryphal Gospel is closer to Jesus than are our canonical Gospels.

Commentary

The Apophthegm

What drove this man to speak to Jesus? Why did Jesus refuse to reply to his question? For what reason did the earliest Christians remember this incident?[21]

---

15 Both are absent in *Gosp. Thom.* 72 and 63.

16 One senses the hand of Luke; see the commentary on 12:15 below.

17 Cf. Schrage (*Thomas-Evangelium*, 153), who recalls that the Gnostic Mark the Magos assigns to the divine substance the attribute ἀμέριστος ("who is not divided"; cf. Irenaeus *Adv. haer.* 1.15.5) and mentions *Gos. Phil.* 78 (= 118.12ff.): *Acts John* 95 ("I want to be one and I want to unite") and *Gos. Truth* 28.28ff. (the fate of the one who is not gnostic is to be divided).

18 See the commentary below on 12:14.

19 See Nestle-Aland[27], ad loc.

20 See Schrage, *Thomas-Evangelium*, 151–53; Schürmann, "Thomasevangelium," 232–33; Eichholz, *Gleichnisse*, 181–83.

21 See Baarda, "Text," 107.

Hebrew law regulated inheritance in the following manner:[22] a man's inheritance was understood to be a whole. Although the law did provide for a division among the inheritors,[23] the ideal norm suggested keeping the inheritance intact through the inheritors sharing a life in common, what the Bible calls "living together" (יָשַׁב יַחַד) or "living among brothers." This solution, which made sense in a nomadic life, was still feasible in a sedentary society. Psalm 133:1 (132:1) recalls that ideal of life in common: "See, what is so good, what is so pleasant, as when brothers live together?"[24] The *Testament of Zebulon* confirms its survival: the streams that are divided into too many channels are swallowed up by the earth and become unproductive. "And you shall be thus if you are divided. Do not be divided into two heads, because everything the Lord has made has a single head. He provides two shoulders, two hands, two feet, but all members obey one head" (*T. Zeb.* 9:3-4).[25] Josephus, who admired the communal life of the Essenes, compared life in common to a united family: "The individual's possessions join the common stock and all, like brothers, enjoy a single patrimony" (*Bell.* 2.8.3 §122). That conception of property and inheritance did not mean that there was complete communism. Shares were provided for, but in practice provisions were not divvied out equally. The older son benefited in particular from the birthright. He received twice what his brothers did, in particular real estate, but, in return, he was obliged to provide for the support of the widow or the widows, as well as the daughters who remained single (see Num 27:11; Deut 12:15-17). Even though it was not viewed favorably, one of the sons could ask at any time for the property to be divided up materially; that is what happened in the parable of the prodigal son (Luke 15:12). Scripture recounts how the patriarch Abraham and Lot, his brother's son (Gen 13:1-18), managed to separate without conflict, thanks to the uncle's thoughtfulness. A rabbinic discussion in the second century of our era dealt specifically with Gen 13:14 (God's order to Abraham, who had just separated from Lot). It appears that Abraham's attitude toward Lot caused a problem for the rabbis, because a separation, even though tolerated, did not fit the highest moral ideal. Rabbi Juda thought that God was unhappy at that time with Abraham, who was unable to get along with his brother's son. Rabbi Nehemiah, however, thought that God was angry as long as Abraham stayed with the unworthy Lot.[26]

The Lukan story, then, fits well into the Jewish context of first-century Palestine.[27] The father is dead. He seems to have had two sons. There is no quarrel with the legal provisions for the dividing up of the inheritance, but the younger son complains about the older son's refusal to carry through on the concrete division provided for in the Law—hence the recourse to an arbitrator, an expert, a reconciler, in order to settle the dispute.[28] It appears that a rabbi was authorized to settle such cases (the anonymous person does, in fact, call Jesus "Teacher").[29]

Jesus refused. The vocative "man" (ἄνθρωπε), translated by "Hey you," perhaps indicates the Master's dissatisfaction and already sets the tone.[30] The rhetorical question that follows indicates that Jesus did not consider himself to have been charged by God with such

---

22 See Daube, "Inheritance"; Derrett, "Fool"; Bovon, *L'oeuvre*, 37–39.

23 See Deut 21:15-17; Num 27:1-22. For rabbinic rules in the matter of inheritance, which developed partly from these two biblical texts, see *m. B. Batra* 8.1–9; cf. Str-B 3:545–49, and the articles mentioned in n. 22 above.

24 Deliberately, I have translated Ps 132 (133):1 according to the LXX; cf. Gen 13:8.

25 In Dupont-Sommer and Philonenko, *Écrits intertestamentaires,* 889. The text aims perhaps first at the division of the kingdom into two; then to Israel as divided by parties. But there is, as the background plan, the idea that an inheritance must remain whole.

26 *Genesis Rabbah* 41.8 on Gen 13:14; Daube, "Inheritance," 328.

27 For other clarifying biblical texts, see Gen 21:10; 38:1; Ezek 46:16-18; Job 42:15; Ruth 4:5, 10; Tob 4:1-21; 1 Macc 15:33-34. For Israel as the inheritance from God, see Deut 4:20; 9:26, 29; 32:9; Josh 13:17.

28 For rules for judges, see Deut 16:18-20; 25:1-3.

29 For rabbis authorized to judge, see Schürer, *History,* 2:1:320–21; 326–28. The figure of Moses is evoked, who wanted to take on the role of judge with the result that is known (Exod 2:11-15; see also below nn. 31 and 39), as well as that of Joshua, appointed for the division of the land at the time of the conquest (Josh 13:1-7); see Gorringe, "Zealot," 269.

30 Cf. Luke 22:58; Rom 2:1; 9:20. Plummer, 322. Lagrange (357) explains why this vocative can reflect diverse interior attitudes, ranging from indignation to embarrassment.

a mission.[31] What does that mean? For some, what may have happened was that Jesus reproached the anonymous person for having confused the material level with the spiritual level.[32] In that case, he had not come to settle such trivial problems. For others, what may have happened was that he refused to play the game of the Zealots, who hoped to inaugurate the eschatological dividing up of the Holy Land.[33] In that case, his anger would have been all the greater in that his message, like that of the Zealots, had a political dimension, but one that was different from their revolutionary ideal. I personally attach considerable importance to the vocabulary associated with dividing up ("to divide with," $\mu\epsilon\rho\acute{\iota}\zeta\omega$, v. 13; "arbitrator," $\mu\epsilon\rho\iota\sigma\tau\acute{\eta}\varsigma$, v. 14).[34] In Luke's eyes, there were different kinds of dividing up. What that man wanted was a dividing up in his own favor: in the end, a carving up of the prey, a dividing up of the booty. This brother let his avarice (what v. 15 will call his "greed," $\pi\lambda\epsilon\text{ov}\epsilon\xi\acute{\iota}\alpha$) be heard. The gospel for which Jesus fought is also an inheritance but an inheritance that is divided up by distributing it to others (cf. vv. 33-34), thus putting into practice the commandment to love one's neighbor (10:25-37). Christ's perspective is neither spiritual in opposition to the material life, nor pacifist in contrast to revolutionary violence. It includes the kingdom[35] and this world; there are inheritances here below; but their being divided up pleases the Master when it is done in the light of the coming kingdom. Jesus compares this kingdom to an inheritance of which everyone receives a sufficient share[36] without giving a raw deal to others, and on which one can live in community. Mary chose the better part, not the spiritual part but the one that corresponds to the kingdom.[37] The life of the earliest Christians as pictured in the Acts of the Apostles (2:42-47; 4:32-35) traces what this eschatological communion would be like, starting in the present (cf. Luke 14:15). What Barnabas did when he sold one of his fields and handed over the proceeds of the sale to the apostles (Acts 4:36-37)[38] is the counter-example to the anonymous inheritor in this passage here in Luke. The early church remembered these two examples in order to teach new converts to look at their possessions in the light of the kingdom (by teaching these examples, it could also help believers manage their possessions in liberty and charitably). Having a share in the kingdom means knowing how to distribute one's income and one's possessions.

There is a text-critical problem in v. 14. Nestle-Aland[27] and Tjitze Baarda, after long study,[39] opt for the reading

---

31 The verb $\kappa\alpha\theta\acute{\iota}\sigma\tau\eta\mu\iota$ signifies "install," "establish," "constitute," "appoint"; see Maurice Carrez and François Morrel, *Dictionnaire grec-français du Nouveau Testament* (Neuchâtel: Delachaux & Niestlé, 1971) s.v.; and BAGD, s.v. It has here a juridical and insitutional sense. As for $\tau\acute{\iota}\varsigma$ ("who?"), it suggests God. The "among you" must designate the anonymous one and his brother. One must then distinguish the "you" of v. 15, which designates hearers of Jesus. Curiously, the reply of Jesus recalls the invective addressed to Moses in Exod 2:14, cited by Luke in Acts 7:27, 35. On the refusal of Jesus, cf., e.g., 11:16, 29-32; Mark 10:39; Mark 13:32; John 2:3-4; John 7:3-6; cf. Gaide, "Riche insensé," 84–85, 86. Jesus, even when he seems to dodge a question, does not repulse anybody. He seeks always to make one reflect, by placing the problem and the situation in its true perspective.

32 This is the current interpretation; see Godet, 2:137; Loisy, 344; Morris, 212: "He [Jesus] comes to bring men to God, not to bring property to men."

33 Gorringe, "Zealot."

34 Note the importance reserved in the OT to the sharing of the holy land (Num 26:52-56; 33:53-56; 34:13; Joshua 12–22) and of spoils (Num 31:25-47). The Hebrews hoped for a new sharing at the end of time, an eternal inheritance: Ezek 45:1-8; 47:13—48:29. On $\mu\epsilon\rho\acute{\iota}\zeta\omega$ and $\mu\epsilon\rho\iota\sigma\tau\acute{\eta}\varsigma$, see BAGD, s.vv. Do not forget either $\mu\epsilon\rho\acute{\iota}\varsigma$ or $\mu\acute{\epsilon}\rho\text{o}\varsigma$, the "part"; see Gottfried Nebe, "$\mu\epsilon\rho\acute{\iota}\zeta\omega$," "$\mu\epsilon\rho\acute{\iota}\varsigma$," "$\mu\acute{\epsilon}\rho\text{o}\varsigma$," *EDNT* 2:408–9; and Horst Balz and Gerhard Schneider, "$\mu\epsilon\rho\iota\sigma\tau\acute{\eta}\varsigma$," *EDNT* 2:409.

35 This kingdom is not divided; cf. 11:17-18 ($\delta\iota\alpha\mu\epsilon\rho\acute{\iota}\zeta\omega$).

36 Cf. Acts 20:32 (*NRSV*): "to give you the inheritance among all who are sanctified"; Acts 2:45 (*NRSV*): "as any had need"; Acts 4:34 (*NRSV*): "There was not a needy person among them."

37 Cf. 10:42 and the commentary on 10:42 above.

38 Bengel (*Gnomon*, 345) considers that an inheritance is something just, but what is not good is the avarice of the anonymous heir.

39 Baarda, "Text"; Metzger, *Textual Commentary*, 135; it is necessary to recognize the contamination by the curious parallel, mentioned above in n. 31, Exod 2:14 LXX, cited twice in Acts (7:27, 35).

"judge or arbitrator" (κριτὴν ἢ μεριστήν), among some ten different variant readings.[40] Δικαστής for "judge," instead of κριτής, can be explained by two different translations of a single Semitic original (the older form of the story must have first been told in Aramaic).[41] The omission of the word "arbitrator" and the presence of a single term "judge" were attested already in the second century, since they are found in Marcion, and later in Codex Bezae (D = 05). What Nestle-Aland[27] fails to mention is that the single word "arbitrator" appears in the *Gospel of Thomas*, Augustine of Hippo (e.g., *Serm.* 107.3),[42] and an Arabic work of Abd al-Gabbār (tenth century), which quotes canonical and apocryphal sayings of Jesus.[43] It is impossible to retrace the entire history of these variants. Since "arbitrator" (μεριστής) is a rare word,[44] it could be that a scribe wanted to explain it by the word "judge," which would mean, then, that the pair μερίζω–μεριστής was original. Or else the term "judge" was the only word used originally in Jesus' reply in Aramaic, and what happened was that in the course of the story's being transmitted the theme of dividing up came to be stressed. In my opinion, Luke wrote "judge or arbitrator" (κριτὴν ἢ μεριστήν), but fluctuations observed in the manuscript tradition of the second to tenth centuries have their origin in the oral transmission of the saying in the first two centuries.

In short, Jesus, according to Luke, refused any human righteousness that was not linked to the order of the kingdom and criticized any relationship to property that, through greed, would neglect one's neighbor. Our human inheritances look so good to us that when we lose touch with our eschatological inheritance, those human inheritances awaken greed in us and provoke division. Jesus wanted sharing rather than division.

The Warning

■ **15** Verse 15 resembles v. 1, so much so that we are tempted to say "in the second place" (δεύτερον) here to match the mention of "in the first place" (πρῶτον) in v. 1.[45] If, in v. 1, one had to protect oneself against "hypocrisy," here what one must be on guard against is "all kinds of greed." The use of two different verbs is not overkill in encouragement to be cautious: "take care" (ὁρᾶτε, literally "see"), and "be on your guard" (φυλάσσεσθε), both present imperatives, as in v. 1,[46] which thus invite us to be vigilant at all times. We have here a rare sense given to the verb "see," which matches a certain corresponding use elsewhere of the verb "listen" (cf. 9:35: "listen to him" [αὐτοῦ ἀκούετε], with the nuance of "pay attention to him," "obey him"). Here, in fact, ὁρᾶτε means "make sure that," "pay attention," "protect yourself from."[47] There is an equivalent in English: "See to it that. . . ." The verb summons the attention of one's sight, and then the attention of the mind. If it is not followed here by a μή with the aorist subjunctive, it is because it is used absolutely with the meaning "Pay attention!" The verb φυλάσσω is usually used by Luke in the active in the proper sense of "keeping watch" during the night (2:8), next of "guarding," for example a prisoner (Acts 12:4; 23:35; cf. 22:20) or, in the figurative sense, of "observing," for example, a law (Luke 11:28; 18:21; Acts 7:53; 16:4; 21:24). The only times this verb is used in the middle voice with the sense "protect oneself against," "avoid," are here and in Acts 21:25. Although it is usually followed by an accusative (cf. Acts 21:25), here it is followed by a preposition (ἀπό).[48] This promenade around the subject "under surveillance," so to speak, leads me to the following conclusion: these two imperatives have nothing Lukan about them. Nor is the word πλεονεξία

---

40 See the listing in Baarda, "Text," 108–14.

41 On the Jewish background plan in this apophthegm, see Daube, "Inheritance," 326–29.

42 *PL* 38:628 twice has *divisor*; cf. Baarda, "Text," 156–62.

43 Cf. Baarda, "Text," 130–56.

44 On μεριστής, see Godet (2:137), who believes that "judge" designates the one who pronounces the sentence and "arbitrator" the one who executes it; Plummer (322) has another opinion: the "judge" who is appointed for a division [of the land] is an "arbitrator"; see also Lagrange, 358.

45 Could it be that 12:1, which has its parallel in Mark

8:15 and Matt 16:6, has also circulated with the commentary related to hypocrisy? For these diverse hypotheses, related to the origin of this verse, see Dupont, "L'après mort," 5 n. 8.

46 The parallels to 12:1, known to be Mark 8:15 and Matt 16:6, each have ὁρᾶτε, "pay attention," before the warning to be on one's guard, as here in 12:15.

47 Cf. Acts 18:15; 22:26, according to Codex Bezae (D) and the majority of manuscripts; BAGD, s.v. ὁράω, 2Bβ, and BDF §149.

48 Cf. 1 John 5:21; 2 Thessalonians 3. It does not necessarily have to do with a Semitism; cf. Plummer,

any more Lukan; it is a part of the ethical vocabulary of the epistles, not of the Gospels.[49] *Πλεονεκτέω* means "to have more than someone else," "to want more," and *πλεονεξία* is the desire to have more than others, whether it be in the form of possessions or privileges—so it is "greed"[50] rather than miserliness; it is the desire to usurp, and the thirst for domination.[51]

The double imperative attributed to Jesus is next justified ("because," *ὅτι* . . .), as is another imperative in 12:40. Although the syntax of this clause is heavy and awkward,[52] its sense is clear: "because, for persons who are affluent, life does not depend on what they themselves possess."[53] Luke may have reworked this saying that he took over from L. He may have added the last words "what they themselves possess" (*ἐκ τῶν ὑπαρχόντων αὐτῷ*)[54] for the sake of clarity.[55] Luke uses *περισσεύω* not only in the sense of "to be affluent" (15:17), but also "to have more than enough" (for example, in the story of the multiplication of the loaves [9:17] or the widow's

coin [21:4]). Did he have the understanding here that what is more than enough is not necessary for life and must be distributed among the poor?[56] That interpretation weakens a theological truth present in the text. Behind "greed" (*πλεονεξία*), there is a fear that causes us to amass more than what others have and more than is necessary to live on. And behind that fear there is a mistaken conviction, namely, that human beings depend on what they possess and, what is even more serious, that their lives are maintained and defy death by virtue of the desire to amass everything for themselves. As if our life derives its breath only from its possessions (*ἐκ τῶν ὑπαρχόντων αὐτῷ*). There was some of that mistaken conviction underlying the anonymous person's request. Hence the virulence of Jesus' reply. Some of that same conviction is to be found also in the plans of the foolish rich man (v. 16). Hence also the transitional function granted this verse; it is not just a structural transition,[57]

322–23. The verbs of fear are normally followed by this preposition; cf. 12:1 and 12:4; BDF §149.

49 Cf. Mark 7:22 (another single usage in the Gospels); Rom 1:29; 2 Cor 9:5; Eph 4:19; 5:3; Col 3:5; 1 Thess 2:5; 2 Pet 2:3, 14. Often in the list of vices. The verb *πλεονεκτέω*, as well as the substantive and the adjective *πλεονέκτης*, are used, in the same contexts, by authors of epistles. In the Apostolic Fathers, see *Did.* 2.6; 5.1; *Barn.* 10.4, 6; 19.6; 20.1; *1 Clem.* 35.5, *Hermas* 36.5 (*Mand.* 6.2, 5); 38.5 (*Mand.* 8.5); 65.5 (*Sim.* 6.4, 5); Polycarp 2.2.

50 Cf. *φιλαργυρία* (1 Tim 6:10); *φιλάργυρος* ("who loves money"; Luke 16:14; cf. Heb 13:5).

51 On the word *πλεονεξία*, see Anton Vögtle, *Die Tugend und Lasterkataloge im Neuen Testament* (Münster: Aschendorff, 1936) 223–25; Gerhard Delling, "*πλεονέκτης κτλ.*," *TDNT* 6 (1969) 266–74; Spicq, *Notes de lexicographie*, 2:704–6; Horn, *Glaube und Handeln*, 60–61.

52 See Loisy, 345; Grundmann, 256; Marshall, 522; Derrett, "Fool," 103.

53 Literally: "his life." See J. Reiling and J. L. Swellengrebel, *A Handbook on The Gospel of Luke* (New York: American Bible Society, 1971) 470. The *TOB* clarifies and simplifies: "It is not the fact that a man is rich that his life has a guarantee by his possessions." According to Sophie Antoniadis (*L'Évangile de Luc: esquisse de grammaire et de style* [Paris: Société Les Belles Lettres, 1930] 110). The Greek phrase "from his possessions" relates to "to become affluent" and

one must understand the text thus: "it is not in the abundance of goods that life consists."

54 The expression *τὰ ὑπάρχοντα* ("possessions") is Lukan (cf. 8:3; 11:21; 12:33; etc.). The dative *αὐτῷ* is correct, if one imagines *ὑπάρχομαι* as "to be there"; "to be." But it is a bit studied (cf. 8:3; 11:21; 12:33, etc.). One would expect the genitive *αὐτοῦ*, "his."

55 Moule ("Acts 4:25") suggests that Luke 12:15 combines here two synonymous expressions and modifies them, which would explain the actual redundancy: *οὐκ ἐν τῷ περισσεύειν τινὶ ἡ ζωή* ("someone's life does not consist in his abundance") and *οὐκ ἐκ τῶν ὑπαρχόντων αὐτοῦ τινὶ ἡ ζωή* ("someone's life does not depend on his possessions").

56 If I understand correctly, this is the subtle interpretation of Derrett ("Fool"), who proposes to translate: "For it is not at the point where he has a superfluity that a person lives on his assets." That is to say, that the life of a person does not depend on his superfluous things. Human life depends on what is necessary. The superfluous should be given away. Jesus attacks the accumulation of riches.

57 Dupont (*Béatitudes*, 3:114–15) distinguishes in 12:15b attention to cupidity, the lesson to be drawn from the apophthegm (12:13-14), and in 12:15c, the abundance of life, a summary of the parable that is

but a transition in the full sense of a conclusion and announcement of the subject matter.[58]

When Christians are motivated by the kingdom of God and not by the fear of being without something, they acquire a proper relationship to money. They know that a vital minimum is indispensable for them, if for no other reason than to witness to the gospel, but they freely dispose of the rest. Nor do they forget—and the two examples in this pericope are there to remind them of the fact—that what is more than enough has the disastrous tendency to appear indispensable in their eyes when they succumb to temptation.

The Parable

■ **16** The words "he told" (literally, "he said . . . to," $\epsilon \hat{\iota} \pi \epsilon \nu$ $\delta \grave{\epsilon}$ . . . $\pi \rho \acute{o} \varsigma$) are Lukan, which is not surprising in an introductory formula (cf. v. 22). "A rich man": such an assignment of social roles is typical of the sapiential and popular literature, of fables or of proverbs. Luke did not hesitate to conform to it. We can picture a large land-holder in Galilee.[59] The "land" ($\chi \acute{\omega} \rho \alpha$) of this man "produced abundantly" ($\epsilon \grave{\upsilon} \varphi \acute{o} \rho \eta \sigma \epsilon \nu$). Neither the noun with this meaning nor the verb is Lukan: elsewhere Luke uses $\chi \acute{\omega} \rho \alpha$ in the larger sense of "region," and the well-chosen $\epsilon \grave{\upsilon} \varphi o \rho \acute{\epsilon} \omega$ is a Lukan *hapax legomenon*, in fact a *hapax* in the entire New Testament. The word $\chi \acute{\omega} \rho \alpha$ can mean the "country," the "(open) country," the "region,"[60] but also the "field," "cultivated land," even the "place."[61] "Produce abundantly" ($\epsilon \grave{\upsilon} \varphi o \rho \acute{\epsilon} \omega$), which is the counterpart of

"bear fruit" ($\kappa \alpha \rho \pi o \varphi o \rho \acute{\epsilon} \omega$) or "bear fruit to maturity" ($\tau \epsilon \lambda \epsilon \sigma \varphi o \rho \acute{\epsilon} \omega$) of the parable of the sower (8:14-15), belongs first of all to medical vocabulary: it means to "be in good health," then "be prosperous," "prosper," and finally "bear good crops," "be fruitful."[62] Up to this point there is nothing reprehensible about this rich person. His possessions were not ill-gained. Note, moreover, that his business was agricultural, which fits the situation in Palestine but also, according to Aristotle, that of most people.[63] It is ahead of the harvest that the landholder forecasts an exceptionally good new crop.

■ **17** After the brief presentation of the flourishing business situation, the landowner lets us in on the debates he is having within himself. In literature, interior monologues function to unmask people's character, their worries, or their intentions. So these monologues have the double advantage of providing the author with a means of expression and the reader with an opening into the meaning. Often, in these monologues—used in the New Testament only by Luke and L,[64] the significant question arises: $\tau \acute{\iota}$ $\pi o \iota \acute{\eta} \sigma \omega$ ("what will I do?" or "what should I do?"—depending on whether the verb is taken to be a future indicative or an aorist subjunctive).

A recent thesis has examined this literary device and discovered its importance in ancient novels, in particular in the writings of Xenophon of Ephesus and in the anonymous Hellenistic Jewish work *Joseph and Aseneth*, as well as in comedies, for example, in the writings of Menander, Plautus, and Terence.[65] This use of mono-

---

going to follow. Elsewhere Dupont ("L'apres mort," 5) has evolved a bit: he suggests that v. 15 does not pass beyond the sapiential point of view. It is the parable, and especially v. 21, that introduces the position dear to Luke: in being generous through life, one is concerned for what is coming after death. See also Horn, *Glaube und Handeln*, 59.

58 For the text-critical problems in this verse, see Tarelli, "Note." In order to understand both the sentence (12:15) and the parable (12:16-21), which is inserted in the sapiential history of Israel, the reader will read Ps 48 (49):7, 11, 17-20; Sir 11:18-19; *T. Jud.* 18–19; *1 Enoch* 94:6-11; 97:8-10; Jas 5:1-6. Do not forget the beatitude for the poor and the curse upon riches in Luke 6:20, 24 and all the Lukan texts about wealth; see the bibliography in Bovon, *Theologian*, 305–7, 442–8; also Seccombe, *Possessions*, 236–75.

59 "A man" (cf. 14:2; 15:11); "a rich man" (cf. 16:1,

19). Compare "a judge" (18:1); "a woman" (15:8); "a woman sinner in the city" (7:37); cf., in the OT, Judg 19:1; 1 Sam (1 Kgdms) 1:1; Job 1:1.

60 See, e.g., 3:1 or 8:26; in the sense of "field," "country"; also 21:21 below.

61 BAGD, s.v.

62 See Plummer, 323; BAGD, s.v.

63 "The more numerous class of humans lives from the land and on its edible fruits," writes Aristotle. *Pol.* I.3.4 (1256A, 39–40); cited by Magass, "Semiotik," 3.

64 Cf. the monologues of the prodigal son (15:17-19); of the dishonest steward (16:3-4; with the same question as here: "What shall I do?" and a similar response, "I know what I shall do"); of the wicked judge (18:4-5); and do not forget the prayers of the Pharisee and the publican (18:9-14).

65 Heininger, *Metaphorik*.

logues was studied by professors of rhetoric.[66] It is known that ancient rhetoric suggested practicing ἠθοποιία, that is, the introduction of characters through speeches. And Quintilian recommended reading the authors of comedies, Menander in particular (*Inst.* 10.1.69).[67] So Luke respected literary and rhetorical custom: his hero asks himself what to do, since, as he points out, he does not have enough room in his barns.[68]

■ **18** After the question and the hesitation comes the result of his thinking it over: the answer and the decision (note the future: "I will do this"). There is nothing wrong here yet. Sin is not located in the exterior, in nature, created by God, nor in the cultivation of the fields, carried out by human beings.[69] It springs up from inside, so much so that the parable illustrates a saying in the Sermon on the Plain: "The good person produces good out of the good treasure of his or her heart, and the evil person produces evil out of his or hers; for out of the abundance of the heart the mouth speaks" (Luke 6:45). A later saying states, "For does it profit people if they gain the whole world, but lose or forfeit themselves?" (9:25). And here is a passage of the invective against the Pharisees: " . . . but inside you are full of greed and wickedness. You fools! . . . So give instead for alms those things that are within; and see, everything

will be pure for you." (11:39-41) The failure of the human project confirms the guilty intention. All of a piece, the person symbolizes the attitude that should not be adopted. His disastrous project belongs first of all to the category of action; carried away by the logic of profit, he wanted to cap the success of his enterprise by the enlargement of his warehouses. This is where he made the wrong choice and demonstrated his sinful nature. By way of response to what he received from nature and obtained through his work, he should have been making donations to others rather than hoarding.[70] God gave, but this person refused to share.

The folly of this landowner is subtly suggested by his first demolishing what had suited him well up to that point.[71] He counted on rebuilding on a larger, grander scale than before. We are talking about the "barns" or "warehouses," or "storehouses" (ἀποθῆκαι)[72] for "wheat"[73] and for other goods ("my goods" is another way of speaking of "my crops" of v. 17).[74] There is no question about there being goods, therefore something positive. But on the landowner's lips, the emphasis is on property, "*my* goods," "*my* crops."[75]

■ **19** As the man concluded his monologue, he looked forward to a brighter and better future. He counted on his production (v. 16), then storage (v. 18) being fol-

---

66 I would add tragedies; cf. monologues destined to inform the spectators and to make them share sufferings, hestitations, or trials of the various heroes, e.g., Sophocles, *Ant.* 898–928.

67 On the ἠθοποιία, see Heininger, *Metaphorik*.

68 For classical usage of ἔχω, cf. οὔτε γὰρ ὅπως βοηθῶ ἔχω, "for I do not know how to succor" (Plato, *Resp.* 2.10 [368B]); BAGD, s.v. ἔχω 1.2d. The verb συνάγω, dear to Luke, as also to Matthew, describes the gathering together—in the active in Acts 14:27; 15:30; mostly in the passive, so Luke 22:66; Acts 4:5, 26, 27, 31; 11:26; etc. The gathering of fruits (of the field) is mostly in the active: Luke 3:17; 11:23; cf. 15:13). Used with "my fruits," "my produce," it confirms the agricultural nature of the enterprise.

69 See Schlatter, 343: "A farmer with his harvest proceeds (unlike what Jesus describes in 12:16) will be scolded and despised by his wife, children, and village." Eichholz, *Gleichnisse*, 184.

70 It is the constant moral teaching of Luke; see 12:33-34; 14:33; 16:9, 9-13; etc.; Neuhäusler, *Exigence de Dieu*, 248–69; Gaide, "Riche insensé," 88–89;

Dupont, "L'après mort," 4–7. See also already Bengel (*Gnomon*, 346), who says that the rich forget the poor. The problem is one of accumulation of wealth and not the fact of not having any of it.

71 One finds again the pair "to build" (οἰκοδομέω) and "to demolish" (καθαιρέω) in the LXX in Jer 49:10.

72 Cf. 3:17; 12:24; BAGD, s.v.; see also the commentary on 3:1-22 (1:116–32).

73 Cf. 3:17; 16:7; 22:31; Acts 27:38.

74 The text is uncertain here: in place of the text of Nestle-Aland²⁷, the majority of manuscripts have either "all my produce" or "all my produce and all my goods." The word that we translate by "produce" is τὸ γένημα, deliberately utilized for the fruit of the vine (22:18). The manuscripts fluctuate, for the rest, between τὰ γενήματα and τὰ γεννήματα; see *New Testament in Greek*, 278.

75 Cf. the case of Nabal, who refuses to share goods and will die for it (1 Sam [1 Kgdms] 25:2-39); Plummer, 324; and Lagrange, 359.

lowed by acquisition of capital for his personal use and especially a hedonistic and narcissistic rest. No one apart from the landowner is mentioned. Everything is concentrated on an encounter between the man and his goods (note the three neuters in a row: πολλὰ ἀγαθὰ κείμενα, "ample goods laid up"). The man was not aware of his solitude. He deluded himself, since he thought of himself as having company, feminine company at that: after the monologue in vv. 17-18, he spoke to his "soul" (in Greek ψυχή, a feminine noun),[76] which, however, is not the company that God wishes for the man (Gen 2:18), but rather his own mirror or reflection. Moreover, he did not picture the comfort that he hoped for (v. 19b) as dependent either on his relationship to others or, especially, on his relationship to God. He did not even associate it with his own being but only with what his soul had ("you have," ἔχεις). What he did not understand was that in withdrawing into himself and doing without a true encounter with others, he remained in error.

In order to express the plan he had for his life, the landowner used conventional terms to invite his soul: "Relax, eat, drink, be merry." The apostle Paul, who was also acquainted with these terms,[77] states that he would subscribe to them if there were no resurrection of the dead (1 Cor 15:32). He refers to an oracle of the prophet Isaiah, who criticized the frivolity of the people in the face of the enemy that threatened them and their forgetfulness of their God. We are given a picture of the people rejoicing during their sacrifices, instead of lamenting:

" . . . killing oxen and slaughtering sheep, eating meat and drinking wine. 'Let us eat and drink, for tomorrow we die'" (Isa 22:13).[78] In fact, although this view of life was evident in Israel,[79] it was especially in Greece that it had become the subject of proverbs, and the Greeks were acquainted with the fact that it had also spread among the Egyptians and the Assyrians. There are countless parallels in the literature, especially in funerary inscriptions.[80] The most famous example is the Sardanapalus inscription, often quoted in antiquity: "There had been engraved on his tomb in Assyrian letters: Sardanapalus, child of Anacyndaraxe, built Tarsus and Anchialè in a single day: eat, drink, and make love, since the rest is worthless."[81] In the list of inscriptions, it is to be noted that although the first two imperatives remain relatively the same, the third one varies: ("enjoy voluptuously" [τρύφησον] and "embrace" [περιλάμβανε] also appear; "be merry" [εὐφραίνου], which occurs frequently in other inscriptions, is rather rare in this series, which, moreover, can also contain two or four terms). The inscriptions then give the brevity of life and the inexorability of death as justification for these imperatives. It is, on the whole, a piece of advice that the dead person gives to the living from beyond the grave. Well then, the Gospel writer puts this pagan wisdom in the heart of a man whom he calls a fool.

■ **20** Now comes the surprise, the unexpected encounter, the interlocutor whom the rich landowner should have taken into consideration. In his isolation, he had

---

76 The commentators diverge in opinion with respect to this word: Godet (2:139), Plummer (324), and Lagrange (359) see in the ψυχή the seat of rejoicing and joyous emotions; Loisy (345), Grundmann (257), and Marshall (523) see the interior being, understood in a Hebraic way (see Ps 41 [42]:6, 12; *Ps. Sol.* 3:1). For Luke, in my opinion, ψυχή has the same meaning in v. 19 as in v. 20. It has to do with the interior being that coincides with the person itself inasmuch as it is a living being and conscious of being (cf. 6:9; 9:24); cf. Dautzenberg, *Leben,* 83–91; Seng, "Tor," 141–42; and Alexander Sand, "ψυχή," *EDNT* 3:500–503.

77 See Ameling ("Parallelen"), on whom I rely; Fitzmyer, 2:973.

78 The end of the verse in the LXX reads φάγωμεν καὶ πίωμεν, αὔριον γὰρ ἀποθνήσκομεν, "let us eat and drink, because tomorrow we will die." It

is interesting to note that the LXX introduces the sentence with the word λέγοντες, "in saying." The LXX is sensitive to the proverbial character of the expression. Further, Eccl 8:15 is acquainted with this wisdom but not the critique: "Because there is for the human being nothing good under the sun, except to eat, to drink, and to rejoice." The same verbs as are in Luke occur in the LXX. On εὐφραίνου, which evokes the rejoicing of banquets, see Ameling, "Parallelen," 35 n. 3, and 40–41; also Seng, "Tor," 142, 146.

79 See Eccl 2:24; 3:12-13; 8:15; 9:7; Tob 7:10; for rabbinic parallels, see Str-B 2:190.

80 Euripides *Alc.* 788–89; *Anthologia palatina* 7.32, 33; 10.87; Herodotus *Hist.* 2.78; Plutarch *Is. Os.* 357E; Lucian *Luct.* 21; Petronius *Sat.* 34.10, etc.; cf. Ameling, "Parallelen," 36–37.

81 Ameling, "Parallelen," 37.

not thought of the network of relationships, wills, and plans—the dialogue he had forgotten to count on! Whether one wishes for solitude or is sorry about it, one is never alone. Here, then, is the opposite of a *deus ex machina.*

Just as Jesus acted with respect to the anonymous inheritor (v. 14), so the God of this parable does not beat around the bush: "You fool!" is the initial vocative.[82] We must delve into Hebraic wisdom in order to understand what kind of madness was involved. For economic logic, and then hedonistic logic, were not lacking in wisdom. In what does the folly consist? Is not the *carpe diem* to be found in this life here below and in this brief existence? Is that not where we get to the bottom of it all? To reason thus is to forget ethics, to forget respect for God, and to pay no attention to the destitution of others. The God of Luke is good: his εὐδοκία ("good pleasure," 10:21) leads to "euphoria" (12:16), his kindness to well-being. But the appropriation of this happiness that is offered is conditioned by the adoption of a gospel attitude. Without that, the God of benefits, if they are not properly administered, becomes the God of punishment (19:21-22). There are irreparable oversights just as there are culpable attachments. The sentence, as precise as one issued by a tribunal, made mention of the only two realities that had counted in the eyes of the man who had been rich for a day: his so-called soul, that is, himself, and his possessions that he had carefully prepared (there is an irony in the use of the verb "prepare," ἑτοιμάζω[83]). From this point on, then, everything is going to happen quickly, according to the word of the God, who is the messenger and prophet of misfortune. As the deep darkness of the night flirts with the shadows of death, all that

will happen "this very night" (cf. Job 27:20). Farewell to the "many years" (v. 19).[84] The fearful impersonal "they" of the Greek "they will demand" (cf. *NRSV*'s "is being demanded"), like agents of secret police forces, probably stands for the angels of death.[85] They will ask him to give back (translated by a present passive: "is being demanded")[86] what had only been a loan: "his soul," that is, this life, this breath of life that will cease to exist. As for his possessions, to whom will they revert? The rhetorical question has at least an implicit answer: in any case, not to you! In antiquity, a joke about greed went the rounds: the height of greed, it was said, is when a man makes out his will and puts down his own name as that of the inheritor![87] The rich man in this parable will lose his possessions and, since he has not lived his life in respect of God, will not have any descendants, or inheritors, which was a great misfortune according to the Hebraic way of thinking.[88]

Here is that parable. It is the story of a bad example, and numerous parallels to it are known, from Seneca to Hofmannsthal to the Midrash and the tales of the Thousand and One Nights.[89] We have here a reminder of the human condition rooted in Hebraic wisdom.[90] Here is a Jewish story with a parallel structure: a man, full of confidence, wants to keep some wine, set aside for the circumcision of his son, and use it for the marriage of that son. At that point the angel of death announces to the father the impending death of his child.[91] Or take the saying of Sirach: "One becomes rich through diligence and self-denial, and the reward allotted to him is this: When he says, 'I have found rest, and now I shall feast on my goods!' he does not know how long it will be until he leaves them to others and dies" (Sir 11:18-19).[92] The

---

82   On ἄφρων and ἀφροσύνη ("unreason"; 11:40) in the Bible, esp. in sapiential literature, see Anton Vögtle, *Die Tugend und Lasterkataloge im Neuen Testament* (Münster: Aschendorff, 1936) 231–32; Seng, "Tor," 142, 145.

83   On this verb, cf. 1:17, 76 and 2:31, where it is utilized in a positive sense with respect to the activity of John the Baptist and even God.

84   Ernst (399) suggests that the number of these years makes allusion to the delay of the parousia. That seems to me unlikely.

85   Others think of the discreet manner of speaking of God in the divine passive; see Godet, 2:140.

86   For ἀπαιτέω, cf. Wis 15:8. For this theme, cf. Wis

2:4-5; Job 20:29; Ps 48 (49):18; Jer 29:32; 1 Sam (1 Kgdms) 15:28.

87   Andreas Thierfelder, ed., *Philogelos: Der Lachfreund von Hierocles und Philagrius* (Munich: Heimeran, 1968) 66; Magass, "Semiotik," 3, 5 n. 3.

88   Cf. Prov 5:10; 13:22; Pss 48 (49):11; Ps 68 (69):37; 108 (109):11; Sir 14:15; Job 20:15, 18.

89   See Bultmann, *History,* 221; Seng, "Tor," 147–50; Heininger, *Metaphorik,* 113–16.

90   That is underlined rightly by Seng, "Tor."

91   *Deuteronomy Rabbah* 9:1 on Deut 31:14; Seng, "Tor," 149.

92   Job, the wise poor man, is the counter-type to our rich fool.

various elements also have their equivalent in Hebraic and Jewish wisdom:[93] speaking to his own soul ($\psi\upsilon\chi\acute{\eta}$); the senselessness of a life without God; the uncertain and passing nature of riches; what the Germans call "*der lachende Erbe,*" "the inheritor who laughs"; the relationship between sin and death; the ill-considered enjoyment of the goods of this world; and the building up of capital with God, rather than here below.

What can be concluded from an examination of all these parallels is that the parable has an ethical orientation and value as paraenesis. It looks at life as a whole, of which the human being is not the owner but only the steward. The God we find in the parable is neither a tyrant nor an iniquitous judge, but the good God of creation and providence who, out of respect for his creatures, expects them to lead a responsible life lived in service to others and to his glory. What is imminent is not the parousia, but individual death, even though the solution of that alternative, which has been debated by commentators,[94] does not modify the fundamental structure of the requirement. In any case, the message of these verses is not limited, as it has been too often said, to an acknowledgment of one's finitude. It also goes beyond reminding us of human dependence on God. It encourages readers to take death into consideration, that is, to define their identities in relation to God, as they construct their lives. The true *memento mori* ("remember that you must die") about which the parable invites us to think consists in being concerned with God and one's neighbor (10:25-37), giving and giving of oneself, because that is how one receives and is received; it means thinking, to quote Dom Dupont,[95] of what comes after death; in Lukan terms, it means placing one's treasure in heaven and becoming rich in God (cf. 12:33-34; 12:21). That is the implicit conclusion that Luke draws from the explicit lesson that he gives in v. 21.[96]

Luke admits that men and women aspire to well-being—in a word, to possessions—that is his anthropology.[97] There are, however, two ways to store up, to amass, to acquire treasures,[98] one of which receives a negative connotation, the other a positive one—that is his ethics. The first is motivated by self-interest: one accumulates for oneself ($\dot{\epsilon}\alpha\upsilon\tau\hat{\omega}$[99]), whatever the nature of the possessions (Luke thinks, in the first instance, of money that has been amassed and all that it represents). The second one is disinterested; it also accumulates, if we dare put it that way, but $\epsilon\dot{\iota}\varsigma$ $\vartheta\epsilon\acute{o}\nu$, literally "with respect to God" (he thinks, in the first instance, of money that is distributed and of all the love that it represents)—that is his theology.[100]

■ **21** Everyone will agree that what the rich man amassed, he amassed for himself. Luke adds the note that he was not "rich in God." $\Pi\lambda o\upsilon\tau\acute{\epsilon}\omega$ means "to be rich" but also "to get rich," which is the dynamic sense that fits here.[101] Throughout his work, but particularly in vv. 33-34 of this twelfth chapter, the Gospel writer teaches us how this enrichment must take place: by the gift of one's possessions (14:33) and by the gift of oneself (9:23).[102] In his eyes, this ethical orientation of life

93   See esp. Seng, "Tor," 141–47.

94   On the one hand, see Jeremias (*Parables*, 164–66), for whom the death of the rich man serves as a parable for the imminence of the end-time; on the other hand, see Seng ("Tor"), Gaide ("Riche insensé," 88 n.16; Dupont ("L'après mort," 4–7) imagines the departure of the individual man. Ernst, 393–99, thinks that, at the traditional level, the parable opposed the good lands to eschatological life and, at the redactional level, it distinguishes the good lands well and badly used.

95   See Dupont, "L'après mort."

96   Cf. the initial $o\ddot{\upsilon}\tau\omega\varsigma$ ("and so") in v. 21.

97   On this anthropology, see Taeger, *Mensch*, 23, 125.

98   The verb $\vartheta\eta\sigma\alpha\upsilon\rho\acute{\iota}\zeta\omega$ does not appear in any other place in Luke-Acts. However, it is present twice in Matt 6:19-20 (= Q), of which Luke 12:33-34 is the parallel. Luke must be inspired already by this passage of Q and rewrites it in his own way

in the forthcoming material; Dupont, *Béatitudes*, 3:114–18.

99   The primitive reading of Codex Sinaiticus ℵ*, which is that also of Codex Vaticanus (B), $\alpha\upsilon\tau\omega$ (= $\alpha\dot{\upsilon}\tau\hat{\omega}$) is only the contracted form of $\dot{\epsilon}\alpha\upsilon\tau\hat{\omega}$ ("for oneself/himself") and does not have another sense.

100   This $\epsilon\dot{\iota}\varsigma$ $\vartheta\epsilon\acute{o}\nu$ is intelligible, but it remains curious. One can understand it either as a substitute for $\dot{\epsilon}\nu$ + dat. (cf. $\dot{\epsilon}\nu$ $\tau o\hat{\iota}\varsigma$ $o\dot{\upsilon}\rho\alpha\nuo\hat{\iota}\varsigma$, "in heaven," 12:33), or, as I prefer, in the sense of "in God," "against God," "toward God." Luke must have used it, other things being equal, because the dative, which is symmetrical to $\dot{\epsilon}\alpha\upsilon\tau\hat{\omega}$, would not have been suitable. Moreover, this enrichment, by being near to God, works in relation to others.

101   With Joüon, "Notes," 353–54.

102   Dupont, *Béatitudes*, 3:113–18; Dupont, "L'après mort," 4–7; Joüon, "Parabole"; Gaide, "Riche insensé"; Degenhardt, *Lukas*, 78–80.

corresponds not to a single act but rather to a daily attitude (cf. the "daily" in 9:23 and Acts 2:46). It is possible only for those who have met God and listened to Jesus. It is not the result of the will alone but also of the mind and the heart, enlightened by the Spirit.

To my way of thinking, v. 21 is secondary. It was born out of a need for the parable to acquire a moral. The first part of v. 21 satisfies that expectation, and the second completes the interpretation by deepening its meaning. It was perhaps Luke himself who added this second part ("but are not rich in God," καὶ μὴ εἰς θεὸν πλουτῶν).[103]

History of Interpretation

I would like to point out the textual hesitations in antiquity concerning the exclamation "Who set me to be a judge or arbitrator between you?" (v. 14). When Marcion retained the single word "judge," he was contrasting Jesus with the Moses of Exod 2:14 and was probably thinking of the judging God of the former order whom he contrasted with the unknown God, a generous Savior.[104] When the *Gospel of Thomas* is interested only in the term "divider" and extends it by the interpretative appendix "I am not a divider, am I?" it witnesses to faith in a Christ who is one and who unifies. Everything that symbolizes division can only be foreign to the Savior. The Gnostic interpretation of the Gospel is a witness to a profound aspiration to unity.[105] Two centuries later, the text of vv. 13-15 was to become a living text for the African bishop Augustine of Hippo when he was locked in a struggle with the Donatists. Augustine suffered in his flesh the division of the church, which was instigated by the intolerant movement of his enemies. In a series of sermons dating from that period,[106] Augustine highlights Jesus' refusal to be an agent of division. He apparently even made reference to a form of the text in which the word "judge" did not occur but which only had "arbitrator," "divider": *Quis me constituit divisorem inter vos?* ("Who made me a divider among you?").[107] The Catholic Church is compared to an inheritance, to the possession promised to the Son according to Ps 2:7-8.[108] This inheritance is quite different from human inheritances.[109] It can be declared heavenly and can be described in terms of love and truth.[110] It also consists of harmony between brothers and sisters in the church.[111] This inheritance, offered while the father is still living, cannot be divided up.[112] In that respect, its distribution is to be distinguished from all other kinds of succession. Alas, notes Augustine, there were, from the very beginning (cf. 1 Cor 1:10ff. and Jude 19) some Christians who favored division and who separated off from the rest of the church. In our time it is the Donatists who are the *divisores*, those who divide up the inheritance, lacking love and harming the unity of the church.[113] Jesus, however, came to gather together, not to divide (*colligere veni, non dividere*).[114] No Christian should ask, as did the anonymous person in the Gospel, to receive his or her share of the inheritance. On the contrary, each one should say: "I want to possess along with you"; "keep the inheritance with me."[115]

---

103 Dupont, *Béatitudes*, 3:113–18; idem, "L'après mort," 4–7; Joüon, "Parabole." On the theology of this verse, see Bovon, *L'oeuvre*, 233–35. For Bengel (*Gnomon*, 346), to be rich in God is to make use of one's temporal goods in order to intensify one's communion with God.

104 On the text of Luke 12:14 in Marcion, see Baarda, "Text," 117–18. The text of the *Diatessaron* of Tatian seems to correspond to that of Marcion, although without the words "or the arbitrator"; see ibid., 115–17.

105 See Baarda, "Text," 121–22; Schrage, *Thomas-Evangelium*, 151–53. A Sahidic manuscript of Luke 12:14 contains the same short text, "Who has established me as arbitrator among you?" according to Baarda, "Text," 121.

106 Baarda ("Text," 156–62) has reviewed six sermons of this period, a few before and a few after the *Col-*

latio Carthaginiensis cum Donatistis of 411 C.E. I call attention especially to *Sermo 107 de verbis Evangelii Lucae*: "I say to you, abstain from all avarice" (Luke 12:13-15) (*PL* 38:627–32).

107 *Serm.* 107.2, 3 (*PL* 38:628), twice.

108 Augustine *Sermo 358 de pace et charitate* 2 (*PL* 39:1586).

109 *Serm.* 358 (*PL* 39:1586–87).

110 *Serm.* 358.2–6 (*PL* 39:1586–89).

111 Augustine *Sermo 359 in Eccl. 25, 2: Concordia fratrum*, etc. 4 (*PL* 39:1593–94).

112 Augustine *Sermo de utilitate ieiunii* 10, 12–11, 13 (CCSL 46:240–41).

113 Augustine *Sermo 265 de ascensione Domini* 9, 10–11.

114 *Serm.* 265.9, 11 (*PL* 38:1224).

115 Augustine *Sermo 358 de pace et charitate* 2–3 (*PL* 39:1586, 1587).

In the same period, Basil "the Great," bishop of Caesarea in Cappadocia, delivered a powerful ethical sermon dealing with the parable of the rich man.[116] He found no allegory in it and concentrated on its ethical meaning. Basil sensitively analyzed the anguish of the rich man, of which he gave a lively depiction. But prior to that, he made a distinction, for the benefit of his listeners, between two kinds of temptations, those arising from adversity and those resulting, as here, from prosperity. Job is the portrait of the person who faces up to misfortune, and the man in this parable is the weak person who is unable to resist abundance. As is known, Basil pictured God as being philanthropic; it was out of affection that God gave all those possessions to the rich man. God wanted to encourage him to be generous. Alas, the unfortunate man forgot the natural community among human beings. The divine philanthropy was not matched by any human philanthropy. In this case, it was the generous patriarch Joseph who was contrasted with the foolish rich man (cf. Gen 47:11): "If Scripture offers us this example [the one of the foolish rich man], it is so that we will avoid behaving similarly." Just as the earth was generous to the landowner in our story, so must we also demonstrate generosity. Basil, who was able to depict the interior anguish of the rich man, next described with fearful harshness the exterior poverty of the poor people of his time, in particular the agony of the poor father who was obliged to sell one of his children in order to feed the rest of the family. Meanwhile, the rich people do not move a muscle. Nothing stops their desire for gold, save death. As for the rich man who refuses to give on the pretext of poverty, he turns out in reality to be poor, spiritually poor. The sin of rich people is believing that their possessions, which are only entrusted to them, constitute their personal property. From that is derived an ethical teaching distinguishing between what is necessary, which is kept for each person, and the surplus, which must be shared.

While the ethical orientation of the example story in Luke matched the concerns of the preacher of antiquity, it was less suited to the intentions of Martin Luther, the Reformer of Wittenberg.[117] In his 1529 sermon, Luther stressed two moments in the pericope, Jesus' refusal of what the anonymous inheritor asked, and the idea of being rich in God. The reason that Jesus refused to intervene is that he stuck to what God had decided, to the state in which each person finds himself or herself (the Lutheran doctrine of states, professions, and social status). Moreover, Jesus respected the will of God, who had made of him a preacher rather than a judge. So much for diverse human activities, which require various professions, the diversity of which is indispensable to justice and good order.

God's domain (the doctrine of the two reigns) is totally different. In this case, the variety of states corresponds to the unity of faith. This is the second moment on which Luther laid stress. To be rich in God—and this is where the reformer parted company with Luke—is to have faith, which does not even proceed from our heart, but from God. The richness in question is entirely the business of the Lord and his initiatives: liberation from sin, justification, sanctification, eternal life, joy, etc. We do not come into possession of these benefits except through the redemption obtained thanks to Christ.

These two moments, each person's personal state and God's action on behalf of all, were so important in Luther's eyes that he could say: "If Christians were to know these two pieces, they would know everything."[118] He himself was so concerned with teaching them that he attacked neither the doctrine of works nor the greed of the rich man. He was satisfied with saying that when faith is received, it must bear fruit: our good works. His attention was limited to this life, and he did not speak of death, which is so decisive in the parable, or of judgment.

Conclusion

By way of personal conclusions, I would say the following: in the apophthegm (vv. 13-14), the reader encounters an uncompromising Christ who had a double reason for refusing to intervene. The time of the judges in Israel and of the dividing up of the country among the tribes, and the age of Moses and of Joshua, all that belonged to the past. And the age of the Messiah, who will carry

---

116 Basil of Caesarea *Hom.* 31 (*PG* 31:261–78).

117 Luther, "Predigt vom 12.10 1529 in Jena," WA 29:587–91, in Mülhaupt, *Luthers Evangelien-Auslegung*, 3:184–89.

118 Mülhaupt, *Luthers Evangelien-Auslegung*, 3:189.

out the final dividing up, has not yet arrived. Moreover, since the request was motivated by the wrong intentions, to honor it would have been tantamount to encouraging dismantlement. But Jesus had in mind dividing up and not dissolution.

It is this root of evils, in one's inner being, that is stigmatized by the first concluding saying (v. 15). This saying orients one's thinking toward the true life that does not depend on what one possesses.

The parable (vv. 16-20) illustrates human finitude and the absurdity of wanting to ensure one's future by capital holdings. Days cannot be bought. Superabundance of possessions is no compensation for penury of time. Economic logic and secular wisdom pale before the wisdom of the gospel. It is curious that death is what brings persons who make the same mistake as the rich landowner to confront true values. Alas, the man in this story had neither the wisdom of Job nor the generosity of Joseph.

To consider death is to contemplate what comes after death and also to think about life (v. 21). How should we live? The Gospel proposes a lifestyle in which happiness is lived out in relationships, and in which giving, usually counted as a loss, becomes the best way to succeed and to be on the receiving end of things. Any possessions we might have at our disposal do not, in the last resort, belong to us. As was the case with the manna, we must not keep for ourselves any more than the minimum necessary for the coming day. The rest is to be shared. This sense of sharing must not curb human dynamism, the joy of producing and being able to contemplate the fruits of one's labor.

If this necessity of sharing proves to be true in connection with money, it also proves to be the case with respect to one's emotions. There is a harmful way of loving that resembles the need to possess expressed by the foolish rich man. Instead of providing the anticipated rest, such an attitude fills one's heart with anxiety and weariness in the face of the infinitude of the task. The person who is loved rebels, and the result is the opposite of the result hoped for. True rest and true rejoicing and being rich toward God stem from a different attitude. That is when loving means trusting in others and giving them freedom, not trying to bring everything back to oneself, putting oneself in the place of another and being related to, but not attached to, what one has.

A Quest without Worries
(12:22-34)
Bibliography

Attridge, Harold W., "The Greek Fragments," in Bentley Layton, ed., *Nag Hammadi Codex II.2–7* (NHS 20; Leiden: Brill, 1989) 1:95–128.

Avanzo, M., "Jesus y la conducción de la comunidad," *RevistB* 37 (1975) 16–22.

Berner, Ursula, *Die Bergpredigt: Rezeption und Auslegung im 20. Jahrhundert* (GTA 12; Göttingen: Vandenhoeck & Ruprecht, 1979).

Black, *Aramaic Approach*.

Bovon, *Theologian*.

Bultmann, *History*, 84, 85, 92, 107, 109, 111, 116, 134; *Geschichte der synoptischen Tradition* (ed. Gerd Theissen and Philipp Vielhauer; 4th ed.; Göttingen: Vandenhoeck & Ruprecht, 1971) 13, 15–16, 20.

Idem, "μεριμνάω κτλ.," *TDNT* 4 (1967) 589–93.

Cameron, Ron, "Parable and Interpretation in the Gospel of Thomas," *Forum* 2.2 (1986) 3–39.

Catchpole, David, "The Ravens, the Lilies, and the Q-Hypothesis: A Form-Critical Perspective on the Source-Critical problem," *SNTU* A 6/7 (1981–82) 77–87.

Chilton, Bruce D., *God in Strength: Jesus' Announcement of the Kingdom* (SNTU B 1; Freistadt: Plöchl, 1979) 231–50.

Degenhardt, *Lukas*, 85–93.

Del Verme, Marcello, *Comunione e condivisione dei beni: Chiesa primitiva e giudaismo esseno-qumranico a confronto* (Brescia: Morcelliana, 1977).

Derrett, J. Duncan M., "Birds of the Air and Lilies of the Field," *DRev* 105 (1987) 181–92.

Dillon, Richard J., "Ravens, Lilies, and the Kingdom of God (Matthew 6:25-33/Luke 12:22-31)," *CBQ* 53 (1991) 604–25.

Dupont, *Béatitudes*, 3:116–24, 272–304.

Edwards, *Theology of Q*, 123–25.

Egger, Wilhelm, "Faktoren der Textkonstitution in der Bergpredigt," *Laurentianum* 19 (1978) 177–98.

Fallon, Francis T., and Ron Cameron, "The Gospel of Thomas: A Forschungsbericht and Analysis," *ANRW* 2.25.6 (1988) 4195–251.

Fieger, Michael, *Das Thomasevangelium: Einleitung, Kommentar und Systematik* (NTAbh 22; Münster: Aschendorff, 1991) 108–10, 127–29, 209–13.

Fuchs, Ernst, "Die Verkündigung Jesu: Der Spruch von den Raben," in Helmut Ristow and Karl Matthiae, eds., *Der historische Jesus und der kerygmatische Christus Beiträge zum Christusverständnis in Forschung und Verkündigung* (Berlin: Evangelische Verlagsanstalt, 1961) 365–88.

George, A., "L'attente du maître qui vient: Lc 12, 32-48," *AsSeign* 50 (1974) 66–76.

Glasson, T. Francis, "Carding and Spinning: Oxyrhynchus Papyrus No. 655," *JTS* 13 (1962) 331–32.

Guelich, Robert A., *The Sermon on the Mount: A Foundation for Understanding* (Waco, Tex.: Word Books, 1982) 369–74 and passim.

Haubst, R., "Eschatologie, 'Der Wetterwinkel'—'Theologie der Hoffnung,'" *TThZ* 11 (1968) 35–65.

Healey, J. F., "Models of Behavior: Matt 6:26; Luke 12:24; Prov 6:6-8," *JBL* 108 (1989) 497–98.

Hendrickx, Herman, *The Sermon on the Mount* (San Francisco: Harper & Row, 1984).

Hoffmann, Paul, "Jesu 'Verbot des Sorgens' und seine Nachgeschichte in der synoptischen Überlieferung," in D. A. Koch, G. Sellin, and A. Lindemann, eds., *Jesu Rede von Gott und ihre Nachgeschichte im frühen Christentum: Beiträge zur Verkündigung Jesu und zum Kerygma der Kirche. Festschrift für Willi Marxsen zum 70. Geburtstag* (Gütersloh, Gütersloher Verlagshaus, 1989) 116–41.

Idem, "Der Q-Text der Sprüche vom Sorgen (Mt 6, 25-33/Lk 12, 22-31): Ein Rekonstructionsversuch," in Ludger Schenke, ed., *Studien zum Matthäusevangelium: Festschrift für Wilhelm Pesch* (SBS; Stuttgart: Katholisches Bibelwerk, 1988) 128–55.

Idem, "Die Sprüche vom Sorgen (Mt 6, 25-33/Lk 12, 22-31) in der vorsynoptischen Überlieferung," in H. Hierdeis and H. S. Rosenbauch, eds., *Artikulation der Wirklichkeit: Festschrift fur Siegfried Oppolzer zum 60. Geburtstag* (New York: Lang, 1989) 73–94.

Horn, *Glaube und Handeln*, 66–68 and passim.

Iwand, *Gegenwart*, 27–38.

Jeremias, *Parables*, passim.

Johnson, *Possessions*, 1–78, 127–71.

Kea, P. V., "Discipleship in the Great Sermon: A Literary-Critical Approach" (Diss. Union Theological Seminary, Richmond, Va., 1983).

Kloppenborg, *Formation*, 216–21.

Idem, "The Q-Sayings on Anxiety (Q 12:2-7)," *Forum* 5.2 (1989) 83–98.

Kraft, R. A., "Oxyrhynchus Papyrus 655 Reconsidered," *HTR* 54 (1961) 253–62.

Laconi, M., "Ricchi devanti a Dio," *SacDoc* 34 (1989) 5–41.

Lambrecht, Jan, *"Eh bien! Moi, je vous dis": Le discours-programme de Jésus (Mt 5–7; Lc 6,20-49)* (LD 125; Paris: Cerf, 1986) 149–78.

Luz, *Matthew*, 1:338–48.

Manson, *Sayings*, 110–14.

Massaux, Edouard, *The Influence of the Gospel of Matthew on Christian Literature before Saint Irenaeus* (3 vols.; New Gospel Studies 5.1–3; Macon, Ga.: Mercer University Press, 1993) 1:22–23; 2:116–19.

Mealand, D. L., "'Paradisial' Elements in the Teaching of Jesus," in E. A. Livingstone, ed., *Studia Biblica 1978: Sixth International Congress on Biblical Studies, Oxford, 3–7 April 1978* (3 vols.; JSOTSup 11; JSNTSup 2–3; Sheffield: University of Sheffield, 1980) 2:179–84.

Mees, M., "Das Sprichwort Matt 6, 21/Lk 12, 34 und seine ausserkanonischen Parallelen," *Aug* 14 (1974) 67–89.

Merkelbach, R., "Logion 36 des Thomas-Evangeliums (die Lilien auf dem Felde)," *ZPE* 54 (1984) 64.

Merklein, *Gottesherrschaft*, 174–83, 207–9.

Meyer, B. F., "Jesus and the Remnant of Israel," *JBL* 84 (1965) 123–30.

Miller, Robert J., "The Lord's Prayer and Other Items from the Sermon on the Mount," *Forum* 5.2 (1989) 177–86.

Molitor, J., "Zur Übersetzung von μετεωρίζεσθε Lk 12, 29," *BZ* 10 (1966) 107–8.

Montgomery, James A., "Some Correspondence between the Elephantine Papyri and the Gospels," *ExpT* 24 (1912–13) 428–29.

Neuhäusler, *Exigence de Dieu*, 77–78.

Nickels, Peter, *Targum and New Testament: A Bibliography, Together with a New Testament Index* (Scripta Pontificii Instituti Biblici 117; Rome: Pontifical Biblical Institute, 1967) 39.

Nickelsburg, George W. E., "Riches, the Rich, and God's Judgement in I Enoch 92–105 and the Gospel according to Luke," *NTS* 25 (1978–79) 324–44.

Nötscher, F., "Das Reich (Gottes) und seine Gerechtigkeit (Mt 6, 33 vgl. Lc 12, 31)," *Bib* 31 (1950) 237–41.

Olsthoorn, M. F., *The Jewish Background and the Synoptic Setting of Mt 6:25-33 and Lk 12:22-31* (Jerusalem: Studium Biblicum Franciscanum, 1975).

Pesch, Rudolf, *Die kleine Herde: Zur Theologie der Gemeinde* (Reihe X; Graz/Cologne: Styria, 1973).

Idem, "'Sei getrost, kleine Herde' (Lk 12,32): Exegetische und ekklesiologische Erwägungen," in Karl Färber, ed., *Krise der Kirche—Chance des Glaubens: Die "Kleine Herde" heute und morgen* (Frankfurt a.M.: Knecht, 1968).

Pesch, W., "Zur Exegese von Mt 6, 19-21 und Lk 12, 33-34," *Bib* 41 (1960) 356–78.

Idem, "Zur Formgeschichte und Exegese von Lk. 12, 32," *Bib* 41 (1960) 25–40.

Riesenfeld, Harold, "Vom Schätzesammeln und Sorgen: Ein Thema urchristlicher Paränese. Zu Mt 6, 19-24," in *Neotestamentica et Patristica: Eine Freundesgabe, Herrn Professor Dr. Oscar Cullmann zu seinem 60. Geburtstag überreicht* (NovTSup 6; Leiden: Brill, 1962).

Sato, *Q und Prophetie*, 57, 173, 218–19, 221–22, 224, 239, 390, 394.

Schlosser, *Règne de Dieu*, 2:573–601 (on verse 32).

Schmid, *Matthäus und Lukas*, 234–37.

Schottroff and Stegemann, *Jesus*, 55–62.

Schrage, *Thomas-Evangelium*, 90, 155–64.

Schulz, *Q*, 142–45, 149–57.

Schweizer, Eduard, *Die Bergpredigt* (Göttingen: Vandenhoeck & Ruprecht, 1982) 73–79.

Seccombe, *Possessions*, 137–38, 146–59.

Sellew, Philip H., "Reconstruction of Q 12:33-59," *SBLSP* (1987) 617–68.

Steinhauser, *Doppelbildworte*, 215–35.

Idem, "The Sayings on Anxieties: Matt 6:25-34 and Luke 12:22-32," *Forum* 6.1 (1990) 67–79.

Tannehill, *Sword*, 60–67.

Wrege, Hans-Theo, *Die Überlieferungsgeschichte der Bergpredigt* (WUNT 9; Tübingen: Mohr Siebeck, 1968).

Zeller, Dieter, *Die weisheitlichen Mahnsprüche bei den Synoptikern* (FB 17; Würzburg: Echter, 1977).

22/ He said to his disciples, "That is why I tell you, do not worry about your life, what will you eat, or about your body, what will you wear? **23/** For life is more than food, and the body more than clothing. **24/** Consider the ravens: they neither sow nor reap, they have neither storeroom nor barn, and God feeds them. Of how much more value are you than the birds! **25/** And can any of you by worrying add a single cubit to your span of life? **26/** If then you are not able to do the minimum, why do you worry about the rest? **27/** Consider the lilies, how they neither spin nor weave;[a] I tell you, even Solomon in all his glory was not clothed like one of these! **28/** If God so clothes the grass, which is alive today in the fields,

a   The text is uncertain. The alternate reading is close to Matthew: "how they grow, they neither toil nor spin."

and tomorrow will be thrown into the oven, how much more will he clothe you—believers of low caliber[b]! 29/ And you, do not keep striving for what you are to eat or what you are to drink, and do not let yourselves be tossed around in every direction. 30/ For it is all the nations of the world that strive after these things, but your Father knows that you need them. 31/ Instead, strive for his kingdom, and these things will be given to you as well. 32/ Do not be afraid, little flock, for it is your Father's good pleasure to give you the kingdom.

33/ Sell your possessions, and give alms with the proceeds. Make purses for yourselves that do not wear out, an unfailing treasure in the heavens, where no thief comes near and no moth destroys. 34/ For where your treasure is, there your heart will be also.

b   Literally, "ye of little faith." For the proposed translation, see below, pp. 218–19 nn. 70–72.

Here the subject is what is necessary, rather than, as in 12:16-21, what is superfluous. But what necessity are we dealing with? The pericope is going to state it, first eliminating popular wisdom, then setting out an indispensable priority. Curiously enough, it is sapiential language that Jesus uses to criticize this wisdom. Since the objective that has priority must be determined, so too the approach that humans must take. What we must fix our attention on (v. 31) is not food or drink but the kingdom; likewise, people can attain it not by increasing their worrying but by intensifying their quest for it. These two contrasting attitudes as well as the two incompatible objectives pick up on the contrasts of vv. 32 and 33-34 between true and false riches, on the one hand, and true and false treasures, on the other.

The wisdom expressed by Jesus in these lines is shocking, even preposterous, because the very attitude that it stigmatizes seems to be the only reasonable one.[1] Do we not have a responsibility to think about what we are going to eat and how we are going to support those who depend on us? Moreover, what resemblance is there between the picture of nature it presents and the reality that we experience in our day? Is it possible for a person to live without any possessions at all? In short, this text, which many have loved from their childhood and which rings true for them, is it not irritating, or at least intriguing?

Analysis

Luke linked this pericope with the preceding one by the admittedly traditional (cf. Matt 6:25) words "that is why" ($\delta\iota\grave{\alpha}\ \tau o\hat{v}\tau o$), which he placed on the lips of Jesus (v. 22). He punctuated this pericope with a consolation (v. 32), before picking up again (vv. 33-34) with the problem dealt with in the preceding pericope, that of money and its proper use (cf. vv. 13-21).[2]

Verses 22-34 constitute a well-knit unit of an ethical nature,[3] by reason of its numerous imperatives, and of a didactic nature, by reason of its various illustrations

---

1   See Luz (*Matthew*, 1:341–42), who indicates several negative reactions with regard to our text; Olsthoorn, *Background*, 5; Lambrecht, "*Eh bien!*," 149.

2   Verse 32 is joined sometimes to vv. 33-34, e.g., by Cyril of Alexandria *Serm. Luc.* 91; see Payne Smith, *Cyril*, 2:419–23.

3   See, e.g., Wrege, *Bergpredigt*, 116–24; Degenhardt, *Lukas*, 80–95. Schulz, *Q*, 149–57; Zeller, *Mahnsprüche*, 82–93; Merklein, *Gottesherrschaft*, 174–83, 207–9; Hoffmann, "Sprüche"; idem, "Sorgen"; idem, "Verbot." Schulz (*Q*, 155) makes this composition address the prophetic movement of primitive Christianity; Merklein (*Gottesherrschaft*, 178) attributes it to Jesus himself.

and logical proofs. The ethical and didactic elements are rooted in the good news of the kingdom. God asks us to be concerned with his business, because he has concerned himself with ours by sending his Son to share our condition (cf. Heb 2:17-18). The radical nature of the ethical imperative is a function of the radical nature of the divine intervention.

To my way of thinking, what we have here is not a teaching in the form of a poem[4] but a lesson in the style of Hebraic wisdom, where there is an alternation between imperatives and indicatives, advice and explanations. The different sayings are linked to each other by a single theme and by linking words (especially the verb μεριμνάω, "worry," "be anxious"). Wisdom and apocalypticism get along well together here, as is often the case in Jesus' teaching.[5] The wisdom in this case is, in fact, religious wisdom, and what attracts our attention is not so much contemplation of nature as the eschatological offer of the kingdom. Since the disciples, who are specifically addressed (v. 22), run the risk of doubting ("believers of low caliber," ὀλιγόπιστοι, v. 28), Jesus suggests to them that they should look at reality intelligently ("consider," κατανοήσατε, vv. 24, 27) and understand not only what is but also what is coming; not only the work of God as creator but also that of the redemptive Father.

Here is my suggestion for an outline of vv. 22-32:[6]

The Gospel writer's introduction, v. 22a
Jesus' metalinguistic expression, v. 22b
First negative command ("do not worry," μὴ μεριμνᾶτε), v. 22c
   First justification ("for," γάρ), v. 23
      First illustration ("consider," κατανοήσατε), v. 24abcd

First deduction ("of how much more," πόσῳ μᾶλλον), v. 24e
   Rhetorical question ("and can any of you," τίς δὲ ἐξ ὑμῶν), v. 25
   Consequence ("if then . . . why do you worry," εἰ οὖν . . . τί . . . μεριμνᾶτε), v. 26
Second illustration ("consider," κατανοήσατε), v. 27
Second deduction ("how much more," πόσῳ μᾶλλον), v. 28
Second negative command ("and you, do not keep striving," καὶ ὑμεῖς μὴ ζητεῖτε), v. 29
   Second justification ("for," γάρ), v. 30
First positive command ("instead, strive for," πλὴν ζητεῖτε), v. 31
Third negative command ("do not be afraid," μὴ φοβοῦ, a singular agreeing with "flock," ποίμνιον), v. 32.

This unit is found also, with the same structure and very often the same words, in Matthew, in the Sermon on the Mount (Matt 6:25-34). The commonly held view,[7] which I share with virtually all commentators, attributes it to Q. Since the saying about treasure is associated with this pericope in both Gospels, Matthew and Luke, coming a little bit before it in Matthew (Matt 6:19-21), and immediately following it in Luke (Luke 12:33-34), it can be conjectured that the two units already followed one after the other in Q. But in what *order*? We should point out that Q had, a little bit before this, a teaching directed at the disciples about confession (Luke 12:1-12 par.) followed by these two units. Luke usually respected Q's order, and the opening expression "that is why" (διὰ τοῦτο, Luke 12:22 par. Matt 6:25) is not surprising, following on the saying about the help of the Holy Spirit (Luke 12:12 par.). Moreover, in a passage that is

---

4   See Grundmann, 259; and Degenhardt (*Lukas*, 80), who speaks of "Lehrgedicht" (didactic poem). Against this, see Schulz, *Q*, 153; and Steinhauser, *Doppelbildworte*, 215. On the style, rhythm, and possible stanzas, see Schulz, *Q*, 153 n. 110; Zeller, *Mahnsprüche*, 83–87. Black (*Aramaic Approach*, 135, 138) notes alliterations and homonyms in a retroversion into Aramaic in 12:33, 27, 24.

5   See Zeller, *Mahnsprüche*, 83–86.

6   The presentation of the structure of the pericope in Q is in Zeller, *Mahnsprüche*, 82.

7   For Wrege (*Bergpredigt*, 116–24) there are, on the contrary, two distinct traditions behind Matthew and Luke, barely having been retouched by the evangelists. The thesis of Luke's dependence by rapport with Matthew is, as one knows, again defended; see several articles in Tuckett, *Synoptic Studies*.

not dependent on Luke, Justin Martyr quotes the saying about treasure right *after* the one about worrying.[8] So it can be accepted that Luke's order corresponds to Q's.[9]

The *contents* of Q can be reconstructed rather easily. The attempts in this regard of Dieter Zeller and Paul Hoffmann are virtually identical.[10] I would like to point out here how Luke has arranged what he got from Q: he provides an introduction to Jesus' speech (v. 22a), which Matthew does not. In this place he does not have the mention of drink (following the text of Q, to which Matthew makes an addition). He has transformed Q's rhetorical question into an affirmation (v. 23). He standardizes the imperative in the illustration (retaining "consider" [κατανοήσατε] twice, vv. 24 and 27, in place of Q's "look" [ἐμβλέψατε] one time and "learn" [καταμάθετε] the other). With Q, Luke speaks of "ravens" (v. 24; Matthew: "birds"), which does not have the same impact, as we will see below. He writes, "they have neither storeroom nor barn" (v. 24; Matthew, following Q, has "nor gather into barns"). Luke retains "God" (v. 24, Q), where Matthew prefers his favorite designation, "your heavenly Father." Here, as in v. 28, Luke uses the phrase "how much more" (πόσῳ μᾶλλον) in his final conclusion. Then, in v. 25, he has improved on the word order, the transition, and the wording of v. 26 ("If then you are not able to do the minimum, why do you worry about the rest?"; Matthew, following Q, has: "and why do you worry about clothing?"). In the second illustration (the lilies, v. 27), if we follow the "Western" text, Luke has omitted the growth, which is noted by Q, and says: "they neither spin nor weave" (Matthew and probably Q: "they neither toil nor spin"). At the end of v. 28, Luke has once again transformed the rhetorical question into an affirmation.[11] In v. 29, he already leads off with the new positive verb "strive" (ζητέω), while Matthew keeps the verb "worry" (μεριμνάω) found in Q. Still in v. 29, Luke prefers indirect discourse to the direct discourse found in Matthew and Q. What is most interesting is that in place

of "what will we wear?" found in Matthew and Q, Luke writes the enigmatic "and do not let yourselves be tossed around in every direction" (καὶ μὴ μετεωρίζεσθε). In v. 30 he adds to Q the genitive "of the world" after "the nations."[12] In v. 31, he adds "instead" (πλήν), of which he is fond[13] and which must be redactional, as also must be, in Matthew, the "first" and "and his righteousness" in the phrase "But strive first for the kingdom of God and his righteousness." Oddly enough, in Matthew and Luke the unit ends with two totally dissimilar sayings, an indication that floating sayings tended to be added at the end of parables or speeches. These two additions are negative imperatives, one of which, the one in Matthew, continues the comment on worries (here, those related to tomorrow); the other, the one in Luke (v. 32) provides a detail about the kingdom that Jesus has just ordered his disciples to strive for (v. 31). The adventitious character of the saying in Luke is revealed in an exterior indication: it is no longer "you (pl.)" that is being addressed but, in the singular, the "little flock." The fact that this saying was a late addition does not mean that it was of recent origin. It must, on the contrary, be an early proclamation. But, like many other sayings, it must have circulated as an isolated saying. Yet, if, from the point of view of the structure, it appears to be tacked on to the verses about worries, it nevertheless fits well with the theological perspective.

The text of Q is a literary composition, as are the statements in Matthew and Luke that follow it. We can attempt to go back behind this composition and reconstruct its origin.[14] At the level of Q, we may take the introduction "that is why I tell you" (v. 22b par.) to be redactional. Likewise, the rhetorical question about the length of life (v. 25 par.), which seems superfluous, must have been added with the passage of time. I would say the same thing about the saying about life and the body (v. 23 par.). The tradition prior to Q issued an invitation to not worry about either food or clothing: the ravens illustrated the case of food; the lilies, that of clothing.

---

8   On the text of Justin, see n. 18 below.

9   Hoffmann ("Sorgen," 131–33) thinks, on the contrary, that Matthew preserves the more original order.

10   Zeller, *Mahnsprüche*, 82; Hoffmann, "Sorgen," 154–55.

11   I do not mention here the other minor differences between Luke 12:28 and Matt 6:30.

12   There are also a few differences between Luke 12:30 and Matt 6:32, e.g., the absence in Luke of the adjective "all" with "these things."

13   See Luke 6:24, 35; 10:11, 14, 20; etc. (nineteen times in Luke-Acts).

14   See Bultmann, *History*, 84, 92, 107, 116; Hoffmann, "Sprüche," 83–89; Zeller, *Mahnsprüche*, 86–87.

The third example, that of grass (v. 28 par.), must not have been a part of the original composition either. The double justification in v. 30 par. has the appearance of a commentary on both what precedes (v. 29 par.) and what follows (v. 31 par.). Verse 29 par. is parallel to v. 22c. These doublets exhorted people to not worry. But instead of their being illustrated, as the first command was, this second exhortation served as the first panel of a diptych. The first was illustrated by two examples, the one about the ravens (v. 24 par.) and the one about the lilies (v. 27 par.); the second was completed by the positive invitation to strive for the kingdom (v. 31 par.). Some justifications or explanations were progressively joined to these two blocks of material: one about life and the body (v. 23 par.), the other about Gentiles and the Father's knowledge (v. 30 par.). Some additional examples about the length of human life (v. 25 par.) and the grass of the fields (v. 28 par.) were added. Our commentary will demonstrate the influence of this history of successive traditions and redactions on the evolution of the meaning.

The *Oxyrhynchus Papyrus* 655 transmits a special form of various sayings in this pericope. The sayings in question are the first negative command (v. 22c), which in the papyrus is immediately followed by the second illustration (v. 27). Then comes the additional example about the length of life (v. 25), which precedes the example of the lilies in Q (v. 27). Finally, after a question from the disciples, Jesus utters a decisive saying about nakedness. This group of sayings is found, in Coptic, in a wording that is shorter in its beginning, in the *Gospel of Thomas* 36–37.[15] Here is the translation of the partially reconstituted text of *P.Oxy.* 655:

> and when you will take your shirts and you will put them under your feet as children do and when you will walk over them, then you will become the sons of the Living One and you will be without fear.[16]

The apocryphal text is clearly interested in clothing. Its retention of only the second illustration, the one about lilies, is understandable. In its omission of the mention of drink it is closer to the text of Luke; in its description of the lilies, to Matthew. In the wording of the question about the length of life, it goes its own way. In my opinion, the *Gospel of Thomas,* which keeps sayings that go back sometimes farther than Q, is based here as much on oral traditions as on the written text of our canonical Gospels.[17]

The same is true of Justin Martyr, who, in his *First Apology* (15.14–16),[18] quotes a parallel passage. He men-

---

15 "Jesus said, "Do not be concerned from morning until evening and from evening until morning about what you will wear" (*Gos. Thom.* 36; trans. Thomas O. Lambdin, in Robinson, *Nag Hammadi Library*, 130. Logion 37 corresponds, at its start, to the text of *Papyrus Oxyrhynchus* 655, and its end permits one to reconstitute the final part of the Greek papyrus, with its lacunae, of the logion from the Greek papyrus.

16 The edition of this papyrus has been the subject of numerous discussions. On one point, the reconstruction that I adopt departs from the text proposed by Aland, *Synopsis*, 286. Following a conjecture suggested by V. Barlet, then by T. C. Skeat, summarized for our day by Kraft ("Oxyrhynchus"), Glasson ("Carding"), Merkelbach ("Logion"), Fallon and Cameron (*Thomas*, 4202), and Attridge ("Greek"), I read ἅτι[να ο]ὐ ξα[ί]νει οὐδὲ ν[ήϑ]ει, "wh[o neith]er card, nor s[pi]n," and not ἅτι[να α]ὐξά-νει οὐδὲ ν[ήϑ]ει, "wh[o g]row but do not s[pi]n." Cf. Schrage, *Thomas-Evangelium*, 90–91. At the end of the citation, which is a modern retroversion from the Coptic, I have rendered the Greek

"as the children" by "as do the children." See also Attridge's translation ("Greek," 127–28): "[Jesus said, 'Do not be concerned] from morning [until evening and] from evening [until] morning, neither [about] your [food] and what [you will] eat, [nor] about [your clothing] and what you [will] wear. [You are far] better than the [lilies] which [neither] card nor [spin]. As for you, when you have no garment, what [will you put on]? Who might add to your stature? He it is who will give you your cloak.' His disciples said to him, 'When will you become revealed to us and when shall we see you?' He said, 'When you disrobe and are not ashamed. . . .'"

17 See Beate Blatz, "Das koptische Thomasevange-lium," in Schneemelcher, *New Testament Apocrypha*, 1:105.

18 Cited by Aland, *Synopsis*, 286–87. "Take no thought what you shall eat, or what you shall put on: are you not better than the birds and the beasts? And God feeds them. Take no thought, therefore, what you shall eat, or what you shall put on; for your heavenly Father knows that you have need of these things. But seek the kingdom of heaven, and all

tions the first negative command (without a mention of drink, Matt 6:25b par. Luke 12:22c); the rhetorical question (superiority of humans over birds, Matt 6:26d par. Luke 12:24e); the assertion that God feeds them (Matt 6:26c par. Luke 12:24d); and the second negative command (without mention of drink, Matt 6:31 par. Luke 12:29), followed by the assertion of God's knowledge (Matt 6:32b par. Luke 12:30b) and of the invitation to strive for the kingdom (in pre-Matthean wording, without "first" ($\pi\rho\hat{\omega}\tau o\nu$) or "and his righteousness"). It all ends with the saying about treasure (Matt 6:21 par. Luke 12:34) with the mention of a person's "mind" (and not "heart"). Although Luke's influence is not present, Matthew's influence does not explain all of Justin's text or his silences. Here, once again, we must appeal to the oral transmission of Jesus' teaching.

In antiquity, there was in circulation an *agraphon* of Jesus, that is, a floating oral saying absent from the Scriptures, that was quoted by Clement of Alexandria and Origen: "Ask for great things, and the little things will be added to you."[19] This saying resembles Luke 12:31 in its caustic contents, while it recalls Luke 16:10 in its structure and its popular wisdom (faithful in the smallest things, faithful in the largest). In Origen, the *agraphon* continues with wording reminiscent of John 3:12 and Wis 9:16: "And ask for heavenly things, and the earthly things will be added to you."[20]

The inventory of these parallels sheds light on the success that the *teaching* of Jesus had in the patristic era,

especially in the second century, and the *absence of strictness* that was characteristic of its oral and written transmission.

Let us move on now to the analysis of vv. 33-34. As is confirmed by the parallel in Justin (*1 Apol.* 15:10–17), this unit, attested by Matthew and Luke, immediately followed the pericope about worries in Q. In the wording of the opening part, the two Gospel writers differ. Matthew preserves the Semitic antithetical parallel of Q (do not amass possessions on earth, but build up treasure for yourself in heaven, Matt 6:19-20), while Luke adapts the text to his language[21] and his theology,[22] being inspired by the wording of surrounding sayings.[23] Luke freely composed v. 33a as a commentator and teacher, while he reworked v. 33b.[24] The two Gospel writers, however, quite close in the final saying about treasure and the heart (Luke 12:34 par. Matt 6:21).[25] This shared faithfulness to even the form of the saying is a witness to the respect that the earliest Christians had for this assertion by their teacher.[26]

From the point of view of structure, we are dealing first with a double command (v. 33), which in Luke is made up of a series of imperatives in the aorist plural, the last of which is continued by a description of heavenly conditions (cf. "where," $\H{o}\pi o\upsilon$), which was supposed to mobilize one's energies. The imperatives are positive in Luke, and the saying is divided into two parts: by acting here and now (v. 33a), the disciples accumulate on high and for tomorrow (v. 33b), while Q (cf. Matt 6:19-20)

---

these things shall be added unto you. For where his treasure is, there also is the mind of a man" (trans. Roberts and Donaldson, in *ANF* vol. 1; Massaux, *Matthew*, 479–81). Justin depends on Matthew in preference to Luke; for the numerous differences with Matthew, Massaux appeals to Justin's own intervention and not the influence of oral tradition. (3:22–23))

19 See Clement of Alexandria *Strom.* 1.24.158.2; Origen *Or.* 14.1; 2.2; texts cited in Aland, *Synopsis*, 286.

20 On this *agraphon*, see Resch, *Agrapha*, 111–12; and Joachim Jeremias, *The Unknown Sayings of Jesus* (trans. Reginald Fuller; London: SPCK, 1957) 87–89 (#18).

21 The words $\pi\omega\lambda\acute{\epsilon}\omega$, $\tau\grave{\alpha}$ $\acute{\upsilon}\pi\acute{\alpha}\rho\chi o\nu\tau\alpha$, and $\grave{\epsilon}\lambda\epsilon\eta\mu o\sigma\acute{\upsilon}\nu\eta$ belong to the Lukan vocabulary.

22 See the commentary on vv. 32-34 below.

23 E.g., "Sell all that you own and distribute the money to the poor, and you will have treasure in heaven"

(18:22 *NRSV*); "make friends for yourselves by means of dishonest wealth" (16:9 *NRSV*); "so therefore, none of you can become my disciple if you do not give up all your possessions" (14:33 *NRSV*).

24 Verse 33a differs totally from Matt 6:19. In v. 33b, the "make purses for yourselves that do not wear out" is redactional; $\beta\alpha\lambda\lambda\acute{\alpha}\nu\tau\iota o\nu$ is peculiar to Luke in the NT; $\pi\alpha\lambda\alpha\iota\acute{o}\omega$ occurs only here in Luke; while $\grave{\alpha}\nu\acute{\epsilon}\kappa\lambda\epsilon\iota\pi\tau o\varsigma$ ("without defect") is a *hapax legomenon* in the NT. It is Luke who must modify the plural "some treasures" into "a treasure" because of his theological preference.

25 Matthew 6:21 is addressed to "you" (sg.); Luke 12:34 to "you" (pl.). Matthew has a tendency to harmonize the text with what comes next (Matt 6:22 "your eye"). *Gospel of Thomas* 76 has, like Luke, the plural. This must be the form of Q.

26 A good synoptic comparison is in Schulz, *Q*, 142–43; and Sellew, "Reconstruction," 621, 623–30.

contrasted bad conduct (negative imperative) with good conduct (positive imperative). This double command is followed, in v. 34, by a justification (cf. the "for," $\gamma \acute{\alpha} \rho$).

In my opinion, the two sayings (vv. 33 and 34) had not always circulated together. They could very well have had an independent existence. Justin Martyr quoted them separated from each other (*1 Apol.* 15.10–17). The *Gospel of Thomas*, for its part, associated only a part of the first saying with the Matthean parable of the pearl: "Jesus said, 'The kingdom of the father is like a merchant who had a consignment of merchandise and who discovered a pearl. That merchant was shrewd. He sold the merchandise and bought the pearl alone for himself. You, too, seek his unfailing and enduring treasure where no moth comes near to devour and no worm destroys'" (76).[27] The wording of the *Gospel of Thomas* is, on the whole, closer to Luke than to Matthew: the treasure is in the singular and it is inexhaustible. The mention of the moth and the worm (Luke was unacquainted with the example of the worm), however, corresponds to Matthew or, rather, to Q.

Historically, the second saying (v. 34), preserved with the greatest of care, must go back to the historical Jesus. When compared with Judaism and Hellenism, it is also the earliest. While the giving of alms, to which v. 33 invites us, fits with Jewish ethical teaching,[28] the renunciation of one's possessions (v. 33) matches the ethical ideal of a branch of early Christianity.

Commentary

■ **22** Luke lets Jesus speak and thus shows the vehicular nature of his literary enterprise. At the beginning of what will be a long quotation,[29] Jesus expresses two realities by a single verb ("I tell you"): he articulates the fact that he is the one who is going to be speaking, and that he is to do so with authority.[30] The phrase is one used by a teacher as much as by a prophet.[31] At the level of redaction, the phrase "that is why" ($\delta \iota \grave{\alpha} \ \tau o \hat{\upsilon} \tau o$) has the following meaning: if one wishes to be rich toward God (v. 21), here is what must be done (v. 22).

Three domains facilitate our understanding of the exhortation "do not worry" ($\mu \grave{\eta} \ \mu \epsilon \rho \iota \mu \nu \hat{\alpha} \tau \epsilon$): Greek philology, the Semitic milieu, and psychological or social modernity.[32] In Greek, $\mu \epsilon \rho \iota \mu \nu \acute{\alpha} \omega$ refers to the worrying that one does about someone and the care that one takes of something; it refers especially to anxious concern, as well as to the inquiries and suffering to which it gives rise.[33] The study of Hebrew sapiential literature provides an ample harvest of examples:[34] in it worries are associated with insomnia, physical exhaustion, the bitterness associated with thankless work, and restlessness and noise.[35] The opposite situation is characterized by rest and peace.[36] Such wisdom acknowledges trouble as being the common lot of human beings and recognizes the fact that daily life, threatened by dangers and death, is the

27 Schrage, *Thomas-Evangelium*, 155–59.

28 Pesch, "Exegese."

29 On the idea of this citation, see Bovon, *L'oeuvre*, 146–51.

30 The text is uncertain in two places: must one read $\alpha \dot{\upsilon} \tau o \hat{\upsilon}$ ("of him") after "the disciples"—or not? Otherwise, the order of the words $\lambda \acute{\epsilon} \gamma \omega \ \dot{\upsilon} \mu \hat{\iota} \nu$ ("I say to you") varies.

31 Exegetes insist usually on the prophetic and charismatic character; see Schulz, *Q*, 57–61; Zeller, *Mahnsprüche*, 93; but one encounters this formula not in the prophetic books of the OT but in apocalyptic writings and Jewish wisdom; see Prov 4:23; *1 Enoch* 91:3; 94:1, 3, 10; 99:13; 109:9; *T. Reu.* 1:7; 4:5; 6:5; *T. Levi* 16:4; *T. Benj.* 9:1; Schulz, *Q*, 58. Kloppenborg (*Formation*, 210 n. 164, 218–19) opts for a sapiential sense of the formula.

32 See the commentary above on 10:41.

33 This vocabulary is absent from Philo, Josephus, and the Stoa (where one has $\varphi \rho o \nu \tau \acute{\iota} \zeta \omega$ and $\varphi \rho o \nu \tau \acute{\iota} \varsigma$). In the LXX, $\mu \acute{\epsilon} \rho \iota \mu \nu \alpha$ (twelve times) and $\mu \epsilon \rho \iota \mu \nu \acute{\alpha} \omega$

(nine times) belongs to customary Greek usage. The substantive renders the Hebrew דְּאָגָה in Sir 30:24; 34[31]:1-2 and 42:9. In the other passages, there is no equivalent in the Hebrew text; see, e.g., Sir 38:29; Job 11:18; Prov 17:12. It applies just as well to Jdt 8:29; Esth 1:11 (Greek) (A13); 1 Macc 6:10; cf. Ps 54 (55):23: "Cast your burden on the Lord and he will sustain you"; see Rudolf Bultmann, "$\mu \epsilon \rho \iota \mu \nu \acute{\alpha} \omega$," *TDNT* 4 (1967) 593–94. Note the present, which marks the duration and repetition of concerns.

34 The background is examined by Zeller, *Mahnsprüche*, 87–92.

35 Cf. 1 Macc 6:10; Sir 40:1-11; 42:9; 29:21-28; Eccl 6:7; 4:4-6.

36 Cf. Eccl 4:6; Sir 1:11-20; 6:28; 51:27.

occasion for all kinds of apprehensions (cf. Gen 3:17-19). Such wisdom suggests a rest that stems from simple living ("Many possessions, many worries," said Hillel [*m. ᵓAbot* 2.7]) and, if possible, the absence of worries. The orientation of one's life is determinative. When it is oriented toward God, one's existence can be blessed and one's worries banished (Prov 16:1-9, 20). Such wisdom is, however, obliged to recognize that happiness does not depend on our efforts alone. It confidently offers to submit itself to God (Prov 3:1-12; 8:32-36; 14:27). Modern life—the third domain—demands autonomy for the world and transforms society into Atlas, who carries the weight of the world, and into Prometheus, who defies the gods. This modern life is in the grips of anxiety confronted with its responsibilities and of hesitations in the presence of its power. At the level of the individual, we have solitude, lack of communication, and an irrational and uncontrollable rise in the level of the anxiety that invades our soul and blocks any reflection or action.[37] Worries are to be found everywhere.

In antiquity, food, clothing, and shelter constituted the triad of indispensable possessions.[38] In a provocative way, Jesus invites us to not worry about what we will eat, nor about what we will wear (Why is shelter neglected here? Cf. 9:58). He thus prepares the way for the saying about the fundamental concern, that is, the kingdom of God (v. 31). But he does not simply contrast two kinds of things to desire; he also distinguishes between different attitudes: unhealthy worries, on the one hand, and legitimate seeking, on the other. In his eyes, a care is illegitimate when it rises to the highest level of our concerns and obscures everything else, and when it causes human beings to be wrapped up in themselves, thus forcing them to neglect God and their neighbors.[39]

■ **23** People are worth more than food or clothing. Verse 23 attempts an explanation. The pair of Greek words $\psi\upsilon\chi\acute{\eta}$–$\sigma\hat{\omega}\mu\alpha$[40] does not have either its Greek meaning of the soul contrasted with body, or its Hebrew Bible meaning of a living soul identified with an active body. Here the soul is fed and the body clothed: one expression relates to our life and the other to our person; the one is more inner; the other, more outer. Such is Lukan anthropology, debtor to both Jerusalem and Athens.[41] When the text says that human beings are worth more than what feeds them or clothes them, it invites readers to be concerned with what is the ultimate basis of their existence rather than with what sustains them temporarily.[42] The third petition of the Lukan version of the Lord's Prayer (request for bread), as well as v. 31b, proves that Jesus did not neglect the indispensable minimum but placed it in second position and made it depend on faith and not on our worries; on God and not on our efforts.[43]

37 See Steinhauser (*Doppelbildworte*, 234–35), who insists on the cognitive and affective character of these two comparisons (ravens and lilies); in his opinion, Luke underlines the intellectual coherence of the images but does not neglect the emotional aspect.

38 See Gen 28:20; Sir 29:21; 1 Tim 6:8; Epictetus *Ench.* 33.7; idem, frg. 18; Philo *Vit. cont.* 4.37–38; Marcus Aurelius 6.30.4; Diogenes Laertius 6.104; other references are in Johann Jakob Wettstein, *Novum Testamentum graecum* (2 vols.; Amsterdam: Dommeriana, 1751–52) 2:349.

39 Jeremias (*Parables*, 214) interprets $\mu\epsilon\rho\iota\mu\nu\acute{\alpha}\omega$ in the sense of pain that one takes. He thinks that Jesus reserves the forces of the disciples for the eschatological mission to which he destines them. Lambrecht ("*Eh bien!*" 163) opposes the pagan attitude, composed of inquietude and anguish, to the Christian attitude, with its confident dynamism. See also James Barr, *Old and New in Interpretation* (New York: Harper & Row, 1966) 34ff. Degenhardt (*Lukas*, 80–81) distinguishes, following the others,

two senses of $\mu\epsilon\rho\iota\mu\nu\acute{\alpha}\omega$, the anxious care that one has, and the pain that one takes; cf. Hoffmann, "Verbot," 120–21. Plummer (326) refers to 1 Sam (1 Kgdms) 9:5 and signals that Paul will take up the teaching of Jesus (1 Cor 7:32-33 and Phil 4:6).

40 One must understand the datives $\tau\hat{\eta}\ \psi\upsilon\chi\hat{\eta}$ and $\tau\hat{\omega}$ $\sigma\acute{\omega}\mu\alpha\tau\iota$ in the sense of "for the soul" and "for the body" and not "in the soul" and "in the body"; see Plummer, 326.

41 On the anthropology of Luke, see Taeger, *Mensch*.

42 See Grundmann, 259; it concerns here the goal of life; is it determined by God or by the proper necessities of the human being? Zeller, *Mahnsprüche*, 89: the one who is concerned only with nourishment and habits conceives the soul and body as an end in itself. Cf. Luke 4:4.

43 See Ernst, 402. I refer to the fact that the $\gamma\acute{\alpha}\rho$ of this verse is missing in a not inconsiderable part of the manuscript tradition.

■ **24** There are multitudinous examples drawn from nature in the sapiential literature: "Go to the ant, you lazybones; consider its ways, and be wise" (Prov 6:6).[44] Such illustrations often serve to praise the providence of God the Creator who watches over his creatures and takes responsibility for maintaining them: "Sing to the LORD with thanksgiving; make melody to our God on the lyre. He covers the heavens with clouds, prepares rain for the earth, makes grass grow on the hills. He gives to the animals their food, and to the young ravens when they cry" (Ps 146 [147]:7-10).[45] When Luke chose the word "raven," he may have been thinking of the Greek proverb that associated ravens with garbage: ἄπαγε εἰς κόρακας, "go away to the ravens!" that is, to the garbage dump, just as we would say: "you can go hang!" or "go jump in the lake!" or "to hell with you!" Although they are despised, the ravens nevertheless receive what they need to live on ("and God feeds them," καὶ ὁ θεὸς τρέφει αὐτούς).[46] "How much more" we, who are different from those birds that make us think of garbage.[47]

So the text contrasts ravens with farmers (a sign that Jesus is speaking to a rural audience or at least to persons accustomed to agricultural images). Unlike people who work the soil, ravens do not have to worry about the three successive steps of country labor—to sow seeds, to harvest, to store up.[48] What is stressed is the third step: storing one's harvest. That precaution is here considered to be a sign of mistrust of providence and ill-considered worrying about the following day. The Israelites received manna from God and did not have the right to keep anything in storage (see Exodus 16). That ideal of total dependence on God in the decisive moment is a theme running through Israelite history, and it is present here.[49] The text thus does not forbid us to eat our fill. God recognizes what we need, but he imposes a restriction. He refuses to allow us to accumulate reserves, which would be a sign of mistrusting him.

■ **25-26** Now comes an additional argument in the form of a rhetorical question and a deduction that is also interrogative, and which separates from each other the two examples drawn from nature (vv. 24 and 27). What is presupposed is our physiological dependence on nature or rather on creation, and consequently ultimately on God. Our ἡλικία, here the "length of our life" rather than our "stature,"[50] does not depend on us. Our worries and troubles will not change anything in that respect.[51]

---

44 The comparison is pursued in Prov 6:7-8. On κατανοέω, see the commentary below on vv. 27-28.

45 In the LXX, the end of v. 9 reads καὶ τοῖς νεοσσοῖς τῶν κοράκων τοῖς ἐπικαλουμένοις αὐτόν, "and to the young ravens when they call for him"—do not forget Luke 12:6-7! See also *Ps. Sol.* 5:9-12: "(9) Birds and fish dost Thou nourish, In that Thou givest rain to the steppes that green grass may spring up, (10) (So) to prepare fodder in the steppe for every living thing; And if they hunger, unto Thee do they lift up their face. (11) Kings and rulers and peoples Thou dost nourish, O God; And who is the help of the poor and needy, if not Thou, O Lord (12)? And Thou wilt hearken—for who is good and gentle but Thou—Making glad the soul of the humble by opening Thine hand in mercy" (trans. G. Buchanan Gray, in *APOT*). Cf. Ps 103 (104):14; 144 (145):15-16; Zeller, *Mahnsprüche*, 89–90; Fuchs, "Raben," 386–87; Str-B, 1:435–37.

46 On the ravens, see Olsthoorn, *Background*, 35.

47 The superiority of the humans to animals is a common theme; cf. 12:7; Paul, still scornful, 1 Cor 9:9. On διαφέρω, in the sense of "to bring upon," see BAGD, s.v. διαφέρω 2b.

48 In place of negations οὐ . . . οὐδέ (Nestle-Aland[27]), some manuscripts have οὔτε . . . οὔτε.

49 On v. 24, see Fuchs, "Raben"; and Steinhauser, *Doppelbildworte*, 215–35. For this latter author, the two examples v. 24 and v. 27 illustrate the necessity to strive not for possessions but for the reign of God.

50 Cf. 2:53 and 19:3, where the word designates the "height," the "stature"; Zeller, *Mahnsprüche*, 89 n. 264. It is possible that, at the level of tradition, it might refer to human height, especially in view of the fact that in v. 27 (as in the parallel in Matt 6:28) the point is the growth of the lilies. There are several Jewish reflections on height—and not only on old age—about Adam and other biblical personages. According to *Numbers Rabbah* (13.2, 13.12), the punishment of Adam was a diminution not only of his longevity but also of his height. Cf. the rabbinic reflections on Lev 26:13 in *b. Sanh.* 110a and *b. B. Batra* 75a; see Olsthoorn, *Background*, 43–44.

51 The form μεριμνῶν here is a present participle: "in worrying"; cf. τί . . . μεριμνᾶτε ("Which concerns are you worrying about?"), which relates to μὴ μεριμνᾶτε ("do not [you pl.] be worried") in v. 22.

Human powerlessness is stressed twice.[52] This extra measure[53] is considered to be a small thing (which, for Luke, is understandable only if the word ἡλικία is given the meaning of "length of life" rather than "stature"!). The most important realities (food and clothing must be understood to be hidden in what is designated by the expression "the rest," περὶ τῶν λοιπῶν) also elude our efforts and our worries. These things do not depend on us.[54] The attitude suggested here is neither one of fatalism, and thus of resignation, nor one of a stoicism[55] aiming for an inner detachment, but rather confident faith in the Creator. What results is not a careless passivity, but rather a free and happy activity that hopes in God[56] and counts on his providence.[57]

■ **27-28** "Consider" (κατανοήσατε) implies both observing and contemplating. It is the verb used in the parable about the splinter and the log (6:41). It means "notice, observe, consider."[58] Lilies[59] do not need clothing, since they are in themselves their own clothing and their corollas outmatch in beauty the most celebrated luxury in the history of Israel, that is, Solomon's.[60] They are not obliged to carry out any of the tasks that are indispensable to the making of cloth, such as spinning and weaving.[61] The text probably does not overlook the complementary work of sewing, since it is possible that the expression "spin and weave" refers, *pars pro toto*, to the whole process, including sewing.[62] In any case, the rabbis took into consideration the labor required from shearing of the wool up to the clothing ready to be worn.[63]

Moreover, we should remember that in Hebrew the verb עמל, the equivalent of κοπιάω ("toil"; cf. Matt 6:28), could refer to human activities; thus, in Ecclesiastes it is used precisely with respect to Solomon. The author of that book in the end was obliged to admit the futility of all his toil, of all his "trouble."[64] The life of the lilies serves as a model for the confident believer, while Solomon's existence is perhaps not so exemplary. It will be recalled that in the milieu of the Jew Tryphon, whom Justin Martyr addressed, certain rabbis identified Solomon with the king of glory of Psalm 24 (23):7 and 10; but others were of the opinion that the "gates" of the Psalm were not lifted up when Solomon arrived and some even

52   In v. 25, τίς . . . δύναται ("who can . . . ?") and in v. 26, οὐδὲ . . . δύνασθε ("you are not able").

53   A cubit, a measure of length—that is, the distance from the elbow to the extremity of the middle finger (about 45 cm).

54   Cf. Eccl 1:15: "What is crooked cannot be made straight, and what is lacking cannot be counted." What is "crooked," that is, perhaps, the old man to whom one cannot give youth. Eccl 7:13: "Who can make straight what he has made crooked"? A similar style of a rhetorical question is in Luke 12:25.

55   Hoffmann, "Verbot," 19.

56   Cf. the appearance of the theme of hope in *Ps. Sol.* 5:11; see n. 45 above.

57   Cf. Psalms 8; 103 (104); 147 (146–147); Sir 42:12; 43:33; *1 Enoch* 1:1—5:4; Zeller, *Mahnsprüche*, 89–90.

58   See BAGD, s.v. This verb is especially Lukan in the NT; see Luke 6:41; 12:24, 27; 20:23; Acts 7:31-32; 11:6; 27:39; but cf. also Matt 7:3; Rom 4:19; Heb 3:1; 10:24; Jas 1:23-24.

59   On lilies, see Olsthoorn, *Background*, 45–49. One thinks of white lilies (*Anemone coronaria*) or of sword lilies (*gladioli*), which can sometimes grow in fields "often overstopping it, and illuminating the broad fields with their various shades of pinkish purple to deep violet-purple and blue truly royal colours" (James Hastings, *Dictionary of the Bible Dealing with*

      Its Language, Literature, and Contents (4 vols.; Edinburgh: T&T Clark, 1898–1902) 3:123.

60   There was a sibilant alliteration in Aramaic between the lilies שׁוֹשַׁנָּן (note the doubling of nun) and Solomon שְׁלֹמֹה; see Black, *Aramaic Approach*, 135; and Olsthoorn, *Background*, 46. One speaks of the glory of Solomon; cf. 1 Kgs (3 Kgdms) 3:13; Josephus *Ant.* 8.7.5. §190; cf. Esth 5:1 LXX: περιεβάλετο τὴν δόξαν αὐτῆς, "Esther is dressed by her glory," at the moment of putting on her royal robe.

61   I follow here the "Western" text, retained by Nestle-Aland[27], οὔτε νήθει οὔτε ὑφαίνει, which is not contaminated by that of Matt 6:28; νήθω, that is, "to spin" wool; ὑφαίνω, "to weave." Nestle-Aland[27] prefers the great number of manuscripts which read: "since they believe, they neither toil nor spin."

62   Olsthoorn, *Background*, 46–47.

63   Cf. *m. Šabb.* 7.2 and *t. Ber* 7.2; see Samuel Krauss, *Talmudische Archäologie* (3 vols.; Leipzig: G. Fock, 1910–12) 1:142–59; Gustaf Dalman, *Arbeit und Sitte in Palästina* (7 vols.; Gütersloh: Bertelsmann, 1928–39) 5:42–144, esp. 60.

64   Eccl 1:3; cf. 3:9; Luke 5:15. The LXX renders this verb by μοχθέω; Aquila uses κοπιόω; see Olsthoorn, *Background*, 47.

wished (a divine voice being opposed to the idea) that he might be excluded from the world to come.[65] When situated in its Jewish context, the contrast between the lilies, which neither spin nor weave, and Solomon takes on substance. What counts, however, is the comparison between believers and the lilies and, thanks to this comparison, the assurance that God pays attention to the little ones. If he gives lilies their splendor and even Solomon his glory, he also takes care of us poor humans, for our good. And that good is not just spiritual.

Although vv. 24 and 27-28 are parallel, the symmetry is not perfect: after two stichs of equal length and equal worth, v. 24 adds some information ("they have neither storeroom nor barn"), while v. 27 uses the same expression ("I tell you") to introduce a comparison (with Solomon). The final conclusion ("how much more") is concentrated in v. 24e and developed in v. 28. In spite of what some say, the text is not a poem, because if it were, it would have a more sustained rhythm and a firmer structure.

Q adds a detail here (v. 28). The dazzling glory of the flowers is given to ordinary plants that will end up in the fire. That reinforces the "how much more . . . you." Ravens were unclean birds. Lilies, in the last analysis, are but short-lived plants. But as for "you," your faith may be little (ὀλιγόπιστοι, v. 28), but God thinks about you and appreciates you.

Luke took care in the formulation of the saying: first of all, he contrasted life "in the fields" (ἐν ἀγρῷ) with death "in(to) the oven" or "in(to) the furnace" (εἰς κλίβανον), and contrasted "today" and "tomorrow." In so doing, he took his place in the sapiential tradition on the brevity of human life, which is similar to that of plants.[66]

In view of the shortage of wood, Israelites used dry grass to light and keep the fire going in their bread ovens.[67] The text describes the lot of grass that flowers in the fields but disappears tomorrow in the fire. When they heard these words, the earliest Christians remembered the brevity of their life and the suddenness of the end of their life.[68] But that is not the point on which the text ends. On the contrary, it continues on an encouraging note, a new reminder of God's providence (cf. Prov 3:1-12; 8:32-36; 14:27).[69] The limits placed before us could cause us to doubt divine kindness, but there is no reason to do so. The intensity and the authenticity of any single life witness to the fact that it is a gift from God.

The Greek word ὀλιγόπιστοι, which is dear to Matthew and is translated here by the expression "believers of low caliber," has its origins in Q.[70] It is not to be found elsewhere in Luke. It refers to believers who waver, overcome by suffering or tempted by riches and pleasures.[71] It is a word that takes the measure of the church after several years have passed, and reports the state of the

---

65 See Justin *Dial.* 36 and 85; *Midr. Ps.* 24:7 (*Midrash Tehillim* 24:10); *b. Sanh.* 104b; Olsthoorn, *Background*, 48–49.

66 Isa 37:27; 40:6-8; 51:12; 2 Kgs (4 Kgdms) 19:26 par.; Pss 36 (37):2; 89 (90):5-6; 101 (102):4-5, 12; 102 (103):15; 128 (129):6; 1 Pet 1:24; Jas 1:9-11; the opposition between today and tomorrow is found in 1 Macc 2:63.

67 "The oven, or תנור used for baking bread, was usually a cylinder shaped firepot, less than a meter high, and some more than a half meter broad at the bottom, whereas narrower at the top; it stood on the ground or was dug in" (Olsthoorn, *Background*, 51 n. 69). The princes of Israel are compared to devouring ovens (Hos 7:4-7; cf. Ps 20 (21):10. The day of judgment is compared to a blazing oven or furnace; cf. Mal 4:1; Isa 31:9; 2 Chr 16:3. On the word ὁ κλίβανος (Attic κρίβανος), see BAGD, s.v. The oven of the potter or the furnace of the blacksmith is called ἡ κάμινος (Matt 13:42, 50).

68 See Olsthoorn, *Background*, 51.

69 See n. 45 above. The verb ἀμφιέζω ("to clothe," "to be dressed") is the Hellenistic form of the classical verb ἀμφιέννυμι, which is used in Matt 6:30 (ἀμφιάζω is the Doric form); see BAGD, s.vv. ἀμφιάζω and ἀμφιέννυμι. It is difficult to say which, Matthew or Luke, corrects the text of Q.

70 This word, a neologism in Greek, corresponds to a Hebraic expression קְטַנֵּי אֱמָנָה "the small in faith." It is reported that Rabbi Eliezer, son of Hyrcanus (around the year 100 C.E.), said to the people, "Whoever has a piece of bread in the bread box and says, 'what am I going to eat tomorrow'? belongs only to those who are small in faith" (*b. Soṭah* 48b); see Olsthoorn, *Background*, 52–53; Grundmann, 261. The translation *"croyants de peu d'envergure"* was suggested by my assistant, Mme Isabelle Chappuis-Juillard.

71 Cf. Luke 8:12-14, especially the third category, v. 14.

faithful who have not been able to persevere in the long haul.[72] It is to them that many of the exhortations and warnings in our Gospels are addressed. The "believers of low caliber" (ὀλιγόπιστοι) lack confidence in God for the following day. Worries have left their mark on them, and they doubt whether they will have sufficient bread. So they correspond exactly to those whom the first (v. 22c) and the second negative commands (v. 29) had in mind.

■ **29-30** Luke uses the "and you" (καὶ ὑμεῖς), absent from the first negative command in v. 22c, to address the "believers of low caliber" and relaunch the paraenesis. In anticipation of the true quest, the one for the kingdom, v. 31 ("strive for," ζητεῖτε), he uses the verb ζητέω here.[73] Unlike what he did in v. 22c, here he brings together drink and food, in faithfulness to Q.

The most curious element is the third one:[74] the famous *crux interpretum*, καὶ μὴ μετεωρίζεσθε.[75] The adjective μετέωρος means "high," "high in the air"; or, in connection with a boat, "whipping on the high sea," with the sails filled out; "inflated," "swollen"; figuratively, "in suspense," "ready to act," or "undecided," "distracted," sometimes "proud," "who goes around stuck up."[76] The verb μετεωρίζω has the following meanings:

"raise to a height"; figuratively, "to lift up hearts," "to fill [them] with vain hopes," or "to incite [them] to revolt"; in nautical language, "put out to sea." In the passive (μετεωρίζομαι) it means "be lifted up," "be bursting with"; figuratively "be up in the air" and "be proud," "be overbearing." It is these two meanings (indecision and pride) that are advanced by commentators.[77] Although the LXX uses the verb in the sense of "to pride oneself," "be overbearing, presumptuous," in which it is followed by the Vulgate,[78] the Syriac versions[79] opt for the other meaning, "be uncertain," "be anxious," "be hovering" between hope and fear,[80] "to worry";[81] the Harclean Syriac version adds "by the pleasures of the flesh," adding an asterisk to it.[82] The philosophy of antiquity can help us make a choice. The ideal of the wise person, whether Epicurean or Stoic, was not to be dependent on one's possessions or worried about one's circumstances or shaken by cares or desires. Ataraxia (stoical indifference) and euthymia (cheerfulness, tranquillity) were the expressions of that ideal and were reflected in the lifestyles that the philosopher adopted.[83] Thinkers seem to be ill at ease when it comes to defining the negative state from which they wish to liberate themselves.[84] They use images that suggest agitation or anxiety of the soul.

---

72   Some writings, for example, the Epistle to the Hebrews or the Gospels of Matthew and of Luke, are addressed to Christians of the third generation, who often behaved as ὀλιγόπιστοι, the "believers of low caliber." Cf. the usage of this word in Matt 6:30, parallel to our passage; see also Matt 8:26; 14:31; 16:8. In Matt 17:20, one encounters the substantive ἡ ὀλιγοπιστία.

73   In the present imperative, ζητεῖτε has iterative and durative force, as in v. 22c. Matt 6:31, faithful to Q, keeps the verb μεριμνάω but in the aorist subjunctive.

74   Matt 6:31, faithful to the tradition, here evokes clothing.

75   On this expression, see Molitor, "Übersetzung"; Olsthoorn, *Background*, 57–58; and esp. Hoffmann, "Sorgen," 143–49; and idem, "Verbot," 134–37.

76   Cicero (*Att.* 15.14) uses the adjective to describe interior agitation, inquietude: "Ita sum μετέωρος et magnis cogitationibus impeditus" ("Thus I am μετέωρος and embarrassed by profound reflexions"). Hoffmann ("Sorgen," 145) refers to other texts of Cicero: *Att.* 16.5; *Tusc.* 1.40 [96]: 4, 16 [35]; *Fam.* 5.13; *Fin.* 1.19; and of Seneca, *Ep.* 5 and 101.

77   Hoffmann ("Verbot," 144 n. 58) furnishes a list of partisans of the various translations.

78   "Nolite in sublime tolli" (Vulgate); "Do not be lifted up in the air" (Luther).

79   The Old Latin witnesses: "Nolite solliciti esse," "Do not be tossed about, agitated, worried." The Latin text of Codex Bezae (D): "Non abalienetis vos" is not easy to translate: "Do not make strangers of yourselves," "isolated," or "dulled."

80   So the Curetonian Syriac version. Curiously, to allow for better understanding, the Sinaitic Syriac version omits some of the verse, as does Tatian, it seems; see Molitor, "Übersetzung," 108.

81   This version lacks what is given in the Peshitta.

82   See Molitor, "Übersetzung," 108.

83   There exist several treatises, of which one is by Plutarch, dedicated to εὐθυμία (here "courage," "confidence," "assurance"). See Hans Dieter Betz, *Plutarch's Ethical Writings and Early Christian Literature* (SCHNT 4; Leiden: Brill, 1978) 198–230.

84   See Ilsetraut Hadot, *Seneca und die griechisch-römische Tradition der Seelenleitung* (Berlin: de Gruyter, 1969) 135–41.

These images are often borrowed from sailing, and one can see the soul compared to a skiff tossed about on the crest of the waves. That is, in my opinion, what the verb μετεωρίζομαι expresses, the state of the anxious soul, in suspense and shaken—that is, tossed about.[85] So I reject the idea of pride, "being overbearing,"[86] as well as the danger of illuminism, "being in the clouds," "pretending to be angels" through a refusal to have one's feet on the ground (cf. Acts 1:11: "why do you stand looking up toward heaven?"), and finally the temptation of astrology (remaining with one's eyes glued to the sky to examine the stars and their message).[87]

Luke seems to be proposing to his hellenized and city-dwelling readers the same ideal as the Greek and Latin sages of his time. Or at least he decided to combat the same vices that they did. But, unlike those thinkers, he did not count on a philosophical meditation or on personal discipline in order to make a success of this liberation and achieve this inner calm; instead, he counted on confidence in God, who is concerned with his creatures in a paternal way.[88] That is what is spelled out in v. 30 in a phrase that reminds us of love for one's enemies (6:32-34) by virtue of the contrast between Christians and the rest of the human race.[89] Everybody strives[90] for "these things,"[91] these possessions, these material realities rep-resented by food and drink,[92] not to mention everything else, clothing, lodging, and pleasures. The text takes such good aim at the essentials that the images strike city-dwellers as much as people who live in the country. Each person has a deep desire to live.

Now in Christian tradition neither Jesus nor Luke nor Matthew looks down on these possessions, which are needed for life on earth. But it is necessary to realize that such possessions are dependent on God, more exactly on the one who is "your Father."[93] He who in 11:13 offered the Spirit is here concerned with all the rest about which it is admitted "that you need them" (ὅτι χρῄζετε τούτων).[94] Although the Father "knows" (οἶδεν), he is not just content with this knowledge. He adds action to the thought, the gift to the knowledge[95] (cf. the "he will give" [δώσει] in 11:13).

■ **31** Anxiety should no more characterize the human being than should inner detachment or fixed indifference. Men and women are, according to Scripture, beings with desires, made of flesh and blood. This desire to live and to do so happily, with accepted pleasure and in an established relationship, has a name, which in Greek is ζήτησις, a quest, a request, an approach, an aspiration, and a movement (ζητεῖτε).[96] The object of this quest is indicated by a single word, βασιλεία

---

85 In his most recent article, Hoffmann ("Verbot," 137) mentions a philosophical treatise attributed today to the Epicurean philosopher Demetrius the Laconian (second century B.C.E.) and transmitted in *Papyrus Herculanensis* 831, which treats explicitly the evil of the soul, called μετεωρισμός ("tossed about") and its therapy. This papyrus has been edited by A. Körte, "Metrodori Epicuri Fragmenta," *Jahrbücher für Classische Philologie Supplement* 17 (1890) 531–97, esp. 571–91. This sense of "to be tossed about," "to be worried," "to be undecided" is found in Polybius 107.6; see Sophie Antoniadis, *L'Évangile de Luc: esquisse de grammaire et de style* (Paris: Société Les Belles Lettres, 1930) 99.

86 This, however, is the sense that has triumphed in the Vulgate and has received a second life by way of the translation of Luther; see BAGD, s.v. The mention of prideful words in Jas 4:16 upholds this translation.

87 I do not know if these two last meanings have been scientifically defended. I find them as possibilities under the pen of A. Maillot, "Bouts de chandelles (3): 'Ne vous tourmentez pas' (Lc 12:29, trad. TOB)," *Reforme*, no. 1912, December 12, 1981, p. 4.

88 See Hoffmann, "Sorgen," 149.

89 The formula is redundant: "All the nations of the world." The majority of translators prefer to reattach πάντα to ταῦτα, as is done in Matt 6:22 (but the text there is not certain), and to translate: "and all these things the nations of the world desire."

90 The verb ἐπιζητῶ is perhaps a little stronger than ζητέω.

91 Ταῦτα is found again at the end of the phrase (χρῄζετε τούτων, "you have need of these") and in v. 31 (ταῦτα προστεθήσεται, "these things will be added").

92 Olsthoorn (*Background*, 57–58), who opts for the sense of "to be prideful," compares the luxury of which many pagans boasted in the rich regions of Palestine with the modesty of means that the majority of Jews enjoyed.

93 On God the Father in Luke, see the commentary above on 11:2 and on 11:13.

94 For χρῄζω, cf. 11:8, the only other Lukan usage.

95 On the knowledge of God, see the commentary above on 10:22.

96 On ζητεῖτε, see Neuhäusler, *Exigence de Dieu*, 76–78; A. George, "L'attente du maître qui vient: Lc

("kingdom"), which is immediately linked to a person, "his," that is, the kingdom of "your Father" (v. 30). All the wisdom that is linked to creation and providence (vv. 22-30) is all of a sudden illumined in a new way.[97] Up to this point one could have been suspicious of such wisdom. But here all at once the reign comes along to restore to creation and providence what the fall and temporality had taken away from them. In Luke's eyes,[98] God's reign is the promise in the process of being fulfilled, hope crystallized in Jesus, in his Word and in the Spirit that has been his since he was raised to heaven (cf. Acts 2:33). God's providence, with its fits and starts and its failures, is drawn away from equivocation toward convincing proof. When threatened, creation groans not in order to complain but in order to get ready (see Rom 8:22). The text gradually moves attention from victory over worrying to the search for the kingdom. Men and women who obey Christ's order and respect the "instead" ($\pi\lambda\acute{\eta}\nu$)[99] and plunge into the search for God, henceforth have the assurance, confidence, and joy of which philosophers have only a premonition. God offers them all the rest, without luxury but unsparingly. Such is the impressive conviction that finds expression here. It is first of all an order, an imperative; but it is also a promise and a certitude.[100]

■ **32** Once this orientation has been adopted, Luke, who listened to Jesus' teaching, is no longer obsessed by worries.[101] The isolated saying that he quotes here[102] allows him to secure his position, since it corresponds to his objective. The Father, who is in relation with his own ("your Father") and who is defined by giving ($\delta o\hat{\upsilon}\nu\alpha\iota$), has expressed his plan of salvation ($\epsilon\vec{\upsilon}\delta\acute{o}\kappa\eta\sigma\epsilon\nu$).[103] The fullness of his love matches the basic essentials of what human beings are looking for and desire ($\zeta\eta\tau\epsilon\hat{\iota}\tau\epsilon$). What we are talking about is the establishment of the divine $\beta\alpha\sigma\iota\lambda\epsilon\acute{\iota}\alpha$, God's reign, which does not correspond to the limited and oppressive powers of this world; God's space, which encompasses creation, surpasses it, and regenerates it; and God's time, which takes over ours and transfigures it. For the time being, this $\beta\alpha\sigma\iota\lambda\epsilon\acute{\iota}\alpha$, associated with Jesus, is experienced only by a minority, a "little flock"—not by isolated individuals or by entire peoples but by those who, scattered all over, acknowledge themselves to be children of this Father and the sheep of this flock. Alfred Loisy said that Jesus preached the kingdom and what came was the church. Our verse proclaims that the kingdom has been offered and what became of it is the church. In order to exclude all triumphalism, the saying[104] defines the flock receiving the kingdom as being doubly small: by the use of the adjective "little" ($\mu\iota\kappa\rho\acute{o}\nu$)

12, 32-48," *AsSeign* 50 (1974) 67 ("to seek it," that is, not to seize it, but to welcome it); Lambrecht, "*Eh bien!*" 150, 163.

97   If the exegesis of the 1970s and early 1980s insisted on the prophetic and apocalyptic character of Q and of our text (see, e.g., Schulz, *Q*, 152–53), that of the 1980s and '90s inserts Q and our pericope into the sapiential tradition (see, e.g., Kloppenborg, *Formation*, 216–21). Several commentators, however, e.g., Zeller (*Mahnsprüche*, 83–87) and Hoffmann ("Verbot," 119) point to the interplay of wisdom and apocalypticism, which was already finely analyzed by Fuchs ("Raben," 387–88): Jesus links Jewish faith in God the creator and ruler to the present. In the same way, eschatological preaching can also be linked to the present moment. "But this means, that the decision to believe can happen only by believing itself" ("Raben, 388"). Jesus does not say something else than Jewish faith; he says "more" not in content but in event.

98   See the commentary on 4:42-43 (1:164–65) and on 6:20-26 (1:220–29); see also the commentary above

on 10:9 and on 11:2; and the brief excursus below on 13:9 and on the kingdom of God; and Bovon, *Theologian*, 1–87.

99   On $\pi\lambda\acute{\eta}\nu$, see the commentary above on 10:11, 14, 20.

100   See Riesenfeld ("Schätzesammeln"), who thinks that the theme of our verses became part of the paraenesis of the nascent church. It could be expressed in form of an instruction to disciples, as here; as a summary, as in Mark 4:18-19 par., or as variations, as in 1 Cor 7:32-34 and 1 John 2:15-17. Riesenfeld refers also to 1 Tim 6:6-11; Jas 5:1-6; 4:4, 7, 12-16; 1 Pet 5:6; Hermas, *Vis.* 4.2.4–6; *Mand.* 5.2.1.

101   In Matt 6:34, the first Gospel returns to this idea.

102   The saying has been studied by W. Pesch, "Formgeschichte"; see also idem, *Herde*; and George, "Attente," 66–67.

103   On $\epsilon\vec{\upsilon}\delta o\kappa\acute{\iota}\alpha$, the "good pleasure" (i.e., "kindness") of God, a fundamental Lukan theme, see Bovon, *L'oeuvre*, 228–31.

104   The verse is composed in three parts: (a) the invitation not to be afraid; (b) the address in the form of

and the diminutive "[little] flock" (ποίμνιον).[105] The parables about the mustard seed and the leaven (13:18-21) are not far removed in thought.

The notion of "flock" suggests the figure of the "shepherd." The ties that exist between Christ and his disciples and the Father and his children are so close that fear can be banned ("do not be afraid," μὴ φοβοῦ). Fear and worries would nevertheless be understandable: this "little flock," like the "remnant" of Israel, remains fragile and threatened. But what is stronger than the threats is the salvific will, the good pleasure (cf. "he took pleasure," "he was well pleased," "he took delight," εὐδόκησεν), the famous "good pleasure," "good will," (εὐδοκία) of 10:21, which has provided an organization for the paradox, the contrast, the promised reversal from the Magnificat (1:49-55) on. It is to this "little flock" that he gives the kingdom; it is this "little flock," subjected and oppressed, which he associates with the reign, that is, with legitimate power, naturally insofar as the sheep remain attached to the shepherd, and the children to their Father.

■ **33** Instead of forbidding enrichment, Luke imposes prodigality. It is well known that Lukan communities counted among their numbers a good number of people with possessions.[106] Throughout Luke-Acts, Luke gives expression to his awareness of the social injustices and his desire to make amends for them, at least in the church.[107] He is, admittedly, convinced that the evil is not inherent in the possessions themselves, but in one's heart being attached to them. Be that as it may, the distance that one is to keep from them does not fall within the province of seeking to please. It corresponds to a theological necessity (one cannot serve two masters, 16:13) and an ethical necessity (woe to the rich, 6:24). The con-

verted persons who turn to God turn away, in the same movement, from their riches. The contrast between the two treasures is drastic. The biblical imperatives, depending on the structure of the sayings in which they occur, require more of humans than they are able to provide. At the level of carrying out the directives, this detachment cannot be limited to the spiritual domain; it must be carried out through acts of material generosity.[108] Luke does not set up a communist program, however. He does not impose the vow of poverty on everyone. What he wants to encourage Christians to do, in the name of his Master, is to make their resources available as a way of expressing their inner detachment and thus facilitate charitable giving that will provide for what any other Christian might lack. That is the manner in which the Christian community practices sharing their possessions. Here, as in 14:33, the imperatives resemble Ebionite requirements, but the examples of Levi and Zacchaeus as well as the apostles' observances show that the Lukan Christ imposes sharing and not poverty. The interpretation we are proposing here[109] differs from the following hypotheses: that Jesus and Luke are encouraging Ebionism; that a vow of poverty is required of only the ministers or a minority of saints; that this is an ideal picture of poor apostles who encourage rich Christians to be generous.[110]

The example of Barnabas (Acts 4:37) carries out Jesus' command in two phases: the relinquishing of the possessions—that is, the sale, then the distribution, of goods, and, in this case, almsgiving.[111] The "possessions" can be of all kinds, either movable assets or real estate. In Jesus' time, Judaism had attached importance to three kinds of good works: fasting, prayer, and almsgiving. Only the Essenes required renunciation of personal pos-

---

a vocative; (c) the justification of the appeal. This structure corresponds to an OT scheme of revelation, which, in a difficult situation, reassures the believer for the future (see Isa 41:8-20); W. Pesch, "Formgeschichte."

105 The word ποίμνιον has perhaps lost its diminutive value. For the shepherd and his flock, cf. Isa 40:9-11 and 49:9b-10; and esp. Mark 14:27.

106 Nickelsburg, "Riches."

107 See Luke 5:11, 28; 6:20, 26, 35; 8:14; 9:25; 11:39-41; 12:13-21; 16:1-14, 19-31; 18:18-30; 19:1-10; 21:1-4; Acts 2:42-47; 4:32-37; 9:36; 11:29.

108 For alms, cf. 11:41; Acts 3:2-3, 10; 9:36; 10:2, 4, 31; 24:17; Matt 6:2-4; *Did.* 1.6; 15.4; *2 Clem.* 16.4;

"to give alms," is "to do mercy." This reverts to the Hebrew "to make the צְדָקָה," via the LXX (Prov 21:21, 26; Dan 4:27; Tob 1:3; Sir 7:10; *2 Enoch* 50:4). That becomes the action of doing good for the poor, as marks of compassion; see Rudolf Bultmann, "ἐλεήμων κτλ.," *TDNT* 2 (1965) 477–87; Ferdinand Staudinger, "ἐλεημοσύνη etc.," *EDNT* 1:428–29; Degenhardt, *Lukas*, 87–88.

109 See Bovon, *L'oeuvre*, 233–35.

110 See Bovon, *Theologian*, 329–48, 442–48.

111 On liberality in Judaism and almsgiving, see W. Pesch, "Exegese," 362–66.

sessions and sharing within the community.[112] We know that in Greece and in Rome, especially in Stoicism, there was an indifference with respect to material possessions, but that inner detachment had more importance than generosity itself.[113] In this chorus of ethical concerns, the Christian option,[114] as attested to by the Lukan Jesus, was marked by his joyous radicalism, his absence of legalism, his concern for his neighbors, and the way he showed interest in the right ways.

To be sure, Luke does not take away from human beings their right to have desires, nor even their right to have possessions, but he redirects these legitimate human inclinations toward God. Thinking of his send-off speech (the forbidding of material purses, 10:4), he speaks of spiritual purses that do not wear out. The advanced decrepitude of this world was a theme common to Jewish apocalyptic writings and Gentile wisdom.[115] The object of that common quest was access to what was unshakable and indefectible.[116] The Lukan Jesus promises that essential element to all those who become selfless and renounce their self-centeredness. Therefore, human beings cannot get to God's eternal world by a mere shifting of the place they put themselves at the center of, even in a spiritual way. It is by giving up their possessions and especially themselves that believers find their way and become rich in their relationship with God (cf. 12:13-21). The message of these verses picks up on the beatitudes and the sayings in chap. 9 (denying oneself, forbidding oneself to gain the whole world) (cf. 6:20, 26; 9:23-25).

The image of the treasure in the heavens recalls the Matthean parable (Matt 13:44), various Pauline texts (e.g., 2 Cor 4:7; Col. 2:3), and Jewish symbolism.[117] The text in Luke also mentions the wearing out of purses, then the threat of thieves and moths.[118] In our day, in Greece or in the Maghreb, even families with the most modest means still have at least a trunk or a chest in which they keep their finest clothing, some pieces of cloth, and one or two pieces of jewelry. Moths are certainly a threat, as are cheese mites. Thieves[119] stand for harmful animals.

■ **34** Jesus' saying, which has the ring of a proverb, brings together the heart and the treasure, the person who values something and what is valued, the one who has desires and what is desired. The saying could be taken in a positive way and be applied to the disciples seated at Christ's feet, to the communion between the faithful and their God, or to communion between brothers and sisters in the faith. Here Luke condemns the ties that are made, not between persons but between people and their possessions (the evil rich man of the parable immediately comes to mind, 12:16-21). While popular wisdom places the heart near to the object it desires, Jesus' wisdom dramatizes the threat: by a kind of magnetization, material possessions attract one's heart to them and alienate it (note the future "will be," which denotes such as irresistible attraction and the inescapable result). What must be done to separate the one from the other? Distribute one's possessions and modify one's heart.[120]

History of Interpretation

The preacher Cyril of Alexandria delivered a sermon on vv. 22-31 (*Serm. Luc.* 90), leaving v. 32, which he took with vv. 33-34, for the following sermon. In English translation his homily takes up four pages. If Cyril delivered

---

112 See Degenhardt, *Lukas*, 188–207; W. Pesch, "Exegese," 364–66.

113 See W. Pesch, "Exegese," 361–62.

114 Cf. the invitations to share in the letters of Paul: Rom 15:25; 1 Cor 7:30; 16:3; 2 Cor 8:4; 9:1.

115 On παλαιόω ("to get old"), e.g. as a piece of clothing, cf. Deut 29:4, 5; 8:4; Josh 9:5; Ps 100 (101):27; Isa 50:9; 51:6; Heb 1:11; 8:13b.

116 On ἀνέκλειπτος, see BAGD, s.v.

117 See the commentary on 6:43-45 (1:250–53).

118 On σής ("mite"), see BAGD, s.v., which refers to Job 4:19 LXX, cited in *1 Clem.* 39.5, as well as *Barn.* 6.2; *Hermas, Sim.* 8.1; etc. With respect to the "moth," see Isa 50:9, referring to the adversaries of the believer,

"as a garment will wear out, the moth (LXX: σής, 'mite') will eat them." In Ps 38 (39):12, it is God himself who, as a moth (LXX: ἀράχνη, "spider"), destroys his creature who is a very small thing. Luke utilizes διαφθείρω ("to corrupt") where Matthew employs ἀφανίζω ("to make disappear").

119 On κλέπτης ("thief"), see the commentary on 12:39 below. The thieves in Matthew "break in" and "steal." The one in Luke simply "approaches." Matthew must preserve the text of Q.

120 According to W. Pesch ("Exegese," 360), Luke has new emphases, which concern social difficulties, the problems of the church, the exercise of virtues, true concerns, and the treasure in heaven.

it as it stands, it did not last more than a quarter of an hour. He began by saying that Christians are blessed (with the help of Bar 4:4, which he quoted and adapted for the members of Christ's church). He placed this ethical text in a theological context. Wisely following Luke rather than Paul, he attributed this benediction not to the role of grace or the cross but to the words of Jesus, the Son spoken of by Heb 1:1-2, which is quoted. So the accent lies first on Jesus, whose spiritual skillfulness Cyril admired. Jesus knew how to guide his apostles and to train them in spiritual excellence in such a way as to make of them examples who could serve as models for all of the human race (he was to interpret, in the following sermon, the small flock as representing all of the human race, less numerous than the race of angels).

Once he made his point about this universality, Cyril spelled out the nature of the worries from which one must be freed: he used the double meaning of μεριμνάω ("to be concerned"): undue concern or justified, active concern. He continued, in the classical manner of his time, by distinguishing between what was necessary and what was superfluous, the latter being declared useless. We must attend to the higher realities: the quest for God, to whom we must devote ourselves (here he cited the parallels to this text that are mentioned by modern commentators, 1 John 2:15 and Jas 4:4).

Being the good orator that he was, Cyril here advanced an objection of a fictitious listener: "Who then will give us what we need to have for our life?" By way of answer, he limited himself to recalling the promise included in the biblical text: the little things will be given to you by God. From that he concluded that God will also offer us the big things, mentioning at that point, side by side, the example of the ravens, the invitation to not be afraid of the one who has a hold merely over the body (quoted according to Matt 10:28-31 rather than Luke 12:4, 6-7), and the example of the sparrows and one's hair. Our preacher would have found it distressing if slaves counted on their masters for their subsistence while Christians doubted the providence of their God. The sermon continues with a traditional critique of

luxury and with praise for the beauty of nature, which has it over the most admirable works of art, which in the last analysis are only copies of the real thing—that by way of commentary on the beauty of the lilies, with which the splendor of Solomon pales by comparison.

At this point Cyril takes a risk: praising Christ's banquets, probably the celebrations of the holy Eucharist. These meals correspond to the life of the faithful who are satisfied with the necessities. They are unassuming, he suggests, but are spiritual and will find their fulfillment in the glory of the kingdom (Phil 3:21 and Matt 13:43 are quoted at this point; they speak of the eschatological glorification of the faithful). Next Cyril explains that it was fitting for the apostles to live—in spite of their prestige—as simply as those whom they sought to win over. Freed of their worries, they thus devoted themselves to their missionary task. They trusted in God to provide the necessities—does not the text call him Father? The sermon ends with a final appeal to be satisfied with the necessities, a warning concerning the last judgment, and an invitation to seek the kingdom.

That is what a parishioner in Alexandria might have heard on a Sunday morning, sometime during the fifth century.[121]

Conclusion

Worries are not just the weeds of the soul. They can also become their inextricable brambles. Only a deep tilling succeeds in eradicating them. There is a way of going about it that not only fails but leaves you more destitute than before: wishing to go about it with a will and ending up adding to one's worries an extra worry, namely, the imperative of having to banish them.

Adopting an attitude of faith is the only way to achieve what must be called a liberation from worries. That attitude is based on confidence in the one who is capable of everything and wishes for our good. When we turn over our worries to God in that way, we feel light, joyous, and free. Our cares henceforth automatically take on different dimensions. To the degree that our worries dissipate,

---

121 See Payne-Smith, *Cyril*, 2:414–18. The reader will find some elements of the history of reception, in particular in Kierkegaard, in the commentary of Luz, *Matthew*, 1:346–48.

they lose their dimension of fantasy. The happiness of faith, that is, companionship with God, our Father, also sets a limit on our desires. Property, luxury, prestige, or power, which were only ersatz substitutes for a missing affection, lose their attraction. We discover that we are given the basic minimum we need to live on; then we want to make a gift of our excess—not out of a sense of duty but because of the pleasure of giving pleasure to others.

In order for this soul therapy to work, we must also love ourselves. We must know that we are different from plants or animals and that our life is more important than food or clothing. We must also listen to that inner pressure of desire, that wish to seek and attain something and to find someone.

On a first reading, what Jesus proposed is crazy. His wording was purposely shocking, but, once we get over the shock, we perceive the wisdom and the truth of it. Perhaps in a strange way, the attitude he proposes becomes attainable and, in the end, reasonable. Even normal, with the normality of the kingdom that joins up with creation. If we get beyond our worries and do not succumb to weakness of faith, we discover God at work in our lives and in nature. It is a discovery of faith that sees beyond murders and dead people. God as Providence is not learned except at the school of the kingdom. Loving him is not just receiving a prophetic revelation from him but also seeking for him by means of inspired wisdom, transmitted from one generation to another.

In making this literary unit relevant to his time, Luke offered it to all his readers: to the little ones whom he freed from the fear of not having enough and the bitterness of not having more, by telling them that God offers them what is essential (v. 32) and what is necessary (v. 30); and to those alleged to be great whom he reori-ented in their philosophical quest, by congratulating them on aspiring to inner peace of mind, but at the same time by also offering them the only sure way to access it. For human counseling (*Seelenleitung*) he substituted Christian spiritual counseling (*Seelsorge*). While Matthew encouraged a faith that attached honor to obeying, Luke called believers to freedom. Matthew ended on the note of calling attention to the malice of the current day that we do well to worry about (Matt 6:34). At this place Luke put the saying about the small flock that rejoices about the offer of the kingdom in the present time.

Selling something is already the same as forgoing it. But there has to be a second act of renunciation. And that is the most difficult step: giving up money. For we are anxious to hold it in our hands. We believe that acquisition and possession help us establish our identity. And that is not entirely wrong. But vv. 33-34 suggest a different way of acting in order to establish it: there is something to be done, to be sure, but to be done in the realm of charity; something to acquire, but the benefit of which will serve others, a profit whose firmness is only derivative. If our treasure is like that, our heart will become attached to it. That is fortunate, in this case, but unfortunate, on the other hand, if we have posses-sions only to keep us company. Only Christ's wisdom, his word in the gospel and his Spirit in our beings, is able to persuade us to practice that ethic that economic science does not recommend. And yet, in the long run, taking into consideration the relationship between quality and price, this practical advice from Jesus is not so weird.

By way of a postscript we would like to point out that v. 34 circulated in the patristic literature either in a form close to the one in our Gospels (Luke 12:34 par. Matt 6:21), or in different forms having as a common charac-teristic the substitution of "mind" for "heart."[122]

---

122 See Mees,"Sprichwort"; and W. Pesch, "Exegese," 376–78.

Bibliography

Betz, Otto, "The Dichotomized Servant and the End of Judas Iscariot (Light on the Dark Passages: Matt 25:51 par.; Acts 1:18)," *RevQ* (1964) 43–58.

Botha, J., "Iser's Wandering Viewpoint: A Reception-Analytical Reading of Luke 12:35-48," *Neot* 22 (1988) 253–68.

Bouttier, Michel, "Les paraboles du Maître dans la tradition synoptique," *EThR* 48 (1973) 175–95.

Clarke, A. K., and N. E. W. Collie, "A Comment on Luke 12:41-58," *JTS* 17 (1916) 299–301.

Combrink, H. J. Bernard, "Readings, Readers, and the Authors: An Orientation," *Neot* 22 (1988) 189–203.

Crossan, John Dominic, *In Parables: The Challenge of the Historical Jesus* (New York: Harper & Row, 1973) 96–120.

Deterding, Paul E., "Eschatological and Eucharistic Motifs in Luke 12:35-40," *Concordia Theological Journal* 5 (1979) 85–94.

Dewey, Arthur J., "A Prophetic Pronouncement: Q12:42-46," *Forum* 5.2 (1989) 99–108.

Dodd, C. H., *The Parables of the Kingdom* (3d ed.; London: Nisbet, 1956) 122–39.

Du Plessis, I. J., "Reading Luke 12:35-48 as Part of the Travel Narrative," *Neot* 22 (1988) 217–34.

Du Plessis, Justus G., "Why Did Peter Ask His Question and How Did Jesus Answer Him? Or: Implicature in Luke 12:35-48," *Neot* 22 (1988) 311–24.

Dupont, Jacques, "La parabole du maître qui rentre tard dans la nuit (Mc 13, 34-36)," in

Idem, *Études*, 1:498–526.

Idem, "Vivere nell'attesta del Signore (Lc 12, 35–48)," *Parola, spirito e vita. Quaderni di lettura biblica*, 8 (1983) 146–58.

Edwards, *Theology of Q*, 125–27.

Ellingworth, Paul, "Lk 12:46—Is There an Anti-Climax Here?" *BT* 31 (1980) 242–43.

Fleddermann, Harry, "The Householder and the Servant Left in Charge," *SBLSP* 25 (1986) 17–26.

George, A., "L'attente du maître qui vient: Lc 12, 32-48," *AsSeign* 50 (1974) 66–76.

Grässer, *Problem*, 86–95 and passim.

Harnisch, Wolfgang, *Eschatologische Existenz: Ein exegetischer Beitrag zum Sachanliegen von 1. Thess. 4,13—5,11* (FRLANT 110; Göttingen: Vandenhoeck und Ruprecht, 1973).

Hartin, P. J., "Angst in the Household: A Deconstructive Reading of the Parable of the Supervising Servant (Lk 12:41-48)," *Neot* 22 (1988) 373–90.

Iwand, *Gegenwart*, 39–44.

Jackson, Bernard S., *Theft in Early Jewish Law* (Oxford: Clarendon, 1972).

Jeremias, *Parables*.

Joüon, Paul, "La parabole du *portier qui doit veiller* (Mc 13, 33-37) et la parabole des *serviteurs qui doivent veiller* (Lc 12, 35-40)," *RSR* 30 (1940) 363–68.

Jülicher, *Gleichnisreden*, 2:137–71.

Kahlefeld, Heinrich, *Parables and Instructions in the Gospels* (trans. A. Swidler; New York: Herder & Herder, 1966) 95–115.

Kollman, B., "Lk 12, 35-38: Ein Gleichnis der Logienquelle," *ZNW* 81 (1990) 254–61.

Lategan, B. C., and J. Rousseau, "Reading Luke 12:25-48: An Empirical Study," *Neot* 22 (1988) 391–413.

Le Déaut, Roger, *La Nuit Pascale: Essai sur la signification de la Pâque juive à partir du Targum d'Exode 12, 42* (AnBib 22; Rome: Institut biblique pontifical, 1963) 263–91.

Lövestam, Evald, *Spiritual Wakefulness in the New Testament* (Lund: C. W. K. Gleerup, 1963) 92–107.

Norelli, Enrico, "AI 4, 16 e la parabola del ritorno del padrone (Lc 12, 36-38)," in idem, *L'Ascensione di Isaia: Studi su un apocrifo al crocevia dei cristianesimi* (Bologna: Dehoniane, 1994) 213–19.

Petzke, *Sondergut*, 120–22.

Prast, Franz, *Presbyter und Evangelium in nachapostolischer Zeit: Die Abschiedsrede des Paulus in Milet (Apg 20,17-38) im Rahmen der lukanischen Konzeption der Evangeliumsverkündigung* (FB 29; Stuttgart: Katholisches Bibelwerk, 1979) 233–48, 260–62.

Preisker, H., "κλέπτω, κλέπτης," *TDNT* 3 (1966) 754–56.

Scheffler, Eben Hans, "A Psychological Reading of Luke 12:35-48," *Neot* 22 (1988) 355–71.

Schmid, *Matthäus und Lukas*, 334–41.

Schneider, Gerhard, *Parusiegleichnisse im Lukas-Evangelium* (SBS 74; Stuttgart: Katholisches Bibelwerk, 1975) 20–37.

Schnell, C.W., "Historical Context in Parable Interpretation: A Criticism of Current Tradition-Historical Interpretations of Luke 12:35-48," *Neot* 22 (1988) 269–82.

Schulz, *Q*, 268–77.

Schürmann Heinz, "Die zwei unterschiedlichen Berufungen, Dienste und Lebensweisen im einen Presbyterium," in H. Boelaars and R. Tremblay, eds., *In Libertatem vocati estis (Ga 5, 13): Miscellanea Bernhard Häring* (Rome: Academia Alfonsiana, 1977) 401–20.

Sebothoma, W., "Luke 12:35-48: A Reading by a Black South African," *Neot* 22 (1988) 325–35.

Sellew, Philip, "Reconstruction of Q 12:33-59," *SBLSP* (1987) 645–68.

Smit, D. J., "Responsible Hermeneutics: A Systematic Theologian's Response to the Readings and Readers of Luke 12:35-48," *Neot* 22 (1988) 441–84.

Idem, "Those Were the Critics, What about the Real Readers? An Analysis of 65 Published Sermons and Sermon Guidelines on Luke 12:35-48," *Neot* 23 (1989) 61–82.

Smitmans, A., "Das Gleichnis vom Dieb," in H. Feld and J. Nolie, eds., *Wort Gottes in der Zeit* (Düsseldorf: Patmos, 1973) 43–68.

Strobel, August, "'In dieser Nacht': Zu einer älteren Form der Erwartung in Lk 17, 20-37," *ZThK* (1961) 16–29.

Tilborg, Sjef van, "An Interpretation from the Ideology of the Text," *Neot* 22 (1988) 205–15.

Tödt, *Son of Man.*

Turner, C. H., "Notes on the Old Latin Version of the Bible," *JTS* 2 (1901) 606–7.

Van Aarde, A. G., "Narrative Point of View: An Ideological Reading of Luke 12:35-48," *Neot* 22 (1988) 235–52.

Van Rensburg, Fika J., "A Syntactical Reading of Luke 12:35-48," *Neot* 22 (1988) 415–38.

Van Staden, P., "A Sociological Reading of Luke 12:35–48," *Neot* 22 (1988) 337–53.

Weder, Hans, *Gleichnisse Jesu als Metaphern: Traditions- und redaktionsgeschichtliche Analysen und Interpretationen* (FRLANT 120; Göttingen: Vandenhoeck & Ruprecht, 1978) 162–68.

Weiser, Alfons, *Die Knechtsgleichnisse der synoptischen Evangelien* (SANT 29; Munich: Kösel, 1971) 123–255.

Wuellner, Wilhelm, "The Rhetorical Structure of Luke 12 in Its Wider Context," *Neot* 22 (1988) 283–310.

35/ "Fasten a belt around your waist and have your lamps lit. 36/ And you, you should be like those who are waiting for their master to return from the wedding banquet, so that they may open the door for him as soon as he comes and knocks. 37/ Happy are those servants whom the master finds alert when he arrives. Amen, I tell you, he will fasten his belt around his waist and have them sit down to eat, and he will come and serve them. 38/ If he comes during the second or third watch of the night and receives such a welcome, happy are those ones. 39/ But know this: if the owner of the house had known at what hour the thief was coming, he would not have let him break into his house. 40/ You also must be ready, for the Son of Man is coming at an unexpected hour."

41/ Then Peter said, "Lord, are you telling this parable for us or for everyone?" 42/ And the Lord said, "Who then is the faithful and prudent manager whom the master will put in charge of his household servants, so that they give the allowance of food at the proper time? 43/ Happy is that servant whom his master will find doing such work when he arrives. 44/ Truly I tell you, he will put that one in charge of all his possessions. 45/ But if that servant says in his heart, 'My master is delayed in coming,' and if he begins to beat the other servants, men and women, and to eat and drink and get drunk, 46/ the master of that servant will come on a day when he does not expect him and at an hour that he does not know, and will cut him in two, and assign him a place among the unbelievers. 47/ That servant who knew what his master wanted, but did not

prepare himself or do what was wanted, will receive a severe beating. 48/ But the one who did not know and did what deserved a beating will receive a light beating. From everyone to whom much has been given,ᵃ much will be required; and from the one to whom much has been entrusted,ᵇ even more will be demanded.

a,b Although these two verbs are close in meaning, they must be distinguished from each other; see the commentary below on vv. 47-48.

"Vigilance" and "service": these two terms come to mind and may sound pious and moralizing. A more modern way of summarizing the biblical passage would be to speak of lucidity and responsibility. So what message is being transmitted in these lines? Is it individual morality or an appeal to ecclesial responsibility? Waiting for the end of the world or one's individual death? A requirement that mobilizes the will and makes the time denser, or an exhausting hope that leads to discouragement? An image of the Lord, absent and present, who demonstrates his love, or who sees to it that retribution is meted out?

Synchronic Analysis

This passage has two major divisions, vv. 35-40 and 41-48, which can in turn be further subdivided.[1] The first division:

A v. 35: invitation to be vigilant
  B v. 36: explanatory comparison
    C v. 37a: beatitude of those who are vigilant
      D v. 37b: oracle of salvation
    C′ v. 38: new beatitude of those who are vigilant
  B′ v. 39: short sapiential parable
A′ v. 40: new invitation to be vigilant.

While vv. 35-37a (A B C) speak of the vigilance of the servants during the absence of their master, vv. 38-40 (C′ B′ A′) stress the unexpected moment of his return. Moreover, the oracle of salvation, v. 37b (D), serves as the basis for the first beatitude, v. 37a (C). The second beatitude, v. 38 (C′) provides a structure that is the opposite of the first one, which forms a small chiasm inside a structure that is itself chiastic.

A question from a listener, who in this case happens to be Peter (v. 41), interrupts the speech and causes it to go off in another direction. Aside from the last two verses (vv. 47-48), the second part of the pericope, the parable of the manager, can be divided into two halves: in the first, it describes the noble task carried out by the responsible manager (v. 42), praises him (v. 43), and then indicates the reward he receives (v. 44); in the second, it contrasts the irresponsible attitude of the same manager (v. 45), his surprise, and then his punishment when his master arrives unexpectedly (v. 46):

E v. 42: task that is entrusted and carried out: correct attitude of the manager
  F v. 43: unexpected and welcome arrival of the master
    G v. 44: oracle of salvation
E′ v. 45: neglected task: guilty attitude of the manager
  F′ v. 46a: unexpected and unsettling arrival of the master
    G′ v. 46b: announcement of the punishment.

This parable has the structure of antithetic parallelism. First it lays out the process for succeeding, and then that for failing. The second half is completely narrative (E′ F′ G′), whereas the first half juxtaposes a story (E), a beatitude (F), and an oracle of salvation (G). In that respect, this first half resembles the first part of the preceding unit (vv. 36-37, B C D) in the same use of narration, beatitude, and oracle with a formal introduction ("amen/truly, I tell you" [ἀμὴν/ἀληθῶς λέγω ὑμῖν]). Moreover, while the manager's work is the focus of attention in the first half of the story (vv. 42-44, E F G), it is the hour of the master's arrival that is at the center of the second half (vv. 45-46, E′ F′ G′). Here and there

---

1 On the context and structure of this unit, see Marshall, 532; Bouttier, "Maître," 186–87.

one finds a similarity of vocabulary with the preceding unit: a "master" who "arrives" and "finds," at least in one case, his people at work, which occasions congratulating "(a) servant(s)." Two well-known differences, accentuated by the distinction Peter makes between "all" and "everyone," are the change from the plural to the singular and the shift from servants, a subordinate position, to the manager, a superior position. Against the background of domestic isotopy (from the beginning to the end, the "house" serves as the setting for the events), a sharing of the positions and the tasks begins to take shape, being confirmed in the last two verses (vv. 47-48). While vv. 47-48a contrast the person who knows what the master wants and the one who does not, v. 48b makes a distinction between the one who *received* ("to whom has been given," $\hat{\psi}$ $\dot{\epsilon}\delta\dot{o}\vartheta\eta$), that is, any servant, and the one to whom the master *entrusted* a particular management ("to whom has been entrusted," $\hat{\psi}$ $\pi\alpha\rho\dot{\epsilon}\vartheta\epsilon\nu\tau o$), that is, every one in charge. The difference consists not in the quantity (there are two mentions of "much") but in the nature of the action (an exacting gift, on the one hand, a responsibility that has been entrusted, on the other) and the ecclesial consequences implied by that nature.

Diachronic Analysis

The genetic analysis of these verses is difficult.[2] Verses 35-36 do not have any true parallel except in *Gos. Thom.* 21 and in *Did.* 16.1. In the *Gospel of Thomas* they follow the parable of the thief, rather than precede it, as here.

In the *Gospel of Thomas* we read: "Therefore I say, if the owner of a house knows that the thief is coming, he will begin his vigil before he comes and will not let him dig through into his house of his domain to carry away his goods. You (pl.), then, be on your guard against the world. Arm yourselves with great strength lest the robbers find a way to come to you."[3] In the *Didache*, the warning not to let one's lamp go out and not to let oneself be unprepared (literally "one's waist be ungirded"; cf. Luke 12:35) is associated with vigilance and the wording of the reference to not knowing the hour also reminds us of Luke 12:40.[4]

Even though the context and the literary genre are different, we should point out, as a parallel in the broader sense, the parable of the ten bridesmaids (Matt 25:1-13), which comes right after the parables of the thief and the servant in the First Gospel (Matt 24:42-51).[5] There we also find the theme of vigilance, the mention of the night, the motif of the lamps (even if Matt 25:1-13 uses $\lambda\alpha\mu\pi\dot{\alpha}\delta\epsilon\varsigma$; and Luke 12:35, $\lambda\dot{\nu}\chi\nu o\iota$), the atmosphere of the wedding, the arrival of the master of the house and the allusion to the door (in Luke, it is the master who, when he comes back, knocks at the door; in Matthew, it is the foolish bridesmaids who ask to be let in). The allegorization is carried much farther in Matthew than in Luke. So it is possible that Matt 25:1-13 is the result of an intense reworking of the parable that Luke (12:36) has preserved almost intact. While Luke drew this short story from L,[6] the scribes of the Matthean school probably reworked it on the basis of an oral tradi-

---

2   See Marshall, 536–37 (possible authenticity); Smitmans, "Dieb," 45–52; Weiser, *Knechtsgleichnisse*, 161–75 (v. 35 is redactional; vv. 36–38 represent not a special tradition of Luke but an elaboration of the evangelist on the basis of elements from Mark and Q); Schneider, *Parusiegleichnisse*, 30–37 (v. 35; v. 36bc; end of v. 37 and v. 38 are secondary, without doubt Lukan); Weder, *Gleichnisse*, 162–68. Kloppenborg (*Formation*, 148 n. 202) opposes the attribution of Luke 12:(35) 36–38 to Q and enumerates the representatives of this hypothesis.

3   The thief is found again in *Gos. Thom.* 103: "Jesus said, 'Fortunate is the man who knows where the brigands will enter, so that he may get up, muster his domain, and arm himself before they invade'" (trans. Thomas O. Lambdin, in Robinson, *Nag Hammadi Library*. The absence of Christology in these

sentences argues in favor of an oral tradition, here not contaminated by the canonical Gospels. See Helmut Koester, "Gnomai Diaphoroi: The Origin and Nature of Diversification in the History of Early Christianity," in Koester and Robinson, *Trajectories*, 114–58. For another opinion, see Schrage, *Thomas-Evangelium*, 67–69, 193; Heinz Schürmann, "Das Thomasevangelium und das lukanische Sondergut," in *Traditionsgeschichtliche Untersuchungen zu den synoptischen Evangelien* (Düsseldorf: Patmos, 1968) 233–34.

4   See Willy Rordorf and André Tuilier, *La Doctrine des douze apôtres: Didachè* (SC 248; Paris: Cerf, 1978) 194–95.

5   Lövestam, *Wakefulness*, 108.

6   Cf. Luke 13:25 (*NRSV*): "When once the owner of the house has got up and shut the door, and you

tion. The call in the Gospels to fasten a belt around one's waist and to have one's lamp lit fits the the symbolism of the Passover (Exod 12:11), a call that was relived during the Jewish feast. The earliest Christians were inspired by it, as is witnessed by, in addition to the texts already mentioned, Eph 6:14 and 1 Pet 1:13 (in connection with the waist), and 1 Thess 5:1-11 (in connection with light).[7] In my opinion, v. 35 (the invitation to be vigilant) and v. 37a (beatitude) are secondary developments that were grafted onto the original parable (v. 36) but which were already known to L. It is probably not the same case with v. 37b, which is so surprising. Christ's waiting at table on his disciples is a theme that Luke (22:27) shares with John (John 13:4-5). Here in this passage in Luke it is a question of an eschatological promise; in John, of a symbolical act. This double perspective is found also, in connection with a meal shared by the believers with Christ, in Revelation (it is symbolic in Rev 3:20 and eschatological in Rev 19:9). The presence of v. 37b can be attributed to Lukan redaction because of the set of themes and the vocabulary, but the possibility that this saying was already present in Q cannot be ruled out, since the *Ascension of Isaiah* apparently refers to it in a different wording that is more traditional than Lukan.[8]

The second beatitude (v. 38), with its mention of the watches of the night and the arrival of the master who "finds" his servants, reminds us of the Markan parable of the doorkeeper (Mark 13:34-36).[9] As the Matthean parallel (24:42, beginning of the parable of the thief) suggests, this saying, in the form of an imperative rather than a beatitude, must have been a part of Q.[10] There it constituted a parallel form of the parable of the doorkeeper (Mark 13:34-36), but, we must add, also of the parable of the servant (Luke 12:42-46 par. Matt 24:45-

51).[11] All of these texts stress lack of knowledge of the hour and the importance of vigilance.

The situation becomes more evident in the parables of the thief (12:39-40) and of the manager (12:42-46). The relationship with Matt 24:42-51, which transmits these same two texts side by side, in the same order and with the same words, or almost the same words, justifies attributing them to Q.[12] Here is how I explain the few differences that there are: in v. 39, Luke improves ($\tau o \hat{v} \tau o$, "this," instead of $\dot{\epsilon} \kappa \epsilon \hat{\imath} \nu o$, "that"; $\dot{\alpha} \phi \acute{\imath} \eta \mu \iota$, "let, allow," instead of $\dot{\epsilon} \acute{\alpha} \omega$, "permit") and prefers "hour" to "part of the night," influenced by the following saying (v. 40). Matthew 24:43-44 adds the verb "stay awake" and "therefore." It is commonly agreed that v. 41 in Luke is redactional: Luke is fond of interrupting a speech of Jesus with a question from a listener (cf., e.g., 11:27, 45). The distinction between "everyone" and "us," moreover, is obviously secondary. Luke imposes it on the text of the second parable in a way that is still noticeable. So it is that the "servant" ($\delta o \hat{v} \lambda o \varsigma$) of Q (Matt 24:45) climbs the social, or rather ecclesial, ladder; in Luke he becomes a "manager" or "steward" ($o \dot{\imath} \kappa o \nu \acute{o} \mu o \varsigma$). In v. 43 Luke leaves the traditional term "servant" in the text. Moreover, he puts everything in the future ("will put in charge" [$\kappa \alpha \tau \alpha \sigma \tau \acute{\eta} \sigma \epsilon \iota$], vv. 42 and 44); he thus places everything in the time of the church, while Matthew (= Q) contrasts the past of the mission that has been received (Matt 24:45) with the future of the recompense (Matt 24:51). Luke, moreover, is sensitive to the alimentary symbolism, since he describes the supplies with care (Matt 24:45: "in charge of his household, to give the other servants their allowance of food at the proper time"; Luke 12:42: "in charge of his household servants, so that they give the allowance of food at the

begin to stand outside and to knock at the door, saying, 'Lord, open to us,' then in reply he will say to you, 'I do not know where you come from'." The two passages, 12:35-36 and 13:25, are similar and both emanate, without doubt, from Luke's special source.

7   See Strobel, "Nacht"; Le Déaut, "Nuit Pascale," 263–338; Weiser, *Knechtsgleichnisse*, 156–58.

8   For the redactional origin of v. 37b, see Weiser, *Knechtsgleichnisse*, 175; Dupont, "Maître," 513 n. 5. The reference to *Asc. Isa.* 4:16 has been conveyed to me by Enrico Norelli; see *Ascensio Isaiae* (2 vols.; vol. 1, *Textus*, ed. Paolo Bettiolo; vol. 2, *Commentarius*, by

Norelli; Corpus Christianorum: Series Apocryphorum 7, 8; Turnhout: Brepols, 1995); see also Norelli, "AI 4, 16."

9   See Dupont, "Maître," 511–16.

10   See Schneider, *Parusiegleichnisse*, 30–32, 35–36.

11   On the ensemble of these parables, see Bouttier, "Maître"; and Crossan, *Parables*, 96–120.

12   Weiser, *Knechtsgleichnisse*, 178–204; Schulz, *Q*, 268–77; Harnisch, *Existenz*, 84–85; Schneider, *Parusiegleichnisse*, 20–29; Fleddermann, "Householder"; Sellew, "Reconstruction," 631–44.

proper time"). I attribute to Luke the order of the words in Greek, ποιοῦντα οὕτως, "at work," literally, "doing such work" (v. 43) and I will explain its importance. In v. 44, Luke avoided the Semitism ἀμήν ("amen") and translated it by ἀληθῶς ("truly"). In the Matthean parallel to v. 45 (Matt 24:48), Matthew, who was fond of descriptive adjectives, added that the servant in this case was "wicked." Or, on the other hand, was it Luke who added "in coming" (ἔρχεσθαι) after the verb "delayed" (χρονίζει), which is not found in Matthew? In any case, it was Luke who noted that the person described was in charge of others and who substituted "the servants" (τοὺς παῖδας καὶ τὰς παιδίσκας, literally, "the male servants and the female servants"), therefore persons who were inferior in status, for Matthew's "fellow servants" (Matt 24:49a), that is, equals. A stylistic consideration (Luke kept the infinitive after having begun to use it) explains a slight grammatical difference between Matthew and Luke in the description of the feasts and the drinking sessions of unsavory character (Luke 12:45c par. Matt 24:49b). The dramatic conclusion to the parable (Luke 12:46 par. Matt 24:50-51) is identical in our Gospels, aside from two small differences. As was his custom, Matthew speaks of "hypocrites"; Luke, of "unbelievers," keeping Q's word. It is also Matthew who, following

another of his customs, added the frightening report of weeping and gnashing of teeth (cf. Matt 8:12; 13:42; etc.). Verses 47-48, which are without parallels, must have come from L.[13] In short, in this pericope, Luke has taken over Q, which he has enriched with sayings from L.

Commentary

■ **35** Fastening one's belt could be an ordinary act or a religious one. A belt[14] hitched up the coat or held in the tunic, which was sometimes long. It thus made it easier for a traveler to walk or for a worker to work.[15] Loosening one's belt, on the other hand, was a sign of relaxation and rest.

"Having one's belt fastened," that is, being ready,[16] also recalled the precipitous departure from Egypt, the nocturnal exodus.[17] Once the simultaneous and paradoxical presence (is not the night supposed to be for rest?) of the belt and the lamp is noticed, the allusion to the Passover is undeniable. It was believed that Passover, as well as the other major events of the history of salvation, took place at night.[18] Jewish hope expected the Messiah at midnight. Jesus' listeners, therefore, were the faithful who counted on the nocturnal arrival of their Messiah, believers in a hostile environment,[19] who had their lamps

---

13 See Weiser, *Knechtsgleichnisse*, 222–24; Sellew, "Reconstruction," 644; Petzge, *Sondergut*, 122.

14 Belts could be made from cloth, leather, or other materials (see Exod 28:4; Rev 1:13; 15:6). The type of belt could correspond to a person's dignity or office. Some belts had spaces to allow money to be slid inside, thus serving as a purse; see 2 Sam (2 Kgdms) 20:8; Ezek 9:2; Matt 10:9. A certain symbolism could be attached to this; see C. Jungbauer, "Gürtel in Hans Bächtold-Stäubli, Eduard Hoffmann-Krayer, and Gerhard Lüdtke, eds., *Handwörterbuch des deutschen Aberglaubens III* (Berlin/Leipzig: de Gruyter, 1930–31) cols. 1210–30. Xavier Léon-Dufour, "Ceinture," in idem, *Dictionnaire du Nouveau Testament* (Paris: Seuil, 1996).

15 Cf. Luke 17:8 and the history of Joseph, from whom the colored tunic is ripped off so that he was dressed only in a loincloth. See Gen 37:23-28; *T. Zeb.* 4:9-10; *T. Benj.* 2:2-3. For putting the belt around the waist, cf. Isa 5:27; Jer 1:17; John 21:18; Eph 6:14; 1QM 15.14; 16.11; Lövestam, *Wakefulness*, 92–93.

16 See 1 Kgs (3 Kgdms) 18:46; 2 Kgs (4 Kgdms) 4:29; Fitzmyer, 2:987.

17 The paschal meal is eaten at night: "your loins girded, your sandals on your feet, and your staff in your hand; and you shall eat it hurriedly" (Exod 12:11). The lamp is not mentioned at this place, but cf. Exod 27:20 and Lev 24:2-4.

18 For this tendency to situate the events at night, at midnight, see Strobel, "Nacht," and Le Déaut, "Nuit Pascale," passim. According to Exod 12:42, the paschal night, when God kept watch in order to save his people, must become one night on watch for Israel.

19 See Eph 6:14; 1 Pet 1:13; *Did.* 16.1; Philo *Sacr.* 63: in order to render thanks to God, it is necessary to be always ready, to have passed through passions to virtue, to have the waist fastened with a belt in a spiritual sense. The sense is not then necessarily eschatological. It can be allegorical.

lit in the night,[20] ready to act while the rest of the world was sleeping.[21]

The requirement of having one's belt fastened completes the list of previous instructions. It brings to a peak the faith of the persons who place their trust in God (12:4-7), who acknowledge the Son of Man (12:8-9), who are on their guard against hypocrisy (12:1) and greed (12:15), and who succeed in overcoming their worries (12:22-32) and building up a treasure in the heavens (12:33-34). Having one's belt fastened and one's lamp lit means knowing the hour through which one is living, focusing on what is essential, freeing oneself from all impediments, forgetting oneself, and getting ready to welcome God's Word.

Verse 35 and the following verse prove that the life of Christians, like the history of salvation, bears the stamp of the καιρός, God's "time." The fullness of time about which the apostle Paul speaks (Gal 4:4) does not affect Jesus alone; it also has an impact on every man or woman who opens himself or herself up to God's presence. The fact that we do not know what is coming at the end—which obliges everyone to be ready—has its place in the correct understanding of the fullness of time. By reminding everyone to be alert, Luke teaches a community that,

because its members remain in the dark, hesitates to wait and neglects the καιρός, the "right time" set by God.

■ 36 The disciples ("you") "are like. . . ." For once it is not the kingdom that "is like. . . ." In fact, what we have here is a simple comparison and not a true parable.[22] The setting is that of a family estate where some agricultural laborers work. The house is perhaps isolated, like a Roman villa,[23] so that the master's absence is noted. The servants do not have any fixed hours for working; they have to be ready all the time.[24] The owner went away some distance, but not too far, since he did not have to spend the night away from home. He left[25] the wedding party—in Scripture, a wedding has religious symbolism—probably the wedding of a friend or relative, since his own wedding would take place at his house (cf. Matt 22:2-4; 25:10-12).[26] He comes home and, when he arrives, knocks on a large door[27] that leads into the courtyard, the door that is closed each evening with a large beam, just as still in our day the entrance to a convent on Mount Athos is bolted each evening. So I picture one of those fortified farms, surrounded by a high wall, such as can be seen in Italy or Tunisia. All of that seems quite natural on Jesus' lips (if v. 36 is authentic). But the earliest Christians also loaded each word with a spiritual sense:[28]

---

20 For the lamp, cf. 8:16; 11:33-34, 36; see the commentary on 8:16-18 (1:313–15). For a simple lamp, clay or metal, see Jülicher, *Gleischnisreden*, 2:79–80, 161–62. For the symbolic value of the lamp and its oil (God's help, life, salvation, the Holy Spirit), see Lövestam (*Wakefulness*, 115–17), who refers to Ps 17 (18):29; Prov 13:9; 20:20; 24:20; Job 18:5-6; *Midr. Ps.* 73 (*Midrash Tehillim* 73:1) (167a) and *Midr. Ps.* 37 (*Midrash Tehillim* 37:1) (126b).

21 The start of v. 35 is in the singular in Codex Bezae (D): "That your waist be fastened with a belt." Otherwise, the periphrastic formula of the verb "to be" followed by a participle is dear to Luke; see BDF §352 and 353.1, esp. n. 4. Marshall (535) proposes translating: "Be the kind of person who . . . ." In v. 36, the verb "to be" is not expressed, and the phrase can be taken as an indicative, "and you, you are similar" or as an imperative, "and you be similar. . . ." I decide on the imperative by reason of v. 35.

22 Jülicher, *Gleischnisreden*, 2:162. On this comparison, see Joüon ("Parabole," 306), who juxtaposes the rose-tinted color of Luke's parable, indicating the expression of confidence, to the somber color of

Mark. See also Dupont, "Maître," 511–26; Weder, *Gleichnisse*, 162–68.

23 On the isolated character of the house, see Gaston Bachelard, *La Poétique de l'espace* (Paris: Presses universitaires de France, 2007) esp. 23–78.

24 See Van Staden, "Sociological," 347.

25 The verb ἀναλύω signifies "to untie," "to weigh anchor," "to break camp," "to leave," often in order to come back. That is the sense to retain here; cf. Wis 2:1; 2 Macc 8:25; 9:1; 13:7. The idea is that of leaving more than of coming back.

26 See Jülicher, *Gleischnisreden*, 2:163; Plummer, 330. Weiser (*Knechtsgleichnisse*, 167) refuses to see here an allusion to the messianic banquet; this is formally correct, although the messianic wedding party could take place only after the parousia. The fact remains that the nuptial atmosphere is apparent; see Marshall, 351 (the plural γάμοι usually is read, for example, in Esth 2:18 and 9:22). See BAGD, s.v.

27 The word "door" is absent, but the verb "to knock" suggests it (11:9-10; 13:25; Acts 12:13, 16).

28 Loisy, 351; Ernst, 408. On the word κύριος, which comes to designate "the Lord" for Christians, see

the "master" is "their Master," "their Lord"; his departure suggests the elevation associated with the Easter event and the absence of the Risen One, which is to be overcome as best as one can;[29] the waiting of the servants (who are called "human beings," "persons," ἄνθρωπος) becomes that of the believers; the unexpected arrival of the master suggests the parousia; finally, the wedding atmosphere makes us think of the kingdom. The frequent occurrence of these motifs in the Gospels[30] is an indication of the intensity of the questioning, the frustration, the expectation, the hope, and the faith of the earliest Christians. "Waiting" (προσδέχομαι) is an attitude that needs to be clarified, since it can be one of joy, eagerness, impatience, or despair, depending on the circumstance. The example given in the text suggests a wait that will not lead to disappointment, and the invitation to be ready, which precedes the mention of waiting, sets it in the context of a joyous liturgical atmosphere.[31] Euphoria and dysphoria, joy and toil cohabit. The conditions are those of work; the setting, that of a liberation and then a feast.

Believers are at work, but they work with the joy of being freed. There is one whose coming they wait for with hope; they will not keep him waiting at the door. They themselves came out of the house of slavery, following the symbolism of the exodus (v. 35). They live henceforth in the house of the Father (v. 36). Eschatological reserve, however, must keep them from an enthusiastic faith: they still have to live in a moral state as they wait for the messianic feast.

■ **37** The beatitude in v. 37a is one produced by Christians that is subtler than it would appear and takes its

inspiration from the beatitude in the following parable (v. 43).[32] The prophet who uttered it, in the light of v. 36 (cf. "when . . . the master . . . arrives," ἐλθὼν ὁ κύριος [v. 37]), has a keen insight into the link between toil and happiness: the people in question are "servants" (the word appears suddenly)[33] who carry out the task they have been given; they keep watch (the present participle, γρηγοροῦνται, "be alert," "stay awake," "be watchful," emphasizes the length, the waiting, which is precisely, at that moment, the task that is to be carried out).[34] But, in the full force of the term in the Gospels, these servants are already "happy" (μακάριοι).[35] That is so not only because they will be rewarded but also because they have adopted the right attitude and are in a good relationship with their master. The verb γρηγορέω ("be alert," "stay awake") is uncommon in Luke, but it is found in certain manuscripts in v. 39, as well as in Acts 20:31 in an ecclesial context (an invitation by the community leaders to be vigilant and to remember—therefore the right attitude with respect to the future and the past).

Luke next inserts (v. 37b) an oracle of salvation[36] whose vocabulary is taken from a later parable (17:8). We are astounded to witness a reversal of roles:[37] Christ, following a move that recalls the Magnificat (1:46-55), changes from being a master to being a servant. This motif, associated by Paul and John with the life and death of Christ,[38] is linked with Christ's coming, which the apocalyptic context leads us to identify with the parousia. At the kingdom feast (14:15), the Lord is the one who will in person wait on tables. The saying in 22:27, "I am among you as one who serves," will in that way have its validity extended. In the move from the time of the

---

Georg Strecker, *Der Weg der Gerechtigkeit: Untersuchung zur Theologie des Matthäus* (FRLANT 82; Göttingen: Vandenhoeck & Ruprecht, 1962) 123–25.

29 Cf. Luke 19:12-15; 24:50-51; Acts 1:9-11; Matt 18:20; 28:20.

30 Cf. Luke 5:35 par.; 12:42-46 par.; 18:8; 19:11-27; Acts 3:19-21; 17:31.

31 Cf. Luke 2:25, 38; 23:51; see also the commentary on 2:25-28 and n. 26 (1:100–101).

32 See Weiser, *Knechtsgleichnisse*, 168–69.

33 On δοῦλος (one who is not juridically free, one who is attached to a master, one who is a slave), cf. 7:2, 3, 8, 10; 14:17, 21-23; 15:22; 17:7, 9; 19:13, 15, 17, 22; 20:10-11; 22:50; Rom 6:16; 2 Pet 2:19, etc.; see Spicq, *Notes de lexicographie*, 1:211–16.

34 See Johannes M. Nützel, "γρηγορέω etc.," *EDNT* 1:364–65.

35 See the commentary on 6:20-26 (1:220–29).

36 Weiser, *Knechtsgleichnisse*, 169–71; Schneider, *Parusiegleichnisse*, 34–35.

37 Rightly, Plummer (330) and Lagrange (367) refuse to see here the influence of the Roman Saturnalia, where, for one day, social roles were inverted and where, for example, a slave could become a master or a king, derisive but short-lived.

38 See already the hymn in Phil 2:6-11; cf. 2 Cor 8:9; Rom 15:7-8.

church to that of the kingdom, the shape of love will not be modified, nor will that of power in the Christian scheme of things. In his farewell speech (22:24-26), the Lukan Christ exhorts Christian ministers to carry out their responsibility by making this Christlike reversal (22:27), which inverts human hierarchical patterns. The Magnificat (1:51-52), which announced such a reversal, is here completed: the new powerful ones, who are the humble ones who have been elevated (1:52), will wield their power not as despots but, following the example of their master, as servants.

This task of service is illustrated by a triple action: being ready for service ("he will fasten his belt around his waist," περιζώσεται, a future middle, which is similar to 17:8 but also to 12:35, where we have the perfect passive; cf. John 13:4); welcoming, in particular seating the guests ("sit down to eat," "place as a guest," ἀνακλίνω, as in banquet stories); and waiting on table ("serve," διακονέω, as in 4:39; 8:3; 17:8; Acts 6:1-6).

■ **38** This second beatitude has the phrase "happy are those . . ." at the end of the sentence in Greek, instead of at the beginning (the usual order, as in the previous verse, v. 37). It was inspired by the parable of the doorkeeper.[39] On the semantic level, it is content with repeating what we already know, thanks to the comparison (v. 36), the first beatitude (v. 37a), and the oracle (v. 37b). It is about the master's coming and what he finds upon arrival. The same elements can be found, including οὕτως ("such"),[40] translated here in v. 38 as "such a welcome," and in the parable of the servant

(v. 43) as "such work." The only new element is the mention here of the "hour," thanks to the precise term "watch of the night" (φυλακή),[41] which Luke will eliminate in v. 39. It should be noticed that only the second and third watches, that is, the middle and perhaps the end of the night, are mentioned. Is this an indication of the consciousness of the delay of the parousia? The first watch is thus not even mentioned.[42]

On the Mount of Olives, only Christ will persevere in being vigilant (22:39-46). Until their Master returns, the disciples will have to adopt the same attitude and fight against sleep. Being awake and being ready are, above all, knowing what it means to *serve*, thanks to the example of Jesus, who was a servant right up until his death (cf. 22:27). Next, it is knowing that, without God's help, human vigilance is uncertain. Finally, it also means getting ready to open the door and to *be served* by the Christ who serves (v. 37b).

■ **39** The question of the hour,[43] introduced in the preceding verse, makes its presence felt insistently in vv. 39-40, where it is associated with the theme of ignorance. In a Socratic manner, Jesus teaches his disciples what they do not know: "but know this" (τοῦτο δὲ γινώσκετε, v. 39),[44] on the one hand, and "unexpected," (οὐ δοκεῖτε, literally "you do not think," v. 40), on the other.[45] Consequently, you must know that you do not know the hour. This awareness of what one does not know is part of what vigilance is about.

So there are those who agree not to know and those who mistakenly want to guess. Among those who agree

---

39   Cf. Mark 13:35 in its traditional, pre-Markan form.

40   The word οὕτως ("such") refers to the vigilant attitude of the servants.

41   On φυλακή in the sense of "watch" of the night, cf. the episode of the shepherds (see the commentary on 2:8-13 and n. 56 [1:86–90]); BAGD, s.v. In ancient times (cf. Judg 7:19), the night of the Hebrews was divided into three watches, then under Roman influence, it was divided into four watches (cf. Mark 13:35; Acts 12:4). It is, without doubt, to the old system that the text refers; see Plummer, 331. Marcion, Irenaeus, Codex Bezae (D), and certain Greek and Latin manuscripts insert "the first" before "watch."

42   One can say, with Plummer (331), that this silence can obviously be otherwise explained. It is during the first watch that the feast unfolds.

43   The word ὥρα can designate a determinate moment

(1:10; 14:17), a part of the day (22:59; 23:44), an important hour (αὐτῇ τῇ ὥρᾳ, 2:38; 24:33; ἐν αὐτῇ τῇ ὥρᾳ 10:21; 12:12), the instant that someone puts a plan in motion, for example, the hour of the adversaries of Jesus (22:53: "the hour and the power of darkness"). In relation to the parousia, cf. 12:39, 40, 46, as in Rev 14:7, 15. The word "hour," then, has in Luke, as in John, great importance.

44   Γινώσκετε can be a present indicative or present imperative. Plummer (331), Lagrange (368), and Delebecque (84) opt for the indicative. Cf. Luke 21:30-31, where one finds the two meanings close together, the indicative and the imperative. The τοῦτο that precedes δέ, and especially the parallel (second person singular of the imperative) in 2 Tim 3:1, prompt me to choose the imperative here, at the suggestion of my assistant David Warren.

not to know, there are also two different attitudes: one, the correct one, consists in living joyously in grace and freedom; the other, the incorrect one, amounts to being taken over by anxiety and placing oneself under the yoke of new constraints in order to manage one's vigilance.

A short parable buttresses Jesus' pedagogical objective.[46] In v. 39, it is, in fact, a parable and not a comparison (v. 40, which is secondary, will draw the lesson: "you also . . . ," καὶ ὑμεῖς . . .). This brief story, we should point out, refers to a situation different from the one in v. 36.[47] It deals with an "owner of the house" (οἰκοδεσπότης), of the same sort as the "master" (κύριος) of v. 36, but this time it is not the master who comes but a "thief" (κλέπτης). Although the setting resembles that of the preceding parable, the incident that takes place is different. It is still a matter of an arrival at an unexpected hour, but this time it is a thief, who does not come in by the main entrance! Unlike the master, who was expected, the thief is not supposed to come.

We should clarify the image of the "thief" in the light of contemporary Jewish reflections that are from the same period as our text. In order to harmonize the various statutes of the Law of Moses and to assign a legal meaning to each of the two Hebrew verbs גנב and גזל, the rabbis of that time worked out an opinion according to which the first referred to the act of "stealing," which takes place at night or secretly, and the second to the act of "robbing," which can take place in broad daylight. Here we have stealing; there, robbery. In Greek the word for "stealing" is κλέπτω, on the one hand; for "robbing," λῃστεύω or ἁρπάζω, on the other. The teachers had to explain in particular why the law was more severe regarding theft than regarding robbery.[48] Acts of robbery, being more serious, were more often the doing of Gentiles than of God's people. They were punished less severely. Acts of thievery, on the other hand, which were less important, were often carried out by Israelites, who were punished more severely. *Noblesse oblige!* The example cited by Jesus is undoubtedly a case of theft, the work of a "thief" (κλέπτης), working at night and without anybody knowing about it; there was a break-in involved, but nobody was hurt.[49] This man was probably a member of the Jewish people. It goes without saying that a landowner is not one to let himself be robbed without reacting.

All of the available studies on the subject say that there was no religious symbolism attached to the thief in contemporary Judaism.[50] What we have in front of us, then, is a live metaphor, one of Jesus' original parables. Not counting the secondary application in v. 40, we can suppose, considering the disturbing image of the theft, that Jesus intended to evoke God's judgment, which was going to fall in an unexpected way on each and every one. Christian tradition took over this parable, the lesson of which is not explicit, and immediately associated it with the Day of the Lord, the parousia, as is proved by 1 Thess 5:2; Rev 3:3, 16:15; 2 Pet 3:10, and, of course, the following verse in the present pericope, 12:40.[51] In my opinion, logia 21 and 103 of the *Gospel of Thomas* are not the late result of a Gnostic de-eschatologizing[52] but the fixing of an early form of the text: the sense that is given is, therefore, that believers must be vigilant in the face of the dangers of the world. The thief does not represent, in this case, God's judgment but rather the threat that the world causes to weigh on believers. The author of

---

45 Delebecque (84) translates: "at the hour when you do not believe." Fitzmyer, 2:983: "at a time when you least expect him."

46 See Jülicher, *Gleichnisreden*, 2:137–45; Kahlefeld, *Parables*, 107–11; Harnisch, *Existenz*, 84–94; Smitmans, "Dieb"; George, "Attente," 68; Schneider, *Parusiegleichnisse*, 20–23; Fleddermann, "Householder," 17–20, 24–25.

47 See Kahlefeld, *Parables*, 107–11.

48 See Jackson (*Theft*, passim), who presents the biblical terminology and then the rabbinic, citing the principal passages of Scripture, esp. Gen 21:25; Lev 5:20-26; Judg 21:23; Isa 3:14-15; Jer 49:9-10; Ezek 18:7-9; Hos 7:1; Ps 68 (69):5-6; Prov 6:30-31; 22:22-23.

49 On the difference between the thief and the brigand, cf. Hos 7:1; Herbert Preisker, "κλέπτω κτλ.," *TDNT* 3 (1966) 754–56.

50 Cf., however, Jer 49:9-10, where God, who comes to judge and punish, is compared, it seems, to a thief: "If thieves came by night, even they would pillage only what they wanted. But as for me, I have stripped Esau bare, I have uncovered his hiding places" (*NRSV*).

51 See Smitmans, "Dieb."

52 See *Gos. Thom.* 21 (cited above); and see the commentary on 12:35-36, p. 229 n. 3. See Shrage, *Thomas-Evangelium*, 68; Smitmans, "Dieb," 53–54; Fieger, *Thomasevangelium*, 93–98.

the *Gospel of Thomas* probably had in mind the temptations that assail the faithful and may cause them to lose their share in the heavenly inheritance. This threatening world probably represents the external and material world.

■ **40** The imperative thrust of the saying is evident here, as in v. 35. We can see the semantic richness of the vocabulary having to do with vigilance: after images of the belt fastened around one's waist and the lamps lit, after the verbs "wait" and "be alert," here comes a new expression: "be ready." The Greek adjective ἕτοιμος[53] can have a passive sense: "prepared," "put in readiness," especially of things (an example in English: the meal is ready in the sense of being served); and an active sense "in readiness," "willing," of persons (an example in English: I am ready, willing to do it). It is this active sense that is to the fore here—an ethical sense encouraging action, and before that, an inner attitude. But Luke was enough of a realist to know that people prepare themselves to be ready and that others play a role in that preparation. He called this to our attention on several occasions: Jesus was the teacher who trained his disciples[54] (which he was doing moreover at this moment by means of his instruction), and a good disciple is a man or woman trained and equipped by Christ.[55] So, to the active and ethical sense that is uppermost in this verse, we must add, in the background, the passive and theological sense.

It is therefore imperative to be ready for the coming of the Son of Man. Up to this point Luke has rarely spoken of apocalyptic events.[56] If he does so now, it is in order to prepare the ground for Christ's passion, as he has been at pains to do since chap. 9.[57] In his opinion, there is no reason to have any doubts or worries. The risen One is,

to be sure, absent, but neither the absence itself nor its length ought to be a cause for alarm, since Christ will certainly come back to establish God's reign in power and glory, to re-create the social and political order, to give each person their reward, to save God's people and all of creation by means of peace and harmony. It will be God's final visitation.

Being ready for these events is, paradoxically, tantamount to not being concerned about them, or at least not having one's eyes glued to heaven in an attitude of passive waiting (cf. Acts 1:11). Being ready means living on earth, where two paths are open to us. Ethical dualism unfolds from the Sermon on the Plain to the parable of the rich man (Luke 6:20-49; 12:16-21). Either you live for your own interest, seeking to enrich yourself for your own sake, or you live in the context of the community of the people of God, for others' sake, thus becoming rich toward God. Not knowing the hour of the arrival of the Son of Man is equivalent to knowing that each hour is an occasion for loving God and one's neighbor,[58] and that his call can be sounded at any moment. The perspective is not only ethical but also spiritual.

■ **41** The Gospel writer spontaneously chose Peter as the spokesman for the Twelve.[59] Behind the question put by the leading apostle, in Luke's eyes, is a binary conception of the church: the parishioners ("everyone"), on the one hand, and the pastors ("us"), on the other. Although Christians are all brothers and sisters, they do not all have the same responsibility and, consequently, do not receive precisely the same teaching.[60] Neither do Jesus' parables all have the same destination in his eyes. Nevertheless, Luke did not dare modify or do too much in the way of completing the Master's words. He

---

53   See BAGD, s.v.; Jülicher, *Gleichnisreden*, 2:139–40.

54   See Luke 6:20-49; 8:9-18; 9:1-6, 46-48; 10:1-11; 11:1-13, etc.

55   See the commentary on 6:39-40 (1:248–49).

56   However, cf. 9:26 and 12:8-9.

57   See Luke 9:22, 31, 44-45; 12:50; 13:31-33; 17:25; 18:31-37.

58   See Iwand, *Gegenwart*, 43–44; only a community that awaits the Son of Man who is coming can receive and recognize him. He arrives like a thief, that is to say, in a way totally incalculable and independent of us.

59   On Peter in Luke-Acts, see the commentary on 5:1–11 (1:166–72); also Wolfgang Dietrich, *Das*

Petrusbild der lukanischen Schriften (BWANT 94; Stuttgart: Kohlhammer, 1972); Bovon, *Theologian*, 388–91.

60   Luke works with two distinctions that should not be confused, that of the crowd (not yet Christian) and of the disciples (already Christians); then that of the faithful and the ministers. Luke 8:4-15 is characteristic of the first distinction. Our passage, of the second. On this question, see Jeremias, *Parables*, 56, 99, 166; Schneider, *Parusiegleichnisse*, 24–25, 28–29; Prast, *Presbyter*, 233–37; Fleddermann, "Householder," 21.

did not furnish an explicit answer to Peter's question. He discreetly adapted the parable,[61] for example, by substituting the term "manager,"[62] which describes leaders, for the term "servant." In so doing, he nevertheless answered the question in an implicit way. By the way he had the question phrased, Luke divided up the subject matter. What comes before and deals with vigilance concerns all believers; what follows and defines the task incumbent upon the leaders refers only to the Twelve, that is, the future ministers.

One should be prudent when drawing inferences from the figure of the Twelve for the ecclesial doctrine of ministry, since Luke's position is about midway between Pauline prophetism and early Catholicism. He made a distinction between the whole group of believers and the smaller group of leaders, without conferring on these ministers a jurisdictional power. He felt that it was the fact of the task being carried out well, rather than any episcopal ordination, that witnessed to a person's being set apart and called by God, who can call each and every one to serve him. The function of the laying on of hands confirms God's choice, expressed by the prophets and acknowledged by the assembled community. So Luke established ministries, but defined them as a service without prerogatives.

■ **42** At the head of God's people, the "small flock" (v. 32), is the Lord, the κύριος, who chooses leaders and vests them with a task. What follows will show that the master goes away as soon as the manager has been entrusted with his mission. A "manager" is not a slave; he has the confidence of the landowner, who charges him with the double task of overseeing the servants and the finances. Here his function is described in precise, but general, terms. The person in charge has as his mission to give (διδόναι) to each person what he needs to live on[63] at the proper time (ἐν καιρῷ). What is the meaning of the words "in charge of his household" (ἐπὶ τῆς θεραπείας αὐτοῦ)? In Greek the word θεραπεία means "service," especially domestic service, but also "treatment" given to the sick and service or "homage" to, or "worship" of, gods. Although it can be an abstract word, it can also refer concretely to the whole team of persons performing these tasks.[64] A manager like Joseph (Gen 47:12, 14) was put in charge of a service, which is tantamount to saying that he was put in charge of the servants. Moreover, although the passage has a domestic denotation, a slight medical connotation cannot be ruled out. In a house, the kitchen is indispensable every day, but a dispensary is sometimes very helpful.[65] Since Luke liked to use more than one meaning at a time, I suppose that he looked on these ways of caring for others as a form of worship of God.

If he successfully carries out this task to his master's satisfaction, the manager is pronounced πιστός and φρόνιμος. The first adjective can have an active meaning, "trusting," or a passive meaning, "trustworthy," "faithful," "inspiring trust/faith," depending on whether it is a matter of the trust that is given or the trust that

---

61 On the word παραβολή in Luke, see the commentary on 8:4 and n. 17 (1:307). The syntax of this parable is curious: a question made up of a main clause and a relative clause, followed not by a response but by a beatitude, reinforced by an oracle; See Jülicher, *Gleichnisreden*, 2:146; Weiser, *Knechtsgleichnisse*, 180–81, followed by Beyer, *Syntax*, 1:287–93. Jesus' question betrays a Semitism and is equivalent to a subordinate clause with a conditional valuation. The question's final relative clause serves as the enunciation of the presuppositions, while the following beatitude serves as the apodosis; cf. Matt 7:9.

62 An οἰκονόμος is etymologically the one who directs a house, then a "financial manager," a "steward," a "governor," but the term designates also, more generally, any person who directs an affair, an enterprise, the finances of a city (Rom 16:23), a "director," an "administrator," a "manager"; the title

can be taken in a figurative sense and is applied sometimes to the head of a religious community. In Luke, one encounters it elsewhere only in another parable (16:1, 3, 8). For a religious sense, see 1 Cor 4:1-2; Titus 1:7; 1 Pet 4:10. See BAGD, s.v.; John Reumann, "'Stewards of God'—Pre-Christian Religious Application of οἰκονόμος in Greek," *JBL* 77 (1958) 339–49; Horst Kuhli, "οἰκονομία etc.," EDNT 2:498–500.

63 On the word σιτομέτριον, a New Testament *hapax legomenon*, see BAGD, s.v.

64 Matthew (25:45), following Q, speaks of ἡ οἰκετεία, which signifies here the "household," the "servants." Luke uses θεραπεία in the sense of "medical care" in 9:11. On this word, see BAGD, s.v.

65 Note the proximity of "medical care" (θεραπεία) and subsistence (ἐπισιτισμός) in 9:11-12; see also 10:34.

is received.[66] It seems to me that the active meaning is the one that fits here in the context of ethical dualism conjured up by the text.[67] The second adjective, "prudent," must be understood not as expressing independent understanding but as a sign of religious wisdom. It describes the wisdom of the Christian minister who carries out God's will in service on behalf of believers and who finds true happiness in the exercise of that service to aid others. The adjective φρόνιμος is used only twice by Luke; it means "prudent," "wise," and corresponds to what is said about it in the Jewish sapiential literature, where believers are "wise in God," and the early Christian literature, where believers are invited to not be "wise in their own wisdom."[68]

■ **43** The manager will be declared "happy," in the sense of the beatitudes,[69] if the "master," who for Luke was Christ on the day of his return, finds him acting that way. Luke improved on the order of words in Q by putting the adverb after the verb (i.e., changing οὕτως ποιοῦντα in Q/Matt 24:46 to ποιοῦντα οὕτως in Luke 12:43), perhaps intending to set off the adverb οὕτως.[70] But he did it also to stress the whole expression "doing such work." In his eyes, what counted was that the manager was not satisfied with good intentions but "acted" (ποιοῦντα) and that he chose the correct kind of activity ("such work," οὕτως).[71]

■ **44** The kind of faithfulness and efficiency demonstrated by the manager is what was to make it possible for God's people to get through the time and to survive (cf. 18:8).[72] This survival of faith, then, was to depend not only on the believers' perseverance but also on the pastors' judicious activity (cf. Col 4:17).[73] In the case of success, the master's satisfaction was to be expressed in terms of a reward.[74] According to v. 44, introduced by formal phrasing, this remuneration was to consist of a new and more important responsibility:[75] managing the master's possessions. The manager first had to take care of men and women; he was henceforth to have the responsibility of managing possessions.[76] What is suggested by the narration is less economic success than an additional honor, the consequence of a trust that has not been betrayed.

■ **45** The second part of the parable swings the story away from normality to scandal, and then to tragedy.[77] To the symmetry of opposite situations must be added certain unexpected elements: a subordinate "if" clause ("if," ἐάν, v. 45; the "but," δέ, being adversative) matches the initial question (v. 42). An inner monologue[78] here matches the direct action of the first part. On the other hand, there is no pejorative indication to match the flattering adjectives of v. 42 (Luke is not speaking here of an "evil" or a "bad"[79] servant). Unlike what he did in

---

66 See Albert Vanhoye, *Situation du Christ: Epître aux Hébreux 1 et 2* (LD 58; Paris: Cerf, 1969) 375–76.

67 On the diverse dualisms, see I. P. Couliano, *I miti dei dualismi occidentali: Dai sistemi gnostici al mondo moderno* (Di Fronte e attraverso 227; Milan: Jaca, 1989), esp. 25–53.

68 See *T. Naph.* 8:10; Rom 11:25; 1 Cor 4:10; Ignatius *Magn.* 3.1; *Pol.* 2.2.

69 See the commentary on 6:20 (1:215–25).

70 BDF §474.2: "to do such" could be a Semitism; cf. Eccl 8:10 LXX: ὅτι οὕτως ἐποίησαν, "because they have done such."

71 See Prast (*Presbyter*, 244), who judges that Luke insists on the present activity of the servant-manager.

72 See Prast, *Presbyter*, 241.

73 See ibid., 237.

74 See Bo Reicke, "The New Testament Conception of Reward," in J. J. von Allmen, ed., *Aux sources de la tradition chrétienne: Melanges offerts a M Maurice Goguel a l'occasion de son soixante-dixième anniversaire* (Neuchâtel/Paris: Delachaux et Niestlé, 1950) 195–206.

75 This recalls the parable of the pounds: Luke 19:17, 19 par. Matt 25:21-23.

76 The first καταστήσει, "he will put in charge" (v. 42), which inscribes the ministerial task in the time of the church, responds to the second καταστήσει, "he will put in charge" (v. 44), which corresponds to the life in the kingdom (cf. 22:29-30); cf. George, "Attente," 68.

77 It is the second part of the parable that contains the decisive message, the point; see Jeremias, *Parables*, 55–58. Crossan (*Parables*, 96–120) is interested in the pair normality–abnormality in the parables. He places, in my opinion wrongly, our parable in the group of those where normality is respected.

78 On the interior monologue, see the commentary on 12:17 above and the bibliography indicated there.

79 The adjective κακός (Matt 24:48) must be a moralizing addition of the first evangelist; see Fleddermann, "Householder," 22; Sellew, "Reconstruction," 641; against Schulz, *Q*, 272; and Schneider, *Parusiegleichnisse*, 26 n. 10.

v. 42, here in v. 45 Luke has not changed his source: the servant remains a servant and does not deserve the title of "manager."

The servant first observed the truth of the situation: "My master is delayed" (Luke added "in coming").[80] This clearheadedness on the part of the servant could have led to a renewal of watchfulness but turned out to be the occasion of his downfall, and he succumbed to temptation (cf. 8:14). Following Q, Luke portrayed the hero's decline in a caricatured way:[81] by beating the other servants, both men and women, the manager first betrayed the trust that his master had placed in him. Instead of giving food to each one of them to live on, he infringed on the physical integrity, and therefore on the dignity and life, of the personnel for whom he bore responsibility. Moreover, entrusted with the finances and the organization of the management, he cornered the food and drink for himself alone.[82] If he had been a good manager, he would have divided things up equally and no one would have been cheated. But when he caved in morally, then he wronged others and treated himself preferentially, betraying his master's trust a second time. There is always the risk of people making abusive use of power in their own self-interest. And it is always the case that the ordinary person, whose basic moral sense is well known, is scandalized by such behavior.

■ **46** In the way this risk is worded, commentators perceive the dangers to which the delay in the arrival of the parousia[83] and more simply the neglect of God expose the church and its ministers. Although this delay is admitted, the certitude of the ultimate coming of the Son of Man is not in doubt. Q, then Luke, ceremoniously emphasized the ignorance on the part of Christians with respect to the date ("on a day when he does not expect him and at an hour that he does not know"). The future "will come" ($\H{\eta}\xi\epsilon\iota$) is the only certitude that no one should fail to know. Notice how this solitary piece of knowledge is stressed by its being placed at the beginning of the clause in Greek; literally: "(he) will come, the master . . ." ($\H{\eta}\xi\epsilon\iota$ ὁ κύριος . . .).

The punishment falls like a guillotine: "and will cut him in pieces."[84] Is the phrasing of this terrible punishment due to a mistake in translation,[85] given the fact that we might perhaps expect an exclusion, a being driven out of the holy community, more than a capital execution? That is what the second part of the saying also suggests: instead of having his share,[86] his eschatological lot, with the righteous, the poor man will share it with

---

80 The delay is not a uniquely Christian theme. Since the time of the prophet Habakkuk, the people of Israel have been confronted by the delay of the ultimate intervention by their God (see Hab 2:1-4). The problem is posed during the epoch when the Qumran commentator reapplied the prophecy of Habakkuk; see 1QpHab 6.12–7.14, e.g., "This means that the Last Days will be long, much longer than the prophets had said; for God's revelations are truly mysterious" (1QpHab 7.7–8, trans. Michael Wise, Martin Abegg, Jr., and Edward Cook, *The Dead Sea Scrolls: A New Translation* (San Francisco: HarperSanFrancisco, 1996) 119; August Strobel, *Untersuchung zum eschatologischen Verzögerungsproblem auf Grund der spätjüdisch-urchristlichen Geschichte von Habakuk 2.2 ff.* (NovTSup 2; Leiden: Brill, 1961) 7–14. The first Christians must confront this delay of the parousia of the Son of Man and must wait. After having maintained, first of all, the imminence, they accept next the delay by arousing vigilance and ethical conduct, as here (12:42-46) or in Matt 25:1-13. Then they invite mission by promising the compensatory presence of the Spirit, as in Mark 13:10 and Acts 1:6-8; cf. Grässer, *Problem*. On the verb χρονίζω ("to delay"), see Weiser, *Knechtsgleich-*

nisse, 216–18. The servant (i.e., servant-manager) supposes not that his master will no longer come back but that he delays, which provides for him, the servant-manager, the period of watching to come.

81 This description recalls the attitude of certain slaves in antique comedies; see J. J. Richard, "Daos, Pseudolus, Mascarille," in Esther Bréguet and Claude Wehrli eds., *Mélanges Esther Bréguet* (Geneva: Typopress SA, 1975) 7–20.

82 See the commentary on 12:19.

83 See n. 80 above.

84 See Betz ("Dichotomized"), who analyzes the verbs διχοτομέω and the phrase τίθημι μέρος τινός, two *hapax legomena* in the NT.

85 This is the opinion of Jeremias, *Parables*, 57 n. 31: "He will give him blows and treat him as a profligate"; cf. Ellingworth ("Anti–Climax"), who refers to Lev 17:10, 14; 20:17; 22:3; Ezek 25:7; Rom 11:22; and Gal 5:12.

86 Cf. 10:42 (ἡ ἀγαθὴ μερίς, "the good part"); 12:13 (μερίσασθαι . . . τὴν κληρονομίαν, "to divide the inheritance"); Acts 8:21 (οὐκ ἔστιν σοι μερὶς οὐδὲ κλῆρος, "there is for you neither part nor lot"); Acts 20:32 (δοῦναι τὴν κληρονομίαν ἐν τοῖς ἡγιασμένοις πᾶσιν, "to assure the inheritance for [or

unbelievers.[87] I believe, however, that there are instead two successive punishments: first the death of the body, sawed in two following the Persian procedure that was applied to a condemned slave,[88] then the final punishment inflicted by God (cf. 12:4-5). Be that as it may, the parable is recounted by Q, then by Luke, in allegorical terms. Its initial wording and the identity of those to whom it was first addressed remain uncertain.[89] Was Jesus speaking to his disciples? Was he talking about the parousia, or the last judgment, or individual death? Or did he have in mind the religious leaders of Israel who proved to be bad shepherds?[90] The ethical dualism reminds us of certain Psalms, and the way the parable ends recalls the lot of the unbelievers in Psalm 37 (36).[91] Readers may ask themselves on which side they are to be found, or whether they are not both faithful and unfaithful.

■ **47-48** Verses 47-48, formerly separate from the parable, are now joined to it.[92] The servant has become "that servant." The description fits: he knew what he had to do, but neither his preparations nor his actions were in line with what his master wanted him to do.[93] Following custom, he was therefore to receive a severe beating.[94] The second character—he is not called a servant, so he is not yet a part of the master's household—did not know what was happening. He did not act any better than the servant. So he, too, deserved (I translate $\ddot{\alpha}\xi\iota\alpha$ ["worthy things"] as "deserving") a punishment, but his was to be a lighter one. In a narrative fashion, what may run through our mind is the beginning of the Epistle to the Romans (Rom 1:1—3:20): the Jew who knows the law and the Gentile who does not know it are both found to be sinners. The person who belongs to the covenant, the household servant, is, however, guiltier, since he knows

---

among] all those who are sanctified"); Rev 20:6; 21:8; 22:19; at Qumran, cf. 1QS 2.11–18 (the notion of "lot" [גּוֹרָל] is very important for Qumran; see Betz, "Dichotomized," 45).

87   The word $\ddot{\alpha}\pi\iota\sigma\tau\sigma\varsigma$ appears only twice in the Gospel (cf. 9:41) and never in Acts. In contrast, Paul uses it often in order to speak of non-Christians, e.g., 1 Cor 7:12-15. If the adjective signifies at first "in whom one cannot have trust" (for a person), "incredible" (for information), it is understood in the sense of "unbeliever," "impiety," "unbelief," sometimes applied to heretics, in the Jewish Hellenistic vocabulary, and then the paleo-Christian; cf. Isa 17:10; Prov 28:25 *v.l.*; Philo *Leg. all.* 3.164; Ignatius *Magn.* 5.2; *Trall.* 10.1; *Smyrn.* 2.1; *2 Clem.* 17.5; BAGD, s.v.

88   On the Persian origin of the punishment, see Grundmann, 268.

89   On the diverse hypotheses of exegetes concerning the primitive meaning and the first audience of the parable, see Weiser, *Knechtsgleichnisse*, 204–12.

90   An analysis of the relationship between masters and servants as found in several parables yields the following features: temporary absence then the return of the master; responsibility and vigilance expected from those waiting for the return; absence but presence hidden among the poor.

91   See Betz, "Dichtomized," 46–47.

92   On the attribution of vv. 47–48 to Luke's special source, and their reciprocal relation, see Petzke, *Sondergut*, 120, 122.

93   For the verb $\dot{\epsilon}\tau\iota\mu\dot{\alpha}\zeta\omega$, see the commentary on 2:31

(1:141–42). It concerns here human preparations, as in 1:17, 76 or 12:20. Luke sometimes uses the verb in the absolute sense of "to make preparations" (thus in 9:52 and 22:9, 12). According to W. Radl "$\dot{\epsilon}\tau\sigma\iota\mu\sigma\varsigma$ $\kappa\tau\lambda$.," *TDNT* 2 [1965] 704–6), the verb in the NT, like the Hebrew verb כוּן, designates less an ethical attitude than a creative action.

94   The verb $\delta\dot{\epsilon}\rho\omega$ (literally, "to skin [to flay]," "to beat in flaying") in the time of the NT signifies "to beat," "to beat black and blue," "to punish harshly"; cf. 20:10-11; 22:63; Acts 5:40; 16:37; 22:19. These blows are here legitimately inflicted by the owner of the slave; Luke distinguishes prohibited blows, for whith he uses the verb $\tau\dot{\upsilon}\pi\tau\omega$ (v. 45). The blow is called $\pi\lambda\eta\gamma\dot{\eta}$ (cf. v. 48), and one must infer that this word is to be understood as plural after $\pi\sigma\lambda\lambda\dot{\alpha}\varsigma$ "many (a great deal)" (v. 47) and $\dot{\sigma}\lambda\iota\gamma\dot{\alpha}\varsigma$ "a few" (v. 48); cf. 10:30; Acts 16:23, 33. Jewish law and Roman law were acquainted with several punishments of this sort, flagellation and caning. Paul mentions the Jewish maximum punishment of forty lashes of the whip ($\mu\dot{\alpha}\sigma\tau\iota\xi$), according to Deut 25:3. One can stop after thirty-nine blows in order not to exceeed the limit prescribed by the law (2 Cor 11:24). In 2 Cor 11:25, Paul speaks of blows of the rod ($\dot{\rho}\dot{\alpha}\beta\delta\sigma\varsigma$) that he has received on three occasions. See Josef Blinzler, *Der Prozess Jesu: Das jüdische und das römische Gerichtsverfahren gegen Jesus Christus auf Grund der ältesten Zeugnisse dargestellt und beurteilt* (3d ed.; Regensburg: Pustet, 1960) 236–40; BAGD, s.vv. $\delta\dot{\epsilon}\rho\omega$, $\pi\lambda\eta\gamma\dot{\eta}$, and $\tau\dot{\upsilon}\pi\tau\omega$.

what his master wants; for that reason he is punished more severely. Ability to do what is right seems to be allowed as a possibility for both of them, but it is not the focus of consideration here.[95] In the present context, was Luke thinking of Jews and Gentiles, or did he have in mind Christian pastors trained to know God's will as made relevant to the contemporary situation by Jesus, on the one hand, and ordinary believers who still have to learn, on the other? Perhaps he was content with distinguishing between Christians and non-Christians. Tradition has grafted a sapiential saying (v. 48b) onto this little parable (vv. 47-48a),[96] a saying of which the structure, but not the content, recalls the saying about the reward of those who have, and the punishment of those who do not have (cf. 8:18; 10:26).

In v. 48b, as in v. 47, it is a question not of opposition but of gradation; not of dualism but of degree of responsibility. To one, "much has been *given* ($\dot{\epsilon}\delta\dot{o}\vartheta\eta$)": for Luke, it is less a matter of the gift of life than of grace and the Spirit. God, who gives "much" ($\pi o\lambda\dot{u}$ plays an important role here) expects much in return. In keeping with apocalyptic vocabulary, at the last judgment, God will come to "seek," to "look for" ($\zeta\eta\tau\dot{\epsilon}\omega$[97]), to harvest the fruits of this collaboration between himself as the giver and human beings who act. He will want to obtain these fruits "from him/her [$\pi\alpha\rho$ ' $\alpha\dot{u}\tauo\hat{u}$]," that is, from the first person mentioned.[98]

To the second person mentioned, much has been *entrusted.* The verb $\pi\alpha\rho\alpha\tau\dot{i}\vartheta\eta\mu\iota$ calls to mind the deposit which, according to the Pastoral Epistles, God has entrusted to his church, to each Christian, and, in particular, to each minister:[99] the gospel has been entrusted to them, but with it also ethical, liturgical, and disciplinary traditions. For Luke, too, the Christians' God has been generous: he has entrusted much to his church (the Gospel writer can think of either Christ or God as the source of these good things). From those to whom God has entrusted a special responsibility he will require "even more."[100] God gives to all, but to certain ones he entrusts, but we must not make this distinction into a hard and fast one. There is a distinction if we think in terms of laypeople and clergy, but there is not one if we think in terms of the believers in Luke's church and their leaders. Nor is there one if we think in terms of other peoples and God's people.

For the sake of variety, the author of the saying resorts here to the verb "demand" ($\alpha\dot{i}\tau\dot{\epsilon}\omega$)[101] and he puts it in the future active third person plural (perhaps a discreet manner of referring to the inquisitor angels, unless it is a sort of plural of majesty referring to God, or a substitute for the so-called divine passive).[102] For Luke, the Christian life and the ecclesial life are unthinkable without a rendering of accounts, to which so many parables allude (e.g., 19:15). Divine kindness, far from eliminating requirements, even seems to make them increase, not in the sense of divine pedagogy (spare the rod and spoil the child[103]), but in the sense of love that has a high image of the person who is loved and does not wish to be disappointed.

History of Interpretation

We read in a fragment of Origen: "Those who live chastely have 'their belts fastened around their waists.'

---

95 One can also imagine the teachers of the law, who know, and people of the earth, now in ignorance; see Petzge, *Sondergut,* 122. One must remember that in Israel sins committed deliberately were punished much more harshly that those committed through ignorance or disregard; see Num 15:27-31; and Fitzmyer (2:992), who refers to Jewish texts.

96 In its form (but not in its content) it recalls the parable of the two brothers (Matt 21:28-32).

97 On the verb $\zeta\eta\tau\dot{\epsilon}\omega$ ("to seek," "to call for"), see the commentary on 11:9 and 11:16 above.

98 For the preposition $\pi\alpha\rho\dot{\alpha}$ followed by the genitive, see BDF §237.

99 The verb form is third person plural of the second

100 On $\pi\epsilon\rho\iota\sigma\sigma\dot{o}\tau\epsilon\rho o\varsigma$, see BAGD, s.v.

101 On the verb $\alpha\dot{i}\tau\dot{\epsilon}\omega$ ("to ask for"), see the commentary on 11:9 above.

102 Cf. 6:38; 12:20; 16:9; 23:31; BDF §130.2, 141; and Fitzmyer, 2:974.

103 "For the Lord disciplines those whom he loves, and chastises every child whom he accepts" (Heb 12:6, citing Prov 3:12 LXX).

aorist middle; cf. Tim 1:18; 2 Tim 2:2; the Pastorals utilize also the word $\pi\alpha\rho\alpha\vartheta\dot{\eta}\kappa\eta$ ("entrusted deposit") in 1 Tim 6:20; 2 Tim 1:12, 14; see Jürgen Roloff, *Der erste Brief an Timotheus* (EKK 15; Zurich: Benziger, 1988) 370–75.

Since our life is a night, we need a lamp, which is our understanding, the eye of our soul."[104] Being vigilant means struggling against enemy powers and making room for God, "opening the door to the Master (δεσπότης) who knocks." Vigilance will be rewarded: the Lord, who will in turn have his belt fastened around his waist, will demonstrate power and righteousness (he will reward everyone according to what they have done).

In a sermon limited to vv. 41-48, Cyril of Alexandria, paying attention to Peter's question, dwells on the notion of spiritual masters to whom more has been given, because they have stronger shoulders, but from whom more will be required (*Serm. Luc.* 93).[105] Their task is to use good judgment in dividing up the spiritual food (cf. Prov 27:23a LXX: "With full knowledge of the facts, you will know the worth of the souls of your flock"). Cyril made a distinction between a basic teaching (fleeing polytheism, becoming attached to the Creator) and an advanced and arcane doctrine (probably referring to Christology and the sacraments).

The commentary by the Venerable Bede (*In Luc.* 4.987–1187)[106] abundantly quotes Gregory the Great: the Lord left for heaven after his resurrection: as in a marriage, he went off, a new man, to engender for himself an angelic multitude. He will come back for the judgment. The watches of the night correspond to the ages of life. We do not know when the thief will come, that is, when death will strike us. The distribution of food stands for the distribution of the Word of God, by both good and bad preachers. We must pay attention and not wish to be among the ignorant people who will be treated more favorably (v. 47). Being ignorant is not the same thing as wishing to be ignorant! The one to whom much has been entrusted is the one to whom also falls, along with his own salvation, the responsibility of feeding the Lord's flock.

A treatise by Meister Eckhart, entitled "*Die Rede der Underscheidunge*" (*Traktate* 2.7)[107] contains the following reflection: continual vigilance consists in watching out for Christ's coming, from wherever he might come. Christ may be present in any circumstance, however surprising it might be. So Christians must develop a special attention, a spiritual understanding, and a particular perception of the Lord.

There are four thinkers of the sixteenth and seventeenth centuries whom we should note: (1) Erasmus associated being ready with doing good on all occasions (*Paraphrasis,* col. 392). (2) Grotius lined up internal cross-references to Scripture and especially quotations of secular authors, from Homer to Xenophanes (*Annotationes* 1.822–24); (3) Luther was wary of sensuality and read "having a belt fastened around one's waist" in v. 35 as a call to be continent.[108] God helps us in this respect by offering us as a belt of righteousness, that is, his grace and his mercy, by which he makes us righteous. He also helps us by transforming our senses through faith in Christ. Finally (4) Zwingli looked at the belt fastened around one's waist from the military perspective.[109] Our life on earth, a long path up to death, is like a military campaign; our service is carried out against the power of the world, sensuality, trickery, and diabolical seductions. The lamp of love helps us in our combat for God. Apostles, prophets, and pastors have a special task: as sentries, they are on watch while the army is resting.

Finally, in the eighteenth century, Johann Albrecht Bengel noted, in connection with v. 37, that the service that Christ will render to his own upon his return is "the greatest promise contained in Scripture."[110]

104 Origen *Hom. in Luc.* (Rauer), frg. 80; 9.310; see too *Hom. in Luc.* (ed. Crouzel et al.), 537.

105 See Payne Smith, *Cyril,* 2:429–34; several fragments of this sermon survive in Greek; see Reuss, *Lukas-Kommentare,* 145–48 (frgs. 184–89). They do not correspond, in all points, to the Syriac text.

106 See The Venerable Bede, *In Lucae Evangelium expositio,* ed. David Hurst (CCSL 120; Turnhout: Brepols, 1960) 255–61.

107 In Josef Quint, ed. and trans., *Meister Eckhart, Die deutschen und lateinischen Werke: Die deutschen Werke,* vol. 5 (Stuttgart: Kohlhammer, 1963).

108 Martin Luther, "Predigt vom 6.12.1519 (aus der Poliander-Nachschrift)," WA 9, 431, 3–28.

109 Zwingli, *Annotationes,* 654–59.

110 Johann Albrecht Bengel, *Gnomon of the New Testament* (trans. Charlton T. Lewis and Marvin R. Vincent; 2 vols.; Philadelphia: Perkinpine & Higgins; New York: Sheldon, 1860, 1862) 1:348.

Conclusion

Jesus' floodlight is trained on believers. In the darkness and the impenetrability of reality, the God of the Jewish Passover, at midnight in the history of salvation, invites each and every one to get ready for the march and then to rest, to be vigilant, and then to participate in the banquet. The disciples are not only equipped but also trained. In spite of Christ's absence, the Christian communities are not devoid of pastors. But ahead of them lie the march, the lengthening of time, and the waiting. Believers run the risk of becoming discouraged, and their ministers of taking what constitutes their pastoral duty to be their privilege. Christ's absence from the scene can act either as a mobilizing factor or as a reducing one. Absence can either sharpen the desire of the person who is loved or prompt them to give up. Christ's departure can be beneficial: the Son returns to the Father in order to get a dwelling place ready for us (cf. John 14:1-4; 16:7); from there, he will send the Spirit (cf. John 14:26); separated from him, we will be called to grow up in our faith (cf. John 16:20).

These anecdotes of a wedding party, a break-in, and a scandal have, over time, acquired an allegorical meaning. Their common setting is the house, that is, the church. Their social organization is that of a family enterprise with its landowner, the Lord, and his servants, who are the Christians. There is a distribution of roles among these believers: the manager (i.e., the pastor) and the servants (i.e., the believers). This Christian community lives in the time that passes from Christ's first coming until his return. It feeds itself, lives, and lasts, torn between hope and resignation, love and scandal, faith and doubt. Will it hold up? If it does, it will renew the experience of the glorious Christ who has once again become a servant. It owes itself henceforth to live out such a reversal of roles: the ministers have as their task to see to it that the word and the bread are distributed equitably. No one is omnipotent, no one is omniscient, no one is infallible. But each one is called to live out in their time the normality of the faith—which is not the normality of the relationships of power of this world—and to avoid scandal. Any believer, or especially any minister, who does not succeed in this will not come out intact but will, following the image, come out cut in two and be rejected as an unbeliever. Neither believers nor pastors are abandoned to their own devices: the ecclesial fellowship facilitates vigilance, and the inspiration of the Spirit makes it possible to confront one's own finitude and one's own fragility, as well as the obstacles that life has in store for each one.

Christian Wisdom
(12:49-59)
Bibliography

Abel, Felix-Marie, *Géographie de la Palestine,* vol. 1: *Géographie physique et historique* (3d ed.; EtB; Paris: Gabalda, 1967) 117–21.

Amiet, P., et alii, *Le feu dans le Proche-Orient antique: Aspects linguistiques, archéologiques, technologiques, littéraires* (Acts du Colloque de Strasbourg, 1972; Leiden: Brill, 1972).

Arens, Eduardo, *The HΛΘΟΝ Sayings in the Synoptic Tradition: A Historico-Critical Investigation* (OBO 10; Freiburg: Universitätsverlag, 1976) 64–90.

Bastin, Marcel, *Jésus devant sa Passion* (LD 92; Paris: Cerf, 1976) 160–64.

Black, Max, "Uncomfortable Words, III: The Violent Word," *ExpT* 81 (1969–70) 115–18.

Boring, *Sayings,* 169–70.

Bovon, François, "La pluie et le beau temps (Luc 12, 54-56)," in idem, *Révélations,* 55–63.

Braumann, Georg, "Leidenskelch und Todestaufe (Mc 10 38f.)," *ZNW* 56 (1965) 178–83.

Bruston, C., "Une parole de Jesus mal comprise," *RHPhR* 5 (1925) 70–71.

Cadbury, Henry Joel, "Some Lukan Expressions of Time," *JBL* 82 (1963) 272–78.

Caird, George B., "Expounding the Parables: 1. The Defendant (Matthew 5.25f; Luke 12.58f)," *ExpT* 77 (1965–66) 36–39.

Carlston, C. E., "Proverbs, Maxims, and the Historical Jesus," *JBL* 99 (1980) 87–105, esp. 100.

Clarke, A. K., and N. E. W. Collie, "A Comment on Luke 12:41-58," *JTS* 17 (1916) 299–301.

Crossan, John Dominic, *In Fragments: The Aphorisms of Jesus* (San Francisco: Harper & Row, 1983) 244–50.

Delling, Gerhard, "καιρός κτλ.," *TDNT* 3 (1966) 455–64.

Derrett, John Duncan M., "Christ's Second Baptism (Luke 12:50; Matt 10:38-40)," *ExpT* 100 (1989) 294–95.

Edsman, C. M., *Le baptême de feu* (ASNU 9; Leipzig/Uppsala: Almqvist & Wiksell, 1940).

Edwards, *Theology of Q,* 127–29.

Feuillet, André, "Le coupe et le baptême de la Passion (Mc 10, 35-40; cf. Matt 20, 20-23; Lc 12, 50)," *RB* 74 (1967) 356–91.

George, A., "'Interpréter ce temps': Luc 12, 54-56," *BVC* 64 (1965) 18–23.

Idem, "La venue de Jésus, cause de division entre les hommes Lc 12,49-53," *AsSeign* 51 (1972) 62–71.

Gnilka, Joachim, *Martyriumsparänese und Sühnetod in synoptischen und jüdischen Traditionen,* in Schnackenburg, *Kirche,* 223–46.

Grässer, *Problem,* 190–92 and passim.

Graystone, G., "I Have Come to Cast Fire on the Earth . . . ," *Scr* 4 (1949–51) 135–41.

Grelot, Pierre, "Michée 7, 6 dans les évangiles et dans la littérature rabbinique," *Bib* 67 (1986) 363–77.

Hampe, Roland, *Kult der Winde in Athen und Kreta* (Heidelberg: Winter, 1967).

Iwand, *Gegenwart,* 45–47.

Jeremias, *Parables.*

Jülicher, *Gleichnisreden,* 2:240–46.

Kaestli, Jean-Daniel, *L'eschatologie dans l'oeuvre de Luc: Ses caractéristiques et sa place dans le développement du christianisme primitif* (Nouvelle série théologique 22; Geneva: Labor et Fides, 1969) 19–23.

Kahlefeld, *Parables,* 103–24.

Klein, G., "Die Prüfung der Zeit (Lukas 12, 54-56)," *ZThK* 61 (1964) 373–90.

Kloppenborg, *Formation,* 151, 161.

Kümmel, *Promise.*

Kuss, Otto, "Zur Frage einer vorpaulinischen Todestaufe," in idem, *Auslegung und Verkündigung: Aufsätze zur Exegese des Neuen Testaments* (3 vols.; Regensburg: Pustet, 1963–71) 1:162–86.

Légasse, S., "Approche de l'épisode préévangélique des fils de Zébédée (Mark 10:35-40 par.)," *NTS* 20 (1973–74) 161–77, esp. 164–70.

Léon–Dufour, Xavier, *Life and Death in the New Testament: The Teachings of Jesus and Paul* (San Francisco: Harper & Row, 1986) passim.

Marz, Claus-Peter, "'Feuer auf die Erde zu werfen, bin ich gekommen . . .': Zum Verständnis und zur Entstehung von Lk 12, 49," in Dupont, *Études,* 479–511.

Idem, "Lk 12,54b-56 par Mt 16, 2b.3 und die Akoluthie der Redequelle," SNTU.A 11 (1986) 83–96.

Mees, Michael, *Ausserkanonische Parallelstellen zu den Herrenworten und ihre Bedeutung* (Quaderni di Vetera christianorum 10; Bari: Istituto di litteratura cristiana antica, 1975) 151–57.

Neusser, Kora, *Anemoi: Studien zur Darstellung der Winde und Windgottheiten in der Antike* (Archaeologica 19; Rome: Bretschneider, 1982).

Patterson, S. J., "Fire and Dissension: Ipsissima Vox Jesu in Q 12:49, 51-53?" *Forum* 5 (1989) 121–39.

Piper, *Wisdom,* 105–7, 113–14, 236–37 and passim.

Polag, *Christologie,* 164–65 and passim.

Roberts, T. A., "Some Comments on Mt 10:34-36 and Luke 12:51-53," *ExpT* 69 (1957–58) 304–6.

Sato, *Q und Prophetie,* 20, 41–42, 58, 183, 292–96.

Schmid, *Matthäus und Lukas,* 276–77, 302.

Schrage, *Thomas-Evangelium,* 57–61.

Schulz, *Q,* 258–60, 421–24.

Schürmann, Heinz, "Eschatologie und Liebesdienst in der Verkündigung Jesu," in idem, *Ursprung und Gestalt: Erörterungen und Besinnungen zum Neuen Testament* (Kommentare und Beiträge zum Alten und Neuen Testament; Düsseldorf: Patmos, 1970) 279–98.

Idem, "Wie hat Jesus seinen Tod bestanden und verstanden? Eine methodenkritische Besinnung," in Hoffmann, *Orientierung*, 325–63.

Sellew, Philip, "Reconstruction of Q 12.33-59," *SBLSP* (1987) 645–68.

Seper, F. H., "*ΚΑΙ ΤΙ ΘΕΛΩ ΕΙ ΗΔΗ ΑΝΗΦΘΗ* (Lc 12:49b)," *VD* 36 (1958) 36–72, esp. 47–51.

Steinhauser, *Doppelbildworte*, 250–58.

Str–B 1:294; 3:461–62.

Streker, G., "Die Antithesen der Bergpredigt (Mt 5, 21-48 par)," *ZNW* 69 (1978) 36–72, esp. 47–51.

Taeger, *Mensch*, 90–94.

Tannehill, *Sword*, 140–47.

Tavernier, M., "La violence de Royaume de Dieu," *AsSeign* 51 (1972) 72–76.

Theissen, Gerd, "Lokalkoloritforschung in den Evangelien," *EvTh* 45 (1985) 481–99, esp. 487–89.

Topel, L. J., "Acquittal: A Redaction-Critical Study of Lk 12:57-59" (Diss., Marquette University, 1973) 27–60.

Visona, G., *Citazioni patristiche e critica testuale neotestamentaria. Il caso di Lc 12, 49* (AnBib 125; Rome: Pontificio Istituto Biblico, 1990).

Vögtle, Anton, "Todesankündigungen und Todesverständnis Jesu," in Karl Kertelge, ed., *Der Tod Jesu: Deutungen im Neuen Testament* (QD 74; Freiburg im B.: Herder, 1976) 51–113.

Ward, R. A., "St. Luke 12:49: καὶ τί θέλω εἰ ἤδη ἀνήφϑη," *ExpT* 63 (1955–56) 92–93.

Wood, H. G., "Interpreting This Time," *NTS* 2 (1955–56) 262–66.

Wrege, Hans-Theo, *Die Überlieferungsgeschichte der Bergpredigt* (WUNT 9; Tübingen: Mohr Siebeck, 1968) 61–64.

49/ "It is a fire that I came to cast upon the earth. And what more do I want if it is already kindled? 50/ It is with a baptism that I am to be baptized, and how oppressed I am until it is completed! 51/ Do you think that I have come to bring peace to the earth? No, I tell you, but rather division! 52/ For from now on five in one household will be divided, three against two and two against three; 53/ they will be divided: father against son and son against father, mother against daughter and daughter against mother, mother-in-law against her daughter-in-law and daughter-in-law against mother-in-law."

54/ And he said to the crowds, "When you see a cloud rising in the west, you immediately say, 'It is going to rain hard'; and that is what happens. 55/ And when you see the south wind blowing, you say, 'There will be scorching heat'; and it happens. 56/ You hypocrites! You know how to interpret the appearance of earth and sky, but why do you not know how to interpret the present time?

57/ "Why do you not succeed in judging for yourselves what is right? 58/ For when you go with your enemy before a magistrate, on the way make an effort to settle with him, or he may drag you before the judge, and the judge hand you over to the officer, and the officer throw you in prison. 59/ I tell you, you will not get out of there until you have paid the last penny."

Verses 49-59 and the preceding verses are linked without any transition. So the previous requests and Jesus' expectations are placed, as we are to discover in this conclusion to the chapter, against a background of violence and division. The beautiful dwelling, which served as a framework for the preceding parables, seems therefore to be threatened by fire or flood. The metaphor of the thief (v. 39), moreover, had already caused a first threat to hang over it. The dangers are spelled out. But they accompany promises of divine presence and beneficial effort. Although vv. 49-59 follow an ecclesial teaching in the form of a parable (12:35-48), they precede a conversion dialogue (13:1-9).

The first verses are still addressed to the disciples (vv. 49-53); the last ones are already addressed to the crowd (vv. 54-59). The first ones root the life of the church in Christology; the last take Jesus' historical presence as their starting point in order to advocate returning to God. The change of audience in v. 54 also constitutes the hinge between Christ's "I" and the "you" referring to those to whom he spoke.[1]

Analysis

Structure
The first part (vv. 49-53) is made up of two parallel sayings (vv. 49-50) with a noun placed at the beginning of each of them ("fire," "baptism"), a verb in the first person singular ("I came," "I am") followed by a telic infinitive ("to cast," "to be baptized"), then an interrogative or exclamatory expression introduced by an "and" ("and what . . . ?" "and how . . . !"). While these two sayings are focused on the single subject, namely, Christ's "I," the following one (v. 51) sets in motion a polemical dialogue with the listeners: the opinion of one of the groups ("you"), declared to be erroneous, contrasts with the opinion of the other one ("I"), which is authorized and correct. While the first word, "fire," stands out in vv. 49 and 50, when we get to v. 51 what counts is the last

word, "division." It is then illustrated by two short scenes with an apocalyptic flavor (vv. 52-53).

In vv. 54-56, it is an existential contradiction that is condemned: Jesus' listeners are accused of knowing how to observe the weather, but remaining blind to the significance of historical events. The two examples cited, rain (v. 54) and scorching heat (v. 55), are easy to understand, while the shortcomings in historical and theological matters are set forth (v. 56b) in contrast to meteorological wisdom (v. 56a). The controversy gets worse at that point, as is indicated by the use of the vocative "you hypocrites" and the scathing rhetorical question "but why do you not know . . . ?"

Finally, a new rhetorical and critical question introduces a short story of a sapiential nature (vv. 58-59). The advice, which is given in the imperative ("make an effort to . . . ," $\delta\grave{o}\varsigma\ \dot{\epsilon}\rho\gamma\alpha\sigma\acute{\iota}\alpha\nu$ . . .), and the analysis of the way the law operates[2] are typical of wisdom literature. The use of the pronoun in the second person singular, found only in this passage, is an indication of the fact that these two verses (vv. 58-59), with the example and its moral, were originally independent.

Origin
It is difficult to know the origin of vv. 49-59 and to know if the present ordering of these materials is the work of Luke or of one of his predecessors. Verse 49 was not created by Luke: signs of the Lukan style are missing and in their place we have one or two Semitisms.[3] Although there is nothing corresponding to this saying in Matthew, it can be read in the *Gospel of Thomas*: "Jesus said, 'I have cast fire upon the world, and see, I am guarding it until it blazes'" (10). Moreover, an *agraphon* that has some resemblance to the saying here in Luke circulated in the patristic period; Origen and Didymus attributed it to the Savior: "The person who is near me is near the fire, but the person who is far from me is far from the kingdom."[4] The *Gospel of Thomas* claims that the promise made in the Gospel of Luke has already been fulfilled: the fire is already kindled. The *Gospel of Thomas* is worried about

---

1   One could imagine that these verses might be divided into two pericopes, as is done, e.g., by Fitzmyer, 2:993–98, 998–1000.

2   "It is a piece of prudential advice, stemming from Jesus," writes Fizmyer, 2:1002.

3   For example, $\tau\acute{\iota}\ \vartheta\acute{\epsilon}\lambda\omega\ \epsilon\grave{\iota}$ . . . ("what can I want more if . . ."); see Seper, "*KAI TI*."

4   I translate here according to the Greek text transmitted by Didymus *Comm. Ps.* 88.8 (*PG* 39:1488D),

what is going to happen to this fire, but Luke does not give much attention to it out of confidence in the divine future. Christ must protect the fire as long as it has not really taken hold, and as long as there are those who have a hostile attitude toward it, wishing to put it out. The *agraphon*, for its part, confers on the believer the responsibility of approaching the fire and the Savior, whereas the Gospel of Luke attributes to Christ the task of spreading the fire on earth. For the Gospel writer, the Kingdom is an eschatological greatness that depends on God, while, according to the isolated saying, it is a spiritual reality that is reached at the end of a quest. The authors of all three of these passages have a positive notion of the fire. It is not the destructive fire of judgment, but the nourishing fire of the good news.

The second saying, concerning baptism (v. 50), seems to have been lined up with the first one.[5] We meet up with it in Mark in another form, inserted into the episode of the dispute among Zebedee's sons (Matthew does not have the saying in question and Luke omits the whole episode): "Are you able to drink the cup that I drink, or be baptized with the baptism that I am baptized with?" (Mark 10:38). I personally believe that these first two sayings were part of L, even if they could also be attributed to Q.[6]

The three other groups of sayings (vv. 51-53, 54-56, 57-59) have their parallel in the Gospel of Matthew. If they are attributed to Q,[7] it would seem that Matthew, as is often the case, had dislocated the original sequence of Q since these parallels are found in the send-off speech (Matt 10:34-36), in the dispute over the sign (Matt 16:2-3), and in the Sermon on the Mount (Matt 5:25-26). In Matt 10:34 par. Luke 12:51, in a saying about peace, Matthew makes use of the expression "do not think," μὴ

νομίσητε, which recalls Matt 5:17. Then he preserves the concrete ruggedness of his source ("bring peace" [*NRSV*], literally, "cast peace"; "the sword"). Luke, however, embellishes the text ("come" [παραγίνομαι] and "bring," literally, "give" [δοῦναι], v. 51) and substitutes "division" for "sword," in order to prepare for what follows (familial divisions).[8] We should point out that there is no parallel in Matthew to v. 52. This verse, with its Lukan characteristics ("from now on," ἀπὸ τοῦ νῦν, for example), could be a redactional transition,[9] as must be the expansion of the quotation of Micah by Matthew (Matt 10:36: "and one's foes will be members of one's own household" [*NRSV*]).[10] There is, in fact, behind vv. 52-53 in Luke a text of Micah (7:6), whose structure Matthew has respected, while Luke, following his source, was satisfied with being inspired by it. Following Micah, Matthew does call attention to the revolt of the younger generation against the older, while Luke pits the young and the old against each other.[11] The *Gospel of Thomas* (16) has knowledge of a text close to Matthew in its beginning and to Luke in what follows. It builds up the earthly effects of Jesus' coming: it mentions "dissension . . . upon the earth: fire, sword, and war"; it knows the distribution of three against two, therefore the contents of Luke 12:52, not known to Matthew; it breaks off with mutual hostility between father and son, found only in Luke, while concluding with an expression that is typical of gnosis: "and they will stand solitary."

It will be noted that Matthew (16:2-3) and Luke are alone in the New Testament in transmitting the following verses (vv. 54-56) concerning the signs of the time. Each of these Gospel writers furnishes an introduction, but they are not the same. Luke: "And he said to the crowds"; Matthew: "He answered them." Nor are the first

---

cited by Aland, *Synopsis*, 291. On this agraphon, see Mees, *Parallelstellen*, 155–56.

5 März, "Feuer," 483–84.

6 Petzke (*Sondergut*, 120) is uncertain about the attribution of these two verses.

7 This is the most widespread opinion for vv. 51-53 and vv. 57-59; see Schulz, *Q*, 258–60. The opinions are more divided for vv. 54-56; see Sellew, "Reconstruction," 646–55. The opinions diverge also regarding the sequence of Q; is it Matthew or Luke who has preserved the context of Q, or neither of the two? See März, "Feuer," 483–84; idem, "Akoluthie."

8 See Schulz, *Q*, 258–59; Sellew ("Reconstruction," 646–49) is undecided about διαμερισμός.

9 See Schulz, *Q*, 258–59.

10 Schulz (*Q*, 259) thinks, on the contrary, that it is Luke who has crossed out the phrase.

11 In 1:17, Luke evokes Mal 3:24 and the eschatological conversation of the fathers toward children; see the commentary on 1:17 (1:37–38).

two sayings attributed to Jesus the same in the two Gospels.[12] Matthew contrasts the evening with the morning, fair weather with stormy weather, and one red sky with another. Luke, on the other hand, makes a distinction between clouds coming from the west and the hot wind from the south, and between rain and scorching heat. It is possible that Matthew is quoting Q and Luke, L. Even though the meteorological descriptions are different, the lesson drawn by Jesus is, in the case of both Gospel writers, identical in its content and close in its form.[13]

The *Gospel of Thomas* also transmits this conclusion of Jesus but adds a christological affirmation to the comment on the weather: "They said to him, 'Tell us who you are so that we may believe in you.' He said to them, 'You read the face of the sky and of the earth, but you have not recognized the one who is before you, and you do not know how to read this moment'" (91). As we can see, the apocryphal text is closer to Luke than to Matthew. It mentions sky and earth, speaks of this moment, and uses the verb "read" instead of "interpret." The *Gospel of Thomas* may be dependent here on Luke, but it could just as well be referring to a special oral tradition of its own. Matthew and Luke, on the other hand, rely on a source; it could be, as I have said above, Q for both of them or Q for Matthew and L for Luke.

In the last verses (vv. 57-59) there is a parallel to Luke in Matthew in the Sermon on the Mount (Matt 5:25-26). As in the case of the previous passage, there are so many differences between the two Gospels that it is possible to conceive of two distinct traditions (e.g., Matthew relying on Q; and Luke, on L).[14] On the other hand, the two Gospel writers were equally scrupulous in their respect

for the lesson drawn by Jesus: the two texts are virtually identical at this point, except for the fact that Luke avoids the foreign word ἀμήν and refers to the coin with the word λέπτον, which I have translated as "penny." Moreover, Luke seems to have taken care in his presentation of the scene and created a moralizing introduction ("Why do you not succeed in judging for yourselves what is right?" v. 57).[15] We should point out that what is a sequence in Luke is dispersed in Matthew and in *Thomas*. Certain studies have attempted to prove that Luke preserved Q's sequence, an eschatological one.[16] Personally, I think that a part of these sayings, if not all, could have come from L rather than from Q. This separate origin could explain the significant differences between Matthew and Luke.

Commentary

The Trial by Fire and Water (vv. 49-50)

■ **49** The saying about fire resembles other testimonies by Jesus to the meaning of his coming.[17] The verb "come" is important: it witnesses to the fact that God sent Jesus and that Jesus agreed to that mission. It also has an eschatological connotation since "the one who is coming" (ὁ ἐρχόμενος) is a designation of the Messiah (cf. 7:19-20). The Greek aorist ἦλθον ("I have come"), with its constative (complexive) and retrospective aspects in connection with the event, might be a reference to the choice of the earliest Christians.[18]

Although Jesus usually thought of his mission in a soteriological way (cf. e.g., 5:32), he did not express it in those terms here. He came "to cast . . . a fire . . . upon

---

12 The divergences are such that their attribution to one and the same source, Q, is uncertain. The question is complicated by the fact that Matt 16:2b-3 is by no means attested by the whole manuscript tradition; see Metzger, *Textual Commentary*, 41; März ("Akoluthie," 90–92) seeks to demonstrate that vv. 2b-3 of Matthew 16 have constituted part of the origin of the Gospel of Matthew and that they are an adaptation of the text of Q. If Luke seems more faithful to the source Q in the examples (Luke 12:54-55), Matthew respects it better in application (Matt 16:3).

13 Luke adds "hypocrites," speaks of "the earth and heaven" (Matt: "of heaven"), uses the verbs οἴδατε ("you know") and δοκιμάζειν ("to evaluate") (Matt: γινώσκετε, "you know," and διακρίνειν, "to

discern"), evokes "this time here" (Matt: "the signs of the times"), and finishes with "how is it that you do not know how to evaluate it?" (Matt: "you cannot").

14 In general, these verses are attributed to Q; see Sellew, "Reconstruction," 661–62.

15 On the redactional character of v. 57, see Bultmann, *History*, 95, 186; and Sellew, "Reconstruction," 660.

16 So, for example, März, "Feuer," 500.

17 Cf. 5:32 par.; 7:34 par.; 9:56 *v.l.*; 12:49; 12:51 par.; 19:10; Matt 5:17; 10:35; 18:11 *v.l.*; Mark 10:45 par.

18 See Bultmann, *History*, 167.

the earth,"[19] which suggests the idea of punishment, a fire that falls from heaven such as the one that the LORD poured out (βρέχω) on Sodom and Gomorrah (Gen 19:24; cf. Luke 17:29), and that Elijah caused to come down (καταβαίνω) on King Ahaziah's servants (2 Kgs [4 Kgdms] 1:10-24).[20] It is this same fire that Jesus' disciples, James and John, wished to call on in order to punish the inhospitable Samaritans (9:54).[21] Josephus used the same verb, "cast" (βαλεῖν), once in speaking of divine anger, in a saying similar to Jesus' saying: "to cast on the earth a wrath unlike any other" (μηδεμίαν ὀργὴν ἐπὶ τὴν γῆν ὁμοίαν βαλεῖν) (Ant. 1.3, 7 §98).[22] In Revelation, John lists all the punishments that the cups pour out on the earth (chap. 16).

These biblical recollections all make one think of the eschatological judgment. Before deciding if v. 49 fits into such a judicial context, however, we must examine the image and the reality of fire. In the Hebrew Bible, fire is a destructive force (if one can purify by fire, it is because fire destroys evil [Lev 13:52; Num 31:23]). Lightning is God's fire, which kills and destroys (Job 1:16). To be sure, fire makes it possible for God to reveal himself (the burning bush; Exod 3:2-3) or to guide his people (column of fire; Exod 13:21-22). Usually, however, the image of fire calls to mind God's judgment (Joel 2:3; Amos 1:4, 7: Mal 3:2), with the result that the intertestamental literature and the New Testament think of eternal punishment as a huge furnace (see *1 Enoch* 91:9; 102:1; 1QpHab 10.5; Matt 13:42; Rev 8:8; 9:17-18; 20:9; etc.), not without some influence from Persian eschatology.[23] Rabbinic literature differentiates among six kinds of fire: normal fire, fever, Elijah's fire (1 Kgs [3 Kgdms] 18:38), the fire of the altar, the fire of the angel who removed the fire

from the furnace (Dan 3:25), and God's fire.[24] Greeks distinguished three virtues of fire: it destroys, it brings light, and it provides warmth. Prometheus stole it from the gods, and Heraclitus declared it to be the original matter, a doctrine that Stoicism brought up to date in its living pantheism. So the Greeks held a rather positive view of fire, unlike the Hebrews.[25]

Let us place ourselves on the level of the historical Jesus.[26] In that case, we must understand the saying without factoring in either the saying about baptism or the sayings about division. The saying would thus correspond to the sometimes enigmatic language of parables of which the Master was fond. He certainly knew that he had been vested with a salvific mission, but he also believed that his God is not weak and that he will punish (hence the image of fire) those who will not think along the lines of the kingdom.[27] Jesus was aware that he had come to light a fire. His presence was an integral part of that event. Fire, which is a decisive factor, can be either beneficial or detrimental, comfort or judgment. Everything depends on the attitude that human beings adopt toward him. His fire is not just a punishment.

On the level of Christian tradition, the saying has given rise to perplexity and commentary. Matthew and Mark omitted it (but did they know it?). The juxtaposition here with the saying about baptism perhaps reveals that there was a desire to shed light on the fire saying with the help of the saying about the two baptisms (3:16; Act 1:5). By so doing, stress was laid on Christology and salvation history: Christ had to suffer and be baptized (v. 50) in order for the new life, the fire (v. 49), to spread. At the same time, the earliest Christians forgot neither eschatology nor judgment: the Gospel will divide fami-

---

19   Usually, something is thrown into the fire (3:9). The expression is not Greek.

20   Cf. Ps 49 (50):3; 77 (78):21; Sir 48:1, 3: "The prophet Elijah arose like a fire and his word burned like a torch. . . . By the word of the Lord, he shut the sky and three times, also, brought down fire" (allusion to 1 Kgs [3 Kgdms] 18:38 and 2 Kgs [4 Kgdms] 1:10-14.

21   See the commentary on 9:54 above.

22   This reading, βαλεῖν, is attested in only a part of the manuscript tradition; the other witnesses read λαβεῖν; cf. Josephus *Bell.* 2.17.6 §427; 3.7.9 §167; *Ant.* 8.13.5 §342; 9.2.1 §23; see Karl Heinrich Rengstorf et al., eds., *A Complete Concordance to Flavius*

Josephus (4 vols.; Leiden: Brill, 1973–97), vol. 3, s.v. πῦρ.

23   On fire among the Persians, see Friedrich Lang, "πῦρ κτλ.," *TDNT* 6 (1969) 928–52, esp. 933–34; on intertestamental and NT literature, see G. Lindeskog, "Feuer," *BHH* 1:479–80.

24   See Friedrich Lang, "πῦρ κτλ.," *TDNT* 6 (1969) 935–37, who refers to *b. Šabb.* 67a; *b. Yeb.* 71b; *b. Yoma* 21b Bar.

25   See Lang, "πῦρ κτλ.," 935–41.

26   On the question of authenticity, see Bultmann, *History*, 164–68.

27   Cf. the end of several parables, e.g., 12:49 and 19:27.

lies, and the Son of Man will come to judge the living and the dead (an old image associated with fire).[28]

Although Luke, on the other hand, did not take the seriousness of the judgment (17:31-35; 18:7; 21:25-28) lightly, here he was thinking instead of the fire of the good news and of the Holy Spirit. This seems to me to be the obvious meaning, especially because of the wish expressed at the end of v. 49 and because of "from now on" ($\dot{\alpha}\pi\grave{o}$ $\tauο\hat{υ}$ $ν\hat{υ}ν$) in v. 52.[29] In its variety, ancient commentary on Luke 11:49 confirms this complex background: Origen read an allusion to active grace in this verse; Pseudo-Macarius, a mention of the Holy Spirit who enlightens the hearts of monks and ascetics; and the Pseudo-Clementine literature and *Pistis Sophia*, an affirmation of inescapable judgment.[30]

There are two ways to understand the end of the verse,[31] as a reality (What more is there to want, since the fire is already kindled?) or as a wish that is still unfulfilled (How I wish that it were already kindled!). The first interpretation relies on Greek syntax;[32] the second, on the Semitic syntax underlying the Greek.[33] I personally think that the saying is authentic and that Jesus expressed here a wish that he was very anxious to have fulfilled (which was later brought together with the saying on "baptism" that is still awaited). But as soon as the saying had been taken over by Christians and reinterpreted, the wish was considered to have been fulfilled and the fire already kindled, in different ways: by the proclamation of the gospel; by Jesus' death, which was the ultimate condemnation of the godless; by the fire of the Spirit that was given at Pentecost; by the division within families and within the people of Israel faced with the Christian mission; and by the incarnation of the Son. In translating Jesus' wish the way they did, Christians made the transition from what could be wished for to what had happened. At the same time, or nearly the same time, they made the transition from Aramaic to Greek.[34]

■ **50** We move on here from the symbolism of fire to that of water. In Mark's version, this "baptism" of Jesus is brought together with the "cup," two ways of speaking of Jesus' death but also of suggesting the two sacraments that remind us of it.[35] $Βάπτισμα$ ("baptism")[36] is a rare word, scarcely used by the Greeks; it is not found at all in the LXX or the literature of Hellenistic Judaism, in which $βαπτισμός$ and $βάπτισις$ do occur. The use of the verbs $βάπτω$ and $βαπτίζω$ ("plunge," "dip," "immerse")[37] directs our attention[38] toward the sym-

---

28 On the sense of v. 49, at the level of Christian tradition, see Kaestli, *Eschatologie*, 20–21; März ("Feuer") sees in this verse a creation of the community of Q; Patterson, "Fire."

29 On the redactional sense, see Grässer, *Problem*, 190–91; Klein, "Prüfung," 375–76; Kaestli, *Eschatologie*, 20–21.

30 See Origen *Hom. in Jer.* 20.8; Pseudo-Macarius *Hom.* 9.9 and 25.9; Pseudo-Clementine *Hom.* 11.3.2 and 19.2; *Pistis Sophia* 116 and 373; Mees, *Parallelstellen*, 152–53.

31 See Fitzmyer, 2:996; Seper, "*KAI TI*."

32 $\vartheta έλω$ can be followed by $εἰ$ (see Herodotus *Hist.* 6.52; 9.14). I take $\vartheta έλω$ as a present indicative, but it can also be a present subjunctive.

33 The interrogative $τί$ ("What?," "Why?") would then be an echo of the Hebrew and Aramaic מָה, and $εἰ$ would be a reflection of the Aramaic הֵן or the Hebrew אִם. One finds parallel syntax in the LXX in Isa 9:14 and Sir 23:14. One can translate thus: "And how I wish that he may be already enlightened!" (*TOB*). In this sense, see BDF §299 3 n. 4; 360, 4; for expressions of wish, cf. Ruth 2:2; John 12:27.

34 Concerning this verse, Ward ("Luke") believes that the phrase expresses a temptation of Jesus; if the work is done, why should I suffer?

35 See Braumann ("Leidenskelch") believes that v. 50 is inauthentic; by the aid of a tradition, Luke expresses his interpretation of the passion and death of Jesus; moreover, he affirms also that this time here is still that of suffering and not yet that of the parousia.

36 See Gerhard Delling, "*ΒΑΠΤΙΣΜΑ ΒΑΠΤΙΣΘΗΝΑΙ*," *Novum Testamentum* 2.2 (1957) 92–115.

37 Even if they can receive different nuances, these two verbs are often synonyms in the sense of "to plunge," "to immerse"; $βαπτίζω$ is a more recent intensive form. See the commentary on 11:27-38 above.

38 The double expression $βάπτισμα$ $βαπτισθῆναι$ (cf. Acts 19:4) is a Greek phrase, but also Hebraic (cf. "to die death": Adam in Gen 2:17; or $\dot{ε}καθμα$-$τίσθησαν$ ... $κα\hat{υ}μα$ $μέγα$, "they were scorched by the fierce heat" in Rev 16:9); cf. BDF §153.

bolism of the trial, toward the threatening waters that inundate or engulf the believer or the psalmist.[39] To be sure, Christian baptism is also understood as a settlement date, a death, explicitly in Rom 6:4 or Col 2:12, implicitly in the account of Jesus' baptism (3:21-22). But the saying here in Luke does not allude to either that first baptism or to the baptism of the Spirit. With the help of an image, that of water, like the preceding one of fire, Jesus foresaw a serious trial. On the horizon here is not the mission to others but his personal fate—in short, an anticipation of his experience on the Mount of Olives (22:39-46), where he had recourse to the image of the cup (22:42). Here he resorts to that of a flood. Death is mentioned each time: the one that kills from the inside like a poison in a cup, and the one that destroys from the outside like a raging sea or a flooding stream.[40] When the earliest Christians took over the saying, they rethought it. To be sure, they understood Christ's anguish,[41] thus taking the incarnation seriously, but they inserted this τέλος ("end," "goal," "completion")[42] into salvation history, as the decisive stage that opens out onto salvation and decision, and also onto the possibility of refusing

to believe. Without respecting the sequence that proceeds from baptism to the laying on of hands, that is, from death to oneself to the gift of new life, the Lukan juxtaposition of the two sayings nevertheless suggests that Jesus' ministry as preacher and martyr opened the eschatological era, where the fire of the Spirit is kindled in believers and the fire of judgment bursts even into families.[43] Luke reports invaluable sayings in which Jesus speaks of his will (v. 49) and his anxieties (v. 50); of his life's plan, tied to fire; and of death, compared to a baptism, into which this plan is likely to drag him. History was to confirm his determination and the danger into which it led him.

In the Land of Dissensions (vv. 51-53)

■ **51** Peace is the state that God wishes for his people, in the full range of their needs and their desires: political security, harmony in the society and the family, well-being (food, health, lodging, climate), balance between town and country, plains and valleys, etc. But prophets who lacked divine inspiration or a divine mission often promised peace to Israel when judgment, God's anger,

39 Cf. Isa 21:4; 43:2; Job 9:31; Ps 41 (42):8; 123 (124):4-5; Josh 7:7; Delling, "*ΒΑΠΤΙΣΜΑ*," 242–45. Légasse ("Approche," 168–69) evokes the eschatological tribulations, under the form of fire and water, which Jewish literature foresees; cf., e.g., *Life of Adam and Eve* 49:3; *Odes Sol.* 24. For "to plunge the soul" in difficulties, cf. in Greek literature Chariton of Aphrodisias *Chaer.* 3.2.6; Libanius *Or.* 18.286 and 54.115.

40 See the commentary on 6:48-49 (1:254–56). G. B. Caird writes with respect to vv. 49-50: "A passionate outburst of impatience at the delay of the crisis which is to end the ministry of Jesus" ("Expounding," 38).

41 Luke loves the verb συνέχω ("to hold together," "to afflict"; in the passive, "to be tormented," "to be tugged at"; Luke 4:38; 8:37, 45; 19:43; 22:63; Acts 7:57; 18:5; 28:8; cf. Phil 1:23). The only usage of the passive in the absolute sense is here and in 2 Esdr 16:10 LXX (Neh 6:10). Helmut Koester ("συνέχω," *TDNT* 7 [1971] 877–87) proposes that this interior oppression is not limited by fear of death. It has to do altogether with the project of realizing life before dying. The sense given to πῶς ("how") has been discussed. Without doubt, it is not necessary to take it as equivalent to the Hellenistic ὡς ("as,"

"how much"), with Delebecque (86) against BDF §436 n. 1; and BAGD, s.v. πῶς 3.

42 On τελέω ("to conduct to its end," "to attain," "to accomplish"), cf. 2:39; 18:31; 22:37; see Gerhard Delling, "τελέω," *TDNT* 8 (1972) 49–87; Hans Hübner, "τελέω, etc.," *EDNT* 3:346–48; Delebecque, 86–87; Samuel Ngayihembako, *Les temps de la fin: Approche exégétique de l'eschatologie du Nouveau Testament* (Geneva: Labor et Fides) 151, 189–205. The form Ὅτου is the Attic form of οὕτινος, gen. of ὅστις. Ἕως ὅτου ("up to," "until," sometimes "while") is a current expression during this epoch; see BAGD, s.v. ἕως 2.1β and γ; see also Henry Joel Cadbury, "The Relative Pronouns in Acts and Elsewhere," *JBL* 42 (1923) 150–57.

43 I do not discuss here the problem of the sense that Jesus himself confers on his death. For my part, I am persuaded that Jesus has a consciousness of the price that he will have to pay for his ministry. He has accepted death, in confidence about the design of God, without explicitly according a redemptive value to his passion (cf. 13:31-33); see also Bastin, *Jésus*, 162–64; Gnilka, *Martyriumparänese*; Xavier Léon-Dufour, *Face à la mort, Jésus et Paul* (Paris: Éditions du Seuil, 1979) 73–90.

was to fall on the land (see Jer 28:8-9). It is always a good sign if a prophet announces misfortune; the chances are in that case that he is a true prophet. For peace is not for today. It will follow on the heels of final tribulations, which will come today and continue on into the morrow. That conviction became a truism for Jewish apocalyptic (see esp. *1 Enoch* 46; 96). Here Jesus, who elsewhere kept his distance from the terrifying apocalyptic visions in order to sow the seeds of the kingdom of God in the here and now, took pains to see that his message was not confused with the utopias of peace instilled by the false prophets. It is, moreover, a matter not of diplomacy but of theology: the presence of the kingdom goes hand in hand with final tensions and divisions. Jesus used still another image here: that of the sword.[44] Since Luke perhaps feared a Zealot interpretation of his Master's message, in his Gospel he preferred to substitute the more abstract word "division" ($\delta\iota\alpha\mu\epsilon\rho\iota\sigma\mu\acute{o}\varsigma$)[45] for the word "sword." In any case, he rewrote the saying inherited from Q in order to give it a more literary expression and to avoid repetitions with the saying about fire (v. 49).

The word "division" conjures up different meanings than the word "sword." Division is caused by several wills each of which bears a share in the responsibility. Division comes up over a period of time. It is caused by passion more than by an intellectual choice. Although vv. 49-50 were concerned with Jesus' fate, vv. 51-53 depict the impact that he had, and that he was to have, on others.

■ **52-53** One of the final tribulations that Jewish apocalyptic consciousness[46] feared most was the degradation of family and social ties, which had heretofore offered a certain level of harmony among the people, reminding them of the golden beginnings of creation and the buoyant prospects of redemption. Why did Jesus, and later, Christians, take over this topos? It was because they were in the process of reestablishing Israel, of gathering it and then reconstituting it. It was to be based on new principles: no longer blood, hereditary privileges, or social customs, but faith, returning to God, and unlimited love without family or ethnic limits. There was also to be a break with one's personal, religious, and patriotic past; membership in a new community (cf. 9:60: one must take sides). This revolutionary reality, of which the disciples became aware (cf. Peter: "Look, we have left our own possessions and followed you"; 18:28), was not going to leave anyone indifferent. Jesus was not such a dreamer that he glossed over the resistance that was going to be organized. This resistance was to set its sights, as always, on the leaders, but reached out to everyone. Jesus, separated from his family, was to be rejected by his people. In the beatitudes, the disciples heard the announcement of their persecutions. The theme of division in families was repeated in Christian preaching, as well as in the earliest Christian writings, e.g., Justin Martyr's *Second Apology*, or the *Martyrdom of Perpetua and Felicitas*, the apocryphal Acts of the Apostles, patristic testimonies, and the earliest non-Christian texts about Christians.[47] They all witness to the fact that when the gospel reached people,

---

44 Cf. the Matthean parallel (Matt 10:34), which is closer to the original. The political orientation of Jesus' ministry has been much discussed; see John Howard Yoder, *The Politics of Jesus: Vicit Agnus noster* (Grand Rapids: Eerdmans, 1972); Richard J. Cassidy, *Jesus, Politics, and Society: A Study of Luke's Gospel* (Maryknoll, N.Y.: Orbis Books, 1978); Oscar Cullmann, *Jésus et les révolutionnaires de son temps: Culte société, politique* (Paris: Neuchâtel, 1970); Martin Hengel, *Christ and Power* (trans. Everett R. Kalin; Philadelphia: Fortress Press, 1977). It is necessary rather to consider the bellicose vocabulary of Jesus as an expression of his apocalyptic battle against the forces of evil; see Otto Betz, "Jesu heiliger Krieg," *NovT* 2 (1957) 116–37; Black, "Violent."

45 See BAGD, s.v.; Gerd Petzke, "$\delta\iota\alpha\mu\epsilon\rho\acute{\iota}\zeta\omega$ etc.," *EDNT* 1:308–9. With this verb, Luke can insist as much on the beneficial sharing (e.g., Acts 2:45) as

on the disastrous division (especially in the passive, e.g., Luke 11:17-18). On $\mathring{\alpha}\lambda\lambda$ '$\mathring{\eta}$, see Plummer, 355.

46 Cf. Mic 7:6; Mal 3:24 (reconciliation after division); Zech 13:23; *Jub.* 23:19; *1 Enoch* 100:2; *4 Esdr.* 6:24; Luke 1:17 (which resumes Mal 3:24); 17:34-35; 21:16-17; Str-B 1:586; 4:2, 977–86.

47 Cf., e.g., Luke 6:22; 1 Cor 7:12-16, where Paul must regulate the case of couples where only one member of the couple becomes Christian; Justin (*Second Apology*) deals with the complaint of a married pagan because his wife, under the influence of a preacher named Ptolemus, has become a believer; in the *Martyrdom of Perpetua and Felicitas*, the father of Perpetua tries to persuade his daughter to renounce her faith by bringing her young son to the prison; *Acts Pet.* 33–34 depicts the irritation of the husbands because of the conversion of their spouses, followed by continence. One must

it divided families; and when it reformed God's people, it tore Israel apart.[48] The question may be asked whether the price was not too high and if it is not disgusting to notice that the message of love intensifies hate. Does not the dark side invade the light side? The answer is tied to the gospel itself: if the Word of God that divides first of all reconstitutes the person, and if Christ who causes divisions[49] develops a true community, we can accept the Christian message, knowing that suffering is an accompaniment to faith. But to accomplish that, there must be prayer, fellowship, and faith that hopes against all hope.

Luke chose the figure five, commonly used to designate a small entity such as the five fingers of the hand, sometimes with a negative connotation because it is an odd number.[50] He hammers away at the reality of division (after the noun "division" in v. 51, the verb "will be divided" occurs twice, once each in v. 52 and v. 53) and chooses three types of precious and precarious relationships: the father with his son,[51] the mother with her daughter,[52] and—picturing the son being married—the daughter-in-law with her mother-in-law.[53] Those who are closely related can get along together the best: in antiquity, the father normally worked in league with his son in an emotional and professional relationship. A daughter-in-law had in common with her mother-in-law that they had both been uprooted from their original family setting. A daughter, like her mother, was prepared for running a house, for marriage, and then for maternity. It is into that resemblance that the sword of the Word brings change, the "division" foreseen by Jesus.[54] For Luke it was to take place "from now on" ($\mathring{\alpha}\pi\grave{o}$ $\tauo\hat{\upsilon}$ $\nu\hat{\upsilon}\nu$), that is, in salvation history, after Christ's ascension, during the time of the church.[55]

The Lukan Christ does not require that there be division. He does not invite members of the same family to rise up against each other. On the contrary, he makes an appeal to humans on behalf of the gospel. But once this fire begins to spread, neutrality is no longer an appropriate stance. Some accept the good news, others reject it, as may be observed even inside families. The existence of evil explains why a message of love gives rise to divisions and troubles social life. The Gospel itself advocates peace and harmony.

Weather and the Present Time (vv. 54-56)

■ **54** The preceding words were addressed to the disciples, to Christians, or even to pastors; the following ones are addressed to the crowds, therefore to those to whom

---

48 The NT, and Luke in particular, is obsessed by the failure of the Christian mission in Israel and by the tearing apart of the people, which was its consequence; see Acts 28:24-25; Bovon, *L'oeuvre*, 145–53.

49 The apocalyptic topos has value also for the religious community, as Paul attests, for which there must be, at the end of time, confessional schisms; see 1 Cor 11:19. If the divergences do have some meaning, the divisions themselves are a scandal, and the apostle struggles for unity; see 1 Cor 1:10; 12:25. See further Jacques Dupont, "L'Église à l'épreuve de ses divisions (1 Cor 11:18-19)," in L. De Lorenzi, ed., *Paul de Tarse, apôtre de notre temps* (Rome: Abbaye de S. Paul, 1979) 687–96. Cf. *T. Jud.* 21:6; 22:1; *T. Zeb.* 9:1-4.

50 See Horst Balz and Gerhard Schneider ("πέντε etc.," *EDNT* 3:70), who do not underline the negative qualification—about which I am not certain.

51 See the commentary on 10:22 above; see also John 5:19-23; and C. H. Dodd, "A Hidden Parable in the Fourth Gospel," in idem, *More New Testament Studies* (Grand Rapids: Eerdmans, 1968) 30–40.

52 "Vis à vis" (i.e., face to face) is somewhat rare in Scripture; see Cant 6:9; 8:1, 5 conceived in the manner of an image; 1 Pet 3:6. The metaphor of the mother is not frequent in Israelite and Jewish piety; see Pieter Arie Hendrik de Boer, *Fatherhood and Motherhood in Israelite and Judean Piety* (Haskell Lectures 1974; Leiden: Brill, 1974) 31–37.

53 Νύμφη: the "fiancée," the "spouse," the "young spouse," the "young woman," the "daughter in law." Each meaning evokes immediately the harmony between Ruth and Naomi (Ruth 1:8-22). Plummer (335) explains thus the transfer of ἐπί, followed by the dative, to ἐπί followed by the accusative: the conflict is more intense between women!

54 On these verses, see Roberts, "Comments"; Black, "Violent." The apparatus of Nestle-Aland[27] attests that there are several small textual problems, but the variants are purely formal and do not touch upon the sense.

55 The phrase ἀπὸ τοῦ νῦν, frequent in the LXX (e.g., Gen 46:30), is proper to Luke in the NT (1:48;

the Christian mission was directed. While believers were caught up in domestic rifts because of their commitment, the crowds clung to their security and remained deaf to the appeals to conversion.[56] Luke was also anxious to point out this change of audience, since the source he used, whether Q or L, indicated a new start here. The parallel in Matthew also suggests the same thing.[57]

The text describes a common attitude, then gives expression to popular wisdom.[58] Everyone in the crowd was interested in the weather. In that time, in an agricultural society, looking at the sky was habitual and necessary. Clouds rose in the west[59] and everyone knew that they forecast rain.[60] Note the singular "cloud" ($\nu\epsilon\varphi\acute{\epsilon}\lambda\eta$; cf. Acts 1:9).[61] All it took was one cloud for an analysis of the situation to be made ("you *immediately* say"). So there is no reason to take this word in the generic sense of a cloud formation. Note also the word $\ddot{o}\mu\beta\rho\sigma\varsigma$;[62] it refers not to "rain" ($\dot{\nu}\epsilon\tau\acute{o}\varsigma$) but to "rainstorm," "thunderstorm," or "downpour."

■ **55** Forecasting was easy, too, when the south wind blew.[63] Whoever has admired the Tower of Winds in Athens knows how much importance people in antiquity attached to Aelous, Boreas, Notus, or Zephyr. Knowledge

of winds was necessary for farmers and indispensable for sailors.[64] There was a rich and exact vocabulary on that subject. Ὁ $\nu\acute{o}\tau o\varsigma$ can refer to the "south wind," which in winter brings rain but in summer is called the "sirocco." Ὁ $\nu\acute{o}\tau o\varsigma$ can also refer to the direction "south."[65] For the author of these biblical verses, the south wind is a scorching one; it brings blistering heat: ὁ $\kappa\alpha\acute{\nu}\sigma\omega\nu$,[66] which means not simply "heat" but "scorching heat."[67]

So as not to tire the reader, Luke worded the second example in a more compact way, making do with confirming the lesson of the first one: everyone, without having to be a prophet, can predict the future, a certain future, if they are willing to pay attention to what surrounds them and if they dare to express themselves.

■ **56** In Lukan terms (v. 56): "You know how to interpret the appearance of earth and sky." The appearance of earth and sky is expressed by the single word $\pi\rho\acute{o}\sigma\omega\pi o\nu$, which means the "face," the "appearance," the "presence," the "person" of someone. You know how to decipher the face of creation, read nature's expressions, and that is good. But you should also, and especially, know how to make analogies and decode the other reality.

5:10; 22:18, 69; Acts 18:6) and occurs once in Paul (2 Cor 5:16); see Plummer, 335.

56 See Godet, 2:164.

57 Matthew integrates these verses into the demand for a sign and preserves, in addition, the remembrance of an introduction in a statement of what becomes, for him, a response (Matt 16:2a).

58 If Luke insists on seeing, leading to the understanding, Matthew enunciates at first the understanding, which is next legitimated by knowledge and is not attributed explicitly to the interlocutors of Jesus.

59 On αἱ δυσμαί ("the setting of the sun," "the setting," the "west"), see BAGD, s.v. The "east" is said to be ἡ ἀνατολή, αἱ ἀνατολαί; cf. 13:29; Matt 24:27; Rev 21:13; BAGD, s.v. The west, symbolically, represents a menacing part of the world, the place of darkness, of death and evil. In antiquity, when the catechumens came to be baptized, they used to renounce Satan and all the pomp, by turning their backs to the west and by entering into the church, while advancing toward the east. Note the kinship to ἀνατέλλω, which makes one think of rising, and ἐπὶ δυσμῶν, which signifies "setting" (i.e., to the west).

60 Ἀνατέλλω, "make arise," "arise," in speaking of the sun or of the star; "to push up," in speaking of a growing plant, of a tree; see the commentary on 1:78 (1:76).

61 My interpretation is supported by a Greek text without an article before νεφέλη.

62 See BAGD, s.v.

63 Note in v. 55 the ellipsis of the verb ἴδητε ("you see"; v. 54), as well as the economy of the adverb εὐθέως ("immediately"; v. 54) and of οὕτως ("and so"; v. 54). 𝔓45 and most of the Old Latin witnesses have read ἴδητε ("you see") equally in v. 55.

64 On the wind in general, see H. W. Hertzberg, "Wind," *BHH* 3:2175; Bovon, "La pluie." On πνέω ("to breathe"), cf. Matt 7:25, 27; John 3:8; John 6:18; Acts 27:40; Rev 7:1; see Eduard Schweizer, "πνέω κτλ.," *TDNT* 6 (1960) 389–455, esp. 452.

65 On νότος, see PW 4:168.

66 Cf. Jas 1:11; Isa 49:10 LXX. In the LXX, ὁ καύσων designates most often the wind blowing from the south; see BAGD, s.v.

67 See Bovon, "La pluie."

Commentators, who are often theologians, plunge into what follows in the text—"but why do you not know how to interpret the present time?"—and unhesitatingly interpret it as: but you don't know how to assess Jesus' mission, or Christ's presence, or the advancement of salvation history, or the delay in the parousia—and I do not know what else.[68] If we examine the plain text, we observe that all these interpretations are based on what is implicit, since, as far as what is explicit is concerned, Luke simply contrasts nature and history: weather, whether storm or sirocco, is contrasted with time, whether future time or past time or "the present time."

Oddly enough, Luke calls those responsible for this distortion "hypocrites." He uses this word on only two other occasions, in 6:42 and 13:15. For him, the hypocrite is less a Tartuffe than a being without self-knowledge who believes that he or she is doing good or knows the truth but remains caught up in evil.[69] Ignorance here involves guilt, since it could have been avoided. All that people have to do is open their eyes to their time.[70] The Lukan Christ does not ask for an escape into another world, as if something supernatural had to be superimposed on nature. What he suggests is being attentive to history as much as to nature. There is "hypocrisy" in the biblical sense of the term, when one reacts correctly to nature while remaining passive in the face of events. Before speaking of theology, Luke 12:54-56 speaks of anthropology: the charge that he levels against human beings who are integrated into nature and conscious of being so is not acknowledging that they are also involved in history. These women and men stifle their potentialities for seeing things clearly, as long as they do not open their eyes to contemplate what is going on in their time. The effort required to do so is not the simple act of looking, since history has a certain obviousness about it, but rather the will to open one's eyes and drop the mask.

What will be the scene before their eyes? In what kind of existence will they be involved? In what time will they see their life unfold? It is at this point that theology has the right to return to the attack, since "the present time" is not just "our time" but also "the present time" contrasted with, and linked to, the time of the kingdom of God. It is the time of the Fall, the time of expectation, the time of revelation, the time of decision, the time of division. The variety of nature, marked by the contrast between rain and heat, has as its matching piece in history a double presence: that of our hypocrisy, a sign of human sins, and that of the voice of Christ, a sign of God's plans. Matthew is not wrong to speak of "signs," and of "signs" in the plural. The *Gospel of Thomas* is not either, when it associates "the present time" with the

---

68 According to Plummer (336), the signs are the birth, preaching, and death of John the Baptist. For Ernst (416). the sign is Israel in the particular time of its history. Marshall (549) speaks of events associated with the ministry of Jesus, and George ("Interpréter," 20) understands this time as the time of the mission of Jesus. According to Grässer (*Problem*, 192), the meaning of the sign is not to allow the delay of the parousia to make an impression. For Kaestli (*Eschatologie*, 21), the meaning is to recognize the decisive character of the present time and not to discern the signs of the imminent end. Klein ("Prüfung") sees the meaning as to consider the facts objectively, in particular the conflicts triggered by Christian preachers, and to arrive at a Christian position (the narrow link between vv. 49-53 and vv. 54-56). Ό καιρὸς οὗτος ("this time") is neither the coming of Jesus nor the messianic present but the history of the world after the coming of Jesus Christ. Wood ("Interpreting") is interested in the meaning of the sentences in the mouth of Jesus. A historical interpretation would suggest that Jesus reproaches his audience for not looking directly at the situation of Palestine, with the Romans and the Zealots. Blind, the interlocutors of Jesus do not see that the war, allegedly messianic, will end in a national disaster. Only the mission of John the Baptist and that of Jesus can allow them to avoid the disaster.

69 Marshall, 550. Luke utilizes the term ὑπόκρισις ("hypocrisy") in 12:1 but ignores the term ὑποκριτής in the discourse against the Pharisees (11:37-54) of which the Matthean parallel is full. See the commentary above on 11:37-54.

70 A good analysis of δοκιμάζω ("to evaluate") is found in Klein, "Prüfung," 378–80: this is neither to know the proximity of the reign nor to grasp the seriousness of the hour of decision; this is, in the context of vv. 49–53, to know how to recognize the actual situation of tension facing Christians and the church. Faith is enriched by this discernment. Conversion and discovery of the meaning of history make a pair.

Savior's presence.[71] Nor are modern commentators, when they see a soteriological, christological, eschatological, and missionary message in Jesus' final saying.

The difference between the texts of Matthew and Luke, so obvious, perhaps derives from what Gerd Theissen calls the "local coloring."[72] The different mentions of red in Matt 16:2-3 correspond to a certain appearance of the sky; in Luke, the threats from the west and the blazing fire from the south, to another climate. Moreover, the absence of Matt 16:2b-3 in certain manuscripts is perhaps the result of the disapproval of Egyptian scribes: they may have thought that, in their country, such meteorological phenomena did not have the significance granted them by the text that they were copying. However that may be, Luke's version raises the following question: under what sky should the phenomena described here be verified? The answer, in my opinion, is obvious. Although the two phenomena that are described do not apply very well to Palestine, they do fit the region of the Aegean Sea and the northern shores of the Mediterranean Sea perfectly.[73] Luke, whose home country I would place north of the Aegean Sea,[74] seems to have adapted Jesus' examples to his own country and to the climate that he knew well.

Good Riddance! (vv. 57-59)

Luke's text contains a redactional introduction, which establishes a link with the preceding passage ("judge what is right" [κρίνω τὸ δίκαιον], which is to be compared with "interpret" [δοκιμάζω] v. 56[75]) and interprets the following parable by way of anticipation.

"Why do you not succeed in judging?" (Τί . . . οὐ κρίνετε . . .). There is in every human being, in Luke's eyes, a block or a brake. What would be normal and human would be to make an assessment or a judgment (it may be remembered that, although Luke forbids condemnatory judgments with respect to other persons, he is very pleased with any demonstration of clearsightedness[76]). The important thing would be for you to judge "for yourselves" (ἀφ' ἑαυτῶν). Luke's attention is centered on these words, which—in Greek—he places before οὐ κρίνετε τὸ δίκαιον, "do you not succeed in judging . . . what is right?" (He adds the same words to his source in a significative way in 21:30b: "you can see *for yourselves* and know that summer is already near").[77] And yet, Luke laments, that is not the case.

What is it that must be judged? Curiously enough, Luke does not have anything more to say about what reality must be known, but only about a value to be promoted. What follows "the present time" of v. 56 here is "what is right," τὸ δίκαιον.[78] The Gospel writer thereby confers an ethical flavor on the whole passage. We probably should take this substantivized adjective in the broader sense of the biblical tradition: not just what is morally right but also what corresponds to God's will, his covenant, and his plan. That means going so far as

---

71   Cf. Matt 16:3; *Gos. Thom.* 91, cited above.

72   See Theissen, "Lokalkoloritforschung," 487–89.

73   In Palestine and in the Hebrew Bible, it is the wind from the east רוּחַ קָדִים that is the hot wind of the desert (cf. Gen 41:6, 23, 27; Exod 10:13; Ezek 17:10; Jonah 4:8). This wind comes sometimes from the southeast or from the west-southwest. In Egypt as in Greece, the hot wind comes from the south; this is the *khamsin* that Philo describes in *Vit. Mos.* 1.120. The translators of the LXX, encountering the hot wind of the Levant in the Hebrew Bible, may have suppressed the mention of its eastern origin or have substituted for it their hot wind from the south, the *khamsin*; see Theissen, "Lokalkoloritforschung," 488.

74   See the Introduction to these volumes (1:1–12).

75   Jülicher, *Gleichnisreden*, 2:244; Taeger (*Mensch*, 92–93) with respect to Gerhard Sellin (*Studien zu den grossen Gleichniserzählung des Lukas-Sondergutes: Die ἄνθρωπός τις-Erzählungen des Lukas-Sondergutes,*

besonders am Beispiel von Lk 10,25-37 und 16,19-31 untersucht [diss., Münster] 86–87) refuses to say that κρίνω is equivalent here to δοκιμάζω.

76   To condemn (6:37); to judge (7:43); see the commentary on 6:37 (1:241–42).

77   See Godet, 2:167. Jülicher (*Gleichnisreden*, 2:244) considers v. 57 scarcely clear; ἀφ' αὐτῶν can signify (a) "by yourselves," without exterior aid; or (b) "from you," and not from someone or the other. As for τί οὐ κρίνετε τὸ δίκαιον, it can have several senses; according to the context, it concerns a reproach addressed to the audience, that they do not judge correctly; following the Bible, it must concern the religious and moral domain. According to Loisy (358) v. 57 is obscure and vexed; see Taeger, *Mensch*, 90–94.

78   On τὸ δίκαιον ("that which is just"), see Godet, 2:167—what there is to do at such a moment. According to Wiefel (250), the parable that follows is shown to be this δίκαιον, "that which is just," and

giving up one's right in favor of God's righteousness, which aims at reconciliation (vv. 58-59) rather than looking for someone who is guilty.[79] Luke thus invites us to make an ethical reading (v. 57) out of our reading of history (v. 56). Daring to contemplate contemporary events already constitutes a moral act. Judging events is a second one. Following up on them is a third.

For Luke, this attitude begins with "conversion," "repentance" (μετάνοια), which will come up in chap. 13.[80] It transforms our image of reality and brings us closer to God. But the plural of the second person (in Greek) should be noted; it sets this passage apart from the parallel in Matthew (Matt 5:25-28), where the singular of the second person is used (in Greek; the difference is not marked in English). It is to "you" (plural) that the criticism and the command are addressed.[81] Discovering what is right certainly concerns the individual person, but also the community of believers. It is in the church that the difficulty is removed and clarity comes back. There is no more distortion of reality, and God's will holds sway: what is right (v. 57) in the present time (v. 56). As the meteorological examples suggest, however, the present time is characterized by the permanence of evil and the opening of the reign. Following Christ, Christians are sources of light in zones of darkness (cf. 11:33-36; 12:35). The parable illustrates what the new existence and the reconstituted community are capable of doing: practicing righteousness in the sense that God gives to that term, that is, knowing how to give up one's right and practice reconciliation. Luke 12:57-59 may be understood as a narrative illustration of what Paul expects from the Christians in Corinth: "If any of you has a dispute with another Christian, how dare you go before heathen judges instead of letting God's people settle the matter?" (1 Cor 6:1 *NRSV*).[82] But the perspective is also larger than that: it is not just a question of infighting in the church but also of a more general predisposition to living harmoniously with others. This is the orientation Luke wished to give to the parable he was going to recount, one that diverges from the meaning that Matthew gave to it by inserting it in the first antithesis of the Sermon on the Mount, the one about anger and murder.[83]

■ **58** The parable has three parts: (a) In a real situation (cf. vv. 54-56), it invites us to adopt a correct ethical attitude (cf. v. 57); in a linking of causes and effects that could keep everyone inactive, a task (ἐργασία) is proposed (v. 58a). (b) Only this course of action can interrupt the apparently inescapable process (cf. "or," "lest," μήποτε, v. 58b). And (c) as if the picture were not dark enough, a solemn saying ("I tell you," λέγω σοι, v. 59) confirms the inexorable weight of reality.[84] If we compare these verses with Matt 5:25-26, we will note that the first part (v. 58a) differs greatly from the Matthean parallel; the second part is closer to it; and the third is almost identical.[85] In the first part, Luke is more explicit and more elegant, even if the situation described is identical: there it is a matter of a legal enemy or opponent, an ἀντίδικος, with whom one is going on the way ("you go," ὑπάγεις; further on, "on the way," ἐν τῇ ὁδῷ). Since the mention of a destination for that common journey would be expected, Luke adds the words "before a magistrate" (ἐπ᾿ ἄρχοντα),[86] who will later be called "the judge" (ὁ κριτής). While in Matthew the reconciliation made it possible to avoid going before the judge, the approach taken in Luke makes it possible to avoid being *dragged*

---

is adapted to the time of decision; the expression is close in Acts 4:19.

79   See BAGD, s.v. δίκαιος; Gerhard Schneider, "δίκαιος, etc.," *EDNT* 1:324–25.

80   Cf. 13:3, 5, 9; see Bovon, *Theologian*, 305–28.

81   This plural must be redactional; the parallel in Matthew has the singular, and Luke himself in vv. 58-59 falls back into the singular of his source.

82   Luke insists on the "by yourselves," on ἀντίδικος, the "adversary," as the Christian coreligionist who has become an opponent, and on the κρίτης, the pagan "judge."

83   See Strecker, "Antithesen," an articulation of the apocalyptic ethic and eschatology.

84   On this parable, see Jülicher, *Gleichnisreden*, 2:240–46; Jeremias, *Parables*, 43–44, 96, 180; Klein, "Prüfung," 380–85; Caird, "Expounding"; Wrege, *Bergpredigt*, 61–64; Topel, *Acquittal*; Taeger, *Mensch*, 90–94; Piper, *Wisdom*, 105–7, 236–37.

85   Wrege, *Bergpredigt*, 62–63.

86   On the Greek judicial and administrative vocabulary of these verses, see J. Duncan M. Derrett, "Law in the New Testament: The Parable of the Unjust Judge," *NTS* 18 (1971–72) 178–91, esp. 183 nn. 1–4; Caird, "Expounding."

before the judge, although Luke hints that this process is already occurring (consequently, in Luke we are dealing with a real risk for someone who is in debt not in the Jewish world, but in the Greek or Roman one).

On the way, there are better things to do than just walk. One can "make" ($\delta\acute{\iota}\delta\omega\mu\iota$, literally "give") an "effort" ($\dot{\epsilon}\rho\gamma\alpha\sigma\acute{\iota}\alpha$): the expression $\delta\grave{o}\varsigma\ \dot{\epsilon}\rho\gamma\alpha\sigma\acute{\iota}\alpha\nu$ is not found anywhere else in Luke.[87] It is considered to be a Latinism (*da operam*). The effort that is worth the trouble is $\dot{\alpha}\pi\eta\lambda\lambda\acute{\alpha}\chi\theta\alpha\iota\ \dot{\alpha}\pi$ ' $\alpha\dot{\upsilon}\tau o\hat{\upsilon}$, which Matthew expresses by the words "come to terms with" him. $\dot{A}\lambda\lambda\acute{\alpha}\sigma\sigma\omega$ means "change"; $\kappa\alpha\tau\alpha\lambda\lambda\acute{\alpha}\sigma\sigma\omega$ (2 Cor 5:18-20), in the active voice in Greek, means "reconcile"; in the middle voice, "to make up," "make peace," in particular in the case of a married couple; in the passive, "be reconciled." Here we read $\dot{\alpha}\pi\alpha\lambda\lambda\acute{\alpha}\sigma\sigma\omega$, which can have different meanings: "(set) free," "release," "deliver," "put away," "get rid of," "dismiss," "send away," etc.; in the passive, in particular, "be rid of someone." That can be done in a more or less dignified fashion, according to the situation or the social relationship.[88] My dictionary gives an example from Demosthenes ("he got rid of his creditors," $\dot{\alpha}\pi\acute{\eta}\lambda\lambda\alpha\xi\epsilon\ \tauo\grave{\upsilon}\varsigma\ \chi\rho\acute{\eta}\sigma\tau\alpha\varsigma$) and adds, in italics, *by paying them*.[89] That is exactly what Luke is thinking of here: the one who is caught in a bad situation, who runs the risk of a lawsuit, must do everything possible to be in a position to get rid of his creditors: in this case the distance is a positive factor and the goodbyes, a blessing. But one does not escape from one's creditors that easily. Luke does not advocate an immoral solution: on the contrary, he proposes an honorable way out for this debtor, a dignified way to avoid ending up before the judge.[90] He does not indicate what concrete step is to be taken, any more than does Matthew, for that matter. The important thing is to act before it is too late.[91]

What doubtless counts is the fact that this person had the necessary intention, cleverness, and sincerity; he was able to calm his creditor[92] either by repaying him or by making new commitments. It does not matter much which solution he pursued. He avoided the worst. The worst would have been (a) a lawsuit and (b) a sentence. It seems that Greek law and Roman law allowed a certain amount of brutality in the case of insolvent debtors: their creditors could literally "drag" ($\kappa\alpha\tau\alpha\sigma\acute{\upsilon}\rho\omega$) them before a judge.[93] If they were insolvent, they ran the risk of being sentenced to "prison" ($\varphi\upsilon\lambda\alpha\kappa\acute{\eta}$), something Jewish law did not provide for. The carrying out of the sentence was entrusted by the judge to an "officer" ($\pi\rho\acute{\alpha}\kappa\tau\omega\rho$). It was the Greek title of a government employee responsible, so it seems, for finances, rather than penal justice (Matthew speaks of a $\dot{\upsilon}\pi\eta\rho\acute{\epsilon}\tau\eta\varsigma$, a "servant," a "helper," or an "assistant," here an "assistant" to the judge; the term is found in references to government employees in charge of carrying out the Sanhedrin's decisions).[94]

For Luke, as for Jesus, wisdom consists in avoiding this world's righteousness and the righteousness of others, in order to determine by oneself and in the church what is righteous. This wisdom relies on common sense when it is a question of imagining unfortunate consequences: you will not get out of there (prison) until you have truly emptied your pockets.[95] You will leave there the smallest coin, the $\lambda\epsilon\pi\tau\acute{o}\nu$ of the Greeks (Matthew speaks of

---

87 But it is neither unanticipated nor shocking; cf. the word $\dot{\epsilon}\rho\gamma\alpha\sigma\acute{\iota}\alpha$ in Acts 16:16, 19; 19:24-25; cf. Godet, 2:168. The Latinism $\delta\acute{\iota}\delta\omega\mu\iota\ \dot{\epsilon}\rho\gamma\alpha\sigma\acute{\iota}\alpha\nu$ has passed into the current language; see BAGD, s.v. $\delta\acute{\iota}\delta\omega\mu\iota$, 7; BDF §5.4 and n. 20.

88 See Godet, 2:168; Jülicher, *Gleichnisreden*, 2:243; Klein, "Prüfung," 383; Marshall, 551.

89 C. Alexandre, *Dictionnaire grec–français* (Paris: Ollendorff, 1888), s.v. $\dot{\alpha}\pi\alpha\lambda\lambda\acute{\alpha}\sigma\sigma\omega$. Does he imagine Demosthenes 36.25? LSJ, s.v., refers to the rhetor Isaeus 5.28 (fourth century B.C.E.) for the same expression.

90 Several commentators believe that Matthew gives the parable a reading that is more moral than Luke's version. So Klein ("Prüfung," 383), who reads in Luke the advice to get rid of his creditor and refuses every idea of reconciliation. Note that,

with exegetical and (doubtless) moral care, Clement of Alexandria (*Strom.* 3.4.36.1) explicates: to take leave "in friendship" from his adversary.

91 Luke insists more on the unfortunate consequences of the trial than on its imminence.

92 It is not explicitly called such, but $\pi\rho\acute{\alpha}\kappa\tau\omega\rho$ (and especially v. 59) suggests that it concerns affairs of debts.

93 See BAGD, s.v.; Fitzmyer, 2:1003. Lagrange (376) thinks that this gesture was not imaginable among the Jews anyway. It seems to me that it is better suited to the world of Luke than to that of Jesus.

94 See Wrege, *Bergpredigt*, 63 n. 3.

95 "That you have paid the last penny." The expression is strong. What I translate as "penny," the *lepta*, a tiny piece of bronze, was the smallest piece of Greek money. Compared to Roman money, it was

a κοδράντης, a Roman coin worth two λεπτά, which circulated widely in Palestine).

Introduced by a critical question (v. 57), which echoes the preceding complaint (vv. 54-56), the parable becomes a variation on the theme of these earlier verses: what you are lacking is eyes to recognize God's righteousness. As far as faith is concerned, true wisdom consists in giving up following human righteousness and putting others' rights before one's own. Otherwise, you will be caught up in the mechanisms of an inexorable world. Although the historical Jesus laid stress on the threat of the eschatological judge, Luke emphasized the attitude one must adopt in the present.

History of Interpretation

Ambrose (*Exp. Luc.* 7.131–33) had this to say about fire and baptism: vv. 49-50 are addressed to the priests responsible for governing God's house, while the preceding verses on vigilance were aimed at all believers. The reason that the Lord came to cast a fire on the earth was so that pastors' zeal might not be forced but free, associated with love rather than duty: he thereby kindled their desire to acquire God. As was his wont, Ambrose then worked in a series of biblical verses on fire. The sadness linked to baptism (v. 50) has nothing to do with the fear of death, but rather with Christ's concern for our redemption.

More than a thousand years later, we find this interpretation of the same vv. 49 and 50 in the writings of Erasmus,[96] who saw in the fire the divine force that purifies at the speed of a runaway fire. Far from extinguishing it, the cross intensifies its effect. It is "fire" by virtue of the gift of life, which is an expression of love, and "baptism" by virtue of the acceptance of death.

Bengel, on the other hand, examined with sensitivity

the two faces of fire: the one that benefits believers, the force of the Holy Spirit (here, in v. 49), and the one that punishes unbelievers, God's anger (reported in 3:16-17).[97]

A fragment of Origen's writings concerning vv. 52-53 explained first of all that five persons can play six roles (for him the daughter-in-law is pitted against both her mother-in-law and her own mother).[98] Then he gave the spiritual meaning of these familial tensions: the house symbolizes the human being; up until the coming of the Divine Word, the five senses did very well at enjoying themselves; from the time that the Word of God sounded in us, two of the five senses turned to the Lord: our vision began to see the order of the universe and to admire the Creator and our hearing began to hear the teaching of the Word. So the three others, which remained servile, rose up against the first two. Hence v. 52.

Origen, who was to be followed by Ambrose, also knew how to give a literal meaning to division within families: he said that it is the separation of believers from unbelievers, that is, the division that sets in between those who follow Christ and those who reject him. In the same way, Ambrose explained that there are moments in life when faith in God is more important than respect for one's parents, and he implies that this faith can create tensions within families (*Exp. Luc.* 7.134–36).[99]

It is from Irenaeus (*Adv. haer.* 1.25.4) that we learn what the explanation of the final parable (vv. 57-59) was in the second century in the Gnostic sect of the Carpocratians.[100] Their doctrine is that their "souls must try out all the ways of living, so that when they leave their bodies they will not have missed anything." Their freedom must not lack anything, or else their souls "would be obliged to return to a body." In the eyes of the Carpocratians, Jesus' parable (Luke 12:58-59 par. Matt 5:25-26) backs up their conception, since the enemy

---

valued at 1/2 *quadrant* and 1/8 *as*; see Plummer, 337; and Xavier Léon-Dufour, ed., *Dictionary of Biblical Theology* (2d ed.; London: Chapman, 1973), s.v. monnaies.

96 Erasmus *Paraphrasis*, col. 394. Between the two, for example, see Bede *In Luc.* 4:1189–1206: the fire is the intensity of the Holy Spirit.

97 Bengel, *Gnomon*, 1:349 and 294.

98 Origen *Hom. in Luc.* (ed. Rauer), frg. 81; 9:314; *Hom. in Luc.* (Couzel), 536–39.

99 For the sake of the audience, Ambrose is concerned to maintain respect owed to parents.

100 In *Adversus haereses*, Irenaeus indicates the interpretation of Luke 12:50 given by the disciples of Mark, the wise man (eastern Valentinianism): this "baptism" corresponds to the "redemption" of Christ descending upon Jesus, and to the pneumatic "redemption" of true Gnostics. It is not to be confused with the psychic "baptism" of the visible Jesus, which accorded only forgiveness.

is the devil, one of the angels of this world, created to lead souls to the archon (cf. "before a magistrate," ἐπ᾽ ἄρχοντα, of Luke 12:58). He is the first of the powers of the world, and he delivers the souls to another angel who is his bailiff so that this latter might shut them away in other bodies, since, as they said, it is the body that is its prison. According to them, v. 59 has the following meaning: "Nobody can free himself or herself from the power of the angels who have made this world, but everyone is constantly passing from one body to another, and that is true as long as he or she has not done all the things that can be done in this world." In the end, when there will be nothing left undone, the soul will rise up to be with God. "Thus all the souls will be saved; either making haste, they will devote themselves to doing everything possible during the course of a single life, or, passing from one body to another, and doing all the kinds of things in them that are required, they will settle their debt and thus be freed from the necessity of returning to be in a body." In my eyes, what is important is the theme of liberation that the Carpocratians conferred on the parable and the meaning that they gave to the verb ἀπαλλάσσω (in the passive, with an active sense): "be quit of, come to a settlement with." The parable is one of deliverance and not of reconciliation.

Using the same parable, Origen (*Hom. in Luc.* 35) offered his listeners an esoteric teaching about the angels (as far as I can see, he nowhere carried on a polemic against the Carpocratians' exegesis). He began by checking out the literal sense: he lined up four characters to represent the "you" and thus distinguished the prince (in our translation the "magistrate") from the judge (35.1). He then quickly established a synoptic comparison with Matthew and pointed out some grammatical ambiguity without resolving it. For example, with regard to "with him" (ἀπ᾽ αὐτου in v. 58, should we take "him" to be the enemy or the prince (i.e., the magistrate)? Who, moreover, is the subject of the verb "he may drag" (κατα-σύρῃ)—the enemy or the prince (i.e., the magistrate)? (35.1–2). Origen next got into the more secret explanation of the various characters (35.3–4), dependent first of all on an apocryphal writing that he does not name and on the *Shepherd of Hermas*, in order to establish his doctrine of the good angels and the bad angels who accompany both Christian and non-Christian human beings. He developed the idea that our guardian angels

have reason to see us keep from sinning and to have us make progress in virtue, while the bad angels lay traps for us. Origen was careful to refrain from saying that the parable does not exactly correspond to his lineup of characters, since it does not mention the guardian angels. In spite of everything, "the enemy is always with us, unfortunate and wretched as we are" (35.5; Couzel, 419).

As for the prince (ἄρχων, which I translate as "magistrate" in v. 58) (35.6–9), according to Deut 32:8-9 he must be the prince of each nation, the angel responsible for a people. "And each one of us has an enemy who is joined to him or her and whose task is to lead that person to a prince" (35.6; Couzel, 419). The enemy's goal is to keep each person in submission to the prince of the nation to which they are subject. While the enemy is the individual's enemy, the prince is the people's prince. As for the judge (Origen pointed out the article before "judge," the absence of an article before "prince," and the possessive "your" before "enemy," which helped him to elaborate his theory), there is only one, that is, Christ, who has conquered all the princes and is the sole and same judge of all.

As Christians, we are still accompanied by our enemy. This enemy wishes to bring us back to his prince, separating us from our new master, Christ. We must try to have done with our enemy; that is our responsibility. But we are still "on the way," that is, following the mystery, with Christ who is himself the way, the truth, and the life (John 14:6). The parable recounts what happens if we do not resist our enemy. The triumph of the enemy and the prince would be complete if they got the judge, that is, Christ, to condemn us to death. Since Christ judges each one according to his or her works, there is, therefore, a considerable risk (35.10–11). Origen considered the agent to be the one who carried out the judge's sentences and condemnations. The logic of divine justice is as implacable as v. 59 describes it to be. Although Christ has the right to pardon, his representatives have but one duty, that of carrying out the sentences. But if I am not in the wrong (35.12–15), I owe nothing to the one who carries out sentences and I can stand up to him (Origen played on the word "penny," λεπτόν, ανδ the neuter of the adjective λεπτός which literally means "light" [in weight], and which thus distinguishes grave sins from light ones, which in turn vary from each other in weight).

At the end of his homily, Origen hesitated to speak of these different eschatological sentences awaiting guilty Christians. He let it be understood that in certain grave cases, the punishment might last for centuries. Hence his final advice: "Let us strive to have done with our enemy' while we are on the way and let us unite ourselves with the Lord Jesus" (35.15; Couzel, 431). In short, the parable allowed Origen to develop an esoteric teaching on the Christian life, which is accompanied by angels, one of whom was a guardian and the other a tempter, and on divine justice applied by Christ the judge. We can sense in this the indispensable and pedagogical joining of God's goodness and distributive divine justice, though it is difficult to express sensitively.[101]

Conclusion

Between a pericope devoted to life in the church (12:35-48) and another focused on Christian commitment (13:1-9), here we have a text in two parts: the first deals with Christ, who speaks of his mission (vv. 49-50) and its consequences (vv. 51-53) in terms of "I." He does this with the help of two terrible images: placing fire on the earth and being engulfed by deep waters. It was a mission on a worldwide scale (what ambition!), of a brutal nature, which was to end tragically. Is that not what happened? After "what is it about?" (v. 49), and "what will it cost?" (v. 50), here we have "for whose benefit?" and "with what repercussions?" (vv. 51-53). First of all, it is for "your" benefit: the ecclesial "you" (plural) follows from the Christ-related "I." Watch out, what you need is not opinions ("you think," δοκεῖτε, v. 51), but convictions. Faith takes delight in the peace of the kingdom, but it is sufficiently perceptive (cf. v. 57) to not cut corners: first comes the gospel in the world, then life in the kingdom. The gospel is not a tranquil balm but a burn; nor is it unbroken fellowship. Next, with what repercussions? Truth, novelty, and the requirement of the gospel, given (δοῦναι, v. 51) by Christ, modify and interrupt the most natural and the strongest relationships. This is God's urgent therapy in the end times, and it does not leave anyone indifferent. Braving division (like separation, further on, in v. 58) goes hand in hand with life in the real world, in peace with God. The apocalyptic rooting of this theme, nevertheless, attests to the fact that these scissions are temporary, and that in the end the reign will reestablish unity, contribute to reconciliation, and assemble God's people. Moreover, although the gospel causes divisions to spring up, some reunions have already been taking place, starting with John the Baptist (1:17), in Christ (7:15), and in the church (Acts 2:42-47).

The second part (vv. 54-59) comes from the same speaker, but it is addressed to many more people, "the crowds" (v. 54). In it Jesus carried out his incendiary mission (v. 49). He lit a fire by shaking up the masses: since wood, a given, is necessary for a fire to get started, Jesus began with self-evident observations, that is, popular wisdom, within everyone's reach. The spark that set everything ablaze: Why remain blind to one's time and history when one has such a keen eye for predicting bad weather and scorching heat? Jesus issued an invitation to "evaluate" and "interpret" (δοκιμάζειν) the present time. He too refuge neither in the past, which he took for granted, nor in the future, which he set in motion; nor did he carry his listeners off into the land of dreams. He encouraged everyone to consider their time as inhabited by God, with all the weight of judgment and of forgiveness that that presence implies. Having established that decisive observation, he invited his listeners to take urgent measures: with respect to oneself, a commitment; with respect to God, trust and hope; with respect to one's neighbor, something other than lawsuits or war.

It is this last point that the following parable (vv. 57-59) brings to light, amassing in a few lines the essentials of an anthropology, an ethic, and an eschatology. Attending to the most urgent things first, Luke did not embellish the situation: he could have spoken of reconciliation, but he spoke more prosaically of a friendly separation. But the essential thing was taken care of: changing tack. Human justice is not described here, following the analogy of faith, as the reflection of divine justice; it appears in the starkness of its correspondence

---

101 Ambrose (*Exp. Luc.* 7.149–58) gives a different explanation of the parable. In his opinion, the adversary, according to Matthew, is virtuous asceticism, while in Luke, it is perverse passion.

to human exploitation. Well then, the logic of human oppression can be interrupted and even overturned. The opposite process, which draws on clearheadedness and faith, is being set in motion. In the world, fire has broken out. It is burning and causing division, but it is also pro-gressively warming things up and bringing them closer. Grace, however, is not cheap. While Jesus has done his part—and at what a price!—he invites each one of us to pitch in: "make an effort," δὸς ἐργασίαν.

The Proper Use of Misfortunes
(13:1-9)

Bibliography

Bartsch, Hans-Werner, "Die 'Verfluchung' des Feigenbaums," *ZNW* 53 (1962) 256–60.

Blinzler, Josef, "Die letzte Gnadenfrist: Lk 13, 5-9," *BLit* 37 (1963) 155–69.

Idem, "Die Niedermetzelung von Galiläern durch Pilatus," *NovT* 2 (1957–58) 24–49.

Bornhäuser, *Sondergut*, 94–102.

Bovon, *Theologian*, 305–28.

Brown, Schuyler, *Apostasy and Perseverance in the Theology of Luke* (AnBib 36; Rome: Pontifical Biblical Institute, 1969).

Bultmann, *History*, 23, 54–55, 61, 63, 204.

Cantrell, Richard A., "The Cursed Fig Tree," *TBT* 29 (1991) 105–8.

Conzelmann, *Theology*, 62 n. 4.

Derrett, J. Duncan M., "Figtrees in the New Testament," *HeyJ* 14 (1973) 249–65; reprinted in idem, *Studies*, 2:148–64.

Goetz, Oswald, *Der Feigenbaum in der religiösen Kunst des Abendlandes* (Berlin: Mann, 1965).

Gourgues, Michel, "Regroupement littéraire et équilibrage théologique: Le cas de Lc 13, 1-9," in van Segbroeck, *Four Gospels*, 2:1591–601.

Heininger, *Metaphorik*, 121–31.

Jeremias, *Parables*, 170–71.

Jülicher, *Gleichnisreden*, 2:433–48.

Kahlefeld, *Parables*, 68–70.

Kahn, Jean G., "La parabole du figuier stérile et les arbres récalcitrants de la Genèse," *NovT* 13 (1971) 38–45.

Laconi, M., "La pazienza di Dio," *SacDoc* 34 (1989) 437–72.

La Potterie, Ignace de, "Les deux noms de Jérusalem dans l'évangile de Luc," in Delorme and Duplacy, *La parole de grâce*, 65.

Lasserre, Jean, *La tour de Siloé: Jésus et la résistance de son temps* (Lyon, 1981) (unavailable to me).

Lémonon, Jean-Pierre, *Pilate et le gouvernement de la Judée: Textes et monuments* (EtB; Paris: Gabalda, 1981).

Linnemann, *Parables*, 15.

Lohmeyer, Ernst, *Galiläa und Jerusalem in den Evangelien* (FRLANT NF 34; Göttingen: Vandenhoeck & Ruprecht, 1936) 41–46 (= Lohmeyer, "Galiläa und Jesus bei Lukas," in *Lukas-Evangelium*, 7–12.

McCown, Chester C., "Gospel Geography: Fiction, Fact, and Truth," *JBL* 60 (1941) 1–25, esp. 14–18.

Michiels, Robert, "La conception lucanienne de la conversion," *EThL* 41 (1965) 42–78, esp. 58–59.

Petzke, *Sondergut*, 122–25.

Pirot, *Paraboles*, 243–49.

Reichmann, Victor, "Feige," *RAC* 7 (1969) 640–89, esp. 671–74, 683–89.

Scholtz, G., "Ästhetische Beobachtungen am Gleichnis vom reichen Mann und armen Lazarus und von drei anderen Gleichnissen (Lk 16, 19-25 [26-31]; 10, 34; 13, 9; 15, 11-32)," *LingBibl* 43 (1978) 67–74.

Schramm, Tim, *Der Markus-Stoff bei Lukas: Eine literarkritische und redaktionsgeschichtliche Untersuchung* (SNTSMS 14; Cambridge: Cambridge University Press, 1971).

Schürer, Emil, *The History of the Jewish People in the Age of Jesus-Christ (175 B.C.–A.D. 135): A New English Version*. Revised (ed. Geza Vermes et al.; 4 vols.; Edinburgh: T. & T. Clark, 1973–87).

Schwarz, Günther, "Lukas 13, 1-5. Eine Emendation," *NovT* 11 (1969) 121–26.

Scott, Bernard Brandon, *Hear Then the Parable: A Commentary on the Parables of Jesus* (Minneapolis: Fortress Press, 1989) 331–42.

Sellin, Gerhard, "Lukas als Gleichniserzähler: Die Erzählung vom barmherzigen Samariter (Lk 10, 25-37)," *ZNW* 65 (1974) 166–89; 66 (1975) 19–60, passim, esp. 178, 184.

Shirock, Robert J., "The Growth of the Kingdom in Light of Israel's Rejection of Jesus: Structure and Theology in Luke 13:1-35," *NovT* 35 (1993) 15–19.

Slee, H. M., "Note on St Luke 13, 6-9 and St Matthew 3, 10 // St Luke 3, 9," *JTS* 21 (1920) 77–78.

Str-B 2:192–98.

Taeger, *Mensch*, 40–41, 136–37.

Telford, William R., *The Barren Temple and the Withered Tree: A Redaction-critical Analysis of the Cursing of the Fig-Tree Pericope in Mark's Gospel and Its Relation to the Cleansing of the Temple Tradition* (JSNTSup 1; Sheffield: JSOT Press, 1980) 224–39.

Ternant, Paul, "Le dernier délai de la conversion (Lc 13, 1-9)," *AsSeign* 16 (1971) 59–72.

Idem, "L'homme ne peut empêcher Dieu d'être bon (Lc 13,6-17)," *AsSeign* 72 (1964) 36–52.

Tiede, *Prophecy*, 71–72, 108–9.

Van Schaik, Alfrink, "De vijgeboom met kans op vruchten (Lc 13, 1-9)," in Bastiaan M. F. van Iersel et al., *Parabelverhalen in Lucas: Van semiotiek naar pragmatiek* (Tilburg: Tilburg University Press, 1987) 110–32.

Wrembek, Christoph, "Fünf Weinberg-Gleichnisse. Eine geistliche Schriftbetrachtung," *GuL* 4 (1989) 260–77.

Young, Franklin W., "Luke 13, 1-9," *Int* 31 (1977) 59–63.

Zeitlin, Solomon, "Who Were the Galileans? New Light on Josephus' Activities in Galilee," *JQR* 4 (1973–74) 189–203.

1/ At that very time there were some people present who had arrived, telling him the story of the Galileans whose blood Pilate had mingled with that of their sacrifices. **2/** He gave them this response, "Do you think that these Galileans were worse sinners than all the other Galileans because they suffered in this way? **3/** No, I tell you; but unless you repent, you will all perish the same way. **4/** Or those eighteen people on whom the tower fell at Siloam, and whom it killed—do you think that they were more in debt than all the others living in Jerusalem? **5/** No, I tell you; but unless you repent, you will all perish the same way."

6/ Then he told them this parable: "A man had a fig tree planted in his vineyard; and he came looking for fruit on it and found none. **7/** So he said to the winegrower, 'See here! For three years I have come looking for fruit on this fig tree, and I find none. Cut it down! Why let it waste the soil?' **8/** He replied, 'Master, let it alone for one more year, until I dig around it and put manure on it. **9/** And if it happens to bear fruit in the future, well and good; but if not, you can cut it down.'"

The untimely arrival of people bearing bad news interrupts Jesus' teaching. Luke is fond of rekindling the reader's interest by incidents of this kind.[1] The Gospel writer, with consummate skill in expressing himself concisely, in a single sentence, explicitly points out the contents of the news and presupposes an implicit question addressed to Jesus (v. 1). The Lukan Christ gives a two-stage answer:[2] in the first stage, he states the opinion,[3] false in his eyes, of those with whom he was talking ("you," v. 2); then he denounces it ("no") before solemnly affirming his own conviction ("I tell you") in the form of threats[4] (v. 3). This polemical contrast between an opinion of outsiders that is criticized and a personal conviction that is displayed corresponds exactly to the structure of a previous episode, 12:51 (division rather than peace), in which we also find "do you think that" ($\delta o \kappa \epsilon \hat{\iota} \tau \epsilon$ $\ddot{o} \tau \iota$), and "no, I tell you" ($o \dot{v} \chi \acute{\iota}, \lambda \acute{\epsilon} \gamma \omega$ $\dot{v} \mu \hat{\iota} \nu$). It also makes a new appearance in the second case (vv. 4-5), which is symmetrical with the first, the only difference being that this time the example is not one that comes from someone else, but one that comes from the lips of Jesus himself (v. 4a). And once again, we encounter "do you think that" ($\delta o \kappa \epsilon \hat{\iota} \tau \epsilon$ $\ddot{o} \tau \iota$) and "no, I tell you" ($o \dot{v} \chi \acute{\iota}, \lambda \acute{\epsilon} \gamma \omega \, \dot{v} \mu \hat{\iota} \nu$), in vv. 4b-5. In these verses (vv. 1-5), we will focus only on the link between an incident that raises a problem and a speech by the master, which is a distinctive feature of an apophthegm.[5] The text does not state if Jesus' answer is a teaching addressed to listeners eager to learn (in that case, the episode would be a scholastic dialogue[6]) or a reply to critics eager to trip Jesus up (a controversy dialogue). We must, moreover, take into account the transmission of the episode and the modifications that that implies: in a first, kerygmatic stage, Jesus was inviting his listeners to convert; in a second, polemical stage, the earliest Christians were attacking an overly facile rabbinic theodicy; then, in a third, didactic stage, the Doctors of

---

1   See, e.g., 7:37; 8:19; 10:25; 11:27, 37.

2   The verb "to respond" is present: $\dot{\alpha} \pi o \kappa \rho \iota \vartheta \epsilon \acute{\iota} \varsigma$.

3   See $\delta o \kappa \epsilon \hat{\iota} \tau \epsilon$, "Do you think?"

4   See Petzke, *Sondergut*, 123.

5   The apothegm is a brief scene in which the principal element is a decisive maxim. See Bultmann, *History*, 11; Schneider, "Antworten," 325.

6   Bultmann (*History*, 56–57) classifies it among the scholastic dialogues because the discussion does not involve a combative attitude of Jesus or of his students, and Jesus' response, in the form of a question, does not take the interlocutors *ad absurdum* or make them appear ridiculous.

the Church were training their catechumens to tie their information about the world to their faith.[7]

Analysis

The absence of any Synoptic parallel leads us to attribute this unit to L.[8] My detailed commentary will enable me to point out the oldest elements of it. Joachim Jeremias detects traditional elements in vv. 2-5 and redactional elements in vv. 1 and 4.[9] The weight of tradition, especially some Semitisms, precludes attributing the entire episode to the pen of the Gospel writer.

As the introduction in v. 6a suggests, the parable (vv. 6b-9) was probably not originally associated with the apophthegm.[10] It was only the theme of conversion that allowed the two pericopes to be brought together. They were probably joined before the Lukan composition, since what is found here is a sequence of L (13:1-17).[11] Luke, on the other hand, must have been responsible for the linking of vv. 1-9 with the preceding sequence (12:49-59), if the latter is attributed to Q; if not, the sequence of L, which probably began in v. 49, would have continued by focusing attention, from v. 54 on, on conversion. By virtue of the distinction and the precision of its *ductus*, its sequence, the parable is a part of L.[12] We are dealing with a parable rather than an allegory, more exactly a parabolic story. Although this account begins with a normal story (vv. 6-7), it ends in a surprising way (vv. 8-9). Unlike the attitude of the landowner, the reaction of the servant is indeed surprising and betrays a certain excess.[13] Located in the country, the episode suggests a plantation such as is still encountered in Palestine or around the Mediterranean Sea: fig trees can cohabit with vines.[14] This parable with two characters depicts a landowner and his agricultural worker. The dialogue between these two characters, the disappointed master's impatience, and the intercession of the winegrower who does not give up constitute the main part of the parable.[15] As is always true in these biblical cases of intercession, it is an inferior person protecting one who is threatened more than the one making the appeal—someone who is inferior to God but who is in a position of responsibility toward the people.[16] The text ends without the master's decision being made known and without any lesson being drawn from this incident. It is not a case of double awkwardness; on the contrary, it is a way of leaving the text open, inviting the reader to reflect and then make a decision.

Since Luke omits the incident of the fruitless fig tree in chap. 19, the conclusion has been drawn that he considered the two texts to be doublets.[17] The Markan episode of the fruitless fig tree, however, is not a parable and ends with a curse that was carried out. Nonetheless, the two pericopes (Mark 11:13-14, 20-21 par. Luke 13:6-9) are perhaps two very divergent recensions of a single initial memory: they have in common the fig tree, the absence of fruit, and the threat. To be sure, the absence of fruit is explained differently (in one case, Mark, it was the wrong season; in the other case, Luke, fruitlessness)

---

7   This is the exegesis (see below) that will permit the justification of this reconstruction of the evolution of the apophthegm.

8   This is the general consensus. See Ernst, 418; Grundmann, 274; Fitzmyer, 2:1004; Petzke, *Sondergut*, 122–25.

9   See Jeremias, *Sprache*, 226–28.

10   See Petzke, *Sondergut*, 123.

11   Schneider (2:237) thinks that the link is the work of Luke, whereas Petzke (*Sondergut*, 124–25) hesitates to say so for want of evidence.

12   This is, again, the general consensus (see n. 8 above).

13   See Bultmann, *History*, 189; Pirot, *Paraboles*, 245. Harnisch (*Gleichniserzählungen Jesu*, 69 nn. 63 and 71, 107–8, 145) wonders whether our story should not be classified as a parable rather than as a parabolic story, in what he calls the *epische Miniaturstücke*, since, despite its dialogical side, it

lacks the dramatic point characteristic of parabolic stories.

14   See Jeremias, *Parables*, 170.

15   See Jacques Dupont, *Pourquoi des paraboles? La méthode parabolique de Jésus* (LiBi 46; Paris: Cerf, 1977) 34–35, 40.

16   Cf. Moses interceding to God on behalf of the guilty people (Exod 32:11-14, 32); other stories with mentions of intercession can be found in Gen 18:16-33; Num 11:2; 1 Sam (1 Kgdms) 7:8-10; 12:19-25; Jer 15:1; Amos 7:1-6; Ps 106 (105):23; 2 Macc 15:12-14; John 17:20. These stories concern men of God (Abraham, for instance) and prophets (Moses and Samuel in particular), who intercede most frequently for the people. James 5:16 makes the point: "the prayer of the righteous is powerful and effective."

17   See, e.g., Schneider, 2:296.

and the threat, although it was carried out in one case (Mark), is only brandished in the other (Luke). Finally, in Mark's story, Jesus takes the place of the impatient master, while in Luke's parable he is the one speaking and possibly, if we allegorize, the winegrower, but in any case not the owner.

We should not forget another text, the "parable" that can be drawn from the fig tree according to Mark 13:28-29 par. Matt 24:32-36 par. Luke 21:29-33: by looking at its branches becoming tender and its leaves sprouting "you know that summer is near" (Mark 13:28b). The reasoning is reminiscent of that in Luke 12:54-56. The fig tree is in good health and it announces a season, summer, that Amos, through a play on words, had once compared to the end (Amos 8:1-3). Nor should we forget Jesus' strange saying about the faith that moves mountains in Mark 11:22-23 and transplants trees in Luke 17:6.[18] We could also call attention to the fact that the *Apocalypse of Peter* used the parable of the fig tree at a time before the Gospel became canonical. It is possible that the author of the *Apocalypse of Peter* was acquainted with an oral form of it that was closer to the original than the literary form of it that we have in the Gospel of Luke.[19] On the other hand, Marcion seems to have omitted Luke 13:1-9, without the reasons for this omission being understood.[20] Finally, let us mention the fact that all sorts of stories about trees were in circulation. The story of Ahiqar[21] contains the story closest to the parable here in Luke:

O my boy! Thou art like the tree which was fruitless beside the water, and its master was fain to cut it down, and it said to him, "Remove me to another place, and if I do not bear fruit, cut me down." And its master said to it, "Thou being beside the water hast not borne fruit, how shalt thou bear fruit when thou art in another place?"

It is possible that Jesus, or the earliest Christians, if the parable is not authentic, may have known such a story and retold it from a new perspective. Jesus' saying (17:6), summarized here, makes possible his knowledge of the story of Ahiqar. Nor is it out of the question to posit that Luke's parable influenced the most recent versions of the story of Ahiqar.

Commentary

From Theodicy to Conversion (13:1-5)

■ **1** Verse 1a indicates an interruption: some anonymous people ($\tau\iota\nu\acute{\epsilon}\varsigma$), probably pilgrims, neither patriots in revolt nor followers of Jesus, "had arrived,"[22] "at that very time" (there is no reason to attribute a theological meaning to the Greek word $\kappa\alpha\iota\rho\acute{o}\varsigma$, "time," here). They told (the same verb, $\grave{\alpha}\pi\alpha\gamma\gamma\acute{\epsilon}\lambda\lambda\omega$,[23] as in the episode of the delegation from John the Baptist [7:18, 22]) him[24] what had happened to the Galileans.[25] It is rather unusual, we should point out, for information to be communicated

---

18 One must distinguish between the fig tree ($\sigma\upsilon\kappa\hat{\eta}$, *Ficus carica*), the sycomore ($\sigma\upsilon\kappa\omicron\mu\omicron\rho\acute{\epsilon}\alpha$, *Ficus sycomorus*), and the mulberry tree ($\sigma\upsilon\kappa\acute{\alpha}\mu\iota\nu\omicron\varsigma$, *Morus nigra*). For a bibliography on the fig tree, see n. 57 below.

19 *Apocalypse of Peter* 2 (Ethiopian version); see Richard Bauckham, "The Two Fig Tree Parables in the Apocalypse of Peter," *JBL* 104 (1985) 269–87.

20 See Adolf Harnack, *Marcion: Das Evangelium vom fremden Gott* (Leipzig: Hinrichs, 1921) 217.

21 Story of Ahiqar 8.39; trans. A. S. Lewis in *APOT* 2:775, cited by Jeremias, *Parables*, 170; on these different versions of this ancient book, see J. M. Lindenberger, "Ahiqar (Seventh to Sixth Century B.C.): A New Translation and Introduction," in *OTP* 2:479–507, esp. 480 and 487. The cited fragment exists in Syriac, Aramaic, and Arabic. The date of these versions is difficult to determine. The Syriac and Armenian versions are the nearest to the original Aramaic.

22 $\Pi\acute{\alpha}\rho\eta\sigma\alpha\nu$ can signify "were present" or "have arrived." See BAGD, s.v. $\pi\acute{\alpha}\rho\epsilon\iota\mu\iota$, and J. Reiling and J. L. Swellengrebel, *A Translator's Handbook on the Gospel of Luke* (Helps for Translators 10; Leiden: Brill, 1971) 499; Blinzler ("Niedermetzelung," 25), who cites Diodorus of Sicily 17.8.2, $\pi\acute{\alpha}\rho\eta\sigma\alpha\nu$ $\tau\iota\nu\epsilon\varsigma$ $\grave{\alpha}\pi\alpha\gamma\gamma\acute{\epsilon}\lambda\lambda\omicron\nu\tau\epsilon\varsigma$ $\pi\omicron\lambda\lambda\omicron\grave{\upsilon}\varsigma$ $\tau\hat{\omega}\nu$ $\acute{E}\lambda\lambda\acute{\eta}\nu\omega\nu$ $\nu\epsilon\omicron\tau\epsilon\rho\acute{\iota}\zeta\epsilon\iota\nu$, "some people arrived announcing that many Greeks were attempting a revolution."

23 This is a typical Lukan verb, found eleven times in the Gospel and fifteen times in Acts. In the LXX it is found in Gen 26:32; Esth 6:2; 1 Macc 14:21. The substance of the message could be information or a proclamation; see I. Broer, "$\grave{\alpha}\gamma\gamma\acute{\epsilon}\lambda\lambda\omega$, $\kappa\tau\lambda$.," *EDNT* 1:12–13.

24 Papyrus 45 omits the pronoun $\alpha\grave{\upsilon}\tau\hat{\omega}$ ("to him").

25 For correct usage of $\pi\epsilon\rho\acute{\iota}$ ("about, on the subject of"), see BAGD, s.vv. $\pi\epsilon\rho\acute{\iota}$ and $\grave{\alpha}\pi\alpha\gamma\gamma\acute{\epsilon}\lambda\lambda\omega$ 1.

to Jesus (the earliest Christians preferred to insist on their Master's omniscience and foreknowledge; see, for example, 5:22 and 9:30-31).

Verse 1b supplies the content of the information. There Pilate is mentioned for the second time in the Gospel, along with his brutal act.[26] Instead of a neutral and secular wording, the text makes uses of a violent and religious expression: the blood of humans and the blood of animals were mingled.[27] Two reasons explain the popular indignation: the mingling of human blood with animal blood and the placing of the abominable tragedy in the holy precinct of the temple. The victims whose blood had been mingled with that of the Galileans must indeed have been animals offered in sacrifice rather than human beings who had been assassinated.[28] Since sacrifices were offered in the temple area, that is where the massacre must have been perpetrated. According to Billerbeck, the responsibility of slitting the victim's throat always belonged to the person who was offering the victim as a sacrifice (cf. Lev 1:5; *m. Zebaḥ.* 3, 1, and *b. Zebaḥ.* 7a-7b).[29] The priest's role was to receive and spill the blood. In that case, the incident could have taken place at any time. According to Josef Blinzler, however, Pilate's act could have been committed only on the day

of preparation for Passover, the only day when laypeople could themselves offer their own sacrifices.[30] In my opinion, the intervention of Pilate's troops must have taken place in the precinct of the temple during Passover, since this time was often the occasion for demonstrations. It is known that the Jewish memory was heightened when repression affected the religious domain and the temple space (cf. 11:51). This mingling of sacrifice and murder profoundly shocked believers' sensitivities. It aroused intensely vigorous disapproval of Pilate and raised the question of theodicy in concrete and painful terms.

The Galileans in question were truly inhabitants of Galilee, even if, in this context, the term suggests Zealots, because of the numerous centers of resistance to the Romans for those who took shelter in Galilee.[31] It is possible that there was unrest in Jerusalem during the feast and that Pilate, personally present, wished to put down a riot. The governors were supposed to go to Jerusalem to maintain order during the feasts (see Josephus *Ant.* 20.5.3 §107; *Bell.* 2.13.2 §§280–81). In his presentation of Pilate, Josephus calls attention to several acts of violent repression carried out by the Roman governor, but none of them exactly matches what Luke reports here.[32]

26   See 3:1; it is in chap. 23 that Pilate intervenes in person; see Acts 3:13; 4:27; 13:28. On this brutal character, see Blinzler, "Niedermetzelung"; and Lémonon, *Pilate.*

27   See *Midr. Ps.* 7 §2 (32a); Philo *Spec.* 3.91; see Blinzler, "Niedermetzelung," 28–29.

28   With Blinzler ("Niedermetzelung," 29, 30) and Fitzmyer (2:1006), contra Oscar Cullmann, *Der Staat im Neuen Testament* (Hewett Lectures; Tübingen: Mohr Siebeck, 1956) 9. One could understand ἡ θυσία in its primary sense of "sacrifice" or in its secondary sense of "sacrificial victim"; see BAGD, s.v., which retains the primary sense. I suggest the word "blood" after "with"; hence: "with the blood of their sacrifices," which I translate "with that of their sacrifices."

29   Str-B 2:192–93.

30   Blinzler, "Niedermetzelung," 31–32. Since, according to him, the second year was the only one of the three years of his ministry in which Jesus did not go up to Jerusalem for the Passover, he sets this drama in this particular year and the date of 14 Nisan of the year 29, which is Monday, April 18!

31   See Acts 5:37: "Judas the Galilean," manifestly a leader of the Zealots; the name "Galilean" could at

some time have designated the Zealots. See Justin *Dial.* 80.4; Hegesippus in Eusebius of Caesaria *Hist. eccl.* 4.22.7; Bultmann, *History,* 55; Bornhäuser, *Sondergut,* 94–96; Blinzler, "Niedermetzelung," 37–40. The definite article before the word "Galileans" in v. 11 indicates that this event was known.

32   For enumerations of these cases, see Marshall, 553; Fitzmyer, 2:1006–7; and Blinzler, "Niedermetzelung," 32–37. The incident that comes closest dates from the year 35 and takes place at the foot of Mount Gerizim and not in Jerusalem; it concerns Samaritans and not Galileans and does not report the blood of sacrifices. It refers to the massacre after which Vitellius, legate of Syria, asked for the return of Pilate to Rome. See Josephus *Ant.* 18.4.1–2 §§85–89. Several authors think that it is necessary to distinguish between these two episodes; see Bultmann (*History,* 57), who hesitates. I agree with Blinzler ("Niedermetzelung," 37): the incident of Luke 13:1 does not correspond to any episode that Josephus mentions. It does nonetheless fit nicely with the image that we have of Pilate.

■ **2** To put it simply, the Lukan Jesus expresses an opinion that could have come to the mind of any pious person. Out of faithfulness to countless biblical affirmations,[33] rabbinic theology did indeed establish a connection between crime and punishment.[34] Does not the degree of violence connected with the death correspond to the gravity of the sin?[35] The adjective that Luke uses here, ἁμαρτωλός ("sinful"),[36] contains two elements: the rupture of the relationship with God and, especially, moral transgression. The guilt or innocence of the victims is not going to cause as much of a problem as the comparison between their sins and those of ordinary people. The idea of punishment is discernible in the verb "suffer," "endure," used to describe the cruel fate of the unfortunate persons mentioned in v. 2 ("because they suffered in this way," ταῦτα πεπόνθασιν).[37] Like many of our contemporaries, those to whom Jesus addressed himself must have thought that by means of this cruel death, God had imposed a sentence for sins that were particularly serious. In their eyes, the punishment was evidence of the scale of the hidden vices. They had in mind other people's sin; Jesus referred them back to their own.

■ **3** Jesus rejects that comparison and the logic that mechanically establishes a link between guilt and punishment. To be sure, he does not deny the guilt of those Galileans, nor that of each and every person, but he does refuse to declare it to be greater because of a more tragic end.[38] He is focused not on the origin of the misfortune but on the future of the living. In Luke's eyes, Jesus rejected any scale of sins and any reasoning concerning deserved fatal outcomes. He was opposed to a conception of blind and cruel divine justice and believed in a God who enters into dialogue with humans.

He contrasted an objectifying and withdrawn doctrine with a faith that recognizes its wrongs and turns toward God, that is, that practices "repentance," "conversion" (μετάνοια). While v. 2 spoke of the wages of sin, v. 3 stresses the statute of faith.

They were talking about other people; he, on the other hand, makes them turn to thinking about themselves: he shifts from the third person to the second person. As with the sayings about the splinter and the log (6:41-42), Jesus offers a change of perspective; he issues an invitation to "conversion." What he says is prophetic, combining information with warning. Your death (literally, your perdition,[39] with the lack of precision inherent in that term) will depend on your decision. Jesus does not contrast grace and retribution, nor does he insist on responsibility alone. He offers something decisive: the possibility of looking at the world and one's own life in another way, not as a satisfied spectator but as an anxious participant. It is not a question of the anxieties associated with obtaining physical necessities (12:22-32), but of healthy concern about not having one's life in order because of not being in order with one's God. Somewhere between the action of the Pharisee and that of the tax collector (18:9-14), those who listened to Jesus were addressed in a vigorous manner and shaken up. They were invited to participate in an intellectual and spiritual displacement, moving up from occupying spectator seats in the theater to being actors on the stage.

Lukan "conversion," "repentance" (μετάνοια) has been the subject of numerous studies.[40] As the positive pole of "sin" (ἁμαρτία), it is in the first instance becoming aware of one's separation from God; next, it involves making a decision, facilitated by the offer of the Christian message, to renew one's relationship with the Lord;

---

33 See J. T. Nelis and A. Lacocque, "rétribution," *DEB*, 1113–17.

34 See Str-B 2:193–94.

35 This popular opinion appears also, with criticism, in John 9:2.

36 See Conzelmann, *Theology*, 227 n. 2; Wolfgang Dietrich, *Das Petrusbild der lukanischen Schriften* (BWANT 94; Stuttgart: Kohlhammer, 1972) 50–51 n. 77; Taeger, *Mensch*, 35–43; see also the excursus, "The Forgiveness of Sins," in volume 1 of this commentary (p. 182).

37 On πάσχω, see J. Kremer, "πάσχω κτλ.," *EDNT* 3: 51–52. Ταῦτα ("these things") is translated as "in

the same way," a pronominal accusative to designate the content of the sufferings; see BDF §154.

38 On this use of παρά ("other than," "more than"), with or without the comparative, see BDF §236.3. The usage seems Semitic; see Fitzmyer, 2:1007; Jeremias, *Sprache*, 226.

39 On ἀπόλλυμι (here the middle Attic future); see A. Kretzer, "ἀπόλλυμι, κτλ.," *EDNT* 1:135–36.

40 See the summaries in Bovon, *Theologian*, 305–28; since then, see Taeger, *Mensch*, 130–47; Horn, *Glaube und Handeln*, 233–35.

it is also a decisive step, more in connection with one's own life and death than with the imminence of the parousia and the last judgment; it is finally and especially a daily requirement of being in solidarity with others (the winegrower in the parable [v. 8] will furnish an example of this).

■ **4-5** Luke was fond of everything that came in pairs.[41] Keeping to the geography of his Gospel, which corresponds to the bipolarity of God's people, he added a tragedy that befell some Jerusalemites to the massacre that some Galileans had suffered. The location of the pool of Siloam is known; it was at the end of the canal built by King Hezekiah, on the southeast side of Jerusalem; this pool was surrounded, in New Testament times, by a portico with colonnades built by Herod the Great.[42] The tower in question must have been located in this area. Josephus spoke of a rampart in this place, which, from the west, "turned southwards above the fountain of Siloam," then to the east (it is what is called the first wall) (*Bell.* 5.4.1–2 §§140, 145).[43] The tower in Luke 13:4 must have been a part of that fortification. We know that during the Jewish War, some fighting and a fire caused deaths in this place (see Josephus *Bell.* 6.7.2 §§363–64),[44] but there is no other ancient witness to this collapse of the tower, probably accidental,[45] or to these eighteen victims.

We know that the original form of the Lord's Prayer spoke of "debts" and "debtors" (cf. Matt 6:12), words that did not evoke guilt and sin for Greeks, hence Luke's effort, partially rewarded, to substitute for them the vocabulary of sin (cf. Luke 11:4).[46] I suppose that the vocabulary of debt in 13:4 ("debtors," "in debt," ὀφειλέται) comes from tradition, while "sinners" (ἁμαρτωλοί) in v. 2 must be redactional.[47] In Luke's eyes, the meaning is the same, since the debt is a debt owed to God.[48]

Here again, Jesus' attitude is liberating, in that it breaks what was believed to be the inexorable link between sin—others' but also our own—and its consequences. It transforms our image of God, who gains in kindness what he loses in omnipotence. For if a meticulously cruel power of retribution is taken away from him, so also is omnipotence over events.[49] For a nosey God as well as for a distant God, Jesus substituted a loving God who waits for us and, even before waiting for us, invites us. Perhaps Protestants feel that Luke did not perceive, as did Paul, the radicalism of forgiveness and grace and that Luke overlooked truly free justification. That is

---

41 See Helmut Flender, *Heil und Geschichte in der Theologie des Lukas* (BEvTh 41; Munich: Kaiser, 1965).

42 See 2 Kgs (4 Kgdms) 20:20; Isa 8:6; 22:11; Sir 48:17; John 9:7, 11.

43 See Pierre Benoit, "Les remparts de Jérusalem," *MB* 1 (1977) 20–35. The definite article designates the fallen tower and does not imply that there was only one at this place; see Lagrange, 380. Ἐν τῷ Σιλωάμ signifies "in the area of Siloam," "at Siloam."

44 Godet, 2:170–71. One wonders whether the accident took place during the public works that included Pilate's construction of an aqueduct; see Josephus *Ant.* 18.3.2 §§60–62; *Bell.* 2.9.4 §175; Marshall, 555; and Wiefel, 252. The verb κατοικέω ("to live") used transitively, is characteristic of Luke; see Jeremias, *Sprache*, 226.

45 To the contrary, Bornhäuser (*Sondergut*, 97) thinks that the fall of the tower was due not to a natural catastrophe but to a punishment of the Romans during a messianic movement. Nothing points to this in the text. I retain the sense of "tower," even if the word πύργος can designate other types of construction. In addition, Demetrius of Kallatis (85 fr. 6), an author from the end of the third century B.C.E. cited by Strabo (1.3.20), describes the fall of a tower that took twenty-five women with it; see BAGD, s.v.; Luke mentions a πύργος, perhaps a shed rather than a tower, in 14:28. On the other hand, in the parable of the murderous winegrowers (20:9), he does not mention the tower that Mark includes (Mark 12:1). We know the importance of the tower in *Hermas*, symbolizing the church on its way to edification (*Vis.* 3.4–7). The word occurs 148 times in *Hermas*.

46 See the commentary above on 11:4.

47 See Jeremias (*Sprache*, 226), who thinks, on the contrary, that the word ἁμαρτωλοί ("sinners") is traditional.

48 See Lagrange, 380. This is the only use of the word ὀφειλέτης ("debtor") in Luke-Acts. Luke twice uses χρεοφειλέτης ("debtor"), in 7:41 and 16:5. The verb ὀφείλω ("to owe") appears in 7:41; 11:4; 16:5, 7; 17:10; Acts 17:29.

49 See Hans Jonas, *Der Gottesbegriff nach Auschwitz: Eine jüdische Stimme* (Frankfurt: Suhrkamp, 1987); Bovon, *L'œuvre*, 221–42.

possible.[50] But Luke did have a positive and relational conception of "conversion," "repentance" ($\mu\epsilon\tau\acute{\alpha}\nu o\iota\alpha$). This turning back to God is not that of a bad conscience alone, but the confident march toward the loved one whom one finds again—reconciliation, the reunion where all contribute something of themselves. The seriousness of the encounter is not eliminated, since if the step is not taken, loss is guaranteed. It is not that God is especially severe but that there is no life without him. The mystery of evil remains, and Luke does not rule out a relationship between suffering and God. In the account of Jesus' passion, Luke was to show the seriousness of the sin and the love of the one who agreed to face it in order to free us from it (22:37, 39-46). In the story of the prodigal child, he was to describe the inescapable requirement of taking stock of oneself (15:17-20). If human beings do not undertake that existential step, they will lose their way.[51] When they repent, they will understand that their fate depends not on their sin but on God's forgiveness. Repenting and believing do not mean avoiding death and judgment but facing death in another way and facing up to God's judgment with confidence.

The Winegrower's Intercession (vv. 6-9)

■ **6** In order to back up the sayings that he addressed to "them," the Lukan Jesus offers them a parable, as in 12:16. Less impassioned than threats, the parable would perhaps encourage reflection and decision, thus getting rid of all defensive tension.[52] The use of the Greek imperfect tense, $\mathring{\epsilon}\lambda\epsilon\gamma\epsilon\nu$ ("he told"), is correct for describing a speech sustained for a certain length of time (the aorist $\epsilon\mathring{\iota}\pi\epsilon\nu$, "he said," on the other hand, serves to introduce a short speech, occurring, for example, in a narrative complex).[53] The entire introduction is typically redactional and recalls both 4:23 and 5:36, as well as 12:16.[54]

The parable itself does not begin with any expression of comparison, so it is left up to readers to make the transfer at their own discretion.[55] What comes first, for emphasis,[56] is the statement of what is at stake: a fig tree ($\sigma\upsilon\kappa\mathring{\eta}$),[57] the property of a man ($\epsilon\mathring{\iota}\chi\epsilon\nu$, "he had," has the strong sense of "he possessed"). The description of the fig tree is as precise as that of the owner is vague.[58] To get an idea of how the story is organized, it suffices for the reader to know that this man did not get what he was expecting. The fig tree, as it happened, was planted[59]

50   See Werner Georg Kümmel, "Luc en accusation dans la théologie contemporaine," in Frans Neirynck, *The Gospel of Luke: Revised and Enlarged Edition of L'Évangile de Luc. Problèmes littéraires et théologiques* (2d ed.; BETL 32; Leuven: Leuven University Press, 1989) 3–19. The reviews analyzed by this author are slightly different from the ones I list, but they are similar in describing the loss of soteriological substance of the cross, the return of natural theology, and most of all the historicization of the message, which bestows guarantees to faith.

51   Young's article ("Luke 13, 1-9," 59–63) is important from a theological point of view. It finds in these verses a new way of seeing time, an interpretation that is neither afraid of the world, nor apolitical. There are historical accidents that can become integrative parts of the gospel message. Luke integrates the problem of evil in the vision of God.

52   On this aspect of the parable, see François Bovon, "Parabole d'Évangile, parabole du Royaume," *RThPh* 122 (1990) 33–41.

53   See BDF §329.

54   See Jeremias, *Sprache*, 227. On the Lukan conception of the parable, see the commentary on 4:23 and 8:4 n. 17 in vol. 1.

55   On this form of parable, see Dupont, *Pourquoi des*

paraboles, 40; Harnisch, *Gleichniserzählungen Jesu*, 67–68, 71–72.

56   See Jülicher, *Gleichnisreden*, 2:433.

57   On this tree, see Reichmann, "Feige," 640–89; Pirot, *Paraboles*, 244–45; Jeremias, *Parables*, 170. For the fig tree in the Bible, see Isa 28:4; Jer 8:13; 24:2-10; Hos 9:10; Joel 1:11-12; Prov 27:18; on the scriptural background, see Ternant, "L'homme," 41; Derrett, "Figtrees," in *Studies*, 2:148–64. For Jeremias (*Parables*, 170–71), the parable of the fig tree is addressed to all Israel; see Godet, 2:171. According to Wrembek ("Fünf Weinberg-Gleichnisse," 270), one ought to distinguish the vine, which represents Israel, from the fig tree, which symbolizes a group, either the disciples or the leaders of the people. For Grundmann (227), the fig tree probably corresponds to Jerusalem.

58   The indefinite $\tau\iota\varsigma$ is similar to the $\mathring{\alpha}\nu\vartheta\rho\omega\pi o\varsigma\ \tau\iota\varsigma$ of other parables (e.g., 12:16; 15:11; 16:1, 19), according to Jülicher, *Gleichnisreden*, 2:433. Origen (*Hom. in Jer.* 18.5) calls the owner $o\mathring{\iota}\kappa o\delta\epsilon\sigma\pi\acute{o}\tau\eta\varsigma$, "the master of the house," or "landlord."

59   The perfect participle aims more at the present situation than the past act; see J Reiling and J. L. Swellengrebel, *A Translator's Handbook on the Gospel of Luke* (Brill Archive; Leiden: Brill, 1971), 502.

in a vineyard. There is nothing unusual about that; Deut 22:9 forbade sowing in a vineyard but not in a mixed plantation,[60] which was commonly done in Palestine. The Greek shifts from an imperfect describing possession ($\epsilon\hat{\iota}\chi\epsilon\nu$, "had," v. 6a) to an aorist describing the unfruitful quest ($\epsilon\hat{\upsilon}\rho\epsilon\nu$, "found," v. 6b).[61] What good is it to own something that will disappoint the hope one has put in it and uselessly occupy a valuable spot? In two juxtaposed clauses, Luke passes from a promising possession to an unfulfilled promise.

■ **7** The opinion of the owner, the character in the parable, then follows that of Jesus, who is speaking. The man tells his winegrower what the listener already knows. These words, which constitute the beginning of the dialogue, are nevertheless not just repetition. They also furnish some details: the owner claims to have waited patiently for a long time (the three years that are mentioned are to be added to the first years of maturation that would normally be expected before the tree would bear fruit [see Lev 19:23]). His words also function as a means of moving the story line along: he adds that he is thinking of cutting the tree down. Codex Bezae (D) inserts the words "bring the ax" before the "cut it down," which makes the outlook even gloomier. The tree is doubly guilty: not only does it not produce the fruit the owner has been counting on but, what is more,[62] it impoverishes the soil with its roots using up resources.[63] So it is useless. What good is a fig tree without figs? The owner's disappointment is understandable; his intention, reasonable.[64] Up to this point everything is within the range of normality.[65]

■ **8** The second part of the parable hides the surprise. It is entirely taken up by the winegrower[66] or, more exactly, by the winegrower's intercession.[67] Corresponding to the

---

60 With Jülicher, *Gleichnisreden*, 2:434, and contra Wrembek, "Fünf Weinberg-Gleichnisse," 270. See Loisy, 362.

61 "To look for," "to go to look for," is the natural activity of a landlord. Jülicher (*Gleichnisreden*, 2:434) advises against allegorizing.

62 One must not forget the $\kappa\alpha\acute{\iota}$, after $\acute{\iota}\nu\alpha\tau\acute{\iota}$: "Why let it *even* use up the soil?"

63 $K\alpha\tau\alpha\rho\gamma\epsilon\hat{\iota}$· The verb $\kappa\alpha\tau\alpha\rho\gamma\acute{\epsilon}\omega$ literally means "to leave land fallow," then "to render inactive," "to render useless," "to abolish." Here the verb is taken in its proper sense: "to deplete" the soil. See BAGD, s.v.; Jeremias, *Parables*, 170: "A figtree absorbs a specially large amount of nourishment." Jülicher (*Gleichnisreden*, 2:436) refers to Theophrastus *De caus. plant.* 2.7.4 and 3.10.6–8 (the roots dry up the soil and the leaves provide shade). Jülicher also points to the irritation of the landlord (*Gleichnisreden*, 2:435). Ἵνα τί ("why?" "for what purpose?") became, at the time, an interrogative particle and could be written as one word; see BAGD, s.v.

64 See Prov 27:18: "He who tends to his fig tree will eat its fruits." Among the rules of war was, "Has anyone planted a vineyard but not yet enjoyed its fruit? He should go back to his house, or he might die in the battle and another be first to enjoy its fruit" (Deut 20:6 *NRSV*). On the reasonable suggestion to cut it down, see Jülicher, *Gleichnisreden*, 2:435; Pirot, *Paraboles*, 243. Another rule of warfare is found in Deut 20:19: "If you besiege a town for a long time . . . you must not destroy its trees by wielding an ax against them. Although you may take food

from them, you must not cut them down" (*NRSV*). In the LXX, this last verbal form is $\acute{\epsilon}\kappa\kappa\acute{o}\psi\epsilon\iota\varsigma$ ("to pull down" or "to cut down"), as in Luke 13:9. One recalls the message of John the Baptist in Luke 3:7-9.

65 See *Gen. Rab.* 5.9 on Gen 1:11: on the curse of the land. From then on, the land that had produced fruit trees only produced trees *bearing* fruit, and not all of which were edible. The disobedience of the land prefigures that of humans. Both are associated with a story involving a tree; see Kahn, "La parabole du figuier," 42–45.

66 The word $\dot{\alpha}\mu\pi\epsilon\lambda o\nu\rho\gamma\acute{o}\varsigma$, literally "one who works [$\acute{\epsilon}\rho\gamma o\nu$, "work"] the vineyard [$\acute{\alpha}\mu\pi\epsilon\lambda o\varsigma$, "vine stock," $\dot{\alpha}\mu\pi\epsilon\lambda\acute{\omega}\nu$, "vineyard"]," hence the "winegrower." It is a *hapax legomenon* in the NT, but the word appears four times in the LXX, always in the plural (2 Kgs [4 Kgdms] 25:12; 2 Chr 26:10; Isa 61:5; Jer 52:16), where it is the translation of כֹּרְם, also in the plural. Philo uses this word in his treatise *De plantatione* 1; Lucian of Samosata (*Philops.* 11) uses it for the slave of a rich man. The word is attested as early as Aristophanes; see Moulton and Milligan, *Vocabulary*, s.v.; BAGD, s.v.; Jülicher, *Gleichnisreden*, 2:434.

67 The introduction ὁ δὲ ἀποκριθεὶς λέγει αὐτῷ ("he, responding, said to him"), translated as "he made this response," is not Lukan; the historical present λέγει ("he said"), in particular, orients the tone to a traditional formula; see Jeremias, *Sprache*, 227.

owner's disappointment, first recounted by Jesus, then expressed by the character himself,[68] is the winegrower's insistent request.[69] The structure of the parable is as follows: (a) a statement of the lamentable situation (b) provokes the disappointment of the owner, who wishes to use harsh measures; (c) then comes the intercession of the winegrower, who wishes to try everything possible in order to save the fig tree and also wishes still to keep all hope alive. The unexpected element is that the story does not end on a note of disappointment; although the intercessor was hierarchically inferior, on the level of the narrative he was the winner. The parable contemporizes the biblical formula of the God who is stronger but who restrains his anger at the generous request of the spokesperson, the prophet, the one who is weaker.[70] Persuasion triumphs over authoritarian decision making, and the lesser causes the greater to relent. It is a case of hope winning out against all hope, of the victory of the last chance that is offered,[71] of the unaccustomed and of surprise.[72] If we were to compare the fig tree to humans,

we would say that the parable expresses the confidence that is still granted them and the hope that they arouse. If, on the other hand, we compare humans with the character of the winegrower, we learn that they bear a great responsibility, that they need to practice solidarity, and that their intercession is always effective.

What makes the character of the winegrower loom large is that he was not satisfied with merely asking the owner[73] for an extension of time, nor was he content with attributing the responsibility to the tree alone. No, he did more than just beg, situated as he was between the property owner and the property. He wanted to get personally involved. Taking as its starting point Israel's love of trees and the peasants' love of what they have sown and planted, the text has the winegrower involved beyond the level of his intercession. He was willing to collaborate in saving the fig tree by performing two tasks that would concretize his solidarity with it, namely, providing drink and food for the tree. By digging[74] around the tree, as is still done in our time in the case

---

68 The present ἔρχομαι ("I am coming") is stronger than "I came." It means "I come regularly." See Jülicher, *Gleichnisreden*, 2:435. Undoubtedly he came back for the fourth time, according to Jülicher (ibid.). Instead I follow Cyril of Alexandria (*Hom. in Luc.* 96; see Reuss, *Lukas-Kommentare*, 152), who thinks that this is his third visit: the master has had enough of this, because since the time that the tree should have borne fruit, our man has come a first time at the end of one year, a second time after two years, and this particular day after three years. He thus expresses his unmet expectations and his discontent.

69 What motivates the winegrower is not his natural optimism but, as in Isa 5:1-7, his affection for his trees and his vineyard, an attachment that is frequently attested and easily comprehensible when one is familiar with the time and effort it requires to cultivate fruit trees. See n. 64 above; and Kahlefeld, *Parables*, 68–70.

70 The intercession begins, in the vocative, with the imperative ἄφες ("leave"), which one finds in the LXX in 2 Kgs [4 Kgdms] 4:27. See Dan 4:15 LXX and Theodotion 23. Philo (*Det. pot. ins.* 105–8) precisely indicates the care that a good cultivator must take with trees.

71 One finds the expression ἕως ὅτου ("until," "as long as," "at the time when") also in 12:50 and 22:16; see 15:8 and 22:18. But it never appears in Acts.

72 Whether influenced by our parable or not, there exists a certain magical practice that one finds in several countries. To make a barren tree produce fruit, two people come to the foot of the tree and play out the following scene: the first person, with ax in hand, prepares to deliver the first blow when the second intercedes on the tree's behalf. The scene is repeated three times. After this, the tree is supposed to have understood what it is supposed to do; see Slee, "Note," 77–78; Derrett, "Figtrees," in *Studies*, 2:158–59.

73 One cannot help but compare the owner and winegrower to God and Christ, as with the parable of the murderous tenants regarding the vineyard owner and his own son (Luke 20:9, 13-15), without, however, equating them, as a proponent of allegory would do.

74 Σκάπτω ("to plow," "to dig"); one plows the soil to break it up before putting a plant or tree in the ground; the verb can also describe the action of a gardener who digs the soil around a tree (or around vegetables before pulling them up). See the first Homeric hymn to Hermes, 90; Xenophon *Oecon.* 20.20; Peter of Alexandria *Ep. can.* 3. Clement of Alexandria (*Strom.* 2.18.95) recalls that this action accompanies another—that of removing suckers. See Ps 80 (79):8-9, in which Israel is compared to a vine: "You brought a vine out of Egypt; you drove out the nations and planted it. You cleared the

of olive trees, the humidity, so rare and so necessary for the growth of the fruit that was counted on, would be retained. By putting manure[75] on it, a very unusual procedure, he would demonstrate[76] the intensity of his commitment and his hope, thereby acting in a way similar to parents of a sick child, who do everything they can to save their child.

If the master were to accept the proposition, he would have to give the winegrower an extension of at least a year,[77] enough time to respect the cycle of seasons. During this time,[78] the tree would have a chance[79] to bear fruit (up to here the point of view presented has been that of the owner, who was looking for fruit without finding any (vv. 6 and 7); here we are now presented with the perspective of the fig tree, which was invited to "bear," literally to "make fruit in the future" (v. 9).[80]

9 After all these efforts, following on the disappointed patience of the owner and the active intercession of the winegrower,[81] what is the result going to be? If it comes to nothing, then the ax will fall. Hope is expressed against a backdrop of risk. The final saying is as cutting as the edge of an ax: "if not,[82] you can cut it down."[83] A word to the wise is sufficient![84] It is up to the tree alone to prevent itself from being cut down.[85]

History of Interpretation

In a chapter in which he defended the worth of the Gospel of Luke, Irenaeus, bishop of Lyons, summarized the parable in a sentence (*Adv. haer.* 3.13.3). Further on, he defended the one God, author of the two testaments, with the help of parables, including the one about the

ground for it; it took deep root and filled the land" (*NRSV*). The LXX, which thinks more of Israel than a tree, translates "clear the ground" with the verb ὁδοποιέω, "to make a path."

75 Codex Bezae (D) specifies a "basket of manure." There exists ἡ κοπρία, ("pile of manure," "manure"), the κόπρος, ("manure"), and τὸ κόπριον ("manure," "the pile of manure," "pile of filth"). In the plural τὰ κόπρια means the same as here, "manure" (from large livestock, undoubtedly, even if they are rare in Palestine). See Jer 25 (LXX 32):33; Sir 22:2; *Hermas Sim.* 9.10.3; Epictetus *Diss.* 2.4.5; Jülicher, *Gleichnisreden,* 2:437; Pirot, *Paraboles,* 245; Jeremias, *Parables,* 170. The fig is a tree that that does not have complicated needs; one should water it from time to time, if possible.

76 On the extravagant side of parabolic stories, see Harnisch, *Gleichniserzählungen Jesu,* 141–51; on the unexpected here, see Pirot, *Paraboles,* 245; Ternant, "L'homme," 37.

77 Some have identified this year with the year of the Lord's favor of 4:19; see Jülicher, *Gleichnisreden,* 2:437.

78 It is about a final granted delay, an ultimatum, that provides an apocalyptic coloring to the parable. Nevertheless, one cannot know if Luke senses an imminence to this year. For him, it is the ultimate event that counts and not the duration of the offer.

79 The subjunctive after κἄν (= καὶ ἐάν "and so") here carries a conditional significance, not concessive; see BDF §374 n. 4. Note the two inverse possibilities, marked by μέν . . . δέ, and the omission of the principal after the first possibility (implying "all is well," "so much the better"), called in rhetoric apo-

siopesis; see Jülicher, *Gleichnisreden,* 2:438; Plummer, 340; Lagrange, 381. Delebecque (89) thinks that this omission corresponds to an Attic turn of phrase for which he provides a list of examples.

80 Numerous manuscripts add the words "in the future" to the rest and places them after "if this is not the case," "if not." It is necessary to keep the order of Nestle-Aland[26] and to observe the seriousness of the expression: the fig tree not only has to provide some fruit one time but must produce it regularly "in the future"; see Jülicher, *Gleichnisreden,* 2:439.

81 Jülicher (*Gleichnisreden,* 438–39) writes, "Die zarteste Nüancierung unterscheidet durch ἄφες und ἐκκόψεις neben σκάψω und βάλω das, was aus der Initiative des Herrn und das, was aus der des Knechtes hervorgehen muss."

82 The words εἰ δὲ μή γε ("if this is not the case," in the sense of "if not") had long been an idiomatic expression.

83 The winegrower, without being explicitly characterized as a servant, nevertheless depends on orders from the owner. It is the latter who is able to give the order to take down the tree.

84 I had written these words spontaneously when I realized that some scribes had reacted in the same way, adding here: "having pronounced these words, he exclaimed to himself: someone who has ears, listen!" See the apparatus of Nestle-Aland[26].

85 The text is interrupted, brusquely, with this proposition of the winegrower: in this way the readers themselves are invited to return to God.

fig tree. He focused on the three visits by the master to pick fruit; these three visits were made, in his opinion, through the intermediary of the prophets. He appears to have presupposed the failure of the final step (still to come in the biblical text) and the cutting down of the tree (4.36.8). This same severity toward the Jewish people is found also in the writings of Ambrose of Milan and Cyril of Alexandria.

For Ambrose (*Exp. Luc.* 7.160–71), the fig tree symbolized the synagogue, the masters of which had nothing to show off but unfruitful leaves. He made two comments on the fig tree: (a) Unlike other trees, the fig tree bears fruit at two different times; the first harvest, which is mediocre, corresponds to what the synagogue has produced; the second, benefiting from summer weather, is more abundant and corresponds to the production of the church. (b) Adam and Eve covered themselves with fig leaves when they became aware of their transgression: they foreshadowed the synagogue, capable of producing leaves but no fruit. Ambrose, whose anti-Judaism is to be criticized, had a lively awareness of salvation history and its stages: to the classical succession of the synagogue and the church, he added some details: the three visits by the master correspond to the visit by God in Abraham (circumcision), in Moses (law) and in Mary (grace). The end of the year (v. 8) designates the decline of the aging world. Ambrose did not give up hope on this synagogue, which he otherwise condemns: the winegrower who digs is Christian preaching that is effective, thanks to the apostles' pickax; and the manure that one puts on it refers to Job, who, seated on a heap of dung and ashes, resisted temptation (Job 2:8), and Paul, who, in order to gain Christ, considered what he had lost as rubbish (Phil 3:8). Ambrose likewise warned the church that it, too, must struggle against fruitlessness.

Cyril of Alexandria (*Hom. in Luc.* 96)[86] used vv. 1-5 to criticize blood sacrifices, and he reeled off a string of biblical quotations relating to vv. 6-9 in order to explain the identity of the fig tree (a process that was often used again). Cyril divided salvation history differently than Ambrose: the first visit of the peasant corresponds to Moses and Aaron; the second, to Joshua and the judges;

the third, to the prophets down to John the Baptist. Intrigued by the story, Cyril wondered who the winegrower was. Touched by the winegrower's plea to his master, he first suggested seeing in him Israel's guardian angel (he quoted Zech 1:12 and Exod 14:19-20), then Christ, who we know is our advocate before the Father (he quoted 1 John 2:1 at this point). It was this intervention by Christ that he stressed, Christ who had come, on a fourth visit, not only to intercede but also to shake up Israel (an allusion to vv. 1-5) and to promise salvation to those who would believe in him. Harsh at first, then happy, he concluded that Christ's last mission to Israel failed, and that the tree was cut down and that the shoot constituted by the church would grow gloriously.

In the Middle Ages, the anti-Jewish controversy faded, at least in the writings of certain authors. The fig tree could represent the human race, as was the case in the writings of the Venerable Bede (*In Luc.* 4.1379–82), or the human soul, especially in Bonaventure's writings (*Comm. in Luc.* 13.11–20). For this Doctor of the Church, while the fig tree is the soul needing to do penance, the vineyard is the ecclesial community (the social and religious reality had changed in a thousand years). Henceforth everything is focused on the fate of the individual: the three years designate childhood, youth, and adulthood; the extension of time is to be seen in the fourth, old age, before death. The individual is helped by the winegrower, who here is not Christ but the preacher, or, better, the ecclesiastical dignitary.[87] It will be noted that in Otto III's Evangeliary, painted in the monastery on Reichenau around the year 1000, the master of the vineyard is represented by Christ followed by Peter and two other apostles, while an agricultural worker is prosaically and energetically taking care of the fig tree, in leaf but without fruit, invaded by the vine branches of the neighboring vineyard. The winegrower, barefoot, turns over the earth around the tree and looks toward the Lord, who is obviously giving him orders. As with Bonaventure, the winegrower represents the preacher or the priest who takes care of the faithful under the orders of his master, Christ.[88]

We have access to a rich trove of materials from the

---

86   See Payne Smith, *Cyril*, 2:446–50.
87   Bonaventure later gives an allegorical meaning, then a moral one, to the parable.
88   See Goetz, *Der Feigenbaum*, 73–74, and illustration no. 41.

sixteenth century, thanks to an unusually helpful reference tool bearing the name *Critici sacri*, published in London in 1660 (a new, augmented, edition appeared in 1698 in Amsterdam).[89] It contained long extracts from some fifteen recent commentaries. In it the reader could find comparisons between the Vulgate and the Greek text, the basic notions of textual criticism, some remarks on style (several commentators call attention to the aposiopesis in v. 9), historical references to Josephus, philological comments (Henri Estienne pointing out the meaning of καταργεῖ [v. 7], which I have translated as "waste"; Drusius unveiling treasures of erudition on Siloam), the lion's share belonging here to Hugo Grotius, who, speaking of the Greek text, impresses us by his judgment and his knowledge. He thought that the vineyard represents the human race, and the fig tree, Israel. He considered the term "debtors" to be a Semitism (*syrismus*, to use his term). He mentioned, in connection with the fate of the fig tree, a parallel in Epictetus *Diss.* 1.15. He thought that the massacre of the Galileans took place during the feast of Passover.

Without their being quoted in the *Critici sacri*, Calvin and Zwingli each have something original to offer. We regret the fact that Zwingli failed to pay attention to the winegrower's efforts; but he did identify (before Wellhausen!) the episode about the Galileans with the massacre on Mount Gerizim ordered by Pilate, as Josephus reported it (*Ant.* 18.4.1–2 §§85–89).[90] Calvin, on the other hand, sensitive to God's patience, to our unfortunate habit of judging others, and to the advantage that there would be to us of preventing God's plagues by being willingly penitent, spoke not about massacred Galileans but about Samaritans.[91] Without explaining his reasons on this point, he must have shared the opinion of Zwingli and the Jesuit scholar Juan Maldonado, since Josephus spoke of a massacre of Samaritans on Mount Gerizim.

Maldonado (*Comm. in quat.* 13.1–9)[92] provided the most impressive commentary on Luke 13:1-9. He wrote six long columns of a magnificent folio on the subject. He discussed in particular the passages from Josephus and Hegesippus concerning the massacre of the Samaritans and concluded that it must have been the same episode as the one spoken of by Luke in 13:1. He explained that Luke's Galileans were in fact Samaritans. As for the parable, he thought that it speaks for itself and that it does not require any long commentary. He did, however, pay attention to three elements: (a) the fact that the fruit that the fig tree was lacking is good works; (b) that God has been patient; and (c) that if humans do not convert, they will end up in the eternal fire. All the rest is but an embellishment, in other words, literature. Nonetheless, he followed up with an impressive series of patristic references to the fig tree, identified with the church, and the like.

In 1653, at Oxford, Henry Hammond published a little-known commentary in English, rather than in Latin, the language previously used for commentaries.[93] When he came to Luke 13:1-9, he did not go beyond repeating the story, here and there adding an explanation, for example, in the case of the Galileans, whose identity bothered him, just as it had intrigued his predecessors. His paraphrase interpreted the parable in a christological sense: the people had been ungrateful; God gave them a time limit during which they had to convert; he sent his Son in order to prune them and to give them fertilizer; if this action remained without effect, then they could expect nothing but destruction.

Conclusion

From 12:54 on, through Jesus' voice, Luke has been inviting readers to become Christians, Christians whose faith bears fruit. In 13:1-9, he works into that urgent invitation a reflection on the times in which they are living.

Christians do not escape history and its vagaries any more than do other human beings. There are, however, both good and bad ways to process accidents and misfor-

89 John Pearson, *Critici sacri sive doctiss. virorum in ss. Biblia annotationes et tractatus* (9 vols.; London: Jacobus Flesher, 1660; new augmented ed., Amsterdam: Henricus & Vidua Theodori Boom, Joannes & Ægidius Janssonii à Waesberge, et al., 1698) 6, *Ann. Ev. Luc.* 13, 551–61 (1698 edition).

90 Zwingli, *Annotationes*, 661–62.

91 Calvin, *Harmony*, 2:94–96.

92 Maldonado, pp. 122–26 of the 1597 edition.

93 Henry Hammond, *A Paraphrase and Annotations upon All the Books of the New Testament* (2d ed.; London: J. Flesher for R. Davis, 1659) 234 on Luke 13:1–9.

tunes. The bad way corresponds to the doctrine of Job's friends;[94] the good way, to Jesus' theology. The bad way seeks to dissociate the thinking subject from the times in which he or she lives and to attribute guilt to other persons by tying them to their own past. The good way consists in getting involved in history and leaving the future up to God. Conversion, if that is what we must call that Copernican revolution of the self that decides to "revolve around" God, does not withdraw us from temporality in order to move us toward some spiritual sanctuary, but transforms our perception of time and awakens our sense of responsibility.

The Lukan perspective is aimed at the individual believer, to be sure, since no one can ask someone else to take his or her place in engaging in "conversion," "repentance" ($\mu\epsilon\tau\acute{a}\nu o\iota\alpha$), but that personal orientation is fruitful only in the context of community. Besides the plurals in Jesus' threats (vv. 3 and 5), there is the juxtaposition of Galileans and Jerusalemites, the two parts of God's people, from the earliest times up to the day Jesus traveled from Galilee toward Judea. And then there are the images of the vineyard and the fig tree.

The Hebrew Bible is rich in metaphors, parables, and allegories that draw a picture of life and death, and the promises and the disappointments of certain plants and certain trees. While the vineyard often stands for the people of Israel[95] (we should not forget that it is in the vineyard that the fig tree grows, in v. 6), the fig tree does not carry the load of that symbolic association in the Hebrew Bible. Joel, describing contemporary misfortunes, spoke of the withered fig tree alongside the starved vine (Joel 1:11-12). Jeremiah distinguished, in his baskets of figs, between the good figs (the deported believers) and the bad ones (the unworthy refugees in the land or in Egypt) (Jer 24:1-10). Micah and Hosea complained that Israel's tree did not bear any good fruit (Mic 7:1; Hos 9:10; 10:1). Here and there, the prophets

of doom announced that Israel, like a tree, would be cut down, uprooted, or burned as a punishment for her ungodliness (e.g., Isa 5:5-7; Ezek 19:10-14; *1 Enoch* 26). Jesus bought into this symbolism, which lends itself to making comparisons between either the people or the believer, on the one hand, and a living tree or a declining one, on the other.[96]

The text of Luke 13:1-9 makes a subtle distinction between the vineyard and the fig tree.[97] As the vineyard moves into the background, attention shifts to the fig tree. Perhaps Luke saw in it a group of humans who are still hesitant or recalcitrant. While he was certainly not thinking of church leaders, could he have been thinking of Gentiles planted in the garden of Israel? Now, according to him, the fig tree was not condemned. On the contrary, the message is such that it was perhaps given another chance. This was an unexpected opportunity that the fig tree needed to take advantage of; it needed to live by its faith, the producer of love.

In my opinion, while the call to commitment is one of the poles of this pericope, especially in the first part, vv. 1-5, it is not the most important one in the second part, vv. 6–9. There Luke, in the guise of the owner and his winegrower, was content to sketch a theology and a soteriology. We would be negligent, in my opinion, if we did not pay attention to this underlying line of thought. On the one hand, we have a Creator God, giver of life, attentive to his people's attitude, who, in the end, was disappointed by the negative responses of his protégé. A God, then, like the one in the prophetic oracles of judgment, whose disappointed love thinks no further than being done with those he had chosen. On the other hand, we have a God who allows himself to yield and who wants to maintain his life plan. To be sure, there were always some prophets who would intercede with God so that he would be merciful.[98] On rare occasions, however, the figure of the intercessor took on the dimensions of

---

94   See, e.g., Job 4:7-9; 8:3-4; 15:34-35.
95   Either the "vine stock" (גֶּפֶן) (Jer 2:21; 5:17; 6:9; Ezek 19:10-14, etc.) or the "vineyard" itself (כֶּרֶם) (Isa 3:14; 5:1-7; 27:2-5; Jer 12:10, etc.). Note that גֶּפֶן, which first signifies the "vine stock," can also designate the "vineyard" by extension. In the NT, see Matt 20:1-16; 21:28-32; 21:33-46 par. Mark 12:1-12 par. Luke 20:9-19; John 15:1-8; 1 Cor 9:7; Rev 14:17-20.

96   See Ps 1:3 for the individual, Ps 80:8-13 (LXX 79:9-14) for the people.
97   The association of the vineyard and the fig tree is, as we have seen, traditional; see Hos 9:10 and, in the NT, Jas 3:12.
98   See n. 16 above.

the winegrower in this pericope who was willing to give the best of himself in order to save the fig tree. This is a Christology of intercessory compassion and of hope, offering good conditions for recovery. The winegrower interceded in order to obtain an extension of time. With the due date being pushed back, the time could become a very positive factor: it could open up the window of opportunity needed for human beings to achieve the necessary transformation of their lives. At this point the winegrower (Christ!) resolves to act and to do everything he can so that the fig tree will escape from its state of fruitlessness. For Luke, Christ needed to intercede first of all in order for God to grant time conducive for salvation to take place. Then God could do what was necessary. This sequence can be explained in terms of the responsibility Luke assigns to human beings: by their "conversion," "repentance" ($\mu\epsilon\tau\acute{\alpha}\nu o\iota\alpha$), they enter into the process of salvation that the Father wills and the Son facilitates, a process in which they take part when they welcome the good news.

In summary, the winegrower fills an important function, which serves no purpose, however, unless the fig tree bears fruit and the owner is willing to be patient for a longer period of time. Will each one do his or her share? The parable ends neither on a note of euphoria nor on one of catastrophe. It remains unfinished, leaving a shadow of uncertainty hanging over the situation, but above all allowing for a large degree of hope.

God Straightens Up Bodies and Liberates People (13:10-17)

Bibliography

Bauer, Andrea, "Lukas 13, 10-17: Die Heilung einer gekrümmten Frau," in Eva Renate Schmidt, Mieke Korenhof and Renate Jost, eds., *Feministisch gelesen*, I: *32 ausgewählte Bibeltexte für Gruppen, Gemeinden und Gottesdienste* (Stuttgart: Kreuz Verlag, 1988) 210–16.

Bernhard, Thomas, Sr., "Women's Ministry in the Church: A Lukan Perspective," *SLJT* 29 (1986) 261–63.

Bultmann, *History*, 12–13, 62.

Burchard, Christoph, "Fussnoten zum neutestamentlichen Griechisch II," *ZNW* 69 (1978) 143–57, esp. 146–49.

Busse, Ulrich, *Die Wunder des Propheten Jesus: Die Rezeption, Komposition und Interpretation der Wundertradition im Evangelium des Lukas* (FB 24; Stuttgart: Katholisches Bibelwerk, 1977).

Derrett, J. Duncan M., "Positive Perspectives on Two Lucan Miracles," *DRev* 104 (1986) 272–87.

Dibelius, *Tradition*, 97–98.

Dietzfelbinger, Christian, "Vom Sinn der Sabbatheilungen Jesu," *EvTh* 38 (1978) 281–98.

Glöckner, Richard, *Neutestamentliche Wundergeschichten und das Lob der Wundertaten Gottes in den Psalmen: Studien zur sprachlichen und theologischen Verwandtschaft zwischen neutestamentlichen Wundergeschichten und Psalmen* (WSAMA. T 13; Mainz: Matthias-Grünewald, 1983) 105–24.

Green, Joel B., "Jesus and a Daughter of Abraham (Luke 13:10-17): Test Case for a Lucan Perspective on Jesus' Miracles," *CBQ* 51 (1989) 643–54.

Haenchen, Ernst, *Der Weg Jesu: Eine Erklärung des Markus-Evangeliums und der kanonischen Parallelen* (2d ed.; De Gruyter Lehrbuch; Berlin: de Gruyter, 1968) 123–29.

Hamm, M. Dennis, "The Freeing of the Bent Woman and the Restoration of Israel: Luke 13:10-17 as Narrative Theology," *JSNT* 31 (1987) 23–44.

Jeremias, *Sprache*, 228–30.

Kirchschläger, *Wirken*, 242–48.

Klein, Hans, *Barmherzigkeit gegenüber der Elenden und Geächteten: Stüdien zur Botschaft des lukanischen Sondergutes* (BThSt 10; Neukirchen-Vluyn: Neukirchener Verlag, 1987) 17–23.

Klinghardt, *Gesetz*, 231–32.

Kopas, Jane, "Jesus and Women in Luke's Gospel," *ThTo* 43 (1986) 192–202.

La Potterie, Ignace de, "Le titre KYRIOS appliqué à Jésus dans l'évangile de Luc," in Descamps and de Halleux, *Mélanges*, 117–46, esp. 132–34.

La Roche, Käthi, "Die Frau mit dem verkrümmten Rücken," *Neue Wege* 7 (1985) 181–83.

Lohse, Eduard, "Jesu Worte über den Sabbat," in Walther Eltester, ed., *Judentum, Urchristentum, Kirche: Festschrift Joachim Jeremias* (BZNW 26; Berlin: Töpelmann, 1960) 79–89.

Loos, Hendrik van der, *The Miracles of Jesus* (NovTSup 9; Leiden: Brill, 1965) 148–50, 216, 520, 522 and passim.

Milot, Louise, "Guérison d'une femme infirme un jour de sabbat (Lc 13, 10-17): L'importance d'une comparaison," *SémBib* 39 (1985) 23–33.

Moltmann-Wendel, Elisabeth, "Die Geschichte von der gekrümmten Frau," *Neue Wege* 7–8 (1983) 193–96.

Neirynck, Frans, "Jesus and the Sabbath: Some Observations on Mark II, 27," in Jacques Dupont et al., eds., *Jésus aux origines de la christologie* (BETL 40; Leuven: Leuven University Press, 1975; 2d ed., 1989) 227–70.

O'Toole, Robert F., "Some Exegetical Reflections on Luke 13,10-17," *Bib* 73 (1992) 84–107.

Petzke, *Sondergut*, 125–28.

Radl, Walter, "Ein 'doppeltes Leiden' in Lk 13, 11? Zu einer Notiz von G. Schwarz," *BN* 31 (1986) 35–36.

Rinaldi, B., "La liberazione di Cristo è da Satana: Gesù e il male," *PaVi* 20 (1975) 96–105.

Roloff, Jürgen, *Das Kerygma und der irdische Jesus: Historische Motive in den Jesus-Erzählungen der Evangelien* (Göttingen: Vandenhoeck & Ruprecht, 1970) 66–69.

Safran, Alexandre, "Le sabbat dans la tradition juive," *RThPh* 3d series 27 (1977) 136–49.

Schüssler Fiorenza, Elisabeth, *But She Said: Feminist Practices of Biblical Interpretation* (Boston: Beacon, 1992) 195–217, 250–55.

Schwarz, Günther, "Καὶ ἦν συγκύπτουσα," *BN* 20 (1983) 58.

Idem, "Λυθῆναι ἀπὸ τοῦ δεσμοῦ τούτου," *BN* 15 (1981) 47.

Steiner, Anton, and Helene Stotzer-Kloo, "Zur Freiheit befreit: Jesus heilt eine behinderte Frau am Sabbat (Lk 13.10-17). Ein Normenwunder," in Anton Steiner and V. Weymann, eds., *Wunder Jesu* (Bibelarbeit in der Gemeinde: Themen und Materialien 2; Zurich/Basel, 1978) 127–46.

Str-B 2:198–200.

Ternant, Paul, "L'homme ne peut empêcher Dieu d'être bon (Lc 13,6-17)," *AsSeign* 72 (1964) 36–52, esp. 48–51.

Theissen, Gerd, *Urchristliche Wundergeschichten: Ein Beitrag zur formgeschichtlichen Erforschung der synoptischen Evangelien* (StNT 8; Gütersloh: Gütersloher Verlagshaus Mohn, 1974) 120–21, 167.

Trautmann, Maria, *Zeichenhafte Handlungen Jesu: Ein Beitrag zur Frage nach dem geschichtlichen Jesu* (FB 37; Würzburg: Echter, 1980) 278–318.

Wahlberg, Rachel C., *Jesus and the Freed Woman* (New York: Paulist Press, 1978).

Wartenberg-Potter, Bärbel von, *Aufrecht und frei: Was Frauen heute in der Bibel entdecken* (2d ed.; Offenbach, 1987) 67–72.

Wilkinson, John, "The Case of the Bent Woman in Luke 13:10-17," *EvQ* 49 (1977) 195–205.

10/ One Sabbath day he was teaching in one of the synagogues. **11/** And just then there appeared a woman having had a spirit of sickness[a] for eighteen years and who was completely bent over and could not stand up straight at all. **12/** Having seen her, Jesus called her over and said to her, "Woman, you are set free from your ailment"; **13/** and he placed his hands on her. Immediately she was straightened up and began praising God. **14/** The leader of the synagogue responded, indignant because Jesus had cured on the Sabbath. He kept saying to the crowd, "There are six days on which work ought to be done; you must come on those days and be cured, and not on the Sabbath day." **15/** But the Lord answered him thus, "You hypocrites! Does not each of you on the Sabbath untie his ox or his donkey from the manger, in order to lead it away to give it water? **16/** But ought not this woman,[b] a daughter of Abraham whom Satan bound for eighteen long years, be set free from this bondage on the Sabbath day?" **17/** And when he said this, all his opponents were put to shame; and the entire crowd was rejoicing at all the wonderful things that were being done by him.

a   Literally: "weakness."
b   Literally: "this one" (feminine singular demonstrative pronoun used as an adjective, in Greek).

After some sayings, dialogues, and parables, Luke inserts a narrative here. We should avoid misjudging it, however; the miracle narrative is but the first duel in a controversy Jesus carried on with the Judaism of his time. While the Lukan Christ did allow bodies to be straightened up, he also attacked bent consciences. In both cases he appears to be the interpreter and executor of God's will. This narrative, moreover, is placed between two plant-based metaphors, between the fig tree and the mustard seed. This proximity has a powerful effect on the narrative.

Analysis

Analysis of the Composition

An introduction moves Jesus and the reader into a sacred space and a sacred time (v. 10). This shift of locale also explains why, although up until that point Jesus had been speaking,[1] now he is teaching (v. 10). Note the periphrastic form of the verb: the event is going to cling to the duration of time.

1   Since 11:17, λέγω ("to say") has been the exclusive verb that defines the activity of Jesus. Here we have διδάσκω ("to teach"); see 4:15, 31; 5:3, 17; 6:6, and 11:1. Since the teaching in Galilee had been related to the synagogue, here in Jerusalem it will be related to the temple; see 19:47; 20:1, and 21:37.

"And just then" (καὶ ἰδού) is a marker of the beginning of a story or an incident (v. 11).[2] There is an element of surprise, nevertheless, since the incident does not consist of anything happening: all that the reader finds in this verse is a Greek present participle indicating duration ("having had," ἔχουσα) and a new imperfect, also indicating duration ("was completely bent over," ἦν συγκύπτουσα).

What sets the event in motion is Jesus' gaze, rather than the woman, who does not ask for anything: this time there is in Greek an aorist participle ("having seen her," ἰδὼν δὲ αὐτὴν, v. 12), then a verb, also an aorist, which get things moving: Jesus called (note the vocative, "Woman," γύναι) and spoke ("you are set free," ἀπολέλυσαι, v. 12). Then he adds an act to his word and placed his hands on her (v. 13a).

Three words in Greek suffice to express what is a confirmation in deed of Jesus' speech and the doing of Another (note the passive): καὶ παραχρῆμα ἀνωρθώθη, "immediately she was straightened up" (v. 13b).

After the woman is cured (this is not explicitly stated in the text), she begins praising God.[3] Once the punctiliar action has been accomplished, the durative aspect comes back into its own and Luke returns to the use of the Greek imperfect, albeit inceptive at first, but also expressing duration, no longer that of bonds, but of praise (v. 13c).

There is a sudden new development that is not indispensable but is nevertheless understandable (the mention of the synagogue and the Sabbath in v. 10 explains the incisive words in v. 14): the leader of the synagogue responds ("answering," ἀποκριθείς, translated as "responded"), annoyed ("indignant," ἀγανακτῶν). He reminds the assembly of the regulation (v. 14), but, curiously or out of cowardice, not Jesus. In his eyes, what has happened resulted from some *work Jesus had done* on *that day*.

In order to stress his authority, at this point (v. 15) Luke calls "Lord" the one he had called "Jesus" up to this point (v. 14).[4] The Lord answered (ἀπεκρίθη) an answer ("responded," ἀποκριθείς) and reacted after having acted (vv. 12-13a). Oddly enough, Jesus' rejoinder was addressed not to one being but to a collective plural, to persons addressed in the critical vocative "you hypocrites," in short "each of you" (v. 15).[5] This rejoinder recalls an authorized and essential custom (note the present "untie," λύει, v. 15). Like the example, the justification that Jesus drew from it was also expressed in the form of a question; but while the example was didactic (v. 15), the justification was rhetorical, if not ironical (v. 16). Moreover, the example and its application match each other thematically and figuratively: in both cases it is a question of the image of the ties one is authorized to break in order to facilitate life.

Verse 16, which shifts from a comparison to reasoning, is presented with a theological connotation; on the one hand, Satan and the bonds that he ties ("bound," ἔδησεν; "from this bondage," ἀπὸ τοῦ δεσμοῦ τούτου); on the other, the plan ("ought," ἔδει) of God (discreetly signaled by the use of the passive "be set free," λυθῆναι), who frees his people, here a "daughter of Abraham."

So there was a controversy between Jesus and the leader of the synagogue about what could be done on the Sabbath. Jesus made a day of deliverance out of this day; "the leader of the synagogue" (ὁ ἀρχισυνάγωγος) thought that the Sabbath should not be a day for healing (v. 14). Such a critical presentation of the opponent and so favorable a one of Jesus naturally fit the apologetic and polemic attitude of Luke and the tradition he took up.[6]

What was the situation at the end of the story? Luke only refers to Jesus and the woman in a discreet manner, him at the beginning of the last verse (v. 17) and her at the end. He focuses his attention on the participants

---

2   See 1:31, 36; 2:25; 5:12; 7:12, 37; 9:39; 10:25; 11:31, 32, etc.

3   The diversity of the genres explains that one has a response of praise here (v. 13), spoken by the woman, and a demonstration of collective joy at the end (v. 17), expressed by the crowd; see Theissen, *Urchristliche Wundergeschichten,* 167; and above, n. 50.

4   See de la Potterie, "Le titre KYRIOS," 132–34 (in the episodic passages, Luke utilizes "Jesus"; when he

comes to principles he uses "the Lord"). However, there are, in my opinion, some exceptions, e.g., 19:9.

5   See Félix-Marie Abel, *Grammaire du grec biblique suivie d'un choix de papyrus* (2d ed.; EtB; Paris: Gabalda, 1927) §55, the present, a2.

6   See Bultmann (*History,* 12), who classifies our pericope among the controversy dialogues and scholastic dialogues.

in the synagogue service whom he divides up into two groups[7] of unequal size: the opponents were not numerous but were hierarchically superior; the crowd was numerous but without much power. On the one hand, we have those designated as opponents, who were reduced to silence by Jesus' power of persuasion but who did not let themselves be convinced for all that. From that point on they were left with nothing but shame. On the other hand, we have the people, who were doubly amazed by the miracle and the convincing line of argumentation and who quite simply rejoiced.[8] The idea of duration appears again here in the narrative (the use of two Greek imperfects).[9] As for the leader of the synagogue, we do not know if he, too, agreed to be freed of his shackles.

This brief presentation of two events, the miracle and the controversy, placed in the context of duration of time, brings to light the unity of the text, a unity that recent commentators have been fond of accepting. Dennis Hamm, for example, thinks that the two "encounters" are organically linked; Joel B. Green refuses to attach more importance to the dialogue than to the miracle; and Jean-Noël Aletti views Jesus' words (vv. 15-16) as the high point of the passage, considering them to be part of the logical link between the performance and the discussion.[10] In order to visualize the scene, I propose the following schema:

Duration
1. Opening, Jesus' situation (v. 10)
2. Description of the woman (v. 11)

Event
3. Jesus' speech (vv. 12-13a)
4. God's act (v. 13b)

Duration
5. Reaction of the cured woman: praise (v. 13c)

Event
6. Reaction on the part of the leader of the synagogue (v. 14)
7. New speech by Jesus (vv. 15-16)

Duration
8. Division among the hearers (shame and joy). Conclusion (v. 17)

Analysis of How the Text Came into Being

This homogeneous text has no exact parallel in the other Gospels. There are, however, other texts related to it by virtue of their treatment of the same problem concerning the Sabbath. They have been preserved by Luke himself or by the other Gospel writers. The ones in question are the accounts of the man with the withered hand (6:6-11 par.), the man suffering from dropsy (14:1-5, without par.), the paralyzed man at the pool of Bethzatha (John 5:1-23), and the man born blind (John 9:1-17), as well as the account of a quarrel about the plucked grain (6:1-5 par.). While the question of place does not play any role, the respect for holy time divided Jesus and his fellow Jews, and later, the earliest Christians and their Jewish counterparts.[11]

Stressing the redactional unity of this story does not prevent us from asking the question of its origin and transmission. There are even several clues that prompt us in our shaping of the question:

- The unusual succession of two distinct episodes: first the miracle, then the controversy concerning the Sabbath, instead of the two elements being interwoven.[12]
- Several tensions or inconsistencies in the story: why did the leader of the synagogue speak to the people rather than directly to Jesus? Why did Jesus, for his

---

7 Luke likes to divide the audience at the end of a sermon or a miracle. This undoubtedly corresponds to the success or failure of the Christian mission; see Luke 7:28 and Acts 28:24-25.

8 The motif of joy instead pertains to the miracle story; see Bultmann, *History*, 12.

9 If one wished to examine the meter, one might compare the length to a long and the events to a short, and the rhythm of the pericope would be expressed thus: – ˘ – ˘. See the schema below.

10 See Hamm, "Freeing of the Bent Woman," 25–26; Green, "Jesus and a Daughter of Abraham," 644–49

(on p. 648 a division of the text); Jean-Noël Aletti, *L'art de raconter Jésus-Christ: L'écriture narrative de l'Évangile de Luc* (ParDi; Paris: Seuil, 1989) 123–31, which includes even 13:18-21 in the unit.

11 The stories are often considered together by the proponents of form criticism; see Lohse, "Jesu Worte über den Sabbat"; Dietzfelbinger, "Vom Sinn der Sabbatheilungen Jesu," 281–98; Trautmann, *Zeichenhafte Handlungen*.

12 See Busse (*Wunder*, 293), who supposes that Luke, drawing inspiration from 14:5, added the discussion to a miracle story; he perceives the caesura between

part, answer in the plural, "you hypocrites," a plural that was kept even as far along as in Luke's conclusion: "all his opponents"?[13]

- The presence of a saying similar to the saying about the ox and the donkey in the related narratives of the man suffering from dropsy (14:5) and the man with the withered hand in its Matthean form (Matt 12:11).[14]
- The style and vocabulary do not belong to Lukan redaction to the same degree throughout the pericope.[15]

In v. 10, while the periphrastic construction and the indication of the locale are characteristic of Luke, the indication of time would appear to come from tradition. So it was told that the miracle took place on the Sabbath. Moreover, since dialogue would be unthinkable without a narrative introduction, it follows that the two parts of the present narrative, miracle and controversy, must have come together early on. They must have already constituted a unit in the tradition that Luke took over.[16]

In vv. 11-13, there are abundant redactional elements: "and just then"; "a woman having had a spirit of . . ." (cf. 4:33; 8:27); the "sickness" referred to in Greek by the same word as the word for "weakness" (cf. 8:2); the word "eighteen" placed *after* the word "years" in Greek (cf. the reverse word order, the traditional one, on the lips of Jesus, v. 16); "having seen her" (cf. 2:17); "call" (cf. 6:13; 23:20; Acts 21:40; 22:2); "immediately" (cf. 1:64); "praise God" (cf. 2:20). But what must have come from tradition would be a verb such as "bend over" ($\sigma\upsilon\gamma\kappa\acute{\upsilon}\pi\tau\omega$), and an expression such as "completely" ($\epsilon\mathit{i}\varsigma$ $\tau\grave{o}$ $\pi\alpha\nu\tau\epsilon\lambda\acute{\epsilon}\varsigma$), a *hapax legomenon* in Luke.

In the controversy, vv. 14-16, the traditional elements predominate: "responded . . . he kept saying" ($\mathit{\mathring{a}}\pi\mathit{o}\kappa\rho\iota\vartheta\epsilon\mathit{i}\varsigma$ . . . $\mathit{\mathring{\epsilon}}\lambda\epsilon\gamma\epsilon\nu$); "to be indignant" ($\mathit{\mathring{a}}\gamma\alpha\nu\alpha\kappa$-$\tau\acute{\epsilon}\omega$, a *hapax legomenon* in Luke); the "absolute" use of the participle $\mathit{\mathring{\epsilon}}\rho\chi\acute{o}\mu\epsilon\nu\mathit{o}\iota$, literally "by coming," translated as "you must come," which is not Lukan; "hypocrites," rare in Luke (cf. 6:42 and 12:56); "daughter of Abraham" (cf. 1:5); "Satan" (Luke prefers, if I dare say so, "the devil"); "eighteen" (literally, "ten and eight") placed this time *before* "years"; "on the Sabbath day" (cf. 4:16); the two successive questions, a literary device that Luke never chose on his own (cf. 2:49). What may be attributed to redaction, on the other hand, is the use of "ought" ($\delta\epsilon\mathit{\hat{\iota}}$) for the respect for ritual regulations (cf. 22:7, compared with Mark 14:12; Luke 2:49; Acts 15:5); possibly resorting to "the Lord" ($\mathit{\acute{o}}$ $\kappa\acute{\upsilon}\rho\iota\mathit{o}\varsigma$), in referring to Jesus; finally, the emphatic use of "this" ($\tau\alpha\acute{\upsilon}\tau\eta\nu$), in v. 16; cf. 12:5.

Verse 17, as is often the case with concluding and introductory verses, displays several Lukan characteristics: reinforcement of the participle by "all" or "entire" ($\pi\acute{\alpha}\nu\tau\epsilon\varsigma$); the substantivized participle "the ones opposing him" ($\mathit{o}\mathit{i}$ $\mathit{\mathring{a}}\nu\tau\iota\kappa\epsilon\acute{\iota}\mu\epsilon\nu\mathit{o}\iota$ $\alpha\mathit{\mathring{\upsilon}}\tau\mathit{\hat{\omega}}$), that is, "his opponents" (cf. 21:15), compared with Mark 13:11; "the entire crowd"; the "all" ($\pi\mathit{\hat{a}}\sigma\iota\nu$), before "the wonderful things"; and finally, the expression "that were being done by him" (cf. 23:8).

In short, Luke did not make it all up himself, but did leave his stamp on a unit that pre-existed and that already associated the miracle with the controversy. The influence of the Gospel writer can be felt especially at both the beginning and the end of the narrative (vv. 10 and 17), then in the account of the miracle (vv. 11-13). As was his custom, Luke paid the greatest respect to the

---

vv. 11-13 and v. 17b first and 14-17a second, despite the redactional effort to rejoin the two based on the root $\lambda\upsilon$- (v. 12, 15, 16). Trautmann (*Zeichenhafte Handlungen*, 292–93) has the same opinion.

13   See Roloff, *Kerygma*, 62 n. 68. In his opinion vv. 12-13, 14a, and 16 are elements of a historical memory; v. 15 was added later and adapted to the significant root $\lambda\upsilon$-. Bultmann (*History*, 12) wonders, on the contrary, whether the apophthegm had not been constructed from an isolated logion v. 15.

14   For Lohse ("Jesu Worte über den Sabbat," 80–81), Luke 13:14-17 is more recent than Luke 14:5 par. Matt 12:11.

15   See Jeremias, *Sprache*, 228–30.

16   On the other hand, several commentators think that it is Luke who created a unity from two parts or broadened a miracle story from a controversy; see nn. 10 and 12 above and n. 18 below. Haenchen (*Weg*, 128) supposes that a healing story had been transformed to the subject of the Sabbath, but he thinks that this evolution was made during the oral phase of transmission.

words of the speakers, particularly those of Jesus (vv. 14-16). The narrative, already linking the woman's deliverance with the problem of the Sabbath day, was probably part of the text of L, following the parable of the fig tree (13:6-9).

A Synoptic comparison of 13:15 (the example suggested by Jesus) with its parallels in 14:5 and Matt 11:12 displays differences in content (untying one's animal in one case, freeing it in the other), in wording (this verse is more literary), and in context (the parallel saying is sufficient by itself without an application and could be adapted to various episodes, while the wording here, playing as it does on the verb "untie" [λύω], cannot be dissociated from the context[17]). The saying in 13:15, then, cannot be attributed either to Luke or to Jesus, but only to the author of L or rather to the oral tradition.

In the present text, the controversy has two persons in confrontation, Jesus and a leader of the synagogue. In the tradition, on the contrary, the sayings of both the leader (v. 14) and Jesus (vv. 15-16) bring into conflict two groups, which, from a *formgeschichtlich* point of view, are Christians versus Jews. I personally think that, as in the story of the plucked grain, the tradition showed the disciples being accused by the Jewish leaders. By his deed and by his word, Jesus flew to their assistance by attacking these opponents (hence the plurals). Luke, or possibly the author of L just before him, may have preferred to bring two persons into conflict, in order to clarify the debate and enliven the narrative.

In their fundamental structure, vv. 10-13 fit the pattern of a miracle narrative: exposition (v. 11), speech by the thaumaturge (vv. 12-13a), healing (v. 13b), and final thanksgiving (v. 13c). By virtue of both its structure and its brevity, this narrative resembles the healing of Peter's mother-in-law (4:38-39). While the vocabulary of the miracle comes from tradition, and the controversy from redaction, an evolution from the simplest to the most complex might be assumed. Since that is not the case, we should think instead of a narrative that had always been recounted with its mixed genres, the miracle introducing the debate, as often happens in the case of certain apophthegms and certain controversies. The successive redactors of L, then of the Gospel, probably followed tradition in allowing themselves more liberty in the rewriting of the narrative than in that of the sayings. While the wording of the narrative by the author of L, then Luke's rewriting of it, are of recent date, the tradition as well, as is attested by the wording of v. 15, corresponds to a recent phase of the Synoptic tradition.[18] Be that as it may, some ancient memories may be hidden behind that tradition.[19]

So the unit was not recounted and then written down as a miracle narrative extolling the thaumaturge. The Christology is discreet, and Jesus legislates just as much as he exercises power. There is, in fact, a legal problem; it concerns the sacred time, the Sabbath day, more exactly, what respecting it implies—still more precisely, the nature of the "work" that is forbidden. This pericope, through sayings of Jesus, does not aim at suppressing the Sabbath day or spiritualizing its observance. It redefines its celebration in terms of liberation rather than rest, thus creating a link with the exodus tradition and parting company with the creation account.[20] "Jesus" cleverly appealed to a Jewish regulation concerning how the Sabbath rule was to be applied, and he carried out and encouraged other kinds of freeing than just those of oxen and donkeys. The deliverance of the woman by Jesus, who did not transgress the Sabbath but rather perfectly respected it, established the Christian offer of the liberating gospel during synagogue services by oral proclamation and the laying on of hands, preaching, and

---

17 I doubt, therefore, that v. 15 was a logion that had had an independent circulation. It is about a secondary adaptation of Luke 14:5 par. Matt 12:11 to the apophthegm Luke 13:10-17.

18 See Trautmann, *Zeichenhafte Handlungen*, 292–93. Dibelius (*Tradition*, 97–98) shows, from dialogues and several fictional elements, that our story is a *Mischform*, still a paradigm (that is to say, an apophthegm) and already "new." Walter Schmithals (*Das Evangelium nach Lukas* [ZBK 3.1; Zurich: Theologischer Verlag, 1980] 152) even wonders if

Luke is not the only one responsible for the parallel story of 6:6-11 (the man with the withered hand).

19 See Roloff (*Kerygma*, 67–68), who notes the wordplay on "to free" (vv. 12 and 16).

20 See Steiner and Stotzer-Kloo ("Zur Freiheit befreit," 128–29), who return, on the one hand, to Genesis 1 and Exod 20:11 and, on the other, to Deut 5:15.

exorcism.[21] The Christianized Sabbath thus became the celebration and the anticipation of eschatological deliverance and the new creation. This pericope belongs to the category of normative miracles (*Normenwunder*) that justify the new Christian allegiance by the charismatic authority of Jesus, the Lord accredited by God.

Commentary

■ **10** A brief introduction interrupted Jesus' previous words (vv. 2-9) in L and interrupts them again in the Lukan Gospel. On the one hand, it makes possible the shift from a speech to a narrative and, on the other hand, prepares for the controversy (hence the synagogue setting and the Sabbath as a temporal indication[22]). By specifying that Jesus was teaching, Luke suggests that his Lord explained God's law. The preaching he talks about must have been the preaching within the liturgy, after the prayers and the reading of the Law and the Prophets.[23]

■ **11** Luke makes a distinction between illness and demon possession and between acts of healing and exorcisms.[24] His view is indicated by his use of the word "spirit" (v. 11), and the dialogue mentions Satan's binding a person (v. 16). That leads the reader to think in terms of demon possession. On the contrary, the narrative outline, which is unacquainted with any expulsion and includes a laying on of hands, suggests a healing and presupposes an illness. There are indeed an illness and a healing; for the author of L—and Luke shares his opinion—illnesses belong to the negative sphere over which Satan reigns.

The expression "having had a spirit of sickness," literally "of weakness" (v. 11) poses a problem. It is found only once in the New Testament, in this verse here in Luke. "To have a spirit," on the other hand, is found three other times in Luke-Acts: in 4:33, in connection with a man who had the spirit of an unclean demon; and in Acts 8:7 and 19:13, once more, in connection with unclean spirits. Nonetheless, here we are dealing not with an unclean spirit but with "a spirit of weakness," that is, "illness."[25] In the eyes of Luke, who took over the expression from his source, the "spirit," the $\pi\nu\epsilon\hat{\upsilon}\mu\alpha$, of this illness had spread in the woman's body in such a way as to bend her over and keep her from being able to change position.[26]

The effects, which were very visible, are indicated in a concise way. There were two of them: on the one hand, the woman had become, and remained, completely bent over. "To stoop together, to bow toward each other, to be bent (over), to be stooped" in Greek is a compound verb, $\sigma\upsilon\gamma\kappa\acute{\upsilon}\pi\tau\omega$.[27] Here it designates a deformed lower,

21 Trautmann (*Zeichenhafte Handlungen*, 280) distinguishes three interests that the Christian community could have had in telling such stories: Jesus' forgiveness of transgressions, the legitimation of Christian practice, and the affirmation of the power and authority of Jesus already during his earthly life. They do not altogether correspond to the one that I have offered. Close to my position, see Klinghardt, *Gesetz*, 238–40. Do not forget the opinion of Origen (*Cels.* 1.6), who teaches us that the Gospel stories, undoubtedly exorcisms, were read in churches during exorcism ceremonies.

22 See 4:31b. The expression ἐν μιᾷ τῶν συναγωγῶν means "in one of the synagogues" of the town or of the region where Jesus was (with Delebecque, 89) and not "in a synagogue" (*TOB* ad loc.); see Christoph Burchard ("Fussnoten zum neutestamentlichen Griechisch II," 146–49), who thinks that the expression ἐν μιᾷ τῶν συναγωγῶν is Lukan, perhaps influenced by the LXX, but not necessarily Semitic. As for ἐν τοῖς σάββασιν, which Luke must

have inherited from the tradition, he understands the phrase as a plural ("on the Sabbaths"), that is to say "every Sabbath." Luke, we know, prefers the singular τὸ σάββατον to the plural to designate a particular Sabbath (see n. 56 below).

23 See the commentary on 4:15 and 4:16–20a in vol. 1.

24 See the commentary on 4:40 and 6:18b in vol. 1.

25 See ἀσθένεια (5:15; 8:2; 13:11-12; 28:9) and ἀσθενέω (4:40; 9:2; Acts 9:37; 19:12; an exception is 20:35, which has to do with the economically weak), ἀσθενής (10:9; Acts 4:9; 5:15-16).

26 It is not about the spirit of the woman, which is depressed from the sickness that has invaded her body, contra Wilkinson, "Case of the Bent Woman," 203. On the expression "who had a spirit of sickness," see Plummer (341), who thinks in terms of a possession, and Lagrange (382), who proposes a demonic influence.

27 Used in the LXX (Sir 12:11; 19:26), this verb means to be bent over in these two places; in one case, it is the posture of the false friend who pretends to be

rather than upper (cerebral), spinal column. On the other hand, since there was nothing that could be done about the problem, and because the bent-over position could not be loosened up, the ill person was rendered unable[28] to straighten up ($\dot{\alpha}\nu\alpha\kappa\dot{\nu}\pi\tau\omega$, "to stand erect," to "straighten oneself").[29]

The adjective $\pi\alpha\nu\tau\epsilon\lambda\dot{\eta}\varsigma$, -$\dot{\epsilon}\varsigma$, means "completed," "complete."[30] The phrase $\epsilon\dot{\iota}\varsigma$ $\tau\dot{o}$ $\pi\alpha\nu\tau\epsilon\lambda\dot{\epsilon}\varsigma$ must be translated as "completely," "totally," "absolutely," "permanently." The expression can be attached to "incapable" in the sense of "completely unable";[31] or to "straighten up," in the sense of "stand completely straight"; or, following a Lukan custom, to both at the same time.[32] Personally, I would translate "not really able to stand up straight any more," "could not stand up straight at all," in order to make palpable the permanent incapacity to stand up completely straight.[33]

What struck men and women in antiquity was the irremediable nature of an illness that did not kill but made it impossible to be in a vertical position. Indeed, Jewish thought held that what distinguished human beings from animals, and brought them closer to angels, was the vertical position, speech, intelligence, and sight permitting foresight (see *Gen. Rab.* 8.11 on Gen 1:27). But that mark of humanity had disappeared in this case. And with it, the power to stand up straight in order to look up (the *sursum* of the Vulgate, of course, suggests the *sursum*

corda, "Lift up your hearts," of the liturgy). The woman was thus deprived of a part of her humanity and the possibility of contact with the divine. Added to her sentiment of incurability she must have felt a personal humiliation, social degradation, and physical pain, on which point the text is silent. This woman symbolizes a human race characterized by the Fall (the good creation, "head held up high," was readily contrasted with the result of the Fall, the birth of humans with their "head downwards"[34]). That reversal of up and down, as well as staring down at lower things on the earth, being unable to rise up toward heaven, could not have escaped the notice of readers in antiquity, who saw in this isolated creature a symbol of all of creation, or at least sinful humanity.

■ **12** The look went beyond simple observation. It both preceded and motivated Jesus' action. His look testified to his receptiveness; his action, to what he said. Both his look and his action indicated, to those having eyes to see and ears to hear, that the Lord did not remain indifferent to unjust destitution and that he acted in order to correct its effects.[35] Luke here describes mercy,[36] an inner attitude, not with abstract terms but with verbs that refer to beneficent actions.[37] We have to admire this capacity of Jesus to express emotion, often discernible in his direct encounters with women. This capacity underlies the criticisms he directed at those who interpreted the law in a restrictive manner.

---

humble; in the other, it is that of the scoundrel who pretends to be sad. Schwarz ("$K\alpha\dot{\iota}$ $\dot{\eta}\nu$ $\sigma\upsilon\gamma\kappa\dot{\nu}\pi$-$\tau\upsilon\upsilon\sigma\alpha$," 58) wants to understand the verb in the sense of "to be hunchbacked"; on the other hand, see Radl, "Ein 'doppeltes Leiden' in Lk 13, 11?" 35–36.

28 $M\dot{\eta}$ $\delta\upsilon\nu\alpha\mu\dot{\epsilon}\nu\eta$ (literally, "was not able"), translated as "incapable." On the desperate situation of this woman, see Steiner and Stotzer-Kloo, "Zur Freiheit befreit," 127–46.

29 Luke uses $\dot{\alpha}\nu\alpha\kappa\dot{\nu}\pi\tau\omega$ ("to straighten up") one more time, in an apocalyptic context: at the end, believers will straighten up and lift their heads (21:28) at the coming of their eschatological redemption. On $\dot{\alpha}\nu\alpha\kappa\dot{\nu}\pi\tau\omega$, see BAGD, s.v. Lagrange (382) thinks of two effects of paralysis, expressed by the two verbs: torso arched and fused together; a head that lifts a little, but not completely.

30 See BAGD, s.v.

31 As the Vulgate puts it: "nec omnino poterat sursum

respicere," "and she absolutely could not look upward."

32 See the commentary on 1:5-7, n. 22, in vol. 1.

33 The description makes one think of the illness named after Bechterew, ankylosing spondylitis (*spondylitis ankylopoietica*); see Wilkinson, "Case of the Bent Woman," 197–200; and Marshall, 557.

34 So in the logion on the high and the low (*Gos. Thom.* 22); one finds theological elaboration on the Fall in *Acts Pet.* 38 and *Acts Phil.* 140.

35 See 7:13, where, between the look and the interjection, Luke situates mercy, which rests implicitly on 13:12.

36 See 10:33-34 (the attitude of the Samaritan, after the idle glances from the priest and the Levite, 10:31-32).

37 Jesus manifests himself here as a benefactor and savior: see Acts 10:38; Luke 5:31; 2:11; 6:9; 8:36; 19:10.

Jesus' calling the woman is expressed in Greek by the verb προσφωνέω ("speak to," "call out," "address," "call by one's name," "call to," "summon")[38] and also by the verb λέγω ("say"). What Luke especially valued in the first of these verbs was the exteriority of the "voice" (φώνη) that one hears (λέγω is used to express the "word" [λόγος] that one listens to). After having been called ("woman," γύναι), the woman must have moved from where she had been in order to learn what Jesus had to say to her, thus accepting dialogue, by her very movement. Up to that point she had kept to the part of the synagogue reserved for women, if the division of synagogues had already made provision for such a separation at that time,[39] or else in a corner where her deformity would not have been too disturbing. As we know from a study of phenomenology of religion, wholeness of body is required of those officiating at religious services and, often, of those attending them (see Lev 22:1-9; Num 5:1-5; Deut 10:10).

The vocative γύναι ("woman") seems to have been current at that time and did not imply any contempt or condescension.[40] The vocative κυρία ("lady") seems to have been used for a woman one already knew and who was of an elevated social rank.[41]

The Lukan Jesus, who asks no questions, asserts himself by announcing a liberation that takes place immediately (Jesus' affirmation is an act of performative language).[42] The woman's "weakness," her "ailment,"[43] matches the "force" that held her captive. To "set free," "loose," "undo" what Satan had done[44] means encouraging the resumption of life, freeing the person.

■ **13** In order for "weakness" to become "strength" again, and for servitude to become a happy deliverance, God's power must come into play. It was with a view to expressing that sudden emergence of the divine power, which was to make of this deliverance a regeneration, that Luke described a laying on of hands, an act that he sometimes associated with the ministry of healing,[45] as here, and sometimes with the liturgical gift of the Holy Spirit.[46] In Luke's eyes, Jesus and, following him, his principal disciples were in possession of God's power,[47] which snatches Satan's victims from him.

The straightening up was instantaneous ("immediately," παραχρῆμα), a narrative device indicating that it came from God.[48] It was as sudden as the infirmity had been lasting, as whole as it was total. Depending on two different meanings of the prefix ἀνα-, "upwards" and "again," the Greek verb ἀνορθόω can mean either "raise," "lift," or "restore," "straighten up." Here, following a description of the infirmity (v. 11), it should be taken in the sense of "straighten up." Used in the passive, it discreetly stresses the divine origin of the healing. What is more, the word is well chosen, since it makes the correction of the cruelest defect all the more visible to

---

38 During the calling of the Twelve, Luke preferred προσφωνέω to the προσκαλέω of Mark 3:13; see the commentary on 6:13 in vol. 1.

39 I do not know when this division occurred; see Wolfgang Schrage, " συναγωγή κτλ.," *TDNT* 7 (1971) 822–23.

40 See Luke 22:57, Matt 15:27-28 (the Syrophoenician calls Jesus κύριε ["Master"]; he calls her γύναι ["woman"]). This occurs frequently in John, e.g., John 2:4 (Jesus to his mother); 4:21 (to the Samaritan woman); 20:13, 15 (to Mary Magdalene); see Col 3:18.

41 In the LXX and Philo this word means the owner of a slave; see BAGD, s.v. κυρία 1.

42 The form ἀπολέλυσαι (perfect passive second person of ἀπολύω, "you have been released") has nuances of the perfect: "you are so now," "see, you are released for good," translated as "you are freed." The verb ἀπολύω is very strong in its use. Plato (*Meno* 245A) uses it to signify the liberation of the Greeks from servitude. On the wordplay with the

root λυ-, see below. On the performative efficacy of Jesus' language, see the commentary on 4:20b-21, n. 25, in vol. 1.

43 Delebecque (89–90) translates it twice (v. 11 and v. 12) as "infirmité."

44 See v. 16.

45 See 4:40; Acts 28:8; in Acts 9:12, 17, the placing of hands onto the converted Saul by Ananias in faith heals him of his blindness and confers the Spirit to him.

46 See Acts 6:6; 8:17, 19; 13:3; 19:6; and Bovon, *Theologian*, 261–70.

47 See 5:17; 6:19; 8:46; 9:1; Acts 3:12; 4:7 (in Acts 3:6 and 4:9-12 Luke reminds the reader that the miraculous power of the apostles does not belong to them: it is Christ who acts as their intermediary); see the commentary on 5:17, n. 23, and 8:48 in vol. 1.

48 See 1:64; 4:39; 5:25; 8:44, 47, 55; 18:43; Acts 3:7; 5:10; 12:23; 13:11; 16:26; see the commentary on 4:21-44, n. 4, in vol. 1.

the reader. It also suggests, in the spiritual and moral sense, the recovery God wishes to offer to his people and its accompanying ethical restoration.[49]

The Greek aorist indicating God's involvement is continued by the inchoative or inceptive imperfect, indicating human praise of God.[50] As a believer, the woman spontaneously attributed the healing to the God of Israel.[51] Her Jewish faith was also a Christian one, since she recognized the Father through the Son's mediation.

■ **14** The man, a "leader of the synagogue" (ἀρχισυνά-γωγος[52]), was the person responsible for the building and the physical arrangements for the worship services (there was only one per synagogue, hence the definite article). This man was indignant (ἀγανακτέω, "be indignant," "aroused," "angry," "express displeasure," "seethe"—an attitude of reaction to something done by someone else).[53] It is an attitude of anger in one who is convinced that the anger is justified; an attitude of moral judgment or condemnation. Luke indicates the motive for this indignation: the choice of the Sabbath day for this healing, which was considered to be work ("cure," "heal" [θεραπεύω] comes back a second time in the verse on the lips of the leader of the synagogue).[54] Now it seems that a physician did not practice medicine on the Sabbath day.[55] So by "working" ("to work" [ἐργά-ζεσθαι], v. 14) Jesus had broken the law. The Jewish leader's anger was justified in his eyes, and, he thought, in God's eyes, too.[56]

---

49 The verb ἀνορθόω means "to build" or "rebuild" a structure (see Acts 15:16) or a person (see Heb 12:12). In the LXX (seventeen instances) it is used, in about half its occurrences, to describe the construction or restoration of a house, a throne, a dynasty, or an entire land, and in the other half to describe the restoration of human beings (Jer 10:12; 40:2; 42:2; Ps 145 (144):14; Ps 146 (145):8; Prov 24:3). God is the great restorer, the Savior. See Ps 20 (19):6-9 LXX, which is especially important in this regard: "They, they are bound and they fall; but we, we arise again and stand firm" (v. 8); see Edwin Hatch and Henry A. Redpath, *A Concordance to the Septuagint and the Other Greek Versions of the Old Testament (Including the Apocryphal Books)* (3 vols.; Oxford: Clarendon, 1897–1906) s.v.; Hermann Cremer, *Biblico–theological Lexicon of New Testament Greek* (trans. W. Urwick; 4th Eng. ed.; Edinburgh: T&T Clark; New York: Scribner, 1892) 807; H. Preisker, "ὀρθός κτλ.," *TDNT* 5 (1967) 449–51; and *ThWNT* 10.2 (1979) 1205 (bibliography); Hamm, "Freeing of the Bent Woman," 35–36.

50 On δοξάζω τὸν θεόν ("to praise God"), see 2:20; 5:25-26 (interesting, because there is cheering from the beneficiary and the witnesses of the miracle, just as there is a response of grace and an explosion of joy in 13:13 and 17); 7:16; 17:15; 18:43; 23:47; Acts 4:21; 11:18; 21:20; see the commentary on 5:25-26 in vol. 1. In praising God the woman expresses a proper response, which contrasts with the mean-spirited reaction of the synagogue ruler.

51 On the miracle stories in Luke, see my commentary on 7:11-17, n. 66. In particular, one must compare this healing to those of the paralytics: 5:17-26 (unable to walk at the beginning, he walks at the end of the story) and Acts 3:1-9 (disabled from

birth, the man has the soles of his feet and his ankles strengthened [στερεόω] by the invocation of Jesus Christ pronounced by the apostle Peter). In these texts, as in Luke 13:10-17, it is not a question of the departure of a spirit, as in the exorcism story.

52 See my commentary on 8:41, n. 34, in vol. 1. The word also appears in 8:49; Acts 13:15; Acts 18:8; 17; and in the famous inscription of Theodotus found in Jerusalem. See Adolf Deissmann, *Light from the Ancient East: The New Testament Illustrated by Recently Discovered Texts of the Graeco-Roman World* (trans. Lionel R. M. Strachan; rev. ed.; New York: George H. Doran, 1927) 439–41; BAGD, s.v. On the organization of the synagogue cult and the distribution of tasks, see Paul Billerbeck, "Ein Synagogengottesdienst in Jesu Tagen," *ZNW* 55 (1964) 143–61.

53 See other uses in the NT: Mark 10:41 par. Matt 20:24; Mark 14:4 par. Matt 21:15; Matt 26:8; Mark 10:14. 2 Corinthians 7:11 uses the substantive ἀγα-νάκτησις ("indignation"). This vocabulary is rare in the LXX; see Wis 5:22; 12:27; Daniel (Theodotion); *Bel and the Dragon* 28. See also 4 Macc 4:21.

54 The insistence placed on the verb "to heal" also signals that Luke does not consider this event an exorcism.

55 On the restrictions imposed by the Sabbath, see *Mekilta de Rabbi Yishmael* 80.1–25, "Shabbata"; Jacob Neusner, *Mekhilta according to Rabbi Ishmael: An Analytical Translation* (2 vols.; Atlanta: Scholars Press, 1988) 2:253–57; Godet, 2:174. Lagrange (383) signals that to build a house was equally forbidden on the Sabbath. Yet Jesus, in a certain manner (see ἀνορθόω, "to rebuild"), reconstructed this woman, as one might assemble a wall.

56 Luke uses the singular τὸ σάββατον (he fears that his Greek readers will not understand a plural that

Why did the Jewish leader not confront the Master directly?[57] What was important to him was the simple division of time and the elimination of work on the seventh day (see Exod 20:8-11; Deut 5:12-15).[58] There is nothing in the Gospel text to say that Christians, Luke, or Jesus disapproved of this faithfulness to the commandment of the law. What Christianity criticized was the interpretation of the healing as a human act, the fruit of a *human transaction*. In their eyes, it was a question instead of *divine deliverance*, what the Sabbath was supposed to encourage, according to its scriptural correspondence to the exodus from Egypt (see Deut 5:15). From Luke's point of view, the leader of the synagogue, ὁ ἀρχισυνάγωγος, who was supposed to be a man of God, seemed to want to prevent Jesus from doing good. When he was unable to keep Jesus from doing it, he considered as a transgression of the law what was, in the eyes of the Gospel writer, the most exemplary obedience possible to God's salvific will. That was a tragic error on his part. Rarely has a reminder of the letter of the law been as contrary to its intention and spirit. According to the leader of the synagogue, there remains nothing that can be done on the Sabbath day ("and not on the Sabbath day," v. 14). So the kind of rest that he suggested could only be the kind appropriate to cemeteries. But the God of Jesus is the God of Abraham, Isaac, and Jacob, the God of the living (20:38), the life-giving God. Luke, who is often taken for a Judeophile,[59] showed himself to be hostile to a certain form of Jewish piety, albeit with a restrained hostility.

■ **15-16** It is this God of deliverances whom the Lukan Jesus reminds us of by way of an example. From 14:5 and Matt 12:11 we know of the case of the animal who fell in a well and who had to be helped urgently.[60] Such a charitable act was allowed in that kind of circumstance, even if it required a certain amount of work. On the other hand, the *Damascus Document*, an Essenian text expressly forbade it (CD 11.13–14). In this case Matt 12:11 and Luke 14:5 must have been referring to the practice of the Pharisees, who were often less strict than the Essenes.[61] The attitude that is attributed here to the Jews (v. 15) seems reasonable.[62] The Jewish religion made adaptations to the requirements of nature, and the teachers of the law authorized shepherds and peasants to water their flocks in an efficient manner yet in such a way as to avoid too seriously violating the ruling about rest. Is a human being not worth more than an animal (12:7)?

What counts most is the vocabulary of deliverance with which the text plays: λύω means "untie," a verb that we encounter in vv. 15 and 16, where it echoes the verb ἀπολύω ("set free," "release," "free") in the miracle narrative (v. 12). Everyone unties their ox or their donkey on the Sabbath day in order to lead it away to give it water to drink. And everyone is justified in doing so.[63]

It would be hypocritical, that is, illogical and falsely religious, to authorize in one case what one refuses

---

designates a singular!); see on v. 10 above, n. 22. The dative τῇ ἡμέρᾳ with temporal signification is classical; see BDF §200 (ἐν followed by the dative [so v. 10] is a Hellenistic and/or Semitic usage; in this case, the formula indicates the moment, and the duration of this moment, *Zeitpunkt* and *Zeitraum*; without the ἐν, the temporal dative indicates only the moment of the action, *Zeitpunkt*).

57   See Fitzmyer (2:1013), who opts for the warning addressed to the people; which would explain the later grief of hypocrisy pronounced by Jesus (v. 15). Maldonado (*Comm. in quat.* 13.15 [p. 127 of the 1597 ed.]), thinks that in speaking to the people, the ruler is in fact attacking Jesus; certainly he is, in a roundabout way.

58   According to Roloff (*Kerygma*, 69): "Eine vom jüdischen Standpunkt aus sachgemässe Reaktion."

59   So Jacob Jervell, *Luke and the People of God: A New Look at Luke-Acts* (Minneapolis: Augsburg, 1972).

60   These texts are analyzed in Lohse, "Jesu Worte über den Sabbat," 86–89; Dietzfelbinger, "Vom Sinn der Sabbatheilungen Jesu," 286; Trautmann, *Zeichenhafte Handlungen*, 309–15.

61   The passage CD 10.14—11:18 provides a list of activites prohibited on the Sabbath. It pays particular attention to the needs of livestock during the Sabbath (11.5–7).

62   See Str-B 2:199. On φάτνη ("feeding trough"), see the commentary on 2:12 in vol. 1.

63   On λύω, see 19:30-35 (the donkey of Palm Sunday, attached, detached, then ridden by Jesus); on the symbolism of liberation, see Hamm, "Freeing of the Bent Woman," 27, 34; Bernard Trémel, "A propos d'Actes 20:7-12: Puissance du thaumaturge ou du témoin?" *RThPh* 112 (1980) 359–69.

in another. All the more so since what is involved, on the one hand, is the survival of an animal and, on the other hand, a human life ("Is it for oxen that God is concerned?" Paul asks ironically in 1 Cor 9:9). So the Sabbath day is not just one on which work can be done if it is for the purpose of providing health care but also the appropriate one for deliverance. A whole theology of the Sabbath is thus overturned. From being a day when obedience results in inaction that tolerates servitude, the Sabbath becomes a feast where love makes itself felt in service to others.[64] The long servitude (Satan was behind Pharaoh in the tightening of the chains) was finally brought to an end on this day.[65] Israel (Abraham and his descendants—sons, and here, daughters) has been freed, delivered, liberated. That task not only had to be tolerated, but it was therefore also the plan of action that providentially matched God's plan ("ought not?" οὐκ ἔδει).[66]

The unusual expression "daughter of Abraham"[67] is a reflection of the strong awareness on the part of God's people. Luke did not invent it. It goes back to a Judeo-Christian tradition or to Jesus himself. The Gospel writer did not reject it but fit it into his Christian concept of God's people. Since Isaac, Abraham's son, was finally untied, so was this daughter of Abraham, who herself was also a descendant of the patriarch.[68]

Probably under the influence of his source, Luke considered the leader of the synagogue to be backed by a group of Jesus' opponents.[69] Confronted by Jesus' word, these "opponents" (ἀντικείμενοι) were overcome with shame, an emotion and state rarely mentioned by Luke. If they did not want to be converted, all they could do was be ashamed.[70] In any case, there was nothing more for them to say. The matter was closed.

Facing these opponents was "the entire crowd,"[71] that is, the congregation in the synagogue, as opposed to their leaders. These people sided with Jesus and turned their backs on their spiritual directors. Luke describes a gathering of people whose opinion had changed drastically. Jesus' success was evident. The Christians who transmitted this story and Luke who gave it a conclusion foresaw, in this happy outcome, the successes of the Christian mission that they counted on. Since Jesus acted, carried on a dialogue, and won people over that way, should Christian missionaries not imitate his example?[72]

---

64 On the day of rest as seen by a rabbinic contemporary, see Alexandre Safran, "Le sabbat dans la tradition juive," 136–49.

65 On Satan, see the excursus "The Devil" in vol. 1, pp. 141–42. See also Taeger, *Mensch,* 72–73. On "to untie this bond," see Schwarz ("Λυθῆναι ἀπὸ τοῦ δεσμοῦ τούτου," 47), who attempts a reverse translation of v. 16 into Aramaic and insists on the figurative sense in Aramaic of "to tie": "to chastise," "to test."

66 Luke contrasts the δεῖ ("it is necessary") of human observance with the δεῖ ("it is necessary") of the divine project of liberation. On this δεῖ, cf. 2:49; 4:43; 9:22, etc.; see the commentary on 9:22 in vol. 1; also Hamm, "Freeing of the Bent Woman," 33.

67 The expression is used in Judaism to designate the people of Israel; see Str-B 2:200, who indicates also the good performance that one expected of women in Israel. On the children of Abraham, cf. 1:54-55; 3:7-9; 16:22-32; 19:1-10; Acts 3:25; see Hamm, "Freeing of the Bent Woman," 34–35; and Fitzmyer (2:1013), who refers to 4 Macc 15:28.

68 On Genesis 22, the "binding" of Isaac, in Jewish exegesis, see Grégoire Rouiller, "The Sacrifice of Isaac (Genesis 22:1-19): First Reading," in François Bovon and Grégoire Rouiller, eds., *Exegesis: Problems of Method and Exegesis in Reading (Genesis 22 and Luke 15)* (trans. Donald G. Miller; PTMS 21; Pittsburgh: Pickwick, 1978) 13–42, and Robert Martin-Achard, *Abraham sacrifiant: De l'épreuve de Moriya à la nuit d'Auschwitz* (Aubonne: Moulin, 1988).

69 See 21:15, the same expression, which diverges from Mark 13:11; these are the only Lukan usages; Paul speaks of adversaries using the same participle in 1 Cor 16:9; Phil 1:28.

70 This is the only usage of καταισχύνομαι ("to be filled with shame") in Luke-Acts; cf. αἰσχύνη ("shame") in 14:9, and αἰσχύνομαι ("to blush") in 16:3. In Paul, who cites Isa 28:16, believers need not have shame (Rom 9:33; 10:11; see 1 Pet 2:6). On the shame of the adversaries of Christianity, see 1 Cor 1:27 and 1 Pet 3:16. In the OT, cf. e.g., Isa 45:16; see Rudolf Bultmann, "αἰδώς," and "αἰσχύνη κτλ.," *TDNT* 1 (1964) 169–71 and 189–91.

71 On ὄχλος in Luke, see the commentary on 6:17 in vol. 1.

72 Compare the stories in Acts in which the apostles experience success and setbacks in the synagogues of the Diaspora, e.g., Acts 13:13-52.

The men and women who saw the woman delivered could not help but rejoice.[73] It was a religious, eschatological joy in the presence of what pointed to the sudden emergence of the kingdom about which the following parable was to speak (vv. 18-21). A joy in the presence of "the wonderful things" ($\tau\grave{\alpha}$ $\check{\epsilon}\nu\delta o\xi\alpha$)—that is, those in which God's glory ($\delta\acute{o}\xi\alpha$) is reflected—that were being done ($\tau\grave{\alpha}$ $\gamma\iota\nu\acute{o}\mu\epsilon\nu\alpha$) by Jesus Christ ($\dot{\upsilon}\pi'\,\alpha\dot{\upsilon}\tau o\hat{\upsilon}$, "by him"). It is in this way that God's plan, the history of deliverance and salvation, is accomplished.[74]

History of Interpretation

For Ambrose, bishop of Milan, the bent-over woman symbolizes the church: "When she has filled the measure of the law and the resurrection, in this rest without end, and she is raised to the summit of grandeur, she will no longer experience the curvature of our infirmity" (*Exp. Luc.* 7.173).[75] The mention of the law and the resurrection is to be explained, according to Ambrose, by the eighteen years of disability: ten years under the law (Ten Commandments) and eight years under grace (according to patristic theology of the eighth day) (ibid.).[76] While this ingenious symbolism of numbers seems artificial, the spiritual exegesis of the curvature does seem to be in line with the text's connotations. Bonaventure was to develop this theme of the soul that is curved and oriented toward temporal possessions (*Comm. in Luc.* 13.24). That interpretation was to enjoy success,[77] as was

the image of the bonds of Satan, the enemy who keeps humans imprisoned.[78] Jerome often stressed this text when explaining that sickness is a metaphor for sin: "Our souls have lots of infirmities. And they have as many sins as they do infirmities" (*In Psalmos* 102.3).[79] And chap. 7 of the Rule of Saint Benedict[80] requires that inner humility be demonstrated even to the point of outward appearance. This position of the head leaning downward toward the ground in this passage does not, however, symbolize the weight of sins but rather the monk's awareness of them in the presence of God his Judge.

The Reformer John Calvin stressed God's power.[81] Satan could not have kept the woman prisoner for eighteen years without God's authorization: there is always someone who will outwit you; the devil, who puts people in chains, is himself curbed by Christ. God's power is manifested also in the complementarity of the law and grace: God's grace could not relax on the Sabbath. On the contrary—and our interpretation agrees with Calvin's—that day is God's special day for saving his people.[82]

The leader of the synagogue, who has often been compared to the barren fig tree, was reprimanded, according to Erasmus,[83] because he did not know the heart of the law, the love of one's neighbor; in fact, he proved himself to be guilty of hypocrisy, which Zwingli explained at length (as a synonym of lying, it is something Christ sees through).[84]

---

73 Luke mentions joy in relation to the truth of the mysteries now revealed (10:20-21); the power conferred on the disciples to vanquish demonic forces (10:17-20) and to offer salvation (2:10; 15:5, 7, 10, 32; 24:52). See K. Berger, "$\chi\alpha\acute{\iota}\rho\omega$, etc.," and "$\chi\alpha\rho\acute{\alpha}$, etc.," *EDNT* 3 (1993) 451–52 and 454–55; Bovon, *Theologian*, 457 n. 118.

74 On $\check{\epsilon}\nu\delta o\xi o\varsigma$ ("glorious," "illustrious," or "brilliant") in the LXX, e.g., Exod 34:10 (the $\check{\epsilon}\nu\delta o\xi\alpha$, the "marvels" that God did); see BAGD, s.v. On $\gamma\acute{\iota}\nu o\mu\alpha\iota$ followed by $\dot{\upsilon}\pi\acute{o}$, see BAGD, s.v. $\gamma\acute{\iota}\nu o\mu\alpha\iota$ 1.2a.

75 Erasmus (*Paraphrasis*, 396) says that she symbolizes the nations, restricted to the affairs of the world and inattentive to heavenly realities. Bede (*In Luc.* 4.1447–64) views the woman as the Jewish community, which will become, thanks to the healing of Christ, the Christian community.

76 They also thought of three periods of six years each in conceiving of the three ages of life.

77 See *Glossa Ordinaria*, *Luc* 13:11 (*PL* 114:303).

78 Maldonado, *Comm. in quat.*, Luke 13:11 (p. 126 of the 1597 ed.).

79 CCSL 78:181, lines 35–36.

80 The chapter is about the twelfth degree of humility; see *Rule of Saint Benedict in English* (trans. Timothy Fry; Collegeville, MN: Liturgical Press, 1982).

81 Calvin, *Harmony*, 2:96–98.

82 Bonaventure (*Comm. in Luc.* 13:22) enumerates Jesus' seven reasons for teaching on the Sabbath (Jewish habit; care for preaching; respect for the rest that this day offered; the desire to show that the Sabbath was a figure of grace; obedience to the order of salvation, which made restoration begin here; the intention of transmitting wisdom; and the concern to show himself to be the master over the law and the Sabbath).

83 Erasmus, *Paraphrasis*, 13.16 (397).

84 Zwingli, *Annotationes*, 662–63.

Christ's actions have also been interpreted thus: the Savior chose to cure the woman in order to unmask the leader of the synagogue.[85] What the Venerable Bede would say was that Christ's seeing the woman meant that he had chosen her by grace; his calling her, that he instructed her; his placing his hands on her, that he showered her with spiritual gifts; and his straightening her up, that he prepared her for praising God by her charitable acts (*In Luc.* 4.1472–75).[86]

Conclusion

The New Testament and especially the Christian interpretation that has been made of it have narrowed Jewish thought about the Sabbath and its observance. To be sure, the Jewish conception was enriched through the centuries, but in the first century it was not the caricature we have made of it. Respecting the Sabbath was and still is nothing less than managing time in a way that factors in God's presence and will.[87]

Luke 13:10-17 is more of a Christian affirmation about the Sabbath than it is a miracle narrative. This conviction is displayed not as an attack on the Sabbath as such but as a rediscovery of its true significance. To be sure, the leader of the synagogue rightly thought of the observance of the Sabbath as respect for a prohibition, but he forgot that it is in the first instance adherence to a positive command.[88] The prohibition of manual labor is matched by the order of spiritual activity. By straightening up this woman, Jesus claimed to be observing the Sabbath in the best way: he offered liberation, life, and rest on that day. He did so not by offering it himself but by proclaiming that such was God's good will. Jew-

ish interpretation of Gen 2:2, which Jesus confirmed, recalls that God completed creation on the seventh day, rather than the sixth.[89] It follows that the woman in our pericope was no longer subject to human time and its constraints. She could henceforth live her life according to God's rhythm, which she began to do right away by praising God (v. 13b).

When a modern reader seeks to discover the theological interest connected with the question of the Sabbath, he or she delves into the origin of illnesses, being unsatisfied with exclusively physiological explanations. This text, however, does not deploy the modern duality of the physical and the psychic but rather the ancient one of the physical and the demonic. Perhaps we should combine the two systems of reference, without identifying them.[90] While one author believed that he read in the woman's illness rheumatism leading to depression, I would submit that there was instead a psychic cause of the physical illness and an interaction between the psychic and the demonic. The woman's condition of being bent over perhaps symbolizes a tendency to turn inward and to limit one's horizon to earthly realities (v. 11).

This text is not just a Christian affirmation about time and how it is to be used, and a biblical reflection on evil and its origin but also a soteriological proclamation: the Son, in referring to the Father, reestablished a creature to the state of her initial wholeness (v. 13b). He personally called her, declared to her the deliverance that God offers and transformed the potentiality of his word (vv. 12-13) into action.

Convinced that he was thereby respecting the Sabbath,[91] the Jesus in our text had a twofold objective: making the woman aware of her status as a regenerated

85   Maldonado, *Comm. in quat.*, Luke 13:2 (p. 126 of the 1597 ed.).

86   Johann Christoph Blumhardt (*Evangelien-Predigten auf alle Sonn- u. Festtage des Kirchenjahres nach dem zweiten Jahrgang der württembergischen Perikopen*, in idem, *Gesammelte Werke*, vol. 2 [Karlsruhe: Evangelischen Schriftenverein für Baden, 1887] 349–61) points out that no other illness is presented in this manner in the Gospels (with the expression "spirit of sickness") and emphasizes that Jesus Christ came to break the power of Satan. Additionally, Bauer ("Lukas 13, 10-17") insists on the fact that Jesus takes the woman seriously, respects her suffering and her desire to live. For him to come to her aid, he breaks several taboos. The woman accepts the

invitation to follow the risky path that Jesus has opened to her. The author emphasizes the marked effect of this text on large numbers of Christians in our time, who feel hobbled under the weight of burdens, marginalized in society and worried about finding their true place. For a feminist exegesis, see Schüssler Fiorenza, *But She Said*, 196–97, 250–55.

87   See Safran, "Le sabbat dans la tradition juive."

88   Ibid., 138–39.

89   Ibid., 139.

90   Wilkinson, "Case of the Bent Woman," 203.

91   See the ἔδει of v. 16 (the interpretation of Jesus), which corrects the δεῖ of v. 14 (the interpretation of the synagogue ruler).

creature and offering a new interpretive truth to the leader of the synagogue as well as to those who were depending on his interpretation. The reference to the ox and the donkey that one unties was not just an argument in favor of the liberation of a human being; it was also the occasion for a spiritual deliverance offered to the listeners, who were given reason to rejoice, and then to the readers.[92]

Confronted with this salvific activity, God's people were going to be divided; it was because Jesus puzzled and upset people in the synagogue for the last time, just as he had the first time (4:22-30). While the woman, like a regenerated Eve, ended up praising God in the presence of "the entire crowd," the leader of the synagogue and his followers got more deeply entangled in hypocrisy (v. 15) and shame (v. 17), which remind us of those qualities in connection with a guilty Adam (Gen 3:7-13). To be a part of Israel meant henceforth being faithful to the Father according to the Son's interpretation.

---

92   See Milot ("Guérison d'une femme infirme un jour de sabbat," 23–33), who insists on the significant discrepancy between the comparison and the event.

The Mustard Seed and the Leaven
(13:18-21)
Bibliography

Allis, Oswald T., "The Parable of the Leaven," *EvQ* 19 (1947) 254–73.

Barclay, William, *And Jesus Said: A Handbook on the Parables of Jesus* (Philadelphia: Westminster, 1970) 52–66.

Black, *Aramaic Approach*, 119–23.

Carlston, Charles E., *The Parables of the Triple Tradition* (Philadelphia: Fortress, 1975) 26–28.

Correns, Dietrich, "Die Verzehntung der Raute, Lk 11,42 und MSchebi 9,1," *NovT* 6 (1963) 110–12.

Crossan, John Dominic, "The Seed Parables of Jesus," *JBL* 92 (1973) 244–66.

Idem, *The Historical Jesus: The Life of a Mediterranean Jewish Peasant* (San Francisco: HarperSanFrancisco, 1991) 276, 280, 284.

Dahl, Nils A., "The Parables of Growth," *StTh* 4 (1951) 132–66; reprinted in idem, *Jesus in the Memory of the Early Church: Essays* (Minneapolis: Augsburg, 1976) 141–66.

Delobel, Joël, "The Sayings of Jesus in the Textual Tradition: Variant Readings in the Greek Manuscripts of the Gospels," in idem, *Logia*, 431–57, esp. 456.

Didier, Marcel, "Les paraboles du grain de sénevé et du levain," *RDN* 15 (1961) 385–94.

Dodd, *Parables*, 141–44.

Donahue, John R., *The Gospel in Parable: Metaphor, Narrative, and Theology in the Synoptic Gospels* (Philadelphia: Fortress, 1988) 36–39.

Dupont, Jacques, "Le couple parabolique du sénevé et du levain," in Georg Strecker, ed., *Jesus Christus in Historie und Theologie: Neutestamentliche Festschrift für Hans Conzelmann zum 60. Geburtstag* (Tübingen: Mohr, 1975) 331–45; reprinted in Dupont, *Études*, 2:609–23 (cited from *Études*).

Idem, "Les paraboles du sénevé et du levain," in idem, *Études*, 2:592–608.

Edwards, *Theology of Q*, 129–30.

Fallon and Cameron, "Gospel of Thomas."

Fleddermann, Harry, "The Mustard Seed and the Leaven in Q, the Synoptics, and Thomas," *SBLSP* (1989) 216–36.

Funk, Robert W., "Beyond Criticism in Quest of Literacy: The Parable of the Leaven," *Int* 25 (1971) 149–70.

Grässer, *Problem*, 141–49.

Haenchen, *Weg*, 180–86.

Harnisch, *Gleichniserzählungen Jesu*, 69 n. 63, 70–71.

Jeremias, *Parables*, 146–49.

Jülicher, *Gleichnisreden*, 2:569–81.

Jüngel, Eberhard, *Paulus und Jesus: Eine Untersuchung zur Präzisierung der Frage nach dem Ursprung der Christologie* (rev. ed.; HUT 2; Tübingen: Mohr Siebeck, 1967) 151–54.

Kahlefeld, *Parables*, 24–28.

Kogler, Franz, *Das Doppelgleichnis vom Senfkorn und vom Sauerteig in seiner traditionsgeschichtlichen Entwicklung: Zur Reich-Gottes-Vorstellung Jesu und ihren Aktualisierungen in der Urkirche* (FB 59; Würzburg: Echter, 1988) esp. 208–16.

Kuss, Otto, "Zum Sinngehalt des Doppelgleichnisses vom Senfkorn und Sauerteig," in idem, *Auslegung*, 85–97.

Idem, "Zur Senfkornparabel," in idem, *Auslegung*, 78–84.

Laufen, "*ΒΑΣΙΛΕΑ* und *ΕΚΚΛΗΣΙΑ*· Eine traditions- und redaktionsgeschichtliche Untersuchung des Gleichnisses vom Senfkorn," in Josef Zmijewski and Ernst Nellessen, eds., *Begegnung mit dem Wort: Festschrift für Heinrich Zimmermann* (BBB 53; Bonn: Hanstein, 1979) 105–40.

Lohfink, G., "Senfkorn und Weltenbaum (Mk 4, 30-32 par.): Zum Verhältnis von Natur und Gesellschaft bei Jesus," in Harald Schweizer, ed., '. . . *Bäume braucht man doch!' Das Symbol des Baumes zwischen Hoffnung und Zerstörung* (Sigmaringen: Thorbecke, 1986) 109–26.

Lohse, Eduard, "Die Gottescherrschaft in den Gleichnissen Jesu," *EvTh* 18 (1958) 145–57, esp. 151–54.

Manson, *Sayings*, 122–24.

Marshall, I. Howard, *Eschatology and the Parables* (London: Tyndale, 1963) 24–28.

McArthur, Harvey K., "The Parable of the Mustard Seed," *CBQ* 33 (1971) 198–210.

Montefiore, Hugh, "A Comparison of the Parables of the Gospel according to Thomas and of the Synoptic Gospels," *NTS* 7 (1960–61) 220–48, esp. 227–29.

Mussner, Franz, "1QHodajoth und das Gleichnis vom Senfkorn (Mk 4,30-32 par.)," *BZ* n.s. 4 (1960) 128–30.

Nebe, Gottfried, *Prophetische Züge im Bilde Jesu bei Lukas* (BWANT 127; Stuttgart: Kohlhammer, 1989) 180–90.

Nolland, 2:726, 729 (bibliography).

Percy, Ernst, *Die Botschaft Jesu: Eine traditionskritische und exegetische Untersuchung* (Lund: Gleerup, 1953) 207–11.

Pirot, Jean, *Paraboles et allégories évangéliques: la pensée de Jésus, les commentaires patristiques* (Paris: Lethielleux, 1949) 125–31.

Ramaroson, Leonard, "'Parole-semence' ou 'Peuple-semence' dans la parabole du Semeur?" *ScEs* 40 (1988) 91–101.

Schmid, *Matthäus und Lukas*, 102–4.

Schnackenburg, Rudolf, *God's Rule and Kingdom* (trans. John Murray; New York: Herder & Herder, 1963) 143–59.

Schrage, *Thomas-Evangelium*, 61–66, 183–85.

Schultze, Bernhard, "Die ekklesiologische Bedeutung des Gleichnisses vom Senfkorn (Mt 13, 31-32; Mk 4, 30-32; Lk 13, 18-19)," *OrChrP* 27 (1961) 362–86.

Schulz, *Q*, 298–309.

Schürmann, Heinz, "Sprachliche Reminiszenzen an abgeänderte oder ausgelassene Bestandteile der Spruchsammlung im Lukas- und Matthäusevangelium," *NTS* 6 (1959–60) 193–210, esp. 206, 209.

Scott, Bernard Brandon, *Hear*, 321–29, 373–87.

Idem, "Parables of Growth Revisited: Notes on the Current State of Parable Research," *BTB* 11 (1981) 3–9.

Seim, Turid Karlsen, "Gudsrikets overraskelse: Parablene om et sennepsfrø og en surdeig," *NTT* 84 (1983) 1–17.

Steiner and Weymann, *Paraboles*, passim.

Tolbert, *Perspectives*, 18, 79–81, 90, 126 n. 12.

Weder, *Gleichnisse*, 104–105, 128–38.

Zimmermann, *Methodenlehre*, 123–27.

Zingg, Paul, *Das Wachsen der Kirche: Beiträge zur Frage der lukanischen Redaktion und Theologie* (OBO 3; Freiburg: Universitätsverlag; Göttingen: Vandenhoeck & Ruprecht, 1974) 100–115.

18/	**He said therefore, "What is the kingdom of God like and to what should I compare it? 19/ It is like a mustard seed that a man took and sowed[a] in his garden. It grew and became a tree, and the birds of the heaven made nests in its branches."**
20/	**And again he said, "To what should I compare the kingdom of God? 21/ It is like leaven that a woman took and hid in three measures of flour until all of it was leavened."**

a   Literally: "threw."

These two parables have held the attention of commentators for a hundred years.[1] Most of them have considered these parables to be authentic and to provide access to the Master's thought.[2] The parables have been viewed as typical of Jesus' teaching and as parables of the kingdom of God. More recently, they have been connected with numerous discussions about eschatology.[3] Being ambiguous, they have also made possible divergent readings by commentators who were anxious to abandon the allegorical method of interpretation but who also were torn between the idea of contrast and that of growth.[4] Should just the proclamation of the gospel be added to that of the kingdom of God, or could the reality of the church be added too? The answers have depended in part on denominational affiliations. The interpretations have also been dependent on each person's system of interpretation,[5] ranging from the allegorical approach of yesteryear to the historical-critical method and from that one to a more literary approach.[6]

---

1   See the above bibliography, which speaks for itself; Kogler, *Doppelgleichnis*, 31–42; Scott, "Parables of Growth Revisited," 3–9.

2   See, as a case in point, McArthur, "Parable of the Mustard Seed," 209–10.

3   Jeremias, *Parables*, 146–49; Dodd, *Parables*, 142–43; Jüngel, *Paulus und Jesus*, 151–54; Grässer, *Problem*, 141–43.

4   On one side, for contrast, see Jeremias, *Parables*, 147; on the other, for growth, see Percy, *Botschaft*, 209– 10. Kuss ("Sinngehalt," 90–94) recognizes contrast but insists on growth; Dahl ("Parables of Growth") emphasizes contrast, but recognizes growth.

5   Growth corresponds to a Catholic sensibility (the evolution of dogma); see, e.g., Kuss, "Sinngehalt"; contrast corresponds to a Protestant sensibility (the rupture effected by revelation), hence Jeremias, *Parables*, 146–49.

6   Jülicher (*Gleichnisreden*, 2:569–81) broke with allegory at the end of the nineteenth century; in

Analysis

The parables of the mustard seed and the leaven are found in juxtaposition and in the same order in both Luke and Matthew. Mark knew just the parable of the mustard seed (Mark 4:30-32), which he placed in his chapter of parables following the similitude of the seed that sprouts and grows all by itself, which is found only in Mark (Mark 4:26-29). The *Gospel of Thomas* has the two parables, but each one in a different place: the mustard seed in the first part (*Gos. Thom.* 20), the leaven in the last (*Gos. Thom.* 96).

In his chap. 8, Luke has no equivalent of the Markan version of the parable of the mustard seed after the similitude of the sower, and here in chap. 13 he quotes the version of the source that he shares with Matthew (Q), rejecting any influence from the Markan version. He is faithful to his practice of avoiding doublets and the contamination of sources. The fact that Luke and Mark both have, in the beginning, a double question is to be explained not by a literary dependence between them but by a habit inherited from rabbinic Judaism. The *Gospel of Thomas* transmits a similar text, but one that has its own particularities: Jesus answers a question put to him by the disciples about the kingdom, and he speaks of a large branch. As for the other parable, the one about the leaven, in *Thomas* it resembles the one found in Matthew and Luke, except for two points: (a) instead of three measures of flour, the *Gospel of Thomas* speaks of large loaves; and (b) following the parable, it adds a command: "Let him who has ears hear."[7]

Rather than imagining a Deutero-Mark,[8] we should suppose that Matthew and Luke are relying here on Q, which must have contained these two parables, one right after the other.[9] Luke appears to have preserved the wording better than Matthew: in the parable of the mustard seed, the double question (v. 18) comes from tradition; so does the parataxis (absence in Luke of subordinate clauses introduced by "when," ὅταν); as well as narration in a past tense ("and it became," καὶ ἐγένετο, in Luke, rather than "and it becomes," καὶ γίνεται, in Matthew). There is one point, however, where Matthew may have preserved a detail from Q: the seed falls "in the field" (Matt 13:31; the words "in his garden," in Luke 13:19, give the impression of a Hellenistic city dweller; they must be redactional).[10] The end of the parable, very similar in Matthew and Luke (Matt 13:32b par. Luke 13:19b; the absence of "in its shade" of Mark 4:32b, the presence of the words "in its branches," which are absent from Mark 4:32b), shows that Q had already connected the parable with certain eschatological passages of Scripture and that that alignment had been made in Greek on the basis of the LXX.[11]

In the parable of the leaven, the introduction, "and again he said" (καὶ πάλιν εἶπεν), of Luke 13:20a, not being Lukan, must fit the text of Q all the more, because the introduction of Matt 13:33, by virtue of its resemblance to Matt 13:24, must be redactional.[12] The interrogative wording of Luke 13:20b could be a redactional assimilation to the opening of the preceding parable, Luke 13:18, since Matt 13:33 and *Gos. Thom.* 96 are both worded affirmatively. The text of the parable is otherwise virtually identical in Matthew and Luke. Since Luke is fond of compound verbs, it can scarcely be imagined that he replaced ἐγκρύπτω ("hide in[side]") (Matthew) with κρύπτω ("hide"). Thus, the Gospel writer must have

---

the 1970s, Funk ("Beyond Criticism," 149–70) and Crossan ("Seed Parables," 244–66) were the first proponents of a literary approach.

7   On these parables in the *Gospel of Thomas*, see Schrage, *Thomas-Evangelium*, 61–66, 183–85; Montefiore, "Comparison," 227–29; Fieger, *Thomasevangelium*, 89–92, 244–46; for a more complete biography, see Fallon and Cameron, "Gospel of Thomas," 4237–52.

8   This is the hypothesis of Kogler (*Doppelgleichnis*), who resumes the argument of his teacher A. Fuchs on pp. 40–42 of his thesis.

9   See the reconstruction of Q in Schulz, *Q*, 298–300, 307; see also Laufen, *Doppelüberlieferungen*, 174–200,

470–90; Edwards, *Theology of Q*, 129–30; Dupont, "Les paraboles du sénevé et du levain," 593–98; Weder, *Gleichnisse*, 128–31.

10   This is not the opinion of Schulz (*Q*, 299), who thinks that the Matthean mention of the field is reminiscent of the parable of the wheat and the chaff (Matt 13:24, 27, 44).

11   See Crossan, "Seed Parables," 255.

12   The expression "kingdom of heaven" is Matthean. Q must have had the words "kingdom of God," which Luke preserves.

taken over κρύπτω from tradition.[13] The relationship here between Matthew and Luke is so clear that we have to conclude that Q was composed in Greek.

Luke attempted to make the two parables as parallel as possible: in each case we read a short introduction with a *verbum dicendi* without any mention of who was addressed, a rhetorical question, an answer beginning with the assertion of the resemblance ("it is like," ὁμοία ἐστίν), the point being compared, a relative clause accompanied by a participial phrase (ὃν λαβὼν ἄνθρωπος ἔβαλεν εἰς . . . ἣν λαβοῦσα γυνὴ [ἐν]έκρυψεν εἰς, "that a man took and sowed in . . . ," "that a woman took and hid in . . ."), and a euphoric outcome (rest for the birds, the rising of all of the dough). Luke may have simplified the first parable slightly in order to make it conform to the second one.[14]

Luke was very pleased to have at his disposal two parables with identical meaning but whose impact was reinforced by this doubling. One of them presents a man, the other a woman (as will again be the case in chap. 15 with the lost sheep and the lost drachma).[15] As is suggested by the initial "therefore" (οὖν), the Gospel writer thought of these parables as the conclusion of the episode of the woman who was paralyzed and then was straightened up,[16] and in a larger sense, of a section of the travel narrative. He probably considered the teaching and the healing that preceded as symbolizing this discreet and active presence of the kingdom of God.

A section comes to a conclusion here, since the narrative summary that immediately follows signals an obvious pause and introduces a new development (13:22). This brief summary reiterates Jesus' activity as a teacher (cf. 11:1-2, 29; 12:1; 13:10) and especially renews the mention of his journey toward Jerusalem (cf. 9:51).

Commentary

■ **18** Five times the Gospel writer has placed on Jesus' lips the vocabulary relating to resemblance.[17] While ἴσος means "being equivalent in number, size, quality; equal," referring to exterior equivalence, ὅμοιος means "of the same kind," referring to the similarity of what is on the interior. Aware that the kingdom of God was not evident, the Gospel writer reckoned that Jesus had understood and explained that divine reality. As a matter of fact, Luke is the only one who used the first person singular:[18] " . . . and to what should I compare it?" The two rhetorical questions that are reported by Luke do not have exactly the same meaning: the objective question ("What is the kingdom of God like . . . ?") is followed by the subjective question (" . . . and to what should I compare it?"). What is understood is that only Christ is Master of the mysteries of the kingdom (cf. 8:9-10; 10:18, 21-22). If the divine reality is to emerge from its enigmatic penumbra, it will have to be by the use of an analogy, which will have the double advantage of limiting the intensity of the epiphany and directing attention to a known reality. Following the biblical tradition and Jesus' message, Luke believed in a noetic correspondence between certain facts of this world and the reality of God's world. That correspondence is equivalent not to an analogy of being but rather to a resemblance rooted in the same plan of the single God who is both Creator and Savior.

---

13 Although hesitant, Schultz (*Q*, 307) is of a different opinion. Note that the text of Luke is not certain: the tradition manuscript hesitates between ἔκρυψεν ("she hid") and ἐνέκρυψεν ("she hid in"). See the apparatus of Nestle-Aland[27].

14 Dupont ("Les paraboles du sénevé et du levain," 597) thinks that Luke's version has been abridged.

15 Of course, Luke writes ἄνθρωπος and not ἀνήρ in v. 19; but ἄνθρωπος here has the sense of "man," a masculine character. On this duality, see Flender, *Heil*, 15–16.

16 See Godet, 2:176; Lagrange, 385; Ernst, 424.

17 Note first the imperfect ἔλεγεν ("he said") (reference to an utterance previously made); see BDF §329. This vocabulary of the resemblance must

be understood in the light of the Jewish tradition of *māšāl* and Greek theories of knowledge; see J. Schneider, "ὁμοιόω κτλ.," *TDNT* 5 (1967) 186–91; G. Haufe, "ὁμοιόω," *EDNT* 2:512. See also Bertil E. Gärtner, "The Pauline and Johannine Idea of 'to know God' against the Hellenistic Background: The Greek Philosophical Principle 'Like by Like' in Paul and John," *NTS* 14 (1967–68) 209–31; Jean Pépin, *Mythe et allégorie: les origines grecques et les contestations judéo-chrétiennes* (rev. ed.; Paris: Études augustiniennes, 1976) 252–57.

18 Matthew uses it once with the verb ὁμοιόω ("to compare"), when Jesus is discussing not the kingdom of God but "this generation"; see Matt 11:16.

Excursus: The Kingdom of God

Luke did not believe that the kingdom of God could be defined.[19] He inherited that concept, knew that it was at the heart of Jesus' message, and attributed it to the apostles as well.[20] Influenced by a certain dualism, he believed that this world is under Satan's power (see 4:5-8; 13:16; Acts 10:38) and that God is trying to regain lost ground, ground that belongs to him. It is to that end that the Father placed his Son on earth. Thanks to the Son's ministry, Satan's power is wavering (see 10:18)[21] and God's is beginning to exert itself (see 2:11; 4:16-21, 43; 6:20; 10:9, 11; 11:20; 17:20-21). For Luke, this revolution takes place at the end of time; God's reign is eschatological (see Acts 2:17). It has come near through the message proclaimed by Jesus and is even already present for those who receive it (see Luke 10:9; 11:20). It will be a while until it is finally established in power and glory (see Acts 1:6-8). This reign of God, linked with the person of Jesus Christ, awaited and mysteriously accessible, constitutes both a temporal greatness, an aeon of God, and a spatial reality, a domain that God liberates and sets up.[22] By means of his parables Jesus announced, explained, and was a manifestation of, this kingdom. The two following parables attempt to do the same.[23]

■ **19** The kingdom of God "is like a mustard seed."[24] The word τὸ σίναπι "can refer to several herbs of the family Cruciferae that provide the condiment bearing the same name, especially those of the genus wild mustard (*Sinapis*), and particularly the *Sinapis nigra L.*, or black mustard, very common in Palestine, notably in the area around Lake Galilee."[25] Famous for its smallness, it allowed rabbis, according to the Talmud,[26] to describe the slightest stain. It serves as an image in the Qur'an:[27] at the time of judgment, on the scales' pan, the mustard seed will be looked at closely. In Q 17:6, the Jesus of Q (cf. Matt 17:20) uses this image again and thus expresses the hope that his disciples will have a minimum of faith. The only problem with that identification is that the adult plant grows to be from four feet to over eight feet tall[28]—therefore the size of a bush, not a tree.[29]

19 On the kingdom of God in Luke, see Martin Völkel, "Zur Deutung des 'Reiches Gottes' bei Lukas," *ZNW* 65 (1974) 57–70; Otto Merk, "Das Reich Gottes in den lukanischen Schriften," in Ellis and Grässer, *Jesus und Paulus*, 201–20; Bovon, *Theologian*, 11–85 (the index on p. 678 under the heading "Kingdom" indicates the most important pages).

20 The βασιλεία τοῦ θεοῦ is an Old Testament and Jewish inheritance, from apocalyptic writings in particular; see Schnackenburg, *God's Rule*, 11–75. The expression was used by Jesus (ibid., 77–258), then recovered by the triple tradition of Mark as well as by the double tradition of the logia. Luke welcomes these gifts and in addition makes the kingdom the content of the apostolic message; see Acts 8:12; 14:22; 19:8; 20:25; 28:23, 31.

21 See the excursus "The Devil," in vol. 1, pp. 141–42.

22 In this sense, ἡ βασιλεία τοῦ θεοῦ ("the kingdom of God") is a reign that is established in time, at the end of time, and a kingdom that stretches through space. On these two aspects, see Schnackenburg, *God's Rule*, 354–57.

23 On the link between parables and the kingdom, see Jüngel, *Paulus*, 139–74.

24 The word ὁ κόκκος (the "seed," "grain") is used here in the sense of "seed that one sows"; see John 12:24; 1 Cor 15:37; O. Michel, "κόκκος κτλ.," *TDNT* 3 (1965) 810–12; BAGD, s.v.

25 Quoted from the article on the mustard seed (Gr. *sinapi*) in Alexandre Westphal, *Dictionnaire encyclopédique de la Bible* (2 vols.; Valence: Imprimeries Réunies, 1932, 1935) 2:195; on the usage of the word σίναπι, see BAGD, s.v.

26 See *y. Ber.* 5.1 (4.C) (Jacob Neusner, ed., *The Talmud of the Land of Israel: A Preliminary Translation and Explanation* [35 vols.; Chicago Studies in the History of Judaism; Chicago: University of Chicago Press, 1982–] 1:193) and *b. Ber.* 5.1 (31a); *m. Nid.* 5.2; see Kogler, *Doppelgleichnis*, 51; and Hans-Josef Klauck, *Allegorie und Allegorese in synoptischen Gleichnistexten* (NTAbh 13; Münster: Aschendorff, 1978) 213 n. 134.

27 Qur'an, Sura 21.48 (47) and 31.15 (16); see Kogler, *Doppelgleichnis*, 51.

28 See Marshall, 560. Pirot (*Paraboles*, 127), cites a rabbinic text (*y. Peʾa* 7.4 [4.N]): "Rabbi Simeon ben Halafta said: 'I have in my garden a wild mustard tree that I can climb on, as on a fig tree.'" Another translation: "Said R. Simeon b. Halafta, 'In my [field] I had this one stalk of mustard. I let it grow until it was just like a bough at the top of a fig tree!'" (Neusner, *Talmud*, 2:287).

29 In light of this difficulty, some botanists have proposed another species, *Salvadora persica*, a tree and not an annual. The proposal is old, dating to the nineteenth century; see Jülicher (*Gleichnisreden*, 2:575), who attributes it to J. Forbes Royle, "On the Identification of the Mustard Tree of Scripture,"

In their enthusiasm, the Christians who told the parable stressed the final success: Mark's version still spoke in terms of a plant, whereas Luke referred to a tree[30] and several manuscripts even mention a large tree. Along with others, the Gospel writer thought of the eschatological tree of life, such as the one referred to in Scripture (cf. Gen 3:22, 24, etc.). He has the birds rest in it, in "biblical" fashion ($\kappa\alpha\tau\alpha\sigma\kappa\eta\nu\acute{o}\omega$, "to tent," "settle").[31]

The rabbinic sources indicate that the mustard seed grows in fields and not in gardens.[32] So why, then, did Luke speak of a garden? In ancient times, a garden[33] was contrasted with the wild state of nature and was distinguished from fields. It was associated with houses and towns and thus with human beings and their urban environment. A garden is maintained and watered, unlike uninhabited places. There are various kinds of gardens and, consequently, of functions—ornamental gardens, vegetable gardens, orchards—some providing cool spots and rest, others providing nourishment and produce. They constitute eminently positive spots where civilizations can combat heat and drought. It is not just by chance that the three great monotheistic religions of the Book, Judaism, Christianity, and Islam, conceive of their paradise as a garden (see Ezek 31:8-9). The Gospel writer uses this reference to stress the plan of the "man" ($\check{\alpha}\nu\vartheta\rho\omega\pi\sigma\varsigma$), the owner, what he was expecting and what he needed; his desire to cultivate drove him to carry on his operation in a special space.

It is noteworthy that such a simple and understandable single parable of Jesus could give rise, in so little time, to such differing interpretations. Mark reinterpreted it in the sense of a *contrast*, as is indicated by the following points: "the smallest of all the seeds on earth" (Mark 4:31b) and "the biggest of all plants" (Mark 4:32b). The parable thus contrasts modest beginnings with a triumphant and miraculous ending. In Q, which Luke followed faithfully, the parable had become an account of a marvelous *growth*. The owner's first act was to take the seed and sow it in the ground. Then came growth, a natural, irresistible, and joyful process. Finally there was the proud result enabling the observation that the "seed" ($\kappa\acute{o}\kappa\kappa\sigma\varsigma$) had turned into a "tree" ($\delta\acute{e}\nu\delta\rho\sigma\nu$).[34] Just as nature has its history, so also does the kingdom of God have its own, which will end in happiness.[35]

Since the story is a simile and not a definition, it is understandable that the lines of comparison were stretched. The stretching was done in differing ways by Mark and Q. And modern commentators have, in turn, also stretched the lines in varying ways. Some say that Jesus sowed the word and that it is the church that grew out of it.[36] In 1961, one author, dependent for his thinking on Luke, rather than Mark, was still able to rejoice in the progressive fulfillment of the kingdom in the sole Catholic Church, visible, hierarchical, and victorious.[37] Since the rediscovery of the eschatological dimension of the message of Jesus at the end of the nineteenth century, however, another explanation has been given, one rooted in Mark, rather than Luke. According to that understanding, what Jesus would have been explaining here is that his message and his actions, albeit in a small but nevertheless real fashion, introduced into our world and our history the reign of God, which, soon and abruptly, without any human collaboration, by a miracle

Journal of the Royal Asiatic Society of Great Britain & Ireland (1844) 259–83, esp. 273–76. One need not endorse this hypothesis, since the tree in question is rare in Palestine.

30 Luke the city dweller has probably not taken account of the difficulty raised in the previous note, unless he took $\delta\acute{e}\nu\delta\rho\sigma\nu$ here to mean "shrub."

31 On $\kappa\alpha\tau\alpha\sigma\kappa\eta\nu\acute{o}\omega$, understood here to mean "to perch" or, even better, "to take shelter in," but not "to make a nest," see Pirot, *Paraboles*, 126–27.

32 See *m. Kil.* 2.9 and 3.2, *b. Kil.* 2.8 and 3.2, Str-B 1:669; Manson, *Sayings*, 123. For an opposing perspective, see Fitzmyer, 2:1017; and Flusser, *Wesen der Gleichnisse*, 201.

33 For $\kappa\hat{\eta}\pi\sigma\varsigma$, cf. John 18:1, 26; 19:41 (then John 20:15, in which Mary Magdalene mistakes the risen Christ for the $\kappa\eta\pi\sigma\nu\rho\gamma\acute{o}\varsigma$, the "gardener"); see McArthur, "Parable of the Mustard Seed," 201; A. Lemaire, "Jardin," *DEB*, 641; H. N. Wallace, "Garden of God," *ABD* (1992) 2:906–7; Émile Mâle, *Rome et ses vieilles églises* (Paris: Flammarion, 1942) 16–17.

34 See Weder, *Gleichnisse*, 129–30.

35 See Jüngel, *Paulus*, 151–54.

36 See Pirot, *Paraboles*, 130; Kuss, "Sinngehalt," 97; Zingg, *Das Wachsen der Kirche*, 106–7.

37 See Schultze, "Die ekklesiologische Bedeutung," 362–86.

of God alone, was going to be transformed into a glorious, powerful, and universal reign.[38]

These two different interpretations, stemming from two different Synoptic traditions, antedate us. What we have to do to advance and get beyond that conflict is to analyze the perception in antiquity of the way growth operates in nature.[39] Portraying people as naively astounded by the miraculous development from the stage of seed to the plant would amount to a caricature. Even if they did not understand the biological process and used the contrast to speak of the resurrection, they were aware that a mysterious but regular process was taking place. They knew that one had to wait, and they were aware that the seed was going to be transformed, to grow, and to become a plant or a tree. They admired the contrast between the miniscule seed that was sown and the final result with its impressive dimensions. They were able to distinguish between this natural process and the historical activity of God (or gods) in the history of their people.[40] They were also aware that human effort was a necessary part of this process, and their art or science of agriculture taught them how to proceed in this matter. By sowing a seed in their vegetable garden, they followed practices, advice, and traditions similar to those propounded in Virgil's *Georgics*.

As is often the case, there is something in the comparison that does not quite correspond to what one intends to say. Although the mustard seed, by virtue of its mention of humble beginnings, suits the beginning of the reasoning perfectly, it does not fit the triumphal end equally well. The reason is that it was the image of the cedar tree and not the mustard seed that the prophetic eschatology of the Hebrew Bible drew on in order to

illustrate paradisiacal endings.[41] Never mind! The reality of the world of nature was going to have to be distorted, under the pressure of allegory, in order to express what one wanted to make it say: the plant became a tree and the birds, which Jewish interpretation identified with Gentiles,[42] found their shelter under its branches. When God got to ruling, he sowed his will and his word, raised up a people practically starting from scratch, and trained them and retrained them to such a point that reconciliation between Israel and the Gentile nations could take place. The end of the parable, beginning with Q, was no longer the expression of a reality of nature but the coded wording of a scriptural hope.[43] Be that as it may, it is symptomatic of Jesus' theology that he chose, in order to ground hope, to depict not the lofty shape of the cedar tree but the modesty of the mustard seed. The first one conjures up the idea of dominating power; the second, perhaps, that of a welcoming community. Could the one be more masculine and the other, more feminine?

Luke decided to place these two parables here, at the end of a development, to serve as a conclusion. From chap. 11 on, he had been indicating, by the portrayal of antithetical attitudes, the true commitment one must make to God. He attacked the Pharisees' hypocrisy (11:37—12:1) and promoted the Christian confession of the Son of Man (12:1-12). He called attention to the invisible world of God, which one must choose, which is imminent, and toward which one must adopt an attitude of vigilance (12:35-48), the reign that one must seek (12:31) and for which one must divest oneself of everything (12:13-21). The Lord is going to arrive (12:36); although he may be delaying in coming (12:45), he will certainly come (12:35-46). This reign of God, which

38 See Jeremias, *Parables*, 146–49. A balanced position respecting contrast and growth is found in Dahl, "Parables of Growth" (see Scott, "Parables of Growth Revisited," 3–5); Weder, *Gleichnisse*, 132.

39 See Kuss, "Senfkornparabel," 78 n. 1; Klauck, *Allegorie und Allegorese*, 214; Lohfink, "Senfkorn und Weltenbaum," 109–26; and see the commentary on 8:4-21 in vol. 1.

40 See Kuss, "Sinngehalt," 93 n. 24.

41 Compare the paradisiacal imagery that is in the background of texts such as Ezekiel 31 or Daniel 4. Mussner ("1QHodajoth und das Gleichnis vom Senfkorn") directs attention to the image of the off-

shoot that became a tree according to the Qumran writings, particularly 1QH 6.14b–17 and 8.4–9.

42 See *1 Enoch* 90:30, 33, 37; Thomas W. Manson, *The Teaching of Jesus: Studies of Its Form and Content* (2d ed.; Cambridge: Cambridge University Press, 1935; reprinted 1963) 133 n. 1; idem, *Sayings*, 123; Kuss, "Sinngehalt," 88–89 n. 14; Jeremias, *Parables*, 147; Zingg, *Das Wachsen der Kirche*, 104.

43 The formulation at the end of v. 19 corresponds to a composite citation of Dan 4:9, 18 (LXX 4:12, 21 and Theodotion in the edition of A. Rahlfs); Ezek 17:23; 31:6, and Ps 103 (102):12a; see Dupont, "Les paraboles du sénevé et du levain," 599–600; Kogler, *Doppelgleichnis*, 149–68.

is associated with Jesus, who has come to cast a fire (12:49), is in some measure already here. Certain of its signs are visible, and it is important to know how to read them (12:54-56). Preparing for it involves repenting and returning to God (13:1-9). God waits for us and helps us: through Jesus' ministry he restores his people, in a way that is still limited and partial, just as the piece of bread in the communion service is ostensibly small. Luke's parable confirms that and serves as a conclusion: by pointing to tiny beginnings, it proleptically affirms the promising process and the tremendous consequences.[44] Luke gives an eschatological interpretation of the parable, but for him there is no eschatology without God's people. The birds in the branches are there to serve as a reminder of that. And even if the Lukan church already counted Gentiles among its members along with Jews and anticipated the reality of the kingdom of God, in the eyes of the Gospel writer it was not to be identified with God's reign. As for the kingdom, we are still closer to the seed than the tree. The church, for its part, is still not made up of good intentions, but of the seed, a divine reality, cast into our garden. This seed, tiny when compared to the planet's needs, is sufficient to cheer hearts. What "the entire crowd" cheered at the end of the story of the woman who was bent over, namely, the wonderful things that Christ was doing (13:17b), is the beginning, a microscopic *sub specie aeternitatis*, of the establishment of God's reign, identified with a life that grows and a resurrection that takes place.[45]

■ **20** Despite Jacques Dupont's conclusions,[46] I do not believe that the two parables were originally twinned. To be sure, Jesus liked to use two examples in succession, but the earliest Christians were also fond of bringing

together what was similar. The superfluous introduction to the second parable, "and again he said" ($\kappa\alpha\grave{\iota}\ \pi\acute{\alpha}\lambda\iota\nu$ $\epsilon\hat{\iota}\pi\epsilon\nu$), the absence of this parable in Mark's triple tradition, and the separation of the two in the *Gospel of Thomas* (logia 20 and 96) are three strong indications in favor of a separate origin. Q brought the two parables together, and Lukan redaction probably further accentuated the resemblance between them.

■ **21** Since a simple repetition would have been monotonous, and equal length fastidious, Luke chose, at the beginning of v. 20, to combine the double question of v. 18 into one. Here again, the Lukan Jesus of course knew the answer to his own rhetorical question. Let us first make clear what the Greek word $\zeta\acute{\upsilon}\mu\eta$ means.[47] We must distinguish between yeast and leaven. Yeast is, first of all, a unicellular microscopic mushroom that multiplies by budding. Then it is the whitish lump of these mushrooms used for making something such as bread. Leaven, on the other hand, is the flour dough that has been left to ferment or to which yeast or old leaven has been added. The process of fermentation, which must take place at a certain temperature, is accelerated by the presence in the fresh dough of yeast or leaven. When Israelites made bread, they used leaven rather than yeast. They obtained this leaven by letting sour grayish dough ferment and then mixing it into the lump to be baked or first mixing it with water. Before baking the new dough, it was necessary to wait several hours in order for the leaven to have time to rise. Here, as elsewhere, then, $\zeta\acute{\upsilon}\mu\eta$ means "leaven."

In spite of this beneficial effect, leaven was considered to be a negative element. In order to understand this fact, we must remember that, for the Israelites, their ideal

---

44 For Dodd (*Parables*, 141–44), the growth of the plant and the rising of the dough are no longer awaited but already realized in the success of the ministry of Jesus, the presence of the reign of God. The time of preparation was the time of the prophets. For Grässer (*Problem*, 141–43), the parable passed from the "how" to the "when" of the reign and its coming, that is to say, from contrast to process. In his opinion, Luke understands the two parables in the sense of the success of evangelism, and not only the coming of the reign.

45 The image of the seed that dies in the ground to return to life is found not only in the Hellenistic tradition of the Eleusinian Mysteries but also in

Jewish tradition and the earliest Christian theology (see John 12:24; 1 Cor 15:37; *1 Clem.* 24.4–5); see Kuss, "Senfkornparabel."

46 See Dupont, "Le couple parabolique du sénevé et du levain," 609–23); Jeremias, *Parables*, 90–94 (Jeremias admits that there are some cases of secondary pairing).

47 On $\zeta\acute{\upsilon}\mu\eta$, see Kogler, *Doppelgleichnis*, 56–60. Kogler thinks that the leaven could also be understood in a neutral fashion, or even positively in Judaism; Str-B 1:728.

48 On unleavened bread, see Kogler, *Doppelgleichnis*, 57.

was their previous existence as nomads, and nomads fed on flat cakes, that is, unleavened bread.[48] This custom was taken over into their worship: the use of leaven was forbidden in the making of ritual oblations intended for the altar. The same was true of the bread of the Presence. The process of fermentation occasioned by the leaven was understood to be an alteration of substances, a corruption. With the approach of Passover, this ban on the use of leaven extended to individual dwellings. It was necessary—and it still is—for each Jewish family to get rid of the old leaven in order to celebrate the big feast by eating only unleavened bread.[49] This ancient custom, preserved in the liturgy and the calendar, had such symbolic significance that the apostle Paul could play on it in order to describe what takes place for Christians on the spiritual level of their belonging to Jesus Christ, "our Passover" (see 1 Cor 5:6-8).

While the choice of the mustard seed was somewhat surprising for a description of the kingdom of God, the choice of leaven was frankly shocking for a Jew.[50] Given our knowledge of Jesus' unconventional style of teaching, both with respect to procedures (frequent absence of reference to the Mosaic law) and choice of examples ("immoral" persons given as models of faith), we must

suppose that the choice of leaven is an indication of authenticity.

Once we skip the spontaneous disapproval aroused by leaven, we are forced to admit the convincing forcefulness of the image. All a woman has to do is put a little leaven in a big lump of dough.[51] Three $\sigma\acute{\alpha}\tau\alpha$ are equivalent to about forty liters,[52] or about a bushel, enough to feed between 100 and 160 persons.[53] This flour is called $\mathring{\alpha}\lambda\epsilon\upsilon\rho o\nu$,[54] a word that means first of all "wheat flour," then any kind of "flour," even "dough made with flour," or "porridge." For Luke, these two examples speak of natural processes, but of a domestic kind directed toward human welfare. The example is eloquent: it is "all" ($\acute{o}\lambda o\nu$) of the lump that is leavened ("was leavened," $\mathring{\epsilon}\zeta\upsilon\mu\acute{\omega}\vartheta\eta$). The contrast is indicated by the hidden leaven[55] and the leavened dough, and the process, by the conjunctive phrase $\acute{\epsilon}\omega\varsigma$ $o\mathring{\upsilon}$ ("until").

Ancient interpretations, such as those of Mark, Q, Luke, and Matthew, were to set the course for later ones, up until the most recent times. To get back to the origins of the Synoptic tradition and Jesus himself, we must strip away two layers: that of early ecclesial appropriation and that of modern hermeneutical predilections.[56] What is revealed by that process is a basic parabolic structure

---

49   On the disappearance of leaven before Passover, see Kogler, *Doppelgleichnis*, 57.

50   McArthur ("Parable of the Mustard Seed," 209) thinks that the comparison with a mustard seed is incongruous; Crossan ("Seed Parables," 259) thinks it frankly ludicrous. On the shocking side of the image of the leaven, see Schulz, *Q*, 309. On the inadequate character of the images sparking frustration, see Scott, "Parables of Growth Revisited," 8.

51   On $\tau\grave{o}$ $\sigma\acute{\alpha}\tau o\nu$, a transliteration of the Aramaic אָתְ[א]ס Hebrew סְאָה, a measure of around thirteen liters (a little more than eight kilograms; see Eduard Schweizer, *Jesus, the Parable of God: What Do We Really Know about Jesus?* [Princeton Theological Monograph Series 37; Allison Park, Pa.: Pickwick, 1994] 32), used for solids. Three $\sigma\acute{\alpha}\tau\alpha$ is the quantity of dough that Abraham and Sarah offered the three visitors of Gen 18:6; three $\sigma\acute{\alpha}\tau\alpha$ is about the same as an *epha*; an *epha* is the offering prepared by Gideon for the angel in Judg 6:19. See 1 Sam (1 Kgdms) 1:24. Could one say with Funk ("Beyond Criticism," 159–61) that this is the quantity that befits an epiphany?

52   See BAGD, s.v.: "about thirty-five liters."

53   Opinions differ on the number of people that these three measures of flour could feed; see Marshall, 560.

54   On $\tau\grave{o}$ $\mathring{\alpha}\lambda\epsilon\upsilon\rho o\nu$, see BAGD, s.v. The verb $\mathring{\alpha}\lambda\acute{\epsilon}\omega$ means "to grind," and the proverbial expression $\beta\acute{\iota}o\varsigma$ $\mathring{\alpha}\lambda\eta\lambda\epsilon\mu\acute{\epsilon}\nu o\varsigma$ or $\mathring{\alpha}\lambda\eta\lambda\epsilon\sigma\mu\acute{\epsilon}\nu o\varsigma$ designates a civilized life (where one grinds grain and where one is no longer content with acorns), then an easy life; see Porphyry *Abst.* 2.6.5; T. Gaisford, ed., *Suidae Lexicon* (Oxford: Typographeo academico, 1834), s.v. $\mathring{\alpha}\lambda\eta\lambda\epsilon\sigma\mu\acute{\epsilon}\nu o\nu$; H. Estienne, ed., *Thesaurus graecae linguae* (8 vols.; Paris: Didot, 1831) 1:1445–46.

55   On the verb $\kappa\rho\acute{\upsilon}\pi\tau\omega$ ("to hide"), see Funk ("Beyond Criticism," 158–59): it is a strange verb to designate "putting" leaven in dough. Deliberately chosen, this verb grabs attention. See Schweizer, *Parable of God*, 32. God is a God who reveals what is hidden. What is hidden is, after all, mysteriously present already.

56   This is what Funk ("Beyond Criticism") proposes for recovering the freshness of the initial connotations.

made up of three constituent elements: the sown seed or the hidden leaven, the plant that grows or the dough that rises, and the final large size or the abundant three measures. The first parable adds a fourth element, perhaps adventitious: the birds. It may be, as Joachim Jeremias has suggested, that these parables were told by Jesus in a polemical context and with an apologetic intention.[57] Had that been the case, the Master would have been defending the not-too-spectacular beginnings of his mission and the small size of his flock up against his own apocalyptic claims. Furthermore, he would have been expressing his sovereign confidence in God's final and imminent intervention. It may also have been the case, as John D. Crossan has suggested,[58] that Jesus wanted to express his experience of God. That is how God acts, Jesus said with the help of daring examples. In place of the protective cedar tree, he chose the unusual image of the mustard seed. And instead of the plentiful bread of life, he spoke of the leaven that was ostensibly hidden, as if to say that God is not at the disposal of those who are the keepers of the revelation. In that case, controversy would have followed on the heels of the proclamation of the parables. Did not such parables shock those who were responsible for what was holy? But what we need to remember, apart from the earlier or later polemics, is Jesus' great hope. Once things are set in motion, the result is inevitable. What happens today is decisive for tomorrow.[59] Jesus' ministry in Israel on behalf of the Word of God was in organic relation with the coming of God's reign.[60]

History of Interpretation

According to Irenaeus of Lyons, the disciples of Marcus the Magician, the leader of eastern Valentinianism, had established a rite in which, by playing with two cups (the contents of the smaller one were poured into the larger one, which was then supposed to overflow), grace's sudden emergence was demonstrated. A formula spelled out that conviction: "May that Charis who is before all things, and who transcends all knowledge and speech, fill thine inner man, and multiply in thee her own knowledge, by sowing the grain of mustard seed in thee as in good soil" (Irenaeus *Adv. haer.* 1.13.1). At that point divine knowledge, overflowing, born of heavenly grace, invaded the believer, who began to prophesy. It was an allegorical interpretation that legitimized these practices: it identified the seed with divine gnosis, born of grace; the ground that receives it, with the inner being (called "good soil" by allusion to another parable, the one about the sower, 8:15); the fantastic result, which is not called a tree or a large plant, apparently with prophecy. The other parable, on the other hand, the one about the leaven, made it possible, by virtue of its mention of the three measures, understood allegorically, to legitimize the division of humanity into three categories, the "hylics," the "psychics," and the "pneumatics," in the interpretation of Ptolemaeus, the leader of the western school of Valentinianism. The woman who hides the leaven is Wisdom, and the leaven, the Savior himself (ibid. 1.8.3).

That interpretation was followed by Origen's, known to us from a fragment: "In another way, one can take the woman to be the Church; the leaven, the Holy Spirit; and the three measures, the body, the spirit, and the soul. They are made holy by the leaven of the Holy Spirit, to such a point that they become one dough with it, in order that 'your whole body, your spirit, and your soul might be kept without reproach until the day of our Lord Jesus Christ' as Saint Paul said" (*Hom. in Luc.* [ed. Rauer] frg. 82, 205, 316).[61] That anthropological interpreta-

---

57 See Jeremias, *Parables*, 149.

58 See Crossan, "Seed Parables," 264–66. For Jüngel (*Paulus*, 154), the occasion of these parables was not the criticisms addressed to Jesus but the prayers of his disciples: Jesus wanted to make them understand the "now." Schnackenburg (*God's Rule*, 154–56), Haenchen (*Weg*, 182), and Ramaroson ("'Parole-semence' ou 'Peuple-semence,'" 91–101) underscore the continuity in God himself, who will bring the modest beginning to a glorious end.

59 See the beautiful formula of Karl Georg Kuhn, "Πειρασμός ἁμαρτία σάρξ im Neuen Testament

und in den damit zusammenhängenden Wortstellungen," *ZThK* 49 (1952) 220 n. 1: "Was *jetzt geschieht, bricht durch* als das *Kommende*," cited by Eichholz, *Gleichnisse*, 74.

60 See Percy, *Botschaft*, 207–11. On the sense of the parable according to the historical Jesus, see Pirot, *Paraboles*, 128–29; Schnackenburg, *God's Rule*, 154–56; Dupont, "Les paraboles du sénevé et du levain"; idem, "Le couple parabolique du sénevé et du levain"; Jeremias, *Parables*, 147–49; Kogler, *Doppelgleichnis*, 188–96.

61 See Origen *Hom. in Luc.* (ed. Rauer) 538–39.

tion resembles the interpretation of the parable of the mustard seed given by Marcus the Magician. The adding on of the quotation of 1 Thess 5:23 was to become a common practice.

If we remain in the East, we can read the developments made by Cyril of Alexandria, who identified the mustard seed with the proclamation of the gospel. So that Church Father was delighted with the success of the Christian mission. The birds, who stand for people compared to God's greatness, find shelter in Christ. This interpretation, a simple one, subsequently became complex by virtue of the quotation of a text from Numbers (Num 10:1-3) speaking of two trumpets, which Cyril identified with the gospel of Christ and the witness of the Law and the Prophets, trumpets that the apostles put to their lips. There follows an explanation of the parable of the leaven that runs along the same lines as Origen's (Cyril *Hom. in Luc.* 98).[62]

In the West, Ambrose, bishop of Milan, commented at length on the two parables. In the light of Matt 17:20, he identified the mustard seed, an image of the kingdom of God, with faith. So having faith is equivalent to having the kingdom. Ambrose reflected on the fate of the seed, crushed but then vigorous, which he compared to Christ: "It is a seed when it is arrested, a tree when it is resurrected, a tree providing shade for the world." The branches are supposed to stand for the apostles, John, Peter, or Paul. Ambrose recalled the previous story, the healing of the woman who was bent over: the Christian life is being straightened up, freed from the law, not in order to live a life of covetousness but freely to perform good works. Ambrose knew that the parable of the leaven was ambiguous. He was acquainted with several explanations of it: for some the leaven stood for Christ, whom the church, the woman, hides "in the most intimate part of our spirits"; for others, the dough is the world, "until it is leavened by the Law, the Prophets, and the gospel." Ambrose himself, however, preferred to say that the leaven is "the spiritual doctrine of the church." "By means of spiritual leaven, the church sanctifies human

beings, who are composed of body, soul, and spirit." We should note that the ministry of the church accomplishes this fermentation through the "teaching of the Scriptures." "So this work of the church is not improvised nor left to chance, but worked out over a long period of time, so that the three elements are but one, without being vitiated by the law of sin." He then quotes 1 Thess 5:23 and refers at length to the unity that the resurrected creature will recover ("we will have the appearance and the charm of a simple creature") (*Exp. Luc.* 7.176–94).[63]

We might cite the testimonies of four other Western Church Fathers. Augustine of Hippo interpreted the woman as the Lord's flesh, the leaven as the gospel, and the three measures as the nations of the world (because of Noah's three sons) (*Tract. Joh.* 9.16–17). Primasius of Hadrumetum had this to say, in his explanation of Rev 6:6: "Thus the Lord said that the leaven is hidden in three measures of flour, thereby demonstrating that the doctrine of Wisdom, starting from little, is consecrated for all the people [retain the variant reading *omni populo*] by the holy figure of the undivided Trinity" (*In Apocalypsin* 2.6). Gregory the Great said that the mustard seed is Christ, small and humble in his flesh, but sturdy as a tree in his majestic power. The branches are the preachers, on which rest the birds, that is, the souls that have risen above terrestrial thoughts and find consolation in the pastors' words (*Moral.* 19.1.3). Finally, the Venerable Bede identified the man of the parable of the mustard seed with Christ, the garden with the church, the growth of the seed with the propagation of the gospel in the world and its growth in the believer's spirit. He concluded, "while in the old vineyard the unfruitful fig tree is cut down, in the garden of the Gospel, the new mustard tree will soon be growing."[64]

Luther interpreted the parable of the mustard seed ecclesiologically and meditated on the church's weakness. That weakness is not associated only with the beginnings of Christianity; it is a constitutive element of the way of God, who causes his kingdom to grow differently than the dictates of this world's reigns, would have

---

62   See Payne Smith, *Cyril*, 456–59. The Greek text of two passages has been edited recently in Reuss, *Lukas-Kommentare*, frg. 153–54, 199–200.

63   The citations are taken successively from Ambrose *Exp. Luc.* §§180, 187, 189, 190, 190, 190, 191, 194; 2:74–82.

64   See Bede *In Luc.* 4.1533–98; CCSL 120:269–71 (citation from page 270 lines 1559–61).

it grow. Luther was thus faithful to his theology of the cross, but, at the same time, he was also partial to the theology of glory, by virtue of the identification he made between the church and the kingdom.[65]

Luther understood the parable of the leaven as a consolation, since in his thinking, once Christ is in us, like the leaven in the dough, nothing can rob us of him. We are one with him, one body, one lump, one cake, one loaf of bread. The enemy can crush us but not separate us from Christ. The enemy can cook us, roast us, and burn us, but cannot withdraw from the dough the leaven that has already caused it to rise. That is our consolation.[66]

Calvin also invited us to draw consolation from the parable or, more exactly, to be doubly encouraged by it. Christians should not be worried about the fact that their ministers are "persons of low social status and of little esteem in the eyes of the world," that those who hear them do not automatically applaud when the gospel is proclaimed, and that the disciples remain few in number and of humble social status. That is not simply a reality to be reckoned with; it is also a way of proceeding that is willed by God: "It is the Lord's express purpose that his kingdom have small and despicable beginnings, so that its power might be all the better known, when unexpected progress is seen to take place." Such an interpretation is theocentric, since it makes the result depend on God's creative power and the initial purpose on his determinative will. By accepting this double encouragement, believers rely on the most solid support there is, that is, God, and thus face up to criticism and ridicule.[67]

Whether the parables have been approached from an ecclesial, an anthropological, a universal, or an eschatological perspective, the history of interpretation has respected God's mysterious wisdom, his lack of conformity to the world, and his invisible power. It also invites believers to welcome God's Word, that is, Christ's gospel, and to hope against all hope. Finally, it gives structure to a vision of the church, its mission in the world, and the kerygmatic responsibility of its ministers.

Conclusion

Only rarely did Luke explicitly link his parables to the kingdom of God. Even though he did so here, let us not precipitously join them to the church or to Christ. So God's reign, compared to a seed that becomes a tree, has a story running from birth to maturity. This seed should not be identified with the tree of life, which matures immediately and just as quickly is lost (Gen 2:9; 3:11-13, 17, 23-24). By means of this new plant, which starts off as a seed buried in the garden, God reestablishes his power. Luke saw the history of God in the form of a history of his Word. This Word, at first hidden, is growing. The Gospel writer was thinking of the ministry of Christ, who preached among us (cf. God's reign among us in 17:20-21). In his time, which was neither the beginning nor the end, the seed had already developed but had not yet become a tree. Following Jesus, Luke stressed smallness. It is not the time for either largeness or triumphalism.

Yet, ever since the good news rang out in Jesus, the newness of God, the eschatological anticipation, has been manifested. The growth of the Word, the current presence of the kingdom, has been sustained, first by Jesus Christ, then by the Holy Spirit. According to Luke, the Gentiles were already responding to the call (Acts 10:1-11, 18; Acts 15) and were entrusting themselves to the fragile protection of the Risen One. The plant grows on its own (as in the parable found only in Mark 4:26-29). But God needs men (v. 19) and women (v. 21): this is a mediation that is necessary at a certain level but useless at another (cf. 17:10). We are talking not about a miracle but about cultivation, in which the human being is involved, and nature, which witnesses to the harmony between creation and redemption. God is the one who makes things grow (cf. 1 Cor 3:6), who wills things (God's plan), who is at work (redemption), and who brings things to completion (eschatology). These parables praise God for his humor (a mustard plant instead of a cedar tree), his love (he loves his garden, he

---

65   Eberle, *Luthers Evangelien-Auslegung*, 448–49.
66   Ibid., 449–50.
67   Calvin, *Harmony*, 2:79–81; quotation from 79–80.

sows life), his way of operating (against human common sense, he prefers to go the way of smallness, make a stop at the lowest level of being, whisper rather than speak loudly), and his desire to work with others (he recruits, he delegates, he collaborates).

Each of these two parables has its own meaning. The first speaks of the action of God, who profits from positive human values, symbolized by the garden and the good soil. The second one proclaims the success of God, who does not refuse to carry out his project of bringing about good, even by means of negative realities, represented here by the leaven. Though at first glance the two parables appear to be twins, each shows its own identity when examined more closely. They are two sisters that should not be confused in spite of their undeniable resemblances.

God is among men, among women, and among children. While the seed is nourished by the earth, the leaven acts on the dough: there is interaction of the Word with faith and of Christ with Christians. It was not by chance that Jesus applied the image of the mustard seed first to the kingdom of God and then to faith (17:6). Nor was it by chance if the image of the leaven was added to that of the seed. The leaven of the gospel works in the world, in churches, and in persons. Bread is prepared and offered, a modest and powerful presence of Christ among his own. Between the winter of the passion and the autumn of the parousia, Luke has placed us in the spring or in summer, each person choosing their season according to their faith and the state of their church.

On the Way to Equity
(13:22-30)
Bibliography

Allison, Dale C., "Who Will Come from East and West? Observations on Matt 8.11-12—Luke 13.28-29," *IBS* 11 (1989) 158–70.

Betz, Hans Dieter, *Essays on the Sermon on the Mount* (Philadelphia: Fortress Press, 1984) 148–49.

Boring, M. Eugene, "A Proposed Reconstruction of Q 13:28-29," *SBLSP* (1989) 1–22.

Brown, *Apostasy*, 140–41.

Chilton, Bruce D., *God in Strength: Jesus' Announcement of the Kingdom* (SNTU B/1; Freistadt: Plöchl, 1979) 179–201; reprinted Sheffield: JSOT Press, 1987.

Corbin, Michel, "La porte étroite, une lecture théologique de Lc 13, 22-30," *Vie chrétienne* 203 (1977) 11–16.

Denaux, Adelbert, "Der Spruch von den zwei Wegen im Rahmen des Epilogs der Bergpredigt (Mt 7, 13-14 par. Lk 13, 23-24)," in Delobel, *Logia*, 305–35.

Derrett, J. Duncan M., "The Merits of the Narrow Gate (Matt 7:13-14, Luke 13:24)," in idem, *Studies*, 4:147–56.

Dupont, Jacques. "'Beaucoup viendront du levant et du couchant . . .' (Mt 8, 11-12; Lc 13, 28-29)," in idem, *Études*, 2:568–82.

Egelkraut, Helmuth L., *Jesus' Mission to Jerusalem: A Redaction Critical Study of the Travel Narrative in the Gospel of Luke, Luke 9:51—19:48* (EHS 80; Frankfurt am Main: Peter Lang, 1976) 169–75.

Giesen, Heinz, "Verantwortung des Christen in der Gegenwart und Heilsvollendung: Ethik und Eschatologie nach Lk 13, 24 und 16, 16," *ThG* 31 (1988) 218–28.

Goulder, *New Paradigm*, 2:571–81.

Grässer, *Problem*, 192–93 and passim.

Grimm, W., "Zum Hintergrund von Mt 8, 11f // Lc 13, 28f," *BZ* n.s. 16 (1972) 255–56.

Gueuret, Agnès, *La mise en discours: Recherches sémiotiques à propos de l'Evangile de Luc* (Theses Cerf; Paris: Cerf, 1987).

Hoffmann, Paul, "Πάντες ἐργάται ἀδικίας: Redaktion und Tradition in Lc 13, 22-30," *ZNW* 58 (1967) 188–214.

Horn, *Glaube und Handeln*, 183–84, 265.

Jeremias, Joachim, *Jesus' Promise to the Nations* (trans. S. H. Hooke; Philadelphia: Fortress Press, 1967).

Kloppenborg, *Formation*, 42 n. 1, 92, 223–27, 237.

L'Eplattenier, Charles, "Lecture d'une sequence lucanienne, Lc 13, 22 à 14, 24," *EThR* 56 (1981) 282–87.

Lambrecht, *"Eh bien!"* 179–94.

Luz, *Matthew*, 1:370–73, 379–81.

Marguerat, *Jugement*, 175–82.

Mees, *Parallelstellen*, 59–71.

Menoud, Philippe H., "Le sens du verbe βιάζεται dans Lc 16, 16," in idem, *Jesus Christ and the Faith: A Collection of Studies* (Eugene, Ore.: Pickwick, 1978).

Mussner, Franz, "Das 'Gleichnis' vom gestrengen Mahlherrn (Lk 13, 22-30): Ein Beitrag zum Redaktionsverfahren und zur Theologie des Lukas," in idem, *Praesentia*, 113–24.

Packett, E. Brian, "Luke 13:25," *ExpT* 67 (1955–56) 178.

Parrott, Rod, "Entering the Narrow Door: Matt 7:13-14 // Luke 13:22-24," *Forum* 5 (1989) 111–20.

Perrin, Norman, *Rediscovering the Teaching of Jesus* (New York/San Francisco: Harper & Row; London: SCM, 1967) 116, 144–45, 161–64.

Polag, *Christologie*, 91–93 and passim.

Quispel, Gilles, "A Diatessaron Reading in a Latin Manichean Codex," *VC* 47 (1993) 374–78.

Rosaz, Monique, "'Passer sur l'autre rive,'" *Christus* 26 (1979) 323–32.

Sampedro Forner, José Carlos, "Historia de la Salvación o Salvación en la Historia: Estudio exegético-teológico de Lc 13, 22-30," *StLeg* 21 (1980) 9–48.

Schlosser, *Règne de Dieu*, 2:603–69.

Schmid, *Matthäus und Lukas*, 254–56.

Schulz, *Q*, 309–12, 323–30, 424–27.

Schürmann, Heinz, *Gottes Reich—Jesu Geschick: Jesu ureigener Tod im Licht seiner Basileia-Verkündigung* (Freiburg im B.: Herder, 1983) 117–22.

Schwarz, Günther, "Matthäus 7, 13a: Ein Alarmruf angesichts höchster Gefahr," *NovT* 12 (1970) 229–32.

Seynaeve, Jaak, "La parabole de la porte étroite: l'acceptation 'pratique' du Christ, Lc 13,22-30," *AsSeign* 52 (1974) 68–77.

Wrege, Hans-Theo, *Die Überlieferungsgeschichte der Bergpredigt* (WUNT 9; Tübingen: Mohr, 1968) 132–35, 146–52.

Zeller, Dieter, "Das Logion Mt 8,11 f / Lk 13,28 f und das Motiv der 'Völkerwallfahrt,'" *BZ* n.s. 15 (1971) 222–37; 16 (1972) 84–93.

Zimmermann, *Methodenlehre*, 145.

22/   **Jesus went through towns and villages,
teaching and making his way to Jerusalem.
23/ Someone said to him, "Master, will only
a few be saved?" He said to them, 24/ "Strive
to enter through the narrow door; for many, I
tell you, will try to enter and will not succeed.
25/ When once the owner of the house has got
up and shut the door, and you, standing outside, begin to knock at the door, saying, 'Lord,
open to us,' then in reply he will say to you, 'I
do not know where you come from.' 26/ Then
you will begin to say, 'We ate and drank with
you, and you taught in our streets.' 27/ And
he will say, 'I do not know where you come
from; go away from me, all you workers of
unrighteousness!' 28/ In that place there will
be weeping and gnashing of teeth when you
see Abraham and Isaac and Jacob and all the
prophets in the kingdom of God, and you yourselves thrown out. 29/ Then people will come
from the east and the west, from the north
and the south, and will dine in the kingdom
of God. 30/ Indeed, some are last who will be
first, and some are first who will be last."**

If this passage had come down to us only on a single
papyrus fragment, detached from its context, it would
present us with a stern image of Jesus' message. Here we
have a teacher who, as in the Gospel of John, does not
directly answer the person questioning him (vv. 23b-24),
who encourages the "everyone for themselves" approach
when confronted with a narrow door (v. 24). Here we
also have a merciless owner of a house who refuses entry
(v. 25), who carries bad faith to the point of pretending
not to know those whom he claims to be in a position
to condemn (vv. 25, 27), who will not be swayed (vv.
26-27), and who proves to be possessed of a judgmental
spirit ("evildoers," v. 27; "you yourselves thrown out," v.
28). Finally, we have a man who predicts weeping and
gnashing of teeth, and who announces, with a touch of
sadism, that those who are damned will have to contemplate the patriarchs' and the prophets' enjoyment (v. 28),
and one who supposes that a door will be miraculously
opened for those who are saved at the last hour as they
come from the four corners of the earth (v. 29), and who
concludes, with apparent satisfaction, that a reversal of
privileges is all that awaits us (v. 30). One has to have the
context of the Gospel to read this passage less pessimisti-
cally. A familiarity with the Bible and its literary genres
is also required in order to perceive that hardness fills a
hortatory function and that the cruel images are perhaps

not God's last word. Be that as it may, this context—the
gospel as good news—must not allow the readers to
take away from these sayings their bitter crudeness. This
passage reminds those who water down the gospel that
access to the kingdom is risky and that God expects specific things from us.

Analysis

The Composition of the Text

For once, the two extremities of the pericope are clearly
marked: the summary in v. 22 serves as a transition and
opens a new section, while in v. 31 a temporal indication
leads us to dissociate what precedes from what follows.
Verses 22-30 thus form a unity, which is composed of a
brief question (v. 23), followed by a long answer by Jesus
that contains sudden new developments (vv. 24-30). A
biting imperative (v. 24a) is flanked by a justification
(v. 24b), itself illustrated by a parabolic, even allegorical,
essentially dialogical, narrative (vv. 25-27): once the situation is laid out (closed door, v. 25a), there comes a first
petition (v. 25b), which is rejected (v. 25c); then a second
entreaty, in the guise of a narrative reminder (v. 26),
receives a new negative response from the master, who
adds his rejection (v. 27b) to his refusal (v. 27a). In v. 28,
we do not know who is speaking, whether it is Jesus (who

has been speaking) or the owner (the character in the story). I opt for Jesus, who draws the consequences from the preceding dialogue of the deaf and sketches a disquieting portrait in chiaroscuro. By way of anticipation, Jesus makes us see the threatening spectacle, whose dualism is not static: the speaker associates enigmatic "last" persons who will have come from the four corners of the earth, and to whom he promises access to the kingdom (v. 29), with the face-to-face encounter of v. 28. Finally, the movement jells: the vocabulary of movement (v. 29) gives way to that of final immobility (v. 30). In short: v. 22, summary; vv. 23-24, dialogue; vv. 25-27, a parabolic narrative; vv. 28-29, final pictures; and v. 30, a final observation.[1] So this biblical passage alternately presents exhortation and evocation, the imperative that wishes us well and the outline of a tragic result. In brief, we have an apophthegm in which the hero's answer is laid out at length, instead of being brief.

The Origin of the Text

It is difficult to tell whether Luke composed this unit himself or whether he took it over as it was from a source.[2] Verses 22-23 are without parallels.[3] Verse 24 is found also, in a different wording, in Matthew's Sermon on the Mount: there what is involved is just entering and not striving to enter; moreover, there the narrow gate is contrasted with a wide gate, in the context of a doctrine of the two ways (Matt 7:13-14). Did the writers of the two Gospels each make his own adaptation of the same Greek text of Q?[4] The parabolic narrative (vv. 25-27) also has its counterpart in the same chapter of Matthew (Matt 7:22-23). The Matthean structure of it is simpler and corresponds, in Luke, to the second petition made by those who were excluded (v. 26) and to the owner's second refusal (v. 27). The scenario of the closed door is absent from Matthew, and the reasons given are quite different: in Matthew, prophecies, exorcisms, and miracles take the place of meals eaten together and teaching. In Matthew, it is Christ who replies in the first person; in Luke, the "owner" of the parable. Although the idea of refusal is the same, expressed in both cases in scriptural terms (Ps 6:9),[5] the English term "workers of unrighteousness" translates a Greek construction in Matthew that is literally "workers of lawlessness"; in Luke, one that is literally "workers of unrighteousness." Considering these differences, can we assume that Luke and Matthew are based, in these two verses, on the same text of Q?[6] We must factor in the oral tradition, in order to be able to

---

1 Preoccupied with the origin of the text, exegetes frequently neglect to research its structure. Corbin, "La porte étroite," 13; L'Eplattenier, "Lecture d'une sequence lucanienne," 282–87; and Meynet, *Saint Luc*, 2:152–53 are exceptions. Corbin, for example, detects here a concentric structure of which the center is v. 26 and the symmetrical parts: A (vv. 23-24a); A´ (v. 30); B (v. 24b); B´ (v. 29); C (v. 25a); C´ (v. 28); D (v. 25b); D´ (v. 27).

2 Two principal hypotheses have been advanced: (a) the unity points back to a source specific to Luke, Proto-Luke or L (e.g., Grundmann, 284; Friedrich Rehkopf, *Die lukanische Sonderquelle: Ihr Umfang und Sprachgebrauch* [WUNT 5; Tübingen: Mohr Siebeck, 1959] 90; Jeremias, *Parables*, 86–87 n. 96 and 110; Wrege, *Überlieferungsgeschichte,* 135 n. 2), and (b) Luke composed this unity with the help of several materials, with Q being the principal source (see, e.g., Bultmann, *History*, 130; Schulz, *Q*, 309–12, 424–27, 323–30; Hoffmann, "Πάντες ἐργάται ἀδικίας," 188–214; Mussner, "Das 'Gleichnis' vom gestrengen Mahlherrn," 113–24.

3 According to Schulz (*Q*, 310) and Hoffmann

("Πάντες ἐργάται ἀδικίας," 192–93), vv. 22 and 23 are redactional.

4 On the analysis of v. 24, see Schulz, *Q*, 309–11 (Matthew has the original form; Luke shortened it); Wrege, *Bergpredigt*, 132–35 (Matthew and Luke have a common kernel, which is developed in a different and independent manner in catechesis); Schwarz, "Matthäus 7, 13a," 229–32 (the logion, by its rhythm, must be isolated); Denaux, "Der Spruch," 305–35 (Luke is closer to Q than is Matthew); Parrott, "Entering the Narrow Door," 111–20 (state of the question and reconstitution of Q).

5 See the commentary below on 13:27.

6 On the connections between the tradition and redaction in these verses (vv. 25–27), see Schulz, *Q*, 424–27 (the text of Q was mistreated by someone, that is to say, by Matthew and by Luke); Mussner, "Das 'Gleichnis' vom gestrengen Mahlherrn" (intelligent rereading and regrouping of verses by Luke—v. 25, on the one hand, and vv. 26-27, on the other, which had no connection together); Hoffmann, "Πάντες ἐργάται ἀδικίας" (an independent origin of v. 25, on the one hand, and of vv.

take into account the parallel quoted in *Second Clement*, which, as we know, is rich in sayings of the Lord transmitted independently of our canonical Gospels: "For this reason, if you do these things, the Lord said, 'If ye be gathered together with me in my bosom, and do not my commandments, I will cast you out, and will say to you, Depart from me, I know not whence ye are, ye workers of lawlessness'" (*2 Clem.* 4.5).[7]

Verses 28-29 also have a parallel in Matthew (Matt 8:11-12). All of Luke's elements are found in Matthew but in a different order. Although Luke begins with weeping and gnashing of teeth, Matthew ends with the mention of them (Matt 8:12b). According to Luke, what has happened to the patriarchs is observed by those who are excluded, whereas in Matthew, the patriarchs' fate is simply alluded to. Luke, moreover, is alone in adding "and all the prophets" to the triad of patriarchs. In Luke, the coming of the last persons to be invited follows the mention of Abraham, Isaac, and Jacob, while in Matthew, it precedes (Matt 8:11a). While Luke points out the four points of the compass, Matthew makes do with "east and west." In Matthew (Matt 8:12a), the mention of those excluded, called the "heirs [literally, sons or children] of the kingdom," is more ceremonious than in Luke. As may be seen, everything is found in both Gospels, but in a different order and worded differently. We must be dealing here with two different, rather free, rereadings of Q.[8]

The conclusion, v. 30, about the first and the last, is found four times in the canonical Gospels: Mark placed it at the end of the teaching on the danger of riches (Mark 10:31). Matthew also quoted it in the same place (Matt 19:30), then reused it at the end of his parable on the workers of the eleventh hour (about five o'clock) (Matt 20:16). Luke, who did not like to use doublets, is the only one who inserted it here; he skipped it at the end of the teaching about riches (18:30). The parable on the workers of the eleventh hour, on the other hand, is missing from his Gospel. These four times, when it is used structurally, fall into two groups: the parallels of Mark 10:31 and 19:30 are virtually identical, while Luke 13:30 and Matt 20:16 are distinctive by virtue of the absence of the word "many" ($\pi o \lambda \lambda o i$) and by the use of the same word order, which invites us to see in these last two verses a rereading of a single Q saying. In it the verb "to be" comes at the beginning and the words follow in the order "last"—"first"—"first"—"last" (even if each of the Gospel writers used as a predicate what was the subject in the other and vice versa, as is proved by the presence or absence of the articles).[9] The *Oxyrhynchus*

26-27, on the other; vv. 26-27 receive an eschatological undertone from v. 25; v. 26 of Luke is nearer to the tradition than the parallel in Matthew; v. 27b is decisive).

7   Cited by Aland, *Synopsis*, 297; the text of Justin (*Dial.* 76.4–5), curiously, seems to testify to familiarity with our written Gospels, but influenced again by oral tradition; see Justin *1 Apol.* 16.11–12. The two texts are cited by Aland, *Synopsis*, 297; Arthur J. Bellinzoni, *The Sayings of Jesus in the Writings of Justin Martyr* (NovTSup 17; Leiden: Brill, 1967) 28–30 (*Dial.* 76.4), 67–69 (*1 Apol.* 16.12), 22–25 (*1 Apol.* 16.11 and *Dial.* 76.5).

8   On the connections of vv. 28-29 with the tradition, see Schmid, *Matthäus und Lukas*, 254–56 (the Matthean context is secondary and redactional; the Lukan elements are the addition of the north and south and the expression "and all the prophets"; Luke's "and you will see," on the other hand, is original); Schulz, *Q*, 323–24 (Matthew has the primitive order; small changes were made only by Matthew); Hoffmann, "$\Pi \acute{a} \nu \tau \epsilon \varsigma \, \grave{\epsilon} \rho \gamma \acute{a} \tau a \iota \, \grave{a} \delta \iota \kappa \acute{\iota} a \varsigma$" (Luke tightly links v. 28 with what precedes; v. 29

is a distinct logion); Zeller, "Logion" (in search of Q, which he proposes went like this: "Many shall come from East and West and recline at table with Abraham, Isaac, and Jacob in the Kingdom of God. But the Sons of the Kingdom will be thrown outside. There there will be wailing and grinding of teeth" [p. 224]); Dupont, "Beaucoup" (the primitive context has been lost, but Matthew has the primitive arrangement; at the beginning this was a single logion; the point of view of Jesus is threat, promise, and contrast; that of Matthew is faith, Israel, and pagans and role of the disciples; that of Luke is the importance of works, Israel, and the Gentiles); Schlosser, *Règne de Dieu* (Luke has the primitive arrangement; in the beginning, this was two logia and not merely one).

9   For Hoffmann ("$\Pi \acute{a} \nu \tau \epsilon \varsigma \, \grave{\epsilon} \rho \gamma \acute{a} \tau a \iota \, \grave{a} \delta \iota \kappa \acute{\iota} a \varsigma$"), v. 30 announced, at the beginning, the conversion of the world at the end of time. Luke makes this saying into a threat and an exhortation: there is no guarantee; one must practice justice.

Papyrus (654, no.3), which corresponds to *Gos. Thom.* 4, transmits the saying in wording identical to Mark 10:31 par. Matt 19:30.[10]

In conclusion, while Matthew has these sayings dispersed, Luke has brought together here sayings originating in the oral tradition that are attested to by Q. He transforms them into a long reply (vv. 24-30) to a question (v. 23) that he constructs after having written a transitional summary (v. 22). The arrangement of this reply takes the double form of an ethical invitation and a dramatic fresco, all of it belonging to the apophthegm genre; but in this apophthegm the reply is more detailed than usual.

Commentary

■ **22** Luke uses this brief summary[11] to indicate a pause, all the while confirming Jesus' double activity—his journey to Jerusalem and his teaching. Reference is also made to 9:52, 57 for the journey, and to the various speeches or recent dialogues for the teaching.[12] His thaumaturgic activity is passed over in silence: while intense in Galilee, it diminished during the journey and was to come virtually to a halt in Jerusalem (cf. 22:51 for an exception).

In Luke's eyes, the proclamation of the gospel was carried out from one town or city to another (Christianity, in his thinking, was an urban phenomenon) (see 4:31, 43; 5:12; 7:1, 11). But the journey necessitated following routes that involved going through villages as well.[13]

The Gospel writer has stressed the journey, to which he called attention twice in v. 22.[14] It is the journey of the Messiah, who advanced toward Jerusalem, the scene of his passion ("to Jerusalem" is stressed, at the end of the sentence).[15] So it is not an insignificant mention, but an important christological, even soteriological, note.

As the present participle "teaching" ($\delta\iota\delta\acute{\alpha}\sigma\kappa\omega\nu$), with durative force, indicates, Luke did not neglect Jesus' teaching. The context of the summary abundantly confirms the didactic nature of Jesus' itinerant activity. This participle is the ecclesial and ethical stamp on the summary.[16]

■ **23** The question of the number of those who would be saved was a contemporary preoccupation in Israel.[17] The

---

10   See Schrage, *Thomas-Evangelium*, 32–34.

11   This summary recalls that of 8:1. Godet (2:179) remarks on the link with 9:51.

12   See "teach us" (11:1); "he began to speak to his disciples" (12:1); "he says to his disciples" (12:22).

13   See 8:1: $\kappa\alpha\grave{\iota}\ \alpha\mathring{\upsilon}\tau\grave{\diamond}\varsigma\ \delta\iota\acute{\omega}\delta\epsilon\upsilon\epsilon\nu\ \kappa\alpha\tau\grave{\alpha}\ \pi\acute{\diamond}\lambda\iota\nu\ \kappa\alpha\grave{\iota}$ $\kappa\acute{\omega}\mu\eta\nu$ ("and he himself went on through cities and villages").

14   The first mention refers to the journeys and travels from cities and villages that he implies. The second insists on the orientation toward Jerusalem that this walk maintained. In $\delta\iota\alpha\pi\diamond\rho\epsilon\acute{\upsilon}\omega\mu\alpha\iota$, one observes the $\delta\iota\acute{\alpha}$ that marks the journey on the land in general, and with the $\kappa\alpha\tau\acute{\alpha}$, which is distributive, one will think of the stopovers in cities and villages. See Godet, 2:179. As for $\pi\diamond\rho\epsilon\acute{\iota}\alpha\nu\ \pi\diamond\iota\acute{\epsilon}\omega$, it is attested in the Greek language (see BAGD, s.v. $\pi\diamond\rho\epsilon\acute{\iota}\alpha$), and does not seem to be a Latinism (*iter facere*).

15   The manuscripts are divided on the spelling of Jerusalem. Nestle-Aland[26], which in particular follows the venerable $\mathfrak{P}^{75}$, $\aleph$, and B, retains the Greek and prosaic form $\hat{I}\epsilon\rho\diamond\sigma\acute{\diamond}\lambda\upsilon\mu\alpha$. Since this is a journey with theological implications, one must have, according to the hypothesis of de La Potterie, "Les deux noms de Jérusalem," 57–70, the Semitic and sacred form ($\hat{I}\epsilon\rho\diamond\upsilon\sigma\alpha\lambda\acute{\eta}\mu$). Not, responds

this author (pp. 68–69), because Luke has in view here in 13:22-30, the hardening of Israel and the condemnation of Jerusalem, which would imply the usage of the Greek and prosaic form.

16   See Hoffmann ("$\Pi\acute{\alpha}\nu\tau\epsilon\varsigma\ \grave{\epsilon}\rho\gamma\acute{\alpha}\tau\alpha\iota\ \grave{\alpha}\delta\iota\kappa\acute{\iota}\alpha\varsigma$," 192), who notes the two aspects, christological and paraenetic, of the summary, v. 22.

17   The survivors seem to be only a few in Isa 37:32 (they are called $\diamond\acute{\iota}\ \sigma\omega\zeta\acute{\diamond}\mu\epsilon\nu\diamond\iota$ in the Septuagint). The motif of the small number of those who are saved is highlighted in *T. Ab.* 11:11 (review A), 2 Esdr 7:47, 8:1-3; v. 1: "The Most High made this world for the sake of many, but the world to come for the sake of only a few"; 9:15-16 ("I said before, and I say now, and will say it again: there are more who perish than those who will be saved, as a wave is greater than a drop of water" [*NRSV*]). But the rabbinic tradition also knows hope for the salvation of all the Israelites; thus *m. Sanh.* 10:1; see Grundmann, 285; Str-B 1:83. In the NT, see Matt 22:14; 25:1-13; John 7:49.

wording of the verse is, however, thoroughly Lukan.[18] As Jesus' reply leads us to understand, what worried the anonymous listener was not the objective question of the quota but his subjective concern about being included in the number. By his answer, Jesus was to confirm the listener's cause for worry: Jesus contrasted the small number ("few," ὀλίγοι) with the acknowledgment of the large number ("many," πολλοί) of those who were unable to enter. Jesus and the person with whom he was speaking were in agreement on one point: few would be saved and many lost. So there was a serious threat.

■ **24** The Matthean parallel confronts everyone with a choice, at the crossroads or at the entrance through two gates (Matt 7:13-14).[19] The Lukan text, on the other hand, invites each believer to engage in a struggle and to persevere (ἀγωνίζεσθε, "strive," is a present imperative with durative or iterative force). That is what the Christian life is like (οἱ σῳζόμενοι [v. 23], a typical Lukan expression, means both "those who are saved" and "those who are being saved").[20] The term ἀγών ("struggle," "fight"; in the context of public games, "contest," "competition," of which the Greeks were fond) was used at that time in the figurative sense by philosophers and missionaries to describe the life of the wise man or the man of God. The author of 1 Timothy used it: "Fight the good fight of the faith; take hold of the eternal life,

. . ." (6:12).[21] That image of the "fight" presupposes an adversary (for Christians, themselves, and behind them Satan, rather than other candidates for salvation), solid training (cf. the theme of the training of the disciples during Jesus' journey from Galilee to Jerusalem), and great strength of character (firmness, intelligence, perseverance, and skillfulness).[22] The competition is not direct, like a scramble in front of a door, but indirect, like a test in school.[23] What takes place is a selection, rather than the sudden appearance of enmity. The only one who will succeed is the one who makes it to the goal (cf. "and [they] will not succeed," καὶ οὐκ ἰσχύσουσιν, v. 24b). And in order to get there, one must have acquired some qualifications (Luke thought in terms of conversion, faith, hope, and the practice of love) and be firmly decided to put them into practice (by being able to renounce everything threatening victory, in order to be able to concentrate on the one thing necessary). So it is not enough to have the right desires (since there are many who are satisfied with looking for a way to enter without any effort, v. 24b). The "struggle," "fight" (ἀγών), is not unrelated to the "anguish when faced with death" (ἀγωνία), which is the ultimate fight, which Jesus himself had to face ("and in his anguish he prayed more earnestly," καὶ γενόμενος ἐν ἀγωνίᾳ ἐκτενέστερον προσηύχετο, 22:44). Salvation is for those who accept

---

18 See οἱ σῳζόμενοι ("the saved," Acts 2:47); εἶπεν πρὸς αὐτοῦ ("he said to them," Luke 12:15; 15:3, etc.; Denaux, "Der Spruch," 326–27; εἰ introduces here a direct question, as in 22:49 and Acts 1:6; 19:2). This turn of phrase is not classical, unless one suggests a verb such as θαυμάζω ("I am amazed"); see Plummer, 346. BDF (§440.3 n. 5) instead thinks of a Semitism: interrogative εἰ in the LXX, e.g., Gen 17:17 LXX.

19 See Deut 11:26-29; 30:15-20; Jer 21:8; Parrott, "Entering the Narrow Door," 116 (references); Luz, *Matthew*, 1:371–72; Schulz, *Q*, 309–12.

20 See Bovon, *L'oeuvre*, 171–74.

21 See ἀγών in the NT: 1 Thess 2:2; Phil 1:30; Col 2:1; 1 Tim 6:12; 2 Tim 4:7; Heb 12:1; ἀγωνίζομαι, John 18:36; 1 Cor 9:25; Col 1:29; 4:12; 1 Tim 4:10; 6:12; 2 Tim 4:7; see Victor C. Pfitzner, *Paul and the Agon Motif: Traditional Athletic Imagery in the Pauline Literature* (NovTSup 16; Leiden: Brill, 1967); G. Dautzenberg, "ἀγών etc.," *EDNT* 1:25–27. The substantive is absent from the Synoptics. Nevertheless, one must

not forget Luke 16:16: "and everyone tries to enter it by force."

22 Corbin ("La porte étroite") reflected on this struggle: it is about a conflict of faith more than of obedience; one must know how to benefit from the present time, an offer of a last chance; one should think about the mystery of Christ. In brief, Jesus (v. 24) modifies and dislodges our questions (v. 23). Rosaz ("'Passer sur l'autre rive,'" 323–32) meditates on the beneficial time to stop before the narrow door, which evokes, according to her, v. 24. Israel stopped on the edge of the Jordan before entering into the promised land (see Deuteronomy 9–10).

23 On the sense of v. 24, see Grässer, *Problem*, 192–93 (the immanence of the kingdom is replaced in Luke by its suddenness); see also Brown, *Apostasy*, 140–41 (salvation is present, and is acquired after a hard-fought struggle); Schwarz, "Matthäus 7, 13a," (v. 24 represents an alarm cry targeted at a people that has lost its way, in view of the gravest danger, which Jesus alone has identified).

God's will, do not succumb at the last moment, and persevere in the almost physical fight of prayer. When he introduced the verb "strive" ($\dot{\alpha}\gamma\omega\nu\acute{\iota}\zeta o\mu\alpha\iota$) into the tradition, Luke was probably inspired by the catechetical teaching of his church, which thought of Christian life as a test or a combat.[24]

If you talk to me about the greatest blessing (salvation, v. 23), I will reply: this is what Jesus' message is like here, expressed in terms of the greatest effort (the struggle, v. 24). It is necessary to be realistic about both life and the kingdom.

Luke may have put this saying and the following ones in this place in order to bring together theocentric parables about the mustard seed and the leaven.[25] In this way, God's initiative and humans' reaction fit together, as do the gift of love and the commitment by way of response. Even though the mustard plant has grown (v. 19), the birds still have to come and light on its branches. Salvation is less a question of will and duty than of dialogue and desire. Faith is not just a struggle.

Structurally, we are dealing here with two sayings (with the "I tell you," $\lambda\acute{\epsilon}\gamma\omega \ \acute{\upsilon}\mu\hat{\iota}\nu$ [v. 24b] clearly setting off the second one). The first one (v. 24a) is an invitation, such as those that Jewish wisdom was capable of issuing. The second (v. 24b), introduced by "for" ($\acute{o}\tau\iota$), stresses, by way of contrast, the importance of the initial imperative.[26]

A word about the narrow door.[27] The tradition that Luke has taken over presupposes the heavy town gate that was closed at nightfall. When that large gate was closed, there was, for latecomers and for emergencies, in that large main gate, or beside it, a small opening accessible to only one person at a time. If that is, in fact, the scenario envisaged by the tradition, our life and the life of the whole world are in the twilight years of the present age and in the dawn of eschatological times (the large gate being already closed). So the decision that needs to be made is one offering a last chance (the narrow door still being accessible). The saying also contains an implicit criticism, that of not having known how to enter in time by the large open gate. Such a scenario corresponds to the theology of Q and to the word $\pi\acute{\upsilon}\lambda\eta$ (city "gate"), which Matthew has preserved. Luke, who wished to construct an allegorical story, thought instead in terms of the "door" ($\vartheta\acute{\upsilon}\rho\alpha$) of a house or of an agricultural estate surrounded by a wall (vv. 25-27; cf. 12:35-48). This change had to be made so that the narrow door (v. 24) could become the door that the owner closes (v. 25). Although eschatology has lost something of its imminence, personal decision has kept its urgency.

■ **25** At the redactional level, then, there is no longer a contradiction between the narrow door of v. 24 and the locked door of v. 25.[28] If the narrow door is indeed that of the last chance, it is logical that at some moment it

---

24 See 1 Tim 6:11-12 and Heb 12:1-3; Dautzenberg, "$\dot{\alpha}\gamma\acute{\omega}\nu$," 64.

25 See Giesen, "Verantwortung des Christen," 218–28, esp. 220.

26 See Denaux, "Der Spruch," 328–29

27 Notions of narrowness (this life) and of breadth (the world to come) appear in 2 Esdr 7:6-15. On the door to a house, or small door ($\vartheta\acute{\upsilon}\rho\alpha$), in contrast to a door to a city, or large door ($\pi\acute{\upsilon}\lambda\eta$), see Schwarz, "Matthäus 7, 13a"; and Derrett, "Merits of the Narrow Gate," 147–56 (for him, one must pass through the little door and enter for free; to pass through the large door would mean to deal with the tax collector!). On the metaphorical or allegorical usage of the door, see K. Praechter, ed., *Kebetos Thebaiou Pinax*, 15.1–3 (Leipzig: Teubner, 1893) 13–14; see Libanius *Or.* 9.12; Ps 118 (117):19-20; Isa 59:14 LXX; Sir 21:10; *T. Ab.* 11 (review A); Matt 25:10-12, *Hermas Sim.* 9.1–16 (references from Derrett, "Merits of the Narrow Gate"); Joachim Jeremias, "$\vartheta\acute{\upsilon}\rho\alpha$," *TDNT* 3 (1965) 173–80. Because of the influence

of the parallel in Matthew, many scribes preferred to write $\pi\acute{\upsilon}\lambda\eta$ rather than $\vartheta\acute{\upsilon}\rho\alpha$ in Luke 13:24. In *Pirqe ʾAbot* 4.21 (16), we read: "Rabbi Jacob said: 'this world is only the lobby of the future world; prepare yourself in the lobby so that you can enter into the ballroom'" (borrowed, slightly altered, from Moïse Schuhl, *Maximes des Pères* [Paris: Librairie Colbo, 1977] 43).

28 One might hesitate on the punctuation to place at the end of v. 24. If one places a period, one brings to mind the distinct origin of the two pieces: instruction on the narrow door and a half-parable on the closed door. If one places a comma, one rejoins the two pieces (they could not enter [v. 24] after the master had closed the door [v. 25]). But in this case, the saying no longer ends satisfactorily; see Lagrange (388), who opts for the comma. In any case, the syntax of vv. 25-27 is clumsy, as scribes and exegetes are well aware. The phrase $\dot{\alpha}\varphi$ ᾽ $o\acute{\upsilon}$ ("as soon as," see BAGD, s.v. $\dot{\alpha}\pi\acute{o}$, 2.2c) is followed by $\ddot{\alpha}\nu$ because if the closing of the door is certain,

is to close once and for all. Night has come. The owner has decided to lock up his house. There are certain acts whose inexorability is tied up with their temporality; some situations are cruel because they cannot be turned around. Too late is too late.

In vv. 25-27, we read a short story composed entirely of a dialogue in two waves. This passage has the air of being a fragment of a story, one that is parallel to that of the wise bridesmaids and the foolish bridesmaids (see Matt 25:10-12). The chronology confers a dramatic effect on events: the owner had already gotten up and already closed the door when "you" stand there, outside, and knock and ask to be let in. You arrive too late. The most the owner might do—if he were to do even that—would be to open up to those he knows.[29] But he pretends at that point not to know you.

■ **26** This is a new attempt (it is the second time the verb "begin" is used).[30] "You" try to get yourself acknowledged, by means of memories that are quite different from the ones Matthew evokes. Luke deliberately refers to a contact between the "owner of the house" and those speaking to him, without any implication of a commitment on their part. These persons were Jesus' contemporaries, his compatriots. They had listened to him, but there is no indication that they had decided to become his disciples. Their spectator attitude is reminiscent of that of the anonymous listener in v. 23.

In that time, what did it mean to speak of "eating and drinking with someone"? Probably not "in your company."[31] Instead, those speaking refer to a proximity, lay claims to a mutual acquaintanceship, and contradict the owner's statement, "I do not know where you come from." They even suggest that they have heard his mes-

sage—but they have not accepted it. So they have scarcely any arguments in their favor, at the most some worthless arguments[32] that are beside the point, from Luke's point of view. Without being aware of it, these persons show that they have not understood the gospel, and they level a glaring accusation against themselves. They had been at Jesus' side but had not understood his message. They had remained at the door of his teaching and had not struggled to fathom its meaning. Hence the owner's reaction: "I do not know where you come from"; that is, I do not know what the source of your life is. Do you live in a communion that can bring you into the kingdom, or do you remain blinded by your egocentricity? Operating out of an allegorical perspective of the history of salvation, Luke perhaps suggests that these persons speaking to the owner represent Jesus' contemporaries.[33] In fact, they represent all those who refuse to commit themselves to serving Christ.

■ **27** The owner then reiterates his refusal and adds to it an expression of rejection.[34] This expression—without anything calling attention to it—is a quotation from Scripture, Ps 6:8[9] LXX: ἀπόστητε ἀπ᾽ ἐμοῦ πάντες οἱ ἐργαζόμενοι τὴν ἀνομίαν, "go away from me, all you who commit lawlessness." While the first part of Luke's text corresponds word for word to the first part of the text of the LXX, it is the second part of the parallel in Matthew (Matt 7:23) that is the exact equivalent of the second part of the text of the LXX. We might call attention to 1 Macc 3:6, which contains the phrase πάντες οἱ ἐργάται τῆς ἀνομίας ("all the evildoers"), which is halfway between Matthew (ἀποχωρεῖτε ἀπ᾽ ἐμοῦ οἱ ἐργαζόμενοι τὴν ἀνομίαν) and Luke (ἀπόστητε ἀπ᾽ ἐμοῦ πάντες ἐργάται ἀδικίας). In the Psalm, it is the suffering righteous

---

the hour is still uncertain (see BAGD, s.v. ἄν, 3). Despite the initial καί ("and"), καὶ ἀποκριθεὶς ἐρεῖ ὑμῖν ("and by way of response he will say to you") must be the main clause. Personally, I place a period between v. 24 and v. 25, but I think, nonetheless, that Luke conceived of vv. 24-30 as a single story. In v. 26, many scribes have written the subjunctive ἄρξησθε because of the influence of the ἄρξησθε of v. 25 and the ἀφ᾽ οὗ ἄν (v. 25).

29 The Bible often uses the verb "to know" to specify the relation of God or Christ with their own: 1 Kgs [3 Kgdms] 18:37; Jer 9:22-23; Ezek 5:13; 2 Chr 6:33; Num 16:5; Isa 63:16; John 7:27; 9:29; 10:14; 1 Cor 8:3; 2 Tim 2:19.

30 On v. 26, see Schulz, Q, 424-27.

31 Contra Reiling and Swellengrebel, *Handbook*, 514. The ensuing formula (5:30) rightly has μετά ("with") and not ἐνώπιον ("before").

32 See Godet, 2:182; and Marshall, 566.

33 See Mussner, "Das 'Gleichnis' vom gestrengen Mahlherrn," 117-18; Seynaeve, "La parabole de la porte étroite," 72-73. Luke's attitude toward Judaism is very controversial; see the survey of contradictory exegetical opinions in François Bovon, "Studies in Luke-Acts: Retrospect and Prospect," *HTR* 85 (1992) 175-96, esp. 186-90.

34 See Hoffmann, "Πάντες ἐργάται ἀδικίας," 202-5.

person who hopes to be relieved of his oppressors. In 1 Maccabees, it is Judas Maccabeus, who frees Israel and gets rid of the evildoers. Here, the eschatological judge is the one who separates the sheep from the goats and applies the procedure of excommunication.[35]

The narrative logic of v. 24 implies zeal in competing to enter through the narrow door. In vv. 25-27 the logic presupposes a reproach addressed to the indecisive spectators. These slight differences, due to the varied origin of the materials, did not keep Luke from producing a well-knit story. A unified theme allowed him to paint an allegorical portrait of the history of God with his people[36] and, ultimately, with all human beings.

■ **28** Those who were turned down had tried everything, so there was nothing left they could do, aside from giving vent "there, in that place" ($\dot{\epsilon}\kappa\epsilon\hat{\iota}$),[37] in front of that closed door, to their desperation ($\kappa\lambda\alpha\upsilon\vartheta\mu\acute{o}\varsigma$ means "weeping," "crying," "moaning") and rage ($\beta\rho\upsilon\gamma\mu\acute{o}\varsigma$ means "gnashing," and $\beta\rho\acute{\upsilon}\chi\omega$, "to crunch," "to gnaw," "devour," sometimes "to gnash" or "grind" [one's teeth]). The expression "weeping and gnashing of teeth" is more Matthean than Lukan (cf. Matt 8:12, the parallel to this text; and Matt 13:42, 50; 22:13; 24:51; and 25:30);[38] but not only does the expression go back to Q, but Luke himself was able to refer elsewhere to the eschatological tears of those who laugh now (6:25) and the hateful grinding of teeth of Stephen's persecutors (Acts 7:54). These expressions of distress and rebellion are rooted in the Hebrew Bible.

The way Luke saw things, although those who were excluded did not get through the door, they did get to look through the windows: just as he did in the case of the exemplary story of the rich man and poor Lazarus, Luke has taken over the Jewish topic of the intensification of the misfortune of the damned when seeing the elect and their delights (16:23).[39] Verse 28 first calls attention to the presence in that reserved space of the patriarchs and all the prophets[40]—in a word, all that was best in the old system. Verse 29 is going to add the presence of the elect of the new covenant.

Following Q, Luke and its parallel in Matthew provide a terrible critique of Israel's privileges. Those who believed themselves to be assured of salvation, but who had not truly opted for God, his Messiah, and conversion, would be inexorably excluded from the kingdom. Such a reversal of situations reflects the experience of the earliest Christians, their hope, and their hostility to Israel. This perspective, which is sociologically understandable, figures in the text of the Gospel, but that is not all there is to the Gospel. Moreover, with *Second Clement*, we should add that Christians are threatened with the same evil, and consequently the same punishment: a knowledge of the gospel that is not followed up on by its application. Luke does not rule out an ethical interpretation of the sayings of Jesus that he has brought together here, along with the perspective sketched by salvation history.[41]

---

35 The term $\dot{\alpha}\delta\iota\kappa\acute{\iota}\alpha$ ("injustice") is important (Ps 6:9, cited, has $\dot{\alpha}\nu o\mu\acute{\iota}\alpha$, "lawlessness"). The word $\dot{\alpha}\delta\iota\kappa\acute{\iota}\alpha$ was a shortcoming for the Greeks (see Aristotle *Eth. nic.* 5.1.19) and, in Israel, was an expression or a summary of sin. The apostle Paul even understood it as the mark of human hostility before God (e.g., our injustice in light of God's justice, Rom 3:5). In Luke also, $\dot{\alpha}\delta\iota\kappa\acute{\iota}\alpha$ has a strong meaning: one who loves and fears God does not know $\dot{\alpha}\delta\iota\kappa\acute{\iota}\alpha$ ("injustice"). The practice of "injustice" excludes the commensality of the Lord in the kingdom. The term, however, is not very common in Luke (see 16:8-9; 18:6; Acts 1:18; 8:23).

36 Mussner ("Das 'Gleichnis' vom gestrengen Mahlherrn") deserves the credit for having established this.

37 The word $\dot{\epsilon}\kappa\epsilon\hat{\iota}$ ("there") can be used in Greek to designate the other world; see Sophocles *Ajax* 1371 and *Antigone* 76 (both cited by Lagrange, 390).

38 See Luz, *Matthew*, 2:11.

39 See the commentary below on 16:23.

40 "And all the prophets" is an obvious addition by Luke. The evangelist thus expresses the caesura within Israel that brings about the coming of the Messiah, Jesus. With the triad of patriarchs and the company of prophets, he presents the whole ensemble of the holy people of the old economy, in the time of promise (see the word "prophet," which recalls this). At the time of its realization, the people and their leaders have faltered. The patriarchs and the prophets also make one think of the two parts of Scripture, the Law and the Prophets (see 24:27, in which one also finds a mention of "all the prophets").

41 Thus, Christians too can lapse into $\dot{\alpha}\delta\iota\kappa\acute{\iota}\alpha$ ("injustice") and risk the rejection of the kingdom; see

■ **29** Contrary to Matthew's presentation, in Luke, the welcoming of the final guests follows the exclusion of the first beggars. Prompted by a literary consideration (bringing the excluded ones [v. 28] closer to the visitors who were turned away [vv. 25-27]), this reversal has a theological effect: the text ends with the procession of the elect, the pilgrimage of the nations (v. 29).

In Matthew, only two directions are indicated: the east, that is, the place of the exile, and the west, that is, the land of slavery under the oppression of Pharaoh (see Zech 8:7; 10:10). The author of the First Gospel had in mind the future of the people of God. Tradition was also probably thinking of the eschatological reassembling of Israel.[42] The four directions in Luke, as well as the organization of all of his work, lead us to give a Christian missionary interpretation of this quadruple pilgrimage.[43] Henceforth, it would be the elect from the nations who were to have access to the kingdom, rather than just the Jews dispersed throughout all the Diaspora.[44] Moreover, the verb "come" is in the future tense. They will arrive and they will be able to enter. The Lukan puzzle of texts that were originally independent of each other produces slight logical tensions: we must forget the "too late" of the bolted door and think instead in terms of "I do not know where you come from." Here the owner recognizes these pilgrims of the last hour, these converts, the fruit of the Christian mission. They can come from far off; they can arrive the very last; they do not know Hebrew; and they probably do not physically belong to Abraham's race. That does not keep God from loving them, welcoming them, and bringing them in and seating them (ἀνακλίνω[45]) at his table in his kingdom. We have here the expression of what is best in the gospel hope and Christian universalism. It is a marvelous message, which, as it broke barriers, was to conquer the ancient world.[46]

■ **30** What the Lukan wording means is this: here we have some persons who arrive in the very last place.[47] They will nevertheless be pronounced to be on a par with those who came first, and they will be considered and treated the same way as the first ones. Why? Not because of any hare-brained idea of the judge, but by virtue of a decision of the arbitrator in consideration of their "struggle" (ἀγών) to enter through the narrow door. And here we have some others who had been first, but who passed up their chance.

Since the wisdom tradition often illustrated truth by means of contrasted images, the relegation to last place of those who were "first" is suggestive. But is that God's final message? Is there not a place for each person in his kingdom? If that were not the case, would it still be his

---

Hoffmann, "Πάντες ἐργάται ἀδικίας," 202–5; Seynaeve, "La parabole de la porte étroite," 73, 75.

42 The biblical tradition awaits an eschatological gathering of the people of God; see Deut 30:4 LXX; Isa 43:5-6; Ps 107 (106):3; Bar 4:37; 5:5; *Ps. Sol.* 11:2; see Allison, "East and West," 158–70. The biblical tradition also knows of an eschatological pilgrimage of the nations to Zion's hill (see Isa 2:2-3; 49:12; 56:6-8; 60; 66:18-20; Jer 3:17; Mic 4:1; Zech 8:20-23; 14; 16; see Joel 4:10-12; see Jeremias, *Jesus' Promise to the Nations*, 55–60; Zeller, "Logion," 222–37 (depending on the circumstances, Israel awaited either the pilgrimage of the nations, or the punishment of the nations; what counts is the glory of God and the glory of Zion).

43 The redactional addition of the north and the south makes sense only if Luke is thinking of the Gentiles and not of dispersed Jews. On this theme of the pilgrimage of the Gentiles, see Grundmann, 286; Dupont, "Beaucoup," 580–81; Schlosser, *Règne de Dieu*, 2:618–20.

44 On v. 29, see Dupont, "Beaucoup"; Zimmermann, *Methodenlehre*, 145; Zeller, "Logion"; Grimm, "Zum

Hintergrund," 255–56 (link with Isa 43:5b-6: coming; direction from heaven; in view of salvation); Schulz, Q, 323–30; Schlosser, *Règne de Dieu*, 2:618–20; Allison, "East and West" (traditional sense: a prophecy about the eschatological gathering of dispersed *Jews*).

45 See 14:15; Rev 19:9; in the OT and Jewish literature: Isa 25:6; see 65:13; Ezek 32:4; *1 Enoch* 62:14; see Marshall, 568; Schlosser, *Règne de Dieu*, 2:618–26.

46 Luke does not envisage here an individual eschatology. He does not reflect further on the actual fate of the patriarchs and prophets. For him, in any case, the feast of the kingdom has not yet begun. On these questions, see Schlosser, *Règne de Dieu*, 618–24.

47 On v. 30, see Horn, *Glaube und Handeln*, 183–84 (from being eschatological in the tradition, the saying becomes paraenetic in Luke); Allison, "East and West," 165 (Jesus, like Paul after him, does not despair over the ultimate fate of Israel, the salvation of "all Israel").

kingdom? The anonymous person in v. 23 was correct: there is a question as to how many will be saved. I will answer that question by saying that, in order to be able to enter the kingdom, one must enter by the door or gate of the gospel and move toward Christ, who, in another place (John 10:7, 9), declared that he was himself the gate. If adherence is a matter of personal responsibility, refusing to believe remains a possibility for this life. Thus, according to the earliest Christians, part of the people of Israel failed to fulfill their responsibility when they did not acknowledge the Messiah (cf. Rom 11:22, 25). After twenty centuries of Christianity, similar withdrawals can invariably be observed in the church. As long as the system of faith remains in force and God's truth is not imposed by what is evident to the eye, the church will remain weak, the Gospel will not be very compelling, and the number of the elect will be limited to the small number of believers, those who carry on the struggle for the faith. This passage has the dark coloring of threat, but it appears in a context of light. The human risk of hardening appears against the light background of the gospel whose door Christ came to open for us, a door that will remain open "as long as it is called 'today'" (Heb 3:13).

History of Interpretation

Cyril of Alexandria's *Sermon* 99[48] begins with an initial conviction: the Word of God guides us the way a captain safely steers his boat to its destination. He then makes one initial observation: Christ did not answer the anonymous person's question. That is how the Lord proceeded: he said nothing apart from what was useful to the listener (here, only that one needs to struggle in order to enter). Then there is a question: Why is the door narrow? Because salvation requires faith and virtue, and nothing less than a combat can win them and keep them for us, and because we must give up everything that might lure us onto the wide road. That is the following point, the one that the story of the owner who bolts his door teaches us. A new question: Who are the excluded people

who had eaten and drunk in his presence? They are the Jews. Their meals in his presence should be understood as a reference to the Israelite worship service. The quotation of the teaching corresponds to the reading of the law in the synagogues. These people who talked with the Master and were rebuffed by him for good are those who had not substituted faith for sacrifices and gospel precepts for Moses' commandments. Cyril added that the saying can apply also to many Christians who have believed in Christ, taken part in Christian feasts, and heard quotations of the Gospels in church but have not retained anything or put anything into practice (in this connection Matt 7:21 is quoted: "Not everyone who says to me, 'Lord, Lord,' . . ."). The penultimate remark is that even so, the Gentiles come from the four corners of the earth to take the Jews' place. Cyril's analysis of v. 30, on those who will be first and those who will be last, made it possible for him—and this is the last point—to put the finishing touches on this sermon of his, which was so hostile to the Jews. In short, we have here an explanatory sermon, which attempted to answer the questions in the text and followed it with units of meaning corresponding to those used in modern interpretation. There is a sensitivity to salvation history and to the theological shifts of emphasis made by Jesus, for example, refusing to answer the question as to how many would be saved. Finally, there is, unfortunately, a well-known anti-Jewish sentiment present in his sermon.

The Venerable Bede's *Commentary on Luke* (*In Luc.* 4.1599–679; CCSL 120:271–73) follows the text of the Gospel. The penetration of the domain of salvation can be done only through the narrow door, that is, through suffering and renunciation. Many are those who would like to enter but cannot, since they are frightened by the ruggedness of the way and are unable to understand that the Lord is gentle and humble in heart. Next, Bede identified the owner of v. 25 as Christ. He thought that Christ is entirely with his own in the heavenly homeland in the process of obtaining joy for them. But, because of his divinity, he can also keep his promise (Matt 28:20) and stay with Christians who are struggling in their

---

48   We know this text from the Syriac version and from some Greek fragments; see Payne Smith, *Cyril,* 2:460–64; and Reuss, *Lukas-Kommentare,* frg. 201–4, 154–56.

earthly journey. In that capacity, he is their secret comforter. The permanent closing of the door is obviously still for another day. Standing outside and knocking at the door amounts to requiring in vain that God show mercy that one has always refused to show to others. Next Bede asked himself how God, who knows what people are thinking, can possibly be unaware of certain human beings. God does not know them, he answered, because he has not been able to put their faith or their love to the test, since these qualities have been nonexistent. Verse 26 (eating and drinking with you, being taught by you) can be taken two ways. On the one hand, it can refer to the Jews (and his explanation resembles Cyril's). These Jews were not able to move on from blood sacrifices and the reading of the prophets to the apostolic teaching that spiritualized obedience and rituals (Rom 14:17 and Phil 3:19 are cited in this connection). On the other hand, it could be talking about us, about our bad way of eating and tasting the Scriptures. The most obscure sacred texts are, in fact, food that must be thoroughly chewed, and the clearest passages are a drink to be swallowed at once. Verse 27 witnesses to the fact that practicing religious ceremonies and knowing the Scriptures amount to nothing unless one's faith accompanies the first, and virtue, the second. Weeping and gnashing of teeth suggested to Bede a comparison with what he imagined Gehenna to be: weeping, because of the extreme heat; chattering of the teeth, on account of the glacial cold. Bede offered two possible explanations of v. 30: one, historical, took note of the bypass of the Jews by the Gentiles; the other, ethical, envisaged a fate contrary to our earthly successes or failures. So, whether in connection with v. 26 or v. 30, Bede offered a double reading of the text: one reading of it as a parable of salvation history; the other, as an ethical and spiritual exhortation. Cyril also gave two explanations of v. 26, along the same lines as Bede. These two perspectives are to be found in the two principal modern interpretations, Franz Mussner's, on the one hand, and Paul Hoffman's, on the other.

If we were at this point to place Erasmus's *Paraphrasis* and Zwingli's *Annotationes* side by side, we would notice the one's enthusiasm and the other's embarrassment. Erasmus read the passage ethically: we must give up the desires of this world and follow the humble Christ; knowing the law and having heard Christ are useless if we continue to hate our brothers and sisters, to prefer our glory to God's, and to put the taste for money ahead of love.[49] Faith alone enables us to put this ethical program into practice and to have access to eternal bliss. It is precisely that happy marrying of faith and works that bothered Zwingli.[50] "Here begin the difficult questions: if it is not faith alone that justifies, once more, we fall again into the way of works; where then is the doctrine of justification by faith?"[51] Zwingli was to attempt to reestablish the priority of faith and to make it clear that "salvation does not accrue to any except those who, with certain faith, throw themselves on God's mercy manifested by Christ."[52] Nevertheless, the only persons who will be saved are those who, from the root of their faith, will cause good works to germinate and will struggle against the number one enemy in their eyes, which is the "flesh." To those who opt for faith, the admonitions to practice good works are pedagogically welcome.

Conclusion

This pericope brings the symbolisms of action and rest together. Jesus is on a journey, on the way of righteousness, where he fulfills God's plan (v. 22). Those persons with whom he enters into conversation are invited to act, to come from the four corners of the earth (v. 29), and to enter by the narrow door into the house of the kingdom (v. 24). A failure to fulfill one's obligations, on the other hand, brings about exclusion (vv. 25-27). God's world resembles a house, a space for rest, joy, and fellowship (vv. 28b, 29b). That space is offered and made accessible to people who work and do things (v. 27b), those who travel (v. 29a), and those who strive for righteousness

---

49   Erasmus, *Paraphrasis*, 398–99.
50   Zwingli, *Annotationes*, 665–67.
51   Ibid., 665.
52   Ibid., 666.

(v. 24a), that is, those who, like Jesus, discover God's plan and do good. The ethics of commitment and the theology of the kingdom go hand in hand. Moreover, from ancient times on, they have made possible two readings of the passage: one, sensitive to salvation history, that is, the fate of Israel and the Gentiles; the other, paying attention to present responsibilities, their risks, and their ethical stakes. It is quite likely that Luke, after having recounted the recent phases of God's plan as a parable, detected the paraenetic undertones of his account. Should the criticism of Israel's privileges not also apply to the status of the church? "You" who are Jesus' Jewish listeners can become the "you" who are the Christian readers of the Gospel. Those who are first are not necessarily those one would think! He who laughs last laughs best! Jesus refused to give a direct answer to a listener's question because he sensed, in the objective distance of that man, his fear of launching into subjective combat. By that means Luke right away ruled out any attitude that would not associate salvation history with personal commitment.

We must say "Luke," because this pericope seems surely to have been constructed by him, since what Luke brought together here Matthew kept separate in four different places (cf. Matt 7:13-14, 22-23; 8:11-12; and 20:16). And what Luke grouped together he also organized into an allegorical story that, as we have seen, is also paraenetic. Jesus' "you" has a double function: it confers a unity on this story of God's people and relates to us by the identification that it establishes with our story.

Whoever speaks of history speaks of temporal relationship. Everything here is concentrated in a brief period of history, but that brevity does not suppress the distinction between the present and the future. In v. 24, we are dealing with the present of the struggle; in v. 25, with the future, the following stage, which is imminent and ultimate, the one that leads to the banquet. What makes possible an existential reading of this parable of the history of God's people is that the present of the text can still be our own. "O that today you would listen to his voice! Do not harden your hearts . . ." (Ps 95[94]:7b-8a [*NRSV*], quoted in Heb 3:7b-8a). As long as there is a "today" (Heb 3:13), the doers (v. 27) can leave behind their iniquity and, by faith, dear to Zwingli, do what is righteous, dear to Erasmus. It will perhaps be the severest combat, but it will also be the finest outcome. This joining of theology and ethics matches the two orientations of the redactional summary in v. 22; does not this summary mention both Jesus' journey to Jerusalem, in line with the divine plan of salvation, and his teaching along the way, aimed at challenging and then training the disciples in the dynamics of the kingdom of God?

It is up to us to receive this teaching in a different way than the negligent listeners in v. 26. Receiving it means, first of all, understanding that our commitment will involve combat (v. 24) and a renunciation along the lines of Jesus' fate. Next, it means knowing "where we come from" (vv. 25, 27) and on what source we draw—our own personal interest or the Word of God. Finally, it means expecting surprises and reversals (v. 30). The reign of God will be different from our expectations, and there we will meet some unexpected guests.

The Fox and the Hen
(13:31–35)

Bibliography

Allison, Dale C., "Matt. 23:39 = Luke 13:35b as a Conditional Prophecy," *JSNT* 18 (1983) 75–84.

Baltzer, Klaus, "The Meaning of the Temple in the Lukan Writings," *HTR* 58 (1965) 263–77, esp. 272–74.

Bastin, Marcel, *Jésus devant sa passion* (LD 92; Paris: Cerf, 1976) 77–81.

Str-B 2:200–202.

Black, *Aramaic Approach*, 205–7.

Blinzler, Josef, "Die literarische Eigenart des sogenannten Reiseberichtes im Lukas-evangelium," in *Synoptische Studien* (Mélanges A. Wikenhauser) (ed. J. Schmid and A. Vögtle; Munich, 1953) 20–52, esp. 42–46.

Idem, *Herodes Antipas und Jesus-Christus: Die Stellung des Heilandes zu seinem Landesherrn* (Bibelwissenschaftliche Reiche 2; Stuttgart: Katholisches Bibelwerk, 1947) 16–20.

Büchele, Anton, *Tod Jesu im Lukasevangelium: Eine redaktionsgeschichtliche Untersuchung zu Lk 23* (FTS 26; Frankfurt am Main: Knecht, 1978) 152–57.

Christ, *Jesus Sophia*, 136–52.

Conzelmann, *Theology*, 61 and passim.

Daube, David, *The New Testament and Rabbinic Judaism* (Jordan Lectures in Comparative Religion 2; London: Athlone, 1956) 190–91.

Denaux, Adelbert, "L'hypocrisie des Pharisiens et le dessein de Dieu: Analyse de Lc 13, 31–33," in Neirynck, *Gospel of Luke*, 155–95, 316–23.

Derrett, J. Duncan M., "The Lucan Christ and Jerusalem: τελειούμαι (Luke 13:32)," *ZNW* 75 (1984) 36–43.

Edwards, *Theology of Q*, 132–33.

Ferraro, Giuseppe, "'Oggi e domani e il terzo giorno' (osservazioni su Lc 13, 32. 33)," *RivB* 16 (1968) 397–407.

Frizzi, Giuseppe, "Carattere originale e rilevanza degli 'apostoli inviati' in Q/Lc 11, 49-51; 13, 34-35 / Mt 23, 34-36. 37-39," *RivB* 21 (1973) 401–12.

Gilbert, Allen H., "Σήμερον καὶ αὔριον, καὶ τῇ τρίτῃ (Luke 13:32)," *JBL* 35 (1916) 315–18.

Grässer, Erich, *Die Naherwartung Jesu* (SBS 61; Stuttgart: Katholisches Bibelwerk, 1973) 109–12.

Idem, *Problem*, 38–40 and passim.

Grimm, Werner, "Eschatologischer Saul wider eschatologischen David: Eine Deutung von Lc 13, 31ff," *NovT* 15 (1973) 114–33.

Gueuret, Agnès, *La mise en discours: Recherches sémiotiques à propos de l'Évangile de Luc* (Theses Cerf; Paris: Cerf, 1987) 109–27.

Havener, Ivan, *Q: The Sayings of Jesus (With a Reconstruction of Q by Athanasius Polag)* (2d ed.; GNS 19; Wilmington, Del.: Glazier, 1987) 24–26.

Herranz Marco, Mariano, "'No me veréis hasta que digáis: bendito el que viene en el nombre del Señor' (Mt 23, 39; Lc 13, 35). Texto griego y sustrato arameo," *CuaBi* 4 (1980) 57–71 (the pagination is out of order; see n. 84 below).

Hoehner, Harold W., *Herod Antipas* (SNTSMS 17; Cambridge: Cambridge University Press, 1972) 214–24, 343–47.

Hoffmann, *Logienquelle*, 171–80.

Jacobson, Arland Dean, "Wisdom Christology in Q" (Ph.D. diss., Claremont Graduate School, 1978).

Jeremias, Joachim, "Die Drei-Tage-Worte der Evangelien," in Gert Jeremias et al., eds., *Tradition und Glaube: Festschrift Karl Georg Kuhn* (Göttingen: Vandenhoeck & Ruprecht, 1971) 221–29.

Kirchschläger, *Wirken*, 28–50.

Kühschelm, Roman, "Verstockung als Gericht: Eine Untersuchung zu Joh 12, 35-42; Lk 13, 34-35; 19, 41-44," *BLit* 57 (1984) 234–43.

Kümmel, *Promise*, 71–74.

Lehmann, *Quellenanalyse*, 146–48.

Marguerat, *Jugement*, 366–72.

Miller, Robert J., "The Rejection of the Prophets in Q," *JBL* 107 (1988) 225–40.

Nickels, *Targum*, 40.

Nolland, 2:737–38 (bibliography).

Physiologus, Der: Tiere und ihre Symbolik (trans. Otto Seel; Zurich/Munich: Artemis, 1987) 26–27.

Plath, Margarete, "Der neutestamentliche Weheruf über Jerusalem (Lk 13, 34-35 // Mt 23, 37-39)," *ThStK* 78 (1905) 455–60.

Polag, *Christologie*, 93–95 and passim.

Prete, Benedetto, "Il testo di Lc 13, 31-33: Unità letteraria ed insegnamento cristologico," in idem, *L'opera*, 225–42.

Idem, "Origine del logion 'Non conviene che un profeta perisca fuori di Gerusalemme' (Lc 13, 33b)," in idem, *L'opera*, 243–60.

Rese, M., "Einige Überlegungen zu Lk 13, 31-33," in Dupont, *Christologie*, 201–25.

Robinson, William C., *The Way of the Lord: A Study of History and Eschatology in the Gospel of Luke* (diss., University of Basel, 1960; Dallas: n.p., 1962) 54–55.

Scheffler, Eben, *Suffering in Luke's Gospel* (AThANT 81; Zurich: Theologischer Verlag, 1993) passim.

Schmid, *Matthäus und Lukas*, 332–34.

Schnackenburg, Rudolf, "Lk 13, 31-33: Eine Studie zur lukanischen Redaktion und Theologie," in Claus Bussmann and Walter Radl, eds., *Der Treue Gottes trauen: Beiträge zum Werk des Lukas. Für Gerhard Schneider* (Freiburg: Herder, 1991) 229–41.

Schnider, Franz, *Jesus der Prophet* (OBO 2; Freiburg: Universitätsverlag; Göttingen: Vandenhoeck & Ruprecht, 1973) 167–72.

Schoeps, Hans Joachim, *Die jüdischen Prophetenmorde* (SymBU 2; Zürich: M. Niehans, 1943); reprinted in idem, *Aus frühchristlicher Zeit, religionsgeschichtliche Untersuchungen* (Tübingen: Mohr Siebeck, 1950) 126–43.

Schulz, *Q*, 346–60.

Schütz, Frieder, *Der leidende Christus: Die angefochtene Gemeinde und das Christuskerygma der lukanischen Schriften* (Stuttgart: Kohlhammer, 1969) 69–73.

Steck, Odil H., *Israel und das gewaltsame Geschick der Propheten: Untersuchungen zur Überlieferung des deuteronomistischen Geschichtsbildes im Alten Testament, Spätjudentum und Urchristentum* (WMANT 23; Neukirchen-Vluyn: Neukirchener Verlag, 1967) 45–50, 53–58, 227–39, 283 n. 1.

Suggs, *Wisdom*, 63–71.

Tiede, *Prophecy*, 70–78.

Tyson, Joseph B., "Jesus and Herod Antipas," *JBL* 79 (1960) 239–46.

Verrall, Arthur W., "Christ before Herod (Luke xxiii. 1-16)," *JTS* 10 (1908–9) 321–53, esp. 352–53.

Weinert, Francis D., "Luke, the Temple and Jesus' Saying about Jerusalem's Abandoned House (Luke 13:34-35)," *CBQ* 44 (1982) 68–76.

Wellmann, M., "Fuchs," PW 7.1 (1910) 189–92.

Wiesner, D., "Fuchs," *Lexicon der Alten Welt* (1965) 1009.

Zeller, Dieter, "Entrückung zur Ankunft als Menschensohn (Lk 13, 34 f; 11, 29 f)," in François Refoulé, ed., *À cause de l'Évangile: Études sur les Synoptiques et les Actes: Festschrift Jacques Dupont* (LD 123; Paris: Cerf, 1985) 513–30.

31/ **At this instant some Pharisees came and said to him, "Get out of here and go far away, for Herod wants to kill you." 32/ And he said to them, "Go and tell that fox, 'See, I am casting out demons and performing cures today and tomorrow, and on the third day I am finished. 33/ Yet today, tomorrow, and the next day I must be on my way, because it is impossible for a prophet to perish outside of Jerusalem.' 34/ Jerusalem, Jerusalem, you who kill the prophets and stone those who are sent to you! How often have I desired to gather your children together as a hen gathers her brood under her wings, and you were not willing! 35/ See, through your fault, your house will be abandoned. I tell you, you surely will not see me until he arrives, when you will say, 'Blessed be he who comes in the name of the Lord.'"**

Here we have a pericope[1] that has posed two principal questions for commentators: What place do these difficult verses occupy in the structuring of the journey narrative, and what meaning should we assign to the interaction they witness to between the Pharisees and Jesus? Put another way, should we grant this passage a central position, at the very heart of a long chiasm?[2] Moreover, is it wise to pay particular attention to Jesus' answer? Since it diverges from the traditional Christian statements (the three days have another meaning here than in them), is the core of it historical, and does it provide us with a rare opening up of the meaning Jesus attached to his destiny?[3]

---

1 Denaux ("Hypocrisie") understands vv. 31–35 as a unity. See the state of the question on these verses in ibid., and the additional note, 316–23; Rese, "Einige Überlegungen," 202–6; Prete, "Testo," 225–42.

2 Denaux ("Hypocrisie") provides an inventory of various hypotheses (additional note, 316–18).

3 See Jeremias, "Drei-Tage-Worte," 221–29; Bastin, *Jésus*, 77–81.

Analysis

As a matter of fact, vv. 31-35 bring together two units hitched to each other (vv. 31-33 and vv. 34-35) by the hook word "Jerusalem." The first is an apophthegm; the second a judgment oracle. Luke, who was fond of dialogues and the initial reactions of those who entered into conversation with the Master, first mentions a piece of advice given by the Pharisees (v. 31). He continues by quoting two symmetrical and complementary replies given by Jesus (vv. 32-33). The first reply is alone in drawing on the metaphor of the fox. The second one is alone in suggesting a justification (every prophet must die in Jerusalem). Common to both is the division into three days, which is noted at the end of the first saying and at the beginning of the second one. Although Jesus' answers were addressed to the tetrarch Herod through the Pharisees (v. 32a), nothing allows us to say that the first summons was dictated by Herod (v. 31). So the Pharisees cannot be considered to have been delegates sent to Jesus;[4] their status remains ambiguous.[5]

The judgment oracle (vv. 34-35) is composed of three parts of unequal length. The first part (v. 34) is a lament, which is introduced by a vocative, whose reduplication is witness to its affective weight, and a double participial phrase in the present, which is durative and/or iterative, with a polemical flavor. This lament ends with a rhetorical question, which recalls Jesus' protective will by means of a new metaphor, that of the hen, before receiving as its only reply the mention of the refusal on the part of the people ("you"). This negative inclination ("you were not willing," οὐκ ἠθελήσατε) is the matching piece to Jesus' positive inclination ("have I desired," ἠθέλησα).

Following this lament, which briefly expressed the divine grievances, comes the brief wording of the judgment, introduced by a recapitulative adverb in Greek, ἰδού ("see"): "see, through your fault, your house will be abandoned" (v. 35a). A final saying, which is also brief and is introduced by a customary phrase, opens onto an enigmatic future; it is not known whether that future will be dark or light (v. 35b).

The literary genre of the apophthegm is well known and is applied here (vv. 31-33):[6] (1) an initial situation, the arrival of the Pharisees, which presupposes a setting and implies a question or an opinion; (2) in counterpoint, a resolute opinion by the hero in the form of a saying. Although the saying here is admittedly decisive, it remains enigmatic.[7] In the text, at its redactional level, the enigma even veers off into obscurity, since two replies by Jesus follow each other, the second (v. 33) seeming to correct rather than explain the first (v. 32b).[8] Verse 33 indeed begins with a reservation expressed by "yet" (πλήν) and distributes the three days differently than v. 32b does. There are several kinds of apophthegms. Although the one here is nourished by the kerygma, it is biographical.[9] In fact, it deals with Jesus' life, but that life and its outcome are considered from the perspective of a ministry in the service of a divine design (cf. the "must," δεῖ, in v. 33). Christology and even soteriology thus invade the biography. For Christians, who are anxious to recall this episode, Jesus' destiny opens up to the dimensions of salvation history, with the themes of the sending of the prophet, his ministry, and his rejection.

The tension between v. 32b and v. 33 facilitates the elucidation of the links between tradition and redaction.[10] Verse 33 is very Lukan in style but also in its

---

4   This point is controversial; Grundmann (288), for instance, thinks it likely that the Pharisees here were emissaries of Herod Antipas.

5   An analysis of the structure of vv. 31–33 is found in Ferraro, "Oggi," 397–407 (showing the parallelism between the end of v. 31 and the beginning of v. 32); Denaux, "Hypocrisie," 256–57 (chiasm and parallelism); Prete, "Testo," 67 (takes the position of Denaux).

6   On this genre in Luke, see Schneider, "Antworten."

7   See Denaux, "Hypocrisie," 253, 255–56.

8   See Karl L. Schmidt (*Der Rahmen der Geschichte Jesu: Literarkritische Untersuchungen zur ältesten Jesusüberlieferung* [Darmstadt: Wissenschaftliche Buchgesell-

schaft, 1964] 265–67), who thinks that the primitive unity ends with the word "tomorrow"; the end of v. 32, a confession of Easter faith, and v. 33 were added by the evangelist.

9   See Bultmann, *History*, 27–39, esp. 35; Denaux, "Hypocrisie," 255–56.

10 The question of the origin of vv. 31-33 has given rise to numerous hypotheses. Two recent authors, Denaux ("Hypocrisie") and Rese ("Einige Überlegungen," 224) conclude that these three verses are redactional (for Rese, the only traditional element is the motif, coming from Q, of the death of the prophets in Jerusalem). The majority of exegetes, particularly the ancients, presuppose a traditional

themes: Jesus' life understood as a journey, as well as the three stages, the three "days," of Galilee, the journey, and Judea. I conclude that in this verse Luke interprets the traditional information of v. 32b, whose vocabulary is scarcely Lukan.[11] Although v. 31 was written by Luke, who was fond of putting the finishing touches on initial descriptions, he drew on information from the tradition.[12] In summary, L (rather than Q, since Matthew was unacquainted with this episode) transmitted a brief biographical apophthegm. In order for the episode to make sense, it had to take place in Galilee or in Perea, Herod's territories, rather than in Samaria, where Jesus had arrived according to 9:52-56, and which at that time was under the jurisdiction of the governor of Judea.[13]

Matthew, too, was acquainted with the beginning of the judgment oracle, the lament over Jerusalem (vv. 34-35), so there is no doubt that this passage belonged to Q.[14] The texts of Luke and Matthew are so close that they must have come from a single Greek version of this source.[15] The few differences between these two Synoptic Gospels can be explained without too much risk of error as follows: the aorist infinitive ἐπισυνάξαι ("gather together"), used by Luke, is popular Greek, compared with the Attic form ἐπισυναγαγεῖν (also "gather together") supplied by Matthew.[16] So here it is Luke who has preserved the text of Q. The same is true with respect to the brood (Luke: τὴν . . . νοσσιάν, "the brood"; Matthew, who was anxious to bring out the parallel with τὰ τέκνα, "the children," corrected that to τὰ νοσσία, "the young").[17] On the other hand, ἑαυτῆς ("her"), which is grammatically more correct, is a Lukan improvement of the text of Q, αὐτῆς ("of hers"), preserved by Matthew. On the contrary, the ἀπ᾽ ἄρτι ("from now on") of Matt 23:39 is redactional (cf. Matt 26:29, 64). The difficult expression ἕως ἥξει ὅτε ("until he arrives when"; Luke 13:35), for which the manuscript evidence is, moreover, poorly attested, is not Lukan and must go back to Q (Matthew finessed it by banalizing it).[18] In the same verse (Matt 23:39 par. Luke 13:35), the γάρ ("for"; Luke: δέ) and the ἄν (absent from Luke) can be attributed to the redaction of the author of the First Gospel. Finally, what context in Q does this lamentation fit? The place that Matthew gives it, at the end of the invective against the Pharisees, after the reminder of the persecution of the prophets, could be the correct one.[19] Instead of inserting it in the same place, or else following 11:49-51, Luke preferred to hold it in order to attach it here to the episode of the Pharisees (vv. 31-33).

The lament over Jerusalem belongs to the literary genre of the judgment oracle,[20] which contrasts the good done by God or his intermediary with the evil done by the people. After this contrasted analysis (v. 34), judgment is pronounced: God will withdraw his salutary presence (v. 35). This saying is introduced, not surprisingly, by "see," ἰδού (in Hebrew הִנֵּה). The repetition of the name Jerusalem, the use of the participle in Greek to refer to the peoples' sin, "who kill . . . and stone," the contrast between divine will and human refusal,

---

substrate. Some use scissors to avoid the repetitions between v. 32 and v. 33 (for references and a critique, see Schmidt, *Rahmen*, 267 n. 1). For Jeremias ("Drei-Tage-Worte," 222–25), the sayings of v. 32b and v. 33 are variants, and they belong to a pre-Easter tradition. According to Prete ("Testo," 66), Jesus' response would be incomplete without v. 33 (the two sayings constitute a unity and are traditional).

11 My solution approaches that of Schnider, *Jesus der Prophet*, 168–69.

12 See Prete, "Testo," 64–65.

13 On the location of the episode, see Fitzmyer, 2:1029. It could be that Herod's threats had played a role in Jesus' decision to leave Galilee to go to Judea.

14 See Havener, *Q: The Sayings*, 24.

15 A written source according to Schmid, *Matthäus und Lukas*, 333.

16 With Schmid (*Matthäus und Lukas*, 333), Schulz (*Q*, 346) thinks it difficult to resolve.

17 With Schulz (*Q*, 346), contra Schmid (*Matthäus und Lukas*, 333).

18 See Schmid (*Matthäus und Lukas*, 333); Schulz (*Q*, 346).

19 According to Schmithals (155), Luke 13:34-35 follows immediately after Luke 11:49-51 in Q: Wisdom continues to speak. According to Marguerat (*Jugement*, 356), it is Luke 13:24-40, 34-35 that represents the sequence of Q. The various hypotheses of scholars are presented and some arguments advanced in John S. Kloppenborg, *Q Parallels: Synopsis, Critical Notes and Concordance* (Sonoma, Calif.: Polebridge, 1988) 158.

20 See Steck, *Israel*, 57–58; Marguerat, *Jugement*, 356.

the mention of repeated salvific actions, as well as the recourse to a comparison[21] all testify to the fact that this lament belongs to the literary genre of the judgment oracle.[22] Compare the following saying, attributed to Yohanan b. Zakkai, a rabbi at the end of the first century of our era: "O Galilee, Galilee, you have hated the Torah. You will end up working for tax farmers."[23]

The judgment oracle, rooted in prophetic literature, was taken up again in the time of Jesus by Jewish wisdom literature. It is precisely into this literature that this lament fits:[24] the use of the name of the capital; the image of the hen and the idea of protection that it suggests;[25] the "I" used by the divine intermediary, rather than by God himself; finally, God's Presence (שְׁכִינָה), closely related to God's Wisdom (הָכְמָה)—all argue in favor of it having such wisdom roots.

The reproach leveled against this generation, that is, the refusal of the divine messenger (v. 34a), provides a clue to the dating. While the rejection of God's envoys was one infamy among many in the time of the Hebrew Bible, in the intertestamental and later rabbinic periods it became the preferred expression of Israel's stubbornness, as attested by Josephus and the Jewish tradition.[26]

Verse 35b, as we are led to understand by the introductory expression "I tell you," stands out clearly against the literary genre of the judgment oracle and is without parallel in Hebraic and Jewish literature.[27] It must be an indication of a wisdom oracle. From a historical point of view, three possibilities come to mind: (1) Jesus made a Jewish wisdom tradition his own (vv. 34-35)

and adapted it to his own case (v. 35b). (2) The earliest Christians quoted a wisdom tradition (vv. 34-35a) and applied it to Jesus (v. 35b). (3) The historical Jesus appealed one day to the wisdom tradition without identifying himself with the Wisdom speaking in the first person singular (vv. 34-35a)[28] and, on another occasion, uttered the saying that v. 35b echoes.[29] Then the earliest Christians made the connection between the quotation and the saying, because they saw a thematic relationship between them. In their eyes there was in both of them a combination of the awareness of the sending and the reality of the refusal. The energy that the early church developed in order to give meaning to the failure of Jesus' mission explains the origin and the preservation of this set of texts. Personally, I opt for the third possibility. The fact that this verse is associated in Luke also with a prophecy about the death of Jesus, and in Matthew with a mention of the prophetic martyrs, can be similarly explained. [30]

Commentary

■ **31** Luke links one dialogue to another and a piece of advice (v. 31) to a question (v. 23).[31] In the previous pericope, a listener was questioning Jesus about the number of people who would be saved, that is, about salvation. Here the Pharisees ask Jesus to go away; they are therefore interested in his person and his fate.

Thus, the advice came from the Pharisees. This Gospel writer was not as hard on this group as Matthew

---

21 On the use of images and comparisons in the sapiential tradition, see S. H. Blank, "Wisdom," *IDB* 4:857.

22 Ezekiel 16 compares the fate of Jerusalem to that of a woman; Hosea 11 compares the destiny of Israel to that of a boy.

23 See *y. Šabb.* 16.8 (3.B) (Neusner, *Talmud,* 11:423); Str-B 1:157.

24 See Christ, *Jesus Sophia,* 136–52; Zeller, "Entrückung," 513–30.

25 See Ps 17 (16):8; Sir 1:15; Steck, *Israel,* 234 n. 14.

26 See 2 Kgs [4 Kgdms] 17:13-14, 23; Neh 9:26-31; Josephus *Ant.* 9.13.2 §§263–67, and 9.14.1 §§277–82; Steck, *Israel,* 81–99.

27 See Schulz, *Q,* 348. There exist, it is true, some oracles of judgment that contain such confirmations with a new introduction, e.g., Ezek 5:1-17; see Marguerat, *Jugement,* 355–56.

28 Following 7:33-35 and 11:49-51, Jesus considered himself to be a child of Wisdom, not Wisdom itself.

29 The reader will observe that v. 35b is not stated christologically in a very direct way.

30 Zeller ("Entrückung," 514) thinks that the lament (Matt 23:37-39 par. Luke 13:34-35) does not immediately follow the citation of Wisdom (Matt 23:34-36 par. Luke 11:49-51) in the source of logia.

31 What exactly does ἐν αὐτῇ τῇ ὥρᾳ signify? In contrast to ἐν ταύτῃ τῇ ὥρᾳ ("in this hour"), the expression marks a precise instant and announces a sudden break in time, a serious incident. See BAGD, s.v. αὐτός. I translate it "at this instant." I do not see a Semitism here (in the sense of "right away"), contra Black, *Aramaic Approach,* 79; and Bastin, *Jésus,* 77.

was.[32] That is not to say that he protected them; in Luke these people serve as opposite numbers and foils for Jesus. They are present in Galilee and during the journey, but disappear from the scene during Jesus' passion (cf. 5:17, the first mention of them in the Gospel, and 19:39, the last). Luke did not want to exclude them from the holy city (they are present there, as Luke 19:39; Acts 5:34; 15:5; 23:6-9; and 26:5 confirm). But he was anxious to spare them during the trial, which was orchestrated by the scribes, the elders, and especially the chief priests. In short, Pharisaism continued, in Luke, to be a force in Judaism that was interested in Jesus and that was sometimes hostile—often criticized but never permanently closed—to the Gospel.

Here the Pharisees give Jesus some advice, namely, to leave the region, because of the tetrarch Herod's intentions. The Greek aorist imperative ἔξελθε ("get out") refers to the moment of departure, and the present imperative πορεύου ("go") encompasses the escape in its continuation.[33] Luke did not think of these men as ambassadors of Herod, so he did not suspect them of being hypocrites.[34] Although they did not have charitable intentions, neither did they seek to get rid of Jesus. The text plays on the motives for the journey to Jerusalem. What the Pharisees said allowed Jesus to affirm that his conduct was not dictated by any human force, not even by the highest political authority.[35] His destiny was in other hands. He would get out and in fact had already gotten out; he would go and in fact he was already going. However, he was not doing so, and would not do so, under human duress, but only in line with God's will, to which he gave his undivided adherence.

Luke refers several times to the Herodian dynasty: he mentions the king of Judea, Herod the Great, at the beginning of the Gospel (1:5) and Herod Agrippa I (Acts 12:1-23) and then Herod Agrippa II (Acts 25:13-26, 32), respectively Herod the Great's grandson and great-grandson, in the Acts of the Apostles. In the main part of the Gospel, he mentions Herod the Great, and Herod Agrippa I's uncle, the tetrarch Herod Antipas.[36] In 9:7-9, this Herod wonders who the Galilean Jesus is and wants to meet him. In 23:8-12, Herod is asked by Pilate—only Luke recounts the episode—to interrogate the accused Jesus. When Luke mentions this Herod, it is not in order to set him up automatically as Jesus' enemy. Even though he was threatening in terms of the fate to which he consigned John the Baptist, Herod Antipas was in the first instance a sovereign, a political man, who wanted to make the most of Jesus, to see him (9:7), and to bring the power of this surprising charismatic (23:8) under his control. During the trial, disappointed by Jesus' silence, Herod was to end up scorning Jesus and insulting him (23:11). Following the advice of Pilate, however, Herod did not consider Jesus to be liable to the death penalty (23:15). From then on Luke brought the Roman governor and the Jewish prince together as friends (23:12) and enemies of God's plan, like the kings of Ps 2:1-2, who conspired against the Lord's anointed (Acts 4:27).

It is quite possible that in this passage (13:31-33) Luke has passed on a solid historical tradition according to which the tetrarch Herod Antipas, during the Galilean period of the ministry of Jesus of Nazareth, wished to nip Jesus' charismatic movement in the bud. We have another, independent witness in the Gospel of Mark (Mark 3:6). So Herod may have wavered between the desire to use Jesus for his own purposes (9:7-9) and the desire to eliminate him in case he could not achieve his ends (here, v. 31) in spite of his princely status. Jesus was, in fact, going to die, but it was not to be either at the hands of Herod or in Galilee. His death was not to come

---

32 On the Pharisees in Luke, see the commentary on 5:17, n. 22, in vol. 1; Denaux, "Hypocrisie," additional note, 321–23. One recalls the role of the priest Amaziah, who both warned King Jeroboam and also advised the prophet Amos to leave the country for Judea (Amos 7:10-17).

33 Together the two imperatives ("come out" and "go") highlight the urgency of the decision to be made and carried out.

34 Certain exegetes, such as Denaux ("Hypocrisie," 262–63 and additional note 322–23), think that the Pharisees act hypocritically, in light of 11:53 and 12:1. Under the pretense of protecting Jesus, they hope for his death in Jerusalem. Verses 31-33 do not validate this hypothesis.

35 Rese ("Einige Überlegungen," 215) emphasizes that, for the first time, Jesus addresses himself to a "grand de la terre." Luke is happy with the public character that the ministry of Jesus thus received.

36 On Herod Antipas in Luke, see Rese, "Einige Überlegungen"; Denaux, "Hypocrisie," 263–64; Blinzler, *Herodes*, 16–20; Hoehner, *Herod*, 214–24, 343–47.

about as a result of Herod's human will ("wants," $\vartheta\acute{\epsilon}\lambda\epsilon\iota$, v. 31).

Jesus drew deeply on his faith in deciding how to act. His conduct was not determined either by what the Pharisees thought or by the power exercised by Herod or Pilate. He took on everyone by relying on God. His ultimate means of opposing those who symbolized traditional resistance to the divine will was to militate on their behalf. These persons might be mistaken about Jesus' identity or might oppose his plans, but in the end they would serve as involuntary agents of God's salvific plan.

■ **32** Jesus retorted; he sent back ("go," $\pi o\rho\epsilon\upsilon\vartheta\acute{\epsilon}\nu\tau\epsilon\varsigma$, literally, "having walked") those who wanted to send him away ("go away," $\pi o\rho\epsilon\acute{\upsilon}o\upsilon$). Let those who had believed they could serve as intermediaries on behalf of another person become Jesus' own messengers! They were the ones who would leave that place. As for Jesus, he was not going to run away. He was to leave serenely at a time of his choosing, submitting to the divine will alone. His itinerary was all laid out, from Galilee to Jerusalem. There is humor in this serious passage, albeit grim humor.

The metaphor of the fox[37] seems to have a double significance: it suggests (a) that Herod resorted to a ruse and (b) that his power was negligible. Often contrasted in antiquity with the lion, the "fox" (here Herod) did not measure up when he was faced with Pilate or the Roman power, or especially Jesus and the divine power. The one who was to scorn Jesus, literally, who would "regard him as having no significance" ($\dot{\epsilon}\xi o\upsilon\vartheta\epsilon\nu\acute{\epsilon}\omega$, 23:11), was in fact an insignificant being who counted on eliminating his enemy by a ruse but who was not to succeed in doing so.

Jesus' saying (v. 32) is invaluable, since it is probably historical. As in 11:20,[38] Jesus laid more stress on his ministry as an exorcist than as a preacher. Admittedly, he did not look down on his prophetic message, but he was anxious to bring out its validation through signs. To exorcisms, he linked healings—or the Gospel writer Luke linked them, since Luke was fond of making a distinction between exorcisms and healings at the same time that he paired them.[39] These two activities, healing and exorcism, witnessed to by two different literary genres, were in fact characteristic of the historical Jesus. That is, moreover, how the memory of Jesus was to be perpetuated in rabbinic literature.[40]

Time is not divided up in the usual way here. Jewish tradition deliberately made a distinction between what takes place today and what will happen tomorrow, in order to indicate sudden upheavals and to serve as a reminder of how precarious human existence is.[41] Here, the mention of two days, "today and tomorrow," symbolically refers to the total but indeterminate duration of Jesus' ministry.[42] It may depend on a Semitic substratum

37 See Verrall, "Christ before Herod," 352–53 (opposes this fox with the chicken and its young of v. 34); Str-B 2:201 (recalls a parable of R. Aqiba of the fox and fish); Grimm, "Eschatologischer Saul," 115–17 (opposes the fox to the lion, Saul to David, Herod to Jesus the Messiah); Hoehner, *Herod*, 343–47 (on the fox in Greek and Jewish literature; confirms the two aspects proposed by Billerbeck, the ruse and the inferior position, but thinks that the Jews insisted above all on the second aspect); Derrett, "Lucan Christ and Jerusalem," 36–43 (refers to Lam 5:18); Wellmann, "Fuchs," 189–92. Isidore of Seville (*Etymologia* 12.2.29; *Physiologus* 15) offers a brief description of the fox (particularly of his ruse); the symbolic Christian interpretation; a comparison with the devil; and then the following argument: he will die who seeks to take part in his flesh; his flesh is lust, avarice, covetousness, and murder; because of this, Herod is compared to a fox. There follows a citation of Matt 8:20 (par. Luke 9:58); Song 2:15; and Ps 63 (62):11.

38 Denaux ("Hypocrisie," 265) thinks that Luke is inspired here by Mark 6:13.

39 On the verb $\dot{\alpha}\pi o\tau\epsilon\lambda\acute{\epsilon}\omega$ ("to finish," "to accomplish"), see BAGD, s.v.; Ferraro, "Oggi," 404. One ought to retain this verb, even if innumerable manuscripts have the more frequent but more suspect verb $\dot{\epsilon}\pi\iota\tau\epsilon\lambda\acute{\epsilon}\omega$, which has practically the same meaning.

40 In rabbinic literature, the memory of Jesus is one of a magician; see Joseph Klausner, *Jesus of Nazareth: His Life, Times, and Teaching* (trans. H. Danby; New York: Macmillan, 1926) 13–65.

41 See Josh 22:18 ("you turn away today from following the Lord! If you rebel against the Lord today, he will be angry with the whole congregation of Israel tomorrow" [*NRSV*]).

42 See Exod 19:10, 16 (the people must be sanctified by Moses today and tomorrow; the third day, God shows himself); Hos 6:2 ("After two days he will revive us; on the third day he will raise us up, that we may live before him").

meaning "day after day."[43] In other words, this ministry might last or it might not.

Contrary to Christian tradition, the expression "the third day" designates the end of Jesus' ministry rather than an immediate resurrection. The fact that it did not match the Christian kerygma is a strong indication in favor of the authenticity of the saying. The symbolic two days of the duration of the ministry are in contrast to the third day, marked by the "end" (in τελειοῦμαι there is τέλος).[44]

The ambivalent character of the verb τελειοῦμαι ("I reach my goal" or "I am finished")[45] is due to Luke's intention. The verb τελειόω does not mean "put an end to" so much as it does "bring to perfection." When expressed by this verb, what comes to an end succeeds in being accomplished, in being brought to perfection. Τέλειος, moreover, means "perfect," that which is not lacking anything. Understood as a middle—yet the absence of a direct object is surprising—this verb marks the completion of exorcisms and healings by Jesus. Understood as a passive, it presupposes the activity of God, who leads his Son to completeness and discreetly alludes to the passion.[46] If God's will—the entire context contrasts different wills—triumphs, it is not at the expense of Jesus' will. On the contrary, Jesus' resistance to Herod's will is an expression of his adherence to the Father's project.

The shape that this accomplishment was to take remains enigmatic. The reader who has read the Gospel through to the end will immediately think of Jesus' death. The use of the verb "accomplish" did not commute this death, in some miraculous or masochistic way, to a happy event; instead, following the rhythm of the saying, it would come in time, in its own time. Jesus would have the time, "today and tomorrow," to live with his life force. He would die "the third day," not a death marked by failure but a death bearing his signature, namely, a mark of the servant's love, the ultimate expression of his service (22:27). It would be less a sacrificial and substitutionary death than one expressing the supreme gift of oneself on behalf of others. This is a fullness that marked a decisive step without interrupting the movement: the canonical book of the Acts of the Apostles and also the apocryphal Acts were to illustrate such a life and such a death by the fate of the disciples. They, too, were to drive out demons and perform healings "today and tomorrow" before arriving, in turn, at that communicative plenitude, that is, their martyrdom.

Be that as it may, the modern Greek expression τελείωσε ("it's finished") is a reminder as hard as steel that this plenitude of the third day, which suggests the resurrection to Christians, corresponds here to an end, to a death. The true gift of self implies, at least for a while, despair, abandonment, breakup, and death. Any experience of death or mourning rightly reminds us of it. It is a question not of advocating suffering but of preparing oneself for it. When reading this passage, Christians who were threatened or even persecuted must have related to it. It answered the question about running away from martyrdom and suggested to them an example of supreme serenity.

■ **33** While v. 32 emphasized the ministry that Jesus carried out through his life, v. 33 stresses the one he fulfilled by his death.[47] In v. 32, Jesus asserts that he is not giving up his ministry in that place. In v. 33, Luke has him say that he will end it in Jerusalem.[48] But before arriving at that point there was a whole life, a whole ministry described by the verb "to walk," "to be on one's

---

43 See Black, *Aramaic Approach*, 79.

44 On these three days, see Gilbert, "Σήμερον καὶ αὔριον," 315–18; Ferraro, "Oggi," 407; Jeremias, "Drei-Tage-Worte," 226–27; Denaux, "Hypocrisie," 278–81; Prete, "Testo," 68–69.

45 See 2:43 (on the subject of days); Acts 20:24 (on the subject of a fate); Heb 2:10; 5:9; 7:28 (on the subject of Christ—the author of Hebrews loves this verb); Plummer, 350; Ferraro, "Oggi," 404–5; Jeremias, "Drei-Tage-Worte," 222; Denaux, "Hypocrisie," 271–74; Schnider, *Jesus der Prophet*, 169–70; Rese, "Einige Überlegungen," 217; Prete, "Testo," 70, 75; Derrett ("Lucan Christ and Jerusalem") proposes

the translation "I am going to die" based on the first definition of the Hebrew verb שלם, "to be finished."

46 See Prete, "Testo," 75–79.

47 See Luke 22:27 for v. 32 and Mark 10:45 (post-Easter parallel of Luke 22:27) for v. 33. Note the δεῖ ("it is necessary"), which expresses the plan of God; see 4:43; 9:22; 13:16, etc.

48 On ἀπόλλυμαι ("to head for his demise," "to die"), see BAGD, s.v.; Ferraro, "Oggi," 406.

way," πορεύεσθαι,[49] in Luke's eyes so rich in connotations. The journey was done according to God's plan, oriented toward his objective, accompanied by proclamation and its signs; it fit into human history, and along it strode God's greatness. The three days in v. 33 have a different significance from those in v. 32. They make up a unit defined by the verb "be on one's way" and express the coherence of a personal plan, in accordance with a vocation. While v. 32, speaking of the first two days, had Jesus' success in mind, v. 33, referring to the period from the first day to the third day, conjured up his obstacles and then his failure. In v. 32, Jesus' death and—according to Luke's way of thinking—its glorious consequences take up the third day. In v. 33, the prophetic ministry fills the three days before ending in death. Verse 33 is to v. 32 what Good Friday is to Easter, and the suffering prophet to the healing Messiah.

Luke may have identified the three days of v. 33 with the three stages of Jesus' life, such as he recounted it. The "next day"[50] would refer to the final stage in Jerusalem, and "tomorrow" would correspond to the journey.[51] So the same concept of three days served, in early Christianity, to describe either, as here, Jesus' career, or, as everywhere else, the resurrection (literally, e.g., Mark 8:31, or figuratively, the reconstruction of the temple, e.g., Mark 14:58).

Here again, Luke takes up the theme of the people who reject God's messengers, more particularly, the theme of Jerusalem killing the prophets. Luke was acquainted with that theme from Q. For him, the title of "prophet"[52] did not appear to be unworthy of Jesus, even if it did not match up with all the aspects of his Jesus' life as Luke understood it. It did, in any case, suit the preacher and the martyr.[53]

Contrary to his usual practice, the Gospel writer used the verb ἐνδέχεται (impersonal use in the sense of "it is possible")[54] in order to avoid the repetition of δεῖ ("it is necessary," "I must," v. 33a). The historical possibilities—since we are on the level of what is possible—come down, according to Luke, to a single one, the one that corresponds to God's will.

Did God really will the death of his messengers? No, but experience led God to expect that. What he wished to do was to warn, protect, and save Israel, of which Jerusalem was the capital. Unfortunately, the people responded to God's kindness with threatening actions, and they rejected the demanding message delivered by the prophets.[55] Martyrdom became the corollary of witnessing. The reason Jesus had to die in Jerusalem was that he faithfully fulfilled his prophetic mission.[56]

■ **34a** In this verse Jesus is no longer speaking to the Pharisees but has turned toward his destination, Jerusa-

49 On this verb, so important in Luke, see the commentary above on 9:51; Ferraro, "Oggi," 405–6; Denaux, "Hypocrisie," 260; Rese, "Einige Überlegungen," 217–18; Prete, "Testo," 72–75.

50 On ἡ ἐχομένη (in the sense of "the following day"), see 1 Chr 10:8 LXX; 2 Macc 12:39; Acts 20:15. The Syriac version (the Peshitta) aligns the chronology of v. 33 with that of v. 32. In v. 33, it adds, in effect, the verb "I must visit (or take care of)" to the words "today and tomorrow," which reserves the departure for the following day; see James Murdock, ed., *The New Testament or the Book of the Holy Gospel of Our Lord and Our God, Jesus the Messiah: A Literal Translation from the Syriac Peshito Version* (New York: Stanford & Swords, 1852) 137; George M. Lamsa, ed., *The New Testament according to the Eastern Text, Translated from the Original Aramaic Sources* (Philadelphia: Holman, 1940) 146. Charles C. Torrey (*The Four Gospels: A New Translation* [New York/London: Harper, 1933] 310–11) draws on this text in his reconstruction of the original Aramaic. Jeremias ("Drei-Tage-Worte,"

223 n. 8) refuses to consider that this reading represents the original text of the Gospel.

51 See Conzelmann, *Theology*, 197 n. 1; Rese, "Einige Überlegungen," 205–6 (on Conzelmann's position). Following this hypothesis, the first day, called "today," must designate the past period of ministry in Galilee, which poses a difficulty.

52 On this title, see the commentary on 7:16, n. 58, in vol. 1.

53 See 4:24: "no prophet is accepted in the prophet's hometown."

54 On ἐνδέχομαι, see BAGD, s.v.

55 See the commentary above on 11:49-51; and the commentary on 6:23 in vol. 1; see also Acts 7:51-53.

56 See Schnider, *Jesus der Prophet*, 171–72; Bastin, *Jésus*, 77–81; Büchele, *Tod Jesu*, 152–57.

lem (cf. 9:51-52; 13:22). The double vocative (cf. "Martha, Martha," 10:41) is freighted with affection,[57] mixed with disappointment. The text continues with a long double participial phrase that inserts the final failure into a series of martyrdoms.[58] Rooted in the prophetic experience, that clause expresses the certitude that in the capital every true prophet ran up against the coalition of the godless king and the false prophet. The plural use of "prophets" and "envoys" ("those who are sent") is a witness not only to an existential awareness but also to a historiographical tradition.[59] Manasseh (2 Kings [4 Kingdoms] 21) had become, in Luke's time, the model of the persecuting king, and Isaiah, that of the martyred prophet (cf. the *Ascension of Isaiah* 1–5). While "kill" gives the idea of a murder, "stone" suggests a capital sentence, the one provided for by the law for God's worst enemies, the idolaters (Deut 17:2-7), the magicians (Lev 20:27), the rebellious children (Deut 21:18-21), and the transgressors of the Sabbath day (Num 15:32-36). By "stoning" God's messengers,[60] Jerusalem perverted the use of the law, was totally mistaken, and changed from being a holy city to being a sinful one. According to the logic expressed in 9:48 and 10:16, by rejecting these messengers, Jerusalem rejected God himself.

The pair "prophets"–"messengers" recalls "prophets"–"apostles" in 11:49. In both cases, what tradition had in mind was the ancient line of men and women of God. In both instances, the redaction thought in terms of, on the one hand, the prophets of the old regime and, on the other, the witnesses (Luke was not thinking of the apostles alone) of the new one, in which the series of martyrdoms began with Jesus' own, as well as Stephen's and James's.[61] While the term "prophets" attests to the role that these messengers played with respect to the people, the participle "are sent" indicates that they are under the orders of the one behind them, God, who has something to say to his people, "to" his people and "against" his people, for those are the two meanings here of the Greek preposition πρός (translated as "to").

■ **34b** The parallel constituted by 11:49-51 explicitly mentioned Wisdom as the one delivering the oracle. For it was the wisdom literature that, feeding on prophetic vehemence, became aware of the permanence of Israel's stubbornness. Here, as in 11:49-51, the lament has a sapiential character; it even proceeds from the mouth of personified Wisdom.[62] So the efforts enumerated by v. 34b were those of that collaborator of God during Israel's history. In a protective mood, she wanted to gather her children and cover them with her wings.[63] Matthew seems to stress the gathering of her children that she wanted to carry out,[64] and Luke, the protection she wanted to offer them.[65] In any case, the "I" of Wisdom was conscious of being charged with a divine mission of salvation.[66] A presupposition of that necessary action was the dispersion of God's people and the threat that hung over them.

The image of the hen[67] is rarely used to speak of God

---

57 See 1 Kgs [3 Kgdms] 13:2; Isa 29:1; Marguerat, *Jugement,* 367.

58 The two participles are parallel and convey the same truth, the second highlighting the gravity of the error; see Marguerat, *Jugement,* 367.

59 This is the tradition of Deuteronomy, which was taken up in sapiential literature. It includes the following elements: first, despite their deliverance into the land offered by God, the people remain disobedient; second, by the voice of the prophets, God, who remains patient, exhorts the people; third, despite it all, the people are hardened; fourth, God therefore pronounces his judgment of condemnation; there is sometimes, in the most recent texts, a fifth element: a hope of repentance and conversion. See Steck, *Israel,* 63–64, 232.

60 See 1 Sam [1 Kgdms] 30:6; 2 Chr 24:21; in the NT, Matt 21:35; Acts 7:58-59; 14:5.

61 See the commentary above on 11:49-51.

62 One finds this in the oration in Prov 1:20-33; for established in Jerusalem, see Sir 24:7-12.

63 See 5 Esdr 1:30 (the first two chapters of 4 Esdras are called 5 Esdras).

64 See Isa 60:4; Zech 10:6-10; in the LXX, ἐπισυνάγω is a technical term to describe the reunion of the dispersed people after the exile or the eschatological reassembly of the nations; see the commentary above on 13:29; Marguerat, *Jugement,* 367.

65 If Steck (*Israel,* 49) is in agreement with these different nuances, Marshall (575) does not accept this opinion.

66 For Caird (174), who refers to Hos 11:8-9 and Isa 65:1-2, it is God who speaks here as "I."

67 In the manuscripts we find the two spellings: ὄρνις, the more common form, and ὄρνιξ, the possibly Doric form. The word first designates a bird in the general sense, then the hen, and the domesticated

or his messengers,[68] but the image of wings has a biblical past.[69] Applied to the protector God, it can refer to the temple, a place serving as both a sanctuary and a locus of divine presence. As a feminine and maternal image, adapted to Wisdom and then to Christ, it offers protection to beings already born, who therefore enjoy a certain degree of autonomy. Their autonomy is so real that they have preferred to turn down the offer. In Luke's eyes, that was absurd, unnatural, and suicidal. This was a tragic opposition of two wills (Jesus' "I desired," and "you were not willing," referring to Jerusalem), even though everything was possible in a holy city, which was a residence for both God and the people, a meeting place for heaven and earth, and a center of the world and a rallying point. The scene also includes a mother and her little ones, a place and a time. Unfortunately, two elements that did not show up for the appointment were a coming together and harmony. The historical Jesus had to resort to this wisdom text to express the predictable failure of his mission.[70] Q, followed in turn by Luke, quotes it, with sadness, to account for the enigmatic rejection of Jesus by his own people.

■ **35a** "See" is the judge's sentence.[71] Note the double "you[r]" ($\dot{\upsilon}\mu\hat{\iota}\nu$ and $\dot{\upsilon}\mu\hat{\omega}\nu$). What belongs to "you" ($\dot{\upsilon}\mu\hat{\omega}\nu$), that is, your house, the temple, will be abandoned. It will be so "to your disadvantage" ($\dot{\upsilon}\mu\hat{\iota}\nu$, *dativus incommodi*, dative of disadvantage), "and that will concern you" (dative of relation), or "by virtue of your attitude" (dative of participation). This dative should probably not be taken for a dative of destination, nor should the verb $\dot{\alpha}\varphi\dot{\iota}\eta\mu\iota$ be understood in the sense of "to leave,"

nor the text translated as "Your house will be left for you." The form $\dot{\alpha}\varphi\dot{\iota}\epsilon\tau\alpha\iota$ is the third person singular of the present passive of $\dot{\alpha}\varphi\dot{\iota}\eta\mu\iota$, a verb with many meanings: "let go," "release," "dismiss," "give back," "remit," "reject," "abandon," "leave," and "pardon."[72] Let us say first of all that the present has the value of an immediate future: although the condemnation is pronounced today, it will take effect very soon. What is it? Several scribes, and probably Matthew himself, sensed a reference here to an oracle of Jeremiah (Jer 22:5: $\epsilon\dot{\iota}\varsigma$ $\dot{\epsilon}\rho\dot{\eta}\mu\omega\sigma\iota\nu$ $\ddot{\epsilon}\sigma\tau\alpha\iota$ $\dot{o}$ $o\dot{\hat{\iota}}\kappa o\varsigma$ $o\dot{\hat{\upsilon}}\tau o\varsigma$, "this house will be reduced to desolation"). So they transcribed the following text: $\dot{\iota}\delta o\dot{\upsilon}$ $\dot{\alpha}\varphi\dot{\iota}\epsilon\tau\alpha\iota$ $\dot{\upsilon}\mu\hat{\iota}\nu$ $\dot{o}$ $o\dot{\hat{\iota}}\kappa o\varsigma$ $\dot{\upsilon}\mu\hat{\omega}\nu$ $\ddot{\epsilon}\rho\eta\mu o\varsigma$, "see, your house is left to you deserted." In this case $\dot{\alpha}\varphi\dot{\iota}\eta\mu\iota$ has the sense of "leave." Luke, who appears to have preserved the text of Q, does not endeavor to emphasize the reference to Jer 22:5. Without resorting to the adjective "deserted" ($\ddot{\epsilon}\rho\eta\mu o\varsigma$), he probably gave the meaning of "forget," "abandon," "reject" to the verb $\dot{\alpha}\varphi\dot{\iota}\eta\mu\iota$. The house will be abandoned; it will be ravaged on the outside or fall into decay on the inside. The house is a protected place that one locks up. It serves as a place for meetings, for family or community life, for common meals; for warmth when it is cold outdoors; for cooling when it is hot outside; in a word, for comfort and well-being. Yet all that holds true only if the house is kept up and the owner looks after it.[73] If the translation and interpretation I have proposed here, and which are admittedly not the first ones that would come to mind, are not accepted, what is left to fall back on is the following translation: "See, your house is left to you" (*NRSV*). Since these words

---

hen in the narrow sense. See LSJ, s.v.; Marguerat, *Jugement*, 368.

68 The expression $\dot{o}\nu$ $\tau\rho\dot{o}\pi o\nu$ ("on the manner of") is frequent in the LXX, translating the Hebrew כַּאֲשֶׁר, etc., e.g., Josh 8:6. On the adverbial use of the accusative (also called the accusative of manner or accusative of relation), see BDF §160, 1, n. 2; and Adolf Kaegi, *Kaegi's Greek Grammar: With Tables for Repetition* (trans. J. A. Kleist; 21st ed.; Wauconda, Ill.: Bolchazy-Carducci, 1995) §135; Steck, *Israel*, 49 n. 2.

69 See Deut 32:11; Ps 17(16):8; 57(56):2; 61(60):5; 91(90):4; *2 Bar.* 41:4 (among the people, "But others again I have seen who have forsaken their vanity, and fled for refuge beneath Your wings" [*APOT*]); Steck, *Israel*, 234 n. 4.

70 Like others, Suggs (*Wisdom*, 60) refuses to attribute this citation to the historical Jesus.

71 The same usage of $\dot{\iota}\delta o\dot{\upsilon}$ is found in the LXX, e.g., Jer 23:19.

72 On this verb, see R. Bultmann, "$\dot{\alpha}\varphi\dot{\iota}\eta\mu\iota$ $\kappa\tau\lambda$.," *TDNT* 1 (1964) 509–12.

73 See Marguerat (*Jugement*, 369), who observes regarding $\dot{\alpha}\varphi\dot{\iota}\epsilon\tau\alpha\iota$ ("is abandoned," or "will be abandoned") that the grammatical tense, the present, is oriented toward the future. One wondered if the "house" did not designate "Jerusalem" instead, because of the "your"; see Marshall, 576. This is to ignore the paradox and tragic irony of a "house" that, from being the temple of God becomes again your house, made by human hands. It will be destroyed shortly by other human hands.

are ambiguous, they will then have to be interpreted in the following way: God is leaving his temple, which will become yours. He is leaving this dwelling without protection and does not want to have anything more to do with it. That being the case, its belonging to you will not do any good, since it will not last.

In the Hebrew Scriptures, the house[74] can refer to any kind of building, that is, the Jerusalem temple (see Ezek 8:14, 16)—perhaps even the city of Jerusalem[75]— and any family, for example, such and such a dynasty, or the entire people. Since the "you" is distinguished from the "house," the house that will be abandoned can only be the city or the temple. In view of the theme of the divine presence,[76] I opt for the temple, whose destruction is thus predicted.[77] The way the oracle is worded, it announces a destruction caused both from the outside, by the Romans, and from the inside, by the Israelites themselves.[78]

To be sure, there were humans who were responsible for the destruction, but, at a deeper level, it had a divine cause. Israel was the root cause of its own loss, and Rome was the instrument of its desolation. But God must have willed these events and caused them to happen. Following on the first two matches of this battle of wills (v. 34) was the third and last match, the deciding one, and alas, the tragic one (v. 35a). The Lord was to abandon those whom he would have liked to connect with; he was to distance himself from those to whom he had assured his presence. As we have seen, there is a biblical tradition about the people who reject God's messengers; there is another one, according to which God's presence is never assured. The risk associated with love is leaving the door open. God's presence can depart from holy places. And various biblical, apocalyptic, and rabbinic accounts speak of those moving departures: at the time of the flood, the exile, or the capture of Jerusalem.[79] Verse 35a, commented on by v. 35b, fits into that tradition (cf. John 1:10-11).

■ **35b** The text of the first half of v. 35b reads quite differently in different manuscripts. Leaving aside minute variants, I focus on one principal problem. Does the text insert the verb ἥξει ("comes/will come") and the conjunction ὅτε ("when") between "you surely will not see me" and "when you say"? Should we read (a) οὐ μὴ ἴδητέ με ἕως ἥξει ὅτε εἴπητε, "you surely will not see me until the day comes when you say" or (b) οὐ μὴ ἴδητέ με ἕως εἴπητε, "you surely will not see me until you say"? Matthew has the following text: οὐ μή με ἴδητε ἀπ᾽ ἄρτι ἕως ἂν εἴπητε, "you surely will not see me from now on until you say . . . ." Since Matthew's wording contains a temporal indication (ἀπ᾽ ἄρτι, "from now on"), I suppose that Luke also has one: ἥξει ὅτε, literally, "will come when." Since the Lukan wording is elliptical, it may have been reworked several different ways by scribes taking their cue from Matthew. I suppose that the implied subject of ἥξει is a substantive indicating the time, "the

---

74 Weinert ("Luke," 75–76) thinks that οἶκος here refers to the rulers of the people rather than the temple.

75 See Jer 12:7 LXX: "I have forsaken my house, I have abandoned my inheritance, I have given my beloved soul into the hands of its enemies."

76 On this theme of the Shekinah, see Str-B 2:314–15; Arnold Goldberg, *Untersuchungen über die Vorstellung von der Schekhinah in der frühen rabbinischen Literatur* (Studia Judaica 5; Berlin: de Gruyter, 1969); Peter Schäfer, *Die Vorstellung vom heiligen Geist in der rabbinischen Literatur* (SANT 28; Munich: Kösel, 1972).

77 See 19:41-44; Mark 13:2. For Weinert ("Luke," 72–74), this is more a prophetic prediction than a prophetic judgment. He argues that Luke is not hostile to the temple (pp. 68–72). A bibliography and presentation of the state of the question on the temple in the Lukan corpus can be found in Alberto Casalegno, *Gesú e il tempio: studio redazionale*

di Luca–Atti (Brescia: Morcelliana, 1984). In the OT, the wrath of God is directed at the house of Israel in Hos 8.

78 See Marguerat, *Jugement*, 369.

79 See Jer 12:7 (see n. 75 above); 22:5; Ezekiel 9–11; 1 Kgs (3 Kgdms) 9:7-8; Ps 69 (68):26; Tob 14:4; *3 Enoch* 4–6; *1 Enoch* 89:55; *2 Bar.* 8:1-2 (a voice from the interior of the temple says, "he who kept the house has forsaken (it)" [*APOT*]); cf. Josephus *Bell.* 6.5.3 §§288–309. On the other hand, see the establishment of Wisdom in Israel, in Jerusalem (Sir 1:15; 24:7-16; Bar 3:15—4:4 [incarnated in the law]) and the absence or departure of Wisdom (Sir 15:7; *1 Enoch* 42; 4 Esdr 5:9b-10; *2 Bar.* 48:33-37). See Steck, *Israel*, 228–30; Marguerat, *Jugement*, 370; and Zeller, "Entrückung," 518–19. Ellis (191) thinks that this is about the departure of the presence of

day," ἡ ἡμέρα; "the moment," ὁ καιρός; or "the time," ὁ χρόνος (in Greek it is normally indicated; cf. Theocritus *Idylles* 23, 33; this particular poem is not considered to be authentic). The double negation οὐ μή[80] followed by the aorist subjunctive lends the air of a curse that is rendered imperfectly by the simple English future. It would be something like "you haven't got a chance of seeing me again," "you surely will not see me."[81] Moreover, ἕως followed by the indicative is possible, even if, used this way, the future indicative is uncommon (cf., however, Jdt 10:15).[82] As for ὅτε, it can be accompanied by a subjunctive when it fills the function of a relative pronoun ("the day when . . .").[83] So Luke's text is not incorrect; it is just elliptical.

Verse 35b[84] begins with a formal introduction, "I tell you," and continues with a saying by Jesus that a Christian prophet had adapted and that Luke placed here: with the enigmatic discretion of oracles, the saying announces first of all that Jesus will be taken away, that he will disappear for a while ("You surely will not see me"). Q, which adopted the oracle (v. 35b), followed by Luke, noticed the link that tied it to the saying about the abandoned house (v. 35a). In their eyes, Jesus' death ("You surely will not see me") will bring about the departure of God's presence from among his people.[85] That will cause the desolation of the house of Israel, concretely the fall of the temple (cf. the saying about the destruction of the sanctuary and the mention of three days, Mark 14:58) and the destruction of Jerusalem.[86]

The saying in v. 35b is not limited to this negative observation; it allows us to catch a glimpse of a future. What will come about then? Your being led to singing the pilgrims' psalm, "Blessed be the one who comes in the name of the Lord" (Ps 118 [117]:26). On what occasion? The arrival of the Lord's messenger? What does that mean? One suggestion is that it refers to Jesus' approach to Jerusalem (19:29-40, but the Matthean parallel [23:37-39] to the saying here in Luke is located after "Palm Sunday"). Another suggestion is that it refers to some other journey by Jesus to the holy city. But what would be the importance of that argument? I prefer to consider an apocalyptic perspective (we know from the use in Ps 2:7 that a single biblical text was applied by Christians to two different stages of salvation history, that is, to Jesus' baptism and to his resurrection). Psalm 118 (117):26, quoted in the "Palm Sunday" pericope (19:38), appears here in an apocalyptic perspective. A welcome was to be extended to an enigmatic traveler. In order to identify this person, we must remember the messianic significance of the verb "come" (cf. John the Baptist's question: "Are you the one who is to come [ὁ ἐρχόμενος]?" 7:19-20). Here, the psalm serves to announce the eschatological coming of the Messiah, God's lieutenant (cf. "in the name of the Lord").[87] The Christian who composed this v. 35b was aware of Jesus' tragic fate, which he compared to a separation (as in the saying about the cup, 22:18), but he did not lose all hope. On the contrary, he felt that Jesus had been taken away to be with God[88] and that,

---

God from the temple made by human hands and its transfer to the temple not made by human hands, the church.

80   On οὐ μή, see BAGD, s.v. μή D; Kaegi, *Grammar*, §177.6.

81   See Kaegi, *Grammar*, §177.6; BDF §365.2.

82   The expression must be traditional, because Luke more readily uses ἕως οὗ (24:49) or ἕως ὅτου (12:50) than ἕως by itself, and he uses the aorist subjunctive (with ἄν, 21:32, or without it, 15:4, 8) more often than the future indicative (9:41).

83   See BAGD, s.v. ὅτε 2b; BDF §382.1–2.

84   For the state of the question, see Herranz Marco, "No me veréis hasta que digáis," 57–62 (incorrect pagination: it must be read in the following order: 57, 62, 61, 60, 59, 58).

85   On the departure of the presence of God, see n. 79 above.

86   On the fall of Jerusalem and the destruction of the temple as divine punishment, see 19:41-44; 21:20-24; Mark 13:1-8; 14-20; Steck, *Israel*, 235 n. 6, 238 n. 4; Pierre Bogaert, *Apocalypse de Baruch. Introduction, traduction du syriaque et commentaire* (2 vols.; SC 144–45; Paris: Cerf, 1969) 1:133–57.

87   For several authors, it is about the Son of Man rather than the Messiah; see Steck, *Israel*, 236–37; Christ, *Jesus Sophia*, 141; Zeller, "Entrückung," 517; cf. *1 Enoch* 61:7 and chaps. 70–71. The argument is that, if the Son of Man is identified with Wisdom, the Messiah is not. Yet the argument loses plausibility if one accepts that v. 35b was altered by a Christian: Jesus being for him the Messiah as well as the Son of Man, he could have identified him with Wisdom.

88   Zeller ("Entrückung," 515–19) insists on the idea of abduction, which he infers from the expression "not

331

from there, as a glorious Messiah, he would come at the end of time to establish God's reign. The historical "I" that disappears is therefore identical to the "he" of the benediction, who—according to what "you" the spectators said—was to come.

If that is the meaning of this verse, we may ask if Luke has not played on the ambiguity of the verb ἥξει ("he will come"), which I have translated as "he arrives." It is, of course, at a banal level, a matter of a *day* that will come; but it is also a question of the arrival of *someone*, of the one who is ὁ ἐρχόμενος "the one who comes."[89]

At a primary level, the text states a tautology: you will not see me[90] when I will be absent. At a secondary level, the text pronounces a judgment: God hides his face until the coming of the Messiah.[91] At a tertiary level, it expresses a tremendous hope: the one who dies has a future in front of him; the one who disappears does not disappear forever.

One last word concerning the "you," as witness to the absence, then to the presence.[92] There is a difficulty with it, since, in v. 34, the "you" refuses to listen to the voice of Wisdom, whereas in v. 35b it sides with God's messenger. The tension is real and may be explained by the interplay between tradition (vv. 34-35a) and redaction (v. 35b). But can a meaning be given to it? Yes, if the hope that is thereby expressed concerning Jesus has repercussions at the level of those who speak with him. In that case—such is the hope of the text—Jesus' fate will transform the witnesses to his life: from being enemies, "you" will become friends at the time of his return. Once favorable to his elimination, "you" will be happy about his return. In the book of Acts, the apostles offer a last chance for conversion to Israel and its leaders, who "through ignorance" were responsible for Jesus' disappearance. In spite of the persistent stubbornness that existed, Luke caused a final offer of pardon to be extended up to the end of Luke-Acts.

History of Interpretation

Let us follow the commentary of the Venerable Bede (*In Luc.* 4.1680–740): in his eyes, Herod was the type of those heretics who mounted the project of killing Christ, that is, of snatching from believers the humility of the Christian faith. The exorcisms and healings refer to the time of the church: the exorcisms took place at the time of the conversion of the Gentiles; the healings, when the commandments were obeyed. The fulfillment on the third day announces the state of eschatological perfection to which the church will attain. Bede then delighted in the image of the hen, which rounded off that of the fox. The coalition of Pilate and Herod against Jesus was that of the true foxes against a hen.

According to the *Glossa ordinaria*,[93] the three days in v. 33 can be understood in an ethical and existential way: the first day, renouncing human vanities by the grace of God; the second, conforming to the truth by one's customs and life; the third, the final glorification. "Your house" (v. 35a), on the other hand, designates the temple or the city of Jerusalem; the "you surely will not see me" (v. 35b) speaks of the absence of penitence and of confession of one's faith. Without such a Christian attitude, humans will not see Christ's face at the time of the second coming. So the announced and acclaimed coming must be taken in the eschatological and mystical sense of the parousia rather than in that of the entry into Jerusalem (that was already Bede's interpretation[94]).

In his commentary, Bonaventure[95] stressed God's plan, fully taken on by Christ: "And since the death

---

to see." He concludes that the category of abduction was the way that Q expressed faith in the resurrection (p. 527).

89 According to Christ (*Jesus Sophia*, 152), Jesus, in our vv. 34-35, makes himself the spokesman for Wisdom and even goes so far as to identify himself with Wisdom.

90 For Herranz Marco ("No me veréis hasta que digáis," 65), "not to see" has a Semitic meaning—not to have an experience, the experience of faith. For Zeller ("Entrückung," 515–17), to say "not to see" is to affirm that Jesus was removed.

91 See Caird, 174.

92 According to Herranz Marco ("No me veréis hasta que digáis," 69–71), Jesus here says with compassion that a better knowledge of his person and his work would help his incredulous hearers to welcome and acclaim him as the messenger of God.

93 *Glossa Ordinaria, Luc 13:33-35* (*PL* 114:306).

94 Cf. Bede the Venerable, *In Luc.* 4.1732–35.

95 Bonaventure, *Comm. in Luc.* 13.67–73, 355–56.

of Christ was not to be accomplished according to the machination of human wickedness, but according to the disposition of Christ's own wisdom and will, the text adds: *Behold, I cast out demons and perform cures today and tomorrow*, through the performance of miracles."[96] Another significant element is the diversity of interpretations of the three days: after having given a chronological interpretation as the literal meaning (the three days represent the three years of Jesus' ministry),[97] Bonaventure refers to various commentators whom he does not name;[98] in the allegorical sense, we are dealing, among other considerations, with the laws of nature, Scripture, and grace; in the ethical sense, we discover contrition (that is, soul-searching, I suppose), confession (of sins), and satisfaction (the good work);[99] in the anagogical[100] sense, the contemplation of God in his traces (*in vestigio*), in image (*in imagine sive in speculo*), and in himself (*in se ipso*).

From the sixteenth century, I would like to call attention to the slightly different emphases of Zwingli and Erasmus. For Zwingli, Christ's *death* was necessary, because he wanted to proclaim the *truth*;[101] for Erasmus, it was Jesus' *ministry*, shorter that some would have liked, which was to lead human beings to *salvation*.[102]

Conclusion

It is true that the exegesis has led me quite a long way from the two questions pointed out in the introduction. While they have troubled other commentators, I have not found them to be important. To take up the first one, I have considerable difficulty seeing in these verses the heart of the travel account or the center of a chiasmus. In the course of these chapters, Luke lined up episodes about Jesus or his words, of equal worth in his eyes, more than he structured them in a symmetrical or parallel fashion. What structuring he did do was in terms of theological themes that he wanted to bring out. This text certainly occurs in about the middle of the travel account and for that reason acquires a particular importance. But the parable of the prodigal son is equally central. Moreover, being located in the middle of a sequence does not necessarily amount to occupying the decisive position in it.

As for the other question, the one about the historical Jesus, let me answer it in the following way: if any passage in the Gospels were to preserve the interpretation that the historical Jesus gave of his ministry and the outcome of his life, it would certainly be this one.

If we concentrate on the text itself, we discover the public character of Jesus' ministry. Confronted with the highest public authority, the Lukan hero was seriously threatened. Warned of this mortal threat, he recalled that the fateful outcome that awaited him was not going to depend on Herod and would not occur in Galilee, but in Jerusalem. He therefore had to continue on the way along which he had made progress (9:51ff.) well before the Pharisees reported to him the ruler's intentions. This journey was not intended to avoid Herod's plot, that is, to flee death, but to accomplish God's plan, that is, to encounter death.

This death was going to confirm not a defeat but a success, the demonstration of the gospel by exorcisms and healings, signs of God's reign. Understood as a final service, it was to lead Jesus to an accomplishment ("I am finished," $\tau\epsilon\lambda\epsilon\iota o\hat{\upsilon}\mu\alpha\iota$). He would reach the state of perfection, to use the language of the Epistle to the Hebrews, which is fond of this verb "bring to accomplishment, completion, perfection" ($\tau\epsilon\lambda\epsilon\iota\acute{o}\omega$, Heb 5:9), but he would also lead his disciples to a state of perfection (Heb 2:10). In doing so, he would condemn the stubbornness of God's people: Jerusalem would be abandoned to its fate; the temple would see God's presence disappear. The protective wings would no longer be

---

96 Ibid., 355.

97 Ibid.

98 Ibid., 356.

99 Another interpretation is that the three days represent the three vows, chastity, obedience, and poverty.

100 Another interpretation: purification, illumination, and perfection; or: contemplation of the hierarchy of what is under heaven, in heaven, and above heaven; or even expulsion of demons, healings, and consummation of all things.

101 Zwingli, *Annotationes*, 668.

102 Erasmus, *Paraphrasis*, 399.

those of the temple but those of Christ, child of the Wisdom of God. Those persons who would refuse to accept that shift would lose that presence and that security. For God would henceforth be found elsewhere than in a sanctuary made with human hands: he would be there in the person of Christ (cf. Mark 14:58; John 2:19-21) and in the life of Christians (cf. 1 Cor 3:16; 6:19).

Is it illegitimate to move on from Christology to ethics? On the basis of these verses, are we not invited to rethink what is given to us to live by? While our tendency is to flee the risks and the threats of the Herods who surround us, Christ appeals to us to follow him. He invites us to fulfill our lives as a mission. Our journey, today, tomorrow, and the third day, will not spare us from dying, but it will fit that dying into a fulfillment about which God will have the last word. This journey will be risky, all the more so since it will take place, it is already taking place, during Christ's long absence.

The Sabbath of the Man with Dropsy (14:1-6)

Bibliography to Luke 14:1–6

Black, Matthew, *Aramaic Approach*, 168–69.

Idem, "The Aramaic Spoken by Christ and Luke 14.5," *JTS* n.s. 1 (1950) 60–62.

Braun, Willi, *Feasting and Social Rhetoric in Luke 14* (SNTSMS 85; Cambridge: Cambridge University Press, 1995).

Idem, "Symposium or Anti–Symposium? Reflections on Luke 14:1-24," *TJT* 8 (1992) 70–84.

Busse, *Wunder*, 304–12.

Daniélou, Jean, "Les repas dans la Bible et leur signification," *La Maison-Dieu* 18 (1949) 7–33.

Derrett, J. Duncan M., "Positive Perspectives on Two Lucan Miracles," *DRev* 104 (1986) 272–87, esp. 277–83.

Dibelius, *Tradition*, 54–56.

Dietzfelbinger, Christian, "Vom Sinn der Sabbatheilungen Jesu," *EvTh* 38 (1978) 281–98.

Ernst, Josef, "Gastmahlgespräche: Lk 14, 1-24," in Schnackenburg, *Kirche*, 57–58.

Falcke, Heino, "17. Sonntag nach Trinitatis: Lk 14, 1-6," *Göttinger Predigtmeditationen* 27 (1973) 424–31.

Finkel, Asher, *The Pharisees and the Teacher of Nazareth: A Study of Their Background, Their Halachic and Midrashic Teachings, the Similarities and Differences* (2d ed.; AGSU 4; Leiden: Brill, 1974) 170–72.

Hemelsoet, B., "'Gezegend hij die komt, de Koning, in de naam des Heren': Rondom Lc 14, 1-6," *ACEBT* 1 (1980) 85–95.

Hirsch, Emanuel, *Frühgeschichte des Evangeliums*, vol. 2, *Die Vorlagen des Lukas und das Sondergut des Matthäus* (Tübingen: Mohr Siebeck, 1941)134–36.

Klein, *Barmherzigkeit*, 16–32.

Klinghardt, *Gesetz*, 232–34.

Liese, H., "Dominus ad cenam invitatus die sabbati: Lc 14,1-12," *VD* 11 (1931) 257–61.

Lohse, Eduard, "Jesu Worte über den Sabbat," in Eltester, *Judentum*, 79–89.

Loos, van der, *Miracles*, 504–8.

Meeûs, Xavier de, "Composition de Lc 14 et le genre symposiaque," *EThL* 37 (1961) 847–70.

Neirynck, Frans, "Luke 14, 1-6: Lukan Composition and Q Saying," in Claus Bussmann and Walter Radl, eds., *Der Treue Gottes trauen: Beiträge zum Werk des Lukas. Festschrift Gerhard Schneider* (Freiburg im B.: Herder, 1991) 243–63.

Nickels, *Targum*, 40.

Petzke, *Sondergut*, 129–32.

Riesenfeld, Harald, "Anteckning till Lk 14, 5," *SEÅ* 49 (1984) 83–88.

Roloff, *Kerygma*, 66–69.

Safran, Alexandre, "Le sabbat dans la tradition juive," *RThPh* 3d series 27 (1977) 136–49.

Schmidt, Francis, "Le pouvoir à table (Essai d'histoire des idéologies à propos de Mc 10, 35-45," *BCPE* Supplement (1978) i–viii.

Simson, P., "L'Évangile (Lc 14, 1-11): le code de bienséance de l'assemblée chrétienne," *AsSeign* 70 (1975) 31–41.

Smith, Dennis E., "Table Fellowship as a Literary Motif in the Gospel of Luke," *JBL* 106 (1987) 613–38.

Staudinger, F., *Die Sabbatkonflikte bei Lukas* (diss., Granz, 1994).

Steele, E. Springs, "Jesus' Table-Fellowship with Pharisees: An Editorial Analysis of Lk 7, 36-50; 11, 37-54, and 14, 1-24" (Ph.D. diss., University of Notre Dame, 1981).

Idem, "Luke 11:37-54: A Modified Hellenistic Symposium," *JBL* 103 (1984) 379–94.

Stöger, Alois, "Sentences sur les repas, Lc 14,1.7-14," *AsSeign* 53 (1970) 78–88.

Str-B 2:202–4; 4.2:617–39.

Tilborg, Sjef van, "De parabel van de grote feestmaaltijd (Lc 14, 1-24)," in Iersel, *Parabelverhalen*, 133–47.

Trautmann, *Zeichenhafte Handlungen*, 286–91.

1/ **And it happened that when he was entering the house of a leader of the Pharisees to eat a meal[a] on the Sabbath, they were watching him closely. 2/ Just then, in front of him, there was a man who had dropsy. 3/ By way of an answer, Jesus said to the experts in the law and the Pharisees, "Is it lawful to cure people on the Sabbath, or not?" 4/ But they remained silent. So he took him and healed him, and sent him away. 5/ Then he said to them, "Which one of you who has a son or an ox that has fallen into a well, will not immediately pull him out on a Sabbath day?" 6/ And they could not reply to this.**

a   Literally: "to eat bread."

Here we find Jesus confronted with an influential person, a representative of the Pharisaic elite, and also with a sick person, an unimportant anonymous person. On the one hand, invited to share a formal meal and, on the other, anxious to perform a healing, Jesus lived this double reality simultaneously, during a Sabbath. Would he be able to take on these contradictory realities? It was a Sabbath day that was not to be a day of rest.

Analysis

Luke had recently reminded us of Jesus' journey (13:22) and pointed out the threats that were weighing down on him if he did not go to Jerusalem (13:31-33). Master of the stages that punctuated his fate, the Lukan Christ here accepts a welcome pause (14:1). This invitation by the Pharisee allowed the Gospel writer to compose a banquet scene. As it happened, the guest of honor jumped at the occasion of this meal to offer a quadruple teaching. While the first lesson deals with the proper use of the Sabbath (14:1-6), the following two have to do with the world of hospitality in which the scene was set. What attitude should one adopt when invited (14:7-11), and to whom should one give hospitality when it is one's turn to do the inviting (14:12-14)? The fourth section deals with God's final invitation to the great dinner in the kingdom (14:15-24).

The Banquet Setting

In every civilization, meals acquire a social and cultural value over time. They become the occasion for welcoming visiting guests and honoring them, then for mining their knowledge and benefiting from the difference that they represent. Rooted in a social reality, the banquet thus also becomes the subject of literary descriptions. The Greeks, in particular, raised physical meals to the rank of intellectual and spiritual delights. From Plato to Macrobius they developed a literary genre with which Luke was acquainted and that he used, for example, the philosophical conversation during a meal.[1] The occasion encourages dialogue; the circumstances or the intention of the host provide the theme for the conversation.

Luke used the banquet motif several times: in chap. 5, it was in Levi's house, during a feast, that Luke made clear what the purpose of Jesus' mission was (5:29-39); in chap. 7, it was during a meal that the woman anointed Jesus and thereby gave the Pharisee a lesson (7:31-50); in chap. 11, it was on the occasion of an invitation that Jesus delivered a philippic against the Pharisees and the experts in the law (11:37-54); here, in chap. 14, a Pharisee is still the one who has invited Jesus; finally, in chap. 22, we are no longer dealing with an invitation, but a Passover meal prepared by the disciples (22:1-13), during which Jesus gives a final teaching (22:14-38). Nor should we forget the meals that the Risen One ate with his disciples (24:30, 41-43). If we remember the welcome extended to Jesus by Martha and Mary (10:38-42), then by Zacchaeus (19:5-6), and the complaint lodged by the Pharisees and the scribes (that he ate with the tax collectors and sinners; 15:1-2), it will be agreed that meals had a literary importance in the Gospel of Luke on a scale without any equivalent in the other Gospels. We should be careful, however, not to attribute all these scenes to the Gospel writer's imagination. Luke was satisfied with amplifying a reality anchored in Jesus' actual life. It should be noted, moreover, that it was the Pharisees, not the Sadducees, their social superiors, who invited Jesus. Even if the relationship between them and Jesus was marked by conflict, it was with them that he had the most natural relationship. This proximity of the Pharisees is important for both the integration of Jesus into history and the sociology of early Christianity. It will also be noted that Jesus often ate with those people who were looked down on by Jewish society and did not seek contacts with the aristocracy of the capital. We have there an indication of Jesus' soteriological intentions, as well as the missionary intentions of the earliest Christians. It is difficult to determine the social standing here of the host, who was "a leader of the Pharisees" (v. 1). Finally, we should be attentive to the link between the meal set-

---

1   See the commentaries on 7:36-50 and 11:37-54 in vol. 1; Hug, "Symposion-Literatur," *RE* 4, A2 (1932), cols. 1273–82; de Meeûs, "Composition de Lc 14," 847–70; Ernst, "Gastmahlgespräche," 57–58; Stöger, "Sentences sur les repas," 78–88; Steele, "Luke 11:37-54," 379–94; Smith, "Table Fellowship," 613–38. On meals in Judaism, see Str-B 4:611–39.

ting and the nature of the lessons that the Lukan Jesus drew from his talks. Here in chap. 14, for example, it was during a meal that problems concerning with whom one should eat were settled, as well as the relationships between daily life and the banquet in the kingdom.[2]

Unlike Greek literary scenes, the Lukan banquets are strikingly brief and simple. In the pericopes brought together in 14:1-24, for example, the dialogues are still implicit or fragmentary. In the episode of the man with dropsy (vv. 1-6), Jesus is the only person to speak. In the following two parts (vv. 7-11 and vv. 12-14), he states his teaching rather than entering into a dialogue. Finally, although the parable of the feast is preceded by a guest's interjection (v. 15), it is not followed by any reaction from Jesus. This rudimentary character is not, however, to be equated with awkwardness. A literary dialogue was often prompted by an incident or an anomaly.[3] Here in v. 2 it is the presence of the man with dropsy that fulfills that function. A little farther on, Luke addresses with sensitivity the sayings about the places of honor granted to the invited guests (vv. 7-11) and those about the choice of those to be invited to the host's home (vv. 12-14). Finally, the decisive shift from worldly receptions to the invitation to the kingdom takes place thanks to a dialogue (vv. 15-16). After having heard a beatitude of Jesus marking eschatological retribution (v. 14), one of the guests, attentive to this perspective ("having heard," ἀκούσας, translated as "having heard these words," v. 15), also replies himself with a beatitude (v. 15), which prompts the account of the parable (vv. 16-24). The composition of the whole unit about the banquet also strikes us by its equilibrium: the parable (vv. 15-24) corresponds to the healing (vv. 2-6), just as the advice given to the hosts who issue invitations (vv. 12-14) corresponds to the instructions given to the guests (vv. 7-11). Finally, the absence of any true dialogue is probably the expression of Luke's inten-tion more than literary awkwardness. Since he repeats for us the fact that the Pharisees did not know what to say when confronted with the miracle (v. 4 and v. 6), right up until the end he keeps them in a silence that, more eloquent than words, expresses their embarrassment and their defeat. Alone in the middle of this embarrassed silence is the voice of the one potential believer. The beatitude that he utters (v. 15) anticipates the confession of Christian faith that was to appear suddenly, as a minor-ity voice, among the recalcitrant people of Israel.

Accounts of Miracles on the Sabbath

The canonical Gospels transmit various accounts of mir-acles performed on the Sabbath day.[4] The triple tradition (cf. Mark 3:1-6 par. Matt 12:9-14 par. Luke 6:6-11) has preserved the healing of the man with a withered hand; the Gospel of John, the healing of the paralytic at the Sheep Gate (John 5:1-16) and the man born blind (John 9:1-23); the Gospel of Luke, those of the woman who was bent over (13:10-17) and of the man with dropsy (14:1-6).

Let us compare the three Lukan accounts, the one that the Gospel writer adapted from Mark (Luke 6:6-11) and those that are peculiar to his Gospel (Luke 13:10-17 and 14:1-6). In none of the three cases did the sickness require urgent attention. Jesus could have waited until the day after the Sabbath, but he did not want to. Each time, the Pharisees were present and made their hostil-ity felt (the verb used is παρατηρέομαι, "watch closely"; 6:7; 14:1). It made a difference where the healing was performed; it was in a synagogue (6:6; 13:10) or the house of a Pharisee (14:1), therefore on unfavorable terrain with religious significance. In each case, the healing accompanied and completed some teaching ("teach," διδάσκειν, 6:6; "teaching," διδάσκων, 13:10; "he told . . . a parable," ἔλεγεν . . . παραβολήν, 14:7). Jesus' instruction—on the true meaning of the Sabbath

---

2 In chap. 7, for example, the incident of the woman allows one to establish a contrast between his actions toward her and the attitude of the Pharisee who invited Jesus.

3 Sometimes even by a miracle; see Busse (*Wunder*, 305), who refers to Plato *Symp.* 172A; Xenophon *Symp.* 1.2–7 (the incident that provokes the discus-sion, an unexpected meeting, takes place just before the meal); and Plutarch, *Symposium* (nine books that comprise part of the *Moralia*). In par-

ticular one should consult the prologue of book 4 and the episode just after (*Moralia, Symposium* 4, prologue and 4.1 §§659E–660E).

4 See the commentary on 6:6-11 in vol. 1, and on 13:10-17 above; Hirsch, *Vorlagen*, 134–36; Lohse, "Jesu Worte über den Sabbat," 79–89; Dietzfelbin-ger, "Vom Sinn der Sabbatheilungen Jesu," 281–98; Busse, *Wunder*, 304–12; Trautmann, *Zeichenhafte Handlungen*, 278–318; Klein, *Barmherzigkeit*, 16–32.

and its observance—counted for more than the miracle itself. A dazzling saying summarizes this specific teaching that Christians made their own: do good and save (6:9); free from Satan (13:16); deliver from water and its threats (14:2, 5). In the face of Jesus' effective action and irrefutable word, his enemies gave in, but grudgingly (6:11; 13:17; 14:4, 6). The narrator adopted Jesus' triumphant solution and rejoiced in this success, albeit aware of the physical threats that that victory would cause for his hero. In his innermost heart, he hoped for the conversion of the Pharisees, that is, that they would be convinced by Jesus' teaching rather than defeated by his arguments.

Although there are many common elements in these accounts, there are differences in their order and in the way they are presented. Here, taking the present pericope as the basis of comparison, is a synoptic comparison (see p. 339):

What changes the most from one account to another is the relationship between Jesus' action as a healer and the words he addresses to his opponents. In the present text, 14:1-6, the healing almost disappears, wedged as it is between two of Jesus' questions. In 13:10-17, the miracle is separated from the controversy that follows it. In 6:6-11, the controversy precedes, then Jesus' opinion wins acceptance thanks to the following miracle. While in chap. 13 one of the questions concerns the Jews' custom and the other, Jesus' liberating act, in chap. 6 Jesus asks the question about what is allowed and answers it by something he does; in chap. 14, Jesus' first saying raises the question of what is allowed and what is forbidden (as in chap. 6), while the second one has to do with the way Jews organized the help they gave people (as in chap. 13).

These differences can be capitalized on in terms of either their structure or their origin. To mention only the present text and its structure, Luke contrasted what Jesus decided to do and the Pharisees' embarrassment and thus answered the question of what is allowed and what is forbidden. Since the second question, the one about how Jews did things, was rhetorical, it did not need an answer; it served as a commentary on what Jesus did and silenced his opponents once and for all. It was in

this way that the Gospel writer brought together on the same historical level the sick person, who represented the neighbor, and the commandment about the Sabbath, which came from God. By this brief interlacing of divergent attitudes, Luke showed how Jesus respected God and his law by helping neighbors in their destitution; the negative side of the coin was the demonstration of how the Pharisees ended up breaking the first great commandment by refusing to obey the second one.

The respective origins of redaction and tradition can be divided up as follows. Luke himself described the situation (v. 1), in this way introducing the miracle account into the setting of the meal.[5] Yet he seems to have relied on Mark for the mention of the Pharisees' vigilance (cf. Mark 3:2), on the beatitude of v. 15 to indicate the meal ("to eat bread"), and perhaps on L for the indication of who had invited Jesus (the expression "a leader of the Pharisees" is not Lukan). The description of the man who was sick (v. 2), on the other hand, is very Lukan, with the possible exception of the word "dropsy," which is found nowhere else in Luke-Acts or, for that matter, in the New Testament. Luke, we must not forget, was capable of using a rare word, such as a precise medical term. The following sequence (vv. 3-4) is a redactional adaptation of the parallel in Mark 3:4-5 par. Luke 6:9-10. Luke probably composed this sequence in imitation of his own earlier text, the one about the person with the withered hand. The second question (v. 5) is found in both Matthew and Luke. It resembles the first question of the account of the woman who was bent over (13:15), but it is especially close to the supplementary saying that Matthew inserted in the account of the man with the withered hand (Matt 12:11). Lacking christological touches and marked by the expression "Which one of you . . . ?" found only on Jesus' lips, it is probably authentic. Our detailed exegesis will examine the question of which one, Matthew or Luke, preserved the earliest form of it. Since the saying did not circulate without a narrative setting, I doubt that Matthew and Luke found it in Q. Transmitted orally, it circulated more readily linked to an account of healing on the Sabbath. It is a part of the triple tradition in Matthew; of L, in Luke.[6] The brief conclusion properly

---

5   One can also imagine that, from v. 1, Luke depends on a story from L that he adapts.

6   See Petzke, *Sondergut*, 130–32. Hirsch (*Vorlagen*,

134–36) and Ernst ("Gastmahlgespräche," 64), on the other hand, attribute the apophthegm in 14:1-6 to Q.

14:1-6	13:10-17	6:6-11
Situation (v. 1)	Situation (v. 10)	Situation (v. 6a)
Incident (v. 2): unexpected presence of a sick person	Incident (v. 11): unexpected presence of a crippled person	Incident (v. 6b): unexpected presence of an invalid
		Jesus' enemies watch him closely
		Jesus calls to the invalid, who obeys (v. 8)
Jesus' first question to the Pharisees (v. 3)		Jesus' rhetorical question to the Pharisees (v. 9)
The Pharisees without an answer for the first time (v. 4a)		
Jesus heals the sick person (v. 4b)	Jesus calls to the woman and heals her (vv. 12-13)	Jesus heals the invalid (v. 10)
	The leader of the synagogue reacts out loud (v. 14)	
Jesus' second question to the Pharisees (v. 5)	Jesus asks his enemies two questions (vv. 15-16)	
The Pharisees without an answer for the second time (v. 6)	Outcome: His enemies are put to shame (v. 17a)	His enemies are filled with fury (v. 11)
	His supporters rejoice (v. 17b)	

attests the hand of the Gospel writer (half of the occurrences in the New Testament of ἰσχύω, "have the power to," "be able to," are Lukan). Nevertheless, neither πρὸς ταῦτα ("to this") nor ἀνταποκρίνομαι ("reply") is characteristic of Luke. These words could be the remains of the original conclusion of the account at the level of tradition.

From the point of view of the literary genre, we are dealing with a miracle account in the form of an apophthegm (note the importance of Jesus' sayings), which Luke inserted into the banquet setting. While in 13:10-17 the miracle is as important as the teaching, in this pericope it fades into the background.[7] The man who

had dropsy did not ask anything of Jesus, who, moreover, did not speak to him. What is more, no sooner was the sick person healed than he was sent away. There was no cry of joy or admiration to emphasize the success of the miracle. So the theological lesson was more important than what was expressed by way of narrative, which puts a recent date on the account.[8] Although admittedly recent, the account in 14:1-6 is not Lukan for all that. It was at the level of L that it took shape. (At the home of a leader of the Pharisees, Jesus healed a man who had dropsy, then justified what he did by a saying. Neither spectators nor enemies knew what to reply.) Luke may have reworked and developed this episode by adding some

---

7 See Klein, *Barmherzigkeit*, 30: if the author of L developed a miracle story from a controversy in 13:10-17, he amplified a controversy in the miracle story in 14:1-6.

8 I am not going so far as to say that Luke 14:1-6 is entirely redactional; see Busse (*Wunder*), who points out three explanations for the origin of our pericope: (a) 14:1-6 is a variant of 6:6-11, (b) 14:1-16 is

elements extracted from the account of the person with the withered hand (the Pharisees' vigilance, the question as to what is allowed on the Sabbath day, and the first embarrassment of the opponents).

Commentary

■ **1** Instead of fleeing, as it had been suggested to him (13:31), Jesus accepted an invitation to eat a meal. Unlike what happened in 7:36 or in 11:37, here Luke only mentions the acceptance of the invitation (v. 1); the later words ("the one who had invited him," v. 12) are a witness to the fact that, unlike in 19:5-6 (Zacchaeus), here Jesus did not impose his presence. By means of this mention of Jesus as a person who consented, the Gospel writer emphasized that the threats (13:31) in no way intimidated the Master.

As was often the case, the Gospel writer used at the beginning of the episode his favorite Semitism καὶ ἐγένετο ἐν τῷ and the infinitive, "and it happened that when. . . ."[9] What happened? First off (v. 1b), Jesus'

enemies were watching him closely; next (v. 2), there was a man there who had dropsy.

The expression "a leader of the Pharisees" is surprising, since the Pharisees were not organized hierarchically.[10] He must have been either a prominent Pharisee, a moral authority in his party, or a Jewish magistrate with Pharisaic leanings, a judge, a president of a synagogue, or a member of a local Sanhedrin. Luke, who was fond of the word ἄρχων ("prince," "ruler"),[11] locates Jesus for once among those who were prominent.

The important word here is obviously σαββάτῳ, "on the Sabbath."[12] Having a formal meal and inviting visiting guests on that day was a part of the current customs.[13] The fact that the Pharisees—they must be the ones referred to by "they"—were watching Jesus closely suggests that experience had taught them to be suspicious.[14] They are portrayed as being on the lookout for something that Jesus might do that was incompatible with their conception of Sabbath rest. The readers are led to ask themselves whether the Pharisees acted that way to protect the law or to trip up their rival.

---

independent of 6:6-11, or (c) 14:1-6 is a redactional composition that incorporates the only traditional element, the floating logion in v. 5. Busse opts for this third hypothesis; similarly Trautmann, *Zeichenhafte Handlungen*, 287.

9   Cf. 5:12 and 11:1. Luke also gladly uses ἐγένετο δέ ("yet it happened") followed by the infinitive, which is itself followed by the subject of the infinitive in the accusative (see 6:1, 12); see the commentary on 1:5-7 in vol. 1; BAGD, s.v. γίνομαι, 1.3f.

10   See Plummer, 354; Lagrange, 397.

11   For ἄρχων in Luke for a Jewish authority, see 8:41; 12:58; 14:1; 18:18; 23:13, 35; 24:20; Acts 3:17; 4:5, 8, 26; 7:27, 35; 13:27; 14:5; 23:5; see the commentary on 8:41, n. 34, in vol. 1.

12   On the classical use of the dative to mark time (*Zeitpunkt*, precise moment, and not *Zeitraum*, duration), see BDF §200; and Kaegi, *Grammar*, §154.1.

13   Like our Sunday, the Sabbath lent itself to celebratory meals, as it still does (the meal had to be prepared the day before by people who were well-versed in the requirements of ritual. Since it could not be reheated, there were means of keeping the food hot; see *m. Šabb.* 4:1–2). Some meals were undoubtedly eaten at midday after services at the synagogue. See *Jub.* 2:21; *b. Pesaḥ.* 6 (68b). According to rabbinic discussion, on the day of the Sabbath and during feasts, one had to divide

up one's time: half for God and half for oneself, that is to say, for rejoicing. According to R. Eliezer, all was for God. See also Josephus *Vita* 54 §279; Str-B 2:202–3; Stöger, "Sentences sur les repas," 80; Fitzmyer, 2:1040–41. The expression φαγεῖν ἄρτον ("to eat bread"), in the sense of "to eat a meal," is a Semitism (see Exod 2:20 LXX). Luke, in this Jewish context, does not hesitate to use it. He borrows it from the traditional beatitude that he is going to cite shortly (14:15); see Str-B 2:207; BAGD, s.v. ἐσθίω, 1a. The expression survives in modern Greek: τρώω ψωμὶ ("to eat together," "to share a meal").

14   Luke uses παρατηρέω in Acts 9:24 to mean "to keep an eye on" the gates of the city, for fear that Saul might escape. In the Gospel, he uses it three times in the pejorative sense to describe the Pharisees who suspect Jesus and are on the lookout (twice in the middle, in 6:7 and here, and once in the active, in the absolute way, in 20:20). On the other hand, the compounds διατηρέω ("to keep with care," "to keep") in 2:51, and συντηρέω ("to preserve," "to retain") in 2:19 have positive connotations. Luke uses the substantive παρατήρησις ("observation," "surveillance") once, in 17:20; see Delebecque, 93.

■ **2** The setting was given in v. 1; v. 2 introduces the person whose presence is going to set the action in motion. The καὶ ἰδού . . . ("just then . . .") is a continuation of καὶ ἐγένετο ("and it happened that") in v. 1. It is a typically Lukan turn of phrase and recalls the way the Gospel writer introduced the old man Simeon (2:25), the man who had the spirit of an unclean demon (4:33), the man covered with "leprosy" (5:12), or the person whose hand was withered (6:6).

Ἔμπροσθεν αὐτοῦ ("in front of him") is rather formal (cf. "before God," Acts 10:4). It is a way of saying that Jesus[15] would have to make a decision. Placed in a situation that had suddenly become uncomfortable, he was going to have either to turn the sick person away by refusing to get involved or else to act with sovereign power, as he had on behalf of the paralyzed man, who was also placed "in front of Jesus" (5:19). In the latter case, he would refuse to rest on the Sabbath day. Is that not what the Pharisees were counting on? Some commentators have suggested that the Pharisees had taken the initiative in order to bring the man who had dropsy to that place, on that day.[16]

The adjective ὑδρωπικός ("suffering from dropsy, edema") belongs to the medical vocabulary of antiquity; it is found also in the writings of physicians of the classical period.[17] It could nevertheless also come to the mind of any educated person; Luke did not have to be a physician to use it.[18]

For people in antiquity, dropsy or edema was a disease whose symptoms were swellings, in particular of the abdomen. As a visible consequence of various kinds of illnesses, it was dreaded. When it became chronic, it weakened the heart and could lead to sudden death.[19] Several different treatments for it were suggested,[20] among them, a stay in the temple of Asclepius in Epidaurus.[21] Greek physicians looked for the cause of this illness in various

---

15   See BAGD, s.v. ἔμπροσθεν 2d; Busse, *Wunder*, 307 (n. 4 on 306): it is a formula inspired by the LXX.

16   He had been brought as a trap for Jesus. This is John Calvin's hypothesis (*Harmony*, 2:102). Against this suggestion, see Plummer, 354.

17   See Hippocrates *Aphorisms* 6.8, 27, 35; *Epidemics* 7.19–21 (if they do not belong to Hippocrates himself, these treatises undoubtedly date to the fourth century B.C.E.); Plutarch (*De vitando aere alieno* 8 [= *Moralia* 831]) (two other passages of Plutarch are mentioned in n. 19 below); Philostratus (*Life of Apollonius of Tyana* 1.6; 3.44). Thanks to the Thesaurus Linguae Grecae, one of my assistants, David Warren, has identified forty-eight uses of the word ὑδρωπικός in the writings attributed to Galen, the second century C.E. doctor. See Karl Gottlob Kühn, ed., *Medicorum graecorum opera quae exstant* (26 vols.; Leipzig: Cnoblochii, 1821–33; vols. 1–22 on Galen) 12:378–1007 and 13:1–361. Book 10 of the treatise assembles all kinds of recipes borrowed from many doctors. More than one purports to treat dropsy. For example (13.262): "For those with dropsy, diet, as appropriate. Make a poultice of heifer dung; dry it carefully and, after having smoothed it over, let it boil in a mixture of water and vinegar in the manner of non-grilled barley flour; after having sprinkled the quarter pound of 'flowers of sulfur' [lit, of sulfur which has not yet been put in the fire], place this poultice over the entire stomach." See Derrett, "Positive Perspectives," 277–83. For other references, see BAGD, s.v.

18   See Henry J. Cadbury, *The Style and Literary Method of Luke* (HTS 6; Cambridge, Mass.: Harvard University Press, 1920) 39–72, esp. 44; Sophie Antoniadis, *L'Évangile de Luc: Esquisse de grammaire et de style* (Collection de l'Institut néohéllenique de l'Université de Paris 7; Paris: Belles Lettres, 1930) 105 (on medical terms; no mention of the substantive adjective "dropsical"). These two books both suffer from the lack of an index.

19   One could point to two, or perhaps three, famous cases of dropsy in antiquity: the philosopher Heraclitus (sixth–fifth century B.C.E.; see Plutarch *De tuenda Sanitate Praecepta* 25 [= *Moralia* 136] and *Comm. Not.* 11 [= *Moralia* 1064]), the Byzantine emperor Heraclius, who died in 641 (see Nicephorus, patriarch of Constantinople, *Breviarium* 27; Cyril Mango, *Short History: Nikephoros, Patriarch of Constantinople* [Corpus fontium historiae Byzantinae 13; Washington, D.C.: Dumbarton Oaks, 1990]), and one might add Herod the Great, according to the description of Josephus (*Bell.* 1.33.5 §§656–57; *Ant.* 17.6.5 §§168–73). On the idea of punishment associated with this illness, see n. 23 below.

20   See Derrett, "Positive Perspectives," 278: "Therapeutic cures of dropsy included control of intake, medicines, and mechanical tapping, squeezing the water out." See n. 17 above.

21   See Rudolf Herzog, *Die Wunderheilungen von Epidauros: Ein Beitrag zur Geschichte der Medizin und der Religion* (Philologus Supplement 22.3; Leipzig: Dieterich, 1931) 16–17, 77 (while asleep in the sanc-

excesses, in particular drinking, and various unwise activities. They provided a rational explanation for it.

Judaism was also acquainted with dropsy and included it in its religious and ethical interpretive system.[22] This disease was considered to be a curse, the consequence of a sin. The book of Numbers reckoned that an adulterous woman would be struck by it (Num 5:21-22),[23] and the Psalmist condemned his enemy to such a punishment (Ps 109 [108]:18). The rabbinical literature passes on sapiential and exegetical reflections on it: according to *Leviticus Rabbah* 15.2 (115c),[24] a person is composed of water and blood. While virtuous persons maintain an equilibrium between these elements, sinners allow one or the other of them to be dominant: either water (in which case they develop dropsy), or blood (in which case they develop "leprosy"). For some rabbis, what caused dropsy was lust; for others, it was slander. For still others, the three kinds of dropsy corresponded to three sins, lust, greed, and witchcraft. Finally, according to Rabbi Levi,[25] the episode of the golden calf resulted in three punishments: the sword, for those who had sacrificed to the calf; the plague, for those who had kissed it; and dropsy, for those who had rejoiced because of it. In my opinion, the link between a scourge associated with water and the golden calf is already suggested in Scripture. Those who worshiped the idol would be punished and would, in fact, have to drink the mixture of crushed gold and stagnant water before being put to the sword (Exod 32:20, 27-28). In short, Jewish feelings and interpretation held dropsy to be a punishment for a sexual sin (adultery, lust) or a religious one (idolatry, witchcraft), or even one of relationships (slander).

Jewish hope, on the other hand, expected that the messianic era would usher in total well-being for the righteous.[26] When the people fasted according to the Lord's wishes and observed the Sabbath righteously, then salvation, probably including physical health, would reach each one.[27] Jewish medicine, for its part, was acquainted with punctures intended to give relief to persons suffering from dropsy, but, according to the current legislation on the matter, practitioners did not have the right to administer punctures on the Sabbath day.[28] When Luke wrote about dropsy, he was probably influenced both by Greek learning and by Jewish beliefs.

■ **3** What Jesus said is described by Luke as a reply ("by way of an answer," $\dot{\alpha}\pi o\kappa\rho\iota\vartheta\epsilon\acute{\iota}\varsigma$). The Master did indeed place himself under the prying scrutiny of his opponents (v. 1) and in the unexpected presence of the man who had dropsy (v. 2). What he really "replied" to was not some words but some eloquent attitudes. As he would continue to do, he considered the Jewish leaders to be the ones to whom he was talking at that moment.

The coupled group of "the experts in the law and the Pharisees" constituted the quintessential Jewish opposition to Jesus' new message, in Galilee and during his journey to Jerusalem. While Luke took over from Mark the term "scribe" ($\gamma\rho\alpha\mu\mu\alpha\tau\epsilon\acute{\upsilon}\varsigma$, 5:21; cf. Mark 2:6), he borrowed from L the term "expert in the law" ($\nu o\mu\iota\kappa\acute{o}\varsigma$; cf. 10:25), which he preferred (cf. 7:30; 11:45, 46, 52).[29] Jesus was to stand up to these opponents and set his interpretation of the commandments and God's will against theirs. In Jerusalem, he was to move into a new locus of operations, the temple, and meet up with other

---

tuary, in her dream a mother sees the treatment and healing of her daughter with dropsy; the latter, staying in Lacedemonia, has the same dream and is cured), 28–29, 82 (a dream suggests a treatment).

22 See Str-B 2:203–4, Derrett, "Positive Perspectives," 278, 285–86 nn. 31–37.

23 See Prov 5:15-23 (the text seems to predict dropsy as a punishment for someone who is not content with his own lawful wife); Josephus *Bell.* 1.33.5 §656; 5.13.4 §549.

24 Cited by Str-B 2:203; see *Midrash Rabbah* 4:189–90.

25 See Str-B 2:203–4.

26 See Isa 57:14-21. The texts from the intertestamental literature that describe the end speak more readily of peace and salvation than of physical healing; see CD, Manuscript B, 2.33–35; 1QH 15.16; 11QPs^a 22.1–15; *T. Dan* 5:9-13; *T. Naph.* 8:1-6; *T. Benj.* 10:5-

11; *Ps. Sol.* 10:3-8; 12:4-6. Nevertheless, the fact remains that the Apocalypse of John hopes for the disappearance of death and the end of suffering (Rev 21:4). For Paul death is also the last enemy (1 Cor 15:25-27). *Letter of Barnabas* 3.4 cites Isa 58:8 and thus invokes eschatological healings.

27 See Isa 58:6-12; Derrett ("Positive Perspectives," 278) insists on the texts of Trito-Isaiah, Isaiah 57–58.

28 See Immanuel Jakobovits, *Jewish Medical Ethics* (New York: Philosophical Library, 1959) 79, cited by Derrett, "Positive Perspectives," 286 n. 33.

29 See the commentary on 7:29-30, n. 54, in vol. 1.

opponents, the chief priests and the elders, but also once again with scribes, this time those of the capital.[30] The confrontation would also take place in reference to other subjects than the interpretation of the Torah.

What was it permissible to do on the Sabbath day? That was the question that confronted everyone who wished to obey the commandment about the Sabbath (Exod 20:8; Deut 5:12-16).[31] It was even so legitimate that the Synoptic tradition sometimes placed it on Jesus' lips (as here and in Mark 3:4), and sometimes on the lips of his interlocutors (Matt 12:10). It was a question that came up naturally, since the Sabbath day was not, in either Scripture or Jewish thought, a day when one did nothing. On the contrary, the text of Gen 2:2 itself states that God completed his work of creation the seventh day and the Jewish commentary *Genesis Rabbah* (7.5; 10.9) meditates on this completeness that was conferred on the Sabbath day.[32] In the eyes of Jewish commentators, the Sabbath was a day when works were performed in the image of God's works, a day of religious activity, of displays of family affection, of friendly gatherings and spiritual conversations. That made it a burning question: Which activities came under the category of things that might be done on the Sabbath day and which ones were to be banned on that day?

Jesus' question was not a general one but a focused one: "Is it lawful to cure people on the Sabbath, or not?"[33] Just as Jesus and his opponents confronted each other, so did two different and contradictory answers face off, two divergent interpretations of the divine commandment. If taking care of people was considered to be secular work, any healing was thereby forbidden; but if it

was looked on as a spiritual task and veritable obedience, even accomplishing messianic work, then the answer could only be yes.[34]

■ **4** "But they remained silent." The verb ἡσυχάζω means "relax from normal activity," then "remain silent." Luke used it to refer to the docile and silent approval of Jerusalem Christians in Acts 11:18 and 21:14 and—oh, what irony—for the application of sabbatical rest in Luke 23:56. As we have seen, Jesus' opponents kept silent from the beginning to the end of the banquet, not knowing what to reply. Here, adding immobility to silence, they remained speechless.[35] They were perplexed as to what meaning to assign to the incident and to what Jesus said. They were conscious of their status as advocates of the law, but, out of prudence, they were afraid to defend it. Finally, they were vexed that they were powerless and had been challenged on their own ground. So in Luke's eyes their quiet was also fed by bad feelings. They were no more forbidden to engage in spiritual dialogue than in charitable acts, which were human ways of making concrete the divine completion of creation on the seventh day. Yet there they were, speechless, whereas they should have been providing the correct interpretation of the law; there they were, at a standstill, whereas they should have been obeying God's salvific will.

Judaism respects times. Attentive to hours, with the utmost energy, it distinguishes between the Sabbath and other days, preferring to lengthen the Sabbath by an hour rather than risk the slightest transgression. But for Jesus, God's will directs that good be done on the Sabbath, and it forbids putting off until the next day what, from another point of view, might wait.[36] What

---

30   See 19:47; 20:1, 19, 27; 22:1-6; etc.

31   Other Old Testament references to the Sabbath include Exod 16:23, 29-30; Lev 19:3; 23:3; and Num 15:32-36.

32   See *Midr. Rab.* 1:52–53, 77–79; Safran, "Le sabbat dans la tradition juive," 136–49; Falcke, "17. Sonntag nach Trinitatis: Lk 14, 1-6," 424–31.

33   The question recalls that of Mark 3:4 par. Luke 6:9. Numerous manuscripts add an εἰ at the beginning of the sentence, which should be taken here as an interrogative particle, Semitic in character; see BDF §440.3.

34   On the position of Jesus, the first Christians, and the evangelists on the subject of the Sabbath and its observance, see Lohse, "Jesu Worte über den Sab-

bat" (authority of the stances of Jesus in the eyes of the first Christians); Dietzfelbinger, "Vom Sinn der Sabbatheilungen Jesu" (link with the teaching of Jesus on the reign of God); Trautmann, *Zeichenhafte Handlungen*, 286–91 (link between Sabbath and synagogue; the mercy of Jesus is opposed to Jewish rigorism).

35   Quite rightly, Lagrange (398) thinks that "they were silent" in Luke 14:4 does not have exactly the same meaning as "they were silent" in Mark 3:4.

36   From a medical point of view, they could have postponed the treatment until the following day; see Dietzfelbinger, "Vom Sinn der Sabbatheilungen Jesu," 281.

would be the point of waiting? In order to "do nothing"? In Christ's eyes, that is not the proper mark of faithfulness. On the contrary, not waiting corresponds to God's will—acting willingly, not to accomplish some work but to participate in creation, in the re-creation of the world, willed and expected by God.[37]

Three verbs describe Jesus' role in this scene: first, $\dot{\epsilon}\pi\iota\lambda\alpha\mu\beta\acute{\alpha}\nu o\mu\alpha\iota$ ("to take hold of"), that is, extending one's hand to help or to be helped (see Heb 2:16), sometimes to take care of someone and help him or her; this is a verb that the New Testament uses more than the LXX does to describe the help or salvation that God provides, or that Jesus extends to unfortunate persons to protect them, sustain them, and keep them from sinking into the abyss of death.[38]

The second verb is $\dot{\iota}\acute{\alpha}o\mu\alpha\iota$ ("heal," "cure").[39] The treatment given by the Messiah ($\vartheta\epsilon\rho\alpha\pi\epsilon\acute{\nu}\omega$, v. 3) produced the cure ($\dot{\iota}\acute{\alpha}o\mu\alpha\iota$, v. 4). In the Gospel of Luke, Jesus is presented not only as the prophet and the messianic king but also as the benefactor and the physician of the "last days" (cf. 4:23, 33-40; 5:31; 6:18; Acts 10:38).[40] A healing power resided in him and went out from his person (5:17 and 8:46). This wonder-working and therapeutic power was not paramedical but a result of the relationship linking Jesus, the Son, to God, his Father (cf. 10:22). It corresponded to God's creative and regenerative power. Even more than that, it was the power conferred on the Son by delegation. And, as 10:19 expressed it, this delegation of power continues in the time of the church, among Jesus' disciples (cf., e.g., the miraculous healings performed by the apostles in Acts 9:34-43 and 20:7-12).

The third verb is the most difficult one of the three to understand: $\dot{\alpha}\pi o\lambda\acute{\nu}\omega$ ("set free," "release," "send away"). We encountered the verb $\lambda\acute{\nu}\omega$ ("untie") and its compound $\dot{\alpha}\pi o\lambda\acute{\nu}\omega$ in the parallel passage, 13:10-17, where they both played an important literary and theological

role.[41] Here $\dot{\alpha}\pi o\lambda\acute{\nu}\omega$ means in the first instance "send away," "dismiss." The case was settled, the matter was closed. The sick person, uncomfortable in the context of a banquet, could go back home. Jesus had given him relief, and order had been restored—not the order of the dead and of cemeteries but that of living persons and their dwellings. The man who had been cured had thus been liberated by Jesus, who expected nothing from him in return. With Christ's permission, he left, delivered of any dependence (illness, demon, Satan; cf. 13:16) and also loosed from any new constraint (with respect to Jesus, his benefactor). The Master's action seems harsh, but it was above all generous, since he treated the man he had healed as an adult and as a free person, as he had done in 8:38-39 with the man from whom the demons had gone, who was sent back home, entrusted with a missionary responsibility.[42]

Luke, we should not forget, was fond of polysemy and cultivated ambiguities loaded with meanings. To the first meaning, "send away," a second one should perhaps be added, that of "free," or "deliver," since $\dot{\alpha}\pi o\lambda\acute{\nu}\omega$ also refers to the setting free of prisoners, their being "pardoned." That is what God did, at the time of the first Passover, by freeing his people from Egypt, which is what was recalled over and over again by the annual freeing of a prisoner, in the context of the feast (23:17-25, five occurrences).[43] So Jesus was here creating something new by healing the sick person and creating a new exodus by freeing him from his slavery.

If this depth of meaning is really to be found in the text, we should probably enlarge the meaning of the preceding verb, "heal," "cure." Healing would also imply being welcomed by Christ and being offered pardon by God. By healing him, Jesus took away the weight that brought his life to a standstill. It follows that it was not a matter of indifference that the healing took place on a Sabbath day. Such an act was not only allowed on a Sab-

---

37   See Kahlefeld, *Parables*, 93.

38   See Jer 31(LXX 38):32; Matt 14:31; Mark 8:23; Heb 2:16; and 8:9 (citation of Jer 31[LXX 38]:32); see Albert Vanhoye, *Situation du Christ:* Hébreux 1–2 (LD 58; Paris: Cerf, 1969) 357–58.

39   Luke uses $\dot{\iota}\acute{\alpha}o\mu\alpha\iota$ fifteen times in his double work; see R. Leivestad, "$\dot{\iota}\acute{\alpha}o\mu\alpha\iota$ etc.," *EDNT* 2:169–70.

40   See the commentary on 4:40-41 in vol. 1.

41   See the commentary above on 13:10-17, n. 42.

42   See the commentary on 8:38-39 in vol. 1.

43   See 6:37c and the commentary on 6:37-38 in vol. 1.

44   On this saying, see the work of Lohse, "Jesu Worte über den Sabbat"; Dietzfelbinger, "Vom Sinn der

bath but had to be done that day because of the double relationship between recovered health at creation, on the one hand, and redemption, on the other.

■ **5** In this verse we have the oldest saying preserved by Luke, one known to Matthew as well, one that must have been pronounced by the historical Jesus.[44] It brings us straight to the point of rabbinic disputes, since both Essene and Pharisaic literature dealt with questions of that nature. While Matt 12:11 and Luke 14:5 transmit the same saying of Jesus, they do not rely on the same Greek source, since the wording is divergent throughout. Instead, they furnish us with two independent translations of the same saying:

Luke 14:5b	*Matt 12:11b*
τίνος ὑμῶν	τίς ἔσται ἐξ ὑμῶν ἄνθρωπος
υἱὸς ἢ βοῦς	ὃς ἔξει πρόβατον ἕν
εἰς φρέαρ πεσεῖται,	καὶ ἐὰν ἐμπέσῃ τοῦτο τοῖς
	σάββασιν εἰς βόθυνον,
καὶ οὐκ εὐθέως	οὐχὶ κρατήσει αὐτὸ καὶ
ἀνασπάσει αὐτὸν ἐν	ἐγερεῖ
ἡμέρᾳ τοῦ σαββάτου	

Among the number of stylistic differences are the following: the subject of the interrogation ("which one of you?" or "what person among you?"), the place into which the fall occurs ("well" or "pit"), the verb used to describe the fall ("fall" or "fall [into]"), the verbs used to describe the rescue ("pull out" or "lay hold of" and "raise up" or "lift"), and finally, the manner of speaking of the Sabbath and the place where that mention is made ("on a Sabbath day," at the end, or "on the Sabbath," before

the end). Among the narrative divergences are the stress Matthew lays on the single sheep and that laid by Luke on the urgency ("immediately"). While Matthew pictures a fall into a natural hole ("a pit") and suggests that the risk of drowning prevented by a strong arm and a well-executed motion, Luke suggests a human-made well and an accident that made it necessary to use a rope (the same verb, ἀνασπάω, "draw" or "pull up," is used in Acts 11:10 to speak of the sheet and the animals, seen by Peter in a vision, being pulled up again to heaven).[45] In short, Luke has accentuated the gravity of the risk and stressed the necessity of immediate assistance.

The most important divergence is certainly the one concerning the animal or the person who falls. Matthew, whose text is certain, thinks in terms of a sheep; Luke, whose text is uncertain, mentions two other living beings: in the second place, an ox (this is the reading of all the manuscripts) and in the first place a "son," a "donkey," or a "sheep," depending on the manuscript.[46] We can eliminate the reading "sheep," of Codex Bezae (D), which, as was the case with the genealogy (Luke 3:23-38), simplifies its task by inserting in Luke the text of Matthew. The reading "donkey" (ὄνος) is well attested and very satisfactory, almost too nice: the donkey (or "ass") and the ox (cf. Luke 13:15; Exod 21:33; Deut 5:14; 22:4; Isa 1:3). The word "son" is undeniably the *lectio difficilior*, the more difficult reading, since the prescriptions of the Hebrew Bible only mention animals and, among them, the donkey and the ox (Deut 22:4; Exod 21:33-34; 23:5). Nevertheless, the Essenes also took up the question of the fall of a human being.[47] In the Pharisaic rabbinic tradition, the case of animals who have fallen was treated in the following manner: the strictest wise men

---

Sabbatheilungen Jesu"; Trautmann, *Zeichenhafte Handlungen*, 309–15; Klein, *Barmherzigkeit*, 26–29.

45 Saul moves in the opposite direction when his friends lower him in a basket by a rope along the walls of Damascus in Acts 9:25. The verb there is χαλάω ("to let down," "to slide down").

46 There is a similar reading "donkey, son," attested in the uncial manuscript Koridethi (Θ) from the ninth century, conserved by Tiflis (= Tbilissi), and by the Syriac version called Cureton. Some also thought of the old poetic word οἶς ("sheep") (Hirsch, *Vorlagen*, 2:135) or of the word ὗς ("pig") (very hesitantly, Fitzmyer, 2:1042).

47 See CD 11.13–14, 16–17: "No-one should help an animal give birth on the sabbath day. And if he makes it fall into a well or a pit, he should not take it out on the sabbath. . . . And any living man who falls into a place of water or into a place <...>, no-one should take him out with a ladder or a rope or a utensil" (in Florentino García Martínez, ed., *The Dead Sea Scrolls Translated* [2d ed.; Leiden: Brill, 1996] 42). The text of the last sentence is so uncertain that one could just as easily read it as a prohibition or an authorization; see Eduard Lohse (*Die Texte aus Qumran* [3d ed.; Munich: Kösel, 1981] 89), who translates the last sentence as: "Einen

said that the animal could be given nourishment but ought not to be delivered on the Sabbath day; the most permissive among them authorized an animal's being hoisted out of a hole on that day.[48] I think that Luke read the words "a son or an ox."[49] His text reflects a saying echoing a liberal Pharisaic interpretation of the kind that Jesus could have encountered in Galilee: a human being, in any case, and even an animal can be saved on the Sabbath day.

Jesus' reasoning, as summarized by the Gospel writer, was as follows: you Pharisees think that God authorizes providing assistance to a being in mortal danger, either a human being or an animal, on the Sabbath day. My interpretation does not differ from yours, and my attitude is similar to yours, since I think that on this Sabbath day there is urgency and mortal danger. Where we differ is with respect to this last analysis of the situation. Nonetheless, I maintain my opinion.

While Luke was content with this reminder (with the two cases), Matthew drew from Jesus' lips the lesson allowed by this example (but the lesson that only the case of the animal allowed): "Now how much more valuable is a human being than an animal!" (Matt 12:12). In spite of their differences, Matthew and Luke defend the same interpretation of the law and even the same liberal Christian way of acting.[50]

By mentioning a father who rushes to help his son, Luke makes a particularly intense relationship come alive before our eyes. Since he was the one who gave life to his son, and since he had visceral emotional attachment to him, the father would do everything in his power to pull his son out of the well into which he had fallen. In that respect he resembles both God the Creator, who gives life to his children, and God the Redeemer, who preserves them. Does he not also intervene through his Son in order to vanquish double death, that is, physical death and existential death? And has it not even happened by the death of his Son?

■ **6** While Jesus did not make his opponents budge by what he said, although his words were very strong, he did, nevertheless, cause them to lose all their willpower: "and they could not," literally, "they couldn't find the strength to" ($οὐκ ἴσχυσαν$). The expression is probably stronger than the mention of silence in v. 4. They did not know what to reply: $ἀνταποκριθῆναι$ ("answer in turn," "reply"), here with a negative connotation, "reply" in a polemical manner.[51] "To this" ($πρὸς ταῦτα$), meaning "against that," "in relation to that," "in view of that," possibly "beyond that." Jesus' opponents had been outshone and could not, by anything they might say, either contradict or surpass Jesus' sayings.

Should we rule out the possibility of their finally having come to an awareness? What would their blocking Jesus at that time lead to? Being too strong for them, Jesus reduced them to silence (note the play on words between $ἡσύχασαν$, "they remained silent," v. 4, and $οὐκ ἴσχυσαν$, "they could not," v. 6). What was to be the outcome of the Master's departure and the evolution of their speechless frustration?

History of Interpretation

According to Ambrose, bishop of Milan, in the West, the soul and spirit of the man with dropsy had been suppressed by his flesh (*Exp. Luc.* 7.205).[52] Cyril, bishop of Alexandria, in the East, however, stressed Christ's

---

lebendigen Menschen, der in ein Wasserloch fällt oder sonst in einen Ort, soll niemand heraufholen mit einer Leiter oder einem Strick oder einem (anderen) Gegenstand."

48 See *b. Šabb.* 128b: a loose application allows one to save the animal; a strict application allows one only to feed it; Str-B 1:629–30; Marshall, 580.

49 Black ("Aramaic Spoken by Christ," 60–62) suggests that the primitive text had a single word בְּעִרָא ("beast of burden"), which was also the original form of the sheep in Matt 12:11, as well as the ox and even the "son" in Luke 14:5. Since the Aramaic word indeed resembles בְּרָא ("son"), it would have

been at the root of the two terms in Luke 14:5. The branching into two happened inadvertently. In addition, the primitive Aramaic text had played on the two words בְּעִרָא ("beast of burden") and בֵּירָא ("well"). Against this hypothesis, see Fitzmyer, 2:1042.

50 On Matt 12:11, see Luz, *Matthew*, 2:187–88.

51 See Busse, *Wunder*, 307; on this verb, see BAGD, s.v.

52 This physiological loss of balance is thus caused by a moral disorder, according to Ambrose; this opinion is reminiscent of the rabbinic interpretation (see n. 24 above).

efficacious gentleness: better than a physician would have, Christ healed the sick person and invited the Pharisees to convert (*Hom. in Luc.* 101). Cyril understood the commandment about the Sabbath and the whole law in a spiritual way. Read this way, the law was not transgressed by Jesus' salvific act. On the contrary, it was the Pharisees' attitude that was condemned as a statutory offense.[53]

The Middle Ages provide us with two interpretations going back probably to patristic times. Dropsy is an ailment that drinking, far from quenching one's thirst, increases.[54] It is therefore an image for avarice. Moreover, the Pharisees' embarrassment in Jesus' presence is easily understandable: if they thought that the healing was allowed, why were they watching Jesus closely? If they considered it to be in conflict with the law, they were accusing themselves, since they often acted on the Sabbath day in the same way Jesus did.[55]

The Reformer Luther preached on several occasions on Luke 14:1-11 (this passage was at that time and had long been the lection from the Gospel on the seventeenth Sunday after Trinity[56]). Luther liked to see in Jesus' attitude a practice of love going beyond all laws, one that did not suspend the order to respect the Sabbath but which, on the contrary, fulfilled it.[57] With perhaps less subtlety than Luke, Luther looked on Jesus' opponents severely. In his eyes, they were the representatives of a humanity wishing others ill instead of wishing them the best.[58] Jesus foiled their schemes and thereby witnessed to the fact that God scatters his opponents.[59]

Conclusion

According to Luke, the gospel teaches that the way to respect the Sabbath consists in taking the miracle, which is the fruit of love, and the life that is thereby reestablished, and fitting them both into the framework of temporal human relations. Here we have, during the Sabbath, a meal and, during that meal, a miraculous healing. By way of contrast, there is the legalistic way of practicing Sabbath regulations exhibited by people with morose spirits who demonstrate suspicion and tacit disapproval.

Such a reversal of the meaning of obedience, such a shift from fear to joyous initiative, from servility to liberty, from silence to speech, from mortal inactivity to spiritual activity, did not take place effortlessly. The person of Christ and his audaciousness were necessary to make it happen. It would have been easy to put the matter off until the next day. But in the eyes of the Gospel writer, that would have signified spoiling the unique opportunity of reestablishing the true order of the Sabbath. In a narrative mode, Luke has made his readers sense the shift from the law to grace, a shift dear to Paul. In performing the healing, Jesus reconnected with God's creative and salvific will.

---

53 See Payne Smith, *Cyril*, 2:471–75.

54 See *Glossa Ordinaria* on Luke 14:2 (*PL* 114:306). The interpretation dates at least to the Venerable Bede, *In Luc.* 4.1748–51; Hurst, 275. The gloss later says, concerning v. 5, that the ox and the donkey (thus read in the Vulgate), having fallen into the well of concupiscence, could represent the Jews and pagans.

55 See Bruno di Segni *Commentaria* 2.14 (*PL* 165, 405). This author also provides a fine explication of the "bread" as the manner of speaking of all food (ibid.).

56 From 1523, WA 11, 184–87; from 1524, WA 15, 689–95; from 1525, WA 17.1, 423–27; from 1526, WA 20, 501–5; from 1528, WA 27, 357–64; from 1531, WA 34.2, 287–98; from 1532, WA 36, 329–33; see Mühlhaupt, 2:195–208.

57 Sermon of 1523 (see preceding note). Calvin (*Harmony*, 2:102) takes the same position.

58 Sermon of 1532 (see n. 56 above).

59 Sermon of 1526 (see n. 56 above). In his *Postillae* (cols. 533–546) Melanchthon tackles three themes: (a) the miracle, (b) the Sabbath (to respect the Sabbath does not mean to do nothing, but to sanctify it by the good), (c) the cause of illness: departing from "the more you drink, the more you are thirsty," Melanchthon identifies dropsy with false doctrine.

As an interpreter of the Scriptures, Christ vigorously asserted his interpretation of the Sabbath and sought to communicate it: hence his rhetorical questions and his efforts at persuasion. The Pharisees were involved in this dialogue. They began by being suspicious, then sank into silence. The vocabulary defining their attitude should be understood, in a first phase, in terms of failure and bitterness. But if, in a second phase, they were to let their defenses down, would they be able to resist for a long time the evidence of God's kindness manifested in his Son Jesus, the eschatological physician?

The Place Chosen and the List of Invited Guests (14:7-14)

Bibliography

Black, *Aramaic Approach*, 94, 171–75, 302.

Cavallin, Caesarius, "'Bienheureux seras-tu . . . *à la résurrection des justes*': Le macarisme de Lc 14, 14," in Refoulé, *À cause*, 531–46.

Conzelmann, *Theology*, 110–11.

Crossan, John Dominic, "Parable and Example in the Teaching of Jesus," *NTS* 18 (1971–72) 285–307, esp. 300–303.

Daniélou, Jean, "Les repas de la Bible et leur signification," *La Maison-Dieu* 18 (1949) 7–33.

Degenhardt, *Lukas*, 97–101.

Dibelius, *Tradition*, 251.

Ernst, Josef, "Gastmahlgespräche: Lk 14, 1-24," in Schnackenburg, *Kirche*, 57–78.

Hug, August, "Symposion-Literatur," PW 4.A2 (1932) 1273–82.

Jeremias, *Parables*, 25–27, 191–92.

Joüon, Paul, "Notes philologiques sur les Évangiles," *RSR* 18 (1928) 354.

Jülicher, *Gleichnisreden*, 2:246–54.

Kahlefeld, *Parables*, 90–93.

Magass, Walter, "Semiotik einer Tischordnung (Lk 14, 7-14)," *LingBibl* 25/26 (1973) 2–8.

Mánek, Jindřich, *. . . und brachte Frucht: Die Gleichnisse Jesu* (Stuttgart: Calwer, 1977) 95–96.

Mara, Maria Grazia, *Ricchezza e povertà nel cristianesimo primitivo* (Studi patristici 1; Rome: Città nuova, 1980) 7–32.

Meeûs, Xavier de, "Composition de Lc 14 et le genre symposiaque," *EThL* 37 (1961) 847–70.

Navone, John, "The Parable of the Banquet," *TBT* 14 (1964) 923–29.

Simson, P., "L'Évangile (Lc 14, 1-11): le code de bienséance de l'assemblée chrétienne," *AsSeign* 70 (1975) 31–41.

Smith, Dennis E., "Table Fellowship as a Literary Motif in the Gospel of Luke," *JBL* 106 (1987) 613–38.

Steele, E. Springs, "Jesus' Table-Fellowship with Pharisees: An Editorial Analysis of Lk 7, 36-50; 11, 37-54, and 14, 1-24" (Ph.D. diss., University of Notre Dame, 1981).

Idem, "Luke 11:37-54: A Modified Hellenistic Symposium," *JBL* 103 (1984) 379–94.

Stöger, Alois, "Sentences sur les repas, Lc 14,1.7-14," *AsSeign* 53 (1970) 78–88.

Str-B 2:204–7; 4:612–39.

7/ When he noticed the manner in which the guests chose the places of honor, he gave them a speech in parables, saying to them: 8/ "When you are invited by someone to a wedding banquet, do not sit down at the place of honor, for fear that someone more distinguished than you has been invited by your host; 9/ and the host who invited both of you may come and say to you, 'Give this person your place,' and then your disgrace would begin when you would have to take the lowest place. 10/ But when you are invited, go and sit down at the lowest place, so that when your host comes, he may say to you, 'Friend, move up higher'; then you will be honored in the presence of all who sit at the table with you. 11/ For all who exalt themselves will be humbled, but those who humble themselves will be exalted." 12/ Then he said to the one who had invited him, "When you give a luncheon or a dinner, do not invite your friends or your brothers or your relatives or rich neighbors, for fear that they may invite you in return, and you would be repaid. 13/ But when you give a banquet, invite the poor, the crippled, the lame, and the blind. 14/ And you will be happy, because they have no means to repay you, for you will be repaid at the resurrection of the righteous."

Should we take these verses literally, and thereby risk reducing Jesus to the rank of an ethics professor?[1] Theologians find it difficult to limit it to that. Or should we think of these instructions as a parable? In the latter case, as a parable about the church and its eucharistic meals,[2] or one about the kingdom and its feast?[3] Philologists balk at shifting to the figurative meaning. The commentary will invite us to marry the literal and figurative senses, and to discover the interaction between the invitation God issues to us and the social relationships that we are encouraged to establish.

Analysis

Structure

After the incident of the man with dropsy, the reader would expect to discover a mention of the meal itself. Instead, Luke provides two short speeches, one addressed to the guests (vv. 7-11), the other to the owner of the house (vv. 12-14). It is not so much a speech that would be expected from one of the honored guests at the end of the meal[4] as it is a lesson about wisdom suggested to Jesus by something the guests did. Catching them out as they were hurriedly claiming the best places for themselves (v. 7b), he challenged them (vv. 8-10). This relationship between what happens and what is going to be said is typical of the apophthegm or of the *chreia*.[5] The first speech, curiously referred to as a "parable,"[6] a "speech in parables," is subdivided into a lesson on how to live, a moral (vv. 8-10), and a theology lesson (v. 11). The moral lesson is itself made up of antithetical parallelism: the first part "when you are invited . . . , do not sit down" (ὅταν κληθῇς . . . μὴ κατακλιθῇς; vv. 8-9) is matched by the second "but when you are invited, go and sit down . . ." (ἀλλ' ὅταν κληθῇς, πορευθεὶς ἀνάπεσε; v. 10). The contrast between the place of honor (ἡ πρωτοκλισία, v. 8) and the lowest place (ὁ ἔσχατος τόπος, v. 9) stresses the difference between the initial

decision and the final outcome that is in store. The same expression "the lowest place," here (v. 9) a humiliating and shameful lot, is used in the second case to define the humble starting point, freely chosen, but which turns out in the end to be a glorious one (v. 10). The unpleasant and pleasant consequences of the ethical choice are well described: "then" the "disgrace" (v. 9) is contrasted with "then you will be honored" (v. 10). The concluding verse, v. 11, like the examples in vv. 8-10, plays on the high and the low; but, with the use of the eschatological future instead of the immediate future, it puts the social and ethical problem into an eschatological and theological perspective (since it is God who is hidden as the implied agent of the passive voice, and his kingdom that is implied in the use of the future tense).

In short, the apophthegm, the first part of this pericope, appears as follows:

a. choosing the places of honor as the occasion for the speech (v. 7)
b. the two examples (vv. 8-10)
—the example not to follow (vv. 8-9)
—the example to follow (v. 10)
c. the reversal of the situations as a theological rule (v. 11).[7]

Jesus' second speech (vv. 12-14), addressed to the host, was not occasioned by any incident. So it is neither an apophthegm nor a *chreia*, but a brief speech that complements the first one. To the invitations that were received Luke adds here the receptions that people give. Two antithetical cases are thus presented in parallelism:

(a) v. 12: "when you give a luncheon or a dinner . . ." (ὅταν ποιῇς ἄριστον ἢ δεῖπνον)
(b) v. 13: "but when you give a banquet . . ." (ἀλλ' ὅταν δοχὴν ποιῇς)

The four likable groups of people that should not be invited are contrasted with four other groups to invite who, at first glance, are unlikable; the contrast between the rich (v. 12) and the poor (v. 13) ties the two series

---

1 Thus, Jülicher, *Gleichnisreden*, 2:251 and 253.
2 Thus, Degenhardt, *Lukas*, 99–101.
3 Thus, Mánek, *Gleichnisse*, 96; combining references to the eucharistic meal and the festival of the kingdom, Stöger, "Sentences sur les repas," 82–83, 87–88; Ernst, "Gastmahlgespräche," 68, 70–71.
4 See de Meeûs, "Composition de Lc 14."
5 Kahlefeld (*Parables*, 89–90) thinks that the entirety,

both the narrative framework and the sayings, is traditional; see also Dibelius, *Tradition*, 151–72, 251.
6 Two questions arise on this issue: (a) What is the meaning of this particular word? And (b) what is the content of the aforementioned "parable," vv. 7–11 or 7–25? See the ensuing commentary.
7 Meynet (*Saint Luc*, 1:145 and 2:157) thinks that v. 11 is the center of the two parts (vv. 7-10 and vv. 12-14).

together. It is recognized that the second series, the one about those who are unfortunate, is an exact anticipation of the series in the following parable (v. 21). The bad example concludes with the possibility of repaying the invitation (v. 12c). The impossibility that ends the good example is picked up in the final beatitude (v. 14), which thus has a double function: concluding the example and enlarging the perspective. As a matter of fact, this last verse (v. 14) lists the moral imperative as part of God's ultimate will. This theological conclusion, which matches v. 11, takes on a literary form different from the one in the first speech; here (v. 14) we have a beatitude,[8] there (v. 11) a proverb, but in both cases there is a clear eschatological orientation.

The second speech has the following structure:

(a) the speech's introductory expression (v. 12a)
(b) the two examples (vv. 12b-13)
—the example not to follow (v. 12bc)
—the example to follow (v. 13)
(c) the final beatitude (v. 14)

Origin

Throughout the Gospel, Luke is sensitive to the danger represented by coveting places of honor. In chap. 11, he reports the criticism that Jesus leveled at the Pharisees: "Woe to you Pharisees! For you love to have the seat of honor (πρωτοκαθεδρία) in the synagogues . . ." (11:43). In 20:46 Jesus warns the disciples against the scribes who are fond of the best seats (πρωτοκαθεδρία) in the synagogues and places of honor (πρωτοκλισία) at banquets. Although the Gospel writer omitted the episode of James and John wanting to have the best places in the kingdom (Mark 10:35-40 par. Matt 20:20-23), he did quote Jesus' sayings criticizing desires for greatness (Luke 9:46-48 and 22:24-27) and love motivated by self-interest (6:32-35).

Although Luke 11:43 comes from Q and Luke 20:46 from Mark 12:38-39, the first part of the present pericope, 14:7-11, which is the most polished from a literary point of view, comes from L.[9] In my opinion, these three traditions have a common origin in the teaching of the historical Jesus. Since the present passage is the only one to place Jesus' sayings in a narrative framework, I draw the conclusion that the apophthegm or the *chreia* is secondary to the sayings.[10] While the text of Q is a critique and the triple tradition a warning, L takes the form of a wisdom teaching.[11] Such lessons on good conduct were not new to the Jewish tradition, as is attested by the book of Proverbs and Sirach.[12] It is worth noting, moreover, that this teaching of Jesus has also been preserved in the Gospel of Matthew by Codex Bezae (D [05]) and Codex Φ (043), by fourteen manuscripts of the Old Latin and three manuscripts of the Vulgate, as well as by the Curetonian Syriac and a marginal reading of the Harclean Syriac, in the form of an independent saying.[13] Matthew 20:28 follows the saying about the Son of Man having come to serve: "And you, you should endeavor to grow from what is small and become smaller from what is great [according to the Curetonian Syriac: "And you, seek to grow from what is small and not to be made small from what is great"]. When you enter and are invited to dine, do not take the places of honor, lest someone more eminent than you should arrive and the host come and say to you, 'Move farther down,' and you would be humiliated. But if you settle down in a lesser place and someone less important than you arrives, the host will say to you, 'Move up the table,' and this will be to your advantage [according to Φ [043] and virtually all of the Latin manuscripts cited: "more advantageous"]." This unexpected parallel allows us to conclude that vv. 8-10 reproduce a tradition. Since v. 7 exhibits several Lukan characteristics, I draw the conclu-

---

8   On this beatitude, where Jesus reveals a double paradox (a declaration of blessedness in the midst of adversity and an invitation to the poor who are incapable of repayment), see Cavallin, "Le macarisme de Lc 14, 14," 536.

9   See Fitzmyer, 2:1044; and Petzke, *Sondergut*, 132–34.

10   Jülicher (*Gleichnisreden*, 2:246) rightly thinks that v. 7 is redactional.

11   Bultmann (*History*, 104–8) insists on the sapiential prosaic Jewish character of these verses. He wonders how they could have been attributed to Jesus ("wie

das Stück überhaupt unter die Worte Jesu geraten ist").

12   See Prov 25:6-7: "Do not put yourself forward in the king's presence or stand in the place of the great; for it is better to be told, 'Come up here,' than to be put lower in the presence of a noble" (NRSV); cf. Sir 1:30; 3:17-18; *Lev. Rab.* 1.5, cited by Str-B 2:204; see nn. 26, 29, and 37 below.

13   On this saying, see Resch, *Agrapha*, 39–40; Jeremias, *Parables*, 191–92; Black, *Aramaic Approach*, 129–33; Fitzmyer, 2:1045–46.

sion that it was the Gospel writer who transformed these sayings into an apophthegm.

Verse 11, for its part, is an independent saying that has been tacked on in various places in the Synoptic tradition:[14] here and in 18:14, at the end of the parable of the tax collector and the Pharisee, as well as in Matt 23:12, in the speech against the Pharisees. It was joined to sayings on the best places, either by Luke or, rather, at an earlier stage by the author of L. As we have seen, by means of this addition, an ethical teaching was granted an added theological dimension. In short, two independent traditions, vv. 8-10 and v. 11, were combined by the author of L. By putting together his large banquet scene, Luke created an introductory narrative (v. 7). He thus strung together two easy-to-read apophthegms (or *chreiae*) one after the other, the interest of which derived from their literary and thematic variety.

In the second speech, vv. 12-14, the division between tradition and redaction is more difficult to establish. This is because there is no parallel to these verses, except for the list of poor in the second invitation, found only in Luke, in the following parable (v. 21) and the list of relatives in 21:16. Since vv. 12-13 are loaded with Lukanisms,[15] and since they are structured in imitation of the preceding verses (vv. 8-10), I conclude that Luke wanted to complete the scene and add to the advice given to those who might be invited a warning to those who might invite them. In order to give substance to this addition, he thought, on the one hand, of the list included in the announcement of betrayals (21:16), and, on the other, he composed the list that he was going to reuse a little later (14:21). That allowed him to contrast relatives and friends (v. 12) with the poor and the unfortunate (v. 13). For the idea of retribution he drew on the saying that he had readied to add in this place, the beatitude of v. 14.

Several non-Lukan elements make it possible for us to say that this beatitude is traditional:[16]

(a) the vocabulary of retribution expressed by the verb ἀνταποδίδωμι ("repay, pay back")

(b) the so-called divine passive ἀνταποδοθήσεται ("will be repaid")

(c) the ἐν ("at," "at the time of") to express a temporal piece of information

(d) the expression "resurrection of the righteous," unique in the entire New Testament

(e) a certain awkwardness resulting from the juxtaposition of hypotaxis (ὅτι, "because," introducing a subordinate clause) and parataxis (γάρ, "for," which adds a coordinate clause).

There is scarcely anything to assign to redaction besides ἔχω ("have") followed by an infinitive (v. 14a), although that construction is not peculiar to the Gospel writer alone. Luke seems, then, to have reworked and adapted (especially in the beginning part) a traditional beatitude transmitted by L that could go back to Jesus himself. The beatitude could not have circulated in its present form. Since it was an independent, floating saying, I assume that in the tradition it had slightly different wording, something like: You will be happy if you give to those who cannot offer you anything in return, and so on. As can be seen, that theme is close to what is found in the sayings about love and retribution that are contained in the Sermon on the Plain (6:32-35).

In short, Luke has created a matching piece (vv. 12-14) to the first speech (vv. 7-11), by composing himself the introduction (v. 12a) and the antithetical parallelism (vv. 12b-13), this last item with the possible help of 21:16 and certainly with the help of the beatitude in 14:14, and then by rewording this independent beatitude (v. 14), in order to place it in this context. In v. 21 he was to pick up again on the list of unfortunate persons (v. 13b).

---

14 See Bultmann, *History*, 81, 103; for Stöger ("Sentences sur les repas," 82) this errant logion could be primitive.

15 Verse 12a resembles v. 7 (here Luke uses the dative after the verb "to say," not, as there, πρός ["to"] and the accusative). "Friends," see 7:16; 11:5-8; 21:16; "brothers," see 8:19-20; 14:26; 21:16; "parents," see 1:36, 58; 2:44; 21:16; Acts 10:24; "neighbors," see 15:6, 9; δοχὴν ποιέω ("to throw a large reception"), see 5:29 (δοχή appears nowhere outside of Luke

in the NT). The ὅταν . . . ἀλλ᾽ ὅταν ("when . . . but when") is certainly not Lukan (see Jeremias, *Sprache*, 238), but Luke borrows it from the tradition that he has just cited (vv. 8-10). As for μήποτε καί . . . καί ("lest . . . also . . . and that"), unlike Jeremias (*Sprache*, 238) I think it is redactional.

16 See Cavallin, "Le macarisme de Lc 14, 14," 531–32, 542–46.

Commentary

■ **7** Jesus spoke to the guests.[17] In fact, he continued to speak to them, since he had been carrying on a discussion (vv. 1-6) with some of them, probably some Pharisees. The Greek imperfect ἔλεγεν, literally "he was saying" (which one could translate "he told"), which can be found in v. 12, is the customary way of introducing a speech, as is also the use of the aorist before the content of a saying or a reply.[18]

He told them a "parable," gave them a "speech in parables." The word παραβολή, which renders the Hebrew מָשָׁל, expresses a reality that is vaguer than our word "parable." It can refer to a proverb, an enigma, a parable, or an allegory, in short any speech inviting us to understand it in the figurative sense. In spite of that indication, the use of this word for paraenetic speech remains curious. I surmise that Luke made use of it for three reasons: (a) By speaking of "a speech in parables" (cf. 5:36; 13:6)[19] he removed from what Jesus said anything that might have been out of place, even impolite (the mention of a "wedding banquet" also turns our attention away from the setting in which the words were spoken, which was, nevertheless, the origin of the sayings).[20] (b) It encourages us, moreover, to not limit the meaning of what Jesus said to just table manners. The rules it states are also those of the Christian life, indeed those of the kingdom (cf. v. 11).[21] (c) By giving to the Greek word the meaning of "speech in parables," he introduced not only vv. 7-11 but also vv. 12-14 and vv. 16-24. Note that vv. 16-24 constitute a true parable.[22]

What gave Jesus the occasion to express himself was the guests' attitude, which was not anything that they should take pride in: "how . . . they chose for themselves" (the Greek imperfect stresses the durative aspect of the action),[23] which I have translated by "the manner in which [they] chose." That is to say, Jesus paid attention[24] not only to the fact but also, and especially, to the manner (πῶς, "how" they went about it, which I translate by "the manner in which").

There were rules governing the procedures to be followed for a meal.[25] Just as we begin with an appetizer, the host could serve a glass of wine and some hors d'oeuvres in a room adjoining the dining room. A servant would bring the guests some water in which they could wash their right hand before serving themselves. At that moment, everyone said a benediction for themselves (that was before they were together at the table). It may have been during such an "appetizer" that the healing of the man with dropsy took place. When all the guests had arrived, they took their places at table in the dining room. Although Jews usually ate their meals seated, when it was a meal to which they had been invited or a feast, when more formality was involved, they ate lying down, according to the traditions of the Greeks and the Romans. The guests reclined on the left side, lying on beds covered with cushions, beds that were placed at angles to the three sides of a low table. In that way the right hand remained free for eating. Since by this time they were together around the table, the head of the house began the meal by pronouncing aloud a benediction over the bread on behalf of the whole group. He also pronounced a benediction over the cup at the end of the meal. At the beginning, in the middle, and at the end of the meal, a servant brought water for them to wash their hands.

---

17 The verb καλέω ("to call by one's name," "to call," "to invite") provides a unity to the whole scene of the meal (vv. 1-24). One finds it very frequently and in strategic places (14:7, 8, 9, 10, 11, 13, 16, 17, 24); see 7:39; Marshall, 581.

18 See BDF §329.

19 Lagrange, 399.

20 See ibid.

21 See Godet, 2:194–95: "Each one must, in his heart . . . always take and retake the last place before God"); Plummer, 358: "The saying here guards against the supposition that Christ is giving mere prudential rules of conduct or of good taste. Humility is the passport to promotion in the Kingdom of God."

22 The same usage of the word in the singular occurs in 12:41 and 15:3 to introduce three parables, thus a "parabolic discourse"; see Bovon, L'oeuvre, 30.

23 The verb is used for the choice of good places, e.g., in Hermas Vis. 3.1.3; see BAGD, s.v. ἐκλέγομαι, 2b.

24 After the verb ἐπέχω ("to direct," "to fix"), the word τὸν νοῦν (his "spirit," his "attention") is implied. But in Greek it is not necessary to include this complement; see Acts 3:5; 1 Tim 4:16.

25 Here I am dependent on an unedited document by M. Durrer, my former assistant, and on an excursus entitled "Ein altjüdisches Gastmahl," in Str-B 4.2:611–39.

The present passage presupposes some margin of freedom in choosing one's place at table. Other texts suggest that the head of the house himself assigned the places of honor to the most important guests (cf. Matt 20:21). We are not informed on all the details of contemporary Jewish protocol. If the host occupied the place in the middle of the horseshoe arrangement, then he must have placed his guests of honor at his sides. Moreover, the head of a table, as well as the middle position, when there were three couches side by side, must have been the best places. A similar uncertainty reigns with respect to what constituted the principal honor: in Christ's time, it seems that it was not one's age but one's social standing that was most important.[26]

■ **8-10** For a Greek, εἰς γάμους meant "to a wedding celebration" (cf. 12:36).[27] A Greek-speaking Jew might have enlarged the meaning of the term, under the influence of the Aramaic word מִשְׁתּוּתָא, and meant by it "to a formal dinner," "to a banquet."[28] Luke, who emphasized the parabolic character of the teaching, had a wedding feast in mind. Since people at that time were already taking such events seriously, certain distinguished guests[29] took care not to be the first to arrive. That is the situation in mind in this passage.

While it is not pleasant to give up one's place, being forced to give it up is humiliating. That is an affront to one's dignity that is experienced with bitterness. The "disgrace" (αἰσχύνη) referred to here[30] includes a subjective aspect (the incident humiliates me) and an objective aspect (I have lost respect in other people's eyes). The verb ἄρξῃ ("you will begin"), here translated as "(your disgrace) would begin," rightly indicates the most degrading moment: it is then that one must begin to move backwards to "the lowest place." That indication thus suggests that one's disgrace is going to increase still more. As a matter of fact, it is always painful to be publicly disgraced. Moreover, Luke rightfully spoke of a "parable," since the incident and its wording suggest all kinds of life situations, all the way from the most banal to the most existential, all of them humiliating and cruel.[31] The Gospel writer was thinking in particular of each person's place in the eyes of God, in the kingdom, and its ecclesial anticipations. To speak of Peter's death, Luke speaks of "to another place" (εἰς ἕτερον τόπον, Acts 12:17). Τόπος is the position one occupies, where one lives, in the community (1 Cor 14:16) or in the kingdom ("I go to prepare a place for you"; John 14:2). It is even sometimes the case that there is no more place (Rev 12:8). As we shall see (vv. 21-23), while the high-ranking people are anxious about their rank, the unfortunate—and with reason—are delighted just to have a place, without consideration for honor. In a hierarchical community such as that of Qumran, the place that each person had was assigned each year, after an examination.[32] When Christ came into the world, there was no room for him (2:7). He came anyway and lived among the poor. It is from that position that he made newness appear, and it was from there that exaltation was able to take place. Human

---

26   See *b. B. Batra* 8 (120a); Str-B 1:774, 914; 2:204–6; 4.2:617–20; Ernst, "Gastmahlgesräche," 67; H. Balz and G. Schneider, "πρωτοκλισία, etc.," *EDNT* 3:187. On the word πρωτοκλισία, see BAGD, s.v.

27   See Godet, 2:195; Plummer, 357; Lagrange, 400, who refers to Esth 9:22.

28   This is how Grundmann (293–94) and Degenhardt (*Lukas*, 98), following Jeremias (*Parables*, 26), understand it.

29   The word ἔντιμος means "honored," "honorable," "worthy of honor," "respected," "distinguished," "valuable"; see BAGD, s.v. We happily return to the example of Rabbi Simeon ben %'Azzai (circa 110 of our era) who said: "keep yourself away from the place of distinction, and seat yourself two or three seats lower, and wait until someone tells you, 'Go higher!' Do not go up (too soon) because someone might tell you, 'Go lower!' It is better for someone to tell you, 'Go higher, go higher!' than for some-

one to tell you 'Go lower, go lower!'" (*Lev. Rab.* 1:5], cited by Str-B 2:204). See also *Letter of Aristeas* 263; Theophrastus *Char.* 21.2; Lucian of Samasota's *Conviv.* 9, not to mention Prov 25:6-7, which is already cited; see Jülicher, *Gleichnisreden*, 2:246–47, who introduces still other references.

30   On αἰσχύνη ("shame"), see A. Horstmann, "αἰσχύνομαι, etc.," *EDNT* 1:42–43.

31   The word τόπος ("place," "space") is important; see G. Haufe, "τόπος etc.," *EDNT* 3:366–67. On ἄρξῃ ("you will begin"), see Plummer, 357: after a short-lived self-promotion comes the long humiliation that begins here.

32   See 1QS 2.19–23, esp. 23: ". . . And no-one shall move down from his rank nor move up from the place of his lot" (García Martínez, *The Dead Sea Scrolls Translated: The Qumranic Texts in English* [Grand Rapids: Eerdmans, 1996] 5).

beings do well to take their place at his side, below, in last place.

For both secular life and ecclesial life, Luke, following Jesus, proposed not a restrictive hierarchy but an ethical order of liberty capable of leading to the choice of certain constraints. Following that order of things, all persons, responsible for their lives, are invited not to consider themselves superior to others (see Phil 2:3-4) but symbolically to take their place, precisely in the meaning of the symbolism, in last place, or at least in their proper place. Just as the Johannine Christ's glory (the same word, $\delta\acute{o}\xi\alpha$, as in v. 10) shines forth in the infamous exaltation on the cross, which is the most humiliating form of torture (John 17:5, 24), likewise here believers, at either a secular wedding feast or a religious one, take last place as their place. That is the way the movement from humility to glory[33] was to take place, the ascension ("move up higher," $\pi\rho o\sigma\alpha\nu\acute{\alpha}\beta\eta\vartheta\iota$ $\mathring{\alpha}\nu\acute{\omega}\tau\epsilon\rho o\nu$, v. 10) offered to the one who received the fine name of "friend" ($\varphi\acute{\iota}\lambda\epsilon$). It was to be a movement in the opposite direction from the movement leading from boasting to embarrassment.[34]

Some people have taken offense at this advice, which appears to be utilitarian and, in the last analysis, selfish.[35] The attitude that Jesus had in mind, which in that respect was faithful to the wisdom tradition (see Prov 25:6-7; Sir 3:17-18), is admittedly self-seeking but based on long-term interest; in the short term, it is, on the contrary, a disinterested lifestyle. It must be said, without a bad conscience, that the God of Scripture invites us to be happy. He is not opposed to our ultimate success. Simply put, he advocates a form of happiness that is not achieved at the expense of others, and he offers a way that includes self-abasement and service. A good dose of faith is required, moreover, in order to be able to follow the advice of that God and the instructions of his Messiah. Without that confidence in the future of the kingdom, humility and self-giving would appear to be quite stupid. The fact that Jesus' exhortations are rarely put into practice is proof that it is not easy to defend one's true interest. But when his exhortations are acted upon, other persons' rights are not infringed upon, we are overcome with joy, and we are even accompanied by social recognition (the "glory," $\delta\acute{o}\xi\alpha$, of v. 10c).[36]

■ 11 The conclusion of this speech expresses a theological consideration of that order. The truth that it puts forward is not new; it even belongs to one of those biblical traditions that are best anchored in the Hebraic conscience.[37] On the one hand, we have the pride of those who rise up (we may think of the Pharaoh of Ezekiel 31),

---

33 The parallel of Matt 20:28 (D et al.), cited above, has "advantageous" or "more advantageous." On a possible common Aramaic original, see the divergent solutions of Black, *Aramaic Approach*, 129–33; and Jeremias, *Parables*, 25–27.

34 Some philological remarks: in the active and in the passive $\kappa\alpha\tau\alpha\kappa\lambda\acute{\iota}\nu\omega$ (7:36; 9:14; 24:30) and $\mathring{\alpha}\nu\alpha\kappa\lambda\acute{\iota}\nu\omega$ (12:37; 13:29) are used with the same meaning of "to recline at table." The $\mathring{\alpha}\nu\alpha$- is explained by the fact that one is on the bed and the $\kappa\alpha\tau\alpha$- by the fact that one must lower oneself to get there; see Jülicher, *Gleichnisreden*, 2:248. In vv. 8-9, the syntax is cluttered, even if the narrative logic is simple: the author has $\mu\acute{\eta}\pi o\tau\epsilon$ ("lest"), followed by the subjunctive $\mathring{\mathring{\eta}}$ $\kappa\epsilon\kappa\lambda\eta\mu\acute{\epsilon}\nu o\varsigma$ ("were invited"), and then takes up the future indicative $\kappa\alpha\grave{\iota}$ $\mathring{\epsilon}\lambda\vartheta\acute{\omega}\nu$ . . . $\mathring{\epsilon}\rho\epsilon\hat{\iota}$ ("and having come . . . he will say"). (Lagrange [400] thinks that this future itself is also dependent on $\mu\acute{\eta}\pi o\tau\epsilon$.) If one takes the second case as a model, the reminder of the invitation of a superior person must have been grammatically subordinated to the mention of the distressing consequence. In v. 10, Luke follows the conjunction $\mathring{\iota}\nu\alpha$ ("so that")

with the future, which is a late and popular construction; see 20:10; BDF §369.2. On $\kappa\alpha\tau\acute{\epsilon}\chi\omega$, with the meaning "to take possession of," "to take," see BAGD, s.v. $\kappa\alpha\tau\acute{\epsilon}\chi\omega$ 1c. On $\mathring{\alpha}\nu\alpha\pi\acute{\iota}\pi\tau\omega$ ("to recline," "to lie down") on the ground or at table, see BAGD, s.v. On $\pi\rho o\sigma\alpha\nu\alpha\beta\alpha\acute{\iota}\nu\omega$ ("to go up," "to move up from one place to another"), see BAGD, s.v. As for the mention of the guests, $\mathring{\epsilon}\nu\acute{\omega}\pi\iota o\nu$ $\pi\acute{\alpha}\nu\tau\omega\nu$ $\tau\hat{\omega}\nu$ $\sigma\upsilon\nu\alpha\nu\alpha\kappa\epsilon\iota\mu\acute{\epsilon}\nu\omega\nu$ $\sigma o\iota$ ("in the presence of all those who sit at the table with you"), we will find another mention of them in v. 24.

35 See Bultmann (*History*, 104); Crossan, "Parable and Example" ("as utterly banal and more accurately as rather immoral," 301).

36 Here $\delta\acute{o}\xi\alpha$ first has the sense of "good reputation," but, taken in the figurative sense suggested by the word "parable" in v. 7 and the theological interpretation of v. 11, it could designate glory before God, which was lost by Adam (Rom 3:23) and regained in Christ (2 Cor 3:18 and Rom 8:30).

37 See Ezek 17:24; 21:31; Job 22:29; Sir 3:18-21; Matt 11:23; 18:4; 23:12; Luke 1:52; 10:15; 16:15; 18:14; 22:26-27; 2 Cor 11:7; Jas 4:6, 10; 1 Pet 5:5-6; *1 Clem.*

then are finally struck down (against their will). On the other hand, there is the humility of those who willingly choose the humblest place (we may think of the Suffering Servant, Isa 52:13—53:12) and end up joyfully receiving places of honor. "Exalt that which is low, abase that which is high," is what Ezekiel had already prophesied concerning King Zedekiah (Ezek 21:26b [31b]). Ethics and doctrine combine in Luke 14:11, which is both a prophetic oracle and a sapiential observation. The major biblical traditions merge in the ministry, message, and existence of Jesus of Nazareth. At the doctrinal level, we are close to the two Adams: the first, the one of the Fall, loses the glory of the Garden of Eden, and the last, the one of the incarnation, gets to the resurrection and the exaltation of Easter. At the ethical level, we are close to the ethical instructions of the wisdom books of the Hebrew Bible, taken over by the ethical instructions of the New Testament epistles.

■ **12a** Luke introduces the second speech without any further explanation. The wording recalls that of v. 7a, just as "the one who had invited him" picks up on "your host," literally, "the one who invited you" (v. 10). By means of such repetitions (cf. v. 12 and v. 21), Luke connects the speeches and associates these parabolic words with Jesus' narrative situation as well as with our own life experiences.[38]

■ **12b-13** The Greek term τὸ ἄριστον is equivalent to the Latin *prandium*; it was the meal eaten early in the day, either in the morning or at noon. Τὸ δεῖπνον, equivalent to the Latin *coena*, on the other hand, was, in antiquity, in particular for the Jews, the main meal of the day, eaten later in the day, usually in the evening.[39] At that time the Jews ate only two meals a day during the week, one in the morning, the other in the evening. On the Sabbath day, they added a noon meal, which they ate after the service in the synagogue; it may have been such a meal to which Jesus had been invited (14.1).[40] If not, they had been invited in the evening (hence the second meaning of δεῖπνον, of a formal meal with guests, "feast," "banquet"). Luke also calls such a formal meal ἡ δοχή (as in v. 13 and 5:29), literally, the "reception" (from δέχομαι, "to receive").[41]

In place of καλέω, Luke here uses the verb φωνέω, "to produce a sound, call." Used by the Greeks in the sense of "call," this verb was rarely used in the sense of "invite." When the invitations were not simply made orally, they were issued by means of the sending of a note, the equivalent of our calling card, of which numerous examples have been found in the sands of Egypt.[42] Moreover, the following parable states that, in addition to the invitation issued in advance, there was also a reminder just before the reception, which was communicated orally by a servant, who was sent out to go around and contact all those who had been invited (v. 17).

Jesus' message was clear and shocking. It disrupted social customs. What could be more natural, more legitimate, than loving those who love us (cf. 6:32-35), inviting those who invite us, and associating ("hanging out") with relatives, friends, and neighbors?[43]

Luke's Jesus would not allow us to give priority and privilege to our relationships with those closest to us. He would have us open up to others and take a new look at each and every person (cf. 8:19-21). He invites us to be truly generous, since only a feast offered to a guest who would not be in a position to return the invitation could have the flavor of a disinterested good work. The Greek verb ἀντικαλέω means just what it says: "invite in return,"[44] such as an invitation to a meal in return for a

---

30.2; Ignatius *Eph.* 10.2; *Lev. Rab.* 1:5: a proverb that dates to Hillel: "my humiliation is my elevation; my elevation is my humiliation"; see the commentary on 1:48 and 52 in vol. 1.

38 This connection between the content of the speeches and their insertion into a banquet is at once an element of the symposium genre and a mark of Luke's literary force; see de Meeûs, "Composition de Lc 14," 859.

39 See Str-B 2:204–6.

40 See the commentary above on 14:1, n. 13.

41 See BAGD, s.v.

42 See the invitations to a meal in honor of the god Serapis in *NewDocs* 1:5–9, and the corrective, *NewDocs* 5:135.

43 See Bernard Berelson and Gary A. Steiner, *Human Behavior: An Inventory of Scientific Findings* (New York: Harcourt, Brace & World, 1964) 65–67.

44 On ἀντικαλέω, see BAGD, s.v. Jewish literature also insists on the hospitality that is to be offered to the poor and downtrodden; see, e.g., Jose ben Jochanan (around 140 B.C.E.), who, according to *Pirqe ʾAbot* 1.44, offers to open his home and to welcome in the poor. Some rabbis have also explained that the four doors of Job's house, oriented toward the four cardinal directions, were designed to welcome

previous invitation. The end of v. 12 with the word ἀντα-
πόδομα ("repayment," "reward," "recompense," "retribution") has given rise to various attempted renderings on
the basis of the literal meaning "and may there thus be a
compensation for you." It has been understood as either
"and may they repay you in kind" or "and may that be
your recompense." Verse 14 favors choosing the idea of
retribution, which is confirmed by the usage of the LXX
and Rom 11:9.[45] The theme is close to the woe to the rich
(6:24), to whom Luke denies any hope since they have
already received their παράκλησις ("consolation"), their
recompense, their retribution.[46] So the second rendering
is to be preferred; it portrays a cruel reality: by inviting
our relatives or our friends, we forfeit our heavenly recompense. Our earthly recompense will be our only hope,
hope of a return invitation.

In v. 26, Jesus will go even further and encourage his
disciples to abandon the human beings dearest to them
in favor of a commitment to the gospel.[47] That teaching
in the following pericope helps us understand the meaning of vv. 12-13. In an excessive and paradoxical manner,
the Gospel expresses an order of priorities: the feast with
the destitute and the unfortunate is more important
than familial relationships and social conventions. This
true charity is expressed not by means of alms but by a
feast (δοχή, "big reception," is used precisely for the invitation of those who are destitute, v. 13). Jesus' disciples
were henceforth to consider those who were excluded
and marginalized as relatives and friends. They were to
stop being afraid of them and considering them a threat.
This attitude would also ease relationships with those
new persons with whom they would be interacting, thus
making it possible to establish more humane relationships.

The feast that "you" give! In Luke's time, that "you"
meant the believer who was well-off socially, and the person who was in charge of the ecclesial community. The
list of those who are unfortunate does in fact recall those
to whom the Gospel was addressed, those for whom
Jesus assumed responsibility, thus fulfilling Isa 61:1-2,
and those for whom the beatitudes were intended.[48] By
sending his Son, God prepared for the imposition of his
reign, which would be the reestablishment of the order
that he willed and the peace that he proposed in his
covenant—peace and happiness for those who are poor,
crippled, lame, or blind, witnesses of the humanity that
was to be regenerated. Those who were rich and well
were invited to associate with them, bringing about an
exacting soul-searching. This good news of the welcome
of those who were excluded and the healing of those who
were sick was confirmed in the meals that Jesus risked
eating with tax collectors and other "sinners," in the
healings that he performed on those who were crippled
and those who were blind, and in the very moving sayings that he delivered. Being a free man, Jesus wanted to
act in the way he did. In a way, he had to, since the state
of humanity required it and God had sent him to carry
out that mission. His disciples and other Christians were
to follow in his way and attempt to make that message
resonate in their social life and their ecclesial communities. It would be reductionist to remember only the social
import or only the ecclesial dimension of these verses.[49]

Two more remarks are offered here: (1) A harmful
conception of physical integrity, which is found in all
religions, including Judaism and Christianity, has led to
the exclusion from the ministry of those who are invalid
or ill.[50] By the welcome extended to these very categories
of persons, the Gospel of Luke fights against a concept of
holiness that would forbid willing to be holy. (2) By favoring their friends and relatives, by not following Jesus'
command (vv. 12b-13), human beings become withdrawn
and forfeit experiencing anything new or having new

refugees and beggars; see Job 31:32 and *T. Job* 9:7-8;
OTP 1:843; Dupont-Sommer and Philonenko, *Écrits
intertestamentaires*, 1615; Ginzberg, *Legends*, 2:229.

45 See Joüon, "Notes philologiques," 354.
46 See the commentary on 6:20, 24 in vol. 1.
47 According to 21:16, it is precisely the ones who are
the closest who will betray the disciples.
48 See 4:18-21 and 6:20-22 and the corresponding
commentaries.
49 Jülicher (*Gleichnisreden*, 2:252) takes the words in

their proper sense here and provides an interpretation that is more ethical than ecclesiastical.
50 See Lev 21:16-23, esp. v. 18: "whether he be blind
or lame;" the curious text 2 Sam [2 Kgdms] 5:8-9:
"the lame and the blind, those whom David hates.
Therefore it is said, 'the blind and the lame shall
not come into the house.'" Matthew 21:14 shows
the overturning of this position. In the Dead Sea
Scrolls, see 1QSa 2.3-10, esp. 6: every person "lame
or blind."

relationships. In their way, these verses combat pernicious homeostasis, parochialism, xenophobia, and intellectual, emotional, and social narrowness.[51]

■ **14** This is an isolated beatitude, like the one pronounced by Elizabeth (1:45). It serves as a matching piece to another beatitude (v. 15). It is addressed in the second person, like the series of the Sermon on the Plain (6:20-23). Here it is in the singular; there, in the plural. It plays on contrast and tautology. The contrast is between promised happiness ("And you will be happy") and present disappointment ("they have no means to repay you").[52] The tautology is in the adequacy of the promised happiness ("And you will be happy") and the announced retribution ("for you will be repaid at the resurrection of the righteous"). In order to be able to understand this beatitude, we need to sort out the temporal indications: beginning with "because" ($\H{o}\tau\iota$), the opposition between the two ages is dominant; there is to be no retribution in the present time, but a recompense at the resurrection of the righteous. Up to "because" ($\H{o}\tau\iota$), the beginning of the sentence gives a Christian meaning to what would otherwise only be a pagan consolation for the beyond. This meaning comes out if the future "you will be" ($\H{e}\sigma\eta$) is properly understood. It is not an eschatological future but refers to the period that will follow the feast of the poor. As soon as you invite those who are excluded and those who are invalid, you will be blessed: it will happen already in the present time, which is the antechamber of a kingdom that your meal, offered to the marginalized people, will have anticipated. In that time, when Christians put into practice the ethics of the kingdom, they will be blessed. On their own, they could scarcely apply Jesus' rules, either as guests or as hosts. But Christ has not only communicated that truth; he has also served as a role model and offered the strength of his Spirit.

Judaism is known to have developed, in Jesus' time, a strong belief in the resurrection, but it had not yet harmonized the various ways in which it was portrayed. On the basis of the theme of the last judgment there developed the necessity of a universal resurrection (a dead person cannot be judged), even if it meant imagining a second death for those who were damned. On the basis of the positive connotations suggested by the very idea of resurrection, another expectation was that this victory over death would be reserved for the righteous alone. Luke was no more successful than was the Judaism of his time in reconciling these two tendencies to which he is a witness, namely, the resurrection of the righteous here in this pericope, and the other concept, in Acts 24:15, that of the resurrection of the righteous and the unrighteous, which is close in its wording but based on a different concept. There is also a difference that shows up elsewhere between the resurrection from among the dead and the resurrection of the dead,[53] or between the first resurrection and the second one.[54] If we want to understand the expression "resurrection of the righteous,"[55] we must read in the Gospel what is said about believers who will have persevered to the end: their reward will be great and they will become children of the Most High (6:35); they will be defended by the Son of Man (12:8), and there will be a final deliverance for them (21:28).

History of Interpretation

The success of ethics in the early church explains the interest that several authors of the patristic period showed in the literal meaning of this pericope. Ambrose of Milan thought that vv. 7-11 provide a "lesson in humility," while vv. 12-14 offer a "lesson in kindness" (*Exp. Luc.* 7.195; 2.83). The preacher John Chrysostom made a distinction between human friendship, of which table

---

51   See Bovon, *L'œuvre*, 136–44.
52   See Cavallin, "Le macarisme de Lc 14, 14." At more than one point my interpretation diverges from his. In my opinion, Luke 14:14 is not concerned with the general resurrection of the dead, and the future $\H{e}\sigma\eta$ ("you will be") is linked not to the kingdom of God but to the time of the church and of the Christian life.
53   Cf. $\H{\eta}$ $\H{a}\nu\H{a}\sigma\tau\alpha\sigma\iota\varsigma$ $\H{\eta}$ $\H{e}\kappa$ $\nu\epsilon\kappa\rho\H{\omega}\nu$, Acts 4:2; $\H{a}\nu\H{a}\sigma\tau\alpha\sigma\iota\varsigma$ $\nu\epsilon\kappa\rho\H{\omega}\nu$, Acts 17:32; 1 Cor 15:12.

54   See Rev 20:5-6 (this text explicitly describes the first death only, but it does add a reference to the second).
55   On the eschatological fate of the "righteous," see *Ps. Sol.* 3.11: $\H{o}\tau\alpha\nu$ $\H{e}\pi\iota\sigma\kappa\H{e}\pi\tau\eta\tau\alpha\iota$ $\delta\iota\kappa\alpha\H{\iota}o\upsilon\varsigma$ ("when he will visit the righteous"). According to this passage, only the righteous will be resurrected; see the note of P. Prigent in Dupont-Sommer and Philonenko, *Écrits intertestamentaires*, 960 on *Ps. Sol.* 3:12.

fellowship is a concrete expression, and friendship in the Holy Spirit, such as vv. 12-13 had in mind. Being a realist, Chrysostom appreciated the fact that such a demand is sometimes beyond our strength. That is no problem: if we cannot welcome those who are crippled or blind to our table, we can at least offer them part of our food. He followed this up with a reflection on indebtedness: since those who are poor cannot pay us back in kind, it is God who becomes our debtor and who will pay us back, which is all to our advantage (*Hom. Col.* 2.3–6).[56] A like ethical concern appears in the two sermons of Cyril of Alexandria, who was, nevertheless, not indifferent to the honors of his episcopal see! But that is just the point; Cyril contrasted a vice with a virtue, misplaced glory with humility, without calling into question the social or hierarchical ecclesial order. In a beautiful statement, he declared that we are born naked, and that only humility corresponds to our real identity and raises us up in God's eyes. Like his adversary, John Chrysostom, Cyril was aware of the radicalism of what Jesus demanded. He interpreted it in such a way as to distort it, saying that Jesus was not opposed to laws of hospitality, just to excessively sumptuous banquets (*Hom. in Luc.* 102–3).[57]

The Venerable Bede also chose the literal sense but dared to supplement it with allegorical reflections: the wedding banquet in v. 8 is that of Christ and his church (*In Luc.* 4.1790–807).[58] We find a similar interpretation in the commentary of Bruno de Segni (*Commentaria* 2.13),[59] the shift from the literal sense to the figurative sense being justified in his eyes by the use, in v. 7, of the word "parable" (Bede [*In Luc.* 4.1841–43] used the generalization in v. 11 as the basis for giving a spiritual sense to vv. 8-10): this is a daily wedding banquet, in Bruno's opinion, since the Lord invites us to his table daily, gaining for himself the souls of the living by baptism or welcoming those of the deceased into his celestial reign. This conclusion follows the same lines as my exegesis: in the face of this Christ-based reality, there is no more reason to choose the best places, since in the kingdom of God, rank no longer counts: in the kingdom there is plenty and enough space for all.

Although the lectionary reading for the Seventeenth Sunday after Trinity covered Luke 14:1-11, the preacher Meister Eckhart preached, in Latin, only on v. 10b, "Friend, move up higher!"[60] What interested him, in the last analysis, was the exaltation and the honor of the believer, soteriology more than ethics. Verse 11 offered him a hermeneutical key capable of fascinating any mystic: those who humble themselves will be exalted. Instead of taking the image of the table, as Luke had, Eckhart chose that of the staircase. To rise, three conditions must be fulfilled: (a) having a staircase under your feet that has a solid base—that is humility; (b) giving up everything you are responsible for—that is poverty; (c) turning your heart toward the summit—that is love. In modern terms that amounts to saying (a) being in your right place; (b) extricating yourself from all your encumbrances; and (c) having others' interest, rather than your own, be your objective. Then Eckhart defined these three terms—humility, poverty, and love—with the help of quotations from Christian and secular authors. Next, he encouraged going up, since it is on the heights that evil has disappeared; this ascension is possible for those who have accepted the three virtues in question. Lastly, this ascent toward glory is legitimate, since it is love shown to God, next a reasonable act of the soul, and finally desire, even burning. Eckhart, who gave a balanced shape to his preaching, pursued a paradoxical meditation: one must know how to descend; it is the best way to rise. To do so, it is necessary to make a break with the order of this world. In short, the preacher detached v. 10b from its context and illuminated it with the help of quotations from Augustine, Cicero, Chrysostom, Seneca, Origen, and others. He pushed the paradox further in a treatise in German:[61] it is not just abasement that results in exaltation but the annihilation of human beings that is equivalent to their higher life in God.[62] When human beings annihilate themselves, they find themselves again

56 *PG* 62:302–10.

57 See Payne Smith, *Cyril*, 2:476–83. Zwingli has the same interpretation (*Annotationes*, 669–70).

58 Hurst, 276.

59 *PL* 165:406.

60 Meister Eckhart, *Sermones*, in E. Benz et al., eds. and trans., *Meister Eckhart: Die deutschen und lateinischen Werke. Die lateinischen Werke*, vol. 4 (2d ed.; Stuttgart: Kohlhammer, 1987) 38.

61 Eckhart, *Traktate* 2, Die rede der underscheidunge, 23, in *Traktate*, 292–94.

62 Luther (Predigt vom 9/27/1523 WA 11, 184–87, esp. 186–87; see Mühlhaupt, 3:199–200) speaks about pride, then material and spiritual goods. He insists

in God. Such an ascetic or mystical interpretation probably goes beyond the ethical and theological meaning of this passage.

Conclusion

Verses 7-14 belong to the literary genre of paraenesis. They recommend avoiding one attitude (vv. 8-9 and v. 12) and adopting its opposite (vv. 10 and 13). What they criticize is not a moral code but an ethos, certain worldly habits. They advocate radical behavior: placing oneself at the bottom end of the social scale and considering those who have been wronged and those who are destitute as one's partners.

Verses vv. 11 and 14 are in the indicative rather than the imperative. They play on the present and the future, generalize on the basis of concrete examples, and lead us to move on from social experience to religious experience. Furthermore, it is that theological reality that explains the demanding nature of the instructions. God alone can impose such a reversal of values. Since it is Christ, moreover, who proposes this theological order, he makes it possible by the example he himself gave and by the strength of his Spirit, which he distributes from his state of exaltation.

Gospel radicalism is here coupled with personal interest as a motive of good deeds. Attaching that much interest to oneself shocks Protestant moralism and probably all moralism attuned to self-denial. God, however, not only tolerates our seeking happiness and honor, but he even proposes it to us as a goal, since what is at stake here, in the final analysis, is is not good or evil in general but our "honor" and "glory" ($\delta \acute{o} \xi \alpha$) or our shame ($\alpha \grave{\iota} \sigma$-$\chi \acute{\upsilon} \nu \eta$). We have a right, says Jesus, to seek our honor.

However paraenetic the verses in this pericope may be, they are also assertoric and even revelatory: they teach us what the true source of our honor is—the place of our dignity. That honor, which is the object of our ambition, is linked less to an ethic of intention than to a practice of commitment. Our "honor" or our "glory" ($\delta \acute{o} \xi \alpha$) depends not on the purity of our soul but on the "place" ($\tau \acute{o} \pi o \varsigma$) that we will have occupied, that we will have "chosen" ($\grave{\epsilon} \kappa \lambda \acute{\epsilon} \gamma o \mu \alpha \iota$). Consequently, the message is clear, on the paradoxical evidence of what is true: it is by taking "the lowest place" ($\tau \grave{o} \nu$ $\acute{\epsilon} \sigma \chi \alpha \tau o \nu$ $\tau \acute{o} \pi o \nu$) that we receive honor—honor, rather than the place of honor, since there is no complicated hierarchy for the competition for the lowest place. All there is to it is the kingdom and the equal welcome extended to all those who will have acted humbly.

By using the word "parable" (v. 7) and by encouraging semantic shifts (v. 11), the text points out that the invitations mentioned apply not only to worldly receptions but also to the Christian life and the ecclesial life. What is suggested is the attitude of believers in the world (vv. 8-10). What is proposed is ministerial and ecclesial practice (vv. 12-13). So there are two kinds of invitations, those received in the context of society, and those received in the context of Christianity. These human and ecclesial relationships are imperative, in their new form, since they are inspired by the rules of the kingdom.

That being the case, living the gospel becomes, in the world, a reflection and an anticipation of the kingdom. The secular domain (the dining room table), an existential image of the religious domain (the communion table), and the religious domain (the transfiguration of the secular domain) both become parables of the kingdom of God.

By "taking his place" in our humanity, Jesus accepted an extreme risk, from which followed the other dangers he had to confront subsequently. What is indeed decisive is the starting place for one's behavior: Christ's, and then ours. He who here reveals and proposes chose the lowest place, that of the servant (22:27). He also managed to invite those who were underprivileged and those who were disabled (15:2), thereby accomplishing what

---

on the difficulty of making oneself low but affirms that it is not impossible. Concentrated on his office as preacher, he remains modest and places himself not above, but at the same level as, his hearers. Thus, he emphasizes ethics in the doctrinal framework of the incarnation of Christ. Some years later (Predigt vom 9/22/1532, WA 36, 329–33, esp. 331–33; see Mühlhaupt, 202–4) he speaks of humility apropos of v. 11: already in this world, one respects the humble and awaits the fall of the proud; he gives some examples from history and from Scripture in this vein. The reward for a humble attitude is often received in this present world. Melanchthon (*Postillae*, cols. 546–48) explains what humility is from definitions and examples.

he said he would do. Following the Easter event, the community of his disciples was faced with the result of that attitude and its options: the glory into which Christ entered (24:26), and the exaltation that Christians were henceforth to confess (Acts 2:33). Counted among the criminals (22:37), their Lord was, from that time on, to direct the procession of the righteous with a view to their resurrection (v. 14).

Bibliography

Abel, Olivier, "De l'obligation de croire: Les objections de Bayle au commentaire augustinien du 'constrains-les d'entrer' (Lc 14, 16-23)," *EThR* 61 (1986) 35–49.

Arens, Edmund, "Ein Tischgespräch über Essen und (Ex)Kommunikation: Das Gleichnis vom Festmahl (Lk 14, 16-24)," *KatBl* 111 (1986) 449–52.

Bailey, *Eyes*, 88–113.

Ballard, Paul H., "Reasons for Refusing the Great Supper," *JTS* 23 (1972) 341–50.

Bataillon, Louis Jacques, "Un sermon de saint Thomas d'Aquin sur la parabole du festin," *RSPhTh* 58 (1974) 451–56.

Beare, Francis W., "The Parable of the Guests at the Banquet: A Sketch of the History of Its Interpretation," in S. Johnson, ed., *The Joy of Study: Papers on New Testament and Related Subjects Presented to Honor Frederick Clifton Grant* (New York: Macmillan, 1951) 1–14.

Beatrice, Pier Franco, "Il significato di Ev. Thom. 64 per la critica letteraria della parabola del banchetto (Mt 22, 1-14 / Lc 14, 15-24)," in Jacques Dupont et al., eds., *La Parabola degli invitati al banchetto: dagli evangelisti a Gesù* (Testi e ricerche di scienze religiose 14; Brescia: Paideia, 1978) 237–78.

Bossuyt, P, "La convocation au festin de Jésus (Lc 14, 1-35)," *Feu nouveau* 17, no. 20 (1974) 1–4.

Brown, *Apostasy*, 90–91.

Bultmann, Rudolf, "Lukas 14, 16-24," in idem, *This World and Beyond: Marburg Sermons* (New York: Scribner, 1960) 126–36.

Crossan, John Dominic, *Four Other Gospels: Shadows on the Contours of Canon* (Minneapolis: Winston, 1985) 39–52.

Idem, "Parable and Example in the Teaching of Jesus," *NTS* 18 (1971–72) 285–307, esp. 302–3.

Degenhardt, *Lukas*, 101–5.

Derrett, J. Duncan M., "The Parable of the Great Supper," in idem, *Law*, 126–55.

Dominic, A. P., "Lukan Source of Religious Life," *ITS* 23 (1986) 273–89.

Donahue, *Gospel in Parable*, 140–46.

Dormeyer, Detlev, "Literarische und theologische Analyse der Parabel Lukas 14, 15-24," *BiLeb* 15 (1974) 206–19.

Dschulnigg, Peter, "Positionen des Gleichnisverständnisses im 20. Jahrhundert," *ThZ* 45 (1989) 335–51.

Dupont, Jacques, *Béatitudes*, 2:258–76.

Idem, "La parabole des invités au festin dans le ministère de Jésus," in idem, *Études*, 2:667–705 (French version of the article published in Italian in Dupont et al., *Parabola*, 279–329).

Dupont, Jacques, et al., eds., *Parabola*.

Edwards, *Theology of Q*, 133–34.

Eichholz, *Gleichnisse*, 126–47.

Erlemann, Kurt, *Das Bild Gottes in den synoptischen Gleichnissen* (BWANT; Stuttgart: Kohlhammer, 1988) 170–95.

Fabris, Rinaldo, "La parabola degli invitati alla cena: Analisi redazionale di Lc 14, 16-24," in Dupont et al., *Parabola*, 127–66.

Fuchs, Eric, "Trace de Dieu: la parabole," *BCPE* nos. 4–5 (1973) 19–39, esp. 26–39.

Funk, Robert W. *Language, Hermeneutic, and Word of God: The Problem of Language in the New Testament and Contemporary Theology* (New York: Harper & Row, 1966) 163–98.

Gaeta, Giancarlo, "Invitati e commensali al banchetto escatologico: Analisi letteraria della parabola di Luca (14, 16-24)," in Dupont et al., *Parabola*, 103–26.

Galbiati, Enrico, "Gli invitati al convito (Lc 14,16-24)," *Bibliotheca Orientalis* 7 (1965) 129–35.

Glombitza, Otto, "Das grosse Abendmahl (Lk 14, 12-24," *NovT* 5 (1962) 10–16.

Goudoever, J. van, "The Place of Israel in Luke's Gospel," *NovT* 8 (1966) 111–23, esp. 118–19; reprinted in J. Smit Sibinga and W. C. van Unnik, eds., *Placita Pleiadia: opstellen aangeboden aan Prof. Dr. G. Sevenster bij zijn afsheid als Hoogleraar te Leiden op 31 Mei 1966* (Leiden: Brill, 1966).

Grässer, *Problem*, 196–98, 200–201.

Haenchen, Ernst, "Das Gleichnis vom grossen Mahl," in idem, *Die Bibel und wir* (Tübingen: Mohr Siebeck, 1968) 135–55.

Hahn, Ferdinand, "Das Gleichnis von der Einladung zum Festmahl," in O. Böcher and K. Haacker, eds., *Verborum veritas: Festschrift für Gustav Stählin zum 70. Geburstag* (Wuppertal: Theologischer Verlag Brockhaus, 1970) 51–82.

Harnisch, *Gleichniserzählungen Jesu*, 230–53.

Hodel, Hans, "Das Festessen (Lk 14, 15-24 / Mt 22, 1-10). Theologisch-didaktische Überlegungen und die Frage nach Medien zur Erschliessung des Gleichnisses," *EvErz* 41 (1989) 439–51.

Jeremias, *Parables*, 63–66, 67–69, 97–100, 180–84.

Jülicher, *Gleichnisreden*, 2:407–33.

Kahlefeld, *Parables*, 84–95.

Karrer, Otto, "Compelle intrare," *LTK* 3 (1959) 27–28.

Koenig, John, *New Testament Hospitality: Partnership with Strangers as Promise and Mission* (OBT 17; Philadelphia: Fortress Press, 1985) 85–123.

Koester, Helmut, "Three Thomas-Parables," in A. H. B. Logan and A. J. M. Wedderburn, eds., *The New Testament and Gnosis: Essays in Honour of Robert McL. Wilson* (Edinburgh: T&T Clark, 1983) 195–203, esp. 197–98.

Kreuzer, Siegfried, "Der Zwang des Boten: Beobachtungen zu Lk 14, 23 und 1 Kor 9, 16," *ZNW* 76 (1985) 123–28.

Lemcio, Eugene E., "The Parables of the Great Supper and the Wedding Feast: History, Redaction, and Canon," *HBT* 8 (1986) 1–26.

Linnemann, Eta, "Überlegungen zur Parabel vom grossen Abendmahl Lc 14, 15-24 / Mt 22, 1-14," *ZNW* 51 (1960) 246–55.

Marguerat, *Jugement*, 324–44.

Meeûs, Xavier de, "Composition de Lc 14 et le genre symposiaque," *EThL* 37 (1961) 847–70.

Navone, John J., "The Parable of the Banquet," *TBT* 14 (1964) 923–29.

Noel, Timothy, "The Parable of the Wedding Guest: A Narrative-Critical Interpretation," *PRSt* 16 (1989) 17–28.

Nolland, 2:752–53 (bibliography).

Norwood, Frederick A., "'Compel Them to Come In': The History of Luke 14, 23," *RelLi* 23 (1953–54) 516–27.

Orbe, *San Ireneo*, 2:220–313.

Palmer, Humphrey, "Just Married, Cannot Come," *NovT* 18 (1976) 241–57.

Pesce, M., "Ricostruzione dell'archetipo litterario comune a Mt 22, 1-10 e Lc 14, 15-24," in Dupont et al., *Parabola*, 167–236.

Pirot, *Paraboles*, 354–60.

Pousset, Edouard, "Les invités du banquet (Lc 14, 15-24)," *Christus* 32, no. 125 (1985) 80–89.

Radl, Walter, "Zur Struktur der eschatologischen Gleichnisse Jesu," *TThZ* 92 (1983) 122–33.

Resenhöfft, Wilhelm, "Jesu Gleichnis von den Talenten, ergänzt durch die Lukas-Fassung," *NTS* 26 (1979–80) 318–31.

Salm, Werner, "Beiträge zur Gleichnisforschung" (Ph.D. diss.; Göttingen, 1953) 208–10.

Sanders, James A., "The Ethic of Election in Luke's Great Banquet Parable," in J. L. Crenshaw and J. T. Willis, eds., *Essays in Old Testament Ethics (J. Philip Hyatt, in memoriam)* (New York: Ktav, 1974) 245–71.

Schlier, Heinrich, "Der Ruf Gottes (Mt 22, 1-4)," *GuL* 28 (1955) 241–47; reprinted in idem, *Besinnung auf das Neue Testament* (Exegetische Aufsätze und Vorträge 2; Freiburg: Herder, 1964) 219–26.

Schottroff, Luise, "Das Gleichnis vom großen Gastmahl in der Logienquelle," *EvTh* 47 (1987) 192–211.

Schrage, *Thomas-Evangelium*, 133–37.

Schulz, *Q*, 391–403.

Schütz, Frieder, *Der leidende Christus: Die angefochtene Gemeinde und das Christuskerygma der lukanischen Schriften* (BWANT 9; Stuttgart: Kohlhammer, 1969) 59–61, 107.

Sellin, "Lukas," 185–86.

Silva, Rafael, and T. Nieto, "Estudio critico-literario e interpretación de la parábola de las bodas y de la gran cena," *Comp* 9 (1964) 349–82.

Stotzer-Kloo, Helen, "Invitation à la fête: L'invitation au grand festin (Lc 14, 15-24)," in Steiner and Weymann, *Paraboles*, 151–69.

Swaeles, R., "L'Évangile (Lc 14, 16-24): La parabole des invités qui se dérobent," *AsSeign* 55 (1962) 32–50.

Tolbert, *Perspectives*, 41–42, 90, 126 n. 12.

Trilling, Wolfgang, "Zur Überlieferungsgeschichte des Gleichnisses vom Hochzeitsmahl (Mt 22, 1-14)," *BZ* 4 (1960) 251–65.

Via, Dan O., "The Relationship of Form to Content in the Parables: The Wedding Feast," *Int* 25 (1971) 171–84.

Vine, Victor E., "Luke 14, 15-24 and Anti-Semitism," *ExpT* 102 (1991) 262–63.

Vögtle, Anton, "Die Einladung zum grossen Gastmahl und zum königlichen Hochzeitsmahl: Ein Paradigma für den Wandel des geschichtlichen Verständnishorizonts," in idem, *Das Evangelium und die Evangelien: Beiträge zur Evangelienforschung* (Kommentare und Beiträge zum Alten und Neuen Testament; Düsseldorf: Patmos, 1971) 171–218.

Wanke, Joachim, *Beobachtungen zum Eucharistieverständnis des Lukas* (EThSt 8; Leipzig: St. Benno, 1973) 57–59.

Weder, *Gleichnisse*, 177–93.

Wegenast, Klaus, "Freiheit ist lernbar: Lukas 14, 15-24 im Unterricht," *EvErz* 40 (1988) 592–600.

Weiser, *Knechtsgleichnisse*, 58–71.

Zimmermann, Heinrich, *Jesus Christus: Geschichte und Verkündigung* (2d ed.; Stuttgart: Katholisches Bibelwerk, 1975) 110–21.

15/   **Paying attention to these words, one of the dinner guests said to him, "Blessed is anyone who will take part in the meal[a] in the kingdom of God!" 16/ He said to him, "Someone was giving a big banquet and invited many people. 17/ At the time for the banquet he sent his servant to say to those who had been invited, 'Come; for it is already ready.'**

a   Literally: "will eat bread."

18/ Then they all alike began to make excuses. The first said to him, 'I have bought a piece of land, and I must go out and see it; please accept my regrets.' **19/** Then another said, 'I have bought five pairs of oxen, and I am going to try them out; please accept my regrets.' **20/** Then another said, 'I have just gotten married, and therefore I cannot come.' **21/** So the servant returned and reported this to his master. Then the owner of the house became angry and said to his servant, 'Go out at once into the squares and alleys of the town and bring in here those who are poor, crippled, blind, or lame.' **22/** And the servant said, 'Master, what you ordered has been done, and there is still room.' **23/** Then the master said to the servant, 'Go out into the roads and hedgerows, and compel those you find[b] to come in, so that my house may be filled. **24/** For I tell you, none of those who were invited will taste my banquet.'"

b   The words "those you find" are not to be found in the Greek but have been added for intelligibility.

Here in vv. 15-24 we have the last scene of banquet discussions that began at the beginning of chap. 14 and that finds its culmination here. Both the initial exclamation by one of the guests (v. 15) and the final saying (v. 24) turn attention away from human and ethical conventions (vv. 7-14) and direct it to the eschatological realities of the kingdom of God. Nevertheless, the decisive motif of the meal links these different realities—the world that is hoped for and this world—to each other. Existential and ethical notes are not absent from this parable (vv. 15-24), just as the preceding sayings (vv. 7-14) did not omit theological and eschatological components. So there are analogies between this life and God's domain that are made visible here to reason and faith.

Analysis

Synchronic Analysis

In line with a method that he often applies (see, e.g., 10:25; 11:27, 45), Luke first reports what one of the guests said when he reacted to Jesus' beatitude (v. 14) by coming up with one of his own (v. 15). While the Master's saying contrasted present destitution with future abundance, the saying of the anonymous man who spoke up neglected the present and focused only on the radiant future. Did this guest prove himself to be a selfish optimist, persuaded that he was on the inside track, or to be a theological realist, convinced of God's ultimate generosity?

Jesus answered him and at the same time addressed not only him but also the wider audience of all those present. He told a story:[1]

1. *The first invitation to many people*
   (a) an invitation to the feast issued by the owner from his house (v. 16)
   (b) a reminder of the invitation by the servant dispatched outside the house (v. 17)
2. *The refusal on the part of all*
   General observation (v. 18a) followed by
   (a) the first specific refusal (the reason being the

---

1   It is a parabolic story. Weder (*Gleichnisse*, 178) insists on the primitive link with the kingdom of God. Kahlefeld (*Parables*, 87–88), on the other hand, emphasizes the threatening prophetic tone. According to Galbiati ("Gli invitati al convito," 129–31), v. 14 makes the story a pure parable, which one can take as mildly allegorizing only from vv. 22-23. For Galbiati, it is the parable that legitimates the exhortation of vv. 12-14 and not vice versa: the link between the poor and the God who welcomes them into his kingdom determines the interest that Christians must have toward them. Jeremias (*Parables*, 64) and Hahn ("Das Gleichnis von der Einladung zum Festmahl," 51–82) consider the Lukan parable to be an example story (*Beispielerzählung*), illustrating the exhortation of vv. 12-14.

"piece of land" and the refrain of the excuse)
(v. 18b)

(b) the second refusal (the reason being "oxen" and
the refrain of the excuse) (v. 19)

(c) the third refusal (the reason being the "wife," but
with modification of the refrain) (v. 20)

3. *The return of the servant and his master's reaction*

(a) once back home, he recounts all that to his master
(v. 21a)

(b) the owner's anger and the new measures he takes;
a new invitation issued to those on the outside:
to the poor and the unfortunate of the town
(v. 21bc)

4. *The last invitation*

(a) the servant alludes to the outside and the inside:
the mission already accomplished and the room
still left (v. 22)

(b) the master gives the order to issue a final invitation, to those outside of the outside, those in the
countryside, the objective being to fill the inside,
that is, of the house (v. 23)

5. *The conclusion in "I"*

In the form of a negative conclusion and a commentary (v. 24). Double inclusion with v.16 (the guests and
the meal).[2]

The person speaking, that is, Jesus, told this story
without interrupting it with subjective comments.
Only the conclusion (v. 24) fails to meet this criterion
of objectivity. The story is linear and takes place with
considerable economy of rhetorical devices. There is, for
example, no flourish concerning the preparations or the
menu. This parsimony goes so far that the carrying out
of the second order (v. 21c) and the third one (v. 23) is
not recounted. We only learn the positive result of the
second invitation (v. 22). As for the third one, the story
breaks off without our learning how the invitation was
issued or how it was welcomed.[3] This final open-ended-
ness certainly made sense to Luke's contemporary readers. It is also explainable in terms of the attention that
the author, in his conclusion (v. 24), pays to the refusal
on the part of the first persons to be invited, rather than
to any acceptance on the part of the last guests. One
more comment on this last verse: in an adroit manner,
characteristic of the dinner genre,[4] the text plays on two
levels, that of the parable and that of reality: the "I" who
expresses himself is both the owner of the parable, which
speaks of the first persons who were invited and the
banquet (cf. v. 16), and the Lukan Christ, who speaks to
"you," guests addressed by him, and then the readers of
the Gospel. He does indeed speak of "his banquet," that
is, the banquet in the kingdom of God (cf. v. 15).[5]

If we confine our attention to just the parable, we
will note the various human relationships exhibited by
the story: to begin with, on the first level, there is the
relationship of the "man" with the persons he invited in
succession, those who refused the invitation, then those
who were invited by chance. The emphasis is placed on
those who declined the offer.[6] Then, on the second level,
there is the functional relationship between the "master"
(v. 21) and his "servant" (v. 17). The servant seemed to
be alone and very busy. He displayed no particular mood
and carried out his mission to the letter. Finally, in the

---

2   Fuchs ("Trace de Dieu," 34–36) provides an
interesting graphic presentation of the parable in
four stages: (a) situation of departure (master and
guests in the same frame, in the same social reality); (b) the guests, by their refusals, exclude the
master from social unity; (c) the master undertakes
a risky response; (d) the master and the new guests
form a new social reality. Funk (*Language*, 163–67)
proposes a threefold structure to the parable: (a)
situation of departure (v. 16), (b) crisis (vv. 17-20),
(c) dénouement (vv. 21-24). Dormeyer ("Literarische und theologische Analyse," 208) is attentive
also to the number three (three excuses, three invitations) as an organizing theme. Dupont (*Études*,
2:672–73), on the other hand, insists on a binary
structure in the parable, even if the sequence of
events is tripartite.

3   See Dupont (*Études*, 2:675), who notes that the parable ends before the banquet has begun: the parable is not about the banquet itself, but the guests
who are going to partake of it.

4   On the various ways an author can locate and drive
his symposium story, see de Meeûs, "Composition
de Lc 14."

5   See Funk, *Language*, 173–74; Hahn, "Das Gleichnis von der Einladung zum Festmahl," 60; Weder,
Gleichnisse, 184.

6   See Fuchs, "Trace de Dieu," 34–36; Dupont, *Études*,
2:673–75.

background, there is the relationship of the master with himself: he was anxious to organize his meal. He decided to invite some friends. Their refusal irritated him and hurt him, since he wanted to have a successful feast. He was, indeed, anxious—the mention of this is certainly important—to fill his house.[7] Success in this matter depended on something other than his past relationships of friendship. It was linked to his possible openness to new relationships. He ran the double risk of losing his friends and rubbing shoulders with marginal persons whose reactions would be unpredictable.

It is interesting to pinpoint the references to a space and a time in which this set of relationships, like all human reality, takes place. First of all, space, which plays a decisive role, even though it is indicated only in a progressive manner: at the beginning, the contrast between the inside (the house) and the outside (the residences of the persons invited) is only hinted at; it becomes explicit only in the case of the second and third invitations: the second takes the servant into town, and the third, into the countryside. The text, which is elsewhere so reserved, does not hesitate to mention in this case squares and alleys in connection with the second invitation, and roads and hedgerows, with the third. The text balances the outside represented by the town and the outside of the outside represented by countryside[8] with the inside, the house (v. 23), and the inside of the inside, the room offered to the guests (v. 22). Note the importance of the intermediary, the mediator, the one who establishes communication and draws the practical conclusions from it. The servant had to "go out" three times in order to

"bring in." The verbs indicating motion play a determinative role in the unfolding of the story.

As for time,[9] its importance is made explicit at the outset: it was the "time for the dinner," when "already" everything was "ready" (v. 17). That situation explained why it was necessary to act "at once" (v. 21c) and even compel those who were hesitant to enter (v. 23). Against a backdrop of the future (v. 15 and v. 24), the present appears as the precise moment for making a decision in the face of an offer and preparations that could not wait beyond that moment.

Diachronic Analysis

Each of three Gospels—Luke, Matthew, and Thomas—transmits a banquet parable.[10] The resemblance among these stories is such that commentators rightly suppose that they have a common origin. Commentators hesitate, however, when it comes to identifying the channels that the transmission of the text followed. Two possibilities have been advanced concerning the links between Luke 14 and Matthew 22: either the Gospel writers made a thoroughgoing adaptation of a single tradition recorded in Q,[11] or they depended on different documents.[12] Luke, in this case, would have picked up again on L. Without being in a position to prove it, I think that it is Luke, and not the author of L, who was responsible for the dinner setting of this chapter (14:1-24). He is the one who inserted the parable of the banquet (vv. 15-24) after the healing of the man suffering from dropsy (vv. 2-6) and the sayings about the invitations (vv. 7-14). He must have taken over the parable from Q.[13] Two beatitudes (v. 14

---

7   Dupont (*Études*, 2:673–75) thinks that the master is the main character in the parable. Linnemann ("Überlegungen," 246–55) is of the view that in the *Bildhälfte* it is the master, not the guests, who is compromised. Fuchs ("Trace de Dieu," 35) asserts that the master is excluded from relationships and that he provisionally loses his identity. Dormeyer ("Literarische und theologische Analyse," 213) mentions a *Lernprozess* in which the master is engaged.

8   See Kahlefeld, *Paraboles*, 90–92; Weder, *Gleichnisse*, 184.

9   See Dupont, *Études*, 2:679–83, esp. 681; Hodel, "Das Festessen," 442.

10 A synoptic comparison can be found in Jeremias, *Parables*; Funk, *Language*, 163–87; Haenchen, "Das Gleichnis vom grossen Mahl," 135–55; Schulz, *Q*,

391–98; Weder, *Gleichnisse*, 177–85; Schottroff, "Das Gleichnis vom grossen Gastmahl," 192–96.

11 This is the majority opinion, it seems to me. A reconstruction of Q occurs in several works mentioned in the preceding note; see Kloppenborg, *Formation*, 229–30. In his opinion, the first invitation, for Q, is addressed to all Israel, which declines it, and the second to the nations.

12 Thus, Linnemann, "Überlegungen," 253–54; Eichholz, *Gleichnisse*, 126–47, esp. 127–29.

13 This is one of those cases in which Matthew and Luke, although parallel, offer divergent texts; see Kloppenborg, *Formation*, 42 n. 1.

and v. 15) helped him join the parts together, while the isotopy of the meal allowed him to lend a certain unity to the whole.

The *Gospel of Thomas* was acquainted with a version of the parable close to the one in Luke,[14] which must have corresponded to the tradition taken over by the author of the Third Gospel, therefore probably to a form of Q, rather than to the exact text of Q that Luke had received. That version was not acquainted with the beatitude that launched the debate (Luke 14:15), or with the doubling of the final invitation (Luke 14:21-23). On the other hand, like Luke but unlike Matthew, *Thomas* mentions various special excuses that are expressed. These resemble those in Luke, although they differ from them in the matter of their number and their nature: there are four of them, against Luke's three, and they relate especially to urban activity and commercial transactions. The first person to be invited, who turned down the invitation, was going to collect a bill that very evening. The second one wanted to take care of his house that he had just bought, and the fourth one, a farm for which he planned to collect the rent. As for the third, who corresponds to the young husband in Luke, he had to organize or prepare a wedding banquet! As in the case of our canonical Gospels, one can distinguish between tradition and redaction in the *Gospel of Thomas*. In its simple structure, the tradition corresponds to Luke's source and probably gives it the same meaning. The redaction, however, is different in one respect: it attacks the buyers and the traders (see the end of the text),[15] probably symbols of a humanity that is too attached to the goods of this world. In any case, the author did not establish any connection between the parable and the theme of the election of Israel. He also avoided speaking of the master's anger, preferring an impassive God to the impassioned God of the Hebraic traditions and of Jesus. In conclusion, the *Gospel of Thomas*, although acquainted with the Gospels of Matthew and Luke, nevertheless preferred to adapt traditional material that was close to the parable the way Q transmitted it.

Matthew, as we know, consistently allegorized the parable.[16] In his rewriting, the "man" became a "king" (even if the word "man" remained attached to his text [ἄνθρωπος βασιλεῦς], Matt 22:2) and the "dinner," the "wedding" banquet for his "son." The servant was multiplied; these "servants" symbolize God's envoys, apostles rather than prophets. They are doubly rebuffed, which leads to their persecution (the equivalent of before and after Easter?). Then the king becomes enraged at "their city," a clear allusion to the fall of Jerusalem in 70 C.E. Then the last invitation is extended to all (that is, to the Gentiles as well). Finally, Matthew balances this universal offer with an alarming warning that is peculiar to him (the expulsion of the bad Christian, the one who did not have a wedding robe). His conclusion, originally a floating saying ("for many are called, but few are chosen"), confirms the meaning of the Matthean rewriting.[17]

The *Gospel of Thomas*, the oldest of the accounts of this story, is witness to the simplest structure: an invitation to some, their refusal, and an invitation extended to others. There is some redundancy in both Matthew and Luke, but they each have it in a different place: Matthew mentions two refusals (Matt 22:3 and 4-5) and one final invitation (Matt 22:8-10). Luke, however, is acquainted with only a single refusal (vv. 18-20) but recounts two last invitations (v. 21 and v. 23).[18] Matthew was thinking of Israel's double refusal either in the time of the prophets and the apostles, or before and after Easter. Luke also gave emphasis to salvation history, but in another way: he was thinking in the first instance of the time of Jesus, characterized by refusal (vv. 17-20); next of the time of the church, characterized by the mission to Israel (symbolized by the town, v. 21) and then to the Gentiles (the countryside, v. 23). Note that Luke did not limit himself to an exegesis faithful to salvation history; he was also capable of pointing out the contemporary risks of stubbornness on the part of Christians.

Finally, Luke provided a setting for the parable: he decided to introduce the story with a beatitude. This beatitude, which helped him write v. 1 (cf. "eat bread"

14 Most of the works mentioned in n. 10 include *Gos. Thom.* 64 in their synoptic comparisons; see Schrage, *Thomas-Evangelium,* 133–37; Koester, "Three Thomas-Parables," 197–98. For bibliography on the *Gospel of Thomas,* see Fallon and Cameron, "Gospel of Thomas," 4237–51.

15 Possible influence of Zeph 1:11; see n. 43 below.

16 See Marguerat, *Jugement,* 325–44.

17 Several manuscripts add this logion to the end of Luke 14:24; see the apparatus of Nestle-Aland[26].

18 See Funk, *Language,* 164.

in both places), must have been a floating saying (of the type of beatitude pronounced by the anonymous woman in 11:27) that came from tradition.[19] We also owe the ambiguity of the conclusion (v. 24) to redactional activity. The parallel in the *Gospel of Thomas* suggests that the original parable ended with a final mention of the refusal on the part of the first persons to be invited. By shifting to the first person and using an introductory phrase ("for I tell you") the writer of the Gospel of Luke proposed here, then, as a conclusion (v. 24), leaving the parabolic level and shifting to the level of eschatological reality mentioned in the beatitude spoken by the anonymous guest (v. 15);[20] this shift also supplied a key to interpreting the parable and finally, it made possible a double inclusion with v. 16.

If we examine the body of the parable, we will note that Luke certainly touched up what was written here and there, but it would be difficult to single out with any degree of certitude the extent and the details of these modifications. The parallel in Matt 22:5, it is true, is a

witness to the fact that the first two excuses (the piece of land and the oxen) came from tradition and the parallel in *Gos. Thom.* 64 would suggest that the third excuse (marriage) did too.[21] On the other hand, the doubling of the final invitation, with which neither Matthew nor Thomas was acquainted, certainly corresponds to a Lukan intention,[22] that of distinguishing between the mission to the Jews and that to the Gentiles.[23] The sending of the servant into the squares and alleys of the town was the result of his redactional activity (v. 21b), while the sending outside town corresponds to tradition (v. 23 // Matt 22:9-10).

Commentary

■ **15** Luke puts a traditional beatitude on the lips of an anonymous guest. In that way he ties the exhortation (vv. 12-14) to the parable (vv. 16-24) and lines up two beatitudes so that they face each other[24] (v. 15 and v. 14).[25] Theologically speaking, the guest neglects the present

---

19 On this logion, see Bultmann, *History*, 109; and Schulz, *Q*, 392 (traditional logion, Luke did not create this macarism).

20 See n. 5 above.

21 Linnemann ("Überlegungen," 250–53) thinks that v. 20, which departs from the excuse formula, is inauthentic. In my opinion, this exegete needs to posit this elimination in order to construct her hypothesis: the guests do not refuse the invitation in an absolute way but want to finish up their affairs before day's end, planning to arrive late.

22 For Linnemann ("Überlegungen," 247), vv. 22-23 are not a redactional addition.

23 Following one of his students (Salm, "Beiträge zur Gleichnisforschung," 208–10), Jeremias (*Parables*, 178–79) presupposes that Jesus knew the story of the rich tax collector Bar Ma'jan and the poor scribe contained in the Palestinian Talmud *y. Sanh.* 6.23c and *y. Ḥag.* 2.77d, as the parable of the rich man and Lazarus (in his opinion) demonstrates (Luke 16:19-31). When he died, the rich tax collector was entitled to a quasi-national funeral. The poor scribe, who died at the same time, was buried in almost complete anonymity. Is this not shocking? No, because the tax collector's elaborate funeral rewarded his one good deed, which he did just before he died: he had organized a banquet for distinguished people, who did not show up, so he invited the poor so that he would not waste the

food. As for the poor scribe, his sad end was punishment for his one sin. But in the other world, the rich man was dying of thirst while the poor man's thirst was quenched. According to Jeremias, this story explains the refusal of the ones who were invited: they did not want to compromise themselves with this *nouveau-riche* host. When he appropriates and corrects this story, Jesus advocates his theology of divine benevolence over against a doctrine of works. For the critical edition, see Gustaf Dalman, *Aramäische Dialektproben* (Leipzig: Hinrichs, 1927) 33–34; for a French translation, see M. Schwab, *Le Talmud de Jérusalem* (repr.; 6 vols.; Paris: G. P. Maisonneuve, 1960) 4:278; for an Italian translation, see Galbiati, "Gli invitati al convito," 134–35; for a German translation, see Str-B 2:231–32. I highly doubt that the Gospel parable draws on this story; Hahn ("Das Gleichnis von der Einladung zum Festmahl," 67) has the same reservations: the parable in the Gospel is not about good works, and to give away food so that it does not go to waste is not equivalent to inviting someone to one's home. With Koester ("Three Thomas-Parables," 197–98), I think that the second invitation (vv. 21b-22) is redactional, not the third.

24 The ἀκούσας ("attentive to these words") emphasizes this link with what comes before.

25 On the genre of the beatitude, see the commentary on 6:20-22 in vol. 1.

and has eyes only for the kingdom banquet.[26] As a member of the elite of Israel (v. 1), he counts on his being that blessed person himself.[27] The beatitude reminds us of the one in Revelation from the point of view of vocabulary, structure, and content: "Blessed are those who are invited to the marriage supper of the Lamb" (Rev 19:9).

■ **16** Even if the "man" here in Luke is not a king, as he is in Matthew, he is not to be pitied. He was planning to have a "big banquet" (I use the second sense of δεῖπνον, which also means "dinner") and invited "many people" (πολλούς). He had a devoted servant and knew the customs (sending out a first invitation, then a final reminder).

Although the theme of the meal serves as a backdrop to the chapter, the motif of the call, that is, of the invitation, also rings out like a refrain. Thus it is that the verb καλέω ("call," "invite") ties the parable to previous remarks (vv. 1, 7-14) and punctuates the story itself (vv. 16, 17, 24; for lack of time and out of a concern for efficiency, the invitation became brusk in v. 21, "bring [them] in here" [εἰσάγαγε ὧδε] and in v. 23, "compel [them] to come in" [ἀνάγκασον εἰσελθεῖν]).

The invitation proper was perhaps made in writing, while the "reminder" would have been oral. Such a convention, practiced only by an elite in Israel,[28] demonstrates the social standing of this man. The practice was common in the East, and Pliny the Elder tells us about these *vocatores*, these servants of the princes, who were in charge of inviting people or reminding them of their invitations. Cyril of Alexandria gives us their name in

Greek: δειπνοκλήτωρ.[29] These marks of respect give a feeling for the honor associated with receiving such a highly esteemed invitation. They also are a reminder of the God of the Scriptures and of prophetic proclamation, who is ever calling his people and inviting them anew.

On the basis of Isa 25:6-8; 55:1-2; 65:13-14, the intertestamental literature conceives of the kingdom of God as a banquet.[30] Various texts in the Gospels share and confirm that Jewish interpretation.[31]

■ **17** Several days, or in any case several hours, separated the official invitation (v. 16) from the simple reminder communicated by the servant (v. 17). So the length of time was followed by the instant, "the time for the banquet." Without developing a theology of the final hour, as did the author of the Gospel of John,[32] Luke was sensitive to the decisive time of Jesus' coming. In the account of the passion, he spoke of "the hour" that arrives (22:14) and of "the hour" and "the power of darkness" (22:53). He also knew how to make the promise and its fulfillment, the preparations and the feast, resound in his soul, which was attuned to typology. In the Infancy Gospel, he used the verb ἑτοιμάζω ("prepare") in connection with salvation, salvation anticipated in the past and fulfilled in the present.[33] Now everything is "ready" (ἕτοιμα); "already" (ἤδη) "ready." "Already," the Gnostics' adverb, suggests not a realized eschatology but such a situation as one in which the decision has to be made immediately. The banquet has not yet begun, but the preparations have already been completed.[34]

---

26 The expression "kingdom of God" is comparable to the "resurrection of the righteous" (v. 14) and to "my dinner" (v. 24). On the kingdom of God in Luke, see the excursus at 13:18-21, as well as the commentary on 6:20 in vol. 1; see also Bovon, *Theologian*, 24–26, 64–72, 77–80, 299–300.

27 The expression "guests" was used in v. 10. According to Jeremias (*Sprache*, 167, 239), it must be traditional. Here Luke borrows it from v. 10, which is traditional.

28 See Str-B 1:880–81; Eichholz, *Gleichnisse*, 129.

29 See Pliny the Elder, *Nat. hist.* 35.10 §89, cited by Lagrange, 403; Cyril of Alexandria, *Hom. in Luc.*, Greek frag. 215 in Reuss, *Lukas-Kommentare*, 160; Prov 9:3-4; Esth 6:14; Philo, *Op. mun.* 78; Lucian of Samosata, *De mercede conductis potentium familiaribus* 14, cited by Jülicher, *Gleichnisreden*, 2:410. The word

δειπνοκλήτωρ appears in the variant of Codex Bezae (D = 05) in Matt 20:28. This variant is cited above.

30 See the list of texts in Bultmann, *History*, 109 n. 1; Schottroff, "Das Gleichnis vom großen Gastmahl," 197–98; Erlemann, *Bild Gottes*, 188–98; Donahue, *Gospel in Parable*, 142. See also *1 Enoch* 62:14; 2 Bar 29:4; b. Šabb. 153a; b. ʾAbot 4.16. Without an eschatological component, large feasts are mentioned in Prov 9:1-6; Esth 1:1-9; 6:14—7:2; Dan 5:1.

31 See Mark 14:25; Luke 13:28-29; 22:16-18, 30; Rev 3:20-21; 19:9, 20-21; Kahlefeld, *Parables*, 87.

32 John 2:4; 4:21, 23; 5:25, 28; 7:30; 8:20; 12:23, 27; 13:1; 16:2, 21, 25, 32; 17:1, 19; 14:27; Giessen, "ὥρα," *EDNT* 3:506–8.

33 See Luke 2:31 and the commentary in vol. 1..

34 See Dupont, *Études*, 2:681.

■ 18-20 The reminder must have been a simple formality, and if there was any serious reason the guest could not come, it would have been made known at the time the official invitation was extended. A refusal at the point the reminder was given would have revealed a lack of proper upbringing.[35] This story is exaggerated, as Eastern parables tended to be; it reveals that the boorish behavior was contagious—all the persons who were invited found an excuse for not accepting the invitation.[36]

The choice of excuses has given rise to numerous commentaries.[37] Influenced by the theme of war in the Matthean text, some have spoken of the dispensations from war conceded by the law.[38] It did indeed exempt and excuse those who had owned some asset for a short while that they had not yet been able to take advantage of, such as a house, a vineyard, or a fiancée. Aside from the fact that the dispensations granted by the law do not exactly correspond to the excuses in the parable, it is hard to see what might be gained from such a parallel:[39] if the persons invited were perhaps excused in the eyes of the law, would they be without an excuse in the eyes of grace?[40] Would those who were committed followers of the Messiah be the only ones who had a right to take part in the eschatological banquet? Is that really what

Jesus' message was?[41] I strongly doubt it. I would say instead that the traditional excuses are no longer valid in this time of urgency and decision. What follows in this chapter (v. 26) will emphasize the absolute priority of following Christ. The parable already affirms that the best reasons pale by comparison with the light of the eschatological banquet.[42]

There is another text in the Hebrew Bible that is perhaps in the background of this parable, the first chapter of Zephaniah,[43] since the reference to the Day of the Lord contains a mention of the "preparation" of a final sacrifice that must doubtless be completed by a meal, and of the "day" of that event and of the "guests" who are expected on it. In that same chapter we also discover a condemnation of the leaders of Israel, who busy themselves with everything except their God,[44] and of merchants and bankers, of which the *Gospel of Thomas* was fond, and an announcement of the ruin of Jerusalem, with which the Gospel of Matthew was also acquainted. It is quite possible that the parable, either originally,[45] or in the course of being transmitted, was developed in the light of this oracle of judgment.[46] As in Zephaniah, in Luke the prophecy of judgment (particularly v. 24) matches the hoped-for blessedness (v. 15); as in Zephaniah, in Matthew the punishment of the city and its reb-

---

35 The text does not in any way suggest that the host is *nouveau-riche* or that the guests are trying to avoid him, contra the view of Jeremias (*Parables*, 179), who suggests this on the basis of the Talmudic parallel; see n. 23 above.

36 Plummer (361) invokes Josephus, *Ant.* 7.8.2 §175.

37 Esp. Derrett, "Parable of the Great Supper," 126–55; Ballard, "Reasons for Refusing the Great Supper," 341–50; Palmer, "Just Married, Cannot Come," 241–57 (hypothesis: "The allusion to Deuteronomy is really there, in Luke, but was intended to be humorous" [p. 242]); Donahue, *Gospel in Parable*, 141–42.

38 See Deut 20:5-7; 24:5; 28:30-33; 1 Macc 3:56; *m. Soṭah* 8.1-7.

39 The text of the Mishnah, to which the preceding note refers, comments on the dispensations anticipated by the law and distinguishes between optional and obligatory war. In the case of obligatory war, holy war, everyone, even the recently married, must fight; see Donahue, *Gospel in Parable*, 141–42.

40 Eichholz (*Gleichnisse*, 136) insists on the grace of the invitation. That grace is so strong that if one

refuses it, one falls, as here, under the "judgment of grace" ("das Gericht der Gnade").

41 See Derrett, "Parable of the Great Supper," 134–36.

42 Beare ("Parable of the Guests at the Banquet," 4) mentions a "general warning against the danger of losing the heavenly by absorption in the ordinary concerns of this world." According to Kahlefeld (*Parables*, 92–93), in Luke the calling of Israel gives way to the soul's communion with God.

43 I owe this reference to the article by Derrett ("Parable of the Great Supper," 127–28).

44 According to Jülicher (*Gleichnisreden*, 2:408), it is the leaders of Israel and not the people themselves whom Jesus' parable attacks.

45 According to Jeremias (*Parables*, 179–80), here Jesus is combating those who are opposed to the proclamation of the good news of the mercy of God, such as he addressed it to the "people of the land" in Israel.

46 On the possibly midrashic nature of the parable, see Derrett, "Parable of the Great Supper," 135–36; Sanders, "Ethic of Election," 248–53, 256–59.

els (Matt 22:6-7) negatively matches the announcement of the kingdom (Matt 22:2).

It has rightly been said that this parable criticized a certain Jewish conception of election and redefined the contours of vocation.[47] The owner's friends do indeed make us think of certain leaders of Israel. Both Jesus and the earliest Christians were opposed to those persons who believed themselves to be righteous and close to God, who felt assured of their place in the kingdom, like the anonymous person in the beatitude (v. 15). Jesus, followed by those who took over the parable, undermined that too-good-to-be-true assurance.

I would like to make a few philological remarks on vv. 18-20. Luke is fond of using the verb "begin" in the inclusive sense (both the beginning of the action and the action itself). The elliptical expression ἀπὸ μιᾶς leads us to supply the implied word γνώμης, ("opinion") or φωνῆς ("voice");[48] so it stresses unanimity more than simultaneity (in that case, we would have had to supply ὥρας, "hour"[49]). The verb παραιτέομαι, in the sense of "make excuses," was common.[50] The expression ἔχε με παρῃτημένον ("consider me excused," "please accept my regrets") should probably not be understood as a Latinism.[51] The expression ἔχω ἀνάγκην ("need to"),[52] which I have translated as "I must," is a familiar expression, albeit absent from the LXX, that is found also in 23:17; 1 Cor 7:37; and Heb 7:27.[53]

■ **21** The three examples, which take up more space than the reference to the banquet and the mention

of the invitation, suffice to make the point. The text continues with the unsuccessful return of the servant. From that point on, the pair κύριος/δοῦλος ("master"/"servant") dominates the scene, and it is their dialogue that counts.[54] The servant's oral report (v. 21a) is mentioned in Lukan terms. It is followed by the blazing characterization of the mood of the one who is this one time called "the owner of the house" (cf. 12:39 and 13:25). He is furious (ὀργισθείς, "became angry"), with the kind of anger that is an indication of sadness, disappointment, and irritation.[55] He held it against those whom he had invited that they knew what he was planning but had not said no to his first invitation. And now, at least temporarily, they were going to spoil his enjoyment of the banquet. Their attitude affected him personally and forced him to change, to modify his plans.[56]

Therefore it was necessary to act "at once" (ταχέως). Luke often uses adverbs or verbs indicating haste or urgency to conjure up God's accomplishments or the attitude of faith that the Lord expects.[57] Those who were invited refused to "come" (v. 20), being busy "going" (v. 19) elsewhere, "going out" (v. 18) for other reasons than the right one. The servant himself was going to "go out at once," as the Word of God "goes out" (see Isa 55:10-11), as Christ "went out" to evangelize (see Luke 4:42-44; 5:27; 8:5; Acts 10:36-38), as the apostles were to "go out" to alert the world (see Acts 14:20; 15:40; 16:10; etc.).[58]

The Christian herald publicly announces the good news: so the parable—and it is not by chance—sends the

---

47 See Sanders ("Ethic of Election," 258), who affirms "that Luke's great concern is with abuses of Deuteronomy's theology and ethic of election." On Matt 22:14, see the subheading of Marguerat, *Jugement*, 331: "L'élection en péril"; Marguerat concludes that in Matthew the sentence of the judge arises between calling and election.

48 With Lagrange, 404.

49 This is the opinion of Jülicher (*Gleichnisreden*, 2:411) because of the verb "to begin."

50 See Jülicher, *Gleichnisreden*, 2:411; and BAGD, s.v. The verb does not mean "to reject the invitation" here, but "to excuse oneself."

51 Contra the position of Grundmann (299), who invokes Martial 2.79: *excusatum habeas me, rogo*, "hold me excused, I ask."

52 The expression is common in the Pseudo-Clementines, according to Jülicher (*Gleichnisreden*, 2:411). On this conflict of interests, see ibid., 413: "Das

Gottesmahl ist das Einzige, an dem teilzunehmen für den irdisch Gesinnten keinen Genuss bietet."

53 Plummer (361) thinks that the guest is clearly exaggerating.

54 Weder (*Gleichnisse*, 184) rightly argues that Luke adds the word κύριος ("master," "lord") to his source, Q, in v. 31, thus making an allusion to God or perhaps to Christ. In fact, Luke uses κύριος three times (vv. 21, 22, and 23), but Matthew not at all.

55 On this anger, see Pirot, *Paraboles*, 356; Weder, *Gleichnisse*, 187; Stotzer-Kloo, "Invitation à la fête," 155–56.

56 See n. 7 above.

57 See the commentary on 1:39 in vol. 1 and above on 12:36.

58 On this missionary component to the parable, see Hahn, "Das Gleichnis von der Einladung zum Festmahl," 82; Weder, *Gleichnisse*, 192.

servant out into the squares and alleys[59] of the town. The readers of the Gospel will not have forgotten the expression in 13:26: ". . . and you taught in our streets." They will also have remembered that Jesus evangelized from one town or city to another (4:43).[60]

The list of those who are unfortunate corresponds exactly to the one in v. 13: those who receive the gospel here are the same as those invited by Christians or the church in that verse.[61] The list fits into a Hebrew Bible tradition about God's mercy and the priority that he grants to those who are powerless, deprived, marginalized, sick, or disabled (see Isa 35:5-6). Commentators on this passage have fluctuated between an interpretation fitting into the framework of salvation history[62] and one oriented toward ethics.[63] As a matter of fact, the two interpretations complement each other: the text criticizes Israel and its leaders, the first ones to be invited, but then it opens out into the lost sheep of the house of Israel, that is, those who are poor and those who are lame in this life.[64] Salvation history, whose most recent stages are hinted at here by Luke, in his eyes concerned those to whom the beatitudes were addressed (6:20-22).

The social dimension[65] cohabits with the religious perspective. The kingdom of *God* is for those who are *poor*.

■ **22** Since time was running out, the account takes shortcuts. The servant has already come back. Proudly, he addresses his "Master" ($\kappa\acute{\upsilon}\rho\iota\epsilon$),[66] claiming to have carried out his orders ($\dot{\epsilon}\pi\iota\tau\acute{\alpha}\sigma\sigma\omega$, "order," "command," is uncommon for expressing God's will[67]). Just as there had been a multiplication of the loaves (9:10-17), here there is a multiplication of the places left at the banquet.[68] In the same way that in giving love one is not impoverished, in welcoming some (v. 21), the owner's household did not deny access to others (v. 23). In line with God's love, exclusivity gives way to inclusivity. As they enter, the first persons invited will leave room for the final guests.

■ **23** The servant's report (which makes use of the word "place" [$\tau\acute{o}\pi o\varsigma$], which is theologically important for Luke[69]), encourages the master to order a final "going out" ($\dot{\epsilon}\xi\epsilon\lambda\vartheta\epsilon$, "go out," in v. 23, as in v. 21). The master enlarged the circle of his beneficiaries: he sent his servant out of town, made him leave the alleys for the roads,[70] the town for the countryside, Israel for the Gentiles.

---

59 See Prov 8:1-3; Isa 15:2-3; Luke 10:10. Luke uses the word $\dot{\rho}\acute{\upsilon}\mu\eta$ ("street") in Acts 9:11 and 12:10.

60 See the felicitous expression of Schlier ("Der Ruf Gottes [Mt 22, 1-4]," 222) on the parallel, Matt 22:3-6: "Es ist die unaufhörliche Leidensgeschichte des Rufes Gottes in seinem Volk."

61 See 7:22, cited by Donahue, *Gospel in Parable*, 142–43. On vv. 12-14 (church of the poor) understood from vv. 15-24 (the poor welcomed by God), see Galbiati, "Gli invitati al convito," 129.

62 See Haenchen, "Das Gleichnis vom grossen Mahl," 147: the first Christian communities discovered in the parable the story of their own origins, especially at the moment of the opening of the church to pagan nations.

63 Funk (*Language*, 172, 175) and Dormeyer ("Literarische und theologische Analyse," 218) feel the tension between these two possible interpretations. Fuchs ("Trace de Dieu," 33–34) mentions three interpretations, not only two: paraenetic (vv. 18-20 warning Christians), missionary (double sending in vv. 21 and 23), and allegorical (illustration of the history of salvation). For Dschulnigg ("Positionen des Gleichnisverständnisses," 335–51) twentieth-century scholarship is German: all the interpretations he summarizes are in German (Jülicher

[1899!], Jeremias, Weder, Arens, and Harnisch). Nevertheless, the survey is valuable.

64 See Kahlefeld, *Parables*, 92–93.

65 Jülicher (*Gleichnisreden*, 2:430) notes a social and antihierarchical tendency in Luke; Galbiati ("Gli invitati al convito," 129, 132–34) does not want to neglect the moral application of the parable and the opening of the church to the poor. Schottroff ("Das Gleichnis vom grossen Gastmahl") interprets it a bit differently: the guests represent the underprivileged sectors, not the children of Israel. See also Erlemann, *Bild Gottes*, 174–75.

66 See n. 54 above.

67 But in Luke it is used to express the imperative will of Jesus (4:46; 8:25, 31, and, of course, here, 14:22). The substantive $\dot{\epsilon}\pi\iota\tau\alpha\gamma\acute{\eta}$ is itself used in the epistles to designate a "command" of God; see Rom 16:26; 1 Tim 1:1; Titus 1:3.

68 See $\kappa\alpha\grave{\iota}\ \ddot{\epsilon}\tau\iota\ \tau\acute{o}\pi o\varsigma\ \dot{\epsilon}\sigma\tau\acute{\iota}\nu$ ("and there is still room"), v. 22.

69 See the commentary above on 14:9-10.

70 In my opinion, in v. 21, $\pi\lambda\alpha\tau\epsilon\acute{\iota}\alpha$ designates a "town square" and not a "wide road," contra BAGD, s.v. In v. 23, $\varphi\rho\alpha\gamma\mu\acute{o}\varsigma$ signifies "fence," "barrier," such as the one that surrounded the vineyard of Isa 5:2 LXX; see BAGD, s.v.

The world had its things it had to do (v. 18); God has his things he has to do. Those two realities are not expressed in the same manner. God wants to bring in the last by persuasion rather than under duress (the servant is not a top sergeant). The apostle Paul spoke sometimes of the obligation of preaching (see 1 Cor 9:16). Here Luke was thinking of the force that goes with it: that of persuading human beings to enter God's house. The vocabulary of necessity or force is admittedly dangerous, not only on the philosophical and religious level but also on the ecclesial or social level. In fact, it has been tragically misunderstood, as we will see below, beginning with Augustine. Be that as it may, here it is rethought in the light of the gospel, Christianized. It is the constraint of love,[71] the gentle violence of the one who convinces hesitant guests and persuades them to enter.

The objective, which had been implicit up to that point, was stated with vigor, in final position. The master wants ($\ddot{\iota}\nu\alpha$, "so that") his house to be full. The house, to be sure, is that of the rich owner, but it is also, for any reader of the Gospel, God's house. Just a little bit earlier (13:35) Luke had transmitted a prophecy of misfortune: the temple, "your house," will be taken away from you.[72] The temple, constructed by human hands, will be

destroyed. But the temple "not made with human hands" ($\dot{\alpha}\chi\epsilon\iota\rho o\pi o\dot{\iota}\eta\tau o\varsigma$; cf. Mark 14:58), remains.[73] Lastly, it is what will welcome the guests; it is what "will be full."

The thoughts of the Pauline school on the pleroma are well known (cf. Eph 1:10, 23; 3:19; 4:13; Col 1:19; 2:9), as are those of the Gnostics. Although, for the Gnostics, it was necessary to reestablish the fullness of the divine world diminished by the fall of Sophia,[74] Christians need to reestablish the fullness of creation impaired by sin, "the pleroma of the Gentiles" (Rom 11:25), that is, of God's people who—this is the great Christian novelty—comprise Jews and Greeks, Israel and the Gentiles (see Rom 11:25-32; Eph 2:11-18). It is that plenitude of which the final expression of the parable speaks:[75] "so that my house may be filled" ($\ddot{\iota}\nu\alpha$ $\gamma\epsilon\mu\iota\sigma\vartheta\hat{\eta}$[76] $\mu o\upsilon$ $\dot{o}$ $o\hat{\iota}\kappa o\varsigma$).[77]

■ **24** Happiness is not the same thing as euphoria. The house will be full, but some will be excluded. That is the final message that Luke draws out of the parable, not joy because of the welcoming of the next to last and the last but sadness because of the exclusion of the first. In solemn terms, "for I tell you," the saying excludes the first persons invited to the "banquet,"[78] undoubtedly also to the house.[79]

---

71 Jülicher (*Gleichnisreden*, 2:414) looks back to Gen 19:3 LXX, which uses the verb $\kappa\alpha\tau\alpha\beta\iota\dot{\alpha}\zeta o\mu\alpha\iota$ ("to constrain"). Kreuzer ("Der Zwang des Boten," 123–28) offers an implausible hypothesis: in the absence of a direct object complement, the constraint could be about the messenger himself, and the text would then be translated: "force yourself to make them to come in." In order for this hypothesis to work, the text would need the verb $\epsilon\dot{\iota}\sigma\alpha\gamma\alpha\gamma\epsilon\hat{\iota}\nu$ ("to bring or lead in") and not, as we have here in v. 23, the verb $\epsilon\dot{\iota}\sigma\epsilon\lambda\vartheta\epsilon\hat{\iota}\nu$ ("to enter"). The variant in $\mathfrak{P}^{45}$, some Greek manuscripts, and two Syriac versions, confirm the customary translation: $\pi o\dot{\iota}\eta\sigma o\nu$ $\epsilon\dot{\iota}\sigma\epsilon\lambda\vartheta\epsilon\hat{\iota}\nu$ ("to make them come in"); see the apparatus of Nestle-Aland[26].

72 See 13:35 and the commentary there.

73 See Acts 7:44-50; Marcel Simon, "Saint Stephen and the Jerusalem Temple," *JEH* 2 (1952) 41–58; reprinted in idem, *Le Christianisme antique et son contexte religieux: Scripta Varia, I* (WUNT 23; Tübingen: Mohr, 1981) 153–68.

74 See Hans Jonas, *The Gnostic Religion: The Message of the Alien God and the Beginnings of Christianity* (2d rev. ed.; Boston: Beacon, 1963) esp. 202.

75 The parable relays part of what Rom 11:25-26

describes as a $\mu\upsilon\sigma\tau\dot{\eta}\rho\iota o\nu$: "So that you may not claim to be wiser than you are, brothers and sisters, I want you to understand this mystery: a hardening has come upon part of Israel, until the full number of the Gentiles has come in. And so all Israel will be saved; as it is written" (*NRSV*).

76 On $\gamma\epsilon\mu\dot{\iota}\zeta\omega$ ("to fill"), see 15:16; it is more concrete than $\pi\lambda\eta\rho\dot{o}\omega$ ("to make complete," "to fulfill," "to fill"); see BAGD, s.vv.

77 It is not by the virtue or the works of the guests that they are invited into the house but by the will and graciousness of the master. It is no longer a question of initial placements (see vv. 7-11). The joy of being on the inside is all the counts; see the commentary above on 14:7-11.

78 We find the word $\delta\epsilon\hat{\iota}\pi\nu o\nu$ describing the messianic banquet in Rev 19:9. There it is used of the "wedding supper of the Lamb." On the verb "to taste" ($\gamma\epsilon\dot{\upsilon}o\mu\alpha\iota$), see Acts 10:10; 20:11; Matt 27:34, etc.; Jülicher, *Gleichnisreden*, 2:415; BAGD, s.v.

79 Some commentators, e.g., Pirot (*Paraboles*, 356) and Erlemann (*Bild Gottes*, 170–72), think that the point of the parable is the substitution of the last invited guests for the first ones to be invited. If this were actually the main intention of the parable, it

Although the saying is clear, the identity of the speaker is less so. In one sense, v. 24 belongs to the last reply of the parable, and the "I" speaking in that verse is the master, who gives his orders. In another sense, as is suggested by the appearance of the "you," v. 24 no longer belongs to the parabolic story. It comments on it, as a saying of the Lord Jesus Christ, directed to the anonymous person of the beatitude (v. 15) and the other persons invited by the leader of the Pharisees (v. 1). Luke was fond of this kind of ambiguity, as may be seen as well in another chapter (16:8-9).[80]

Was Luke as intransigent as the conclusion of his parable?[81] To be sure, he was forever announcing the calling of the Gentiles and seeing in them the true persons addressed in the Gospel. "They will listen" (Acts 28:28). Did he really conclude that a recalcitrant Israel would be permanently rejected? I hope not and I read a final ray of hope in the terrible finale of Acts ("and I would heal them," Acts 28:27).[82] All the same, in this parabolic portrait, half allegorical, the judgment falls, inexorably.

Israel or its leaders are not explicitly mentioned: the threat could therefore affect other chosen people, as Matthew points out narratively, by means of the episode of the wedding robe. Moreover, the parable is not a report but a picture. It makes one reflect, it "compels" dialogue. Readers, whether Jews or Gentiles, will ask themselves, "What am I going to do?" Into what category am I going to put myself? For that is the nature of parabolic language: on the one hand, it makes the reign of God a present reality;[83] on the other, it invites one to opt for the gospel.[84] Even such a pessimistic conclusion does not want "sinners to die," but rather that they be converted and live.

History of Interpretation

The earliest interpretations we know about, those of Irenaeus (*Adv. haer.* 4.36.5–6),[85] or Origen (*Comm. in Matt.* 17.15–16),[86] focused on Matthew's version. They were allegorical; Origen's had twice as much exegetical vigor as usual. To the allegorical sense, which was evident to his eyes, he added a spiritual sense, which it would be impossible to find without the help of the Holy Spirit (17.17–24):[87] the "person," the ἄνθρωπος, for example, who represents God is a bulwark against those who have contempt for the Hebrew Bible. The New Testament confirms here the value of anthropomorphisms, the eternal powerlessness of human words to speak of God, and the no less lasting necessity of having recourse to our language in order to refer to God. I offer another example: the parable, thanks to this squared allegory, points out, through the different persons invited, the variety of souls and their incorporation. If we shift from the *Commentary on Matthew* to the only Greek fragment that has been preserved of the *Homilies on Luke 14:15-24*,[88] we read there an allegorical interpretation of the

---

would not, according to Haenchen ("Das Gleichnis vom grossen Mahl"), be about Jesus. Hahn ("Das Gleichnis von der Einladung zum Festmahl") is more cautious. Dupont (*Études,* 2:697–98) criticizes Haenchen's position.

80　See n. 5 above.

81　See Vögtle, "Die Einladung zum grossen Gastmahl," 199–204: v. 16 to v. 21a describe Israel's negative attitude before and after Easter; v. 21c and following are about pagans, those from the first times and from Luke's time. Verse 24 is a condemnation of Israel.

82　See Bovon, *L'oeuvre,* 150; Marion Soards, *The Speeches in Acts: Their Content, Context, and Concerns* (Louisville: Westminster John Knox Press, 1994) 206–8; Daniel Marguerat, "Juifs et chrétiens selon Luc-Actes: une quête d'identité. Surmonter le conflit des lectures," *Bib* 75 (1994) 126–46, esp. 143–44.

83　God is present in the meal, according to Hahn ("Das Gleichnis von der Einladung zum Festmahl," 82).

84　See Funk, *Language,* 190; Fuchs ("Trace de Dieu," 38–39), citing Bernard Rordorf: the parable invites us to "habiter le monde poétiquement"; Weder, *Gleichnisse,* 189–90. For Harnisch (*Gleichniserzählungen Jesu,* 250–53) this parable, departing from the real (lacking time, the weight of worries), opens us to the possible, the possibility of freedom.

85　On the exegesis of the Fathers, see Pirot, *Paraboles,* 360; on the entirety of the history of exegesis, see Beare, "Parable of the Guests at the Banquet."

86　*Origenes Werke,* 1:628–34.

87　Ibid., 1:634–53; see Beare, "Parable of the Guests at the Banquet," 7–8.

88　*Hom. in Luc.,* frg. 84; see Origen, *Hom. in Luc.,* 540–43. The fragment, which begins at the second excuse, is shorter than that edited by Rauer in his first edition of GCS from 1930 and shorter still than

excuses: the owner of the five oxen, according to Origen, neglected what is accessible to one's intelligence in favor of what was just accessible to the senses (Origen must have been thinking of the five senses). The man who got married must be either the one who becomes enamored of false wisdom or else the one who becomes attached to pleasure ("eager for pleasures," φιλήδονος), rather than to God ("friend of God," φιλόθεος).

If we continue in the East, we can read the preacher Cyril of Alexandria's *Sermon 104*, which is both ethical and spiritual.[89] Here the Lord Jesus attacks the Pharisees' pride and their attachment to material realities, while offering a spiritual reward for virtue and good works. By next advocating an allegorical reading of the parable, Cyril reckons that he is following his Master. Note that he interprets the use of force in v. 23 as the irresistible force of God's call (he quotes John 6:44), and not as the automatic recourse to the secular arm in matters of faith.

In the West, we should point out the commentary by Ambrose, bishop of Milan, a sermon by Augustine, then the interpretation of Gregory the Great and the Venerable Bede. According to Ambrose (*Exp. Luc.* 8.197–205),[90] the three people who were excused may symbolize, successively, the Gentiles (their principal character trait being miserliness, a scourge of his time), the Jews (from oxen the transition is naturally made to the yoke of the law, which this people understands, in the opinion of Ambrose, in a material way), and the heretics (heresy being experienced as a dangerous and seductive woman). Ambrose next thought of the second invitation as the welcome of the Gentiles into the church (the presence of good and evil—this touch is Matthean—can be observed in Constantinian Christianity, which was in its initial stage). Because of this interpretation, Ambrose made little distinction between the second and the third

invitations. He preferred to allegorize alleys, squares, roads, and hedgerows (*saepes* is Ambrose's and the Vulgate's translation of φραγμός, and also means "fence," "hedge") in order to emphasize the universal proclamation offered to those who are already on the way toward the kingdom because they follow their good will and their moral judgment. Oddly, his commentary ends with an explanation of the end of the parable in its Matthean version (the episode of the robe and the mention of gnashing of teeth).

In the year 411, a decisive conference was held in Carthage that was called by the emperor to decide between the Catholics and the Donatists. In the context of that polemic, which ended with the triumph of the Catholic cause, the pastoral, episcopal, and theological activity of Augustine, bishop of Hippo, was considerable. From the texts that have been preserved from that conference, it appears that Augustine at that time legitimized having recourse to the secular arm by the imperative command of the master of the parable to his servant: "Compel [them] to come in!" (v. 23).[91] Augustine's *Epistula 185*, entitled *De correctione Donatistarum*, which dates from the beginning of 417, makes a distinction between the easygoing invitation of v. 21 and the invitation accompanied by force in v. 23, just as obedience differs from disobedience. "Wherefore, if the power which the Church has received by divine appointment in its due season, through the religious character and the faith of kings, be the instrument by which those who are found in the highways and hedges—that is, in heresies and schisms—are compelled to come in, then let them not find fault with being compelled, but consider to what they be so compelled. The supper of the Lord is the unity of the body of Christ, not only in the sacrament of the altar, but also in the bond of peace" (*Epist.* 185.6.24).[92] The

that published in *PG* 13:1903–5. The rest comes from other sources, in particular from Origen's *Commentary on Matthew*.

89 See Payne Smith, *Cyril*, 2:484–89; there are fragments from this sermon, frgs. 214–18, in Reuss, *Lukas-Kommentare*, 160–62.

90 At the same time Jerome commented on the Matthean version of the parable; see Jerome *Comm. in Matt.* 3.22.1–98.

91 The Latin versions alternate between *compelle* (Vulgate and part of the Vetus Latina) and *coge* (part of the Vetus Latina and the African recension). Augus-

tine (see next note) is also familiar with the plural *cogite*; see P. Sabatier, ed., *Bibliorum sacrorum Latinae versions antiquae seu Vetus Italica* (3 vols.; Rheims, 1743; repr. Turnhout: Brepols, 1976) 3:331.

92 "Quapropter, is potestate quam per religionem ac fidem regum, tempore quo debuit, divino muere accepit ecclesia, hi qui inveniuntur in viis et in sepibus, id est in haeresibus et schismatibus, coguntur intrare; non quia coguntur reprehendant, sed quo cogantur, attendant. Convivium Domini, unitas est corporis Christi, non solum in sacramento altaris, sed etiam in vinculo pacis" (CSEL 57:23).

same recourse to Luke 14:23 is to be found in the *Contra Gaudentium* (ca. 420). Augustine, believing he could rely on his pastoral experience, believed that the church knows what is good for its faithful better than they understand it themselves: "Therefore this imperial order, to which you respond by voluntarily seeking death, offers many the occasion to be assured of the salvation that is in Christ: even when brought by force to the banquet of such a noble father and forced to enter, they nevertheless find inside what they need to make them happy that they have gotten there" (1.25.28).[93] It may be asked whether Augustine's theology of grace did not encourage him, by an unfortunate analogy between divine power and the imperial power, to legitimatize force used to lead people to happiness. Irresistible grace was materialized in the irresistible sword.[94] In the presence of such exegetical abuse, Scripture is as powerless as Christ was on Good Friday.[95]

From the Middle Ages, leaving aside the *Glossa ordinaria* or Bruno de Segni's commentary,[96] I might single out the homiletical efforts of someone like Thomas Aquinas or Meister Eckhart. Thomas Aquinas treated the necessity of spiritual food and of the two stages of that divine feeding, suggested by the parable, that is, preparation and communication.[97] The "man" who does the inviting is Christ and his "big banquet" points to the three kinds of meals, represented by the eucharistic meal, the intellectual meal, and the emotional meal. For each of those meals, Christ prepares, one might say, two servings or sittings, the *prandium*, breakfast or lunch, to which all are invited, and the *coena*, the dinner, in which only the master's friends can take part.[98] The first sitting,

the breakfast or lunch, includes the sacrifices of the old law, the doctrines of philosophy, and the efforts of grace, which correspond to the three orders: eucharistic, intellectual, and emotional. The second sitting, the dinner, the only one to be called "big," is the Eucharist, Holy Scripture, and heavenly glory (in which the three orders given by the master to his servant come up again). When it is communicated to human beings, it is a double invitation: from inside, by God; from outside, by an angel or a human being. The invitation does not necessarily work, as is indicated by the three refusals, understood, in the light of 1 John 2:16, as pride, avarice, and fleshly weakness. The three waves of persons invited correspond less to the stages of salvation history than to contemporary social realities: the first invitation is turned down by those who succumb to pride, to riches, and to fleshly desires; the second one is intended for those lacking in moral judgment; the third, for nonbelievers, pagans, heretics, and Jews. The use of constraint stands for either the evidence of miracles or the *vexatio*, the "torment," that is, I suppose, the power of the secular arm, according to the fatal Augustinian interpretation.

Here is the essence of the homiletical commentary of Meister Eckhart (especially from homily 20a on):[99] (a) God invites those whom he loves to the evening banquet; it is a love feast. (b) The one who agrees to take part in it must be pure (influence of Matt 22:11-13). (c) The fact of its being in the evening deserves our attention; it is only to be understood in terms of the movement of the sun. Since the sun rises and increases in size up until noon, in the same way the divine light invades the soul and lights up its moods. (d) The invitation is

93   In Augustine, *Works of Saint Augustine*; *NPNF¹, Anti-Donatist Treatises*, 5; see Bovon, *L'oeuvre*, 231 n. 36.

94   On the parable elsewhere in Augustine, see *Sermo* 112 (*PL* 38:647); *Quaest. Ev.* 2.30 (CCSL 44B, 70).

95   From the end of antiquity, the interpretations of Gregory the Great (*Hom. Ev.* 36 [*PL* 76:1265–74]) and the Venerable Bede (*In Luc.* 4.1889–2023; Hurst, 278–81) survive (Bede copies Gregory, only adding some personal phrases to the beginning).

96   See *Glossa ordinaria* Luke 14:15-24 (*PL* 114:308–9); Bruno de Segni *Comm. Luc.* 2.33 (*PL* 165:407–10).

97   Unpublished sermon discussed by Bataillon, "Sermon."

98   This distinction, common in the Middle Ages, justified Matthew's version, since it ends with the dis-

missal of an intruder who had successfully entered the feast, whereas in Luke's version no one is sent away from the banquet hall; see *Glossa ordinaria* Luke 14:16 (*PL* 114:308).

99   There are two very similar sermons in old German and one sermon or sermon preparation in Latin: *Predigt* 20a and *Predigt* 20b in Meister Eckhart, *Predigten*, 1:322–52 and *Dominica secundo post Trinitatem de Evangelio* (Luke 14:16-24), in Meister Eckhart, *Sermones*, 1:80–91. One can read a translation into modern German of these two sermons in Meister Eckhart, *Deutsche Predigten und Traktate*, ed. and trans. Josef Quint (Munich: Hanser, 1978) 241–50 (numbered here 20 and 21).

for the evening, that is, the hour when the soul becomes detached from the world and comes to rest. (e) The evening meal is the last meal of the day; whoever tastes it does not want another one. (f) The host is nameless, which reminds us that it is impossible to find any appropriate way to express God. (g) The three excuses correspond respectively to a triple servitude: submission to worries, slavery to the senses, and being deprived of God (when the soul is turned toward God, it is "man"; when it turns away from him, it is "woman"). Squares and alleys, roads and hedgerows symbolize the various forces that guide the soul (Eckhart at this point develops a theory, difficult to understand, of these forces, mobile or fixed, wide or narrow, upper or lower). Sermon 20a closes with a prayer: may God help us to reject poor excuses and to become "male." In short, the invitation to the banquet symbolizes the appeal that God makes to the soul so that he might become united with it. Although the eucharistic meal appears discreetly in the background, the point of the parable is, above all, a matter of the sending of the divine light into the soul in order to win over its living forces and reprove its pernicious tendencies.[100]

In the sixteenth century, the humanist Erasmus reckoned that the anonymous author of the beatitude (v. 15) "as in a dream, was struck by the desire to take part in this celestial banquet."[101] Since the author of the beatitude believed that there was a minimal number of persons on the list of those who were invited to this magnificent banquet and that the list was restricted to Jews like himself, Jesus offered him this parable. Erasmus said that the reticent among those who were invited were detained by "worldly possessions" or "frivolous realities." He contrasted them with eternal life, that banquet whose abundance and scope he understood.

Luther identified Jesus' opponents with the papists whom he chided.[102] If the man (God) issues invitations to his banquet (the gospel, Jesus Christ, the sacrament), this banquet deserves to be called "big," that is, infinite and eternal, since it is to be distinguished from meals given by the Pharisees. Luther's pointed anti-Jewish and anti-Catholic remarks did not, however, prevent him from engaging in self-criticism or issuing warnings. The excuses that made it possible to dodge the invitation can, in fact, become our own. So watch out! These excuses can, moreover, take on a new coloration, with the field suggesting to Luther the clerical danger; the oxen, political oppression; the wife, not lust but attachment to earthly goods. Luther, who scarcely tolerated here the radicalism of the gospel, sought a compromise between the spirit of the gospel (self-abnegation) and the ethics of his day (a reasonable use of the goods of this world).[103]

Among Calvin's explanations I would only point out an allegiance to the medieval mentality, inherited from Augustine. With the help of the phrase "compel them to come in," Calvin justified having recourse to the secular arm against heretics and infidels. To be sure, he began by understanding that saying by using as his basis God, who puts all his energy into bringing us back to him. But he added, slightly embarrassed: "But I do not think Augustine was wrong in often using this testimony against the Donatists to prove that the disobedient and rebellious might legitimately be forced by the edicts of godly princes to the worship of the true God and to unity in the faith; because, although faith is voluntary, yet we see that these are useful means to tame the obstinacy of those who will not obey unless they are forced."[104]

One hundred fifty years later, at the time of the Revocation of the Edict of Nantes, Reformed Protestants

---

100 There also exists a sermon of Tauler on our parable, *Sermo* 60g (= I n. 34), in Johannes Tauler, *Die Predigten Taulers: Aus der Engelberger und der Freiburger Handschrift sowie aus Schmidts Abschriften der ehemaligen Strassburger Handschriften* (ed. Ferdinand Vetter; Deutsche Texte des Mittelalters 11; Berlin: Weidmann, 1910; reprinted Frankfurt am Main: Weidmann, 1968) 317–21. He is scarcely interested in the series of ideas but prefers to let the various words of the text resonate. He concentrates on the three kinds of meals to which the human being is invited: the interior knowledge of God, the Eucharist, and eternal life.

101 Erasmus, *Paraphrasis*, 402–3.

102 Luther, Predigt vom. 5/30/1535, WA 41, 280–92; Mühlhaupt, 12:208–19.

103 See Melanchthon (*Postillae*, 42–45), who gladly conveys to the youth the classical heritage about feasts and the good uses that must accompany them, but who does not forget at the beginning to bring to mind the meaning of the parable. Later (45–50), the humanist Reformer speaks at length about the church.

104 Calvin, *Harmony*, 2:109.

were to pay dearly for that Augustinian interpretation that Calvin had approved. On October 21, 1685, in the presence of the king, Bossuet legitimized the use of constraint against Protestants by the phrase *compelle intrare* understood in the Augustinian sense. Shortly afterwards, two letters of Augustine, including the one in question, the *Epistula 185*, were translated and published in order to show that in bringing Protestants back into the fold by force, the French Catholic Church was in conformity with the stance of the ancient Church of North Africa faced with the threat of the Donatists.[105] It was to combat that Augustinian interpretation that was still so much alive that Pierre Bayle anonymously wrote and published his famous *Commentaire philosophique*,[106] while he was still suffering from the blow of the death of his brother, who had refused to recant at the time of the Revocation. Bayle rejected the literal sense of "compel them to come in" and instead preferred the metaphorical sense, which alone fits a parable. In a modern way, he refuted the religious justification of violence and asserted that moral or physical obligation would never result in belief. "If the Ruler thinks he can compel consciences, religion becomes a farce and political life a bloody theater."[107] Finally, conversely, belief, as understood by Bayle, could never authorize constraint: "And I say to my readers . . . that we should not focus on what one forces people to do or believe in the case of religion, but on whether force is used, and if it is, one thereby commits a deed that is very wicked and very much in opposition to what is distinctive to all religion, and especially the Gospel."[108] Bayle thus opted for a nondogmatic attitude in doctrinal matters, and for a nonskeptical attitude in ethics. He thus defended the unconditional and transcendent character of the moral conscience.

It was the same battle that Alexandre Vinet was to wage 150 years later in order to obtain freedom of worship in the Swiss Canton of Vaud.[109] He deplored the fact that St. Augustine, "one of the most perfect Christians," was to be counted "among the patrons of intolerance," "he who gave to *compelle intrare* the horrible and disastrous sense on which so many people hastened to pride themselves."[110] He was acquainted, albeit indirectly, with Bayle's refutation of it, and he was delighted with this refutation, before finding in Augustine's own writings certain passages proving that "although a mistaken doctrine misled Augustine's thinking, tolerance had been inscribed in his heart by the same heavenly hand that had engraved faith."[111]

Conclusion

The hesitations of commentators as to the literary genre of this text, which comes under the heading of a judgment oracle and a warning, are revealing as to its polysemy. But there is also an impressive load of hope in this offended God's loving. In order to make it possible to endure the shock of this divine mercy and this human ingratitude, the parabolic story selects the opposite of a languorous lament; it opts for a sober, even elliptical, description. So elliptical that, although the text is closed on the one hand (v. 24), it is open on the other (v. 23). The opening is to human freedom; are the last persons to be invited going to accept the master's final offer?[112]

The passage distinguishes three groups or circles. The first circle refers to the closest friends of the owner of the house. On the register of the history of election, it is a question of God's people, in particular the leaders of Israel, whose persistent reticence Luke records. On the

105 I am relying on Abel, "Obligation," 35–49; previously, see Bovon, *L'oeuvre*, 231–32.
106 Pierre Bayle, *Commentaire philosophique sur ces paroles de Jesus-Christ "Contrain-les d'entrer" ou Traité de la tolérance universelle* (3 vols.; Canterbury [in fact the work was published in Holland], 1686–88).
107 Abel, "Obligation," 42.
108 Bayle, *Commentaire philosophique*, 3:121–22; cited by Abel, "Obligation," 42.
109 Alexandre Vinet, "Mémoire en faveur de la liberté des cultes" (1826), notes 18:2 (in idem, *La liberté des cultes* [2d ed.; Paris, 1852] 298–306).
110 Ibid., 298–99.
111 Ibid., 300.
112 Reflecting on the way the parable has been presented in religious history, Hodel ("Das Festessen") points to the work of the Swiss painter Willy Fries, commissioned by the Gossner Mission of Berlin and painted in 1965 to hang in the great room of what had been formerly a center of the Confessing Church of Germany. He also points out several short plays including one by M. Graff (*Das Fest*, Südwestfunk, Baden-Baden, 1989) in which the lead role, a female pastor, is played by Marianne Sägebrecht.

register of the truth referred to by the text, there is no hesitation either: the most zealous Christians, the believers of all the ages, are at stake, constantly threatened by themselves. The second circle, those who dwell in town, is composed of those less close to the owner: these are the lost sheep of Israel, that is, the poor people for whom Jesus intended the good news and the Jews whom the apostles were to call together as soon as the elevation of the Son took place. The third circle was further removed in time and space: the nations in salvation history, human beings who were subject to the universal calling. The owner invited "many people" (v. 16), his house was to be filled with many people (v. 23). There is a theological problem here: the first persons to be invited were excluded from the banquet. Compare that with what the apostle Paul said. For him, it was a "mystery," a truth that only God knows and reveals (Rom 11:25). What he was able to say about it himself was that, historically linked to Israel's stubbornness (Rom 11:11-12), the conversion of all nations would take place, and that that next event would finally lead not to Israel's perdition but to its salvation (Rom 11:26). By comparison, Luke did not go that far: he told of the stubbornness of one group, then the welcome extended to a second, and the enrichment of a third. He closed his parable on the note of the failure of the initial invitation, the disjunction between the owner and those whom he invited first. Nary a word about their salvation *in extremis*.[113]

We should note, however, that Luke wrote a parable and not a theological statement. His parable was not a preview snapshot of eschatological reality but a tool with which to transform the present reality, a word spoken in order to elicit a response. Sometimes the word condemns (v. 24), sometimes it observes (vv. 18-20). The narrator states in particular that the excuses can all be understood as expressions of the desire to possess ("I have bought," v. 18; "I have bought," v. 19; "I have just gotten married," v. 20). He does not have anything against desire, nor the possessions toward which that desire is directed. What is exposed, and then condemned, is the orientation that desire takes on, that is, the lack of respect for true priorities.

The parable offers another advantage; it issues an invitation to a feast, not to the solitary possession of material acquisitions but to community sharing of treasures of relationship. This is everything that a person who is poor or crippled (v. 21b) or distant or lost (v. 23) lacks. It is this lack that is made up and this sharing that is offered, in the symbolic form of a meal. Our communion services and our eucharistic celebrations are an anticipation and a representation of the banquet of the kingdom in a way that is awkward yet at the same time adequate. How could we fail to link this parable to the Lord's Supper? Do not the mention of bread, the context of the kingdom, and the expression "for it is already ready," encourage us to do so?

"Someone," ἄνθρωπός τις (v. 16), this omnipresent, omnipotent, omnifragile person, dominates the parable from start to finish. He wants his meal (the word occurs three times), he prepares his meal, he is to have his feast. He expects many people and he will have a full house. He is single-minded: in both breadth and intensity of scope, his positive willpower prevails over his aggressive disappointment. His availability outdoes his authority as a "master," κύριος.

God, who is unknowable and unnamable, is represented by a "person." The Word of God, Son of God, is referred to as a "servant." The radiation of being is described with the complementary vocabulary of "sending" and "inviting." Humankind is ambivalent, torn between selfish desire and the desire for God, between primary rejection and unreserved commitment. The offer is made to all. Who will persist in their stubbornness forever?

---

113 See n. 82 above.

Reflect before Speaking or Acting
(14:25-35)

Bibliography

Bultmann, *History*, 160–63; *Ergänzungsheft*, 37, 64.

Carlston, *Triple Tradition*, 87–89.

Coulot, *Jésus et le disciple*, 43–45.

Cullmann, Oscar, "Que signifie le sel dans la parabole de Jésus? Les évangélistes, premiers commentateurs du logion," *RHPhR* 37 (1957) 36–43.

Degenhardt, *Lukas*, 105–13.

Derrett, J. Duncan M., "Nisi dominus aedificaverit domum: Towers and Wars (Lk 14, 28-32)," *NovT* 19 (1977) 241–61; reprinted in idem, *Studies*, 3:85–106.

Dinkler, Erich, "Jesu Wort vom Kreuztragen," in idem, *Signum crucis: Aufsätze zum Neuen Testament und zur christlichen Archäologie* (Tübingen: Mohr Siebeck, 1967) 77–98.

Dupont, Jacques, "Renoncer à tous ses biens (Lc 14, 33)," in idem, *Études*, 2:1076–97.

Edwards, *Theology of Q*, 134–36.

Eichholz, *Gleichnisse*, 192–99.

Fletcher, Donald R., "Condemned to Die: The Logion on Cross-Bearing: What Does It Mean?" *Int* 18 (1964) 156–64.

Gough, Louis F., "A Study on Luke 14:26: Jesus Calls His Disciples to a Life of Supreme Commitment," *ATJ* 3 (1970) 23–30.

Guardini, Romano, *Der Herr: Betrachtungen über die Person und das Leben Jesu Christi* (15th ed.; Freiburg: Herder, 1985) 210–13.

Heininger, *Metaphorik*, 132–39.

Hellestam, Sigvard, "Mysteriet med saltet," *SEÅ* 55 (1990) 59–63.

Hempel, J., "Lk 14, 25-33: Eine 'Fall-Studie,'" in H. Seidel, ed., *Das Lebendige Wort: Beiträge zur kirchlichen Verkündigung. Festgabe für Gottfried Voigt zum 65. Geburtstag* (Berlin: Evangelische Verlagsanstalt, 1982) 255–69.

Hommel, Hildebrecht, "Herrenworte im Lichte sokratischer Überlieferung," *ZNW* 57 (1966) 1–23.

Hunzinger, Claus-Hunno, "Unbekannte Gleichnisse Jesu aus dem Thomas-Evangelium," in Eltester, *Judentum*, 209–20.

Jarvis, Peter G., "Expounding the Parables, V: The Tower-Builder and the King Going to War (Lk 14, 25-33)," *ExpT* 77 (1965–66) 196–98.

Jeremias, *Parables*, passim.

Jülicher, *Gleichnisreden*, 2:67–69, 202–14.

Kahlefeld, *Parables*, 126–31.

Kea, Perry V., "Salting the Salt: Q 14:34-35 and Mark 9:49-50," *Forum* 6 (1990) 239–44.

Kloppenborg, *Formation*, 230–37.

Lambrecht, Jan, "Q-Influence on Mark 8, 34—9, 1," in Delobel, *Logia*, 277–304.

Laufen, *Doppelüberlieferungen*, 302–42.

Mánek, *Gleichnisse*, 97–98.

Moore, T. V., "The Tower-Builder and the King: A Suggested Exposition of Luke 14, 25-35," *Exp* 8/7 (1914) 519–37.

Mundhenk, Norman, "Problems Involving Illustrations in Luke," *BT* 44 (1993) 247–48.

Nauck, Wolfgang, "Salt as a Metaphor in Instructions for Discipleship," *StTh* 6 (1953) 165–78.

Nolland, 2:759–60 (bibliography).

Panimolle, Salvatore A., "Se uno non 'odia' la moglie e i figli, non puo essere mio discepolo (Lc 14, 26)," *PSV* 12 (1984) 143–65.

Perles, Felix, "Zwei Übersetzungsfehler im Text der Evangelien," *ZNW* 19 (1919–20) 96.

Petzke, *Sondergut*, 134–35.

Piper, *Wisdom*, 130–31, 197–202, 248, 272–76.

Polag, *Christologie*, 85–86 and passim.

Schmidt, Thomas E., "Burden, Barrier, Blasphemy: Wealth in Matt 6:33, Luke 14:33, and Luke 16:15," *TJT* 9 (1988) 171–89.

Schroeder, Hans-Hartmut, *Eltern und Kinder in der Verkündigung Jesu: Eine hermeneutische und exegetische Untersuchung* (TF 53; Hamburg-Bergstedt: Reich, 1972) 90–110.

Schulz, *Q*, 430–33, 446–49, 470–74.

Schwarz, Gunther, "Der Nachfolgespruch Markus 8, 34bc Parr.: Emendation und Rückübersetzung," *NTS* 33 (1987) 255–65.

Seccombe, *Possessions*, 99–117, 133–34.

Seeley, David, "Blessings and Boundaries: Interpretations of Jesus' Death in Q," *Semeia* 55 (1991) 131–46.

Idem, "Jesus' Death in Q," *NTS* 38 (1992) 222–34.

Seynaeve, Jaak, "Exigences de la condition chrétienne: Lc 14," *AsSeign* 54 (1972) 64–75.

Stein, Robert H., "Luke 14:26 and the Question of Authenticity," *Forum* 5/2 (1989) 187–92.

Stock, Augustine, *Counting the Cost: New Testament Teaching on Discipleship* (Collegeville, Minn.: Liturgical Press, 1977).

Thackeray, Henry St. John, "A Study in the Parable of the Two Kings," *JTS* 14 (1913) 389–99.

Theissen, Gerd, "'Wir haben alles verlassen' (Mk 10, 28): Nachfolge und soziale Entwurzelung in der jüdisch-palästinischen Gesellschaft des 1. Jahrhunderts nach Ch.," *NovT* 19 (1977) 161–96.

Vaage, Leif E., "Q[1] and the Historical Jesus: Some Peculiar Sayings (7, 33–34; 9, 57–58, 59–60; 14, 26–27," *Forum* 5/2 (1989) 159–76.

25/ Large crowds were traveling with him. So turning to them, he said to them, 26/ "Whoever comes to me and does not hate their father, their mother, their wife, their children, their brothers and sisters, yes, and even their own self, cannot be my disciple. 27/ Whoever does not carry their own cross and follow me cannot be my disciple.

28/ For which of you, intending to build a tower, does not first sit down and estimate the cost, to see whether you have enough to see your job through to completion? 29/ Otherwise, when you have laid the foundation and are not able to finish, all who observe it will begin to ridicule you, 30/ saying, 'This person began to build and did not have the means to finish.'

31/ Or what king, going out to wage war against another king, will not sit down first and consider whether he is able with ten thousand to oppose the one who comes against him with twenty thousand? 32/ If he cannot, then, while the other is still far away, he sends a delegation and asks for the terms of peace. 33/ So, therefore, none of you can become my disciple if you do not give up all your possessions.

34/ Salt, therefore, is good. But if even salt has lost its taste, how can its saltiness be restored? 35/ It is fit neither for the soil nor for the manure pile; it is thrown away. Let anyone with ears to hear listen!"

Just as both nature and Scripture require an alternation of work and rest, so does the Gospel mention in turn Jesus' itinerant activity and beneficial stops. The Pharisee's banquet (14:1-24) is followed here by travel with others (14:25), in accordance with an alternation between something previously encountered (travel, 13:22) and something that comes later (the meal, 15:1-2). Nothing keeps the Master from teaching, whether trips or stops along the way, since he actually uses both occasions to deliver his divine wisdom. This is the picture Luke paints of Jesus: a man of God, a sage, and a prophet who interprets sabbatical rest, social life, the banquet of the kingdom, and Christian calling in the framework of an invitation and a meal, and who then uses the occasion of collective travel to define the conditions of being his follower. Although Luke joined Jesus' message to the present activity of his hero, it was in order to capture the attention of his readers and impress lasting memories on them.

The conditions for being Jesus' follower are enumerated in a way that is alternately shocking and intriguing. The champion of love (10:25-28) here becomes the one who praises hate (v. 26). The Master, whose call to "follow me" (5:27-28) brooked no hesitation, encourages his listeners to sit down and take the time to reflect (vv. 28-32). Finally, the one who invites people to listen (v. 35b) leaves it vague what it is that he intends for them to understand (vv. 34-35a).

Luke thus displayed the quality of his art and the weight of his theology by the relationships that he established between the content of the message and the way it was expressed, as well as by the connections he suggested between the narrative framework and the wisdom that was dispensed. His witness to these features is all the more skillful in that he was limited in his freedom of action and was obliged to respect what came to him from tradition. His margin of liberty, then, was limited to some adjustments and some slight personal touches.

Analysis

The pericope is divided into six parts of unequal length:

- *The description of the situation*: Jesus traveling, accompanied by crowds (v. 25).
- A *pair of sayings*: one on hate, another on the cross (vv. 26-27).
- A *pair of parables*: one on the tower, another on war (vv. 28-32).
- A *concluding saying*: on giving up all one's possessions (v. 33).
- A *new development*: on salt (vv. 34-35a).
- A *last appeal*: invitation to listen (v. 35b).

We should not be fooled by this listing. The passage highlights three of Jesus' teachings (vv. 26-27, 28-33, 34-35a), framed by a mention of the situation (v. 25) and a final exhortation (v. 35b).[1]

As is often the case with introductions and summaries, the opening part of the pericope, v. 25, bears obvious Lukan marks: the travel, the crowds, and Jesus' attitude.[2] Thus, it is a creation of the Gospel writer, who provides a reminder of the current trip toward Jerusalem (cf. 9:51 and 13:22).[3]

The two sayings, about hate and the cross, respectively (vv. 26-27), are constructed in a similar fashion:

a conditional subordinate clause, followed by a main clause. Nevertheless, although the apodosis in both cases is identical ("[they] cannot be my disciple"), the protases are different (in Greek, literally: "if anyone . . ." [v. 26]; "whoever . . . ," [v. 27]).[4] This observation suggests that the sayings had different origins but were linked by a growing concern—up to, and including, Luke—to bring them together (v. 33 confirms this feeling; it is redactional and ends exactly the same way).[5] These two sayings of Jesus, originally independent of each other, had already been combined by the tradition, as is proved by the parallel in Matt 10:37-38, where we find them side by side in the same order, signaled, as here, by identical endings and different beginnings.[6] Even if the wording does not agree (in the first saying, Matthew uses the comparative "love . . . more than," where Luke does not hesitate to say "hate"), I nevertheless suppose that these sayings are parallels that came down to these two Gospel writers via their common source, Q.[7]

The initial independence of the two sayings is confirmed by the triple tradition and the *Gospel of Thomas*, since Mark quotes the first saying, albeit worded a little differently, in one place (Mark 10:29-30), and the second one, in another (Mark 8:34).[8] Given the importance of the theme of these words of Jesus, Matthew and Luke preserved them in two different wordings, Q's and Mark's: the passage from Q is read here and in Matt

---

1   Already in 1914, T. V. Moore ("Tower-Builder and the King," 519–37) proposed such a division, except that he groups points 5 and 6 together; see also Seynaeve ("Exigences de la condition chrétienne," 66), who counts four parts up through v. 33; and Coulot (*Jésus et le disciple*, 43–45), who observes here a catechesis in three stages: vv. 26-27, vv. 28-33, vv. 34-35.

2   On συμπορεύομαι ("to go with"), see 7:11 and 24:15 (the only other usage in the NT is Mark 10:1). The word ὄχλοι is common in Luke but also in Matthew and Mark. The use of "many crowds" occurs only here and in 5:15 in Luke's work, but it is common in Matthew. The singular ὄχλος πολύς, on the other hand, appears more frequently in Luke, e.g., in 5:29 and 6:17. On στραφεὶς εἶπεν πρὸς αὐτούς ("turning, he said to them"), a typically Lukan formula, see 7:44; 10:22, 23; 23:28. On the other hand, Jeremias (*Sprache*, 241) argues that στραφείς is traditional, referring to 7:9.

3   Note the imperfect, typical of summaries.

4   A similar phenomenon occurs in the parallel in Matthew. Although the two sayings finish in the same way ("is not worthy of me"), they begin differently ("whoever loves," Matt 10:37; "whoever does not take...," Matt 10:38).

5   See Dupont, "Renoncer," 1083–85.

6   See n. 4 above.

7   Sato (*Q und Prophetie*, 23–24, 43, 52–53) calls for caution. He is not certain that the verses between Luke 14:26 and 17:6 belong to Q, as is usually thought: not only does the order of these verses differ substantially between Luke and Matthew, but also the order of Luke, which typically aligns with Q, hardly makes sense. It could be a question of oral statements ("mündliches Überlieferungsgut von Q," 53), or elements of Q-Matt having influenced Q-Luke or vice versa (Sato thinks that the written form of Q received a Matthean and a Lukan form).

8   See Ernst, 447–48.

10:37-38; Mark 10:29-30 is found in Matt 19:29 and Luke 18:29-30; and Mark 8:34, in Matt 16:24 and Luke 9:23. On one occasion the *Gospel of Thomas* quotes the two sayings together (55) and another time quotes just the first one by itself (101).[9]

The appeal to hypothetical Q leads us to a double search: the quest for the traditional wording of the sayings, an effort that has been going on for a long time,[10] and the search for the order of the sayings in tradition, therefore for the context of Q, which is a recent approach on the part of commentators.[11] I will undertake the first of these tasks in the commentary in order to bring out more meaning in the rereading of Luke. But at this point, let me say a word about the second task.

The Matthean parallel to these two sayings in Luke (Matt 10:37-38) is followed by a third saying, on the loss of one's life (Matt 10:39). That saying, however, also shows up in Luke, but much later (17:33).[12] Did Matthew for once perhaps preserve Q's order? To have in mind all the components of the problem, we must remember *Gos. Thom.* 55 and 101, as well as John 12:25, and especially remember that the triple tradition also juxtaposed the sayings about bearing the cross and losing one's life (see Mark 8:34-25 par. Matt 16:24-25 par. Luke 9:23-24). The situation can be presented graphically thus:

	Matt 10	Luke 14	Mark 8//Matt 16//Luke 9	Luke 17	John 12	*Gos. Thom.* 55	*Gos. Thom.* 101
1. Rejection of one's family:	x		x	x	x	x	x
2. Bearing the cross:	x	x	x			x	
3. Loss of one's life:	x	x					

From this graphic presentation it appears that the logia kept the strength they originally had as autonomous sayings (e.g., John 12, for the third; and *Gos.Thom.* 101, for the first). Another, didactic force tended to bring them together (e.g., the triple tradition for the last two; Luke 14 and *Gos. Thom.* 55, for the first two). Was the bringing together of the three, witnessed to by Matthew alone, due to tradition or redaction? John S. Kloppenborg believes that it was tradition.[13] In that case, we need to explain why Luke dislocated them (did Luke keep alive the memory of this trio by creating a third saying, v. 33, on the theme that was dear to his heart, giving up all one's possessions?). As for me, I do not see why he would have moved

the third saying from chap. 14 to chap. 17. So I think that the saying on the loss of one's life circulated independently (cf. John 12) and was deposited somewhere in Q (cf. Matt 10 and Luke 17). In that case, it was Matthew, influenced by Mark 8, who joined it to the other two.[14] Both the double tradition (with sayings 1 and 2) and the triple tradition (with sayings 2 and 3) brought the sayings together in order to give expression to the requirements of being Jesus' follower: one of them stressing the inexorable consequence (martyrdom), the other the favorable outcome (true life).

The two parables are true parables,[15] of a type characteristic of L.[16] Each of them was made up of a rhetorical

---

9 See Schrage, *Thomas-Evangelium*, 120–23.

10 See Bultmann, *History*, 160–63; Schulz, *Q*, 446–47, 430–31.

11 See Kloppenborg, *Formation*, 230–32; Sato, *Q und Prophetie*, 23–24, 43, 52–53.

12 See Xavier Léon-Dufour, "Luke 17,33," in Delorme and Duplacy, *La parole de grâce*, 101–12. According to Leon-Dufour, the insertion of the saying in the little apocalypse (Luke 17:22-37) is obviously redactional.

13. Kloppenborg, *Formation*, 230–32.

14 Lambrecht ("Q-Influence," 277–304) thinks, on the

contrary, that Mark 8:34—9:1 is under the influence of Q.

15 See Jülicher, *Gleichnisreden*, 2:vii; Bultmann, *History*, 170–71; Harnisch, *Gleichniserzählungen Jesu*, 67 and 69 n. 63.

16 See Heinrich Greeven, "Wer unter euch . . . ?" *WD* 3 (1952) 86–101; reprinted in Wolfgang Harnisch, ed., *Gleichnisse Jesu: Positionen der Auslegung von A. Jülicher bis zur Formgeschichte* (WdF 366; Darmstadt: Wissenschaftliche Buchgesellschaft, 1982) 238–55; Harnisch, "Wer unter euch," 106; Jeremias, *Parables*,

question (v. 28 and v. 31), followed by the statement of the unfortunate consequences that would result from a bad decision, one of them in a long wording using "otherwise . . ." (vv. 29-30), the other with "if . . . not" (v. 32).[17] As it sometimes happens,[18] these parables are not worded in terms of any comparison. Nor did they, in their traditional state, include any application. The analogy remained implicit, and the meaning was left up to the wisdom of the listener. At the redactional level, Luke sensed this lack and filled the gap with an application, v. 33 ("So therefore, none of you . . .").[19] Moreover, he may have added v. 30. Not only is this verse Lukan in its wording, but it also teaches us nothing new. It may have simply fulfilled an internal requirement of Luke, that of recalling the essentials and spelling things out.

We know that the author of L was fond of stories or examples that were paired (such as the two short parables of the lost sheep and the lost drachma in 15:3-10).[20] But we have there something brought into being by the will of the redactor; the different grammatical constructions and situations envisaged suggest that those two stories came into being separately. They circulated separately, unless one of them served as a model for the creation of the other.[21] A text from the book of Proverbs may have favored their being brought together or even their creation, lending a midrashic flavor to these parables: "Wisdom builds the house, . . . victory is the fruit of detailed planning" (Prov 24:3-6 REB).[22]

Evidently, the possibility of these two parables having been spoken by Jesus on the same occasion cannot be ruled out, since he appeared to be fond of the *Doppelgleichnisse*, paired parables.[23] If that was the case, we would have to add a sapiential component to the apocalyptic character of Jesus' teaching, since the prudence that the parables have in mind seems more proverbial than prophetic, more Greek than Hebraic[24]—unless, of course, being elliptical, on Jesus' lips they have to do with God's reliability rather than with human responsibility. In that case, on the pattern of "which of you?" answered by "no one," the Master would have meant to speak of God and his kingdom.[25] And it would have been the author of L or, rather, even the Gospel writer himself, who transformed the meaning, shifting from eschatology to wisdom, from the kingdom of God to the disciples' commitment. To complicate the problem, we should mention a third parable, found only in the *Gospel of Thomas*. Having a different wording than the pair here in Luke, it is similar in its content. And curiously, it is linked to the kingdom of God and not to being a follower, as if the Father imposed his power the way the Zealots did: "Jesus said, 'The Kingdom of the father is like a certain man who wanted to kill a powerful man. In his own house he drew his sword and stuck it into the wall in order to find out whether his hand could carry through. Then he slew the powerful man'" (*Gos. Thom.* 98). Several commentators have wondered if this parable,

---

196; Klaus Berger, "Materialien zu Form und Überlieferungsgeschichte neutestamentlicher Gleichnisse," *NovT* 15 (1973) 25–33.

17 See Petzke (*Sondergut*, 134–35), who presents things a bit differently.

18 This is the case in parables that develop the form not of comparison but of metaphor, e.g., Luke 12:42-46.

19 See Bultmann, *History*, 170–71. It is quite possible that the comparison formula ("The kingdom of the Father is like") in *Gos. Thom.* 98, which we will discuss in more detail later, is itself also secondary.

20 On double parables, see Jeremias, *Parables*, 90–92.

21 There is not, to my knowledge, a study on the prehistory of these parables; we have only the conclusion that they belong to L; see Petzke, *Sondergut*, 134.

22 See Derrett, "Nisi Dominus," 245–46.

23 See Jeremias (*Parables*, 90), who favors this hypothesis.

24 We know that several American scholars insist on the sapiential character of Jesus (e.g., Burton L. Mack, *A Myth of Innocence: Mark and Christian Origins* [Philadelphia: Fortress, 1985]) or of Q (e.g., Kloppenborg, *Formation*).

25 Moore ("Tower-Builder and the King," 528) supposes that Christ is the builder and the king; Hunzinger ("Unbekannte Gleichnisse," 214–15) thinks that God himself is; he is criticized by Jeremias in the sixth edition of the *Gleichnisse Jesu* (195–96 n. 7; this critique is absent from the fifth edition that I normally use, and from the French translation; it is, however, included in the English [sixth] edition [197 n. 23]). Jarvis ("Expounding the Parables," 198) follows Hunzinger cautiously.

which has scarcely any trace of Gnosticism, might not be authentic.[26] It would have been eliminated from the gospel tradition because it reeked of the Zealots. That is quite possible. I doubt, however, if it circulated alongside these two Lukan parables; both the difference in literary form and the success of paired texts tell against that possibility.

Luke was anxious to provide an unambiguous application of these two enigmatic parables. He did so by composing a saying that he made up himself (v. 33), which was influenced by the wording of vv. 26-27 and which, with its "[each one of] you" ($\pi\hat{\alpha}\varsigma\ \dot{\epsilon}\xi\ \dot{\upsilon}\mu\hat{\omega}\nu$), corresponds to "which of you . . . ?" ($\tau\dot{\iota}\varsigma\ .\ .\ .\ \dot{\epsilon}\xi\ \dot{\upsilon}\mu\hat{\omega}\nu$) of the first parable. In doing so, he explicitly associated the parables with the problem of discipleship (cf. v. 33, which matches the failures in vv. 26 and 27: "[that person] cannot be my disciple"). The Lukan radicalism shows up once more: future disciples must part with all their possessions (cf. 9:62 and 12:33).[27]

For no apparent reason,[28] and without any transition, Luke then adds something about salt. These sayings have been transmitted to us by the three Synoptic Gospels (Mark 9:49-50; Matt 5:13; Luke 14:34-35). The agreements between Matthew and Luke are so numerous and so obvious (e.g., the curious use of the verb $\mu\omega\rho\alpha\dot{\iota}\nu\omega$ [intransitive: "be dazed"; transitive: "to dull," "make foolish"]) that we must suppose that there was a Q wording in addition to the Markan wording.[29] Unlike the sayings about hating one's family and bearing the cross, the development of the theme of salt did not have the honor of appearing in a doublet: Matthew and Luke were content to mention it a single time, combining as best they could the triple tradition (Mark 9:49-50) and the double tradition (which is to be found underlying Matt 5:13 and Luke 14:34-35).

Luke started off by following Mark but added a "therefore" ($o\hat{\upsilon}\nu$) in order to link the sayings to the preceding parables: "Salt, therefore, is good." In the second clause, he adopted the text of Q (except for two details: the addition of an "even" [$\kappa\alpha\dot{\iota}$] and the adoption of the verb "to season," or "restore saltiness to" [$\dot{\alpha}\rho\tau\dot{\upsilon}\omega$], which comes from Mark): "But if even salt has lost its taste, how can it be seasoned?" In what follows next, he stuck to Q, as is proved by the parallel in Matthew and by Mark's silence, but he did not follow Q slavishly: "It is fit neither for the soil nor for the manure pile";[30] "it is thrown away" (Luke probably kept Q's text here, which Matthew embellished in this way: "It is thrown out and trampled underfoot by people.")[31] Finally, an all-purpose phrase allows Luke to establish a unity between v. 25 and v. 35 and to come to a conclusion before moving on to something else (15:1-2). That phrase, "Let anyone with ears to hear listen!" circulated independently in the Synoptic tradition. Luke made use of it elsewhere (cf. 8:8).[32] The way the phrase was worded was whispered in Luke's ear here by Mark, to whom he returns at the end of the pericope (there is no parallel in Matthew), since Mark's conclusion used an imperative: "Have salt in yourselves, and be at peace with one another."[33] Luke, in other words, borrowed that exhortative mood from Mark. In short, Luke inserted a set of three clauses from Q into a framework inspired by Mark:

(a) salt is good (Mark)
(b) if the salt loses its taste . . . (Q)
(c) it is fit neither . . . (Q)
(d) it is thrown away (Q)
(e) let anyone with ears . . . (cf. Mark)

---

26 In particular, Hunziger, "Unbekannte Gleichnisse."
27 On this verse, see Dupont, "Renoncer." Jeremias (*Sprache*, 243) is undoubtedly wrong to identify traditional elements in v. 33.
28 According to the Roman Missal, the pericope ends at v. 33.
29 See Schulz, *Q*, 470–71; Carlston, *Triple Tradition*, 87; Steinhauser, *Doppelbildworte*, 332 (reconstruction only of v. 34); Coulot, *Jésus et le disciple*, 45; Kloppenborg, *Formation*, 232–34.
30 Some commentators have drawn attention to the thematic and formal connection with 9:61-62 (the same usage of $\epsilon\dot{\upsilon}\vartheta\epsilon\tau o\varsigma$, "suitable"); Kloppenborg, *Formation*, 232–34.
31 Cf. Matt 7:6: "lest they trample them underfoot" (concerning pearls thrown to pigs; this is the same verb, $\kappa\alpha\tau\alpha\pi\alpha\tau\dot{\epsilon}\omega$ ["to trample underfoot"], redactional).
32 The formula, as we have seen, is added in certain manuscripts to the end of the parable of the rich man (12:21) and in others to the end of the parable of the barren fig tree (13:9).
33 This formula from Mark may have inspired Matthew at the beginning of his passage: "you, you are the salt of the earth."

In spite of a rhetorical sequence and a logical unity that are somewhat chaotic, Luke 14:25-35 constitutes a literary and thematic unity. We attribute this composition, focused on the conditions of discipleship, to the redaction of Luke, who put it together starting with elements from Q, L, and, to a lesser extent, Mark. The view that this composition comes from tradition is held by some, but I do not subscribe to that opinion; others attribute it to Q[34] and still others to L.[35]

Commentary

■ **25** The meal scene inside the house is concluded at this point; a new stage has begun, and it takes place outside, on the road. The brief summary that introduces it[36] draws one's attention more to those to whom Jesus speaks than to Jesus himself.[37] He was no longer speaking to enemies or disciples but to the crowds, who were probably favorable and who were traveling with him,[38] without yet being committed to following him for good. And for a good reason: they still did not know what was involved in becoming a disciple. By visualizing these crowds on the road, v. 25 prepares for Jesus' instruction on the conditions of discipleship. The literary composition proves that in Luke's eyes there was not just one form of vocation, the call immediately followed by a result (5:1-11, 27-28). There was also the kind of joining up that was prepared for and was the result of a decision. Far from being negative, this journey with Jesus does not belong to just the previous verses. The sayings will specify what the later, decisive stage is.

■ **16-27** Verse 26 makes an excellent connection with v. 25: it is not enough to "come to me," that is, to "travel with me"; one must also have broken with one's past. A person must not have a divided heart, pulled in opposite directions, and cannot serve two masters at the same time. The disciple must make a choice. Choosing means knowing how to give things up, and especially how to part with them (see 9:61-62; 16:13).

By making use of the verb "hate," the text shocks and outrages us. The more pedagogical Matthean parallel is argued by means of a comparison: we must prefer Christ to our family. The Lukan text, on the other hand, works through contrast and opposition. And it has its truth: "For where your treasure is, there your heart will be also" (see 12:34). Believing that we could love everything at the same time would be tantamount to succumbing to the fantasy of being all-powerful. There are unconditional attachments that can be lived only to the detriment of other ties.[39] To be sure, the verb "hate" probably reflects a Semitic origin, and the Semitic languages often use contrasts to express things our languages would express by a comparative degree of preferences (so in that case Matthew made a satisfactory "translation").[40] But by refusing to "translate," the Hellenist Luke preserved the power of the truth that he expressed through the use of emotive opposition. He knew that everything that does not belong to the world of the being who is loved becomes a source of irritation and the breaking of relationships. How, then, can one reconcile this new order with the old commandment to love one's parents and quite simply with the commandment to love one's neighbor? There are four complementary answers: (1) The Decalogue also lays down a love of God that sets priorities and is exclusive (the first commandment). (2) The family circle, like every reality of this world, can

---

34   Thus Marshall, 591.

35   Jülicher (*Gleichnisreden*, 2:209 and 2:70) thinks that the arrangement of vv. 26-35 is traditional. When speaking of a "source" (2:209), he must be thinking of Luke's L. In his opinion, Luke added a γάρ ("for") to v. 28, and all of v. 33.

36   On the Lukan technique of summarizing, see the introduction.

37   The first main clause has the "crowds" as its subject.

38   See Gen 13:5 LXX: Lot travels with Abraham.

39   We read the contrast "to hate"–"to love" in the saying about the two masters in 16:13.

40   See Deut 21:15: "If a man has two wives, one of whom he loves and the other he hates . . ."; Gen

29:30 expresses preference differently: Jacob "loved Rachel" מֵלֵאָה, literally: "from Leah," that is, "more than Leah" (מִן, "from," marks the comparative). The LXX renders the expression with the comparative adverb μᾶλλον ἤ ("more than"). The subsequent verse, Gen 29:31, uses contrast: "When the Lord saw that Leah was unloved"; see Lagrange, 409; Fitzmyer, 2:1063. The sermon cited by Hempel ("Lk 14, 25-33," 255–69) takes it to mean the choice between priorities, weakening the meaning of the verb μισέω ("to hate"). Grundmann (303) also takes it this way.

turn inward, excluding transcendence and one's neighbor. It then becomes idolatrous, and thus God's enemy.[41] In that case, the rupture with that social reality[42] signifies liberation and especially faithfulness to God. (3) Next, the aforementioned hate does not attack persons, but what they represent (social isolation, hierarchical roles). It finds its culmination, let us not forget, in "hating" oneself. (4) Set apart for God, the Levites also had to leave their families (Deut 33:9-10). Jesus may have been influenced by that requirement, as were the monks of Qumran (cf. 4QTestimonia [4Q175] 15–17). So Jesus did not suggest subjecting one's family to public contempt in order to favor the blossoming of one's own personality. Instead, he considered dying to one's family and to oneself to represent the negative aspect of becoming a disciple, just as Good Friday is necessary for Easter.

Nevertheless, like certain philosophers, Jesus advocated breaking family ties—in an age when one's aged parents needed the support of their adult children and when children who were minors depended on their parents.[43]

What, then, does it mean to "be a disciple"? We should note that the text does not speak of "becoming a disciple," since that expression would suggest that such becoming depended on ourselves. Rather, "being a disciple" means being accepted by the Master. For that to happen, we must be here and not elsewhere; attentive and not distracted. One must be ready to learn, not from human but from divine wisdom; not in the course of an intellectual learning, but a global one, involving the head, heart, will, and body.[44] What a tremendous event! To explain this, the New Testament appeals to various images: undressing, dying, leaving, not turning back, and hating.[45]

"Hating" is tantamount to "leaving."[46] The crowds who came to him (v. 26), traveled with him (v. 25). What had to be added, in order for them to join him and to have fellowship with him that was genuine and lasting, was the unavoidable element of parting with what was closest to their hearts. In this connection hate is not, in the first instance, an emotion;[47] it is an act.[48] Once the break has been made and we have gone through the tunnel of Good Friday, the light of Easter can make possible loving others, including our family, no longer as a closed circle but as relatives in Christ and as God's creatures. But we must not cut corners.

The list of family members differs from one tradition to another, from one Gospel to another. The triple tradi-

---

41   See Ps 139 (138):21-22: "Do I not hate those who hate you, O Lord?" In the Qumran writings also, the believer hates what God hates (see 1QH 14.10-11; 17.24), in particular those who are not members of the community (see 1QS 1.10; 9.21-22; 19.17-21). According to Josephus (*Bell.* 2.8.7 §139), the Essenes promised under oath to hate evildoers; see Krister Stendhal, "Hate, Non-Retaliation, and Love: 1QS 10:17-20 and Rom. 12:10-21," *HTR* 55 (1962) 343–55, and Fitzmyer, 2:1063.

42   On the importance of family relations in Israel, see Schroeder, *Eltern und Kinder in der Verkündigung Jesu*, 90–110, esp. 97–102.

43   As the parable of the prodigal son (15:11-32) and the constitution of the Christian community prove, it was possible, despite a still-living patriarchate, to remove oneself from a family; see Theissen, "Wir haben alles verlassen," 161–96; François Bovon, "Communauté familiale et communauté ecclésiale dans le Nouveau Testament," *Les Cahiers Protestants* 6 (1974) 61–72.

44   On μαθητής in Luke, see the commentary on 5:29-32 in vol. 1, n. 20. There is no study of the verb μανθάνω ("to learn") in its Christian sense; see G. Nebe, "μανθάνω etc.," *EDNT* 2:383–84.

45   "To strip off" (Col 3:9); "to put to death" (Col 3:5); "to die" (Rom 6:2); "to crucify" (Gal 6:14); "to leave" (Mark 10:29); "to forget what is behind" (Phil 3:13); "to hate" (here, Luke 14:26; perhaps Jude 23). See Anton Vögtle, *Der Judasbrief: Der zweite Petrusbrief* (EKKNT 22; Neukirchen-Vluyn: Neukirchener Verlag, 1994) 106–7; Ernst Fuchs and Pierre Reymond, *La deuxième épître de saint Pierre. L'épître de saint Jude* (2d ed.; CNT 13b; Geneva: Labor et Fides, 1988) 186–87.

46   The parallel in the triple tradition has ἀφῆκεν ("left") (see Mark 10:29 par. Luke 18:29).

47   See Schweizer, 159.

48   One should read Guardini, *Der Herr*, 210–13: "Und nun sagt Jesus: In allem, was dich umgibt, ist ein Feind. Nicht nur die unerlaubten, die niedrigen, die bösen, auch die guten, grossen und schönen Dinge tragen den Feind in sich" (p. 212). He proceeds to say that the human being notices this as soon as he or she hears the call of Christ and discovers in himself or herself the worst enemy.

tion (Matt 19:29 par. Mark 10:29 par. Luke 18:29) begins with the inclusive notion of "house," before proceeding to distinguish generations and curiously fitting "fields" into the enumeration. The double tradition was unacquainted with the house and the fields but began with father and mother and ended with children. Brothers and sisters, absent from the parallel in Matthew, were probably imported here by Luke from the triple tradition (since logically they should have come before rather than after children).[49] Luke's originality,[50] the mark of his radicalism, is the mention of the wife and oneself: the wife that a man chose, even if the choice was not as free then as it is today, and oneself, the person one prefers.[51] The mention of "oneself" also serves as a hermeneutical safeguard. Make no mistake about it, the hate in question does not correspond to the break made by the prodigal son, since he acted out of self-love (15:13).

Luke did not create the phrase "cannot be my disciple" (it was Matthew who interpreted it as "is not worthy of me").[52] Luke took it up here and made it explicit in terms of "coming" to Christ,[53] of accompanying him and loving him.

In v. 27, Q's negative wording ("whoever does not carry their own cross") must have been older than Mark's positive wording (Mark 10:29).[54] The carrying of the cross is still a precondition and does not yet have intrinsic worth.[55] Q's content can be found by reading Matthew at the beginning of the verse and Luke at the end.[56] In the first half of the saying, Luke did, in fact, improve on Q's Greek: he wrote ὅστις ("whoever"; Matthew: καὶ ὅς, "and the one who"), βαστάζει ("carry"; Matthew has the less precise λαμβάνει, "take"), ἑαυτοῦ, ("their [literally: "his"] own"; Matthew: αὐτοῦ, "their" [literally: "his"]), and ἔρχεται ὀπίσω μου ("follow me" [literally: "comes after me"]; Matthew, pleonastically, ἀκολουθεῖ ὀπίσω μου, literally: "accompanies after me").[57] As in the preceding verse, Luke respected the end of the saying as Q had worded it ("cannot be my disciple").

Although the triple tradition increased the number of verbs and spiritualized the matter of following as well as the bearing of the cross, the double tradition visualized in a concrete way the martyrdom experienced because of faithfulness to Christ.[58] Luke stressed that picture by the use of the verb βαστάζω ("carry a burden," "carry"), which he was to apply in Acts to Paul and his sufferings on behalf of Christ's name (see Acts 9:15).[59] The saying must originally have lacked any christological trait. The use of that trait was to spread among the Christian com-

---

49   On the reconstitution of the text of Q, see Bultmann, *History*, 160–63; Schulz, *Q*, 446–47; Vaage, "Q¹ and the Historical Jesus," 171–72.

50   See Stein ("Luke 14:26 and the Question of Authenticity," 190–92), who points out five Lukan elements in this verse, slightly different from the ones that I have retained.

51   We recall the mention in 9:24, in an expression borrowed from Mark 8:35. The text is uncertain: like Fitzmyer (2:1064), I prefer the reading ἔτι δὲ καί, which is better attested than ἔτι τε καί. The first is found in Acts 2:26 in a citation; the second in Acts 21:28.

52   Even if he often reflects on the condition of a disciple, Luke rarely does so using the word μαθητής ("disciple"); see 6:40, however.

53   The words "come after me," which are absent from the Matthean parallel, are Lukan. We find them inserted by the evangelist in the introduction to the parable of the two houses in 6:47.

54   See Ernst, 448. Verse 27 has disappeared from part of the tradition of manuscripts, a good example of homoioteleuton (v. 27 ends like v. 26).

55   See Bultmann, *History*, 163.

56   On the reconstitution of Q, see Schulz, *Q*, 430–31; Laufen, *Doppelüberlieferungen*, 304; Lambrecht, "Q-Influence," 279–82.

57   On the other hand, Lambrecht ("Q-Influence," 279) retains Luke's formula for Q.

58   *Gospel of Thomas* 55 reads simply, "who does not carry his cross like me." The Manichean Psalms called *Sarakoton* ("Psalms of Itinerants"), adding the rejection of the world, juxtapose carrying one's cross and the leaving of family, like the canonical Gospels. See C. R. C. Allberry, ed., *A Manichaean Psalm Book, 2* (Manichaean Manuscripts in the Chester Beatty Collection 2; Stuttgart: Kohlhammer, 1938) 167, lines 47–53, 175, lines 25–27. In the first citation, carrying one's cross precedes leaving family. In the second it is the reverse. The mood is imperative in the first instance (second person singular), assertoric in the second (first person singular). In both cases, the references to the Gospel are separated from each other by a third element.

59   Paul himself is particularly fond of this verb to define Christian ethics and the condition of the believer; see Rom 15:1; Gal 6:2, 5, 17.

munity, and it is found, in various wordings, everywhere, including in the *Gospel of Thomas*.[60]

Sentencing to death by crucifixion, which was perhaps of Persian origin but was a Roman practice, was known in Palestine.[61] Various revolts had been quelled by means of such executions.[62] Although the vertical bar remained fixed in the ground, it appears that the condemned persons had to carry the mobile horizontal part, the *patibulum*, to the place where they would be executed. The horror of this punishment was well known. Many Zealots, whose fanatical devotion to God did not fail to make an impression, had experienced it. So we do not have to see here an allusion to Jesus' cross, which would move the origin of the saying to the post-Easter period. Various rabbinic texts indicate a didactic and metaphorical use of the image of the cross.[63] The historical Jesus, then, could have said: "The person who does not carry their own cross cannot be my disciple." In the course of the saying's being transmitted in the church, it was natural for a relationship of it with Jesus' cross to be established.[64] The Master's authority, noticeable from the start in the "my" in "my disciple," needed to be stressed. Hence the appearance of the theme of following Christ, attested to by all the witnesses to this saying.[65]

If we compare the thrust of the saying here in v. 27 with that in 9:23, we notice a difference in tone. In 9:23, Luke stressed the continuing aspect of Christian existence, the constant sharing in Christ's sufferings, and concrete expressions, right down to the details of daily life (cf. the "daily," which he insisted on adding). Here it is a matter of the initial, overall, and permanent commitment, paraded in front of the crowds who had been attracted but were hesitant.

Verses 26 and 27, which v. 33 will supplement, tell what it takes to "be able to be his disciple."[66] Each party has a share in any given relationship. Nevertheless, the text does not consider here what Christ does (the Gospel often has occasion to speak of it; see chap. 15). It frankly states what is expected of the man or woman who wishes to follow Christ. "Being a disciple" means being taught by someone else, accepting to be trained by the Other. In order to accept being a disciple—that is the bottom line of these two sayings—one must agree to make a break with one's origin and expect a future that is counter to common sense.[67] If the past no longer is the determining factor for human beings and if the future is not what mobilizes their hopes, as it usually is, then what arises is an unexpected present existence. Is there not henceforth

---

60   See Mark 8:34 par. Matt 16:24 par. Luke 9:23; Luke 14:27 par. Matt 10:38; *Gos. Thom.* 55. Nevertheless, in Luke 17:33 and John 12:25, unlike in Mark 8:35 par. Matt 16:24 par. Luke 9:24, the christological references are absent.

61   See Martin Hengel, *Crucifixion in the Ancient World and the Folly of the Message of the Cross* (Philadelphia: Fortress, 1977) 10–13.

62   See the classic example of Alexander Jannaeus crucifying eight hundred Pharisees, given not without exaggeration by Josephus (*Ant.* 13.14.2 §380), or that of James and Simon, the sons of the Zealot Judas of Gaulanitis, who were crucified in the context of the uprising occasioned by the Roman occupation after the deposition of Archelaus (see Josephus *Ant.* 18.1.1 §4; 20.5.2 §102; also *Bell.* 2.8.1 §118 and Acts 5:37).

63   See Bultmann (*History*, 161 n. 1), who refers to *Gen. Rab.* 56.3 (36c): "'Abraham took the wood for the burnt offering and laid it on his son Isaac' (Gen 22:6). Just as one does who carries his cross on his shoulder" (his translation). See Jon D. Levenson, *The Death and Resurrection of the Beloved Son: The Transformation of Child Sacrifice in Judaism and Christi-

anity* (New Haven: Yale University Press, 1993) 104, 132. Other interpretations, such as that in Str-B (1:587) and that of Fletcher ("Condemned to Die," 162), argue that carrying one's cross was not a Jewish metaphor.

64   On the original meaning of the saying in Aramaic, the supposed errors of its translation into Greek, and its Christian misinterpretation, see Schwarz, "Der Nachfolgespruch Markus 8, 34bc Parr," 255–65. On the cross and its symbolism, see the first entries in the collection of Dinkler ("Jesu Wort vom Kreuztragen," 1–118).

65   On the Christianization of the saying, see Degenhardt, *Lukas*, 107–9.

66   On the theology of these two verses, see Seynaeve, "Exigences de la condition chrétienne," 69–72 (the majesty of Jesus, absolute detachment, and the walk with Christ to the cross); see Coulot, *Jésus et le disciple*, 43–45.

67   See Fletcher ("Condemned to Die," 164): "Let the disciple refuse himself; let him think constantly as one who feels the weight of the hateful beam across his back and knows himself condemned to die. This

some wisdom in reflecting before deciding to take such a step?

■ **28-30** A few preliminary detailed comments. In v. 28, the "for" ($\gamma\acute{\alpha}\rho$) serves as a link between the parables and the preceding sayings, following a logic that is not self-evident.[68] Phrases of the type "which of you . . . ?" are frequent in L and Q.[69] They create a unanimity of opinion among the hearers in order to persuade them better of the gospel truth that is to be discovered by analogy. The will of the builder is expressed by the translation "intending" (the article $\acute{o}$, found in many Greek manuscripts, should not, however, be retained[70]). The word $\pi\acute{v}\rho\gamma\sigma\varsigma$ has turned more than one commentator's hair white.[71] It can refer to either a wide or tall watchtower or a small structure built by a farmer for his protection. It can even be applied—but this meaning is contested—to a construction of another shape, for example, a barn (*Wirtschaftsgebäude*). As in the parable about the two houses (6:48), the plans provide for a "foundation" ($\vartheta\epsilon\mu\acute{\epsilon}\lambda\iota\sigma\nu$). It must, then, have been a rather ambitious project, at least for the man in this story, who probably did not have the means of the king in the second par-able.[72] I opt for a farmer who wants to build a "tower" in his vineyard for watchmen who will protect his farm workers, and where he can store his tools and his goods in a place where thieves and mice would not be able to get at them. And why not also a place for a wine press and a drying shed? And a wine cellar?[73] Luke was fond of the interrogative particle $\sigma\grave{v}\chi\acute{\iota}$, used in rhetorical questions expecting an affirmative answer.[74] The adverb $\pi\rho\hat{\omega}\tau\sigma\nu$ here has its chronological meaning, "first" (see, e.g., 4:22; 17:8; 24:26). The participle $\kappa\alpha\vartheta\acute{\iota}\sigma\alpha\varsigma$, which I have translated as "sit down," is probably one of the most important words in the parable. Moreover, it is found also in the second parable (v. 31). It allows us to picture the process that is in mind (reflection and calculations) and sets up a contrast with the verbs of movement in vv. 25-27. The verb $\psi\eta\phi\acute{\iota}\zeta\omega$ ("estimate," "count up," "reckon," "calculate") comes from the word $\psi\hat{\eta}\phi\sigma\varsigma$ ("pebble"); pebbles were originally used for counting (see Rev 13:18).[75] The word for "cost," $\delta\alpha\pi\acute{\alpha}\nu\eta$, was a common word but is not used elsewhere in the New Testament.[76] Before the words $\epsilon\grave{\iota}$ $\acute{\epsilon}\chi\epsilon\iota$ ("whether he has [= you have]") I supply an implicit "to see." After $\acute{\epsilon}\chi\epsilon\iota$ ("he

---

68 See above.

69 In Luke: 11:5; 14:28, 31; 15:4, 8; 17:7; in the Source of the logia: Luke 11:11 par. Matt 7:9; Luke 12:25 par. Matt 6:27; Luke 15:4 par. Matt 12:11; see n. 16 above.

70 In effect it has to do with an assumption, and not a description. The article before the participle is absent, for example, in 15:4 and 8; see Jülicher, *Gleichnisreden*, 2:202.

71 All the commentators mention it. In addition, see Jülicher (*Gleichnisreden*, 2:202), who, despite Horace *Carm.* 1.4.13 ("pauperum tabernas regumque turris" ["the shacks of the poor and the palaces of the kings"]), keeps the meaning of a personal tower of protection like that of Mark 12:1; see Derrett, "Nisi Dominus," 251–54; Spicq, *Lexicon*, 3:213–18; Jeremias, *Parables*, 196 n. 19; Str-B 1:868–69; Balz and Schneider, "$\pi\acute{v}\rho\gamma\sigma\varsigma$, etc.," *EDNT* 3:200.

72 Luke recalls the construction mentioned in 6:47-49 (parable of the two houses) and in 12:16-21 (parable of the foolish rich man who arranged the construction of new barns ($\alpha\pi\sigma\vartheta\hat{\eta}\kappa\alpha\iota$). He mentions the Tower of Siloam in 13:4. Unlike Mark 12:1 par. Matt 21:33, he does not mention a tower in the

vineyard in the parable of the murderous tenants in 20:9. I do not see an allusion here to the Tower of Babel (Gen 11:1-9). See the towers mentioned in Isa 5:2 (in the vineyard) and 2 Chr 26:9-10. In these three texts, the LXX associates (as in Luke 14:28) the verb $\sigma\grave{\iota}\kappa\sigma\delta\sigma\mu\acute{\epsilon}\omega$ ("to construct") with $\pi\acute{v}\rho\gamma\sigma\varsigma$ ("tower," in the singular and in the plural). Josephus of course often speaks of towers of defense, e.g., *Bell.* 5.4.3–4 §§156–83. One ought not forget the allegory of the tower in *Hermas Vis.* 3.2–8 and *Sim.* 8.2–9.30.

73 The choice of a tower is justified: it is an important construction but less essential than the residence would be for this man.

74 Cf. Sir 11:7: "Do not find fault before you investigate; examine first [$\pi\rho\hat{\omega}\tau\sigma\nu$] and then criticize."

75 G. Braumann, "$\psi\hat{\eta}\phi\sigma\varsigma$ $\kappa\tau\lambda$.," *TDNT* 9 (1974) 604–7. The English words "calculation" and "to calculate" derive from the Latin *calculus*, "pebble."

76 The verb $\delta\alpha\pi\alpha\nu\acute{\alpha}\omega$ ("to spend") is derived from $\delta\acute{\alpha}\pi\tau\omega$ ("to devour," "to tear up," "to waste"). It appears five times in the NT, including in 15:14.

77 I therefore disagree with the translations proposed both by BAGD, s.v. ("Vollendung"), and by Delebecque, 96 ("aller jusqu'au bout"). The word appears in Chrysippus, frg. 509, according to Hans von Arnim, *Stoicorum veterum fragmenta* (4 vols.;

has [= you have]"), I supply "enough," that is, the necessary money (cf. "enough money" in Moffatt and *Today's English Version/Good News Bible/Good News Translation*). The noun ἀπαρτισμός ("enterprise") suggests "adjustment" or "finishing touches" more than "completion."[77] It is concerned with the organization of the job and the layout of the construction itself. Everything needs to be coordinated: expenses with the owner's means, the work with the plans, the stages of construction in proper sequence, and finally the parts of the tower with each other. So I translate the expression by "see your job through to completion."

In 6:48 we encounter the same correct use of τίθημι ("lay") with θεμέλιον ("foundation")[78] as here in 14:29. What does μήποτε negate? Not θέντος ("[you] have laid") but ἄρξωνται ("will begin to"). So the words ἵνα μήποτε are to be taken together, meaning "otherwise."[79] The subordination is thus interrupted by two genitive absolutes, one of them positive, in the aorist (you have laid a foundation), and the other negative, in the present (you do not have enough to see your job through to completion). The verb ἰσχύω ("have the strength [to]") naturally suggests economic strength, "have the means (to)."[80] The idea of completion appears here only in the verb ἐκτελέω ("to bring to completion with implication of a job well done," "to finish").[81] The outcome is

that, in the countryside, people keep an eye on each other; the farmer's neighbors, the people in the village, had been watching his digging in the earth and laying a foundation. And they continued to watch (notice the present participle, θεωροῦντες, "who see it,"[82] and the choice of the verb, θεωρέω, "look at," "observe," rather than βλέπω, "see," or ὁράω, "notice," "witness"). Confronted with the cessation of work, they "begin to" (that is, continue to) ridicule. The spotlight is on the verb ἐμπαίζειν ("ridicule") by its being placed at the end of the sentence. Although the work stops, the mocking does not.[83] Thoughts turn to the seat of scoffers and to Ps 22 (21):7: "All who see me mock at me; they make mouths at me, they shake their heads" (*NRSV*). If the man in this story does not sit down and estimate the cost, he is doubly punished for his lack of foresight. Not only does he not have his tower, but he also has to be the butt of his neighbors' sarcastic remarks. In v. 30 we should notice the pejorative nuance of "this person," "that is the person who . . ." (οὗτος ὁ ἄνθρωπος) and the contrast between the beginning and the end, the initial power and the final powerlessness.

Here we have a story of what could happen, an example that no one wants to follow; a lesson whose persuasive force is obvious. It is, moreover, a story that has been very well crafted: its intention is set out at the outset ("intend-

---

Leipzig: Teubner, 1903) 2:164; frg. 808, according to Karlheinz Hülser, *Die Fragmente zur Dialektik der Stoiker* (4 vols.; Stuttgart: Frommann-Holzboog, 1987) 3:968; it also appears in Dionysius of Halicarnassus *Comp.* 24.2. It is a *hapax legomenon* in the NT. See Derrett, "Nisi Dominus," 248.

78   On this stage of construction, see my commentary at 6:47-48.

79   Luke consistently uses μήποτε as a subordinating conjunction. Here, on the other hand, is the primitive adverbial usage of this conjunction (μή negation and ποτέ indefinite adverb of time), which is not exactly synonymous with μή by reason of the indefinite nuance. Μήποτε in effect contains the nuance of "if ever" or "if perhaps" and expresses a sentiment of apprehension.

80   The verb ἰσχύω can have several meanings: "to have the force of," "to be strong," "to be in good health," "to have the means to," "to be in control," "to be worth" (especially for money) and even, coming close to δύναμαι, "to be able to"; see LSJ, s.v., and BAGD, s.v.

81   The two occurrences in 14:29-30 are the only ones in the NT. In the LXX, see Deut 32:45 (B = Codex Vaticanus); 2 Chr 4:5; 2 Macc 15:9 (for fighting). See BAGD, s.v.

82   The same form is used for the mockers in Ps 22 (21):8, which is cited later in this paragraph.

83   On ἐμπαίζω, see BAGD, s.v.; F. G. Untergassmair, "ἐμπαίζω etc.," *EDNT* 1:444–45. With the exception of our passage, the other NT uses relate to the mocking directed at Jesus (e.g., Luke 18:32; 22:63; 23:11, 36). The other verb for "to mock" is ἐκμυκτηρίζω, which is used in Ps 21:8 [22:8], cited in the text. We find the substantives ἐμπαιγμός ("mockery") in *Ps. Sol.* 2:11 and Heb 11:36; ἐμπαιγμονή ("mockery") in 2 Pet 3:3; and ἐμπαίκτης ("mocker") in 2 Pet 3:3 and Jude 18. The verb ἐμπαίζω first signifies "to play," "to gamble," then, more frequently, "to have fun at the expense of," "to laugh at," "to mock."

ing," θέλων); the foreseeable failure, at the end ("did not have the means to finish," οὐκ ἴσχυσεν ἐκτελέσαι). The project in question was a construction: the verb "build" appears in the beginning and at the end of the parable. In the beginning, the verb is in the aorist infinitive: the construction is considered to be an act whose completion is foreseen. At the end, it is in the present infinitive: it has not been possible either to continue or to complete the construction. We learn nothing from the observers' ridicule at the end (v. 30), but the ending does function as a reminder to us of what is important: a given space, the time available, from the beginning (ἀρχή, in ἄρχομαι, "begin") to the end (τέλος, in ἐκτελέω, "finish," "complete" [a job]); a free space, but only in the framework of what is possible. The person in the story must give thought to the matter, and use their reflection to estimate the cost. Besides the time available and the material goods, there is a third force that should not be neglected: the necessary taking stock, assessment, and calculation. To do that, one must sit down and take one's time. Wisdom lies in allowing for a moment before the beginning of the action, and in fitting in a stage between intention and action. Wisdom consists in sitting down (καθίσας) in order to reflect and write, and mentally and concretely to calculate the cost of the undertaking.[84]

I have called it a story, but it is especially a story cast in the form of a personalized question: "Which of you . . . ?" It is up to us to write a positive version of it in our lives.

Building is a distinctively human trait.[85] It is not the only one but is the most significant one. The Gospel offers each person a kind of building: becoming a "disciple" and "believing." In this way, Jesus, followed by tradition and the Gospel writer, encourages the listener

to be wise. Confronted with a project so serious and ambitious that it turns one's life upside down (cf. vv. 26-27), wisdom requires not only knowledge of whether one wants to carry through one's project to completion but also an assessment of whether one has the means to do so. This wisdom message is what is called for in the context of the journey to Jerusalem, marked by the prediction of the passion and the strict commitment of the disciples. It does not contradict, but rather complements, the Galilean prophetic message, the Messiah's urgent call offering salvation and inviting persons to follow him.

Even though the parables using the question "which of you?" often have God as the ultimate subject, I reject the interpretation that sees God behind the farmer and behind the king waging war.[86] That idea would then be that human beings would not surround themselves with so few precautions. Nor would God: he wants to complete the building of his reign and win his final battle. That is why he only takes on workers and soldiers ready to leave everything to serve him. Nor do I believe that there was a severe distortion of the meaning during the transmission of the parables. According to that view, the parables would have been told by Jesus in a theocentric sense, but would have been completely reinterpreted by either the author of L or Luke himself. Originally parables of confidence in God, they became parables of self-examination.

■ **31-32** The case of the king caught up in a war is told simply, but precisely.[87] The Greek, like the English, says that a king "goes out" (πορευόμενος) (see 1 Macc 5:39) against his enemy, that he "opposes" him (ὑπαντῆσαι),[88] or that his enemy "comes against him" (ἐρχομένῳ ἐπ' αὐτόν).[89] Συμβάλλω εἰς μάχειν is a common expression for "to join battle."[90] The Lukan expression "to wage

<hr />

84 Several exegetes think that the two demands, to reflect before deciding for Christ and to follow without delay, are incompatible. They think, therefore, that the call to follow immediately is authentic and the call to careful reflection is secondary, marked by the seriousness of philosophical engagement. In this context, two texts are regularly cited: Epictetus *Diss.* 3.15.8–13 and Philo *Abr.* 105–6.

85 According to Derrett ("Nisi Dominus," 243), the Jewish symbolism evokes the construction of a house for training in the Torah. For construction in the OT, see 2 Chr 2:5; Isa 28:16; Prov 24:3-6.

86 I see this proposed with more or less force by Moore, "Tower-Builder and the King," 528–37;

Hunzinger, "Unbekannte Gleichnisse"; Jarvis, "Expounding the Parables," 198; Derrett, "Nisi Dominus," 248–50; see n. 25 above.

87 Jülicher (*Gleichnisreden*, 2:202) thinks that, of the double parables, none surpasses this one in simplicity and clarity ("Schlichtheit und Durchsichtigkeit").

88 Συναντάω in the more ordinary sense of "to meet" is more common; see 1 Macc 4:29.

89 See 1 Macc 5:9 ("ready to come and fight against you").

90 See Josephus *Ant.* 12.4.9 §222; for συμβάλλω τινί for a debate, see Acts 17:18; for fighting, 1 Macc 4:34; 2 Macc 8:23; 14:17.

war (against)" (συμβαλεῖν εἰς πόλεμον), although less common, is perfectly understandable.[91] It simply has a larger situation in mind, not the battle of that day but the season's campaign.[92] Sending a delegation when the enemy approaches ("while the other is still far away," ἔτι αὐτοῦ πόρρω ὄντος!) is a reaction that everyone knows well.[93] It is the only reasonable way out in the case of obvious numerical inferiority. The expression ἐρωτάω τὰ πρὸς εἰρήνην ("ask for the terms of peace"[94]) belongs to diplomatic and military language and is more Semitic than Greek. It is a modest, elegant, discreet, and explicit way of announcing one's submission.[95] The incorporation of "thousands" of soldiers into an army was the

practice in various armies in antiquity, among the Persians, the Macedonians, and the Hebrews, for example.[96] The title χιλίαρχος, originally given to the "commander of a corps of a thousand soldiers," during Macedonian times designated superior officers; then, for a short while after the death of Alexander the Great, it was given to the officer who had the highest rank, just below the king. The term was also used as the Greek equivalent of the Roman "military tribune."[97] In Israel, the "thousands" were the troops corresponding to clans (see Num 1:16). In the *War Scroll* and the *Rule of the Community* (*Manual of Discipline*) discovered at Qumran,[98] we find reference to "thousands" and "hundreds," as well as to the leaders

---

91 We find the expression εἰς πόλεμον ("to make war," literally: "toward war") in 1 Macc 4:13; 5:39; 10:78; cf. Zech 14:2 LXX.

92 We find the same expression "with ten thousand men" in 1 Macc 4:29 (note that ἐν in the Semitic sense of "with" is exceptional in Luke). On this military vocabulary, see Plummer, 365; Jülicher, *Gleichnisreden*, 2:204–6; Lagrange, 411.

93 In another context, 19:14 uses the same expression for sending a delegation.

94 The text is uncertain; we find τὰ πρός, τὰ εἰς, πρός, εἰς, or nothing; see the apparatus of Nestle-Aland[26], 210; Fitzmyer, 2:1065–66; *New Testament in Greek*, 2:34.

95 On the subject of ἐρωτάω, we note the evolution of the primary meaning of "to ask," "to question," to the derived sense "to ask for," "to request," "to invite"; see 7:3 and 11:37. Much ink has been spilled over the expression ἐρωτάω τὰ πρὸς εἰρήνην (see 19:42; Acts 12:20). There is no exact Greek parallel (see Polybius 5.29.4). On the other hand, there is a Hebraic expression שׁאל לשׁלום, which is translated in the LXX as ἐρωτάω τὰ εἰς εἰρήνην (see Judg 18:15 [B = Codex Vaticanus], 1 Sam [1 Kgdms] 30:21 [with or without τά following the manuscripts]; 2 Sam [2 Kgdms] 8:10; 11:7; Ps 122 [121]:6; 1 Chr 18:10). In intertestamental literature see *T. Jud.* 9:7 (cf. 7:7). The expression does not have the same meaning everywhere; it could mean "to subdue," that is, "to ask for conditions of peace"—payment of tribute, or simple surrender, etc.; or "to greet," "to wish the well-being of someone," "to pay one's respects," for example, from one king to another king. In a context of war such as ours, it must have to do with the act of submission. 1 Maccabees 6:57-62 depicts an attempt at peace that ends badly. There is also the homage paid to King David

by Toi, king of Hamath, which signifies an act of allegiance (2 Sam [2 Kgdms] 8:9-12). Not only does Toi submit, but he also offers gifts to David. One also recalls the trouble that Herod Antipas had with his father-in-law Aretas, king of the Nabataeans. See Loisy, 389–90; Jülicher, *Gleichnisreden*, 2:205; Thackeray, "Study in the Parable of the Two Kings," 389–99; W. Foerster, "εἰρήνη κτλ.," *TDNT* 2 (1964) 400–417; Jeremias, *Parables*, 196 n. 20; Fitzmyer, 2:1065–66.

96 Argos and Athens each had, at one point, a company of a thousand men in active service. The Persians divided their armies into companies of six thousand, one thousand, and one hundred men. Israel had units of a thousand men led by a commanding officer (see 1 Sam [1 Kgdms] 17:18 and 18:33). If the Roman legion numbered five or six thousand men and the cohort around four hundred eighty, auxiliary troops were divided into cohorts of a thousand men beginning in the time of Nero. The same was true of the Pretorian guard, of the special troops installed in Rome (*equites singulares Augusti*), and of isolated cohorts stationed in various places. See E. Lammert and F. Lammert, "Kriegskunst," PW 11 (1922) 1831–32; C. G. Brandis, "Chiliarchos," PW 3 (1899) 2275–76; W. H. Mare, "Armor, arms," in Merrill C. Tenney, ed., *Zondervan Pictorial Encyclopedia of the Bible* (5 vols.; Grand Rapids: Zondervan, 1975) 1:314; D. Kennedy, "Roman Army," *ABD* 5:789–92.

97 See BAGD, s.v.

98 See 1QM 3.16-17; 4:1; 1QS 2.21 (about organization and community); see Dupont-Sommer and Philonenko, *Écrits intertestamentaires*, 1876.

of thousands and the leaders of hundreds. The heavenly armies, following contemporary Jewish beliefs, also were organized by thousands (see Rev 5:11).

The example has in mind not the siege of a city but the imminent confrontation between two armies. The king in the story, like the farmer just mentioned, was going first to sit down, then to deliberate ("will consider," $\beta ov\lambda εύσεται$).[99] The issue under discussion was not on the level of will, but of capability ("whether he is able," $εἰ$ $δυνατός ἐστιν$). He had numbers against him (he was outnumbered two to one), but there might have been other arguments to take into consideration.[100] If he was not unreasonable, he was going to make his decision on the basis of the best of the possibilities available to him. As may be seen, this second example is a little different from the first one. While the farmer would have done well to take time to reflect before breaking ground, the king had to take the proper steps in the course of the war, just before the decisive battle. Moreover, while the builder did his reflecting on his own, the king was surrounded by advisors.

The lesson of the second example is clear: whoever wants to "go out" with Christ against God's enemies must do so wisely. Power without wisdom is useless. For neither power nor reflection is without limits. Faith is lived out on earth and not in heaven. It factors in deliberation and presupposes other persons' advice. What is absolute and what is contingent coexist. And what lies in wait for Jesus' disciples is formidable.

■ **33** At the point where the parables invite readers to take stock of the means at their disposal to find out what their capacities are and take the measure of them, v. 33 concludes ("so therefore," $ovτως ovν$) paradoxically with an order of renunciation:[101] the farmer had to count his pennies; the king, his troops. In order to imitate them, Lukan Christians needed to get rid of their false securities. The "possessions"[102] that were such a concern to the Gospel writer are false supports. They had to be bid farewell: $ἀποτάσσομαι$ means "take leave of," "say goodbye to," in the literal sense; "renounce," "give up," in the figurative sense.[103] Beginning with the beatitudes and the woes (6:20, 24), Luke had unmasked the pernicious power of money, the false confidence attributed to it. At the end of the parable of the foolish rich man (12:21), he had contrasted riches directed toward God and riches for oneself. At the conclusion of the pericope about worries (12:33-34), he had joined the quest of the kingdom of God to the giving up of one's possessions. There is, then, an awesome consistency to the radicalism of Luke's Gospel message: the power of "being Jesus' disciple" (vv. 26, 27, 33) depends, on the human end, on giving up power, whether the power of money, of circumstances of birth, of religious affiliation, or of weapons. The Gospel is as clear as springwater, as simple as the language of children. Limiting the application of the requirement to certain persons (the leaders of the community or an ascetic elite) or to a period of time (the generation of the apostles), or transforming it into a simple provision for leaving everything or into a choice of the single priority, is to trouble this clear water and this simple language.[104] The problem is theological and ethical, rather than exegetical. Can we believe that God, the God of Lukan

---

99 The present $\beta ov\lambda εύεται$ ("deliberates"), which corresponds to the present $ἐρωτάω$ ("asks") in v. 32, is attested by the vast majority of Byzantine manuscripts, several uncials, and a good number of manuscripts in the Latin tradition. I have retained the future because of the weight of the Bodmer papyrus ($\mathfrak{P}^{75}$), Sinaiticus (א), and Vaticanus (B).

100 1 Maccabees 4:28-35 describes a victory despite an overwhelming numerical disadvantage (the ratio is ten thousand men against sixty thousand infantrymen and five thousand cavalry).

101 On v. 33, see principally Dupont ("Renoncer") and Schmidt ("Burden, Barrier, Blasphemy," 171–89), who both resist spiritualizing the need. Lagrange (412) and some others note the tension, the *inconcinnitas* as they said then, between vv. 28-32 and v. 33, which is supposed to draw a conclusion. For

Lagrange, one has to explain it at the level of Jesus, who is enigmatic, and not of Luke, reinterpreting traditions.

102 On $τὰ ὑπάρχοντα$ ("goods"), see 8:3; 11:21; 12:15, 33; 16:1; 19:8; Acts 4:3; Dupont, "Renoncer," 1086; Del Verme, *Comunione*; Johnson, *Possessions*; Seccombe, *Possessions*; Bovon, *Theologian*, 442–48.

103 See 9:61; Acts 18:18 ("to take leave"); Philo *Leg. all.* 3.142–45; *Deus* 147–51; Jülicher, *Gleichnisreden*, 2:206; Degenhardt, *Lukas*, 111–12; Brown, *Apostasy*, 104–5; Schmidt, "Burden, Barrier, Blasphemy," 182.

104 See Dupont, "Renoncer," 1085–87.

mercy, really wills this extravagant renunciation? Must we follow the order and complicate the social task of our government officials by a radical Christian stance, these officials who are already confronted with the misery of the Third World and the rise of the Fourth World?

■ **34-35a** Luke weaves in here, at the end of the conclusion, the passage about salt. The "therefore" (οὖν) of v. 34 has the same logical function as the one in v. 33;[105] it links up with what precedes. On the one hand, the conclusion of v. 33 stresses the necessity of being totally devoted to Christ and not at all any more to this world—to put it clearly, giving up everything in order to become a disciple. On the other hand, vv. 34-35 envisage the long-term risks.[106] Becoming a disciple is not enough; one must remain one. Relapsing, which is a function of human responsibility, leads to rejection, which is a function of the divine will.

The noun phrase "salt, therefore, is good" (rather than "salt is something good") was borrowed from Mark. In the Lukan context, it means that "being a disciple" is a good thing, in the full sense that the adjective καλός ("good") and the adverb καλῶς ("well") assumed on the lips of Christians: that is, in accordance with God's will, in harmony with what is ultimately good, in symmetry with the biblical promises, and in controversy with the dominant Jewish interpretation.[107]

Luke next picks up on the text of Q (cf. the parallel in Matt 5:13). If we do not pay attention to the reality of nature,[108] there is no problem in the text. We are dealing with a rhetorical question that presupposes a negative answer: if even salt is no longer what it was, how can its flavor be restored? The answer: it is impossible. It would be as difficult as bringing a dead person back to life,

because salt, like human beings, has but one life. The subject of the passive verb "will be prepared," "will be seasoned," ἀρτυθήσεται, is "salt" ("with what will *it* be seasoned?" that is, "with what will one season *it*?").[109] The use of the active in Mark ("with what will you season it?") favors this interpretation.

Salt is no longer salt! Disciples who have been able to estimate their costs (vv. 28-32), who have given up their own people, their possessions and themselves (vv. 26, 33), who have prepared themselves for martyrdom (v. 27), and who are therefore capable of being disciples (vv. 26, 27, and 33), "good" disciples, just as salt is good—if these disciples cease being what they have chosen to be, they are "finished" beings. If they have lost their "edge," the wisdom of the gospel, they are no longer good for anything. The adjective εὔθετος ("well-placed," "suitable," "usable," "fit"),[110] which was used in 9:62, is found also here: the disciples who cease to be disciples, salt without salt, are like a foolish person who, instead of looking ahead toward the kingdom of God, looks backwards to the fleshpots of the Egyptians (see 9:62; Phil 3:13; Exod 16:3). They are not good, not "fit"(εὔθετος), for anything except ending up outside. "Be thrown outside" is an apocalyptic and disciplinary way of saying: be cast into Gehenna or excommunicated.[111] Matthew states: "it is no longer good for anything, but is thrown out and trampled under foot" (*NRSV*). Luke—whence does he get these expressions?—says: "It is fit neither for the soil nor for the manure pile; it is thrown away." Luke states that if salt no longer has its properties, it of necessity loses all its efficacy, therefore its usefulness. It is the same with the disciples who would no longer be disciples, who would have lost that taste, that inner order, that capacity,

---

105 See Carlston, *Triple Tradition*, 87. Another interpretation of this οὖν ("therefore") is given in Plummer, 366 (οὖν might recall other moments when the saying was also pronounced).

106 Schweizer (160) argues for the following sense: a disciple who is not a disciple through and through is more useless than an unbeliever. For several commentators, including Cullmann ("Que signifie le sel dans la parabole de Jésus?" 36–43), the quality that each disciple must retain is his or her fortitude in suffering.

107 See Bovon, *L'oeuvre*, 151–52.

108 See below.

109 See Godet, 2:208. The choice of the verb comes

from Mark, and that of the voice comes from Q. On this verb ἀρτύω, see Marshall, 595. One finds this verb for seasoning fish and meat in Artemidorus of Ephesus *Oneirocrit.* 2.18; the word "salt" is associated with this verb in Col 4:6; see Clement of Alexandria *Strom.* 2.14.61.

110 See the commentary above on 9:62.

111 See 13:28; 20:12, 15; Matt 22:13; John 6:37; 9:34; 12:31; 3 John 10; see F. Annen, "ἐκβάλλω etc.," *EDNT* 1:405–6.

and that wisdom.[112] In the present context, it can only be a matter of the disciples. The same must have been true in the tradition. I do not believe that the saying about salt ever concerned an Israel threatened by unfaithfulness.[113]

In antiquity,[114] salt had a double function: preserving food and seasoning dishes. For an ancient orator or author, that image conjured up the preservation of what was good as much as its seasoning.[115] That was true in particular for Luke, who showed concern for duration, both in the sense of continuity of doctrine (cf. 5:39) and perseverance in the faith (cf. 18:8).

It appears that it is chemically impossible for salt to lose its taste. R. Joshua ben Hananiah, perhaps attacking the Gospel, is alleged to have said that salt can no more lose its flavor than a mule can give birth to offspring (*b. Bek.* 8b).[116] What was Jesus' meaning? Four answers can be given to that question:[117] (1) Jesus was alluding to a local situation: in Palestine. Salt was obtained from the Dead Sea by a process of evaporation, by which blocks made of a mixture of salt crystals and carnallite were extracted. In case there was too great a proportion of carnallite as a result of bad extraction, the "salt"—or what was called "salt"[118]—did not salt. (2) Another explanation is that the salt in question here sometimes referred to blocks used as catalysts for stoves. Over time,

they lost their effectiveness and were thrown away. (3) In cooking, what was used was pure salt, or else salt with condiments. In the latter case, the seasoned salt, called ἅλες ἡδυσμένοι, could lose its taste and cease to create just the right balance with condiments. It became contemptible. (4) Finally, the oldest and, in my opinion, the best explanation is that Jesus used an exaggerated example. Popular wisdom knew that salt never loses its taste. Jesus suggested imagining the impossible (note the "even," καί: "if even salt . . ."): salt that does not salt, desalinated salt. Well, in that case it is no longer good for anything. The damage cannot be repaired; it is irreversible.

What did Luke have in mind in using the words "soil" and "manure"?[119] Was it the ignorance of a city dweller who believed that salt can be used as fertilizer? Or the awkwardness of an author who took over a saying that had been badly translated from Aramaic into Greek (the original would have read: "neither as condiment, nor as fertilizer")?[120] Luke must have known that salt thrown on the ground was a sign of a curse: the Israelites sowed salt on the conquered city of Shechem and condemned it to sterility.[121] I confess that I do not understand v. 35a.

The final enigma is the use of the verb μωραίνω.[122] Since μωρός seems to sometimes literally mean "flat," "insipid," I suppose that the verb μωραίνω, in the pas-

---

112 Taste is contained in the word ἅλας ("salt") and in the verb ἀρτύω ("to arrange," "to season"); interior order is indicated by the same verb ἀρτύω, aptitude by the adjective εὔθετος ("useful," "suitable"), and folly by the verb μωραίνω ("to become dull," "to make tasteless").

113 Contra Dodd (*Parables*, 103–6) and Schulz (*Q*, 471–72). Regarding the comparison of the disciple to salt, Godet writes, "C'est de meme un beau role que celui du disciple de Christ exerçant, par l'âpre et austere saveur de l'Évangile don't il est pénétré, une action purifiante et vivifiante sur la vie fade ou souillée de l'humanité qui l'entoure" (2:209).

114 The Gospels use the newer form τὸ ἅλας (genitive ἅλατος). The classical term is ὁ ἅλς (genitive ἁλός). On the importance of salt for humans, see Sir 39:26; Job 6:6; J. A. E. van Dodewaard and J. Argaud, "Sel," *DEB*, 1185–86.

115 For the use that evokes flavor, see Col 4:6.

116 See Str-B 1:236.

117 For helpful explanations, see Cullmann, "Que signifie le sel dans la parabole de Jésus?" 37–40;

Carlston, *Triple Tradition*, 88; Bultmann, *Geschichte, Ergänzungsheft* 37 (discussion of several commentators on the body of questions related to these two verses).

118 The first meaning of the word ἅλς is "block of salt," "rock of salt."

119 See Marshall, 596–97.

120 See Perles, "Zwei Übersetzungsfehler," 96: behind the word γή is the Aramaic verb חבל ("to season"), which the translator, out of ignorance, took for the Hebrew word חֵבֶל ("land"), often translated as γή ("land," "earth") in the LXX, e.g., Isa 14:21. The "earth" and the "dunghill" are used together in 1 Sam [1Kgdms] 2:8 = Ps 113 (112):7 to designate one who is lowly and humble. See Epictetus *Diss.* 2.4.4–7.

121 See Judg 9:45; and M. Weippert, "Salz," in Kurt Galling, ed., *Biblisches Reallexikon* (Tübingen: Mohr Siebeck, 1977) 265.

122 See Marshall (595), who proposes a translation error; he thinks of the Hebrew verb תפל, which first means "to be without flavor" (Job 6:6) and can also mean "to be shocking," or even "to be mad"

sive, could be understood in the sense of "become flat," "lose its taste." Luke used the figurative sense of the saying: "to become foolish," that is, lose that wisdom of the gospel of which the apostle Paul spoke in 1 Cor 1:18-25.

■ **35b** Luke's Jesus addressed a final imperative to his listeners/readers. He made clear to them that they had to pay the closest attention possible. While the risk is great, so is the promise. Let the disciples' decision be commensurate with their master's confidence.

History of Interpretation

The path that commentators have followed in interpreting these verses through the centuries of the history of the church has been full of embarrassments and temptations. Tertullian still followed in Luke's path. He found it normal for a convinced Christian to be confronted with deprivation and suffering. The parable of the builder served as a warning to such a Christian that reflection was a necessary prelude to commitment. After making the big decision, it would be worthless to turn back (Luke 9:62 and Matt 6:24 par. Luke 16:13 were quoted) and complain. "If you wish to be the Lord's disciple, it is necessary you "take your cross, and follow the Lord:" *your cross*; that is, your own *straights* and *tortures*, or your *body* only, which is after the manner of a *cross*. Parents, wives, children, will have to be left behind, for God's sake" (*Idol.* 12.1-3, here 2).

According to Cyril of Alexandria (*Hom. in Luc.* 105),[123] it would be a mistake to follow the literal sense, an error that the parallel in Matthew invites us not to commit. We should prefer God to the human beings that are dearest to us. It is to him that the greatest honor redounds. We must turn away from honors when God calls us and strive for the blessings to come.

The order to "hate," then, requires an interpretation

that would make it compatible with the command to love.[124] Citing Gregory the Great (*Hom euang.* 37.1–2),[125] the Venerable Bede attempted to reconcile love and hate (*In Luc.* 4.2025–26). There is a hate that draws on love rather than resentment, as is suggested by the indication to hate oneself. That hate with which we must first hate ourselves cannot concern our persons, but the carnal desires that thwart the salvation of our souls. To put it simply, what we must hate is not other people, or even ourselves, but the evil that is in them and in us. "So then, when these things have been spurned, we are led in the direction of what is best, as if we were arriving at love through hate" (2043–44).

The two parables succeeded in eliciting ethical and allegorical interpretations that were in no way mutually exclusive. This is how the *Glossa ordinaria* summarizes in one sentence the ethical meaning it finds in vv. 26-27 and vv. 28-32: "After the Lord had given those who had been following him to Jerusalem wonderful precepts concerning contempt for the world and rejection of the body, he put forward a precept concerning perseverance, for which patience with humility are necessary."[126] Allegory could, with a joyful heart, have a field day: building a tower is developing virtue; the mockers are the demons; the king is God as judge, whom one must get ready to face on the day of the last judgment, etc. We may once again quote the *Glossa ordinaria*: "In order to be able to implore the severe judge for peace, we must send our tears, our good works, and our pious sentiments on ahead of us, as ambassadors."[127]

As the Reformer Calvin knew well, thousands of men and women have taken these sayings (vv. 26-27) literally, leaving the world and abandoning those closest to them. Somewhat facilely, he reproached them for their naïveté in wanting to be monks.[128] Even in our day, the monastic life still establishes a separation between monks

---

(Jer 23:13). The original translator of Q must have retained the first sense, as did Mark. He unfortunately opted for the second. On μωραίνω, see Spicq, *Lexicon*, 2:536–41.

123 See Payne Smith, *Cyril*, 2:490–93.

124 In his *Book of Sentences*, Prosper of Aquitane, as we know, draws on the works of Augustine. We read there the following: "sic diligendi sunt homines, ut eorum non diligamus errores, quia aliud est amare quod facti sunt, aliud odisse quod faciunt" ("human beings must be loved in such a way that their faults

are not loved, because it is one thing to love the fact that they have been created, and another to hate what they do"). This sentence, which is not a literal citation, draws from a passage from the *Enarrations in Psalmos*, Ps 100:5. It is taken up, by way of Luke 14:26, by Bonaventure *Comm. Luke* 14.53, 2.1374.

125 *PL* 76:1275–76.

126 *Glossa ordinaria*, Luke 14:28.

127 Ibid.

128 Calvin, *Harmony*, 1:312.

and the world (the famous *clausura* of the convents) and regulates the minimal contact they are authorized to have with their families. These men and women are a reminder to other humans of the radical gospel requirement. Moreover, it is that aspect that impressed Zwingli:[129] the gospel requires obedience not just in words but also in deeds.[130]

Conclusion

Luke has pursued a double objective here. As an author, he meant to bring a particular touch to the portrait that he was painting: Jesus, prophet and wise man, Messiah on a journey to his passion, conveyed to the crowds a logical and metaphorical teaching on the only way to become his disciple. As missionary and pastor, the Gospel writer encouraged his readers not to be satisfied with a reading that would distract them. "Let anyone with ears to hear listen!" (v. 35b). This move from an agreeable knowledge to a real approval represents the decisive step that the contemporary crowds (v. 25), and then readers today, are invited to take.

The two parables (vv. 28-32) encourage everyone to realize how costly the enterprise is. This enterprise is on the level of the banquet to which everyone is invited (14:15-24). On the one hand, we have the absolute requirement (vv. 25-35); on the other (vv. 15-24), the absolute gift. Although the requirement, clearly expressed (vv. 26, 27, 33), is radical, it does not serve to make a selection or favor the courageous. It corresponds to an inner necessity. God does not need saints; he

needs supporters. This passage expects all to decide to belong to Christ. As salt is salt or is nothing (vv. 34-35), it is a matter here of unwavering confidence. Doctrinal weakness would be a lukewarm or hesitant faith; moral weakness, a compromising attitude and insufficient perseverance.

Can we be unfailing? In response to that question, Luke completed the portrait of Jesus that he was painting. And the reader will discover that the painter's model himself left his family at the beginning of his ministry (v. 26) and carried his cross at the end of his journey (v. 27). The temptations (4:1-13) had made it possible to take the measure of the stakes and to estimate the cost of the commitment. The response is ambiguous, with two senses, neither of which excludes the other. The first sense is this: since the readers are not Christ, they are invited to locate themselves, to take stock of their possessions and appraise their means. That way they will not fall into the trap of improperly identifying themselves with Christ, which would, in the long run, prove to be destructive. The second sense is that, since Christ, as Son of God, has received the Spirit and the Word, they are available to him so that human beings can make decisions and not get discouraged. Christians are thus involved in a relationship, an interrelational becoming. For that reason they accept their responsibilities, including necessary separations, and make their possessions and their gifts available to others. According to Luke, Jesus Christ is thus the Savior and the model for all believers.

---

129 Zwingli, *Annotationes*, 640.
130 Bengel (*Gnomon*, 1:361) presents, regarding v. 26, an intelligent reflection on hatred. He describes a hatred utterly bereft of bitterness of someone who is disgusted with himself or herself and wants for every creature subjected to vanity, saved as he is by God and heavenly good by a detailed knowledge, a taste of and nostalgia for God.

(15:1-2)

Bibliography

Adam, A., "Gnostische Züge in der patristischen Exegese von Lk 15," in F. L. Cross, ed., *Studia evangelica*, vols. 2–3: *Papers presented to the Second International Congress on New Testament Studies held at Christ Church, Oxford, 1961* (TU 88; Berlin: Akademie-Verlag, 1964) 299–305.

Bailey, Kenneth E., *Finding the Lost: Cultural Keys to Luke 15* (Concordia Scholarship Today; St. Louis: Concordia, 1992).

Idem, *Poet and Peasant; and, Through Peasant Eyes: A Literary-Cultural Approach to the Parables in Luke* (combined ed.; Grand Rapids: Eerdmans, 1983) 142–206.

Idem, "Psalm 23 and Luke 15: A Vision Expanded," *IBS* 12 (1990) 54–71.

Barth, Carola, *Die Interpretation des Neuen Testaments in der valentinianischen Gnosis* (TU 37; Leipzig: Hinrichs, 1911) 60–61.

Bartolomé, Juan J., "Comer en común: Una costumbre típica de Jesús y su proprio comentario (Lc 15)," *Sal* 44 (1982) 669–712.

Idem, "Συνεσθίειν en la obra lucana (Lc 15,2; Hch 10,41;11,3): A propósito de una tesis sobre la escencia del Cristianismo," *Sal* 46 (1984) 269–88.

Bonnard, Pierre, "Approche historico-critique de Lc 15," *CBFV* 12 (1973) 25–37; reprinted in idem, *Anamnesis: Recherches sur le Nouveau Testament* (CRThPh 3; Geneva: Revue de théologie et de philosophie, 1980) 93–103.

Bovon, François, "The Parable of the Prodigal Son (Luke 15:11-32): First Reading," in Bovon and Rouiller, *Exegesis*, 43–73.

Bovon and Rouiller, *Exegesis*.

Braun, Herbert, *Qumran und das Neue Testament* (2 vols.; Tübingen: Mohr Siebeck, 1966) 1:90.

Cantinat, Jean, "Les paraboles de la miséricorde (Lc 15,1-32)," *NRTh* 77 (1955) 246–64.

Dodd, Charles H., *The Parables of the Kingdom* (London: Nisbet, 1935) 89–90 and passim.

Donahue, *Gospel in Parable*, 146–62.

Dupont, Jacques, "Réjouissez-vous avec moi! Lc 15,1-32," *AsSeign* 55 (1954) 70–79.

Entrevernes, Groupe d', *Signs and Parables: Semiotics and Gospel Texts* (trans. G. Phillips; Pittsburgh: Pickwick, 1978) 121–83.

Farmer, William R., "Notes on a Literary and Form-Critical Analysis of Some of the Synoptic Material Peculiar to Luke," *NTS* 8 (1961–62) 301–16.

Fiedler, Peter, *Jesus und die Sünder* (BBET 3; Frankfurt am Main: Peter Lang, 1976) 148–72.

Giblin, Charles H., "Structural and Theological Considerations on Lk 15," *CBQ* 24 (1962) 15–31.

Goppelt, Leonhard, *Theologie des Neuen Testaments*, vol. 1: *Jesu Wirken in seiner theologischen Bedeutung* (GTL; Göttingen: Vandenhoeck & Ruprecht, 1975) 177–85.

Grasset, G., "Les 99 et le fils aîné," *PenCath* 232–33 (1988) 77–85.

Heininger, *Metaphorik*, 140–66.

Hofer, Peter, *Untersuchungen zur literarischen Gestalt und kompositorischen Einordnung von Lk 15,1-32* (Salzburg, 1976).

Jeremias, Joachim, "Tradition und Redaktion in Lk 15," *ZNW* 62 (1971) 172–89.

Jülicher, *Gleichnisreden*, 2:314–65.

Kahlefeld, *Paraboles*, 2:17–22, 35–43.

Klein, Hans, *Barmherzigkeit gegenüber den Elenden und Geächteten: Studien zur Botschaft des lukanischen Sondergutes* (BThSt 10; Neukirchen-Vluyn: Neukirchener Verlag, 1987) 48–56.

Kossen, Hendrik B., "Quelques remarques sur l'ordre des paraboles dans Lc 15 et sur la structure de Mt 18,8-14," *NovT* 1 (1956) 75–80.

Krüger, René, "La sustitución del tener por el ser: Lectura semiótica de Lc 15,1-32," *RevistB* 49 (1987) 65–97.

Lambrecht, *Once More Astonished*, 24–56.

Landau, R., "Vom gewinnenden Vater (Lk 15,11-32)," *ThBei* 22 (1991) 1–6.

Linnemann, *Parables*, 65–81.

Mánek, *Gleichnisse*, 51–53, 98–104.

Meynet, Roland, "Deux paraboles parallèles: Analyse 'rhétorique' de Lc 15,1-32," *AnPh* 2 (1981) 89–105.

Neale, David A., *"None but the Sinners": Religious Categories in the Gospel of Luke* (JSNTSup 58; Sheffield: JSOT Press, 1991) 100, 151, 154–64, 188.

Pirot, Jean, *Paraboles et allégories évangéliques: La pensée de Jésus, les commentaires patristiques* (Paris: Lethielleux, 1949) 250–98, 473–99.

Ramaroson, Léonard, "Le cœur du troisième Evangile: Lc 15," *Bib* 60 (1979) 348–60.

Ramsey, George W., "Plots, Gaps, and Ambiguity in Lk 15," *PRSt* 17 (1990) 33–42.

Rasco, E., "Les paraboles de Lc 15, une invitation à la joie de Dieu dans le Christ," in I. de la Potterie, ed., *De Jésus aux Evangiles: Tradition et Rédaction dans les Évangiles synoptiques* (BETL 25; Gembloux: Duculot, 1967) 165–83.

Réau, Louis, *Iconographie de l'art chrétien*, vol. 2: *Iconographie de la Bible* (2 vols.; Paris: Presses universitaires de France, 1957) 2:333–39.

Sanders, E. P., "Jesus and the Sinners," *JSNT* 19 (1983) 5–36.

Scott, Bernard B., *Hear Then the Parable: A Commentary on the Parables of Jesus* (Minneapolis: Fortress, 1989) 99–125, 129, 149, 223, 308–13, 407–17.

Siniscalco, Paolo, *Mito e storia della salvezza: Ricerche sulle piu antiche interpretazioni di alcune parabole evangeliche* (Filologia classica e glottologia 5; Turin: Giappichelli, 1971).

Tolbert, *Perspectives*, 55–57, 94–114, 126 n.12, and passim.

Trilling, Wolfgang, *Christusverkündigung in den synoptischen Evangelien: Beispiele gattungsgemässer Auslegung* (Biblische Handbibliothek 4; Munich: Kösel, 1969) 105–19.

Völkel, Martin. "Freund der Zöllner und Sünder," *ZNW* 69 (1978) 1–10.

Waelkens, Robert, "L'analyse structurale des paraboles: Deux essais: Lc 15,1-32 et Mt 13,44-46," *RThL* 8 (1977) 160–78.

Weder, *Gleichnisse*, 168–77, 252–62.

Welzen, P. H. M., "Beschrijving van de methode," in B. van Iersel et al., eds., *Parabelverhalen in Lucas: Van semiotiek naar pragmatiek* (TFT Studies 8; Tilburg: Tilburg University Press, 1987) 1–21.

Idem, *Lucas, evangelist van gemeenschap: Een onderzoek naar het pragmatisch effect van Lc 15,1—17,10* (Diss., Nijmegen, 1986).

1/ **All the tax collectors and sinners kept approaching him to listen to him. 2/ And the Pharisees and the scribes were grumbling, saying, "This fellow welcomes sinners and eats with them."**

Chapter 15 starts out with a short scene that makes a distinction between two groups. One of these groups lodges a complaint against Jesus, namely, that he has shared meals with the other group. The three parables that follow constitute a single speech, the Master's apologetic and didactic retort; in v. 3 Luke uses the singular "this parable," "this parabolic speech." The unity of this defense is evident: finding again what has been lost gives rise to legitimate joy. Eating with others (v. 2) must therefore be related to the act of finding again what was lost (vv. 6, 9, 24, and 32). We should remember that a banquet scene constituted the essential part of the preceding chapter (14:1-24) and confirms the importance of meals, along with the scene related to the journey (14:25). Even if readers read the three parables of mercy and forgiveness as a single unit, they should be careful to note what distinguishes each one with respect to both form and content:[1] the first two are twin parables illustrating searching, whereas the third, which is much more developed, omits any element of search on the part of the father, thereby giving a more dramatic turn to the lot of the son. Furthermore, this last parable focuses, in its conclusion, on the other son, whose recriminations— note the subtle inclusion—recall the grumbling on the part of Jesus' adversaries in the beginning of the chapter. Luke 15 displays another element of imbalance: the preponderant place given over to the speech (vv. 3-32) as over against the extremely condensed description of the scene (vv. 1-2). In chap. 16, Jesus will continue to speak but to a different audience. From there on it will be his disciples who will be listening to his words. That will continue to hold true for chap. 17.

Analysis

We would do well to look back as far as chap. 13 in order to find a structure analogous to the one in chap. 15.[2] What corresponds to the initial situation in both of these chapters (13:1 par. 15:1-2) is a double, symmetrical, illustration that takes the form of a question using the same Greek coordinating conjunction, $\ddot{\eta}$ (13:2-5 par. 15:3-10), which is followed by a more developed parable (13:6-9 par. 15:11-32). Each time the orator draws a lesson from the illustration he has offered, introducing it by "I tell you" (13:3, 5 par. 15:7, 10). We should, however, note one difference: the passage in chap. 13 with that structure is three or four times shorter than chap. 15. The kinship of the two passages is nevertheless significant and calls for

---

1   On these distinctions, see Waelkens, "Analyse," 164–65.

2   See Farmer, "Notes," 305–6; followed by Dupont, "Réjouissez-vous," 74.

an explanation. Luke presents Jesus as a teacher throughout the journey narrative that takes him from Galilee to Jerusalem. Certain teachings take the oratorical style as their starting point and take on the form of a revelation or an exhortation. Others, such as the passages we have been examining, serve as reactions to puzzling or offending situations. In those cases, in Luke's depiction, Jesus comes off as a commentator or a lawyer.

The rhetoric of antiquity had a fondness for resolving such cases. If the little composition in chap. 13 called for conversion as a top priority, the one in chap. 15 invites us, at a different, higher level of interpretation, not to become irritated by other people's conversions, however despicable those persons might be. A reading of these two passages leads to the conclusion that what is called for on Jesus' part is more than a single response or argument. To prove our point, we will need to run the risk of repeating our line of reasoning, obviously in such a way as to avoid being monotonous, and then deepen it. The parable of the drachma repeats the parable of the lost sheep, and the parable of the prodigal son enlarges the perspective. This enlargement produces an unexpected result. It does not dilute the solution of the problem in a demobilizing generalization but brings together the subjectivity common to those who ask questions: the older son grumbles (vv. 28-30), as do the Pharisees and the scribes (v. 2). What is more, the text ends without our knowing if this son is going to take part in the celebration. In his teaching Jesus has dealt on the objective level; he leaves it up to his listeners to make the appropriate subjective response.[3]

What is involved in chap. 15 is conversion, just as it was in chap. 13. This conversion is obviously that of sinners but also of righteous persons, and it involves the bringing together of sinners who have repented and righteous persons, that is to say, the entire flock, as well as the reunion of the money with its owner, and the reuniting of the family. We might therefore ask if the structure of the chapter is not inspired by a biblical model centered on the theme of God's people. The models that have been suggested are Psalm 23[4] and especially Jeremiah 31. Long ago, commentators made the connection between the prodigal son and Jer 31:18-20 (Ephraim, the beloved son, who, after having distanced himself, wants to come back to God, whose paternal heart is stirred).[5] More recently, connections have been made between the lost sheep and Jer 31:10-14 (he who scattered [the people of] Israel will gather them together again and will watch over them as a shepherd watches over his flock) and, less obviously, the lost drachma and Jer 31:15-17 (Rachel, a woman, weeps for her children and the Lord promises her a reward—money, that is, for her work).[6] Luke's quoting or alluding to Scripture is not always evident. Since there is no explicit quotation of Scripture here, I find it more probable that he is drawing on a general symbolism, that of the flock or the family, than that he is making use of a specific passage. If such be the case, any reading inherited from pietism that emphasizes the individual might well be anachronistic. But we should not get ahead of ourselves by going into a detailed exegesis of the passage at this point and neglect the attention given to the single sheep, which represents the single sinner who repents. There are many advantages to the parabolic language. It stirs the reader's imagination and encourages the discovering of new meanings in the text. Readers may concentrate their attention on either the family[7] or on each one of its members.[8] No angle of approach is out of bounds. To this subjective variety of approaches we should add

---

3 Regarding the absence of a conclusion (Jesus takes the same position toward the Pharisees that the father takes in opposition to the elder son), see Groupe d'Entrevernes, *Signs*, 172.

4 See Bailey ("Psalm 23 and Luke 15," 54–71), who insists on several elements of overlap: the good shepherd, repentance, dangers and death, the help that God provides more by virtue of his holiness than his love, and the reference to a feast. What is a mere image in the psalm becomes a story at the hand of Luke.

5 See Gottfried Quell, "πατήρ," *TDNT* 5 (1967) 973.

6 See Kossen, "Quelques remarques," 75–80; several scholars agree, including Jacques Dupont, "La parabole de la brebis perdue (Mt 18,12-14; Lc 15,4-7)," in idem, Études, 2:624–46. Others, e.g., Fitzmyer (2:1072), remain skeptical.

7 See, in the bibliography of Luke 15:11-32, Derrett, "Law in the New Testament"; Pöhlmann, *Der verlorene Sohn*, 19, 51–52; Schnider, *Söhne*, 37; see also Donahue, *Gospel in Parable*, 152–57.

8 For attention given to the father, see Jeremias, *Parables*, 130–31; Donahue, *Gospel in Parable*, 152–53; and in the bibliography of Luke 15:11-32, Patte, "Structural Analysis," 77; Pesch, "Exegese," 174–76; Fusco, "Narrazione," 59. For attention given to the

the multiplicity of methods that have been applied to the reading of the biblical text. To the classical pair of historical-critical and theological readings[9] we have added in our day structural and rhetorical approaches,[10] and all of these ways of reading the text have, by virtue of the text and its context, revealed (new) religious senses. The length of the bibliography is an indication of the abundance of meanings that have been found in this parabolic text. Some interpreters have even gone so far as to count the number of syllables in order to be able to admire the balance in the structure of the writing, and to note the number of verbs in order to discover what is essential in the text.[11] The participle ἀναστάς (v. 18) thus occupies a pivotal position, since the verb ἀνίστημι, which elsewhere affirms the resurrection, might here mean more than "get up." Do not vv. 24 and 32 say that the young man was dead and that he came back to life?[12]

Even though Luke has already drawn on the Markan tradition reporting the grumbling of the Pharisees and the scribes (5:29-32 par. Mark 2:15-17), he makes new use of it here, in vv. 1-2; he reworks it in his own way and, above all, generalizes the criticism addressed to Jesus. The Gospel writer is thus most definitely responsible for the description of the scene.[13]

The Gospels of Matthew and *Thomas* are the only ones, besides Luke, to transmit the parable of the lost sheep. We will need to compare these three versions, but we can already submit that Luke, like Matthew, derives the parable from his Sayings Source, Q, rather than from his special material, L.[14] As for the twin parable of the drachma, certain stylistic elements[15] invite us to consider it not as Luke's creation but as a traditional duplication of the first parable. There are such double parables in both Q (Luke 13:18-21) and L (Luke 14:28-32). The second parable here must not have been found in the copy of Q that Matthew had at hand. We can find no good reason why the Gospel writer would have eliminated it, if it had been in his copy.[16] If it had, he could have adapted it to his ecclesial and pastoral perspective in the same way he had treated the first parable. Moreover, since Luke was not afraid to use doublets, it is he who has drawn this "feminine" version, which complements the "masculine" story of the shepherd, either from his version of Q, or from an oral tradition, or from L.[17] It is even possible that this parable of the lost sheep was in both Q and L. We should not even exclude the possibility that Luke himself was the one who composed the second parable. In other words, we really do not know for sure. There are two definite indications of the secondary character of the parable of the drachma: (a) The sequence is hardly logical; a natural crescendo would have been created by the following sequence: the object (the drachma), the animal (the sheep), and finally the human being (the son). (b) Verse 10 studiously avoids repetitions and skips any explanation, the reason being that the moral of the story has already been fully drawn in v. 7.[18]

Luke did not "invent" the parable of the prodigal son,[19] nor, for that matter, is he responsible for the

elder brother, see Denis Buzy, "Enseignements paraboliques," *RB* 14 (1917) 168–207, esp. 191, cited by Lagrange, 420. For attention given to both brothers, see, in the bibliography of Luke 15:11-32, Fuchs, "Das Fest," 402–15; and idem, "Jesus' Understanding of Time," 160–62. For attention given to the younger brother, see, among many others (in the bibliography of Luke 15:11-32), Via, "Prodigal Son," 21–43.

9   See Cantinat, "Paraboles," 246–64; Dupont, "Réjouissez-vous"; Ramaroson, "Cœur," 348–60; Lambrecht, *Once More Astonished*, 24–56.

10   See Giblin, "Considerations," 15–31; Waelkens, "Analyse"; Groupe d'Entrevernes, *Signs*, 121–83; Meynet, "Deux paraboles," 89–105; idem, *Saint Luc*, 2:161–65; Krüger, "Sustitución," 65–97.

11   See, in the bibliography of Luke 15:11-32, Sibinga, "Kompositionstechnik," 97–113.

12   Ibid., 104–5.

13   See Schulz, *Q*, 387; Fiedler, *Sünder*, 148; Jeremias, *Sprache*, 243–44; Merklein, *Gottesherrschaft*, 187.

14   See Schulz, *Q*, 387–91; Detlev Dormeyer, "Textpragmatische Analyse und Unterrichtsplanung zum Gleichnis vom verlorenen Schaf: Lk 15,1-7," *EvErz* 27 (1975) 352; Sasagu Arai, "Das Gleichnis vom verlorenen Schaf: Eine traditionsgeschichtliche Untersuchung," *AJBI* 2 (1976) 122–32; Weder, *Gleichnisse*, 171–72; Merklein, *Gottesherrschaft*, 186–89.

15   See Jeremias, *Sprache*, 247–48.

16   With Fitzmyer, 2:1073. According to Trilling (*Christusverkündigung*, 107) and Merklein (*Gottesherrschaft*, 186), the parable of the drachma may already have been associated in Q with that of the lost sheep.

17   On all of these possibilities, see Fitzmyer, 2:1073.

18   The commentaries insist more on the similarities between v. 7 and v. 10 than on the differences.

19   While Rudolf Pesch ("Zur Exegese Gottes durch Jesus von Nazaret: Eine Auslegung des Gleichnisses

second part of the parable (vv. 25-32).[20] The episode of the older son is not there only by chance, and the parable had two parts from the start. It is even true that the second part prompted the Gospel writer to develop the initial scenario of the Pharisaic resistance to pardoning sinners and eating with them (vv. 1–2). Luke found this parable in L, whose literary quality is once more a source of admiration. The third parable, for that matter, matches, on the aesthetic plane, the most beautiful pages of L, such as the story of the good Samaritan or the story of the disciples on the road to Emmaus.

As in chap. 14, the Gospel writer has created here a fine collection with the help of extracts from Q (the lost sheep) and L (the prodigal son), to which he has added a simple doublet of unknown origin and has evened out the overall style of the entire chapter. In order to do that, he has taken as his model the beginning of chap. 13 (vv. 1-9 of chap. 15)[21] and has perhaps thought of biblical parallels, most notably Jer 31:10-20.[22]

The Scenario (vv. 1-2)

Commentary

■ **1-2** In the spirit of a true popular storyteller, Luke submits that "all" the tax collectors and sinners kept approaching Jesus (literally "him"), the hero whom it is no longer necessary to introduce. They approach him in a friendly manner, as the parallel of the Sermon on the Plain suggests ("whoever comes to me," 6:47). This is an approach to "him" ($\alpha\dot{v}\tau\hat{\omega}$, v. 1)[23] that is associated with the realization of the distance to be overcome and with an obedience that begins by "listening" (the same verb $\dot{\alpha}\kappa o\dot{v}\epsilon\iota\nu$ is used in 6:47 and here in v. 1). It involves not just any kind of listening but listening to "his words," as in 6:47, and here in v. 1, "to him." What is more, since the tax collectors' and sinners' actions were repeated, the tense used had to be the imperfect, and it is the periphrastic imperfect that was used: ($\hat{\eta}\sigma\alpha\nu\ \dot{\epsilon}\gamma\gamma\dot{\iota}\zeta o\nu\tau\epsilon\varsigma$, "they kept approaching"). The one and only difficulty in v. 1 is the social or religious identity of these persons who were listening to Jesus.[24] The "tax collectors" are assuredly a social group, but it is their symbolic identity that counts. They represent human beings separated from God, those who are attached to material possessions without regard for doing harm to their peers. Like their cohorts, the "sinners," they constitute the reserve supply of future converts, the potential source of future joy for heaven (vv. 7 and 10). Eschewing too strict a distinction between the social sector and the religious world, Luke uses a single symbolic expression to describe all those persons who oppress their neighbors and are separated from God. We have here those persons who need Jesus and those for whom he has gone to bat. The Pharisees and the scribes also constitute a symbolic element: placed in a historical and social reality, they represent a constant hostility to the message of liberation. The readers have been encountering them for a long time.[25] Although they

vom Vater und den beiden Söhnen [Lk 15, 11-32]," in B. Casper, ed., *Jesus: Ort der Erfahrung Gottes* [Freiburg im B.: Herder, 1976] 145–49) believes that it came practically verbatim from the mouth of Jesus, Heikki Räisänen ("The Prodigal Gentile and His Jewish Christian Brother [Lk 15,11-32]," in van Segbroeck, *Four Gospels*, 2:1617–36), considers it entirely the creation of Luke.

20 In the wake of Julius Wellhausen and Alfred Loisy, Eduard Schweizer ("Antwort an Joachim Jeremias, S. 228–231," *ThZ* 5 [1949] 231–33) and Jack T. Sanders ("Tradition and Redaction in Lk 15,11-32," *NTS* 15 [1968–69] 433–38) have attempted to show that the episode of the elder brother is external and foreign in origin. Similarly, see Heininger, *Metaphorik*, 146–50. Against this hypothesis, see Jeremias, "Tradition und Redaktion," 172–81.

21 See n. 2 above.

22 See n. 6 above.

23 See Jülicher, *Gleichnisreden*, 2:315: "Es soll ohne Nebengedanken durch $\dot{\alpha}\kappa o\dot{v}\epsilon\iota\nu\ \alpha\dot{v}\tau o\hat{v}$ nur wie 5, 15; 6, 17 die Heilsbedürftigkeit und das herzliche Vertrauen als Motiv ihres Andrängens bezeichnet werden."

24 See the commentary on Luke 5:30 and 7:34 in vol. 1; ; Völkel, "Freund," 1–10; Sanders ("Jesus and the Sinners," 5–36), who argues against the identification of "sinners" with the "people of the earth." The "sinners" are not the multitude of poor people but are the men and women who publicly flout the commandments of God. Neale (*Sinners*, 191–94) insists on the redactional character of the passages relating to "sinners" in the Third Gospel.

25 See Luke 5:17, 21, 30; 6:7; 11:53; see the commentary on Luke 5:17-19 in vol. 1.

are defenders of the religious tradition, they interpret it in such a way as to appropriate its meaning for their own benefit. They are Jesus' prime adversaries in the eyes of Luke the historian, the contemporary Jewish leaders in the eyes of Luke the Christian theologian, and finally the conservative wing of early Christianity about whom the Gospel writer will speak in Acts 15:5. As was often the case in the course of the history of God's chosen people, in Luke's view, the leaders of the people did not understand God's plan of salvation and therefore expressed their opposition to this plan.[26] Their "grumbling" was their expressive manner of making their presence felt; they believed that in that way they were keeping track of the situation, whereas in fact they did not have any control over it (note the simple verb $\gamma o\gamma\gamma\acute{u}\zeta\omega$ in 5:30, the compound verb, as here and in 19:7, and the theme of resistance to God in Acts 7:51-53 or Luke 6:22-23).[27] On their lips "this fellow" ($o\hat{v}\tau o\varsigma$) is pejorative, just as "him" ($\alpha\mathring{v}\tau\acute{o}\varsigma$) is complimentary from the point of view of the tax collectors and sinners. The leaders reproach "this fellow" for "welcoming sinners" (the word "sinners" by itself suffices to denote those being criticized by the leaders, since the tax collectors are included among the sinners). The welcome in question here[28] does not involve material hospitality but rather the attentive listening that Jesus directs their way and which is expressed here in the context of meals in common. Just as Jesus had accepted the Pharisees' invitation (7:36 and 14:1), he did not refuse that of the tax collectors (5:27, 29 and here).

Not without exaggeration, some have found in these communal meals "the essence of Christianity."[29] It remains true, however, that the social, ethical, and religious reality demonstrated by these meals is of prime importance to Luke.[30] In place of the word "essence," I would prefer to speak of a test, a criterion, or a password/"shibboleth" (Judg 12:5-6). Whether the church stands or falls depends on whether it practices or refuses to practice communal meals that are both material sharing and spiritual communion. Luke recorded the practice here for the people of Israel in the time of Jesus and was to reveal its programmatic implementation in the case of the period of the church (Acts 11:3). The church in Jerusalem barely practiced it; the church accepted the principle of meals in common with Gentiles, who were henceforth integrated into Christendom. The church was to give its approval to Peter's gesture in this direction, which was inspired by God. The decisive theological function of Luke 15, which corresponds to its central position in the narrative, is to explain the link between meals in common and conversion.[31] Since Jesus meets the sinners where they are, they can meet him where he is. That was Jesus' practice from the beginning, and the practice he advocated for his disciples (10:7-9 speaks of entering houses, sitting down together with the people, and then announcing the kingdom of God). That is the practice required here, the one that God suggests and that he makes visible in Jesus' acts and in the true stories he tells, namely, the parables.

Verses 1-2 recall Jesus' historical practice, but they also reveal above all Luke's theological perspective. Whereas the historical Jesus accepted invitations from sinners (5:29-32), here it is he who receives them (v. 2). What is more, the meals he shared with them occupy a secondary position (v. 2); what is of prime importance is listening to the Master (v. 1).

---

26   See Bovon, *Theologian*, 300–302.

27   See the commentary on Luke 5:29-32 in vol. 1.

28   On the verb $\pi\rho o\sigma\delta\acute{e}\chi o\mu\alpha\iota$ ("to welcome"), which Luke uses six times elsewhere as "to wait," see Jeremias, "Tradition und Redaktion," 187–88.

29   Franz Mussner, *Der Galaterbrief* (5th ed.; HThKNT 9; Freiburg im Breisgau: Herder, 1988) 423.

30   See Bartolomé, "Comer en común"; and idem, "$\Sigma v\nu\epsilon\sigma\vartheta\acute{\iota}\epsilon\iota\nu$," two important articles on community meals in the work of Luke; see also Fiedler, *Sünder*, 149–51.

31   The third use of the verb $\sigma v\nu\epsilon\sigma\vartheta\acute{\iota}\epsilon\iota\nu$: after Easter, the resurrection meal with Jesus' disciples (Acts 10:41) follows the testimony that Luke attributes to Peter. See Acts 1:4.

The Lost Sheep and the Lost Drachma (15:3-10)

Bibliography

Arai, Sasagu, "Das Gleichnis vom verlorenen Schaf: Eine traditionsgeschichtliche Untersuchung," *AJBI* 2 (1976) 111–37.

Buzy, Denis, "La brebis perdue," *RB* 39 (1930) 47–61.

Derrett, J. Duncan M., "Fresh Light on the Lost Sheep and the Lost Coin," *NTS* 26 (1979–80) 36–60; reprinted in idem, *Studies*, 3:59–84.

Dolto, *Psychanalyse*, 2:21–35.

Dormeyer, Detlev, "Textpragmatische Analyse und Unterrichtsplanung zum Gleichnis vom verlorenen Schaf, Lk 15,1-7," *EvErz* 27 (1975) 347–57.

Dulaey, Martine, "La parabole de la brebis perdue dans l'Eglise ancienne: De l'exégèse à l'iconographie," *REA* 39 (1993) 3–22.

Dupont, Jacques, "Les implications christologiques de la parabole de la brebis perdue," in idem, *Christologie*, 331–50, 430–31; reprinted in idem, Études, 2:647–66.

Idem, "La parabole de la brebis perdue (Mt 18,12-14; Lc 15,4-7)," in idem, Études, 2:624–46.

Faccio, H., "De ove perdita (Lc. 15,3-7)," *VD* 26 (1958) 221–28.

Focant, Camille, "La parabole de la brebis perdue: Lecture historico-critique et réflexions théologiques," *FoiTe* 13 (1983) 52–79.

Fonck, Leopold, "Ovis perdita et inventa," *VD* 1 (1921) 113–77.

Galbiati, Enrico, "La parabola della pecora e della dramma ritrovate (Lc 15,1-10)," *BeO* 6 (1964) 129–33.

Güttgemanns, Erhart, "Struktural-generative Analyse des Bildworts 'Die verlorene Drachme' (Lk 15, 8-10)," *LingBibl* 6 (1971) 2–17.

Leclercq, Jean, "'Scopis mundatam' (Mt 12,44; Lc 11,25): Le balai dans la Bible et dans la liturgie d'après la tradition latine," in J. Fontaine and C. Kannengiesser, eds., *Epektasis: mélanges patristiques offerts au cardinal Jean Daniélou* (Paris: Beauchesne, 1972) 129–37.

Loewenich, Walther von, *Luther als Ausleger der Synoptiker* (FGLP 10/5; Munich: Kaiser, 1954) 48–50.

Mara, Maria G., "Parabole lucane della misericordia nel Commento di Origene alla lettera ai Romani," *Aug* 18 (1978) 311–19.

Merklein, *Gottesherrschaft*, 186–92.

Monnier, Jean, "Sur la Grâce, à propos de la parabole de la brebis perdue," *RHPhR* 16 (1936) 191–95.

Mourlon Beernaert, Pierre, "Quatre lectures méthodiques de la 'brebis perdue' (Lc 15,1-7)," *FoiTe* 9 (1979) 387–418.

Orbe, *San Ireneo*, 2:117–81.

Perkins, Pheme, *Hearing the Parables* (New York: Paulist Press, 1981) 29–33, 38, 47, 52.

Petersen, William L., "The Parable of the Lost Sheep in the Gospel of Thomas and the Synoptics," *NovT* 23 (1981) 128–47.

Poirier, Paul-Hubert, "L'Evangile de Vérité, Ephrem le Syrien et le comput digital," *REAug* 25 (1979) 27–34.

Ruether, Rosemary Radford, *Sexism and God-Talk: Toward a Feminist Theology* (Boston: Beacon, 1983) 67–71.

Schmidt, Wilhelm, "Der gute Hirte: Biblische Besinnung über Lk 15,1-7," *EvTh* 24 (1964) 173–77.

Schnider, Franz, "Das Gleichnis vom verlorenen Schaf und seine Redaktoren: Ein intertextueller Vergleich," *Kairos* 19 (1977) 146–54.

Schrage, *Thomas-Evangelium*, 193–96.

Schulz, *Q*, 387–91.

Schweizer, *Parable of God*, 36–38.

Tooley, Wilfred, "The Shepherd and Sheep Image in the Teaching of Jesus," *NovT* 7 (1964–65) 15–25.

Topel, John, "On Being 'Parabled,'" *TBT* 87 (1976) 1010–17.

Walls, Andrew F., "'In the Presence of the Angels' (Lk 15,10)," *NovT* 3 (1959) 314–16.

3/ **So he told them this parable: 4/ "Which one of you, having a hundred sheep and having lost just one of them, does not leave the ninety-nine others in the wilderness and go after the one that is lost until he finds it? 5/ And when he has found it, he lays it on his shoulders, rejoicing. 6/ And when he arrives home, he invites his friends and neighbors, saying to them, 'Rejoice with me, for I have found my sheep that was lost!' 7/ I tell you, just so, there will be more joy in heaven over just one sinner who is converted than over ninety-nine righteous persons who need no conversion.**

8/ Or what woman having ten drachmas, if she loses so much as a single drachma, does not light a lamp, sweep the house, and search carefully until she finds it? **9/** And when she has found it, she calls together her female friends and neighbors, saying, 'Rejoice with me, because I have found the drachma that I had lost.' **10/** Thus, I tell you, there occurs joy before God's angels over just one sinner who is converted."

The Lost Sheep (vv. 3-7)

Analysis

By the scenario he set up in vv. 1-2, the Gospel writer lent an apologetic character to the parable[1] of the lost sheep.[2] He was also responsible for the introduction he placed before the parable. The vocabulary of v. 3 and the turns of phrase[3] are indicative of this.

Luke was not the only one to transmit this parable.[4] The Gospels of Matthew and *Thomas* as well as the *Gospel of Truth* were also acquainted with it. As this latter version constitutes more of a commentary on the parable than a quotation of it, it will suffice for us to compare the three recensions found in Luke, Matthew, and *Thomas*. A different setting is given for the parable in each of these: kerygmatic in *Thomas*, where an introduction speaks of the kingdom; ecclesiastical in Matthew, where chap. 18 is concerned with discipline; and apologetic in Luke, as we have seen. This very variety betrays the indiffer-

ence of the early tradition to any attempt to put this short account into a historical setting. The differences in content also prove that no one of these versions of the parable corresponds exactly to the original. As we know, the various movements in early Christianity kept up their devotion to Jesus' teaching, but each of them adapted it to its peculiar needs in its own way.[5]

The most condensed version is found in the *Gospel of Thomas* (107): "Jesus said, The kingdom is like a shepherd who had a hundred sheep. One of them, the largest, went astray. He left the ninety-nine and looked for that one until he found it. When he had gone to such trouble, he said to the sheep, I care for you more than the ninety-nine."[6] This version differs from the two others in its description of the sheep as "the largest" and in its indication of the special affection that the shepherd had for it (Luke also indicates this preference but does it in the lesson drawn in v. 7, rather than in the parable itself). These features have been understood as the expression of a Gnostic interpretation.[7] But that is

---

1   Mourlon Beernaert ("Lectures," 387–418) summarizes four different didactic interpretations of this text: historical-critical, structural, christological, and psychoanalytical.

2   On the intersection of the parable and its narrative framework, Dormeyer ("Analyse," 352) suggests that the literary unity constitutes a *Mischgattung*.

3   The expression εἶπεν δέ occurs fifty-nine times in the Gospel, fifteen times in Acts, and elsewhere in the NT only in John 12:6); πρός followed by the accusative after *verba dicendi* occurs ninety-two times in the Gospel, forty-nine times in Acts, and not at all in Matthew or Mark. "To tell" a parable is specific to Luke (fourteen occurrences) except for one instance in Mark 12:12; on "this parable," see Luke 20:19 compared to Mark 12:12; see Jeremias,

"Tradition und Redaktion," 187, 180, and 181, from which I have taken these statistics.

4   Galbiati ("Parabola," 130) recognizes the same fourfold structure in Luke and Matthew: (1) the loss of the individual in the midst of the many, (2) the anxious search, (3) the invitation to rejoice, and (4) application. According to Schnider ("Gleichnis," 147), the structure is tripartite: (1) losing a part from the midst of the whole, (2) leaving the group to go on the search, and (3) finding the lost part and reuniting the group.

5   Getting back to the teaching of Jesus remains the objective of many exegetes (thus, Arai, "Schaf").

6   Translation of Puech, *Gnose*, 2:26.

7   See, among others, Arai, "Schaf," 119–22; cautiously, Schrage, *Thomas-Evangelium*, 193–96.

not certain; it could be a question of a Judeo-Christian way of expressing Israel's status as the chosen people, as God's beloved child.[8] On the other hand, the mention of the ninety-nine others, a constant feature in all the versions of the parable, scarcely fits the nations, whose traditional number in the Bible is seventy or seventy-two.[9] To summarize: the version in the *Gospel of Thomas* is not necessarily Gnostic, nor does it depend on the canonical Gospels. It is a valuable witness to the oral transmission of Jesus' teaching far into the second century. The author of the *Gospel of Thomas* understood this text as a parable of the kingdom, in a spiritual rather than an eschatological sense, as he understood that term. Probably following a certain tradition, he saw in the size of the sheep a sign of its choice and in the exertion of the shepherd[10] an expression of the Savior's love. The shepherd's statement would appear to be an ancient addition to the original text, along the lines of the lesson drawn in Matt 18:14 and Luke 15:7.

Along with many others, I consider the parallel texts in Matthew and Luke to be new redactional readings of a single version having its origin in Q.[11] That source did not place the parable in any narrative context, nor did it have a long introduction. On the other hand, it did already draw a lesson from the parable, but a lesson that is difficult to reconstruct with precision (cf. Matt 18:14 par. Luke 15:7).[12]

Matthew and Luke have preserved a trace of an interrogative wording. Since the Matthean phrase "What do you think?" is redactional, Luke must have preserved a wording that is closer to that of Q. Both Luke and Matthew also remember the questioning that conveyed the parable, since they both refer to a "you" (plural). But where they part ways is with respect to the verb: "lose" (in the active, in Luke) or "be lost" (in the passive, in Matthew).[13] Both wordings are suspect, for the first corresponds to Luke's soteriology, and the second to Matthew's ecclesiastical perspective. There is also a difference between the two Gospels as to where the sheep gets lost: "in the wilderness" (Luke) or "on the mountains" (Matthew).[14] It is interesting to note that in Ezekiel 34, the chapter on the shepherds of Israel, we find a mention of both ("the wilderness," Ezek 34:25; "the mountains," Ezek 34:6). Matthew and Luke do not use the same verb to say that the shepherd leaves his flock; in this case it is probably Matthew who preserves Q's verb ("leaves" ἀφίημι)[15] and Luke who improves on the style ("leaves [behind]" καταλείπω). Both Matthew and Luke stress the search, but they express it in different terms: "go in search of" (Matthew), "go after . . . until he finds

---

8   See 2 Sam (2 Kgdms) 12:3; and Petersen ("Parable," 130–35), who shows that the adjective "large" to describe the "sheep" is not necessarily Gnostic. It could be a description of Israel.

9   Luke seems to think of them in 10:1 with the sending of the seventy-two.

10 Is it necessary to understand the labor of the shepherd as an allusion to the Savior's suffering? Arai ("Schaf," 124) thinks so. Schrage (*Thomas-Evangelium*, 196) thinks instead of the efforts of the Gnostics or of the Savior to salvage what was lost.

11 For research on Q, see particularly Schulz, *Q*, 387–91; Arai, "Schaf," 122–32; and Milton C. Moreland and James M. Robinson, "The International Q Project: Work Sessions 23–27 May, 22–26 August, 17–18 November 1994," *JBL* 114 (1995) 475–85, esp. 483.

12 On these two parallel verses, see Arai, "Schaf," 113–19.

13 The Matthean formulation could have reflected Ps 119 (118):176; see Arai, "Schaf," 124.

14 Some have explained these two different expressions as translations of the same original Aramaic word שׁוּרָא, which designates a mountainous and barren place. Some have also assimilated this word with another Aramaic word, דּוּרָא (pronounced almost identically by the Galileans), which signifies the enclosure in which the sheep were brought together. See Jeremias, *Parables*, 133; resumed by Mánek (*Gleichnisse*, 51–52), who adds another explanation: Matthew appreciates the "mountain" as a place of communion between Jesus and his disciples; Luke, on the other hand, construes it as a dangerous place, and does not concede to it any place in the age to come!

15 Dupont ("Parabole," 275) does not hesitate to translate this verb as "to desert," or "abandon." Scholars have often debated whether the shepherd abandoned the ninety-nine sheep altogether, if he left them with a servant, or if he hurried to lock them up in a pen. Obviously the narrator is not interested in the question, and it would be unwarranted to ask it; see Pirot, *Paraboles*, 251.

it" (Luke). In this case, it is probably Luke who seeks to improve the wording.[16] We should also attribute to Lukan redaction a suggestive detail that recalls Hermes Criophorus: "he lays it on his shoulders."[17] The two recensions lead up to the same high point in the parable: the "joy," more specifically the verb "rejoice." Curiously, Matthew puts the phrase "truly I tell you . . ." on Jesus' lips, with the result that in his Gospel we first read Jesus' conclusion (Matt 18:13b), then a lesson he himself draws (Matt 18:14). There are also redundancies in Luke, but different ones: under the influence of the second parable, the one about the drachma (v. 9), Luke describes a return to the "home" of the shepherd, an invitation to the friends/relatives and neighbors (same expression in the two parables), and a joyous celebration (the same expression: συγχάρητέ μοι, "rejoice with me"). It is significant that in Luke, Matthew, and *Thomas*, the shepherd has something to say, even if the wording is different from one version to another. We should therefore conclude that there was an expression of joy on his lips in the original parable. The lesson that Q drew from the parable can be reconstructed thanks to the statement by the shepherd in Matthew and the conclusion drawn by Luke: this lesson spoke of the joy occasioned by the single sheep being found again, a joy greater than that occasioned by the ninety-nine others. In the final lesson, the Matthean redaction thinks in terms of a church and its members who are in danger of going astray (Matt 18:14); the Lukan redaction, on the other hand, thinks in terms of salvation and sinners called to repent (here, in v. 7,

and later, in v. 10).[18] Finally, there is a syntactical difference between Luke and Matthew in that the hypothetical wording of the First Gospel (Matt 18:12-13) must be secondary, for it corresponds to the casuistic character of ecclesiastical discipline worked out by that Gospel in chap. 18. Furthermore, there is a confirmation of Luke's narrative style in the *Gospel of Thomas*.[19]

Commentary

■ **3-4** Luke, the city-dweller, speaks of a Jesus who preaches in the countryside: "Which one of you, having a hundred sheep . . . ?" This is a fairly big flock,[20] but it provides a special contrast between the whole and the "just one of them." "Is it really necessary to leave everything for that single sheep?" readers will ask themselves.[21] The disappearance is described by the single verb "lose."[22] But this verb brings to mind a scenario that suggests the loss of an animal by accident or through sickness, its falling into a ravine, or its being attacked by a wild animal or suffering from some sort of fever. As the flock moves on, any laggard risks being the victim of some catastrophe.[23] The animal's misfortune begins with being left alone and abandoned. What is more, in Christian usage ἀπόλλυμι ("being lost") is the antonym of "being saved." This Christian sociolect draws on the vocabulary of its Jewish roots. Mindful of the role of Adam and of personal transgressions, Jesus' disciples ask themselves what they should do. They recall their Master's statements on various subjects, some of which ring the note of intran-

---

16 On the contrary, according to Arai ("Schaf," 126), v. 4b of Luke belongs to the oldest layer of the tradition because it does not demonstrate the influence of Ps 119 (118).

17 If carrying a sheep on one's shoulders could become an artistic motif, it is only because it was first a concrete, even prosaic reality; see Buzy, "Brebis," 51.

18 According to Dupont ("Implications"), the parable has the same structure as Matthew and Luke: "The first describes the shepherd's behavior; the second demonstrates his joy." See also Schweizer, *Parable of God*, 36–38.

19 Dupont ("Implications," 336) and Merklein (*Gottesherrschaft*, 188) each propose an "archetype" of the parable. These two models resemble each other; that of Dupont retains the hypothetical form, and

that of Merklein takes the interrogative form. The former uses the verb "to lose," the latter "to be lost."

20 *Realien*, as the Germans say concerning herds and the life of shepherds and sheep; see Jülicher, *Gleichnisreden*, 2:316–17; Buzy, "Brebis," 48; and Mourlon Beernaert ("Lectures," 395–96).

21 Among the most important responsibilities of the shepherd is to count his sheep when evening comes; see Mourlon Beernaert ("Lectures," 395–96): "The number 99 indicates that the counting had already taken place" (p. 396).

22 On this verb, see Dupont ("Parabole," 274). This is the same verb that is used in the LXX to describe the loss of the donkeys of Kish, 1 Sam (1 Kgdms) 9:3, 20. See Ezek 34:4, 16 LXX.

23 See Buzy, "Brebis," 49.

24 Monnier ("Sur la Grâce," 191–95) insists on the

sigence ("Struggle to enter through the narrow door!" 13:24), and others of which speak of comfort. This is the case with this parable, which, although it uses only one word to speak of loss, uses many to affirm the act of coming to the rescue. Two expressions are significant: (a) the shepherd "leaves" ($\kappa\alpha\tau\alpha\lambda\epsilon\acute{\iota}\pi\epsilon\iota$) what he is doing at the moment and (b) concentrates on the task he considers to be most important ($\pi o\rho\epsilon\acute{\upsilon}\epsilon\tau\alpha\iota$, "goes"). He does this with his mind set unshakably on a goal ("until he finds it"). Most important of all, following Luther's theological grammar (*justitia passiva*), the passive sheep is looked for, then found, and finally carried.[24] All the activity is carried on by the shepherd.[25] If religion has succeeded in providing a sickeningly sweet portrayal of this scene, this is to be contrasted with the ruggedness of the rural reality: the lost animal is frightened and exhausted[26] and in no way facilitates the job of its rescuer. It is heavier than one would think and does not smell good! As is often the case, Jesus' language captures the reality on the spot and at the same time contemporizes Israel's religious symbolism.[27]

■ **5-6** All the shepherd's exertion fails to exhaust his energy or extinguish his joy. Luke uses numerous participles and other verbs: to his utter delight, the shepherd finds the sheep and lays it on his shoulders. Then the Gospel writer pictures a festive scene—a joyous party with friends and neighbors.[28] He draws the picture with the vocabulary of joy,[29] which is colored with a community hue. In addition to the mention of the collective element of friends and neighbors, he twice uses the Greek preposition $\sigma\acute{\upsilon}\nu$ ("with") in compound forms: the shepherd "calls together," "invites" ($\sigma\upsilon\gamma\kappa\alpha\lambda\epsilon\hat{\iota}$) his friends and neighbors, then exclaims: "Rejoice with me!" ($\sigma\upsilon\gamma\chi\acute{\alpha}\rho\eta\tau\acute{\epsilon}\ \mu o\iota$).[30]

Advocates of structural analysis have the time of their lives with this story;[31] they set the loss over against the reunion, the single sheep against the rest of the flock, and the going away against the return; they find a paradoxical relationship between joy and sinners and between the absence of joy and righteous persons.[32] They esteem that Jesus issues an "invitation to understand," that is, to find here (vv. 4-7) an answer to the question posed by his attitude (vv. 1-2). "Jesus," they write, "becomes the actant of an auto-interpretative and persuasive manifestation."[33] To their way of thinking, the parable implements a single narrative program

---

merciful work of God that precedes even repentance and ignores the double decree of Calvinist theology! Merklein (*Gottesherrschaft*, 191) admires the divine initiative that, without any prior condition, overtakes the sinner.

25 See Weder, *Gleichnisse*, 174. Tooley ("Shepherd and Sheep Image," 15–25) analyzes the image of the shepherd. Jesus resorts to this image to illustrate his ministry, not his passion.

26 See Mánek, *Gleichnisse*, 52.

27 For the images of the people of Israel as a flock or as sheep; the sin of Israel compared to the folly of sheep; God as a shepherd who protects his flock, see Pss 23 (22):1; 79 (78):2; Isa 40:11; Jer 31:10; Ezek 34:12. Jülicher (*Gleichnisreden*, 2:317) refers to many passages in the OT that describe the loss of animals; Derrett ("Fresh Light," 42–47) says that the parable is a "re-enactment of the great finding and reclaiming which was the central point of the Jewish conception of history" (p. 43); Galbiati ("Parabola") points forcefully to Ezekiel 34. Dupont ("Implications," 340) invokes the parables of the OT in the interpretation of those in the NT.

28 With good reason, Linnemann (*Parables*, 67–68) is surprised at this invitation to celebrate at his house.

She considers it an addition from the second parable, that of the lost drachma. Likewise, Merklein (*Gottesherrschaft*, 187–88). Nestle-Aland retains the active $\sigma\upsilon\gamma\kappa\alpha\lambda\epsilon\hat{\iota}$ ("convoke" or "invite") in vv. 6 and 9. Here, as there, the middle $\sigma\upsilon\gamma\kappa\alpha\lambda\epsilon\hat{\iota}\tau\alpha\iota$ is also attested, which carries the nuance that the shepherd or the woman invites friends, and that this in itself gives them pleasure.

29 See Mourlon Beernaert ("Lectures," 397), resuming the position of Jeremias (*Parables*, 135–36): the main point of the parable is not the quest, but the joy. Jülicher (*Gleichnisreden*, 2:320) provides a series of parallel passages that express the same joy.

30 Dormeyer ("Analyse," 353–54) laments the gulf that separates religion from the common life: that a man or a woman rejoices after having found a precious object is normal in secular life. A similar dynamic should also be at work in religious life.

31 See Giblin, "Considerations" (bibliography of Luke 15:1-2); Dormeyer, "Analyse," 350; Krüger, "Sustitución" (bibliography of Luke 15:1-2); Meynet, *Saint Luc*, 2:161–70.

32 See Waelkens, "Analyse," 161–64.

33 See Groupe d'Entrevernes, *Signs*, 100.

(although the sheep's getting lost, in my opinion, presupposes another one): establishment of a subject, qualification, performance, and gratitude. The shepherd does more than one would think: in addition to the somatic performance (he recovers the animal), there is his persuasive performance (he invites his friends and neighbors), as well as his assertive performance (he expresses his joy). As for the program of Jesus as speaker, it continues through v. 7: it "thus produces an interpretation of his own behavior and annuls the relevance of the grumbling of his adversaries."[34]

■ **7** We still have to explain v. 7, a Lukan theological commentary that is both simple and enigmatic.[35] In Luke's eyes, the parable is both paraenetic (it invites decision)[36] and doctrinal (it invites belief and understanding). "Just so" (οὕτως) leads to the transfer, to the passing over to the other reality, to "allegory." "Just so, there will be (more) joy" (the logic of this is that the future as well is encouraging). In Luke it is usually Christians who experience joy. But here in this passage it has taken over God's heart.[37] It is from that very source that it will well up to water the world of human beings. The joy is complete, that of a person overcome with happiness, springing from the supreme good that is neither material, nor spiritual, but relational. In the lost sheep God finds a vis-à-vis.[38] People can see for themselves that the

loss of an object renders that object more valuable, and it is often the case that a fixation takes hold of the person who goes in search of it.[39] The only thing that can equal the anxiety connected with having lost something is the joy associated with finding it again. For Jesus the loss of the sheep was a passive event, which becomes strangely active in Luke's narration.[40] Sinners must be converted,[41] must repent, and must make their way back on their own to God—in a word, must respond to the call of the gospel.[42] This response is not just an affair of the moment, however decisive that moment may be; it must last. The present participle of the verb (μετανοοῦντι, "who is converted")[43] stresses the length of the effort. Note Luke's double structure: "to be converted" is to accept the work of the shepherd on our behalf. And that work involves Jesus, who is the image of the Father.[44]

The second part of v. 7 is difficult to interpret. Does Luke really think that there are that many righteous persons? And for that matter are they really righteous (see 16:15 and 18:9)? Are there really, to his way of thinking, beings "who need no conversion"? Are we dealing here with a hyperbole or an ironic exclamation?[45] In any case, Luke dares to make a comparison between beings. He does not lump them all together in the same category. In chap. 18, he will be distinguishing between the tax collector and the Pharisee (18:14); in chap. 7, he set off

---

34   Ibid., 104.
35   See above.
36   On the parable as interpellation, see Schnider, "Gleichnis," 148; and Focant, "Parabole," 56.
37   On this joy of God himself, see Pirot, *Paraboles*, 253; Linnemann, *Parables*, 72–73; Trilling, *Christusverkündigung*, 119 (bibliography of Luke 15:1-2); Dupont, "Implications," 332; Arai, "Schaf," 117; Merklein, *Gottesherrschaft*, 190.
38   On the metaphor of the sheep as applied at times to Israel, see Derrett, "Fresh Light," 37; and Weder, *Gleichnisse*, 173.
39   Linnemann (*Parables*, 65) mentions the everyday objects toward which human behavior is universally the same. Dupont ("Implications," 341) reminds the reader of the concrete circumstances and real-life situations to which the parables make reference.
40   Arai, "Schaf," 112–13. Luke's suggestion does not correspond, however, to the theology (advocated by certain rabbis) that insists that initial conversion must precede reinstatement; see Mánek, *Gleichnisse*, 51.

41   It is clear that Luke is the only one who explains this demand for conversion and repentance; see Arai, "Schaf," 115–16.
42   For a psychoanalytical treatment (driven by desire and not marked by morality, the subject finds his or her personal coherence), see Dolto, *Psychanalyse*, 2:21–35; and a summary by Mourlon Beernaert, "Lectures," 411–15.
43   On the Lukan use of μετάνοια, see Focant, "Parabole," 65–67; and Bovon, *Theologian*, 305–28.
44   While few exegetes express the first articulation, several elucidate the second: see Trilling, *Christusverkündigung*, 116 (bibliography of Luke 15:1-2), Schnider, "Gleichnis," 148; Weder, *Gleichnisse*, 174; Dupont, "Implications," 346–50; Mourlon Beernaert, "Lectures," 399, 401–4; Focant, "Parabole," 70.
45   Linnemann describes this parable as "hyperbole" (*Parables*, 66). Melanchthon (*Postillae*, col. 69) speaks of "bitter irony."

410

the good attitude of certain persons against the negative attitude of others (7:29-30). Narration, like the theater, requires the use of contrasts. But is that true also of theology? In my opinion, Luke does not press his line of reasoning that far; in Luke's account, Christianity, which was in the position of a minority by comparison with the Judaism of its day, defends the value of converted sinners in the eyes of God. Although they were certainly in the minority, they could lay claim—such was their conviction—to divine approval. And the social, racial, and religious origin of these people in the minority was of no importance. Here, as elsewhere, the expression "the tax collectors and sinners" characterizes them as Christians coming from a guilty past.[46]

Luke is not interested in the "ninety-nine" others. But these persons are nevertheless present in Luke's text. As we have seen, they do not correspond to Gentiles as distinguished from the true people of Israel. Be that as it may, the commentators of the second century, especially the Gnostics,[47] understood one piece of evidence that has escaped our notice in this century. In antiquity, people used to count on the fingers of their hands. And changing from ninety-nine to one hundred meant changing from the left hand (considered as the bad one) to the right (the good one). In other words, this change from ninety-nine to one hundred signified attaining what is good. The lost unit brought the total to the left side.[48] When the sheep was found again, it became the source of blessing to the whole. There may have been in the tradition, quite possibly also in Jesus' thinking, then later in both Gnostic and orthodox interpretation, a perception of totality and a sensitivity to the cosmic dimension associated with the figure 100. The sheep, first lost, and then found again, brings along with it in its destiny, by way of solidarity, the whole flock.[49] Jesus no doubt had in mind the people of Israel, for whom he cared so much, that he could even focus on those who were excluded.[50] Even in our time we should perhaps not rule out thinking about this parable in terms of the destiny of the whole human race. While Luke thought of his readers as sinners, represented by the lost sheep, whom he was inviting to be converted, let us not forget that Matthew identified the shepherd with the pastors of his church.[51] Both rank-and-file Christians and Christian leaders are summoned to remember their responsibility toward the whole human race and even toward all of God's creation.[52]

The Lost Drachma (vv. 8-10)

Analysis

We should note the close resemblance between the second parable (vv. 8-10) and the first (vv. 4-7). The use of ἤ ("or") suggests that the second parable serves as another way of expressing what was in the first parable.[53] The few characteristic differences that distinguish them from

---

46 According to Schnider ("Gleichnis," 149), the Lukan rewriting of the parable is a retroactive historicization of the intervention of Christ in Israel.

47 See *Gos. Truth* 31:35—32:30 and the Gnostic perspective that Irenaeus describes (*Adv. haer.* 1.16.2).

48 On these arithmetic considerations, see Schrage, *Thomas-Evangelium*, 195–96; Poirier, "Evangile," 27–34; and Focant, "Parabole," 61–62.

49 Several others emphasize that the saving of the sheep does not harm the herd—on the contrary, it benefits the herd. Thus, Galbiati, "Parabola," 123; and Derrett, "Fresh Light," 37.

50 Various exegetes are of the opinion that there is a relationship in the tradition between the framework (v. 2, the criticism of Jesus) and the parable itself (v. 4, the shepherd's search for the lost sheep), e.g., Weder, *Gleichnisse*, 168–69, 174–75; Arai, "Schaf," 135–36. Distinguishing "historisch" from "geschichtlich," Linnemann (*Parables*, 69) takes this view.

51 On the perspective of Matthew, see Arai, "Schaf," 117–19; and Pierre Bonnard, "Composition et signification historique de Matthieu 18," in idem, *Anamnesis: Recherches sur le Nouveau Testament* (CRThPh 3; Geneva: Revue de théologie et de philosophie, 1980) 115.

52 The various rewritings demonstrate several different images of Jesus. According to Arai ("Schaf," 132), the two layers of Q show the oldest images of him: Jesus as a critical companion who meets with the excluded and, the more recent, Jesus as the Christ of grace. In Luke he is the herald of conversion; in Matthew, the shepherd of the church; and in *Thomas*, the Savior of the soul.

53 The studies of the second parable are infinitely fewer than those of the first; see Walls, "In the Presence of the Angels," 314–16; Galbiati, "Parabola"; Güttgemanns, "Struktural-generative Analyse," 2–17; Derrett, "Fresh Light"; Ruether, *Sexism and God-Talk*.

each other and the literary need for repetition also merit our attention.

As common elements we may count the following: a rhetorical question; the stories of a loss, an intense search, and a finding again associated with a shared rejoicing; and the presence of an application that is introduced by the phrase "I tell you" and that is centered on the theme of "joy."

As differences we may count the absence of the words "one of you" (v. 4), which simplifies the text;[54] the figure "ten" following the word drachmas, in Greek, whereas "a hundred" precedes the word for "sheep" in the Greek of v. 4 (we should also note the elegant presence of the word ἔχουσα ["having"] between the words in Greek for "drachmas" and the figure "ten");[55] the hypotaxis (hypothetical clause: "if she loses . . .") in place of the parataxis used in v. 4.[56] Moreover, the sheep "is lost" (τὸ ἀπολωλός), whereas it is the woman who loses her drachma (ἣν ἀπώλεσα, "that I had lost").[57] While the shepherd (v. 6) invites "his friends and neighbors," the woman, not surprisingly, calls together her women friends and neighbors (v. 9). "Before God's angels" (v. 10) is more mythological than "in heaven" (v. 7).[58] Finally, the application in v. 10, unlike the one in v. 7, contains no element of comparison. The only dominant note is that of absolute joy.[59]

Commentary

■ **8-10** The tradition represented in the Gospels sometimes communicates the same message of Jesus through repetition. Readers have already encountered this technique, which applies to prose the use of *parallelismus membrorum* (poetical parallelism). In chap. 13, they have read two parables, one concerning the mustard seed and one concerning yeast (13:18-21; in that case also, there is first a man's work, and then a woman's);[60] in chap. 14, the parable of the property owner who thinks about building a tower, followed by the parable of the king who gets ready to wage a military campaign (14:28-32). Here in chap. 15, what a woman does confirms what a man has done. This housewife is perhaps somewhat poorer than her male counterpart, since her ten drachmas represent only modest assets, which explains why she is so anxious to find the lost coin. There is nothing in the story that would indicate that her coins represented her dowry or that they had been set in a tiara or in a necklace.[61] The drachma is a silver coin whose weight could vary from one region to another, from one period in time to another (this is the only place in the New Testament where it is mentioned). Its worth, therefore, is hard to establish; according to Josephus, the Attic drachma would have been worth a quarter of the Jewish shekel

---

54   As a whole, the second parable is shorter than the first, which is logical because the reader, knowing the first, more quickly grasps the second. The attention here is on a woman (rather than a man, the shepherd), but the absence of the words "among you" does not necessarily indicate an absence of women in Jesus' audience, contra Godet, 2:218; Loisy, 395; and Plummer, 371 (hesitantly).

55   The second parable is written with the care one would attribute to the author of L, or perhaps Luke himself.

56   Curiously, Matthew uses a hypotaxis of this kind in his version of the lost sheep (Matt 18:12-14).

57   It seems that it is v. 9 that inspired v. 6, and not vice versa. The invitation of the neighbors and relatives fits better in the second parable. If this is in fact the case, then the second parable is not a purely Lukan creation. It must have enjoyed its own circulation, undoubtedly within L. But since it became only the sister of the first parable, it is likely that the first figured not only in Q but also in L.

58   The expression "before the angels of God" occurs

also in 12:9. The words "the angels" must go back to tradition; see Jeremias, *Sprache*, 248. One wonders if Luke added the words "of God" to a traditional expression; see Grundmann, 308; and Wiefel (284), who compares Luke 22:69 to Mark 14:62.

59   I suppose, here also, that the formulation of v. 10 is older than that of v. 7. Luke must have drawn from it in his composition of v. 7. The vocabulary of conversion used in the two verses must be attributed to the evangelist himself. The tradition, logically, would have spoken of a "saved one," a "saint," or an "elected one."

60   Helmut Flender (*Heil und Geschichte in der Theologie des Lukas* [BEvTh 41; Munich: Kaiser, 1965]) is sensitive to Lukan thought, which is fond of including both sexes, men and women, in the design of God. See Wiefel, 284; and Mánek, *Gleichnisse*, 98.

61   This hypothesis, which Jeremias (*Parables*, 134–35) has cautiously put forward, has encountered opposition, most notably from Fitzmyer (2:1081 in particular), who nevertheless refers to such a gem. See

used in Palestine (*Ant.* 3.8.2 §195).[62] According to the same author, Herod the Great offered 150 drachmas to each of his soldiers and even more to their officers (*Bell.* 1.16.3 §308).[63] According to Appian (*Bel. civ.* 3.7.43 §177), Mark Anthony's soldiers would have considered a gift of only one hundred drachmas a sign of his stinginess.[64] At one time, the drachma had considerable purchasing power: it could buy a sheep or a fifth of a cow;[65] it amounted to a day's wages. Dio Chrysostom (70[20].5) reports that anyone would have had reason to be upset with oneself over having lost even a single drachma.[66] In the time of Nero, the denarius would have replaced the drachma.[67] In speaking of "drachmas" rather than denarii, was Luke hoping to suggest a past era, the time of Jesus?

The woman is sure of what she must do;[68] since the room had no window and the door did not let in enough light, she "lights a lamp" (this is the same word for "lamp" [λύχνος] and the same verb for "light" [ἅπτω] as in 11:33). Then she sweeps the house, the same activity mentioned in 11:25 (there, the house had been cleared of its burdensome visitor and was swept in order to make it clean again). What is most important is that the woman "searches." The adverb "carefully" (ἐπιμελῶς) stresses the intensity and the nature of the search.[69] There was no equivalent to this adverb in the preceding parable. On the other hand, the insistence and goal are worded in both places in language that is nearly identical: "until he/she finds it."[70] She finds it by seeing it or hearing it,

since the coin would shine and/or ring. The author does not take the time to say that the housewife rejoices (the term he used in connection with the shepherd); he specifies, however, that the woman is also anxious to share her joy immediately. The invitation is appropriate in the second parable, which is not the case with the first parable, since here we can picture a village where relatives and neighbors are within earshot.

The application is simple: joy "occurs" (γίνεται) when a sinner is converted, when a human being acknowledges that God is looking for him or her. It is not possible to ascertain the exact meaning of the pious phrase "before God's angels." My understanding of it is that it refers to a joy that reaches the entire heavenly court (rather than to God's joy, which only the angels witness). Ἐνώπιον means "before," "in the presence of," and, in a judicial context, "in the judgment of."[71]

There is no doubt that Luke appreciates the welcoming of women into the Christian community on an equal basis with men.[72] He sees in that welcoming the application of a truth aired from 12:22-32 on, namely, that every human being has an irreplaceable worth in God's eyes (cf. the stress put on "just one" in the phrase "just one sinner who is converted," vv. 7 and 10). Moreover, he delights in choosing money, a reality taken from the economic world, as his second example, after the sheep, taken from the rural setting. As he does elsewhere, the Gospel writer thus widens his horizons: he speaks to country folk and city-dwellers, to those who are rich and

Shelagh Weir, "A Bridal Headdress from Southern Palestine," *PEQ* 105 (1973) 101–9.

62   Mentioned by Fitzmyer, 2:1081.

63   Mentioned by Fitzmyer, 2:1081.

64   See BAGD, s.v.

65   Ibid.

66   Ibid.

67   See Fitzmyer (2:1081), who points to his bibliography; and Marshall, 603. Formerly, Plummer, 370; and, before all of them, Melanchthon, *Postillae*, cols. 70–71.

68   The commentaries point out a Jewish parallel in which the attentive study of the law is compared with the meticulous labor of a man who searches for a valuable object (*Midr. Cant.* 1.1.9 (79b); see *Midrash Rabbah* 9.2, 10–11; Marshall, 603. Since Wettstein (*Novum Testamentum graecum*, 1:757), scholars have cited a parallel in Greek literature: Theophrastus *Char.* 10.6: καὶ τῆς γυναικὸς ἐκβα-

λούσης τρίχαλκον οἷος μεταφέρειν τὰ σκεύη καὶ τὰς κιβωτοὺς καὶ διφᾶν τὰ καλύμματα ("And if his wife drops a coin worth three coppers, he is capable of moving the dishes, beds, and chests, and of searching in the cracks of the floorboards"). See Güttgemanns, "Struktural-generative Analyse," 11–12.

69   On this adverb, which implies care and zeal for accomplishing a task, see BAGD, s.v.

70   Bengel (*Gnomon*, 1:363) makes much of this expression: Jesus pursues the sinner in his everyday life. Jesus even goes to his table, where, in Bengel's opinion, we sin the most (by gossip or by gluttony?).

71   See Plummer, 371. Lagrange (418) sees a rabbinic caution in this phrase (a discreet way of speaking about God, I suppose).

72   See Ruether, *Sexism and God-Talk*.

to those who are poor, to Jews and Gentiles, to men and women.

History of Interpretation

Patristic exegesis spoke of the parable of the hundred sheep or that of the ten drachmas and not of the parable of the lost sheep or that of the lost drachma.[73] In that respect it was tuned to the totality, fractured and then reestablished. Patristic authors read in this parable the history of the Fall and redemption. The Christian adoption of the image of the good shepherd, moreover, explains the greater success of the first parable as compared to the second.[74] Gnostics made use of the parable of the lost sheep.[75] The *Gospel of Truth* (31:35—32:30) identified the shepherd with the Savior and applied the above-mentioned rules of arithmology to the parable.[76] We should compare this text with what Irenaeus and Hippolytus had to say about it. The Valentinians considered the lost sheep to be their mother, Sophia, and its loss to be the sojourn of Sophia outside the *Pleroma* (Irenaeus *Adv. haer.* 1.8.4). The followers of Mark Magus associated speculation on numbers with our text.[77] A similar relation between the parable and the doctrine of salvation is found, in the third century, in the Manichaean Psalms: "I also am one in the number of thy hundred sheep which thy Father gave into thy hands that thou mightest feed them."[78]

Valentinus also drew support from the parable, which he interpreted as follows: "Moreover, that Achamoth wandered beyond the Pleroma, and received form from Christ, and was sought after by the Savior, they declare that He indicated when He said, that He had come after that sheep which was gone astray. For they explain the wandering sheep to mean their mother, by whom they represent the Church as having been sown. The wandering itself denotes her stay outside the Pleroma in a state of varied passion, from which they maintain that matter derived its origin" (Irenaeus *Adv. haer.* 1.8.4 [trans. *ANF*]).

In the third century, Origen makes reference to our parables in his commentary on the Epistle to the Romans.[79] In his opinion, it is the same doctrine that was set forth in both Luke 15 and in Romans.[80] The Romans' faith, proclaimed throughout the world (Rom 1:8), corresponds to joy in the presence of God's angels (Luke 15:10) (Origen *Comm. in Rom.* 1.9).[81] In connection with Rom 2:12-13 (condemnation of both those who know the law and those who do not), the parable of the drachma recalls God's salvific will (ibid. 2.9).[82] Finally, Origen refers to the two parables when he comments on Rom 10:17-21 (ibid. 8.6).[83] He maintains that the same conception of salvation is present everywhere: the lost sheep and the lost drachma represent in a special way the Gentiles for whom the good shepherd and Wisdom came to seek.[84]

At the end of the fourth century, Ambrose preached on these two parables (*Exp. Luc.* 7.207–11). He noted that Luke 14 underlined the hesitancy that human beings manifest in this world. Chapter 15 offers God's creatures "remedies for getting lost" (207). This divine

73   See Adam, "Gnostische Züge" (bibliography of Luke 15:1-2), 299.

74   Ibid.

75   See ibid.; Schrage, *Thomas-Evangelium*, 195–96; Siniscalco, *Mito e storia della salvezza* (bibliography of Luke 15:1-2), 35–67; Orbe, *San Ireneo*, 2:117–81 and passim; Schnider, "Gleichnis," 150–54; Poirier, "Evangile"; Petersen, "Parable."

76   The Savior of the lost sheep is compared to Jesus healing on the Sabbath, invoking the precedent of the animal that had fallen into a well (Matt 12:11).

77   See Irenaeus *Adv. haer.* 1.16.1; and Hippolytus *Ref.* 6.52.4–5; see Miroslav Marcovich, ed., *Hippolytus, Refutatio omnium haeresium* (PTS 25; Berlin/New York: de Gruyter, 1986) 273. See Heracleon, frg. 23. Simon the Magician might have identified the lost sheep with Helen. See Irenaeus *Adv. haer.* 1.16.2; 1.23.2; Hippolytus *Ref.* 6.19.2.

78   Psalms to Jesus, 273; C. R. C. Allberry, ed., *A Manichaean Psalm-Book*, vol. 2 (Stuttgart: Kohlhammer, 1938) 93. See Ψαλμοὶ Σαρακωτῶν, ibid., 181, lines 30–33.

79   See Mara, "Parabole," 311–19.

80   This is also the opinion of Cyril of Alexandria *Hom. in Luc.* 106. See Payne Smith (*Cyril*, 2:499), who compares our two parables with 2 Cor 3:18 and Gal 4:19.

81   *PG* 14:854–55.

82   *PG* 14:890–92.

83   *PG* 14:1170.

84   Such is the conclusion of Mara, "Parabole."

aid that is available is triple: from God, the father in the last parable; from Christ, the shepherd in the first parable; and from the church, the woman in the second parable (208). But it always involves the same mercy. Moreover, the single sheep by itself represents the whole human race (the ninety-nine other sheep correspond to the countless angelic hosts who evidently do not need to repent; v. 7). The shepherd who lays the sheep on his shoulders is Christ, whose arms are fastened to the cross (209). While human beings can be compared in some way to the animal (the sheep), they also resemble the drachma, since they bear the likeness of their king (the image of God) and constitute capital (the assets of the church) (211). Ambrose was not alone in developing such interpretations. He depended on an exegetical trend, especially of Origen. The interest afforded by such identifications resides in their suggestive character as well as in the success they have enjoyed through the centuries.

With some slight differences, we find Cyril of Alexandria using certain aspects of this exegesis at the end of the fifth century (*Hom. in Luc.* 106).[85] In his interpretation we, like the sheep, are God's property; like the drachma, we bear the image of our Creator.[86] The two parables have the same meaning. They express the goodness of God, who has found us, thanks to the incarnation of his Son, which was misunderstood by the Jews, just as was Jesus' attitude, according to Luke 15:2.[87] He furnishes a new, original example to combat the idea of a God who would play favorites: when someone is sick in a house, that person is given preferential treatment,

and no one draws the conclusion that others are being treated unfairly.[88] Finally, we find in Cyril an explanation that has continued to be popular through the centuries: the lamp that the woman lights symbolizes the light that God causes to shine on our behalf.[89]

The Venerable Bede, as we know, made the most of the treasures of patristic exegesis for the West in the Middle Ages (*In Luc.* 4.2163–276, 284–87). Several allegories that we have found in the East have turned up in the West as well.[90] On the other hand, one detail that Bede borrowed from Gregory the Great is perhaps original, namely, the observation that the text does not say "Rejoice with the lost sheep," but "with me." That can only mean that the Shepherd's joy consists in saving our life and bringing it back to heaven (4.2206–8, 286).

Bonaventure thought of the three parables as one unit, the first suggesting reconciliation, the second redemption, and the third adoption (*Comm. Luc.* 15.6, 383). Albert the Great detected a progression through the three texts in their description of repentance: the first parable refers to the patient calling back the sinner, the second, to the active search for the lost image (of God?), and the third, to the reconciliation offered by the Father (*Enarr. Luc.* 15.4, 382).[91] Sermons in the vernacular languages confirm at the homiletical level[92] the content of medieval exegesis in Latin. In the eyes of those preachers, the parables are more a description of penitence than conversion.[93] Certain pastors in particular castigated persons who did not consider themselves to be sinners and neglected practicing penitence.[94]

On at least two occasions Luther preached on the text

---

85 See Payne Smith, *Cyril*, 2:495–99.

86 Ibid., 2:498.

87 Ibid., 2:495–96.

88 Ibid., 2:498.

89 Ibid., 2:499.

90 See *Glossa ordinaria* (*PL* 14:310–11).

91 Bengel (*Gnomon*, 363) discovers three characteristics of the sinner in the parables of the sheep, the drachma, and the lost son: foolishness, carelessness, and stubbornness.

92 See Anton Emanuel Schönbach, ed., *Altdeutsche Predigten, Texte* (3 vols.; Graz: Styria, 1886–91; reprinted Darmstadt: Wissenschaftliche Buchgesellschaft, 1964) 46, 2:124–26.

93 This is the case with Eckhart, *Sermones*, 10, 103–11, 98–104.

94 Thus Tauler (*Predigten* 36 [34.25] and 37, 131–47),

who delivered two sermons on the same day in German, one on the first parable, and the other on the second. Whether one becomes a Christian (first sermon) or remains one (second sermon), suffering is unavoidable. It is by his two natures (he explains in the first sermon) that Christ saves us (the shoulders of the shepherd are located between his body, which signifies his humanity, and his head, which signifies his divinity). With mystical superlatives, Tauler describes the warmth and well-being of the recovered sheep, the joy mentioned in the Gospel. A translation of these sermons into modern German can be found in Tauler, *Predigten* (ed. Walter Lehmann; 2 vols.; Jena: Diederichs, 1913) 1:140–54.

of the first two of these parables.[95] His sermon of 1524 had a certain élan; in it Christ paints his own portrait. He comes not to make demands but to save, just as the shepherd and the woman do. His coming was welcome, since human beings, who, like the sheep and the drachma, are lost, had not succeeded in staying on the right path and had been sinking further and further into darkness. These two parables are therefore the expression of an offer of true consolation to the human race. These parables should ring as familiar a note as bread and cheese.[96] What was a living communication of the gospel on the part of Luther, however, became a hard doctrine when it came to Melanchthon.[97] The subtitles of his *Annotationes* alone suffice to indicate this character. The first was "On mercy and the promise of grace." In that paragraph[98] he dealt with Adam's sin, God's salvific will, and the inability of human reason to understand anything but the (Mosaic) law. On the other hand,

grace alone opens the way to the gospel. Thus, the three parables of mercy contain "a sweet meaning of Christ's passion."[99] Zwingli also found a narrativization of the work of salvation and a resurgence of major theological themes in these two parables.[100] Calvin, however, was sensitive to what set the Matthean version apart from the Lukan version. He found an ecclesiastical note in Matthew and a missionary thrust in Luke.[101] Erasmus, on the other hand, took pains to line up these two parables with the life of the church and believers' psychology.[102] Every human being is a sinner, but, as Paul's example demonstrates, everyone can benefit from divine mercy. In our time it is bishops, the successors of the apostles, who play the part of the shepherd that Jesus did in his time. Although they hate sin, they love sinners, knowing that the greatest sinners among them can become the most fervent believers in Christ and the "new life."

---

95 Predigt vom 16.6 1524 (WA 15, 1524), pp. 633–34; Predigt vom 2.7 1525 (WA 17.1), pp. 317–20.

96 The sermon of 1525 elaborates on the Pharisees and tax collectors, past and present.

97 Melanchthon, *Annotationes on Luke 15*, cols. 304–17.

98 Ibid., cols. 305–7.

99 Ibid. col. 307. Melanchthon has several other excursuses, particularly on penitence and contrition, in the *Postillae*, cols. 60–73. Note the Reformer's persistent interest in money!

100 Zwingli, *Annotationes*, 670–71.

101 Calvin, *Harmony*, 219–20.

102 Erasmus, *Paraphrasis on Luke 15*, cols. 404–6.

The Two Sons
(15:11-32)
Bibliography

Bovon, *L'œuvre*, 48–51; reprinted in Bovon and Rouiller, *Exegesis*, 52–54.

Fitzmyer, 2:1092–94.

Kissinger, Warren S., *The Parables of Jesus: A History of Interpretation and Bibliography* (ATLA.BS 4; Metuchen, N.J.: Scarecrow, 1979) 419 (index "Prodigal Son"), esp. 351–70.

Metzger, Bruce M., *Index to Periodical Literature on Christ and the Gospels* (NTTS 6; Leiden: Brill, 1966) 316–18.

Pöhlmann, Wolfgang, *Der verlorene Sohn und das Haus: Studien zu Lk 15,11-32 im Horizont der antiken Lehre von Haus, Erziehung und Ackerbau* (WUNT 68; Tübingen: Mohr Siebeck, 1993) 190–207.

van Segbroeck, *Cumulative Bibliography*, 235 (index 15,11-32).

Bibliography on Verses 11-32

Alemany, José J., "Lc 15,11-32: Una sugerencia de análisis estructural," in A. Vargas-Machuca and G. Ruiz, eds., *Palabra y vida: homenaje a José Alonzo Díaz en su 70 cumpleaños* (Madrid: Universidad Pontificia Comillas de Madrid, 1984) 167–76.

Alonso Díaz, José, "Paralelos entre la narración del libro de Jonás y la parábola del hijo pródigo," *Bib* 40 (1959) 632–40.

Aus, Roger David, "Luke 15,11-32 and R. Eliezer Ben Hyrcanus's Rise to Fame," *JBL* 104 (1985) 443–69.

Idem, *Weihnachtsgeschichte – Barmherziger Samariter – Verlorener Sohn: Studien zu ihrem jüdischen Hintergrund* (ANTZ 2; Berlin: Institut Kirche und Judentum, 1988) 126–73.

Barry, Phillips, "On Luke xv. 25, συμφωνία: Bagpipe," *JBL* 23 (1904) 180–90.

Basset, Lytta, *La joie imprenable: Pour une théologie de la prodigalité* (LiTh 30; Geneva: Labor et Fides, 1996).

Baumgartner, H., "Christologie (Soteriologie) und Parabel vom verlorenen Sohn," *ThZ.S* 4 (1887) 178–99.

Berder, Michel, and Jean-Luc-Marie Foerster, *La parabole du fils prodigue (Luc 15, 11-32)* (Cahiers Evangile, Supplément 101; Paris: Cerf, 1997).

Billy, Dennis J., "Conversion and the Franciscan Preacher: Bonaventure's Commentary on the Prodigal Son," *CFr* 58 (1988) 259–75.

Blumenkranz, Bernhard, "La parabole de l'enfant prodigue chez saint Augustin et saint Césaire d'Arles," *VC* 2 (1948) 102–5.

Idem, "'Siliquae porcorum' (Lc 15, 16)," in idem, *L'exégèse médiévale et les sciences profanes: Mélanges d'histoire du Moyen Âge dédiés à la mémoire de Louis Halphen* (Paris: Presses universitaires de France, 1951) 11–17.

Bonus, Albert, "Luke xv.30," *ExpT* 31 (1919–20) 476.

Braumann, Georg, "'Tot-Lebendig, verlorengefunden' (Lk 15, 24 und 32)," in W. Haubeck and M. Bachmann, eds., *Wort in der Zeit: neutestamentliche Studien. Festgabe für Karl Heinrich Rengstorf zum 75. Geburtstag* (Leiden: Brill, 1980) 156–64.

Brettschneider, Werner, *Die Parabel vom verlorenen Sohn: Das biblische Gleichnis in der Entwicklung der europäischen Literatur* (Berlin: Schmidt, 1978).

Broer, Ingo, "Das Gleichnis vom verlorenen Sohn und die Theologie des Lukas," *NTS* 20 (1973–74) 453–62.

Burchard, Christoph, "Fußnoten zum neutestamentlichen Griechisch," *ZNW* 61 (1970) 157–71, esp. 159–60.

Carlston, Charles E., "Reminiscence and Redaction in Lk 15,11-32," *JBL* 94 (1975) 368–90.

Cattaneo, Enrico, "L'interpretazione di Lc 15,11-32 nei Padri della Chiesa," in Galli, *Interpretazione e invenzione*, 69–96.

Cerfaux, Lucien, "Trois réhabilitations dans l'Evangile," *BFCL* 72 (1950) 5–13; reprinted in idem, *Recueil*, 2:51–59.

Coppens, Joseph, "Le péché, offense de Dieu ou du prochain? Note sur le psaume 51,6 et Lc 15,18-21," in J. Coppens, ed., *La notion biblique de Dieu* (2d ed.; BETL 41; Gembloux: J. Duculot, 1985) 163–67.

Corlett, Tom, "'This Brother of Yours,'" *ExpT* 100 (1989) 216.

Crespy, Georges, "Psychanalyse et foi," *EThR* 41 (1966) 241–51; reprinted in idem, *Essais sur la situation actuelle de la foi* (Paris: Cerf, 1970) 41–56.

Crossan, John Dominic, ed., *Polyvalent Narration* (Semeia 9; Missoula, Mont.: Scholars Press, 1977) 1–73 (see Scott, Tolbert, Via).

Daube, David, "Inheritance in Two Lukan Pericopes," *ZSRR* 72 (1955) 326–34.

Dauvillier, Jean, "Le partage d'ascendant et la parabole du fils prodigue," in *Actes du Congrès de Droit Canonique: cinquantenaire de la Faculté de droit canonique, Paris, 22–26 avril 1947* (Bibliothèque de la Faculté de droit canonique de Paris; Paris: Letouzey et Ané, 1950) 223–28.

Deissmann, Adolf, "The Parable of the Prodigal Son," *RelLi* 1 (1932) 331–38.

Derrett, J. Duncan M., "Law in the New Testament: The Parable of the Prodigal Son," *NTS* 14 (1967–68) 56–74; reprinted in idem, *Law*, 100–125.

Idem, "The Parable of the Prodigal Son: Patristic Allegories and Jewish Midrashim," in F. L. Cross, ed., *Studia Patristica*, vol. 10 (TU 107; Berlin: Akademie-Verlag, 1970) 219–24.

DeWitt, John R., *Amazing Love: The Parable of the Prodigal Son* (Edinburgh: Banner of Truth, 1982).

Dolfini, Giorgio, *La parabola del figliol prodigo nella tradizione germanica* (Milan: La Goliardica, 1968).

Dolto, *Psychanalyse*, 2:59–76.

Dronke, Peter, "Platonic-Christian Allegories in Homilies of Hildegard von Bingen," in H. J. Westra, ed., *From Athens to Chartres: Neoplatonism and Medieval Thought: Studies in Honour of Edouard Jeauneau* (STGMA 35; Leiden: Brill, 1992) 381–96.

Dumais, Marcel, "Approche historico-critique d'un texte: La parabole du père et de ses deux fils (Lc 15,11-32)," *ScEs* 33 (1981) 191–214.

Dupont, Jacques, "L'enfant prodigue," *AsSeign* 17 (1969) 64–72.

Ehrich-Haefeli, Verena, "Sécularisation, langue et structure familiale: Le père dans le théâtre de Lessing et de Diderot," *Coll Helv* 4 (1986) 33–72, esp. 54–60.

Erlemann, Kurt, *Das Bild Gottes in den synoptischen Gleichnissen* (BWANT 126; Stuttgart: Kohlhammer, 1988) 131–50.

Faral, Edmond, ed., *Courtois d'Arras: Jeu du XIIIe siècle* (Paris: Champion, 1911).

Frenzel, Elisabeth, *Stoffe der Weltliteratur: Ein Lexikon dichtungsgeschichtlicher Längsschnitte, Stuttgart* (6th ed.; Stuttgart: Kröner, 1983) 702–5.

Fuchs, Ernst, "Das Fest der Verlorenen: Existentiale Interpretation des Gleichnisses vom verlorenen Sohn," in idem, *Glaube und Erfahrung: Zum christologischen Problem im Neuen Testament* (Tübingen: Mohr Siebeck, 1965) 402–15.

Idem, "Jesus' Understanding of Time," in idem, *Studies of the Historical Jesus* (trans. A. Scobie; SBT 42; London: SCM, 1964) 104–66, esp. 160–62.

Funk, Robert W., *The Poetics of Biblical Narrative* (FF; Sonoma, Calif.: Polebridge, 1988) 177–83.

Fusco, V., "Narrazione e dialogo nella parabola detta del figliol prodigo," in Galli, *Interpretazione e invenzione,* 17–67.

Galli, G., ed., *Interpretazione e invenzione: La parabola del Figliol Prodigo tra interpretazioni scientifiche e invenzioni artistiche* (Università degli studi di Macerata, Pubblicazioni della Facoltà di lettere e filosofia 37; Genoa: Marietti, 1987).

Giblet, J., "La parabole de l'accueil messianique (Lc 15,11-32)," *BVC* 47 (1962) 17–28.

Greenwood, David C., *Structuralism and the Biblical Text* (RaR 32; Berlin/New York: Mouton, 1985) 129–38.

Grelot, Pierre, "Le père et ses deux fils: Lc 15,11-32.

Essai d'analyse structurale" and "De l'analyse structurale à l'herméneutique," *RB* 84 (1977) 321–48, 538–65.

Güttgemanns, Erhart, "Narrative Analyse synoptischer Texte," *LingBibl* 25–26 (1973) 50–73, esp. 62–63.

Hasenclever, Walter, *Der Sohn: Ein Drama* (2d ed.; Leipzig: Wolff, 1917).

Hilgenfeld, Adolf, "Das Gleichnis von dem verlorenen Sohne (Lk 15,11-32)," *ZWTh* 45 (1902) 449–64.

Hofius, Otfried, "Alttestamentliche Motive im Gleichnis vom verlorenen Sohn," *NTS* 24 (1977–78) 240–48.

Holstein, Hugo, *Das Drama vom verlorenen Sohn: Ein Beitrag zur Geschichte des Dramas* (Programm des Progymnasiums zu Geestemünde; Halle: Hendel, 1880).

Hoppe, Rudolf, "Gleichnis und Situation: Zu den Gleichnissen vom guten Vater (Lk 15,11-32) und gütigen Hausherrn (Mt 20,1-15)," *BZ* 28 (1984) 1–21.

Jeremias, Joachim, "Zum Gleichnis vom verlorenen Sohn, Lk 15,11-32," *ThZ* 5 (1949) 228–31.

Kallensee, Kurt, *Die Liebe des Vaters: Das Gleichnis vom verlorenen Sohn in der christlichen Dichtung und bildenden Kunst* (Berlin: Evangelische Verlagsanstalt, 1960).

Kelley, Robert L., "The Significance of the Parable of the Prodigal Son for Three Major Issues in Current Synoptic Study" (Diss., Princeton University, 1972); see *DAI.A* 33 (1972) 390.

Kienzle, Beverly Mayne, "Hildegard of Bingen's Gospel Homilies and Her Exegesis of The Parable of the Prodigal Son," in Rainer Berndt, ed., *"Im Angesicht Gottes suche der Mensch sich selbst." Hildegard von Bingen (1098–1179)* (Erudiri Sapientia 2; Berlin: Akademie-Verlag, 2001) 299–318.

Kirschbaum, Engelbert, *Lexikon der christlichen Ikonographie*, vol. 4 (Rome: Herder, 1972) cols. 172–74.

Klötzl, W., *Ein Vater hatte zwei Söhne: Eine Auslegung von Lk 15, 11-32* (Zurich, 1966).

Kruse, Heinz, "The Return of the Prodigal: Fortunes of a Parable on Its Way to the Far East," *Or* 47 (1978) 163–214.

Le Du, Jean, *Le fils prodigue ou les chances de la transgression* (Série Évangile 1; Paris: S.O.F.E.C., 1977).

Lohfink, Gerhard, "'Ich habe gesündigt gegen den Himmel und gegen dich . . .': Eine Exegese von Lk 15,18.21," *ThQ* 155 (1975) 51–52.

Magass, Walter, "Geben, Nehmen, Teilen als Tischsequenz in Lk 15,11-32," *LingBibl* 37 (1976) 31–48.

Mangey, Thomas, *Philonis Judaei opera quae reperiri potuerunt omnia* (4 vols.; London: G. Bowyer, 1742) 2:676.

Marion, Jean-Luc, *God without Being: Hors-Texte* (trans. T. A. Carlson; Religion and Postmodernism; Chicago: University of Chicago Press, 1991) 95–101.

Marsch, Edgar, "Die verlorenen Söhne: Konstitution und Redaktion in der Parabel," in J. Brantschen and P. Selvatico, eds., *Unterwegs zur Einheit: Festschrift für Heinrich Stirnimann* (Freiburg, Schweiz: Universitätsverlag; Vienna: Herder, 1980) 29–45.

Méroz, Christianne, *Le visage maternel de Dieu* (Le Mont-sur-Lausanne: Ouverture, 1989) 55–60.

Moore, George F., "συμφωνία – Not a Bagpipe," *JBL* 24 (1905) 166–75.

Niebuhr, Karl-Wilhelm, "Kommunikationsebenen im Gleichnis vom verlorenen Sohn," *ThLZ* 116 (1991) cols. 481–94.

Patte, Daniel, "Structural Analysis of the Parable of the Prodigal Son: Toward a Method," in idem, ed., *Semiology and Parables: Explorations of the Possibilities Offered by Structuralism for Exegesis* (PTMS 9; Pittsburgh: Pickwick, 1976) 71–149 (reactions and discussion, 151–78).

Pesch, Rudolf, "Zur Exegese Gottes durch Jesus von Nazaret: Eine Auslegung des Gleichnisses vom Vater und den beiden Söhnen (Lk 15,11-32)," in B. Casper, ed., *Jesus: Ort der Erfahrung Gottes: Festschrift für Bernhard Welte* (Freiburg im Breisgau: Herder, 1976) 140–89.

Pirot, Jean, *Paraboles et allégories évangéliques: la pensée de Jésus, les commentaires patristiques* (Paris: P. Lethielleux, 1949) 279–98.

Pöhlmann, Wolfgang, "Die Abschichtung des verlorenen Sohnes (Lk 15,12f.) und die erzählte Welt der Parabel," *ZNW* 70 (1979) 194–213.

Idem, *Der verlorene Sohn und das Haus: Studien zur Lk 15,11-32 im Horizont der antiken Lehre von Haus, Erziehung und Ackerbau* (WUNT 68; Tübingen: Mohr Siebeck, 1993).

Pokorný, Petr, "Lk 15,11-32 und die lukanische Soteriologie," in K. Kertelge, T. Holtz, and C.-P. März, eds., *Christus bezeugen: Festschrift für Wolfgang Trilling zum 65. Geburtstag* (Leipzig: St. Benno-Verlag, 1989) 179–92.

Price, James L., "Luke 15,11-32," *Int* 31 (1977) 64–69.

Räisänen, Heikki, "The Prodigal Gentile and His Jewish Christian Brother (Lk 15,11-32)," in van Segbroeck, *Four Gospels*, 2:1617–36.

Rengstorf, Karl H., *Die Re-Investitur des verlorenen Sohnes in der Gleichniserzählung Jesu Lk 15,11-32* (VAFLNW.G 137; Cologne: Westdeutscher Verlag, 1967).

Rickards, Raymond R., "Some Points to Consider in Translating the Parable of the Prodigal Son (Lk 15,11-32)," *BT* 31 (1980) 243–45.

Rilke, Rainer M., "Der Auszug des verlorenen Sohnes," in Rainer, *Neue Gedichte* (Leipzig: Insel-Verlag, 1923) 17–18.

Robbins, Jill, *Prodigal Son—Elder Brother: Interpretation and Alterity in Augustine, Petrarch, Kafka, Levinas* (Religion and Postmodernism; Chicago/London: University of Chicago Press, 1991).

Rosenkranz, G., "Das Gleichnis vom verlorenen Sohn im Lotos-Sûtra und im Lukasevangelium," *ThLZ* 79 (1954) cols. 281–82.

Sahl, Hans, "Der verlorene Sohn," in *Der Ruf: Unabhängige Blätter der jungen Generation, 1, 1* (München, August 15, 1946) 11.

Sanders, Jack T., "Tradition and Redaction in Lk 15,11-32," *NTS* 15 (1968–69) 433–38.

Schlienger-Stähli, Hildegard, *Rainer Maria Rilke – André Gide: Der verlorene Sohn. Vergleichende Betrachtung* (Zurich: Juris-Verlag, 1974).

Schnider, Franz, *Die verlorenen Söhne: Strukturanalytische und historisch-kritische Untersuchungen zu Lk 15* (OBO 17; Freiburg, Schweiz: Universitätsverlag; Göttingen: Vandenhoeck & Ruprecht, 1977).

Schniewind, Julius, "Das Gleichnis vom verlorenen Sohn," in Schniewind, *Die Freude der Busse: Zur Grundfrage der Bibel* (2d ed.; Göttingen: Vandenhoeck & Ruprecht, 1960) 34–87.

Scholz, Günter, "Ästhetische Beobachtungen am Gleichnis vom reichen Mann und armen Lazarus und an drei anderen Gleichnissen (Lk 16,19-25 [26-31]; 10,34; 13,9; 15,11-32)," *LingBibl* 43 (1978) 67–74.

Schöttgen, Christian, *Christiani Schoettgenii Horae Hebraicae et Talmudicae in universum Novum Testamentum*, vol. 1 (Dresden-Leipzig: Hekelii B. Filium, 1733) 296–97.

Schottroff, Luise, "Das Gleichnis vom verlorenen Sohn," *ZThK* 68 (1971) 27–52.

Schwab, Claude, *Un père prodigue: Variations sur une parabole de Jésus* (Aubonne: du Moulin, 1985).

Schweizer, Eduard, "Antwort an Joachim Jeremias, S. 228–231," *ThZ* 5 (1949) 231–33.

Idem, "Zur Frage der Lukasquellen: Analyse von Lk 15,11-32," *ThZ* 4 (1948) 469–71.

Scobel, Gert, "Das Gleichnis vom verlorenen Sohn als metakommunikativer Text: Überlegungen zur Verständigungsproblematik in Lk 15," *FZPhTh* 35 (1988) 21–67.

Scott, Bernard B., "The Prodigal Son: A Structuralist Interpretation," in Crossan, *Polyvalent Narration*, 45–73.

Sellew, Philip, "Interior Monolog as a Narrative Device in the Parables of Luke," *JBL* 111 (1992) 239–53.

Sibinga, Joost Smit, "Zur Kompositionstechnik des Lukas in Lk 15,11–32," in J. W. Van Henten et al., eds., *Tradition and Re-Interpretation in Jewish* and Early Christian Literature: Essays in Honour of Jürgen C. H. Lebram (StPB 36; Leiden: Brill, 1986) 97–113.

Siniscalco, Paolo, "La parabola del figlio prodigo (Lc 15, 11-32) in Ireneo," in *Studi in onore di A. Pincherle* (2 vols.; SMSR 38; Rome: Ateneo, 1967) 2:536–53.

Stein, Dominique, *Lectures psychanalytiques de la Bible: L'enfant prodigue, Marie, saint Paul et les femmes* (Paris: Cerf, 1985) 49–66.

Stock, Alex, *Textentfaltungen: Semiotische Experimente mit einer biblischen Geschichte* (Düsseldorf: Patmos, 1978).

Str-B 2:212–18.

Strunk, R., and M. Mausshardt, "Leitung des Schöpferischen (Lk 15,11-32)," in Y. Spiegel, ed., *Doppeldeutlich: Tiefendimensionen biblischer Texte* (Munich: Kaiser, 1978) 59–78.

Thieme, K., "Augustinus und der ältere Bruder: Zur patristischen Auslegung von Lk 15,25-32," in H. Berg, ed., *Universitas, Dienst an Wahrheit und Leben: Festschrift für Bischof Dr. Albert Stohr im Auftrag der Katholisch-Theologischen Fakultät der Johannes Gutenberg-Universität Mainz* (2 vols.; Mainz: Gruenwald, 1960) 1:79–85.

Tissot, Yves, "Allégories patristiques de la parabole lucanienne des deux fils (Lc 15,11-32)," in Bovon and Rouiller, *Exegesis*, 243–72.

Tolbert, Mary A., "The Prodigal Son: An Essay in Literary Criticism from a Psychoanalytic Perspective," in Crossan, *Polyvalent Narration*, 1–20.

Vasse, Denis, *Le temps du désir: Essai sur le corps et la parole* (Paris: Seuil, 1969) 31–34.

Vazques Medel, Manuel Angel, "El perdón libera del odio: Lectura estructural de Lc 15,11-32," *Communio* 11 (1978) 271–312.

Via, Dan O., *The Parables: Their Literary and Existential Dimension* (Philadelphia: Fortress, 1967) 162–76 and passim.

Idem, "The Prodigal Son: A Jungian Reading," in Crossan, *Polyvalent Narration*, 21–43.

Visser't Hooft, W. A., *La paternité de Dieu dans un monde sécularisé* (trans. C. de Morawitz and E. de Peyer; Publications de la Faculté de théologie de l'Université de Genève 8; Geneva, 1984).

Vogel, H.-J., "Der verlorene Sohn: Lk 15,11-32," *TeKo* 18 (1983) 27–34.

Vogler, W., "Die Parabel von der grenzenlosen Güte eines Vaters (Lk 15,11-32)," *Die Christenlehre* 43 (1990) 324–34.

Voltaire, *L'enfant prodigue: comedie en vers dissillabes, représentée sur le Théatre de la Comédie française le 10 octobre 1736* (Paris: Chez Prault fils, 1738).

Walser, Robert, *Phantasieren: Prosa aus der Berliner und Bieler Zeit*, in Walser, *Das Gesamtwerk* (ed. J. Greven; 2d ed.; 12 vols.; Geneva: H. Kossodo, 1975) 6:258–61.

Idem, *Prosa aus der Berner Zeit*, vol. 2: *Maskerade, 1927–1928*, in Walser, *Das Gesamtwerk* (ed. J. Greven; 2d ed.; 12 vols.; Geneva: H. Kossodo, 1978) 9:112–15.

Weiser, Alfons, "Zuvorkommendes Erbarmen (Lk 15,20)," in K. Backhaus and F. G. Untergassmair, eds., *Schrift und Tradition: Festschrift für Josef Ernst zum 70. Geburtstag* (Paderborn: Ferdinand Schöningh, 1996) 259–71.

Weymann, V., "Invitation à une vie digne de ce nom: La fête qu'un père offre à ses fils (Lc 15,11-32)," in *Paraboles de Jésus*, 59–77.

Witwitzky, Willibald, *Das Gleichnis vom verlorenene Sohn in der bildenden Kunst bis Rembrandt* (Diss., Heidelberg, 1930).

11/ Then he said, "A man had two sons. **12/** And the younger of them said to the father, 'Father, give me that share of the fortune that belongs to me.' And the father divided his estate between them. **13/** And, not many days later, having collected everything, the younger son emigrated to a distant region, and there he squandered his fortune by living without any hope of being saved. **14/** And when he had spent all he owned, a severe famine came upon all that region, and as for him, he began to be in need. **15/** He set off and hired himself out to one of the citizens of that region, who sent him off to his fields to look after the pigs. **16/** And he would gladly have filled his stomach[a] with the carob pods that the pigs were eating; but no one gave him any of them. **17/** But when he came to himself he said, 'How many of my father's hired hands

a   This is the reading I follow.

have plenty of bread, but as for me, I'm lost because of this famine. 18/ Getting up, I will go to my father, and I will say to him, "I have sinned against heaven and against you; 19/ I am no longer worthy to be called your son; treat me like one of your hired hands."' 20/ So getting up, he went to his father. While he was still a long way off, his father saw him and was filled with compassion, and he ran and threw himself on his neck and smothered him with kisses. 21/ The son said to him, 'Father, I have sinned against heaven and against you; I am no longer worthy to be called your son.' 22/ But the father said to his servants, 'Quick, bring the finest robe and put it on him; and put a ring on his finger[b], and shoes[c] on his feet. 23/ And bring the fatted calf and slaughter it, and let us celebrate as we eat. 24/ For this son of mine was dead and has come back to life; he was lost and has been found!' And they began to celebrate. 25/ Now his elder son was in the fields. When, on his return, he approached the house, he heard strains of music and the singing of a choir. 26/ And he called one of the young servants and asked what this meant. 27/ This young servant said to him, 'Your brother has come, and your father has slaughtered the fatted calf, because he has got him back safe and sound.' 28/ Then he became angry and refused to go in, but his father went out and pleaded with him. 29/ But he answered his father in these words: 'I've been working like a slave for you for many years now, and I have never disobeyed any of your orders. Yet, as for me, you have never given me even a young goat so that I might dine[d] with my friends. 30/ But when this son of yours arrived on the scene, he who has devoured your property with prostitutes, you slaughtered the fatted calf for him!' 31/ He said to him, '(My) child, you are always with me, and all that is mine is yours. 32/ It was only right for us to celebrate and rejoice, because this brother of yours was dead and has come to life; he was lost and has been found.'"

b   Literally: "on his hand."
c   Or, "sandals."
d   This is the reading I follow.

The Two Sons (vv. 11-32)

We might hesitate as to what title to give to this parable, and behind the question of the title is that of the content. Our hesitation cannot be eradicated, for is not every attempt to synthesize bound to lead to simplification? Should we complain about the variety of readings of this text?[1] Is it not the text itself that is responsible for the multiplicity of interpretations of it? Interpreters are embarrassed, perhaps even frozen, in the face of such a wealth of commentaries, both those they know and those they do not, and from both past centuries and the present.

1   See Scobel, "Gleichnis," 21–67.

In Luke 15:11-32, what is involved is nothing less than the essence of Christianity and the true picture of human society. We have God, who is the Father in the Gospel; Christ, who is the unassuming and incisive speaker; and the church, divided into two groups, both of which are guilty. There is also the absence, either intentional or unintentional, of any mention of women; they are present only in the sense of being not mentioned. Note also the man who is moved by compassion when he finds his son still alive. The two brothers in the story are purposely assigned different fates and are rivals, just as Cain and Abel were. We also find the major categories of Christian doctrine: the Fall and reconciliation and the people of God divided and, in their sin, dependent on grace alone. The will to live, autonomy, rivalry, and dependence are further elements in the story. Does this parable legitimize parental authority and give support to a certain concept of family life? Does this story encourage the realization of one's desires and bring this realization into conflict with reality? After pointing us to heaven, does this tale then redirect our gaze toward earth and uphold the values of both personal and property law?

Analysis

Let us begin by establishing the Greek text. In v. 16 I prefer the reading $\gamma\epsilon\mu\acute{\iota}\sigma\alpha\iota$ $\tau\grave{\eta}\nu$ $\kappa o\iota\lambda\acute{\iota}\alpha\nu$ $\alpha\mathring{v}\tauo\hat{v}$ ("to fill his belly"), a wording whose coarseness shocked the scribes early on in the transmission. The third-century Papyrus Bodmer XIV–XV, $\mathfrak{P}^{75}$, reads $\chi o\rho\tau\alpha\sigma\vartheta\hat{\eta}\nu\alpha\iota$ ("to have his fill"). This reading was also followed by the most famous later witnesses.[2] At the end of v. 21, which contains the answer of the younger brother to his father, several manuscripts have a longer reading that repeats v. 19b word for word. It is probably a secondary development of the tradition. Certain scribes were anxious to have the prodigal son follow through on his plans by having him finish the speech he had planned to give. In v. 22, I propose retaining the word $\tau\alpha\chi\acute{v}$ ("quick[ly]") in the text. Luke loves to use the motif of haste in order to suggest a divine intervention (see 1:39). The father's haste clashed with the desire of theologians who favored a

penitential discipline involving a certain delay before the granting of absolution. Finally, in v. 29, I am in favor of retaining the verb $\mathring{a}\rho\iota\sigma\tau\acute{\eta}\sigma\omega$ ([so that] "I might dine"), a reading whose manuscript attestation is admittedly weak but whose semantic value is more original than that of $\epsilon\mathring{v}\varphi\rho\alpha\nu\vartheta\hat{\omega}$ ([so that] "I might celebrate"), a wording already used twice, in vv. 23 and 24b.

Now let us follow the story line, which could not be introduced in a manner any briefer than it is: $E\mathring{\iota}\pi\epsilon\nu$ $\delta\acute{\epsilon}$ ("Then he said"). There is also a very concise description of the family's situation, which turns to a family story, because the members of the family "say" things to each other ($\kappa\alpha\grave{\iota}$ $\epsilon\mathring{\iota}\pi\epsilon\nu$ ["and he said"], which inserts a quotation into Jesus' words; there will naturally be other cases to point out that are similar).

The first episode presents a son and his father in a face-to-face encounter in which the father, out of either strength or weakness of character, gives in without batting an eye. The second and subsequent episodes involve only the son. To speak of a narrative is also to speak of a time line, which in this case unfolds in linear fashion and with a sustained rhythm. "And not many days later" (v. 13), "the younger son" (the text stresses this designation, which it has already used in almost the same wording: "the younger of them" in v. 12) advances the story with an act that corresponds to the verb used at the outset. The son's liberty of action would assuredly have been negligible if his father had not given in to his imperious request. The son is the subject of the verbs: after having collected [everything] ($\sigma\upsilon\nu\alpha\gamma\alpha\gamma\acute{\omega}\nu$, "having brought together"), he dispersed it. Every narrative also needs some reference to the space in which the story takes place. There are two parts to this space, and the distance is incrementally increased ($\epsilon\mathring{\iota}\varsigma$ $\chi\acute{\omega}\rho\alpha\nu$ $\mu\alpha\kappa\rho\acute{\alpha}\nu$, "to a distant region," v. 13; $\kappa\alpha\grave{\iota}$ $\pi o\rho\epsilon\upsilon\vartheta\epsilon\grave{\iota}\varsigma$ . . . $\grave{\epsilon}\nu\grave{\iota}$ $\tau\hat{\omega}\nu$ $\pi o\lambda\iota\tau\hat{\omega}\nu$ $\tau\hat{\eta}\varsigma$ $\chi\acute{\omega}\rho\alpha\varsigma$ $\grave{\epsilon}\kappa\epsilon\acute{\iota}\nu\eta\varsigma$, "He set off, . . . one of the citizens of that [other] region," v. 15). The narrator assumes a moralizing, disapproving tone and uses a vocabulary critical of the son. This distancing coincides with a decline, accompanied by a progressive shortage ($\mathring{\eta}\rho\xi\alpha\tauo$ $\mathring{v}\sigma\tau\epsilon\rho\epsilon\hat{\iota}\sigma\vartheta\alpha\iota$, "he began to be in need"; v. 14), and an unsatisfied desire ($\grave{\epsilon}\pi\epsilon\vartheta\acute{v}\mu\epsilon\iota$ $\gamma\epsilon\mu\acute{\iota}\sigma\alpha\iota$ $\tau\grave{\eta}\nu$ $\kappa o\iota\lambda\acute{\iota}\alpha\nu$ $\alpha\mathring{v}\tauo\hat{v}$, "and he would have gladly filled his

---

2   The manuscripts ℵ, B, D, L, et al.; see the apparatus of Nestle-Aland.

stomach"; v. 16). His father had given him the better part of his estate (v. 12), but from now on no one gives him anything (v. 16). Once he takes stock of his material situation, he begins an inward spiritual pilgrimage, which turns the story around (v. 17).[3] After making a comparison (v. 17), the young man decides on a new course of action (vv. 18-19). But his ambition is now on a reduced scale, since he thinks of the only counterpart to his last job. This provides symmetry between his job looking after pigs, v. 15, and the job he plans to ask for, vv. 18-19. No one can reproach the son of having shilly-shallied; no sooner said than done. The participle ἀναστάς ("getting up," v. 20) indicates the beginning of the new action that the monologue had anticipated; the same participle is used in v. 18. Even though the young man has come full circle, the narrative has only reached the halfway point (or advanced a third of the way, since we still have to take into consideration the older son). The younger son has used up his options. With some degree of courage, he comes before his father empty-handed (v. 20a) and offers himself as an object to his father. The usualness and ordinariness stop there.

At this point an element of surprise crops up in the story. It is not the father's taking matters into his own hands that is surprising but the way he does it. The narrator, who is anxious to indicate that the father is the new subject of the verbs, highlights the father's compassion, the haste occasioned by his emotion, the hugs, and the kisses. Once again, Luke hides neither his feelings nor his opinions; having condemned what is evil, he approves what is good. The son has time to run through only half of what he had promised to himself to say: v. 21 puts in motion vv. 18b-19a, just as v. 20a makes good on the plan formulated in v. 18a. Verse 19b (the offer to work) is not accomplished and loses all of its raison d'être. This is because the father also has a new plan of action, which short-circuits his son's plans. This plan amounts to a garland of superlatives and—it is as if the son should not be spoken to until all the preparations have been made—the father does not speak to his son but gives orders instead to his servants and, in his role

as wise boss, furnishes an explanation for his orders (vv. 22-24). The firm insistence of v. 24a, with its suggestive parallelism ("for this son of mine was dead . . . he was lost . . ."), leads into a narrative pause—in fact, almost to a conclusion. Verse 24b closes this second part of the narrative with the father having the advantage. But—and this is where the narration is tricky—when it says that "they began to celebrate," the author gives the reader the idea that the story is not yet over. And the reader, who has not forgotten the opening words of the story ("A man had two sons," v. 11), is led to wonder what has become of the older son.

So the third part of the story is quite naturally allotted to this third person. The fact that only one part is devoted to him suggests that there is some unfinished business to take care of. The story gives the younger son the time to go away and come back but allows the older son only the time necessary to give vent to his bad temper. The refrain of v. 32, which picks up on the joyful announcement in v. 24, nevertheless leaves the door partly open to the future. If the older son will just agree to take part in the dancing, the beginning of the rejoicing (v. 24b) can be followed by a corresponding conclusion. The narrator continues to express his personal views, as he talks first about the younger son's dissolute life (v. 13), then the father's compassion (v. 20), and finally the older son's anger (v. 28). He takes note also of the father's disappointment ("we had to celebrate and rejoice") in the imperfect tense in Greek, which denotes a continued action in the past. Could the lights still be lit again and the party start all over again? The tone of v. 32 is not very optimistic. This third part of the story has been skillfully crafted; the older son also is situated outside the house, albeit not far away, as had been the younger son (v. 13), but in the fields (v. 25). He, too, comes back (v. 25b), but that is where the resemblance ends: a dialogue between the older son and a young servant (vv. 26-27) picks up on the monologue of the younger son with himself (vv. 17-19). The silent hugging and kissing of v. 20 is replaced here by a bitter dialogue (vv. 28-32).[4]

---

3   Two works that are almost contemporaneous analyze Lukan monologues: Heininger, *Metaphorik*, 31–82; and Sellew, "Interior Monolog," 239–53.

4   The sheer number of authors who analyze the structure of the parable prevents me from engaging with each individually. See, e.g., Via, *Parables*, 164–72; Patte, "Structural Analysis"; Pesch, "Exegese"; Schnider, *Söhne*, esp. 37; Greenwood, *Structuralism and the Biblical Text*, 129–38 (this remains inac-

This long story bears signs of Lukan redaction in both its style and its convictions. That is why some authors have alleged that the Gospel writer made it up out of whole cloth.[5] Nevertheless, it resembles those elegant and well-honed literary units of L. For that reason many exegetes attribute it to that talented anonymous author.[6] The tripartite structure of the text raises a question: Is not the matter of the older son a conjectural addition, a way to settle some score? The hypothesis becomes more believable if we make a distinction between the vocabulary and the phrasing of the two parts, the earlier one being more Semitic, the latter one more Greek. For more than a century now, various famous scholars have added their support to this ingenious solution.[7] Other commentators, every bit as erudite as the first group, have called our attention to one characteristic of Jesus' teaching that is rare but significant, the keyword being "*zweigipfelig*" ("double-peaked").[8] The Master's parables do not always have a single point or focus; they may have "two heads," since they proclaim a message with two complementary aspects.[9] This is how it is here with the same good news, which is addressed to one group of people but does not make others immediately happy. But this same message must be conveyed to this latter group. If this analysis is correct, then we are dealing with the development of Jesus' thinking rather than the history of the Synoptic tradition. My own choice is the following hypothesis: behind our present text lies an original oral parable told by Jesus and preserved in the memory of the early Christians, which the author of L took the trouble to put down in writing. This is the parable that Luke received from the tradition and integrated into his central chapter. He put it in an appropriate place in his Gospel:[10] after the success of Jesus' ministry in Galilee, "his" Jesus came up against increasing opposition. The message is well suited to the line of argument, and the kerygma and defense go hand in hand.

Commentary

■ **11** The expression "a certain person" (ἄνθρωπός τις) has a Semitic flavor that is not Lukan (Luke's customary expression is "a certain man" [ἀνήρ τις]). "A certain person" is characteristic of L.[11]

The phrase "had two sons" (v. 11) prepares the way for the three parts of the parable, especially the last one, which deals with the older son.

■ **12** When reading the words "the younger of them," the reader will do well to focus on the composition of the family, even if the adjective "younger" (νεώτερος) was a designation in the early church (see Acts 5:6; 1 Pet 5:5) for a new convert (the new converts sometimes made up a distinct group). Our text stands in a long line of scriptural tradition that places more value on the youngest child than on the oldest. In spite of his shortcomings and his excesses, the youngest son incarnates divine election and receives the paternal blessing.[12]

Nothing indicates that the younger son went beyond his rights in making the request he did to his father. At most he lacked wisdom and probably consideration. As more than one papyrus has shown, the expression "that share of the fortune that belongs to someone" (τὸ ἐπιβάλλον μέρος) was certainly precise—and even legal—language that was widespread and intelligible. It can also be found in documents that are neither liter-

cessible to me); Sibinga, "Kompositionstechnik"; Meynet, *Saint Luc*, 2:162–64.

5   See Schottroff, "Gleichnis," 27–52; and Räisänen, "Prodigal Gentile."

6   Petzke (*Sondergut*, 140–41) is cautious. He considers it difficult to distinguish here between tradition and redaction but nevertheless presupposes that Luke reworked a prior text.

7   The hypothesis discussed in the past by Jülicher (*Gleichnisreden*, 2:360–63) and defended by Loisy (402–3) has been revived by Schweizer ("Zur Frage der Lukasquellen," 469–71; and idem, "Antwort") and then by Sanders ("Tradition and Redaction"). Schweizer seems to have revised his interpretation;

see idem, "Wer ist Jesus Christus?" *ThLZ* 99 (1974) 724–25; and idem, *Parable of God*, 33, 66–70.

8   Principally Jeremias, *Parables*, 115; and idem, *Sprache*, 252–55.

9   See Dupont, *Pourquoi des paraboles*, 60.

10 Fusco ("Narrazione," 26–27) has addressed the parable's placement in the body of the Gospel.

11 The exposition that I am providing here relies on pages I have written in Bovon and Rouiller, *Exegesis*, 36–51. The reader will kindly forgive me for having limited the references to the approximately fifty recent articles with which I am familiar.

12 See Derrett, "Law in the New Testament," 68–70.

ary nor legal, and it can refer to other "shares" than just those having to do with inheritance.[13]

When the young man speaks of οὐσία, he is referring to his father's fortune. Luke says that the father divided his estate (βίος) between them (vv. 12 and 30). Is there a distinction to be made between the two Greek terms (οὐσία and βίος)? We should remember that οὐσία is the word for "existence," "substance," and whatever "possessions" there are. The son can speak of them because they do exist. In the agrarian context of the parable, we should think first of all of real estate, beginning with the land. The Greek word βίος has as its first meaning "life," then "means of subsistence," "resources." So the father gives his son the means to make a living.[14]

The ideal in ancient Israel was to live in the context of an extended family. As time went on, it was impossible to prevent the breakup of the inheritance. It would appear that in the first century of our era it was possible, according to Jewish law, to divide up one's possessions during one's life. It was discouraged, since it was considered undesirable to have aged parents reduced to begging from their children.[15] We are not dealing here with the carrying out of a last will and testament, which required the death of the testator, or of a dividing up of the estate among the living, which would not take effect until the death of the one giving away the estate. What is involved is the dividing up of an estate by an ancestor, in which case the descendants forfeit any further claim to the estate, in German, *Abschichtung*, the existence of which is presupposed by Wis 33:20-24 and Tobit 8:21. Although foreign to Roman law, this solution was not unknown in Hellenistic law. So readers coming from a Jewish or Hellenistic background would have understood what was

being done. Normally the son, enriched by this process, was held responsible for the welfare of his parents. By already claiming his part of the estate, the young man may not have shown much filial sensitivity, but he did not commit any crime against the law. The younger son's having received his share did not mean that the older son received his. By staying in his father's house, the older son would not be in a position to receive his share of the inheritance, which, by law (Deut 21:15-17), was twice that of his brother's, until his father's death. In the parable, as a matter of fact, the father has free use of his goods right up until the end. The narrative does not tell us how the father arranged for his younger son to get his share of the inheritance.[16]

■ **13** The verb συνάγω, which means "assemble," "bring together," "consolidate," or "gather," here means "collect his belongings," or "gather his belongings together" before his departure; it may also have the meaning of "converting everything into cash."[17]

"Not many days later" is one of those litotes of which Luke was fond. In other words, the younger son was in a hurry to take off.[18] "Living without hope of salvation" (ζῶν ἀσώτως). Etymologically ἀσώτως means "without hope of salvation" (ἀ-privative + σῴζω). Here the expression suggests in the first instance an irreversible squandering (cf. v. 14a: "when he had spent all he owned"). But when the readers recall Luke's interest in the vocabulary of salvation, they will also detect an ethical connotation in this adverb (ἀσωτία belonged to moral language at that time).[19] The younger son's wrong consisted less in his request or his departure than in his misuse of the inheritance from his father.[20] Money plays

---

13 See BAGD, s.v. ἐπιβάλλω; and above all Pöhlmann, "Abschichtung," 194–213.

14 On οὐσία and βίος, see BAGD, s.vv.

15 See Sir 33:21-22: "While you are still alive . . . do not let anyone take your place. It is better that your children should ask from you than that you should look to the hand of your children" (*NRSV*).

16 Dauvillier ("Le partage d'ascendant," 223–28) has studied these complex legal problems with care. On the other hand, Daube ("Inheritance in Two Lukan Pericopes," 326–34), Pöhlmann ("Abschichtung"), Schottroff ("Gleichnis"), and Pesch ("Exegese") argue against overemphasizing the

legal aspects of the text; for them the human aspect is most important.

17 See Moulton and Milligan (*Vocabulary*, s.v.), BAGD (s.v.), and Fitzmyer (2:1088), who cite the example of Plutarch *Min.* 6, 7 §672c: κληρονομίαν εἰς ἀργύριον συναγαγών (but we must observe that Plutarch took pains to specify εἰς ἀργύριον).

18 See Fitzmyer, 2:1087.

19 References to secular authors (who use this word) are in Fitzmyer, 2:1088. Pesch ("Exegese") points to Prov 28:7 LXX.

20 The elder son will say (v. 30) that his younger brother squandered this money "with prostitutes."

a big role in the story, and the economic situation of this or that character plays out throughout the story.[21]

"A severe famine came upon (all that region)." People in antiquity kept alive the memory of the famines that had caused them suffering. These famines were usually local in scope by reason of the limits of commercial trading in those days.[22] On the other hand, Luke calls attention to one famine in the book of Acts that was worldwide in scope (Acts 11:28). Memory of biblical history also plays a role here, since the expression "there was a famine" (ἐγένετο λιμός) occurs in the LXX.[23] The story of the prodigal son recalls Joseph's saga,[24] or the story of Tobias.

■ 14 The vocabulary of "being in need"[25] was not the exclusive domain of the Gnostics. It was available to all those whose basic needs were not met. In Heb 11:37 we read of "the destitute," "the poor" (ὑστερούμενοι). For Paul, that theologian of Jewish origin, one's current human condition is determined by what one lacks. Since the Fall, human beings have been deprived (ὑστεροῦνται) of God's glory (Rom 3:23). The son's degradation continues: after having squandered his fortune he experiences such severe pangs of famine that he feels lost: "but as for me, I am lost because of this famine" (ἐγὼ δὲ λιμῷ ὧδε ἀπόλλυμαι, v. 17).

■ 15 He has just enough gumption left, however, to move him to try something new. He decides to hire himself out (ἐκολλήθη) to a stranger (v. 15). This man, who was a citizen (πολίτης) of that region, owned a herd of pigs, so he must not have been a Jew. Reading this verse alongside Acts 10:28, which uses the same verb (κολλᾶσθαι),[26] we may conclude that the prodigal son made himself ritually impure.[27]

"He sent him off to his fields": without warning, the narrator has changed the subject of the verb; although this is awkward in Greek, it is a common way of speaking in Hebrew and Aramaic.[28]

■ 16 The word κεράτιον, diminutive of κέρας ("horn"), is used in the plural to designate carob pods, the fruits of the carob tree. The Alexandrian poet Lycophron confirms this usage: any kind of leguminous food, such as remainders of olives or grapes, crushed, and mixed with grass, could be used to feed pigs (675–78). According to one modern scholar, "the carobs (keratia), as big as large beans, horned (keras), bumpy and dark-colored, with a bittersweet flavor when they are dry, have always been used as food for animals in the Near East and are often nibbled on by the natives of the region themselves, on a par with chickpeas, peanuts, or watermelon seeds."[29]

■ 17 "He came to himself" (εἰς ἑαυτὸν δὲ ἐλθών)." One of the primary meanings of the Greek verb (ἔρχομαι) is "come back" (cf. John 9:7). The expression "come to oneself" was a part of the religious and philosophical vocabulary of the period. We encounter it in both the *Testament of Joseph* (3:9) and Epictetus (*Disc.* 3.1.15). For Hellenistic Judaism and early Christianity it expressed a decisive step of "conversion" (μετάνοια), a return to God.[30]

"He said," or more correctly "he said to himself." Here as often, Luke or L, which Luke takes over, resorts to an interior monologue. This literary convention permits the author to describe the spiritual evolution of the characters in the story and to give the story a new twist.

"I am lost": the Greek verb (ἀπόλλυμι) meaning "spoil," "lose," "destroy" is used in the middle voice (ἀπόλλυμαι) with the meaning "be lost" or "die."[31] The risks of death were real and numerous: war, famine, and accidents on both land and sea. These dangers had acquired a symbolic connotation in the Scriptures. The prophets would mention their disappearance when they wanted to signal the ultimate salvation: "I will raise up for them a tree of peace and they will no more be annihilated by famine on earth and they will no longer be reproached by the Gentiles" (Ezek 34:29 LXX).

21 See Jülicher, *Gleichnisreden*, 2:341.
22 See Cantinat, "Paraboles," 262.
23 See Gen 47:13 LXX and Ruth 1:1 LXX; Fitzmyer (2:1088) also mentions some secular texts.
24 On these similarities with the story of Joseph, see Aus, *Weihnachtsgeschichte*, 126–73.
25 See Bovon in Bovon and Rouiller, *Exegesis*, 45.
26 On κολλᾶσθαι, see Burchard, "Fußnoten," 159–60. In his opinion, the verb does not always imply a permanent relationship in the Lukan corpus; it can also describe an occasional contract.
27 On the impurity of pigs, see Lev 11:7; Deut 14:8; 1 Macc 1:47; Fitzmyer, 2:1088.
28 See Jülicher, *Gleichnisreden*, 2:343.
29 Cantinat, "Paraboles," 262.
30 See Pokorný, "Soteriologie," 179–92. Sellew ("Interior Monolog," 246) offers another interpretation.
31 See BAGD, s.v.

The young man no longer even dares to think about his status as "son." What he hopes for at most is to be a "hired hand," a "worker" ($\mu\acute{\iota}\sigma\vartheta\iota o\varsigma$)[32] on his father's estate. With such a status he would be better off than being poor, although he would still be very much looked down upon.

■ **18** We have already called attention to the importance of the participle "getting up" ($\mathring{\alpha}\nu\alpha\sigma\tau\acute{\alpha}\varsigma$, vv. 18, 20). Redundant and with a Semitic flavor,[33] this participle is used with verbs of action and movement. It indicates the beginning of an action or a departure. It would be inappropriate to give it an independent meaning or to see in it an act of straightening out and therefore to give it a moral or allegorical interpretation.

The future tense "I will go" ($\pi o\rho\epsilon\acute{\upsilon}\sigma o\mu\alpha\iota$) does not refer only to the future; it also hints at the son's intention and will to carry out this costly project. He intends to make a true confession of his sin. The verb "miss" ($\mathring{\alpha}\mu\alpha\rho\tau\acute{\alpha}\nu\omega$), which is often followed by the object "target, mark" ($\sigma\kappa o\pi o\hat{\upsilon}$), took on the religious meaning of "sin" in the LXX. It has been demonstrated that the double meaning of "sinning against (both) heaven (God) and a person" is to be found in the Bible, and that it did not involve two different acts, but one. A single act can hurt humans and wound God.[34] Without specifying what his sin was, the younger son realized that he had at the same time violated the order established by God and had been detrimental to his father's interests. The Shepherd of *Hermas* asserts that sinning against the Lord and against one's parents is a serious sin (*Vis.* 1.3.1). We do not have to identify the father with God to find analogies between the fate of the younger son and the destiny of human beings.[35]

■ **19** The son is not interested in talking about his legal status. He knows that he can no longer make any filial claim to his father's possessions. He declares that he has lost his honor, his identity, and even the right to be called "son." The Greek verb ($\kappa\alpha\lambda\acute{\epsilon}\omega$) means "call," but in the passive ("to be called") becomes almost a synonym of the verb "to be." That does not keep readers of the Bible from remembering that human beings are not children of God by nature. They can become God's children only if they are "called" (see Matt 5:9; and cf. Luke 6:35).

■ **20-21** The style of vv. 20-21 reminds us of the narrative prose of the Hebrew Bible. The repetition is a help for the reader: the announced plan (vv. 18-19) is carried out (vv. 20-21). But the fact that the repetition remains incomplete keeps the story from being monotonous. The father interrupts his repentant son's speech and expresses his paternal affection, which Luke, or the author of L before him, called "(to be filled with) compassion." This verb ($\sigma\pi\lambda\alpha\gamma\chi\nu\acute{\iota}\zeta o\mu\alpha\iota$) is rare in Greek but was used by the LXX and is present in the *Testaments of the Twelve Patriarchs*. It took on the sense of "having pity, compassion," which we encounter also in early Christian literature.[36] The Gospel writer or his source situates it in strategic places, both here and in the parable of the Good Samaritan (10:33). Different features underline this paternal love, which at last finds expression: the father runs, which is indecorous behavior for the head of the family; he hugs his son and smothers him with kisses (cf. Gen 33:4). Luke is careful to call our attention to similar actions in relation to the older son: in v. 28, the father goes out to meet him and encourages him.

■ **22-23** It is evident that for Luke the father remains in control of that part of his estate that he has not already given to his younger son. The older son does not complain about that fact. Without being entirely clear, the orders that the father gives are impressive; they prove that he refuses to accept the shameful state of his younger son. Instead he keeps him or reestablishes him in his status as son. The Greek adjective $\pi\rho\acute{\omega}\tau\eta$ can have two different meanings. It can mean (literally) "first" chronologically; in that case, it would refer to the "son's" robe, which the father would have been careful not to throw away or give away. He would have "brought it out" ($\mathring{\epsilon}\xi\epsilon\nu\acute{\epsilon}\gamma\kappa\alpha\tau\epsilon$) of the closet or the trunk in which he had been keeping it (cf. 2 Kgs [4 Kgdms] 10:22). The other

---

32   The New Testament also uses the term $\mu\iota\sigma\vartheta\omega\tau\acute{o}\varsigma$, e.g., Mark 1:20.

33   See Fitzmyer (2:1089), who rightly specifies that this is a Septuagintalism.

34   See Lohfink ("Ich habe gesündigt," 51–52), who returns especially to Exod 10:16 LXX and adds that sin undermines relationships.

35   Pokorný ("Soteriologie," 184) reminds us that the tax collector in the parable utters a confession of sins that is almost identical (see Luke 18:13b).

36   *T. Zeb.* 6:4; 7:1-2; 8:3. See the commentary above on 10:33; and Helmut Koester, "$\sigma\pi\lambda\acute{\alpha}\gamma\chi\nu o\nu$," *TDNT* 7 (1971) 548–59. See also Spicq, *Lexicon*, 1409–12.

meaning is "first" in the sense of quality, that is, "best," "the most beautiful," the robe reserved for honored guests.[37] The further mention of the ring and the shoes favors the first interpretation. The young man is reestablished in his status as son. The ring is not a gift to be given to a visitor but a symbol of power: "Removing his signet ring from his hand, Pharaoh put it on Joseph's hand; he arrayed him in garments of fine linen, and put a gold chain around his neck" (Gen 41:42 *NRSV*). Unlike guests who take their shoes off upon arrival, the younger son is going to have shoes put on him. In the symbolic language of actions, in Israel the act of walking around with shoes on while surveying a plot of land indicated that one was taking possession of it. So the father is anxious to completely reintegrate his son into the family.[38]

This reintegration will be celebrated by a banquet and rejoicing. Luke has spoken several times of the importance of meals eaten in common (see 5:29-32; 7:36-50; 14:1-24; 15:1-2). Since meat was not eaten every day, the fatted calf[39] was saved for special occasions.

■ **24ab** Like v. 32, v. 24ab expresses the Lukan interpretation of the event. In Luke's eyes, the parable depicts salvation and a restored life, a redemption, and a resurrection. The vocabulary used makes possible this transfer from the human level to the divine sphere.[40]

■ **24c-25** The end of v. 24 (v. 24c) should be joined to what follows: those noisy festivities that have begun are going to trigger the wrath of the older son. That he himself works the land—an observation mentioned in passing—is an indication that the father is not a large landowner of a great landed estate (*latifundia*) but someone who exploits an estate of medium size. In spite of

the double meaning of v. 24ab, we should stay within the setting of the story and not too readily identify the older son with "the Pharisee busily observing the Law while the hearts of the repentant sinners blossom in the joyous light of divine grace."[41]

We should, nevertheless, understand the Greek word $\sigma\upsilon\mu\varphi\omega\nu\iota\alpha$ (v. 25) in the sense of musical harmony of voices or musical instruments, even if the word can sometimes refer to a musical instrument.[42] The $\chi\upsilon\rho\upsilon\iota$ can be understood in two ways: either dances or choral singing.[43] I prefer this latter sense, because I find the following explanation too subtle: the older son first hears the sound of music ($\sigma\upsilon\mu\varphi\omega\nu\iota\alpha$), then the noise of the dancers' feet ($\chi\upsilon\rho\upsilon\iota$).[44]

■ **26-27** We should probably group the "servants" ($\pi\alpha\hat{\iota}\delta\epsilon\varsigma$) (v. 26) with the "servants" ($\delta\upsilon\hat{\upsilon}\lambda\upsilon\iota$) of v. 22; all of them are the master's servants, except that the ones in v. 26 ($\pi\alpha\hat{\iota}\delta\epsilon\varsigma$) are probably the younger servants (cf. 7:7). The young servant gives an accurate description of the welcome of the son who has been found again. The verbs "to be safe, in good health" ($\hat{\upsilon}\gamma\iota\alpha\iota\nu\omega$) and "to get back" ($\hat{\alpha}\pi\upsilon\lambda\alpha\mu\beta\hat{\alpha}\nu\omega$) merit a comment. In Luke's time the verb "to be safe, in good health" ($\hat{\upsilon}\gamma\iota\alpha\iota\nu\omega$) and the adjective "healthy, sound" ($\hat{\upsilon}\gamma\iota\eta\varsigma$) could refer to a Christian attribute, not just one's physical health.[45] Several decades later, the verb "to get back" ($\hat{\alpha}\pi\upsilon\lambda\alpha\mu\beta\hat{\alpha}\nu\omega$) acquired a spiritual sense: "And then the Son of God shall rejoice and be glad in them when he has received his people in purity" (*Hermas Sim.* 9.18.4).

■ **28** The parable describes each character with a verb chosen specifically for that person: the older son "became angry" (v. 28). We know of a series of people

37 This is Fitzmyer's understanding (2:1090).
38 See Ps 60 (59):10; Deut 1:36; 11:24-25; Josh 1:3; 14:9; Ruth 4:7; see also Rengstorf, *Re-Investitur*, 46–50.
39 See Judg 6:28 (LXX; Codex Alexandrinus) and Jer 46 (LXX 26):21; also Fitzmyer, 2:1090.
40 On vv. 24 and 32, see Pokorný, "Soteriologie," 189–91. In Hellenistic Judaism, this contrast between death and life was used to illustrate conversion; in early Christianity it was used to express the meaning of baptism and new life in Christ. In Stoicism, anyone who was not awakened to Stoic philosophy was called "dead," $\nu\epsilon\kappa\rho\acute{\upsilon}\varsigma$, see Rudolf Bultmann, "$\vartheta\acute{\alpha}\nu\alpha\tau\upsilon\varsigma$ $\kappa\tau\lambda$.," *TWNT* 3 (1965) 7, 11–21; and Sibinga, "Kompositionstechnik," 104 n. 30.

41 Godet, *Commentaire*, 2:230.
42 Barry ("On Luke xv. 25," 180–90) has suggested that the $\sigma\upsilon\mu\varphi\omega\nu\iota\alpha$ is a bagpipe. Moore ("$\sigma\upsilon\mu\varphi\omega\nu\iota\alpha$," 166–75) concedes that this word may refer to a musical instrument but not a bagpipe. See BAGD, s.v.; and Fitzmyer, 2:1090.
43 See BAGD, s.v. Plato (*Resp.* 5.19 §475d) associates $\hat{\epsilon}\pi\alpha\kappa\upsilon\acute{\upsilon}\omega$ with $\chi\upsilon\rho\upsilon\iota$.
44 See Jülicher, *Gleichnisreden*, 2:354.
45 For the verb, see 1 Tim 1:10; 2 Tim 4:3; Titus 1:9, 13; 2:1, 2; for the adjective, see Titus 2:8. See also the excursus by Martin Dibelius, *The Pastoral Epistles: A Commentary on the Pastoral Epistles* (Hermeneia; Philadelphia: Fortress, 1972) 24–25.

who were angry in the Hebrew Bible. There is the anger of Samuel when Saul was rejected as king (1 Sam [1 Kgdms] 15:11); of David when Uzzah died (2 Sam [2 Kgdms] 6:8); of Job when facing his destiny (spoken of by Bildad, in Job 18:4); of Jonah when opposing the mercy that God had on Nineveh (Jonah 4:1, 4, 9). Another example is the anger that the righteous people may feel in the face of the success of the wicked (Ps 37 [36]:1, 7-8; Prov 3:31-32). Numerous biblical texts speak of anger on the part of righteous persons in the face of what seems to be the favorable treatment given to guilty persons. This jealousy and, more generally, any form of anger were already criticized in the Hebrew Bible and are condemned in the New Testament (see Matt 5:22; Jas 1:20).[46]

■ **29** It would be nice to know exactly how the father pleaded with his older son ($\pi\alpha\rho\epsilon\kappa\acute{\alpha}\lambda\epsilon\iota\ \alpha\grave{\upsilon}\tau\acute{o}\nu$). In any case, it did not work. This son thought of his life as work, perhaps also as submission ($\delta o\upsilon\lambda\epsilon\acute{\upsilon}\omega$ can have both of these meanings; we probably should not speak here of servility or try to discover an allusion to the Pharisees).[47] His relation to his father is governed more by duty than by affection: "And I have never disobeyed any of your orders." He feels very strongly that he has been treated unfairly; he has been faithful to his position, and yet he has never had the right to have a special meal, not even the slightest young goat (to say nothing of a fatted calf!).

■ **30** In spite of the phrasing of the news ("your brother has come"), the older brother refuses to call the one who came back "brother." The prodigal son is at best called "your son."[48] "This" ($o\grave{\upsilon}\tau o\varsigma$), in "this son of yours," is pejorative. The older son reproaches the younger son especially for having "devoured your property" (the use of $\kappa\alpha\tau\epsilon\sigma\vartheta\acute{\iota}\omega$ in the figurative sense is attested in one of Aesop's fables[49]) in squandering, and his mounting bitterness causes him to add "with prostitutes."[50]

■ **31** The father's answer was moving but insufficient. It was moving because of the use of the affectionate vocative "(my) child" ($\tau\acute{\epsilon}\kappa\nu o\nu$).[51] It was insufficient from the point of view of the older brother, who had not profited from this sharing of property. The expression "all that is mine is yours" ($\pi\acute{\alpha}\nu\tau\alpha\ \tau\grave{\alpha}\ \grave{\epsilon}\mu\grave{\alpha}\ \sigma\acute{\alpha}\ \grave{\epsilon}\sigma\tau\iota\nu$) can be read on two levels.[52] On the juridical level it indicates that, because of the younger son's request, the rest of the father's possessions will be reserved for the older son and, since he is still living on the property, he can already use them. On the affective level, the father says to his son: feel free (to do what you want with the possessions), since you are at home. Personally, I would prefer not opposing these two levels: even if the father is right in considering his possessions as still belonging to him, he is not wrong in offering his older son the unconditional power to use these possessions. But this son does not understand that all of these possessions are his.

■ **32** The father continues, tactfully; without insistence, he says: "It was only right for us to celebrate and rejoice," and not "it was only right for you. . . ." His paternal sensitivity, however, does not keep him from making a correction: the person that the older brother calls "your son," he calls "your brother."[53] "Celebrate" ($\epsilon\grave{\upsilon}\varphi\rho\alpha\acute{\iota}\nu o\mu\alpha\iota$)

---

46   There are more studies on the wrath of God than on that of humans; nevertheless, see "Zorn," *BHH* 3 (1966) cols. 2246–48.

47   On $\delta o\upsilon\lambda\epsilon\acute{\upsilon}\omega$, see BAGD, s.v.; and Fitzmyer, 2:1091.

48   In v. 32, the father will correct him: "because this brother of yours. . . ." See Corlett, "This Brother," 216.

49   I am referring to the fable entitled "The Young Man and the Swallow," which begins with these words: $\nu\epsilon\grave{o}\varsigma\ \check{\alpha}\sigma\omega\tau o\varsigma\ \kappa\alpha\tau\alpha\varphi\alpha\gamma\grave{\omega}\nu\ \tau\grave{\alpha}\ \pi\alpha\tau\rho\grave{\omega}\alpha$ . . . "a young, profligate man, having spent his inheritance. . . ." See the critical edition by Émile Chambry, *Aesopi Fabulae* (2 vols.; Paris: Belles lettres, 1926) 2:405–6, at where she places the numeral 249; in another edition and translation by the same author (*Esope Fables* [Paris: Belles lettres, 1967] 110), the same place is marked by 248. See also the slightly differ-ent rendering of the story found in *Aesop's Fables* 274 (in *Fables: Babrius and Phaedrus* [trans. Ben E. Perry; LCL; Cambridge, Mass.: Harvard University Press, 1965] 171).

50   It is better to favor the feminine reading, $\mu\epsilon\tau\grave{\alpha}\ \pi o\rho\nu\hat{\omega}\nu$ ("with prostitutes") than the masculine $\mu\epsilon\tau\grave{\alpha}\ \pi\acute{o}\rho\nu\omega\nu$.

51   For references to parallels, see Fitzmyer, 2:1091. The $\sigma\acute{\upsilon}$ is the counterpart to $\acute{o}\ \grave{\alpha}\delta\epsilon\lambda\varphi\acute{o}\varsigma\ \sigma o\upsilon\ o\grave{\upsilon}\tau o\varsigma$.

52   It is reminiscent of a Greek proverbial expression: "among friends, all is common." Luke echoes this formula to describe the communion among Christians in Acts 4:32.

53   See n. 48 above.

and "rejoice" (χαίρω, χαίρομαι) are often mentioned side by side in the LXX (albeit in the reverse order).[54]

Karl Heinrich Rengstorf has concluded that vv. 24 and 32 belonged to the tradition.[55] When his son left home, the father would have carried out a solemn rite, declaring him dead in his eyes. To make a public announcement of this amputation of a member of the family, "the reunited clan publicly broke a jar full of roasted wheat, and nuts, all the while crying out, in order to publicize the fact that so or so would henceforth by separated, lost, that is to say dead, as far as the clan was concerned."[56] It follows that, for Rengstorf, vv. 24 and 32 have a juridical character, that of an official reinstatement. In my view, however, vv. 24 and 32 are characteristic of Lukan redaction. They are on neither the juridical nor the ethical level. They are to be understood on the religious level, which goes beyond the narrative setting of the parable. They use the verbs "be dead" and "live," "be lost," and "be found," which bring the third parable closer to the other two parables, provide a thematic unity to ch. 15 and serve as a hermeneutical key to the whole, just as vv. 7 and 10 do. Along with the three salient verbs of the parable ("come to oneself" [v. 17], "be filled with compassion" [v. 20], and "become angry" [v. 28]), vv. 24 and 32, which speak about the passage from death to life and from perdition to salvation, provide a meaningful summary of the parable.[57]

History of Interpretation

The Church Fathers realized how many different interpretations of the parable of the two sons were possible. The oldest exegesis, which can be reconstituted indirectly, seems to be that of the Valentinians (second century C.E.).[58] Its originality was in seeing in the older son angels who were jealous of the redemption of the human race, represented by the ultimate fate of the younger son.[59] In the view of the Valentinians, the perdition of the young man corresponded to the fall of humanity or of the soul in the world of matter.[60] The Gnostics focused on the reasons for the emigration of the younger son and his subsequent being in need, and they lent a Platonic coloration to these elements that we also find in certain Church Fathers.[61]

The theologians of the "Great Church," for their part, defended other points of view that were not always incompatible. Their first interpretation has been called ethical; it could also be labeled soteriological. Irenaeus, for example, concentrated his attention on the younger brother, whose return represented the salvation of the human race.[62] He was followed by Titus of Bostra, Jerome, Pseudo-Jerome (the author of *Epistula* 35), and Cyril of Alexandria, four authors whose interpretation may be summarized as follows: "God grants people the liberty of serving him, but they misuse it and forget their

---

54 Joel 2:21-34; Lam 4:21; and Esth 9:17 (this last example has the substantives χαρά and εὐφροσύνη).

55 Rengstorf, *Re-Investitur.*

56 I cite a statement from the French summary of Rengstorf's study (*Re-Investitur*).

57 I have already cited several passages from the Old Testament that clarify this aspect of the parable; there are others, which I enumerate here: Gen 2:24 (leaving one's parents; see Fusco, "Narrazione," 32); Jonah (see Alonso Díaz, "Paralelos," 632–40); Exod 33:19 ("I have compassion on whom I have compassion"; see Méroz, *Le visage maternel de Dieu*, 55); Hos 2:4-17 (the prostitute wife); and Gen 33:4 (the kisses of Jacob and Esau). See Hofius ("Alttestamentliche Motive," 240–48), who emphasizes these Hebrew Bible parallels and surmises that the creator of this parable (Jesus, not Luke) depended on the Hebrew text and not the Greek of the LXX. Additionally, see Ezek 18:23 and 33:11 (God hoping for the conversion of the sinner); Scobel ("Gleichnis," 53) argues

that an allusion to these verses is discernible in v. 32 but even more in vv. 7 and 10. Finally, see Prov 29:3; and Pokorný, "Soteriologie," 182.

58 For unknown reasons Marcion seems to have expunged the parable of the two sons from his Gospel. See Harnack, *Marcion*, 219* (text and notes); and Tissot, "Allégories," 267 (esp. n. 4).

59 See Adam, "Gnostische Züge"; Tissot, "Allégories," 248–49; and Cattaneo, "Interpretazione," 90–92.

60 See Ps.-Jerome, *Epistle* 35 (*PL* 30:249); and Ps.-Macarius, *Logos* 22.4–18, in Heinz Berthold, ed., *Makarios/Symeon, Reden und Briefe: Die Sammlung I des Vaticanus Graecus 694 (B)* (2 vols.; GCS; Berlin: Akademie-Verlag, 1973) 1:222–25; see also Cattaneo, "Interpretazione," 92 n. 80.

61 See Cattaneo, "Interpretazione," 92.

62 Yet he names this pericope "the parable of the two sons" and combines this interpretation with an ethnic solution (*Adv. haer.* 4.36.7 and 14.2; see below); see Tissot, "Allégories," 250; Cattaneo, "Interpretazione," 83–86.

Creator. They sink into debauchery and dedicate themselves to demons. But if, in the depths of their poverty, they recognize their Creator, God will come to their aid. He will restore to them their lost dignity by forearming them against the Devil and will welcome them to the Eucharist."[63] As Jerome noted, this interpretation is all-encompassing: the figure of the younger brother stands for all human beings, both Gentiles and Jews, all of whom are equally guilty (*Epistula ad Damasum* 21.3). The difficulty of this reading of the texts is that of identifying with whom the older son is to be associated.

The second way of interpreting this passage was also allegorical and apparently contemporaneous with the first interpretation, with which it was often combined. It dealt with the Gentiles, and has been described as ethnic. It saw in the younger brother a reference to the Gentiles, and in the older brother a reference to people of Israel. The mention (v. 11) and the presence (vv. 13-24, 25-32) of two sons explains the origin of this second interpretation. The sin of the younger brother, thus of the Gentiles, is precisely idolatry. The older brother's sin is equally clear: it consists in hardening. The difficulty of this reading is that of knowing how to understand the older brother's profession of obedience (v. 29). Two options were open to the Church Fathers: one, anti-Jewish, called this profession of obedience a lie; the other, favorable to Israel, saw it as a resolute commitment to monotheism.[64]

There was a third interpretation, closely related to these two, that can be called penitential or sacramental. It resembles the ethical explanation but modifies the chronology of salvation. On the narrative level of the parable, the new life that is offered at the moment of baptism begins not with the son's reinstatement in v. 22 but already in v. 12, when the father's possessions are divided up. In that case, the younger son's wandering symbolizes the guilty life of Christians who have lost their way but finally repent and return to the bosom of the church. The intransigent wing of early Christianity, which did not feel comfortable accepting a church made up of sinners, represented in their time the jealous older son.[65]

We need to make clear that the Greek Fathers' exegesis (on the Alexandrian side, Clement's *Hypotyposes* and Origen's five *Tomes* on Luke; and on the Antiochian side, Theodore of Mopsuestia's commentary) has largely disappeared. The exegesis of the Latin Fathers, on the other hand, is better represented and dealt particularly with an ethnic reading of the two brothers, as in the writings of Maximus of Turin, Augustine of Hippo, Caesarius of Arles, and others.[66] Finally, to our surprise, Christian writers in antiquity did not reproach the younger brother for having laid claim to his share of the inheritance. On the contrary, in his role as son, by making this request, he expressed his refusal of servile obedience and his legitimate desire for liberty.[67]

We have two continuous patristic expositions of our parable that are both homiletical. The Western one is by Ambrose, the Latin bishop and preacher of Milan (*Exp. Luc.* 7.212–42), and the Eastern one is by Cyril of Alexandria. True to himself, Ambrose was eager not to lose even a tiny piece of meaning. He was more interested in accumulating interpretations than in imposing any logical scheme on them. Beginning with the penitential perspective, he declared that, although one squanders one's baptismal patrimony by distancing oneself from the church, there is no depth to which one can sink that makes faith and pardon impossible. He then allegorizes the distancing (from oneself and from Christ). The famine is the absence of good works apart from the Word of God. The owner of the pigs is doubtless the Devil and demons; the food for the pigs stands for vain verbiage,

---

63 These lines are quoted from Tissot ("Allégories," 251), who also cites the relevant references of the adherents of this interpretation.

64 See Tissot ("Allégories," 252–54) and Cattaneo ("Interpretazione," 89, esp. nn. 71 and 72), who provide numerous patristic references. We have already encountered this ethnic interpretation in Irenaeus, in conjunction with the ethical interpretation (*Adv. haer.* 4.36.7), and then in Tertullian, whose interpretation evolved because of his adherence to Montanism. The African abandoned the penitential interpretation of his catholic period (*Paen.* 8.6–9 and 12.7) in favor of the ethical solution and one or two elements of the ethnic solution (*Pud.* 8–9); see Tissot ("Allégories," 267–71) and Cattaneo ("Interpretazione," 73–79).

65 See Tissot, "Allégories," 254; Cattaneo, "Interpretazione," 73–79.

66 For references, see Tissot, "Allégories," 252 n. 4; Cattaneo, "Interpretazione," 83, 90.

67 See Tissot, "Allégories," 251 n. 3.

doubtless philosophy. "No one to give him any of the food" represents pagans, of whom ancient exegesis spoke as being "nonexistent." "Coming to oneself" stands for coming to the Lord. The father's hired hands were the Jews.[68] Ambrose followed this up with a spiritual meditation in which coming to God entails confessing one's transgression, since divine mercy is attendant on confession of sins. Without such an admission there can be no intercession on the part of either Christ or the church. Ambrose identified Christ with the father who runs and hugs his penitent son. Without hesitation, but not without tension with his previous exegesis of v. 2, Ambrose thought of the reinstatement of v. 22 and the slaughter of v. 23 as allusions to baptism and the Lord's Supper. He thus slid in the direction of an ethical or soteriological interpretation. When the younger son "dies," he resembles Adam; when he "regains his life," he symbolizes saved humanity, whose image of God is restored. To finish up, compelled by the biblical text, in which the older son makes his appearance in v. 25, Ambrose modified his perspective and progressively fell into line with the ethnic interpretation: the older son was, first of all, a person who was hostile to the forgiveness of sins after penitence (Ambrose thought of Christians, perhaps the Novatianists); but next he had in mind the Jewish people who preferred the sacrifice of a foul-smelling kid to that of Christ, who was a good-smelling lamb (identified, I presume, with the fatted calf!). As we reread Ambrose's entire exposition,[69] we note that he was much more interested in the younger son than in the older one.

Cyril, patriarch of Alexandria, devoted one of his sermons to this parable, which he considered the best composed of all parables (*Serm. Luc.* 107).[70] Unlike Ambrose, he trimmed the tree of interpretation by shunning both the Gnostic interpretation (defended by "certain people") and the ethnic interpretation, which he said

was highlighted by "some among us" (the orthodox). He attacked the Gnostic interpretation by advocating the truth of dogma (unlike the older son, the angels rejoiced in the redemption of humanity). He assailed the ethnic interpretation by pointing out the truth of history (Israel had never led the exemplary life that the older son had). Just as Tertullian had done,[71] Cyril recalled the literary context in order to establish the ethical or soteriological sense as the only one: those who make recriminations when God shows mercy (he had in mind the Pharisees and the scribes of v. 2, as well as the older son of v. 28) are wrong in not rejoicing over the conversion and pardon that are always possible. So he defended the ethical or soteriological interpretation, putting special emphasis on the reactions of the older son. His adversaries seemed to be less those Jews who were hostile to the calling of Gentiles than intolerant Christians opposed to divine mercy.

The Latin exegesis of later centuries is once more better known to us than Greek or Eastern exegesis. The Venerable Bede's commentary (*In Luc.* 4.2277–583)[72] drew on Augustine and Ambrose; the *Glossa ordinaria*[73] drew on Bede and his predecessors; and Bonaventure (*Comm. Luc.* 15.21–52), the seraphic Doctor of the Church, in turn, drew on all those who preceded him. The numerous repetitions did not appear, for all that, as monotonous rehashes but rather as multiple confirmations of the truth. For a sample, let us follow Bonaventure's exegesis.[74] He offers a logical structuring of the parable and looks for the validity of the meaning obtained by comparison of the intertextuality of parallel passages in the Bible as well as by authoritative citations of patristic authors. For him, the parable has four parts: the first describes the insolent prodigality of the prodigal son; the second, his destitution; the third, his penitence; the fourth, the father's mercy. Then each part is analyzed in turn. The

---

68   "One is a son by baptism, a friend by virtue, a mercenary by work, a slave by fear," wrote Ambrose (*Exp. Luc.* 7.228).

69   Tissot ("Allégories," 255–59) analyzes this exposition.

70   See Payne-Smith, *Cyril,* 2:500–510. Several Greek fragments of this sermon survive; see Reuss, *Lukas-Kommentare,* 166–68 (frgs. 226–30).

71   See Tertullian *Pud.* 7.2, in which the word *materia* designates the concrete situation in which the par-

able was spoken. See Tissot, "Allégories," 269, esp. n. 3.

72   The fourth volume of Bede's commentary concludes here, at the end of his explication of Luke 15.

73   *Glossa ordinaria* Luke 15:11–32 (*PL* 114:311–14).

74   With help from Billy, "Conversion and the Franciscan Preacher," 259–75.

prodigal son's insolence, for example, is clarified from three angles: human freedom, witting sin, and the squandering of grace and nature. This logical network favors certain observations. On the theme of human freedom we have the fact that the father's children are called "sons"; that confirms their free will and their calling to the eternal heritage. The younger son asks for his part of the inheritance, which proves that he wants to trust his own judgment. Believing that he is asking for something for himself, he is in fact asking for something against himself. With respect to the squandering, Bonaventure draws up a list of spiritual sins (pride, vanity, envy, quick-temperedness, weariness or lassitude)—all of which lead to carnal vices (a taste for luxury, gluttony, lust). Each time, he confirms the existence of the sin or vice in question by quoting a verse of Scripture, and the same method shows up in the analysis of each section. When he interprets the third quarter of the parable, the one having to do with penitence, Bonaventure once more divides up the matter and discovers what he calls the *ordo reparationis animae* (*Comm. Luc.* 15.33); this order includes contrition, confession, and gratification. As Augustinian tradition would have it, penitence is impossible without God's initiative and activity, so we are dealing not simply with a moral order but also with a theological one. No one comes to the Father who is not drawn by him; the Johannine verses on predestination (John 14:6 and 6:44) are quoted in this connection. It is significant that the fourth part of the parable, the one that has to do with God's grace, includes what constitutes two parts, according to our literary criteria. For Bonaventure's theological criteria these two parts ("now this part is divided into two parts" [*dividitur autem haec pars in duas*]) correspond to two faces of what is one and the same divine quality: mercy. According to him, mercy, which is the point of the parable, applies to each of the sons—through the acceptance of the guilty son's conversion and the calming of the faithful son's indignation. For Bonaventure, the father has a capital role, and his love applies to each

of the sons, perhaps in different ways, but surely in equitable measure. In the case of the younger son, this applies by means of a triple grace: prevenient grace (the father sees his son while the son is still a long way off), concomitant grace (the father throws himself on his son's neck), and subsequent grace (the father smothers his son with kisses). In the case of the older son, this love applies through the "father's most generous response" (15.51).[75]

We owe the *Paraphrases* of the humanist Erasmus to the Renaissance.[76] Erasmus was aware of the difference between a paraphrase and a commentary. In the case of a paraphrase, there is no change of persons, since the modern author intends to reproduce the voice of the author of antiquity. In the case of a commentary, however, there is a change of persons, since a second voice adds itself to the first. In his paraphrase of this parable, Erasmus retells the story according to a rhetoric that he intends to be based on the Gospel, all the while striving to be faithful to classical criteria. At the very moment that the author of *Paraphrases* reads that the father sees his son, he sets forth a series of rhetorical questions that are based on the predictable reactions of a human father: Is not the father going to menace, judge, and condemn his son? Is he not going to regret his generosity and recall his son's wrongs? Yet "he does not remember anything of all that" (*nihil horum meminit*).[77] He follows that up with a laying out of a triple contrast between before and after, the son's degeneration, and his rehabilitation by his father. Every paraphrase involves an interpretation. Erasmus emphasizes the importance of penitence.[78] It calls the son "a young man" and understands his sins as youthful sins. If he was able to get rid of them, it was because he remembered, and that was the first step on the way to salvation. Since Erasmus respected the Augustinian tradition concerning the father's role, which scarcely has any support in the biblical text, he held that the father facilitated his son's return; the sinner's coming to himself was "thanks to the silent breathing on the part of his benevolent father." Although the son went away,

75 For another medieval interpretation, see Albert the Great *Enarr. Luc.* 15.11–32, and an anonymous sermon in old German (Altdeutsche Predigten, 24 [Schönbach, *Altdeutsche Predigten*, 2:64–66]).

76 Erasmus *Paraphrasis* 15.11–32 (ed. Vander, 406–10). On this work, and the exegetical method of Eras-

mus, see Jacques Chomarat, *Grammaire et rhétorique chez Erasme* (Paris: Belles lettres, 1981) 1:587–710.

77 Erasmus *Paraphrasis* (ed. Vander, 408).

78 Erasmus speaks of *resipiscentia*, where Melanchthon (see n. 84 below) speaks of *poenitentia*.

the father, on the other hand, was never absent. "And the son did not come back home without the father's working himself into the memory of the son, who had been reduced to the direst straits."[79] What is most striking in the following development of this rewriting of the story is the spiritualization of the divine goods and the contrast between them and the goods of this world. Everything—whether it be the house, the fields, or the calf—has been dematerialized. So, unlike Calvin,[80] Erasmus remained faithful to the allegorical interpretation of this parable.

Certain passages in Luther's debate with Eck recall to the modern reader the fact that there was a discussion concerning the beginning of faith (the *initium fidei*), just as there had been in the time of the semi-Pelagian quarrel.[81] Erasmus's artistic looseness is perhaps a reflection of his refusal to get involved in a theological dispute that would spoil the rhetorical beauty of this parable. For Luther, penitence did not begin with a fear of punishment nor by the son's remembering what a good salary his father's hired hands received. No, the real starting point for him was the interior attraction that the father exercised over his son and the love of home that he had instilled in him. Even more than Erasmus, Luther accentuated this Augustinian legacy, according to which conversion and faith cannot be dependent on either human will or any human power of decision.[82] Zwingli even went so far as to declare that anyone who does not hate every part of himself or herself is an unbeliever.[83] This concern for imposing grace alone and refusing any human participation in the process of salvation creates a distortion; although the parable does speak of salva-tion or pardon, it no longer recounts a spiritual progression. For the Reformer Melanchthon, in his *Annotationes*, the parable shows a contrast between the man's sin and the regeneration that God offers to him.[84] And in his *Postillae* Melanchthon explained what these three things are: ἀσωτία, life without hope of salvation; στοργή, unfailing paternal love; and—this is what is original with him—fraternal love that has been so poorly dealt with in this story.[85] Although putting the accent on the father's attitude is not an unattractive approach, defending a particular doctrinal position caused Melanchthon to distance himself from Luke's text.

Calvin may have been sensitive to this tension between the parable and doctrine.[86] In any case, he strove to come back to the letter of the text and urged an interpretation that did not allegorize each detail. As much as he was able, he attempted to read the parable as a concrete human story that encourages those who hear it and read it to adhere to the following line of reasoning: if human beings, sinful as we are,[87] can generously forgive our children, should we not expect much more from God's kindness? Naturally, Calvin did not rule out moving from the human level to the divine level, but he limited it to this line of reasoning. Having done that, he divided the parable in a different way than many other commentators. He saw a story in two parts. The first part (all of the story of the younger son) "shows how ready and willing God is to pardon our sins." The second part (the older son's attitude) "shows how maliciously and perversely they act who disparage His mercy."[88] The younger son's straying did not inspire Calvin very much,[89] and, unlike Bonaventure,

---

79 Erasmus *Paraphrasis* (ed. Vander, 407, 409).
80 See below.
81 On the exegesis of Luther, see Luther, *Evangelien-Auslegung*, 798–807; and Mülhaupt, *Luthers Evangelien-Auslegung*, 234–35. It is surprising that this parable did not receive more attention from the Reformer.
82 Martin Luther, Disputation at Leipzig, 12.7.1519, WA 2:362; Mülhaupt, *Luthers Evangelien-Auslegung*, 234.
83 Zwingli, *Annotationes*, 671–75, esp. 673. Zwingli adds together the ethical and ethnic meanings. At the beginning of his annotation on ch. 15 (670), he affirms that Christ here reveals the reason God sent his Son into the world.
84 Melanchthon, *Annotationes* (ed. Bretschneider, 309–13); in col. 309, he shows his knowledge of

the alternative interpretation, although he prefers the ethical interpretation for its more widespread application. Zwingli holds the same opinion.
85 Melanchthon *Postillae* 71–77. Melanchthon also includes a philological and botanical analysis of carobs in these developments.
86 Calvin, *Harmony*, 2:220–25.
87 Toward others, a human being surrenders nothing, except by force. He is only naturally generous where his own children are concerned (Calvin, *Harmony*, 2:223).
88 Ibid., 221.
89 The same cannot be said of Johannes Butzbach, who falls back on the parable of the prodigal son at the end of his autobiography of 1506. The modern editor placed Dürer's engraving of the prodigal child at the beginning of his edition of Butzbach's

Calvin paid little attention to the father's attempts to show his affection for his older son. Moreover, we should note that Calvin, as well as other Reformers, considered the younger son's initial act to have been sinful. Like Melanchthon, but unlike numerous Church Fathers, he condemned the young man's request as expressing covetousness and not a legitimate desire for freedom.[90]

The parable of the prodigal son is one of those passages in the New Testament that has left its mark as much on literature as on theology, on art as on liturgy, on culture as on religion.[91] Playwrights laid claim to this story. Already around 1220, an anonymous author in Picardy wrote a work in French verse called *Courtois d'Arras*.[92] The subject matter of this play, which must have been a drama by virtue of its dialogical character, is as follows.[93] "*Courtois d'Arras* is an adaptation of the parable of the Prodigal Son (Luke 15). The young man, who is the hero in the story, leaves his father's house (1–90). A tavern, whose landlord and servant boast of its comforts, looks to him like a pleasant place to stay (91–147). There he meets two women, Manchevaire and Pourette, who flatter him (148–245), conspire to rob him (246–78), and pull it off (279–340). After that, he is kicked out by his host (341–430). Then he bemoans his misfortune (431–50). A burgher gives him some pigs to look after (451–85), and his extreme poverty drives him to repent (486–599). He makes up his mind to return home to beg his father to forgive him, and his father does (600–631), in spite of the advice of his older son (632–44)." The play follows the story line of the biblical story except that it *ends* with the mention by the father of the lost sheep, spoken of in the parable that *precedes* the parable of the prodigal son in the Gospel of Luke. The adaptation also modifies the relative importance of the elements by giving more lines to the dissipation of the younger son than the Gospel does. What is more, the beginning of the adaptation is characterized by a heated exchange between the two brothers, during which the older son already complains about how hard he has to work and how lazy his brother is. Curiously, the feast that followed the younger son's return is not described.[94] Moreover, as is the case with those who read Luke, the spectators of the play are not told what the older brother's final decision was. But they themselves are involved by being invited to sing a *Te deum*!

There were a number of dramas or epics between the thirteenth and the fifteenth centuries that rewrote the story, but there was a veritable avalanche in the sixteenth century, which continued right up to the middle of the seventeenth. These works were written in several vernacular languages: Italian, French, Spanish, Dutch, English, and German. Sometimes satirical, these stories or plays were were usually didactic, religious, or moralizing. The Reformation, which seized on the parables of Luke 15 to illustrate its doctrine of justification, was admittedly no stranger to this intense output.[95] By way of example, we might mention the work of Burkhard Waldis,[96] a Franciscan who became a Protestant pastor.

---

autobiography. See Johannes Butzbach, *Odeporicon: zweisprachige Ausgabe* (ed. Andreas Beriger; VCH Acta humaniora; Weinheim: VCH Acta Humaniora, 1991).

90   In this regard Melanchthon (*Annotationes*, ed. Vander, 310) is clearer still: "the son sins twice; he demands his inheritance prematurely . . . and then he spurns paternal authority."

91   The pages that follow rely on a preliminary work of Emi Bätschmann, who was then my assistant. For orientation, see Frenzel, *Stoffe der Weltliteratur*, 334, 702–5. Brettschneider (*Die Parabel vom verlorenen Sohn*) should be used with caution.

92   Courtois is here the name of the hero, the prodigal son. He is called "from Arras" because in line 81 the author mentions a historical figure whom the critic could locate at Arras, France; see Faral, *Courtois d'Arras*. I thank my colleague Beverly Kienzle, who helped me understand this text.

93   One wonders, rather, if the play might have been one of the dramatic monologues that the jugglers were fond of reciting; see Faral, *Courtois d'Arras*, III.

94   In the series, perhaps incomplete, of seven tapestries from Tournai from the beginning of the sixteenth century, preserved at the Hôtel-Dieu de Beaune in France, the portrait of an indulgent party thrown by the prodigal son who squandered his resources hangs opposite the generous welcome of his parents (the mother is present) and the banquet of reconciliation prepared for him; see R. de Narbonne and M. Tiziou, *Hôtel-Dieu, Beaune* (Paris: Société d'Éditions Régionales, 1990) 40–41.

95   Frenzel (*Stoffe der Weltliteratur,* 705) provides a bibliography germane to this subject.

96   See Holstein, *Das Drama.*

His play was put on for the first time in 1527. A narrator introduces the action, then comments on it at the end of each of the two acts of the play. A child reads the Gospel at the beginning and pronounces a benediction at the end. The singing of hymns puts the finishing touches on the religious dimension of the performance. In this case as well, the first act begins with a dialogue between the two brothers; then follow unsuccessful attempts on the part of the father to keep his younger son with him and a tedious dividing up of the money. Next we have the squandering of the inheritance (once again we have the inn of ill repute and the two young women of dubious virtue; the play depicts also the discovery of the pleasures of gambling, pleasures that end up disastrously, namely, with a beating and the young man being kicked out). The first act ends with the prodigal son looking after pigs, which reduces him to utter destitution. The second act follows the text of Luke (unlike in the *Courtois d'Arras*, the celebration associated with the reunion is not made to disappear). We should note one difference from the Gospel, however: after a long dialogue with his father, the elder son, who is intractably wedded to a religion of works, himself leaves home and takes holy orders, a move disparaged by the author. The narrator, by way of commentary, sets forth the Protestant doctrine of justification by faith alone. At this point, the innkeeper makes his appearance and implores God's mercy, while the elder brother reappears to trumpet the merits of his three monastic vows. The narrator concludes by saying that all those who humble themselves will be made great.[97]

From the end of the seventeenth century on, the interpretation of the parable was linked to the history of ideas, the claims of the Enlightenment, the evolution of the history of the family, and the blows struck at the paternal image of God. As a sign of emancipation, Voltaire dared to treat the subject flippantly; he wrote a comedy that combined the Lukan account with a love story.[98] In this case, it is the woman engaged to the younger son who secures the father's pardon for her

beloved. As for the elder son, he is wicked on two counts: he wants the entire inheritance for himself and lusts after his brother's girlfriend. Nevertheless, the downfall has a Lukan ring to it, in that the father invites his two sons to be reconciled to each other. It is interesting to compare this play with the more or less contemporary tragedy *Miss Sara Sampson,* written by Gotthold Ephraim Lessing, which was completed in 1755.[99] Even if the title does not recall the biblical parable, the work draws heavily on the Gospel of Luke, for it uses elements of the parables of the prodigal son and of the lost sheep. In this work, the child is a daughter, Sara, who leaves her family's home after being seduced and kidnapped by Mellefont. She rots in a dingy inn, overcome with remorse. Her father sets out to find his lost daughter, and when he does, brings her back home and forgives her. His intention is to bring back his daughter's lover as well. In the meantime, Sara dies, poisoned by a woman whom Mellefont had loved before Sara, following which Mellefont kills himself. According to Emi Bätschmann's explanation, these two persons represent the two sides of the prodigal son, one that represents squandering (Mellefont has a burdened past) and one that has a conscience that comes alive (Sara regrets what she has done). As in the Gospel of Luke, the father's house is seen in a positive light, as the place of virtue and goodness. Whoever abandons it gets lost. By way of contrast, the outside world represents evil and vices. Sarah does not come home of her own accord. It is her father, playing the part of the good shepherd, who finds her at the end of a long search. There is no elder brother. In place of the joyous feast is the tragic double death of the lovers. But we should not forget that that death can be understood as a return to the Father's house. In German, *heimgehen* is a euphemism for dying. Emi Bätschmann has noted that, although the theatrical treatment has secularized the parable, Lessing's language has preserved numerous biblical reminiscences. What is more, since the drama centers on the father and his only child, the spectators are moved to transpose it onto the relationship of humans with God,

---

97 Among many other works of this period, an anonymous Italian piece, *La rappresentazione del figliuol prodigo,* from the beginning of the sixteenth century is worth mentioning, as is a Spanish work, *El hijo pródigo,* from 1604, and an English play, *The London Prodigal* of 1605, which is pseudo-Shakespearean.

98 Voltaire's prodigal child was performed for the first time in 1736 and edited in 1738.

99 See Ehrich-Haefeli, "Sécularisation, langue et structure familiale," 33–72.

wherein they discover the dangers of human autonomy with respect to the Heavenly Father.[100]

In Friedrich Schiller's *Räuber* (*Robbers*), which appeared in 1781, the parable is structured around a love story, just as in the case of Voltaire and Lessing. Here, too, the action begins with an act of repentance, as in the previous examples. Karl, the son who gets lost, writes to his father asking to be forgiven by him (we have passed from direct communication to the use of letters). Franz, the elder brother, who is jealous of his brilliant younger brother, intercepts the letter. By a subterfuge, the elder brother answers the letter, in the name of the father, issuing a curse. Furious at receiving such a missive, Karl sinks into criminality and becomes the captain of a band of bandits (hence the name of the play—the author had first thought of entitling the work *The Prodigal Son*). Karl thus distances himself from a society and a patriarchal order of which he is critical. It is the woman he loves who is to bring him back to his father's home, where dramatic incidents unfold. The elder brother, eager to receive his inheritance, causes his father's death by announcing to him his younger brother's death. But it turns out to be a death only in appearance, a subterfuge, since the elder brother has locked up his father in a tower, where his robber son meets up with him. That son is pardoned, but the father dies, nevertheless—this time for real— when he learns the identity of the robber. After having a dream in which the torments of the last judgment are revealed to him, the elder son commits suicide. At that point, Karl, the robber, kills his beloved, at her request, then turns himself in, in order to be judged by other human beings. The tragedy ends with this last scene. The spectator observes that the two brothers have each killed or wanted to kill their father, a father who is in the last analysis a weak one. There is scarcely any correspondence any more between the human level and the divine level, which ceases to be personal and merciful and becomes a superior and vindictive force. There is an absence of faith; the two brothers represent types bearing the marks of modernity. It is no longer a question of putting one's life in harmony with the parable, but, as one critic has remarked, "getting out of it."[101]

Other, more recent authors also felt the need to struggle with this parable. In *Le retour de l'enfant prodigue* (1907), André Gide invented a third son; when we have come full circle and the prodigal son gets back home, resigned to his fate, he takes up again with his family and finds out that a younger brother had been born after he left home. It so happens that this youngest brother tells him that he also plans to leave home. At this point, the prodigal son, who had left home not to enjoy life but to find himself, urges his brother to carry out his intentions to the hilt: "Leave home without making a fuss. Come here and kiss me, my little brother; you leave bearing with you all of my hopes. Be brave; forget us, forget me. May you not come back."[102]

Rainer Maria Rilke entitled one of his poems "Der Auszug des verlorenen Sohnes" (1906).[103] The main theme of this poem is not returning home but leaving. Around 1910, Rilke wrote a more important work, a rewriting in prose of this parable, which he placed at the end of the *Aufzeichnungen des Malte Laurids Brigge* (The Notebook of Malta Laurids Brigge). This is how the text begins: "You would have a hard time convincing me that the story of the prodigal child is anything other than the legend of someone who did not want to be loved."[104] The reason he leaves home is that his family's love hems him in and betrays his identity. He also goes away to

---

100 We should not forget that Lessing was the son of a pastor and that, after much reflection, he did not end up following in his father's footsteps. Another pastor's son who could have identified with the prodigal son, H. J. M. R. Lenz, authored a comedy inspired by the parable entitled *Der Hofmeister, oder Vorteile der Privaterziehung* (1774).

101 See K. Weimar, "Vom Leben in Texten: Zu Schillers 'Räubern,'" *Merkur: Deutsche Zeitschrift für europäisches Denken* 42 (1988) 461–71, esp. 464.

102 André Gide, *Le retour de l'enfant prodigue . . .* (Folio; Paris: Gallimard, 1991) 182; see Schlienger-Stähli, *Rainer Maria Rilke—André Gide.*

103 Published in Rilke, *Neue Gedichte*, 2:17–18. Rilke could have been inspired by a tapestry of the Elizabeth-Kirche of Marburg, or by Rodin's statue entitled *Prière*.

104 "Man wird mich schwer davon überzeugen, daß die Geschichte des verlorenen Sohnes nicht die Legende dessen ist, der nicht geliebt werden wollte" ("Aufzeichnungen des Malte Laurids Brigge" [1910], in Rainer Marie Rilke, *Sämtliche Werke* [12 vols.; Frankfurt am Main: Insel Verlag, 1956–66] 6:938). The second quotation comes from p. 945.

free himself from his projections. What he is looking for in the last analysis is the love of God, of God not as an object but as the "direction of his love." For insofar as God is limited, he is no longer infinite, he is no longer God. But insofar as he is not limited, he is also infinitely difficult to love and is understood as "extreme distance." The extreme poverty of the prodigal son is no longer understood in terms of shame; instead of taking care of pigs, the son becomes a shepherd, a job that symbolizes, in the poet's work, the occasion for a fresh start and an experience of God that is possible. If the shepherd comes home, it is not because he is doing penance or because he remembers his father, but because he wants to accept his role as son. When he comes home, his relatives, who have aged, recognize him and forgive him. Forgive him out of what motive? Out of love. "My God, love." This exclamation, which wavers between a flat phrase and the full meaning of the expression, summarizes, in a provocative way, according to Emi Bätschmann, the gulf between false love and true love.[105] By throwing himself at the feet of his family, he pleads with them not to love him any longer with a deceitful love. The path that the prodigal son follows is a path toward God, a God who has ceased to be a Father, just as the man has lost his status of being a son. It is a journey toward a God who no longer comes to us.

Much could be said about the way the theme of the prodigal son has been handled in art.[106] Dürer's engraving and Rembrandt's paternal hands are well known. It has been suggested that Georges de La Tour's *Tricheur* was intended to represent how a courtesan, a swindler, and a servant-woman conspired to "fleece" the prodigal son. There are also complete cycles of tapestries and engravings having as their subject matter the different episodes of the story of the prodigal son. Unfortunately I am obliged to give up the idea of recounting them. I am also, sadly, obliged to bypass a discussion of the importance of the parable in the liturgy (such as the role it plays in the ceremony in which an Orthodox believer becomes a monk).

Conclusion

In conclusion, I would like to quote Charles Péguy, who was very fond of the three parables in Luke 15, and who went against the current of modernity by interpreting them in a biblical sense. He gave these parables an important place in *Le porche du mystère de la deuxième vertu*, published in 1911.[107] He celebrates hope, the second virtue; he celebrates Jesus, the shepherd of the parable;[108] he imagines the shepherd's anguish at not finding the lost sheep;[109] and, above all, he stresses the hope that directs the shepherd's steps.[110] In the poet's eyes, Jesus "did not come to recount twaddle,"[111] but the living words of parables—the lost sheep, the lost drachma, and especially the lost son. "Unaged. Not worn-out or aged."[112] "These three parables, may God forgive us for saying so, occupy a secret place in one's heart."[113] Especially the third: "But for fourteen hundred years, for two thousand years now that it has been retold to countless persons (since the first time it was told), to countless Christians, one would have to have a heart of stone, my child, to hear it without crying."[114] "Unique. So it has had a unique role to play."[115] "*A man had two sons.* That story is beautiful in Luke; it is beautiful everywhere. It is not just in Luke, it is everywhere."[116] "It is the word of Jesus that has had the most repercussions of any, in the whole world."[117]

---

105 One should also read two passages from the prose of Robert Walser, one from 1917, the other from 1927: "Die Geschichte vom verlorenen Sohn," in idem, *Phantasieren*, 258–61; and "Der verlorene Sohn," in idem, *Maskerade*, 112–15.

106 See Witwitzky, *Das Gleichnis vom verlorenen Sohn*, an invaluable resource; Kallensee, *Die Liebe des Vaters* (he places his emphasis on art, especially from the twentieth century), and Kirschbaum, *Lexikon*, 4:172–74.

107 I am referring to Charles Péguy, *Œuvres poétiques complètes* (intro. F. Porché; La Pléiade; Paris: Gallimard, 1975) 527–670.

108 Ibid., 570, 577.

109 Ibid., 577: "La dévorante inquiétude au cœur de Jésus."

110 Ibid., 578.

111 Ibid., 587.

112 Ibid., 622.

113 Ibid., 623.

114 Personally, I would prefer to put a question mark, rather than a period, at the end of this sentence.

115 Ibid., 624.

116 Ibid.

117 Ibid., 625.

The Dishonest Manager
(16:1-9)

Bibliography

Arnott, William, "The Unjust Steward in a New Light," *ExpT* 24 (1912–13) 510.

Bailey, *Poet*, 86–118.

Barth, Markus, "The Dishonest Steward and His Lord: Reflections on Luke 16:1-13," in D. Y. Hadidian, ed., *From Faith to Faith* (PTMS 31; Pittsburgh: Pickwick, 1979) 65–73.

Baudler, Georg, "Das Gleichnis vom 'betrügerischen Verwalter' (Lk 16, 1-8a) als Ausdruck der 'inneren Biographie' Jesu: Beispiel einer existenz-biographischen Gleichnisinterpretation im religions-pädagogischer Absicht," *ThGl* 28 (1985) 65–76.

Baverstock, A. H., "The Parable of the Unjust Steward: An Interpretation," *Theol* 35 (1937) 78–83.

Beames, Frederick, "The Unrighteous Steward," *ExpT* 24 (1912–13) 150–55.

Beavis, Mary Ann, "Ancient Slavery as an Interpretive Context for the New Testament Servant Parables with Special Reference to the Unjust Steward (Luke 16:1-8)," *JBL* 111 (1992) 37–54.

Bigo, Pierre, "La richesse comme intendance, dans l'évangile: A propos de Luc 16:1-9," *NRTh* 87 (1965) 267–71.

Blinzler, J., "Kluge Ausnützung der Gegenwart zur Sicherung der Zukunft: Lk 16, 1-8," *BLit* 37 (1963–64) 357–68.

Boyd, William F., "The Parable of the Unjust Steward (Luke xvi.1ff)," *ExpT* 50 (1938–39) 46.

Breech, James, *The Silence of Jesus: The Authentic Voice of the Historical Man* (Philadelphia: Fortress Press, 1983) 101–13.

Bretscher, Paul G., "Brief Studies: The Parable of the Unjust Steward—A New Approach to Luke 16:1-9," *CTM* 22 (1951) 756–62.

Brown, Colin, "The Unjust Steward: A New Twist?" in Michael J. Wilkins and Terence Paige, eds., *Worship, Theology and Ministry in the Early Church: Essays in Honor of Ralph P. Martin* (JSOTSup 87; Sheffield: JSOT Press, 1992) 121–45.

Burgos Núñez, Miguel, de, "El Escándalo de la Justicia del Reino en Lucas XVI," *Communio* 21 (1988) 167–90.

Byrne, Brendan, "Forceful Stewardship and Neglectful Wealth: A Contemporary Reading of Luke 16," *Pacifica* 1 (1988) 1–14.

Bultmann, *History*, 175–76, 199–200, 422.

Buzy, Denis, *Les Paraboles* (VS 6; Paris: Beauchesne, 1932) 671–95.

Caemmerer, Richard R., "Investment for Eternity: A Study of Luke 16:1-13," *CTM* 34 (1963) 69–76.

Camps, Guiu M., and Bartomeu M. Ubach, "Un sentido bíblico de *adikos, adikia* y la interpretación de Lc 16, 1-13," *EstBib* 25 (1966) 75–82.

Clavier, Henri, "L'ironie dans l'enseignement de Jésus," *NovT* 1 (1956) 3–20.

Colella, Pasquale, "De mamona iniquitatis," *RivB* 19 (1971) 427–28.

Idem, "Zu Lk 16,7," *ZNW* 64 (1973) 124–26.

Collins, R. L., "Is the Parable of the Unjust Steward Pure Sarcasm?" *ExpT* 22 (1910–11) 525–26.

Comiskey, John P., "The Unjust Steward," *TBT* 52 (1971) 229–35.

Coutts, John, "Studies in Texts: The Unjust Steward, Lk. xvi, 1-8a," *Theol* 52 (1949) 54–60.

Daube, David, "Neglected Nuances of Exposition in Luke-Acts," *ANRW* 2.25.3 (1984) 2329–57, particularly 2334–39.

Davidson, J. A., "A 'Conjecture' about the Parable of the Unjust Steward," *ExpT* 66 (1954–55) 31.

Degenhardt, Hans Joachim, *Lukas, Evangelist der Armen: Besitz und Besitzverzicht in den lukanischen Schriften. Eine traditions- und redaktionsgeschichtliche Untersuchung* (Stuttgart: Katholisches Bibelwerk, 1965) 114–20.

Delebecque, Edouard, "Le régisseur infidèle (16, 1-13)," in idem, *Évangile de Luc*, 89–97.

Derrett, J. Duncan M., "Fresh Light on St. Luke xvi: I. The Parable of the Unjust Steward," *NTS* 7 (1960–61) 198–219.

Idem, *Law*, 49, 55, 79–80.

Idem, "'Take thy Bond . . . and Write Fifty' (Luke xvi.6): The Nature of the Bond," *JTS* 23 (1972) 438–40.

Drexler, H., "Miszellen zu Lukas 16, 1-7," *ZNW* 58 (1967) 286–88.

Du Plessis, Isak J., "Philanthropy or Sarcasm?— Another Look at the Parable of the Dishonest Manager (Lk 16:1-13)," *Neot* 24 (1990) 1–20.

Dupont, Jacques, *Les Béatitudes* (3 vols.; Bruges: Abbaye de Saint-André, 1958–73) 1:107–11, 2:118–22, 168–72.

Idem, "L'exemple de l'intendant débrouillard: Lc 16, 1-13," *AsSeign* 56 (1974) 67–78.

Idem, "La parabole de l'intendant avisé (Luc 16, 1-13)," LV (B) *ParLi* 12 (1953) 13–19.

Dutton, F. G., "The Unjust Steward," *ExpT* 16 (1904–05) 44.

Erlemann, *Bild Gottes*, 151–69.

Essig, K.-G. "Anmerkungen zur Bildebene des Gleichnisses vom ungerechten Verwalter (Lk 16, 1-9)," in Luise Schottroff and Willy Schottroff, eds., *Die Auslegung Gottes durch Jesus: Festgabe für Herbert Braun zum 80. Geburtstag am 4 Mai 1983* (Mainz: n.p., 1983) 116–41.

Fassl, Peter, "'Und er lobte den ungerechten Verwalter' (Lk 16,8a): Komposition und Redaktion in Lk 16," in R. Killian, K. Funk, and P. Fassl, eds., *Eschatologie, Bibeltheologische und philoso-*

phische Studien zum Verhältnis von Erlösungswelt und Wirklichkeitsbewältigung: Festschrift für Engelbert Neuhäusler zur Emeritierung gewidmet von Kollegen, Freunden und Schülern (St. Ottilien: EOS, 1981) 109–43.

Feuillet, André, "La parabole du mauvais riche et du pauvre Lazare (Lc 16, 19-31) antithèse de la parabole de l'intendant astucieux (Lc 16, 1-9)," NRTh 101 (1979) 212–23.

Idem, "Les riches intendants du Christ (Luc xvi, 1-13)," RSR 34 (1947) 30–54.

Firth, C. B., "The Parable of the Unrighteous Steward (Luke xvi. 1-9)," ExpT 63 (1951–52) 93–95.

Firth, H., "The Unjust Steward," ExpT 15 (1903–4) 426–27.

Fitzmyer, Joseph A., "The Story of the Dishonest Manager (Lk 16:1-13)," TS 25 (1964) 23–42; reprinted in idem, Essays on the Semitic Background of the New Testament (SBibSt 5; Missoula, Mont.: Scholars Press, 1974) 161–84.

Fletcher, Donald R., "The Riddle of the Unjust Steward: Is Irony the Key?" JBL 82 (1963) 15–30.

Flusser, David, "Jesus and the Essenes," Jerusalem Perspective 3 (1990) 3–5, 13.

Focant, Camille, "Tromper le Mammon d'iniquité (Lc 16:1-13)," in Refoulé, À cause, 547–69.

Fonck, Leopold, Parables, 464, 592–608, 664, 667, 674.

Fossion, A., "Tromper l'argent trompeur: Lecture structurale de la parabole du gérant habile, Luc 16,1-9," FoiTe 13 (1983) 342–60.

Friedel, Lawrence M., "The Parable of the Unjust Steward," CBQ 3 (1941) 337–48.

Fuchs, Éric, and Marc Faessler, "L'Évangile et l'argent: la parabole de l'intendant intelligent," BCPE 30 (1978) 3–14.

Fyot, Jean-Louis, "Sur la parabole de l'intendant infidèle," Christus 6 (1959) 500–504.

Gächter, Paul, "Die Parabel vom ungetreuen Verwalter (Lk 16, 1-8)," Orien 27 (1963) 149–50.

Idem, "The Parable of the Dishonest Steward after Oriental Conceptions," CBQ 12 (1950) 121–31.

Galbiati, Enrico, "Il fattore infedele (Luca 16, 1-9)," BeO 3 (1961) 92–96.

Gander, Georges, "Le procédé de l'économe infidèle, décrit Luc 16.5-7, est-il répréhensible ou louable?" VC 7 (1953) 128–41.

Genuyt, François, "Luc 16: Le porche du Royaume," SémBib 9 (1978) 10–35.

Gibson, Margaret D., "On the Parable of the Unjust Steward," ExpT 14 (1902–3) 334.

Grant, John, and F. W. S. O'Neill, "The Unjust Steward," ExpT 16 (1904–5) 239–40.

Hampden-Cook, E., "The Unjust Steward," ExpT 16 (1904–5) 44.

Heininger, Metaphorik, 167–77.

Herranz Marco, Mariano, "La predicación de Jesús: Parabola del administrador infidel (Lc 16, 1-13)," Cuadernos Evangelica 14 (1975) 5–26.

Herrmann, Johannes, "Rechtsgeschichtliche Überlegungen zum Gleichnis vom ungerechten Verwalter (Lk. 16:1-8)," TRG 38 (1970) 389–402.

Hiers, Richard H., "Friends by Unrighteous Mammon: The Eschatological Proletariat (Luke 16:9)," JAAR 38 (1970) 30–36.

Hoeren, Thomas, "Das Gleichnis vom ungerechten Verwalter (Lukas 16,1-8a): Zugleich ein Beitrag zur Geschichte der Restschuldbefreiung," NTS 41 (1995) 620–25.

Hof, Otto, "Luthers Auslegung von Lukas 16, 9," EvTh 8 (1948–49) 151–66.

Hooley, B. A., and A. J. Mason, "Some Thoughts on the Parable of the Unjust Steward (Luke 16:1-13)," ABR 6 (1958) 47–59.

Horn, Glaube und Handeln, 72–80.

Hüttermann, Fritz, "Stand das Gleichnis vom ungerechten Verwalter in Q?" ThGl 27 (1935) 739–42.

Ireland, Dennis J., "A History of Recent Interpretation of the Parable of the Unjust Steward (Luke 16:1-13)," WTJ 51 (1989) 293–318.

Idem, Stewardship and the Kingdom of God: An Historical, Exegetical, and Contextual Study of the Parable of the Unjust Steward in Luke 16:1-13 (NovTSup 70; Leiden/New York: Brill, 1992).

Jalland, Trevor G., "A Note on Luke 16, 1-9," StEv 1 (TU 73) (1959) 503–5.

Javelet, Robert, Les paraboles contre la loi (Paris: Éditions Saint-Paul, 1967) 147–62.

Jeremias, Parables, 45–48, 181–82.

Jülicher, Gleichnisreden, 2:495–514.

Jüngel, Eberhard, Paulus und Jesus: Eine Untersuchung zur Präzisierung der Frage nach dem Ursprung der Christologie (4th ed.; HUT 2; Tübingen: Mohr Siebeck, 1972) 157–60.

Kahlefeld, Paraboles, 2:90–91.

Kamlah, Ehrhard, "Die Parabel vom ungerechten Verwalter (Luk. 16, 1ff.) im Rahmen der Knechtsgleichnisse," in Otto Betz et al., eds., Abraham unser Vater: Juden und Christen im Gespräch über die Bibel. Festschrift Otto Michel (AGSU 5; Leiden: Brill, 1963) 276–94.

Kannengiesser, Charles, "L'intendant malhonnête," Christus 18 (1971) 213–18.

King, Alexander, "The Parable of the Unjust Steward," ExpT 50 (1938–39) 474–76.

Kistemaker, Simon, "Shrewd Manager. An Exposition of Luke 16:1-9," Evangel 2, no. 2 (1984) 135.

Kloppenborg, John S., "The Dishonored Master (Luke 16, 1-8a)," Bib 70 (1989) 474–95.

Knox, Wilfred L., *The Sources of the Synoptic Gospels* (2 vols.; Cambridge: Cambridge University Press, 1957) 2:93–96.

Kosmala, Hans, "The Parable of the Unjust Steward in the Light of Qumran," *ASTI* 3 (1964) 114–21.

Krämer, Michael, "Ad parabolam de villico iniquo: Lc 16, 8.9," *VD* 38 (1960) 278–91.

Idem, *Das Rätsel der Parabel vom ungerechten Verwalter, Lk 16:1-13: Auslegungsgeschichte – Umfang – Sinn. Eine Diskussion der Probleme und Lösungsvorschläge der Verwalterparabel von den Vätern bis heute* (BSRel 5; Zurich: Pas-Verlag, 1972).

Krüger, Gerda, "Die geistesgeschichtlichen Grundlagen des Gleichnisses vom ungerechten Verwalter Lk 16, 1-9," *BZ* 21 (1933) 170–81.

Kümmel, *Heilsgeschehen*, 271–77, esp. 274.

Latham, Henry, *Pastor Pastorum or the Schooling of the Apostles by Our Lord* (Cambridge: Deighton, Bell; London: George Bell, 1890) 386–98.

Ledrus, M., "Il fattore infedele (Lc 16, 1-9): Stralciato da uno studio in preparazione sulla modestia (epieikeia) evangelistica," *PalCl* 50 (1971) 978–82.

Lenwood, Frank, "An Alternative Interpretation of the Parable of the Unjust Steward," *ConQ* 6 (1928) 366–73.

Lévy, Jean-Philippe, "Sur trois textes bibliques concernant des actes écrits," in M.-H. Prevost and M. Humbert, eds., *Mélanges à la mémoire de Marcel-Henri Prévost: droit biblique, interprétation rabbinique, communautés et société* (Paris: Presses universitaires de France, 1982) 23–48.

Liese, H., "Villicus iniquitatis: Lc. 16, 1-9," *VD* 12 (1932) 193–98.

Lindars, Barnabas, "Jesus and the Pharisees," in E. Bammel, C. K. Barrett, and W. D. Davies, eds., *Donum gentilicium: New Testament Studies in Honour of David Daube* (Oxford: Clarendon, 1978) 51–63, esp. 53–56.

Loader, William, "Jesus and the Rogue in Luke 16, 1-8A: The Parable of the Unjust Steward," *RB* 96 (1989) 518–32.

Lunt, Ronald G., "Expounding the Parables, III: The Parable of the Unjust Steward (Luke 16:1-15)," *ExpT* 77 (1965–66) 132–36.

Idem, "Towards an Interpretation of the Parable of the Unjust Steward (Luke xvi. 1-18," *ExpT* 66 (1954–55) 335–37.

Maass, Fritz, "Das Gleichnis vom ungerechten Haushalter, Lukas 16, 1-8," *ThViat* 8 (1961–62) 173–84.

Maillot, Alphonse, "Notules sur Luc 16, 8b-9," *EThR* 44 (1969) 127–30.

Maiworm, J., "Die Verwalterparabel," *BK* 13 (1958) 11–18.

Mann, C. S., "Unjust Steward or Prudent Manager?" *ExpT* 102 (1991) 234–35.

Mara, Maria G., *Ricchezza e povertà nel cristianesimo primitivo* (Studi Patristici 1; Rome: Città nuova, 1980).

Marshall, H. S., "The Parable of the Untrustworthy Steward," *ExpT* 39 (1927–28) 120–22.

Marshall, I. Howard, "Luke xvi, 8: Who Commended the Unjust Steward?" *JTS* 19 (1968) 617–19.

Martin-Achard, Robert, "Notes sur Mammon et la parabole de l'économe infidèle," *EThR* 28 (1953) 137–41.

McFayden, J. F., "The Parable of the Unjust Steward," *ExpT* 37 (1925–26) 535–39.

Meier, A., *Das Gleichnis vom gerechtfertigten Verwalter, Lk 16,1-14* (8th ed.; Lübeck: Schmidt, 1885; reprinted in Krämer, *Rätsel*, 250–57.

Menoud, Philippe Henri, "Riches injustes et biens véritables," *RThPh* n.s. 31 (1943) 5–17.

Merkelbach, Reinhold, "Über das Gleichnis vom ungerechten Haushalter (Lucas 16, 1-13)," *VC* 33 (1979) 180–81.

Middleton, R. D., "St. Luke xvi. 9," *Theol* 29 (1934) 41.

Miller, W. D., "The Unjust Steward," *ExpT* 15 (1903–4) 332–34.

Molina, Jean-Pierre, "Luc 16/1 à 13. L'injuste Mamon," *EThR* 53 (1978) 371–76.

Monat, Pierre, "L'exégèse de la parabole de 'l'intendant infidèle', du IIe au XIIe siècle," *REAug* 38 (1992) 89–123.

Moore, Francis J., "The Parable of the Unjust Steward," *ATR* 47 (1965) 103–5.

Moxnes, *Economy*, 139–46.

Murray, George, "The Unjust Steward," *ExpT* 15 (1903–4) 307–10.

Noonan, John T., Jr., "The Devious Employees," *Commonweal* 104 (1977) 681–83.

Oesterley, William O. E., "The Parable of the 'Unjust' Steward," *Exp.* 6/7 (1903) 273–83.

Paliard, Charles, *Lire l'Écriture, écouter la Parole: La parabole de l'économe infidèle* (LiBi 53; Paris: Éditions du Cerf, 1980).

Pargiter, Frederick E., "The Parable of the Unrighteous Steward," *ExpT* 32 (1920–21) 136–37.

Parrott, Douglas M., "The Dishonest Steward (Luke 16.1-8a) and Luke's Special Parable Collection," *NTS* 37 (1991) 499–515.

Paterson, W. P., "The Example of the Unjust Steward," *ExpT* 35 (1923–24) 391–95.

Paul, Geoffrey, "The Unjust Steward and the Interpretation of Luke 16:9," *Theol.* 61 (1958) 189–93.

Pauly, Dieter, *Die Bibel gehört nicht uns* (Munich: Kaiser, 1990).

Pautrel, Raymond, "'Aeterna tabernacula' (Luc xvi, 9)," *RSR* 30 (1940) 307–22.

Perkins, Pheme, *Hearing the Parables* (New York: Paulist Press, 1981) 165–71, 185.

Petzke, *Sondergut*, 141–47.

Pickar, Charles H., "The Unjust Steward," *CBQ* 1 (1939) 250–52.

Pirot, Jean, *Jésus et la richesse: Parabole de l'intendant astucieux* (Marseille: Imprimerie Marseillaise, 1944).

Porter, Stanley E., "The Parable of the Unjust Steward (Luke 16:1-13): Irony is the Key," in David J. A. Clines et al., eds., *The Bible in Three Dimensions: Essays in Celebration of Forty Years of Biblical Studies in the University of Sheffield* (JSOTSup 87; Sheffield: JSOT Press, 1990) 127–53.

Preisker, Herbert, "Lukas 16, 1-7," *ThLZ* 74 (1949) 85–92.

Riggenbach, Eduard, "Villicus inquitatis: Duo filii Mt 21, 28-32," in K. Bornhäuser et al., eds., *Aus Schrift und Geschichte: Theologische Abhandlungen Adolf Schlatter zu seinem 70. Geburtstage* (Stuttgart: Calwer, 1922) 17–34.

Rouiller, G., "Un saint de la terre: L'économe infidèle (Lc 16, 1-13)," Échos de Saint-*Maurice* n.s. 15 (1985) 49–56.

Rücker, Adolf, "Über das Gleichnis vom ungerechten Verwalter, Lc 16:1-13" (BibS[N] 17/5; Freiburg/St. Louis: Herder, 1912).

Salvoni, F., "L'economo falsario (Lc 16, 8-9)," *RBR* 4 (1969) 207–16.

Samain, Etienne, "Approche littéraire de Luc 16" (bibliography and appendix by T. Snoy), *FoiVie* 72 (1973) 39–68.

Idem, "Le bon usage des richesses, en Luc XVI, 1-12," *RDT* 2 (1947) 330–35.

Schmahl, G., "Das Gleichnis vom ungerechten Verwalter (Lk 16, 1-9): Ein Beispiel aktualisierter Tradition," *PBl* 25 (1973) 135.

Schwarz, Günther, "'. . . lobte den betrügerischen Verwalter'? (Lukas 16,8a)," *BZ* 18 (1974) 94–95.

Scott, Bernard B., "A Master's Praise: Luke 16, 1-8a," *Bib* 64 (1983) 173–88.

Scott, R. B. Y., "The Parable of the Unjust Steward (Luke xvi. 1ff.)," *ExpT* 49 (1937–38) 234–35.

Seccombe, David P., *Possessions and the Poor in Luke-Acts* (SNTU B 6; Linz: Fuchs, 1982) 158–72.

Seibert, H. W., *Der ungerechte Haushalter: Versuch einer Rechtfertigung desselben nach Lukas 16, 1-13* (Leipzig: Wallmann, 1913).

Sellew, Philip, "Interior Monologue as a Narrative Device in the Parables of Luke," *JBL* 111 (1992) 239–53.

Smith, B. T. D., *The Parables of the Synoptic Gospels: A Critical Study* (Cambridge: Cambridge University Press, 1937) 108–12.

Sorger, Karlheinz, and Georg Baudler, "Der 'ungetreue Verwalter' (Lk 16, 1-13)," 15 (1985) 82–84.

Steele, J., "The Unjust Steward," *ExpT* 39 (1927–28) 236.

Steinhauser, Michael G., "Noah in his Generation: An Allusion in Luke 16:8b, εἰς τὴν γενεὰν τὴν ἑαυτῶν," *ZNW* 79 (1988) 152–57.

Stoll, Raymond, "The Unjust Steward: A Problem in Interpretation," *EcR* 105 (1941) 16–27.

Thomas, W. H. Griffith, "The Unjust Steward," *ExpT* 25 (1913–14) 44.

Tillmann, Fritz, "Zum Gleichnis vom ungerechten Verwalter. Lk 16, 1-9," *BZ* 9 (1911) 171–84.

Topel, L. John, "On the Injustice of the Unjust Steward: Lk 16:1-13," *CBQ* 37 (1975) 216–27.

Velte, D., "Das eschatologische Heute im Gleichnis vom ungerechten Haushalter," *MPTh* 27 (1931) 213–14.

Vögtle, Anton, "Das Gleichnis vom ungetreuen Verwalter," *ORPB* 53 (1952) 263–70.

Volckaert, J., "The Parable of the Clever Steward (Luke xvi. 1-9)," *CleM* 17 (1953) 332–41.

Wansey, J. C., "The Parable of the Unjust Steward: An Interpretation," *ExpT* 47 (1935–36) 39–40.

Weber, Simon, "Revision gegen die Freisprechung des ungerechten Verwalters Luk. 16, 5-8," *ThQ* 93 (1911) 339–63.

Weder, *Gleichnisse*, 262–67.

Williams, Francis E., "Is Almsgiving the Point of the 'Unjust Steward'?" *JBL* 83 (1964) 293–97.

Idem, "The Parable of the Unjust Steward (Luke xvi. 1-9)," *ExpT* 66 (1954–55) 371–72.

Wilson, Paul S., "The Lost Parable of the Generous Landowner and Other Texts for Imaginative Preaching," *QR* 9 (1989) 80–99.

Wright, A., "The Parable of the Unjust Steward," *Interpreter* 7 (1911) 279–87.

Zerwick, M., "De villico iniquo," *VD* 25 (1947) 54–55, 172–76.

Zimmermann, Heinrich, "Die Botschaft der Gleichnisse Jesu," *BiLeb* (1961) 92–105, 171–74, 254–61, esp. 254–61.

1/ **And he said to the disciples, "There was a rich man who had a manager, and charges were brought to him that this man was squandering his property. 2/ Having summoned him, he said to him, 'What is this that I hear about you? Give an accounting of your management, because you cannot manage the business**[a] **any longer.' 3/ Then the manager said to himself, 'What could I possibly do, since my master is taking the management away from me? I am not able to dig, and I am ashamed to beg. 4/ I have decided what to do so that, when I am dismissed as manager, they may welcome me into their homes.' 5/ And, summoning his master's debtors one by one, he said to the first, 'How much do you owe my master?' 6/ He said, 'A hundred baths**[b] **of oil.' He said to him, 'Here are your papers, and sit down and quickly write fifty.' 7/ Then he said to another, 'And you, how much do you owe?' He said, 'A hundred cors**[b] **of wheat.' He said to him, 'Here are your papers; write eighty.' 8/ And the Lord commended the manager of dishonesty**[c] **for having acted intelligently; for the children of this age are more intelligent than the children of light are in dealing with their own generation. 9/ And as for me, I tell you, make friends for yourselves by means of the mammon of dishonesty**[d] **so that when it is gone**[e] **they may welcome you into the eternal tents."**

a   Literally: "manage"
b   On these measures, see p. 448 below.
c   That is, the dishonest manager
d   That is, deceitful money
e   On this ambiguous expression, see p. 451 below.

The parable of the dishonest manager (vv. 1-9), which has given rise to innumerable commentaries and which is in fact a parabolic narrative, has been considered a *crux interpretum*. So what does it indeed mean? Does it stress the proper use of material goods? Or is the stress on insolent resourcefulness, which is rewarded in the end? Or on the existential stance to take in the face of the imminence of the parousia or death? In addition to that general question, there are further particular questions: Is the κύριος ("lord," "master") of v. 8 the rich owner of the parable or the Lord Jesus Christ? How is the parable to be subdivided? Does the pericope end with v. 8, v. 9, or v. 13? In v. 9, who are the "friends" that one should make

and what is the "mammon of dishonesty"? In the same verse, what do the "eternal tents" represent?[1]

Analysis

Synchronic Analysis

Although chap. 15 was addressed to the Pharisees and the scribes, chap. 16 is aimed first of all at the disciples, who must understand and live the good news (chap. 15) in community and in the world (chap. 16).[2]

In v. 14, what Jesus says is interrupted by a comment on the part of the narrator, who calls our attention to the decisive presence of the Pharisees, described as lovers

---

1   See Bultmann (*History*, 422) and Ireland (*Stewardship*, 5–47), who provide valuable summaries of the various interpretations of the parable. Taking law and money as the keys to its interpretation, Paliard (*Lire l'Écriture, écouter la Parole*) surmises that the sense of the parable changes depending on whether one reads it on its own (as an enigmatic tribute to shrewdness), in light of what comes after (as the

defiance of the unjust order of money and security by love), or in light of what comes before (as the transition in Jesus Christ from law to gospel).

2   See de Burgos Núñez, "El Escándalo de la Justicia," 167–90. According to Zwingli (*Annotationes*, 676), the first parable in Luke 16 teaches us to meet our neighbor with the same love that God shows in Luke 15.

of money. At this point Jesus speaks to them (v. 15). I assume that it is also to them that Jesus addresses the following aphorisms on the law (vv. 16-17) and divorce (v. 18) and, finally, the parable of the rich man and the poor man, Lazarus (vv. 19-31). But just as the Pharisees, along with the disciples, had been the audience for the first parable, the disciples are, in turn, along with the Pharisees, the audience for the second one.[3]

The two parables are found at opposite ends of chap. 16 (vv. 1-9 and vv. 19-31).[4] They both call attention to a rich man (vv. 1 and 19), one of whom was in dialogue with his manager (v. 1); the other, having to deal with a beggar (v. 20). While the second parable ends without commentary (v. 31), the first one gathered to it, at the end, a series of explanatory maxims, first in vv. 8b and 9, then in vv. 10-13, which, linked to each other and to what precedes by the linking word "mammon," provide a variation on the theme of the first parable. If we think of this chapter as a balanced construction, the small block of material concerning the Pharisees (vv. 14-15), by reason of its content, serves not only as a conclusion to the first parable but also as an introduction to the second. We should probably also link vv. 16-18 to the second parable, even though the connection between these passages and that parable is not immediately obvious. A reading of the chapter as a whole reveals that the crucial theme is material goods; but the reader will also sense the fact that money is the visible face of what constitutes the human being, his or her righteousness before God (v. 15).

Diachronic Analysis

The two parables, which are without Synoptic parallels, come from Luke's special material, L, as is suggested also by some structural and stylistic indications.[5] These parables, which begin with the characteristic expression ἄνθρωπός τις, "a man,"[6] effortlessly recount a story.

The vocabulary is simple but not without precision. In the first parable, the manager carries on an interior monologue, which is characteristic of L.[7] The sayings of vv. 10-12, however, have a completely different style, and in their sapiential manner of expression resemble some of the maxims of the preceding chapters (cf., e.g., 11:36; 12:2-3; etc.). As they have no Synoptic parallels, commentators usually attribute them to L.[8] Verses 13 and 16-18, on the other hand, with parallels in Matthew (Matt 6:24; 11:12-13; 5:18; 5:32; and 19:9) and, in part, in the *Gospel of Thomas* (*Gos. Thom.* 47 and 11), come from Q. This last sequence is interrupted by a brief apophthegm (vv. 14-15), whose construction would appear to be redactional, since we know that this Gospel writer was fond of emphasizing a maxim by inserting it into a narrative context. Verse 14 is redactional and creates a scenario for Jesus and the Pharisees. It introduces a maxim the first half of which has a Lukan ring to it (v. 15a) and the second half of which could well be from the tradition (the word βδέλυγμα, "abomination," is not characteristic of the Third Gospel).

If we concentrate on vv. 1-9, we will see the hand of the author of the Gospel of Luke in the summary introduction to the parable (v. 1a).[9] Luke may have retouched the parable, but it is essentially the work of the gifted author of L, who drew on an oral parable whose rural flavor is proof of an ancient origin (which may have been Palestinian, since later Diaspora Christianity was primarily urban). Verse 8a provided a conclusion for the parable and the "master" (κύριος) mentioned there stood originally for the owner in the parable.[10] As was often the case in the Synoptic tradition,[11] the early Christians were anxious to add their interpretation in the form of a saying by Jesus. Verse 8b, which fulfills this function, is obviously outside the parable, since it can in no way pass for a word of commendation from the owner. What is more, the two

---

3   Chapter 17, addressed to Jesus' disciples (see vv. 1 and 22), continues this teaching on the Christian life in the church.

4   According to Bigo ("La richesse comme intendance," 271), the two parables in Luke 16 are sister parables and present the doctrine, which becomes traditional, of the apt usage of riches.

5   See Jeremias, *Sprache*, 255–57, 260–62; Fitzmyer, 1:84; Petzke, *Sondergut*, 141–51.

6   See Sellin, "Lukas."

7   See Heiniger, *Metaphorik;* Sellew, "Interior Monologue," 239–53.

8   For example, Fitzmyer, 1:84.

9   See Jeremias, *Sprache*, 255.

10 Contra Bultmann (*History*, 175–76), I do not imagine the parable without this conclusion composed in the style of the parable.

11 See Jeremias, *Parables*, 110–13.

successive occurrences of ὅτι ("that," "because," "for") are awkward; the first belongs to the parable and the second to the commentary. This commentary grew out of a double embarrassment: ascertaining the point of the parable, and dealing with the implication that the story might encourage dishonest conduct. The vocabulary having to do with intelligence (φρονίμως, "shrewdly," in v. 8a; φρονιμώτεροι, "shrewder," in v. 8b) takes care of linking the parable to this first addition to it. The double ambiguity is thus resolved by the opposition, typical of earliest Jewish Christianity, between "children of this age" and "children of light." The saying rebukes the "children of light" by forcing them to look at the example of the "children of this age."[12]

Taking as focus a wisdom stance, this commentary was not sufficient. It was necessary to spell out its ethical content[13]—hence the addition of a second saying, ceremoniously introduced by the words: "And as for me, I say to you." That the claim of authenticity is made so pointedly indicates that the saying is unlikely to be genuine. The person speaking here is not the historical Jesus but a Christian prophet. Believing himself to be inspired, he takes care to direct the practical wisdom of the disciples toward others, undoubtedly the poor, at the same time flashing a heavenly reward before their eyes (we will come across this same contrast in the second parable). The archaic vocabulary of v. 9 is a clear indication that it dates back to an oral Aramaic phase of the earliest

church in Palestine. The two successive commentaries (vv. 8b and 9) doubtless come from the same period.[14]

The sayings in vv. 10-12 can also function as commentaries, but, unlike vv. 8b and 9, they had an independent existence before being joined to the parable and its commentaries by reason of similarities of a thematic order (the management motif) and structural order (the words "mammon" and "unjust"). What is more, this joining was not accomplished without problems, since vv. 10-12 extol honesty, while the parable itself praises a certain kind of dishonesty.[15] But it was for that very reason that Christians of that time drew on these two verses to resolve the double ambiguity of the parable in a more satisfactory way than vv. 8a, 8b, and 9 did. Furthermore, this bringing together of these elements required some structural adjustment: v. 10b, which borders on improbability (one does not entrust large amounts of property to someone who has proved incapable of managing small amounts!), may have been created at the time when v. 10a was joined to the parable, to make it more appropriate.[16]

Commentary

■ **1a** Luke is just as likely to use the Greek imperfect as the Greek aorist to introduce Jesus' words.[17] The imperfect is better suited to a relatively long utterance.[18] Moreover, Luke is witness to the evolution of the language: he often shuns the classical use of the dative after the verb

---

12   See Degenhardt, *Lukas*, 119: "Der Vers 8b ist die erste Deutung der christlichen Gemeinde, aber schon vor Lukas formuliert."

13   Verses 9-13, which are Lukan, shift the emphasis from eschatology (vv. 1-8) to ethics, according to Degenhardt, *Lukas*, 120.

14   I place myself between Fletcher ("Riddle of the Unjust Steward," 19), who thinks that v. 9 is a commentary on the parable given by Jesus himself, and Degenhardt (*Lukas*, 119–20), who thinks that it comes from Luke.

15   Feuillet ("Les riches intendants du Christ," 30–54) provides an elegant attempt to harmonize the message of these verses, all attributed to the historical Jesus. There is a strong link between v. 4 and v. 9; furthermore, vv. 9-13 form a unity (only v. 13 may have come from another context). From v. 1 to v. 13 there is a single, unified teaching on wealth (viz., that the wealthy are the stewards of the goods of God). Emphasizing only the invitation to almsgiv-

ing limits the meaning; the poor are the managers of spiritual goods. In the same vein, see Jalland ("Note," 505) and Pickar ("Unjust Steward," 251). For Lunt ("Expounding the Parables," 133) on the other hand, "it simply will not do to attempt to wring from this parable Christian teaching about money." According to Degenhardt (*Lukas*, 118–19), the parable demonstrates the characteristics of the leadership of Israel and is not concerned with wealth; it attacks the religious leaders who demand too much from the people of God.

16   See Williams, "Almsgiving," 296–97.

17   For the use of an introduction with an imperfect (ἔλεγεν, "he was saying"), see 9:23; 10:2; 12:54; 13:6, 18; 14:7, 12, et al. For the aorist (εἶπεν, "he said"), see 9:43; 10:23, 30; 11:2, 5, 46; 12:15-16, 22, et al.

18   See the commentary above on 13:6.

"to say" in favor of the preposition πρός followed by the accusative, which would normally mean "toward," or "to" (e.g., 17:1). Furthermore, most manuscripts made the text smoother by speaking of "his disciples" rather than just "the disciples."[19]

The story that is told respects the rules of oral literature in that it never has more than two people interacting at a time.[20] The opening situation, which is summarily described in v. 1b, allows the action to get off to a running start. The first scene is laid out in v. 2: when the master is informed of the scandal, he does not even wait to get any explanation from his manager but asks immediately for a rendering of the accounts and fires him. Verses 3-4 portray the second scene: left to fend for himself, the manager asks himself what he will do; then he suddenly hits on a solution. Scenes three (vv. 5-6) and four (v. 7) are symmetrical; the manager is placed opposite two of his debtors (of course, to avoid repetition, the second encounter, in v. 7, is more compact than the first, vv. 5-6). There is symmetry of the last scene (v. 8a) with the beginning, in that this last scene again mentions the owner and his manager. Here once more, only the master is permitted to speak.[21]

This summary does not give expression to one essential element, brought up by the manager himself in v. 6: ταχέως, "quickly." Everything takes place very quickly, as would be expected in such a circumstance. As one novelist has written, "Quick reaction is essential for anyone who wants to clear their name."[22] The rich man takes action just as soon as he learns of the scandal. For his part, the manager does not have a moment to lose before his master's orders go into effect. Our own day, marked by numerous scandals, is very much aware of what is going on here, even if two modern factors were missing in ancient times: the role of the media and the intervention of governmental authorities. The fact that they are absent from this story only makes the story line still purer.

■ **1b** The manager acted in a manner similar to the prodigal son, in that he squandered his master's possessions.[23] This text is even more restrained than the one in the preceding chapter (15:13-14, 30), and provides no spicy details. Nor is it interested in the rich man's source of information.[24]

■ **2** The past is of little importance. The master's present decision[25] puts the manager at bay; he must hit on an immediate solution in order to assure himself of a safe future. Otherwise, he will be lost. To be sure, he is not threatened with legal action; nevertheless, when he is fired[26] he loses his salary and his reputation. Unless . . .

The manager's first offense was all the more serious in that his master had placed his confidence in him and his critical task was to manage his master's possessions.[27] He was a "manager," "steward" (οἰκονόμος); his work was one of "management," "administration"

---

19   See the apparatus of Nestle-Aland.

20   See Rudolf Bultmann, "The Study of the Synoptic Gospels," in *Form Criticism: A New Method of New Testament Research; Including The Study of the Synoptic Gospels, by Rudolf Bultmann, and Primitive Christianity in the Light of Gospel Research, by Karl Kundsin* (trans. F. C. Grant; Chicago/New York: Willett, Clark, 1934) 22.

21   Dupont offers a good presentation of the parable ("L'exemple de l'intendant débrouillard," 67–68); see also Zimmermann, "Die Botschaft der Gleichnisse Jesu," 254–58.

22   Jacques Neirynck, *Le manuscrit du Saint-Sépulcre* (3rd ed.; Paris: Cerf, 1995) 277; Bailey himself (*Poet*, 99) also insists on this haste.

23   The same verb (διασκορπίζω, "to squander") is used here (16:1) as there (15:13). The term τὰ ὑπάρχοντα ("goods") is common in the work of

Luke (see 8:3; 11:21; 12:15, 33, 44; 14:33; 19:8; Acts 4:32).

24   On the verb διαβάλλω ("to denounce"), see Godet, 2:162; Marshall, 617; Topel, "Injustice," 217. What is the precise meaning of the question τί τοῦτο ἀκούω περὶ σοῦ? According to Plummer (382), it is: "Why do I hear this of thee?"

25   On φωνήσας ("having called in"), which we find also in v. 24, see Godet, 2:162; Plummer, 382.

26   On μεταστᾳϑῶ ("I am dismissed"), which is an aorist subjunctive signaling action (and not a perfect, which would describe the final state), see Drexler ("Miszellen zu Lukas 16, 1-7," 286–88), who understands this phrase to mean "when I will have been dismissed." In my opinion the story is only about the activity of the steward. Determined by the surrendering of accounts, compelled by the discovery of his trickery, an action is still possible.

27   See Jülicher (*Gleichnisreden*, 2:498) and Zimmer-

($οἰκονομία$); and his job was to "manage," "administer" ($οἰκονομεῖν$). These terms,[28] which are obviously stressed in this text, are familiar to the reader of Luke, who will remember a similar story, that of the manager at a fork in the road who is called on to choose between wisdom and folly (12:42-46). In a Christian community in the process of organization, stewardship represented a primary concern. Wise organization and good leadership are for that matter of concern not only to the church but also to the family, society in general, and especially the private sector.

The rich man's power was not absolute; to be sure, he was in a position to fire his manager ("because you cannot[29] manage the business any longer"), but he was still dependent on his collaborator for one last service: "Give an accounting of your management!" Although he was the boss, he had seen fit to delegate authority. Therefore, he was obliged to ask his subordinate to step down. The manager's stroke of genius is seen in the way he carried out this last job in a way that would serve his own interests, namely, using to his own benefit the fine margin of maneuverability remaining to him. The clause $ἀπόδος\ τὸν\ λόγον\ τῆς\ οἰκονομίας\ σου$ probably does not mean "turn in your accounts to me," which could be

done immediately, but rather "give me an accounting of your management."[30]

■ **3** The interior monologue is typical of L.[31] It enables the hero to express his embarrassment and then to communicate his decision out loud. A management type, he could not picture himself performing pick-and-shovel work.[32] Furthermore, he no longer had the physical strength for manual labor. He belonged to the well-off middle class and therefore could not stoop to begging, for which he lacked the moral fiber.[33] He did not want to be reduced to either of these extreme alternatives.

■ **4** The monologue skillfully avoids indicating the content of the action the man had decided on. He was content with triumphantly announcing that he had found the best solution. That is the meaning of $ἔγνων$—"I've got it," "I've got a solution," "I have decided."[34] The words "I have decided what I am going to do" ($ἔγνων\ τί\ ποιήσω$, v. 4) are of course the answer to the question "what could I possibly do?" ($τί\ ποιήσω$, in v. 3). Leapfrogging over the solution, as I have indicated, the sentence nevertheless tells us to what favorable conclusion the right answer will lead. It does so via a subordinate final clause that defines a final state that symmetrically balances the initial state: "so that, when I am dismissed as manager,[35] they

---

mann ("Die Botschaft der Gleichnisse Jesu," 255), who each insist on trust.

28   On the vocabulary of $οἰκονομία$, see John Reumann, "Heilsgeschichte in Luke. Some Remarks on Its Background and Comparison with Paul," *StEv* 4 (TU 102) (1957) 86–115; and Ireland (*Stewardship*, 114–15), who concludes that the parable is addressed to the disciples, and it exhorts them to utilize material goods with prudence and honesty.

29   The Byzantine text, that is, the majority of manuscripts, following several uncials (A, L, Θ, along with the Vulgate and part of the Vetus Latina) has the future $δυνήσῃ$ ("you will be able"). The present $δύνῃ$ ("you can"), which connotes a sense of an immediate future, makes better sense of the urgency of the situation.

30   On this expression, see Plummer, 382.

31   The expression $τί\ ποιήσω$ can be understood as a future ("what will I do?") or, even better, as a deliberative aorist subjunctive ("what could I do?"); thus, Delebecque, 90. On this interior monologue, see n. 7 above.

32   On $σκάπτω$ ("to dig," "to plough," "to hoe," the jobs of a gardener, peasant, and winemaker), see 13:8. "I

am not able to dig" might be a proverbial expression; we hear an echo of Aristophanes *Birds* 1432: $τί\ γὰρ\ παθῶ\ σκάπτειν\ γὰρ\ οὐκ\ ἐπίσταμαι$ ("What will become of me? Because I do not know how to dig").

33   On "to beg," see Plummer, 383; see Gerd Theissen, "'We Have Left Everything . . .' (Mark 10:28): Discipleship and Social Uprooting in the Jewish-Palestinian Society of the First Century," in idem, *Social Reality and the Early Christians: Theology, Ethics, and the World of the New Testament* (trans. Margaret Kohl; Minneapolis: Fortress, 1992) 60–93, esp. 86. Shame was in antiquity—and is still—a very strong sentiment and a very powerful motivator for action. See Sir 40:28.

34   The aorist $ἔγνων$ takes its meaning from its aspect; see Delebecque, 90–91. Weder (*Gleichnisse*, 266) observes that the future here is not so much threatening as it is malleable.

35   On the precise meaning of $μετασταθῶ$, see n. 26 above.

may welcome me into their homes." Continuing to have a welcome[36] is equivalent to preserving one's dignity, not losing one's social status, maintaining a sense to one's life, getting off easy after an emotional struggle.

■ **5-7** The solution decided on seems simple enough but nevertheless poses a legal problem that compounds the literary problem. Does the proposition offered to the various debtors by the manager, who seemed to enjoy a certain autonomy, imply dishonesty or not?[37] At first blush, it seems to recommend making false entries. On the other hand, it could be that the manager simply decided to forgo his own commission. It would appear that such a custom was in effect in antiquity (even if the Torah forbade lending at interest). It was not uncommon for managers, like tax collectors, to be able to add a large margin of profit to what had to be repaid to the owner who made loans. Everyone knew perfectly well that a large amount that was included for commission, and which was tantamount to usury, ended up in the pocket of the manager. It has even been demonstrated that the rate of that commission, not so much in cash as in kind, could reach astronomical levels.[38] Although that hypothesis is attractive, I do not subscribe to it, for I feel that the manager's "dishonesty" ($\dot{\alpha}\delta\iota\kappa\acute{\iota}\alpha$, v. 8a) consisted not only in squandering his master's property but also in falsifying the "documents" ($\gamma\rho\acute{\alpha}\mu\mu\alpha\tau\alpha$), the promissory notes or tenant contracts. I also feel that the commentary on v. 8b has successfully unearthed a "child of this age" in our main character rather than a manager who, after having given in to the weakness of squandering, shapes up and acts honestly (vv. 5-7).

As always, the author of L, followed in this by Luke, prefers good narrative to legal precision. He does not tell us exactly what these "documents" ($\gamma\rho\acute{\alpha}\mu\mu\alpha\tau\alpha$) are.[39] Nor does he tell us if the debtors are merchants or farmers.[40] In either case the figures speak volumes: 100 baths of oil correspond to 450 liters or the equivalent of the pay for 500 to 600 days of a laborer's work.[41] An explanation has also been found for the more modest reduction in the amount owed for the wheat.[42]

---

36   The reader must wait for vv. 5-7 to discover that the "they" in question are the debtors with whom the manager also maintained social relationships which provided meaning in his life. The third person plural could, it is true, have a more general meaning, quasi-impersonal: "so that people might receive me."

37   Some have offered the hypothesis that the manager did not make any accounting errors but gave up his own portion of the profits: Gibson, "On the Parable of the Unjust Steward," 334 (the thrifty manager renounces his part of the profits and hence does not steal from his master); Gächter, "Parable of the Dishonest Steward," 124–28 (the servant renounces his exorbitant profits); Derrett, "Fresh Light on St. Luke xvi: I," 198–219; idem, "Take thy Bond . . . and Write Fifty," 438, 440 ("Under oriental conditions, loans of comestibles were made subject to a much higher interest-rate than loans of money. . . . Thus, Luke's hearers knew at once that the debtors had signed acknowledgements including additional sums which were, whether called 'compensation' or 'interest,' unquestionably exigible in the Hellenistic courts and equally unquestionably contrary to the spirit (but perhaps not the letter) of the biblical prohibition of 'usury'"); Fitzmyer, "Story of the Dishonest Manager," 161–84 (the servant kills two birds with one stone: by renouncing usury, he obeys the

law, and, by doing good makes friends for himself); Hoeren, "Das Gleichnis," 620–25.

38   See Derrett, "Take thy Bond . . . and Write Fifty." But here, in my opinion, the interest for the oil would be not 50 percent but 100 percent!

39   On the $\gamma\rho\acute{\alpha}\mu\mu\alpha\tau\alpha$, see Lagrange, 433. In the margin of my manuscript, Bertrand Bouvier observed, "The presence of these documents contradicts the reputation (perhaps usurped) that one attributes to the Orientals to conclude important contracts orally, with a simple handshake."

40   For Gächter ("Parable of the Dishonest Steward," 124–28), these are farmers. For Lunt ("Expounding the Parables," 132), they are merchants. According to Zimmermann ("Die Botschaft der Gleichnisse Jesu," 256), the question is of no importance.

41   The 100 baths of oil correspond to 100 barrels of 45 liters each, the product of around 140 olive trees. See Dupont ("L'exemple de l'intendant débrouillard," 68) and Grundmann, 318; see Josephus *Ant.* 8.2.9 §57 (cited by Marshall, 618). The discount on the oil has the value of the discount on the wheat; see Lunt ("Expounding the Parables," 132).

42   The kor is worth 10 baths according to Dupont ("L'exemple de l'intendant débrouillard," 68); this is a measure of 589 liters, according to Lagrange (433); 364 liters, according to Grundmann (318); and 220 liters, according to Marshall (619), who

■ **8a** If we identify the "lord" (ὁ κύριος) of v. 8a with the rich man (he is also called by the same Greek word in vv. 3 and 5, where we have translated it by "master"),[43] we have to be surprised at his reaction. Should he not be doubly furious over (a) the squandering and then (b) the forgery of the documents? There is much truth in that, and Günther Schwarz, appealing to the Semitic substratum, has reconstructed an original text that says the direct opposite of what our passage says. In this reconstruction we read, "And the owner cursed the unrighteous manager, because this manager had tricked him"![44] Likewise, another scholar, basing his reconstruction on the fact that the earliest manuscripts lacked punctuation, has proposed reading v. 8a as a question or, at least, an exclamation: "So then, is the owner going to congratulate the manager for having acted wisely?" The implicit answer to that would be "No, of course not."[45] I refuse to resort to these exegetical stratagems and call our attention to the fact that the owner does not congratulate the manager in an unqualified manner but simply praises him for having acted intelligently, that is, in a self-interested way for his own profit (which is the way a rich man would see things). The "owner" (ὁ κύριος) is a good loser and, as such, takes off his hat to his manager's class act. It was neither the first nor the last time that Luke's Jesus shocked middle-class sensitivities[46] and advocated unworthy conduct in order to bring out better what one Spanish commentator has called "the scandal of the righteousness of God's reign."[47] This is done by an argument from the lesser to the greater.[48]

■ **8b** This verdict is given in a style that is quite different from that of the parable. On the heels of a surprising detail in the story comes a severe observation, an implicit warning. Ancient Judaism, followed in this by early Christianity, opposed two worlds and two ages: "this aeon," "this time" (ὁ αἰὼν οὗτος),[49] and the aeon to come, the one of God and his reign, referred to here as "light" (τὸ φῶς).[50] Believers, "children of light" who are still encircled by darkness, must at all times and in all places be put on their guard. Paul, who makes use of the same dualism, speaks in the same vein in 1 Thess 5:5-6: "For you are all children of light and children of the day; we are not of the night or of darkness. So then let us not fall asleep as others [understood as the

---

identifies it with the homer of the Hebrew Bible and who doubts the value of the measures provided by Josephus *Ant.* 15.9.2 §314.

43 According to Lunt ("Expounding the Parables," 132), the κύριος of v. 8 certainly refers to the owner, and not to Jesus; Zimmerman ("Botschaft," 256–58) enumerates the various possible interpretations. Pautrel ("Tabernacula," 317–18) suggests that the ancient versions are unclear on this question.

44 Schwarz (". . . lobte den betrügerischen Verwalter'?" 94–95) believes that he has discovered a double error in translation from Aramaic to Greek, caused by the ambiguity of two words: בְּרַךְ ("to praise," "to curse"); and עָרִים ("intelligent," "treacherous"). He proposes the translation: "And the master cursed the dishonest manager, since he had acted treacherously."

45 Merkelbach, "Über das Gleichnis vom ungerechten Haushalter," 181: "Der Satz ist nicht affirmativ gemeint, sondern eine Frage (oder auch ein indignierter Ausruf)."

46 Jesus offends: see Luke 4:28; 5:21; 6:2, 11; 7:39; 11:15, 45; etc.

47 De Burgos Núñez, "El Escándalo de la Justicia." Topel ("Injustice") proposes that the parable speaks of forgiveness, which seems unjust in the eyes of people but corresponds to the will of God. Bailey (*Poet,* 98) thinks that the text plays with the ideas of pity and pardon; if the master accepts the reductions, he must likewise pardon his manager. On the contrary, Preisker ("Lukas 16, 1-7," 85–92) thinks that the manager is fundamentally corrupt and behaves in harmony with the god of this world.

48 Krüger ("Die geistesgeschichtlichen Grundlagen," 170–81) analyzes this argument and finds its roots in ancient wisdom literature. The author refers to, among other texts, Prov 18:16 ("The gift of a man puts him at ease and welcomes him into the company of the great") and to *Midr. Exod.* 22.1. Par. 30 (*Midras rabbot . . .* [New York/Berlin, 1924], II, fol. 78ᵛ, 1.7–21): Nebuchadnezzar was rewarded for a single good work (having given supplies to Israel out of his own means). How much more so . . . ; see also Eccl 5:9-16.

49 The same expression occurs in Luke 20:34.

50 On "children of the light," see John 12:36; Eph 5:8; 1 Thess 5:5. On the motif of "light" in the Lukan corpus, see Luke 2:32; 8:16; 11:33, 35; 12:3; Acts 9:3; 12:7; 13:47; 22:6, 9, 11; 26:13, 18, 23. On the motif of "darkness," see Luke 1:79; 11:35; 22:44; 22:53.

children of darkness] do, but let us keep awake and be sober" (*NRSV*). Here in Luke, as in Paul, the atmosphere is apocalyptic and the believers know that they are living in the last days. What is daring in Luke 16:8b is that "the children of this age" are hailed—albeit in certain limited circumstances—as an example for the "children of light." This is a little like the "owner" (κύριος, who, for the early Christians, gradually became the Lord God or better the Lord Jesus), who praised the unworthy manager for having demonstrated the wisdom that rightly belongs to God's reign alone.[51] This is close to the thought of the Matthean maxim: "Be wise (φρόνιμοι, another form of the same Greek word that we find in Luke 16:8) as serpents . . ." (Matt 10:16, *NRSV*).

■ **9** Verse 9 raises four difficult questions, but the overall meaning that we can draw from it is simple.[52] With all his authority ("And as for me, I tell you"), the Lukan Christ invites his readers to make friends for themselves with their material wealth and promises them in return spiritual benefits in the world to come.[53]

Let us examine each of the four questions in turn:

(a) The "friends" have been taken to be the poor to whom you grant favors.[54] The difficulty with that identification is the necessity of affirming that it is the poor who will welcome those who are saved into the kingdom of God ("the eternal tents"). So other solutions have been proposed: that it is the angels who hide behind the beneficiaries of your generosity,[55] or even that your personified alms will serve as your intercessors in the other world (this is a Jewish and early Christian concept).[56] In my opinion, the "friends" are those persons who benefit from the sharing of your goods and who, in a symbolism of the eschatological banquet, will welcome you to that eschatological table and who will not shut the door in your face (cf. 13:23-30).

(b) The "mammon of dishonesty." "Mammon" is a word of Semitic origin yet absent from the Hebrew Bible; it came into general use in New Testament times. Its etymology is uncertain, but it might very well be from the same root as our word "amen," what one can have confidence in, what one can trust.[57] Since human beings count on their money, the word came to refer to material goods. In line with the critical stance toward money adopted by various currents of early Christianity, the term is consistently used in a negative sense in the New Testament. The expression "mammon of dishonesty" is not very precise and needs to be explained on the basis of the origin of the maxim (a prophetic commentary on the parable). In this case it definitely has to do with money acquired in a dishonest way.[58] But it should not be deduced from this that money is inherently evil, even if there is—from the point of view of the kingdom, not

51   On φρόνιμος ("intelligent") and this vocabulary in the work of Luke, see Plummer, 383; Pautrel, "Tabernacula," 318; and Fletcher ("Riddle of the Unjust Steward," 23–24), who describes some irony in the parable (pp. 27–30). Williams ("Almsgiving"), on the other hand, argues against the presence of irony in this parable.

52   Colella ("Zu Lk 16,7" [although in fact the article is about v. 9]) proposes interpreting v. 9 as: "Make friends for yourselves, and not unjust wealth!" He offers this proposal because of a possible meaning of the Hebrew particle מן ("rather than," or "and not"), which is, in his opinion, incorrectly rendered here with the Greek ἐκ ("outside of").

53   Krämer (*Rätsel*, 234) argues that the parable, according to its primitive meaning, invited the disciples to distribute their goods before following Jesus; according to a more recent meaning, it encourages mistrust in mammon, with all its dangers.

54   See Bigo, "La richesse comme intendance," 269; and Topel ("Injustice," 220), who opts for this solution but mentions the others.

55   See Grundmann, 321.

56   See Williams, "Almsgiving," 295–96.

57   For a reflection on the system of mammon in its opposition to the system of God, see Molina, "Luc 16/1 à 13: L'injuste Mamon," 371–76; de Burgos Núñez, "El Escándalo de la Justicia," 173. On mammon, see Delebecque, *Études grecques sur l'Évangile de Luc* (CEA; Paris: Belles lettres, 1976) 93, 95; Degenhardt, *Lukas*, 120–23; see the Targums cited by Str-B 2:220, and *1 Enoch* 63:10; Jalland, "Note," 504. On true riches, see Philo *Fug.* 3ff. (16ff.); *Praem. poen.* 17f. (103f.).

58   Camps and Ubach ("Un sentido bíblico de *adikos, adikia*," 75–82) analyze the vocabulary of ἀδικία ("injustice, iniquity") and argue that it refers not only to injustice but also to falsehood; see Hos 10:13a. On the Semitic genitive (τῆς ἀδικίας), see Delebecque, 92 n. 1.

of earthly justice—no clean money. Giving it away is the only way to make dirty money clean; that is in fact the main point of our text.[59]

(c) "When it is gone": the Greek verb ἐκλείπω is often used without a direct object with the intransitive meaning "to be missing," "to be absent," "to disappear." The meaning is thus clear: when there is no more money.[60] But that raises a question: can your money not be missing before you arrive in the kingdom of God, before the end of your life? Here again, we must find an explanation by drawing on the exegetical character of the maxim. The text plays on the idea of virtue that is rewarded and is expressed in the manager's language: "so that, when I am dismissed as manager, they may welcome me into their homes" (v. 4b). We encounter once more the verb "receive," the image of welcome into a home, the observation that there has been a rupture, and the idea of finality. Since the commentary in v. 9 opens up the perspective to the divine world, the stopping place ("when it is gone," ὅταν ἐκλίπη) is delightfully ambiguous. Money loses its usefulness at the moment of our death, which is the very time when one is the most deprived of a single cent. Yet it is also the moment when, as in the parable, it is good to be able to count on one's friends.

(d) The "eternal tents" have caused a lot of ink to flow, no doubt in vain.[61] Just as the Johannine Christ speaks of "many rooms" reserved for believers in the "Father's house" (John 14:2), so does the Lukan Christ draw on the same divine reality. The "tent" (which we find again in the singular in Rev 13:6) was one of the blessings of the blessed time of the exodus. In the first instance, it was the place where one could meet God, the "tent of meeting" (see Exodus 25–27; 33:7); later it became the family living space where the Israelites were wont to live in a time when sedentary life and domestic comfort represented the dangers of idolatry.[62] Here the tents are eternal, which means that they are to be taken in a figurative sense. Two different kinds of spiritual meaning are obviously possible: the "eternal tents" are either the place believers go to at death or the place where the faithful will be welcomed at the time of the parousia.

The prophet who uttered this oracle must have been speaking in a figurative way about the kingdom of God. For the author of L and especially for Luke himself, we see a shift in focus due to the individualization of eschatology, so the dwelling place in mind is no doubt the one to which Christians will go at the time of their death.[63] The second parable, with its contrast between this life and the life after death, confirms this interpretation. This is, moreover, the way in which the parable was understood early on in the history of its interpretation.

History of Interpretation

One curious ancient interpretation is the one that Jerome attributed to Theophilus, bishop of Antioch.[64] Not surprisingly, Theophilus interpreted the parable allegorically

---

59 Or, as Bengel (*Gnomon*, 1:367) has argued, genuine accumulation of wealth (to ascend to the skies) is actually distribution (for the benefit of others).

60 There are two other variants, which are related: ὅταν ἐκλείπητε ("when you die") and ὅταν ἐκλίπητε ("when you come to die"), which are no longer recorded in Nestle-Aland, but are nevertheless part of the *textus receptus*; see Wettstein, *Novum Testamentum graecum*, 1:764; 2:55–56.

61 Pautrel ("Tabernacula") wants to understand "to receive in his tent" in the sense of "to take as hostage." The unfaithful steward justifies himself by playing games with the bookkeeping, but he is still at the mercy of his debtors, who are able to blackmail him—thus the Pharisees, who are prisoners of their role. The reader who does not adopt this interpretation will nevertheless find many biblical and ancient references in this article on the subject

of tents in which one dwells, whether wittingly or as a hostage!

62 On σκηνή, see W. Michaelis, "σκηνή κτλ.," *TDNT* 7 (1971) 368–94.

63 See Dupont, "L'après-mort dans l'oeuvre de Luc," *Revue théologique de Louvain* 3 (1972) 3–21.

64 See Jerome, *Epist.* 121.6. Tatian sees vv. 1-12 as a unit, according to Pautrel ("Tabernacula," 317). Bigo ("La richesse comme intendance," 268) observes that the Church Fathers frequently comment on this parable and that they take it in the same way (sharing one's goods with the poor). In the same vein, see Pautrel ("Tabernacula," 308–9). See also Pickar, "Unjust Steward," 252. There are two sermons of Augustine on this biblical passage: Sermon 113 (*PL* 38:648–52) and *Sermo Lambot* 4 (*PLS* 2:759–69, esp. 765–69).

but, more surprisingly, applied it to the apostle Paul.[65] Did not Paul, for a long time, cheat God, whom the "rich man" stands for? When the manager is abruptly unmasked, this represents the Damascus road and Christ stopping Paul with these words: "Why are you persecuting me?" What could I possibly do, Paul asks himself, in order for Christians to welcome me when I will be relieved of my status as a Jewish teacher? The answer: change the requirement for Gentiles by replacing the Law and the Prophets with conversion or penance, and help Jews, sustained by divine mercy, by reducing their debts (all they have to do is believe henceforth in the resurrection of Christ, which took place on the eighth day, and which is referred to by the eighty measures).

For Jerome (*Epist.* 121.6), who stated that he had discovered no explanation of the parable in the writings of Origen or Didymus, the parable calls to mind the fate of sinners who find the way to be saved. But, he wrote, we should be warned that this parable is only a shadow of truth (Jerome was doubtless anxious to rein in allegorical flights of fancy). In his opinion, we should note the presence of an argument from the lesser to the greater. If the manager, sinner that he was, knew how to act intelligently before being praised by his master, how much more will not Christ praise his disciples? (ibid.).

For his part, Ambrose emphatically declared that wealth is foreign to human beings (*Exp. Luc.* 7.246). It is neither born with them nor dies with them. That is one more reason for not coming under its influence.

Albert the Great saw in the manager a rascal who nevertheless acted with a wisdom worthy of God's own wisdom; did he not send the debtor away freed of his burden, after the debtor had taken good stock of the situation? (*Enarr. in Luc.* 16.1–9 [416–25]). The measures of oil, which the man kept for himself instead of giving them to their rightful owner, are the food intended for widows and orphans. According to Albert, the debtor's burden is not entirely lifted, since the faithful, once they are pardoned, still have responsibilities to shoulder and must still bear a moral share.

According to Anselm of Canterbury (ca. 1033–1109) the manager's fate is in the first instance an image of malice, and then of the progress that it is possible for any holder of an ecclesiastical charge to make (*Hom.* 12).[66] Since priests are to have no authority after death, the critical moment is not death but an illness or some difficult moment in their life. The miraculous solution is authentic preaching that moves its hearers to repentance. Typical of the exegetes of his time, Anselm delighted in attaching symbolic meaning to various numbers. The manager was iniquitous only in his earlier actions. His later action (equivalent to his preaching), on the other hand, was wise and intelligent. If the text calls him the "manager of iniquity," it does so with reference to his past, just as the Gospel continues to call Matthew a "tax collector" when he no longer is one.

In one sermon in Old German, we find the purest example of the classical explanation:[67] the steward is praised not because he has been unfaithful to God but because he has proved wise with respect to himself. This assertion holds good for anyone and everyone. The parable exhorts one and all to get ready for death or rather to foresee what their personal and financial situation will be at that decisive moment.

According to Erasmus, in this parable the Lord invites his disciples to demonstrate as much gentleness as possible and to do good on all occasions, all the while knowing that our kindness is never wasted but has lasting value for the future.[68] In Erasmus's way of thinking, the time when the Master strikes is at the hour of our death—and life is short. That is one more reason for preparing without delay for our eternal life. Our material goods have been entrusted to us not for our personal advantage but to be used for the benefit of our neighbors. It is spiritual riches that are the true ones.[69]

Luther felt obliged to explain once more justification

---

65 A sermon in Old German provides another identification of the steward with Paul. But in this case, it is the second debtor and not the first who is identified with the pagans. See Predigt 52, in Dominica 9 (Schönbach, *Altdeutsche Predigten,* 2:141–43).

66 *PL* 158:655–60; see Krämer, *Rätsel,* 241–57.

67 Reference in n. 65 above.

68 Erasmus, *Paraphrasis,* 411.

69 We find this traditional Catholic doctrine in the work of Feuillet, "Les riches intendants du Christ." Williams ("Almsgiving") cites the biblical and rabbinic texts that associate the good work, almsgiving, with heavenly reward. In his opinion, the hospitable "friends" in v. 9 are a personification of almsgiving.

by faith alone since, said he, there are biblical texts, such as Luke 16, that people never stop quoting in a way that is contrary to the meaning of the text, as an argument in favor of justification by works.[70] For Luther, only the believer who is freely made righteous by God's grace is in a position to act in the way intended by Christ in this passage in Luke. Only the Word of God makes people aware of the tragic nature of their sinfulness and makes it possible for them to change their lives in such a way that they can act intelligently. Luther also refused to admit that the mention of "friends" in v. 9 could justify the heavenly role of "saints."

There are few pericopes on which Bengel commented as carefully as this one.[71] It is difficult to see why. He insisted on the links with the preceding chapter: after the love of God for us (Luke 15) comes our love for our neighbor (Luke 16); after the feast, daily life resumes. Criticism is not aimed at all managers,[72] but only unfaithful ones. When the manager is dismissed, he is unable to dig because it is work he is not used to, or beg because of excess modesty.[73] He is triply guilty (squandering of his master's goods, falsification of the accounts, and love of self instead of love for God). Here, as in Luke 15, God, in his generosity, gives up his rights and values the one who even wastes what belongs to God himself.[74]

In the middle of the nineteenth century, H. Bauer interpreted the parable allegorically by deciphering in it the unfolding history of early Christianity.[75] According to him, what Luke had in mind was the movement away from Jewish particularism toward Christian universalism. The owner represents the theocratic leaders of the people of Israel; the manager, the apostles, who were incapable of keeping for themselves the spiritual benefits that had been entrusted to them (the benefits of the covenant, the law, and the theocracy) and who shared them with the Gentiles.[76]

Conclusion

The reason Jesus chose to shock his audience was that it made it possible for him to engage them more effectively. He told a scandalous story in order to invite each listener to take steps that were existentially sound. In this story a spendthrift manager has no hesitation about becoming openly dishonest in order to limit the damage of his personal ruin. Instead of panicking, this imaginary person finds within himself what we dare to call the moral resources necessary to avoid a catastrophe. It is the character of this last-minute effort that Jesus invests with a parabolic virtue. The setting furnished by the rendering of the accounts suggests in particular the imminent arrival of the last judgment.

Christian tradition has preserved this parable in spite of the fact that it was a source of embarrassment. It has attempted to offer an acceptable interpretation of it. First of all, it noted, with a certain displeasure, that pagans sometimes act more intelligently than Christians (v. 8b). Next, when prompted to reflect on the spiritual func-

---

70 Predigt vom 8/17/1522 (WA 10.3:283–92); see Mülhaupt, *Luthers Evangelien-Auslegung*, 236–44.

71 Bengel, *Gnomon*, 1:476–79.

72 For Melanchthon (*Annotationes*, col. 345), on the contrary, since all people are sinners, the criticism is addressed to everyone.

73 Zwingli (*Annotationes*, 676–77) interprets the interior dialogue of the unfaithful manager differently: the manager acts like any victim of misfortune who is inclined to survive by any means, even dishonesty.

74 In this contrast between oneself and God, Bengel, unlike Erasmus (*Paraphrasis*, 411–12), loses sight of others.

75 H. Bauer, *Versuch*; summarized by Krämer, *Rätsel*, 246–50. In 1885, Meier (*Das Gleichnis*) commented on Luke 16:1-14, looking for a way to harmonize the parable with the overall teaching and message of Jesus. He was interested in the state of the soul of the steward who was surprised by his master; in the discount given to the debtors, which he did not regard as dishonest; in the children of the light, whom he interprets as "idealists"; and in the children of the darkness, whom he considers "pragmatic"! See the summary by Krämer, *Rätsel*, 250–57.

76 We find elements of the history of interpretation in the work of Krämer (*Rätsel*, 241–57) and Monat ("L'exégèse," 89–123). See also Pautrel, "Tabernacula," 317; Fletcher, "Riddle of the Unjust Steward," 18; Bigo, "La richesse comme intendance," 268 n. 3; Pickar, "Unjust Steward," 252; see also n. 64 above.

tion of money, it introduced here the interpretation of a Christian prophet faithful to the wisdom of Israel who encouraged generosity (v. 9).

Luke, who inherited this composition as part of L, offers this parable and its earliest interpretations to the disciples, therefore to Christians themselves (v. 1a). He is also happy that he has vv. 10-12, which rule out understanding the parable as an incitement to deception and which stress each person's personal responsibility.[77]

---

77 I had already finished this exegesis by the time I encountered Hoeren, "Das Gleichnis." According to this author, the steward had not yet been relieved of his responsibilities when he acted out of panic. In addition, according to the Jewish law of that time, he did not have the right to change the debts without consulting his master. Even though he was praised by his master, it was by virtue not of his presumptuous deception but rather a well-ordered piety: he had applied, at least partially, his religious obligation to reduce the debts at regular intervals (see Deut 15:1-5; Leviticus 25). Hoeren insists particularly on Neh 5:11 as a parallel to our parable.

Rules of Faithfulness
(16:10-18)

Bibliography: Verses 10-13

Anderson, Fred C., "Luke xvi. 10," *ExpT* 59 (1947–48) 278–79.

Descamps, Albert, "La composition littéraire de Luc XVI 9-13," *NovT* 1 (1956) 47–53.

Dupont, Jacques, "Dieu ou Mammon (Mt 6, 24; Lc 16, 13)," *CNS* 5 (1984) 441–61.

Honeyman, Alexander M., "The Etymology of Mammon," *ArLg* 4 (1952) 60–65.

Mastin, Brian A., "Latin Mam(m)ona and the Semitic Languages: A False Trail and a Suggestion," *Bib* 65 (1984) 87–90.

Rüger, Hans P., "Μαμωνᾶ," *ZNW* 64 (1973) 127–31.

Safrai, Shemuel, and David Flusser, "The Slave of Two Masters," *Imm* 6 (1976) 30–33.

Samain, Etienne, "Approche littéraire de Luc 16," *CBFV* 12 (1973) 39–62.

Schlögl, Nivard, "Die Fabel vom 'ungerechten Reichtum' und die Aufforderung Jesu, sich damit Schätze für den Himmel zu sammeln," *BZ* 14 (1916–17) 41–43.

Schulz, *Q*, 459–61.

Snoy, T., "Le problème de la finale de la parabole de l'intendant avisé," *FoiVie* 72 (1973) 66–68.

Stegemann, *Zwischen Synagoge und Obrigkeit*, 158–72.

Str-B 2:220–22.

Bibliography: Verses 14-15

Degenhardt, *Lukas*, 131–33.

Hanson, R. P. C., "A Note on Luke xvi. 14-31," *ExpT* 55 (1943–44) 221–22.

Klinghardt, *Gesetz*, 14–40.

McConaughy, Daniel L., "A Recently Discovered Folio of the Old Syriac (Syc) Text of Luke 16, 13-17," *Bib* 68 (1987) 85–88.

Moxnes, *Economy*, 1–9, 146–48, 151–53.

Schmidt, Thomas E., "Burden, Barrier and Blasphemy: Wealth in Matt 6:33, Luke 14:33, and Luke 16:15," *TJT* 9 (1988) 171–89.

Bibliography: Verses 16-18

Bachmann, Michael, "Johannes der Täufer bei Lukas: Nachzügler oder Vorläufer," in W. Haubeck and M. Bachmann, eds., *Wort in der Zeit: Neutestamentliche Studien. Festgabe für Karl Heinrich Rengstorf zum 75. Geburtstag* (Leiden: Brill, 1980) 123–55, esp. 137–50.

Baltensweiler, Heinrich, *Die Ehe im Neuen Testament: Exegetische Untersuchungen über Ehe, Ehelosigkeit und Ehescheidung* (AThANT 52; Zurich: Zwingli, 1967).

Bammel, Ernst, "Is Luke 16, 16-18 of Baptist's Provenience?" *HTR* 51 (1958) 101–6.

Idem, "Markus 10,11f. und das jüdische Eherecht," *ZNW* 61 (1970) 95–101.

Banks, Robert J., *Jesus and the Law in the Synoptic Tradition* (SNTSMS 28; Cambridge: Cambridge University Press, 1975) 203–26.

Barnett, Paul W., "The Jewish Eschatological Prophets" (Ph.D. diss.; University of London, 1977) 145–210.

Berrouard, Marie-François, "L'indissolubilité du mariage dans le Nouveau Testament," *LV(L)* 4 (1952) 21–40.

Betz, Otto, "Jesu heiliger Krieg," *NovT* 2 (1957) 117–37.

Bockmuehl, Markus, "Matthew 5.32; 19.9 in the Light of Pre-rabbinic Halakhah," *NTS* 35 (1989) 291–95.

Bonsirven, Joseph, *Le divorce dans le Nouveau Testament* (Paris/Tournai: Desclée, 1948).

Bovon, François, "The Law in Luke-Acts," in idem, *Studies in Early Christianity* (WUNT 161; Tübingen: Mohr Siebeck, 2003) 59–73.

Braumann, Georg, "'Dem Himmelreich wird Gewalt angetan,'" *ZNW* 52 (1961) 104–9.

Burchard, Christoph, "Zu Lukas 16,16," in C. Burchard and G. Theissen, eds., *Lese-Zeichen für Annelies Findeiss: zum 65. Geburtstag am 15. März 1984* (Dielheimer Blätter zum Alten Testament und seiner Rezeption in der Alten Kirche 3; Heidelberg: Wissenschaftlich-Theologisches Seminar, 1984) 113–20.

Cameron, Peter S., *Violence and the Kingdom: The Interpretation of Matthew 11:12* (2d ed.; ANTJ 5; Frankfurt/New York: Lang, 1988) 124–25.

Catchpole, David R., "The Law and the Prophets in Q," in G. F. Hawthorne and O. Betz, eds., *Tradition and Interpretation in the New Testament: Essays in Honor of E. Earle Ellis for His 60th Birthday* (Grand Rapids: Eerdmans, 1987) 95–109.

Idem, "On Doing Violence to the Kingdom," *JTSA* 25 (1978) 50–61.

Idem, "The Synoptic Divorce Material as a Traditio-Historical Problem," *BJRL* 57 (1974–75) 92–127.

Chamblin, Knox, "John the Baptist and the Kingdom of God," *TynBul* 15 (1964) 10–16.

Chilton, *God in Strength*, 203–30.

Coiner, Harry G., "Those 'Divorce and Remarriage' Passages (Matt 5:32; 19:9; 1 Cor 7:10-16), with Brief Reference to the Mark and Luke Passages," *CTM* 39 (1968) 367–84.

Cortès, Juan B., and Florence M. Gatti, "On the Meaning of Luke 16:16," *JBL* 77 (1958) 231–43.

Crouzel, Henri, *L'église primitive face au divorce, du premier au cinquième siècle* (Paris: Beauchesne, 1971).

Idem, "Séparation ou remariage selon les Pères anciens," *Greg* 47 (1966) 472–94.

D'Angelo, Mary Rose, "Remarriage and the Divorce Sayings Attributed to Jesus," in W. D. Roberts, ed., *Divorce and Remarriage: Religious and Psychological Perspectives* (Kansas City: Sheed & Ward, 1990) 78–106.

Danker, Frederick W., "Luke 16:16—An Opposition Logion," *JBL* 77 (1958) 231–43.

Daube, *Rabbinic Judaism*, 285–300.

Delling, Gerhard, "Das Logion Mk X.11 (und seine Abwandlungen) im Neuen Testament," *NovT* 1 (1956) 263–74.

Derrett, *Law*, 363–88.

Descamps, Albert L., "The New Testament Doctrine on Marriage," in R. Malone and J. R. Connery, eds., *Contemporary Perspectives on Christian Marriage* (Chicago: Loyola University Press, 1984) 217–73, 347–63.

Idem, "Les textes évangéliques sur le mariage," *RThL* 9 (1978) 259–86; 11 (1980) 5–50.

Dewey, Arthur J., "Quibbling over Serifs: Observations on Matt 5:18/Luke 16:17," *Forum* 5 (1989) 109–20.

Donahue, John R., "Divorce: New Testament Perspectives," *Month* 242 (1981) 113–20.

Down, M. J., "The Sayings of Jesus about Marriage and Divorce," *ExpT* 95 (1984) 332–34.

Dungan, David L., "Jesus and Violence," in E. P. Sanders, ed., *Jesus, the Gospels, and the Church: Essays in Honor of William R. Farmer* (Macon, Ga.: Mercer University Press, 1987) 135–62.

Dupont, Jacques, *Mariage et divorce dans l'évangile: Matthieu 19,3-12 et parallèles* (Abbaye de Saint-André: Desclee de Brouwer, 1959) 45–88, 124–53.

Fitzmyer, Joseph A., "Divorce among First-Century Palestinian Jews," *ErIsr* 14 (1978) 103–10, 193.

Idem, "The Matthean Divorce Texts and Some New Palestinian Evidence," *TS* 37 (1976) 197–226.

Force, Paul, "Encore les incises de Matthieu!" *BLE* 94 (1993) 315–27.

Giesen, Heinz, "Verantwortung des Christen in der Gegenwart und Heilsvollendung: Ethik und Eschatologie nach Lk 13,24 und 16,16," *ThGl* 31 (1988) 218–28.

Greeven, Heinrich, "Ehe nach dem Neuen Testament," *NTS* 15 (1968–69) 365–88.

Guelich, Robert A., *The Sermon on the Mount: A Foundation for Understanding* (Waco, Tex.: Word, 1982) 143–49.

Haacker, Klaus, "Ehescheidung und Wiederverheiratung im Neuen Testament," *ThQ* 151 (1971) 28–38.

Harrington, Wilfrid, "Jesus' Attitude toward Divorce," *ITQ* 37 (1970) 199–209.

Haudebert, Pierre, "Abrogation ou accomplissement de la loi mosaïque? (Luc 16, 16-18)," *Impacts* 4 (1984) 15–26.

Hoffmann, Paul, "Jesus' Saying about Divorce and Its Interpretation in the New Testament Tradition," *Conc* 55 (1970) 51–66.

Idem, *Logienquelle*, 50–79.

Honeyman, Alexander M., "Matthew V.18 and the Validity of the Law," *NTS* 1 (1954–55) 141–42.

Isaksson, Abel, *Marriage and Ministry in the New Testament* (ASNU 24; Lund: Gleerup, 1965) 67–74.

Jensen, Joseph, "Does Porneia Mean Fornication? A Critique of Bruce Malina," *NovT* 20 (1978) 161–84.

Kaestli, *L'eschatologie*, 24–27.

Kilgallen, John J., "The Purpose of Luke's Divorce Text (16,18)," *Bib* 76 (1995) 229–39.

Idem, "To What Are the Matthean Exception-Texts (5,32 and 19,9) an Exception," *Bib* 61 (1980) 102–5.

Klinghardt, *Gesetz*, 371.

Kornfeld, Walter, and Henri Cazelles, "Mariage," *DBSup* 5 (1957) cols. 905–35, esp. cols. 926–35.

Kosch, Daniel, *Die eschatologische Tora des Menschensohnes: Untersuchungen zur Rezeption der Stellung Jesu zur Tora in Q* (NTOA 12; Fribourg, Switzerland: Universitätsverlag, Göttingen: Vandenhoeck & Ruprecht, 1989) 427–44.

Idem, *Die Gottesherrschaft im Zeichen des Widerspruchs: Traditions- und redaktionsgeschichtliche Untersuchung von Lk 16,16//Mt 11,12f bei Jesus, Q, and Lukas* (EHS 23/257; Bern/New York: Lang, 1985).

Kretzer, Armin, "Die Frage: Ehe auf Dauer und ihre mögliche Trennung nach Mt 19,3-12," in H. Merklein and J. Lange, eds., *Biblische Randbemerkungen: Schülerfestschrift für Rudolf Schnackenburg zum 60. Geburtstag* (Würzburg: Echter, 1974) 218–30.

Kümmel, Werner Georg, "'Das Gesetz und die Propheten gehen bis Johannes'—Lukas 16,16 im Zusammenhang der heilsgeschichtlichen Theologie der Lukasschriften," in idem, *Heilsgeschehen*, 2:75–86; and in Georg Braumann, ed., *Das Lukas-Evangelium: Die redaktions- und kompositionsgeschichtliche Forschung* (WdF 280; Darmstadt: Wissenschaftliche Buchgesellschaft, 1974) 398–415.

Idem, *Promise*, 121–24.

Laufen, *Doppelüberlieferungen*, 343–60.

Ligier, Louis, *Péché d'Adam et péché du monde* (2 vols.; Theol [P] 43, 48; Paris: Aubier, 1960, 1961) 2:74–116.

Lohfink, Gerhard, "Jesus und die Ehescheidung: Zur Gattung und Sprachintention von Mt 5,32," in H. Merklein and J. Lange, eds., *Biblische Randbemerkungen: Schülerfestschrift für Rudolf Schnackenburg zum 60. Geburtstag* (Würzburg: Echter, 1974) 207–17.

Lövestam, Evald, "Die funktionale Bedeutung der synoptischen Jesusworte über Ehescheidung und Wiederheirat [Mk 10, 2-12; Mt 19, 3-9; Lk 16,18; Mt 5,31f]," *SNTU* 2 (1977) 19–28.

Idem, "De synoptiska Jesus-orden om skilsmässa och omgifte: Referensramar och implikationer," *SEÅ* 43 (1978) 65–73.

MacRae, George W., "New Testament Perspectives on Marriage and Divorce," in L. G. Wrenn, ed., *Divorce and Remarriage in the Catholic Church* (New York: Newman, 1973) 1–15.

Mahoney, Aidan, "A New Look at the Divorce Clauses in Mt 5,32 and 19,9," *CBQ* 30 (1968) 29–38.

Malina, Bruce, "Does Porneia Mean Fornication?" *NovT* 14 (1972) 10–17.

Mearns, Chris, "Realized Eschatology in Q? A Consideration of the Sayings in Luke 7.22, 11.20 and 16.16," *SJT* 40 (1987) 189–210.

Menoud, Philippe Henri, "De la manière d'entrer dans le Royaume," *Flambeau* 55 (1979) 271–75.

Idem, "The Meaning of the Verb βιάζεται in Luke 16.16," in idem, *Jesus Christ and the Faith: A Collection of Studies* (trans. E. M. Paul; PTMS 18; Pittsburgh: Pickwick, 1978) 192–201.

Moore, W. Ernest, "Βιάζω, ἁρπάζω and Cognates in Josephus," *NTS* 21 (1974–75) 519–43.

Idem, "Violence to the Kingdom: Josephus and the Syrian Churches," *ExpT* 100 (1989) 174–77.

Mueller, James R., "The Temple Scroll and the Gospel Divorce Texts," *RevQ* 10 (1979–81) 1–15.

Myre, A., "Dix ans d'exégèse sur le divorce dans le Nouveau Testament," in Société canadienne de théologie, ed., *Le divorce: L'Église catholique ne devrait-elle pas modifier son attitude séculaire à l'égard de l'indissolubilité du mariage? Travaux du Congrès de la Société canadienne de théologie tenu à Montréal du 21 au 24 août 1972* (CTHP 6; Montreal: Fides, 1973) 139–62.

Neirynck, Frans, "De Jezuswoorden over Echtscheiding," in V. Heylen, ed., *Mislukt Huwelijk en Echtscheiding: Een multidisciplinaire Benadering* (Sociologische Verkenningen 2; Antwerp: Patmos; Louvain: Leuven University Press, 1972) 127–41.

Idem, "Huwelijk en Echtscheiding in het Evangelie," *CBG* 6 (1960) 123–30.

Nembach, Ulrich, "Ehescheidung nach alttestamentlichem und jüdischem Recht," *TZ(W)* 26 (1970) 161–71.

Olsen, V. Norskov, *The New Testament Logia on Divorce* (BGBE 10; Tübingen: Mohr Siebeck, 1971) 72, 113.

Parker, David, "The Early Traditions of Jesus' Sayings on Divorce," *Theol* 96 (1993) 372–83.

Perrin, *Rediscovering*, 74–77.

Pesch, Rudolf, *Freie Treue: Die Christen und die Ehescheidung* (Freiburg: Herder, 1971) 56–60.

Idem, "Die neutestamentliche Weisung für die Ehe," *BiLeb* 9 (1968) 208–21.

Prast, Franz, *Presbyter und Evangelium in nachapostolischer Zeit: Die Abschiedsrede des Paulus in Milet (Apg. 20, 17-38) im Rahmen der lukanischen Konzeption der Evangeliumsverkündigung* (FB 29; Stuttgart: Katholisches Bibelwerk, 1979) 278–81.

Prete, B., "Le epoche o i tempi della 'storia della salvezza,'" *PaVi* 27 (1982) 29–32.

Przybyla, Alfons Edward, "List rozwodowy w prawie Mojzesza (Lettre de divorce dans la loi mosaïque)," *Zycie i Mysl* [Warsaw] 26 (1976) 54–64.

Richards, Hubert J., "Christ on Divorce," *Scr* 11 (1959) 22–32.

Ruckstuhl, Eugen, "Hat Jesus die Unauflösligkeit der Ehe gelehrt?" in idem, *Jesus im Horizont der Evangelien* (SBAB 3; Stuttgart: Katholisches Bibelwerk, 1988) 49–68.

Sabourin, Léopold, "The Divorce Clauses (Mt 5,32; 19,9)," *BTB* 2 (1972) 80–86.

Saraggi, G., "Il Matrimonio: sacramento dell'unità. Messagio del Nuovo Testamento," *PalCl* 49 (1970) 1166–74.

Idem, "Il messagio biblico attraverso i secoli," *PalCl* 49 (1970) 1278–86.

Schaller, Berndt, "Die Sprüche über die Ehescheidung und Wiederheirat in der synoptischen Überlieferung," in Lohse, *Ruf Jesu*, 226–46.

Schlosser, *Règne de Dieu*, 2.509–39.

Schnackenburg, Rudolf, *Gottes Herrschaft und Reich: Eine biblisch-theologische Studie* (Freiburg: Herder, 1959) 88–90.

Schneider, Gerhard, "Jesu Wort über die Ehescheidung in der Überlieferung des Neuen Testaments," *TThZ* 80 (1971) 65–87.

Schrenk, Gottlob, "βιάζομαι, κτλ.," *TDNT* 1 (1964) 609–14.

Schubert, Kurt, "Ehescheidung im Judentum zur Zeit Jesu," *ThQ* 151 (1971) 23–27.

Schulz, *Q*, 114–20, 261–67.

Schürmann, Heinz, *Gottes Reich*, 124–29.

Idem, "Neutestamentliche Marginalien zur Frage nach der Institutionalität, Unauflösbarkeit und Sakramentalität der Ehe," in O. Bocher et al., eds., *Kirche und Bibel: Festgabe für Bischof Eduard Schick* (Paderborn/Munich/Vienna/Zurich: Schöningh, 1979) 409–30.

Idem, "'Wer daher eines dieser geringsten Gebote auflöst . . .': Wo fand Matthäus das Logion Mt. 5,19?" *BZ* 4 (1960) 238–50.

Schwarz, Gunther, "ἰῶτα ἐν ἢ μία κεραία," *ZNW* 66 (1975) 268–69.

Schweizer, Eduard, "Matth. 5, 17-20. Anmerkungen zum Gesetzverständnis des Matthäus," in idem, *Neotestamentica: Deutsche und Englische Aufsätze 1951–1963* (Zurich: Zwingli, 1963) 399–406.

Idem, "Noch einmal Mt 5, 17-20," in idem, *Matthäus und seine Gemeinde* (SBS 71; Stuttgart: Katholisches Bibelwerk, 1974) 78–85.

Smith, Don T., "The Matthean Exception Clauses in the Light of Matthew's Theology and Community," *SBTh* 17 (1989) 55–82.

Stenger, Werner, "Zur Rekonstruktion eines Jesusworts anhand der synoptischen Ehescheidungslogien," *Kairos* 26 (1984) 194–205.

Stock, Augustine, "Matthean Divorce Texts," *BTB* 8 (1978) 24–33.

Strecker, Georg, "Die Makarismen der Bergpredigt," in idem, *Eschaton und Historie: Aufsätze* (Göttingen: Vandenhoeck & Ruprecht, 1979) 108–31.

Thiering, Barbara E., "Are the 'Violent Men' False Teachers?" *NovT* 21 (1979) 293–97.

Tosato, Angelo, "The Law of Leviticus 18:18: A Reexamination," *CBQ* 46 (1984) 199–214.

Idem, *Il matrimonio nel giudaismo antico e nel Nuovo Testamento* (Rome: Città nuova, 1976).

Trevijano Etcheverría, Ramon, "Matrimonio y divorcio en Mc 10, 2-12 y par.," *Burg* 18 (1977) 113–51.

Vargas-Machuca, Antonio, "Divorcio e indisolubilidad del matrimonio en la Sagrada Escritura," *EstBib* 39 (1981) 19–61.

Vawter, Bruce, "The Biblical Theology of Divorce," *PCTSA* 22 (1967) 223–43.

Idem, "Divorce and the New Testament," *CBQ* 39 (1977) 528–42.

Idem, "The Divorce Clauses in Matt 5:32 and 19:9," *CBQ* 46 (1984) 199–214.

Wiebe, Phillip H., "Jesus' Divorce Exception," *JETS* 32 (1989) 327–33.

Wijngards, J. N. M., "Do Jesus' Words on Divorce (Lk 16:18) Admit of No Exception," *Jeevadhara* 5 (1975) 399–411.

Wilson, Stephen G., *Luke and the Law* (SNTSMS 50; Cambridge/New York: Cambridge University Press, 1984) 43–51.

Wink, Walter, *John the Baptist in the Gospel Tradition* (SNTSMS 7; London: Cambridge University Press, 1968) 20–23.

Witherington, Ben, III, "Jesus and the Baptist—Two of a Kind?" in D. J. Lull, ed., *SBLSP* 27 (Atlanta: Scholars Press, 1988) 225–44, esp. 237–38.

Wrege, Hans-Theo, *Die Überlieferungsgeschichte der Bergpredigt* (WUNT 9; Tübingen: Mohr Siebeck, 1968) 66–70.

10/ "Whoever is faithful in the least matter is also faithful in the greatest; and whoever is dishonest in the least matter is also dishonest in the greatest. 11/ If then you have not been faithful with respect to dishonest mammon, who will entrust to you what is true? 12/ And if you have not been faithful with respect to what does not belong to you, who will give you what is yours?

13/ "No servant can serve two masters; for he will either hate the one and love the other, or he will be devoted to the one and despise the other. You cannot serve God and mammon."

14/ The Pharisees, who are greedy, heard all this and sneered at him. 15/ And he said to them, "You are those who justify yourselves in the sight of other human beings; but God knows your hearts; for what is prized by human beings is an abomination in the sight of God.

16/ "The law and the prophets were in effect until John; since then, the good news of the kingdom of God is proclaimed, and everyone strives to enter it. 17/ It is easier for heaven and earth to pass away, than for one stroke of a letter in the law to be dropped.

18/ "Anyone who divorces his wife and marries another commits adultery, and whoever marries a woman divorced by her husband commits adultery."

One of the problems in architecture is that of empty spaces. What does one do with the empty space that separates two constructions in the same style? Should the similarity be preserved, or, on the contrary, should an entirely different element be introduced?[1] When he was putting together what we call chap. 16, Luke was confronted with a similar problem. Having decided to place a parable at either end of the chapter, what was he going to put between them? With his choice of the material in vv. 10-13, he opted for similarity (the same theme of the faithful stewardship of possessions); with vv. 14-18, he chose dissimilarity, for that matter a dissimilarity composed of disparate materials (one's own righteousness, stages in the history of salvation, the law, and divorce). The resemblance suggests a consecutive reading and confers a coherent meaning to the passage. The contrasting materials, on the other hand, encourage one to pay attention to isolated elements.

Analysis

As I suggested in my analysis of vv. 1-9, vv. 10-12 serve as commentaries on the parable of the dishonest manager, but they had an independent existence and meaning before being inserted in the present context. Verse 10a is a proverb that Luke has perhaps split in two in order to give it a negative counterpart, thus making it easier to bring it together with the parable of the dishonest manager. In doing this, the Gospel writer gave in to his didactic inclinations[2] and repeated a single truth by presenting it in two guises. Nevertheless, since Hebraic wisdom also favored repetition and symmetry, it is not certain that all of the repetition is due to the redaction. It could have been that the anonymous proverb (v. 10a or v. 10a and b) served as a point of departure for a more personal and more theological reflection (vv. 11 and 12). The author

of this reflection may have been the historical Jesus, whose parable of the talents also makes mention of faithfulness in small things that is rewarded in a big way ("He said to him, 'Well done, good servant! Because you have been trustworthy in a very small thing, take charge of ten cities'" [Luke 19:17]). We would then have here (in vv. 11-12) a hypothetical example of the opposite scenario.[3] A part of the vocabulary of these verses, with its use of the Greek neuter gender, translated as "what is true," "what does not belong to you," and "what is yours," seems alien to the Master's vocabulary. So we can assume that there has been a substantial reworking of Jesus' words. This rereading must have taken place in the milieu of the author of L, to whom I attribute the redaction of these verses, which are absent from the other Gospels.[4]

It is easier to determine the origin of the maxim on the two masters (v. 13): this is from the Sayings Source (Q), as is attested by its presence in the parallel passage in Matt 6:24. The relationship between these two Synoptic Gospels—Luke and Matthew—is such here that they are based on a single Greek formulation of Q that was written, rather than oral. The only difference is that Luke, still employing figurative language, specifically states that the person who is unable to serve two masters is a servant ($o\grave{\imath}\kappa\acute{\epsilon}\tau\eta\varsigma$). The presence of this saying of Jesus in the *Gospel of Thomas* is a confirmation of its success and its wide circulation, since the author of that Gospel does not seem to have come by his knowledge of it through the Synoptic Gospels alone.[5] The location of this maxim in Q is difficult to determine. Its position here in the Gospel of Luke seems to be due to redactional aims; the Gospel writer himself (or, before him, the author of L) has constructed a complex of sayings concerning the faithful stewardship of material possessions hinging on the use of the linking word "mammon" (vv. 9, 11, and 13).

1   This comparison with architecture was suggested to me by my former assistant Marcel Durrer.

2   He likes to explain, and to explain to everyone: for example, he clarifies for the benefit of his Greek readers (in 22:70) what may only have been clear to his Jewish audience (22:67).

3   Matthew 25:21 gives a slightly different formulation: "Well done, good and faithful servant, you have been faithful with few things; I will put you in charge of many things."

4   Their absence in Matthew in particular makes their presence in Q unlikely. Furthermore, their vocabulary is not typically Lukan.

5   On *Gos. Thom.* 47, see Schrage, *Thomas-Evangelium*, 109–16; Fieger, *Thomasevangelium*, 149–53; Robert W. Funk, R. W. Hoover, and the Jesus Seminar, eds., *The Five Gospels: The Search for the Authentic Words of Jesus. New Translation and Commentry* (New York: Macmillan, 1993) 499–500.

Verses 14 and 15, as is often the case with narrative settings or literary articulations, can undoubtedly be assigned to Lukan redaction. This is proved by both the form and the content of these verses: the verb "to hear" (ἀκούω, v. 14), the use of the participle of the Greek verb ὑπάρχω in the sense of "being" = "who are" (ὑπάρχοντες, v. 14), the vocabulary referring to one's own righteousness, as well as the idea that the Pharisees might have been greedy.[6] The contrast between what is high (ὑψηλόν, translated by "prized") and what is low, between what pleases human beings and what pleases God, is also very Lukan (see 1:52; 10:15; 14:11; 18:14; 22:26-27), but Luke is obliged to use a traditional expression to express this idea here ("an abomination in the sight of God," βδέλυγμα ἐνώπιον τοῦ θεοῦ, v. 15c) (see Prov 16:5).

Verses 16-17, which are so important for Luke's theology, come from Q.[7] In the course of my exegesis, I will make a comparison of the Gospels of Matthew and Luke because of the theological repercussions of such a study. I do not know what the place of these sayings was in the Q source. Luke seems to have introduced them here without fearing the contrast that they create with their context. At the most, he may be suggesting a thematic link with the story of the poor man Lazarus; the end of that parable (v. 31) does in fact reaffirm the permanent validity of Holy Scripture, the Law and the Prophets together, even beyond Christ's coming, his resurrection, and therefore the proclamation of God's reign (cf. vv. 16-17).[8]

Even if certain commentators attribute the saying on divorce to L and make a big point of its primitive character,[9] v. 18 must also come from Q. As is known, the sayings of Jesus on this subject are reported, not without significant differences, by the triple tradition (Mark 10:2-12 and parallels), the double tradition (Q), the apostle Paul (1 Cor 7:10-11), and even *Hermas Man.* 4, 1, 6.[10] While Q transmits only Jesus' opinion, Mark's version places a dispute (Mark 10:2-9) before this statement on the subject of marriage and divorce (Mark 10:10-12). Like Luke, and unlike Matthew, Mark is unaware of any exception to the rule of the indissolubility of marriage. But, unlike Luke, in these verses, couched in legal language, he also thinks of the case of a divorce sought by the wife (Mark 10:12—with an eye, it would seem, on the possibilities open in Roman law).

In the Lukan version, the double verdict, which allows of no exception, is concerned with the sole responsibility of the husband and betrays no knowledge of any steps that a wife could initiate in the matter. As for the husband, the Lukan text considers two possibilities: a man's divorce of his wife followed by his remarriage, and marriage with a divorced woman. While Matt 19:3-9 repeats Mark 10:2-12, Matt 5:31-32 quotes and adapts Q, inserting it into a new setting, one of the famous antitheses of the Sermon on the Mount. The text in Matthew 5 is thus parallel to Luke 16:18. The two parallel verses (Matt 5:32 and Luke 16:18), which are very similar (they both mention divorce followed by remarriage and then marriage with a divorced woman), differ in three respects: (a) Luke does not know of the Matthean exception in the case of "unfaithfulness," πορνεία. (b) Matthew says that when a divorce is initiated by the husband, it is the wife who is exposed to the danger of adultery. For Luke, it is the divorcing husband who commits adultery. (c) Finally, Luke has in mind a situation in which divorce will be followed by remarriage. This wording parallels Mark's. As has been pointed out in countless studies on these biblical passages, the early Christians, in various ways and on various occasions, took up Jesus' teaching on divorce and adapted it to their own cultural and legal situations.[11]

---

6 The rare verb ἐκμυκτηρίζω ("to sneer") may be pre-Lukan. See Jeremias, *Sprache*, 258–59.

7 There is a widespread agreement among exegetes on this point; see Kloppenborg, *Q Parallels*, 178.

8 On the ordinance of vv. 16-18, see Klinghardt, *Gesetz*, 14–23.

9 Schaller, "Ehescheidung," 230–31.

10 There are innumerable studies on the origins of these passages; see Luz, *Matthew*, 1:250–51; Greeven, "Ehe nach dem Neuen Testament," 365–

88; Schneider, "Ehescheidung," 65–87; Schaller, "Ehescheidung"; Bockmuehl, "Matthew 5.32," 291–95.

11 See Schaller ("Ehescheidung," 244–46), who suggests that in their homiletical teaching (more than in their casuistic law), the first Christian communities softened Jesus' teaching on divorce by rendering it a prohibition of remarriage.

Commentary

■ **10** This verse is a proverb, and parallels can doubtless be found in other literatures.[12] This secular wisdom is here enlisted in support of religious wisdom. The one who is "faithful" (πιστός) here is not the person who is "accredited" but the "faithful" one to whom a deposit has been entrusted.[13] It is only one step from faithfulness to faith, but in the context, this faithfulness is instead expressed in terms of honesty. This person is faithful and honest in "what is least" (ἐν ἐλαχίστῳ), which is a superlative. Some have said "in the least moment"; I prefer "in the least matter."[14] This person is or will be faithful "in the largest" (ἐν πολλῷ), which is not necessarily to be understood in the quantitative sense of "in many things," but in the qualitative sense of "in an important matter," or "in the greatest (matter)."[15] In the present context, it must be a question either of spiritual goods, entrusted already in the present to Christians and to the leaders of the community, or else of eschatological goods to be managed in the kingdom of God.[16]

The person pronouncing this maxim considers honesty to be of a piece; that is to say, human beings are consistent, stable, integrated beings.[17] He himself demonstrates a brave confidence in this part of humanity, a confidence that no doubt corresponds less to an anthropological optimism than to a faith in God's creative and redemptive power. The maxim is also loaded with an implicit challenge equivalent to an imperative. The sentence does not stop there, however; it has a negative counterpart: the "dishonest" (ἄδικος) person is less one who is "unrighteous" or "unfair" than one who practices what is "unrighteous," the "dishonest" person on whom one cannot count.[18] In the background of this verse there is a rather strict dualism, which is nevertheless more ethical than ontological and more popular than scholarly.

■ **11-12** Verses 11 and 12 foresee an exclusively catastrophic scenario and, in their own way, prolong the paraenetic thrust of v. 10. Those who fail to manage material goods conscientiously (the expression "dishonest mammon" must be a rereading, aimed at Greek-speaking readers, of the expression "mammon of dishonesty" in v. 9) can be anyone in general, but particularly the leaders of local churches. The objective and subjective dangers, as well as the temptations and suspicions and slanders, that the religious leaders of that time had to confront are only too well known. We may remind ourselves of the precautions that the apostle Paul exercised in the matter of the management of the offering he took up on behalf of the poor Christians in Jerusalem.[19] Mammon is said to be "dishonest" (ἄδικος); that is, it is deceptive and cannot be trusted. Verse 12 restates what money is, in the eyes of the author, namely, a possession that is "alien" to human beings, that we should learn to become independent of and to deprive ourselves of. The text powerfully states that money has a disastrous effect in that it alienates human beings from their true identity as God's creatures.[20] Conversely, real possessions are declared to be "true" (τὸ ἀληθινόν) and "yours" (τὸ ὑμέτερον). What is "true" has its intrinsic truth in that it is rooted in God's will; and it is "yours" in the sense that it is what constitutes your true possession.[21] The text looks at the future in a holistic fashion, without distinguishing "during this life" and "after death" or "in this time" and "in the kingdom of God." The double question that is asked is evidently a rhetorical one. No one entrusts anything greater to the person who has proved to be a poor manager of what is less—especially not God, who is both hidden and revealed in the "who?" (τίς). As in the case of the parable of the ten minas (19:11-27), the author no doubt has in mind the eschatological distribution of goods that the Lord will make.

---

12 See the Jewish examples in Wettstein, *Novum Testamentum graecum*, 2:764–65.

13 See Lagrange (436), who naturally refers to 19:17 (the parable of the minas: "Well done, good servant! Because you have been trustworthy in a very small thing . . .").

14 Plummer (386): "'In very little' rather than 'in what is least.'"

15 See BAGD, s.v. πολύς, I, 2c.

16 See the commentary on vv. 11 and 12 below.

17 Thus, Lagrange, 436.

18 See Marshall, 623.

19 On the collection, see Keith F. Nickle, *The Collection: A Study in Paul's Strategy* (SBT 48; Naperville, Ill.: Allenson, 1966); Dieter Georgi, *Remembering the Poor: The History of Paul's Collection for Jerusalem* (Nashville: Abingdon, 1992); Hans Dieter Betz, *2 Corinthians 8 and 9: A Commentary on Two Administrative Letters of the Apostle Paul* (Hermeneia; Philadelphia: Fortress Press, 1985).

20 On ἀλλότριος, see BAGD, s.v.

21 See Godet, 2:169.

One thing that is surprising in these verses is their abstract, almost philosophical, vocabulary: "what is true," "what does not belong to you," "yours" (your share). This is in some ways a Hellenic intellectual counterbalance to the Semitic and mythological term "mammon." The author of the source used here by Luke ought to be congratulated on this hermeneutical effort, which was no doubt indispensable.[22] One final observation. We know what a lively relationship the *Second Epistle of Clement* maintained, in the middle of the second century, with the oral tradition of its time,[23] and it was acquainted with a form of vv. 10-11 that inverts the order of vv. 10 and 11-12. The letter was unacquainted with the doubling in vv. 11 and 12, and modified its vocabulary: "For the Lord says in the Gospel, 'If ye did not guard that which is small, who shall give you that which is great? For I tell you that he who is faithful in that which is least, is faithful also in that which is much'" (*2 Clem.* 8.5).[24] And in place of material goods, the author of *2 Clement* saw, in the smallest things, Christian life here on earth, characterized by keeping the flesh pure and by the seal of baptism. We have here a wider horizon, and the danger comes no longer from "mammon" but from "the flesh."[25]

■ **13** The "servant" (οἰκέτης)—which is a Lukan addition to Q (Matt 6:24)—is one who works in his master's house (cf. Acts 10:7). In a figurative sense, the term can refer to any believer who is active in this world, or rather to any leader of a Christian community.[26] We are struck by the sharp and surprising dualism of Jesus, who is the "Master" in Luke, but the one who speaks in Q. According to succession and property laws in Judaism at that time, it was possible to belong to two masters.[27] Moreover,

rabbis, meditating on the earthly world and the heavenly world, joked that most people had two masters, one human, the other divine.[28] It is in this cultural context that we must understand Jesus' maxim. But even if Jesus' saying is phrased as a maxim, it also has the force of a commandment. Aramaic, like Hebrew, opposes "love" and "hate" in order to express the idea "prefer" or "opt for" or "have as one's priority."[29] Jesus invites people to side with God—this is a personal matter.

If one wants to belong to God, it is not enough to be born into the people of Israel. The maxim therefore presupposes the emergence of the notions of "personhood" and "free choice." But life is understood as work, and free choice is not identical with autonomy, since a person always depends on a "master" (κύριος). Life's structure corresponds to what Paul describes in Romans 6 (shifting from one master to another), but the two poles have different names in the two cases. Here in Luke we are dealing with God and mammon; in Romans, with sin and righteousness.[30] While Paul is concerned with shifting from one master to another,[31] the Jesus we find in the Gospels contrasts the two extremes. We should scarcely speculate on the slight differences that the verbs "devoted to"[32] and "despise"[33] make in v. 13b, compared with the verbs in v. 13a. We have here the use of parallelism that was common in Hebraic and Aramaic literatures.[34] Although "mammon" was the word that linked the parable and the maxims, it does not have the same meaning in all cases. Here in v. 13, it stands more for mythological importance than for material reality.[35] The apostle Paul may have been acquainted with this maxim of Jesus; in any case he pondered its truth. He knew that

22 On vv. 10-12, see Descamps, "Composition," 51–52.

23 See Koester, *Ancient Christian Gospels*, 18, 353–55.

24 See Klaus Wengst, *Didache (Apostellehre), Barnabasbrief, Zweiter Klemensbrief, Schrift an Diognet, eingeleitet, herausgegeben, übertragen und erläutert* (Schriften des Urchristentums 2; Darmstadt: Wissenschaftliche Buchgesellschaft; Munich: Kösel, 1984) 220–21, 248–49.

25 We find in the work of Irenaeus (*Adv. haer.* 2.34.3) and Hilary (*Epistola seu libellus* 1 [*PL* 10:733]) a Latin form that joins v. 10 (the opposition between the lesser and greater) and vv. 11-12 (the second person plural and a hypothetical case): "Si in modico fideles non fuistis, quod magnum est quis dabit vobis?" Cited by Aland, *Synopsis*, 308.

26 See Descamps, "Composition," 51.

27 See Degenhardt, *Lukas*, 128.

28 See Safrai and Flusser ("Slave of Two Masters," 30–33), who think that Jesus brings about a synthesis of Pharisaic elements (a theory of two desires) and Essene elements (radicalization of evil in the figure of the Devil).

29 See Str-B 1:434; Luz, *Matthew*, 1:335.

30 Or sin and God (Rom 6:10-11).

31 Through a death and a new life obtained by the work of Christ.

32 On ἀντέχομαι, see Moulton and Milligan, s.v.

33 On καταφρονέω, see Spicq, *Lexicon*, 2:280–84.

34 See BDF §§477, 2; 489–92.

35 See the exegesis of v. 9 above.

it is not possible to "please" God and people at the same time (1 Thess 2:4; Gal 1:10),[36] and he considered celibacy preferable to the married state because of a similar incompatibility of interests (1 Cor 7:32-35).

If we were to dare to resort to using Paul to explain Jesus, we might say that trying to serve two masters divides a person in two (1 Cor 7:34: "and he is divided" [καὶ μεμέρισται]) and unleashes frightful anxieties (1 Cor 7:32: "I want you to be free from anxieties" [θέλω δὲ ὑμᾶς ἀμερίμνους εἶναι]). While the preceding verses stressed the threats posed by material possessions, v. 13 reveals a further danger associated with an interpersonal relationship (there will be another instance of it in v. 18 in connection with divorce). In fact, in vv. 10-18, what is placed in relationship to God is all of human existence—not just money but also sexuality, as well as one's selfish relationship to oneself. Serving God (v. 13) in this life (the "smallest thing" in v. 10) consists in being faithful (vv. 10-12) in all areas of life, personal (vv. 10, 15), economic (vv. 11-12), and interpersonal (vv. 13, 18). Jesus invites us to opt for God, with the insistent conviction of one who speaks in terms of determinism or predestination. Paul will spell out Jesus' thought by saying that in Christ God has made possible this shift of belonging, this transfer from mammon to God. Instead of servitude, submission thus becomes freedom.

■ **14-15** There is a break at this point in the story, and the narrator speaks again in order to mention, in addition to the disciples (cf. v. 1), other listeners, the Pharisees ("the Pharisees . . . heard all this" [ἤκουον δὲ ταῦτα πάντα οἱ Φαρισαῖοι], v. 14). It is especially to the latter group that Jesus addresses his next words (vv. 15-31).[37] But he will turn again to the disciples (17:1).[38] These shifts in the persons whom Jesus addresses imply

that the Gospel, which is addressed to the church, has a paraenetic thrust and fills an apologetic and polemical function for outsiders. As a matter of fact, these shifts of audience can give a special tone to one and the same message, for it is often the same readers who are disciples and Pharisees at the same time.

Luke speaks of the Pharisees in a negative way: he calls them "greedy," literally, "lovers of money" (φιλάργυροι—this is the only time he makes this accusation with reference to them).[39] In ancient times, just as today, when making accusations, supplementary complaints were unfortunately readily piled on top of the principal ones. One of the traits that was readily targeted was greed. Just as in a bullfight, the decorated barbed dart that the banderillero thrusts into the neck or shoulder of the bull precedes its being put to death. The reproach that the Christians leveled here at the Pharisees is the same one that the Pharisees themselves found a way to use in their writings, perhaps with the Sadducees in mind.[40] The presence of the adjective "greedy" is a significant indication of the degree to which this text is polemical, rather than an accurate reflection of the social or psychological reality of the Pharisees. The fact that this reproach comes up here is also readily explicable in terms of the subject matter of this chapter.[41]

The verb "sneer" (ἐκμυκτηρίζω) is expressive; its literal meaning is "to turn up one's nose (ὁ μυκτήρ is the Greek word for "nostril") as a sign of scorn," thus "to sneer." It is not necessary to know why the Pharisees sneered.[42] Luke is interested only in indicating their opposition. Jesus' reply is scathing and upholds (cf. vv. 10-13) the dichotomy between the world of created beings and that of their Creator. From Jesus' point of view, the Pharisees' attitude was humanly guilty, since

---

36 See François Bovon, "L'éthique des premiers chrétiens entre la mémoire et l'oubli," in idem, *Révélations*, 206–7.

37 Innumerable manuscripts, including Alexandrinus (A), add a καί ("and," "also") before "the Pharisees" (with the meaning "the Pharisees, themselves also") in order to emphasize that the Pharisees were only the secondary hearers of Jesus words.

38 We note the alternation of hearers from ch. 15; see 15:1-3; 16:1; and 17:1.

39 See 2 Tim 3:2; and, for the verb φιλαργυρέω ("to love money," or "to be greedy"), 2 Macc 10:20.

40 See *Ps. Sol.* 1:4 (I consider this book to be of Phari-

saic origin); Marshall, 625; and Klinghardt, *Gesetz*, 33.

41 To designate a personal condition, Luke can utilize the simple verb "to be" (e.g., 1:6), the periphrastic form of the imperfect (e.g., 2:8), or, as here, the verb ὑπάρχω ("to be disposed to," "to exist," "to be"; see 8:41 and 23:50).

42 We could say: in their eyes, Jesus forgets that it is wealth and not poverty that, according to the law, is the expression of divine blessing; or, it is easy to condemn wealth if one has none.

they ought to have conformed to God. Instead of admitting the transcendent truth of Jesus' words and recognizing their guilt, these men[43]—following a well-known psychological reaction—reared up and counterattacked with their derisive laughter. They feared losing face and, forgetting that God knows our hearts, they only thought of their own righteousness (v. 15a). This criticism of self-righteousness is a theme dear to Luke.[44] But in his usage, the Gospel writer seems to have been influenced by both the Pauline terminology of justification and a topos of Jewish ethical literature that brought together as the object of one and the same criticism both the love of riches and self-righteousness.[45]

Luke uses another Jewish topos in order to destabilize his adversaries, namely, that of God's knowledge of people's hearts (v. 15b).[46] This idea goes beyond appearances to link up with being.[47] Note the adversative "but" (δέ): you think you can wiggle out of it, "but" God will unmask you. Next comes a new proverb (v. 15c; cf. v. 10a),[48] a veritable *coup de grâce*.[49] Ever since the Magnificat (1:48, 51-52), Luke has been proclaiming the reversal of values. Those who exalt themselves (cf. 14:7-11) and believe that they can thereby become important are on the wrong track.[50] In the eyes of God, this is something abominable, an "abomination" (βδέλυγμα). This is a very strong term in Greek and refers in the LXX to an "abomination" (Gen 43:32; Isa 1:13) or a sign of idolatry (cf. Matt 24:15 par. Mark 13:14, quoting Deut 9:27 and 11:31).[51]

Even though the text does not necessarily have to be read from an eschatological perspective,[52] the motif of judgment results from the negative divine evaluation.[53] There is no place here for half-measures or half-heartedness. The only path to salvation is humility (to know that one is "low"; cf. 1:48 and 18:9-14) and being merciful (giving to those who are humble; cf. 10:30-37; 16:19-31), two stances that are characteristic of faith and that reckon what is "high" or exalted according to God's criteria. The end of v. 15 must be the taking up by Luke of a Jewish proverb that he has adapted to his own purpose. If this is indeed the case, the Gospel writer piles up Jewish sapiential material in order to ensure the triumph of Jesus' wisdom (see Prov 16:5).

■ **16** Luke 16:16 is the one verse in the Third Gospel whose interpretation has been the most disputed because of its enigmas and its strategic importance for Luke's theology. Summarizing Hans Conzelmann, Siegfried Schulz was able to put it this way:

Luke was the first to understand in a consistent way the life of Jesus as a phenomenon of past history. His first book . . . lays out the story of Jesus as the middle of a vast history of salvation, of which Luke 16:16 is a programmatic attestation. Luke 16:16 (along with 13:25) represents the "key to the definition of the *heilsgeschichtliche* [according to salvation history] place" of Luke's double work.

43   On the expression ἐνώπιον τῶν ἀνθρώπων ("in the sight of other human beings"), see Job 10:4; Ps 31 (30):20; Luke 12:9; Rev 13:13. See the commentary on 2:31 in vol. 1.

44   See 10:29; 18:9; 20:20; Matt 23:28. Luke is also, of course, well aware of a positive use of the vocabulary of justice and justification (see 1:6; 7:29; 23:47; Acts 13:38-39). See Bovon, *Theologian*, 105, 167, 288 n. 43.

45   See *T. Mos.* 7:6, *1 Enoch* 96:4, *1 Enoch* (Greek) 102:10; Klinghardt, *Gesetz*, 30–40. We should note that "to justify oneself" is not always seen negatively; it all depends on the way in which one justifies oneself.

46   See Prov 24:12; 1 Sam (1 Kgdms) 16:7; 1 Kgs (3 Kgdms) 8:39; 1 Chr 28:9. It is necessary to understand γινώσκει, whose primary meaning is "to arrive at a knowledge of," in the sense of εἰδέναι ("to have knowledge of," "to know"); see Plummer (388), who refers to John 2:24-25 and 10:14, 17.

47   See Ernst, 469.

48   One piece of evidence in favor of a quotation is the words ἐνώπιον τοῦ θεοῦ ("before God") at the end of the sentence, instead of ἐνώπιον αὐτοῦ ("before him"). See Ps 138 (137): 6; Lagrange, 439.

49   The ὅτι that follows does not have to be causal but could be explanatory. According to Plummer (388), it is necessary to assume something before this ὅτι, such as "God does not see as humans see."

50   See the commentary on 14:7-11 above, esp. 14:11. See also Isa 2:11-19; 5:14-16; Ezek 28:17; 31:1-18; Ernst, 470.

51   On βδέλυγμα, see W. Foerster, "βδελύσσομαι," *TDNT* 1 (1964) 598–600; and Marshall, 626.

52   This is what Ernst (470) does by connecting eschatology to ethics.

53   Thus, Godet, 2:171–72.

Others, such as Paul Minear, have countered this assertion: "Rarely has a scholar [i.e., Hans Conzelmann] placed so much weight on so dubious an interpretation of so difficult a logion."[54]

Interpreters have a hard time understanding why the Gospel writer put this saying in this spot (the parallel is found in Matt 11:12-13). It is easier to see why he bracketed v. 17, which speaks of the intangible law, and which Matthew quotes in another context (Matt 5:18), together with it. In both cases we are dealing with the law, and the second saying keeps us from giving an antinomian meaning to the first.[55] The differences between Luke and Matthew are important. Unlike Matthew, who takes as his starting point the kingdom and then works back to the Law and the Prophets, Luke offers us a chronological order corresponding to his theological vision of history. In so doing, he seems to have preserved the simple order and wording of Q, which Matthew modified by insisting on prophecy.[56] Luke is interested in temporal considerations—note the "until" ($\mu \acute{\epsilon} \chi \rho \iota$)[57] and the "since then" ($\grave{\alpha} \pi \grave{o} \ \tau \acute{o} \tau \epsilon$)[58]—and makes a distinction between two major periods of history. The first is that of "the Law and the Prophets." This expression, which was Jewish in origin, was taken over by Christians.[59] Given their common attachment to the doctrine of two eons, Jews and Christians are at one in acknowledging that there must be a time limit to such a period. Where Christianity, following Jesus, parts company with Judaism is in affirming that the first period has come to its end and the second, in a form that remains to be determined, has already begun.

There has been considerable struggle over the question of deciding on what side of the barrier to put John the Baptist.[60] It is not possible to decide the question on philological grounds; both "until" and "since then" can have either an exclusive or an inclusive meaning. The situation is no clearer on the literary level, since Luke begins his Gospel with John the Baptist (who thereby belongs to the new age), but, unlike Matt 3:1-2, never grants him the privilege of preaching the kingdom (which thus keeps John the Baptist in the old age). But, in point of fact, that is not what is important. What does matter, in Luke's eyes, is that, since the time of John the Baptist and Jesus, the history of salvation has entered its final phase. Luke, moreover, insists on the transitions: John the Baptist stands on the threshold: he rounds out the series of "prophets" (cf. 1:76) and inaugurates the procession of witnesses (cf. 3:18, where he "proclaimed the good news"). Luke is not at pains to distinguish here between the time of Jesus and that of the church; that difference will be marked by the passage from the

---

54   Siegfried Schulz, *Die Stunde der Botschaft: Einführung in die Theologie der vier Evangelisten* (Hamburg: Furche, 1967) 284 (indeed, 13:25 refers not to Luke 13:25, but to Acts 13:25, as Kümmel notes ["Gesetz," 398 n. 1 (in Braumann, *Lukas-Evangelium*)]); Conzelmann, *Theology*, 16, 20–27; Paul S. Minear, "Luke's Use of the Birth Stories," in L. E. Keck and J. L. Martyn, eds., *Studies in Luke-Acts: Essays Presented in Honor of Paul Schubert* (Nashville: Abingdon, 1966) 122 (the two quotations adopted from Kümmel, "Gesetz," 398–99 [in Braumann, *Lukas-Evangelium*]); Bovon, *Theologian*, 30–31, 54, 78–79. In addition to the decisive study by Kümmel ("Gesetz"), see on v. 16, Danker, "Luke 16:16," 231–43; Perrin, *Rediscovering*, 74–77; Schulz, *Q*, 261–67; Schlosser, *Règne de Dieu*, 2:509–28; Burchard, "Zu Lukas 16,16," 113–20; Klinghardt, *Gesetz*, 16–17.

55   See Kümmel, "Gesetz," 403 (in Braumann, *Lukas-Evangelium*).

56   Matthew argues; he adds a $\gamma \acute{\alpha} \rho$ ("because"). He speaks of "*all* the prophets," which he places before "the Law." He is interested in the Scriptures as prophecies ("have prophesied").

57   Matthew has $\acute{\epsilon} \omega \varsigma$, which is less elegant. Luke uses $\mu \acute{\epsilon} \chi \rho \iota$ again in Acts 10:30 and 20:7. See Kümmel, "Gesetz," 405 (in Braumann, *Lukas-Evangelium*).

58   Luke does not use this expression elsewhere; he is usually content with $\tau \acute{o} \tau \epsilon$, whose meaning changed over the course of the Hellenistic era (from "then" to "from this point on"); see BAGD, s.v. $\tau \acute{o} \tau \epsilon$. Matthew has "since the days of John the Baptist," a redactional formula; see Schlosser, *Règne de Dieu*, 2:511.

59   The expression is common in Luke-Acts (Luke 16:29, 31; 24:27, 44; Acts 13:15; 24:14; 28:23) and in Matthew (Matt 5:17; 7:12; 11:13; 22:40). Elsewhere in the New Testament, only John 1:45 and Rom 3:21 use it. It has to do with a formulation of Jewish origin; see Kümmel, *Heilsgeschehen*, 1:20 n. 23; idem, "Gesetz," 405 (in Braumann, *Lukas-Evangelium*).

60   See Kümmel, "Gesetz"; Bovon, *Theologian*, 14–15, 150, 236–37 and passim; Conzelmann, *Theology*, 18–27.

Gospel to the book of Acts. Those two latter times are subdivisions within the new age.[61] Note that even if he shows respect for his Q source in v. 16a, he later proceeds to rework it in a very personal way in v. 16b.

One word needs to be said about the law: v. 17 serves to inform the reader that it is not the requirements of the law that have ended, since the law is a permanent expression of God's will. So what is it, then, that has ended? For Matthew, it was the prophetic nature of the law that found its fulfillment in Christ. For Luke, however, the period of the law was a time of waiting, a stage in the history of the people, marked by an earthly existence lacking the resurrection, by a Scripture that waited to be read in a spiritual fashion, and by a people who were not yet defined in universal terms.[62]

"Since then": Luke is thinking above all of the ministry of Jesus, who proclaimed, and still proclaims, the good news, thus putting himself in opposition to the political "good news" of the imperial propaganda and to the "good news" of the contemporary religions of salvation.[63] The wording is redactional; Q must have still lacked the verb "to proclaim the good news" and had to link the enigmatic verb "is violently treated" ($\beta\iota\acute{\alpha}\zeta\epsilon\tau\alpha\iota$) to the kingdom of God in a construction that Matt 11:12 has preserved.[64]

The end of Luke 16:16 is difficult, since the Greek verb ($\beta\iota\acute{\alpha}\zeta\epsilon\tau\alpha\iota$) may be taken either as a passive ("is violently treated") or, more likely, middle ("strives to") and either in a good sense "everyone," "each one" ($\pi\hat{\alpha}\varsigma$ is in that case a believer), or in a bad sense (the "whoever" [$\pi\hat{\alpha}\varsigma$] is in that case an enemy).[65] If we take a look at Matthew (11:12), where admittedly the verb is in another part of the sentence, it is used in the passive ("has been

subjected to violence") and the following phrase ("the violent take it by force") has a negative sense. Can this Matthean rereading of Q serve as a crutch for the interpretation of Luke? It is to be noted that in speaking of the kingdom, Luke has interpreted the pessimistic judgment of Q, which is preserved in Matthew, in an optimistic sense.[66] I personally understand Luke as having followed through on his reinterpretation *in bonam partem*, "everyone strives to enter it," literally "puts all their violence toward it (that is, toward the kingdom of God)." In that case the verb would refer to the same struggles as those carried on by those competitors who are invited to enter through the narrow door in 13:24 (where the verb used is "struggle," $\alpha\gamma\omega\nu\acute{\iota}\zeta\omega\mu\alpha\iota$). It may seem incongruous to speak of violence in connection with a faith decision, but we should take this expression in a figurative sense. If understood this way, does the sentence correspond to reality? Enthusiastic faith was not more generally valued in the first century than in our day. I see this saying either as an implicit imperative (in the same way that the invitation to go through the narrow door is in 13:24), or as a shortened wording of the following truth: those who have welcomed the good news of the kingdom put all their moral and spiritual strength into entering it. In that case the pronoun $\pi\hat{\alpha}\varsigma$ refers to each person longing to be saved and not just anybody or everybody.

The first one to have pronounced the words we find in Luke 16:16 par. Matt 11:12-13 (Jesus or some Christian prophet) backs off from the immediate reality in order to take in the entire sweep of history.[67] That represented no small intellectual effort, but others in that day, in Jewish apocalyptic, Roman literature, or the earliest Christian theology, were equal to the task.[68] Although the temporal

---

61 He no longer has the parousia in view as the final stage before the attainment of the kingdom "in power."

62 See Bovon, "Law in Luke-Acts," 59–73.

63 On the proclamation of the gospel, see the commentary on 4:43 in vol. 1. On the notion of the kingdom of God (which Matthew renders as kingdom of heaven, as is his custom), see the excursus on the kingdom of God on page 297 above.

64 According to Schulz (*Q*, 265–67), Q here mentions the enemies of the gospel, the persecutors of Christians.

65 On this verb, see G. Schrenk, "$\beta\iota\acute{\alpha}\zeta\omega\mu\alpha\iota \ \kappa\tau\lambda$.," *TDNT* 1 (1964) 609–14; Menoud, "Meaning of the

Verb $\beta\iota\acute{\alpha}\zeta\epsilon\tau\alpha\iota$, 192–201; Kümmel, "Gesetz," 407–8 (in Braumann, *Lukas-Evangelium*). In modern Greek, the verb means "to hurry," "to be pressed for time."

66 See Schlosser, *Règne de Dieu*, 2:517–22.

67 The same overarching vision, and with vision from above, is found in the sayings with $\mathring{\eta}\lambda\vartheta o\nu$ ("I have come"); see Bultmann, *History*, 152–56, 163.

68 As an example, see the view of the entire history of Israel in the grand vision of animals, *1 Enoch* 85–90; the idea of the present "age" as opposed to the past in the work of Horace, *Carmen saeculare*. Or these two verses of Catullus 1.5–6, which mention the effort of Cornelius Nepos to write a universal history: *iam tum, cum ausus es unus Italorum / omne*

dimension is amply considered, the cultural horizon is more limited; the (dare I say ethnocentric?) judgment is focused on the history of Israel and so does not include the past history of other peoples.[69]

■ **17** Matthew 5:18 and Luke 16:17 say the same thing with the same vocabulary but using a totally different syntax.[70] Luke's syntax is that used in Luke 18:25 (the camel going through the eye of a needle), and the wisdom that emerges from the saying in each case underscores one and the same impossibility, using the same literary procedure. Far from being apocalyptic (since that which is apocalyptic awaits the end of the world[71]), the maxim presupposes instead the stability of the world. Faithful to a tradition he did not dare criticize, Luke has transmitted the saying just as he had conveyed 11:42 (where the end of the verse upholds respect for all the commandments, whether minor or major, ritual or ethical). In the rest of his literary work, especially in the book of Acts, he will reveal his true face: although agreeing not to tamper with any detail whatsoever of the law, he is not willing to interpret it literally. Although for the tradition the maxim prescribed a scrupulous obedience, in the Lukan redaction there is an obligatory respect for the text without any servile application of it. Without being hypocritical, one can, according to Luke, scrupulously recopy and respect the book of Leviticus without literally observing it oneself.[72] The shift of milieu (from Q's community to Luke's) has occasioned a profound modification in the interpretation and application of one and the same maxim.

■ **18** As Kierkegaard has said, the Gospel is clear and simple.[73] It condemns divorce and even looking with lust (Matt 5:27-28). Then does not the good news get transformed in the process into a new law, even stricter than the old one? Monogamy, which had not always been the rule in Israel, is here presupposed. It is not said that by his attitude the man in question in this passage "undermines God" or causes his wife or wives to "suffer" but that he "commits adultery" (μοιχεύει). In order to understand this verb we must try to disregard puritanical ethics and light comedy. How exactly are we to interpret this verb in Greek? Does it have in view the act itself, and if so, precisely which one (not all extra-conjugal relations were labeled "adulterous")? Or was it its consequences that were in mind, and in that case, which ones (ethical, with respect to oneself, others, and God; legal, with respect to the legal bond and property rights; or religious, with respect to the divine order)?[74] The maxim has its setting in a Greek-speaking Jewish world, so it is not surprising that it is interested only in the lot of the man. Its particular setting is the ascetic current that was taking shape in the time of Christ (refusal to grant divorce and honoring of celibacy).[75] The law already prescribed the death penalty for the adulterous woman (Lev 20:10; Gen 38:24; Deut 22:22-24; Exod 20:14). Here the Gospel condemns as adulterous the man who

aeuum tribus explicare chartis, "you, the only one among the Romans who dared to explain the universal story in three volumes."

69 The parallel in Justin Martyr *Dial.* 51.3 seems to preserve a text close to Q, which is to say, a first part of the verse similar to Luke and a second similar to Matthew.

70 In Matthew the saying is introduced by a solemn formula: "For truly I declare to you" (Matt 5:18), which could have been a part of Q (see Schulz, *Q,* 114). At the end of the saying, Matthew adds to Q the cumbersome words "until everything is accomplished." Luke, on the other hand, modifies Q by opting for the elegant comparative (see 5:23 and 18:25; Matthew has "until . . . not a single . . ."). It is difficult to determine which of the two texts, whether the Matthean ἰῶτα ("iota") and κεραία ("stroke of a pen"), which has Semitic overtones, or the simpler Lukan version (with κεραία by itself) represents the text of Q.

71 See 1 Cor 7:31: the form of this world is passing away.

72 My exegesis here rejoins that of Zwingli, *Annotationes,* 679–81.

73 Søren Kierkegaard, *For Self-Examination: Judge for Yourself!* (ed. and trans. Howard V. Hong and Edna H. Hong; Princeton, N.J.: Princeton University Press, 1990) 166–67. I am indebted to Gabriel-Ph. Widmer, who helped me find this passage.

74 On this verb, see Friedrich Hauck, "μοιχεύω κτλ.," *TDNT* 4 (1967) 729–35. For Justin (*1 Apol.* 15.1–4), the σωφροσύνη of the first Christians was at stake.

75 See Peter Brown, *The Body and Society: Men, Women, and Sexual Renunciation in Early Christianity* (Lectures on the History of Religions 13; New York: Columbia University Press, 1988).

undermines someone else's marriage or his own.[76] This is more than a reminder of the law, since the law had several different levels and had added the possibility of divorce to the severity of the Decalogue. And it was also more than a reminder of the law in that a man could escape the condemnation of the Decalogue by refusing to let his act be called adultery. A skilled interpreter of the Torah could, in fact, say the opposite of what v. 18 says; he could say that the man who spurns his wife is not an adulterer and the man who marries a woman who has been spurned is not one either. Luke's Jesus here takes a stand in a dispute over the interpretation of the law, and more particularly over the definition of adultery. As far as v. 18 is concerned, adultery is less a sexual act than one of interpersonal and legal relations. We may question, however, whether Luke's definition was primarily legal. In passing on the maxim he has given it an ethical coloring, as Justin Martyr was to do somewhat later: the law of the kingdom, strict as it is about money (cf. 12:33 and 14:33), is just as strict about the relations of men and women (*1 Apol.* 15.1-4). Luke's Jesus asks us to remain in our present state (just as Paul does in 1 Cor 7:20) and not to rush to help—a help that could be suspicious—an abandoned woman. But why does he not consider either the covetousness of the man whose desire is directed at the woman married to another man, or the women's point of view, that is to say, what they might want or what they might do? Probably it is because he has taken over a maxim that must have been the answer to a precise question having arisen in the course of an exegetical dispute

the memory of which had been lost. The solution, in any case, is clear: sending the woman back to her own family, in other words divorcing her and taking another wife, is equivalent—in spite of the Torah's level of tolerance—to adultery, that is, to an intimate relation with the wife of another man.[77] That holds for the first case. As for the second one, venturing to take as one's wife a divorced woman, also is a form of adultery, since it makes impossible any reconciliation between the dismissed wife and the husband who dismissed her.[78]

History of Interpretation

The principal interpreter we will mention is Ambrose, bishop of Milan (*Exp. Luc.* 7.244–46). In commenting on vv. 10-13, he said that human beings are not owners but stewards. In fact, the only true master is God; the other, mammon, can only fill the role of a despot to whom human beings submit themselves as slaves. Money is said to be sinful since it stimulates our tendency to be avaricious and incites us to become slaves to it. We are strangers to riches, since they are of a different nature than we are, neither being born nor dying with us. Christ, on the other hand, is ours, since he is life.

In commenting on vv. 14-15, Ambrose gave an allegorical interpretation of the Pharisees' avarice that was hostile to Judaism, saying that their greed symbolizes the attitude of the Jews, who were unable to share the riches that rightfully belong to all peoples and who consequently were not worthy of receiving Christ.

76　As we know, the bibliography on this subject is immense; see Luz, *Matthew*, 1:242, 249; Greeven, "Ehe nach dem Neuen Testament"; Bockmuehl, "Matthew 5.32"; Rudolf Pesch, *Freie Treue: Die Christen und die Ehescheidung* (Freiburg: Herder, 1971) 56–60; and the works that I indicate in the section bibliography.

77　Here I agree once again with Greeven, "Ehe nach dem Neuen Testament," 381.

78　In my opinion, vv. 16-18 have hardly any link either between them or with their context. Daube (*Rabbinic Judaism*, 294–300) disagrees because he identifies aspects of John the Baptist in v. 16 with Elijah, to whom the rabbis attributed a particular authority concerning the law (v. 17). Further, he recalls that in heterodox Judaism the sanctity of the law led to a rejection of remarriage (v. 18). Kümmel

("Gesetz," 403) shows the fragility of this construction. Kilgallen ("Luke's Divorce Text," 229–39) tries to understand v. 18 figuratively: the law (v. 17) is as indissoluble as marriage (v. 18). According to Johnson (255), vv. 14-18 are centered on the themes of idolatry, avarice, and divorce, which constitute all three abominations ($\beta\delta\acute{\epsilon}\lambda\upsilon\gamma\mu\alpha$, v. 15). We also see these three juxtaposed in the Hebrew Bible and in Qumran documents (CD 4.14–5.10). Before all of these researchers, Bengel (*Gnomon*, 1:481) tried to establish the coherence of chap. 16 of Luke, and that of vv. 15-18 in particular, by pointing out that the Pharisees, in their own peculiar justice and their pride, who have heard vv. 1-13, make fun of heavenly simplicity (v. 15), scorn the gospel (v. 16), strip the law of its worth (v. 17), of which an example of improper religious practice is provided.

In his commentary on vv. 16-17, Ambrose compared the law with nature and contrasted both with the Gospel. The law did not end with John the Baptist but was eclipsed by the arrival of what was better. It is right to fight for this better thing, namely, in order to enter the kingdom of God. And here Ambrose, as a preacher, praises holy violence: "In matters of faith violence is religion, whereas nonchalance is a sin." And again, "So let us be violent toward nature, so that it might not sink into what is terrestrial, but rather rise up to the heights" (8.1).

On v. 18, we can even go back as far as the exegesis of the second century, since Tertullian tells us what Marcion's exegesis was in order to combat it more effectively (*Adv. Marc.* 4.34). According to Marcion, although Moses allowed divorce, Christ forbade it. Tertullian recognized that there was a difference between the respective teachings of the two divine messages, but that the differences are softened in the Gospel of Matthew. Following his practice, Tertullian limited his discussion to Luke, the only Gospel approved by his adversary, that is, to Luke 16:18 in particular. He maintained that this verse does not forbid all cases of divorce but only those involving a new marriage. So Christ—and this is the thrust of his argument—did not directly contradict Moses. Christ directed the Mosaic law toward the original intention of the Creator God.[79]

Conclusion

For Luke, being "faithful in the least matter" (v. 10a) means adopting the attitude toward money that Jesus expects from his disciples. As for being "faithful in the greatest" (v. 10a), this means becoming a follower of God. Basically, v. 10 repeats in its own language the double commandment to love (10:27).

Hidden behind the "who?" ($\tau i \varsigma$) of v. 11 is God, who wants to entrust Christians, the $\pi\iota\sigma\tau o i$ ("faithful" and "honest" believers), with what truly belongs to them ($\tau \grave{o}$ $\grave{a}\lambda\eta\vartheta\iota\nu\acute{o}\nu$, "what is true," v. 11), not in the sense of an abstract truth, but of a concrete reality that will withstand perishability and lies. What is being talked about is the place reserved for each person in the kingdom, the place reserved for you, which is "yours" (v. 12).

In order for that to happen, one must avoid confusing issues, confusing the least matters with the greatest ones (vv. 10-12), mammon with God (v. 13), what is an abomination with what is prized (v. 15). Anxious Christians who are pulled every which way place themselves in an intolerable, literally an untenable, situation. There are certainly two worlds, but it is impossible to inhabit them both at the same time and in the same way. One must opt for God's world and then, on the basis of that option, structure one's life in the world of the present.

That is equivalent to renouncing the establishment of one's own independent identity (v. 15) and letting oneself be caught up in God's plan, which pertains to both one's person (God knows your hearts, v. 15) and the universe (God has his plan for saving it, v. 16).

God, who revealed himself in the past through the Law and the Prophets (v. 16a) has now revealed himself in the message of the kingdom proclaimed by Jesus (v. 16b). Human response must be impassioned (v. 16c), but this passion for the kingdom does not imply a forsaking of the law (v. 17), since both correspond to the will of one and the same God, albeit in two distinct periods of time. Respect for God, moreover, implies respect for other persons (v. 18).[80]

---

79 I did not have time to offer a history of interpretation of Luke 16:16. But one should consult Zwingli (*Annotationes*, 679–81) on this question (see above, n. 74): this verse is not concerned with the letter of the law. One should certainly not despise this letter of the law, but the letter of the Scriptures is the door to the Spirit. Without the letter, each follows his own inclination. It is the same with the letter as with the rites of the Old Testament which, understood figuratively, point toward the greatest commandment, the double commandment of love.

80 See Olsen (*New Testament Logia on Divorce*), who highlights the importance of Augustine in the controversy between Catholics and Protestants on the question of divorce. Olsen presents a cross-section of the opinions of humanists, Reformers, and Catholic theologians of the sixteenth century. The reader will find an anthology of Protestant texts on this subject also in the work of Erasmus Sacerius, *Corpus iuris matrimonialis* (Frankfurt: Feyerabend, 1569).

The Parable of the Rich Man and the Poor Man Lazarus (16:19-31)

Bibliography

Aalen, Svere, "St. Luke's Gospel and the Last Chapters of I Enoch," *NTS* 13 (1966–67) 1–13.

Alexandre, Monique, "L'interprétation de Luc 16, 19-31 chez Grégoire de Nysse," in J. Fontaine and C. Kannengiesser, eds., *Epektasis:* Mélanges patristiques offerts au Cardinal Jean Daniélou (Paris: Beauchesne, 1972) 425–41.

Amjad-Ali, Charles M., "No Name for the Rich: The Parable of Lazarus," *Al-Mushir* 32 (1990) 22–27.

Barth, Karl, "Miserable Lazarus (Text: Luke 16:19-31)," *UTSR* 46 (1934–35) 259–68.

Bartsch, Hans Werner, *Entmythologisierende Auslegung: Aufsätze aus den Jahren 1940 bis 1960* (TF 26; Hamburg: Reich, 1962) 183–87.

Batiffol, Pierre, "Trois notes exégétiques: Sur Luc 16,19," *RB* 9 (1912) 541.

Bauckham, Richard, "The Rich Man and Lazarus: The Parable and the Parallels," *NTS* 37 (1991) 225–46.

Bishop, E. F., "A Yawning Chasm," *EvQ* 45 (1973) 3–5.

Bornhäuser, Karl, *Sondergut,* 138–60.

Idem, "Zum Verständnis der Geschichte vom reichen Mann und armen Lazarus: Lukas 16, 19-31," *NKZ* 39 (1928) 833–43.

Bouvier, Bertrand, and François Bovon, "Actes de Philippe, I, d'après un manuscrit inédit," in W. A. Bienert, D. Papandreou, and K. Schäferdiek, eds., *Oecumenica et Patristica: Festschrift für Wilhelm Schneemelcher zum 75. Geburtstag* (Stuttgart: Kohlhammer, 1989) 367–94.

Boyd, W. J. P., "Apocalyptic and Life after Death," *StEv* 5 (TU 103; Berlin: Akademie-Verlag, 1968) 39–56.

Bretherton, Donald J., "Lazarus of Bethany: Resurrection or Resuscitation?" *ExpT* 104 (1993) 169–73.

Bruyne, Donatien de, "Chasma, Lc 16, 26," *RB* 30 (1921) 400–405.

Bultmann, *History,* 193, 212, 220.

Cadbury, Henry J., "The Name of Dives," *JBL* 84 (1965) 73.

Idem, "A Proper Name for Dives: Lexical Notes on Luke-Acts VI," *JBL* 81 (1962) 399–402.

Cadron, F. Hugh, "'Son' in the Parable of the Rich Man and Lazarus," *ExpT* 13 (1901–2) 523.

Cantinat, Jean, "Le mauvais riche et Lazare," *BVC* 48 (1962) 19–26.

Cavallin, Hans C., "Leben nach dem Tode im Spätjudentum," in *ANRW* 2.19.1 (1979) 240–345.

Cave, Cyril H., "Lazarus and the Lukan Deuteronomy," *NTS* 15 (1968–69) 319–25.

Charlesworth, James H., *The Old Testament Pseudepigrapha and the New Testament: Prolegomena for the Study of Christian Origins* (SNTSMS 54; Cambridge: Cambridge University Press, 1985) 106–7.

Cölle, R., "Zur Exegese und zur homiletischen Verwertung des Gleichnisses vom reichen Mann und armen Lazarus, Luk 16, 19-31," *ThStK* 75 (1902) 652–65.

Collins, Adela Yarbro, "Early Christian Apocalyptic Literature (bibliography)," *ANRW* 2.25.2 (1984) 4665–711.

Czesz, B., "La parabola del 'Ricco epulone' in S. Ireneo," *Aug* 17 (1977) 107–11.

Degenhardt, *Lukas,* 133–35.

Derrett, J. Duncan M., "Fresh Light on St Luke xvi, II: Dives and Lazarus and the Preceding Sayings," *NTS* 7 (1960–61) 364–80; reprinted in idem, *Law,* 78–99.

Díaz, Jesús, "La discriminación y retribución inmediatas después de la muerte (Precisiones neotestamentarias y de la literatura judía contemporánea)," in *La escatología individual neotestamentaria a la luz de las ideas en los tiempos apostólicos [y] otros estudios* (Semana Bíblica Española 16; Madrid: Instituto Francisco Suárez, 1956) 85–157.

Dunkerley, Roderic, "Lazarus," *NTS* 5 (1958–59) 321–27.

Dupont, Jacques, "L'après-mort dans l'œuvre de Luc," *RThL* 3 (1972) 3–21; reprinted in idem, *Nouvelles études sur les Actes des Apôtres* (Paris: Cerf, 1984) 358–79.

Idem, *Béatitudes,* 3:60–64, 111–12, 162–82.

Idem, Eichholz, *Gleichnisse,* 221–28.

Eliade, Mircea, "Locum refrigerii . . . ," *Zalmoxis* 1 (1938) 203–8.

Evans, Christopher F., "Uncomfortable Words, V: '. . . Neither Will They Be Convinced,'" *ExpT* 81 (1969–70) 228–31.

Feuillet, André, "La parabole du mauvais riche et du pauvre Lazare (Lc 16, 19-31) antithèse de la parabole de l'intendant astucieux (Lc 16, 1-9)," *NRTh* 101 (1979) 212–23.

George, A., "La parabole du riche et de Lazare, Lc 16, 19-31," *AsSeign* n.s. 57 (1971) 80–93.

Glombitza, Otto, "Der reiche Mann und der arme Lazarus, Luk. xvi 19-31: Zur Frage nach der Botschaft des Textes," *NovT* 12 (1970) 166–80.

Grensted, L. W., "The Use of Enoch in St. Luke XVI, 19-31," *ExpT* 26 (1914–15) 333–34.

Gressmann, Hugo, "Vom reichen Mann und armen Lazarus: Eine literargeschichtliche Studie," *APAW. PH* 7 (1918) 1–91.

Griffiths, J. Gwyn, "Cross-Cultural Eschatology with Dives and Lazarus," *ExpT* 105 (1993) 7–12.

Grobel, Kendrick, "'. . . Whose Name Was Neves,'" *NTS* 10 (1963–64) 373–82.

Hafer, R. A., "Dives and Poor Lazarus in the Light of Today," *LQ* 53 (1923) 476–81.

Hanhart, Karel, *The Intermediate State in the New Testa-*

ment (Groningen: Druk. V. R. B. Kleine, 1966) 10–42.

Hanson, R. P. C., "A Note on Luke XVI, 14-31," *ExpT* 55 (1943–44) 221–22.

Harnack, Adolf, *Der Name des reichen Mannes in Luc. 16,19* (TU 13,1; Leipzig: Hinrichs, 1895) 75–78.

Haupt, Paul, "Abraham's Bosom," *AJP* 42 (1921) 162–67.

Heininger, *Metaphorik*, 177–91.

Himmelfarb, Martha, *Tours of Hell: An Apocalyptic Form in Jewish and Christian Literature* (Philadelphia: Fortress Press, 1983).

Hintzen, Johannes, *Verkündigung und Wahrnehmung: Über das Verhältnis von Evangelium und Leser am Beispiel Lk 16, 19-31 im Rahmen des lukanischen Doppelwerkes* (BBB 81; Frankfurt: Hain, 1991).

Hock, Ronald F., "Lazarus and Micyllus: Greco-Roman Backgrounds to Luke 16:19-31," *JBL* 106 (1987) 447–63.

Hoffmann, Paul, "Auferstehung, I/3: Neues Testament," in *TRE* 4 (1979) 450–67.

Idem, *Die Toten in Christus: Eine religionsgeschichtliche und exegetische Untersuchung zur paulinischen Eschatologie* (NTAbh 2; Münster: Aschendorff, 1966) 25–174.

Horn, *Glaube und Handeln*, 81–85, 144–49, 181.

Huie, Wade P., "The Poverty of Abundance: From Text to Sermon on Luke 16:19-31," *Int* 22 (1968) 403–20.

Jensen, Hans J. L., "Diesseits und Jenseits des Raumes eines Textes: Textsemiotische Bemerkungen zur Erzählung 'Vom reichen Mann und armen Lazarus' (Lk 16, 19-31)," *LingBibl* 47 (1980) 39–60.

Jeremias, *Parables*, 182–87.

Jervell, Jacob, "Der Sohn des Volkes," in C. Breytenbach and H. Paulsen, eds., *Anfänge der Christologie: Festschrift für Ferdinand Hahn zum 65. Geburtstag* (Göttingen: Vandenhoeck & Ruprecht, 1991) 245–54.

Joüon, Paul, "Notes philologiques sur les Évangiles, Luc 16,30," *RSR* 18 (1928) 354.

Jülicher, *Gleichnisreden*, 2:617–41.

Kilgallen, John J., "A Consideration of Some of the Women in the Gospel of Luke," *StMiss* 40 (1991) 27–55.

Kissinger, Warren S., *The Parables of Jesus: A History of Interpretation and Bibliography* (ATLA.BS 4; Metuchen, N.J.: Scarecrow, 1979) 419–20 (index: "Rich Man and Lazarus"), esp. 371–76.

Köhler, Konrad, "Zu Luk. 16,10-12," *ThStK* 94 (1922) 173–78.

Kreitzer, Larry, "Luke 16:19-31 and 1 Enoch 22," *ExpT* 103 (1992) 139–42.

Kremer, Jacob, "Der arme Lazarus: Lazarus, der Freund Jesu. Beobachtung zur Beziehung

zwischen Lk 16, 19-31 und Joh 11, 1-46," in Refoulé, *À cause*, 571–84.

Idem, *Lazarus: Die Geschichte einer Auferstehung. Text, Wirkungsgeschichte und Botschaft von Joh 11, 1-46* (Stuttgart: Katholisches Bibelwerk, 1985), esp. 92–93.

Künstlinger, David, "Im Schosse Abrahams," *OLZ* 36 (1933) 408.

Kvalbein, Hans, "Jesus and the Poor: Two Texts and a Tentative Conclusion," *Themelios* 12 (1986–87) 80–87.

Langkammer, Helmut, "Das Lukasevangelium, das Evangelium vom Erlöser und vom universalen Heil," *RTK* 36 (1989) 43–59.

Lefort, L.-Th., "Le nom du mauvais riche (Luc 16.19) et la tradition copte," *ZNW* 37 (1938) 65–72.

Lorenzen, Thorwald, "A Biblical Meditation on Luke 16:19-31: From the Text toward a Sermon," *ExpT* 87 (1974–75) 39–43.

Manns, Frederic, "Luc 24,32 et son contexte juif," *Anton* 60 (1985) 225–32.

Manrique, A., "La parábola del rico epulón y de Lázaro y la justicia social en la época de Jesús (Lc 16, 19-31)," *CDios* 191 (1978) 207–15.

Mieses, Matthias, "Im Schosse Abrahams," *OLZ* 34 (1931) 1018–21.

Nardi, C., "La quinta omelia su Lazzaro di S. Giovanni Crisostomo, traduzione e commento," *RAMi* 10 (1985) 37–53.

Nickelsburg, George W. E., "Riches, the Rich, and God's Judgment in I Enoch 92–105 and the Gospel according to Luke," *NTS* 25 (1979) 324–44.

North, Brownlow, *The Rich Man and Lazarus: A Practical Exposition of Luke xvi, 19-31* (London: Banner of Truth Trust, 1960).

Obermüller, Rodolfo, "La miseria de un rico: un juicio neotestamentario—Lucas 16, 19-31," in L. Brummel et al., eds., *Los pobres: Encuentro y compromiso* (Buenos Aires: Editorial La Aurora, 1978) 45–66.

Omanson, Roger, "Lazarus and Simon," *BT* 40 (1989) 416–19.

Osei-Bonsu, Joseph, "The Intermediate State in Luke-Acts," *IBS* 9 (1987) 115–30.

Osiek, Carolyn, *Rich and Poor in the Shepherd of Hermas: An Exegetical-Social Investigation* (CBQMS 15; Washington, D.C.: Catholic Biblical Association of America, 1983) 24, 30, 68.

Palma Becerra, Juan, "El rico y el pobre llamado Lázaro (Análisis narrativo de Lc 16, 19-31)," in *Anunciaré tu verdad: homenaje a los profesores Antonio Moreno y Beltrán Villegas* (AFTC 39; Santiago: Pontificia Universidad Católica de Chile, 1990) 105–13.

Pax, Elpidius, "Der Reiche und der arme Lazarus: Eine Milieustudie," *SBFLA* 25 (1975) 254–68.

Pearce, Keith, "The Lucan Origins of the Raising of Lazarus," *ExpT* 96 (1984–85) 359–61.

Perkins, Pheme, *Hearing the Parables* (New York: Paulist Press, 1981) 53–62, 64–66, 134–38, 140–42, 156, 171.

Powell, W., "The Parable of Dives and Lazarus (Luke XVI, 19-31)," *ExpT* 66 (1954–55) 350–51.

Reinmuth, Eckart, "Ps.-Philo, Liber Antiquitatum Biblicarum 33,1–5 und die Auslegung der Parabel Lk 16:19-31," *NovT* 31 (1989) 16–38.

Reiser, Mario, "Das Leben nach dem Tod in der Verkündigung Jesu," *EuA* 66 (1990) 381–90.

Renié, J., "Le mauvais riche (Lc., xvi, 19-31)," *ATh* 6 (1945) 268–75.

Rimmer, N., "Parable of Dives and Lazarus (Luke xvi. 19-31)," *ExpT* 66 (1954–55) 215–16.

Rohrbaugh, Richard L., *The Biblical Interpreter: An Agrarian Bible in an Industrial World* (Philadelphia: Fortress Press, 1978) 97–120.

Roy, M., "Jugement, sanction et évangile; Matthieu 25, 31-46; Luc 15, 11-32; 16, 19-31," *Christus* 28 (1981) 440–49.

Sahlin, H., "Lasarus-gestalten I Lk 16 och Joh 11," *SEÅ* 37–38 (1972–73) 167–74.

Sauzède, Jean-Paul, "Une série pour le carême," *EThR* 58 (1983) 59–71.

Schnider, Franz, and Werner Stenger, "Die offene Tür und die unüberschreitbare Kluft. Strukturanalytische Überlegungen zum Gleichnis vom reichen Mann und armen Lazarus (Lk 16, 19-31)," *NTS* 25 (1978–79) 273–83.

Scholz, Günter, "Aesthetische Beobachtungen am Gleichnis vom reichen Mann und armen Lazarus und von drei anderen Gleichnissen (Lk 16,19-25; 10,34; 13,9; 15,11-32)," *LingBibl* 43 (1978) 67–74.

Schottroff, Luise, and Wolfgang Stegemann, *Jesus von Nazareth, Hoffnung der Armen* (Stuttgart/Berlin/ Cologne/Mainz: Kohlhammer, 1978) 38–41, 133–35.

Schurhammer, G., "Eine Parabel Christi im Götzentempel," *KM* 49 (1920–21) 134–38.

Seccombe, David P., *Possessions and the Poor in Luke-Acts* (SNTU B 6; Linz: Fuchs, 1982) 173–81.

Sellin, *Gleichniserzählungen*.

Standen, A. O., "The Parable of Dives and Lazarus and Enoch 22," *ExpT* 33 (1921–22) 523.

Stemberger, Günter, *Der Leib der Auferstehung: Studien zur Anthropologie und Eschatologie des palästinischen Judentums im neutestamentlischen Zeitalter (ca. 170 v. Chr. – 100 n. Chr.)* (AnBib 56; Rome: Biblical Institute Press, 1972) 37, 44.

Str-B 2:222–33.

Tanghe, Vincent, "Abraham, son fils et son envoyé (Luc 16, 19-31)," *RB* 91 (1984) 557–77.

Trudinger, Paul, "A 'Lazarus Motif' in Primitive Christian Preaching?" *ANQ* 7 (1966) 29–32.

Vogels, Walter, "Having or Longing: A Semiotic Analysis of Luke 16:19-31," *EeT* 20 (1989) 27–46.

Wehrli, Eugene S., "Luke 16:19-31," *Int* 31 (1977) 276–80.

Welzen, Paulus Hubertus Mechtildis, "Lucas, evangelist van gemeenschap: Eee onderzoek naar de pragmatische effecten in Lc 15, 1-17, 10" (Ph.D. diss., Nijmegen, 1986) 151–90.

Westra, Abe, "De gelijkenis van de rijke man en de arme Lazarus (Lk. 16, 19-31) bij de vroefchristelijke Griekse Schrijvers tot en met Johannes Chrysostomos" (Ph.D. diss., Leiden, 1987).

Wieser, Friedrich Emanuel, *Die Abrahamvorstellungen im Neuen Testament* (EHS.T 137; Frankfurt a. M./ New York: Lang, 1987) 22–25.

Zaleski, Carol, *Otherworld Journeys: Accounts of Near Death Experience in Medieval and Modern Times* (New York: Oxford University Press, 1987).

19/ "Now there was a rich man who was dressed in purple and fine linen who feasted sumptuously every day. **20/** A poor man named Lazarus lay[a] at his gate, covered with sores, **21/** who longed to satisfy his hunger with what fell from the rich man's table; but even the dogs would come and lick his sores. **22/** Now it happened that the poor man died and was carried away by the angels to be in Abraham's bosom. The rich man also died and was buried. **23/** And in Hades, looking up, and being tormented, he saw Abraham far away with Lazarus in his bosom. **24/** And he called out to him, 'Father Abraham, have mercy on me, and send Lazarus to dip the tip of his

a   Literally: "had been thrown."

finger in water and cool my tongue; for I am in agony in these flames[b].' 25/ Abraham said, 'My child, remember that during your lifetime you received your share of good things, and Lazarus in like manner evil things. Now he is comforted here, while you, you are in agony. 26/ And in all these regions, between us and you a great chasm has been fixed, so that those who might want to pass from here to you cannot do so, and no one can cross from there to us.' 27/ He said, 'Then, father, I beg you to send him to my father's house, 28/ for I have five brothers, so that he may call out to them, so that they will not also come into this place of torment.' 29/ But Abraham said to him[c], 'They have Moses and the prophets. Let them listen to them.' 30/ He said, 'No, father Abraham; but if someone comes to them from the dead, they will repent.' 31/ He said to him, 'If they do not listen to Moses or the prophets, neither will they be convinced even if someone rises from the dead.' "

b   Literally: "in this flame."
c   Literally: "But Abraham said."

Here we have a carefully told, beautiful, sad, and imaginary story.[1] Like the companion parables of the Good Samaritan and the prodigal son, this parable invites us, here implicitly, to do good and to imitate Lazarus, to repent and to follow the ethical example of Jesus' earliest disciples. Hence its classification as an "example" story.[2]

In spite of the story's simplicity and beauty, its readers have been either intrigued or shocked by various elements of it.[3] Is Abraham's severity compatible with Christian pity? Is the description of life beyond death true and normative? Is there an allusion to Jesus Christ's resurrection in v. 31? Was Lazarus consoled because of his poverty or because of his piety? Conversely, was the rich man punished for being rich or because of his lack of charity? Why did the poor man have a name, but not the rich man? Is this story truly a unit? Are we not dealing instead with an original story (vv. 19-26) to which a dialogue has been added (vv. 27-31)? Is not Jesus quoting a well-known Egyptian, Jewish, or Greek story that would be the basis of his own? Is it possible to attribute a story this unusual to the historical Jesus?

All these questions have obviously given rise to innumerable commentaries.[4] Commentators have long been struck by the impressive study by Hugo Gressmann, who, in 1918, called our attention to a parallel tale told in Egypt and known in Israel.[5] Since the final dialogue is missing from this foreign tale, many have concluded that the second part of the parable was secondary, a solution

1   As Hintzen (*Verkündigung*, 121) has noted, the indefinite τις (v. 19, "there was once *a* man") indicates fiction writing. Contra Tertullian (*An.* 7.2), who, because of the proper name Lazarus, surmises that the sufferings of the rich man in hell are real and presupposes that this parable narrates events that really occurred. On the aesthetic quality of the parable, see Scholz, "Aesthetische Beobachtungen," 67–74.

2   See Jülicher, *Gleichnisreden*, 2:585, 641; Loisy, 414; Grundmann, 324–25.

3   See the list of questions in Grobel, "'. . . Whose Name Was Neves,'" 374–75; Hock, "Lazarus," 448, 455.

4   I have consulted ten commentaries and more than twenty-five articles. The bibliography itself is longer still. There is one entire book dedicated to this parable (Hintzen, *Verkündigung*). Hock ("Lazarus," 447) thinks, however, that, compared to others, our parable has certainly not monopolized commentators' attention. The situation seems to me to have changed over the last twenty years.

5   Gressmann, "Vom reichen Mann und armen Lazarus," 1–91. Scholars frequently summarize the position of this author; see, e.g., Schottroff and Stegemann, *Jesus von Nazareth*, 39; George, "Parabole," 80–82; Bauckham, "Rich Man and Lazarus," 225–31.

that had been proposed already by Adolf Jülicher.[6] In 1921, Rudolf Bultmann rejected the authenticity of both parts of the parable, and his opinion has been influential.[7] According to Bultmann, it was the early church that put a traditional story, which was Jewish rather than Egyptian, on Jesus' lips, not without adapting it to the Christian outlook.[8] Recent studies have sought to break loose from this prestigious exegetical past. Various literary or structural analyses have reaffirmed the unity of the narrative.[9] Others have looked for different parallels, for example, in Greco-Roman rhetoric.[10] We should mention finally still other studies that have been interested in ancient descriptions of life beyond death and in accounts of travels beyond the grave.[11]

Analysis

The reversal of fortunes and the contrast between riches and poverty are familiar to readers of the Gospel of Luke. The Magnificat announced the first (1:46-55); the beatitudes, followed by the woes, the second (6:20-26). In the course of the travel narrative, drawing on L, Luke recalled the dangers of riches and the Christian ideal of giving them up (12:33-34, 14:33). He also transmitted a parable whose unfortunate hero is a rich man who forgets how precarious life is (12:16-21).[12] Finally, as we have seen,[13] he skillfully constructed chap. 16, by placing a parable defending generosity (vv. 1-9) next to another that shows the fatal outcome of selfish ownership (vv. 19-31). Between the two, Luke placed some of Jesus' maxims (one of which reminds us that the divine scale of values is contrary to human conceptions, v. 15), and a redactional introduction that mentions the Pharisees' greed (v. 14).

With a lean style, the story begins by sketching out the two characters and defines their respective situations: first the rich man (v. 19); then, more generously, the poor man (vv. 20-21). The contrasts between the two men present us in turn with the social status, physical aspect, lifestyle, and characteristic setting of each of them.[14] It is curious that, though they were contemporaries and neighbors, the two men appear not to have known each other or to have ever met. Then the story begins ("Now it happened that . . ." [ἐγένετο δέ])at the point where most stories end—death (v. 22). What is surprising is the coincidence that they share the same fate of dying (the same Greek verb for dying—ἀποθνῄσκω—is used for both men), although they had had nothing in common up to that point. Now, however, on the day of their death, their paths cross ineluctably, since one of them, the poor man Lazarus, is immediately carried off by the angels to be in Abraham's mysterious bosom, while the other, the anonymous rich man, who is buried unceremoniously, ends up in the land of the dead (the designation "in Hades" (ἐν τῷ ᾅδῃ) should probably be taken as a proper noun). This is the point at which the symmetrical construction ends. The rest of the story is concerned with the rich man, the depiction of his new situation and the requests that he makes to Abraham, all of which will be turned down. The narrator delineates the uncomfortable situation of the rich man "being tormented," who nevertheless could see "Abraham far away, with Lazarus in his bosom" (v. 23). He sees the poor man and calls out to Abraham for help. The rich man had not been able to look at Lazarus on earth but now has been reduced to a humbler state. The request he makes is also a humble one, that of having his infernal sufferings lightened (v. 24). Abraham refuses his request, however, giving two reasons: one theological (people's destinies are determined by the principle of equality; v. 25), and the other topographical (the two localities are not contiguous; v. 26). The rich man does not admit defeat but

---

6   Jülicher, *Gleichnisreden*, 2:634.

7   Bultmann, *History*, 178, 196–97, 203–4.

8   Loisy (414, 419, 421) is not so sure; he thinks that the evangelist could be the author of the entire parable, although he recognizes that the theological perspective changes at v. 27 (the theology becomes more profound and allegorization more pronounced).

9   For example, Schnider and Stenger, "Die offene Tür," 273–83.

10 See Hock ("Lazarus," 455–63), who devotes his attention especially to two treatises of Lucian of Samosata, *Gallus* and *Cataplus*.

11 See Bauckham, "Rich Man and Lazarus," 226 n. 4, 236–44; Himmelfarb, *Tours of Hell*.

12 See especially the commentary on 1:46-55 and 6:20-26 in vol. 1, and above on 12:33-34; 14:33.

13 See pp. 443–44 above.

14 See Tanghe, "Abraham," 566.

attempts a second request, this one less selfish than the first, on behalf of his brothers (vv. 27-28). Abraham turns him down a second time, saying that his brothers have all they need with Moses and the prophets (v. 29). The last attempt made by the rich man (v. 30) meets with practically the same negative response from Abraham (v. 31).[15] This provides the following schema:

The state of the living
    The rich man (v. 19)
    Lazarus (vv. 20-21)
The deaths of the living
    The death of the poor man (v. 22a)
    The death of the rich man (v. 22b)
The dead rich man in his misfortune facing Abraham
    The rich man looks on the poor man in his good
        fortune (v. 23)
    The rich man's first request (v. 24)
    Abraham turns him down the first time (vv. 25-26)
    The second request (vv. 27-28)
    The second refusal (v. 29)
    The third request (v. 30)
    The third refusal (v. 31)

It is not easy to specify exactly what the literary genre of this story is: it is not introduced by a formula of comparison (cf. 13:18, 20), and it does not end with a moral (cf. 12:21) or an invitation to imitate someone or something (cf. 10:37). The story begins with the presentation of a fictional character ("Now there was a . . . man" [ἄνθρωπος δέ τις]), similar to those we find in the beginning of several parables in L (cf. 14:16; 15:11; 16:1; and the close examples in 12:16; 13:6; 18:2). It

continues on with the introduction of a second character. The meaning of the story is drawn from the comparison between the two characters, as in the parable of the Pharisee and the tax collector (18:9-14). In the strict sense, we are dealing not with a parable but rather a story whose exemplary element is evident without being explicit.[16]

As it is, the narrative does not have only a single climax.[17] Like fireworks, it first lights up the shape of the reversed fortunes, and then, in three salvos, it hammers out the inexorable decisions. While speaking of the deceased, the story addresses itself to the living; unlike the rich man, who has no out, since it is truly too late for him, the living, when they hear this story, still have time, time to repent. Do they not have the Law and the Prophets, illustrated and actualized by Jesus' teaching in parables? Even in the first part, the description is not subject to a single interpretation, and the reversal of fortunes is as much a defense of God, who has been accused of being inequitable, as it is an enhancement of the status and virtue of poor people.

An analysis of the vocabulary, style, and intrigue of the Lukan story makes it possible to work our way back from it to previous literary strata.[18] As is often the case, the further developments have been gathered together at the end; vv. 30-31 are redactional, as proved by the vocabulary (e.g., "repent," μετανοέω), the syntax (the way "he said" is expressed in Greek [ὁ δὲ εἶπεν]), and the theology (the same link between the Hebrew Bible and Jesus' resurrection as in 24:44-46). Here and there, moreover, Luke was able to make alterations to the traditional text he had inherited from L.[19] He wrote this example story expressly for his rich readers, who were

---

15 A number of critics divide the text into two parts, most frequently making the division between v. 26 and v. 27, influenced as they are by the Egyptian parallel. See Hock ("Lazarus," 449), who provides a list of scholars who share this view. Godet (2:184), without bothering here with the question of sources, divides the material into three sections: (a) vv. 19-21, the sin of the rich man; (b) vv. 22-26, the punishment of the rich man; and (c) vv. 27-31, the cause of evil. But he speaks of two corresponding scenes: one on earth (vv. 19-22) and the other in Hades (vv. 23-31) (p. 176). Vogels ("Having or Longing," 27–46) suggests that if the rich pass from having to not having (and to wanting), the poor

pass from not having (and from wanting) to not wanting and having.

16 The parable is most often classified among the example stories; see Jülicher, *Gleichnisreden*, 2:585 and 641; Loisy, 414; Grundmann, 324–25.

17 Ernst (472) speaks of two peaks: life without God (and its result) and the permanence of the law (and ethical conversion).

18 The most important work in this vein is that of Hintzen, *Verkündigung*, 271–347.

19 Luke could have insisted (καθ' ἡμέραν, "every day," v. 19), launched the story (ἐγένετο δέ, "now it happened that," v. 22), added an element ("and was buried," v. 22), given precision ("looking up," v. 23).

outsiders rather than insiders, Gentiles rather than Jews, and who were in danger of neglecting both the poor in front of their door and "the poor people" who made up the Christian community.

The author of L, a writer of considerable stature, is most likely the one who gave a literary form to the oral story. It is probably to him that we owe the mention of purple and fine linen,[20] as well as the use of his own term, "the bosom" of Abraham (in the plural in Greek, in v. 23 [ἐν τοῖς κόλποις], compared with the singular in v. 22), the special reworking of the end of the story (v. 26), and the supplying of the first redundancy (the request on behalf of the rich man's brothers, vv. 27-29). He aimed the parable at rich people, Jews rather than Gentiles, insiders rather than outsiders, reminded them of their social obligation—enunciated by the prophets— to be merciful and generous, and invited them, following the Deuteronomistic tradition, not to be stingy.[21]

My thesis that an original story has been amplified by two successive developments (vv. 27-29, then vv. 30-31) does not depend on the supposition of a borrowing, for the first part, from an Egyptian tale.[22] I do not believe that the author drew slavishly on a single source. On the contrary, the original narrator constructed his story by drawing on various traditional materials that can be found in Egypt, Greece,[23] and especially Palestine. These materials are concerned not only with the opposite fates of the rich man and the poor man but also with their different deaths, the geography of the land of the dead,[24] and the possibility of a dialogue between the living and the dead. No, the evolution from the tradition to the composition of L, and finally to the Lukan redaction,

is tied not to the character of one source but to the successive reinterpretations of the story that proved to be necessary through the years and to different audiences hearing or reading the story. The persons responsible for these rereadings were in the first instance the narrators, and later the authors. These persons did not betray the original simplicity of the story by heterogeneous additions but were simply attempting to keep the meaning at the same time they were enriching it. Nevertheless, in so doing, they inevitably modified it.

The Egyptian tale that reminds us of this parable has been preserved in the Demotic language[25] on a papyrus from the second half of the first century of our era.[26] It is part of a narrative collection attested in the fourth century B.C.E.[27] that could go back as far as the sixth century B.C.E. Here, in summary, is the part that is of interest to us. A father, Satme, and his son, Si-Osiris, attended, on a mountain, the solemn funeral of a rich man and the pitiful burial of a poor man. The father wished to share the fate of the rich man in the land of the dead. His son, however, wished for him to share the fate of the poor man and, in order to convince him, took his father on a tour of Amᶜnte, the Egyptian Hades. There they observed the reversal of fortunes resulting from the divine weighing of a person's soul, their good deeds, and their wrongdoing. The person wearing the fine linen was the poor man, who received the funeral attire of the rich man as a compensation for his good deeds. He was also the one who had the privilege of standing near Osiris. As for the rich man, he was cruelly punished by having the hinge of Amᶜnte's door, which kept opening and closing, fixed in his right eye.

     Some of these suggestions correspond to those of Hintzen (*Verkündigung*, 346–47), whose list is even longer.

20 Hintzen (*Verkündigung*, 346), on the contrary, prefers to attribute these words to Lukan redaction.

21 With Hintzen, *Verkündigung*, passim.

22 See Gressmann, "Vom reichen Mann und armen Lazarus," and below.

23 On Greco-Latin parallels, see Hock, "Lazarus," and below.

24 With Bauckham, "Rich Man and Lazarus."

25 Demotic is a late Egyptian language, dating from the last centuries of pagan Egypt; it is written in a cursive style that is also called Demotic, which simplifies the hieratic writing.

26 British Museum Papyrus DCIV, in F. L. Griffith, ed., *Stories of the High Priests of Memphis: The Sethon of Herodotus and the Demotic Tales of Khamuas* (Oxford: Clarendon, 1900) 42–81, 142–207. The first to have made the connection with our parable is Gaston Maspero, *Popular Stories of Ancient Egypt* (trans. A. S. Johns from the 4th French ed.; New Hyde Park, N.Y.: University Books, 1967) 154–81; see G. Möller, "Die ägyptische Rezension," in Gressmann, "Vom reichen Mann und armen Lazarus," 62.

27 George, "Parabole," 81.

There are several analogous tales in Jewish literature. The oldest one is the story of the rich Maʿyan's son, preserved in the Palestinian Talmud.[28] Here is a summary of it: Two men die at the same time, at Ashkelon. One of them is a pious Jew, who is given a private, bare-bones burial, and the other is the son of a rich tax collector, named Maʿyan, whose impressive funeral is attended by the entire city. A friend of the pious Jew, who is himself an attentive reader of the law, laments such an injustice. He is calmed down by two successive dreams. The first one explains to him that all that was required to enable Maʿyan's son to receive such an honorable funeral was one good work (having offered to some poor folk the food that was meant for some guests who were invited but did not show up) and all that was required to explain why the pious Jew deserved such a pitiful burial was one bad deed (having once put on his head tefillin before putting on his hand tefillin). The second dream was a revelation to him of the land of the dead, where the pious Jew rests in a garden beside a spring, while the rich man's son is by the bank of a river, thirsty, desperately sticking out his tongue without being able to quench his thirst.

We should also consult the examples suggested by the rhetoricians or the sages of ancient Greece. It was considered good manners to compare various persons in order to better praise some and denounce others.[29] Rich people and poor people figured frequently in speeches as well as in comedies (see Philostratus *Vit. soph.* 481).[30] For example, the Greek Cynic writer and philosopher Lucian of Samosata, in his treatise *Gallus* (14 and 7), contrasts a "poor man" (πτωχός), the cobbler Micyllus, with a "rich man" (πλούσιος) named Eucrates.[31] In another treatise, *Cataplus* (13–14), the same Micyllus is put side by side with the rich tyrant Megapenthes. Even though the poor man in this story is not a beggar lying at the gate of the rich man, he still is his neighbor.[32] Sometimes he wants to share in the rich man's banquet (*Gallus* 9), since he is attracted by the good odors coming out of the prepared dishes of food (*Cataplus* 16). So we have at the same time a conventional way of describing a poor man and a rich man and a moralizing description of the fate of good people and bad people. The reversal of fortunes was part of the rhetorical store with a philosophical flavor. In *Cataplus,* the trip to Hades makes such a retribution visible; Micyllus and Megapenthes meet up the same day with Charon, the boatman who ferries dead people to Hades (1–3, 14). Micyllus is taken away by death while hard at work, while Megapenthes is poisoned during a banquet (15, 11). While the judgment of the cobbler Micyllus is settled quickly by virtue of his purity, Megapenthes' drags on (26–28), for he did not let himself be taken away by death without a struggle. His efforts and his bargaining (4, 8–10, 12–13) remind us of the second part of the Lukan parable, the very part for which there are no Egyptian or Jewish parallels.[33] Finally, it is a reversal of fortunes indeed that the reader encounters, since Micyllus reaches the island of the blessed (*Cataplus* 24), while Megapenthes is denied the waters of the Lethe River, which would confer on him the gift of forgetfulness. He is obliged to recall his past continuously (28–29). The thing that saved Micyllus was his self-control and his "wisdom" (σωφροσύνη) in the midst of poverty. What caused the ruin of Megapenthes was his vice and his lack of self-control (ἀκρασία).[34]

---

28   *Y. Ḥag.* 2.2 (77d, 38) and *y. Sanh.* 6.6 (23c, 26) (Neusner, *Talmud,* §20 [57] and §31 [181–82]); Str-B 2:231–32; George, "Parabole," 82–83.

29   See Theon of Alexandria *Progymnasmata,* 9–10; see Christian Walz, *Rhetores Graeci* (9 vols.; Stuttgart: J. G. Cottae, 1832) 1:231–39; James R. Butts, "The 'Progymnasmata' of Theon: A New Text with Translation and Commentary" (Ph.D. diss., Claremont Graduate School, 1987) 446–89; and Hermogenes of Tarsus *Progymnasmata* 8; see H. Rabe, ed., *Hermogenis opera* (Rhetores Graeci 6; Stuttgart: Teubner, 1969) 18–20; Hock, "Lazarus," 456. The "comparison" was called σύγκρισις; the "moral characterization" ἠθοποιία. See the commentary above on 12:17.

30   Mentioned by Hock, "Lazarus," 456–57.

31   He also encounters other rich persons, Simonides and Gniphon.

32   *Gallus* 14 (neighbor of Simonides) and *Cataplus* 16 (neighbor of Megapenthes).

33   With Hock, "Lazarus," 459–60; contra Bauckham, "Rich Man and Lazarus," 236.

34   The parallels with Lucian of Samosata were known before the study of Hock ("Lazarus"), but they were used only to illustrate one detail (thus, Rudolf Helm, *Lucian und Menipp* [Leipzig: Teubner, 1906] 66; Hans Dieter Betz, *Lukian von Samosata und das Neue Testament: Religionsgeschichtliche und paränetische Parallelen. Ein Beitrag zum Corpus Hellenisticum Novi Testamenti* [TU 76; Berlin: Akademie-Verlag, 1961]

The mention of the hereafter does not necessarily imply that the story had an Egyptian origin.[35] In New Testament times, all the peoples of the Mediterranean world thought of the world of the dead along similar structural lines, which did not keep them from representing it differently in certain details.[36] There was some tension in the evolution of the conceptions within Judaism, which awaited a last judgment and the resurrection of the dead but began to believe in a land of the dead in the hereafter whose relative comfort or lack of comfort depended on one's morality in this life.[37] This perspective came to coexist with that of the last judgment and the final resurrection by conferring precise topography on the old idea of Sheol and by transforming the life beyond the grave into one of a long waiting period.[38] The apocalyptic literature is a good source of information on this subject. *Ethiopian Enoch* (*1 Enoch*) 22 contains a description of the land of the dead, but it is far from being alone in this respect; the *Apocalypse of Peter* (6–12) and the *Apocalypse of Paul* (11.19–51) follow suit. 1 Peter, contemporaneous with the Gospel of Luke, may be acquainted with the existence of a place where the souls or the spirits of the dead are watched over and held back until the last judgment and the resurrection of the dead (3:19).[39] We are not dealing with a belief peculiar to any one writing, but rather with one that had come to be held generally.[40] To be sure, the geography of life beyond the grave could, and did, vary from one writing to another, from

one religious group to another, and perhaps even from one believer to another, but everyone's consciousness was filled with the same expectation. By way of example we might mention *1 Enoch*, which appeared to divide the land of the dead into four deep, large, and smooth pits. The first three were dark and reserved for sinners; the fourth, decorated with an illuminated fountain of water, was reserved for the righteous.

Commentary

■ **19-21** The description of the rich man is a conventional one, having to do with his appearance and his lifestyle. His clothes were cut from the most expensive fabrics; the Greek word ($\pi o\rho\varphi\acute{v}\rho\alpha$) translated "purple" refers first of all to a sea snail (*murex*) from which a liquid is extracted; then to the secretion itself, the purple dye; and finally to any outer garment or overcoat dyed with that warm color. In the rabbinic literature, "purple" (the Hebrew word used is a transliteration of the Greek) is used only for kings and God. In the Roman empire, and later in the Byzantine, purple became exclusively the color of the emperors.[41] As for the "fine linen" ($\beta\acute{v}\sigma\sigma o\varsigma$), this was a particularly fine linen of Egyptian or Indian origin from which undergarments were made.[42] In time the word came to refer to the clothes themselves.[43] The color of the "byssus" (from the Latin word for fine linen, derived from the Greek) appears to have varied between

---

82, 97, 195) or were disparaged by the very ones who advanced them (thus Schottroff and Stegemann, *Jesus von Nazareth*, 133–35). See Hock, "Lazarus," 457; Bauckham, "Rich Man and Lazarus," 234–36.

35 Despite Gressmann ("Vom reichen Mann und armen Lazarus," 43, 53 and passim), who detects some Greek elements in the Egyptian story.

36 Zaleski, *Otherworld Journeys*, 11–25; Hoffmann, *Die Toten in Christus*, 25–174.

37 See Cavallin, "Leben nach dem Tode," 240–345; Himmelfarb, *Tours of Hell*, 41–126; Stemberger, *Der Leib der Auferstehung*, passim; Hanhart, *Intermediate State in the New Testament*, passim.

38 See Alan E. Bernstein, *The Formation of Hell: Death and Retribution in the Ancient and Early Christian Worlds* (Ithaca, N.Y.: Cornell University Press, 1993) 133–202.

39 On this difficult verse, see Paul J. Achtemeier, *1 Peter: A Commentary on First Peter* (Hermeneia; Minneapolis: Fortress Press, 1996) 252–62. Achtemeier

does not identify the "spirits" of 1 Pet 3:19 with the souls of the dead.

40 See, e.g., the Greek recensions, short and long, of the *Testament of Abraham*; see Francis Schmidt, *Le Testament d'Abraham* (TSAJ 11; Tübingen: Mohr Siebeck, 1986).

41 See 1 Macc 4:23 on dyes, and Mark 15:17-20 on materials and clothes (outer garments). See Plummer, 391; Str-B 2:222; Hintzen, *Verkündigung*, 122–23.

42 According to Str-B (2:222–23), the Hebrew term בּוּץ could just as easily refer to wool. Further, the costliest linen came from Beth Shean (Scythopolis); see Pax, "Der Reiche," 256–57.

43 Batiffol ("Trois notes exégétiques," 541) directs our attention to a passage from Philostratus (*Vit. Ap.* 2.20): ". . . while the upper class dressed in cotton [$\beta\acute{v}\sigma\sigma\omega$, better translated as 'fine linen']. This, they relate, grows on a tree with a trunk like a poplar and with leaves like a willow. Apollonius says he was

white and reddish-brown. The luxurious clothes of the rich man, namely, his purple coat and his tunic made out of byssus, were in perfect taste and of harmonious colors. The use of the imperfect tense in Greek ($\dot{\epsilon}\nu\epsilon\delta\iota\delta\dot{\upsilon}\sigma\kappa\epsilon\tau o$) to tell us how "he was dressed" indicates his customary, not his exceptional, attire and confirms the fact that he was scandalously rich. We may recall the rich man in the previous parable who said to his soul (himself): "Relax, eat, drink, and be merry ($\epsilon\dot{\upsilon}\varphi\rho\alpha\dot{\iota}\nu o\upsilon$)" (12:19). We find the same Greek verb ($\epsilon\dot{\upsilon}\varphi\rho\alpha\dot{\iota}\nu o\mu\alpha\iota$) "be merry" used here in chap. 16, where it is translated "to feast," which brings together the joys of the flesh and the pleasures of good food.[44] Only very well-off persons, so the story suggests, are able to afford such satisfactions on a daily basis. And to complete the picture, the text adds the adverb "sumptuously" ($\lambda\alpha\mu\pi\rho\tilde{\omega}\varsigma$), "magnificently," "luxuriously," "lavishly."[45]

Certainly nowhere does the parable express the guilt of the rich man.[46] But—and this is the art of parables—a successful description alone suffices in building up a severe case for the prosecution. Any reader is immediately on to what is going on. A Jew will recall that the Law and the Prophets call us to be merciful (see Isa 58:7)[47] and forbid ostentatious arrogance.[48] A Greek-speaking Gentile would have in mind encouragements to practice moderation.[49] What the rich man did wrong was not just

that he did not take care of the poor man Lazarus, but that he also lived in excessive luxury.[50]

Christian tradition has been anxious to provide a name for the person who shrugged off his responsibility for Lazarus.[51] In English they have given him a name derived from the word used to describe his state in the Latin Vulgate, namely, "Dives," the word for "rich" in Latin. The New Testament in Sahidic Coptic calls him "Nineveh." In the fourth century, Priscillian called him "Finees."[52] In the third century, a Latin author called him "Finaeus."[53] The oldest of the Greek manuscripts of the Gospel, Papyrus Bodmer XIV/XV ($\mathfrak{P}^{75}$), from the third century, calls him "Neues" ($\dot{o}\nu\dot{o}\mu\alpha\tau\iota$ $N\epsilon\dot{\upsilon}\eta\varsigma$).[54] This variety of ancient witnesses seems to boil down to two different possible names: (a) Phineus ($\Phi\iota\nu\epsilon\dot{\upsilon}\varsigma$), the name of a hero of the legend about the Argonauts who was punished beyond the grave by the Harpies, who carried him off or polluted the food allotted to him because he had abused his powers of divination,[55] and (b) Neues ($N\epsilon\dot{\upsilon}\eta\varsigma$), a shortened form of $N\iota\nu\epsilon\nu\dot{\eta}\varsigma$ (the name of the city of Nineveh in Greek is $N\iota\nu\epsilon\upsilon\dot{\eta}$, and the name of its inhabitants, the Ninevites, is $N\iota\nu\epsilon\upsilon\dot{\iota}\tau\eta\varsigma$ in the singular). The story was told that the son of Ninos (the founder of the city of Nineveh) and his wife (the queen Semiramis) was named Ninyas ($N\iota\nu\dot{\upsilon}\alpha\varsigma$) and that he lived a life of pleasure and debauchery, with no thought of the cost.

---

pleased by the cotton [$\beta\dot{\upsilon}\sigma\sigma\omega$], since it looked like a gray philosopher's cloak. In fact, cotton [$\beta\dot{\upsilon}\sigma\sigma o\varsigma$] comes from India to many of the sanctuaries in Egypt" (trans. Jones, LCL). On the conventional connections between wealth and clothes, see Hintzen, *Verkündigung*, 176.

44 See the commentary above on 12:19.

45 The adverb, which is not exceptional, is nevertheless absent from the LXX and appears nowhere else in the New Testament.

46 Several exegetes have wrongly taken from this silence a refusal to read in this parable a criticism of wealth and its inappropriate usage; see the long list of exegetes in Hock ("Lazarus," 453 n. 28).

47 Quoted by Bornhäuser, *Sondergut*, 143.

48 Our text is part of the Jewish sapiential and apocalyptic tradition, which vigorously attacks the wealthy: see *1 Enoch* 89:2; 102:9; 103:5-8; *T. Mos.* 7:8; Jas 2:2-3; 5:1-6; see Reinmuth, "Ps.-Philo, Liber Antiquitatum Biblicarum 33,1–5," 29 (bibliography in n. 51).

49 See Hock, "Lazarus," 461.

50 With Hock, "Lazarus."

51 Several studies mention this point: see Harnack, *Der Name des reichen Mannes*; Zahn, 583–84; Gressmann, "Vom reichen Mann und armen Lazarus," 6–8; Lefort, "Le nom du mauvais riche," 65–72; Grobel, "'. . . Whose Name Was Neves'"; Cadbury, "Name of Dives," 73; Hintzen, *Verkündigung*, 79–82.

52 Priscillian *Tractatus ad populum* 1 (= *Tractatus* 9) (CSEL 18:91).

53 Pseudo-Cyprian *De pasca computus* 17 (CSEL 3/3, 265; *PL* 4:1043); see George Ogg, *The Pseudo-Cyprianic De pascha computus: Translated with Brief Annotations* (London: SPCK, 1955) 15, 37. The name "Finaeus" is omitted by one of the two manuscripts.

54 See the apparatus of Nestle-Aland. This name is close to the one that the Sahidic provides for this verse, mentioned above.

55 Hintzen, *Verkündigung*, 80–81. It is not necessary to compare this name with Phinehas (LXX $\Phi\iota\nu\epsilon\epsilon\varsigma$) in Num 25:1-13.

The most famous quotation of the proverb "Eat, drink . . ." orients us also in the direction of Nineveh, since it is engraved on Sardanapalus's tomb.[56] In short, the parable originally gave the rich man no name, but very quickly people wanted to give him one to match the name of the poor man Lazarus, perhaps because of oral performance that was carried on parallel to the written narration. Some of these people, in Egypt, turned toward Nineveh; others, in the West, were reminded of the expedition of the Argonauts.

There is a richer description of the poor man than of the wealthy one. Even if the Greek word for "throw" ($\beta \acute{\alpha} \lambda \lambda \omega$) lost some of the notion of violence in late Greek,[57] it nevertheless lends a negative connotation to the situation, as the presence of the Greek participle translated "covered with sores" ($\epsilon \acute{i} \lambda \kappa \omega \mu \acute{\epsilon} \nu o \varsigma$) confirms. Lazarus was not therefore in control of his destiny; like a piece of wreckage tossed about by the waves, he finally washed up at the door of the rich man.[58] The poor man's wounds are stressed: the initial mention of them ("covered with sores" [$\epsilon \acute{i} \lambda \kappa \omega \mu \acute{\epsilon} \nu o \varsigma$], v. 20) is matched by a corresponding notice in the following verse ("his sores" [$\tau \grave{\alpha}$ $\acute{\epsilon} \lambda \kappa \eta$ $\alpha \grave{v} \tau o \hat{v}$], v. 21).[59] What is more, the rich man's feasts are matched by the unsatisfied hunger of the poor man, and this is worded in such a way as to bring to mind the situation of the prodigal son who also "would gladly

have filled his stomach" ($\epsilon \pi \epsilon \vartheta \acute{v} \mu \epsilon \iota$ $\chi o \rho \tau \alpha \sigma \vartheta \hat{\eta} \nu \alpha \iota$, 15:16),[60] as well as the figure of speech used by the Syro-Phoenician woman (cf. Matt 15:27, "for even [little] dogs eat the crumbs that fall from their masters' table," rather than Mark 7:28; although Luke does not report the incident, he must have known it).[61] The figure of the crumbs and the dogs must have become a proverbial one[62] and explains the presence of dogs after the mention of what fell from the table. In fact, what was involved must have been more the soft part of the bread used to wipe one's hands than the crumbs.[63] Western attachment to dogs is at variance with the negative prejudice against them in the ancient Orient, where they were considered to be unclean animals.[64] Even if this last point is in dispute, the mention of the licking by dogs, who must have been stray dogs, is intended to make the picture even darker.[65]

The wealth of the poor man consists in the fact that he bears a name and, what is more, one that is promising. "Lazarus" means—for the person interested in knowing (and who knows a little bit of Hebrew!)—"God helps."[66] The author of L often enjoys giving names to certain persons. Besides Lazarus, we might mention Zacchaeus (19:2) and Cleopas (24:18). It could be that this author was the one who added the name Lazarus, all the more since Lazarus is the only hero in a parable who is given a name. Or then again it could have come from the

---

56 See above, and the commentary on 12:19.

57 See Plummer (391), who refers to 5:37; John 5:7; 12:6; 18:11, etc. Godet (2:177) is conscious of the negative tone that this verb introduces.

58 Since the house of the rich man must be spacious, it has a porch or gate ($\pi v \lambda \acute{\omega} \nu$) and not a mere door ($\vartheta \acute{v} \rho \alpha$); on these two words, see the commentary above on 13:24. See also Plummer (391), who suggests that the $\pi v \lambda \acute{\omega} \nu$ could form a part of the house or could be detached, citing Acts 10:17; 12:14; Matt 26:71; 2 Chr 3:7; and Zeph 2:14.

59 The term $\acute{\epsilon} \lambda \kappa o \varsigma$ designates an abscess or a tumor of the skin, which can arise from various causes: sickness, infection, cuts, or even a snakebite (see LSJ, s.v.). The term is used in the LXX to designate the sixth plague in Egypt (Exod 9:9-11; Deut 28:27, 35), the malady that afflicted Job (Job 2:7), and the ailment that nearly killed King Hezekiah (2 Kgs [4 Kgdms] 20:7. The Greek word corresponds to the Hebrew שְׁחִין, from the root שׁחן, which means "to be warm" or "to burn." See Julius Preuss, *Biblisch-talmudische Medizin: Beiträge zur Geschichte der*

Heilkunde und der Kultur überhaupt (3d ed.; Berlin: S. Karger, 1923). I am grateful to David Warren for this information.

60 On the motif of satiation in the story of the feeding of the five thousand, see the commentary on 9:17 in vol. 1.

61 See Luke 9:10 compared to Mark 6:45: Bethsaida. See the commentary on 9:10 in vol. 1.

62 Erich Klostermann (*Das Markusevangelium* [4th ed.; HNT 3; Tübingen: Mohr Siebeck, 1950] 82) mentions a Jewish parallel and two Greek parallels.

63 See Jeremias, *Parables*, 152.

64 See already Godet (2:265) and Loisy (415); since then, Pax, "Der Reiche," 260.

65 See Plummer, 392; Lagrange, 444; Grundmann, 327. The $\acute{\alpha} \lambda \lambda \alpha$ ' $\kappa \alpha \acute{i}$ ("but even") favors this interpretation. Pax ("Der Reiche," 261) offers another point of view. This is the sole biblical usage of $\epsilon \pi \iota \lambda \epsilon \acute{i} \chi \omega$ ("to lick"); see Plummer, 392.

66 All the commentators note this point; see, e.g., Ernst, 473–74.

tradition while it was still in its oral phase. Lazarus is the hellenized form of Eliezer. Should we think of Abraham's servant Eliezer, who almost became Abraham's heir (Gen 15:2-4)?[67] Moreover, he was afraid of being poorly received before he met Rebekah near the well (Gen 24:10-21). This person was famous in Jewish Haggadah.[68] In my view, there is no reason to think of the Lukan text as an allusion to this Eliezer. What is more, Luke is scarcely interested in the etymology[69] of proper names.

■ **22** For once the two men meet the same fate. They both die—and at the same moment. But at this critical, fatal moment their destinies only intersect, rather than coincide; for these two men, the paths diverge with respect to both language and the facts. One of them— and Luke talks first the poor man (v. 22a), whose story he is following throughout (vv. 20-21)—is immediately carried away by the angels. The other one— and here Luke picks up (v. 22b) on a previous description (v. 19)—is buried. This contrast is only one aspect of the different fates awaiting the two dead men. The warm connotation (the support of the angels who carry off souls,[70] and Abraham's welcoming bosom) contrasts with the cold indication, concerning the rich man, "and he was buried."

The poor man was not carried off in the same way as Enoch and Elijah, since those two heroes of the Hebrew Bible escaped death.[71] On the other hand, his being carried off does correspond to the fate of the righteous after their death; what remains of their personality is led off toward the place reserved for the righteous. It is not said that the poor man was lifted up to the heights ($\dot{\alpha}\pi o\varphi\acute{\epsilon}\rho\omega$ means "to carry off" or "to transport," rather than "lift up to the heights"). Popular Judaism and Hellenistic religion had both adopted this belief in angels who carried off souls.[72] Funeral epigrams and inscriptions on tombs both witness to parallels to the Lukan expression "in the bosom (of)" ($\epsilon\dot{\iota}\varsigma\ \tau\dot{o}\nu\ \kappa\acute{o}\lambda\pi o\nu$).[73]

For example, it was hoped that a dead child would be welcomed "into his mother's bosom."[74] The patriarch's name appears here, since the story is told from a Jewish point of view and therefore presupposes that Abraham is the father of believers and the protector of the righteous.[75] In my opinion, Lazarus did not reach "paradise" and will not escape the last judgment.[76] His awaiting of

---

67 The connection between Lazarus of our parable and Eliezer in Gen 15:2 goes back at least as far as Wettstein, *Novum Testamentum graecum* (1:767) and John Lightfoot, *A Commentary on the New Testament from the Talmud and Hebraica* (4 vols.; 1675; repr., Peabody, Mass.: Hendrickson, 1997) 3:166; see Derrett, "Fresh Light on St Luke xvi: II," in idem, *Law*, 86–87.

68 See Ginzberg, *Legends*, 1:292–97 and passim; Cave, "Lazarus and the Lukan Deuteronomy," 323–24.

69 See the commentary on 1:13-14 in vol. 1.

70 On these angels and their function, see Wettstein, *Novum Testamentum graecum*, 1:767; and Fitzmyer, 2:1132.

71 See the commentary on 9:30-31 in vol. 1; and Bovon, *Theologian*, 192–93.

72 *Tg. Canticles* 4:12; Alexander Sperber, *The Bible in Aramaic Based on Old Manuscripts and Printed Texts* (5 vols.; Leiden/New York: Brill, 1992) 4a (134); for the English translation of H. Gollancz, dating to 1908, see Bernard Grossfeld, ed. and introd., *The Targum to the Five Megilloth* (New York: Hermon, 1973) 215; Str-B 2:223–25; Pax, "Der Reiche," 262; Plummer, 392–93.

73 It is most frequently used in the dative plural ($\kappa\acute{o}\lambda\pi o\iota\varsigma$), either preceded by the preposition $\dot{\epsilon}\nu$ or not. The bosom that welcomes the deceased

is most often the earth itself. Thus: $\sigma\hat{\omega}\mu\alpha\ \mu\grave{\epsilon}\nu\ \dot{\epsilon}\nu\ \kappa\acute{o}\lambda\pi o\iota\varsigma\ \kappa\alpha\tau\acute{\epsilon}\chi\epsilon\iota\ \tau\acute{o}\delta\epsilon\ \gamma\alpha\hat{\iota}\alpha\ \Pi\lambda\acute{\alpha}\tau\omega\nu o\varsigma,\ \psi\upsilon\chi\grave{\eta}\ \delta'\ \iota\sigma\acute{o}\vartheta\epsilon o\varsigma\ \tau\acute{\alpha}\xi\iota\nu\ \dot{\epsilon}\chi\epsilon\iota\ \mu\alpha\kappa\acute{\alpha}\rho\omega\nu$ ("the earth retains in its bosom the body of Plato while the soul, equal to the gods, takes its place among the blessed"). Attributed to Speusippos in Hugo Stadtmueller, ed., *Anthologia graeca epigrammatum palatina cum Planudea* (3 vols.; Leipzig: Teubner, 1894–1906) 16.31; see 7.61, 321, 368, 476. See Hock, "Lazarus," 456; Richmond A. Lattimore, *Themes in Greek and Latin Epitaphs* (Urbana: University of Illinois Press, 1962) 211–12, 243, 302, 304; Hoffman, *Toten*, 173 n. 13, who mentions *LAB* 40:4.

74 In Stadtmueller, *Anthologia graeca (palatina)*, 7:387, a father who has lost his wife, then his son, a little boy, asks Persephone to place the child into the bosom of his deceased mother ($\dot{\epsilon}\varsigma\ \kappa\acute{o}\lambda\pi o\upsilon\varsigma$). See Hock, "Lazarus," 456 n. 36.

75 By connecting this Lukan expression with traditional Jewish ones, such as "to rest with one's fathers," or "to rejoin his fathers" (Gen 15:15; 47:30; Judg 2:10; 1 Kgs [3 Kgdms LXX] 1:21), Str-B 2:225 trivializes this phrase, because, to my knowledge, the expression "the bosom of Abraham" is unknown in the Judaism of the time.

76 Strictly speaking, one could understand the bosom of Abraham in two ways: first, in a familial and

the events of the end-time is simply an agreeable one, at the opposite extreme from his earthly life.

■ **23** The expression "in Hades," meaning "in the land of the dead" (ἐν τῷ ᾅδη),[77] follows the mention of the tomb ("and he was buried" [καὶ ἐτάφη]).[78] The rich man gets to the land of the dead via his tomb, just as Lazarus does. However, in the rich man's case, he arrives—probably alone—in a very different place in the land of the dead, since he is in the throes of torment (this is a traditional expression in descriptions of Hades).[79] At this point he looks up in the hope of gaining some relief. He sees (note the use of the historic present in Greek, "he sees" [ὁρᾷ], which stresses the painful duration of this spectacle)[80] Lazarus's good fortune. What he sees provokes his jealousy, awakens his sense of guilt, and gives him an idea! The text makes it clear that what he sees is far away,[81] since the land of the dead is immense and its compartments are distant from each other.

■ **24** So the rich man, who has lost his arrogance, begins to beg. Being either prudent or manipulative, he takes over the language of pious people: "Father Abraham," he says ("father" in the sense of "ancestor," rather than spiritual father).[82] In apocalyptic literature, those who are damned often suffer from either a furnace or frost, famine or thirst. As a consequence, they beg their keepers or their visitors to grant them some respite or relief (see, e.g., *Apoc. Paul* 17). Faithful to these stereotypes, our author puts a request on the lips of the rich man but does so artfully; the rich man, who seems to have interiorized his guilt, does not demand to be freed but is content to ask for some small measure of relief (the reader discovers that he suffers from being burned by "this flame"; in spite of the mention later of his tongue, what the flames act on is his body rather than his mouth).[83] The Greek verb ὀδυνάω, here used in the passive voice (ὀδυνῶμαι), meaning "suffer," belongs to the apocalyptic vocabulary.[84] All Abraham would have to do

---

emotional sense, which corresponds to Johannine usage (according to John 1:18, the Son rests εἰς τὸν κόλπον τοῦ πατρός, according to John 13:23 and 25, the beloved disciple is reclining ἐν τῷ κόλπῳ τοῦ Ἰησοῦ, and ἐπὶ τὸ στῆθος τοῦ Ἰησοῦ); and, second, in a social and honorary sense (at a banquet in which the cushions are set out in a diagonal arrangement, the head of one finds himself at the bosom of the other). I prefer the first interpretation; I do not imagine here either a banquet or a place of honor. See Str-B 2:225–26; Hock, "Lazarus," 456 n. 35. On the idea of an eschatological feast, see Lorenzen, "Meditation," 40.

77 On Hades, a term that appears around a hundred times in the LXX, see Acts 2:27, 31; and Luke 8:31, which mentions ἡ ἄβυσσος ("the abyss"); see Gressmann, "Vom reichen Mann und armen Lazarus," 34–43; Str-B 2:228; Himmelfarb, *Tours of Hell*, 48–49, 68, 76, 84, 96, 106–7, 110–11, 116, 119–20. We must most probably distinguish Hades from Gehenna. On Gehenna, absent in the LXX, see Luke 12:5; cf. seven uses in Matthew, three in Mark, and one in the Epistle of James. See the commentary on 8:30-31 in vol. 1.

78 See Pax ("Der Reiche," 262–63), who speaks of "an abrupt staccato" (p. 262).

79 See the mentions of the Christ among the dead in Acts 2:24, 27, 31, where we find Hades and ὠδίνες ("pains of childbirth"); here in Luke 16:24 we have the related verb ὀδυνῶμαι ("to suffer").

80 Cf. 13:28; Marshall, 636–37.

81 The expression ἀπὸ μακρόθεν ("from afar") is pleonastic but common in this later period (see ἀπὸ ὄπισθεν, "from behind," "next," in the LXX of 1 and 2 Samuel [1 and 2 Kingdms]); see Plummer, 394.

82 Luke 13:17 describes a "daughter of Abraham"; see the commentary above on 13:15-16. On "Father Abraham," see Plummer, 394; Cave, "Lazarus and the Lukan Deuteronomy," 324. For Abraham in Luke-Acts, apart from our text, see Luke 1:55-73; 3:8, 34; 13:16, 28; 19:9; 20:37; Acts 3:13, 25; 7:2, 16, 17, 32; 13:26; Bovon, *Theologian*, 99–101, 119.

83 On torture by fire, see Isa 66:24; Sir 7:17; 21:9-10; *1 Enoch* 10:13; 1QH 17.13 (lacunary text); and Matt 5:22.

84 See Zech 9:5 LXX; 12:10 LXX; Isa 21:10 LXX; Lam 1:13-14 LXX. See also ὀδύνη ("pain") in, e.g., Gen 44:31 LXX; Isa 30:26 LXX; Amos 8:10 LXX; Wis 4:19. The word ὠδίς (late form: ὠδίν) means "pain" of childbirth, and later all cruel suffering, such as that of death; on ὠδίνω ("to feel pain"), see Hatch and Redpath, *Concordance*, s.v. See also the Latin *dolor* in, e.g., Albert-Marie Denis, *Concordance latine des Pseudépigraphes d'Ancien Testament: Concordance, corpus des textes, indices* (Corpur Christianorum Thesaurus Patrum Latinorum, Supplementum; Turhout: Brepols, 19983) s.v.

would be, first, to have Lazarus dip the tip of his finger in water (the reader discovers that Lazarus's stay in Hades is made pleasant by the presence of a cool spring or fountain)[85] and, second, to have Lazarus touch the rich man's painful tongue with this water in order to soothe the burning sensation.[86] Without explicitly drawing out the parallel, the author describes acts that resemble those that the rich man might easily have carried out during his lifetime on behalf of Lazarus, namely, relieving the latter's suffering by sharing some water and bread from his table.[87]

■ **25** But (the Greek particle δέ is adversative and prepares us for a negative answer) Abraham answers him by saying, "My child" (τέκνον), literally "child" (Abraham accepts his paternal, ancestral role and does not refuse to grant the rich man his rights as a member of the people of the covenant).[88] "Remember" (in the sense of "become aware of," "realize," and not "recall," or "bring to mind").[89] In a didactic manner, the text contemplates the fates of these two men and contrasts them: for you "the good things" (τὰ ἀγαθά) in your earthly life; for him ("in like fashion," ὁμοίως, symmetrically, in his earthly life) "evil things" (τὰ κακά).[90] We now have the reverse situation, since the roles have had to be reversed

here and now: "now" (νῦν) and "here" (ὧδε). Why?[91] In order to reestablish equality and to encourage the reader to opt for a fate that will resemble neither that of the rich man in the afterlife nor that of the poor man in this life. The strategy of the text is to lead readers to make their moral choice, namely, that of deciding in favor of sharing and fairness. Depending on your response, you will either be carried off by the angel to be in Abraham's bosom or you will go down the path that plunges you into the torments of Hades. According to Luke, comfort ("he is comforted" [παρακαλεῖται]) is the reestablishment of the fairness that creates in you the feeling of well-being and justice; Luke used the word "comfort" in the pericope on the beatitudes and the woes (6:24) in order to say that rich people are in fact the unfortunate ones who have had their "comfort" during their earthly life.[92] Lazarus is fortunate in that he enjoys his good fortune beyond the grave.

■ **26** There is an objective separation between the two men, which Abraham's subjectivity can in no way change. A great "chasm" (χάσμα)[93] "has been fixed" (the Greek verb ἐστήρικται is somewhat awkward but vivid; it indicates that the division is intentional, fixed, and that nothing is going to reduce the space between them).[94]

---

85   See *1 Enoch* 22; Marshall, 637–38; ὕδατος is a "genitive of material" (Lagrange, 446).

86   The verb καταψύχω is a *hapax legomenon* in the New Testament; see the expected time of respite (ἀνάψυξις) in Acts 3:20. Eduard Schweizer and Albrecht Dihle, "ψυχή κτλ.," *TDNT* 9 (1974) 663–65.

87   Godet, 2:180: the drop of water here mirrors the crumbs in v. 21.

88   On τέκνον ("child"), see Plummer, 395: the refusal is as polite as it is final. The expression εἶπεν δέ is characteristic of Luke; see Dupont, "Après-mort," 16 n. 47.

89   In Hades, according to the Greeks, there were two rivers: one of forgetfulness and the other of remembrance; see Plummer, 395.

90   The word ἀπολαμβάνω ("to receive one's portion," "to receive fully") here carries the nuance "not to expect anything else." Luke uses this verb five times in the Gospel (if one includes 18:30); Bornhäuser (*Sondergut*, 149) proposes translating this verb as "to grasp," "to monopolize," or "to seize" (coming from a hypothetical original Semitic root). The form ὀδυνᾶσαι is common (halfway between ὀδυνᾷ and ὀδυνάεσαι). Note the expression "your good things" concerning the rich man, who considers

them to be his own, as opposed to "the bad things," external to Lazarus, who had to endure them. He has not cursed, unlike the poor of Sir 4:5-6.

91   On these adverbs, see Plummer, 395; Dupont, "Après-mort," 17.

92   On παρακαλέω, see the commentary on 6:20-24 in vol. 1. On reversals of status, see the Magnificat (commentary on 1:51-53). In Judaism, see *'Abot R. Nat.* 12:6 (recension A): individual fate is not shared with another, neither here below nor in the hereafter; there is no consolation in the afterlife for those who eat and drink in this world. See Jacob Neusner, *The Fathers according to Rabbi Nathan: An Analytical Translation and Explanation* (BJS 114; Atlanta: Scholars Press, 1986) 94; Str-B 2:232.

93   On this χάσμα, see Grundmann (329), who envisions it filled with water. According to Bishop ("Yawning Chasm," 3–5), the original Palestinian hearers would have thought of a wadi, deeper than it was wide. To say that two parties are not in agreement or that they are having difficulty communicating, Palestinians often say, "You are in one wadi, and we are in another wadi."

94   On στηρίζω, see BAGD, s.v.

Communication between them is no longer possible nor allowed in either direction.[95] No bridge can be thrown between the two sides; the "chasm" is too "great" ($\mu\acute{\epsilon}\gamma\alpha$). No one can cross it. The text is insistent on the impossibility of crossing ("to pass" [$\delta\iota\alpha\beta\alpha\acute{\iota}\nu\omega$], "to cross" [$\delta\iota\alpha\pi\epsilon\rho\acute{\alpha}\omega$]). It is also insistent on the difference between the two places ("between us and you" [$\mu\epsilon\tau\alpha\xi\grave{\upsilon}\ \acute{\eta}\mu\hat{\omega}\nu\ \kappa\alpha\grave{\iota}\ \acute{\upsilon}\mu\hat{\omega}\nu$]). What are we to make of "in all these" (regions of Hades) ($\acute{\epsilon}\nu\ \pi\hat{\alpha}\sigma\iota\ \tauo\acute{\upsilon}\tauo\iota\varsigma$)?[96] "With all that,"[97] or "in spite of all that"?[98] This situation, although inescapable, is not necessarily to be eternally so. Although undeniably implacable, its validity holds for the time during which one awaits the events of the end-time, the last judgment, and the resurrection of the dead.[99]

■ **27-28** The story could have ended there, but it continues further, doubtless because the author of L wished it to.[100] The rich man does not give up and makes a new request to Abraham.[101] Even if this new petition is less selfish, it is no less motivated by self-interest, since the rich man is anxious to protect his clan or his extended family ("my father's house," where he has "five brothers," presumably all younger than himself, for whom he has been responsible since the death of their father.[102] What the rich man is asking for is not Lazarus's resurrection but an appearance of the ghost of this dead man.[103] There are good reasons for the difference in wording here from that in v. 24. It is no longer a question of having mercy on the rich man ("have mercy on me" [$\acute{\epsilon}\lambda\acute{\epsilon}\eta\sigma\acute{o}\nu\ \mu\epsilon$], v. 24), but rather of responding to his entreaty ("Then . . . I beg you" [$\acute{\epsilon}\rho\omega\tau\hat{\omega}\ \sigma\epsilon\ o\mathring{\upsilon}\nu$], v. 27). The sentence is ponderous, but the sequence of subordinate clauses in Greek introduced by $\acute{\iota}\nu\alpha$ and $\acute{\iota}\nu\alpha\ \mu\acute{\eta}$[104] itself clearly indicates what the dead man is after: having Lazarus sent back to earth to warn his five brothers[105] so that they can escape a fate as disastrous as the rich man's. The expression "this place of torment" is perfectly suited to a description of the land of the dead. It is in fact a "place" ($\tau\acute{o}\pi o\varsigma$, v. 28) where people receive their punishment in the form of torment.[106]

■ **29** Abraham responds in a Jewish fashion. One must listen, as always, to Moses and the prophets. Scripture, as represented by its two essential divisions,[107] is still per

---

95   It is impossible for the righteous ($\acute{o}\pi\omega\varsigma\ o\acute{\iota}\ \vartheta\acute{\epsilon}\lambda o\nu\tau\epsilon\varsigma\ \delta\iota\alpha\beta\hat{\eta}\nu\alpha\iota\ \mu\grave{\eta}\ \delta\acute{\upsilon}\nu\omega\nu\tau\alpha\iota$, "so that those who want to cross over . . . cannot do so") and forbidden for the reprobate ($\mu\eta\delta\grave{\epsilon}\ \delta\iota\alpha\pi\epsilon\rho\hat{\omega}\sigma\iota\nu$, "nor . . . cross over"), according to Plummer, 396. This is too subtle in my opinion; transfer is both forbidden and impossible for both groups.

96   Lagrange, 447.

97   Loisy, 418–19.

98   See Evans, "Uncomfortable Words," 229.

99   The fact remains that the good thief is expected immediately in paradise (and not in a pleasant region of rest for the dead) (23:43).

100   See p. 476 above.

101   He is simply called "father." Numerous manuscripts add "Abraham" to "father" to make it correspond to the vocatives in vv. 24 and 30.

102   The father of the rich man does not seem to appear among the living to whom Lazarus's witness should be directed.

103   On the desire to communicate with the dead, see Lorenzen, "Meditation," 40. Because of this eventual return of Lazarus to life, some have linked our parable with the raising of Lazarus in John 11; see Fitzmyer (2:1129), who rejects this comparison. In my opinion, the texts have only the name "Lazarus" in common. On the risks and successes of necromancy in ancient Israel, see W. Beillner, "Die Totenbeschwörung im ersten Buch Samuel (1 Sam. 28:3-25)" (Ph.D. diss., University of Vienna, 1954); Joanne K. Kuemmerlin-McLean, "Magic: Old Testament," *ABD* 4:468–71.

104   The first $\acute{\iota}\nu\alpha$ (v. 27) is complementary, the second final.

105   The wording is well chosen: "so that they will not also ($\kappa\alpha\grave{\iota}\ \alpha\mathring{\upsilon}\tauo\acute{\iota}$) come into this place of torment." Pax ("Der Reiche," 266) correctly notes that this elder brother would have had to instruct his five brothers on the proper respect for the law, rather than the pleasures of life; on this obligation to instruct one's family, see *b. Ber.* 7.31 (47b): the ignorant are especially the ones who do not educate their children in the law. See Jacob Neusner, *The Talmud of Babylonia: An American Translation* (30 vols.; Chico, Calif.: Scholars Press, 1984) 1:320.

106   Luke utilizes the singular $\acute{\eta}\ \beta\acute{\alpha}\sigma\alpha\nu o\varsigma$, which means "testing," "investigation," "punishment," or "torment."

107   On the Law and the Prophets, cf. Luke 24:44, where the Gospel writer uses a tripartite division: Law of Moses, Prophets, and Psalms. The canon of the Hebrew Scriptures, composed traditionally of two parts, becomes the definitive Jewish canon in three parts. See Jean-Daniel Kaestli and Otto Wermelinger, eds., *Le Canon de l'Ancien Testament: Sa formation et son histoire* (Geneva: Labor et Fides, 1984).

ceived as an oral message conveyed by witnesses that God has chosen to represent him. The listening that the patriarch calls on the rich man to enact joins obedience to hearing (cf. 9:35).[108] So the tormented rich man makes three successive requests. Although the first one is a part of the original parable, the second one—to be found in vv. 27-29—corresponds to a first stage of evolution of the parable in a Judeo-Christian environment, where obedience to the law was a condition of salvation.[109] The efficacious witness that the rich man was counting on ("so that he may call out" [ὅπως διαμαρτύρηται], v. 28) was neither a reminder of God's commandments nor a recalling of the Christian message, but a miracle that would provide a convincing demonstration. Abraham refuses to grant any miraculous sign that would be divorced from faith, and especially one that would not involve any obedience.[110]

■ **30-31** The last two verses seem to have been added, this time by Luke himself, who was anxious to give the story a Christian touch and to spell out the authentic impact of the gospel message. These verses, we might add, were written under the influence of the failure of Christian proclamation in Israel; even Jesus' resurrection ("if someone comes to them from the dead . . .") did not bring about repentance and the conversion of the chosen people (the verb "they will repent" [μετανοήσουσιν] is Lukan). Transmitted via human speech, namely, the proclamation of the gospel, Jesus' resurrection does not convince by virtue of the strength of the evidence or the intrinsic compulsion of the miracle. Just as obedience to the law is necessarily a free choice, so too are conversion and faith matters left to the risk of choice. Since the resurrection, Jesus is accessible only through preaching, and one accepts him or refuses him by faith and not by sight.[111]

The risen Christ does not allow human beings access to God without their practicing obedience and love of neighbor any more than Moses and the prophets did. Conviction ("will they be convinced" [πεισθήσονται]) is not solely dependent on exterior factors (the Law, the Prophets, Christ) but also, and particularly, on the inner attitude of those who decide to believe, to place their trust in God, and to love him.[112]

History of Interpretation

Marcion preserved the parable in his Gospel.[113] Nevertheless, his characteristic dualism led him to make some distinctions. On the one hand, there was retribution in the form of torments and comfort given by the Demiurge to those who worshiped the Law and the Prophets; on the other, Abraham's bosom and the share in heaven were destined for the true worshipers of Christ and his God.

The African theologian Tertullian, of course, refused to distinguish between two gods. In his eyes it would be wrong, in particular, to contrast the comfort offered those who obey the law with Abraham's bosom promised to those who believe in the Son of God. On the other hand, as Tertullian was at pains to stress, Lazarus's fate, as described in the parable, is still not equivalent to eternal salvation. We should understand Abraham's bosom in the sense of "some temporary receptacle of faithful souls, wherein is even now delineated an image of the future" (*Adv. Marc.* 4.34.14). In this way, Tertullian made a chronological distinction between comfort immediately after one's death and later eternal salvation after the

---

108 See the commentary on 9:34-35 in vol. 1.

109 On διαμαρτύρομαι ("to protest by taking the gods and man as witness," "to adjure," "to call out," "to provide testimony"), see BAGD, s.v.

110 On this second refusal of Abraham, see Lagrange, 447.

111 Bartsch (*Entmythologisierende Auslegung*, 184–85) emphasizes the importance of the end of the parable and observes that the New Testament reflection on signs refers to the reading of the Scriptures; see Lorenzen, "Meditation," 40.

112 There are two textual problems in v. 31: Nestle-Aland retains ἀναστῇ ("resurrects"), while 𝔓⁷⁵ and some other manuscripts read ἐγερθῇ ("awak-

ens," "revives"), and W it and sy^s.c read ἀπέλθῃ ("to go away"), Dr¹ and (Ir^lat) read ἀναστῇ καὶ ἀπέλθῃ πρὸς αὐτούς ("resurrected and went away with them"). They propose moreover to read πεισθήσονται ("they were persuaded") and reject πιστεύσουσιν ("they believe"), attested by D^lat sy^s.c.p. and Ir^lat. On these variants, see Tanghe, "Abraham," 557–63.

113 See Adolf Harnack, *Marcion: Das Evangelium vom fremden Gott* (Bibliothek Klassischer Texte; repr., Darmstadt: Wissenschaftliche Buchgesellschaft, 1996) 220*–22*.

last judgment,[114] whereas Marcion contrasted the comfort granted by the Demiurge with the eternal salvation offered by the true God. Tertullian did, however, stress the fact that there is a resemblance between this temporary protection and eternal salvation.

There are two more comments that need to be made about Tertullian's interpretation. On the one hand, all nations can gather in "Abraham's bosom," since the patriarch is called "the ancestor of a multitude of nations" (Gen 17:4 NRSV) (*Adv. Marc.* 4.34.12). On the other hand, in spite of the abrupt transition, there is a thematic continuity in Luke 16, a relationship between the parable and the preceding verses (dealing with the time of John the Baptist [v. 16] and divorce [v. 18]). This relationship is one of theological correspondence: Lazarus is to John the Baptist what the rich man is to Herod (did not that king put to death the prophet who had been accusing him of entering into an ungodly marriage?) (*Adv. Marc.* 4.34.9). We might say that Lazarus corresponds to the oppressed righteous.

The parable got dragged into another controversy, the one about the nature and the destiny of the soul. Origen held that after death the soul puts on another body, which serves it as both medium and clothing. To his way of thinking Lazarus's temporary fate between his earthly life and his final resurrection illustrated how this other body operated.[115]

The story of Lazarus and the evil rich man has remained topical in succeeding centuries. The Cappa-

docian father Gregory of Nyssa used the parable in his theological treatises and his liturgical practice in order to call to mind the afterlife and to exhort believers to practice a purification which, if not accomplished here below, has to be done after death. Christians must decide if they want to have their possessions in this world or the next. For Gregory, as for Origen or Tertullian, the parable calls to mind a state that is intermediary between this life and the resurrection. Unlike the Alexandrian father Origen, however, he did not conceive of the souls of the deceased as receiving a body to serve as clothing and medium for this transitory stage. For him, all the description of the beyond found in Luke 16 applies to the fate of the soul.[116]

Gregory of Nyssa was also a preacher, so for him, as for many other bishops and priests, the story of Lazarus and the evil rich man could not fail to demand attention.[117] What he got out of the story as a pastor was somewhat different from what he read in it as a theologian.[118] The contrast between the rich and the poor struck him. The poor man, with his sores, represents the countless disinherited here below, whereas the rich man, with his greed, his contempt for the poor, and his forgetting God, serves as a negative example. Gregory spoke in the context of the last judgment, where the situations will be reversed.[119]

Here, by way of example, are certain striking elements in the exegesis of a Western theologian of the Middle Ages, Albert the Great, whose commentaries were

---

114   In the same paragraph, Tertullian can also say that the bosom of Abraham is superior to hell but inferior to heaven. He proposes an intermediary stay for the souls of the righteous until the consummation of all things.

115   The opinion of Origen is preserved in Methodius of Olympius's work, "De resur., III. 17–18" in G. N. Bonwetsch, ed., *Methodius* (GCS 27; Leipzig: Deichert, 1917) 413–16. See Alexandre, "Interprétation," 430–31. In the same passage, Origen criticizes the "simple" who believe that Lazarus and the rich man merely continue their own existence after death within their bodies. He situates himself on the side of the "rigorous" who place the retribution of the two men before the final resurrection.

116   Gregory of Nyssa, *De anima et resurrectione* (*PG* 46:80b–88a); *De hominis opificio* 27 (*PG* 44:225–29).

117   There are no fewer than six homilies of John Chrysostom related to our parable: *PG* 48:963–1016,

1027–54. See Hermann Josef Sieben (*Kirchenväter-homilien zum Neuen Testament: Ein Repertorium der Textausgaben und Übersetzungen, mit einem Anhang der Kirchenväterkommentare* [Instrumenta patristica 22; Steenbrugis: Abbatia S. Petri; The Hague: Nijhoff, 1991] 80–81), who also mentions around ten other preachers. The article by Alexandre ("Interprétation," 425) further expands the list.

118   My presentation of Gregory of Nyssa is inspired by Alexandre's study, "Interpretation." In these pages on the history of interpretation I also draw on the preparatory work of Ms. Denise Jornod, who was my assistant in Geneva.

119   He does this in two sermons: *De pauperibus amandis*, I (*PG* 46:468CD), and ibid., II (*PG* 46:484D–485B). See the edition of A. van Heck in G. Heil et al., ed., *Gregorii Nysseni Opera IX* (Leiden: Brill, 1969) 106, 122–23; see also two relevant texts on the beati-

obviously based on the Vulgate (*Evang. Luc.* 16.19–31 [435–54]). This Doctor of the Church was careful to first sketch out each argument that he was going to develop. Next, he made sure to buttress each interpretation with quotations from Holy Scripture. He also strove to bring out the parable's structure. Finally, he proceeded step by step through a word-by-word exegesis of the text. The use of the Latin word *homo* in referring to the rich man gave Albert the chance to describe this character as being composed of "earth" and "intellect" (this intellect permitting him to choose between good and evil), inclined to follow what is earthly, and at the same time attracted upwards by his arrogance (435). The reason that this man had no name was that he deserved none. His richness was an evil richness, the kind that keeps one from entering God's kingdom. There are five reasons for criticizing his extravagant clothing, criticisms that Albert found a way to relate to the prelates of his own time. As for the banquets organized by the rich man, they are to be taken in either a literal or a figurative sense (435–38). Albert next applied the same kind of exegesis to Lazarus, who was not only a poor man but also a beggar; he was put to the test by God, introduced to the rich man to incite the latter's generosity, supplied with a name, and covered with sores in order to test the mercy of passersby. The dogs functioned as a curse that God transformed into a blessing (Albert also had in mind the "Lord's dogs," that is, the preachers of his time). When offered by God, death can be a blessing; as a matter of fact, Lazarus's death was an end not only to his life but also to his pitiful state. The angels, who corroborated his merits, carried him to be in Abraham's bosom, which is not paradise but the place where the patriarchs and the prophet wait for the Lord (here Albert cited Jerome and Gregory; besides this limbo for the fathers, he mentions a limbo for children, and purgatory) (438–45). As for the other character, he turned from being rich in material goods to being rich in punishments. His exegesis goes on in the same style: the man who was punished appealed to Abraham, since he remembered the patriarch's intercession on behalf of Sodom (Genesis 18). If he hoped for Lazarus's finger to do something for him, it was because he counted on the Holy Spirit (cf. Luke 11:20). He was to receive nothing from the tip of that finger, just as Lazarus had not received the slightest crumb from the rich man's table (445–49). Finally, Albert was surprised at the sudden interest the rich man showed in his five brothers. In Albert's view, when this man thought of his family, he was still protecting his own interest (he would suffer even more in the event that his brothers were to join him) (452).[120]

Finally, let me note that Melanchthon drew the following conclusions from the parable.[121] There is solace in the face of the scandal of the cross, in that extreme suffering does not mean that God abandons or rejects his own.[122] Lazarus is the symbol of the church in all ages when it is poor and humiliated. Yet God protects faithful believers and stays with them even through their death.[123] The bosom of Abraham does not refer to the limbo for the fathers but rather to eternal beatitude offered to those who, like Abraham, are justified by faith.[124] Even if the comforts and punishments in the parable are not to be taken literally, their reality is not to be questioned.[125]

---

tudes, *Oratio* III (*PG* 44:1229C–1232B) and *Oratio* V (PG 44:1261D).

120 Eckhart, Sermon 7 (*Sermones*, 75–79), concentrates his attention on v. 19; an anonymous sermon for the First Sunday after Pentecost in Old German (number 44, Altdeutsche Predigten, II, 117–20) identifies the rich man with the Jewish people and Lazarus with the Gentiles.

121 Melanchthon, *Annotationes*, cols. 300–302, 523–28; *Postillae*, cols. 28–42.

122 Melanchthon, *Annotationes*, cols. 301–2; *Postillae*, col. 28.

123 Melanchthon, *Annotationes*, cols. 523–25. Melanchthon is interested in the etymology of the name Lazarus ("God comes to help," "Gotthelf") (ibid., col. 524; and *Postillae*, col. 33).

124 Melanchthon, *Annotationes*, col. 525.

125 Melanchthon, *Postillae*, col. 35. In addition, there exist several sermons of Luther: Predigt vom 6/22/1522 (WA 10.3, 176–200; Mülhaupt, 3:251–61); Predigt vom 6/6/1535 (WA 41, 293–300; Mülhaupt, 3:261–68). For other excerpts, see Mülhaupt, 3:268–73.

Conclusion

Like any parable, the story of the rich man and poor Lazarus describes one reality in order to point to another. Each of these two realities is always different from the other. The first one, the one that is explicit, has to do with the world of the dead, whereas the second, the one that is implicit, has to do with the world of the living. Nevertheless, the language of parables brings these two together and is not alone in doing so. Divine will and human responsibility also deal with them. The narrator and the reader in his wake understand that they have in hand what they need to know about the problem, as well as the keys to paradise. Their main advantage is that they are still alive.

So they recall "Moses and the prophets" and the ethical imperatives that these latter lay on each and every one (v. 29). Moreover, they know, thanks to the Christian message, that someone has risen from the dead (v. 31). They also are not unaware of the risk associated with the gravity of their situation, in which they are reluctant to believe and resist being "convinced" (v. 31). Finally, they have the parable right under their noses. But the text is worthless unless it triggers the operation of the will, and this triggering will not happen apart from God's help, directly through his Spirit, and indirectly through Scripture. They are thereby reminded of the ethical dimension of their lives: "You will always have the poor with you" (John 12:8). The author of L and, following him, Luke, hope that the readers will follow their invitation. For the description of the fate of the rich man is not just a parable. The God who pardons will also ask for a reckoning. Even Paul, the proponent of justification by faith, does not sidestep the theme of retribution (cf. Rom 14:10-12 and 2 Cor 5:10). There is no cheap grace.

Luke 17:1-10
Scandals, Pardon, Faith, and Service
Bibliography Verses 1-6

Barth, Gerhard, "Auseinandersetzungen um die Kirchenzucht im Umkreis des Matthäusevangeliums," *ZNW* 69 (1978) 158–77, esp. 169–74.

Caba, *Oración de petición*, 124–46.

Catchpole, David R., "Reproof and Reconciliation in the Q Community: A Study of the Tradition-History of Mt 18,15-17.21-22/Lk 17,3-4," SNTU 8 (1983) 79–90.

Dagron, Alain, *Aux jours du Fils de l'Homme: Essai sur le service de la parole. Luc XVII 1 à XVIII 8* (Lecture Sémiotique et Propositions Théologiques Série Biblique 2; Lyon: Profac, 1990).

Idem, "De la lecture ou propos sur le texte en quête de lecteur," *SémBib* 51 (1988) 35–40.

Delebecque, Édouard, *Études grecques sur l'Évangile de Luc* (Collection d'études anciennes; Paris: Belles Lettres, 1976) 99–107.

Delobel, Joel, "Sayings," 456.

Deming, Will, "Mark 9:41—10:12, Matthew 5:27-32, and B. Nid. 13b: A First Century Discussion of Male Sexuality," *NTS* 36 (1990) 130–41.

Derrett, J. Duncan M., "Moving Mountains and Uprooting Trees (Mk 11:22; Mt 17:20; Lk 17:6)," *BO* 30 (1988) 231–44.

Idem, "Two 'Harsh' Sayings of Christ Explained," *DRev* 103 (1985) 218–29.

Duplacy, Jean, "La foi qui déplace les montagnes (Mt 17,20; 21,21 et par.)," in M. Jourjon et al., eds., *A la rencontre de Dieu: Mémorial Albert Gelin* (BFCTL 8; Le Puy: X. Mappus, 1961) 273–87.

Frizzi, Giuseppe, "L'ἀπόστολος delle tradizioni sinottiche (Mc, Q, Mt, Lc e Atti)," *RivB* 22 (1974) 3–37.

George, A., "La foi des apôtres, efficacité et gratuité: Lc 17, 5-10," *AsSeign* 58 (1974) 68–77.

Hahn, Ferdinand, "Jesu Wort vom bergversetzenden Glauben," *ZNW* 76 (1985) 149–69.

Houzet, P., "Les serviteurs de l'Évangile (Luc 17, 5-10) sont-ils inutiles? Ou un contresens traditionnel," *RB* 99 (1992) 335–72.

Kafka, Gustav, "Bild und Wort in den Evangelien," *MThZ* 2 (1951) 263–65.

Klein, *Barmherzigkeit*, 120–21.

Lafon, Guy, "Loi, promesse, grâce: une lecture de Luc 17, 5-10," in idem, *Esquisses pour un christianisme* (Cogitatio fidei 96; Paris: Cerf, 1979) 203–9.

Lührmann, Dieter, *Glaube im frühen Christentum* (Gütersloh: Gütersloher Verlagshaus Mohn, 1976) 17–30.

Idem, *Logienquelle*, 111–14.

MacGillivray, "Luke xvii. 3," *ExpT* 25 (1913–14) 333.

Michel, Otto, "'Diese Kleinen'—eine Jüngerbezeichnung Jesu," *ThStK* 108 (1937–38) 401–15.

Moffatt, James, "Jesus upon 'Stumbling Blocks,'" *ExpT* 26 (1914–15) 407–9.

Müller, Karlheinz, *Anstoss und Gericht: Eine Studie zum jüdischen Hintergrund des paulinischen Skandalon-Begriffes* (SANT 19; Munich: Kösel, 1969) 42–45.

Pesch, Wilhelm, *Matthäus der Seelsorger: Das neue Verständnis der Evangelien dargestellt am Beispiel von Matthäus 18* (SBS 2; Stuttgart: Katholisches Bibelwerk, 1966) 21–25.

Schlosser, Jacques, "Lk 17,2 und die Logienquelle," SNTU 8 (1983) 70–78.

Schmid, *Matthäus und Lukas*, 304–5, 308–9.

Schulz, *Q*, 320–22.

Schwarz, Günther, "πίστιν ὡς κόκκον σινάπεως," *BN* 25 (1984) 27–35.

Shelton, Robert M., "Luke 17:1-10," *Int* 31 (1977) 280–85.

Trilling, Wolfgang, *Hausordnung Gottes: Eine Auslegung von Matthäus 18* (Die Welt der Bibel 10; Düsseldorf: Patmos, 1960) 30–35, 57–60.

Wilhelms, Eino K., *Die Tempelsteuerperikope Matthäus 17, 17-24 in der Exegese der griechischen Väter der Alten Kirche* (SESJ 34; Helsinki: Kirjapaino, 1980).

Zmijewski, Josef, "Der Glaube und seine Macht: Eine traditionsgeschichtliche Untersuchung zu Mt 17,20; 21,21; Mk 11,23; Lk 17,6," in idem and Ernst Nellessen, eds., *Begegnung mit dem Wort: Festschrift für Heinrich Zimmermann* (BBB 53; Bonn: Hanstein, 1980) 81–103.

Bibliography Verses 7-10

Bailey, *Eyes*, 114–26.

Beyer, *Syntax*, 1:287–93.

Bornhäuser, Karl, "Das Gleichnis von den 'unützen' Knechten: Bemerkungen zu Lk 17, 5-10," *PBl* 82 (1939–40) 455–58.

Bultmann, *Marburg Sermons*, 148–58.

Derrett, J. Duncan M., "The Parable of the Profitable Servant (Luke xvii. 7-10)," in idem, *Studies*, 4:157–66.

Dupont, Jacques, "Le maître et son serviteur (Lc 17,7-10)," *EThL* 60 (1984) 233–51.

Eichholz, Georg, "Meditation über das Gleichnis von Lk. 17, 7-10," in K. Halaski and W. Herrenbrück, eds., *Kirche, Konfession, Ökumene: Festschrift für Professor D. Dr. Wilhelm Niesel Moderator des Reformierten Bundes zum 70. Geburtstag* (Neukirchen-Vluyn: Neukirchener Verlag, 1973) 25–33.

George, A., "La foi des apôtres, efficacité et gratuité: Lc 17,5-10," *AsSeign* 58 (1974) 68–77.

Greeven, Heinrich, "Wer unter euch . . . ?," *WD* 3 (1952) 86–101.

Heininger, *Metaphorik*, 191–97.

Holstein, H., "Serviteurs inutiles?" *BVC* 48 (1962) 39–45.

Houzet, Pierre, "Les serviteurs de l'Évangile (Luc 17, 5-10) sont-ils inutiles? Ou un contresens traditionnel," *RB* 99 (1992) 335–72.

Jeremias, *Parables*, 193.

Jülicher, *Gleichnisreden*, 2:11–23.

Kilgallen, John J., "What Kind of Servants Are We? (Luke 17,10)," *Bib* 63 (1982) 549–51.

Maasewerd, T., "Unbekanntes Evangelium," *BLit* 28 (1960–61) 291–96.

Minear, Paul S., "A Note on Luke 17:7-10," *JBL* 93 (1974) 82–87.

Moffatt, James, "The Story of the Farmer and His Man," *Exp* 8/23 (1922) 1–16.

Neuhäusler, Engelbert, *Anspruch und Antwort Gottes: Zur Lehre von den Weisungen innerhalb der synoptischen Jesusverkündigung* (Düsseldorf: Patmos, 1962) 34–36.

Pesch, Wilhelm, *Der Lohngedanke in der Lehre Jesu verglichen mit der religiösen Lohnlehre des Spätjudentums* (MThS 7; Munich: Zink, 1955) 20–22.

Prast, Franz, *Presbyter und Evangelium in nachapostolischer Zeit: Die Abschiedsrede des Paulus in Milet (Apg. 20, 17-38) im Rahmen der lukanischen Konzeption der Evangeliumsverkündigung* (FB 29; Stuttgart: Katholisches Bibelwerk, 1979) 249–53.

Riggenbach, Eduard, "Ein Beitrag zum Verständnis der Parabel vom arbeitenden Knecht Luk. 17, 7-10," *NKZ* 34 (1923) 439–43.

Schmid, Josef, "Zwei unbekannte Gleichnisse Jesu," *GuL* 33 (1960) 428–33, esp. 431–33.

Sudbrack, Josef, "'Armselige Knechte sind wir. Unsere Schuldigkeit war es, was wir taten': Meditation über Lk 17,1-10," *GuL* 41 (1968) 308–12.

Ward, A. Marcus, "Uncomfortable Words, IV: Unprofitable Servants," *ExpT* 81 (1969–70) 200–203.

Weiser, *Knechtsgleichnisse*, 105–20.

1/ He said to his disciples, "It is impossible for causes of stumbling not to come, but woe to the person by whom they come! 2/ It would be better for that person if a millstone were to be hung around their neck and they were to be thrown into the sea than for them to cause one of these little ones to stumble. 3/ Be on your guard!

"If another disciple sins, you must rebuke the offender, and if there is repentance, you must forgive them. 4/ And if the same person sins against you seven times a day, and turns back to you seven times and says, 'I repent,' you must forgive them." 5/ The apostles said to the Lord, "Increase our faith!" 6/ The Lord replied, "If you had faith the size of a mustard seed, you could say to this mulberry tree, 'Uproot yourself and go plant yourself in the sea,' and it would obey you.

7/ "Who among you would say to your slave who has just come in from plowing or tending sheep in the field, 'Come here at once and take your place at the table'? 8/ Would you not rather say to him, 'Prepare a dinner for me, put on your apron and serve me while I eat and drink; later you yourself may eat and drink'? 9/ Are you grateful to the slave for doing what was commanded? 10/ So you also, when you have done all that you were ordered to do, say, 'We are worthless slaves; we have done what we ought to have done!'"

After having spoken to his enemies (cf. 16:14-15), Jesus resumes (cf. 16:1) the teaching that he aims at his disciples (v. 1). There are four themes—causes of stumbling, forgiveness, faith, and service—that are taken up one after the other, without any apparent sign of a logical sequence. Once one becomes better acquainted with these verses, however, they do hang together, and one sees the theme of community life with the personal responsibilities and ministerial duties that they imply.

Analysis

Verses 1-3a, which deal with causes of stumbling, have parallels in Mark 9:42 and Matt 18:6-7. However, Luke is probably not dependent here on the triple tradition, whose main witness is Mark, but rather on L or Q.[1] Had he been following Mark, he would probably not have omitted the mention of the believers from Mark 9:42 ("one of these little ones who believe" [ἕνα τῶν μικρῶν τούτων τῶν πιστευόντων]).[2] Moreover, he is at pains to follow the order of his source by first calling attention to the inevitability of causes of stumbling (v. 1), and then the deadly but nevertheless preferable fate of the person who is drowned (v. 2). Matthew, who combines Mark and another tradition, perhaps Q, has the elements in reverse order (cf. Matt 18:6-7).

It is not easy to specify what, in these first verses of the chapter, is due to the personal rewriting of the Gospel author. The introduction (v. 1a) and the exhortation (v. 3a), without parallels, are from his hand, as well as the studied expression ἀνένδεκτόν ἐστιν, "it is impossible"[3] (v. 1b; Luke was perhaps anxious to avoid misunderstandings that might arise if he used the word ἀνάγκη, "necessity," Matt 18:7). In v. 2, on the other hand, the

Greek verbs for "it would be better" (λυσιτελεῖ), "to be hung" (περίκειμαι),[4] and "throw" (ῥίπτω) are not typical Lukan words. They must come from his source. If Luke has followed Q[5] rather than L here, then he is more faithful to it than Matthew. The "millstone" (λίθος μυλικός) must also come from tradition. Matthew 18:6, here following Mark 9:42, uses another Greek expression for "millstone" (μύλος ὀνικός, "a millstone turned by a donkey").

The teaching about causes of stumbling belonged to the oral catechetical teaching of the early church. Paul had already referred to it in Rom 14:13b ("one must never put an obstacle or stumbling block in the way of a fellow Christian")[6]; *1 Clem.* 46.8 has its own version of the maxim on the millstone,[7] and the *Pseudo-Clementine Homilies* transmit a form of the maxim on the inexorable that includes repetition.[8]

The two parallel sentences on forgiveness (vv. 3b-4) that are transmitted by Matthew, at some distance from each other, in the same chapter (Matt 18:15 and 18:21-22) are generally attributed to Q.[9] David R. Catchpole has reconstructed the text of Q with the help of Matt 18:15-17 (without the scriptural quotation of v. 16b) and 18:22, has compared the fragment to various Jewish disciplinary texts (*T. Gad* 6; 1QS 5–6; CD 9.2–8), and sees it as an application of Lev 19:17 ("You are not to nurse hatred toward your brother. Reprove your fellow-countryman frankly, and so you will have no share in his guilt." [*REB*]). Even though this analysis of the literary genre is interesting, it is not convincing once one examines the history of the tradition. It would be better to admit that the Jewish Christian Matthew reworked the sayings in Q in the direction of ecclesiastical discipline.[10] And it is Luke who has most faithfully preserved the original

---

1   See Schmid, *Matthäus und Lukas*, 305; and Ernst, 477–78.

2   See Schlosser, "Lk 17,2," 74–76.

3   See n. 31 below.

4   This verb reappears in Acts 28:20, referring to a chain.

5   This is the opinion of Schlosser, "Lk 17,2."

6   See Müller, *Anstoss und Gericht*, 42–45.

7   "Malheur à cet homme-là! Il vaudrait mieux pour lui n'être pas né que de scandaliser un seul de mes élus: il serait meilleur pour lui qu'on lui attaché une meule et qu'on le précipite au fond de la mer que de détourner un seul de mes élus" (A. Jaubert).

8   *Pseudo-Clementine Homilies* 12.29.1: "The prophet of truth has said: The good things must come and blessedness (he said) to him on whom they come. Likewise, bad things must come as well, and woe to him to whom they come."

9   See Kloppenborg, *Q Parallels*, 184–85; Funk, *Five Gospels*, 362. Schmid (*Matthäus und Lukas*, 308–9) offers a helpful synoptic comparison.

10   See Luz, *Matthew*, 2:421–23, 448–50, 465.

wording of Q.[11] To be sure, the Gospel writer has taken some liberties, which are hard to detect, with respect to Q.[12] The two maxims (vv. 3b and 4) must always have circulated together, for it is from their juxtaposition that the meaning derives its energy.[13] The guilty person who repents must be forgiven without limit ("seven times").

This obligation to forgive also constituted part of the catechetical equipment which each Christian was provided. One ancient Christian text has preserved a trace of this oral teaching (*Did.* 15.3). There is nothing to indicate that this rule about forgiveness was always linked to the comment on causes of stumbling (vv. 1-3a) or to the one about faith (vv. 5-6).

This third unit (vv. 5-6) is composed of an interjection by the disciples and Jesus' reply. The vocabulary and style of v. 5 betray a creation on the part of the Gospel writer. The terms "apostles" and "Lord," used here, are of late origin,[14] and the interruption of a speech by a question or a request made by the listeners is characteristic of Luke's style (see 11:45; 14:15). The introduction in v. 6 ("The Lord replied") also belongs to Luke's redactional activity.

Jesus' maxim itself (v. 6) obviously came from tradition. It was even so popular that it is found in the triple tradition (Mark), in the double tradition (Q), and in the *Gospel of Thomas* (*Gos. Thom.* 48 and 106).[15] Mark and Matthew attach the sentence from the triple tradition to the episode of the withered fig tree (Mark 11:22-23 par. Matt 21:21). As for the parallel in the double tradition, Matthew, who is not reluctant to use doublets, quotes it in the conclusion that Jesus gives to the story of the healing of the "lunatic" (that is, the man suffering from epilepsy [Matt 17:20]) and he is the only one to place it in this location (it is absent from Mark 9:14-29 and Luke 9:37-43). Luke alone keeps Q's wording, which he fits into a speech by Jesus (here, in Luke 17:6). It is not out of the question, however, that the verse quoted by Luke comes from L rather than from Q.[16] There are, in fact, two significant differences between Matt 17:20 and Luke 17:6; in Matthew we are dealing with a mountain, whereas in Luke we have a mulberry tree with solid roots.[17] Moreover, the mountain is asked to move itself "from here to there," while the mulberry tree is asked to uproot itself and plant itself "in the sea." It may be, however, that the mulberry tree corresponds to Q and that Matthew, by speaking of the mountain twice (Matt 17:20 and 21:21),[18] harmonized here with the other wording of the maxim, the one in the triple tradition. There is, then, considerable variation in the vocabulary between the two Gospels, even though the sentence structure is identical in Matthew and Luke. The stability of the expression "have faith the size of a mustard seed" alone is sufficient testimony to the fact that these words had a decisive importance for the early Christians.

The version found in *Gos. Thom.* 48, which is simple and apparently archaic, reminds us, by its structure, of the wording of Q. However, it suggests the fate of a mountain rather than of a tree. What is curious about it is that it does not bring up the theme of faith in God, but rather that of harmony among human beings. In this

11 See Schulz, *Q*, 320–22.

12 The words ὕπαγε ("go") and μεταξὺ σοῦ καὶ αὐτοῦ μόνου ("just between you and him") are Matthew's additions, just as the dialogue that follows is redactional (Matt 18:21-22). On the other hand, Luke preferred to write "if he repents" (v. 3b) rather than to copy out the phrase from Q "if he listens to you" (Matt 18:15). The same is undoubtedly true for the injunction "forgive him" (Luke 17:3b; Q has "you have won your brother over" [Matt 18:15]). The words "in a day" (Luke 17:4), which intensify both the problem and its solution, must also be the result of a decision Luke made. *Didache* 15.3 (ἐλέγχετε δὲ ἀλλήλους) suggests that ἔλεγξον αὐτόν ("show him his fault," Matt 18:15) is the traditional wording, while its Lukan counterpart ἐπιτίμησον αὐτῷ ("rebuke him," Luke 17:3b) is redactional.

13 I diverge from Bultmann (*History*, 86), who argues that v. 4 was a secondary development apart from v. 3. Nevertheless, one detail breaks the symmetry: v. 3b ends with an imperative, but v. 4 ends with a future.

14 For apostles, see 9:10; 11:49; 22:14; 24:10. For Lord, see, e.g., 10:1; 24:3. See also Bovon, *Theologian*, 214–18, 407–16.

15 See Kloppenborg, *Q Parallels*, 186–87.

16 I am unaware if another commentator has already offered this suggestion.

17 On the mulberry tree, see the commentary below.

18 See Schulz, *Q*, 466.

case we are dealing with peace that is reestablished in the home and that is able to move mountains. How can we explain this ethical orientation?[19]

The parable of the slave (vv. 7-10) is transmitted only by Luke. That is why scholars ordinarily attribute its origin to L.[20] There are four questions that need to be asked about this parable. How much did Luke rewrite it? What was the structure of the story in tradition before the rewriting? To what literary genre does this brief piece belong? Is it possible to speak of authenticity in connection with this parable?

Although it is not obvious, Luke's hand is nevertheless recognizable throughout the story,[21] as witnessed by the following indications: the way the story is introduced (cf. 11:5) and the adverb "at once" (εὐθέως; cf. 12:36) in v. 7; the felicitous use of the Greek participle in the elegant expression translated "put on your apron and serve me" (περιζωσάμενος διακόνει μοι; cf. 12:37b), as well as the expression "later" (μετὰ ταῦτα; cf. 5:27) and the pair of verbs "eat" and "drink" (cf. 5:30, 33) in v. 8; the Greek noun χάρις, here used in the accusative in the sense of "gratitude" (cf. 6:32-34), and the verb "command" (διατάσσω; cf. 8:55) in v. 9; and finally, the generalizing phrase "all that you were ordered to do" (πάντα τὰ διαταχθέντα ὑμῖν) in v. 10. We may conclude this point by quoting Jacques Dupont: "The traces left by his [Luke's] reworking are real but limited."[22]

There is no doubt that vv. 7-10 form a unity. It may be asked, however, if, in the course of the parable's transmission, certain elements have not come to be acciden-

tally attached to the earliest form of it.[23] It is likely that a parable consisting of successive questions came from tradition and had its origin in a Semitic environment. By their weightiness, vv. 8-9 appear to be early. The same cannot be said about v. 10, which is not essential to the speaker's didactic purpose.[24] The first part of this verse lazily leans on the preceding verse, and its second part turns the perspective around (the listeners have to change from thinking of themselves as masters to thinking of themselves as slaves). This reversal of roles could be a narrative subtlety[25] or it could be an indication of a secondary development.[26] In my opinion, the moralizing perspective of the context of the sentence confirms that this conclusion is an addition. If this hypothesis proves to be correct, then—as usual—it is the end of the story that has been subjected to elaboration.[27] As we will explain in our exegesis, this elaboration must have taken place before Luke's redaction.

As is the case with several other parables derived from L,[28] the story begins with a question: "Who among you . . . ?" This first question (v. 7), a rhetorical one, expects a negative answer: "No one does." The second question (v. 8), which is also rhetorical, once more appeals to the listeners' good sense. Here, it says, is what everyone is used to doing. A third question draws the conclusion: a master is not especially grateful to his slave when the slave correctly carries out his task (v. 9). Originally, the transfer from the social sphere to the religious one was left up to the listeners' initiative. The parable was content to provoke a responsible reaction[29] by virtue of a rheto-

---

19 On *Gos. Thom.* 48, see Fieger (*Thomasevangelium,* 153–55, 263–65), who, in the light of *Gos. Thom.* 106, understands the logion in a Gnostic rather than an ethical sense: the house is the Gnostic himself, which seeks unity with himself. See also Crossan, *Fragments,* 294–99.

20 See Petzke, *Sondergut,* 151–53; Fitzmyer, 2:1145.

21 On the Lukisms of these verses, see Weiser, *Knechtsgleichnisse,* 108–13; Wilhelm Bruners, *Die Reinigung der zehn Aussätzigen und die Heilung des Samariters: Lk 17, 11-19. Ein Beitrag zur lukanischen Interpretation der Reinigung von Aussätzigen* (FB 23; Stuttgart: Katholisches Bibelwerk, 1977) 313–16; Dupont, "Le maître," 239–43.

22 Dupont, "Le maître," 242.

23 Several opinions have been offered on this subject. According to John Dominic Crossan (*In Parables: The Challenge of the Historical Jesus* [New York: Harper

& Row, 1973] 107–8), vv. 8-10 are secondary. According to George ("La foi des apôtres," 73–74), vv. 8b-9 are secondary. Weiser (*Knechtsgleichnisse,* 107–10) argues for v. 8 only; Schweizer (175) thinks that part of v. 8 and v. 10 are secondary, while Minear ("Note on Luke 17:7-10") thinks that only v. 10 is secondary. See Dupont, "Le maître," 239.

24 I diverge from Dupont, "Le maître," 234, 238–39, 242, 243.

25 See Dupont, "Le maître," 238.

26 See the opinions of Minear and Schweizer mentioned above in n. 23.

27 Another example of lengthening at the end of a speech is Luke 15:7, 10.

28 See, e.g., 11:5-8; 15:4-7, 8-10; for bibliography on this subject, see the commentary above on 11:5-6.

29 See François Bovon, "Parabole d'Evangile, parabole du Royaume," *RThPh* 122 (1990) 33–41.

ric of dialogue. Verse 10 represents a response—a good response—to what the original speaker expected from the listeners.

The scathing realism of the speaker and the parable's Semitic structure and style are arguments in favor of the authenticity of this teaching attributed to Jesus. The fact that Luke is the only Gospel to report it does not constitute a decisive argument against its authenticity.[30]

Commentary

■ **1-3a** The etymological meaning of the uncommon Greek adjective ἀνένδεκτος is "unacceptable," "inadmissible." But as it is used here, it can take on the meaning "impossible."[31] This studied expression was perhaps not the happiest choice, since, by the very ethical connotation associated with it, it suggests that causes of stumbling are not tolerable. The sentence taken as a whole, however, affirms that causes of stumbling are impossible to avoid[32] because of the presence of evil in the world.[33]

The Greek word meaning "cause of stumbling" (σκάνδαλον) appears only here in Luke-Acts (we encounter the verb "cause to stumble" [σκανδαλίζω] only twice,

in 7:23 and 17:2). The Greek noun, whose etymological meaning is "what springs," is in the first instance the "stick" of a trap, then the "trap" itself used to capture animals, then the "snare" used to cause the enemy to fall, and finally "the cause of stumbling."[34] The term is used in the figurative sense in the LXX and the New Testament.[35] Here it has to do with an act that causes the downfall of someone else, of a sin that causes someone to sin.[36] So this presupposes the setting of a community: the disciples (perhaps considered as ministers) shock other believers (called "little ones" in v. 2) by their scandalous behavior; by taking advantage of their power, embezzling funds, betraying conjugal fidelity, giving up serving God alone, and so on.[37] When believers see such scandalous behavior, they "stumble," that is, they are in danger either of letting themselves be carried along by such behavior, or beginning to doubt God's power, or condemning others with an excessive anger.[38]

Personal responsibility is underscored by the use of the singular in the phrase "but woe[39] to the person by whom they come." The fate awaiting this guilty one resembles a punishment. And, as a matter of fact, just such executions by drowning were carried out in certain places.[40] Nevertheless, the flow of the text suggests

---

30 Likewise Bultmann does not appear to doubt the authenticity of this parable (*History*, 141, 201–5); see also idem, *Jesus* (Berlin: Deutsche Bibliothek, 1926; reprinted Tübingen: Mohr Siebeck, 1958) 64–66.

31 This word does not appear in the LXX or in the rest of the New Testament. It is late and very rare in non-Christian Greek texts; see Chrysippus *Fragmenta logica et physica*, *SVF* 55.5; Artemidorus of Ephesus *Oneirocr.* 2.70; Diogenes Laertus 7.50; Aristophanes of Byzantium, frag. 13.6 (A. Nauck, ed.); London Papyrus 1404.8; see BAGD, s.v.; and the CD-ROM Thesaurus Linguae Graecae, which, in addition, provides about twenty other references from Christian authors. Its usage escalates in the patristic period; see Lampe, s.v. Thanks to David Warren for this information.

32 The manuscript tradition fluctuates between "to the disciples" (without αὐτοῦ) and "to his disciples" (with αὐτοῦ). It also alternates the order of the words "for causes of stumbling not to come."

33 See Godet, 2:279; Paul Ricœur, *Le mal: un défi à la philosophie et à la théologie* (Autres temps 5; Geneva: Labor et Fides, 1996).

34 See Lagrange, 451; Stählin, "σκάνδαλον κτλ.," *TDNT* 7 (1971) 339–40.

35 See, e.g., Josh 23:13; 1 Sam (1 Kgdms) 18:21; Ps 69 (68):23; Matt 18:7 (the parallel to our passage); Rom 11:9 (quotation of Ps 69 [68]:23); 1 Pet 2:7.

36 In 7:23, it was Jesus himself who provided occasion for a fall; see the commentary on 7:18-23 in vol. 1.

37 It is not difficult to enumerate other examples by consulting one of the numerous vice lists in the epistles, for example, Gal 5:19-21. Grundmann (331–32) recalls the "scandalous" attitude of the rich man toward Lazarus in the preceding pericope.

38 First Corinthians illustrates the way in which the apostle Paul reacted to scandals; see 1 Cor 1:10-17; 5:1-13; 6:1-11; 8:1-13; 11:17-22.

39 The same expression, πλὴν οὐαί, occurs in 6:24; see Plummer, 398.

40 "When you finish reading this scroll, tie a stone to it, and throw it into the middle of the Euphrates, and say, 'Thus shall Babylon sink, to rise no more, because of the disasters that I am bringing on her'" (Jer 51:63-64 *NRSV*). The Code of Hammurabi (e.g., in §2) already foresees these punishments; see André Finet, *Le code de Hammurapi: Introduction, traduction et annotation* (Littératures anciennes du Proche-Orient 6; Paris: Cerf, 1973) 45; see Godet, 2:279; and Marshall, 641.

instead a preventive measure: it would be better[41] to eliminate such a public danger before it becomes rampant. The image of the millstone[42] suggests the countryside, and the preventive punishment presupposes the presence of deep water.[43] Such a verdict could have been rendered in Galilee, not far from the lake.

Luke summons his readers to personal vigilance several times in Luke-Acts. The very same words that he puts on Jesus' lips here—"Be on your guard!" (v. 3a)—are found also in 21:34 and in Acts 5:35 and 20:28.[44]

■ **3b-4** There is an abrupt shift from drastic prevention by drowning (vv. 1-3a) to generous forgiveness (vv. 3b-4). This is because Luke, following the early Christians and probably Jesus himself, expected believers, especially ministers, to respond to different situations in different ways: while one must know how to protect the weak by getting rid of the guilty ones, one must also know how to strive relentlessly to bring sinners back into the community the minute they repent. The manuscript evidence is uncertain in v. 3b: in one reading, the sin is not spelled out ("if another disciple sins"); in the other, the sin is directed against someone ("if another disciple sins against you").[45] It could be that the generalization implied in the absence of the words "against you" corresponded to an institutionalization of the maxim; intended by Jesus to apply to all believers, the sentence may have been progressively restricted to the point where it applied only to ministers. In any case, repentance ("if [t]he[y] repent[s]" [ἐὰν μετανοήσῃ]) is no longer

a matter of initial conversion but ecclesiastical repentance.[46]

There were several different ways in which the requirement of forgiveness could be radicalized: speaking of seven times, seven times a day (is Luke here influenced by Ps 119 [118]:164?), or seventy times seven times (or seventy-seven times; Matt 18:22). There is even an apocryphal development in which we read, "That is why your brother Peter (the risen Christ is speaking to the apostle Philip) remembered what Noah did on the day the sinners were punished, when he told me, 'Do you want me to forgive my brother as many as seven times, the way Noah forgave?' And I answered him, 'I don't want you to be satisfied with following Noah's example; no, I want you to forgive seventy times seven times'" (*Acts Phil.* 8.12).[47] The main idea is obviously that there must be no limit to forgiveness.

The text inserts a decisive step between the guilty action on the part of the one person and the forgiveness offered by the other; it is the reproach ("rebuke the offender [= him]," ἐπιτίμησον αὐτῷ), which should lead to repentance ("if there is repentance [he repents]," ἐὰν μετανοήσῃ). This risky dialogue provided the origins of pastoral conversations with parishioners, ecclesiastical discipline, and the ritual practice of penitence.[48] This kind of dialogue itself had its roots in the prophetic tradition (the prophet had to take up guard duty in Israel).[49] Several texts make it clear that the conversation must be fraternal, devoid of anger, and in an irenic spirit:

---

41 The verb λυσιτελέω literally means "to pay the tax" (λύει τὰ τέλη). When used in the third person singular in an impersonal manner, as it is here, it means "it is beneficial," sometimes with a comparative nuance. This verb is used only here in the New Testament, although it occurs several times in the LXX (Tob 3:6; Sir 20:10, 14; 29:11) and is common in Greek literature.

42 On the "millstone," see Str-B 1:775–78; and H. Balz and G. Schneider, "μυλικός, etc." and "μύλος, etc.," *EDNT* 2:445, who refer to *b. Qidd.* 29b.

43 In the Synoptic tradition, θάλασσα can be used for the "Sea" of Galilee (Mark 1:16; 4:39). Luke avoids this incorrect usage of the word "sea" (he prefers λίμνη, "pond" or "lake"; see 5:1; 8:22, 23, 33). See the commentary on 5:1 in vol. 1 and n. 9 there.

44 Luke records other expressions of exhortation or warning, e.g., "He who has ears to hear, let him hear!" (8:8; 14:35), or "listen to him!" (9:35).

45 The parallel to v. 4 contains the words "against you" after the phrase "he has sinned." On the other hand, there is hesitation in the manuscript tradition about this same v. 4 concerning the words "to you," which follow the phrase "he returns."

46 On the vocabulary of μετάνοια, see Bovon, *Theologian*, 305–28.

47 See François Bovon, Bertrand Bouvier, and Frédéric Amsler, *Acta Philippi* (2 vols.; CCSA 11, 12; Turnhout: Brepols, 1999) 1:261. Another parallel is *Gos. Naz.* 15a, cited by Jerome *Pelag.* 3.2 (*PL* 23:598); Schneemelcher, *New Testament Apocrypha*, 1:161; and Kloppenborg, *Q Parallels*, 185.

48 See Grundmann, 332. On penitence of Christians in antiquity, see C. Vogel, "Pénitence," *DECA* 2:1983–86.

49 See Ezek 3:16-21; *T. Gad* 6; 1QS 5.25—6.1; CD 9.2–8; Catchpole, "Reproof," 81–82.

"And reprove one another not in wrath but in peace as you find in the Gospel" (*Did.* 15.3).

■ **5-6** As if to underscore the contemporary relevance of Jesus' words for the church, Luke here makes use of the Christian vocabulary of "apostles" and their "Lord." Feeling powerless in the face of the magnitude of the task, especially that of forgiving, those whom Jesus was talking to[50] asked him for his help. Are they begging him to give them faith or some measure of faith, or an increase in their level of faith? The absence of an article before the Greek word for "faith" (πίστιν) would suggest a renewed amount of confidence in God:[51] "Increase our faith!" (Πρόσθες ἡμῖν πίστιν).

According to Luke, Jesus replied that not much faith was required to work miracles. The image of the mustard seed is a traditional one, and the reader will remember that it described the presence of the kingdom of God.[52] He or she will also recall the contrast between the seed and the tree and then apply it here to faith and its fruits. Usually the Greek word συκάμινος refers to the mulberry tree, whose thorns and roots make it difficult to uproot it. In the LXX, however, this same word seems to render another kind of tree, the sycamore, which also was considered difficult or impossible to uproot and whose size provides a more marked contrast with the mustard seed.[53] However that may be, the hyperbole is a rhetorical device, the kind of rhetorical exaggeration in favor in the East. The thematic content is also enigmatic and reflects the style of the historical Jesus. In Jesus' way of thinking, what was necessary was less a supplementary measure of faith (as a precondition to faith) than a living and active faith (resulting from faith).[54] To have faith is tantamount to entering into God's domain—and everything is possible for God. What is more, when divine power is given to human beings, it is always tied to a mission.[55] The Greek conjunction εἰ ("if"), followed by the present indicative in the subordinate clause, corresponds to a real condition, but the situation becomes unreal in the main clause, where we have an unreal condition (expressed by the Greek imperfect and aorist used with the particle ἄν), the kind of sentence we find also in authors of classical Greek.[56] You do have faith, but your faith does not uproot any tree. If your faith were living, that faith, which is obedience, according to the apostle Paul (ὑπακοή, Rom 1:5), ought to make itself obeyed ("and it would obey you," καὶ ὑπήκουσεν ἂν ὑμῖν, v. 6).

■ **7-10** The parable gets slightly modified in the shift from Jesus to Luke. In the freshness of the original version, it portrays the daily life of a simple peasant and his slave.[57] The latter's daily work did not end in the fields, but in the house, where he still had to fix and serve the dinner. In so doing the slave was only carrying out his duty, and his master had no special reason to show him gratitude. This recall of social customs was transformed into a parable on Jesus' lips, an enigmatic parable whose significance had to be discovered by the ones who listened to it. My hypothesis is that the moral that we read in v. 10 was not yet a part of the story. Because of Jesus' person, those who heard those words could understand the story to mean that God has given meaning to our lives. When we live according to his law ("what was commanded"), we have no reason to boast, no claim to make,

---

50 The "apostles" in v. 5 are either the same as the disciples of v. 1, or else they comprise a small inner circle within a larger body of disciples (thus George, "La foi des apôtres," 69).

51 See Godet, 2:282; Grundmann, 332. In 18:8, Luke shows concern about the future of the faith (with the definite article): "But when the Son of Man comes, will he find the faith on the earth?"

52 See Luke 13:19 and the commentary above on that verse.

53 On this tree, see Str-B 1:795, 2:234; C.-H. Hunzinger, "συκῆ, κτλ." *TDNT* 7 (1971) 751–57; George, "La foi des apôtres," 70 n. 10; Hahn, "Jesu Wort," 156–57.

54 On vv. 5-6, see Jean Duplacy, "Foi," 273–87; George, "La foi des apôtres."

55 See Duplacy ("Foi," 282–87), who refers to (among other passages) Job 42:2; Num 20:12; Sir 48:4-10, 12-16.

56 See Godet, 2:282; Smyth, *Greek Grammar* §2300b.

57 Should δοῦλος be translated as servant or slave? Did a Galilean peasant in Jesus' day own a slave, or did he have a servant at his disposal? Weiser (*Knechtsgleichnisse*, 105–6) thinks that slavery is in view here, but he points out that ancient Judaism afforded a slave more rights than did Greek or Roman systems; see Muhammed A. Dandamayev, "Slavery (OT)," and S. Scott Bartchy, "Slavery (Greco-Roman)," *ABD* 6:64–66.

and deserve no special credit. Understood this way, the parable can either instruct those who hear it, or fulfill a polemical function.[58]

With the addition of v. 10, it is basically this meaning that is made explicit, but a moralizing note is added that was missing from the original, as well as a wording that in my view is overdone. The moralizing element is that what one does should be not only in harmony with orders ("doing what was commanded") but should also be the carrying out of a duty ("what we ought to have done"). The part that is overdone is the description of the slaves. The Greek adjective ἀχρεῖος means "useless," "unusable," "good for nothing," "worthless."[59] If the slave proved useful to his master by doing his duty, was it not going too far to make the moral of the parable our worthlessness? Since Luke stressed God's need for human beings to cooperate with him and to participate in events,[60] I attribute the birth of v. 10 to the oral tradition or to the author of L.

We must look elsewhere for the redactional element in the story, namely, in what has to do with the ecclesiastical dimension that Luke prepared for in v. 5 by the use of such terms as "apostles" and "Lord,"[61] a dimension that can be discerned in the parable itself. For the Gospel writer, the relistening or rereading of the parable is accompanied by an allegorical coloration in that the vocabulary can in fact take on a second meaning and hint at ecclesiastical realities. The Greek term δοῦλος ("slave" or "servant") often also refers to a "minister" of the church;[62] the verb διακονέω ("to serve") sometimes calls to mind table "service" (see Luke 10:40; Acts 6:2);[63]

ποιμαίνω ("to tend [sheep]") is the main function of pastors of the church;[64] ἐσθίω ("to eat") and πίνω ("to drink") suggest the Eucharist.[65] This extends even to the word ἀγρός ("field"), which suggests the world where the missionary task of the church is carried out (see Matt 13:38), and to the verb ἀροτριάω ("to plow"), which refers to the spreading of the word of God (see Luke 9:62; 1 Cor 9:10). So Luke expects the leaders of the church to carry out their tasks with zeal and faithfulness, without expecting to receive any special congratulations or reward in return. God needs men and women but considers those who believe themselves particularly indispensable to be useless for the task. What matters—and the repetition of the Greek verb "to do" (ποιέω) confirms it—is action in the service of God and inside the community of the church. The tasks carried out inside the house (for the edification of the community) are, moreover, the indispensable complement to activity on the outside, in the fields (the evangelization of the world).[66] As the expression "put on your apron and serve me" (περιζωσάμενος διακόνει μοι) sounds like a christological phrase peculiar to Luke ("he will fasten his belt . . . and . . . serve them" [NRSV], περιζώσεται . . . καὶ . . . διακονήσει αὐτοῖς; 12:37b), it is likely that Luke thought of the service offered by Christ as the model of the service carried out by the ministers of the church.[67]

History of Interpretation

According to Albert the Great (d. 1280), vv. 5-6 deal with the power and the humility of all living faith. This faith

---

58 On the polemical aspect, see Dupont ("Le maître," 246–47), who thinks that v. 10 is part of the original. We find similar warnings in Judaism; see the sayings of Antigone of Socho (m. ʾAbot 1:3) and Johanan ben Zakkai (m. ʾAbot 2:8).

59 On this adjective, see Godet, 2:285–86; Ward, "Uncomfortable Words," 200–203. The only other New Testament usage of this adjective is in Matt 25:30 ("As for this worthless slave, throw him into the outer darkness"), which illustrates the contempt and condemnation that the adjective ἀχρεῖος connotes.

60 See Bovon, "L'importance des médiations dans le projet théologique de Luc," in idem, L'œuvre, 181–203.

61 Minear ("Note on Luke 17:7-10") has made this point.

62 See, e.g., Acts 4:29; 16:17; Rom 1:1; Phil 1:1; Rev 1:1.

63 See the commentary above on 10:40.

64 See Matt 2:6; John 21:16; Acts 20:28; 1 Cor 9:7; 1 Pet 5:2-3; Marshall, 646.

65 See Luke 9:13, 17; 22:14-20; Marshall, 646.

66 See Minear, "Note on Luke 17:7-10," 85.

67 See Grundmann, 333. Observe, in addition, that the text of vv. 7-10 is not certain everywhere. Numerous manuscripts add αὐτῷ ("to him") to the verb "to command" in v. 9 and answer the rhetorical question with the words οὐ δοκέω ("I think not"). See Metzger (Textual Commentary, 166), who assigns the letter C, which means "that there is a considerable degree of doubt whether the text or the apparatus contains the superior reading" (definition given on xxviii). As for v. 10b, Marcion seems to have omitted it from his Gospel.

resembles a mustard seed; its smallness suggests humility; its delicacy, wisdom; its strong taste, breaking through into the heart; and its heat (mustard plasters were made from mustard seeds), love that goes hand in hand with faith. The mulberry tree, on the other hand, understood in a negative sense, stood for the bearing of the fruit of the devil. Its fruit is black. The grubs that feed on its leaves produce silk that confirms the arrogance of the world. The flies that alight on its fruit symbolize carnal temptations. So faith must uproot that small tree and throw it into the bitterness of hell, or better still, the bitterness of penitence. Medieval botany entered in this way into the service of exegesis and theology (*Enarr. in Luc.* 17.6 [464–65]).

Erasmus linked the verses on faith (vv. 5-6) to the parable of the slave (vv. 7-10). To his way of thinking, Christ expects of us a faith that is both powerful and humble. The image of the mustard seed and its application in Luke 13:18-19 and 17:5-6 gave the humanistic scholar the opportunity to link the fate of Christ to the faith of his disciples. Jesus was humble like the tiny mustard seed since he accepted his incarnation and his crucifixion. In the present he demonstrates his power through his disciples. The parable of the slave invites these disciples to not misuse this power they have received and to carry out the orders of their Master in humble and faithful service.[68]

Bengel (1687–1752) attached importance to the worthless slave. If he proves to be guilty, he deserves to be punished. If, on the other hand, he does his duty, he deserves no credit. God, who alone is good, does not need our help. With sensitivity, Bengel noted that if being called "a worthless slave" by God is a misfortune, then calling oneself one is a blessing.[69]

Conclusion

The rich man in the parable (16:19-31) had had an attitude that caused stumbling. So the fact that the question of causes of stumbling comes up at the beginning of chap. 17 is no surprise to the reader. Nor is the severity of the measures taken with respect to those persons by whom causes of stumbling come, when compared with the punishment meted out to the rich man in the land of the dead. From a cause of stumbling that has already happened, in chap. 16, the text moves on to a threatening cause of stumbling in chap. 17. And the threat is all the more serious in that "these little ones," that is, the faithful, who are delicate and powerless, also run the risk of stumbling. The cause of stumbling par excellence is that of sweeping up others into one's own stumbling; that means provoking others into sinning by one's own example.

Sin is not the last word in life, however. Forgiveness encircles it and offers itself to those persons who, realizing that they have sinned, get a grip on themselves, and repent. The limitless offer of forgiveness corresponds here to the harshness of the condemnation of those by whom stumbling comes.

There is no taking stock of oneself without there being a relationship with God, without a springing up of faith. All faith, however modest, is rigorous and efficacious, and able to uproot and displace trees, symbols of solidity and stability.

Since it is marked by the forgiveness that frees one from causes of stumbling, the life of faith places believers in a communal relationship with God. Whether in the context of work or rest, when we are in God's company, the relationship is that of a farmer and his farmhand. It is a communion respected by differences of status and origin, a common life presented here as intense and demanding.

The first part of this pericope (vv. 1-4) is concerned with interpersonal relationships among human beings. The second part (vv. 5-10) illuminates the relationships between believers and God. By virtue of its very structure, it intersects the two parts of the Decalogue and the double commandment to love. The only difference is the order, since here the relationship with God appears in second position.

---

68   Erasmus, *Paraphrasis,* 418.
69   Bengel, *Gnomon,* 1:376; see Lagrange, 456.

Ten Men Suffering from "Leprosy" (17:11-19)

Bibliography

Betz, Hans Dieter, "The Cleansing of the Ten Lepers (Luke 17:11-19)," *JBL* 90 (1971) 314–28.

Blinzler, Josef, "Die literarische Eigenart des sogenannten Reiseberichts im Lukasevangelium," in J. Schmid and A. Vögtle, eds., *Synoptische Studien: A. Wikenhauser zum 70. Geburtstag* (Munich: Zink, 1953) 20–52, esp. 46–52.

Bours, Johannes, "Vom dankbaren Samariter: Eine Meditation über Lk 17, 11-19," *BiLeb* 1 (1960) 193–98.

Bruners, Wilhelm, *Die Reinigung der zehn Aussätzigen und die Heilung des Samariters: Lk 17, 11-19. Ein Beitrag zur lukanischen Interpretation der Reinigung von Aussätzigen* (FB 23; Stuttgart: Katholisches Bibelwerk, 1977).

Bultmann, *History*, 33.

Busse, *Wunder*, 313–27.

Charpentier, Étienne, "L'Évangile (Lc 17, 11-19): L'étranger appelé au salut," *AsSeign* 67 (1965) 36–57.

Conzelmann, *Theology*, 68–73.

Delobel, "Sayings," 456.

Dibelius, *Tradition*, 120.

Domergue, Marcel, "Les dix lépreux: Guérir et sauver," *Christus* 40 (1993) 272–80.

Elliott, J. K., "Seven Recently Published New Testament Fragments from Oxyrhynchus," *NovT* 42 (2000) 209–13.

Enslin, Morton S., "Luke and Matthew, Compilers or Authors?" *ANRW* 2.25.3 (1985) 2357–88, esp. 2378–84.

Glöckner, *Neutestamentliche Wundergeschichten*, 125–60.

Glombitza, Otto, "Der dankbare Samariter, Luk. xvii 11-19," *NovT* 11 (1969) 241–46.

Heutger, Nicolaus, "Die lukanischen Samaritanererzählungen in religionspädagogischer Sicht," in Haubeck and Bauchmann, *Wort*, 275–87.

Jervell, Jacob, "The Lost Sheep of the House of Israel," in idem, *Luke and the People of God: A New Look at Luke-Acts* (Minneapolis: Augsburg, 1972) 113–22.

Klein, *Barmherzigkeit*, 38–42, 73, 104.

Liese, H., "Decem leprosi mundantur, Lc. 17, 11-19," *VD* 12 (1932) 225–31.

Meltzer, H., "Die Gleichnisse vom dankbaren Samariter und von der wunderbaren Speisung," *PrM* 25 (1921) 198–206.

Paul, Andre, "La guérison d'un lépreux," *NRTh* 92 (1970) 592–604.

Pesch, Rudolf, *Jesu ureigene Taten? Ein Beitrag zur Wunderfrage* (QD 52; Freiburg: Herder, 1970) 114–34.

Roloff, *Kerygma*, 157–58.

Strelan, John G., "Preparing to Preach: Reflections on Luke 17:11-19," *LTJ* 16 (1982) 83–87.

Wilson, Paul Scott, "The Lost Parable of the Generous Landowner and Other Texts for Imaginative Preaching [Lk 16:1-13]," *QR* 9 (1989) 80–99.

11/ Now it happened, as he was walking toward Jerusalem, that he was going along the border between Samaria and Galilee. **12/** As he was entering a certain village, ten men suffering from "leprosy"[a] approached him[b], stopped while they were at some distance from him[c], **13/** and they[d] called out, saying, "Jesus, Master, have mercy on us!" **14/** When he saw them, he said to them, "Go and show yourselves in person[e] to the priests." Now it happened that, as they went, they were made clean. **15/** One of them, when he saw that he was healed, turned back, glorifying God with a loud voice. **16/** Then he prostrated himself at Jesus' feet and thanked him. And he was a Samaritan. **17/** Jesus answered and said, "Were not ten made clean? And the nine, where are they? **18/** Was none of them found to return and glorify God[f] except this foreigner?" **19/** Then he said to him, "Get up and walk. Your faith has saved you."

a   Literally: "ten 'leprous' men."
b   The Greek word αὐτῷ ("him") must have been part of the original text; see below, p. 503 n. 33.
c   Literally: "who stood far off."
d   Literally: "they" or "themselves."
e   Literally: "Having gone, show yourselves."
f   Literally: "were they not found, returning to give glory to God?"

Should we put the stress on the ten men suffering from "leprosy" who were healed or on the single Samaritan who gave thanks? Should we emphasize the victory of Christ the miracle-worker or the man's saving faith? Is the final gratitude more decisive than the initial trust? Is the fact that the man healed of his "leprosy" was a Samaritan just an anecdotal detail, or was it a decisive factor? Was the story the memory of a historical event, an imitation of Scripture, or the development of another gospel episode?

Analysis

Verse 11 has distinct characteristics and fills a double function: by its use of the Greek infinitive in the phrase ἐν τῷ πορεύεσθαι ("as he was walking") and the imperfect διήρχετο ("he was going along between") it corresponds to a summary and, like 8:1 or 13:22, it supplies a caesura in the journey narrative.[1] But the initial καὶ ἐγένετο ("now it happened") prepares the reader for the discovery of a new episode.

There are two phases to the anecdote itself, as the medieval illustrator of the Evangelistary of Echternach saw so clearly.[2] In the first phase, Jesus directly confronts the ten men suffering from "leprosy" (vv. 12-14). In the second, we see the healed Samaritan returning to Jesus (vv. 15-19).[3] In the midst of this second part, the narrator interrupts his telling of the story to slip in an aside: "And he was a Samaritan." The importance of this gloss is witnessed to by the use of the term "foreigner" (ἀλλογενής) in v. 18, and the significance is further confirmed by the mention of Samaria in v. 11.

Although a saying of Jesus often gives meaning to a novel situation,[4] what counts here is what the Samaritan did in response to the new situation created by the miracle. Jesus' final words are limited to emphasizing the Samaritan's worthy faith. This highlighting of the thankful Samaritan establishes a link between this story and the one about Zacchaeus (19:1-10) or the one about the woman with the ointment (7:36-50). Even though the story begins with Jesus' success as a miracle-worker, the emphasis is on another aspect, the attitude demonstrated by the Samaritan.[5] This text is neither an apophthegm nor an account of a miracle; by praising the Samaritan, it encourages us to imitate him.[6] By its theatrical schematization and its use of round numbers (10 and 1), it looks like a tale, or perhaps even a parable.[7]

The episode may be outlined as follows:

Setting of the episode:	v. 11	Summary and localization
First part	vv. 12-13	The ten men suffering from "leprosy" call for help
	v. 14a	Jesus' response
	v. 14b	Healing of the ten men on the way
Second part	vv. 15-16	The one man's reaction
	vv. 17-18	Jesus' triple rhetorical question
	v. 19	Jesus' final command

What may have been the origin of this story? The redactional character of vv. 11 and 19 is evident, even though the statement "he was going along the border between Samaria and Galilee" (διήρχετο διὰ μέσον Σαμαρείας καὶ Γαλιλαίας)[8] is a curious expression

---

1 See the commentary on 8:1 in vol. 1 and above on 13:22.

2 The scene is divided into two parts: on the left, Jesus blessing the ten lepers, and on the right, the Samaritan who returned throwing himself at Jesus' feet. Illustration 535 in Schiller, *Ikonographie*, 1:463. This Evangelistary dates to 1020–1030.

3 See Pesch, *Taten*, 124; Bruners, *Reinigung*, 68–79.

4 In this case it is about apophthegms. Bultmann (*History*, 33, 60–61, 218–44) considers this passage to be a biographical apophthegm put together from Mark 1:40-45 (an episode that was itself influenced by 2 Kgs [4 Kgdms] 5:9-19).

5 According to Dibelius (*Tradition*, 58 n. 1, 120–21) the story is not news, since the miraculous is not

emphasized, but is a legend whose focus is not the Samaritan but Jesus, who recognized the man's piety. See Pesch, *Taten*, 123–24.

6 Nolland (2:845) writes: "The narrative defies standard form-critical classification."

7 Bruners (*Reinigung*, 118) reaches the conclusion that this story is analogous to 2 Kgs (4 Kgdms) 5, "eine 'nachgeahmte prophetische Erzählung' mit überbietendem Charakter."

8 Because it is unusual, the expression διὰ μέσον inspired the intervention of scribes; see n. 22 below. Additionally, Luke prefers to use the article before proper names of regions (see 2:39; 3:1; 1:39 is an exception). See Glombitza, "Samariter," 241,

with a surprising meaning.[9] What is Lukan is the concern with punctuating the speeches and the stories with summaries, as well as the language (the expression "now it happened" [καὶ ἐγένετο] and the verb "walking" [πορεύομαι]) and the themes (en route to Jerusalem and the faith that saves).

Some authors maintain that the entire story is redactional. Bruners, in particular, is of the opinion that Luke invented the whole story by drawing on the story of Elisha and Naaman (2 Kings [4 Kingdoms] 5) and the Markan miracle (Mark 1:40-45) that is reproduced in Luke 5:12-16.[10] Other commentators posit a tradition behind the story, in spite of the absence of Synoptic parallels. Rudolf Pesch, for example, would eliminate certain redactional elements (principally vv. 11-12 and v. 19) and restore an original text whose structure would correspond to the Lukan text. The second part of the story, in particular, would be original, as well as the Samaritan identity of the man healed of his "leprosy."[11] More recently, commentators have shifted the emphasis. Hans Klein assigns the better part of 17:11-19 to L and sees characteristic theological concerns in it. Interest in place-names, attention to foreigners, and the distinction between healing and salvation are all typical of the author of L. Moreover, according to Klein, the author of L did not create this story but merely reworked it. The original episode must have been a miracle story corresponding by and large to the first half of the present story.[12] Earlier, Hans Dieter Betz had suggested the possibility that the story was transmitted orally, without much in the way of Christian connotations, in a form that emphasized Jesus as a divine miracle-worker and already

included the element of the return of the man healed of his "leprosy." This story was later adapted to a doctrinal concern and a polemical intention, that of understanding the miracle's true importance, in terms of Christian salvation. Giving preference to the conversion over the miracle amounted to creating the outline of a Christian orthodoxy.[13]

One fact is clear: as he did everywhere else, Luke did not take over a text from L without rewriting it or adapting it. Besides the reworking of the beginning and the end,[14] we should reckon with a series of Lukanisms throughout the story. The genitive absolute at the beginning of v. 12 ("As he was entering a certain village," εἰσερχομένου αὐτοῦ εἴς τινα κώμην) is characteristic of Luke, as is the use of the title "Master" (ἐπιστάτης) in v. 13, and the expressions "glorifying God" and "with a loud voice" in v. 15. Moreover, the biblical style and the scriptural reminiscences are very much in Luke's mode of expression. However, we should not overemphasize the Gospel writer's narrative creativity. Every episode that he recounts is determined by three considerations: the memory of the facts, memories of biblical stories, and, finally, the contemporaneous needs of the Christian community. It is obvious that Luke knew the story of Elisha and Naaman, the king who suffered from "leprosy" (2 Kings [4 Kingdoms] 5) (see Luke 4:27).[15] In telling the story, Luke drew on the biblical text, but the narrative he wrote was his own. He also remembered the account of the man suffering from "leprosy" that he took over from Mark (Mark 1:40-45), which he had told several pages earlier (Luke 5:12-16).[16] Here again it is another story that he tells, and he got this one from L.

245–46; Pesch, *Taten*, 117–19; Bruners, *Reinigung*, 124–63.

9   If this expression is traditional, it is not necessarily part of the primitive story itself.

10   Bruners, *Reinigung*, 123–382. The position of Busse (*Wunder*, 321) is not different from that of Bruners. According to Bruners (*Reinigung*, 118), Luke also has the problem of surpassing his Old Testament model; see n. 7 above. For a critique, see point 3 of the criticism of Hans Dieter Betz in his critical review in *ThLZ* 106 (1981) 399.

11   Pesch, *Taten*, 116–23 (reconstruction of the traditional story on 122–23). Glöckner (*Neutestamentliche Wundergeschichten*, 125–31) criticizes the opinion of Bruners and arrives at a conclusion similar to that of Pesch.

12   Klein, *Barmherzigkeit*, 38–42.

13   Betz, "Cleansing," 314–28.

14   See above.

15   See Bruners, *Reinigung*, 113–18.

16   See Bultmann (*History*, 33) and Bruners (*Reinigung*, 93–103), who point to common elements of structure and similarities in vocabulary. Additionally, we see lines 32–41 of *Papyrus Egerton 2*, which also recount the healing of a leper. The story is close to Mark 1:40-45, except that in this story the man to be healed by a miracle mentions other contagious lepers (as here in Luke 17:12-14). See Daniel A. Bertrand, "Papyrus Egerton 2," in Bovon and Geoltrain, *Écrits apocryphes*, 1:411–16.

All the episodes and parables of the L document have a remarkable literary quality and have stylistic characteristics in common. Indications of this sort appear in both parts of the present story, from interest in Samaria (v. 11), Samaritans (v. 16), and foreigners (v. 18), to salvation (symbolized by miracles or parables and given immediacy by Jesus' active presence),[17] to say nothing of a characteristic way of writing: "they called out" (ἦραν φωνήν), "have mercy on us" (ἐλέησον ἡμᾶς), "when he saw (literally, having seen)" (ἰδών), and twice "to thank" (εὐχαριστέω). To these constructions could be added the non-Lukan vocabulary: "to approach, come to meet" (ἀπαντάω), "at some distance" (πόρρωθεν), and "a foreigner" (ἀλλογενής).[18]

It is possible—at least hypothetically—to go back behind L to the oral tradition. At that level, the link with Samaria and the Samaritan identity of the good man healed of his "leprosy" was still missing. The christological title "Master" (ἐπιστάτης) was not yet a part of the story. But the story already included the return of a single man and therefore also already comprised a second part, ending on the note of Jesus' surprise at the different reactions of the men healed of their "leprosy" (v. 17).[19] Like the story of the centurion from Capernaum (7:1-10), this narrative had a single episode that was an example story and was characteristic of the new relationships established by the Gospel.

Commentary

■ **11** Luke here reminds us that Jesus is on a journey, the goal of which is the Holy City (see 9:51, 53; 13:22; 18:31; 10:28). As was the case in 13:22, the Gospel writer does not succeed in establishing an explicit organic link between that destination and the following episode.[20]

The second part of v. 11 begins with "and he" (καὶ αὐτός), which has a christological flavor,[21] and ends with a difficult expression. The Greek expression διὰ μέσον already creates a problem in that the manuscripts have different readings: either "through the midst of" (διὰ μέσου), which is common in Greek; "in the midst of" (μέσον); or even "between" (ἀνὰ μέσον).[22] This construction, which was probably present already at the level of L, no doubt used the preposition διά, followed by the accusative, in the locative sense, as did the poets.[23] The second difficulty is that we cannot be sure whether διὰ μέσον means "between" (that is, "along," "on the border with," "in the middle of") or "across." If the author of L knowingly made use of this studied construction, it must have been because he had something definite to say, not a trivial "across" but "going along the border between." The third difficulty arises from the fact that Samaria is mentioned before Galilee. Why is this so, if travelers would have had to leave Galilee first before going through Samaria on the way to Judah? To be sure, they could have gone over to the other side of the Jordan and gone through Perea if, as pious Jews, they had wanted to avoid contact with Samaritans (cf. John 4:9). But, in the first place, it is not certain that Luke conceived of this trip the way the author of L did. It is also possible that Luke's knowledge of Palestinian geography may have been approximate.[24] Finally, Samaria must have been uppermost in his thinking, since he was going to be talking next about a Samaritan.[25] Luke and, before him, the author of L must have known that one had to leave Galilee for Samaria before arriving in Judea. It was the

17   See Klein, *Barmherzigkeit*, 38–42, 73, 104.

18   See Glöckner, *Neutestamentliche Wundergeschichten*, 129–31.

19   On this point, I agree with Betz ("Cleansing," 321), contra Klein, *Barmherzigkeit*, 41.

20   The wording of v. 11a is Lukan through and through; see καὶ ἐγένετο ἐν τῷ ("now it happened that while he . . . "), inspired by the LXX and Luke 5:12; 9:18, 29, 33, et al. The verb πορεύομαι ("to walk") occurs here in its present infinitive form and so emphasizes the duration of the action; see the indicative, imperative, or present participles in 7:8, 50; 8:14. See also Bruners (*Reinigung*, 128–30) and the commentary on 8:7 and 14 in vol. 1.

21   See 6:20; 9:51, etc.; Jeremias, *Sprache*, 37–38, 264.

22   See LSJ, s.v. μέσος 3d, 5, and 3e. The majority of manuscripts emend the text to read διὰ μέσου, while some others read either ἀνὰ μέσον or simply μέσον. See the apparatus of Nestle-Aland; Wettstein, *Novum Testamentum graecum*, 2:76; Bruners, *Reinigung*, 149–50.

23   See LSJ, s.v. διά b1.1–2.

24   This is the famous opinion of Conzelmann, *Theology*, 71–72 and passim.

25   See Marshall, 650.

easiest way to get there, as traveling by way of Perea was more uncomfortable.[26] The authors were happy not to have Jesus avoid Samaria (cf. 9:52). It could be that Luke was thinking that Jesus simply crossed the two regions. The author of L, on the other hand, was probably more nuanced and conceived of Jesus traveling along the border between them. Did the ancient route actually follow the border between Galilee and Samaria for a part of the distance?[27]

■ **12-13** The men suffering from "leprosy" stopped at the distance imposed upon them by those who were well.[28] They could call out to Jesus at the very moment he was entering[29] a certain village.[30] Even though, unlike in 5:13, Jesus is not said to have touched the men suffering from "leprosy," the text uses the vocabulary of encounter. The Greek word ἀπαντάω here means "to come toward," "to meet" in a friendly way; in other contexts it can mean "confront" an enemy in battle, or "appear" in court.[31] In Luke's time, the noun ἀπάντησις ("meeting") took on a technical sense; it referred to the encounter with the risen Christ at the time of the parousia (see 1 Thess 4:17; Matt 25:6).[32] A Christian reading of this text would immediately think that the men suffering from "leprosy"

would benefit from encountering Jesus.[33] The fact that there were ten of them derives from the popular way of telling stories, as in the parable of the wise and the foolish bridesmaids (Matt 25:1); it simply means that there was a large number of them. In spite of what Albert the Great said (*Enarr. in Luc.* 17.2), we should not be looking for a symbolic significance in the number.

These ten sick men called out to Jesus the way one would address someone who is divine.[34] They gave him an honorific title of which Luke was fond and which he had perhaps found in his source,[35] namely, "Master," "Boss," "Chief" (ἐπιστάτα) (designating someone in power rather than someone possessing special knowledge).[36] But we should note that each time a disciple addressed Jesus using this title, it was when the disciple demonstrated that his faith was weak or his understanding limited. In the development of the story, these ten men suffering from "leprosy" were, with one exception, to reveal the limits of their appropriate initial confidence.

By insisting on the parallels with certain other passages (2 Kings [4 Kingdoms] 5 and Luke 5:12-16), commentators have not paid sufficient attention to the

---

26 See Josephus *Vita* 269; and *Ant.* 20.6.1 §118; Bruners, *Reinigung*, 152.

27 On the difficulties of v. 11b, see Plummer, 403; Lagrange, 457; Ernst, 483; and Darell L. Bock, *Luke* (2 vols.; BECNT 3A–B; Grand Rapids: Baker, 1994, 1996) 2:1400–1401.

28 The aorist ἔστησαν signifies that they stop at a distance (punctiliar aspect); see BDF §318. On the attitude of the Israelites toward leprosy, see the commentary on 5:12 in vol. 1.

29 The present participle suggests that the approach and arrival in which the intervention of the lepers comes interrupt the duration.

30 The name of the village is not provided (unlike in 19:1, which mentions Jericho), because the details of the place that the author of L often likes to supply were given in v. 11b.

31 See LSJ, s.v. The New Testament sees only one other occurrence of ἀπαντάω apart from our passage: Mark 14:13. We also find ὑπαντάω as a synonym, for instance in Luke 8:27; 14:31; and Acts 16:16. Here in 17:12 and elsewhere, the manuscripts fluctuate between the two verbs; 𝔓[111] reads ἀπήντησαν.

32 See Lucien Cerfaux, *Le Christ dans la théologie de Saint Paul* (2d rev. ed.; LD 6; Paris: Cerf, 1954)

33–38. Cautiously, M. Lattke, "ἀπαντάω etc.," *EDNT* 1:114–15.

33 Following a genitive absolute of which Jesus is the subject (αὐτοῦ), it is grammatically incorrect to say that the lepers encounter him (αὐτῷ), but the classical rule was not always followed at the time the Gospels were written. The removal of the αὐτῷ is more plausible than its addition: it is explained by a purist response on the part of many scribes. See Lagrange, 457.

34 Betz ("Cleansing," 321) insists on this characteristic of Jesus in this episode. Charpentier ("L'étranger," 36–57) observes that the vocative "Jesus" is rare in the New Testament (eight instances in all, five of which are in Luke: Luke 4:34; 8:28; 18:38; 23:42, and here, 17:13).

35 The title is peculiar to the Gospel of Luke (see 5:5; 8:24, 45; 9:33, 49), but everywhere else it comes out of the mouths of the disciples. See Bovon, *Theologian*, 204–5. With Betz ("Cleansing," 316) and contra Bruners (*Reinigung*, 191), I think that here it is traditional.

36 See the commentary on 5:5 in vol. 1, n. 15 (amend Luke 17:33 to Luke 17:11, twice); Glombitza, "Samariter," 241–42; Bruners, *Reinigung*, 184–89.

fact that the tone of the episode recalls the piety of the Psalms. Jesus,[37] like God himself, was confidently called on to help in a prayer in which there was no hesitation: "Have mercy on me, heal me!" (Ps 41:4 [LXX 40:5]: Κύριε, ἐλέησόν με, ἴασαι τὴν ψυχήν μου) is a standard phrase in the individual laments in the Psalms. Note also Ps 51:1-2: "Have mercy on me, O God, . . . and cleanse me from my sins" (= LXX 50:3-4 Ἐλέησόν με, ὁ θεός, . . . καὶ ἀπὸ τῆς ἁμαρτίας μου καθάρισόν με) and Isa 33:2: "Lord, have mercy on us" (Κύριε, ἐλέησον ἡμᾶς).[38]

■ **14** Just as God could look on people with compassion,[39] so did Jesus ("When he saw them," literally, "having seen," ἰδών).[40] The words accompanying the description seem enigmatic to modern readers and may have been so to readers in antiquity as well. In Israel, "leprosy" was considered to be a state of uncleanness, and the priest who diagnosed it ordered the isolation of the sick person. A ritual resembling a funeral service marked the departure of the person suffering from "leprosy" from the community of those who were well. The law of Moses somewhat optimistically advocated another ritual in case the sick person was healed. When the person who had been suffering from "leprosy" was healed and followed that ritual, he or she was declared to be "clean" and was reinstated in the family.[41] Jesus invited the ten men suffering from "leprosy" to have their cases diagnosed according to the provisions of the law. He confirmed their initial confidence by inviting them to believe that they were already healed and to show themselves to the priests. He tested their faith in his power by sending them off before they were healed.[42] As the phrase "Now it happened that" (καὶ ἐγένετο, v. 14c) indicates, according to Luke, Jesus did indeed possess this power that the ten men believed was his. On the way (ἐν τῷ ὑπάγειν), they were miraculously healed; in biblical terms, they were made "clean."[43] Their faith healed them.

The second part of the story (vv. 15-19) will demonstrate that, although this faith of theirs made them "clean," it still was not sufficient to "save" them. Only the Samaritan did in fact hear Jesus' famous phrase ring in his ears: "Your faith has saved you" (v. 19). This second part of the story, the peak of the narrative, invites the reader to discover the truth that if one's faith is not accompanied by gratitude,[44] but remains unidimensional, it is not true faith. It remains stuck on the level of the miracle and never reaches up to the level of salvation.[45]

Moving ahead rapidly to the essential point, the story does not take the time necessary to satisfy us on all the points we might be curious about. For one thing, it does not say what kind of priests they were: were they local priests, or ones from Jerusalem? Nor does it take an interest in telling us everywhere the man who was healed went, so readers are left asking themselves if he is also going to end up showing himself to the priests. Finally, the author of the story neglected to tell us what Jesus' schedule was during the time that the men suffering from "leprosy" were on their way.[46] If these silences are considered to be clumsy, then they are explained as the

---

37 Luke is not necessarily thinking of the etymological import of the proper name Jesus, which in Hebrew means "Yahweh saves" (יֵשׁוּעַ); see Bruners (*Reinigung*, 184), who is not as negative as I am (he points to v. 19, where we encounter the verb σῴζω, "to save").

38 See Bruners (*Reinigung*, 189–90), who provides a list of references in the Psalms, and especially Glöckner (*Neutestamentliche Wundergeschichten*, 139–55), who connects our pericope to the hymns of David.

39 The motif of divine compassion occurs frequently in the Hebrew Bible and the LXX; see Exod 3:7; Ps 33 (32):13-19; etc. Or, for one telling example, see Ps 119 (118):132: ἐπίβλεψον ἐπ᾽ ἐμὲ καὶ ἐλεησόν με ("turn your face to me and have mercy on me!"). See D. Vetter, "ראה r'h sehen," *THAT* 2 (1976) 696–97.

40 The reader will also recall the compassion of the

Good Samaritan (10:33) and of the father of the prodigal son (15:20).

41 See Leviticus 14 and the commentary on Luke 5:12 in vol. 1.

42 See Lagrange, 458; Charpentier, "L'étranger," 72.

43 The order resembles the one that Jesus gave earlier to another leper (5:14). In the Psalms we find "purify me" next to "have mercy," e.g., Ps 51 (50):1-2, cited above.

44 See Lagrange, 458; Glöckner, *Neutestamentliche Wundergeschichten*, 145–48.

45 See Charpentier ("L'étranger," 70), who points out the two thieves (23:39-43), one of whom requests mere physical deliverance, and the other true salvation.

46 The story does not explain precisely how Jesus knows that this man is a Samaritan. Does he recognize him by his clothing, or perhaps his accent?

result of successive rereadings.[47] But if they are taken to constitute a successful pruning, they compel our admiration.

■ **15** There is a visual contrast provided by the fact that ten men had asked Jesus to help them and had obtained satisfaction, whereas only one of them[48] reacted positively. The first thing that man did was to see—that is, to notice—that he had been healed. This visual realization was a response to Jesus' looking, which in turn was a response to the appeal made by the men suffering from "leprosy." There is an affectionate gratefulness in the expression "when he [that man] saw" ($i\delta\omega\nu$, v. 15) in the gaze of the Samaritan, who thanks Jesus for having seen him too ("When he [Jesus] saw," $i\delta\omega\nu$, v. 14).

What the book of Leviticus calls a cleansing ("to make clean," $\kappa\alpha\vartheta\alpha\rho\iota\zeta\omega$, vv. 14 and 17), the Gospel of Luke here calls, as did the Greeks, a healing ("to heal," $i\alpha\omega\mu\alpha\iota$, v. 15).[49] Without hesitation or delay, that is to say without first going to the priests, the man who was healed of his "leprosy" returns to Jesus. The Greek word $\dot{\upsilon}\pi\sigma\sigma\tau\rho\epsilon\phi\omega$ for "to turn back" has a locative sense here (the man healed of his "leprosy" retraced his steps).[50] In its association with joy and praise, however, it also suggests a spiritual reality: the man healed of his "leprosy" interiorized his healing, intensified his initial trust, deepened his faith, and completed his conversion.[51] Yet we should not get ahead of schedule; before finding *Jesus*, the man healed of his "leprosy," who had made up his mind to return, praised *God* with all his heart. The story skillfully remains within a biblical atmosphere. An individual lament in the Psalms often leads to thanksgiving, which is directed to the God of Israel.[52] Moreover,

the strength of the sentiment requires that one speak out with a loud voice.[53]

■ **16** This story, which began with an appeal directed to Jesus, brings the man healed of his "leprosy" back to the miracle-working Master. So the perspective is not just biblical but also, and especially, Christian. The initial faith of the Samaritan was addressed imploringly to Jesus, and now his mature faith is once again addressed to him. The Christian creed, albeit underlying, is certainly present. The doxology addressed to God the Father ("glorifying," $\delta\sigma\xi\alpha\zeta\omega$, v. 15) is accompanied, from the perspective of the narrators, by thanksgiving ("to thank," $\epsilon\dot{\upsilon}\chi\alpha\rho\iota\sigma\tau\epsilon\omega$, v. 16) directed to Jesus, the Son. The veneration surrounding Jesus is precisely and fully detailed: "prostrated himself at Jesus' feet" (v. 16).[54] We are, to be sure, not yet dealing with true worship (the Greek word for that, $\pi\rho\sigma\sigma\kappa\upsilon\nu\epsilon\omega$ "[fall down and] worship," is used in connection with Jesus only after his resurrection; 24:52).[55]

The author of L added one detail to the story he took over from tradition, and Luke in turn adopted that alteration. The man who was healed of his "leprosy" was a Samaritan. Luke used that addition to call attention to the fact that God's mercy in Jesus Christ has broken religious barriers and called into question any and every particularistic definition of Israel's election. The gospel is intended to be shared with the whole earth, beginning in Jerusalem, going on to Samaria, and spreading out to the ends of the earth (cf. Acts 1:8; 8:1; 9:31). Samaritans and Gentiles, moreover, respond with more faith and gratefulness to the call of the gospel than do the Israelites themselves, they who were the first to be called (see Luke 14:16-24; Acts 13:46; 18:6; 28:25-28).[56]

See Bock, 2:1404. It is not until v. 18 that the reader realizes that Jesus is not alone; see n. 57 below.

47　See Klein, *Barmherzigkeit*, 41–42.

48　Does the word $\epsilon\hat{i}\varsigma$ ("one") carry the nuance here of "a single one?"

49　On $i\alpha\omega\mu\alpha\iota$, see Bruners, *Reinigung*, 218–20.

50　On $\dot{\upsilon}\pi\sigma\sigma\tau\rho\epsilon\phi\omega$, one of Luke's favorite verbs, see Bruners, *Reinigung*, 220–22.

51　Of course these are the verbs $\dot{\epsilon}\pi\iota\sigma\tau\rho\epsilon\phi\omega$ and $\mu\epsilon\tau\alpha\nu\sigma\epsilon\omega$, and not the verb $\dot{\upsilon}\pi\sigma\sigma\tau\rho\epsilon\phi\omega$, which Luke uses to speak of the return to God; see Bovon, *Theologian*, 305–28.

52　One can reread Psalm 22 (21) in this light; see Glöckner, *Neutestamentliche Wundergeschichten*, 147–48. Luke loves to include praise addressed to

God after a miracle story or a surprising episode; see Luke 2:20; 5:25-26; 7:16; 13:13; 18:43; 23:47.

53　A cry at the top of one's voice occurs also in Luke 4:33; 8:28; 19:37; 23:23 (in the plural, to express hostility), and Acts 8:7 (to describe the shriek of the exorcised demons).

54　The leper in the earlier story (5:12) also falls prostrate, but he does so before, not after, his healing, at the moment when he begs to be cleansed.

55　See Gerhard Lohfink, *Die Himmelfahrt Jesu* (SANT 26; Munich: Kösel, 1971) 171–74; Bruners, *Reinigung*, 229–40.

56　On Samaria and the Samaritans in Luke-Acts, see Jacob Jervell, *Luke and the People of God: A New Look at Luke-Acts* (Minneapolis: Augsburg, 1972) 113–32;

■ **17** The rhetorical questions attributed to Jesus are more theological than psychological. Far from being addressed to the Samaritan by way of congratulations, they are addressed to all who listen to and read the text,[57] and they establish a new diagnosis, no longer that of "leprosy" but that of stagnant faith. The first two questions tell of the same sad reality, namely, that out of ten who benefited, nine slipped away without letting us see them express their thanks.

■ **18** The third question begins by repeating the same truth: none of them was found to return and glorify God. But it is extended by the addition of a supplementary element: only one[58] man took the trouble to express his gratitude, and he was a foreigner.[59] The words "this foreigner"[60] evidently echo the gloss "And he was a Samaritan" in v. 16. This third question (v. 18) reflects a concern of the author of L to show the receptivity of the Samaritans, who were considered to be foreigners. In the book of Acts, Luke raises the question as a problem and ostensibly develops the thesis of the divine offer to all nations.[61] The Gospel writer could not help but be happy with this addition made by the author of L, and he goes on to confirm its worth by what he says in v. 19.

■ **19** Luke was also anxious not to have the story end without a personal statement by Jesus to the Samaritan himself (note here the second person singular of the imperative). That is why he himself added a final response, v. 19, in which he used an expression[62] emphasizing the relationship between the miracle and faith,[63] as well as the more than physical reality offered by Jesus to the one whom he had healed. By this legitimate insistence on salvation by faith, Luke nonetheless modified the initial perspective that the author of L had in mind, namely, that of the gratitude that accompanied faith, the dialogical character of one's relationship to Christ, and the capacity to perceive that there was a deliverance that went beyond the physical healing. These fine points tend to disappear in Luke's redaction in favor of an expression about which there is evidently nothing to restate. It was indeed his faith, that is to say the confidence he placed in Jesus' divine power, that saved the Samaritan, by going beyond the physical healing. The man who had been healed of his "leprosy" was invited to get up[64] and walk, a walking modeled on that of Jesus.[65]

History of Interpretation

This text was known as early as the second half of the second century. Marcion included it in his Gospel (see Tertullian *Adv. Marc.* 4.35.4),[66] Irenaeus knew that it was found only in the Gospel of Luke (*Adv. haer.* 3.14.3), and the *Pseudo-Clementine Homilies* (1.6.4) report the story in a listing of Jesus' miracles.[67]

Bovon, *Theologian*, 383; Klein, *Barmherzigkeit*, 73–80. The author of L and Luke the evangelist share this interest in Samaria with the author of the Fourth Gospel (see John 4 and 8:48).

57. In v. 18, Jesus speaks of the Samaritan in the third person singular; he does not address him directly in the second person singular.

58. The same usage of εὑρίσκω ("to find") in the passive occurs only in Acts 5:39 and perhaps in Luke 9:36; see Bruners, *Reinigung*, 263–64.

59. The authors of the story deliberately attribute words to Jesus (vv. 17-18) that, without monotony, exactly correspond to the vocabulary of the story itself ("ten," "were cleansed," "returned," and "give glory to God").

60. The word ἀλλογενής ("foreigner") is a *hapax legomenon* in the New Testament. Nevertheless, Acts 10:28 speaks similarly of an ἀλλόφυλος, that is, "someone from another tribe," a "foreigner."

61. This is the theological function of stories such as the conversion of Cornelius (Acts 10:1-11, 18) or the Jerusalem Council (Acts 15); see Dupont, "Le salut des Gentils et la signification théologique du livre des Actes," in idem, *Études*, 393–419; Bovon, "Tradition et redaction en Actes 10,1—11, 18," in idem, *L'œuvre*, 97–120.

62. On the formula "your faith has saved you," used in 7:50; 8:48; 18:42, and here, see the commentary on 7:48-50 in vol. 1.

63. Charpentier ("L'étranger," 77–78) insists on this aspect.

64. Literally, "Get up and walk!" or "Walk!" On the use of the participle ἀναστάς in Luke's writings, see Ernst Haenchen, *The Acts of the Apostles: A Commentary* (trans. B. Noble and G. Shinn; Philadelphia: Westminster, 1971) 159 n. 2.

65. The imperative πορεύου ("walk") in v. 19 forms an *inclusio* with the infinitive πορεύεσθαι ("to walk") in v. 11.

66. Harnack, *Marcion*, 88.

67. In the third century, see Origen, *Comm. in Rom. 2* (*PG* 14:906); A. Ramsbotham, "The Commentary of

Medieval iconography, doubtless dependent on patristic exegesis,[68] had a good understanding of the literary structure and theological significance of this Gospel story. Two scenes are represented side by side, for example, in the Evangelistary of Echternach. In the first scene, Jesus heals the ten men suffering from "leprosy" at some distance. In the second, he blesses and speaks to the Samaritan, who had come back to prostrate himself at Jesus' feet, while the nine others went away turning their back.[69]

In the twelfth century, the medieval Doctor of the Church Albert the Great developed an allegorical interpretation of the story (*Enarr. in Luc.* 17.11-19). In the Vulgate, the Latin word used to translate the Greek word for the "village" (κώμη) that Jesus entered was *castellum*. Albert gave a spiritual sense to this fortified village, then concluded from the existence of ten men suffering from "leprosy" that there were ten different kinds of "leprosy" that affected ten persons in the Bible,[70] some of whom were affected exteriorly and others interiorly, with respect to virtue, perfection, and salvation. Carrying this through into his exegesis of v. 14 ("go and show yourselves in person to the priests"), Albert emphasized *obedience* as faith's companion, an obedience that turns out to be indispensable for obtaining salvation.

Leaving aside exegesis for medieval homiletics, readers can find a sermon by a preacher in Old German[71] who also understood "leprosy" in the figurative sense of a sign of sin. Moreover, this sermon explains that, when Jesus sent the ten men who were suffering from "leprosy" to the priests, he was demonstrating his obedience to the law of Moses. The healing that preceded that visit witnessed to the one who was the true healer. The Samaritan who came back to Jesus stands for the pagan world that is welcomed into the faith. Finally, the nine ungrateful men prompt the preacher to predict a gloomy future for the Jews. In the Western church, Luke 17:11-19 was used at that time as a liturgical reading for the Fourteenth Sunday after Trinity.

The Reformer Luther wrote a commentary and on several occasions preached on this biblical passage.[72] This pericope was important to Luther, who drew from it a confirmation of his doctrine of justification by faith. In general, his commentary was polemical and identified the priests, to whom the men suffering from "leprosy" were supposed to show themselves, with the Catholic hierarchy. It was the priests who incited the nine men not to return to Jesus![73] The ten men suffering from "leprosy" demonstrated faith; and Christ, love; faith and love constitute the essence of being a Christian.[74] When human beings have faith, they behave as did the men suffering from "leprosy," firm in the face of doubt and focused on Christ. By calling out, the ten sick men showed how serious their request was.[75] In Luther's time, it was still known that when a person suffering from "leprosy" was in a weakened state, he or she could no longer speak in a loud voice.[76] In a further polemical vein, Luther's commentary used this biblical passage to condemn justification by works (if such a doctrine had been applied, the nine ungrateful men who had suffered

---

Origen on the Epistle to the Romans," *JTS* 13 (1912) 217.

68 In the fourth century, two passages from Epiphanius of Salamis's *Panarion* (42.11.6 and 42.11.17) help reconstruct a part of a text of Marcion and, thanks to the second, to discover a refutation. In the same work (*Panarion* 66.41.1), Epiphanius uses Luke 17:11-19 in his polemic against the Manicheans.

69 See n. 2 above.

70 Did the evangelistic tradition choose the number ten, as Albert the Great supposed, because of the number of lepers mentioned in the Bible?

71 Sermon no. 57, Dominica 14, in Schönbach, *Altdeutsche Predigten*, 2:156–58.

72 Luther, "Evangelium von den zehn Aussätzigen verdeutscht und ausgelegt," Wittenberg: Melchior Lotther 1521 (WA 8:340–97). See his Sermon from 9/6/1523 (WA 12:662–65), Sermon from 9/10/1531

(WA 34 2:184–95), Sermon from 9/14/1533 (WA 37:146–48). The case of the grateful Samaritan is also discussed in the Tischreden of Luther (WA TR 4, 702; No. 5183, Mülhaupt, *Luthers Evangelien-Auslegung*, 274–309).

73 Luther, "Evangelium" (WA 8:373), Mülhaupt, *Luthers Evangelien-Auslegung*, 293.

74 Luther, "Evangelium" (WA 8:355), Mülhaupt, *Luthers Evangelien-Auslegung*, 277. For Albert the Great, the obedience necessary for salvation must accompany faith; here it is love and gratitude—which do not determine salvation—that accompany faith.

75 Luther, "Evangelium" (WA 8:356), Mülhaupt, *Luthers Evangelien-Auslegung*, 278.

76 Luther, "Evangelium" (WA 8:355), Mülhaupt, *Luthers Evangelien-Auslegung*, 277.

from "leprosy" but were healed would have come down again with their merciless disease).[77] Like the painters in the Middle Ages, Luther knew that this story represented a diptych, the first *volet* relating to the beginnings of faith, and the second to its being put to the test and being perfected.[78] For Luther, a faith that is solid is one that is capable of expressing gratitude and persevering in patience. The Samaritan who turned back and came and prostrated himself at the Lord's feet defined what true worship is by his attitude.[79] Luther refused to identify "leprosy" with sin and showing oneself to the priests with oral confession.[80]

In the eighteenth century, Bengel was interested in listening to what both sides had to say. The voice that came out of the ten unfortunate men (v. 13) was a product of a labored effort on their part, since it was weak, as is always the case with a person suffering from "leprosy"; the loud voice of the healed Samaritan (v. 15) stands for the correct use of a recovered organ.[81]

In the first half of the nineteenth century, Wilhelm Martin Leberecht de Wette preached on this text in a clear, measured, conventional manner, without refusing to give vent to his emotions. What stood out for him in the episode of the ten men suffering from "leprosy" was the necessity of both public worship of God and personal piety. The individual gratitude expressed by the man healed of his "leprosy" fits into a collective step laid down by Christ, that of going to the priests.[82]

Conclusion

The binary structure of the story speaks for itself. The initial confidence of the ten men suffering from "leprosy," and the look, then the intervention of the healer, are followed by the new relationship between the one who is more than just someone who has been miraculously cured and the one who is much more than a healer. Thanks to his faith, his gratefulness, and his praise, the Samaritan truly encountered God's spokesman, the Messiah, and, through him, God himself. The fact that this grateful man who was healed of his "leprosy" was a Samaritan is also significant. Samaria appears as the symbol of nations who henceforth have access to salvation, which is more important than health. Distance has given way to proximity,[83] and silence to dialogue. For Luke, this Samaritan, who was as good as the other "Good Samaritan" (Luke 10:30-37), has also become a role model for future generations of readers to follow.

77 Luther, "Evangelium" (WA 8:355, 365), Mülhaupt, *Luthers Evangelien-Auslegung*, 277, 286.

78 Luther, "Evangelium" (WA 8:360, 368), Mülhaupt, *Luthers Evangelien-Auslegung*, 282, 288.

79 Luther, "Evangelium" (WA 8:378), Mülhaupt, *Luthers Evangelien-Auslegung*, 297.

80 Luther, "Evangelium" (WA 8:344–45), Mülhaupt, *Luthers Evangelien-Auslegung*, 274–75. Erasmus (*Paraphrasis*, 419) identifies the leper with heresy and insists on the trust (*fiducia*) of the ten lepers. Melanchthon (*Postillae*, 425–35) mostly discusses the following points: the miracle qua miracle is accomplished by love; it represents the promise of grace; it manifests divine power; it comes from divine compassion. Ingratitude is endemic to human beings (Adam is the archetype) and is opposed to the gratitude of faith (personified by the healed Samaritan). Priests are representatives not of the sacrament of penance (here he is with Luther) but of baptism and the Eucharist, of the evangelistic ministry and true worship (here he differs from Luther with whom he does not share such severity).

81 Bengel, *Gnomon*, 1:377.

82 Wilhelm Martin Leberecht de Wette, *Predigten, theils auslegender, theils abhandelnder Art. I–II* (Basel: Neukirch, 1825, 1827) 2:96–114.

83 See Eph 2:13: "But now by Jesus Christ you who were once *far* have been brought *near* by the blood of Christ." See also Acts 2:21, 39.

Bibliography Verses 20-21

Allen, P. M. S., "Luke xvii. 21: ἰδοὺ γὰρ ἡ βασιλεία τοῦ θεοῦ ἐντὸς ὑμῶν ἐστιν," *ExpT* 49 (1937–38) 476–77.

Ballard, Frank, "Luke xvii. 21," *ExpT* 38 (1926–27) 331.

Bauer, U., "Der Anfang der Endzeitrede in der Logienquelle (Q 17): Probleme der Rekonstruktion und Interpretation des Q-Textes," in Stefan H. Brandenburger and Thomas Hieke, eds., *Wenn drei das Gleiche sagen: Studien zu den drei Evangelien: Mit einer Werkstattübersetzung des Q-Textes* (Theologie 14; Münster i. W.: Lit, 1998) 79–101.

Beasley-Murray, George R., *Jesus and the Kingdom of God* (Grand Rapids: Eerdmans, 1986) 313–21.

Braun, Herbert, "Der Irrtum der Naherwartung," in idem, *Jesus—der Mann aus Nazareth und seine Zeit* (Stuttgart: Kreuz-Verlag, 1969) 201–13.

Bretscher, Paul M., "Luke 17:20-21 in Recent Investigations," *CTM* 22 (1951) 895–907.

Cadbury, Henry J., "The Kingdom of God and Ourselves," *ChrCent* 67 (1950) 172–73.

Carroll, John T., *Response to the End of History: Eschatology and Situation in Luke-Acts* (SBLDS 92; Atlanta: Scholars Press, 1988) 76–87.

Catchpole, David R., "The Law and the Prophets in Q," in G. F. Hawthorne and O. Betz, eds., *Tradition and Interpretation in the New Testament: Essays in Honor of E. Earle Ellis for His 60th Birthday* (Grand Rapids: Eerdmans, 1987) 95–109.

Conzelmann, *Theology*, 120–25.

Dalman, Gustaf, *Die Worte Jesu: Mit Berücksichtigung des nachkanonischen jüdischen Schrifttums und der aramäischen Sprache* (Leipzig: Hinrichs, 1898) 116–19.

Dodd, *Parables*, 62, 83, 87, 155.

Easton, Burton Scott, "Luke 17:20-21: An Exegetical Study," *AJT* 16 (1912) 275–83.

Elliott, J. K., "Seven Recently Published New Testament Fragments from Oxyrhynchus," *NovT* 42 (2000) 209–13.

Feuillet, André, "La double venue du règne de Dieu et du Fils de l'homme en Luc xvii, 20—xviii, 8: Recherches sur l'eschatologie des Synoptiques," *RThom* 81 (1981) 5–33.

Idem, "La venue du règne de Dieu et du Fils de l'homme (d'après Luc, XVII, 20 à XVIII, 8)," *RSR* 35 (1948) 544–65.

Glasson, Thomas Francis, "The Gospel of Thomas, Saying 3, and Deuteronomy xxx. 11-14," *ExpT* 78 (1966–67) 151–52.

Grässer, *Problem*, 170–72.

Griffiths, J. Gwyn, "ἐντὸς ὑμῶν (Luke xvii. 21)," *ExpT* 63 (1951–52) 30–31.

Grimm, Werner, *Jesus und das Danielbuch, I: Jesu Einspruch gegen das Offenbarungssystem Daniels: Mt 11, 25-27; Lk 17, 20-21* (ANTJ 6; Frankfurt/New York: Lang, 1984) 70–90.

Hampel, *Menschensohn*, 51–70.

Hartl, Hedda, "Die Aktualität des Gottesreiches nach Lk 17, 20f.," in H. Merklein and J. Lange, eds., *Biblische Randbemerkungen: Schülerfestschrift für Rudolf Schnackenburg zum 60. Geburtstag* (Würzburg: Echter, 1974) 25–30.

Hawthorne, G. F., "The Essential Nature of the Kingdom of God," *WTJ* 25 (1962–63) 35–47.

Héring, Jean, *Le royaume de Dieu et sa venue: Études sur l'espérance de Jésus et de l'apôtre Paul* (Bibliothèque théologique; Neuchâtel: Delachaux & Niestlé, 1959) 42–45.

Hiers, Richard H., "Why Will They Not Say, 'Lo, Here!' or 'There!'" *JAAR* 35 (1967) 379–84.

Jeremias, Joachim, "L'attente de la fin prochaine dans les paroles de Jésus," in E. Castelli, ed., *L'Infallibilità: L'aspetto filosofico e teologico. Atti del convegno indetto dal Centro internazionale di studi umanistici e dall'Istituto di studi filosofici. Roma, 5–12 gennaio 1970* (Rome: Istituto di studi filosofici, 1970) 185–94.

Joüon, Paul, "Notes philologiques sur les Évangiles, Luc 17:20-21," *RSR* 18 (1928) 354–55.

Kaestli, *L'eschatologie*, 28–37.

King, Karen, "Kingdom in the Gospel of Thomas," *Forum* 3 (1987) 48–97.

Kümmel, *Promise*, 32–36, 90–91, 103, 105, 151.

Lebourlier, Jean, "Entos hymon: Le sens 'au milieu de vous' est-il possible?" *Bib* 73 (1992) 259–62.

Lewis, F. W., "Luke xvii. 21," *ExpT* 38 (1926–27) 187–88.

Michaels, J. Ramsey, "Almsgiving and the Kingdom Within: Tertullian on Luke 17:21," *CBQ* 60 (1998) 475–83.

Morgen, Michele, "Lc 17,20 37 et Lc 21,8-11.20-24: Arrière-fond scripturaire," in Christopher Mark Tuckett, ed., *The Scriptures in the Gospels* (BETL 131; Leuven: Leuven University Press, 1997) 307–26.

Müller, Dieter, "Kingdom of Heaven or Kingdom of God?" *VC* 27 (1973) 266–76.

Mussner, Franz, "'Wann kommt das Reich Gottes?' Die Antwort Jesu nach Lk 17, 20b-21," *BZ* 6 (1962) 107–11.

Nicklin, T., "With Observation," *ExpT* 27 (1915–16) 475.

Noack, Bent, *Das Gottesreich bei Lukas: Eine Studie zu Luk. 17,20-24* (SymBU 10; Uppsala: Gleerup, 1948).

Percy, *Botschaft*, 216–33.

Perrin, *Rediscovering*, 58, 68–74, 77, 193–96.

Proctor, K. S., "Luke 17, 20.21," *BT* 33 (1982) 245.

Proost, K. F., "Lukas 17,21, ἐντὸς ὑμῶν," *TT* 48 (1914) 246–53.

Read, David, "Christ Comes Unexpectedly," *ExpT* 98 (1986) 21.

Riesenfeld, Harald, "ἐμβολεύειν ἐντός," *NSNU* 2 (1949) 11–12.

Idem, "Gudsriket-här eller där, mitt ibland människor eller inom dem? Till Luk 17:20-21," *SEÅ* 47 (1982) 93–101.

Idem, "Le Règne de Dieu parmi vous ou en vous? (Luc 17,20-21)," *RB* 98 (1991) 190–98.

Roberts, Colin H., "The Kingdom of Heaven (Lk. xvii. 21)," *HTR* 41 (1948) 1–8.

Robinson, James M., "The Study of the Historical Jesus after Nag Hammadi," *Semeia* 44 (1988) 45–55, esp. 53–55.

Rüstow, Alexander, "*ΕΝΤΟΣ ΥΜΩΝ ΕΣΤΙΝ*: Zur Deutung von Lukas 17.20-21," *ZNW* 51 (1960) 197–224.

Schlosser, *Règne de Dieu*, 1:179–243.

Schnackenburg, Rudolf, "Der eschatologische Abschnitt Lk 17, 20-37," in Descamps and de Halleux, *Mélanges*, 213–34.

Schrey, Heinz H., "Zu Luk. 17,21," *ThLZ* 74 (1949) 759.

Schwarz, Günther, "οὐκ μετὰ παρατηρήσεως?" *BN* 59 (1991) 45–48.

Sledd, Andrew, "The Interpretation of Luke 17, 21," *ExpT* 50 (1938–39) 235–37.

Smith, Albert G., "'The Kingdom of God Is within You,'" *ExpT* 43 (1931–32) 378–79.

Sneed, Richard, "'The Kingdom of God Is within You' (Luke 17,21)," *CBQ* 24 (1962) 363–82.

Strobel, August, "A. Merx über Lc. 17, 20f," *ZNW* 51 (1960) 133–34.

Idem, "In dieser Nacht (Luk 17,34): Zu einer älteren Form der Erwartung in Luk 17,20-37," *ZThK* 58 (1961) 16–29.

Idem, "Die Passa-Erwartung als urchristliches Problem in Lc 17,20f.," *ZNW* 49 (1958) 157–96.

Idem, "Zu Lk 17,20f," *BZ* 7 (1963) 111–13.

Tödt, *Son of Man*, 101, 104–8, 262.

Uro, Risto, *Neither Here Nor There: Lk 17:20-21 and Related Sayings in Thomas, Mark and Q* (Occasional Papers of the Institute for Antiquity and Christianity 20; Claremont, Calif.: Institute for Antiquity and Christianity, 1990).

Wabnitz, Auguste, "Note supplémentaire sur Luc XVII, 21," *RThQR* 18 (1909) 289–94.

Idem, "Note sur Luc XVII, 21," *RThQR* 18 (1909) 234–38.

Idem, "Seconde note supplémentaire sur Luc XVII, 21," *RThQR* 18 (1909) 456–66.

Waggett, P. N., "Studies in Texts," *Theol* 8 (1924) 163–66.

Weiss, Johannes, *Die Idee des Reiches Gottes in der Theologie* (VTKG 16; Giessen: Ricker, 1901) 4–6, 30, 48–49.

Wenham, David, *The Rediscovery of Jesus' Eschatological Discourse* (Gospel Perspectives 4; Sheffield: JSOT Press, 1984) 107–9, 135–74.

Wikgren, Allen, "ENTOS," *NSNU* 4 (1950) 27–28.

Bibliography Verses 22-37

Allen, H. J., "The Apocalyptic Discourse in S. Luke XVII," *Exp* 4/9 (1925) 59–61.

Ashby, E., "The Days of the Son of Man," *ExpT* 67 (1955–56) 124–25.

Black, M., "The Aramaic Dimensions in Q with Notes on Luke 17.22 and Matthew 24.26 (Luke 17.23)," *JSNT* 40 (1990) 33–41.

Borsch, Frederick H., *The Son of Man in Myth and History* (NTL; London: SCM, 1967) 307–8, 343, 347–57, 380–82, 399.

Bover, José M., "Desearéis ver uno de los días del hijo del hombre (Luc. 17,22)," in *Valoración sobrenatural del "cosmos": La inspiración bíblica. Otros estudios. XIV Semana bíblica española (21–26 Sept. 1953)* (Madrid: Consejo Superior de Investigaciones Científicas, Instituto Francisco Suárez, 1954) 391–97.

Bovon, *Theologian*, 23–28, 58 n. 59, 65–67.

Brunec, Michael, "Sermo eschatologicus," *VD* 30 (1952) 214–18, 265–77, 321–31; 31 (1953) 13–20, 83–94, 156–63, 211–20, 282–90, 344–51.

Carroll, *Response*, 87–96.

Catchpole, David R., "The Law and the Prophets in Q," in G. F. Hawthorne and O. Betz, eds., *Tradition and Interpretation in the New Testament: Essays in Honor of E. Earle Ellis for His 60th Birthday* (Grand Rapids: Eerdmans, 1987) 95–109.

Colpe, C., "ὁ υἱὸς τοῦ ἀνθρώπου," *TDNT* 8 (1972) 400–77.

Delobel, "Sayings," 456–57.

Dupont, Jacques, *Les trois apocalypses synoptiques, Marc 13, Matthieu 24–25, Luc 21* (LD 121; Paris: Cerf, 1985) 99, 145–46.

Feuillet, André, "La double venue du Règne de Dieu et du Fils de l'homme en Luc XVII, 20—XVIII, 8: Recherches sur l'eschatologie des Synoptiques," *RThom* 81 (1981) 5–33.

Geiger, Ruthild, *Die lukanischen Endzeitreden: Studien zur Eschatologie des Lukas-Evangeliums* (EHS.T 16; Bern: Herbert Lang; Frankfurt: Lang, 1973).

Guenther, Heinz O., "A Fair Face Is Half the Portion: The Lot Saying in Luke 17:28-29," *Forum* 6 (1990) 56–66.

Idem, "When 'Eagles' Draw Together," *Forum* 5 (1989) 140–50.

Hemelsoet, Ben, "Jesus en Jeruzalem niet gescheiden, niet gedeeld [17,37]," *ACEBT* 3 (1982) 86–98.

Higgins, Angus J. B., *Jesus and the Son of Man* (London: Lutterworth, 1964) 162–65.

Hoffmann, *Logienquelle*, 37–42, 44, 269, 284.

Jefford, Clayton N., "The Dangers of Lying in Bed: Luke 17:34-35 and Parallels," *Forum* 5 (1989) 106–10.

Kloppenborg, *Formation*, 154–66.

Kümmel, *Promise*, 29, 38.

Lambrecht, Jan, "Q-Influence on Mark 8,34—9,1 [12,8-9; 14,27; 17,33]," in Delobel, *Logia*, 456–57.

Laufen, *Doppelüberlieferungen*, 315–36, 361–84.

Leaney, Robert, "The Days of the Son of Man (Luke xvii. 22)," *ExpT* 67 (1955–56) 28–29.

Léon-Dufour, Xavier, "Luc 17,33," *RSR* 69 (1981) 101–12.

Leroy, Herbert, "'Wer sein Leben gewinnen will . . .': Erlöste Existenz heute," *FZPhTh* 25 (1978) 171–86.

Lührmann, *Logienquelle*, 71–83.

Idem, "Noah und Lot (Lk 17:26-29)—Ein Nachtrag," *ZNW* 63 (1972) 130–32.

Manson, *Sayings*, 141–47.

Marchi, J. de., "'Ubicumque fuerit corpus, ibi congregabuntur et aquilae' (Mt. 24, 28; Lc. 17, 37)," *VD* 18 (1938) 329–33.

Meyer, Dieter, "πολλὰ παθείν," *ZNW* 55 (1964) 132.

Mundhenk, Norman, "Problems Involving Illustrations in Luke," *BT* 44 (1993) 247–48.

Oñate Ojeda, Juan A., "Nota exegética: Pues, así como el relámpago," *Burg* 32 (1991) 569–72.

Pesch, Rudolf, *Naherwartungen: Tradition und Redaktion in Mk 13* (KBANT; Düsseldorf: Patmos, 1968), 112, 147–48.

Powell, W., "The Days of the Son of Man," *ExpT* 67 (1955–56) 219.

Rigaux, Béda, "La petite apocalypse de Luc (XVII, 22-37)," in *Ecclesia a Spiritu Sancto edocta: Mélanges théologiques, hommages à Mgr Gérard Philips* (BETL 27; Gembloux: J. Duculot, 1970) 407–38.

Sabourin, Leopold, "The Eschatology of Luke," *BTB* 12 (1982) 73–76.

Schlosser, Jacques, "Les jours de Noé et de Lot: A propos de Luc, xvii, 26-30," *RB* 80 (1973) 13–36.

Schnackenburg, Rudolf, "Der eschatologische Abschnitt Lk 17, 20-37," in Descamps and de Halleux, *Mélanges*, 213–34.

Schneider, Gerhard, "Anbruch des Heils und Hoffnung auf Vollendung bei Jesus, Paulus und Lukas," in idem, *Lukas, Theologe der Heilsgeschichte: Aufsätze zum lukanischen Doppelwerk* (Bonn: Hanstein, 1985) 35–60.

Idem, *Parusiegleichnisse im Lukasevangelium* (SBS 74; Stuttgart: Katholisches Bibelwerk, 1975) 42–46.

Schulz, *Q*, 277–87.

Souza, Bernard de, "The Coming of the Lord," *SBFLA* 20 (1970) 166–208.

Steinhauser, *Doppelbildworte*, 197–214.

Tannehill, *Sword*, 118–22.

Tödt, *Son of Man*, 47–51, 104–12, 259–62.

Vielhauer, *Aufsätze*, 74–76, 108–10.

Wenham, *Rediscovery*.

Winstanley, Edward W., "Days of the Son of Man," *ExpT* 24 (1912–13) 533–38.

Zmijewski, Josef, *Die Eschatologiereden des Lukas-Evangeliums: Eine traditions- und redaktionsgeschichtliche Untersuchung zu Lk 21, 5-36 und Lk 17, 20-37* (BBB 40; Bonn: Hanstein, 1972) 326–540.

Idem, "Die Eschatologiereden Luk 21 und Lk 17: Überlegungen zum Verständnis und zur Einordnung der lukanischen Eschatologie," *BiLeb* 14 (1973) 30–40.

20/ **When questioned by the Pharisees, who consulted him in order to find out when the kingdom of God was coming, he replied in these words[a], "The kingdom of God is not coming in a way that can be observed; 21/ they will not say, 'Look, here it is!' or 'There it is!' For, in fact, the kingdom of God is in the space that belongs to you."**

22/ **Then he said to the disciples, "The days are coming when you will long to see one of the days of the Son of Man, and you will not see it. 23/ And they will say to you, 'Look there!' or 'Look here!' Do not go[b], do not set off in pursuit! 24/ For as the lightning flashes and lights up the sky from one side to the other, so it will be with the Son of Man in his day[c]. 25/ But**

a Literally: "Consulted by the Pharisees, when will the kingdom of God come, he answered them and said."

b Literally: "Do not go away."

c The words "in his day" are not found in all the manuscripts; see below, p. 518.

first he must endure much suffering and be rejected by this generation. 26/ Just as it was in the days of Noah, so too will it be in the days of the Son of Man. 27/ They were eating and drinking, and marrying and being given in marriage, until the day Noah entered the ark, and the flood came and destroyed all of them. 28/ Likewise, just as it was in the days of Lot: they were eating and drinking, buying and selling, planting and building; 29/ on the day that Lot left Sodom, it rained fire and sulfur from heaven and destroyed all of them. 30/ It will be like that on the day that the Son of Man will be revealed[d]. 31/ On that day, anyone on the housetop who has belongings[e] in the house must not come down to take them away; and likewise anyone in the field must not turn back toward what is behind him. 32/ Remember Lot's wife. 33/ Those who try to acquire their life[f] will lose it, but those who lose their life will keep it. 34/ I tell you, on that night there will be two men in one bed; one will be taken and the other left. 35/ There will be two women grinding meal together; one will be taken and the other left[g]." 37/ And answering, they said to him, "Where, Lord?" He said to them, "Where the corpse is, there the eagles will gather."

d   Literally: "is revealed"
e   Literally: "and his belongings"
f   Literally: "his soul"
g   Verse 36 ("Two will be in the field; one will be taken, the other left") was not a part of the original text of the Gospel of Luke; see below, p. 524.

The categories of time and space are dominant in these verses and constitute its framework. In fact, we ought to talk about times and spaces, since this text offers a solution to the problem of the relationship between the human present and the divine future, between created space and hoped-for space, although the logic of this relationship is in part enigmatic. The difference between each of these pairs and among them all is not just a question of duration or distance, since these categories intermingle at the same time that each spreads out in its own way. The Son of Man has his days and his day; he will come and he has come. As for "you," you must act clearheadedly as you consider examples from the past in Scripture and Jesus' teaching in the present. If you do so, you will overcome your disappointments, avoid traps, and, in the end, save your lives.

Analysis

Synchronic Analysis

Here Luke places his first apocalyptic discourse, between a miracle story (the ten men suffering from "leprosy," 17:12-19) and a parable (the widow and the unjust judge, 18:1-8). In fact, vv. 20-37 are made up of three units of unequal length: an answer by Jesus aimed at the Pharisees (vv. 20-21), followed by a prophecy intended for the disciples (vv. 22-35), and a final maxim in answer to a question asked by the disciples (v. 37).[1]

Verses 20-21 resemble an apophthegm (or *chreia*).[2] On the one hand, there is the question attributed to Jesus' adversaries about when the kingdom of God will come; on the other, the decisive answer, which unfolds in three waves, two negative and one positive.[3] The positive part

---

1   On the inauthenticity of v. 36, see below.
2   In contrast to a pure apophthegm, the text does not make the Pharisees the subject of the first verb and is content to report their question.

3   More interested in Jesus' last saying (v. 21b), Luke does not report the Pharisees' reaction.

of the answer ("for, in fact, the kingdom of God is in the space that belongs to you"; v. 21b) justifies the double negative part of it ("The kingdom of God is not coming in a way that can be observed; they will not say, 'Look, here it is!' or 'There it is!'; vv. 20b-21a). There is, in fact, a tension between the Pharisees' question and Jesus' answer, insofar as the question has to do with the date, and the answer with the nature of its coming.

Verses 22-35 represent a collection of the Master's apocalyptic maxims, whose effect on the disciples is pointed out by Luke in v. 37a. In these verses it is no longer a question of the kingdom of God, but of the Son of Man. Moreover, although Jesus' answer to the Pharisees avoided verbs in the future tense, here they are omnipresent.

Even if the terms "day," "days," and the title "Son of Man" provide the passage with a definite consistency, it is not easy to group the sentences in it into units of meaning; v. 22 evokes a melancholic future frustration (the period during which the Son of Man will be absent); v. 23 gives a good piece of advice (beware of false messages localizing the presence of the Son of Man); v. 24 makes use of a comparison, namely, lightning (to describe the coming Son of Man); v. 25 claims, in another style, that there will be an event (the passion) that must necessarily precede the end-time (the parousia); vv. 26-27 and vv. 28-30, which are symmetrical, provide a double comparison, one with Noah's time and one with Lot's; v. 31 supplies a second double piece of advice (face up to the situation and do not turn back); v. 32 confirms v. 31 by the use of an example that connects with Lot's time, already mentioned (in vv. 28-29); v. 33, which is in another style, justifies in its own way the previous advice (given in v. 31): by accepting to lose one's life, one gains it; vv. 34-35, which are concrete in the same way that v. 31 is, describe the apocalyptic selection process (one is taken, the other left behind), deliver an implicit menace, and indirectly issue an invitation to adopt a satisfactory stance.

By its structure and its set of themes, v. 37 resembles vv. 20-21. This verse, which is a little apophthegm (or *chreia*), first reports a question asked by the listeners (v. 37a), then mentions the Master's answer in the form of a proverb or an enigma (the corpse and the birds of prey, v. 37b). By the inclusion thus created with the beginning of the pericope (vv. 20-21), Luke sought to unify the whole passage. But he was also at pains to note the evolution of the problem: while the Pharisees were worried about the date ("when?" [πότε], v. 20), the disciples asked about the place ("where?" [ποῦ], v. 37a).

Diachronic Analysis

As was the case with the send-off speeches (9:3-5 and 10:2-12), Luke keeps the apocalyptic speech that he derives from Mark separate from the one that he gets from Q. Although he saves the one from Mark 13 for the eve of the passion (Luke 21:5-33), he places the one from Q here, namely, at the end of the travel narrative.

In fact, Luke is not satisfied with recopying Q when he offers us this collection of sayings. He reworks it in various ways: by quoting, not without adapting, a maxim that probably comes from L, which he places at the beginning of his composition (vv. 20b-21, on the kingdom of God);[4] by incorporating a passage from Mark's apocalypse (v. 31 par. Mark 13:15-16, on the one who must not come down from the roof); by moving to this place a maxim from Q (v. 33 par. Matt 10:39, on the loss of one's life), which he considered a useful commentary on the difficult saying he had just mentioned (v. 31); by composing himself certain sentences to use as an introduction (v. 22, on the longing to see one of the days of the Son of Man) or as a theological supplement (v. 25, on the necessity of the passion) and ethical supplement (v. 32, on Lot's wife); and by reworking everything derived from Q in order to adapt it to the orientation and tone of his work.

Even if this reconstruction of the prehistory of the text remains hypothetical, an exegetical consensus emerges on several points:[5] the verses that have a parallel in Mat-

---

4   Because of the parallels in *Gos. Thom.* 3 (= *P.Oxy.* 654), *Gos. Thom.* 113, *Gos. Mary* 8.15-22; and Matt 24:26, the inclusion of Luke 17:20-21 in Q has attracted scholars' attention anew; see Robinson, "Study," 50–53; King, "Kingdom," 59–67; Uro, *Neither Here Nor There*; Bauer, "Der Anfang," 79–101.

5   See the commentaries of, for example, Schweizer, and the principal studies mentioned in the two bibliographies on this pericope, such as Kaestli, Zmijewski, Geiger, Kloppenborg.

thew (vv. 23, 24, 26-27, 30, 34-35, 37) come from Q;[6] v. 31 comes from Mark; the introductions (vv. 20a, 22a, and 37a) and certain sentences (vv. 25 and 32) are redactional. There remain some doubts: Do vv. 20b-21 really belong to L, or were they, in one form or another, from Q? Verse 22 (on the longing to see one of the days of the Son of Man) is certainly redactional, but may be the reformulating of a tradition by Luke.[7] What is the relationship between v. 21a ("they will not say, 'Look, here it is!' or 'There it is!'"), v. 23 ("And they will say to you, 'Look there!' or 'Look here!' Do not go, do not set off in pursuit."), and Matt 24:26 ("So, if they say to you, 'Look! He is in the wilderness,' do not go out. If they say, 'Look! He is in the inner rooms,' do not believe it." [NRSV])? The second example, the one about Lot (vv. 28-29) has no parallel in Matthew; it could be redactional, but Luke is not known to create doublets willingly.[8] So these verses could come from the tradition, going back to either Q or L or to an oral tradition. As was his habit, Luke respected Q's order, but did permit himself an exception: in order to achieve the equilibrium he was hoping to create and provide something to match vv. 20-21 (on the "when?"), the Gospel writer created a final apophthegm (v. 37, on the "where?"), which he filled with a maxim from Q on the corpse and the eagles (v. 37b), which Matthew had maintained in its original position (between the maxim about lightning and the example of Noah; Matt 24:28).[9] Finally, we should note that Luke has here abandoned one of his principles, that of concentrating on one source at a time.[10] To be sure, he did not mix Mark's apocalypse and Q's, as Matthew 24 did. Nevertheless, he did sandwich several foreign elements into Q. I will highlight the details of the relation between tradition and redaction as I develop the exegesis of the passage, as they are decisive for arriving at its meaning.

Commentary

The Presence of the Kingdom of God

■ **20-21** In Luke, when the Pharisees question Jesus, are they spying on him and setting a trap for him? In 15:2; 16:14; and 18:9-14, passages similar to this one, Luke presents a negative image of them. However, this context is not sufficient to categorize their question as an inquisition or a trap. Ἐπερωτάω here means "consult" rather than "interrogate."[11] Jesus is going to correct the Pharisees' information, not thwart their evil plot.

Jewish faith, following the Royal Psalms (Psalms 47; 93; 96–99; etc.), attests to God's present, but celestial, royalty. What Israel hopes for is the earthly realization of this power. Hence we have an alternation of impatience, confidence, and disappointment. The question of the delay of the end-time is not just a Christian one. It was first a Jewish one, as witnessed to by both the book of the prophet Habakkuk and the commentary on it provided by the Qumran pesher (Hab 2:2-3; 1QpHab 6.12–7.14).[12] When the Pharisees in Luke asked about the date, they were wondering about the earthly eschatological manifestation of God's royal power. The Gospel writer was not unaware that that question, combined with faith in the risen Christ, is also a Christian question, which will be echoed by the parable in the next chapter (18:1-8), the Emmaus disciples' complaint (24:21), and the eleven disciples' post-Easter question (Acts 1:6).[13]

6   See "International Q Project," in Brandenburger and Hieke, *Studien*, 119–20. Kloppenborg (*Formation*, 154–66) attributes the second example, that of Lot (vv. 28-29) to Q as well, but refuses, rightly, to include vv. 20b-21 as an integral part of Q.

7   See Schnackenburg, "Der eschatologische Abschnitt Lk 17, 20-37," 219–22 (only the words "the days are coming" are traditional).

8   See Henry J. Cadbury, *The Style and Literary Method of Luke* (HTS 6; Cambridge, Mass.: Harvard University Press, 1920) 85–88. On the other hand, Schulz (*Q*, 279–80) and Lührmann (*Logienquelle*, 71–83; idem, "Noah und Lot," 130–32), think that Matthew retained the original text of Q and that Luke's text reflects the secondary influence of the Jewish tradition (the flood from the days of Noah and fire raining down on Sodom in the days of Lot as examples of divine punishment). Guenther ("Fair Face," 56–66) offers several reasons why vv. 28-29 are inauthentic, principally that, as examples of early Christian, post-Easter exegesis, these two verses could not go back to the historical Jesus.

9   On this displacement, I share the opinion of Kloppenborg, *Formation*, 155–56.

10   See the introduction in vol. 1.

11   On ἐπερωτάω, see Spicq, *Lexicon*, 2:32–33; Moulton and Milligan, *Vocabulary*, s.v.

12   Strobel, *Verzögerungsproblem*, 7–19.

13   See Grässer, *Problem*, 21 n. 2, 23, 36–38, 204–7; and Bovon, *Theologian*, 13–33.

The question of the date cannot be separated from the question of the knowledge of the date, nor even, for that matter, from the very question of knowledge itself and the ways of obtaining knowledge. Jesus replied that external means of acquiring knowledge, such as observing the stars or other visible signs, are of no use. The Greek word translated "be observed" ($\pi\alpha\rho\alpha\tau\acute{\eta}\rho\eta\sigma\iota\varsigma$), a *hapax legomenon* in the New Testament, belongs to the vocabulary of persons who are educated, or even learned; it was used by astronomers and in the observations necessary for fixing a religious calendar or the esoteric calculations of astrologers.[14] This Greek term appears in several Greek translations—those of Aquila, Theodotion, and Symmachus—of the Hebrew for "night of vigil" (לֵיל שִׁמֻּרִים) in Exod 12:42. The night of Passover is a night that must be observed by accurately calculating it and by carefully respecting it. Now the end of the world was also supposed to take place at night, like the liberation of Israel from Egypt—hence the apocalyptic excitement in certain Jewish circles in Jesus' time when they calculated the date of Passover. Some commentators have wanted to limit the meaning of the expression "in a way that can be observed" ($\mu\epsilon\tau\grave{\alpha}\ \pi\alpha\rho\alpha\tau\eta\rho\acute{\eta}\sigma\epsilon\omega\varsigma$) to the calculation of the date and the observance of the night of Passover.[15] That ought not to be true at the redactional level, since Luke attacks, in the maxim he attributes to Jesus, any examination of exterior signs or any apocalyptic speculation, whether Jewish, Christian, Greek, or Roman. Diodore of Sicily used the term to refer to Celtic, Egyptian, or Babylonian religious or astrological practices (5.31.3; 1.9.6; 1.28.1). The apostle Paul corrected errors, perhaps of Jewish origin, that led people to "observe" ($\pi\alpha\rho\alpha\tau\eta\rho\acute{\epsilon}o\mu\alpha\iota$) special days, months, seasons, and years (Gal 4:10).[16] Luke, like Paul (1 Thess 5:1-2) or Mark (Mark 13:32), felt that no one could know the date of the end of the world, of the parousia of the Son of Man, or of the arrival of the kingdom of God; that no one could know, or should try to know these times (Acts 1:7: "It is not for you to know the times or periods that the Father has set by his own authority"). There are better things to do: live attentively as Christians, proclaiming the gospel to the uttermost ends of the earth, in the hope of the arrival of a kingdom that would come without warning.[17]

Even if the wording of the Pharisees' question (v. 20a) is Lukan, Jesus' answer must trace back to L. Indeed, Luke does not use the vocabulary of "observing" ($\pi\alpha\rho\alpha\tau\acute{\eta}\rho\eta\sigma\iota\varsigma$) anywhere else.[18] L is fond of using the vocabulary of cultured people; the words "they will not say, 'Look, here it is!' or 'There it is!'"[19] seem to be less an imitation of v. 23 than a borrowing from a tradition parallel to Q (if Q, according to Luke 17:23, probably dealt with the Son of Man, this other tradition was probably concerned with the kingdom of God).[20] The meaning of Jesus' second assertion is not obvious; either (a) no one can tell if the kingdom of God is here or if it is there, since it provides no precursory warning; or (b) one cannot tell if it is here or if it is there, since it has already arrived (in some imperceptible way).[21]

Then we have the decisive maxim: "For, in fact, the kingdom of God is in the space that belongs to you." Even if the translation of this sentence is problematic, that is less the result of the intention of an author who loved enigmas[22] than of our inability to translate the

---

14 Rüstow, "Deutung," 197–201.

15 Strobel, "Passa-Erwartung," 157–96; idem, "A. Merx über Lc. 17, 20f," 133–34; idem, "Zu Lk 17,20f," 111–13.

16 See Harald Riesenfeld, "$\tau\eta\rho\acute{\epsilon}\omega\ \kappa\tau\lambda.$," *TDNT* 8 (1972) 140–46.

17 See Acts 1:6-8, 11; Luke 12:35-40 (the ignorance is indicated in v. 39); and Luke 13:23-30. Even though $\acute{\epsilon}\rho\chi\epsilon\tau\alpha\iota$ is in the present tense, it must have a future connotation; see Schlosser, *Règne de Dieu*, 1:189.

18 Undoubtedly mistaken, Schwarz ("$o\grave{\upsilon}\kappa\ \mu\epsilon\tau\grave{\alpha}$ $\pi\alpha\rho\alpha\tau\eta\rho\acute{\eta}\sigma\epsilon\omega\varsigma$?" 46) considers the words $\mu\epsilon\tau\grave{\alpha}$ $\pi\alpha\rho\alpha\tau\eta\rho\acute{\eta}\sigma\epsilon\omega\varsigma$ to be a translation of the Aramaic כְּנָטִיר ("insgeheim," meaning "in secret"). In his opinion, the kingdom of God does not come in a hidden manner.

19 Innumerable manuscripts have the words $\mathring{\eta}\ i\delta o\grave{\upsilon}$ $\acute{\epsilon}\kappa\epsilon\hat{\iota}$ ("or here it is"); see the apparatus of Nestle-Aland.

20 On Q 17:23, see Kloppenborg, *Q Parallels*, 190–92.

21 Grimm (*Danielbuch*, 70–90) wonders if Jesus is attacking two different adversaries: in v. 20b, he addresses an apocalyptic group inspired by the book of Daniel, whereas in v. 21a he denounces a zealot group attempting to establish the kingdom of God on earth here and now.

22 François Bovon, "The Effect of Realism and Prophetic Ambiguity in the Works of Luke," in idem, *Traditions*, 97–104.

Greek word ἐντός with certitude. Three different translations have been suggested for this adverb, improperly used as a preposition: "within/inside/in the heart of," "among/in the midst of," and "within the reach/grasp/possession of." The commonest meaning is the first one, "within." It fits well here, since the text contrasts the exterior to the interior, the visible to the imperceptible.[23] It is the meaning that has been favored for many centuries by commentators sensitive to the inner and spiritual nature of the Christian faith. The objection that can be made to this translation is that it would be strange of Luke to affirm the presence of the kingdom of God inside the Pharisees' hearts! On the other hand, in favor of this translation we can point to the wording of this maxim in *Gos. Thom.* 3, which makes a play on the opposition of the exterior to the interior.[24] When ἐντός is used with a noun or a pronoun in the genitive plural referring to persons, it becomes ambiguous: either "within you," with "you" referring to a collection of individuals (that is, "within each one of you"); or "within you," taking "you" as a group (that is, "in your midst," "among you").[25] Many recent commentators have opted for this last translation, as have several translations of the Bible.[26] It has appealed to theologians and other Christians

who associate the kingdom with Christ's presence in the church. Objections that can be made to this translation are that it flies in the face of the many passages in Luke that insist on the apocalyptic character of the kingdom of God,[27] and that it forgets the normal use in Luke-Acts of another expression, ἐν μέσῳ, followed by the genitive, with the meaning "in the midst of," "among."[28] A third translation, "within your reach/grasp/purview," would respect the Lukan interest in ethics, conversion, and decision making. This is the meaning we find in a papyrus that is approximately contemporaneous with Luke, telling of a woman who had a reserve supply of wine locked up that was ἐντὸς αὐτῆς, "at her disposal," "in her possession," "in/at her house."[29] Objections that can be made to this translation are that it accepts a marginal use of ἐντός and that it suggests a theory of the availability of the reign of God that is poorly attested in Luke-Acts.[30]

It is hard to make up one's mind. Personally, I prefer the present meaning (rather than the immediate future) of the verb "it is" (ἐστίν). Moreover, I believe that ἐντός is not absolutely synonymous with ἐν. The adverb, used as a preposition, has the concrete meaning of "in the space of."[31] Finally, I would like to connect Jesus' state-

---

23   Riesenfeld ("Le Règne de Dieu," 190–98) has argued vigorously in favor of this translation; see his articles from 1949 and 1982 in the bibliography.

24   "If those who lead you tell you: 'See, the kingdom is in heaven,' then the birds of the sky will be there ahead of you. If they tell you, 'It is in the sea,' then the fish will be there ahead of you. But the kingdom is inside you and outside you." The corresponding Greek text is included in *P.Oxy.* 654, which is cited by Aland, *Synopsis*, 315; see King, "Kingdom," 59–65. One should also consult *Gos. Thom.* 113: "His disciples said to him, 'On which day will the kingdom come?' [Jesus said:] 'It will not come by expecting it. No one will say "Here it is" or "There it is." But the Kingdom of the Father is spread out over the earth and men do not see it.'" See also *Gos. Mary* 8.15-22: "Be careful lest someone mislead you and tell you 'here he is' or 'there he is' because the Son of Man is within you; follow after him. Those who seek him will find him. Go then and proclaim the gospel of the kingdom." The question of the timing of the kingdom's arrival crops up also in *2 Clem.* 12.2, as it does in Luke 17:20a, but with a response that deviates from Luke 17:20b-21: "When someone asked the Lord when the kingdom would come, he

said, 'when the two are one and the outside like the inside and the male with the female, neither male nor female.'"

25   See Schlosser, *Règne de Dieu*, 1:202; Lebourlier ("Entos hymon," 259–62) defends the possibility of it, contra Riesenfeld, "Le Règne."

26   See, e.g., *NRSV, NAB, NJB, REB, TNIV,* Segond, and *TOB.*

27   Beginning with the second request of the Lord's Prayer (11:2).

28   For example, Jesus at twelve years old among the elders: ἐν μέσῳ τῶν διδασκάλων (Luke 2:46); see also 22:27; 24:36; Acts 1:15; 2:22; 6:15; and 27:21; Rüstow, "Deutung," 212–13.

29   *Papyrus Oxyrhynchus* 2342, 1:7–8 (London, 1954, 124–27), cited by Rüstow ("Deutung," 214), who provides other examples (pp. 214–16). See previously Roberts, "Kingdom of Heaven," 1–8; Griffiths, "ἐντὸς ὑμῶν," 30–31.

30   It only complicates the oldest interpretations, such as Tertullian's (*Adv. Marc.* 4.34) and Origen's (*Hom. Num.* 24.2); Origen *Or.* 2.25.1 takes on this meaning; see below.

31   See Lebourlier, "Entos hymon," 259.

ment with the Hebrew Bible theology of God's presence among his people.[32] Deuteronomy 30:11-14 declares that the divine commandment is hidden neither in heaven nor beyond the sea. According to Exod 17:7, the guilty Israelites doubted God's presence among them at Massah and Meribah. In Exod 34:9, Moses asked God to help him by being present among a stubborn people. According to Zephaniah (3:14-20), the daughter of Zion can rejoice, since "the king of Israel, the LORD, is in your midst" (v. 15b; cf. v. 17a).[33] It would appear, then, that in 17:21 Luke wished to turn our attention away from apocalyptic calculations, expressing doubt and mistrust, in order to orient our attention toward God's presence among his people, a presence requiring faith to make it real. It is not just a question of what is inside us believers, even if God's presence—which is exterior to us, linked to the person of Christ, and opposed to the people of Israel when they rebel—implies an interior attitude of one's heart. We can compare Luke 17:21 with Rom 10:5-13, where it is said that the Word of God, Christ's presence, and the righteousness of faith are not far from us, that they are on our lips and in our hearts. In Jesus, the kingdom of God has come to us (cf. 11:20). It still happens in our day in apostolic preaching (cf. 10:9). So the kingdom of God is not just an apocalyptic category (cf. Acts 28:31). It and its coming must be distinguished from the Son of Man and his eschatological coming, about which vv. 22-37 speak. The two realities are certainly associated, but there is a tension between them, between the sending of the Son and his ultimate parousia, between the inconspicuous presence of the kingdom already in the present and its powerful manifestation at the end of time.[34] Luke 17:21 asserts the kingdom's presence in order to allow the following verses better to set out the future.[35]

While Waiting for the Son of Man

■ **22-23** Verses 22-24 form a small unit that is somewhat reminiscent of vv. 20-21. The change of audience indicates only a slight pause.[36] The disciples long to live through an eschatological day, just as the Pharisees hoped to see the coming of the kingdom of God. Christian hope is patterned on Jewish hope. There will be misleading rumors circulating among Christians similar to those that have circulated among Jews. The truth is that the Son of Man will come in the unlimited effervescence of a dazzling flash of lightning, just as the kingdom is already present in the limited space that is your own. Luke attempts to set out the category of the kingdom, which he draws from the side of the present, and that of the Son of Man, which he draws from the side of the future.[37]

Even though the disciples already participate in the joy of the present kingdom, they will not be satisfied with that anticipatory joy. Their future in the church, in the present, in this world, will remain oriented toward its eschatological completion. The "until he comes" of the eucharistic liturgy (1 Cor 11:26) comes to mind, as does the beatitude in Luke 14:15 ("Blessed is anyone who will dine in the kingdom of God"), and the *Marana tha,* "Our Lord, come" (1 Cor 16:22).

Luke sets the plural ("the days are coming") against the singular ("one of the days"),[38] and duration against a moment in time. The church is going through a long period of dissatisfaction and aspiration. It misses the Son of Man and would like to know the joy of his presence, if only for a short while, just as it did, perhaps, when Jesus was there,[39] or when, most certainly, he will return. The desire to see the promised land or the blessings of the end-time is a theme of Jewish hope that the early

---

32 With Schlosser (*Règne de Dieu,* 1:179–243) and Grimm (*Danielbuch,* 70–90).

33 See Grimm, *Danielbuch,* 84–90.

34 On the kingdom of God, see the brief excursus in the commentary above on 13:18.

35 For me the most helpful studies on Luke 17:20-21 have been Noack, *Gottesreich;* Strobel, "Passa-Erwartung"; Rüstow, "Deutung"; Mussner, "'Wann kommt das Reich Gottes?'" 107–11; and Schlosser, *Règne de Dieu,* 1:179–243.

36 See Noack, *Gottesreich,* 40; Conzelmann, *Theology,* 123.

37 See Geiger, *Die lukanischen Endzeitreden,* 37–76; and Bovon, *Theologian,* 25–28.

38 The expression "the days of the Son of man" is ambiguous. It could refer to the messianic era, the time of the parousia, or the period of the earthly ministry of Jesus; see Kaestli, *L'eschatologie,* 31.

39 Kaestli (*L'eschatologie,* 31) limits the aspiration of the disciples to the past. The expression "the days of the Son of Man" in v. 26, which has an eschatological orientation, seems to me to prevent limiting v. 22 to the past, historical Jesus alone.

Christians, especially Luke, took over for themselves.[40] But for the time being (which is a time that stretches out into the future), there is nothing to hope for except waiting and perseverance: "you will not see it" (καὶ οὐκ ὄψεσθε). The sentence, right down to the wording "the days are coming" (ἐλεύσονται ἡμέραι, v. 22), recalls 5:35: "when the bridegroom will be taken away," that will be the beginning of a period of fasting.[41] The time of the church is just as much a period of separation as it is a time of communion.

Luke nips enthusiastic impulses in the bud. The false prophets who announce the coming and the presence of the Son of Man are not to be believed. In early Christianity that risk, which is removed here, was serious enough that a warning had to be given in the Gospel of Mark (13:21-23) and, probably, in Q (Luke 17:23; Matt 24:26).[42] We may reconstruct the text of Q with a certain degree of probability: "They will say to you, 'Look, he is in the wilderness, do not go out; look, he is in one of the inner rooms, do not follow him there'" (ἐροῦσιν ὑμῖν· ἰδοὺ ἐν τῇ ἐρήμῳ ἐστίν, μὴ ἐξέλθητε· ἰδοὺ ἐν τοῖς ταμείοις, μὴ διώξητε).[43] Luke takes over and adapts the text that has been attributed with probability to Q; he mentions neither the wilderness nor the inner rooms, but is content with a vague "here or . . . there" (moreover, the text of Luke is particularly uncertain in this verse).[44]

As for the double prohibition (the text of which is also uncertain),[45] it is difficult to picture: Where is it that we are not supposed to go away from? And in what direction are we not supposed to set off? Luke is content with vague wording. The first verb "go away" (ἀπέρχομαι, translated here as "go there") asks us not to leave the place we are; the second, "set off in pursuit" (διώκω), not to chase rainbows.

■ **24** Matthew and Luke have different wordings of the text about the coming of the Son of Man like a flash of lightning, but they are in significant agreement as to the meaning. It is unlikely that Luke transformed an elegant turn of phrase into a cumbersome one. So we may conclude that the awkward Lukan text reproduces Q without major changes.[46] Among the variants that affect the text,[47] there is one that is important: Should we or should we not read the words "in his day" (ἐν τῇ ἡμέρᾳ αὐτοῦ)? The external evidence, that is, the weight of the manuscripts, is divided. Personally speaking, for reasons of internal evidence, I would prefer retaining the words in the Lukan text. They must have been omitted because of the tension they create with "one of the days" (μία τῶν ἡμερῶν) in v. 22. In fact, "the day of the Son of Man" (cf. v. 24: "the Son of Man in his day"; see also v. 30) must represent a conventional way of speaking, whereas "the days of the Son of Man" (v. 22) must

---

40   See 2:30 (Simeon, who saw the salvation of God); 3:6 (all flesh will see the salvation of God); 1 Pet 1:9-12 (the prophets have not yet been able to see what has been reserved for Christians); Rev 1:7 ("every eye will see him"). On the text of 𝔓[111] (τοῦ ἐπιθυμῆσαι), see Elliott, "Fragments from Oxyrhynchus," 209–13.

41   Here, as there, the word "days" is mentioned in two separate places, but here in 17:22 the first describes the time of the church and the second, the time of the Son of Man.

42   See above; and Laufen, *Doppelüberlieferung*, 361–69.

43   I follow the reconstruction of Laufen, *Doppelüberlieferung*, 363; along similar lines, see "International Q Project," in Brandenburger and Hieke, *Studien*, 119.

44   The critical apparatus of Nestle-Aland (217) scrupulously specifies the numerous variants. The differences principally concern the order of the adverbs "here" and "there," as well as the presence or absence of the title "the Christ" (with uncertainty undoubtedly arising from Mark 13:21).

45   Certain manuscripts, such as 𝔓[75], have only one prohibition: "Do not follow him!"; others are content with "Do not believe him," inspired by Mark 13:21. Others have the double prohibition but with slight variations.

46   Why did Luke not bother to improve the style of this saying?

47   Innumerable manuscripts add the article ἡ before the participle ἀστράπτουσα. The participle with the article ("the flash of lightning") indicates a permanent quality. Without the article, it replaces a subordinate circumstantial ("the lightning, when it strikes"), which is the better construction. Other manuscripts, probably accidentally (by haplography), omit the words εἰς τὴν ὑπ᾽ οὐρανόν. Codex D, always distinctive, reads ἀστράπτει ("hurls lightning") precisely where the others have λάμπει ("shines").

represent a redactional formulation (the first expression is apocalyptic; the second expresses the period of the history of salvation).[48]

There are several kinds of lightning, and the way they were described in antiquity does not correspond to modern scientific observations. Moreover, the wording in Luke is strange.[49] Nonetheless, the comparison that Luke makes clearly brings home his point about the universality and visibility of the final coming of the Son of Man. There are to be no precursory signs; Christians are called on to display only vigilance and perseverance during this period when things will not be seen (v. 22) and they must live by faith alone. When the final moment comes, there will be no room for doubt, since the evidence will be indisputable. Like the image of the thief (12:39), that of lightning is an old one and could go back to Jesus himself, speaking, to be sure, not of himself but of the coming of the eschatological judge, God in person, similar to the face of a human being, the Son of Man. After Easter and later, in the time of Q, the identification of the Son of Man with Jesus gained the field. Nor is there any doubt that Luke himself took that identification for granted.

First the Passion

■ **25** Once again, the Gospel writer is anxious to avoid impatience and apocalyptic fever; so there is to be no parousia without crucifixion, no future without a past, no glory without humility. The wording and the content of the redaction of v. 25 are modeled on the other Lukan announcements of the passion.[50] The implicit warning in the face of false anticipations is akin to the one in 21:9b ("for these things must take place first" [*NRSV*], δεῖ γὰρ ταῦτα γενέσθαι πρῶτον).

Two Examples

■ **26-30** Following Q, Luke distinguishes and sets out different periods of Christian history. In v. 22, he men-

tions the days to come of the church, as well as the days, both past and future, of the Son of Man; in v. 24 he speaks of the exact day of the parousia; next, in v. 25, of Christ's generation. At this point he brings up the days of Noah and then those of Lot, with which he compares the eschatological period of the Son of Man. Dividing history into such periods makes it easier to understand the existential, religious, and ethical significance of reality.

Verse 26 offers a simple comparison with the days of Noah, while v. 27 mentions what there was in the past that can serve as an example for the future. There is no explicit lesson drawn, however; that is left up to the reader's imagination and reasoning. In v. 26, Luke respected the text of Q (perhaps substituting "just as" [καθώς] for "as" [ὥσπερ]), whereas Matthew inserted the term "coming" ("parousia") of which he was fond (Matt 24:37; cf. Matt 24:27).[51] The text of Q is more difficult to reconstruct in v. 27. Luke may have simplified the beginning by avoiding the repetition of the word "flood" (κατακλυσμός, which is repeated in Matt 24:38-39).[52] There is no value judgment made; the only thing that is pointed out is the abrupt and catastrophic end of a period of apparently normal activity. The account in Genesis (chaps. 6–8) has been drastically compressed: there is no indication of emotions in either the human activity or the divine decision. It is not that the editors of Q or the author of the Gospel were averse to such indications; they simply presupposed knowledge of them. In Genesis, moreover, attention is focused on Noah, his family, and the animals that were spared; here it is directed toward the victims of the catastrophe. The biblical story thus becomes an example of an unforeseen catastrophe and probably of a deserved judgment as well.[53] This is because there was a long period, from the time of the writing of the story in Genesis to the redaction of Q, during which the scriptural data were being appropriated and being used in paraenesis. Although it is not mentioned that frequently in biblical texts,[54] the example

48 See Kaestli, *L'eschatologie*, 30–35.
49 How does one make sense of the curious feminine in the expression ἐκ τῆς ὑπὸ τὸν οὐρανὸν εἰς τὴν ὑπ᾽ οὐρανόν? For more on lightning, see H. Prinz, "Lightning in History," and K. Berger, "The Earth Flash," in R. H. Golde, ed., *Lightning, I: Physics of Lightning* (London/New York/San Francisco: Academic Press, 1977) 1–21, 119–38. On Luke's formulation, see Fitzmyer, 2:1169–70.
50 Particularly that of 9:22.
51 Schulz, *Q*, 279. I am not certain that the plural "days" is a Lukan correction of Q which originally had the singular.
52 Ibid.
53 With Schlosser, "Jours," 35–36.
54 See Isa 24:18; 54:9; Ezek 13:11, 13; 14:14, 20; 38:22; Ps 29 (28):10; Sir 40:10; 44:17; Wis 10:4; 14:6; Schlosser, "Jours," 13 n. 2.

of the flood is often mentioned in extrabiblical Jewish literature.[55] It is frequently proposed as a moral lesson to warn readers of the risks they run if they live lives of indolence, carelessness, or debauchery. At the time that Jesus, Q, and Luke were using it as an example, the shift in attention from righteous Noah to his guilty contemporaries, to which I called attention above, had already been operating for a long time.[56] All one has to do to be convinced of this is to read *3 Macc.* 2:4 and 2 Pet 2:4-5. Although many commentators draw only one lesson from it, namely, the unforeseen character of the parousia, I am tempted to draw two: in addition to that unforeseen character of the parousia there is the legitimate condemnation of the ungodly.

Like Greek rhetoric, Jewish paraenesis is fond of using series of examples. Lot's contemporaries (Gen 13:12-13, 18-19) have often been compared with Noah's generation (Genesis 6–8); they are often found in proximity to each other and sometimes accompanied by Pharaoh (Exodus 1–15; see *3 Macc.* 2:3-7). So the linking of the two generations was probably made in a Judeo-Christian environment before any such activity on the part of the writer of the Gospel of Luke. If food is a common element in the two examples, marriage is distinctive of the first example, the time of Noah (vv. 26-27). In the second, Lot's generation (vv. 28-29), economical activities—commerce, agriculture, and building—are stressed.

As with marriage in v. 27, there is nothing wrong with these activities in and of themselves. But when carried on in the wrong fashion, as was the case in Sodom and Gomorrah, they give rise to excesses that are subject to divine judgment. On the heels of the flood (v. 26) came the rain ("it rained," ἔβρεξεν) of fire and sulfur (v. 29). The result was exactly the same in both cases: "and [it] destroyed all of them" (καὶ ἀπώλεσεν πάντας; vv. 27, 29). The history of salvation has its setbacks.

Verse 30 spells out the comparison just as v. 26 had and does it in similar terms. We come full circle: "like that" (κατὰ τὰ αὐτά) picks up on "just as it was" (καθὼς ἐγένετο); "it will be" (ἔσται), echoes "so . . . it will be" (οὕτως ἔσται); etc. Verse 30 has two peculiarities, however. Whereas v. 26 spoke about a period of time ("the days of the Son of Man"), v. 30 focuses on a point in time ("on the day of the Son of Man"). Faithful to the tradition of Q (cf. Matt 24:37 and 39), Luke has in mind here the moment of the parousia, just as the examples, in turn, highlighted the exact moment of the catastrophe. In v. 26, as in v. 22, on the other hand, Luke was speaking of the days of the Son of Man, as of the eschatological period. Is there any importance to be attached to this difference? It would seem so, since Luke not only distinguishes between periods[57] but also contrasts a period of time with a moment in time. The period of time is that in which human responsibility is operative; the moment in time is when divine judgment comes into play. For Luke, one's personal life would seem to be made up of "days" to live in faithfulness to God and of the "day" when that faithfulness (or lack of it) meets up with its reward (or punishment). In the same way, the collective life of the people of God and of the nations of the earth plays out in different periods of time ("the days of," "this generation," etc.), which also have a terminal point. This end is not equivalent to a nothingness; it is rather equivalent to a judgment, because of the God who is master of history.

The other distinctive feature of v. 30 is the appearance of the verb "to reveal" (ἀποκαλύπτω). Along with Q and other early Christians, what Luke was waiting for was a final revelation of Christ Jesus with the features of the Son of Man. He not only says it here; he also repeats it often,[58] for example, in a colorful way in the parable of the minas (Luke 19:12), and in the beginning of the book of Acts in the account of the ascension (Acts 1:11). As it will be abrupt and radiant, the final appearance of the Son of Man can rightfully be labeled an "unveiling," a "revelation," and an "apocalypse."[59]

---

55   The article by Schlosser, "Jours," points out and explains the texts, as do the works of Lührmann (*Logienquelle,* 71–83; and "Noah und Lot," 130–32).

56   Schlosser, "Jours," 16.

57   See above.

58   Luke 9:26; 12:36-40; 13:25; 21:27; Acts 3:19-21; 10:42; 17:31.

59   Several New Testament texts utilize the same vocabulary in describing the same event, e.g., Rom 8:18; 1 Cor 3:13; 1 Pet 1:5; 5:1, which all use the verb ἀποκαλύπτω; Rom 2:5; 8:19; 1 Cor 1:7; 2 Thess 1:7; 1 Pet 1:8, 13; 4:13, which use the substantive ἀποκάλυψις.

The "D" Day

■ **31-32** The saying (v. 31) belongs to the triple tradition (Mark 13:15) and to the oldest and the most apocalyptic stock of material in it. Whereas Mark uses the advice for the antepenultimate day of the "abomination of desolation," Luke saves it for the final day of the parousia of the Son of Man. In this way, Luke links this maxim with the previous sentence by the use of the words "on that day"; improves on Mark's "the one" (ὁ) by using "anyone who will be" (ὃς ἔσται); changes the location of people and specifies the personal belongings that every person fleeing would like to take along ("and their belongings in the house," καὶ τὰ σκεύη αὐτοῦ ἐν τῇ οἰκίᾳ);[60] and, like Matthew, avoids the words "or go back down into," μηδὲ εἰσελθάτω (thus avoiding the suggestion of a Palestinian house in which one must go back down into the house when descending from the roof by the exterior staircase).[61] The persons on the roof or rather on the terrace of the roof may be there because of their anxiety. Sensing a danger in the offing, they may have gone up to look out for what might happen or in order to take refuge higher up. Or they may simply have been doing something that took them there, such as drying out plants or fruits.

In any case, the peasants in the field in the following saying (v. 31b) are quite simply at work. From a grammatical point of view, Luke is right in preferring the Greek ὁ ἐν ἀγρῷ ("the one who will be in the field") to Mark's ὁ εἰς τὸν ἀγρόν (Mark 13:16), which, if literally translated as if it were classical Greek, would be "the one who will go into the field," but which, in more popular (Koine) Greek, actually had the meaning of "the one who will be in the field."[62] Luke is less elegant than Matthew, who simply has "back" (ὀπίσω); Luke faithfully follows Mark, who has, literally, "toward what is behind" (εἰς τὰ ὀπίσω; Mark 13:16). In doing this, Luke is not at all

giving in to the tendency to be intellectually lazy. Since he has just called attention to personal belongings, he is here noting the reality of the belongings to which everyone is tempted to return (the Greek article τά represents "what," "that which," "the things"). The reader will be reminded of the triple renunciation required of attentive disciples (9:57-62). In connection with the third example, Jesus had declared, by way of a threat, that every plowman who "looks back" (βλέπων εἰς τὰ ὀπίσω) is unfit for the kingdom of God. The category of "(what is) back" is not just a manner of speaking; it is a very concrete concept and defines the earthly belongings that one is in danger of preferring to eschatological benefits. "What is back" represents the previous life that must be given up in order to obtain life with God.[63] When he wrote these words "must not turn back toward what is behind him," Luke was looking beyond the image to the real world, which, as a Christian, he had renounced. Paul also drew inspiration from the metaphor of plowing to urge the Philippians to look straight ahead of them without turning back (Phil 3:13). Taking their inspiration from Jesus' maxim, the first-century Christian catechists used the metaphor in their teaching.

Luke rightly explains the threat in v. 32, whose redactional character is incontestable.[64] In a paraenetic fashion, the Gospel writer makes a connection with the story of Lot in order to tell one episode of it that is dramatic and consequently exemplary at the same time. It was precisely Lot's wife's wanting to turn back because of her care for the possessions she had left behind that turned her into a pillar of salt (Gen 19:17, 26).

How to Live?

■ **33** At this point Luke inserts a Q maxim that most certainly was not part of the apocalyptic paragraph of Q.[65] Matthew respected Q's order by quoting it after the

---

60   Mark mentions "something in his house," which he places after the verb "to take away" (Mark 13:15). The word σκεῦος is vague; it could designate an "object," a "vase," "personal belongings," an "instrument," a "utensil," or a "thing."

61   See Rigaux, "Apocalypse," 423–24.

62   See BAGD, s.v. εἰς 1. δ; and BDF #205 on the use of εἰς for ἐν (BAGD [ibid.]: "used where ἐν would be expected . . . Mk . . . εἰς τὸν ἀγρόν [ὤν] 'he who is in the field' 13:16"; BDF #205: "εἰς instead of ἐν in

a local sense . . . Mk . . . 13:16 εἰς τὸν ἀγρόν] [ἐν Mt 24:18; Lk 17:34])."

63   The Lukan antithesis between earthly and divine wealth is well known to his readers: see 5:11, 28; 9:57-62; 12:16-21; 12:33-34; 14:33; and the commentary above on 14:33, esp. n. 102.

64   See Rigaux, "Apocalypse," 424.

65   On this verse, see Leroy, "'Wer sein Leben gewinnen will . . . ,'" 171–86; and Laufen, Doppelüberlieferungen, 315–36.

commandment to hate (to use the Q/Lukan wording) one's own family and to carry one's cross (Matt 10:37-39). The saying was also included in Mark in a similar wording, and Luke did not shy away from producing a doublet (the parallel to Mark 8:35 is found in Luke 9:24). By placing the Q maxim here, the Gospel writer created a small unit: first he quotes Mark in v. 31 ("on the housetop" and "in the field"); then he tacks on a redactional piece of advice drawn from the Bible (v. 32); and finally he provides the profound meaning by quoting a Q maxim on true life (v. 33).[66]

Luke undoubtedly preferred to paraphrase Q[67] (which had "find one's life") by writing "try to acquire one's life."[68] Moreover, he used the Greek verb ζῳογονέω, which has several meanings: "engender," "give life to," "make alive," perhaps "keep/preserve alive." In 5:10 the Gospel writer had already stressed the quality of life in Christ: when the apostles became "fishers of men" they took on the responsibility of bringing in a "live catch," keeping alive the fish/Christians that they would catch in the nets of the gospel (the Greek verb being in that case ζωγρέω "to capture alive").[69] So Luke begins by criticizing attempts to acquire life based on a capitalization of oft-criticized earthly possessions (they have been mentioned above in v. 31), then reminds us that the only way to acquire the true life is by giving of oneself, by losing oneself. Luke finds expression of salvation in terms of life, life that is new and genuine.

Among the numerous variants of this saying of Jesus, Luke 17:33 is, along with John 12:25, the only parallel that is innocent of any christological justification; the expression "for my sake" (ἕνεκεν ἐμοῦ) is missing here,

and that absence may be seen a sign of antiquity, I might even say of authenticity.[70]

Jesus' teaching, to which Luke remains faithful, is not doctrinal but practical; it is more a matter of experience than of knowledge.[71] The saying is a paradox on the formal level. It basically expresses something obvious, namely, that in freeing oneself from what constitutes one's life, the believer finds life that is authentic. This is nonetheless a radical requirement, and there is a part of each one of us that reacts negatively in a visceral way to such teaching.

The Night of Sorting Out

■ **34-35** The "I tell you" is a marker that, from a genetic perspective, signals the distinct and independent origin of vv. 34-35; from a literary perspective it expresses the conviction of the one speaking and his concern to be convincing.[72]

The words "on that night" are surprising, since up to this point it has always been a question of "day" or "days." In v. 31, Luke spoke of "that day." Does "that night" refer to some other point in time? I do not think so; the last day will be one of total darkness that will be broken by the sudden light of the Son of Man. The apocalyptic tradition is acquainted with this final darkness (cf. Mark 13:24), and Luke has just indicated that the sudden emergence of the Son of Man will resemble lightning cleaving the sky, which is presumed to be dark.[73]

Jewish hope was multifaceted, expecting not only the "day of the Lord" but also the "night" of redemption, the final counterpart of the night of the exodus.[74] A new image does not invalidate an older one.

---

66 See Laufen, *Doppelüberlieferungen*, 315–22.

67 The ὃς ἐάν and ὃς δ' ἄν, followed by the aorist subjunctive, must be redactional (Q must have had participles preceding the article: ὁ εὑρών ("whoever has found") and ὁ ἀπολέσας ("whoever has lost"); see Matt 10:39. Contra Laufen, *Doppelüberlieferungen*, 315–22.

68 On the importance of the verb περιποιοῦμαι ("to acquire for onseself"), see Spicq, *Lexicon*, 3:100–102.

69 See the commentary on 5:8-11 in vol. 1.

70 With Leroy, "'Wer sein Leben gewinnen will . . . ,'" 171–73.

71 Ibid., passim.

72 On the rhetorical and solemn usage of λέγω ("I say"), see the commentary on 4:23 in vol. 1.

73 On a nocturnal parousia, see the image of the thief in the night: Luke 12:39-40; Matt 24:43; and 1 Thess 5:2.

74 In several articles mentioned in the bibliography, Strobel insists on the importance of this "night," which reflects an ancient, early Christian tradition rooted in Jewish apocalypticism according to which ultimate redemption will begin during one of the last nights of Easter. He thinks that in 17:20-21 Luke is struggling against all efforts to calculate the date of this last Easter night. Strobel recounts several patristic accounts of the parousia taking place at night.

The two expressions are matched in the Gospel of Matthew and the *Gospel of Thomas*. But in neither of these parallels is there this chronological information. Matthew 24:40 simply says "then" ($\tau\acute{o}\tau\epsilon$) and *Gos. Thom.* 61 makes no mention of the hour. I believe nevertheless that Luke did not think up this mention of the night but took it over from his apocalyptic tradition.[75] Furthermore, it suits his purposes, since the mention of the bed suggests nocturnal sleep. But we would be mistaken to conclude from this that Luke has consciously taken over for his own purposes a Jewish idea according to which the parousia was going to take place during a Passover night. In this speech, the Gospel writer insists on the unpredictable nature of the end of time and, elsewhere, on the delay in the arrival of the parousia, which will be like a final night and a last day.

The event is of greater importance for Luke than the timing, and he has two examples at hand to illustrate this, the bed and the millstone. Matthew, like Luke, also mentions the millstone but, not knowing about the night, speaks of a field rather than a bed. *Gospel of Thomas* 61 knows only of the shared bed. The fact that this Gospel shares knowledge of the bed with Luke speaks in favor of the antiquity of this saying. I would suggest that Q was worded as follows: "I tell you, there will be two men in the same bed; one is taken and one is left; two women will be grinding at the mill; one is taken and one is left."[76]

In saying that two men[77] share a single bed,[78] Luke was probably not thinking of lovers in the Greek sense of love but rather of those low-income homes where several members of the same family occupied the same bed. The reader will be reminded of the parable of the troublesome friend, where the father says that he and his children are in bed ($\epsilon\dot{\iota}\varsigma$ $\tau\dot{\eta}\nu$ $\kappa o\acute{\iota}\tau\eta\nu$), perhaps in a single family bed.[79]

In the case of this example, as in the following one, what matters most to the Gospel writer is the mention of the greatest proximity; he speaks of a single bed and points out that the women grind meal "in the same place" ($\dot{\epsilon}\pi\dot{\iota}$ $\tau\dot{o}$ $\alpha\dot{\upsilon}\tau\acute{o}$, v. 35). Division appears even when family unity is the strongest and when professional cohesion is the most visible. For Luke, the sudden appearance on the scene of the Son of Man shatters the most visible symbols of unity, fellowship, and collaboration.[80]

In Jewish society, as in many other agrarian societies, the women were the ones responsible for grinding the grain that the men had grown. This work could be done in the evening or early in the morning, before sunrise.[81] By speaking of the work in the fields, then the grinding near the house, Matthew gives us a unified picture of the scene. Did Luke break that unity in v. 34 by substituting the bed for the field?[82] That is unlikely.[83]

"Taking" and "leaving"[84] have an apocalyptic flavor to them here.[85] There are parallels that indicate that at the end of time the angels "will take" the elect in order to lead them to their peaceful dwelling place and "will leave" the damned, thus giving them over to their punishment.[86] Why does he say that here? In order to stress the inexorable harshness of the end (there are situations that nothing more can be done about). In order to remind us that the parousia will coincide with the last judgment (the image of sorting out is widely attested, as is confirmed by the Matthean allegory of the sheep put at the right hand of the king and the goats put at his left [Matt 25:32-33]). In order to motivate readers to take the

---

75 With Strobel, "Nacht," 19–21.

76 I follow the reconstruction of Steinhauser, *Doppel-bildworte*, 197–214.

77 "One" ($\dot{o}$ $\epsilon\dot{\iota}\varsigma$) and "the other" ($\dot{o}$ $\ddot{\epsilon}\tau\epsilon\rho o\varsigma$) are both masculine.

78 The use of $\mu\iota\hat{\alpha}\varsigma$ ("one") in the expression $\dot{\epsilon}\pi\dot{\iota}$ $\kappa\lambda\acute{\iota}\nu\eta\varsigma$ $\mu\iota\hat{\alpha}\varsigma$ ("in one bed") expresses this singularity.

79 See Luke 11:7 and the commentary above on 11:7.

80 The expressions $\dot{\epsilon}\pi\dot{\iota}$ $\tau\dot{o}$ $\alpha\dot{\upsilon}\tau\acute{o}$ ("in the same place"; Acts 1:15; 2:1, 44, 47) and $\dot{o}\mu o\vartheta\upsilon\mu\alpha\delta\acute{o}\nu$ ("of one accord"; Acts 1:14; 2:46; 4:24; 5:12) describe the fraternal unity of the first Christians.

81 According to Strobel ("Nacht," 21), Palestinian women, in our day as well as Jesus' time, are at their millstones early in the morning, before sunrise.

82 Schulz (*Q*, 280) thinks that Matthew substituted the field for the bed, perhaps influenced by Matt 24:18.

83 *Gospel of Thomas* 61, as we have seen, is part of a tradition that includes only the bed.

84 See John 14:3: $\pi\alpha\rho\alpha\lambda\acute{\eta}\mu\psi o\mu\alpha\iota$ $\dot{\upsilon}\mu\hat{\alpha}\varsigma$ $\pi\rho\dot{o}\varsigma$ $\dot{\epsilon}\mu\alpha\upsilon\tau\acute{o}\nu$ ("I will take you to myself").

85 Matthew 24:40-41, following Q, has the present; Luke the grammarian and stylist substitutes the future (which is more correct) for the present in v. 34 and v. 35; see Schulz, *Q*, 280.

86 See Matt 13:49: "The angels will come and separate the wicked from the righteous."

necessary existential steps and to be on the right side at the crucial moment of the parousia. If we take into consideration the whole of Luke's work, what distinguishes one person from another is neither virtue alone nor predestination, but a harmonious plan of election that relies on believers' committed and lively response.[87] In the present, the "just," the "elect" cannot be distinguished from other people. They will all be taken by surprise at the very moment the Son of Man arrives.[88]

■ **36** Verse 36, which is present in the *textus receptus*,[89] has been relegated as a variant to the critical apparatus in recent editions of Luke, and rightly so.[90] It is, in effect, the result of contamination of Luke's Gospel by Matthew's. Ancient scribes inserted here Matthew's first example (Matt 24:40), the one with the two men in the fields, which they missed in Luke. So in these manuscripts of Luke we are dealing with three different cases: what takes place in bed, at the millstone, and in the fields.[91] Several modern translations have maintained v. 36 in their text.[92]

The Eagles Gathered around the Corpse

■ **37** Luke derived an enigmatic maxim from Q. It is known that the Greek word for "body," $\sigma\hat{\omega}\mu\alpha$, originally meant a "dead body" or "corpse." In the parallel in Matthew (Matt 24:28), we read $\pi\tau\hat{\omega}\mu\alpha$, which originally meant "that which has fallen," and then, as here in the Matthean parallel, "corpse."[93] So the idea of "corpse" is common to the two parallel verses.

The Greek word for "eagle" is $\dot{\alpha}\epsilon\tau\acute{o}\varsigma$ and for "vulture," $\gamma\acute{v}\psi$. Now when corpses are involved, we think of vultures rather than eagles. To be sure, there have been exceptions noted in both directions: starved eagles rushing at carrion and hard-up vultures attacking living prey. In antiquity especially, it was believed that eagles also eat dead animals and that vultures eat prey captured live.[94] In Hebrew נֶשֶׁר is the word for "eagle" and פֶּרֶס for "vulture," or more precisely, the (great) bearded vulture. Leviticus 11:13-19 and Deut 14:13-18 each furnish a list of unclean birds, among which several are birds of prey, with the eagle and vulture at the head of both lists.[95]

The image of the eagle swooping down on its prey is used by the prophet Habakkuk to describe the Chaldeans' dazzling invasion (Hab 1:8) and by the author of the book of Job to speak of the rapidity with which days go by (Job 9:26). The same book of Job cites the example of the eagle that "mounts up and makes its nest on high . . . from [which it] spies its prey [and lets] its young suck up blood" (Job 39:27-30). The author adds, by way of conclusion: "and where the slain is, there it is" (Job 39:30). The LXX renders this verse as "Wherever there may be carcasses, they [the eagle's young] are to be found there immediately." The saying in Q must refer to this passage of Scripture.

The image of the corpse must have shocked Luke, since he replaced the specific word for "corpse" ($\pi\tau\hat{\omega}\mu\alpha$) by the generic word for "body" ($\sigma\hat{\omega}\mu\alpha$), which can be used for one that is either living or dead and which he

---

87 See Bovon, *L'œuvre*, 165–79.

88 Verses 34-35 evidence very slight textual differences that have no real consequence. The absence of $\mu\iota\hat{\alpha}\varsigma$ ("one") in Codex Vaticanus (B) and its Latin equivalent in the Latin manuscript c as well as some Vulgate manuscripts does not change the meaning but mutes Luke's insistence on one bed only. Additionally, the absence of all of v. 35 in the first section of Codex Sinaiticus (א) and some other witnesses can be explained by homoioteleuton, with the same word at the end of both v. 34 and v. 35 ($\dot{\alpha}\varphi\epsilon\vartheta\acute{\eta}\sigma\epsilon\tau\alpha\iota$, "will be left").

89 That is, in the text edited in the Renaissance and accepted across the centuries; see Wettstein, *Novum Testamentum graecum*, 1:vi–vii.

90 For example Nestle-Aland, 218.

91 We encounter a similar phenomenon in Luke 11:11-12.

92 Hence, the Louis Segond Bible, which I use and which dates to 1935.

93 Is it Matthew who clarifies this by writing $\dot{\epsilon}\grave{\alpha}\nu$ $\acute{\eta}$ ("wherever there is") or Luke who expresses it proverbially by omitting the verb "to be" in the subordinate clause?

94 See Guenther, "Eagles," 146–47.

95 The LXX (Lev 11:13 and Deut 14:12) translates the first word as $\dot{\alpha}\epsilon\tau\acute{o}\varsigma$ ("eagle") and the second as $\gamma\rho\acute{v}\psi$, which is surprising because the Greek word $\gamma\rho\acute{v}\psi$ usually refers to a mythical bird, the "griffin." The word $\gamma\acute{v}\psi$ ("vulture") appears in the fourth position on the LXX list, a translation of דָּאָה ("kite"). The MT of Lev 11:13 has a textual problem.

could agree to apply to Christ. At the level of Q, this maxim must have followed the one about lightning (Matthew must have preserved the original sequence: Matt 24:27, lightning; 24:28, eagles).[96] This maxim stresses the speed with which God's judgment was going to be carried out. Luke has removed the saying from its context, created a little apophthegm, and put the question of "where" on the lips of Jesus' disciples. In Luke's writing, the saying about the eagles takes on a new character. Worrying about the location of the events of the end-time would be as absurd as wearing oneself out attempting to calculate their chronology. The arrival of the Son of Man will be as unpredictable as it will be sudden, and it will be as obvious as lightning and will draw attention just as quickly as birds of prey are attracted to their prey.

The passive verb in Greek ἐπισυναχθήσονται (which translates as "will gather"), which Luke has taken over from his source, must have been to his liking. At the end of time, believers will be attracted by the Son of Man in person (σῶμα), but it will be more a question of their being gathered to him by the angels than of their joining him on their own. To say that is to admit the presence of a slight allegory in Luke's words.[97] Is it not already to be found in the end of the saying in 11:23: "Whoever does not gather with me scatters"?

History of Interpretation

The *Gospel of Thomas* provides a spiritual interpretation of v. 21b or of its tradition.[98] By rewording the maxim, the author of that Gospel understood ἐντός in the sense of *intra*, "inside," rather than with the meaning *inter*, "among." The various Latin versions of the New Testament also understood it the same way: "For lo, the kingdom of God is within you" ("*Ecce enim regnum Dei intra vos est*" [Vulgate]). Although the Syriac and Ethiopic versions are ambiguous,[99] the quotations, paraphrases, and commentaries by ecclesiastical authors in those languages interpreted it along the same lines. That way of understanding it enabled an ethical development, especially in the interpretation of the African theologian Tertullian. If the kingdom of God is "within you," you are in charge of it, and it is up to you to carry out God's will. In Tertullian's interpretation, the kingdom of God is therefore available to you (*Adv. Marc.* 4.35).[100] Tertullian tied the verse in Luke to Deut 30:11-14. We know that God's commandment in Deuteronomy, which is "not too far away," which is "in your heart," is quoted in the Epistle to the Romans (Rom 10:8). So it is not surprising that an exegetical tradition that was to last more than a millennium associated Deut 30:11-14 and Rom 10:8 with Luke 17:21.[101]

The eschatological understanding of the kingdom of God was transformed into a spiritual and ethical way of perceiving in Origen's case as well.[102] This patristic interpretation is confirmed by Ambrose of Milan's homilies on Luke: "Questioned by his disciples as to the hour when the kingdom of God would come, the Lord said, 'The kingdom of God is inside you.' Yes, by the reality of his grace, not by slavery to sin. Thus, whoever wishes to be free must be a servant in the Lord (cf. 1 Cor 7:22); for in so far as we share in bondage, we also share in the kingdom" (*Exp. Luc.* 8.33).[103] The homilies of Cyril of Alexandria were along the same line; he was one of the first to note the tension between the Pharisees' question concerning the *date* of the coming of the kingdom and

---

96   With Guenther ("Eagles," 144–46), who also mentions the supporters of the opposing opinion.

97   Polag (*Christologie*, 95) offers an allegorical touch at the level of Q: Israel becomes a prey for the false Messiahs.

98   See above. See also Noack (*Gottesreich*, 4–5), who offers a remarkable synopsis of the interpretations of vv. 20-21 from the beginning of the second century through the end of the nineteenth (pp. 4–38).

99   See Noack, *Gottesreich*, 5–7.

100   This interpretation appears in the context of an attack on Marcion. Tertullian refuses once again to establish an opposition between the good God and the Creator. The "reign of God" concerns the only and unique God.

101   See Noack, *Gottesreich*, 8–9.

102   Origen *De Princ.* 1.3.6; *Hom. in Luc.* 36.2–3; *Hom. in Jer.* 18.2; *Hom. in Num.* 24.2. See Noack, *Gottesreich*, 9.

103   Ambrose simultaneously emphasizes the grace of God (it is by his intermediary that the reign of God reaches us) and the responsibility of Christians (it is by their service that believers take part in this reign).

Jesus' answer settling the question of the *place* where it would arrive (*Hom. in Luc.* 117).[104] Reflecting on Jesus' answer, Cyril felt himself obliged to explain how the kingdom of God could be inside the Pharisees (the "you" at whom Jesus' answer was aimed). Cyril—if the passage is genuine—was able to do it by adding to the first interpretation another interpretation,[105] the one that was to become the second classic interpretation of this Lukan verse: even if you are not aware of the fact, the kingdom of God is in your midst, among you.[106]

All we have to do is read the commentary by the Venerable Bede[107] or the *Glossa ordinaria* to notice that the spiritual and ethical interpretation—in other words, the first of the two above-mentioned interpretations—was ascendant in both the West and the East.[108] The kingdom that is within you cannot be dissociated from Christ's spiritual presence, his word, and his divine commandments.

The exegetical situation was not modified by the Renaissance or the Reformation.[109] The second interpretation did not gain ground until Juan Maldonado's philological comments at the end of the sixteenth century. According to him, these words were addressed to the Pharisees; God's reign is not future but present; and the Pharisees themselves could welcome the kingdom,

since it was present "among them."[110] From that time on, it became common to understand the expression ἐντὸς ὑμῶν in the sense of "among you," all the while continuing to translate it by "in you," under the influence of the Vulgate.[111] Hugo Grotius, for example, was of the opinion that ἐντὸς ὑμῶν means "*in ipso populo Judaico*" ("among the Jewish people") and declared that it was among that people, in the midst of those who were not noticing it, that God's reign had begun to demonstrate its power through Jesus' miracles and exorcisms.[112] And there were other, later commentators who also threw their weight behind that position. In the eighteenth century, in particular, we can see how the two interpretations in question clashed in arguments made on philological grounds.[113] There were also recurring defenses of the respective positions as the nineteenth century drew to a close.

It was not until the end of the nineteenth century, with the entry on the stage of defenders of an imminent eschatology, that there came to be a renewal of interest in Luke 17:21. Johannes Weiss could only conceive of a present orientation as an exception, one of those exclamations that a future winner lets escape from his lips in a moment of enthusiasm.[114] He refused to see ἐντὸς ὑμῶν as a spiritual reality present only in one's heart and

104 Reuss, *Lukas-Kommentare*, 178–79 (frg. 251); Payne-Smith, *Cyril*, 2:542; Noack, *Gottesreich*, 11–12.

105 "For 'it is within you,' that is, it depends upon your own wills, and is in your own power, whether or not you receive it. For every man who has attained to justification by means of faith in Christ, and is adorned by all virtue, is counted worthy of the kingdom of heavens" (Cyril, *Hom. in Luc.* 117; see Reuss, *Lukas-Kommentare*, 179 [frg. 251]; Payne-Smith, *Cyril*, 2:542).

106 *PG* 72:841. John 1:26b ("Among you stands one whom you do not know") is summoned to the rescue in order to support this interpretation. This verse from John will be henceforth integrated into scriptural orchestration. Since these lines do not appear in the Syriac, Reuss (*Lukas-Kommentare*, 179) does not include them. One must in fact admit that the authenticity of this passage is not certain.

107 Bede, *In Luc.* 794–96: "Regnum Dei se ipsum dicit intra illos utique positum, hoc est in codibus eorum ubi credidere regnantem" ("The reign of God breaks out, placed, in a way, in their midst, reigning in their hearts where they have found faith").

108 See Noack, *Gottesreich*, 15–16.

109 Ibid., 16–19.

110 This is one of the interpretations that Maldonado (*Comm. in quat.* 4.106) finds amenable. He attributes it to Euthymius *Commentarius* 17:21 (*PG* 129:1048); see Plummer, 406.

111 Noack (*Gottesreich*, 21) gives the impressive example of Johannes Piscator, *Commentarii in omnes libros Noui Testamenti* (Herborn, 1613) 529–30.

112 Grotius, *Annotationes*, 869. According to Noack (*Gottesreich*, 24–25), in the middle of the eighteenth century two monographs were devoted to Luke 17:21: Hannecken, *Disputatio de regno Dei in nobis* (Wittenberg, 1705), and J. A. Gnilius, *Tentamen exegeseos ad dictum Salvatoris Luc. XVII. 20.21 de Regno Dei in terris instituto* (Strasbourg, 1733). Unfortunately I have been unsuccessful at gaining access to these two works. While Hannecken, contrary to the prevailing opinion of his day, understands the ἐντὸς ὑμῶν spiritually, Gnilius understands it materially.

113 Noack, *Gottesreich*, 26–37.

114 Weiss, *Die Idee des Reiches Gottes in der Theologie*, 4–6, 30, 48–49.

believed that there were portents of God's reign implemented by Jesus, who was, moreover, opposed to any apocalyptic calculations concerning the end-time.

Ancient authors I have consulted lacked inspiration with respect to vv. 22-37. They had a patent contempt for apocalyptic scenarios. For example, Ambrose, bishop of Milan, one of the principal commentators on Luke in the patristic era, preferred allegory, moralizing, and harmonization. Ambrose spent a fair amount of energy on emphasizing the fact that the Lord, on different occasions, refused to communicate any information whatsoever concerning the date when God's reign would burst on the scene. What is more, even when he was preaching on a passage in the Gospel of Luke, what Ambrose was actually commenting on was its parallel in the Gospel of Matthew. "Flee to the mountains" (Matt 24:16) for him meant seeking refuge with an apostle: "Your mountain, he exclaimed, is Paul; your mountain is Peter. Take the stand of your spirit on their faith" (*Exp. Luc.* 8.39). After that, everything lent itself to his allegorizing exercise, whether it was a bed, a roof, the night, or grinding grain. One of these interpretations merits special attention, the one of v. 37. The "eagles" symbolize the souls of the righteous who are carried off on high, such as the three Marys and the apostles standing around Christ's tomb. The "body" represents Christ in his threefold manifestation, first as the incarnate Son whose remains are welcomed on Good Friday; then as the Son of Man awaited on the clouds in heaven; and finally as the life-giving bread that is shared in the eucharistic meal (*Exp. Luc.* 8.54–55).

Conclusion

The literary unit Luke 17:20-37 broaches the thorny question of the kingdom of God, the Son of Man, and the end of time. By reading these verses, readers learn to avoid the worst and to opt for what is right. The date of the parousia (vv. 20-21) or the localization of the coming of the Son of Man (vv. 22-25) must neither worry them nor obsess them. Luke stresses here that the kingdom of God is near and even, in a certain sense, already present (v. 21). He maintains that when the Son of Man, who is still awaited, does come, his coming will be marked by unquestionable visibility (v. 24). Since Christians find themselves situated altogether in time and between the times, they must respect the relevance of reality (vv. 23, 32-33). The happiness with which we are endowed by the kingdom of God does not eclipse the tragedy of Jesus' crucifixion (v. 25). All the faith in the world is unable to take away the unpredictable character of the parousia (vv. 20, 24, 30). God's goodness, manifested by the coming of his kingdom, does not eliminate the punishment that results from his justice (v. 26). Confronted by the divine purpose, human beings are divided, even within the most united of families (vv. 34-35). What is most important for each one is to get ready and to make up one's mind (vv. 31-33), not with reference to a specific moment in time (vv. 20-21), nor to a particular place (v. 23), but with respect to the encounter with God, which can happen at any time but always unexpectedly (v. 24) and which, at the same time, will always be a welcome one (v. 22).

The Parable of the Unjust Judge and the Insistent Widow (18:1-8)

Bibliography 18:1-8

Bailey, *Eyes*, 127–41.

Benjamin, Don C., "The Persistent Widow," *TBT* 28 (1990) 213–19.

Bindemann, Walther, "Die Parabel vom ungerechten Richter," *ThV* 13 (1983) 91–97.

Binder, Hermann, *Das Gleichnis von dem Richter und der Witwe. Lk 18, 1-8* (Neukirchen-Vluyn: Neukirchener Verlag, 1988).

Bornhäuser, *Sondergut*, 161–70.

Bovon, François, "Apocalyptic Traditions in the Lucan Special Material: Reading Luke 18:1-8," *HTR* 90 (1997) 383–91.

Buzy, Denis, "Le juge inique," *RB* 39 (1930) 378–91.

Caba, *Oración de petición*, 26–62.

Catchpole, David R., "The Son of Man's Search for Faith (Luke xviii 8b)," *NovT* 19 (1977) 81–104.

Cranfield, C. E. B., "The Parable of the Unjust Judge and the Eschatology of Luke-Acts," *SJT* 16 (1963) 297–301.

Daube, David, "Neglected Nuances of Exposition in Luke-Acts," *ANRW* 2.25.3 (1984) 2329–57, esp. 2339–40.

Delling, Gerhard, "Das Gleichnis vom gottlosen Richter," in idem, *Studien zum Neuen Testament und zum hellenistischen Judentum* (Göttingen: Vandenhoeck & Ruprecht, 1970) 203–25.

Derrett, J. Duncan M., "Law in the New Testament: The Parable of the Unjust Judge," in idem, *Studies*, 1:32–47.

Deschryver, Richard, "La parabole du juge malveillant (Luc 18, 1-8)," *RHPhR* 48 (1968) 355–66.

Freed, Edwin D., "The Parable of the Judge and the Widow (Luke 18.1-8)," *NTS* 33 (1987) 38–60.

George, Augustin, "La parabole du juge qui fait attendre le jugement (Lc 18,1-8)," *AsSeign* 60 (1975) 68–79.

Grässer, *Problem*, 36–38.

Harnisch, Wolfgang, "Die Ironie als Stilmittel in Gleichnissen Jesu," *EvTh* 32 (1972) 421–36.

Heininger, *Metaphorik*, 198–208.

Hicks, John M., "The Parable of the Persistent Widow (Luke 18:1-8)," *ResQ* 33 (1991) 209–23.

Huhn, Karl, *Das Gleichnis von der 'bittenden Witwe': Gebetsaufruf Jesu an die Gemeinde der Endzeit* (Hamburg: Bethel, 1946).

Iersel, Bastiaan van, "De rechter en de weduwe (Lc 18,1-8)," in idem, *Parabelverhalen*, 168–93.

Jeremias, *Parables*, 153–57.

Jülicher, *Gleichnisreden*, 2:276–90.

Kissinger, Warren S., *The Parables of Jesus: A History of Interpretation and Bibliography* (ATLA.BS 4; Metuchen, N.J.: Scarecrow Press, 1979) 397–98.

Leal, Juan, "La oración y la crisis de fe," *Manresa* 39 (1967) 213–20.

Linnemann, *Parables*, 119–24.

Ljungvik, Herman, "Zur Erklärung einer Lukas-Stelle (Luk. xviii. 7)," *NTS* 10 (1963–64) 289–94.

Meecham, Henry G., "The Parable of the Unjust Judge," *ExpT* 57 (1945–46) 306–7.

Moessner, *Banquet*, 166–68.

Monloubou, Louis, *La prière selon Saint Luc: recherche d'une structure* (LD 89; Paris: Cerf, 1976) 80–81.

Muñoz León, Domingo, "Jesús y la apocalíptica pesimista (A propósito de Lc 18,8b y Mt 24,12)," *EstBib* 46 (1988) 457–95.

Ott, *Gebet und Heil*, 19, 32–72.

Panizo, Rosanna, "The Method of the Parables: More Contemporary Than You Would Think," *QR* 12 (1992) 91–110.

Paulsen, Henning, "Die Witwe und der Richter (Lk 18,1-8)," *ThGl* 74 (1984) 13–39.

Perkins, Pheme, *Hearing the Parables of Jesus* (New York: Paulist Press, 1981) 176, 194–95.

Perrin, *Rediscovering*, 129–30.

Praeder, Susan Marie, *The Word in Women's Worlds: Four Parables* (Zacchaeus Studies; Wilmington, Del.: Glazier, 1988) 51–71.

Puzo, Félix, "¿Un texto escatológico? (Lc 18,8b)," *EstEcl* 19 (1945) 273–334.

Reid, Barbara, "The Ethics of Luke," *TBT* 31 (1993) 283–87.

Riesenfeld, Harald, "Zu μακροθυμεῖν (Lk 18,7)," in J. Blinzler, ed., *Neutestamentliche Aufsätze: Festschrift für Prof. Josef Schmid zum 70. Geburtstag* (Regensburg: Pustet, 1963) 214–17.

Robertson, G. Philip, "Luke xviii. 8," *ExpT* 40 (1928–29) 525–26.

Robertson, J. A., "The Parable of the Unjust Judge (Luke xviii. 1-8)," *ExpT* 38 (1926–27) 389–92.

Ru, G. de, "De gelijkenis van de onrechtvaardige Rechter (Lucas 18:1-8)," *NedThT* 25 (1971) 379–92.

Sabbe, Maurits, "Het eschatologisch Gebed in Lc 18,1-8," *Collationes Brugenses et Gandavenses* 1 (1955) 361–69.

Sacchi, Alessandro, "Pazienza di Dio e ritardo della parusia (Lc 18,7)," *RivB* 36 (1988) 299–327.

Sahlin, Harald, *Zwei Lukas-Stellen: Lk 6:43-45; 18:7* (SymBU 4; Uppsala: Wretmans Boktryckeri, 1945) 9–20.

Schneider, Gerhard, *Parusiegleichnisse im Lukasevangelium* (SBS 74; Stuttgart: Katholisches Bibelwerk, 1975) 71–78.

Spicq, Ceslas, "La parabole de la veuve obstinée et du juge inerte, aux décisions impromptues (Lc. xviii,1-8)," *RB* 68 (1961) 68–90.

Stähhlin, Gustav, "Das Bild der Witwe: Ein Beitrag zur Bildersprache der Bibel und zum Phänomenon der Personifikation in der Antike," *JAC* 17 (1974) 5–20.

Stramare, Tarcisio, "Oportet semper orare et non deficere (Lc 18,1): Espressione di comando o segreto di successo?" *Lat* 48 (1982) 155–66.

Via, Dan O., "The Parable of the Unjust Judge: A Metaphor of the Unrealized Self," in Daniel Patte, ed., *Semiology and Parables: Exploration of the Possibilities Offered by Structuralism for Exegesis* (PTMS 9; Pittsburgh: Pickwick, 1976) 1–32 (responses and discussion, 33–70).

Warfield, Benjamin B., "The Importunate Widow and the Alleged Failure of Faith," *ExpT* 25 (1913–14) 69–72, 136–39.

Weder, *Gleichnisse*, 267–73.

Wenham, David, *The Parables of Jesus: Pictures of Revolution* (London/Sydney: Hodder & Stoughton, 1989) 185–90.

Idem, *Rediscovery*, 107–9, 137.

Weiss, K., "ὑπωριάζω," *TDNT* 8 (1972) 590–91.

Wifstrand, Albert, "Lukas xviii. 7," *NTS* 11 (1964–65) 72–74.

Zimmermann, Heinrich, "Das Gleichnis vom Richter und der Witwe (Lk 18, 1-8)," in Schnackenburg, *Kirche*, 79–96.

1/ **He told them a parable to show them that they need to pray always and not lose heart[a]. 2/ He said, "In a certain city there was a judge who neither feared God nor had respect for people[b]. 3/ In that city there was also a widow who kept coming to him and saying, 'Grant me justice against my opponent.' 4/ And, for a while he refused; but later he said to himself[c], 'Though I have no fear of God and no respect for anyone, 5/ yet because this widow keeps bothering me[d], I will grant her justice, so that she may not finally wear me out by continually coming.'"**

6/ **Then the Lord said, "Listen to what the unjust judge[e] says. 7/ And will not God grant justice to his chosen ones who cry to him day and night? And he delays with respect to them[f]. 8/ I tell you, he will quickly[g] grant justice to them. Nevertheless, when the Son of Man comes, will he find faith on earth?"**

a   Literally: "so that it might be necessary for them always to pray and not lose heart, saying."

b   Literally: "person" (without article, in the singular).

c   Literally: "he said in himself."

d   Literally: "giving me trouble"

e   Literally: "the judge of unrighteousness"

f   Other possible translations: "Will he delay with respect to them?" *or* "He is patient with them." *or* "But does he not exercise forbearance with respect to them?"

g   Another possible translation: "soon."

Following the first apocalyptic speech (17:22-37), Luke again picks up on the communication of Jesus' teaching to his disciples (cf. 17:22). In a parable,[1] he presents two characters, an unjust judge and a widow who insistently defends herself, drawing our attention first to the one, and then the other. Next he mentions certain of the Master's explanations, before concluding with a double moral, which, by analogy, encompasses both divine action (v. 8a) and the attitude of human beings (v. 8b).

The speech continues with a second parable, which also presents two characters, this time two men, each one very different from the other, a Pharisee and a tax collector (18:9-14).

Analysis

In introducing the parable (v. 1a) Luke takes care to convey the meaning he gives it (v. 1b): ceaseless praying

---

1   On the Lukan use of the term παραβολή, see the commentary on 8:4 in vol. 1.

2   The action: ἤρχετο πρὸς αὐτόν ("she kept coming to him"). The speaking: λέγουσα ("saying").

is indispensable, as is the struggle against discouragement. The reason he is anxious to decode the message at the very outset is that in his eyes this message is either ambiguous or controversial.

The narrator begins the parable itself (cf. the "he said," λέγων, v. 2) by giving a brief description of the immoral judge (v. 2). He refrains from calling attention to any action, thereby suggesting that the judge has been doing exactly nothing. On the other hand, he does not describe the widow's character at all but concentrates instead on what she does: she goes to the judge and makes him take up her case (v. 3). This move, in both its acts and its words,[2] is repeated, as is indicated by the use of the imperfect tense in Greek.[3] This leads to an impasse: while she wants him to act, he obstinately turns a deaf ear (v. 4a). There is then a pause in the story, since, for the time being, the situation is deadlocked; an hour that lasts hours and days.[4]

What kept the judge from acting[5] was not absence of willpower. On the contrary, the judge was not lacking in forcefulness. He had his priorities, but his wish in this case was wishing to do nothing ("and . . . he refused" [καὶ οὐκ ἤθελεν], v. 4a).

What got things going again was not a move on the widow's part, but the judge's thinking things over. We know that interior monologues play an important role in the parables found only in Luke (see 12:17; 15:17; 16:3; 18:4).[6] We are first reminded of the judge's sinfulness ("Though I have no fear of God and no respect for anyone"; v. 4b) and then are told right away that he has finally decided to do something and that he is going to do it for the wrong reasons (v. 5). This monologue, plunging as it does into the miasma of the human soul, fills a performative function: things start happening again when the judge intervenes, and the widow's rights are about to be restored. The long wait has as its coun-

terpart: the judge's sudden decision, which comes up in a definite time frame. And the matching piece for lasting frustration is the welcome satisfaction that will also last. So we have a happy ending, albeit for a rather dubious reason.

Beginning with v. 6, the reader learns of several commentaries on the story. The "Lord" who is speaking must be the narrator of the parable, who, by changing roles, becomes first a preacher and later, a professor of exegesis. As a preacher, he issues an invitation (v. 6) to "listen" to the person called an "unjust judge," literally a "judge of injustice."[7] This does not yet amount to a commentary, but it does already provide an exhortation serving as a moral to be drawn from the story.

Verse 7 provides a theological commentary[8] on the story and a promise of vindication of God's "chosen ones," who prove their faithfulness by praying without ceasing ("who cry to him day and night").

The end of v. 7 is enigmatic, and its meaning depends on the translation given for the Greek verb μακροθυμέω. As will be seen in the detailed commentary on the passage, it is probably best to translate this verb as "to delay" and to understand v. 7b as a commentary on the commentary, as a Lukan gloss ("And he delays with respect to them.").

A new introductory expression, λέγω ὑμῖν (" I tell you," v. 8a),[9] makes it possible to introduce a new commentary, which is a repetition of the first one (v. 7a),[10] with a supplementary piece of information: ἐν τάχει, which may be understood to have the sense of either "quickly," "at once," "without delay," or "soon," "shortly."[11]

This series of commentaries ends up with an impressive display of reserve, introduced by one of Luke's favorite adverbs, "nevertheless" (πλήν). All of that is perfectly fine, he admits, *but* . . . ; the chosen ones have indeed been promised that they will obtain justice. *Be that as it*

---

3   Ἤρχετο ("she kept coming").

4   Ἐπὶ χρόνον ("for a long time").

5   Μετὰ ταῦτα ("after this"); finally, after a long period of inaction.

6   See the commentary above on 12:17.

7   For the phrase ὁ κριτὴς τῆς ἀδικίας, see 16:8, where the unfaithful manager is given a similar title, ὁ οἰκονόμος τῆς ἀδικίας. In 16:8, the storyteller who meditates on the parable is called ὁ κύριος, as here in 18:6.

8   Ὁ δὲ θεός . . . ("and God . . ."), 18:7.

9   Cf. v. 6: εἶπεν δὲ ὁ κύριος ("then the Lord said").

10 In v. 8a, we find the verb ποιέω ("to do") and the notion of ἐκδίκησις ("retribution," "punishment," "justice").

11 Luke must understand these words to mean "immediately," while the source from which he reworked them understood them as "soon"; see below.

may, they must continue to be faithful to the end. This interrogative conclusion[12] picks up again on the homiletical style of v. 6 and is addressed to the circle of readers.

There are few passages in the Gospels that witness as keenly as this one to the trajectory a teaching may have followed from its first expression to its final wording.[13] Even in the absence of any parallel in the other Synoptic Gospels, it is possible to retrace the stages of development from the final redaction by the Gospel writer all the way back to the oral stage of tradition.

In the view of many commentators,[14] vv. 1 and 8b, which frame the parable, are redactional. The vocabulary is already a first attestation to that: "it is necessary," "to need to" ($\delta\epsilon\hat{\iota}\nu$), "to pray" ($\pi\rho\sigma\epsilon\acute{\nu}\chi\epsilon\sigma\vartheta\alpha\iota$) in v. 1; "nevertheless" ($\pi\lambda\acute{\eta}\nu$), "when he comes" ($\acute{\epsilon}\lambda\vartheta\acute{\omega}\nu$) in v. 8b. The theological categories used confirm it: the importance of sustained prayer, personal responsibility, the role of faith, the mediation of the Son of Man, the delay in the arrival of the parousia, and the pastoral orientation. For the Gospel writer, the widow is the principal character in the parable; she is a living illustration of the believer's unceasing prayer.

It would appear that it was also Luke who was anxious to clip certain apocalyptic wings through the expression of the realistic observation in v. 7b: "And he delays with respect to them." The Gospel writer was thoroughly convinced that God would come to avenge his chosen ones but that he would take his time in doing so. For the time being, he would put it off.[15]

What Luke reworked and adapted must have been a written text, a portion of what is called L, or material peculiar to Luke (in German, *Sondergut*). A chain of proofs in favor of this hypothesis is constituted by the accumulative evidence of the literary quality of the parable, the recourse to interior monologue, the use of certain expressions,[16] and the thematic content.[17] The narrative finesse, the attention given to states of the soul,

and the observation that a good deed can result from an evil intention all attest to a well-schooled intellectual capacity—and all of this corresponds to what results from the successful testing that can be applied to the author of L. For him, as for Luke, in spite of the way the judge is described, what counts is the widow and her fate. The injustice done to her must be corrected, and this is what the author of L is anxious to emphasize. Verse 8a, with its introductory expression "I tell you," which serves as a marker, is a proof of it. God is soon going to grant "them" justice; that is the conviction of this author, who seems to accord a collective value to the widow, as a representative of the community of chosen ones.

The author of L did not invent this parable, since the meaning he gives it changes the significance of the parable itself somewhat. Tradition, insofar as we can reconstruct it, reflected on the relationship between the widow and the judge. Verse 7a seems to express the meaning it lent to the story, namely, that the widow represents God's chosen ones, the community of believers. Influenced by apocalyptic thought, the community took over the parable and applied it to its own destiny. The members of the community suffered from God's absence and were impatiently waiting for eschatological retribution. Their biggest hope was "retribution," "justice" ($\acute{\epsilon}\kappa\delta\acute{\iota}\kappa\eta\sigma\iota\varsigma$). The attitude that the community adopted during that long period of waiting was one of supplication, crying out to God. The members knew that the parable that they had received featured a sinful judge. That did not keep them from reasoning from the lesser to the greater (*a minori ad maius*), and counting on an ultimate and imminent intervention on the part of God, the formidable Judge.[18]

Going back a step further, one gets to the oldest commentary on the parable, which deals with the judge and ignores the widow; this begins in v. 6. More an exhortation than a commentary, perhaps an expression on the

---

12 Note the interrogative particle $\acute{\alpha}\rho\alpha$: "However when the Son of Man comes, will he find the faith on the earth?"

13 See Bovon, "Apocalyptic Traditions," 383–91.

14 See, e.g., Fitzmyer, 2:1176–77; Heininger, *Metaphorik,* 199–200.

15 See below.

16 The expression "neither feared God nor had respect for people" (v. 2; see v. 4b) recalls an expression in L, the confession of the prodigal son who claims

to have sinned "against heaven and against you" (15:18, 21).

17 The connection between our parable and the parable of the tiresome friend (11:7-8), which also appears in L, has been pointed out frequently; see Jülicher, *Gleichnisreden,* 2:268.

18 See below.

part of a Christian prophet, the imperative is an invitation to listen to the judge's monologue. If one listens to him carefully, according to the opinion of this prophetic voice, one realizes that God will rectify the situation of his people and will offer these believers the retribution that is rightfully theirs.[19]

The parable itself, vv. 2–5, may go back substantially to the historical Jesus (although it is true that some of the wording results from successive rereadings). The irony of the situation, the shocking character of the judge whose belated judgment nevertheless serves as an example, the succinctness of the story, and the simplicity of the plot do, in fact, correspond to what may be known about Jesus' teaching in parables.[20]

Commentary

■ **1** Perseverance in praying is a motif we encounter not only in Luke but also in the Pauline and Deutero-Pauline epistles. Readers will remember the prayers of Jesus in Luke at critical moments in his life[21] and invitations to prayer.[22] They will also have in mind repeated exhortations in the epistles, such as "pray without ceasing" (ἀδιαλείπτως προσεύχεσθε) in 1 Thessalonians (5:17).[23] In their desire to pray, the faithful are confronted with a double threat: the risk of internal doubting and weariness (indicated here by the expression "lose heart" [ἐγκακεῖν]),[24] and the external danger of worldly distractions and the disappointing delay in the arrival of the parousia that Luke reports elsewhere.[25]

The Lukan prayer reflects the practice of the early Christians, especially the Hellenists and the followers of the apostle Paul. It is composed of petition, intercession, thanksgiving, and sometimes confession of sins. It also has its own strains by virtue of the links it makes with the stages of salvation history, its being integrated into the tradition of the Psalms, and its christological stamp (more an imitation of Jesus' praying than intercession in the name of Christ).[26]

Corresponding to the "economic" use of "it is necessary" (δεῖ), which expresses God's plan,[27] there is a corresponding "ethical" use of "it is necessary" (δεῖ) here, which encourages the faithful to be constant in their practice. Just as the Father's will and the Son's finally concur in the scene in the garden (22:39-46), so must the wills of the Father and his children finally form a single will within the community of believers.

■ **2** The story begins with the mention of a judge. He was not connected with either a synagogue or the temple but rather with a municipality. He was a part of the secular judicial system, which, in Israel in Jesus' time, seems to have coexisted with the religious one.[28] The judge was in the city (and we know that Luke was fond of thinking in terms of cities).[29] What interests the narrator is not what belongs to the world of the law but what belongs to the world of ethics; the professional conscience and ethics of our man were nonexistent. Luke expresses this sad reality using biblical vocabulary:[30] the judge "neither feared God nor had respect for people." He disobeyed the two most important commandments that Luke set out at the beginning of his book. He was at the opposite pole from the ideal of Zechariah, who sang the praises of

---

19   See Bovon, "Apocalyptic Traditions," 388–89.

20   Several recent books on the historical Jesus either neglect or ignore this parable entirely. Yet L is important on this subject; see Kim Paffenroth, *The Story of Jesus according to L* (JSNTSup 147; Sheffield: Sheffield Academic Press, 1997) 23 n. 62.

21   See 3:21; 5:16; 9:18, 28; 11:1; 22:41; 23:34, 36.

22   See 11:1-13; 21:36; 22:40, 46; Acts 2:42; 6:3; 28:10.

23   See also Rom 12:12; Phil 4:6; Col 4:2; Eph 6:18; 1 Tim 2:1-2. Ignatius *Eph.* 20.1; *Hermas, Sim.* 9.11.7. Grotius (*Annotationes*, 872) cites 1 Thess 5:17 in his interpretation of Luke 18:1.

24   Ephesians 3:13 and 2 Thess 3:13 use the verb ἐγ-κακέω, following Paul (Gal 6:9 and 2 Cor 4:1). The danger of discouragement is particularly noticeable in the Scriptures from the third Christian genera-

tion at the end of the first century, e.g., Hebrews, the Deutero-Pauline letters, and *1 Clement*.

25   Luke is conscious of this risk; see 8:14; 18:8; 21:36; 24:21; and Acts 1:6-8.

26   See n. 21 above and the commentary above on 11:4; see also Bovon, *Theologian*, 454–57.

27   See Luke 2:49; 4:43; 9:22; 13:16, 33; 19:5; 22:37; 24:44; Acts 1:16, 21; 3:21; 4:12; 9:16; 19:21; 23:11; 24:19; 25:10; 27:24, 26.

28   See Derrett, "Law"; contra Heininger, *Metaphorik*, 203.

29   The woman who had lived a sinful life was also part of the social fabric of the town; see 7:37.

30   See the prior biblical instances of the double expression "to fear God" and "to respect human beings"; cf., e.g., Exod 10:16.

those who serve God "in holiness and righteousness" (ἐν ὁσιότητι καὶ δικαιοσύνη, 1:74-75). He contravened the double imperative that the legal expert knew well and that he quoted in reply to Jesus' question (10:27).[31]

Even if readers in Luke's time would have had no trouble understanding the meaning of the expression "to fear God," namely, respect for the Master of the covenant and the will to conform to his ethical law, they might have wondered what the exact meaning of the Greek verb ἐντρέπομαι was. The passive voice of ἐντρέπω means "to turn into oneself," "to be afraid," "to be ashamed," or "to be moved." Followed by the accusative case, it means "to pay attention to," "to be interested in," "to fear," "respect." In this context, respect for others implies attention paid to them and even affection. It is just such respect that the judge singularly lacks. In fact, his attitude toward the widow perfectly illustrates the expression "not having respect for people" (καὶ ἄνθρωπον μὴ ἐντρεπόμενος).[32]

■ 3 The second character is a widow, who represents the incarnation of dependence and social fragility. Deprived of her husband, she does not appear here to have been surrounded by any offspring. So she was alone, at the mercy of the excesses, self-interests, and pressures exerted on her by those people who were powerful in her society. Luke, who was interested in the weak, the poor, and the "little people," was concerned about widows. He made of them the symbolic beneficiaries of Christ's activity as healer and Savior.[33] He also saw in them a category of believers to whom the Christian community owed particular respect (see Acts 6:1-6; also Isa 1:17). Finally, he admired them as models for the practice of charity,

which was all the more alive because it took place in the context of deprivation, frustration, and poverty (see Luke 21:1-4).[34]

As was the case with the judge, the widow is not located with respect to either synagogue or family connections, but rather in relation to the city where she lived. So the city does indeed represent the social context in which the action takes place. It is the widow who makes the first move by going to the judge. The use of the imperfect tense of the verb in Greek, ἤρχετο ("who kept coming"),[35] is an indication that she does not balk at approaching him more than once with her request, a necessary move as far as she is concerned but one that is in vain.

She asks for her rights and proclaims them ("saying," λέγουσα). She holds the judge to making a decision that will grant her "justice," the "pursuit in justice" (ἐκδίκησις) with regard to the guilty third party, and the "righting of the wrong" committed—the "punishment" of the guilty person and the "retribution" due to that person—in a word, "justice." All of this hope is expressed by a scathing imperative: "grant me justice" (ἐκδίκησόν με).[36]

In the background, scarcely mentioned, is the guilty one, "the opposite party," "one's opponent in justice," "the adversary" (the ἀντίδικος).[37] In the narrator's perspective, this person is in the wrong. He has abused the legitimate rights of this widow and is still benefiting from this illegitimate advantage.

■ 4a The judge does not flinch. He puts himself out of reach and will not even hear of considering this case.[38] He is powerful enough to be in a position to refuse to

---

31   See the commentary on 1:74-75 in vol. 1, and the commentary above on 10:27.

32   On ἐντρέπομαι, see H. Balz and G. Schneider, "ἐντρέπω, etc.," EDNT 1:461.

33   Cf. the widow in 7:11-17; see also Deut 10:18; Ps 68 (67):6; and BAGD, s.v.

34   On widows in the Lukan corpus, see Robert W. Price, The Widow Traditions in Luke-Acts: A Feminist-Critical Scrutiny (SBLDS 155; Atlanta: Scholars Press, 1997).

35   In the iterative imperative; see BDF §325.

36   We find the term in Luke 21:22, in which all the Scriptures will be accomplished in the days of ἐκδίκησις (used in an absolute fashion without the article). We also see it in Acts 7:24, in another con-

text (Moses avenges an oppressed Israelite brother). See also Ps 43 (42):1. On ἐκδικέω and ἐκδίκησις, see G. Schrenk, "ἐκδικέω κτλ.," TDNT 2 (1964) 442–46.

37   Luke has presented us with other instances of lawsuits, for example, the parable of 12:57-58 in which the plaintiff and his ἀντίδικος ("adversary") walk side by side to meet the judge, or the episode of the brother who wants Jesus to judge between him and his brother (Luke 12:13-15).

38   We must highlight the severity of the judge's stubbornness: καὶ οὐκ ἤθελεν ἐπὶ χρόνον ("for a long time he refused").

get involved in this matter. Although he takes advantage of the woman's situation, there is no check or recourse available her. And it goes on and on that way.[39]

■ **4b** What separates the two stages of the story is temporality or, better, chronology. There is first the long time ("for a while" [ἐπὶ χρόνον]) of inactivity (v. 4a). And then there is the moment in time ("he said" [εἶπεν], a punctiliar aorist) that follows the period of inactivity ("later" [μετὰ δὲ ταῦτα], v. 4b).[40]

■ **5** In the beginning of the interior monologue,[41] the judge reasserts his personal liberty of action, based on a cheeky and selfish sense of autonomy: "Though I have no fear of God and no respect for anyone" (v. 4b). But what follows shows the limits imposed on his range of options by the principle of reality that shows up the precariousness of his independence: "yet because this widow keeps bothering me" (v. 5). The judge is unable to escape his human condition, his position as municipal judge, the widow's legitimate persistence, what he calls the "trouble," "bother," "fatigue" (κόπος, from κόπτω, "beat," in the vernacular "to clobber") to which the widow has been subjecting him.[42] Indirectly, it is the existence of others and their right to life and justice that limit the judge's own freedom of action, whether he likes it or not.

Just as the imperative "grant me justice" (ἐκδίκησόν με) sums up the widow's agenda, the "I will grant her justice" (ἐκδικήσω αὐτήν) in turn summarizes the judge's new plan of action. In fact, he capitulates and sides with the widow, giving her what she wanted, thus conforming to the wishes of someone other than himself. So, after having first refused (v. 4a), he now is willing. This decision, which is also a confession, is preceded, as we have seen, by a motive that is not very honorable ("yet because this widow keeps bothering me"). Then another motive is mentioned immediately following, and this one is nothing to be proud of either: "so that she may not wear me out by continually coming." In order to provide himself double protection, the judge agrees to satisfy the widow's wishes. On the one hand, he is afraid not only of the woman's insistence in the present but also that she will step up her harassment in the future ("finally" [εἰς τέλος]),[43] which is a possibility he cannot rule out.

The verb ὑπωπιάζω is well chosen. It means, literally, "give a black eye," "strike in the face," or figuratively "wear down," "browbeat," "bring someone into submission by constant annoyance."[44] Commentators have wondered whether it should be taken here in the literal sense or the figurative sense. For my part, I take it in the figurative sense and see in it a possible undermining of the judge's honor. Just like the father who had gone to sleep in the parallel parable (11:5–8), the judge finally condescends to giving the victim her rights in order to avoid an external discomfort and to spare himself a personal humiliation. What the widow could do to him would probably damage his professional reputation.[45]

It is with this unexpected twist that the parable comes to an end. The story is told with narrative economy; we are not told what most certainly was the outcome of a plan of action that has now been decided on.

■ **6** In v. 1, Luke used ἔλεγεν ("he said"), the imperfect tense of the Greek verb λέγω, to indicate speaking that lasted some time. Here, in v. 6, he resorts to εἶπεν, the aorist tense of the same verb, also translated "he said" in English, but the Greek tense indicates speaking that was

---

39 On the temporal usage of ἐπί followed by the accusative, see BDF §233.3 n. 5, and 455.3 n. 5. We find related, though different, usages of the accusative of duration χρόνον in Acts 15:33 and 19:22. According to Grotius (*Annotationes*, 873), it refers to "a certain amount of time," neither too long nor too short. In my opinion, Luke insists on a long period of time.

40 We find μετὰ . . . ταῦτα elsewhere in Luke, e.g., 5:27 and 10:1.

41 Other interior monologues are introduced by the same formula (see 7:39; 16:3) or similar ones (see 12:17; 15:17).

42 See Alexandre, *Dictionnaire*, s.v. κόπος; and BAGD, s.v. κόπος.

43 On εἰς τέλος, which is not eschatological here, see Grotius (*Annotationes*, 873), who thinks that the expression comes from the Hebrew לָנֶצַח and means "continually." He refers to Pss 9:7; 79(78):5; 103 (102):9, where the LXX translates the Hebrew as εἰς τέλος.

44 See Alexandre (*Dictionnaire*, s.v.); Grotius (*Annotationes*, 873) sees this as a Latinism (which he frequently finds in Luke): *obrundere* means, among other things, "to complain or cry out about something to the point of disgust." He cites Terence *Andria* 348, "Obrundis, tametsi intelligo" ("You keep complaining, even though I'm well aware").

45 See Daube, "Neglected Nuances of Exposition in Luke-Acts," 2339–40.

of short duration. Luke's reference here to the "Lord" (ὁ κύριος, as in 10:1 or 16:8) as the subject of the verb has as its purpose to emphasize of the christological authority underlying the injunction "Listen to what the unjust judge says."[46]

The use of the indicative present λέγει ("he [the unjust judge] says") constitutes something of a problem. This verb could initiate a new speech and refer to what follows (v. 7, maybe even vv. 7-8),[47] but that seems improbable to me. I prefer to understand this verb as a reference to the decision the judge has just made (vv. 4b-5).

"Listen" (ἀκούσατε) does not simply involve the act of hearing; it also means "listen to," "pay attention to," "heed," "understand," sometimes even "obey."[48] In the account of the transfiguration (9:35), the heavenly voice issues an invitation to listen to a person, the Son of God, in the present imperative ("listen to him" [αὐτοῦ ἀκούετε], with the idea of duration, "obey him").[49] Here the imperative is worded with the aorist and pertains to the content of the message ("what" [τί]). What the unjust judge "says" is that, out of weariness and for reasons of personal comfort, he is going to end up giving the widow her rights. As they "listen to" that, and as they understand the meaning of it, the Lord's (ὁ κύριος) faithful ones will realize what the parable is about. If, in the end, such a judge dispenses justice, how much more is God going to restore the rights of believers.

■ **7a** It is this meaning, implicit in v. 6, that is going to come to the fore in v. 7a. The author of this interpretation must have been a Christian prophet; he had in mind a Christian community to which he referred with the ecclesiastically important and beautiful name of God's "chosen ones" (οἱ ἐκλεκτοί). The widow, who in biblical symbolism may stand for Israel (see Isa 54:4) or those persons to whose rescue God comes, is interpreted here collectively as the community of the "chosen ones."[50] The expression "chosen ones," with an ecclesiastical meaning, has its roots in the Hebrew Bible and was developed in Jewish apocalyptic writing and its conception of the remnant of Israel.[51] It was taken up in the earliest Christian literature.[52] The Pauline epistles are particularly familiar with the expression "those who are called" (οἱ κλητοί, Rom 1:6-7). The expression the "chosen ones" must have been a popular ecclesiastical title (see 1 Cor 1:2, 24) in the community to which the author of L belonged.[53]

In the "unjust judge" (v. 6), readers will recognize, with some trepidation, an illustration of "God" himself (v. 7a). If such a positive attitude can be displayed by an immoral judge, it will certainly be the same with the Supreme Judge.[54] In Israel, the judge was essentially the one who defended people's rights against those people who would try to bend those rights or violate them. So, depending on the circumstances, the judge would either acquit people or punish them. As judge, God is the one who inspires confidence, since his secure position scares away enemies on all sides. Beginning with the passage on the beatitudes, Luke has managed to provide hope for the poor, since the God who is to establish his reign will at the same time restore justice and condemn oppression (6:20, 24). The same conviction is to be found in v. 7a: God is going to come to judge, to restore justice, and in particular to offer to his chosen ones an eschatological rehabilitation. This ultimate vindication in the legal sphere is tantamount to eternal salvation.[55]

---

46   See BDF §329.

47   See Bock, 2:1450.

48   The verb ἀκούω is one of the great Lukan verbs. As Jacques Dupont (Études sur les *Actes des apôtres* [LD 45; Paris: Cerf, 1967]) has helpfully pointed out, the evangelist uses ἀκούω frequently at the end of his work as a final encouragement to listen to the Word of God; see Acts 28:22, 26, 27, 28.

49   See the commentary on 9:34-35 in vol. 1, as well as Isa 65:12; Sir 17:7; Wis 3:9.

50   For more on widows, see Deut 10:18 and Ps 68 (67):6; on God's elect, see Ps 105 (104):6; 106 (105):6; Sir 46:1.

51   Grotius (*Annotationes*, 398–400) provides a serious study of this expression, based on Matt 20:16.

52   See Rom 16:13 (in the singular); Col. 3:12; *1 Clem.* 49.5; *Hermas, Vis.* 3.8.3. In the LXX, see, e.g., 1 Sam 2:9 (γένος ἐκλεκτόν).

53   See preceding note, as well as Matt 22:14; 24:22, 24, 31; Mark 13:20, 22, 27; Rom 8:33; 2 Tim 2:10; Titus 1:1; 1 Pet 1:1; 2:9; 2 John 13; Rev 17:14; see also the commentary on 9:35 in vol. 1.

54   God is conceived of as a judge as early as the book of Genesis; see Gen 16:5; 18:25; 31:53; Ps 7:11; et al.

55   Paul, to whom Luke is close theologically, also uses juridical vocabulary to describe the ultimate goods offered by God. Nevertheless, he prefers language of justice (δικαιοσύνη) to that of retribution (ἐκδίκησις or μισθός).

Next, the comparison between the "widow" and the "chosen ones" is spelled out. What they have in common is a shared supplication. This prayer on the part of the community of the chosen ones has been described as a "cry."[56] It has been said by at least one author that "faith is not a cry."[57] It is certainly not just that, since it must be expressed in terms of a thoughtful and articulate confession. But it is still also a cry, a cry arising out of suffering, an appeal for help, and even for God to be personally present. If God's "chosen ones" cry to him "day and night," it is because they are still deprived of their rights, their legitimate existence, and their true life, and they suffer in a hostile world that marginalizes them.[58] They therefore appeal to God to console them and satisfy their needs—in a word, to hear them out. If they must listen to the Word (v. 6), then God needs to listen to them, which he will certainly do, in response to their unremitting cries.[59]

In concrete terms, what the prophet who has provided this commentary on the parable had in mind was not only individual and liturgical prayers but also the entire life of the community, which can be compared to a prayer. Is this not what the apostle Paul did, in Rom 12:1, when he asked Christians in the capital city "to present [their] bodies as a living sacrifice, holy and acceptable to God, which is your 'worship.'"[60]

■ **7b** The words "and he delays with respect to them" (καὶ μακροθυμεῖ ἐπ' αὐτοῖς) appear to be a Lukan gloss.[61] Their meaning is scarcely explicable without reference to a passage in Sirach (Ecclesiasticus 34:21-22); in the passage in question the verb μακροθυμέω, which may mean "show patience," clearly has the meaning here "delay."[62] It occurs in a context of hope, where the believer expects God to intervene and see that justice is done to the righteous, without delay. Luke distances himself from such a hope, which is nevertheless shared by the author of L, who makes it clear that the retribution will come "quickly" (v. 8a). Luke corrects that: no, the Lord will come, to be sure, to judge "quickly," but for the time being he "delays."[63] The strange construction in Greek, ἐπ' αὐτοῖς, literally "on them" (the believers), that is "with respect to them," is also to be explained as an influence of that same Deuterocanonical book, since that same construction is joined to the same verb, in Sir 35:19.[64]

■ **8a** The community whose voice has just been heard (v. 7a) was stamped by apocalyptic expectation, as we have seen. But the members of that community did not

---

56   The verb βοάω ("to cry out") can be used in Greek to describe prayer; see BAGD, s.v., citing *Barn.* 3.5 (Isa 58:9 LXX) and *1 Clem.* 34.7.

57   This is the title of a book by Henry Duméry, *La foi n'est pas un cri: Suivi de Foi et institution* (Paris: Seuil, 1959).

58   The first Christians often felt like strangers on this earth; they were afflicted by tribulations, temptations, and other persecutions; see Mark 10:30; John 17:14-15; Acts 14:22; 1 Pet 4:12-19; Rev 2:13. They knew that if the reign of God must come, this world, while it waits, can be thought of very negatively (see Gal 1:4; Rom 12:2; Eph 5:16; 1 John 5:19).

59   The spirituality of the Psalms insists on the attentiveness of the God for whom the Psalmist yearns with all his being (see Helmer Ringgren, *The Faith of the Psalmists* [Philadelphia: Fortress Press, 1963] 3, 76).

60   See Ernst Käsemann, "Gottesdienst im Alltag der Welt," in *Exegetische Versuche*, 2:198–204.

61   One variant is attested by W, family 13 of minuscules, and the majority of Byzantine witnesses: καὶ μακροθυμῶν ἐπ' αὐτοῖς ("all while manifesting his patience toward them"). Because of its grammatical

position, the present participle μακροθυμῶν can hardly mean "delaying," except if by that one means "even if he delays."

62   Meanings of μακροθυμέω· include (a) "to have patience," "to have compassion" (in the case of debts, e.g., Matt 18:26, 29), and (b) "to be slow to." See BAGD, s.v.

63   On the delay of the Lord, see Hab 2:2-4; see also the commentary above on 12:45.

64   On ἐπ' αὐτοῖς, see Fitzmyer, 2:1180. I prefer to interpret μακροθυμέω as meaning "to delay" rather than "to have patience" (see n. 62 above). According to this last interpretation, v. 7 has only one question in two parts: Will God not do justice, and will God not show his forbearance? The difference in mood between the two verbs does not preclude this interpretation because ποιήσῃ (formally an aorist subjunctive) is equivalent to a punctual future indicative, and μακροθυμεῖ is a present indicative with a durative value. Personally, I still think there is a tension between the idea of retribution and that of forbearance. Thus, I prefer the first interpretation which understands μακροθυμέω to mean "to delay" and v. 7b to be an affirmation.

feel it necessary to make that imminence explicit, since for them it was self-evident. The mention of the chosen ones' unremitting cries was sufficient to bring it to mind. The author of L, however, preferred to spell it out.[65] To his way of thinking, this final retribution—and he was not embarrassed to repeat the essence of v. 7a—would take place "quickly" ($\dot{\epsilon}\nu$ $\tau\acute{\alpha}\chi\epsilon\iota$). When L wrote these words, for him they meant "soon,"[66] but when Luke rewrote this material he shifted their sense to another possible meaning in Greek: "quickly," "at once." Although Luke did not expect the parousia to arrive overnight, he nevertheless expressed his conviction that it would arrive with a dazzling flash like lightning (cf. 17:24) and that the last judgment would take place very quickly (cf. 21:28-32).[67]

■ **8b** Luke did not stop there in his reinterpretation. He was also careful to give voice to his own apprehension. Since we have to count on waiting for some length of time, is there not a danger of faith cooling off?[68] "Nevertheless, when the Son of Man comes, will he find faith on earth?" This anguished questioning is interesting for more than one reason.[69] In the first place, it confirms the Lukan opinion that the eschatological judgment, a prerogative of God according to the prophets and the early Christians (cf. vv. 7-8a),[70] would be carried out through the mediation of the Son of Man (note how frequently this title is used in 17:22-37 and 21:25-36, the two apocalyptic speeches in Luke). In the second place, it confirms the close links that are to be found between prayer (v. 1) and faith (here, in v. 8b). The attitude that the chosen assume in prayer is an expression of their religious conviction. Where there is faith, there also will be prayer.[71] Next, this question contemplates an uncertain future in which only the duration is assured. Luke

has reinterpreted the early eschatology of imminence as a patient waiting for a distant end of the history of salvation.[72] Finally, this question, which is not rhetorical, admits that the Christian faith runs the risk of failure. It was possible for a book to appear bearing the title: *"Is Christianity going to die?"* (the original in French: *Le christianisme va-t-il mourir?*).[73] This is the very question that Luke was asking himself. And he was worried about it, since he assigned a share of responsibility in the carrying out of this salvation to human beings, although the main share of responsibility is God's.[74]

History of Interpretation

Tertullian, who rejected the dichotomy that Marcion made between a God of love and a God of vengeance, was happy, as was frequently the case, to read in Luke 18:1-8 that the good God, witnessed to by Christ, is also the God of complete righteousness (*Adv. Marc.* 4.36).

Another Church Father, Cyril of Alexandria, in his sermon on Luke 18:1-8, explained to his parishioners the nature and function of prayer (*Hom. in Luc.* 119).[75] It is a direct, easy, and unhoped-for means of access to God, and a privilege that human beings ought not to neglect. It is, moreover, as the parable assures us, a sure path, since God answers prayers that are serious and steadfast. In the next part of his speech, Cyril mentioned the enemies of authentic prayer and above all charged his parishioners not to combat these enemies with anger or violence but to love them and to petition God on their behalf. He buttressed his point of view with numerous examples drawn from the Scriptures, such as Num 10:35 (Moses' prayer).[76]

---

65   By beginning the saying with $\lambda\acute{\epsilon}\gamma\omega$ $\dot{\upsilon}\mu\hat{\iota}\nu$ ("I tell you"), the author of L signals an addition.

66   Several authors think that this is also the meaning that Luke gives to these words; this seems unlikely to me. For more on this question, see Bornhäuser, *Sondergut*, 167–68; Fitzmyer, 2:1180–81.

67   On Lukan eschatology, see Bovon, *Theologian*, 11–85.

68   Numerous Christian authors from the end of the first century and the beginning of the second century share this fear, for example, the author of Revelation and that of the Epistle to the Hebrews (see Rev 2:4-5; 3:15-16; Heb 10:32-36).

69   See Bovon, *L'œuvre*, 203.

70   See Marguerat, *Jugement*, 14–17.

71   See above.

72   On this reinterpretation, which, in my opinion, is not a betrayal, see Bovon, *Theologian*, 28–30.

73   This meditation, in the faith, on the past and the future of Christianity is the work of the historian Jean Delumeau, *Le christianisme va-t-il mourir?* (Paris: Hachette, 1977).

74   See Taeger, *Mensch*, 225–28; Bovon, *L'œuvre*, 165–79.

75   See Payne-Smith, *Cyril*, 2:551–55.

76   Actually, the prayer of Moses, which does not lack a spirit of revenge, radiates violence.

Albert the Great analyzed the text of the parable step by step (*Enarr. in Luc.* [ed. Borgnet] 18.1-8).[77] Commenting on v. 1, he too reflected on prayer and, like Cyril, defined its main characteristics with the help of the Scriptures, which he interpreted in dependence on tradition, especially on Augustine. For him, prayer is more than a moment in one's life or one act among many. It is the attitude of the human spirit, which, filled with piety, directs its attention to God.[78] And this *affectus* ("disposition"), this frame of mind, this willpower, this attitude is demonstrated in thought, speech, and act. With the help of the parable, Albert laid principal emphasis on two characteristics of Christian prayer, the *instantia* ("earnest supplication") and the *devotio* ("devotion"). The *instantia* must be understood as an intense, insistent, and persevering supplication on the part of the chosen; the *devotio*, as humble confidence in God that is also translated into good deeds toward one's neighbor.

In his *Paraphrases*, Erasmus spoke of prayer in a less theoretical manner and inserted his reflection into a commentary that took into consideration the Lukan context.[79] Jesus' teaching in Luke 18:1-8 must not be taken out of the apocalyptic context in which the Gospel writer inserted it (cf. Luke 17:20-37). It was also to be understood with reference to the continuous situation of persecution. Such points of view explain the interest the humanist had in v. 8 (will the Son of Man find faith on earth?). In fact, in his view, the answer to that agonizing question depends as much on God as on human beings. For God reacts to prayer; in particular, he answers the requests of persecuted believers. To be sure, sometimes he responds to the cries of his chosen ones in an indirect manner. Nevertheless, what he does accomplish is to detach their souls from evil and bring his chosen ones to a state of repose. Erasmus thought that in this manner God participates in the protection and the maintaining of faith on earth. When the Son of Man comes, the apocalyptic forces of evil will have reached a climax and will be caught off guard by the sudden and dazzling

character of his arrival. Faith in God, which implies confidence and steadfastness, will turn God's anger away from believers.

Hugo Grotius's *Annotationes* need to be mentioned here.[80] They come the closest to what in our day is called a critical commentary. This Dutch master of jurisprudence was admittedly not interested in literary genres or the history of tradition, but he did apply a highly perfected philological method that was carried out with adroitness and precision. All understanding of a text necessarily presupposes an analysis of its vocabulary and syntax, and Grotius was particularly brilliant in the area of philological competence. He also knew the biblical parallels, often those of the LXX, as well as how Greek authors wrote (and he even refers to Syriac, Latin, and Arabic authors, in the cases where a knowledge of them sheds some light on a passage). For example, he assigned the meaning "for a while" to ἐπὶ χρόνον in v. 4 and "continually" to εἰς τέλος in v. 5. He relied on the Lukan use of the accusative of χρόνος in the first case (Acts 15:33; 19:22) and the way the expression εἰς τέλος is used in the LXX, in the second.[81] His explanations of the verb ὑπωπιάζω "give a black eye," "mistreat," in v. 5 and the expression "his chosen ones" in v. 7 (which appears in his commentary on Matt 20:16) are of the utmost interest. In discussing the variants[82] of v. 7b, he used various Greek manuscripts, as well as Syriac and Arabic versions. In order to translate the difficult verb μακροθυμέω, he relied not only on his contemporary commentators but also on the passage in Ecclesiasticus (Sir 35:21-22).[83] Instead of the ideas of patience or compassion, he ended up preferring that of delay. But once the delay and the tribulations that accompanied it are a thing of the past (cf. 2 Cor 4:17), the Son of Man will act quickly (cf. Hab 2:3 and Rev 22:20).

A word concerning the Pietist commentator Bengel. His interpretation of the widow confirms his interest in the community of believers. The widow does not represent the human soul, as certain allegorists had pro-

---

77 The explanations of the Dominican scholar are often paraphrases, whose validity he ensures by numerous scriptural quotations.

78 "Oratio est, ut dicit Augustinus, pius affectus mentis in Deum directus" (*Enarr. in Luc.* [ed. Borgnet, 495]).

79 Erasmus, *Paraphrasis*, 421–22.

80 Grotius, *Annotationes*, 372–75.

81 Even though I admire his knowledge, I have not followed it in these two cases.

82 See above, 536.

83 On this point I share Grotius's opinion.

posed,[84] but the community of the faithful. Bengel was all the more interested in this character because, like the community of the chosen, a widow is often alone and destitute.[85]

Conclusion

God's chosen ones, that is, those whom he prefers, are here compared to a widow. That means that the Christian community sees its election as placed under the sign of the cross, with God absent and the community being in a state of social powerlessness.

In that respect, the widow resembles the tired and famished traveler in the parable in Luke 11:5-8, which is a twin of the one in this chapter. However powerless they were, both the widow and the traveler were not left to their fate. A voice, that of Jesus, speaking messianically, announces to them that retribution is promised and bread is to be offered. In the Gospel teaching given here, we see the resurgence of the structure of the beati-tudes: the widow is happy, since a protector will suddenly appear; the traveler is happy, since a host will sustain him.[86] From now on, one is allowed to have hope, and God is present in a certain way, in spite of the distance.

Be that as it may, the New Testament, in particular this passage, is not just the revelation of a divine glory. It is also fraught with human doubts. Luke and, before him, the author of L, several Christian prophets, and Jesus himself, knew that, like a widow, they were at the mercy of an arbitrary and oppressive power. Luke himself went so far as to correct what he felt to be the excessive hope of those who were expecting an imminent correction of the path leading to misfortune: Luke recognizes, in a muted fashion, that God is going to delay. But the Gospel writer compensates for this feeling of helplessness by clinging to Jesus' legacy: there is such a thing as prayer, and it behooves us to pray. God is faithful and, however far off he may be, he is sure to intervene in the end.

---

84   This interpretation was offered with some reservations by Theophylactus *Enarr. Luc.* 18.1-8 (*PG* 123:1001); see Christopher Stade, *The Explanation by Blessed Theophylact of the Holy Gospel according to St. Luke* (House Springs, MO: Chrysostom Press, 1997) 233.

85   Bengel, *Gnomon*, 1:380–82.

86   We find this structure a little later in 18:28-30; see below.

The Parable of the Pharisee and
the Tax Collector
(18:9-14)

Bibliography 18:9-14

Bailey, *Eyes*, 142–56.

Böhl, Felix, "Das Fasten an Montagen und Donnerstagen: Zur Geschichte einer pharisäischen Praxis (Lk 18,12)," *BZ* 31 (1987) 247–50.

Bruce, F. F., "'Justification by Faith' in the Non-Pauline Writings of the New Testament," *EvQ* 24 (1952) 66–69.

Bultmann, *Marburg Sermons*, 107–17.

Cerfaux, Lucien, "Trois réhabilitations dans l'Évangile," in idem, *Recueil*, 2:51–59, esp. 53–55.

Charpentier, Étienne, "Le chrétien: un homme 'juste' ou 'justifié'? Lc 18,9-14," *AsSeign* 61 (1972) 66–78.

Cortés, Juan B., "The Greek Text of Luke 18:14a: A Contribution to the Method of Reasoned Eclecticism," *CBQ* 46 (1984) 255–73.

Crossan, John Dominic, "Parable and Example in the Teaching of Jesus," *NTS* 18 (1971–72) 285–307, esp. 299–300.

Del Verme, Marcello, "Le decime del fariseo orante (Lc 18, 11-12): Filologia e storia," *VetChr* 21 (1984) 253–83.

Downing, Francis Gerald, "The Ambiguity of 'The Pharisee and the Toll-Collector': Luke (18:9-14) in the Greco-Roman World of Late Antiquity," *CBQ* 54 (1992) 80–99.

Dreher, B., "Der Pharisäer: Biblisch-homiletische Besinnung zum Evangelium des 10. Sonntags nach Pfingsten (Lk 18,9-14)," *BiLeb* 8 (1967) 128–32.

Fernández, J., "La oración del publicano (Lc 18,9-14)," *CB* 5 (1948) 193–99.

Feuillet, André, "Le pharisien et le publicain (Luc 18,9-14): La manifestation de la miséricorde divine en Jésus Serviteur souffrant," *EeV* 48 (1981) 657–65.

Idem, "La signification christologique de Luc 18,14 et les références des évangiles au Serviteur souffrant," *NV* 55 (1980) 188–229.

Fiedler, *Sünder*, 228–33.

Fry, Euan, "The Temple in the Gospels and Acts," *BT* 38 (1987) 213–21.

Green, Lowell C., "Justification in Luther's Preaching on Luke 18:9-14," *CTM* 42 (1972) 732–47.

Gueuret, Agnès, "Le pharisien et le publicain (Lc 18,9-14)," in Jean Delorme, ed., *Les Paraboles évangéliques: Perspectives nouvelles, XIIe Congrès de l'ACFEB, Lyon (1987)* (LD 135; Paris: Cerf, 1989) 289–307.

Harnisch, *Gleichniserzählungen Jesu*, 82–85, 90–92, and passim.

Heimbrock, Hans-Günter, "Meditation: Das Gleichnis vom Pharisäer und Zöllner (Lk 18,9-14)," in

Y. Spiegel, ed., *Doppeldeutlich: Tiefendimensionen biblischer Texte* (Munich: Kaiser, 1978) 171–78.

Heimler, Adolf, "Meditation: Das Gleichnis vom Pharisäer und Zöllner (Lk 18,9-14)," in Y. Spiegel, ed., *Doppeldeutlich: Tiefendimensionen biblischer Texte* (Munich: Kaiser, 1978) 179–85.

Heininger, *Metaphorik*, 208–18.

Hengel, Martin, "Die ganz andere Gerechtigkeit: Bibelarbeit über Lk 18,9-14," *ThBei* 5 (1974) 1–13.

Hoerber, Robert G., "'God Be Merciful to Me a Sinner': A Note on Luke 18:13," *CTM* 33 (1962) 283–86.

Holleran, J. Warren, "The Saint and the Scoundrel," *TBT* 25 (1987) 375–79.

Jeremias, *Parables*, 139–44.

Jülicher, *Gleichnisreden*, 2:598–608.

Kilgallen, John J., "The Importance of the Redactor in Luke 18,9-14," *Bib* 79 (1998) 69–75.

Kissinger, *Parables*, 347–48.

Klein, *Barmherzigkeit*, 64–68.

Kodell, Jerome, "Luke and the Children: The Beginning and End of the Great Interpolation (Luke 9:46-56; 18:9-23)," *CBQ* 49 (1987) 415–30.

Krüger, René, "El desenmascaramiento de un despreciador prestigioso: Lectura semiótica de la parábola del fariseo y el publicano. Lucas 18, 9-14," *RivB* 49 (1987) 155–67.

Linnemann, *Parables*, 58–64, 143–46.

Lorenzen, Thorwald, "The Radicality of Grace: The Pharisee and the Tax Collector (Luke 18:9-14) as a Parable of Jesus," *Faith and Mission* 3 (1986) 66–75.

Lüpke, Rolf, "Gemeinde im Anbruch des Reiches Gottes (Lk 14,15-23 und 18,9-14)," *Die Christenlehre* 40 (1987) 49–64.

Magass, Walter, *Hermeneutik und Semiotik: Schrift—Predigt—Emblematik* (FThL 15; Bonn: Linguistica Biblica, 1983) 44–54.

Idem, "Die magistralen Schlusssignale der Gleichnisse Jesu," *LingBibl* 36 (1975) 1–20.

Mahr, Franz, "Der Antipharisäer: Ein Kapitel 'Bibel verfremdet' zu Lk 18,10-14," *BK* 32 (1977) 47.

Merklein, Helmut, "Dieser ging als Gerechter nach Hause . . .': Das Gottesbild Jesu und die Haltung der Menschen nach Lk 18,9-14," *BK* 32 (1977) 34–42.

Mottu, Henry, "The Pharisee and the Tax Collector: Sartrian Notions as Applied to the Reading of Scripture," *USQR* 29 (1973–74) 195–212.

Nützel, *Offenbarer Gottes*, 255–63.

Perkins, Pheme, *Hearing the Parables* (New York: Paulist Press, 1981) 38–39, 171–76.

Pesch, Rudolf, "Jesus, a Free Man," in E. Schillebeeckx and B. van Iersel, eds., *Jesus Christ and*

Human Freedom (Concilium n.s. 3/10; New York: Herder & Herder, 1974) 56–70.

Ramsauer, Helene, and Jürgen Weitz, *Schüleraus-legung-theologische Auslegung: Ein Versuch* (Gütersloh, 1969) 299–308.

Schlosser, Jacques, "Le pharisien et le publicain (Lc 18,9-14)," in Delorme, *Paraboles évangéliques*, 271–88.

Schmitz, S., "Psychologische Hilfen zum Verstehen biblischer Texte? Zum Beispiel Lk 18, 9-14," *BK* 38 (1983) 112–18.

Schnider, Franz, "Ausschliessen und ausgeschlossen werden: Beobachtungen zur Struktur des Gleichnisses vom Pharisäer und Zöllner Lk 18,10-14a," *BZ* 24 (1980) 42–56.

Schottroff, Luise, "Die Erzählung vom Pharisäer und Zöllner als Beispiel für die theologische Kunst des Überredens," in L. Schottroff and H. D. Betz, eds., *Neues Testament und christliche Existenz: Festschrift für Herbert Braun zum 70. Geburtstag am 4. Mai 1973* (Tübingen: Mohr Siebeck, 1973) 439–61.

Schweizer, Harald, "Wovon reden die Exegeten? Zum Verständnis der Exegese als verstehender und deskriptiver Wissenschaft," *ThQ* 164 (1984) 161–85.

Stemm, Sönke von, "Der betende Sünder vor Gott: Lk 18,9-14. Zur Rezeption von Psalm 51(50),19," in Tuckett, *Scriptures*, 579–89.

Stoyiannos, V. R., "Ἡ παραβολή του τελώνου και φαρισαίου εἰς την ἑλληνικήν πατερικήν παράδοσιν," *Kleronomia* 2 (1970) 1–41.

Tankersley, Arthur J., "Preaching the Christian Deuteronomy: Luke 9:51; 18:14" (Ph.D. diss.; Claremont School of Theology, 1983).

Völkel, Martin, "Freund der Zöllner und Sünder," *ZNW* 69 (1978) 1–10.

Vogt, Ernst, "Hat 'Sabbat' im A.T. den Sinn von 'Woche'?" *Bib* 40 (1959) 1008–11.

Watkins, Owen C., ed., John Bunyan [1628–1688], *Seasonable Counsel: A Discourse upon the Pharisee and the Publicane* (Miscellaneous works of Bunyan 10; Oxford: Clarendon; New York: Oxford University Press, 1988).

Wimmer, Joseph F., *Fasting in the New Testament: A Study in Biblical Theology* (Theological Inquiries; New York: Paulist Press, 1982) 79–84.

Young, Norman H., "'Hilaskesthai' and Related Words in the New Testament," *EvQ* 55 (1983) 169–76.

Zimmermann, Heinrich, *Jesus Christus: Geschichte und Verkündigung* (Stuttgart: Katholisches Bibelwerk, 1975) 105–10.

9/ **Then he told[a] this parable to certain persons who were sure that they were righteous and regarded others with contempt: 10/ "Two men[b] went up to the temple to pray, one a Pharisee and the other a tax collector. 11/ The Pharisee, taking a stance, spoke this prayer[c] to himself, 'O God, I thank you that I am not like other[d] people[b]: rapacious, iniquitous, adulterers, or even like this tax collector. 12/ I fast twice a week; I give a tenth of all my income.' 13/ But the tax collector, standing far off, would not even look up to heaven, but was beating his breast and saying, 'O God, be reconciled to me, a sinner!' 14/ I tell you, this man went back down[e] to his home[f] justified rather than the other; for all who exalt themselves will be humbled, but all who humble themselves will be exalted."**

a   Literally: "he said."
b   Literally: "human beings."
c   Literally: "these things."
d   Literally: "the rest," the same word translated as "others" in v. 9.
e   Literally: "descended."
f   Literally: "to his house."

Is this parable not doubly difficult to explain? On the one hand, is not the story both too simple and too well known to bear comment? On the other, how is it possible to comment on it without taking over centuries of criticism of Jews and their piety that Christians have drawn out of the story? To overcome the first obstacle, some commentators perform amazing feats of imagination, saying, for example, that in the original text, Jesus attacked both the tax collector and the Pharisee. The tax collector should have overcome his embarrassment and dared to come close to God, instead of standing far off.[1] To overcome the second obstacle, other readers would spare Jesus by declaring that the parable is not genuine. The Galilean Jesus would never have risked caricaturing a Pharisee that way, nor broken the commandment to love one's enemies that he himself had prescribed.[2]

It is no doubt preferable to meditate on this biblical passage as one applies it to oneself, to understand the anthropological structure of the two characters in the story, and to listen to what the Lukan Jesus has to say implicitly about God.[3]

Analysis

Synchronic Analysis

Verse 9 marks a new point of departure by introducing a new parable ("Then he told this parable," Εἶπεν δὲ καὶ . . . τὴν παραβολὴν ταύτην) and by mentioning the persons addressed, albeit without naming them. The person speaking can only be Jesus, but the text, which is once again unspecific, does not refer to him by name. The way the people addressed are presented is complex and even ponderous, but not without cleverness; in its two participial clauses (in Greek), it introduces the two parts of the story and suggests in advance a key to the interpretation of the two characters.

Verses 10–13 set out the brief story, which is told with a skillfully unbalanced symmetry. We should enumerate several parallel elements: the presence of two characters in the temple (v. 10); interest shown in both the places they are found and their respective attitudes (v. 11a and v. 13ab); the prayers they offer (vv. 11b-12 and v. 13c), and their respective mentions of God ("O God" [Ὁ θεός], v. 11b and v. 13c). On the other hand, we need to point out the elements that indicate differences or upset the balance: the length of the Pharisee's prayer (vv. 11b-12) as compared to the tax collector's short exclamation (v. 13c), and the length of the description of the tax collector (v. 13ab) as compared with the short mention of the other character (v. 11a).

Verse 14a tells us what we should learn from this episode. By having Jesus pronounce the words "I tell you" (λέγω ὑμῖν), Luke has him stress the importance that must be attached to his [Jesus'] doctrinal judgment.[4]

Verse 14b serves as a generalizing commentary (note the "all who" [πᾶς ὁ]), which is added to the indication of how the situation has just been sized up (v. 14a). In this last part of the verse, to describe the same reality, a different vocabulary is used: the text here substitutes the verb "exalt" (ὑψόω) for the verb "justify" (δικαιόω). The tenses of the verbs vary as well and shift the reality in mind from the present to the future. Present justification (such is the force of the perfect passive participle "justified" [δεδικαιωμένος]) is replaced by an exaltation that is still awaited ("will be exalted," ὑψωθήσεται). Finally, the maxim resorts to the categories of high and low, absent from both the judgment delivered in v. 14a and the parable itself (vv. 10-13).

It is understandable that this story found its place following the episode of the widow and the sinful judge. Do not the two texts both have to do with prayer?[5] However, the structure of the present story enables us to make comparisons with still other stories, such as that of the rich man and the poor man Lazarus (16:19-31). And its subject matter recalls the story of the Samaritan (10:30-37) and the one about Martha and Mary (10:38-42).

---

1   See Downing, "Ambiguity," 80–99.

2   Fiedler, *Sünder*, 228–33.

3   Schweizer (188) thinks that v. 14 directs attention to a wholly other God, who corresponds neither to the Pharisee nor to the tax collector.

4   Note the presence here of the verb δικαιόω ("to justify") used in the theological sense.

5   The same verb, προσεύχομαι ("to pray"), occurs at the beginning of each parable (18:1 and 18:10), but it does not serve exactly the same function: in the first instance, it constitutes part of the introduction to the parable and provides the key to interpretation; in the second, however, it is part of the parable itself.

The parable of the Pharisee and the tax collector is followed not by a new speech but by a narrative episode, the children sent away by the disciples, one that occasioned a double pronouncement by Jesus (18:15-17). One and the same message is conveyed by the two pericopes, and it has to do with access to God, described in the present passage in terms of justification and elevation and in the other, in terms of welcome and entrance into the kingdom of God.[6]

Some commentators have attempted to make a structural analysis of the Gospel of Luke.[7] Agnès Gueuret, in particular, attributes a special position to the present pericope in the travel narrative.[8] This passage belongs to the third part of this narrative (17:11—19:28) and to the second of three subsections of this part. It precedes the last stage, the one connected with Jericho, which in turn precedes the entry into Jerusalem. While Jerusalem is the city that excludes, Jericho is the one that welcomes: the tax collector in the parable in that way heralds Zacchaeus (19:1-10) and the Pharisee anticipates the Pharisees who are overruled by Jesus in the same chapter (19:39-40).[9]

Diachronic Analysis

This parable was undeniably a part of L that the Gospel writer took over and adapted. Luke's hand can be seen in the beginning and the end of the pericope. Even if it cannot be ruled out that v. 9 is due to L,[10] it is more likely that Luke once more emphasized here the self-righteousness for which he reproached the Pharisees (see 16:15).[11] It would then be he who added, as was often done, a floating maxim attributed to Jesus, in the form of a generalizing conclusion (v. 14b). He had already made use of this saying, rooted in Scripture (see Ezek 21:31), several chapters earlier (14:11).[12] Both the introduction (v. 9) and the final commentary (v. 14b) mention those persons, such as the tax collector, who begin "badly" (the "others" who are regarded with contempt [v. 9]; those "who humble themselves" [v. 14b]). But they put primary focus on those persons, such as the Pharisee, who believe themselves to be off on the "right" track ("certain persons who were sure that they were righteous" [v. 9]; "all who exalt themselves" [v. 14b]). If Luke aimed the preceding pericope at Christians who were tired of praying, he aimed this one at readers, both Christians and Jews, who were themselves facing another danger, the sin of being spiritually proud.

Verse 14a, a moral derived from the parable, must go back to tradition, for the text does not work without this analysis, which is above all good news. This maxim, which is both narrative and theological, has preserved the redactional stamp of the author of L.

As for the parable itself (vv. 10-13), it belongs to the genre known as σύγκρισις, the "comparison" of two opposite situations, dear to Greek rhetoric. The prose of these verses has been classified as Semitic on the basis of the judgment that it has more parataxis (juxtaposing short clauses) than hypotaxis (subordinating some clauses to others).[13] This opinion must be qualified, since although the style is simple, as is fitting for a story, it is not lacking in elegance and the text does not sug-

---

6   Bailey (*Eyes*, 142–43) calls our story a "parabolic ballad" composed, like others (e.g., 10:30-35; 14:16-23, and 16:1-8), of seven "strophes": (1) the two men; (2) the attitude of the Pharisee and the beginning of his prayer; (3) the remainder of the prayer in which he attacks those who resemble the tax collector; (4) the end of the prayer and the mention of the Pharisee's good works; (5) the attitude of the tax collector; (6) the end of the description of the tax collector and his prayer; (7) the moral or lesson to be learned. This ballad is preceded by an introduction (v. 9) and followed by a conclusion (v. 14b). This division into seven "strophes" seems quite problematic to me.

7   See Meynet, *Saint Luc*, 1:177, 2:172–73.

8   See Gueuret, "Le pharisien et le publicain," 296–97.

9   Gueuret writes: "Nous voyons ainsi ce court passage

du ch. 18 apporter sa pierre à la construction de l'univers figurative et thématique du livre entire de Luc" (ibid., 303).

10   Bailey (*Eyes*, 144) is uncertain: v. 9 could stem from oral tradition, from redaction of L, or from Luke himself. Many exegetes attribute v. 9 to Lukan redaction; see Jülicher (*Gleichnisreden*, 2:598), for example, who thinks it is muddled ("umständlich").

11   See the commentary above on 16:15.

12   See the commentary above on 14:11. The two statements are identical, with one very small and inconsequential difference: the second half begins with καὶ ὁ ("and the one who") in 14:11, but with ὁ δέ ("but the one who") in 18:14.

13   For example, Grundmann, 349; and most of all Jeremias, *Parables*, 139–44.

gest a translation. We find in it an infinitive of purpose (προσεύξασθαι, "[in order] to pray," v. 10); the correct use of ὁ εἷς . . . ὁ ἕτερος ("one . . . the other"); and two contrasting participles, σταθείς ("taking a stance," v. 11) and ἑστώς ("standing," v. 13). The text admittedly contains some grammatical difficulties that are reflected in the uncertainties of the manuscript tradition.[14] But on the whole, the story is strikingly compact, and the picture that can be drawn from it resembles an impressive diptych. It matches what is known of the artistic and literary characteristics of the author of L.[15]

Even if this author has left his stamp on this story, he did not invent it. It fits doubly into what is known of the life of the historical Jesus of Galilee, who was indeed criticized for having contacts with tax collectors,[16] which he defended by calling upon and even authoritatively offering the love of God, who wishes to save sinners.[17] The parable appropriately fits into what some commentators call the "Jesus situation."[18]

This story, which was linked to a context of conflict, corresponded on the Master's lips to a polemical reaction; that is, it encouraged those who heard it to change their attitude and to put their lives in God's hands. With the passage of time, the parable lost its direct relation to Jesus and took on a theological coloration. Although it is indeed an example story, to reduce it to that would be to forget that it is also a vehicle for the proclamation of the gospel.[19] A theological reading of it is compatible with reading it as a moral.

Commentary

■ **9** Πρός τινας may be understood in one of two ways: either Jesus spoke "to certain persons" or he spoke "about certain persons." The usual way that the verb "say," "tell," is used in the Third Gospel when it is followed by πρός plus the accusative favors the first translation. The context of communication[20] thus initiated does not rule out the possibility that there were other persons around who were listening, in particular disciples (cf. 17:22; 18:1). On two previous occasions it was noted that Pharisees were present (16:14; 17:20).

Luke describes those persons to whom Jesus spoke. The verb πέποιθα, which is the second perfect active of the verb πείθω, functions as a synonym of πέπεισμαι, the perfect middle-passive of the same verb. And, although the verb means "persuade, appeal to" in the active, in the middle-passive it means "believe, to be persuaded," and the perfect active πέποιθα often even means "to have confidence."[21] As for the preposition ἐπί followed by the dative, it can express several different kinds of relationships, which are often difficult to distinguish: "near," "for the purpose of," but also "about," which must be the meaning that fits here—these persons[22] were sure (about themselves) that they were righteous. In this sentence, we are dealing not with a legitimate self-confidence but with a fragile arrogance that perpetuates itself only by criticizing others ("and regarded others with contempt," καὶ ἐξουθενοῦντας

---

14 The difficulties principally concern the beginning of v. 11: σταθεὶς πρὸς ἑαυτὸν ταῦτα προσηύχετο ("standing up straight he prayed this prayer about himself") and the end of v. 14a: δεδικαιωμένος . . . παρ᾽ ἐκεῖνον ("justified . . . as opposed to the other one").

15 See Petzke, *Sondergut*, 161–65.

16 See, e.g., Mark 2:14-15 par. Matt 9:9-13 and Luke 5:27-30; Mark 11:19 par. Luke 7:34; Luke 15:2; 19:7.

17 See Luke 5:32 and 19:10: in both of these cases, the mention of the calling of sinners to conversion and the mention of finding what was lost places these stories, along with ours here (18:9-14), in a controversy sparked by Jesus' relationship to tax collectors.

18 See, e.g., Zimmermann (*Jesus Christus*, 105–10), who notes the difference between the audience of Jesus (the Galilean taking on his adversaries) and that of Luke (the evangelist addressing Christians). Zim-

merman writes that at the time of their transmission the parables had lost the memory of their original foundation. It is worth noting that Schottroff ("Erzählung," 439–61) has presented a vigorous argument against authenticity; she is followed by Fiedler, *Sünder*, 228–33.

19 See Schottroff, "Erzählung," 445–46.

20 Julicher (*Gleichnisreden*, 2:599) observs that, in Luke's writings, εἶπεν δὲ καί marks a change of audience.

21 On πείθω, especially in Luke's usage, see Rudolf Bultmann, "πείθω," *TDNT* 6 (1968) 1–7.

22 Τινές is often used disparagingly for adversaries whom the author does not want to name explicitly; see 1 Cor 15:12 or Gal 1:7.

τοὺς λοιποὺς); by a pretension, more social than psychological, to belonging to a superior class of the population; and by seeking to impress others. The parallel expression in 16:15 indicates, moreover, that these persons claimed to be righteous "in the sight of other human beings" and not just in God's eyes. In neither case does the righteousness in question distinguish between the private and public spheres or between secular life and religious life.[23] The people spoken to are excessively confident that their conscience is clear and that they belong to a superior class. Their conscience is determined by how they live rather than having their life determined by their conscience.[24] Their ostentation itself is an indication that they are perhaps less sure of themselves than it appears. We already learn this from the prophet Ezekiel on whom Luke may be drawing. The righteousness of the righteous is not fool-proof insurance: "Though I say to the righteous that they shall surely live, yet if they trust in their righteousness and commit iniquity, none of their righteous deeds shall be remembered; but in the iniquity that they have committed they shall die" (Ezek 33:13 NRSV). Here in Luke 18:9, the contempt for others (these same people are to be mentioned again in the Pharisee's prayer in v. 11) already compromises the righteousness that these people purport to possess.[25] The Greek verb ἐξουθενέω (the form ἐξουδενέω is also attested) is a strong one, since etymologically it means "to hold to be of no account, nothing" (οὐδέν); "to scorn" as it were with a mortal scorn. The LXX, the *Testaments of the Twelve Patriarchs*,

and Paul all use this verb.[26] Luke will use it again in the passion narrative: Herod will treat Jesus with just such scorn (ἐξουθενήσας δὲ αὐτόν, literally, "having held him to be nothing," 23:11). Now, according to the structure of Luke's narrative, it is to just such persons, so sure of themselves and so scornful, that Jesus spoke this parable.[27]

■ **10** The verb that the Jews commonly used, and with reason, to indicate that they were going to Jerusalem or to the temple, was "go up" (see Josephus *Ant.* 12.4.2 §§164–65). Luke himself adopted this usage; in Acts 3:1 he wrote that Peter and John were on their way up (the same Greek verb ἀναβαίνω) to the temple.

The two men[28] headed for the temple, that is, to the temple precinct. They stood in one of its courts, presumably the court of the Israelites, rather than in the one reserved for the priests.[29] Given the compactness of the account, we should pay attention to every detail. The placing of the action in the "temple" space contrasts with the tax collector's return "home," literally "to his house" (v. 14). As a public place, the temple assuredly provided a welcome place for the people of Israel to worship God. But by virtue of its social function, it also reinforced individuals in their role in society and even conferred on them a status that had repercussions on their identity and even their conscience. The house, the scene of more intimate personal relationships, allowed for more authenticity and a more transparent sense of who one was.[30] The earliest Christians met in house churches.[31]

"To pray" (προσεύχομαι) is one of Luke's favorite

---

23   Bailey (*Eyes*, 144) appreciates the introduction that v. 9 constitutes, particularly its theological dimension: "Thus this introduction is clearly appropriate to the internal message of the parable."

24   On the subject of v. 10, see Mottu ("Pharisee," 198), who draws on a distinction from Karl Marx.

25   The theme is close to that of Rom 10:3: "For, being ignorant of the righteousness that comes from God, and seeking to establish their own, they have not submitted to God's righteousness" (*NRSV*).

26   See Amos 6:1 LXX, which uses πεποιθότες ("persuaded") and ἐξουθενοῦντες ("contemptuous"); see Jülicher, *Gleichnisreden*, 2:599.

27   On the term "parable" in Luke, see the commentary on 8:4 in vol. 1, n. 17.

28   Literally, "human beings." The presence of the number after the noun conforms to classical Greek usage; see James Hope Moulton, *A Grammar of New*

Testament Greek (4 vols.; Edinburgh: T&T Clark, 1906–63) 2:172. We also find the construction ὁ εἷς . . . ὁ ἕτερος ("the one . . . the other") in 7:41 and 16:13. Does it come from a parallel Semitic usage, as N. Turner suggests in Moulton, *Grammar*, 3:36? Probably not.

29   On the space of the temple in the larger sense, see Francis Schmidt, *La pensée du Temple: De Jérusalem à Qoumrân. Identité et lien social dans le judaïsme ancien* (Paris: Seuil, 1994).

30   Mottu ("Pharisee," 199–200) insists on this point.

31   For example, one recalls the home of Simon Peter and his mother-in-law (Luke 4:38-39), that of Cornelius the centurion (Acts 10:2, 22; 11:12-14), or that of the Philippian jailer (Acts 16:30-34). On house churches, see Hans-Josef Klauck, *Gemeinde zwischen Haus und Stadt: Kirche bei Paulus* (Freiburg: Herder, 1992).

verbs. It not only specifies the act of worship, but also expresses the entire religious life or, better still, a human being's identity before God.[32] The aorist infinitive used here indicates a single act, whereas in 18:1 the present infinitive refers to a customary action. In the present verse we could be dealing with an individual prayer at one of the hours at which Jews customarily prayed[33] or else a prayer that, although certainly also private, could have been said in the public context of the morning or evening expiatory sacrifice.[34]

Readers of Luke will by this time have become accustomed to seeing, through the glasses of the Gospel writer, people whom Jesus criticizes face to face (from 5:17 on) in the same scene as those for whom he showed his concern (from 5:17 on). So these readers will not be surprised to encounter here, side by side, a Pharisee, a designation referring to a militant member of a religious movement,[35] and a tax collector, referring to a profession.[36] In order to make the fundamental disparity[37] between the two prayers stand out better, the narrator perfectly lines up what is common to the two characters, namely, the place, the time, and the intention.[38]

■ **11a** The first aorist passive participle σταθείς (from ἵστημι, "to cause to stand") is more studied than the commoner forms στάς (7:38; Matt 20:32) or ἑστώς (v. 13). The customary position for prayer was standing,[39] except, of course, for the cases where one was required to be prostrate. In calling attention to this position, did Luke wish to add a slight polemical note to suggest that the Pharisee was too confident of his relation to God?

What follows in the text creates a difficulty; we should probably read σταθεὶς πρὸς ἑαυτὸν ταῦτα προσηύχετο, even if the order of the words or their presence in the text is not absolutely textually certain.[40] Yet there remains the question of what we should attach πρὸς ἑαυτόν to: to what precedes, σταθείς, which would yield the translation "taking a stance, to himself," literally, "standing for himself"; or to what follows, προσηύχετο, which yields the translation "he prayed to himself." According to the first interpretation, the localization is precise and the prayer was probably spoken out loud. According to the second interpretation, we are not told where the Pharisee spoke his prayer, and it was not spoken in such a way as to be heard by other persons.[41] The proximity of the words πρὸς ἑαυτόν and σταθείς, as well as the parallel expression, referring to the tax collector, "standing far off" (μακρόθεν ἑστώς, v. 13), favor our opting for the first interpretation.[42] On the other hand,

32 See Luke 1:10; 3:21; 5:16; 6:12; 9:18, 28-29; 11:1-2; 18:1-10, 11; 20:47; 22:40-41, 44; see also the commentary on 6:12 in vol. 1.

33 Luke himself knew these Jewish prayers at the third, sixth, and ninth hours; see Acts 3:1 and 10:9. See François Bovon, *De Vocatione Gentium, histoire de l'interprétation d'Act 10, 1—11, 18 dans les six premiers siècles* (BGBE 8; Tübingen: Mohr Siebeck, 1967). The oldest mention of these hours of prayer seems to be the LXX version of Dan 6:10-11, 16.

34 See Sir 50:19; Bailey (*Eyes*, 146) resolutely chooses this solution. This prayer accompanied the sacrifice and benefited from its efficaciousness.

35 See Del Verme, "Le decime del fariseo orante," 253–58; see also the commentary on 5:17-19 in vol. 1.

36 See Herrenbrück, *Zöllner*.

37 Jülicher (*Gleichnisreden*, 2:601) speaks in this regard of *Gespreiztheit* ("self-conceit") and of *Zuversichtlichkeit* ("trust").

38 See Jülicher, *Gleichnisreden*, 2:600.

39 The prayer of the Eighteen Benedictions is also called *Amidah*, that is, a prayer that is given while standing up. It is recited standing up, heels

together, in silence. I am grateful to my colleague Jon Levenson for this information. We must imagine that the Christians whom the author of 1 Tim 2:1-8 invited to pray did so standing up. The first early Christian frescoes on the walls of the catacombs portrayed supplicants praying while standing upright with their hands extended above their heads, for example, in the catacomb of Saint Priscilla in Rome; see G. Seib, "Orans, Orante," Engelbert Kirschbaum et al., eds., *Lexikon der christlichen Ikonographie* (8 vols.; Rome/Freiburg: Herder, 1968–76) 3:352–54.

40 Some good manuscripts have the order ταῦτα πρὸς ἑαυτόν, which settles the grammatical problem by hooking πρὸς ἑαυτόν to προσεύχετο ("he prayed about himself"). Some other manuscripts and some versions either contain ταῦτα only, or else omit this pronoun altogether. On all this, see the critical apparatus of Nestle-Aland.

41 Jülicher (*Gleichnisreden*, 2:601) writes: ". . . um das Gebet als ein stilles zu bezeichnen."

42 Certainly one would normally prefer πρός followed by a dative with a verb without movement, but the dative was already losing currency in Luke's day.

the existence of a common Greek expression for "say to oneself" and the potential irony in suggesting that, in the last analysis, this prayer, intended for God, did not travel farther than the person who spoke it, favor opting for the second interpretation. In my opinion, we should not make a choice, since we are dealing with an amphibology characteristic of the Gospel of Luke. The Gospel writer wanted the reader to understand that by acting as he did, the Pharisee cut himself off from both other persons and God.

■ **11b-12** Three texts have been proposed as ancient parallels to the Pharisee's prayer. One is a prayer found in the Babylonian Talmud, in which God is praised because he has kept the person praying from sharing the lot of the ungodly (*b. Ber.* 28b).[43] Another is one of Aesop's fables, which probably reproduces the text of a true prayer but allows us to deduce that the person offering it is a hypocrite.[44] Still another is a dialogue, probably pseudo-Platonic, entitled *Alcibiades II*,[45] which compares the prayers of the Athenians and the Spartans and leads readers to give good thought to what they want to ask of the deity. A reading of these parallels enables us to settle one contentious question: Does Luke's text furnish his readers with a prayer to read that corresponds to Pharisaic piety or one that caricatures it? The answer is inescapable: using some authentic elements (the sense of being chosen, comfort drawn from being protected, and pride in having respected moral values), the Lukan text is a caricature that weights the text in the direction of an unflattering comparison. It is to be strongly regretted that for centuries Christian interpretation of this

brief story has been along the lines of an anti-Semitic reading, but we must not forget either that caricaturing one's adversary was part of the polemical arsenal in ancient times. Although Luke himself was admittedly less virulent than Matthew (see Matthew 23), he is still heavy-handed in the speech against the Pharisees (Luke 11:16-54), in certain anecdotes (e.g., 5:29-32; 16:14-15). Nor does he beat around the bush here.

We should count as part of the caricature the omnipresence of the first person singular, the highlighting of supererogatory works (namely, fasting twice a week and tithing all of one's income—supererogatory practices when compared with the requirements of the Mosaic law), and the general disdain in which the rest of humanity was held, in particular the tax collector present here. The parable is careful not to mention truly good works of charity; in so doing, it picks up on the complaint in 11:42 (you tithe excessively and you neglect what is essential, judgment and the love of God).

So the Pharisee drowns his piety, which could be obedience, in a wave of spiritual pride and hypocrisy. He represents, to be sure, the negative pole of the comparison, a character with whom no one would want to identify.[46] Even if the redaction of the text is due to the author of L, and later to Luke, I do not see why we should exclude the possibility of there having been a Jesus who, as a polemicist, created a caricature that served both to protect him and to make his listeners reflect.

Let us mention four special problems by way of conclusion to our analysis of the Pharisee's prayer.

---

43   This text is quoted, in translation, in Jeremias, *Parables*, 142. Bailey (*Eyes*, 145) notes other Jewish texts that criticize the spiritual leaders of Israel; see, e.g., *As. Mos.* 7.9-10: "And though their hands and their minds touch unclean things, yet their mouth shall speak great things, and they shall say furthermore: 'Do not touch me lest you should pollute me in the place (where I stand)'" (*APOT*); see also *m.* ʾ*Abot* 2:5.

44   *Aesop's Fables* 666 (in *Fables: Babrius and Phaedrus* [trans. Ben E. Perry; LCL; Cambridge, Mass.: Harvard University Press, 1965] 575). The fable is discussed by Schottroff, "Erzählung," 448–49.

45   Especially 148d–149c. This treatise is most often published among the works of Plato, next to the dialogue entitled *Alcibiades I,* e.g., in vol. 8 of the LCL.

46   On this point I disagree with Jeremias (*Parables*, 143–44), who thinks that the portrait of the Phari-

see is not a caricature and thus the original audience would have had to hear Jesus' verdict (v. 14a) in order to understand the Pharisee's culpability. Rather, on this point I am closer to Schottroff ("Erzählung," 444) and to Harnisch (*Gleichniserzählungen Jesu*, 90). Recall the useful Christian self-criticism: many Christians read the parable in a Pharisaic way, praising God for not being like this Pharisee! See Walter Wink, *The Bible in Human Transformation: Toward a New Paradigm for Biblical Study* (Philadelphia: Fortress Press, 1973) 55 n. 43, cited by Mottu, "Pharisee," 196 n. 3.

(1) How should we understand the end of v. 11? Are the words "or even like" ($\mathring{\eta}$ $\kappa\alpha\grave{\iota}$ $\acute{\omega}\varsigma$) parallel to the preceding "like" ($\mathring{\omega}\sigma\pi\epsilon\rho$), and do they introduce a counterpart to the first list? Or do they simply continue the one and only list by offering an example? In most cases, during the travel narrative the Greek conjunction translated "or" ($\mathring{\eta}$) links similar phenomena rather than contrasting ones. Moreover, "like" ($\acute{\omega}\varsigma$) may be used before giving an example. These two observations lead us to the following conclusion: the tax collector is an example of the "other people" and not a new kind of sinner.[47] So we may translate "or even like this tax collector."

(2) The list "rapacious, iniquitous, adulterers" (v. 11) belongs to a genre known from Jewish and Christian sources: lists of vices (and virtues) or vicious persons (and virtuous persons) drawn up for paraenetic or catechetical purposes. This list belongs to a simple and didactic division of humanity into two camps, the good people (the community using the list) and the bad people (those termed the "outsiders").[48] Other lists are longer, since this list does not aim at being exhaustive. There are no two that follow the same order.[49]

(3) The fast connected with Yom Kippur, the great Day of Atonement, and the fasts mentioned in Zech 8:18-19, as well as the Ninth Day of Ab, commemorating the destruction of the First, and later the Second, Temple,

constituted a national duty. This Lukan text is, along with the *Didache* (8:1), one of the oldest witnesses concerning fasting, which was optional for Jews, on Monday and Thursday.[50] The expansion of personal piety favored the establishment of these two days of weekly fasting. Reading Luke, we would conclude that first-century Pharisees appeared to have respected that custom. By way of contrast, Christians were to choose Wednesday and Friday as their days for fasting.[51]

(4) In 11:42, Luke had already reproached the Pharisees for their meticulous implementation of tithing and their neglect of the most important commandments.[52] There is an implicit criticism to be found in the word "all" ($\pi\acute{\alpha}\nu\tau\alpha$). And it should be noted that $\kappa\tau\mathring{\omega}\mu\alpha\iota$ means "acquire" (hence the translation "income") rather than "possess."[53]

■ **13** Readers are told neither the name of the second character in the story nor anything much about him. They had learned from the beginning of the story (v. 10) that he was a tax collector, but not what level he had attained in the professional hierarchy. Two other positive figures in the Gospel are named Lazarus (16:20) and Zacchaeus (19:1), and Zacchaeus was a chief tax collector ($\mathring{\alpha}\rho\chi\iota\tau\epsilon\lambda\acute{\omega}\nu\eta\varsigma$). While Christians today look sympathetically on the tax collector in this story as someone who adhered to the same religion that they do, people in

47 Here I follow the analysis of Bailey, *Eyes*, 150–52. On $\acute{\omega}\varsigma$ to introduce an example, see BAGD, s.v. $\acute{\omega}\varsigma$ 2.

48 The commentaries readily point out the etymology (though uncertain) of the word "Pharisee," which means "one who sets oneself apart," "one who separates," "one who removes oneself."

49 On these lists, see Anton Vögtle, *Die Tugend- und Laster-Kataloge im Neuen Testament* (NTAbh 16/4–5; Münster: Aschendorff, 1936); Siegfried Wibbing, *Die Tugend- und Lasterkataloge im Neuen Testament* (BZNW 25; Berlin: Töpelmann, 1959). Nestle-Aland provides references to the New Testament lists in the margin of Rom 1:29. Jülicher (*Gleichnisreden*, 2:602) advises taking this rejection of the rest of humanity *cum grano salis*. He is not wrong!

50 See Wimmer, *Fasting*, 79–84; and especially Böhl ("Das Fasten," 247–50), who provides all the pertinent references to Jewish sources from antiquity and offers an explanation for the historical origin of these twice-weekly fasts (not because Monday and Thursday were the market days but because they permitted one—under the impetus of the Hasidim

[ancestors of the Pharisees and Essenes]—to do penance after the name of God and the honor of the Torah were profaned under Antiochus IV Ephiphanes).

51 In a letter dated June 21, 1999, Jon Levenson, to whom I am grateful for these insights, adds, "In any event, in rabbinic Judaism, fasting on Monday and Thursday is seen as not compulsory, but one has to be very careful about assuming uniformity of practice and norm, even in the rabbinic community, esp. in the first century." On fasting in Luke's writings, see 5:33-35, and the commentary on 5:33-34 in vol. 1.

52 See the commentary above on 11:42; Del Verme, "Le decime del fariseo orante." In his opinion, the tithe played an important role for the Pharisees and was not, in their eyes, a supererogatory work.

53 See Jülicher, *Gleichnisreden*, 2:603. This is the perfect $\kappa\acute{\epsilon}\kappa\tau\eta\mu\alpha\iota$, which has the present sense of "to possess" (that which one has acquired!).

ancient times had good reasons for distrusting tax collectors. On the one hand, Jews did not like these revenue officers in the service of a prince of doubtful morality or of a foreign occupying force; on the other, Greeks and Romans had a visceral antipathy to the members of this profession, whom they considered to be greedy and inflexible.[54] Bucking the prevailing opinions, Jesus, and the disciples after him, deliberately chose tax collectors, not in order to praise them but in order to cite them as examples of the reversal that the gospel produces and of the previously unheard-of operation of grace and hope. This tax collector appears on the visible level, but readers, looking for the meaning behind the text they read, are witnesses to the birth of a relationship of love that is the beginning of a personal rehabilitation, called here "justification," and elsewhere "pardon" or "salvation."[55]

What exactly do readers see? A man, standing "far off." "Far off" from what? From the Pharisee? From other believers? It was rather a question of the holiest space. And why that distance? Out of fear, shame, or modesty? None of that was of any importance; the only thing that counted was the distance by which he expressed his respect for God, as God, and his awareness of his own humanity and his having been created and having become a sinner. The consideration of distance is scorned only by those who dream of fusions and symbioses that rob human beings of their responsibilities. In the

Jewish and Christian biblical tradition, keeping a certain distance was tantamount to preserving the possibility of an encounter or a dialogue. In order to be able to enjoy another person's face, one must remain at a certain distance from it.[56]

The Greek language is not averse to double negations that often reinforce each other. Here we have "οὐκ . . . οὐδέ" ("not . . . not even").[57] The tax collector would not even look up to heaven.[58] Too little attention is often paid to this verb "would," "want." This man carefully kept his glance lowered.[59] Whereas the temple was the place where, by tradition, one customarily raised one's eyes in order to gaze upon the divine glory, the tax collector did not allow himself to partake of that joy.[60] On certain occasions, however, Jews would pray with their head bowed and their arms crossed across their breast.[61]

Perhaps out of misplaced pride, men in ancient times left it up to women to beat their breasts as a sign of mourning or of repentance.[62] To express the same gesture, Luke uses the same expression in 23:48 (seeing the crucifixion take place, the crowds literally beat their breasts); and he uses the verb κόπτεσθαι ("mourn," literally, "beat" one's breast) in 8:52 (as a sign of mourning, when Jairus's daughter died) and in 23:27 (the women who accompanied Jesus on the way to his crucifixion).[63] There is a clear contrast between the Pharisee's posture and the tax collector's attitude; it brings to mind another

---

54 The tax collectors are among the first characters to appear in the Gospel of Luke: Luke is concerned about them as early as 3:12. On the workings of taxation and duties, see the bibliographical references given in n. 36 above.

55 The social image of tax collectors is more important to the evangelists than their professional activity. This is why they are often put into the same category as the "sinners," e.g., in Luke 7:34; Matt 11:19; and Luke 15:1. In the Gospels, "prostitutes" are the counterparts of the "tax collectors"; see Luz, *Matthew*, 3:30–31.

56 Bernard Munono Muyembe, *Le regard et le visage: de l'altérité chez Jean-Paul Sartre et Emmanuel Levinas* (EHS. Philosophy 148; Bern/New York: Lang, 1991). One must also know the occasion to stand at a distance from one's partner, opponent, or judge; see Rev 18:10, 15-18.

57 See Jülicher, *Gleichnisreden*, 2:604; BDF §431.2.

58 For the idea of the sky for God, see *4 Macc.* 6:26 (also see 4:11 and 6:6).

59 See Jülicher (*Gleichnisreden*, 2:604), who refers to Josphus *Ant.* 11.5.3 §143 and to *1 Enoch* 13:5, ὅτι αὐτοί οὐκ ἔτι δύνανται λαλῆσαι, οὐδὲ ἀπᾶραι αὐτῶν τοὺς ὀφθαλμοὺς εἰς τὸν οὐρανὸν ἀπὸ αἰσχύνης περὶ ὧν ἡμαρτήκεισαν καὶ κατεκρίθησαν ("because they are not yet able to speak, nor to lift up their eyes to heaven from shame concerning the things they had sinned and been condemned" [*APOT*]).

60 We find the expression "to lift one's eyes" in Luke 6:20 and 16:23. For gestures in prayer, Greek most often uses "to extend" (ἐκτεῖναι) for the hands, or ἀνατεῖναι for the hands or the eyes; see U. Borse, "ἐπαίρω, etc.," *EDNT* 2:17. In 1 Tim 2:8, it is the hands that men must "lift" (ἐπαίροντας) in prayer. In *T. Jud.* 20:5 we read ἄρια πρόσωπον πρὸς τὸν κριτήν ("lift one's face to the judge").

61 Bailey, *Eyes*, 153.

62 Ibid.

63 See the commentary on 8:52-53 in vol. 1.

contrast, the one between Simon the Pharisee and the sinful woman (7:36-50).

The tax-collector's invocation, "O God" (Ὀ θεός),[64] is identical to the Pharisee's (v. 11), but the content and, if we "listen" carefully, the tone of the prayer are completely different. The tax collector, a twin of the prodigal son, considers himself to have nothing to his credit and hopes only to be the object of mercy. He asks God to be favorable to him. In the middle voice, the Greek verb ἱλάσκομαι means "propitiate," "appease" the gods by one's prayers and libations. In the passive, as here, it means "be propitiated," "be merciful," "be gracious." In the biblical tradition, which reversed the tradition of Greek religion, this passive implied an activity on God's own part rather than activity or piety on the part of human beings. By virtue of his grace and love, God agrees to be favorably disposed once more toward his people.[65] The imperative "be reconciled to me" (ἱλάσθητί μοι) is not exactly equivalent to "have mercy on me" (ἐλέησόν με, 18:39).[66] It suggests more the end of vindictiveness and the reestablishment of a relationship than compassion. That was also the purpose of the morning expiatory sacrifice offered in the temple: to have God hold out the offer to persons to rejoin his people and benefit from his pardon. The text does not indicate that the tax collector was trying to pray at the hour of the sacrifice and thus benefit from this expiatory rite.[67] The imperative "be reconciled to me" (ἱλάσθητί

μοι) corresponds to a request from someone whose faith has spiritualized his relation to God and who has no need of ritual mediation.

■ **14a** The demonstrative pronoun οὗτος ("this man") makes clear that, contrary to all expectations, it is this man, and not the other, who was to go back down to his home "justified." By the use of the verb "justify" (δικαιόω), the text shifts from a religious category to a legal one. It is well known that the Hebrew faith was capable of changing its language in order to define the links between the people of Israel and their God. The apostle Paul reflected in a special way on the domain of law and justice. And so does Luke's Jesus. Since v. 14a comes from the tradition, it is probable that the verb "to justify" (δικαιόω) also goes back to L, and maybe even to the oral tradition.[68] Luke himself was inspired by it to write the introduction to the parable (v. 9, the "persons who were sure that they were righteous"). The tax collector went back down to his home and so did not escape the human condition. But he did not go back in the state he had been in previously. A transformation in God, moving from anger to affection, from condemnation to acquittal, necessarily implies, even if that is not immediately visible, a transformation in the man or woman. This modification not only concerns the interior sphere but also has repercussions on one's entire life, whether social or religious. The tax collector's "home" was to become one of those liberated zones, one of those house churches.[69] In keeping

---

64 We notice the absence of the vocative θεέ and the usage of the nominative with the article (ὁ θεός); see Matt 27:46 and Mark 15:34; BDF §147.

65 The verb ἱλάσκομαι ("to make expiation") is used in the New Testament only in Heb 2:17, but the substantive ἱλαστήριον is used twice (Rom 3:25 and Heb 2:27), and the term ἱλασμός two additional times (1 John 2:2 and 4:10), always in relation to the sacrifice of Christ.

66 With Bailey, *Eyes*, 153.

67 Contra Bailey, *Eyes*, 153. There is no further reference to the expiatory sacrifice of Christ. As in the parable of the prodigal son (15:11-32), redemption operates without reference to the work of Christ. The role of Christ is limited to the proclamation of a possible pardon.

68 Schneider (2:365) quite rightly affirms that the verb δικαιόω ("to justify") does not have to be taken in the technical sense in which the apostle Paul uses it.

69 The end of v. 14a presents a textual problem.

Among all the different variants proposed by the manuscripts, two present themselves as serious candidates. The first is the one retained by Nestle-Aland and that I follow as well: παρ᾽ ἐκεῖνον ("more than that one" or "rather than that one"), which is principally the reading of the uncials from Egypt and the codices from Sinai (ℵ) and the Vatican (B). The second, ἢ γὰρ ἐκεῖνος ("and not that one"), corresponds to the Antiochian and then Byzantine texts. Although this last variant is ancient, it is so "difficult" (ἢ γάρ does not appear elsewhere in Luke, nor anywhere in the New Testament) as to be practically impossible. Paleographically, one can understand how a *ΠΑΡΕΚΕΙΝΟΝ* could become *ΗΓΑΡΕΚΕΙΝΟΣ*. One could also understand the variant ἢ γὰρ ἐκεῖνος as the work of a purist reader who wanted to correct the popular turn of phrase παρ᾽ ἐκεῖνον. I keep my distance from the position adopted by Cortés, "Greek Text," 255–73.

with the meaning I find in the end of v. 14a, the controversy remains: it is a question not of degree (the tax collector more than the Pharisee) but of contrast (the tax collector rather than the Pharisee).[70]

■ **14b** The Gospel writer had already used this floating saying in 14:11, where, to tell the truth, it fits better than it does here.[71] Nevertheless, to test its relevance here, we would have to admit that there had been a new semantic shift: from religion (vv. 10-13) and the judicial system (v. 14a) to space. But it goes without saying that the categories of high and low had belonged for a long time, in both Israel and Greece,[72] to the language of both the judicial system and society, to both ethics and religion. Here it definitely has to do with ethics and religion. Following his basic practice, Luke places us here at the intersection of the theology having to do with God, who comes to our aid, and the human race in need of assuming its responsibilities.[73] The tax collector, without any good works to his credit, has nevertheless done what God wished for him to do: he repented.[74] And God, speaking through Jesus, has indeed revealed himself as he is in the Scriptures and in the Gospel,[75] namely, the one who does not wish for the sinner to die.[76] From a historical point of view, in spite of the Lukan polemic, we should make it clear that the semantic content of v. 14 also corresponds to a Pharisaically-inspired Jewish theology.

History of Interpretation

A sermon by Augustine of Hippo dating from the year 413 (Sermon 115) took the preceding pericope, 18:1-9, as its starting point, in order to assert the complementarity of prayer and faith.[77] "So then, in order to pray we must believe, and in order to keep the faith that makes prayer, we must pray" (115.1).[78] The text goes on to an expected attack on pride, which goes as far as insulting the other person who prays. Then it deals with the tax collector, who ran no risk in standing far off in that God looks down favorably on the humble. Next he attacks the Pelagians and explains to them that the Pharisee's error was not in thanking God for his righteousness but in having imagined that he was lacking nothing.

In his commentary on Luke, the theologian Albert the Great interpreted the two characters allegorically (*Enarr. in Luc.* [ed. Borgnet] 18.9-14). Human nature is at the same time both spiritual interiority and material exteriority (just as Abraham had both a son and a donkey according to Gen 22:3!). It seeks to ascend to God, who revealed himself as the two men were going up to the temple. Albert modified his first allegorization by viewing the Pharisee as the incarnation of the observance of the law and the tax collector as that of its transgression. He went on to assign a meaning to every detail in the text. He stressed the vileness of the Pharisee, who did not let the Holy Spirit pray in him (cf. Rom 8:26) but instead gave free rein to his earthly instinct (by treating the tax collector like an animal). And he admired the modesty of the tax collector, whom he compared with the prodigal son (cf. Luke 15:21), and expressed appreciation for the tax collector's penitence, which was the reason for his being justified.

Luther, however, rose up against the dangers of just such an interpretation of justification.[79] He refused to find the origin of justification in any human attitude,

---

70 The variant παρ' ἐκεῖνον, above all because of context, insists on this contrast: "rather than that one," "and not that one." See Schneider, 2:365.

71 See the commentary above on 14:11.

72 On the metaphor of height and depth in the Old Testament, see e.g., the episode of the Tower of Babel (Gen 11:1-9) or the fall of the king of Tyre (Ezek 28:12-19). In Greece, of course, the greatest gods lived in the heights, on the summit of Mount Olympus!

73 See Bovon, *L'œuvre*, 170–74.

74 We know the importance of repentance and return to God in Luke; see Bovon, *Theologian*, 305–28. For Schweizer (188), v. 14b corresponds to the renunciation of all self-justification. For Schneider (2:365),

this is a characteristic that is essential to God and which he manifests.

75 Cf. the father in the parable of the prodigal son (15:20) or the merciful God of the prophets (e.g., Ezek 18:29-32).

76 For a more detailed commentary on the floating logion, see the commentary above on 14:11.

77 *PL* 38:655–57.

78 *PL* 38:655.

79 Numerous sermons of Luther on our pericope have survived (from 1516 to 1538 or even 1544). At the time, Luke 18:9-14 served as the Gospel text for the Eleventh Sunday after Trinity Sunday. Luther's sermons are introduced, enumerated, and evaluated by Green, "Justification in Luther's Preach-

whether humility or repentance. He did recognize that the Gospel of Luke was the most likely place to find support for the idea of justification by works. That impression could be explained by the combat that the Gospel writer had to wage against those who are content with a faith that they do not allow to bear fruit. For Luther, the parable defines true piety, and he contrasts it with hypocritical piety. What the Pharisee did can be said to be good, but what was not good was his heart. And it was there that everything played out; consequently what he did was contaminated and it all amounted in the end to blasphemy. The Pharisee did not in fact know God, that God is nothing but grace, favor, and mercy. Nor did he love his neighbor. In the last analysis, he was even guiltier than the tax collector. Implicitly applying his theory of the two reigns, I suppose, Luther refused to draw any social consequence from his theology; as a result we must not attribute any state to the souls of the political authorities, God's lieutenants. The criticism that Jesus leveled at the Pharisee ought not to keep them, albeit knowingly sinners, from going about their work and passing sentences.

In the middle of World War II, on August 4, 1940, Rudolf Bultmann preached on this text without making a single mention of the international situation or the existence of anti-Semitism in Germany.[80] There is one excuse, or at least one explanation, for this attitude: this Marburg professor did at least declare that the Pharisee stood not for the Jews but for all of humanity in its ignorance of God. His sermon was rooted in the Lutheran tradition: the Pharisee did not lie. What he was wrong about was believing that he could be justified by God on the basis of what he did. Bultmann was thus looking for a new interpretation based on modern psychology.[81] A correct understanding of the text, he was saying, depends on one's feeling personally hurt by Jesus' attack on the Pharisee. If one does happen to feel psychologically and socially at ease and secure in one's status, then suddenly the presence of a marginal or a delinquent person along side us upsets our sense of security. The need to have one's worth recognized is a legitimate one, but it must not be exercised at the expense of others. But that is just what happens in the parable. Looking on the *Sache*, the matter, was replaced, in the Pharisee's case, by looking sideways on others. As a result he was insufficiently serious in his relation to God and lacking in love for his neighbor. In such a case, the community fades from view and isolation sets in. One moves from being the strong person one believes oneself to be to becoming weak. What holds true for our relationships with other human beings holds true also for our relationship with God. In this interpretation, we find the basic Bultmannian thesis of the interdependence of theology and anthropology. Trying to impress other human beings the wrong way corresponds to trying to impress God the wrong way. The solution we find in the Gospel is to copy the attitude of the tax collector, who showed that he had a true knowledge of who he was in God's sight.

Conclusion

Religion is a matter for the "temple" and the "house." When faith becomes ecclesiastical and social (the "temple"), it is rendered more fragile by virtue of the presence of other people. When the tax collector focused his prayer on God and on himself, he nevertheless managed to show who he truly was and made it possible for God to be himself.[82] He was not ashamed to be ashamed. He trusted in God in the knowledge that he had nothing to offer but his failure.[83] That is why he received what was essential: acknowledgment and rehabilitation. That made it possible for him to go back down to his home

---

ing on Luke 18:9-14." I have focused my attention on the sermon from August 1522, edited in 1523, WA 10.3:293–303; Mülhaupt, *Luthers Evangelien-Auslegung*, 309–16.

80   Bultmann, *Marburg Sermons*, 107–17.

81   One should also read the psychological lectures of Heimbrock ("Meditation") and of Heimler ("Meditation").

82   The tax collector is undoubtedly the figure in the story with whom the reader identifies. See Schottroff, "Erzählung."

83   See Monloubou, *La prière selon Saint Luc*, 80–81.

(the "house") and to rediscover his place in the secular
reality, his personal circumstances, his relationships with
his family and loved ones. He was still the same person,
and yet everything had changed. That was because God
had looked on him with favor.[84]

---

84   With good reason one can say, with Dreher ("Der
     Pharisäer," 128–32), that the prayer attributed to
     the Pharisee is a perversion of Psalm 119 (LXX 118)
     and that the prayer of the tax collector is a realiza-
     tion of Psalm 51 (LXX 50).

Jesus and the Children
(18:15-17)
Bibliography 18:15-17

Aland, Kurt, *Die Säuglingstaufe im Neuen Testament und in der alten Kirche* (TEH 86; Munich: Kaiser, 1961) 67–71.

Idem, *Die Stellung der Kinder in den frühen christlichen Gemeinden—und ihre Taufe* (Munich: Kaiser, 1967) 11–17.

Idem, *Taufe und Kindertaufe* (Gütersloh: Gütersloher Verlagshaus, 1971) 29–39.

Beasley-Murray, George R., *Baptism in the New Testament* (London: Macmillan, 1962) 320–29.

Berger, Klaus, *Die Amen-Worte Jesu: Eine Untersuchung zum Problem der Legitimation in apokalyptischer Rede* (BZNW 39; Berlin: de Gruyter, 1970) 41–46.

Brown, Robert N., "Jesus and the Child as a Model of Spirituality," *IBS* 4 (1982) 178–92.

Crossan, John Dominic, "Kingdom and Children: A Study in the Aphoristic Tradition," *Semeia* 29 (1983) 75–95.

Cullmann, Oscar, *Le baptême des enfants et la doctrine biblique du baptême* (CThAP 19/20; Paris: Delachaux & Niestlé, 1948) 35–37, 67–69.

Idem, *Des sources de l'évangile à la formation de la théologie chrétienne* (Neuchâtel: Delachaux et Niestlé, 1969) 142–48.

Derrett, J. Duncan M., "Why Jesus Blessed the Children (Mk 10:13-16 par.)," *NovT* 25 (1983) 1–18.

Fowl, Stephen, "Receiving the Kingdom of God as a Child: Children and Riches in Luke 18:15ff," *NTS* 39 (1993) 153–58.

Hahn, Ferdinand, "Kindersegnung und Kindertaufe im ältesten Christentum," in H. Frankemölle and K. Kertelge, eds., *Vom Urchristentum zu Jesus: Für Joachim Gnilka* (Freiburg/Basel/Vienna: Herder, 1989) 497–507.

Jeremias, Joachim, *Die Kindertaufe in den ersten vier Jahrhunderten* (Göttingen: Vandenhoeck & Ruprecht, 1958) 61–68.

Idem, *Nochmals: Die Anfänge der Kindertaufe. Eine Replik auf Kurt Alands Schrift: "Die Säuglingstaufe im Neuen Testament und in der alten Kirche"* (TEH 101; Munich: Kaiser, 1962) 66–72.

Klein, G., "Bibelarbeit über Markus 10,13-16," in G. Krause, ed., *Die Kinder und das Evangelium* (PSA 10; Stuttgart/Göttingen: Klotz, 1973) 12–30.

Kodell, J., "Luke and the Children: The Beginning and the End of the 'Great Interpolation' (Luke 9:46-56; 18:9-23)," *CBQ* 49 (1987) 415–30.

Krause, Gerhard, ed., *Die Kinder im Evangelium* (PSA 10; Stuttgart/Göttingen: Klotz, 1973).

Légasse, Simon, "L'enfant dans l' Évangile," VS 122 (1970) 407–21.

Idem, *Jésus et l'enfant. "Enfants," "petits" et "simples" dans la tradition synoptique* (EtB; Paris: Gabalda, 1969) 36–43, 195–209, 326–33.

Lindars, Barnabas, "John and the Synoptic Gospels: A Test Case," *NTS* 27 (1981) 287–94.

Ludolphy, Ingetraut, "Zur Geschichte der Auslegung des Evangelium infantium," in Krause, *Kinder,* 31–51.

McDonald, James H., "Receiving and Entering the Kingdom," *StEv* 6 [TU 112] (1973) 328–32.

Michaelis, Wilhelm, "Lukas und die Anfänge der Kindertaufe," in Walter Eltester, ed., *Apophoreta: Festschrift für Ernst Haenchen zu seinem siebzigsten Geburtstag am 10. Dezember 1964* (BZNW 30; Berlin: Töpelmann, 1964) 187–93.

Patte, Daniel, "Jesus' Pronouncement about Entering the Kingdom Like a Child: A Structural Exegesis," *Semeia* 29 (1983) 3–42.

Percy, *Botschaft,* 31–37.

Perrot, Charles, "La lecture d'un texte évangélique: Essai méthodologique à partir de Marc 10,13-16," in Institut catholique de Paris, *Recherches actuelles* (2 vols.; PoTh 2; Paris: Beauchesne, 1972) 2:51–130.

Pesch, Wilhelm, "Die sogenannte Gemeindeordnung Mt 18," *BZ* 7 (1963) 220–35.

Ringshausen, Gerhard, "Die Kinder der Weisheit: Zur Auslegung von Mk 10:13-16 par.," *ZNW* 77 (1986) 34–63.

Robbins, Vernon K., "Pronouncement Stories and Jesus' Blessing of the Children: A Rhetorical Approach," *Semeia* 29 (1983) 43–74.

Sauer, Jürgen, "Der ursprüngliche 'Sitz im Leben' von Mk 10,13-16," *ZNW* 72 (1981) 27–50.

Schilling, Frederick A., "What Means the Saying about Receiving the Kingdom of God as a Little Child? Mk. x 15; Lk xviii. 17," *ExpT* 77 (1965–66) 56–58.

Schramm, *Markus-Stoff,* 141–42.

Weber, Hans Ruedi, *Jesus and the Children: Biblical Resources for Study and Preaching* (Geneva: World Council of Churches, 1979) 22–33.

Windisch, Hans, "Die Sprüche vom Eingehen in das Reich Gottes," *ZNW* 27 (1928) 163–92.

15/ **People also introduced to him**[a] **some newborn children so that he might touch them. When the disciples saw it, they rebuffed them. 16/ But Jesus called the newborn children**[b] **to him, saying, "Let the children come to me, and do not stop them; for it is to such beings as these that the kingdom of God belongs**[c]. **17/ Truly I tell you, whoever does not receive the kingdom of God as a child will not enter it."**

a   Literally: "They brought him"
b   Literally: "called them"
c   Literally: "is theirs"

Just as the episode about the ten men suffering from "leprosy" (17:12-19) interrupted one of Jesus' speeches, so does the episode about the children (18:15-17) interrupt another of the Master's speeches (18:1-14). This incident will be followed by an important person's question of Jesus (18:18), just as the miracle concerning the persons suffering from "leprosy" was followed by a question from the Pharisees (17:20). By using such rudimentary literary procedures, Luke endeavored both to integrate the material he had received and to avoid monotony. Above all, he attempted to make the whole into a thematic unity, and here he has succeeded, by indicating the ways one can gain access to God (18:14) and his kingdom (18:16-17).[1]

Analysis

Here Luke leaves L and again makes contact with the outline of Mark, from which he had departed a long time before. He had, in fact, completed his rewriting of his previous portion of Mark[2] at the end of chap. 9 (the foreign exorcist [9:49-50 par. Mark 9:38-40]). He does not return to Mark 9:41 but picks up again at Mark 10:13. He had quoted certain intermediary verses elsewhere,[3] and he was not anxious to take over the rest of them. There is one surprising omission,[4] though, the pericope on divorce

(Mark 10:1-12), and it is not clear what might have shocked him in this Markan passage. Did Luke figure that his brief mention of divorce in 16:18 was sufficient instruction for his readers? Or did his decision to omit this Markan unit result from a literary practice?[5] Any time a transition is made from one source to another certain adaptations must be made, and they sometimes spoil things. Whatever the reason, from this point on Luke follows the Gospel of Mark for a while: after the episode about the children, he mentions the dialogue with the rich man (18:18-23 par. Mark 10:17-22), the danger of riches (18:24-27 par. Mark 10:23-27), the disciples' renunciation of their possessions (18:28-30 par. Mark 10:28-30), a prediction of the passion (18:31-34 par. Mark 10:32-34), and, after a new omission,[6] the blind man in Jericho (18:35-43 par. Mark 10:46-52). Consistent with his system of alternating sources, Luke picks up again on L in 19:1 (the episode concerning Zacchaeus). He shows that he is a well-informed and competent author by the way in which he succeeds in hiding this dependence on older documents and his transitions from one source to another.

The episode about the children has been transmitted by the three Synoptic Gospels and by the *Gospel of Thomas.* The Gospels of Luke and *Thomas* are not acquainted with Jesus' final gesture (the laying on of hands), which is found in the other two Gospels (Mark

---

1   See Grundmann, 353; Frederick W. Danker, *Jesus and the New Age: A Commentary on St. Luke's Gospel* (2d ed.; Philadelphia: Fortress Press, 1988) 97. According to Schneider (2:367), the pericope in 18:9-14 gives an *example* of true piety; 18:15-17 presents a *symbol* of it.

2   In 10:16; 11:14-22; 12:10; 13:18-19; 14:34-35; 17:1-12, 31-32 Luke does not draw his inspiration from Mark (or not primarily from Mark).

3   The saying about the millstone (Mark 9:42) also occurs in Luke 17:1-2; those on salt (Mark 9:50) correspond to Luke 14:34.

4   Mark 9:41 (the cup of water) and Mark 9:43-49 (cutting off one's hand or foot) do not occur in Luke; one wonders why.

5   See the inverted and abridged version of Mark 3:7-21 in Luke 6:12-16; see further the commentary on 6:12-16 in vol. 1.

6   That is, the misplaced request of the sons of Zebedee and the call to service in Mark 10:35-45 (Mark 10:41-45 have their parallel in Luke 22:24-27, in L).

10:16 par. Matt 19:15). For Luke and *Thomas*, the pericope did not need this conclusion. It represented an
apophthegm emphasizing a decisive maxim rather than
a significant action. In this way, these Gospels adopted
a conservative stance and went back behind Mark and
recovered the earliest structure of the episode.[7]

Mark himself did not ignore Jesus' words, since he
was not satisfied with having a single maxim; the famous
sentence, "Let the little children come to me; do not stop
them," is accompanied by a justification, "for it is to such
as these that the kingdom of God belongs" (Mark 10:14
NRSV), and followed by an independent saying, "Truly I
tell you, whoever does not receive the Kingdom of God as
a little child will never enter it" (Mark 10:15 *NRSV*). This
last sentence, omitted by Matthew, constitutes a characteristic exegetical addition of the Synoptic tradition. It is
probably early and came to be added to the apophthegm
in order to enrich its meaning.[8] Luke accepted this additional maxim and took it over without modification.[9] The
author of *Gos. Thom.* 22, for his part, worded the episode
and its maxims in his own way. The children are not
brought to Jesus; Jesus is the one who sees them being
suckled. The disciples do not scold the parents. Instead
of saying "Let the children . . . ," Jesus says, "These children who are being suckled are like those who enter the
kingdom." Next the disciples question the Master (here
the author of the *Gospel of Thomas* adapts another maxim
on the children, similar to Matt 18:3): "Shall we then,
being children, enter the kingdom?" Jesus replies to
them at length with the apocryphal maxim concerning
the left and the right and the above and the below.[10]

The Synoptic apophthegm composes an ideal scene.
At the level of the redaction, the children, whom Luke
calls "newborn children" in v. 16a,[11] stand for all the
children of the world. Still the expression that Luke
uses in v. 16b, "the children" ($\tau\grave{\alpha}$ $\pi\alpha\iota\delta\acute{\iota}\alpha$), originally
indicated the same children who had been brought to
Jesus (in that case the definite article "the" [$\tau\acute{\alpha}$] had
its original demonstrative sense, "these"[12]). Just as the
collective memory carefully preserves certain memories
of great men, such as rabbis, generals, or emperors, so
did the earliest Christians remember an unexpected
attitude on the part of their Master[13] (in ancient times
no special attention was normally paid to children).[14] I
would therefore question the view according to which
this apophthegm would have originated as a narrative
development of a maxim such as the one in Mark 10:15
par. Luke 18:17: "Truly I tell you, whoever does not
receive the kingdom of God as a child will not enter it."
This maxim lays stress on welcoming into the kingdom,
whereas the story stresses welcoming of the children.[15]
Nor am I any more inclined to believe that the pericope
had its roots (*Sitz im Leben*) in the practice or the defense
of the baptism of children.[16] In order to give shape to
their memory, the bearers of the Christian tradition may
have been inspired by the biblical example of Elisha who,
in spite of his servant Gehazi's recrimination, welcomed
the Shunammite woman (2 Kgs [4 Kgdms] 4:27).[17]

It is perhaps this same memory that is at the origin of
another apophthegm, the one in which Jesus takes the
initiative of placing a child in the midst of his disciples
in order to show them the true greatness and the proper

---

7   Grundmann (352–53), Schneider (2:366–68) and
     Klein ("Bibelarbeit," 14–15) offer helpful compari-
     sons of the Markan and Lukan parallels. I agree
     with Klein on the essentials of his reconstruction.
8   See Klein, "Bibelarbeit," 19–20.
9   The fact that Luke 18:17 and Mark 10:5 are identi-
     cal shows the respect Luke had for the sayings of
     Jesus.
10   This saying is quoted also at the end of *Acts Phil.* 34
     (140).
11   See the explanation below.
12   On the definite article keeping its demonstrative
     value, see BAGD, s.v. ὁ, ἡ, τό, 1.
13   Percy (*Botschaft*, 31–37) and Légasse (*Jésus et l'enfant*,
     326–33) root the episode in the life of the historical
     Jesus.
14   On children in antiquity, see n. 36 below.

15   Bultmann (*History*, 32) thinks that Mark 10:15 par.
     Luke 18:17 is an archaic, independent saying (hence
     it did not originate from reflections on the episode
     with the children). He also thinks that this passage
     does not have to be considered a legendary narra-
     tive development.
16   See Schneider (2:366), who presents this hypothesis
     as a possibility. In his three works mentioned in the
     bibliography, Aland opposes all baptismal read-
     ings of this pericope, as does Michaelis, "Anfänge,"
     187–93. In my opinion, neither the historical Jesus
     nor oral tradition nor Markan or Lukan redaction
     establishes a link between this story and the sacra-
     ment of baptism; see the history of interpretation
     below.
17   See Bultmann, *History*, 32. For a rabbinic parallel,
     see Str-B 1:808.

way to welcome God and his envoy (Mark 9:33-37 par. Matt 18:1-5 par. Luke 9:46-48).[18] In the context of that other apophthegm, Matthew has transmitted a maxim of Jesus that encourages not only welcoming the kingdom of God as a child but also becoming like a child oneself (Matt 18:3). This requirement is known also from the *Gospel of Thomas*, in the maxim put on the lips of the disciples and quoted above (*Gos. Thom.* 22), from the Gospel of John (John 3:5), from Justin Martyr, and from the *Apostolic Constitutions*,[19] in varied forms. These wordings correspond to hermeneutical efforts to make intelligible the new life of believers desirous of attaining God's eschatological world.

Commentary

■ **15** In this scenario, Luke has replaced the "children" ($\pi\alpha\iota\delta\acute{\iota}\alpha$) of Mark 10:13 with "newborn children" ($\beta\rho\acute{\epsilon}\varphi\eta$) for two or perhaps three reasons. Noticing that they were "brought" and not "led" to Jesus, he thinks of very small children. Moreover, that is what he wants them to be, for he is anxious to stress their state of total dependence. Lastly, thinking of the Christianity of his own time, perhaps he had an ecclesiastical reason for preferring the term "newborn child" ($\beta\rho\acute{\epsilon}\varphi\circ\varsigma$) here to "child" ($\pi\alpha\iota\delta\acute{\iota}\circ\nu$).[20] The parents' intention, about which the story is silent, was to obtain some physical contact of their little ones with Jesus. In the eyes of the Gospel writer, the verb "touch" was important; he used it in connection with Jesus in front of the widow of Nain's son's coffin (7:14), with the woman who anointed Jesus (7:39), and with the sinful woman who had been suffering from

hemorrhages (8:44-47).[21] The parents hoped that if Jesus "touched" their babies he would transmit a spiritual force or a blessing to them (on two occasions, 6:19 and 8:46, Luke has asserted, without batting an eye, that a miraculous "power" [$\delta\acute{\upsilon}\nu\alpha\mu\iota\varsigma$] had flowed from Jesus to heal the sick). The request is, to say the least, ambiguous. It brings to mind the hopes that people in ancient times placed in the worship of healing gods, the protective presence of sacred places or magical practices.[22] On a more moderate level, it resembles the requests for blessing that adult children made of their aged parents.[23] In any case, the parents wanted to make the most of the occasion.

At that point, the disciples intervened, playing the roles of both security service and bodyguards. They rebuffed the parents, in an attempt to deny them access to Jesus. Were they shocked by these families' mixing up religion with magic in their minds? Did they wish to have Jesus retain the initiative with respect to his charitable deeds?[24]

The question has been raised as to whether the term "newborn children" ($\beta\rho\acute{\epsilon}\varphi\eta$) might not have been a title used for themselves by a group of Christians, for example, some itinerant prophets. According to that theory, the "disciples" ($\mu\alpha\vartheta\eta\tau\alpha\acute{\iota}$) stood for the ministers of the Great Church, or of the majority community, anxious to maintain their authority and their privileges.[25] This would not appear to be the hermeneutical level on which the Gospel writer operated. To be sure, the "infants" had a symbolic value for him. Like the "poor" in the beatitudes, they stood for those who are the object of divine solicitude, the beneficiaries of the kingdom of God; here,

18 See the commentary on 9:46-48 in vol. 1.
19 Justin *1 Apol.* 61.4; *Apos. Con.* 6.15.5 (the new birth is replaced here with baptism); see Jeremias, *Kindertaufe*, 61–68.
20 See below. On the subsitution of $\beta\rho\acute{\epsilon}\varphi\circ\varsigma$ for $\pi\alpha\iota\delta\acute{\iota}\circ\nu$, see Michaelis, "Anfänge," 189–90; by this substitution, Luke accentuates the meaning of the story.
21 See the commentary on 8:43-48 in vol. 1.
22 See Weber, *Jesus and the Children*, 15: since Jesus was considered a man of God, it is not surprising that parents would have brought their children to him for him to touch. The story does not say that the children were sick; not a single problem is mentioned.
23 It is Mark (10:16) who mentions a blessing con-

ferred by an imposition of the hands. We know that the Judaism of antiquity celebrated a benediction of the children on the evening of a day of fasting; see Soferim 18.15; Str-B 1:807–8; 2:138; and Jeremias, *Kindertaufe*, 61.
24 According to Haenchen (*Weg Jesu*, 344), the laying on of hands must have signified, for the readers, the communication of divine power and blessing.
25 See Ringshausen ("Kinder der Weisheit," 34–63), who defends this hypothesis at the traditional, Markan and Matthean level. In his opinion, the Lukan alterations and the new context in which the evangelist inserts this pericope show that Luke is not interested any longer in this interpretation of the episode.

as in 6:20, the kingdom of God is said to belong to them. Jesus' tenderness toward them was not just a matter of human kindness. The Gospel writer, once more—this time using a different metaphor—attempts to communicate the semantic and even ontological reversal that the Gospel proposes and banks on a new sense given to life, a new being in God.[26] Perhaps the entire Lukan community enjoyed using for themselves the title "newborn children" ($\beta\rho\acute{\epsilon}\varphi\eta$), a term that Luke applied to Jesus in the infancy narrative.[27]

■ **16** Luke's Jesus, unlike Mark's, does not get angry[28] (Luke avoids picturing a master who is unable to keep his emotions under control). He calls, even summons, the very small children. The verb "call to oneself" ($\pi\rho\sigma\sigma\kappa\alpha\text{-}\lambda\acute{\epsilon}\sigma\mu\alpha\iota$) is carefully chosen and is a felicitous replacement for the banal "say" in Mark 10:14.[29] What Jesus says next aimed neither at the parents, in truth very much in the background, nor at the children, who appear more as an occasion for what is said than the ones who are actually being spoken to, but at the disciples, therefore—in Luke's time—at Christians and their pastors. In Luke, Jesus has the children come to him not in order to speak to them but to use them as an example.

The sentence uttered by Jesus comprises three phrases, which in fact divide up into two parts. The first two phrases express the same obligation, first positively ("let the children[30] come to me"), then negatively ("do not stop them"). The third phrase supplies a justification (note the "for" [$\gamma\acute{\alpha}\rho$]) for this double imperative: "for it is to such beings as these that the kingdom of God belongs."

The verb "let" ($\check{\alpha}\varphi\epsilon\tau\epsilon$) blows a wind of freedom that excludes any constraint. "Come to me" is an expression rooted in sapiential literature that Luke had already applied to Jesus (6:47).[31] "Come to him" or "go to him" is a personalized manner of approaching God, turning away from one's egocentric way of living, subscribing to the Word, and practicing repentance/conversion ($\mu\epsilon\tau\acute{\alpha}\nu\sigma\iota\alpha$).[32] Obedience here means the path of following; "principles" are ruled out in favor of relations of person ("you") to person ("me"). Life is understood as a walk; religion, as a movement.[33]

"Stop" ($\kappa\omega\lambda\acute{\upsilon}\epsilon\tau\epsilon$)[34] brings to mind ecclesiastical discipline, the power not to admit, the right to exclude. A religious community necessarily has an identity and its limits.[35] The maxim attributed to Jesus redefines this notion of limits. The negative imperative means that no human authority can or must regulate access to Christ or God. If there are to be any limits to the community, they will be neither exterior nor formal. They will depend on the One who calls each person—here, using a living metaphor, who invites the "children." And if there is to be any human participation, it will be only that of the persons concerned. The Gospel proclaims that the kingdom of God is reserved for children, just as it is for the

---

26 See the commentary on 1:51-53 in vol. 1.

27 See 1:41, 44; 2:12, 16. On the other hand, Michaelis ("Anfänge," 189) thinks that $\beta\rho\acute{\epsilon}\varphi\sigma\varsigma$ is not a favorite word of the evangelist.

28 Every exegete points out this absence in the Lukan corpus of the verb $\grave{\alpha}\gamma\alpha\nu\alpha\kappa\tau\acute{\epsilon}\omega$, which appears in Mark 10:14 and whose meaning is quite strong: "to grow impatient," "to grow angry," "to complain," "to be indignant."

29 In the calling of the disciples (6:13) Luke had substituted the verb $\pi\rho\sigma\sigma\varphi\omega\nu\acute{\epsilon}\omega$ for the Markan $\pi\rho\sigma\sigma\kappa\alpha\lambda\sigma\tilde{\upsilon}\mu\alpha\iota$.

30 Since it is a word of Jesus himself, Luke does not dare modify it. In distinction to the introduction (v. 15), he keeps the word $\pi\alpha\iota\delta\acute{\iota}\alpha$ ("children"), which came from Mark and the tradition.

31 See the commentary on 6:47-49 in vol. 1.

32 See Bovon, *Theologian*, 305–28.

33 This is close to the verb $\pi\epsilon\rho\iota\pi\alpha\tau\acute{\epsilon}\omega$ ("to walk") used by the apostle Paul (see Rom 6:4), $\pi\rho\sigma\sigma\text{-}$ $\acute{\epsilon}\rho\chi\sigma\mu\alpha\iota$ used by the author of the Epistle to the Hebrews (see Heb 10:22), and $\grave{\alpha}\kappa\sigma\lambda\sigma\upsilon\vartheta\acute{\epsilon}\omega$ ("to follow") used by the Synoptic tradition (see Luke 5:27).

34 Much ink has been spilled over this verb $\kappa\omega\lambda\acute{\upsilon}\omega$ ("to hinder"); see Cullmann, *Des sources*, 142–48; Aland, *Die Säuglingstaufe*, 68–69; Michaelis, "Anfänge," 188–89. Although it could be used in the framework of baptism (see Acts 8:36), it was used by Christians also on other occasions. One link to baptism here does not make it a rule.

35 See E. P. Sanders, ed., *Jewish and Christian Self-Definition* (3 vols.; Philadelphia: Fortress Press, 1980–82).

36 Légasse (*Jésus et l'enfant*, 195–209) situates the episode within the larger theological project of Luke: the child symbolizes trust and humility. Percy (*Botschaft*, 31–37) insists on the receptivity of children and refuses to accept the thesis of their innocence. Aland (*Taufe*, 33–36) lays out an impressive list of patristic texts from the first two

poor, for those who have nothing to offer and who do not count in society.[36]

The New Testament itself, by virtue of the meager place it allots to children, is a witness to those ancient times that neglected boys and girls and did not think of them except as a mass to shape into their adult state through education and the inculcation of obedience.[37] Luke himself runs the risk of neglecting children, whose worth he brings out in other respects. Like Mark before him, he does not consider the children to be the ones Jesus was speaking to, but as moving examples.[38] Fortunately, this is the end of the maxim (v. 16) that promises them the kingdom of God.[39] The expression "to such beings" refers in the first instance to the children, and then to those who are like them. There was an understandable shift from that sentence to the more explicit version about becoming like children in order to enter into the kingdom of God.[40]

■ 17 The solemn introduction, "Truly I tell you,"[41] shows (a) the esteem in which the earliest Christians held the contents of the following sentence and (b) the independent status of this maxim in relation to the apophthegm.

From a thematic point of view, the apophthegm and the maxim are close. Nevertheless, this last sentence is more of a completion than a repetition of the apophthegm's message. By calling the children to him, Jesus demonstrated to his listeners God's method of making the welcoming of the infants with open arms a priority. He explained what approach to adopt in order to "enter" the kingdom of God.[42] The apophthegm says: God welcomes children. The maxim, introduced by "truly" (in Greek ἀμήν, from which we get our "amen"), goes on to say: become like children and you will enter it (see Matt 18:3). The phrase "as a child" specifies the subject of the verb rather than its direct object.[43] Luke 9:48 ("as a child," using the same figure of a child) said something else: welcoming a child is tantamount to welcoming Christ. But the fact that these three messages overlap in Christians' memories is in the last analysis a good sign, a proof that everything is connected: the attitude of God, who welcomes human beings (18:15-16); the attitude of human beings who hope to be welcomed by God (18:17); and the attitude offered to them as a way of welcoming both Christ and his Father (9:48). Children are God's

---

centuries that mention the innocence of children. In addition, the same Aland (*Die Stellung der Kinder*, 11–13) argues that the readers of the Gospels from the first and second centuries took the text literally, and so they believed that the little children possessed the kingdom. For them, the issue is less clear for Jesus himself, who could choose the children as examples. Personally, I would rather say the opposite: the literal meaning refers to Jesus (thus Weber, *Jesus and the Children*, 18), followed by a subsequent tendency to give a figurative meaning. On children in antiquity, see Légasse, *Jésus et l'enfant*, 267–87; Weber, *Jesus and the Children*, 65–76. In Sparta, a boy's worth was decided according to his future ability to render military service. The elders, not the father, decided the fate of a newborn baby, whose survival depended on its health and strength. In Athens, the child was seen as valuable only after its education. In Rome, the father could refuse to recognize his own child and had the right to expose it at birth. In Israelite society, a child was a gift of God, and fertility was a blessing. But outside of the covenant setting, a child did not have any particular importance and no one worried about its individuality.

37 See Aland, *Taufe*, 29–39.

38 See Weber, *Jesus and the Children*, 34, 66.

39 The kingdom is promised to them and those who are like them; contra André Malet in his French translation of Rudolf Bultmann, *L'histoire de la tradition synoptique* (Paris: Seuil, 1971) 50 n. 3.

40 Cf. Matt 18:3: "Truly I tell you, unless you change and become like children, you will never enter the kingdom of heaven." There is a moving Jewish text (*Tanna debe Eliyyahu* 5, trans. William G. Braude and Israel J. Kapstein, *Tanna D'be Eliyyahu: The Lore of the School of Elijah* [Philadelphia: Jewish Publication Society of America, 1981] 91) that says that at the resurrection God will embrace the souls who inherit life, will take them on his knees, press them to his heart, kiss them, and then take them to life in the world to come. Another Jewish text is worth mentioning: there was a dispute between Rabbi Gamaliel II and Rabbi Josua: Gamaliel forbade foreign children who were born in Israel to enter to the kingdom of God, whereas Josua granted entry to them (*t. Sanh.* 13.1–2; see Str-B 1:786).

41 See Berger, *Die Amen-Worte*, 42–44.

42 See Windisch, "Sprüche," 177, 187; Henri Clavier, *L'accès au Royaume de Dieu* (EHPhR 40; Paris: Clermont-Ferrand, 1943).

43 Even if one cannot distinguish a nominative neuter from an accusative grammatically. Here, παιδίον certainly has merit as a subject.

children. Human beings must rediscover their childhood. They must favor the child as a picture of the Son, the Father's envoy.

History of Interpretation

It was not until the fourth century of our era that a connection was made between this text and the practice of infant baptism.[44] It became important at that time for a doctrinal and liturgical reason. The Christians in that period were increasingly skeptical of children's innocence, so they sought to remove infants from the sphere of sin by making pedobaptism a general practice. As a result, canonical or dogmatic liturgical texts used this passage to justify and impose infant baptism. The *Apostolic Constitutions* (6.15.7) and Pope Innocent I seem to have been the first witnesses to this new orientation.[45] Up to that point, Christian commentators of the earliest centuries had been silent on the subject.[46] Both the commentators and the preachers were to remain quiet on this subject.[47] It was not until the arguments with the Anabaptists in the sixteenth century that there were commentators anxious to give this biblical passage a sacramental interpretation.[48]

In the twentieth century, it was Joachim Jeremias who thought that he had discovered traces of pedobaptism at the end of the first century by relying not on tradition but on various redactions of this passage. To his way of thinking, these redactions refer to a liturgical use of this passage in a baptismal setting.[49] Jeremias was supported by Oscar Cullmann but vigorously criticized by Wilhelm Michaelis and especially Kurt Aland.[50]

Conclusion

Simeon welcomed the child Jesus in his arms and thus saw the promised salvation (2:25-35). The adult Jesus welcomed children and assured them that the kingdom of God would be theirs (18:15-17). It is between these two poles of welcome that the divine plan and its success are acted out, in God's coming to us and our going to him. The church's task is to support Christ strongly by "inviting" the children and to avoid hindering or "stopping" his efforts (18:16).

44 See the well-informed article by Ludolphy, "Geschichte," 31–51.

45 Innocent I *Epistulae* 30.5 (*PL* 20:592); see Ludolphy, "Geschichte," 35–36.

46 Tertullian, on the other hand, quotes Matt 19:14 (corresponding to our v. 16) to discourage baptism for children who are too young. Clement of Alexandria (*Paed.* 1.5.3–4) refers to this pericope; in his opinion, Matt 18:3, which does not allude to baptism, clarifies the meaning given to Matt 19:14 par. Mark 10:14 par. Luke 18:16. The author of *De Baptismo* 2.4.3, attributed to Basil of Caesarea (*PG* 31:1589–92), quotes Mark 10:15 (corresponding to our v. 17) on the subject of obedient faith, not baptism. Augustine (*De peccatorum meritis et remissione et de baptismo paruulorum ad Marcellinum* 1.19.24 [*CSEL* 60:23–24]) refers to Matt 19:14 (corresponding to our v. 16), on the subject of the alleged innocence of children; see Ludolphy, "Geschichte," 32–36.

47 Ludolphy, "Geschichte," 32: "Weder in der alten Kirche noch im Mittelalter konnte in den untersuchten Kommentaren, bzw. einer Homilie eine Verbindung zwischen unserem Text und der Kindertaufe festgestellt werden."

48 See Ludolphy, "Geschichte," 37–45. The Anabaptism movement alleges that the Reformers appropriated our pericope to defend child baptism. But, even here, the exegesis is slow to follow the dogmatics. For example, if Luther hardly refers to our biblical passage in his struggles against the Anabaptists, Melanchthon is less reserved in his *Annotationes* and *Conciones in Evangelium Matthaei* (CR 14:924–26). As for Calvin (*Harmony*, 2:251–52), he infers from our passage that grace is promised to children and that, consequently, they should be baptized.

49 Jeremias (*Kindertaufe*, 61–68) emphasizes John 3:5 (being born of water and the Spirit), a parallel rereading of our v. 17, as well as the disciplinary usage of the verb κωλύω ("to hinder"), and Luke's use of the term βρέφη ("newborn").

50 Cullmann (*Le baptême*, 63–69) insists on the baptismal import of the verb κωλύω ("to hinder"). See also Michaelis, "Anfänge"; and Aland, *Die Säuglingstaufe*, 67–71; idem, *Taufe*, 29–39; idem, *Die Stellung der Kinder*, 11–17. Hahn ("Kindersegnung," 497–507) thinks that the demand for the baptism of children corresponds to the evolution of the doctrine of sin and the forgiveness of sins. I am grateful to J. Gnilka for this reference.

Inheriting Eternal Life
(18:18-30)

Bibliography Verses 18-23

Bailey, *Eyes*, 157–70.

Berger, Klaus, *Die Gesetzauslegung Jesu: Ihr historischer Hintergrund im Judentum und im Alten Testament, I: Markus und Parallelen* (WMANT 40; Neukirchen-Vluyn: Neukirchener Verlag, 1972) 396–460.

Bivin, David, "A Hebraic Nuance of *lego*: Key to Understanding Luke 18:18-19," *Jerusalem Perspective* 42–44 (1994) 37–45.

Caspari, A., "Der gute Meister," *CuW* 8 (1932) 218–31.

Coulot, Claude, *Jésus et le disciple: Étude sur l'autorité messianique de Jésus* (EtB n.s. 8; Paris: Gabalda, 1987) 103, 109, 122–24.

Idem, "La structuration de la péricope de l'homme riche et ses différentes lectures (Mc 10,17-31; Mt 19,16-30; Lc 18,18-30)," *RevSR* 56 (1982) 240–52.

Degenhardt, *Lukas*, 139–59.

Degenhardt, Johannes J., "Was muß ich tun, um das ewige Leben zu gewinnen?" in H. Merklein and J. Lange, eds., *Biblische Randbemerkungen: Schülerfestschrift für Rudolf Schnackenburg zum 60. Geburtstag* (Würzburg: Echter, 1974) 159–68.

Dupont, *Béatitudes*, 3:153–60.

Galot, Jean, "Le fondement évangélique du vœu religieux de pauvreté," *Greg* 56 (1975) 441–67.

Huuhtanen, P., "Die Perikope vom 'Reichen Jüngling' unter Berücksichtigung der Akzentuierungen des Lukas," in A. Fuchs, ed., *Theologie aus dem Norden* (SNTU A2; Linz: Plöchl, 1977) 79–98.

Kessler, Andreas, *Reichtumskritik und Pelagianismus: Die pelagianische Diatribe de divitiis: Situierung, Lesetext, Übersetzung, Kommentar* (Paradosis 43; Freiburg: Universitätsverlag, 1999).

Klijn, Albertus F. J., "The Question of the Rich Young Man in a Jewish-Christian Gospel," *NovT* 8 (1966) 149–55.

Klinghardt, *Gesetz*, 124–36.

Krüger, Rene, "El precio economico del discipulado: Exégesis semiótica de Lucas 18,18-30," *RevistB* 49 (1987) 193–207.

Légasse, Simon, *L'appel du riche (Marc 10,17-31 et parallèles): Contribution à l'étude des fondements scripturaires de l'état religieux* (VS n.s. 1; Paris: Beauchesne, 1966) 97–110, 184–214.

Idem, "L'appel du riche," in A. George et al., eds., *La Pauvreté évangélique* (LiBi 27; Paris: Cerf, 1971) 65–91.

Luck, Ulrich, "Die Frage nach dem Guten: Zu Mt 19,16-30 und Par," in W. Schrage, ed., *Studien zum Text und zur Ethik des Neuen Testaments: Festschrift zum 80. Geburtstag von Heinrich Greeven* (BZNW 47; Berlin/New York: de Gruyter, 1986) 282–97.

Mara, Maria G., *Ricchezza e povertà nel cristianesimo primitivo* (Studi Patristici 1; Rome: Città nuova, 1980).

Matura, Thaddée, *Le radicalisme évangélique: Aux sources de la vie chrétienne* (LD 97; Paris: Cerf, 1978) 69–82.

Mees, Michael, "Das Paradigma vom reichen Mann und seiner Berufung nach den Synoptikern und dem Nazaräerevangelium," *VetChr* 9 (1972) 245–65.

Murray, Gregory, "The Rich Young Man," *DRev* 103 (1985) 144–46.

Neuhäusler, *Anspruch*, 170–85.

O'Hara, Mary Louise, "Jesus' Reflections on a Psalm," *TBT* 90 (1977) 1237–40.

Radl, 121–22.

Raja, R. J., "'A Costly Commitment': Discipleship in the Gospel of Luke. An Exegetico–Theological Investigation of Lk 9,23-27; 9,57-62; 14,25-35; 18,18-30" (Ph.D. diss., Pontifical Gregorian University, 1982).

Riga, Peter J., "Poverty as Counsel and as Precept," *TBT* 65 (1973) 1123–28.

Sanders, E. P., "Priorités et dependences dans la tradition synoptique," *RSR* 60 (1972) 519–40.

Schmid, *Matthäus und Lukas*, 129–31.

Schramm, *Markus-Stoff*, 142.

Spitta, Friedrich, "Jesu Weigerung, sich als 'gut' bezeichnen zu lassen," *ZNW* 9 (1908) 12–20.

Swezey, Charles M., "Luke 18:18-30," *Int* 37 (1983) 68–73.

Thomas, Kenneth J., "Liturgical Citations in the Synoptics," *NTS* 22 (1975–76) 205–14.

Tillard, Jean-Marie R., "Le propos de pauvreté et l'exigence évangélique," *NRTh* 100 (1978) 207–32, 359–72.

Trilling, *Christusverkündigung*, 123–45.

Wagner, Wilhelm, "In welchem Sinne hat Jesus das Prädikat ΑΓΑΘΟΣ von sich abgewiesen?" *ZNW* 8 (1907) 143–61.

Walter, Nikolaus, "Zur Analyse von Mc 10,17-31," *ZNW* 53 (1962) 206–18.

Ward, Ronald A., "Pin-Points and Panoramas: The Preacher's Use of the Aorist," *ExpT* 71 (1959–60) 267–70.

Weiss, J., "'Zum reichen Jüngling' Mk 10,13-27," *ZNW* 11 (1910) 79–83.

Wenham, J. W., "Why Do You Ask about the Good? A Study of the Relation between Text and Source Criticism," *NTS* 28 (1982) 116–25.

Zimmerli, Walther, "Die Frage des Reichen nach dem ewigen Leben," *EvTh* 19 (1959) 90–97.

Bibliography Verses 24-30

Aicher, Georg, *Kamel und Nadelöhr: Eine kritisch-exegetische Studie über Mt 19,24 und Parallelen* (NTAbh 5; Münster: Aschendorff, 1908).

Bivin, David, "Counting the Cost of Discipleship: Lindsey's Reconstruction of the Rich Young Ruler Complex," *Jerusalem Perspective* 42–44 (1994) 23–35.

Idem, ed., "Jerusalem Synoptic Commentary Preview: The Rich Young Ruler Story," *Jerusalem Perspective* 38–39 (1993) 3–31.

Celada, Benito, "Más acerca del camello y la aguja (Mt 19,24; Mc 10,25; Lc 18,25)," *CB* 26 (1969) 157–58.

Denk, Josef, "Camelus: 1. Kamel, 2. Schiffstau," *ZNW* 5 (1904) 256–57.

Idem, "Suum cuique," *BZ* 3 (1905) 367.

Fürst, Heinrich, "Verlust der Familie – Gewinn einer neuen Familie (Mk 10,29f. Parr.)," in I. Vázquez, ed., *Studia historico-ecclesiastica: Festgabe für L. G. Spätling* (BPAA 19; Rome: Pontificium Athenaeum Antonianum, 1977) 17–47.

Galot, Jean, "La motivation évangélique du célibat," *Greg* 53 (1972) 731–58, esp. 750–56.

García Burillo, Jesús, "El ciento por uno (Mc 10,29-30 par): Historia de las interpretaciones y exégesis," *EstBib* 37 (1978) 29–55.

Goguel, Maurice, "Avec des persécutions," *RHPhR* 8 (1928) 264–77.

Herklotz, F., "Miszelle zu Mt 19,24 und Parall.," *BZ* 2 (1904) 176–77.

Kilpatrick, George Dunbar, "Some Problems in New Testament Text and Language," in E. E. Ellis, ed., *Neotestamentica et Semitica: Studies in Honour of Matthew Black* (Edinburgh: T&T Clark, 1969) 203.

Köbert, Raimund, "Kamel und Schiffstau: Zu Markus 10,25 (Par.) und Koran 7,40/38," *Bib* 53 (1972) 229–33.

Lattey, Cuthbert, "Camelus per foramen acus," *VD* 31 (1953) 291–92.

Legrand, Lucien, "Christian Celibacy and the Cross," *Scr* 14 (1962) 1–12.

Lehmann, R., "Zum Gleichnis vom Kamel und Nadelöhr und Verwandtes," *ThBl* 11 (1932) 336–38.

May, David M., "Leaving and Receiving: A Social-Scientific Exegesis of Mark 10:29-31," *PRSt* 17 (1990) 131–51, 154.

Minear, Paul S., "The Needle's Eye: A Study in Form Criticism," *JBL* 61 (1942) 157–69.

O'Callaghan, José, "Examen crítico de Mt 19,24," *Bib* 69 (1988) 401–5.

Theissen, Gerd, "'Wir haben alles verlassen' (Mk 10,28): Nachfolge und soziale Entwurzelung in der jüdisch-palästinischen Gesellschaft des 1. Jahrhunderts nach Chr.," *NovT* 19 (1977) 161–96.

18/ Then a certain ruler questioned him thus[a], "Good Teacher, what must I do to inherit eternal life?"[b] **19/** Jesus said to him, "Why do you call me[c] good? No one is good but God alone. **20/** You know the commandments: 'Do not commit adultery; Do not kill; Do not steal; Do not bear false witness; Honor your father and mother.'" **21/** He said, "I have kept all these since my youth[d]." **22/** When Jesus heard these words, he said to him, "There is still one thing remaining for you to do[e]. Sell all that you own and distribute it to the poor, and you will have a treasure in the heavens; then come, follow me." **23/** When he heard this, he became sad; for he was very rich.

24/ Having seen him become very sad[f] he said, "How hard it is for those who have wealth to enter the kingdom of God! **25/** For it is easier for a camel to go through the eye of a needle than for someone who is rich to enter the kingdom of God." **26/** Those who heard it said to him, "but who can be saved?" **27/** He said, "What is impossible for mortals is possible for God."[g]

a Literally: "saying."
b Literally: "doing what, will I inherit eternal life?"
c Literally: "say I am?"
d Literally: "since youth."
e Literally: "there is still one thing remaining for you."
f Literally: "having become very sad."
g Literally: "at the side of . . . at the side of God."

28/   **Then Peter said, "Look, we have left our own possessions and followed you." 29/ He said to them, "Truly I tell you, there is no one who has left house or wife or brothers or parents or children, for the sake of the kingdom of God, 30/ who will not get back very much more in this age, and in the age to come, eternal life."**

There are many polemic texts in the New Testament. So knowing against what adversaries outside the church they are directed facilitates the interpretation of these texts. On the other hand, there are other passages that were written to overcome the internal contradictions in the Christian communities. The latter seems to be the raison d'être for the verses we are considering here (18:18-30). Their function is to resolve a logical and theological contradiction; in other words, how can one reconcile a salvation that is inaccessible to human beings, and that depends on God alone, with a salvation that is accessible to human beings, and that God gives as a reward to those living lives that honor divine requirements?

Analysis

Commentators do not group vv. 18-30 of Luke 18 together as a single literary unit without some hesitation, since they might well study as isolated units the dialogue with the rich man, the maxim about the camel and the eye of a needle, the maxim about salvation being impossible, and the conversation Jesus carried on with his disciples about what they needed to leave behind.[1] Those who end up deciding in favor of a single unit do so on the basis of the redaction of the Gospels. Both Mark and Luke did in fact take these verses to be interdependent, as parts of one homogenous whole. But those who exam-

ine the origin of these episodes or maxims in the oral tradition end up finding fragments that were originally autonomous.

It is from Mark (Mark 10:17-31) that Luke has taken these verses. Like Mark, he has placed this unit between the pericope about the children (Mark 10:13-16 par. Luke 18:15-17)[2] and the announcement of the passion (Mark 10:32-34 par. Luke 18:31-34). Like Mark, he has fashioned a literary unit here by an elegant *inclusio*: "eternal life" is mentioned at the beginning (v. 18) and it reappears at the end (v. 30). Like Mark, he has established a double coupling with the previous unit. He knew that "to receive the kingdom of God" (v. 17) is synonymous with "to inherit eternal life" (v. 18), and so he couples the episode about the rich man with the one about children, emphasizing the thematic continuity by the use of a contrast (this poor rich man, unlike in Matt 19:22, is obviously not a young man!). He establishes the second point of coupling in v. 25, at the point where he makes use of the same vocabulary as in v. 17, namely, entrance into the kingdom of God.[3]

The link with what follows is less evident; it is more theological than literary. No linking word appears on the surface of the text, and the introduction to v. 31 pauses to point out that the following words of Jesus, the announcement of the passion, are addressed to the disciples whom he has taken aside.[4]

---

1   See Minear, "Needle's Eye," 160, 168–69. According to Trilling (*Christusverkündigung*, 126–27), Luke links the episodes more closely than Mark. While Trilling sees three conjoined episodes here, Huuhtanen ("Perikope," 79–98) divides the passage into four and, moreover, refuses to subsume the variety of subjects into one thematic unity. On this last point, see, before him, Walter, "Zur Analyse von Mc 10,17-31," 209.

2   Dupont (*Béatitudes*, 3:153) emphasizes that Luke makes a stronger connection (compared to Mark)

between the story of the children and that of the rich man.

3   For a useful comparison of Luke and Mark, see Grundmann, 353–55; Schneider, 2:369; Schweizer, 189–90; Légasse, *L'appel*, 97–110; Trilling, *Christusverkündigung*, 123–32; Dupont, *Béatitudes*, 3:153–60; Huuhtanen, "Perikope," 97–98.

4   For a structural analysis of the section within a larger whole, see Meynet, *Saint Luc*, 1:168–70, 174–75; 2:175–78; and Bailey, *Eyes*, 157–58. According to Bailey, vv. 18-30 form a chiasm: (A) to inherit

As always, Luke felt free to give himself plenty of elbow room in order to rewrite transitions, introductions, and conclusions. Here (v. 18a), he preferred emphasizing the prominence of the person speaking rather than that person's activity. To the question concerning eternal life, identical in Mark and Luke (v. 18b), he put on Jesus' lips (vv. 19-20) an answer very similar to the one in Mark. Jesus simply quotes the Decalogue according to the LXX, more literally than did the Second Gospel.[5] Why, in v. 21, did Luke prefer to use the active voice of the verb φυλάσσω ("keep") in place of the middle found in Mark?[6] In v. 22, he does not allow Jesus to show affection for a person who does not, in the end, adhere to the gospel.[7] Then he speaks prospectively of what remains to be done, where Mark retrospectively notes what is lacking. Luke, who is always wary of riches, speaks of "all that you own,"[8] creating a suggestive contrast with "all" that the man had kept since his youth. Luke's "distribute it" (διάδος) is more precise than Mark's simple "give it" (δός). The narrative conclusion (v. 23) naturally offered

Luke more liberty than the dialogue; out of lack of sympathy for the rich man, the Gospel writer summarized in a single word how he felt ("very sad" [περίλυπος], where Mark specifies that he "was shocked . . . sad" [στυγνάσας . . . λυπούμενος]). By way of preparation for the following episode, Luke calls the person "rich,"[9] a term found again in the maxim about the camel, v. 25.[10]

In order better to connect the two incidents (vv. 18-23 and vv. 24-27), Luke, if we are to read the words omitted in certain important manuscripts in v. 24,[11] once more mentions the speaker's sadness, albeit in a somewhat mechanical way. As was his wont, Luke scarcely dared retouch the wording of Jesus' maxims that he had inherited; Luke 18:24b is practically[12] identical to Mark 10:23b. Since, unlike the Second Gospel, Luke does not remind us of the presence of the disciples, he also omits Mark's statement about their stupefaction and thereby also omits the repetition of one of Jesus' maxims (in fact, he omits all of Mark 10:24[13]) and thus directly moves on to the enigmatic and dazzling sentence about the camel

---

eternal life (v. 18); (B) five examples from the commandments (vv. 19-21); (C) a new obedience (v. 22); (D) it seems too difficult (vv. 26-27); (E and E′) the parable of the camel and the needle (vv. 24-25); (D′) the new obedience seems too difficult (vv. 26-27); (C′) it has been realized nevertheless (v. 28); (B′) five examples of the new obedience (v. 29); (A′) receiving eternal life (v. 30). Coulot ("Structuration," 240–52) provides a very similar analysis. Krüger ("El precio economico," 193–207) analyzes the pericope structurally, and his work is also conducive to a chiastic reading.

5   In Exod 20:12-16 and Deut 5:16-20, the commandment "honor your father and your mother" precedes the prohibitions. The sequence of adultery, murder, theft, and false testimony corresponds to Deut 5:17-20 LXX and not to Exod 20:13-16 LXX. The two versions of the Decalogue in the LXX as well as Matt 19:18-19 use the negative particle οὐ with the future indicative, whereas Luke 18:20 and Mark 10:19 use μή with the aorist subjunctive.

6   By choosing the active, Luke accords with its most common usage, since the meaning "to observe" in the middle voice is rare or poetic. Normally the middle signifies "to keep watch over one's own security," or "to guard against."

7   He leaves out the words "Jesus, looking at him, loved him" from Mark 10:21. Matthew also omits this detail. Did the copy of Mark that Matthew and Luke used no longer contain these words?

8   The expression πάντα ὅσα combines the ideas of "all that" and "as much as"; see LSJ, s.v. ὅσος. On this demand to give away everything, see Matura, Le radicalisme évangélique, 69–82. Swezey ("Luke 18:18-30," 68–73) explains why possessions are illusory and why dispossessing oneself of them, as Abraham and Moses did, corresponds to a choice of true loyalty.

9   The Markan parallel (Mark 10:22) reads, "for he had many possessions."

10   On the episode of the rich man and its structure, see Coulot, "Structuration."

11   See Nestle-Aland and critical apparatus.

12   The difference, and it would be significant, would concern the tense of the main verb if one read the present tense in Luke (as Nestle-Aland has it, attested by some important manuscripts). I prefer the future tense, as in Mark.

13   Curiously, Matthew also ignores this verse; see Frans Neirynck et al., eds., *The Minor Agreements of Matthew and Luke against Mark with a Cumulative List* (BETL 37; Leuven: Leuven University Press, 1974) 137. Instead of invoking another source here, it is better to say that Matthew and Luke revised Mark in the same way; see Coulot, "Structuration," 241–42.

and the eye of the needle (v. 25), which has provided no end of difficulty—you can say that again!—to scribes and commentators from ancient times on down to the present. The external manuscript attestation of this sentence is in fact poor.[14] Furthermore, unlike Mark 10:26, Luke does not inform us that the question[15] about the possibility of salvation came from surprised disciples. As for Jesus' answer, Luke, in this instance, has allowed himself the privilege of rewording it in order to give it more impact.[16]

The Gospel writer has slightly reworked the material in the last part of the pericope (vv. 28-30). He has linked the disciples' two decisions in a single clause in Greek (in which they have left their own possessions to follow Jesus[17]). Anxious to modify the list of what they have given up, he adds—and this is significant—the wife to the members of the family, as he had done in 14:26.[18] He prefers mentioning pairs instead of spelling out details,[19] and, being the good city dweller that he is, leaves out Mark's "fields" (Mark 10:29).[20] Whereas Mark gives Christ and the gospel as motives for renunciation (Mark 10:29), Luke mentions the kingdom of God. This modification is probably not as small as it seems. The promise (v. 30) is different from Mark's version in more than one way. These differences could be classified as stylistic: Luke avoids repeating the list of possessions and relatives[21] and prefers ὅς οὐχὶ μή ("who will not") to Mark's ἐάν ("if"), a compound verb to a simple one, a vague "much more" to "a hundredfold," and a single temporal phrase to two such phrases juxtaposed.[22] Or they could be classified as thematic: surprisingly, Luke considers only the positive aspect of recompense and disregards the mention of persecutions in the present age. Finally, Luke omits Mark 10:31, with its maxim about the first and the last, probably because he has already included it in 13:30.

On the whole—and it is a curious result—Luke's modifications are not always improvements, and they are more limited than Matthew's.[23] As for the content, I will call special attention to the following: Luke thinks of the rich man as a "ruler" (ἄρχων); he does not stress the feelings of his characters (whether of Jesus, the rich man, or the disciples); he adds the wife to the list of those whom one must leave and eliminates persecutions in the present age. As a motive for renunciation, he prefers to mention the kingdom of God.

---

14 See the explanation below.

15 Identical in Mark and Luke.

16 In Luke the response gains balance and brevity; translated literally, Mark 10:27b would read, "impossible with men, but not with God; for everything is possible with God."

17 Mark 10:28 juxtaposed: "Look, we have left everything and we have followed you."

18 See the commentary above on 14:26.

19 He brings together the "brothers" and "sisters" of Mark 10:29 into a single rubric of "brothers," which he no doubt intends in an inclusive sense. He prefers "parents" to "father" and "mother." He is satisfied with the Markan mention of "children."

20 The manuscript tradition of this list is not certain. Some scribes tended to harmonize the text of Luke with that of the two other Synoptics; others sought to respect the natural chronology of familial relations (one has parents before one has a wife and children).

21 Cf. Mark 10:30: "houses and brothers and sisters and mothers and children and fields"; Mark's text has variants, such as the insertion of "father" and the substitution of the singular "mother" for the plural.

22 Luke loves compound verbs, hence his preference for ἀπολαμβάνω. He also appreciates the temporal adverb νῦν ("now"), which, for example, he adds to some beatitudes (6:21). Here, however, he omits a νῦν, which he thinks superfluous next to "in this age." Note that there are differences between the manuscripts in this verse as well; the simple λάβη is very well attested, for example.

23 Matthew gladly adds details: he specifies that it is a young man (Matt 19:20); he emphasizes the importance of observing the commandments (Matt 19:17b); he adds the love of neighbor to the list from the Decalogue (Matt 19:19); he identifies being "perfect" as selling one's goods and following Jesus (Matt 19:21a); he adds a mention of the end of the age (called "the renewal of all things," the final rule of the Son; logion on the twelve thrones; Matt 19:28). The episode of the rich man appears also in a Judeo-Christian Gospel, probably the *Gospel of the Nazarenes*; see Trilling, *Christusverkündigung*, 135; Klijn, "Rich Young Man," 149–55; Mees, "Das Paradigma," 245–65; Minear, "Needle's Eye," 164; Daniel A. Bertrand, "Fragments évangéliques," in Bovon and Geoltrain, *Écrits apocryphes*, 1:442–43.

If we go back behind the Markan redaction of our verses (Mark 18:23) to their prehistory, the episode of the rich man probably circulated as an independent unit.[24] The same could be said of the saying about the camel (vv. 24-25), whose shocking radicalism was mitigated over a period of time by a theocentric consolation (everything is possible for God, vv. 26-27), rooted in Scripture.[25] The dialogue about rewards for following and renunciation (vv. 29-30) also existed separately. Told by preachers or catechists, these examples illustrated how serious Christian engagement was and how specific it was by comparison with the other types of Jewish observance.[26] The memory of paradoxical or outrageous statements by Jesus was, to be sure, preserved, but it occasioned discussions and required, for its survival, certain adjustments. Since there was a thematic unity to these different statements, they were logically attracted to each other and in the end came to form a literary unit[27] that Mark placed in the context of Jesus' journey (cf. Mark 10:17), on his way up to Jerusalem (cf. Mark 10:32).[28] For Luke also, these dialogues were to be located during Jesus' trip from Galilee to Judea.[29]

Commentary

■ **18** Since Luke was usually precise in his use of titles, we can assume that here he was not using the Greek word ἄρχων in the popular sense of "prince" that we would find in a story. What he had in mind was rather a member of the Sanhedrin or one of the leaders of the Pharisaic movement.[30] He was especially proud to point out that the most prominent people did not hesitate to consult Jesus, whose reputation as a "teacher" was well established in Israel in their opinion.

This reputation that Jesus possessed derived from an authority that was religious, intellectual, and spiritual all at the same time. Such consultations were not rare and were even the impetus behind a literary genre.[31] Moreover, Luke had already furnished such a discussion about access to eternal life in an earlier chapter.[32]

■ **19** Before getting to the heart of the matter, the Synoptic Jesus reprimands this man he is talking with for having used excessive language. Jesus understands the adjective "good" in a surprisingly absolute sense and insists on saving that virtue for God. Even if, at a certain level, Jesus picks a quarrel with this man for no reason at all, at another level, he is right in referring him to God rather than to God's subordinates. Such is the suggested intention; the answer to the question that has been asked is to be supplied not by the interpreters of the law but by God alone (εἷς ὁ θεός), who alone is good.[33] In doing this, Jesus, followed by the earliest Christians, demonstrated his uniqueness in a Judaism concerned with the correct interpretation of the law. Jesus refused to be an

---

24 A *Schulgespräch* or *Lehrgespräch*; see Zimmerli, "Frage," 91–92, 96–97; Trilling, *Christusverkündigung*, 134–38. On the several meanings that this episode acquired before Markan redaction, see Minear, "Needle's Eye," 162–63.

25 See the commentary on 1:37 in vol. 1. On the evolution of the unity from the primitive stage, see Minear, "Needle's Eye," 165–67.

26 See Schneider, 2:370; Zimmerli, "Frage"; Minear, "Needle's Eye," 167–68.

27 See Walter, "Zur Analyse von Mc 10,17-31," 206.

28 On the structure of the voyage from Galilee to Jerusalem, see Schmidt, *Rahmen*, 238–39, 246–54; Dieter Lührmann, *Das Markusevangelium* (HNT 3; Tübingen: Mohr Siebeck, 1987) 141–42; Robert A. Guelich, *Mark 1–8:26* (Word Biblical Commentary 34A; Dallas: Word, 1989) xxxvi.

29 See Swezey, "Luke 18:18-30," 68–70.

30 The Pharasaic movement used this term to designate their own "ruler" (see Luke 14:1). The Jewish authorities also have their ἄρχοντες, their "rulers,"

according to the passion narrative (Luke 23:13 and 24:20) or the story of the church's origins (Acts 4:5). See BAGD, s.v. ἄρχων 2a; see also the commentary above on 14:1.

31 See *b. Ber.* 28b; Isidore Epstein, ed., *The Babylonian Talmud* (18 vols.; London: Soncino, 1978), Seder Zera'im 173; Str-B 1:808; Zimmerli, "Frage," 93–96. As for the *Sitz im Leben* of this question of "life" (as the root of this literary genre), Zimmerli ("Frage," 95–96) proposes *Tempeltor-Liturgie*, the ritual of admission to the temple, of which the Hebrew Bible maintains traces (see Ezek 44:9; 18:9; Exod 19:10-11; Ps 15:1). At the threshold of the sanctuary, the Israelite would ask: "What must I do to have the right to enter and to share in life?"

32 It is the case of the lawyer who likewise hoped to inherit eternal life (Luke 10:25).

33 See Wagner ("In welchem Sinne," 143–61), Spitta ("Jesu Weigerung," 12–20), Bailey (*Eyes*, 162), who refer to *b. Taʿan.* 24. See Epstein, *Babylonian Talmud*, Seder Moʿed 4.126, one of the rare passages

expert, of whom there were so many, since what his God needed at that time was prophets who would act rather than interpreters who ran the danger of never getting past the level of words.[34]

■ **20** Like Jesus, the earliest Christians (in particular Luke) did not doubt—the era of suspicion and of the bad conscience had not yet dawned— that it was possible to observe the law,[35] and that obeying it would make life accessible. This Christian double conviction had its roots in Judaism.

■ **21-22** Everyone will recognize that the "ruler's" reply was truthful; he had in truth successfully observed the law since his youth. Nevertheless, this observance was not enough. Jesus added something to it—not a commentary that would smooth away the difficulties but an extra requirement, adapted to the person making the request. This requirement of an external radical practice proves to be the best test of an interior commitment. Obedience to the Torah—about which Luke is happy—is put to the test on the terrain of renunciation. The apophthegm's message is clear, even if it manifestly appears to be a "deviant" orientation within Judaism. In order to inherit eternal life and build up a treasure for oneself in heaven, it is necessary to observe a new practice, namely, making all one's possessions available and adhering to the prophet Jesus.[36]

■ **23** Jesus, whose omniscience is discreetly hinted at, has found our man's Achilles' heel. The "ruler" had not been expecting such practical advice. Not willing to subscribe to this plan of action, he sinks into sadness rather than anger. And that is what makes him a moving figure.

■ **24** In ancient Israel, murder, adultery, theft, and false witness were a threat to moral purity, as v. 20 reminds us in its quotation of the ancient Decalogue. Either the religious situation had changed, or Jesus had introduced a new kind of asceticism, since possession of riches has become the danger par excellence, the principal difficulty ($\delta\nu\sigma\kappa\acute{o}\lambda\omega\varsigma$, "with difficulty," here translated as "hard").

■ **25** In order to make the outrageous comparison with the camel more tolerable, the suggestion has been made, from ancient times on down to the present,[37] of reading $\kappa\acute{\alpha}\mu\iota\lambda o\varsigma$, "rope" or "ship's cable," used to tie an anchor to a boat, instead of $\kappa\acute{\alpha}\mu\eta\lambda o\varsigma$, "camel" (the two words were probably already pronounced the same way, due to the phenomenon known as itacism).[38] In fact, if this image is thus rendered more logical, it still loses none of its radicalness. It is not any easier for a large rope than a camel to go through the eye of a needle.[39]

$T\rho\acute{\eta}\mu\alpha$ means "opening" or "hole"[40] (certain manuscripts preferred to substitute a synonym, such as $\tau\rho\acute{\nu}\pi\eta\mu\alpha$, "hole," as in Matthew, or $\tau\rho\nu\mu\alpha\lambda\iota\acute{\alpha}$, also "hole,"

---

of rabbinic literature in which a master is called "good." On the relation between vv. 18-19 and their divergent parallel in Matt 19:16-17, especially from the perspective of textual criticism, see Wenham, "Why Do You Ask about the Good?" 116–25. On the other hand, see Murray ("Rich Young Man," 144–46), who advocates for Matthean precedence.

34 Zimmerli ("Frage," 96) insists on the difference, within the same literary genre, between what Jesus says and how a rabbi would have responded.

35 See Degenhardt, "Was muß ich tun?" 161–62.

36 See Légasse, "L'appel du riche," 77.

37 See Denk, "Camelus," 256–57; Lehmann, "Zum Gleichnis vom Kamel," 336–38; Köbert, "Kamel und Schiffstau," 229–33; Bailey, *Eyes*, 165–66; Kessler (*Reichtumskritik*, 406–16) provides a record of patristic references. See Origen *Comm. in Matt.* 19:24, frg. 390, 12.3.1 (GCS 41.1), 166. Is the fragment authentic? See also Cyril of Alexandria *Hom. in Luc.* 123; Payne-Smith, *Cyril*, 2:571–72. On the state of the question, see Aicher, *Kamel*, 6–16.

38 On $\kappa\acute{\alpha}\mu\iota\lambda o\varsigma$, a "large cable," or "large rope," a rare and late term, see BAGD, s.v.

39 There is a rabbinic parallel: human dreams, according to Rabbi Samuel b. Nahmani, are reflections of human thoughts. Thus, has not one ever seen a man dream of a golden date palm tree or an elephant passing through the hole in a needle? (*b. Ber.* 55b; Epstein, *Babylonian Talmud*, Seder Zeraʿim 342; see Bailey, *Eyes*, 166).

40 On the word $\tau\rho\hat{\eta}\mu\alpha$ ("opening," "hole," or "eye" of a needle), see Moulton and Milligan, *Vocabulary*, s.v.; BAGD, s.v.

41 On the variants, see Wettstein, *Novum Testamentum graecum*, 2:103, and the apparatus of Nestle-Aland. To understand the saying more easily, some have understood the eye of the needle in the sense of a door; see Minear, "Needle's Eye," 158; Bailey, *Eyes*, 167. For the state of the question, see Aicher, *Kamel*, 16–21.

as in Mark).[41] While Matthew and Mark read the word ῥαφίς ("sewing needle") Luke preferred βελόνη, a variant form of βέλος, which referred in the first instance to anything with a sharp point but later often came to refer to a "needle."[42] Here again, numerous scribes attempted to harmonize the Third Gospel with the two other Synoptic Gospels by choosing to use ῥαφίς ("sewing needle") in Luke as well.[43] However that may be, the maxim is clear: there is no entrance into the kingdom of God for rich people. Their only "out" is to distribute their riches (cf. the expression διάδος πτωχοῖς, "distribute it to the poor," in the previous episode, v. 22).[44]

■ **26-27** Verses 26–27 seem not to go as far as this radical requirement, and this is not just an appearance but a fact. Yet if we look at other expressions that are attributed to Jesus and echoed by the Gospel writers or the apostle Paul, it is evident that God alone is the cause of salvation. The Gospels are the very expression of this good news and the Epistle of Romans points out that the only way out, the only way to go through the eye of the needle, if one may put it that way, is to be found in God and in Jesus Christ (Rom 3:20, 23-24; 7:24-25). Verses 26-27 are on a different level than vv. 24-25; it is no longer a question of a radical requirement, but rather of something else no less radical, the omnipotence of evil, the incapacity of human beings to do good. The only solution, which is a part of the divine plan and which consists of the manifestation of righteousness being freely imputed, is expressed in the phrases "what is impossible for mortals" (τὰ ἀδύνατα παρὰ ἀνθρώποις) and "what is . . . possible for God" (δυνατὰ παρὰ τῷ θεῷ).

The rich man's sadness (vv. 23 and 24) was probably an allusion. As we read the account of the passion, we come across another man who was sad, Peter, who was distressed over having denied his master (22:62). Such sadness is not the last word in history; instead, it is one of its first words. Indeed, like the prodigal son's return to his senses (15:17), it constitutes the first act of conversion: the tears that one sheds over one's irremediably guilty past. And nothing in us, or nothing we do, can restore that past, transform the evil that we have done into good, or renew the ties that we have broken. There is no going back in time. As v. 27 says, there are some things that are "impossible" for mortals. On the other hand, the God of Scripture, who does not desire to see sinners die, has conceived of what used to be called means of grace, a turning back of time, the objective expiation in Christ, the subjective pardon offered human beings, and imputed righteousness, if we wish to make our own theological vocabulary that has drawn on biblical texts like the present passage. Peter's sadness, the sifter through which he had to pass (22:31), in the Acts of the Apostles ran into the community's joy, which was a regenerative inspiration and a source of unfailing confidence. Peter did get converted (Luke 22:32), for he did return in the end.[45]

■ **28** Luke's erasing of the disciples' presence from vv. 24-27 is understandable; since they had left everything to follow Jesus and had therefore carried out the ambitious program set forth in these verses, it would have been an insult to the logic of the narrative to have them surprised or have them ask the question "But who can be saved?"[46] For that reason, what Peter says in v. 28 occurs not as an objection but rather as a concrete proof that, however ambitious Jesus' program was, it was still capable of being carried out and was in fact carried out by certain people.[47]

■ **29-30** The apostle's exclamation, which is not lacking in pride (note the pronoun "we" [ἡμεῖς] in v. 28), allows the Lukan Jesus to reiterate the truth of his argument. He had defended his point of view in vv. 22 and 24-25.

---

42   On the word βελόνη ("the point of a spear," "needle"), see LSJ, s.v.; Moulton and Milligan, *Vocabulary*, s.v.; BAGD, s.v.

43   On the variants, see Wettstein, *Novum Testamentum graecum*, 2:103, and the apparatus of Nestle-Aland.

44   On v. 25, see Minear, "Needle's Eye"; Celada, "Más acerca del camello," 157–58; O'Callaghan, "Examen crítico," 401–5.

45   See Schweizer, 190.

46   Mark either does not perceive the contradiction or has not succeeded in reconciling it; see Walter ("Zur Analyse von Mc 10,17-31," 209), who discusses the absence of coherence in the sequence of ideas in Mark.

47   On the early Christians' surrender of all their goods and their itinerancy, see Theissen ("'Wir haben alles verlassen,'"161–96), who compares this phenomenon to others from antiquity, especially some Jews.

He recalls it once more here, in vv. 29-30, in other words, and vigorously.

We only have to go back to chap. 14 to find an enumeration similar to the one in v. 29. Such a list of indispensable renunciations was associated at that time with the status of being a "disciple" and was an expression of the condition for entrance into the circle of the faithful (cf. 14:26).[48] In this chapter, it is associated with the same reality worded in terms of being a follower. It was a matter of "hating," which was another way of saying "leaving" or "giving up," the verb used here by Peter (v. 28) and Jesus (v. 29).[49] Although the two lists are fundamentally identical (it should be noted that in both cases the mention of the wife is specific to Luke), they differ in some details. We may note the absence in 18:29 of one's own self, which appeared in 14:26, as well as the mention here, in 18:29, of a reason for all these renunciations, namely, "for the sake of the kingdom of God," an expression missing from 14:26. Let us not forget that this passage belongs to Mark's triple tradition and that the passage in chap. 14 belongs to the double tradition of "Q." We may also recall a related text (9:24), the maxim about the loss of one's life, which also belongs to the triple tradition. In that sentence, a reason was offered: "for my sake," which is what corresponds to "for the sake of the kingdom of God" in this chapter (v. 29).[50]

Whereas 14:26 emphasized the initial requirement, 18:29-30 takes pleasure in stressing the final reward. As a matter of fact, the condition of being a disciple is lived out in two successive stages,[51] which correspond to the two periods of time in the Jewish way of thinking, which later became the Christian one. In spite of the presence of Jesus and the proclamation of the kingdom of God, the change of aeons has not yet taken place. The followers of the gospel are still subject to the vagaries of the present time and are still waiting for the arrival of the coming aeon. Nevertheless, within that inherited binary structure, there is a new and happy situation that the maxim proclaims:[52] from now on, any losses agreed to are to be abundantly compensated for. Jesus' message is thus to be distinguished from a facile promise of bliss in the beyond. It was in the here and now that Peter and those who made commitments similar to his were to receive in abundance. To be sure, Luke refused to enumerate these benefits. Was Luke already afraid of a too millenarian reading of these rewards (in other words, a literal interpretation of what Mark enumerated)?[53] Luke's abstract wording "very much more" ($\pi o\lambda\lambda a\pi\lambda a\sigma\acute{\iota}ova$) seems pale compared to the concrete list in Mark 10:30.[54] However that may be, Luke, like Mark and the Synoptic tradition, was of the opinion that life as a Christian offers new relationships in the spiritual family constituted by the ecclesial community.[55] While through the centuries Christian civilization has praised family values to the skies, Christianity in the first century, following Jesus' example, was sensitive to how much family ties

---

48 See the commentary above on 14:26-27. On $\tau\grave{a}$ $\acute{\iota}\delta\iota a$ ("our own"), see John 1:11. Bailey (*Eyes*, 167–68) thinks that the expression implies goods and people.

49 On $\acute{a}\varphi\acute{\iota}\eta\mu\iota$, in the sense of "to leave" or "to abandon," see 5:11; on this verb, see the commentary above on 13:35a.

50 In Mark 10:29, which corresponds to Luke 18:29, we read "for my sake and for the sake of the good news." Why did Luke modify this formula in favor of "for the sake of the kingdom of God"?

51 For "this age," Luke, following Mark here, uses the term $\kappa a\iota\rho\acute{o}\varsigma$ ("present state," "time," "epoch"). For the "time to come," he uses the term $a\grave{\iota}\acute{\omega}v$ ("time," "life," "length of time," "eternity," "eon"). The difference of the two words suggests the qualitative difference between these two periods, which divide time. On this vocabulary, see James Barr, *Biblical Words for Time* (SBT 33; Naperville, Ill.: Allenson, 1962).

52 Here we find once again the structure that we analyzed in the exegesis of the beatitudes; see the commentary on 6:20, 24 in vol. 1.

53 We know that in the second century certain Christians, such as Papias, took the prophecies and promises of the Apocalypse of John literally, especially the statements about the reign of the thousand years; see the witness of Papias, preserved and critiqued by Eusebius of Caesarea *Hist. eccl.* 3.39.11–13; see García Burillo, "El ciento por uno," 49–50.

54 On the term $\pi o\lambda\lambda a\pi\lambda a\sigma\acute{\iota}ova$ ("much more"), the variants "seven times more" (under the probable influence of the LXX version of Sir 35:10 and other numberings in 35:11 or 35:13), and "one hundred times more" (under the influence of Matt 19:29 and Mark 10:30), see Fitzmyer, 2:1205; Moulton and Milligan, *Vocabulary*, s.v.; BAGD, s.v.

55 See François Bovon, "Communauté familiale et communauté ecclésiale dans le Nouveau Testament," *Cahiers Protestants* n.s. 6 (1974) 66–68; Fürst,

could lead to being weighed down and restricted. What the gospel offers, and what the commitment of disciples who have distanced themselves from their past and their belongings leads to, is a new way of life in the context of a network of unexpected relationships. The Christian community, according to this passage in Luke, creates a new family. And what it offers is a matter not just of the spiritual or affective sphere but of the material and social sphere as well. The "house" that one has left (v. 29) is offset by the houses one finds, which are a part of that "much more" (v. 30).[56]

Oddly enough, Luke, who nevertheless knew that we enter the kingdom of God "through many persecutions" (Acts 14:22), fails to reproduce Mark's realistic diagnosis, namely, that the life of a Christian is not fulfilled "in this age" without being accompanied by persecutions ("with persecutions" [$\mu\epsilon\tau\grave{\alpha}$ $\delta\iota\omega\gamma\mu\hat{\omega}\nu$], Mark 10:30).[57] Since the parallel in Matthew (Matt 19:29) does not have it either, we may wonder whether the copy of Mark that these two Gospel writers had available to them was missing this piece of information. The question may also be raised whether Luke and Matthew preferred to point out only the beneficial results of following Christ, saving the listing of ultimate tribulations for another chapter, the one with the eschatological speech. Luke already pointed out several of these tribulations in his first eschatological speech (17:22-37), without, however, pointing out that Christians would bear the special brunt of them. Other tribulations, more specifically aimed at the followers of the Gospel, are mentioned in chap. 21, the second eschatological speech (see especially 21:12-

29). Finally, Luke did not mind sprinkling his work with very realistic warnings. We need think only of 12:11, where there is an explicit announcement of persecutions: "When they bring you before the synagogues, the rulers, and the authorities, do not worry about how you are to defend yourselves or what you are to say . . ." (*NRSV*). In other words, the fact that Luke did not mention persecutions here in 18:30 does not mean that Luke censored Mark for a doctrinal reason.[58] If the copy of Mark that he read mentioned persecutions but he preferred not to reproduce that mention, he did so for reasons of literary suitability and theological progression.[59]

History of Interpretation

The study of two texts involves us in a dispute over different interpretations of this pericope. The first one is a treatise written in Rome at the beginning of the fifth century of our era, the *De divitiis, On riches*; the second is an apocryphal text, written in Greek, of uncertain dating, the *Acts of Andrew and Peter*. Both of these works betray the attention that was paid in the first centuries of the church to the maxim about the camel and the eye of a needle.

Composed in an aristocratic setting, the *De divitiis*[60] defends a literal interpretation of the text and corresponds to the ascetic tendency of numerous Christians in the capital. These Christians took seriously Christ's order to leave one's possessions and follow him. These athletes of the faith, in their attempt to attain a state of holiness, were shocked by all attempts—and they were numerous

"Verlust der Familie," 17–47; Légasse (*Contribution*) insists on the ecclesial dimension that Luke gives to his rereading.

56   Luke keeps the house in the list of goods to surrender but does not include it among the goods that are restored in abundance. This is hardly surprising, since, as we have seen, Luke does not draw up the list at this point.

57   On the Markan expression "with persecutions," see Goguel, "Avec des persécutions," 264–77; and Joachim Gnilka, *Das Evangelium nach Markus* (2 vols.; EKKNT 2; Neukirchen-Vluyn: Neukirchener Verlag, 1978–79) 2:93.

58   On the time of the church as a time of trials, see Conzelmann, *Theology*, 200–201, 209–11.

59   On vv. 29-30, see García Burillo, "El ciento por uno."

60   The best edition is found in Kessler (*Reichtumskritik*, 241–331). The text was attributed to Pope Sixtus III (432–440), to Agricolus, to Fastidius, to Pelagius, and to an anonymous Sicilian. Recently Kessler (pp. 104–44) has criticized these attributions and proposed an anonymous author from the middle of the Pelagian reformist movements. According to Kessler (pp. 186–219), the writing expresses the ascetic mentality that is hostile to material goods and that materialized with the renunciations of Melany and Pinien.

at that time—at watering down the radical requirement laid out by Jesus.

Chapter 18 of *De divitiis* first lays into those who understood *camelus* in the sense of a ship's cable (18.2).[61] The variant reading κάμιλος ("ship's cable"), read by late Greek manuscripts, is therefore an ancient reading that had been taken over by the Latin manuscripts. It satisfied two requirements: logical, by maintaining the consistency of the images, and doctrinal, by making Christ's implicit commandment less extravagant. The author of *De divitiis* attributed this exegetical trick to rich Christians who were unable to bring themselves to give up their possessions. He furthermore refused to ease the requirement of poverty by referring to the following statement by Jesus about what is impossible for mortals compared with what is possible for God (18.3–4). At that time there must have already been some commentators who consoled themselves in that fashion. In his opinion, the maxim about what is possible for God must be understood as follows: God accepts even poor people, who, unlike rich people, do not have the means to acquire a treasure in heaven through generous almsgiving. The author then pits himself against another explanation according to which God bars rich people from the reign of heaven but not from eternal life (18.5). He goes on to attack an allegorical interpretation that we know from other texts (ibid.).[62] In this interpretation, the camel, an obedient animal, in spite of his load of sins and his far-from-straight shape, represents Gentile people who become believers. Entrance into the kingdom through the eye of a needle, understood as a narrow gate, is easier for them than for rich people—in other words, the Jewish people, who have received so much. The author suggests two arguments in order to reject that allegorical interpretation: (1) The camel's curves, which correspond to his nature, cannot refer to human beings' sins, which correspond to their free will. (2) Scripture does indeed compare human beings to certain animals, such as dogs, foxes, lambs, or wolves but never to camels! There is a reason for that; Scripture compares one character to another but not animal shapes to human proclivities.

What emerges from these arguments is that early Christianity developed various mutually incompatible interpretations in order to render a revered maxim acceptable.[63] In this case, the literal interpretation of the ascetics, monks, and the saints met the theological tricks (recourse to the maxim that everything is possible for God) and to exegetical tricks (recourse to allegorization).

The *Acts of Andrew and Peter* (13–21) also provides a supplementary explanation, this time in the form of a narrative, which follows the same line. During one of their missionary voyages, the apostles Andrew and Peter met a rich man. In order to convince him to give up everything, Peter, informed by an appearance of the Savior, stages a series of miracles, which consist in making a

---

61 See Kessler, *Reichtumskritik*, 306–14. The author of *De divitiis* refers to this saying of the Lord without specifying which Gospel he cites. His quotation corresponds to Matt 19:24; Mark 10:25; and Luke 18:25, but is not identical to the Old Latin text or the Vulgate.

62 See Kessler, *Reichtumskritik*, 412–13. Ambrose of Milan (*Exp. Luc.* 8.70–71), after having noted the literal interpretation, quite vigorously, moves on to the figurative meaning, identifying the camel with the Gentiles and the rich with the Jewish people, rich in the law. Hilary of Poitiers offers the same interpretation, with one caveat (to possess in itself is not wrong, but to possess while doing wrong to others is) (Hilary, *Comm. in Matt.* 19.9–11).

63 Clement of Alexandria (*Strom.* 2.5.22.3), writes "Much more, then, is the Scripture to be believed which says, It is easier for a camel to go through the eye of a needle, than for a rich man to be a philosopher." To be a philosopher for him means to be a Christian; Clement substitutes the Christian life for access to the kingdom of God. In his *Quis div.* 2.2, Clement, favoring, it seems, the literal meaning, points out two attitudes of rich people in light of Matt 19:24 par. Luke 18:25: either to throw oneself into the pleasures of the world or recognize the demand without giving oneself the means to observe it. Clement writes to encourage the rich to find ways of successfully living the Christian life. See Basil of Caesarea *Homilia in divites* (PG 31:271–304). For patristic interpretations of Luke 18:25 par. Matt 19:24 (selection based on Centre d'analyse, *Biblia Patristica*, vols. 1–6), see *Passio Mariani and Jacobi* 8.11; Methodius of Olympus *De lepra* 16.7; Origen *Comm. in Matt.* 15.14, 20; Epiphanius *Panarion* 66, 69.5–8; Gregory of Nazianzus *Orationes theologicae* 30.10; Ambrose of Milan *Expositio Psalmi* 118.2, 18 (CSEL 62:30). On Ambrose and Hilary, see n. 62 above.

camel go through the eye of a needle that is miraculously extendable. What emerges from this attractive story, where, as in a fairy tale, there is no limit to what is possible, is this: God's antecedence is respected (the miracle precedes the act of faith); the maxim on what is possible provides comfort and not a watering down of the maxim about the camel; finally, the criticism of riches loses nothing of the force of its truth.

Conclusion

"To inherit eternal life" is the human hope par excellence, whether expressed in these terms or in others; it is the theme of almost all religions. "What must be done?" to receive such an inheritance is the question asked by several religions, in particular Judaism and Christianity, which put responsibility at the heart of their message. The Jesus of this pericope, as of all of the Gospel, offered a paradoxical answer. On the one hand, he remained faithful to the tradition of Israel and advocated obedience to the divine law. He was even in favor of a reform that, different from Pharisaism but parallel to Essenism, recommended an ethics of renunciation, especially of material goods. On the other hand, he knew that salvation was a matter exceeding human capacity. Women and men cannot "make" their own salvation. The only way they can hope to obtain it is through God's initiative and intervention. In this pericope what is emphasized is the first aspect, the energetic reminder of the requirement of obedience (the disciples are examples of those who have practiced it successfully; the rich man is a negative example of failure). But the second aspect is not beyond the horizon. This biblical passage does not succeed in resolving the paradox of this logically irreconcilable position. Only faith, which experiences love, readily admits that God, our opposite number, provides what he orders; it also willingly acts facing him and in response to him.

A New Passion Prediction
(18:31-34)

Bibliography 18:31-34

Bennett, Wilbert J., "'The Son of Man must . . . ,'" *NovT* 17 (1975) 113–29.

Büchele, Anton, *Der Tod Jesu im Lukasevangelium: Eine redaktionsgeschichtliche Untersuchung zu Lk 23* (FTS 26; Frankfurt: Knecht, 1978) 132–35.

Farmer, William R., "The Passion Prediction Passages and the Synoptic Problem: A Test Case," *NTS* 36 (1990) 558–70, esp. 563–66.

George, Augustin, "Comment Jésus a-t-il perçu sa propre mort?," *Lumière et vie* 101 (1971) 35–41.

Haenchen, *Weg Jesu*, 360–62.

Kariamadam, Paul, "The End of the Travel Narrative (Luke 18,31—19,46): A Redaction-Critical Investigation" (Ph.D. diss.; Institut Biblique Pontifical, Rome, 1979).

Lambrecht, Jan, "Reading and Rereading Lk 18, 31—22,6," in Refoulé, *À cause*, 585–612.

Perry, John M., "The Three Days in the Synoptic Passion Predictions," *CBQ* 48 (1986) 637–54.

Schmid, *Matthäus und Lukas*, 133–34.

Schneider, Gerhard, *Verleugnung, Verspottung und Verhör Jesu nach Lukas, 22, 54-71: Studien zur lukanischen Darstellung der Passion* (SANT 22; Munich: Kösel, 1969) 36–39.

Schramm, *Markus-Stoff*, 133–36.

Varro, R., "Annonce de la Passion et guérison de l'aveugle de Jéricho selon s. Luc, 18,31-43," *AmiCl* 78 (1968) 25–27.

Zimmermann, Heinrich, *Jesus Christus: Geschichte und Verkündigung* (Stuttgart: Katholisches Bibelwerk, 1973) 263–69.

31/ Having taken the Twelve with him, he said to them, "See, we are going up to Jerusalem, and everything that has been written by the instrumentality of the prophets[a] will be accomplished for the Son of Man. 32/ For he will be handed over to the Gentiles; and he will be mocked and insulted and spat upon. 33/ And, after they have flogged him, they will kill him, and on the third day he will rise again." 34/ But they understood nothing about all these things and what he said was hidden from them, and they did not grasp what was said.

a And not "by the prophets," which would have been ὑπὸ τῶν προφητῶν. In saying διὰ τῶν προφητῶν, which limits the role of the prophets, the text subtly suggests that God is the author who stands behind his spokespersons.

The question put to Jesus by other people did not sidetrack him from the project of his life, which once more he declared to be a project of death. Although the Twelve had been told about it, they had no understanding of it at all. But Jesus himself knew the way in which what was written needed to be linked to what was going to happen. According to Luke, the proof of this is what he said.

Analysis

In this passage Luke pursues his rereading of the Gospel of Mark (Mark 10:13-52),[1] respecting the linking between the episode about the children (18:15-17), the pericope of the rich man and the disciples who had become poor (18:18-30), the new passion prediction (18:31-34), and the healing of the blind man in Jericho (18:35-43).

In fact, however, the Gospel writer has reworked his source quite a bit. Just as he had struck out the mention of the disciples' astonishment (Mark 10:24a and 26a) in the preceding pericope (18:24 and 26), here he erases the holy fear of those who accompanied Jesus (Mark 10:32),[2] which, we must admit, pops up in Mark for no apparent reason. Luke is going to replace it, in his con-

---

1 Luke does not seem to be influenced here by a source other than Mark; see Schneider, 2:372.
2 See ibid.

clusion, by a mention of the Twelve's lack of understanding of their Master's words (v. 34). By way of introduction (v. 31b), he is content to rewrite two of Mark's statements, namely, that Jesus took the Twelve with him and that he spoke to them (Mark 10:32b).[3]

Since he lays emphasis in these chapters on the travel theme,[4] he turns (v. 31b) with satisfaction to the words that Mark placed on Jesus' lips: "See, we are going up to Jerusalem" (Mark 10:33a). Anxious to provide precise wording for his scriptural theology of the history of salvation, he writes: "and everything that has been written by the instrumentality of the prophets will be accomplished for the Son of Man" (v. 31c)[5] in place of Mark's implicit and even vague wording: "what was going to happen to him" (Mark 10:32) . . . "and the Son of Man" (Mark 10:33).

Curiously enough, Luke is interested here in the Roman part of Jesus' trial and passes up the Jewish part. He eliminates the appearance before the high priests and the scribes as well as the death sentence pronounced by these authorities (Mark 10:33). Why? Our detailed commentary will attempt to answer that question. In Luke, the verbal form "he will be handed over" ($\pi\alpha\rho\alpha$-$\delta o\theta\dot{\eta}\sigma\epsilon\tau\alpha\iota$) is not followed, as in Mark, by "to the chief priests and the scribes" (Mark 10:33) but immediately by "to the Gentiles." Luke has skipped almost two lines.[6]

In his account of the trial before the Roman authority (vv. 32-33a), Luke, like Mark (Mark 10:34), speaks not about the grounds for the accusation or the arguments for the defense—in other words anything objective—but rather only about episodes that strike the imagination and sadden the heart, in other words, what is highly subjective. After having mentioned Jesus' transfer to the Gentiles, using a first verb in the passive voice, he lines up three other verbs to define not the stages of the trial but the various ways in which a martyr is tortured; these three verbs, all of them also in the passive voice, emphasize how Jesus was treated: "to be mocked" ($\dot{\epsilon}\mu$-$\pi\alpha\dot{\iota}\zeta o\mu\alpha\iota$), "to be insulted" ($\dot{\upsilon}\beta\rho\dot{\iota}\zeta o\mu\alpha\iota$), and "to be spat upon" ($\dot{\epsilon}\mu\pi\tau\dot{\upsilon}o\mu\alpha\iota$) (v. 32). Two of these three verbs have been borrowed from Mark; the third, the most characteristically Greek in its reference to the excessive insolence involved, is peculiar to Luke ($\dot{\upsilon}\beta\rho\dot{\iota}\zeta o\mu\alpha\iota$, "to be insulted"). In Mark, this excessive violence follows the death sentence; in Luke, interested in the crude reality of the facts, they precede the capital execution.

In v. 33a, Luke modifies the grammatical construction of v. 32 and returns to Mark's active voice. The "Gentiles" ($\ddot{\epsilon}\theta\nu\eta$)—in other words, the Romans (further humiliation and insult)—will flog Jesus, then kill him.[7] Since he has not mentioned the death sentence, the Gospel writer takes away the judicial dimension from Jesus' trial. What he makes of it is virtually a collective murder.[8]

Whereas he has poured out his feelings about the tortures, he announces the resurrection in a laconic statement: "and on the third day he will rise again" (v. 33b). Luke's brevity is in fact Mark's, which he only corrects on one point: he prefers here, as he has elsewhere, the expression "the third day" to Mark's "after three days" (Mark 10:34b).[9] Finally, there are, in Luke, passion predictions that do not even mention the favorable outcome provided by the resurrection (see 9:44; 13:31-33; 17:25).

While Mark's text stops with the prediction of the resurrection, Luke adds to this announcement a narrative comment (v. 34). He emphatically points out the Twelve's lack of understanding. This comment both

---

3   In Greek: $\kappa\alpha\dot{\iota}$ $\pi\alpha\rho\alpha\lambda\alpha\beta\dot{\omega}\nu$ $\pi\dot{\alpha}\lambda\iota\nu$ $\tau o\dot{\upsilon}\varsigma$ $\delta\dot{\omega}\delta\epsilon\kappa\alpha$ $\ddot{\eta}\rho\xi\alpha\tau o$ $\alpha\dot{\upsilon}\tau o\hat{\iota}\varsigma$ $\lambda\dot{\epsilon}\gamma\epsilon\iota\nu$ (Mark 10:32b).

4   See 9:51, 53; 13:22; 17:11; and, later on, 19:28.

5   In Greek: $\kappa\alpha\dot{\iota}$ $\tau\epsilon\lambda\epsilon\sigma\theta\dot{\eta}\sigma\epsilon\tau\alpha\iota$ $\pi\dot{\alpha}\nu\tau\alpha$ $\tau\dot{\alpha}$ $\gamma\epsilon\gamma\rho\alpha\mu$-$\mu\dot{\epsilon}\nu\alpha$ $\delta\iota\dot{\alpha}$ $\tau\hat{\omega}\nu$ $\pi\rho o\phi\eta\tau\hat{\omega}\nu$ $\tau\hat{\omega}$ $\upsilon\dot{\iota}\hat{\omega}$ $\tau o\hat{\upsilon}$ $\dot{\alpha}\nu\theta\rho\dot{\omega}\pi o\upsilon$.

6   The phrase $\pi\alpha\rho\alpha\delta o\theta\dot{\eta}\sigma\epsilon\tau\alpha\iota$ $\tau o\hat{\iota}\varsigma$ $\dot{\alpha}\rho\chi\iota\epsilon\rho\epsilon\hat{\upsilon}\sigma\iota\nu$ $\kappa\alpha\dot{\iota}$ $\tau o\hat{\iota}\varsigma$ $\gamma\rho\alpha\mu\mu\alpha\tau\epsilon\hat{\upsilon}\sigma\iota\nu$, $\kappa\alpha\dot{\iota}$ $\kappa\alpha\tau\alpha\kappa\rho\iota\nu o\hat{\upsilon}\sigma\iota\nu$ $\alpha\dot{\upsilon}\tau\dot{o}\nu$ $\theta\alpha\nu\dot{\alpha}\tau\omega$ $\kappa\alpha\dot{\iota}$ $\pi\alpha\rho\alpha\delta\dot{\omega}\sigma o\upsilon\sigma\iota\nu$ $\alpha\dot{\upsilon}\tau\dot{o}\nu$ $\tau o\hat{\iota}\varsigma$ $\ddot{\epsilon}\theta\nu\epsilon\sigma\iota\nu$ (Mark 10:33) becomes $\pi\alpha\rho\alpha\delta o\theta\dot{\eta}\sigma\epsilon\tau\alpha\iota$ $\gamma\dot{\alpha}\rho$ $\tau o\hat{\iota}\varsigma$ $\ddot{\epsilon}\theta\nu\epsilon\sigma\iota\nu$ in Luke (v. 32).

7   In Greek: $\kappa\alpha\dot{\iota}$ $\mu\alpha\sigma\tau\iota\gamma\dot{\omega}\sigma\alpha\nu\tau\epsilon\varsigma$ $\dot{\alpha}\pi o\kappa\tau\epsilon\nu o\hat{\upsilon}\sigma\iota\nu$ $\alpha\dot{\upsilon}\tau\dot{o}\nu$ ("and after they beat him they will kill him"; v. 33); $\kappa\alpha\dot{\iota}$ $\mu\alpha\sigma\tau\iota\gamma\dot{\omega}\sigma o\upsilon\sigma\iota\nu$ $\alpha\dot{\upsilon}\tau\dot{o}\nu$ $\kappa\alpha\dot{\iota}$ $\dot{\alpha}\pi o\kappa\tau\epsilon\nu o\hat{\upsilon}\sigma\iota\nu$ ("and they will beat him and kill him"; Mark 10:34a).

8   In 9:22, the list of Jewish authorities, as well as the use of the verb $\dot{\alpha}\pi o\delta o\kappa\iota\mu\dot{\alpha}\zeta\omega$ ("to reject after a test," "to reject"), suggests a judicial framework. In 9:44; 13:31-33; 17:25; and 24:7, 26, 46, however, reference to the trial is practically absent. The mention of suffering, on the other hand, is central to these verses.

9   See 9:22; 24:7, 46; Acts 10:40. Luke can place the ordinal adjective before the substantive or after the substantive with repetition of the article, which highlights the adjective.

adapts and moves to a different place Mark's mention of the disciples' astonishment (Mark 10:32a).[10] In Luke, this mention is made where it should be, that is, *after* Jesus' announcement of his alarming future. Its wording is nonetheless surprising; the reader will have trouble figuring out why the Twelve did not understand such a precise description.[11] The reason is that Luke was thinking less of the evidence of the facts than of their significance according to God's plan. The narrative and historical lines (vv. 32-33) must be considered against the scriptural and theological background (v. 31b and v. 34). Luke has weighed his words in order to express this divine plan foreshadowed in Scripture that was so dear to him. Verse 34, like v. 31b, abounds in terms that are highly redactional and theologically loaded.[12]

Commentary

■ **31** Since Jesus began traveling, he had been surrounded not only by disciples (16:1; 17:1, 5, 22), both men and women (8:1-3), but also by Pharisees (13:31; 14:1; 15:2; 16:14; 17:20; perhaps 18:9); sympathizers, either in a crowd (14:25) or individually (13:23; 18:18); and even tax collectors, "sinners" (15:1), persons suffering from "leprosy" (17:12), and children (17:15). In these chapters devoted to the travel narrative, Luke seems not always to have been at pains to identify who Jesus' listeners were or to restrict the thrust of his words to specific persons. Here, however, he has taken the trouble to have Jesus and the Twelve off by themselves. What Luke is thereby suggesting is that what Jesus is going to communicate is destined for the Twelve alone. Luke is, in fact, consistent, since he has the passion predictions restricted to the narrow circle of the disciples.[13] This intention attributed to Jesus has a doctrinal basis that

will be confirmed by the speeches in Acts—only Christians have the right to know the meaning of Jesus' death. The speech in Miletus, the only speech in Acts addressed to Christians, the elders of Ephesus whom Paul had gathered together in Miletus, mentions the expiatory quality of the cross, about which the missionary speeches, aimed at Jews or Gentiles, are eloquent in their silence.[14] So we should take the verb "take with oneself" ($\pi\alpha\rho\alpha\lambda\alpha\mu$-$\beta\acute{\alpha}\nu\omega$, v. 31) seriously.[15] By drawing the Twelve to himself, Jesus excluded the rest of his listeners, because what he was communicating belonged in a way to the realm of mysteries.

The trip up to Jerusalem, about which Luke's readers would be thinking and which the disciples can feel in their legs, has an "end" ($\tau\acute{\epsilon}\lambda o\varsigma$), an objective that will also be an accomplishment. By the use of the verb "finish," "bring to an end" ($\tau\epsilon\lambda\acute{\epsilon}\omega$),[16] Luke confers a meaning on what would appear to be devoid of meaning. If he has not used here the traditional "it is necessary" ($\delta\epsilon\hat{\iota}$), he still spells out the theological necessity with which the contingent events are fraught. The unknown and apparently meaningless future becomes known thanks to Jesus' inspiration in the present and is laden with meaning thanks to the reference to the prophetic writings.[17]

One of Luke's constant concerns is to have recourse to the Scriptures to explain Jesus' coming, his ministry, and especially his passion. To be sure, he was not the only one to look for correspondences between what was found in Scripture and what befell the Son of Man. But he was one of those who insisted most vigorously on the fact that what happened to Jesus[18] was rooted in Scripture. The less meaning there was to the story and the less logic to the events, the more necessary it was to ensure that they had cohesion and that there was a reason to them[19] by putting them into the thinking of a mysterious God who

---

10   See Grundmann, 357.

11   Schweizer (191) notes this point.

12   One would also search in vain in Mark's Gospel for a counterpart to "everything that is written by the instrumentality of the prophets" and which "will be accomplished" (v. 31b).

13   See 9:18 (before 9:22); 9:43 (before 9:44); and 17:22 (before 17:25).

14   See Bovon, *Theologian*, 203.

15   On $\pi\alpha\rho\alpha\lambda\alpha\mu\beta\acute{\alpha}\nu\omega$ in Luke, see A. Kretzer, "$\pi\alpha\rho\alpha$-$\lambda\alpha\mu\beta\acute{\alpha}\nu\omega$, etc.," in *EDNT* 3:29–30.

16   On this verb, which we also find in 12:50 and 22:37

(in 13:32 we find the compound form $\grave{\alpha}\pi o\tau\epsilon\lambda\acute{\epsilon}\omega$), and its theological import, see Grundmann, 355; see also the commentary above on 12:50, esp. n. 50.

17   See Grundmann, 356.

18   See Bovon, *Theologian*, 94–96, 120.

19   Bennett ("'The Son of Man must . . . ,'" 113–29) insists on this point and rightly argues that the mention of $\delta\epsilon\hat{\iota}$ ("it is necessary") or the reference to the prophetic Scriptures not only places the future in the hands of God but also affirms God's "regularity" (this word appears, for example, on p. 121 of Bennett's article).

lifted the corner of the veil for those whom he called his prophets. And we may imagine that Luke, in saying "by the instrumentality of the prophets," was thinking of all of Scripture: he considered Moses (the Law) and David (the Psalms) to be prophets in the same way that Isaiah and Jeremiah were.

■ **32-33** In his book, the Gospel writer has constantly predicted the passion, whose shadow has hung over Jesus' life from his birth. Did Mary not already learn of it from Simeon's oracle (2:35) and from Jesus himself, already at the beginning of his ministry (4:28-29)?[20] In the predictions of the passion, the Gospel writer did not attempt to decide how much of Jesus' death was the responsibility of the Jews and how much that of the Romans. Sometimes he mentions the authorities in Jerusalem, sometimes the Gentile leaders; sometimes he is content with calling attention to the role of "humans" or "this generation."[21] His failure to mention the Jewish phase of the trial here was not in order to spare the judges of Israel[22] but in order to go directly to the point, so as to mention the Son of Man's sufferings. It is he who is the center of all our attention.[23] It is a picture of his fate as a suffering righteous person that Luke wishes to draw with several strokes of his pen.[24] What interested the Gospel writer

was not the mystery of human justice but the relentlessness of the physical attack on Jesus. He was first of all handed over to the Gentiles,[25] which meant that he was abandoned to those who had no reason to spare him.

Next he was to become the plaything of cruel forces.[26] They were to mock him, to make sport of him, to ridicule him, to scoff at him—these are the different nuances of the verb ἐμπαίζω; ironically, the nouns παῖγμα ("play, sport") and παίγνιον ("plaything, toy") come from the same root.[27] After that he was to be insulted (ὑβρισθήσεται), that is, treated with "insolence" (ὕβρις).[28] Then he was to be spat upon (ἐμπτυσθήσεται), in the literal sense, or, in the figurative sense, to be covered with opprobrium. Next he was to be flogged. The verb μαστιγόω ("whip, flog, scourge") could be used in many ways: Roman law distinguished between different types of punishment, those used during a procedure as a means of intimidating and weakening the accused person, or as a minor punishment before release, or as the first step of a capital punishment.[29] In this verse, the proximity of the verb "to kill"[30] suggests a link with capital punishment. This, says Luke to his readers, is the fate that was awaiting the "good teacher" of Galilee, the "wise master" of the trip to Jerusalem: in human terms, it did

---

20 In veiled terms; see 5:35; 9:31, 51; 12:50; see Bovon, *Révélations*, 71.

21 Luke 9:22 mentions only Jewish authorities; 9:44, which is vague, describes a delivery into the hands of men; 13:33 speaks of the death of the prophet in Jerusalem; 17:25, which is also vague, mentions "this generation"; 24:7 refers to a delivery into the hands of sinful men; 24:26 and 46 refer to the sufferings of Christ without indicating their origin.

22 See Schweizer, 191.

23 In the predictions of the passion, Luke insists not only on the death of Christ but also on his suffering; the infinitive παθεῖν ("to suffer") occurs in 9:22; 17:25; 24:26, 46. On this verb and Luke's usage of it, see the commentary on 9:22 in vol. 1; and Bovon, *Theologian*, 177.

24 See nn. 31 and 34 below.

25 Psalm 94 (93):2-7 enumerates the sinful works of the proud. Zephaniah 3:11-13 and Sir 10:12-18, on the other hand, proclaim the victory of God over the proud infidels and the divine protection granted to the humble.

26 Here begins the most detailed prophecy of Jesus' sufferings in the book of Luke. The Lukan story

of the passion does not describe these events in a mechanical way. Should we be surprised? See Ps 123 (122):3-4a: "Mercy, Lord, Mercy! For we have had more than enough of contempt; we have had more than our fill, we are surfeited with it."

27 The verb ἐμπαίζω ("to deceive," "to ridicule") appears twenty-six times in the LXX: see, e.g., Gen 39:14, 17; 2 Macc 7:10.

28 Although the substantive ὕβρις ("pride," "arrogance") is common in the LXX, the verb ὑβρίζω ("to insult") only appears six times. Grundmann (356) notes the ties that this verb maintains with ancient tragedy and applies them to our passage: "Am Martyrium des Menschensohnes vollzieht sich die Tragödie der Völker, die an ihm freveln."

29 See Josef Blinzler, *The Trial of Jesus: The Jewish and Roman Proceedings against Jesus Christ Described and Assessed from the Oldest Accounts* (Westminster, Md.: Newman, 1959) 277–93.

30 In Greek, it is ἀποκτείνω. Luke uses this verb in 6:9 *v.l.*; 9:22; 11:47-49; 12:4-5; 13:4, 41, 34; 18:33 (here); 20:14-15; Acts 3:15; 7:52; 21:31; 23:12, 14; 27:42. See H. Frankemölle, "ἀποκτείνω, etc.," in *EDNT* 1:134.

not make sense. But this meaninglessness is expressed by verbs that, in the LXX and according to the piety of the Psalms, describe the fate met by those who, in this cruel and unjust world, worship God and love their neighbor.[31] At the moment Luke has Jesus express himself, Jesus places himself between the Scripture impatient to be fulfilled and the history of salvation expecting to be written imminently.

"On the third day," there will be the resurrection. There is not a word of explanation, only an affirmation that is explicit but enigmatic. "The third day" of Scripture, such as it is found in the wording quoted by Paul in 1 Cor 15:3-5, is a date that is more theological than chronological.[32] In the active, $\dot{\alpha}\nu\dot{\iota}\sigma\tau\eta\mu\iota$ means "raise," "raise up," "bring back to life," as a transitive verb. In the intransitive form, $\dot{\alpha}\nu\dot{\iota}\sigma\tau\alpha\mu\alpha\iota$, here in the future ($\dot{\alpha}\nu\alpha\sigma\tau\dot{\eta}\sigma\epsilon\tau\alpha\iota$), means "rise," "stand up," "come back from the dead."[33] Luke was acquainted with other verbs expressing God's restoration of the righteous sufferer:[34] $\dot{\epsilon}\gamma\epsilon\dot{\iota}\rho\omega$ ("rouse"), which suggests coming out of death as one would come out of sleep;[35] $\dot{\upsilon}\psi\dot{o}\omega$ ("raise high"), which defines the resurrection in terms of elevation (see Acts 2:33); $\dot{\alpha}\nu\alpha\lambda\alpha\mu\beta\dot{\alpha}\nu\omega$ ("take up"), which brings to mind the ascension (see Acts 1:2, 11);[36] $\epsilon\dot{\iota}\sigma\dot{\epsilon}\rho\chi\rho\mu\alpha\iota$ $\epsilon\dot{\iota}\varsigma$ $\tau\dot{\eta}\nu$ $\delta\dot{o}\xi\alpha\nu$ ("enter into [one's] glory"), which puts the resurrection in the same category as an enthronement

and restores to Christ the estate Adam had lost at the time of the Fall (see Luke 24:26; 9:26, 32; 21:27).

■ **34** The contrast is so great between Jesus, alive and giving, and the Son of Man, tortured and dispossessed, and between the present and the future that, according to Luke, even the scriptural bridge the Master offers his disciples does not help them understand. It would take the resurrection itself, not just Jesus' prophecy, to make the disciples grasp it, to have their eyes opened, and to have the Scriptures also opened. For the moment, however, they are in a state of incomprehension.

"Nothing about all these things" ($o\dot{\upsilon}\delta\dot{\epsilon}\nu$ $\tau o\dot{\upsilon}\tau\omega\nu$) is obviously a strong expression. The Greek verb used, $\sigma\upsilon\nu\dot{\iota}\eta\mu\iota$, also has a powerful meaning. It refers here to the act of intelligence that grasps—that is, that is capable of bringing together—distinctly different kinds of reality and of understanding.[37] Well, as for the Twelve, however much they had been Jesus' protégés, they still had not caught on to anything of all this[38] (just as Mary and Joseph had not understood one of Jesus' enigmatic utterances when he was twelve years old; 2:50).[39]

"What he said" (literally, "this word," $\tau\dot{o}$ $\dot{\rho}\dot{\eta}\mu\alpha$ $\tau o\dot{\upsilon}\tau o$), an expression on which Luke confers a biblical seriousness, refers here, as in 2:50, to something Jesus said.[40] But the expression is also used by Luke in a wider sense to report something said by an apostle or even by God.[41]

---

31 On the suffering of the righteous person, see Eduard Lohse, *Märtyrer und Gottesknecht: Untersuchungen zur urchristlichen Verkündigung vom Sühnetod Jesu Christi* (Göttingen: Vandenhoeck & Ruprecht, 1955); Karl T. Kleinknecht, *Der leidende Gerechtfertigte: Die alttestamentlich-jüdische Tradition vom "leidenden Gerechten" und ihre Rezeption bei Paulus* (WUNT 2/13; Tübingen: Mohr Siebeck, 1982). See n. 34 below.

32 See Dupont, "Ressuscité 'le troisième jour,'" in idem, Études, 321–36; see also n. 9 above.

33 On $\dot{\alpha}\nu\dot{\iota}\sigma\tau\eta\mu\iota$ and $\dot{\alpha}\nu\dot{\iota}\sigma\tau\alpha\mu\alpha\iota$, see Xavier Léon-Dufour, *Résurrection de Jésus et message pascal* (ParDi; Paris: Seuil, 1971) 32–33.

34 Restoration is already announced in the Servant Songs, Isa 50:8-9; 53:12 (see n. 25 above). On the suffering of the righteous, see n. 31 above.

35 See J. Kremer, "$\dot{\epsilon}\gamma\epsilon\dot{\iota}\rho\omega$ etc.," *EDNT* 1:372–76.

36 Luke 24:51 uses $\dot{\alpha}\nu\alpha\phi\dot{\epsilon}\rho\omega$ ("to take up").

37 On $\sigma\upsilon\nu\dot{\iota}\eta\mu\iota$, which Luke also uses in 2:50; 8:19; 24:45; Acts 7:25 (twice); 28:26-27; see H. Balz, "$\sigma\upsilon\nu\dot{\iota}\eta\mu\iota$, etc.," in *EDNT* 3:307–8.

38 As we know, the incredulity of the disciples is a motif that is dear to Mark, which he interprets as callousness; see Mark 6:52 (where we find the same verbal form $o\dot{\upsilon}$ $\gamma\dot{\alpha}\rho$ $\sigma\upsilon\nu\dot{\eta}\kappa\alpha\nu$, "for they did not understand") and Mark 9:32 (where we find $o\dot{\iota}$ $\delta\dot{\epsilon}$ $\dot{\eta}\gamma\nu\dot{o}o\upsilon\nu$ $\tau\dot{o}$ $\dot{\rho}\dot{\eta}\mu\alpha$, "they did not understand this statement"); see Joachim Gnilka, *Die Verstockung Israels: Isaias 6, 9-10 in der Theologie der Synoptiker* (SANT 3; Munich: Kösel, 1961); Bovon, *Theologian*, 371–73.

39 $\kappa\alpha\dot{\iota}$ $\alpha\dot{\upsilon}\tau o\dot{\iota}$ $o\dot{\upsilon}$ $\sigma\upsilon\nu\dot{\eta}\kappa\alpha\nu$ $\tau\dot{o}$ $\dot{\rho}\dot{\eta}\mu\alpha$ $\dot{o}$ $\dot{\epsilon}\lambda\dot{\alpha}\lambda\eta\sigma\epsilon\nu$ $\alpha\dot{\upsilon}\tau o\hat{\iota}\varsigma$ ("but they did not understand the word that he spoke to them"); see the commentary on 2:50 in vol. 1.

40 The term $\dot{\rho}\dot{\eta}\mu\alpha$, for a remark of Jesus, is found also in 5:5; 7:1; 9:45 (twice); 20:26; 22:61; 24:8; and Acts 11:16.

41 For a word of God, see 2:29; 3:2. For a word of an apostle, see Acts 28:25. The expression $\tau\dot{o}$ $\gamma\epsilon\nu\dot{o}\mu\epsilon$-$\nu o\nu$ $\dot{\rho}\dot{\eta}\mu\alpha$ in Acts 10:37 is rich and complex: it refers all at once to the story of Jesus and the apostolic

This is another way of saying that the Twelve had not caught on to anything of all this;[42] what Jesus said was still "hidden" to them.[43] Its meaning was "sealed," as it were, and far from their comprehension.[44] Thus, for Luke, a saying could be present and readable, but its meaning absent and concealed. Luke was not a theologian concerned only with singleness of meaning. He did not believe that a meaning was always readable on the surface. Glory is concealed behind agony. There was something of the idea of the "hidden God" (*deus absconditus*) in Luke's writings.[45] And as if a double affirmation were not enough, Luke goes on to say "and they did not grasp[46] what was said." So there are moments when Luke shares Mark's harsh treatment of the Twelve.[47]

As readers are to discover, the Son of Man's resurrection and his being spiritually present to his followers on Easter will remedy this dramatic deficiency. The eyes of both the mind (νοῦς) and the heart (καρδία) will be opened (see Luke 24:32, 45).[48] The disciples will understand what they had not been able to understand during Jesus' lifetime. They will get to that phase when the Risen One, spiritually present, will repeat what he had told them at that time, namely, that "everything written about me in the law of Moses, the prophets, and the Psalms must be fulfilled" (24:44). Luke develops a biblical theology of divine salvation that is foretold, fulfilled, and proclaimed by means of, first, a contrast between a "before" characterized by lack of understanding and an "after" characterized by understanding, and then by the setting forth of different poles: the Scriptures; Jesus the righteous one who suffered and then was raised; and the disciples, first weak and then strong.

History of Interpretation

While Ambrose of Milan did not comment on these verses,[49] Calvin attached great importance to them.[50] He felt that Christ was armed with the invincible strength of the Spirit that enabled him to venture into Jerusalem knowing what was awaiting him: "in order to be spat upon by them, mocked, insulted, whipped, and finally tortured on the cross." He considered that the Master was right in repeating the predictions of the passion, given his disciples' terror. Jesus used two means to encourage them: first, his foreknowledge was a testimony to his divinity that helped them "find a solution for the scandal of the cross"; second, the perspective of the resurrection gave them assurance. Calvin also wondered why Christ limited his prophecies only to the circle of the Twelve and concluded that it was not to favor them but to make future witnesses of them. Noting that here Luke was "ampler than the others," the Reformer declared that the harmony between the voice of the biblical prophets and Jesus' fate represents "a very neat remedy for overcoming temptation." Finally, he saw the disciples' weaknesses and strengths side by side. Although they

---

proclamation of him; see the commentary on 9:45 in vol. 1, n. 33; Bovon, *Theologian*, 82–85.

42 Luke makes a similar observation in 9:45, expressing it in similar terms directly following another prediction of the passion: οἱ δὲ ἠγνόουν τὸ ῥῆμα τοῦτο καὶ ἦν παρακεκαλυμμένον ἀπ' αὐτῶν ἵνα μὴ αἴσθωνται αὐτό ("But they did not understand this saying; and it was hidden from them, so that they could not perceive it"). See the commentary on 9:45 in vol. 1.

43 On κρύπτω in Luke, see 11:52 *v.l.*; 12:2; 19:42; as well as H.-J. Ritz, "κρύπτω, etc.," *EDNT* 2:322–23; see also the commentary above on 12:2.

44 Note the ἀπ' αὐτῶν, literally, "away from them," translated as "from them." We find the same expression in 9:45, after the verb παρακαλύπτω in the passive; see n. 42 above, where the passage is quoted.

45 See Bovon, *Theologian*, 83–84.

46 On γινώσκω in Luke, see the commentary above on 10:22.

47 See Mark 6:52; 8:17, 32-33; 9:32; see n. 38 above.

48 On this opening of the minds of the disciples and of the Scriptures themselves, see Gerhard Delling, ". . . als er uns die Schrift aufschloss.' Zur lukanischen Terminologie der Auslegung des Alten Testaments," in H. Balz and S. Schulz, eds., *Das Wort und die Wörter: Festschrift Gerhard Friedrich zum 65. Geburtstag* (Stuttgart: Kohlhammer, 1973) 75–83; Bovon, *Theologian*, 117 n. 79.

49 See Ambrose of Milan *Exp. Luc.* 8.65–79 (treatise on Luke 18:18-30) and 8.80–90 (on Luke 18:35—19:10).

50 Calvin, *Harmony*, 2:267–69.

were frightened, they nevertheless followed their Lord. Therefore, they are "rightfully to be praised for having preferred to act counter to their emotions rather than abandoning him."[51]

Conclusion

On the way to Jerusalem, the Lukan Jesus had a premonition of his destiny and announced it once more to his disciples. The Gospel writer preferred to stress theology rather than psychological interaction. He conceived of this tragic fate as a fulfillment of the prophetic books, stressing here the suffering more than the triumphant outcome, and the role of the Romans more than that of the Jews in Jesus' trial. Like the parents of the twelve-year-old boy (2:50), the disciples did not understand this harmony between Scripture and imminent history. Luke felt that this lack of understanding was more a matter of obduracy than of stupidity. Jesus' resurrection (24:36-43) and the gift of the Holy Spirit (Acts 2:1-4) were to transform their hearts and open their minds (24:45). But the story has not yet reached that stage in the history of salvation.

---

51   Ibid., 507–8.

The Blind Man near Jericho
(18:35-43)

Bibliography 18:35-43

Achtemeier, Paul J., "'And he followed him': Miracles and Discipleship in Mark 10:46-52," *Semeia* 11 (1978) 115–45.

Betz, Hans Dieter, "The Cleansing of the Ten Lepers (Luke 17:11-19)," *JBL* 90 (1971) 314–28, esp. 323–27.

Idem, "The Early Christian Miracle Story: Some Observations on the Form Critical Problem," *Semeia* 11 (1978) 69–81.

Burger, Christoph, *Jesus als Davidssohn: Eine traditionsgeschichtliche Untersuchung* (FRLANT 98; Göttingen: Vandenhoeck & Ruprecht, 1970) 42–46, 107–12.

Busse, *Wunder*, 227–34.

Duling, Dennis C., "Solomon, Exorcism, and the Son of David," *HTR* 68 (1975) 235–52.

Dupont, Jacques, "L'aveugle de Jéricho recouvre la vue et suit Jésus (Marc 10,46-52)," *RAT* 8 (1984) 165–81.

Fisher, Loren R., "'Can This Be the Son of David?'" in F. T. Trotter, ed., *Jesus and the Historian: Written in Honor of Ernest Cadman Colwell* (Philadelphia: Westminster, 1968) 82–97.

Fuchs, Albert, *Sprachliche Untersuchungen zum Matthäus und Lukas: Ein Beitrag zur Quellenkritik* (AnBib 49; Rome: Biblical Institute Press, 1971) 45–170.

Haenchen, *Weg Jesu*, 369–72.

Johnson, Earl S., Jr., "Mark 10:46-52: Blind Bartimaeus," *CBQ* 40 (1978) 191–204.

Kertelge, Karl, *Die Wunder Jesu im Markusevangelium: Eine redaktionsgeschichtliche Untersuchung* (SANT 33; Munich: Kösel, 1970) 179–82.

Ketter, P. "Zur Lokalisierung der Blindenheilung bei Jericho," *Bib* 15 (1934) 411–18.

Kodell, Jerome, "Luke's Use of Laos, 'People,' Especially in the Jerusalem Narrative (Lk 19,28—24,53)," *CBQ* 31 (1969) 327–43.

Lövestam, Evald, "Jésus Fils de David chez les Synoptiques," *StTh* 28 (1974) 97–109.

Meynet, Roland, "Au cœur du texte: Analyse rhétorique de l'aveugle de Jéricho selon saint Luc," *NRTh* 103 (1981) 696–710.

Mirro, Joseph A., "Bartimaeus: The Miraculous Cure," *TBT* 20 (1982) 221–25.

Paul, André, "La guérison de l'aveugle (des aveugles) de Jéricho," *CBFV* 9 (1970) 44–69.

Idem, *Parcours évangéliques: Perspectives nouvelles* (La foi en acte; Paris: Cerf, 1973) 40–66.

Pillarella, G., "Sedebat secus viam mendicans (Luc. 18,35)," *PalCl* 38 (1959) 1085–87.

Porter, Stanley E., "'In the Vicinity of Jericho': Luke 18:35 in the Light of Its Synoptic Parallels," *BBR* 2 (1992) 91–104.

Reist, Thomas, *Saint Bonaventure as a Biblical Commentator: A Translation and Analysis of His Commentary on Luke XVIII, 34—XIX, 42* (Lanham, Md.: University Press of America, 1985).

Robbins, Vernon K., "The Healing of Blind Bartimaeus (10:46-52) in the Marcan Theology," *JBL* 92 (1973) 224–43.

Roloff, *Kerygma*, 121–26.

Rossi de Gasperis, Francesco, and Ignace de la Potterie, "'Signore, che io veda!' (Lc 18,41); il discernimento spirituale del cristiano oggi," *Ritiri ed esercizi* 3 (1984) (inaccessible to me).

Schramm, *Markus-Stoff*, 143–45.

Steinhauser, Michael G., "The Form of the Bartimaeus Narrative (Mark 10.46-52)," *NTS* 32 (1986) 583–95.

Trilling, *Christusverkündigung*, 145–63.

van der Loos, *Miracles*, 422–25.

Varro, R., "Annonce de la Passion et guérison de l'aveugle de Jéricho selon s. Luc 18, 31-43," *AmiCl* 78 (1968) 25–27.

35/ It happened that, as he was approaching Jericho, a blind man was sitting by the roadside begging. 36/ When he heard a crowd going by, he asked what was happening. 37/ They told him that it was Jesus the Nazorean who was passing by[a]. 38/ And he cried out, "Jesus, Son of David, have mercy on me!" 39/ But those who were in front sternly ordered him to be quiet. But he shouted even more loudly, "Son of David, have mercy on me!" 40/ When Jesus stood still[b] he ordered the man to be brought to him. When the man[c] came near, he asked him[d], 41/ "What do you want me to do for you?" He said, "Lord, let me see again."[e] 42/ Jesus said to him, "Receive your sight;[f] your

a   Literally: "that Jesus the Nazorean is passing by."

b   In 18:11, with reference to the Pharisee, the same participle has the meaning of "taking a stance."

c   In Greek: "he."

d   It is Jesus who asked the question. In 18:18, the same verbal form was used with reference to the ruler who questioned Jesus.

e   Another possible, but less probable, translation: "let me see."

f   Or: "See."

faith has saved you." 43/ And immediately he regained his sight[g] and followed him, glorifying God. And all the people, when they saw it, praised God.

Here we have the story of a person of solid will who spoke with faith to the person passing by at the beginning and, at the end, gave glory to God with the same degree of confidence. We also have here the story of the transformation of a blind man, a destitute beggar sitting by the roadside, who miraculously recovered his sight.[1] In describing this beneficial change effected by a persevering faith, the Gospel writer also introduced the readers to God and Christ, to whom that faith was directed. In these few verses, Jesus is as active as the blind man.

Analysis

After the redactional conclusion in v. 34,[2] Luke picks up again on the Markan narrative,[3] more particularly on the story of the blind man near Jericho (Mark 10:46-52).[4] According to his custom, Luke makes the narrative parts conform to his personal style. In vv. 35-37, he writes this way: "it happened that, as . . ." ($\dot{\epsilon}\gamma\dot{\epsilon}\nu\epsilon\tau o\ \delta\dot{\epsilon}\ \dot{\epsilon}\nu\ \tau\hat{\omega}$), which is typical of his style of writing. He gives to the genitive a succinctness lacking in Mark: "when . . . a

crowd going by" ($\ddot{o}\chi\lambda ov\ \delta\iota a\pi o\rho\epsilon vo\mu\dot{\epsilon}vov$).[5] He chooses a precise verb, after which he uses a subordinate clause in the optative mood in Greek:[6] "he asked what was happening" ($\dot{\epsilon}\pi vv\vartheta\dot{a}v\epsilon\tau o\ \tau\dot{\iota}\ \epsilon\ddot{\iota}\eta\ \tau o\hat{v}\tau o$). He prefers the participle "begging" ($\dot{\epsilon}\pi a\iota\tau\hat{\omega}v$) to the noun "beggar" ($\pi\rho o\sigma a\dot{\iota}\tau\eta\varsigma$, Mark 10:46), which he may have found too familiar.[7]

The Gospel writer has not limited his activity to these formal changes. He also dares to modify—albeit ever so slightly—the time and place of the story, placing the incident at the point in time when Jesus and the procession accompanying him are approaching Jericho.[8] Then he sacrifices the disciples in his rewriting of the Greek genitive before omitting the name of the blind man, Bartimaeus (Mark 10:46).[9] It is hard to see why. Finally, Luke intensifies the dialogical character of the scene:[10] he modifies the function of the participle "hearing/when he heard" ($\dot{a}\kappa o\dot{v}\sigma a\varsigma$), which gives the beggar a chance to ask a question, and provides an opportunity for the crowd to answer ("they told him" [$\dot{a}\pi\dot{\eta}\gamma\gamma\epsilon\iota\lambda av\ \delta\dot{\epsilon}\ a\dot{v}\tau\hat{\omega}$], found only in Luke, is well chosen). In our

---

1   Mark 8:22-26 tells the story of another healing of a blind man, which took place at Bethsaida. Luke is unaware of or simply ignores this story, which is located at the end of the great omission of Mark 6:45—8:26.

2   Varro ("Annonce," 25) considers v. 34 a hinge and insists on similarities between 18:31-34 and 18:35-43, two texts that already steer the reader's attention toward the passion. He also notes certain differences between the two (Son of Man, on the one hand; Son of David, on the other; the incredulity of the apostles, on the one hand; the faith of the blind man on the other; etc.).

3   With Schneider (2:374), here one must consider whether Luke uses any source besides Mark.

4   As we have seen (see above), Luke omits the pericope of the dispute between the apostles (Mark 10:35-45). According to Schneider (2:374), we do not know why. According to Varro ("Annonce"), it was to tie together the prediction of the passion with the faith of the blind man. According to

Burger (*Davidssohn*, 107–12) and Trilling (*Christusverkündigung*, 147–48), Luke clarifies the text of Mark.

5   Translated as: "a crowd going by."

6   The use of the optative tends to disappear at this time; see BDF §65.2 and 384–86. Quite a few manuscripts add an $\ddot{a}v$ and read $\tau\dot{\iota}\ \ddot{a}v\ \epsilon\ddot{\iota}\eta\ \tau o\hat{v}\tau o$ ("what could have been happening").

7   On $\pi\rho o\sigma a\dot{\iota}\tau\eta\varsigma$ ("begger"), see BAGD, s.v. Because of the influence from Mark, numerous manuscripts of Luke have $\pi\rho o\sigma a\iota\tau\hat{\omega}v$ ("begging").

8   Mark, who noted the entrance of Jesus and his disciples into Jericho, awkwardly narrates this story just as they are leaving the city (Mark 10:46).

9   Luke perhaps fears foreign names; but this does not prevent him from mentioning Bar–Jesus (Acts 13:6), Barabbas (Luke 23:18), or Barnabas (Acts 4:4, 36).

10   See Burger, *Davidssohn*, 108.

commentary we will focus on the change involved in having Jesus called "Nazorean" ($N\alpha\zeta\omega\rho\alpha\hat{\iota}o\varsigma$).[11]

Elsewhere Luke uses the proper name "Jesus" sparingly, but in this pericope he uses it more freely than does his source, Mark.[12] Furthermore, he avoids the Markan repetition of the Greek verb for "cry out, shout" ($\kappa\rho\acute{\alpha}\zeta\omega$) by using the synonymous Greek verb $\beta o\acute{\alpha}\omega$ the first time (v. 38).[13] For the vague "many" in Mark 10:48, Luke substitutes the precise phrase "those who were in front" ($o\acute{\iota}\ \pi\rho o\acute{\alpha}\gamma o\nu\tau\epsilon\varsigma$), which is both logical and suggestive at the same time. He also prefers "be quiet" ($\sigma\iota\gamma\acute{\alpha}\omega$) to Mark's "keep silent" ($\sigma\iota\omega\pi\acute{\alpha}\omega$).[14] The end of v. 39, on the other hand, is identical to the end of the corresponding verse in the Second Gospel.

In v. 40, Luke prefers the imposing participle "standing still" ($\sigma\tau\alpha\theta\epsilon\acute{\iota}\varsigma$) and elegantly depicts what is happening—Jesus' command, its execution, and the Master's question.[15] In doing so, he omits the encouragement given the blind man by the crowds,[16] thus forfeiting in the process a concrete detail found in Mark.[17] He also omits another detail, the beggar's throwing off his cloak (Mark 10:50).[18]

As usual, Luke respects the wording of what Jesus says.[19] In fact, he takes over all of the following Markan dialogue almost intact.[20] On one point, however, he was anxious to correct his source. In Luke, the beggar calls Jesus "Lord" ($\kappa\acute{\upsilon}\rho\iota\epsilon$) instead of "Rabbi" ($\dot{\rho}\alpha\beta\beta o\upsilon\nu\acute{\iota}$).[21]

The end of the story varies from one Gospel to another. Mark's account stops at the point at which the blind man follows Jesus,[22] while Luke goes on to mention a double act of praise: the beggar's, then that of all the "people" ($\lambda\alpha\acute{o}\varsigma$—a term that indicates here a progression from the "crowd" [$\ddot{o}\chi\lambda o\varsigma$], used at the beginning of the story, v. 36).[23]

What is the organization of the episode from the point of view of formal analysis?[24] Verses 35 and 39 have *the blind man* as subject, in dialogue with the crowd. He was there when Jesus was approaching Jericho (v. 35). When the crowd went by, he asked what was happening (v. 36). Once he found out (v. 37), he cried out for help (v. 38). Although rebuffed (v. 39a), he persisted in his call for help (v. 39b).[25] Verses 40 to 42, for their part, have *Jesus* as subject, in dialogue with the blind man; he ordered him to be brought to him (v. 40a), then

---

11 Matthew simplifies the beginning of the episode, keeps the location at the exit from Jericho, omits the name Bartimaeus (as does Luke), describes two blind men but fails to mention that they are beggars (Matt 20:29-34).

12 Luke inverts the wording of Mark 10:47; Luke has Ἰησοῦ υἱὲ Δαυίδ ("Jesus, Son of David," 18:38) where Mark has υἱὲ Δαυὶδ Ἰησοῦ ("Son of David, Jesus"). And he has no counterpart to "Jesus" in Mark 10:50.

13 The disappearance of this verb causes the loss of ἤρξατο ("he began," Mark 10:47), a verb that Luke usually likes to use.

14 There is no essential difference in meaning between σιγάω and σιωπάω. It is simply a stylistic variation.

15 The Markan counterpart (Mark 10:49) does not lack character but still has an awkward repetition of the verb φωνέω ("to speak," "to raise one's voice," "to call"), which occurs three times.

16 Mark 10:49b: θάρσει, ἔγειρε, φωνεῖ σε ("Take courage, stand up; he is calling you").

17 See Burger, *Davidssohn*, 107–12; Trilling, *Christusverkündigung*, 148.

18 The beggar, who used the cloak as clothing and as a blanket, must have thought it too dirty. The usage of the verb ἀποβάλλω, in the sense of "to take off" clothing (Mark 10:50), is not attested in the LXX or

in the rest of the New Testament, but it is common in Greek literature; see Achtemeier, "Miracles," 115–45, esp. 138 n. 19.

19 In v. 42, however, there is a Lukan addition: ἀνάβλεψον ("to receive sight"); see Schweizer, 192.

20 In v. 41, Luke simply writes ὁ δὲ ("and he"), where Mark 10:50 has ὁ δὲ τυφλός ("and the blind man"). In v. 43 Luke substitutes the precise word that he likes, παραχρῆμα (see the commentary on 8:43-48 in vol. 1, and above on 13:13) for Mark's εὐθύς.

21 See the explanation below.

22 Mark 10:52 contains the detail "on the road," which Luke omits.

23 Matthew simplifies the sequence of events, but he relays the emotional condition of Jesus, who responds favorably to the blind man because he is σπλαγχνισθείς ("moved with compassion," Matt 20:34).

24 See the double analysis of Meynet ("Cœur," 696–710), who distinguishes the syntagmatic and paradigmatic frameworks.

25 Meynet ("Cœur," 699–701) insists on the double cry of the blind man and advocates a chiastic structure (vv. 35b-36a and v. 43 correspond to each other, as do vv. 36b-38 and vv. 41b-42, on the one hand, and v. 39ab and vv. 40-41a, on the other hand; the shout in v. 39c is the centerpiece).

questioned him (vv. 40b-41a). By way of an answer to the blind man's reply (v. 41b), he spoke to him a second time in the imperative, justified by the blind man's faith (v. 42b). The result of this double movement back and forth, from the blind man to Jesus (vv. 35-39)[26] and of Jesus to the blind man (vv. 40-42), suddenly appears in v. 43a:[27] Jesus' will asserted itself through the miracle, which was followed by the determination of the healed beggar, who wanted to follow Jesus and glorify God. The "crowd," which had become the "people," expressed their praise to God. Luke's elimination of the disciples from the scene is understandable. Their presence would have complicated the unfolding of the story. The crowd, on the other hand, serves a useful purpose. First of all, its negative reaction brings out the perseverance of the blind man, who had to repeat his cry for help. Next, although the function of the crowd in the first part of the story was to prevent something from happening, in the second part, the crowd served to encourage the action, on Jesus' orders, since it was the crowd who brought the blind man to Jesus. In the final part of the story, the crowd joined in the praise of the person who had been miraculously cured.[28]

The question has been asked whether this episode actually corresponds to a miracle story, because of the dialogues that give it its structure.[29] The question has also been raised as to who the principal character is,

the blind man or Jesus, and whether the perspective was anthropocentric or Christocentric. It has also been noted that the connotations would suggest a Palestinian origin rather than a Hellenistic one. Aside from the localization, which appears to be pre-Markan, mention has also been made of the adjective denoting Jesus' origin (Nazarene in Mark, Nazorean in Luke), as well as the title Son of David.

To my way of thinking, what we have here is a miracle story, at least in its original form.[30] In the course of being transmitted orally, however, the emphasis shifted from Christ, who intervened in a sovereign way, to the one who, thanks to his voluntary faith,[31] recovered his sight. His two cries for help, his brush with the crowd, and his way of responding to what Jesus said and did had become exemplary, and his being healed, symbolic. We can imagine that certain preachers and, even more, certain catechists might have recounted this story to sympathizers or neophytes. Those telling the story, moreover, did not make their listeners opt for one character as opposed to another. The blind man was catechetically usable[32]—if that expression is acceptable—for the sole purpose of serving as a model of crying for help, following, and causing others to follow the Son of David.[33] Mark linked the end of this episode to the following pericope on the entry into Jerusalem,[34] where the "kingdom of our father David" (Mark 11:10) echoes the repeated title "Son of

---

26 Varro ("Annonce," 25) writes: "La question centrale est donc bien de savoir pourquoi on marche derrière Jésus et où l'on va, en vérité."

27 Robbins ("Healing," 224–43) insists on the two aspects of the story: to become a disciple and the activity of Christ.

28 According to Betz ("Miracle Story," 72–75), who analyzes the text of Mark, the story has three parts: the opening (which is long compared to others of the genre, Mark 10:46-50 par. Luke 18:35-40a), the middle section (Mark 10:51-52b par. Luke 18:40b-43a), and the conclusion (Mark 10:52c par. Luke 18:43bc).

29 Dibelius (*Tradition*, 51–52) sees the story as a paradigm of an imperfect kind. According to Bultmann (*History*, 213), the composition of the Markan story is so late that it is not possible to reconstruct the original miracle account. Varro ("Annonce," 25) describes this biblical passage as a miracle story. Betz ("Miracle Story") sees it as a miracle story, enriched by another literary genre, a story of call-

ing. Following Achtemeier ("Miracles"), Steinhauser ("Bartimaeus Narrative," 583–95) sees it as a "call story," arguing that the account conforms to the pattern of Old Testament stories of calling (Gideon, Judg 6:11b-17; Moses, Exod 3:1-12).

30 With Trilling, *Christusverkündigung*, 146–50; and Robbins, "Healing," 232. According to Achtemeier ("Miracles," 120–25), on the other hand, the traditional account constituted not a miracle story but a personal legend that showed how one became a disciple. Mark, in his opinion, respected this genre, while Matthew and Luke made it into a miracle story.

31 Robbins ("Healing," 239) underscores this will and faith.

32 Trilling (*Christusverkündigung*, 158) suggests the catechism as the *Sitz im Leben* and as the socio-ecclesial root of the story.

33 The movement of faith and the movement of Christ the healer accumulate; see Robbins, "Healing."

34 See Haenchen, *Weg Jesu*, 372.

David" (Mark 10:47-48), and he linked its beginning to the previous pericope concerning true greatness, where "what do you want me to do for you (plural)?" (Mark 10:36) was a prelude to Jesus' question "what do you want me to do for you (singular)?" (Mark 10:51). Luke, on the other hand, removed the tie with the Jerusalem episode, was not interested in its messianic connotations, and had in mind instead the definition of true disciples, who resemble children (18:15-17), can divest themselves of their possessions (18:18-30), and can welcome Jesus (19:1-10).[35]

Commentary

■ **35** The following harmonization of the Synoptic Gospels has been attempted: Jesus passed the *Old* Jericho on his left,[36] which at that time was in ruins, and the town of Ain es-Sultan or Elisha's Spring on the right (this to follow Matthew and Mark),[37] and having gotten back onto the pilgrimage route linking Besan to Jericho through the valley of the Jordan, Jesus was at this point covering the half hour of walking that would bring him to the *New* Jericho, the one built by the Herods (this to follow Luke).[38] It has even been supposed that Jesus stopped at Elisha's Spring and whipped up the crowds, who began

following him at that point, and that the blind man had carefully chosen his spot, since that was on the pilgrimage route.[39] The question has also been raised[40] as to what the nature of the beggar's blindness was, whether he was born that way or whether it was due to an accident or an illness, so-called functional blindness or blindness due to hysteria. All of that, which witnesses to a kind of devotion to Scripture that is today out-of-date, must not distract us from focusing on what is essential.

Luke suggests that Jesus was continuing his journey[41] toward Jerusalem. On the way, he planned to stop in Jericho, which was to represent an oasis of calm before the storm.[42] This proximity of a town with a positive connotation will permit the staging of a final miracle story. The Gospel writer has mentioned the fulfillment of Isaiah's prophecy, quoted in connection with the inaugural speech delivered in Nazareth (4:18-19). He has mentioned the proclamation of the good news to the poor and recounted some instances of healing, purification, and even resurrection. In a summary in chap. 7, he mentioned some miraculous recoveries of sight (7:21). Here he illustrates the fulfillment of the prophetic words καὶ τυφλοῖς ἀνάβλεψιν, "and recovery of sight to the blind" (Isa 61:1 LXX, quoted in 4:18).[43]

35   It is, in Luke as in Mark, the last miraculous healing story before the passion; see Dupont, "L'aveugle de Jericho," 165.

36   See Josephus *Bell.* 4.8.3 §459. The author of the Bordeaux Itinerary, the oldest Christian itinerary of sacred places, knows that the city of Jericho is located a mile and a half from the Israelite city of Jericho (Paul Geyer, ed., *Itinera Hierosolymitana* [CSEL 39; Vienna: F. Tempsky, 1898] 24); see Ketter, "Lokalisierung," 416; van der Loos, *Miracles,* 423.

37   See 2 Kgs (4 Kgdms) 2:19-22; Ketter, "Lokalisierung," 415. This spring was supposed to help pregnant women.

38   To reconcile the Synoptics, some have imagined two distinct miracles (Augustine *Quaest. ev.* 2.48 [*PL* 35:1360–61]), or one miracle at two different times (Calvin, *Harmony,* 2:279), and still other solutions. Porter ("Vicinity," 91–104), who enumerates these options, comes to the following opinion himself: "In conclusion, I argue that the apparent contradiction of Luke 18:35 with Mark 10:46 and Matt 20:29 is caused by failure to appreciate the semantic range

of Luke's use of ἐγγίζω. This may be a verb of motion for Luke, but it seems much more likely that it is primarily a verb of location. Thus Luke 18:35 should be rendered 'when he was in the vicinity of Jericho'" (p. 104). I have not been convinced.

39   All this is presented by Ketter, "Lokalisierung." According to Pillarella ("Sedebat," 1085), this was a road for passersby; it had become a second home for the begging blind man.

40   See van der Loos, *Miracles,* 425.

41   The verb ἐγγίζω can mean "to go near" or "to be near"; εἰς ("to," "in") does not always imply movement in the language of the day; see Porter, "Vicinity." The fact remains that in a story that involves travel, the most natural meaning is that Jesus went near to Jericho. See n. 38 above.

42   It would be incorrect to posit a second source here (besides Mark); see Burger, *Davidssohn,* 109–12.

43   See Isa 29:18; 35:5; Grundmann, 357. Note that the Masoretic Text of Isaiah 61 does not include these words.

■ **36-37** What could be more normal than having a blind man[44] make an inquiry and having the persons to whom he speaks reply? There is nothing less usual, however, than the term Ναζωραῖος.[45] We need to remember that Nazareth was an unimportant and little-known town. It would be difficult to have Ναζωραῖος mean "from Nazareth." It would appear that, rather early on, this enigmatic term was associated with the Hebraic institution of the nazirite. In any case, Luke alluded to this institution in his infancy stories. He introduced John the Baptist as an ascetic, as a nazirite who had taken vows (1:15). However, although holiness was one of Jesus' attributes, his love of life did not correspond to the asceticism expected of a nazirite. Moreover, the text does not read Ναζιραῖος but Ναζωραῖος, a Lukan form found as well in Acts 2:22; 3:6; 4:10; etc. The Gospels of Matthew and John are not unacquainted with the term Ναζωραῖος; according to John 19:19, this word was part of the inscription on the cross; according to Matt 2:23, when Joseph came back from Egypt, he settled with his family in Nazareth "so that what had been spoken through the prophets might be fulfilled, 'He will be called a Nazorean'" (NRSV).[46]

■ **38-39** The man in our story is deprived of his sight but not his voice. He is able to communicate; he had made an inquiry shortly before (v. 36), and now he cries out. There is a book entitled *La foi n'est pas un cri* (*Faith Is Not a Cry*).[47] The title is right, for one's faith must be expressed in reasoned utterances. It may nonetheless on occasion be expressed by crying out. All of the anguished waiting of the human being who is affected is able to be expressed in that way, whether it is someone who has been hurt or someone who is an invalid. There is no faith without crying out. The call for help ἐλέησόν με ("have mercy on me") was to become one of the most popular of all Christians prayers. Was it already a characteristic expression of Jewish piety? Here the words are addressed not to God but to Jesus, called "Son of David."[48] A miracle story rooted in a Greek setting would have spoken of the "Son of God." The title "Son of David" obviously brings us back to Israel. It suggests the Jewish messianism, the famous promise made to David according to 2 Samuel 7. The Infancy Gospel (Luke 1–2) is immersed in this messianic climate.[49] Yet, if the blind man confers that royal connotation on this title, it poses a problem. To be sure, Israel was expecting its future sovereign to bring peace but did not dream of that person accomplishing miracles. If the blind man nevertheless addressed Jesus as the Messiah, it was because he had followed his own line of reasoning, namely, that if the Son of David was going to restore Israel, he could also give him back his sight.[50]

There is, however, another explanation. Solomon had been the son of David, and he was credited with many aptitudes and abilities. In the course of time, through the centuries, the Hebrew tradition had extended his wisdom to include science, medicine, and even magic. It is possible, then, that the blind man called on Jesus to help him more as a doctor or healer than as a messiah. By calling him "Son of David," he linked Jesus with Solomon and counted on being cured miraculously. If that was the traditional meaning associated with the term "Messiah," the question is whether Luke was still aware of it.[51]

■ **40-41** Christianity always raises two questions: "What should we do?" (cf. 3:10-14; Acts 2:37) and "What do you

---

44   Luke therefore fails to mention the proper name of the blind man—Bartimaeus, according to Mark 10:46.

45   Burger (*Davidssohn*, 108) also retains Ναζαρηνός for Luke, who, upon hearing this word, must have heard the echo of an honorific title.

46   On this title, see H. Kuhli, "Ναζαρηνός, etc.," in *EDNT* 2:454–56; Luz, *Matthew*, 1:122–24. Joachim Gnilka (*Das Matthäusevangelium* [2 vols.; HThKNT 1; Freiburg: Herder, 1986, 1988] 1:56–57) wonders if the term Ναζωραῖος has something to do with the Hebrew נֵצֶר ("shoot"), as in the messianic shoot (see Isa 11:1).

47   See Henry Duméry, *La foi n'est pas un cri: Suivi de Foi et institution* (Paris: Seuil, 1959).

48   According to Burger (*Davidssohn*, 111), Luke, unlike Mark, does not insist on this title. According to Trilling (*Christusverkündigung*, 150–51), this title has an eschatological dignity (and not a genealogical value). It has soteriological import for the individual more than for the community. It is rooted in the Palestinian Christianity. See Robbins, "Healing," 226, 233–34.

49   Schweizer, 192.

50   See Achtemeier, "Miracles," 125. Achtemeier also thinks that Mark is wary of the title "Son of David" (pp. 127–32).

51   See Fisher ("'Son of David?'" 82–91), who presents this hypothesis as a possibility.

want me to do for you?" (v. 41), the ethical and soteriological questions. To Luke's way of thinking, when
Jesus asks the soteriological question, he already knows
the answer. His only reason for asking it is to allow the
request to be articulated. Between the two questions
mentioned there is therefore room for the request, which
moves from a shout to a specific petition: "Lord, let me
see again" (Κύριε, ἵνα ἀναβλέψω). "Lord," in the vocative case in Greek, is typically Lukan, since for Luke, the
"Son of David" is the "Lord"[52] on whom the members of
the Christian community call for their salvation (Joel
3:5 LXX, quoted in Acts 2:21). Our man asks for his
salvation packaged as healing. To put it another way,
Luke's readers interpret the blind man's request as an
illustration of the hope of being saved. For the Christians of antiquity—to this the frescoes of the catacombs
are a witness—a blind man who recovered his sight
represented an example of a restoration due to a divine
force, and a hope of eternal salvation, above and beyond
the precariousness of human existence. "See" became
synonymous with "seeing what is invisible," moving from
the state of humanity that is blind because it has been
blinded to the state of a Christianity that both believes
and is open to what is essential in what appears around
them. In this way Luke links a provisional blindness
with Paul's conversion (the same Greek word for "seeing
again" [ἀναβλέπω] is used twice in Acts 22:13).[53] And in
Acts 26, which contains another reminder of Paul's conversion, Luke has the Resurrected One who appears to
the apostle on the Damascus road say: the apostolic ministry that is now incumbent on you consists in "open[ing]
their eyes so that they may turn from darkness to light
and from the power of Satan to God" (Acts 26:18 NRSV).

The meaning of ἀναβλέπω is nevertheless not
certain. The verb can have three different meanings. It
normally means "look up" (ἀνά in the sense of "up"); it
can also mean "regain (one's) sight" (ἀνά in the sense
of "again"). However, it can also, without any thought
of "up" or "again," simply mean "receive sight, become
able to see." It might be, then, that the theme here is just
"sight," rather than the more precise theme of *recovered*
sight.[54] The preposition ἀνά, when used as a prefix to a
compound verb, may, however, have a meaning implying
repetition (the author of the Fourth Gospel is known to
have played on this ambiguity in speaking of Nicodemus
who had to "be born from above" and "be born again").
If this is the correct meaning here, we should translate
the verb as "regain one's sight." Since the compound verb
ἀναβλέπω is used in all three Synoptic Gospels and the
simple verb βλέπω is not found in this story, we must
accept the meaning "regain one's sight."[55] The miracle is
not, for all that, diminished in any way; it is simply more
precise. The blind man found again what the Creator
had conferred on his creatures at the beginning; salvation is essentially a restoration, the fulfillment of a divine
plan that goes beyond the Fall and links up, by means
of an eschatological redemption, with God's beneficent
original intention.

■ **42** There is no salvation for a humanity that refuses to
accept it. The formula "your faith has saved you,"[56] which
Luke quotes on several occasions, links salvation to faith,
and divine power to human beings' willingness to receive
it and petition for help.[57]

■ **43** The adverb παραχρῆμα ("immediately")—by
now Luke's readers are acquainted with it—serves as a
marker. Whatever took place that quickly could only have
had a divine origin. The blind man recovered his sight
(this is the third use of the verb in these few lines) and
began to follow Jesus[58] (the use of the imperfect tense
of the Greek verb ἠκολούθει can express both the wish

52 According to Trilling (*Christusverkündigung*, 148),
   we should observe a crescendo from "Son of David"
   to "Lord."

53 The verb ἀναβλέπω appears three times in Luke's
   version of this passage (but only twice in Mark's);
   see Schweizer, 192.

54 On this question, see van der Loos, *Miracles*, 425,
   esp. n. 1.

55 We recall the miraculous healing of blind Tobit, the
   father of Tobias, who finally has joy at seeing the
   face of his son again; see Tob 2:9-10; 3:17; 5:10; 11:1-
   14.

56 According to Schneider (2:375), by giving sight
   Jesus enables faith (see v. 34, which precedes, as well
   as 9:45; 24:45; Acts 9:16-18; 26:28). According to
   Dupont ("Aveugle," 174–75), faith transforms the
   human being. To convince oneself of this, one need
   only compare the blind man at the beginning of the
   story with the man at the end.

57 Achtemeier ("Miracles," 134) thinks that, according
   to Luke, unlike Mark, a miracle can serve as a legitimate point of departure for becoming a disciple.

58 Meynet ("Cœur," 704) insists that a crescendo
   characterizes the blind man: he progresses from

of the one doing the following[59] and the duration of the activity).[60] This following was accompanied by thanksgiving.[61] The miracle, following the rule of the literary genre, produced an admiring reaction on the part of the spectators, who responded in a religious mode by praising God.[62] As we have seen, the crowd was also transformed by becoming God's people ($\lambda\alpha\acute{o}\varsigma$).[63]

History of Interpretation

The African theologian Tertullian reproached Marcion for being a docetist, in particular for the fact that Marcion did not give Jesus any ancestors (*Adv. Marc.* 4.36). On the other hand, Tertullian could congratulate the blind man of Jericho on knowing Christ, since this man provided Jesus with a human lineage by calling him the Son of David. Tertullian went on to transfer our attention from the blind man, who was given his sight, to the readers of the Gospel, who would lose their spiritual blindness by learning the rule of faith.

Ambrose of Milan (*Exp. Luc.* 8.80–84) was not able to admit that Jesus lacked knowledge of anything.[64] So if the Master questioned the blind man, that was for our instruction. For him, as for Tertullian, the healing of the blind man had a spiritual significance. The blind man

and Zacchaeus represent a type of person "to whom the Lord's mysterious power restored the power they had lost of seeing the light." By comparing the blind man with Zacchaeus, Ambrose leaned in the direction of harmonizing Luke's version with Matthew's, which mentions two blind men.[65] He stresses the verb "to see." He concluded from the example of Zacchaeus that it is not easy to "see" Jesus and that to do so, one must go up higher. From the example of the blind man he drew the following conclusion: "He could only see insofar as he followed Christ, praised the Lord, and overcame the world."[66]

When Cyril of Alexandria preached on Luke 18:35-43 (*Hom. in Luc.* 126),[67] his main concern was Christology. He felt that the blind man of Jericho did not share his adversaries' errors, for he did not divide Christ up. By calling Jesus "Lord" and asking him to do something that only God could do, he respected his divine nature; by calling him "Son of David" he acknowledged his human nature. What Jesus did confirmed the blind man's faith; the Master did not need to call on the divine authority to help him in order to perform his miracle.

The *Glossa ordinaria*[68] and Bonaventure's commentary[69] testify to the fact that the sermon that Pope Gregory the Great had preached on the blind man of Jericho had a lasting impact in the West.[70] This bishop

---

seeing to walking to praising: "L'homme est trois fois guéri" (705). In my opinion Luke does not insist on the third element, the recovery of praise. He does not mention a radical change in the function of the mouth; instead he believes in the continuity between the initial call for help and the final expression of gratitude.

59 See BDF §326.

60 Varro ("Annonce," 26) articulates three elements of the "ascent to Jerusalem" found in Luke 18:31-43: "l'appel aux Ecritures, les titres du Christ, la cécité et sa guérison."

61 The double mention of praise by the healed man and of the crowd of onlookers is typical of Luke; see 5:25-26; and Trilling, *Christusverkündigung*, 148. On $\delta o\xi\acute{a}\zeta\omega$ ("to glorify"), see 5:25-26; 7:16; 13:13; 17:15; 23:47; Acts 3:13; 4:21; 11:18; 13:48; 21:20; and the commentary on 5:25-26 in vol. 1.

62 On $\alpha\hat{\iota}\nu o\varsigma$ ("praise") and $\alpha\grave{\iota}\nu\acute{e}\omega$ ("to approve," "to praise") in Luke, see H. Balz, "$\alpha\grave{\iota}\nu\acute{e}\omega$, etc.," in *EDNT* 1:39.

63 Several exegetes, among them Meynet ("Cœur," 705), note the change from $\check{o}\chi\lambda o\varsigma$ ("crowd," v. 36)

to $\lambda\alpha\acute{o}\varsigma$ ("people," v. 43); curiously, Kodell ("Luke's Use of Laos," 327–43) insists on a distinction between these two terms in Luke-Acts ($\lambda\alpha\acute{o}\varsigma$, "people" of God in salvation history), and argues (p. 327) that here, conversely, the two words are used synonymously.

64 The quotations come from paragraphs 80 and 84.

65 Yet Ambrose does not go so far as to make Zacchaeus the second blind man; see the note by G. Tissot (Ambrose, *Traité*, 2:135 n. 1). The case of Zacchaeus the rich man, following the story of the poor blind man, allows Ambrose to extend his sympathies to the rich as well.

66 This is the translation of G. Tissot. The verb translated in French as "louer" is *praedicare*, which could imply more than praise: testimony, that is, proclamation and preaching.

67 See Payne Smith, *Cyril*, 2:583–86, and the three Greek fragments edited by Reuss, *Lukas-Kommentare*, 190–91 (frgs. 278–80).

68 *Glossa ordinaria*, 18:35–43 (*PL* 114:324–25).

69 See below.

70 Gregory the Great, Sermon 2 (*PL* 76:1081–86).

of Rome tied this episode to the immediately preceding announcements of the passion. The miracle (vv. 35-43) confirmed the announcement of the resurrection (v. 33). It also was an invitation to those who read about it to turn their eyes toward the supernatural, in other words, to look for the hidden meaning of the text. This meaning is allegorical. The blind man stands for the human race blinded by sin. Jericho represents the moon, which signifies the flesh doomed to die. As Jesus was approaching Jericho, he reminded us that through his incarnation he had come close to human beings and wished to restore their sight. While he was walking, he was demonstrating his compassionate humanity. When he stopped, he gave an indication of his immutable divinity. Jesus was compassionate by virtue of his human nature and possessed power by virtue of his divine nature. The blind man was right to want the light, the light of the invisible. He added discipleship to his faith. He never detached the memory of his repentance from his joy. Those who rebuffed the blind man stand for the desires that assail human beings. But the blind man's desire was stronger than their assaults, and his repeated crying out truly proclaimed his faith.

The commentator Bonaventure (*Comm. in Luc.* 18.58–66), who owed a large debt to Gregory the Great, the *Glossa ordinaria*, and Hugh of St-Cher, divided his explanation up into four parts. First of all, he stressed the aptness of the blind man, who is a symbol of defective humanity, unstable and blinded by its desire for possessions, calling out to Jesus for help. Second, he called attention to the tenacity of this man, who refused to let himself be put down. The reason he kept making his requests and questioning people was that he knew how to persevere in his faith and in his prayers. Moreover, the fact that he cried out repeatedly was a confirmation of his faith, and the crowd's answer to him showed that those creatures knew how to direct their attention to their Creator. In using the title "Son of David" advisedly, the blind man also demonstrated the quality of his faith. Third, Bonaventure turned his attention to Christ in order to sing the praises of his generosity. Even though human beings call out to Christ to come to them, it is in fact he who draws them to himself. Fourth, the commentator emphasized how complete the recovery was. Praising God ensued, on the part of the healed blind man, who henceforth obeyed, and on the part of the people, who admired a sinner's conversion.[71]

For his part, Calvin was of the opinion that, in spite of their difference, the three Synoptic Gospels report one and the same story.[72] He would not admit that they contradicted each other; instead, he suggested that one Gospel might have omitted a detail here and there, and that another might have told the story with greater clarity. Reconstructing a historical development, he supposed that the blind man tried in vain to meet up with Jesus when the latter entered Jericho and that, without being discouraged by the failure of his first attempt, he ran toward the way out of town so that he could finally meet the Master. By deliberately putting off offering help, Jesus imposed a spiritual discipline on the blind man that Jesus was keen on. The blind man willingly accepted that discipline and cried out all the more loudly. "This 'cry' showed how fervent and ardent his affection was." It also was a witness to the lack of fear on the part of the person who had nevertheless been reprimanded. Calvin followed this up with a reflection on prayer. He affirmed that there is a "rule" in the church establishing the acceptable wish list of things that believers have the right to ask God for in their prayers. This list, which he unfortunately did not supply here, is, in his eyes, immutable. Only the Holy Spirit can step in and modify it, and that, he tells us, happens only rarely! Following Ambrose's example, Calvin reckoned that the reason Jesus questioned the blind man was in order to wake up the people who had been dozing in the presence of God's marvelous deeds. Finally, Calvin mentions the pity the blind man asked for and the pity offered by Christ. He concludes his commentary by noting what was stressed by each Gospel. For example, Luke added the people's praise "to ensure a more definite endorsement of the miracle."[73]

---

71   On Bonaventure's exegesis, his commentary on Luke, and his interpretation of Luke 18:35-43, see Reist, *Bonaventure*, 29–78, 142–47, 164–68.

72   Calvin, *Harmony*, 2:278–81.

73   At the end of his article, Meynet ("Cœur," 706–10) is interested in the new texts that the evangelical text can engender. In particular he presents a song, with verses and refrains, written in the Sara language by Christians in Chad. Thus we read, "Fils de David, aie pitié de moi! Ouvre mes yeux, que je te

Conclusion

Since the blind man and Jesus alternate as grammatical subjects of the verbs, the pericope directs our attention toward human beings in search of their recovery and toward Christ, who, when he hears the petition, answers it. The blind person is one of those listed among the categories of unfortunate persons needing comfort (Isa 61:1 LXX) enumerated by Luke at the beginning of his Gospel (4:18; 7:22). The scene of the action, "Jericho," becomes a locus for salvation to take place, and the "Son of David," a title designating the Savior. The miracle was capable of convincing a Greek audience; it also edified the Christian community. As is often the case, it becomes an illustration of salvation, and what is visible becomes a metaphor for what is invisible. By his determination, the blind man answers the classic question: "What should we do?" (Luke 3:10, 12, 14; Acts 2:37). Jesus' mercy in turn poses another question: "What do you want me to do for you?" (v. 41) and furnishes a response to the answer: "Lord, let me see again" (v. 41). The Jericho episode, which is a symbol of redemption, also sketches, in Luke's pen, the portrait of the disciples. Conscious that the moment was auspicious, the blind man took advantage of the opportunity, expressed his wish without hesitation, never gave up, displayed his confidence, and, once his wish was granted, did not sink into thanklessness. According to the Gospel writer, this ideal portrait was going to take on the flesh of a concrete existence and not be limited to a spiritual life detached from earthly contingencies.

---

connaisse! Appelle-moi à toi, que je te suive! Ouvre ma bouche, que je loue Dieu! Fils de David, aie pitié de moi!" ("Son of David, have mercy on me! Open my eyes that I may know you! Call me to you that I may follow you! Open my mouth that I may praise God! Son of David, have mercy on me!") (p. 706).

A Visit to Zacchaeus
(19:1-10)
Bibliography

Ahern, Barnabas M., "The Zacchaeus Incident," *TBT* 25 (1987) 348–51.

Aletti, *Art de raconter*, 17–38.

Bizer, C., "Die Geschichte von Zachäus (Lk 19,1-10) – religionsunterrichtlich, religionskundlich und alternativisch buchstabiert: Ein durchaus subjektiver Versuch," *EvErz* 28 (1976) 217–24.

Borghi, Ernesto, "Leggere un testo, leggere un testo biblico," *ScC* 124 (1996) 351–61.

Burgos Núñez, Miguel de, "El relato de Zaqueo (Lc 19,1-10). Un pacto de justicia," *Comm* 26 (1993) 165–84.

Cadbury, Henry J., "Lexical Notes on Luke-Acts, III: Luke's Interest in Lodging," *JBL* 45 (1926) 305–22.

Contreras Molinà, Francisco, "El relato de Zaqueo en el evangelio de Lucas," *Comm* 21 (1988) 3–47.

Idem, "Zaqueo, una historia del Evangelio," *Proy* 34 (1987) 3–16.

Cocagnac, A. Maurice, "L'Évangile de Luc (Lc 19,10): Zachée, l'église et la maison des pécheurs," *AsSeign* 91(1964), 39–51; n.s. 62 (1970) 81–91.

Costen, James H., "Viewing Life from High Places: Psalm 139,1-18, Luke 19,1-10," *JITC* 24 (1996) 183–88.

Dauvillier, Jean, "Le texte évangélique de Zachée et les obligations des publicains," *Recueil de l'Académie de législation* 5/1 (1952) 27–32.

Derrett, *Law*, 278–85.

Dupont, Jacques, "Le riche publicain Zachée est aussi un fils d'Abraham (Luc 19,1-10)," in Bussmann and Radl, *Treue Gottes*, 265–76.

D'Sa, Thomas, "Exploiter Evangelized: Reflections Based on the Episode of Zacchaeus and Pastoral Practice," *VJTR* 60 (1996) 194–206.

Ebel, Basilius, "Das Evangelium der Kirchweihmesse (Lukas 19,1-10) gedeutet im Geist der Väter," in H. Emonds, ed., *Enkainia: Gesammelte Arbeiten zum 800 jährigen Weihegedächtnis der Abteikirche Maria Laach am 24. August 1956* (Düsseldorf: Patmos, 1956) 110–22.

Fiedler, *Sünder*, 127–35.

Garland, J. M., "Retrospect," *ExpT* 95 (1983–84) 371–73.

Garriot, C., "Land, Sin, and Repentance," *The Other Side* 21 (1985) 22–25.

Gianto, A., "Darstellung der Geschichte von Jesus und Zacchäus," *Orientasi* 16 (1984) 99–109.

Grindlay, Bruce W., "Zacchaeus and David," *ExpT* 99 (1987–88) 46–47.

Hamm, Dennis, "Luke 19:8 Once Again: Does Zacchaeus Defend or Resolve?" *JBL* 107 (1988) 431–37.

Idem, "Zacchaeus Revisited Once More: A Story of Vindication or Conversion?" *Bib* 72 (1991) 248–52.

Hassold, Michael J., "Eyes to See: Reflections on Luke 19,1-10," *LTJ* 29 (1995) 68–73.

Henry, Jim, *Une véritable conversion* (Craponne: Viens et Vois, 1983).

Hobbie, F. Wellford, "Luke 19,1-10," *Int* 31 (1977) 285–90.

Hollenweger, Walter J., *Besuch bei Lukas: Vier narrative Exegesen zu 2. Mose 14, Lukas 2,1-14, 2. Kor. 6,4-11 und Lukas 19,1-10* (KT 64; Munich: Kaiser, 1981) 43–48.

Howell-Jones, D., "Lost and Found [Luke 19:10]," *ExpT* 92 (1980–81) 371–72.

Hunzinger, C.-H., "συκοφαντέω," *TDNT* 7 (1971) 759.

Kariamadam, Paul, *The Zacchaeus Story, Lk 19,1-10: A Redaction-Critical Investigation* (Alwaye, Kerala, India: Pontifical Institute of Theology and Philosophy, 1985).

Karris, Robert J., "God's Boundary-Breaking Mercy [Lk 7,10; 19,1-10; 12,15-21]," *TBT* 24 (1986) 24–30.

Kerr, Alastair J., "Zacchaeus's Decision to Make Fourfold Restitution," *ExpT* 98 (1986–87) 68–71.

Klein, *Barmherzigkeit*, 68–71.

Lance, H. Darrell, "Some Thoughts on Maintaining Fellowship," *ABQ* 16 (1997) 154–60.

Laverdiere, Eugene A., "Zacchaeus," *Emmanuel* 90 (1984) 461–65.

Leroy, François, "Les sermons africains pseudo-augustiniens: Caillau S.Y. 1,46 et [E]scorialensis 19 (Chrysostomus Latinus) sur l'épisode de Zachée (Lc 19)," *Wst* 105 (1993) 215–22.

Loewe, William P., "Towards an Interpretation of Lk 19,1-10," *CBQ* 36 (1974) 321–31.

Löning, Karl, "Ein Platz für die Verlorenen: Zur Formkritik zweier neutestamentlicher Legenden (Lk 7,36-50; 19,1-10)," *BiLeb* 12 (1971) 198–208.

Mitchell, Alan C., "The Use of συκοφαντεῖν in Luke 19,8: Further Evidence for Zacchaeus's Defense," *Bib* 72 (1991) 546–47.

Idem, "Zacchaeus Revisited: Luke 19.8 as a Defense," *Bib* 71 (1990) 153–76.

Nestle, Eberhard, "Sykophantia im biblischen Griechisch," *ZNW* 4 (1903) 271–72.

O'Hanlon, John, "The Story of Zacchaeus and the Lucan Ethic," *JSNT* 12 (1981) 2–26.

O'Toole, Robert F., "The Literary Form of Luke 19:1-10," *JBL* 110 (1991) 107–16.

Raber, F., "Furtum," *Der Kleine Pauly*, 2:647–49.

Raja, R. J., "Seeking God, Sought by God: A Dhvani-Reading of the Episode of Zacchaeus (Luke 19,10)," *Jeev* 25 (1995) 139–48.

Ravens, D. A. S., "Zacchaeus: The Final Part of a Lucan Triptych," *JSNT* 41 (1991) 19–32.

Röckel, Gerhard, "Die Geschichte von Zachäus (Lk 19,1-10)—im Unterricht gemalt: Ein Versuch in der Eingangsstufe des Gymnasiums," *Religionsunterricht an höheren Schulen* 36 (1993) 311–14.

Rouillard, Philippe, "Zachée, descends vite," *VSpir* 112 (1965) 300–306.

Salom, A. P., "Was Zacchaeus Really Reforming? (Reply to N. M. Watson)," *ExpT* 78 (1966–67) 87.

Schibilsky, Michael, "Dann bist Du ja einer von uns: Bericht über die Zachäusgeschichte als Bibliodrama," *Religionsunterricht an höheren Schulen* 34 (1991) 258–60.

Schottroff and Stegemann, *Jesus*, 136–40.

Schwank, B., "Die Frömmigkeit des Zachäus," *EuA* 54 (1978) 64–66.

Schwarz, G., "ὅτι τῇ ἡλικίᾳ μικρὸς ἦν [Lk 19,3]," *BN* 8 (1979) 23–24.

Tannehill, Robert C., "The Story of Zacchaeus as Rhetoric: Luke 19,1-10," *Semeia* 64 (1993) 201–11.

Vitório, Jaldemar, "E procurava ver quem era Jesus: Análise do sentido teológico de 'ver' em Lc 19,1-10," *PerTeol* 19 (1987) 9–26.

Vogels, Walter, "Structural Analysis and Pastoral Work: The Story of Zacchaeus," *LV* 33 (1978) 482–92.

Völkel, Martin, "Freund der Zöllner und Sünder," *ZNW* 69 (1978) 1–10.

Vos, Geerhardus, "Seeking and Saving the Lost," *Kerux* 7 (1992) 1–19.

Watson, Nigel M., "Was Zacchaeus Really Reforming?" *ExpT* 77 (1965–66) 282–85.

Weymann, Volker, "Vom Zwiespalt befreit im Zwiespalt leben: Biblisch-theologische Beobachtungen zur Erfahrung der Befreiung vom Bösen inmitten des Bösen (Lk 19,1-10; Gen 32, 23-33)," *Ref* 26 (1977) 333–42.

White, Richard C., "A Good Word for Zacchaeus? Exegetical Comment on Lk 19,1-10," *LTQ* 14 (1979) 89–96.

Idem, "Vindication for Zacchaeus," *ExpT* 91 (1979–80) 21.

1/ **After entering Jericho, he was passing through it. 2/ Now there was a man there called by the name Zacchaeus. And he was a chief tax collector and he was rich. 3/ And he was trying to see who Jesus was[a], but on account of the crowd he could not, because he was short of stature. 4/ So, having gone ahead of him, he ran ahead and climbed a sycamore tree in order to see him, because he was going to pass that way. 5/ And when Jesus came to the place, he lifted up his eyes and said to him, "Zacchaeus, hurry and come down; for I must stay at your house today." 6/ And he hurried down and was happy to welcome him. 7/ And all who saw it began to grumble, saying that he was going to be the guest of a sinner. 8/ Zacchaeus stood there and said to the Lord, "Look, Lord, half of my possessions I will give to the poor; and if I have defrauded anyone of anything, I will pay back four times as much." 9/ Jesus said to him, "Today salvation has come to this house. And he is a son of Abraham[b]. 10/ For the Son of Man came to seek out and to save the lost."**

a   Literally: "to see Jesus who he was."

b   Or: "And he too, he is a son of Abraham."

This very well known story, localized in Jericho, is the matching piece to the healing of the blind man at the entrance to that same town (18:35-43). The Gospel writer has placed this story at the end of the travel narrative recounting the trip from Galilee to Jerusalem (9:51—19:27), in a section that has been named "the Gospel of the outcast."[1] It is a story that in its structure and function resembles the account of the calling of another tax-collector, Levi (5:27-32). It is a story in which multiple Lukan themes jostle and link up together: walking, wealth, the desire to see, the reversal of values, encounters, salvation as a current event, and Jesus' identity and mission.

In spite of an evident narrative quality and characteristic theological motifs, the episode has been interpreted in two different ways in recent years. The traditional interpretation stresses the salvation offered to the tax collector Zacchaeus and the consequences that he drew from it; the other interpretation, first proposed by Frédéric Godet, accepts the misunderstood moral value of the hero, who deserves to hear the Master's oracle of salvation (v. 9a) and to be called a "son of Abraham" (v. 9b).[2] As will be seen, the differences between these two interpretations are manifest[3] and have important implications. One interpretation latches onto God's grace demonstrated on that day by the salvific presence of the Son of Man (see v. 10). The other stresses the ethical commitment of the one who, in a sense, has earned his salvation (see v. 8). One speaks of repentance and pardon; the other, of good deeds and rewards. The one sees in Zacchaeus a scorned sinner; the other, a misunderstood righteous man. The one understands v. 8 as a commitment to follow Jesus that takes shape "today" (the present tense of the verbs has the force here of an immediate future). The other reads in this text an ancient custom that is still practiced "today" (with the present tense of the verbs having an iterative or durative force). In the first case, Zacchaeus is a "son of Abraham," since he is a true Jew. In the second, he is declared to

be such, either by once again finding, through sin and redemption, God's initial promise to the patriarch, or by benefiting from an eschatological redefinition of who is Abraham's descendant.

Analysis

Synchronic Analysis

A laconic initial sentence (v. 1) mentions Jesus' arrival and his passing through Jericho, with a curious omission of his name.[4] A Greek expression (καὶ ἰδού, "Now") serving as a marker, draws our attention to another character and sets in motion the story of an encounter. After Zacchaeus is introduced (in three phases: name, profession, and social status, v. 2), he does not succeed in getting his wish answered (v. 3). Refusing to admit defeat, he conceives of an alternate strategy (v. 4).

The moviemaker once more trains his camera on the first character and also provides a microphone; we hear Jesus invite himself to the house of Zacchaeus (v. 5), who accepts with alacrity (v. 6).

A new obstacle prevents the visit from taking place in a harmonious atmosphere. The third party, "all" (that is, "the crowd" of v. 2), expresses its disapproval (v. 7). At that point Zacchaeus speaks up, and what he says, even if it is addressed to the "Lord," takes account of the spectators' criticism (v. 8). Finally, Jesus expresses himself[5] through a two-part saying. He addresses himself to Zacchaeus but speaks about him in the third person singular (v. 9b), and what he says thus takes account of the critical audience's point of view.[6]

Such a presentation would be incomplete without the following details: the verb "pass" (διέρχομαι, in v. 1), reappears in v. 4. The expression "and he" (καὶ αὐτός), which appears twice in v. 2, reappears in v. 9, each time referring to Zacchaeus. Zacchaeus, moreover, wished to "see" (ἰδεῖν) Jesus in v. 3. Verse 4 confirms his intention by saying "in order to see him" (ἵνα ἴδη αὐτόν). While Zacchaeus was satisfied with learning that Jesus

---

1. The expression "the Gospel of the outcast," applied to Luke 15-19, comes from Manson, *Sayings*, 282.
2. See Godet, 2:336–38.
3. See nn. 67–68 below.
4. Luke seems to go out of his way to mention Jericho (see 18:35), while elsewhere the names of towns are rarely recorded.
5. See O'Toole: "Jesus has the last word" ("Literary Form," 105).
6. See ibid., 115.

"was going to pass that way" (ἤμελλεν διέρχεσθαι, v. 4), for his part Jesus thought that he must stay (δεῖ με μεῖναι, v. 5). The haste that was asked for by Jesus ("hurry," σπεύσας, v. 5) is matched by the haste actually used by Zacchaeus (the same σπεύσας, with the same verb καταβαίνω, "he hurried down," v. 6). "Your house" (v. 5) is balanced by "this house" (v. 9). Zacchaeus's wish ("he was trying to" [ἐζήτει], v. 3) serves as a matching piece to the wish of the Son of Man ("For the Son of Man came to seek out . . ." [ζητῆσαι], v. 10). The "today" (σήμερον) of Jesus' stay (v. 5), is equivalent to the one (the same σήμερον) in v. 9, the "today" of "salvation." The "rich man" Zacchaeus (v. 2) took care of "the poor"

(v. 8). The encounter was made possible by the convergence of horizontal and vertical movements (cf. "he . . . climbed" [ἀνέβη], v. 4, and "(hurried) down" [κατέβη], v. 6). At the outset, Zacchaeus wanted to know "who Jesus is" (translated as "who Jesus was," v. 3). At the conclusion of the story, he knows him and uses the Greek vocative κύριε (probably to be translated as "Lord," v. 8). Jesus himself resorts to another christological title, "the Son of Man," ὁ υἱὸς τοῦ ἀνθρώπου (v. 10).

Several commentators have ventured to make a graphic presentation of the pericope.[7] One of the proposed presentations is in the form of a diptych.[8] Here is the diagram I propose:

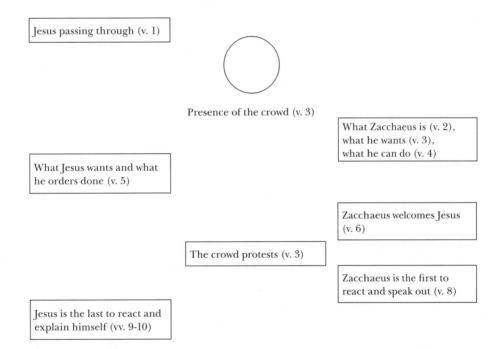

Jesus passing through (v. 1)

Presence of the crowd (v. 3)

What Zacchaeus is (v. 2), what he wants (v. 3), what he can do (v. 4)

What Jesus wants and what he orders done (v. 5)

Zacchaeus welcomes Jesus (v. 6)

The crowd protests (v. 3)

Zacchaeus is the first to react and speak out (v. 8)

Jesus is the last to react and explain himself (vv. 9-10)

As may be seen, the crowd, threatening from the outset (v. 3), occupies center stage.[9] The story revolves around their grumblings, and it is because of them that the encounter between the two persons shifts from the level of the event to that of its meaning.[10]

Diachronic Analysis

Once we have clarified the structure of the story, is it possible to define its literary genre? When commentators take Zacchaeus to be the principal player, they alternately understand the story as a biographical

7   For example, Meynet, *Saint Luc*, 2:179; Kariama-dam, *Zacchaeus Story*, 54; Bock, 2:1515.

8   See O'Toole, "Literary Form," 112–16. Equally for a division into two parts, see Klein, *Barmherzigkeit*, 68.

9   Tannehill, *Narrative Unity*, 1:111–13, 122–24: sus-

pense because of the barrier that the crowd creates; O'Toole, "Literary Form," 114.

10   See Petzke, *Sondergut*, 166: "Ab V. 7 wird die Begegnung kommentiert."

apophthegm, a personal legend, a conversion story, or an account of a quest/seeking.[11] If, on the other hand, they are impressed by the Master's attitude and maxims, they speak instead of a story about Jesus.[12] But when they are most impressed by the polemical side of the episode, they classify the scene among the controversy or apologetical stories.[13]

In my opinion, the problem of determining the literary genre cannot be dissociated from the history of the tradition and of the evolution of the story. In its final, redactional shape, the episode about Zacchaeus does not have a pure form. Instead, it displays the characteristics of various literary genres; it can be viewed as a conversion, pardon, salvation, or controversy story.

Although the procedure entails risks, we must dare to trace the development back from the final product, the Lukan story, to its antecedent drafts. Even if the Gospel writer's stamp, his vocabulary, and his style are to be felt from one end to the other,[14] certain verses seem nevertheless more redactional than others. Commentators are generally agreed that vv. 1 and 10 are redactional.[15]

Although v. 1 situates the scene in a spatial sense, it also serves as a link with the preceding story, and v. 10 hitches to the story a generalizing saying that, although admittedly welcome, is not indispensable to the plot. When they read this final word of Jesus, readers will note that the Gospel writer has taken the story of Zacchaeus to be a salvation story. In it, Jesus plays the salvific role of the shepherd of a lost sheep of the house of Israel.[16] As we will see, in so doing Luke has probably recovered the original meaning, the one the story had in its earliest stage.

The Gospel writer inherited the story from the community and from the author of L.[17] The quality of the plot and the level of language are the indications of this. At that stage, controversy seems to have been an important element,[18] showing up among Christians—the "crowd" of v. 3, and those designated as "all" in v. 7.[19] Zacchaeus's reply (v. 8), which must belong to this stage,[20] is a witness to the problem caused in that period by the status of rich Christians. The story had as its function defending their presence in the community as long as they truly desired to encounter Christ and decided to

11   Bultmann (*History*, 56) thinks that the story is a biographical apophthegm centered on the final words of Jesus. Dibelius (*Tradition*, 118) thinks it is the personal legend of Zacchaeus. According to Hamm ("Luke 19:8 Once Again," 436–37), it is a history of conversion. Tannehill ("Zacchaeus," 205) argues for a quest narrative (particularly an apophthegm or pronouncement story), noting a double quest: that of Zacchaeus, of course, but also that of Jesus; see O'Toole, "Literary Form"; Bock, 2:1515.

12   See Vincent Taylor, *The Formation of the Gospel Tradition: Eight Lectures* (London: MacMillan, 1933) 75–76, 153.

13   A controversy, according to Talbert (176–77); an apologetical narrative, a "vindication story," according to White, "Vindication for Zacchaeus," *ExpT* 91 (1979–80) 21.

14   O'Hanlon ("Zacchaeus," 2–4) and Fiedler (*Sünder*, 127–35) offer an analysis of vocabulary and style. Loewe ("Towards an Interpretation," 321) and Tannehill ("Zacchaeus," 201) also insist on the Lukan character of this pericope. Kariamadam's monograph, *Zacchaeus Story,* is entirely dedicated to the redactional perspective of Luke in these ten verses.

15   Certain about v. 10, the authors hesitate on v. 1; see Bultmann, *History*, 34, 64; Fitzmyer, 2:1219; Schnei-

der, 2:377; Wiefel, 326; Petzke, *Sondergut*, 168–69; Dupont, "Le riche publicain Zachée," 265–66.

16   See n. 83 below, which discusses the ties between this verse and Ezekiel 34 (the shepherd of Israel); Luke 15:3-7.

17   Most exegetes share this opinion, e.g., Grundmann, 358; Petzke, *Sondergut*, 165; and Fitzmyer, 2:1218.

18   Klein (*Barmherzigkeit*, 69) is one of the few commentators to suppose that v. 7 is secondary. But, distinguishing fewer layers than I do, he considers v. 8 to be primitive and reconstructs a chain consisting of vv. 6, 8, and 9a: Jesus declares salvation to the one who is first converted and who begins to practice charity.

19   I admit that for Luke the "crowd" does not always consist of Christians. Schottroff and Stegemann (*Jesus*, 136–40) think that Luke is especially interested in rich people in the Christian community. Löning ("Platz für die Verlorenen," 206–8) thinks that in legends the characters represent attitudes within a community.

20   Numerous exegetes declare v. 8 to be secondary and most frequently attribute it to Luke himself; see Bultmann, *History*, 33; Petzke, *Sondergut*, 168; Fitzmyer, 2:1219; Dupont, "Le riche publicain Zachée," 266.

make their possessions available to help others. Verse 8 belongs to this layer of the history of the text, and the vocabulary and syntax are a confirmation of this.[21]

The story about Zacchaeus can be traced back even further, and at this earliest stage it resembled calling and controversy stories, such as the one about Levi (5:27-32) or the one about the paralyzed man in Capernaum (5:17-26).[22] In that time, the earliest Christians remembered how freely grace was dispensed by Jesus, and how generously he offered pardon. They also remembered that that attitude did not go unchallenged by a hostile reaction on the part of many people in Israel. The "crowd" in v. 3 and the "all" in v. 7 stand for that part of the chosen people who at that stage repeated the expression of displeasure ("grumble," $\delta\iota\alpha\gamma o\gamma\gamma\acute{\upsilon}\zeta\omega$) first expressed by the chosen people in the desert, as reported in the book of Exodus.[23] The story of Zacchaeus furnished a weapon to Christians, who were a minority group within the people of Israel, and sketched out a reply that they could use in answering the criticisms that were coming thick and fast about their missionary efforts. Verses 7 and 9 (perhaps only v. 9b, v. 9a probably being a Lukan gloss[24]) arose at this stage in the evolution of the story.

It is possible to imagine that the whole story originated at that time.[25] That seems probable to me, since the first part of the story has an anecdotal quality that was not indispensable to the line of controversy and that is absent from other stories of a similar nature.

We must then postulate an early, fourth stage that only recounted what happened to Zacchaeus, which was worth mentioning.[26] The short but powerful chief tax collector had gone all out to see Jesus. He was remembered because Jesus had honored this tax collector with his presence. My opinion is—and in this I am opposed to one of the (very Protestant) principles of *Formgeschichte*—that attention was also focused from the very start on the believers, not just on Christ.[27] Consequently, it is possible that some biographical memories may have been preserved, such as the conversion of Cornelius in Peter's presence or the unexpected encounter between Zacchaeus and Jesus. Operating as a good historian, pastor, and author, Luke forgot so little of the original story that he recovered its original meaning.

Commentary

■ **1** There is nothing surprising about the intransitive use of the Greek verb $\epsilon\iota\sigma\acute{\epsilon}\rho\chi o\mu\alpha\iota$ ("enter") and the transitive use of $\delta\iota\acute{\epsilon}\rho\chi o\mu\alpha\iota$ ("pass through") in Luke's writing.[28] Having the episode take place in Jericho[29] may have been the result of a literary decision on the part of the Gospel writer, but if we take into account the interest L had in

---

21 The verb $\sigma\upsilon\kappa o\phi\alpha\nu\tau\acute{\epsilon}\omega$ ("to make a false statement") is used in only one other passage in L, 3:14. The words $\tau\grave{\alpha}$ $\acute{\eta}\mu\acute{\iota}\sigma\iota\alpha$ ("half") appear only here (we would expect, for "half," $\acute{\eta}$ $\acute{\eta}\mu\acute{\iota}\sigma\epsilon\iota\alpha$ or $\tau\grave{o}$ $\acute{\eta}\mu\iota\sigma\acute{\upsilon}$; $\tau\grave{\alpha}$ $\acute{\eta}\mu\acute{\iota}\sigma\epsilon\alpha$ and $\tau\grave{\alpha}$ $\acute{\eta}\mu\acute{\iota}\sigma\eta$ mean "halves"). We should note that the manuscripts differ on the spelling of these words. Bertrand Bouvier has suggested to me that the plural $\tau\grave{\alpha}$ $\acute{\eta}\mu\acute{\iota}\sigma\iota\alpha$ might come from the influence of $\tau\hat{\omega}\nu$ $\acute{\upsilon}\pi\alpha\rho\chi\acute{o}\nu\tau\omega\nu$. If Luke was the author of v. 8, he risks contradicting himself, since he requires a disciple to make all his goods available (see 12:33; 14:33; and 18:22). Furthermore, the insertion of $\mu o\upsilon$ ("my") between "half" and "goods," which is foreign to Luke's style, makes it seem affected. Finally, $\tau\epsilon\tau\rho\alpha\pi\lambda o\hat{\upsilon}\nu$ ("quadruple") is a *hapax legomenon* in the New Testament.

22 See O'Toole, "Literary Form," 109. Bultmann (*History*, 34) has even suggested that the story of Zacchaeus, considered as an ideal scene, was composed from the episode of Levi (Mark 2:14 par. Luke 5:27-28) and from its coupling with the dispute of Mark 2:15-17 par. Luke 5:29-32.

23 See Luke 5:30 and the commentary on 5:29-32 in vol. 1; see also 7:34; 15:2 and the commentary above on 15:1-2.

24 See Dupont, "Le riche publicain Zachée," 266.

25 On the possible fictiveness of the story, see Bultmann, *History*, 59; and Fiedler, *Sünder*, 127–35. The latter thinks that the story is Luke's creation.

26 See Evans (*Saint Luke*, 660), who mentions the "lively human touches."

27 See François Bovon, *L'Évangile et l'Apôtre: Le Christ inséparable de ses témoins* (Aubonne: Editions du Moulin, 1993).

28 See 11:52; 13:24b; 14:23; 24:29 for this usage of $\epsilon\iota\sigma\acute{\epsilon}\rho\chi o\mu\alpha\iota$, and Acts 14:24 and 15:3, 41 for this usage of $\delta\iota\acute{\epsilon}\rho\chi o\mu\alpha\iota$.

29 On Jericho, see de Burgos Núñez, "Zaqueo," 168–69; see also the commentary above on 18:35.

arch- tax collector could be "boss" or "very good"

personal and place names,[30] it is possible to suppose—and this is the solution I prefer—that the story about Zacchaeus was already located in Jericho in Luke's source.[31]

■ **2** The Greek of v. 2 strings together a pleonasm and a repetition.[32] It corresponds to the literary particularities of neither L nor Luke. The pleonasm involved in "called by the name" is uncharacteristic of the Third Gospel,[33] and the repetition "and he . . . and he" appears awkward.[34]

Even if there are some Christian families in Cyprus bearing the name Zakchaiou,[35] the name Zacchaeus is a Semitic one, and its bearer must have been Jewish.[36] According to its etymology, the name means "the pure one," "the innocent one."[37] Luke does not pay any more attention to this etymology than to others. Zacchaeus[38] was not only a tax collector[39] but a chief tax collector (ἀρχιτελώνης), a term that did not appear to be known in the Greek language of that time.[40] The text stresses this man's professional success.[41]

■ **3** In taking over this old story, Luke has left his stamp on it. He knew that human beings have desires and a sense of quest. So Zacchaeus "was trying" to see Jesus. His wish was in collaboration with his hope. The verb ζητέω ("try to find, seek, search, look for") is an important one for Luke and can refer to the quest for truth, for health, for a meaning to life, or for salvation.[42] In

p) from searches 25x!

---

30   See Petzke (*Sondergut*, 166), who had insisted on this point.

31   See Fitzmyer, 2:1222.

32   See Evans, *Saint Luke*, 661. Some have seen traces of Aramaic origins in these awkward wordings; see Wilfred L. Knox, *The Sources of the Synoptic Gospels* (ed. H. Chadwick; 2 vols.; Cambridge: Cambridge University Press, 1953, 1957) 2:112.

33   See, for comparison, Acts 10:1: ἀνὴρ δέ τις ἐν Καισαρέᾳ ὀνόματι Κορνήλιος, ἑκατοντάρχης ("In Caesarea there was a man named Cornelius, a centurion"). One part of the manuscript tradition, in Luke 19:2, omits the unnecessary word καλού-μενος "called"; see the apparatus of Nestle-Aland.

34   Applied to Christ, the expression "and he" is laudatory; see 5:1 and the commentary on that verse in vol. 1. Without a particular connotation, it can be applied to anyone, e.g., Zechariah in 1:22. Delebecque (118) understands the second καὶ αὐτός in v. 2 to mean "moreover."

35   Bertrand Bouvier, to whom I am grateful, told me this fact.

36   The majority of commentators presuppose this, as do I, even if the text does not say so explicitly. Tertullian (*Adv. Marc.* 4.37.1), on the other hand, seems to think that Zacchaeus is pagan. We know of other instances of Zacchaeus, such as the one in 2 Macc 10:19 and in Josephus *Vita* 46 §239; see Str-B 2:249; BAGD, s.v.; Fitzmyer, 2:1223; and Bock, 2:1516.

37   The Hebrew was זַכַּי ("Zakkai"). We find this name in Ezra 2:9 and Neh 7:14. Its Greek equivalent in the LXX is Ζάκχος (2 Esdr 2:9; 17:14). There are some textual variants for this name; see Fitzmyer (2:1223), who explains that the name did not have to be an abbreviation of "Zachariah." We recall also the famous rabbi at the end of the first century C.E., Yochanan ben Zakkai.

38   The memory of Zacchaeus is preserved in the Pseudo-Clementine writings, in which he becomes the bishop of Caesarea (*Ps.-Clem. Hom.* 3.63.1; *Ps.-Clem. Rec.* 3.66.4) and in Clement of Alexandria *Strom.* 4.6.35. The latter identifies him with Matthew. See Walter Bauer, *Das Leben Jesu im Zeitalter der neutestamentlichen Apokryphen* (Tübingen: Mohr Siebeck, 1909; reprinted Darmstadt: Wissenschaftliche Buchgesellschaft, 1967) 344; Bovon and Geoltrain, *Écrits apocryphes*, 1:1630 (index).

39   Garland ("Retrospect," 372) makes Zacchaeus say "I have learned to count," more than to read. On collectors of duties and taxes, see Völkel, "Freund," 1–10; Herrenbrück, *Zöllner*. See also 3:12; 5:27-30; 7:29, 34; 15:1; and the commentary on 5:27-28 in vol. 1. Jericho was not at the border but had always represented an important stop on the way to Jerusalem. To my knowledge, we are unaware of the organization of taxes and duties in this city; see Fitzmyer, 2:1223.

40   See Herrenbrück, *Zöllner*, 276–77. The term ἀρχι-τελώνης, like its counterparts ἀρχισυνάγωγος ("ruler of the synagogue," 8:49) and ἀρχιερεύς ("high priest," 3:2), designates a hierarchical leader, the boss of tax collectors; see BAGD, s.v. O'Hanlon ("Zacchaeus," 12) and Nolland (3:904) think otherwise; they see in him an excellent tax collector.

41   On the Lukan vocabulary of poverty and wealth, see Tannehill, "Zacchaeus," 202; Bovon, *Theologian*, 442–48; see also the commentary on 6:20, 24 in vol. 1. On the fate of another rich man, see the commentary above on 12:16 and 21.

42   The verb ζητέω occurs frequently in the Gospel (twenty-five or twenty-six times). In its strong sense, in addition to the passages mentioned in the body of the text, see 5:18; 11:10; 12:31; 13:24; 15:8; 17:33; 24:5; see also the commentary above on 11:9-10; and Raja, "Seeking God," 139–48.

11:9, Jesus declared, "Search, and you will find." In 9:9, we have the most interesting parallel: Herod was "trying, looking for a way" to see Jesus, a desire that was rekindled during the period of the passion (23:8, with the verb "want": "he had been wanting to see him" [ϑέλων ἰδεῖν αὐτόν]). The fate of Herod Antipas (Acts 12:20-23) will turn out to be the opposite of Zacchaeus's, since the monarch simply wanted to witness some miracles (23:8),[43] while the chief tax collector, who was looking for Jesus himself, was called upon personally to participate in the salvific action.

Zacchaeus had, to be sure, heard talk of the Master, but he did not really know him. Unlike Peter and the other disciples (9:18-22), at this point in time he still could not answer the question "Who is he?" (τίς ἐστιν; v. 3). So he wanted to see him in order to know who he was. The Gospel writer, who was a man who depended on sight as well as the spoken word,[44] considered the verb "to see" a metaphor for knowledge, love, and faith.[45]

Zacchaeus's climbing a tree is obviously to be explained by his shortness of stature.[46] But what is surprising is that this physical detail is not picked up on in Jesus' concluding statements.[47] When the Gospel writer is interested in someone's physical appearance, it is to point out some defect or, as here, a limitation.[48]

■ **4** Compared to v. 2, v. 4 is written in an elegant style.[49] Zacchaeus ran ahead[50] and climbed a sycamore tree. He hoped in that way to see Jesus pass that way.[51] Had he taken into consideration the fact that it is not always easy to look through a tree's foliage? Was he also afraid of being seen—did he wish to see without being seen? Luke, who mentioned a "mulberry tree" (συκάμινος)[52] in 17:6, here speaks of a "sycamore tree" (συκομορέα). He probably has a different tree in mind here from the one in 17:6. This particular kind of sycamore tree, a sycamore fig tree, which is unknown in the West, is a species that grows in plains, does not lose its foliage, possesses a short, wide trunk and has thick low branches that spread wide. So it was not hard to climb it.

■ **5** The plan of action that Zacchaeus had drawn up plays out for him beyond all his expectations. Jesus did in fact pass that way,[53] but he did not just pass that way. He

---

43 On the various fates that await humans, see the Lukan typology of four kinds of death: François Bovon, "The Lukan Story of the Passion of Jesus (Luke 22–23)," in idem, *Studies in Early Christianity* (WUNT 161; Tübingen: Mohr Siebeck, 2003) 85.

44 See Stephen D. Moore, "The Gospel of the Look," *Semeia* 54 (1991) 159–96.

45 On the strong sense of the verb "to see," see Loewe, "Towards an Interpretation," 324–25; O'Hanlon, "Zacchaeus," 13; Ahern, "Zacchaeus Incident," 348–51; Vitório, "E procurava," 9–26; Aletti, *Art de raconter*, 31–33; Hassold, "Eyes to See," 68–73.

46 The term ἡλικία signifies one's "age" first, and "stature" second. Luke used it in 2:52 to describe Jesus' growth. Here he clearly uses it again to describe physical "size." See BAGD, s.v.

47 See Tannehill, "Zacchaeus," 201–2.

48 One thinks of, among other things, the withered hand (6:6) or the loss of blood (8:43).

49 Εἰς τὸ ἔμπροσθεν ("ahead"); ἀναβαίνω ἐπί ("climbed up"); and ἤμελλεν (in the sense of "he was about to," "he was going to") are more elegant expressions. See Evans, *Saint Luke*, 662.

50 The manuscript tradition alternates between προδραμών ("having run in advance," "having preceded") and προσδραμών ("having run ahead"). It is better to retain the first of the two verbs, which

is better attested. The expression εἰς τὸ ἔμπροσθεν ("ahead," with movement) is common in Greek; see BAGD, s.v., which gives some references from secular literature. Criticized as pleonastic (see BDF §484), the expression προδραμών εἰς τὸ ἔμπροσθεν nevertheless makes sense: Zacchaeus preceded Jesus in time because he moved forward in space!

51 The adjective ἐκείνης takes the place of the complete expression ἐκείνης τῆς ὁδοῦ ("on the way"). In Classical Greek, the genitive of place designates all the space inside of which an action takes place. Luke is the only New Testament author to use this genitive (which he uses also in 5:19). Here it seems to me to be used wittingly (despite BDF §186.1).

52 On the sycamore, see BAGD, s.v., which refers to Immanuel Löw, *Die Flora der Juden* (4 vols.; Vienna/Leipzig: Löwit, 1924–34; reprinted Hildesheim: G. Olms, 1967) 1:274–80; see also Nogah Hareuveni, *Tree and Shrub in Our Biblical Heritage* (trans. and adapted by Helen Frenkley; Kiryat Ono, Israel: Neot Kedumin, 1984) 82–92. The term is not used in the LXX. Some argue over whether the city of Jericho really contained sycamores and whether Zacchaeus may have climbed onto a roof instead! See Fitzmyer, 2:1224, who summarizes the discussion.

53 Observe the precise ἐπὶ τὸν τόπον ("to that place," v. 5).

he saw Zacchaeus

lifted his eyes and saw[54] Zacchaeus, just as Zacchaeus had himself counted on seeing Jesus (vv. 3-4). In addition to having Jesus exchange glances with Zacchaeus, Luke has him speak to him, and in that way Jesus articulates what he wants Zacchaeus to do in the form of an imperative. Zacchaeus, whose name Jesus knew by virtue of his superhuman omniscience, was obliged to hurry down. Following a biblical literary convention, the invitation to hurry suggests a divine intention.[55] The adverb "today"[56] and the verb "must"[57] confirm the setting in motion of a salvific strategy. God's representative interrupted his travel to "stay"[58] at Zacchaeus's house. All these prosaic terms take on a holy connotation here.

■ **6** According to Luke, responding to Jesus' request was no chore for Zacchaeus. The chief tax collector hurried down and was happy to welcome the traveler who was passing through town. The verb "welcome" ($\dot{v}\pi o\delta \acute{e}\chi o\mu\alpha\iota$) into one's home bears all the meaning implied by hospitality in that time.[59] It also bears witness to the theological attention that Luke paid to encounters and visits.[60] The fact that Zacchaeus opened the door to his house with joy reflects a conviction on the part of the Gospel writer that God's presence inevitably gladdens

the human heart.[61] A contrast is established between Zacchaeus and another rich man, the one who went away very sad (18:23).

■ **7** What makes one person happy makes another bitter.[62] Luke has accustomed his readers to jealous recriminations situated near scenes of pardon, reconciliation, healing, and deliverance.[63] All those who here expressed their disapproval belonged to the category of those who were sure that they were righteous (18:9). They allowed themselves to judge and condemn both Zacchaeus, confirmed in his state as a sinner,[64] and Jesus, whose daring and carefree attitude made him guilty in their eyes.[65] Behind this sketch is hidden the experience of the earliest Christians, who witnessed Israel's resistance to the new message.[66]

■ **8** Verse 8 has given rise to intense debates. The Greek verbs in the present tense, $\delta \acute{\iota}\delta\omega\mu\iota$ and $\dot{\alpha}\pi o\delta \acute{\iota}\delta\omega\mu\iota$, can be understood either as futuristic presents indicating the immediate future, "I am going to give," "I am going to pay back," or as iterative or durative presents, "it is my custom to give," "it is my custom to pay back." If we choose the first option, as I am inclined to do, with Hamm and many others,[67] what motivated

---

54 The text of Nestle-Aland is content to read $\dot{\alpha}\nu\alpha\beta\lambda\acute{e}\psi\alpha\varsigma$ ("having looked up"), but innumerable manuscripts add "he saw him and"; see the apparatus of Nestle-Aland. Lance ("Some Thoughts," 154–60) insists on Jesus who allows contact with sinners.

55 Compare the haste that marks another providential encounter, that between Mary and Elizabeth in 1:39; see the commentary on 1:39 in vol. 1.

56 The readers of Luke recall the "today" of the birth of Jesus (2:11); see the commentary on 2:11 in vol. 1.

57 The word $\delta\epsilon\hat{\iota}$ ("it is necessary") is a term characteristic of the economics of salvation to which Luke tries hard to bear witness: see 2:49; 4:43; 9:22; etc.; see also the commentary on 2:49b; 4:43, and 9:22 in vol. 1. The verb $\mu\acute{e}\lambda\lambda\omega$ ("to be about to do," v. 4) itself undoubtedly has a theological connotation as well.

58 Like John (see, e.g., John 1:38-39), Luke devotes considerable attention to this verb: see 1:56; 8:27; 9:4; 10:7; 24:29.

59 See BAGD, s.v.; Helga Rusche, "Gastfreundschaft und Mission in Apostelgeschichte und Apostelbriefen," *Zeitschrift für Missionswissenschaft und Religionswissenschaft* 41 (1957) 250–68; Bock, 2:1518. Elsewhere Luke also uses $\dot{\alpha}\pi o\delta \acute{e}\chi o\mu\alpha\iota$, which

60 means "to welcome" but is more general and does not imply receiving someone into one's home.

60 See Henry J. Cadbury, *The Making of Luke-Acts* (New York: Macmillan, 1927) 249–53; idem, "Lexical Notes," 305–10.

61 On joy in Luke, see Schwank, "Frömmigkeit," 64–66; Bovon, *Theologian*, 457 n. 118.

62 René Girard (*La violence et le sacré* [Paris: B. Grasset, 1972] 93–101) has described this psychological mechanism, which is characteristic of antagonistic siblings and is a source of violence. Borghi ("Leggere un testo," 360) distinguishes between the blameworthy inertness of the crowd and the impetus toward movement that Jesus confers on Zacchaeus.

63 See n. 23 above.

64 On $\dot{\alpha}\mu\alpha\rho\tau\omega\lambda\acute{o}\varsigma$ in Luke, see Schottroff and Stegemann, *Jesus*, 136–40; see also the excursus on the pardon of sinners in vol. 1 of the commentary, and the commentary above on 13:2.

65 See 15:1-2; and de Burgos Núñez, "Zaqueo," 171–73.

66 On $\kappa\alpha\tau\alpha\lambda\acute{v}\omega$ ("to detach," or "to lodge"), see the commentary on 2:7b and 9:12 in vol. 1.

67 Watson, "Was Zacchaeus Really Reforming?" 282–85; Salom, "Was Zacchaeus Really Reforming?" 87;

and transformed Zacchaeus's ethical decision was the encounter with Jesus. If we retain the second option, as White, Mitchell, and Fitzmyer do,[68] then Zacchaeus was a righteous man who, on the defensive, recalled his good deeds. The vocabulary of loss and of salvation in vv. 9 and 10 tips the balance in favor of the first option, since it clearly suggests that Zacchaeus was "lost" and that he was subsequently "saved" by the Son of Man, who effected this transformation at the moment he entered Zacchaeus's house.

Up to this point, the Lukan Jesus has required persons to make all of their possessions available (see 12:33; 14:33; 18:22). Zacchaeus's intention seems to fall short of this requirement and resembles the limited generosity of a Barnabas (Acts 4:36-37) or the hospitality of a Lydia, who kept her house (Acts 16:15, 40) in the Acts of the Apostles. The emphasis in this passage, however, is on the size of the gift and the worth of the gesture. It has even been suggested that if the chief tax collector did not give everything to the poor, it was in order to fulfill his second promise, namely, to pay back four times as much.[69]

The Greek verb συκοφαντέω had as its first meaning a precise one: "accuse falsely, slander," during a trial; then, in a more general sense, "speak evil of," "to quibble with," "jeer at," "extort through slander." Luke used it in chap. 3 in reference to soldiers who, anxious about their fate, opened up to John the Baptist.[70] If we take into consideration the way in which duties and taxes were levied, it is probably this precise, legal sense that must prevail here. For when a tax collector did not get what he wanted, he could pursue in court the person who had not paid up and could even be tempted to produce false evidence.[71] The "four times as much," moreover, could have been dictated by reference to a single, isolated commandment in the law of Moses[72] but was more probably suggested by a rule of Roman law whose use could have spread in the fiscal administration of the procuratorial province of Judea where these events took place.[73] Nevertheless, the text puts less stress on the respect of laws than on Zacchaeus's generosity.

The scene recalls two biblical episodes, the hospitality Abraham extended to three angels (Genesis 18)[74] and the hospitality extended by Rahab to Israelite spies (Josh 2:1).[75] These biblical stories, which were known at the time, facilitated the redaction of the story about Zacchaeus.

■ **9** Luke was responsible for the first saying in v. 9 ("Today salvation has come to this house."). At the same time that he imitated the saying in v. 5b, he provided the hermeneutical key to it: Jesus' presence (v. 5b) is equivalent to the sudden emergence of salvation (v. 9a), a salvation that, beginning "today," gives Zacchaeus a reason to be, to believe, and to act charitably. This salvation is both

---

Hamm, "Luke 19:8 Once Again"; idem, "Zacchaeus Revisited," 248–52; Nolland, 3:906; Tannehill, "Zacchaeus."

68   White, "Vindication for Zacchaeus"; Mitchell, "Zacchaeus Revisited," 153–76; idem, "συκοφαντεῖν," 546–47; Fitzmyer, 2:1220–21.

69   Tannehill ("Zacchaeus," 203). Ahern ("Zacchaeus Incident," 350) notes that Zacchaeus at first is inert and stands his ground (v. 8a), before becoming actively engaged (v. 8b).

70   Note that in chap. 3 the verb is applied not to tax collectors, who are rarely mentioned before 3:12-13, but to soldiers in 3:14; see the commentary on 3:14 in vol. 1.

71   See Nestle, "Sykophantia," 271–72; Kerr, "Decision," 68–71.

72   This may allude to the restitution of four lambs for a stolen lamb (Exod 22:1; see 2 Sam 12:6). Josephus may refer to this rule in *Ant.* 16.1.1 §3. Numbers 5:6-7 lays down another general rule that is much

less demanding: one must make restitution for the stolen object in addition to 20 percent of the object's value. See Str-B 2:249–51; Fitzmyer, 2:1225; and esp. Dauvillier, "Le texte évangélique," 27–32.

73   See Kerr, "Decision"; Raber, "Furtum," 647–49.

74   The hospitality of Abraham is legendary; see *Gen. Rab.* 48.1–20; 54.4; 56.5; *1 Clem.* 10.7; Mitchell, "Zacchaeus Revisited," 164–75.

75   Bear in mind that in Greek Joshua and Jesus share the same name, Ἰησοῦς. The episode takes place at Jericho, where Rahab offers hospitality to Ἰησοῦς, to Joshua. James 2:20-26 mentions the examples of Abraham and Rahab side by side; see John Drury, *Tradition and Design in Luke's Gospel: A Study in Early Christian Historiography* (London: Darton, Longman & Todd, 1976) 73–74; Mitchell, "Zacchaeus Revisited," 164–65. Note the reservations of O'Hanlon, "Zacchaeus," 6–9.

eschatological and grounded in history, and its spiritual dimension is an integral part of its material component.[76]

It is not easy to interpret v. 9b, which, though it derived from tradition, was able to take on a new meaning at the level of its redaction by Luke. It would probably be misleading to understand descent from Abraham in the Pauline sense of being chosen through belonging to Christ (Gal 3:6-18; Rom 4:1-25). Luke had another conception of Israel's identity; in his eyes, the historical Jewish people remained Abraham's descendants. But this people had to show itself worthy of its status; if not, it would lose that privilege. What Jesus had to do, in the case of these "lost" sheep of Israel, was to find them, reestablish them, "save" them, and thus permit them to fulfill the obligations associated with their Jewish identity. That is what is going on here with Zacchaeus, who, both welcoming and welcomed, bore the fruit of repentance, that is, showed by what he did that he had repented. In this way, the Gospel writer confirmed what he had John the Baptist say: "Bear fruits worthy of repentance. And do not begin to say to yourselves, 'We have Abraham as our father'; for I tell you, God is able from these stones to raise up children to Abraham" (3:8). Luke seems to me to be theologically situated between the apostle Paul and James, the author of the epistle bearing that name.[77]

■ **10** Verse 10 picks up on a christological affirmation already encountered in the Third Gospel: "I am here to call not the righteous but sinners to repentance" (5:32).[78] If it could be said that the story about Zacchaeus represents the essence of the entire Gospel,[79] then that characterization can be applied even more aptly to the single v. 10. The vocabulary of "losing" and "finding again" is basic to the theological thought of Luke and dominates chap. 15, which is so central (see esp. vv. 24 and 32).[80] The function attributed here to the Son of Man[81] corresponds to the one that God, the shepherd of Israel, assumes by identifying with David, his servant in the prophecy in Ezekiel (see Ezek 34:15-16, 23-24).[82] It was perhaps not just coincidental that the title "Son of David" appeared in the pericope about the blind man who was healed (18:35-43), the section that immediately precedes the one about Zacchaeus.

History of Interpretation

It did not take long for the story about Zacchaeus to attract the attention of Christian artists.[83] Several sarcophaguses from the end of the fourth century present, among other episodes, the encounter between Christ and Zacchaeus, naturally without forgetting the tree. The same is true of a fragment from around the year 400, which is a leaf of a diptych preserved in Castello Sforzesco in Milan.

The iconographic success of the story during the Middle Ages may also be explained by the use of the pericope as a Gospel lection in the ceremony of consecration of every new church.[84] There are numerous representations of this story in Psalters and Evangeliaries, for instance, one belonging to Emperor Otto III, painted on the island of Reichenau, and lectionaries, such as the one that came from the Lake Constance convent and belonged to Emperor Henry II. Western fresco art turned to the story of Zacchaeus less frequently. We should note, however, the medieval fresco in the nave

76   See de Burgos Núñez, "Zaqueo," 170–71; Bovon, "Le salut dans les écrits de Luc. Essai," in idem, *L'œuvre*, 165–79.

77   On v. 9b and the expression "son of Abraham," see Mitchell ("Zacchaeus Revisited," 164–75), who thinks that the everyday works of Zacchaeus earn him the title of "son of Abraham"; the salvation of the tax collector is therefore a matter of ethical commitment. It is unclear, in this view, what role Jesus plays. I am closer to Dupont ("Le riche publicain Zachée," 269–73). Aletti (*Art de raconter*, 22) insists, unlike Mitchell, on Jesus as the agent of Zacchaeus's transformation.

78   See the commentary on 5:32 in vol. 1.

79   Loewe ("Towards an Interpretation," 321) writes,

"It does seem to condense much that is peculiarly characteristic of Lk."

80   See the commentary above on 15:24 and 32.

81   On this title in Luke, see the commentary above on 12:8-9.

82   See Ezek 34:15-16, 23-24; O'Hanlon, "Zacchaeus," 18–19; Aletti, *Art de raconter*, 27–29.

83   I rely principally on Kirschbaum (*Lexikon*, 4:559–60); see also Schiller, *Ikonographie*, 1:165; Louis Réau, *Iconographie de l'art chrétien* (3 vols.; Paris: Presses universitaires de France, 1955–59) 2.2:397, 400.

84   Ebel ("Das Evangelium der Kirchweihmesse," 111) insists on this point.

of Sant'Angelo in Formis, near Capua and the ceiling of the Church of Zillis in Grisons (in Switzerland). There we see Zacchaeus, with his arms outstretched, clinging to the branches of a tree and holding a sickle in one of his hands. That way the tax collector could prune the branches in order to have a better view. Byzantine illumination art readily added the banquet organized in Zacchaeus's house to the encounter near the tree; this was the case with the Psalter from the Pantokrator Monastery (on Mount Athos).

Ambrose, the bishop of Milan (*Exp. Luc.* 8.80–90), was intrigued by Zacchaeus, whom he compared to the blind man in the preceding pericope.[85] He took him, like the blind man, to be a Gentile, but in this case one "born noble, but of meager merit." By climbing a tree, he put right "the errors of his past life" and, by virtue of his faith, outstripped his previous useless actions. "Nobody can see Jesus while standing on the ground," he said. And "in this way he was host to Jesus in his interior dwelling place." Whereas Zacchaeus was rich, the blind man was poor. Ambrose wanted to set at ease the rich people of his time, who were liable to be "upset and offended" by certain stories in the Gospels. We may recall the lesson he drew from chap. 18 of Luke: "Let them learn that there is nothing wrong with being rich, only with not knowing how to use one's riches."

Ambrose also gave free rein to the associations that the metaphor of the tree inspired. In antiquity, the sycamore tree was considered to be a wild fig tree that did not bear fruit and was therefore barren and useless. This gave rise to the idea that Zacchaeus trampled on what he unfortunately called the "uselessness of the Jews." Since the root of the tree was holy (Rom 11:16) but its branches were useless (see Rom 11:17; John 15:2), Zacchaeus was, as it were, grafted onto the good olive tree (Rom 11:17). He became a healthy tree bearing good fruit (Matt 7:17; cf. Matt 7:18 par. Luke 6:43). Nathanael, under the tree (John 1:48), looked for Christ under the law; Zacchaeus, up in the tree, "higher than the Law, gave up his possessions and followed the Lord."

In the Middle Ages, Albert the Great insistently portrayed the extent of Zacchaeus's sins. Before Jesus came, the tax collector's house resembled an inferno. Zacchaeus's short stature was a symbolic indication of his lack of stature in matters of faith and courage. But by climbing the tree, which recalls the cross, he practiced the imitation of Christ and became an example. In addition, by coming down again from the tree, he was humbly made aware of his earthly nature. When Christ entered that home of vice, he who called Zacchaeus to life, as he had done for Lazarus, drove the Evil One out of it. Albert also stressed grace and actions. Zacchaeus became[86] a son of Abraham thanks to what Christ did and to the ethical steps he himself took. Finally, Albert elaborated on the two meanings of the word "house," the house used for secular life and the one consecrated to God, the church building, of which he gave a long spiritual description, larded with biblical quotations (*Enarr. in Luc.* 19.1–10).

The humanist Erasmus of Rotterdam, unlike Albert the Great, was content to underline Zacchaeus's virtues, which he contrasted with the vices of the Pharisee of the parable (Luke 18:9-14) from a viewpoint that was distinctly hostile to Judaism.[87] Zacchaeus's righteousness was completely interior. Carried forward by his fervent desire for righteousness, the head tax collector wanted with all his heart to see Jesus. Erasmus, who portrayed him as a Christian before there was such a category by that name, was of the opinion that Zacchaeus wanted to verify *de visu* the incarnate identity of the Son of God. With no fear of allegorizing, he explained Zacchaeus's shortness as indicating humility, and the sycamore tree as a fig tree that would have become barren had it not been for Zacchaeus's faith and the spiritual fruit of his love (this is the way Erasmus understood Zacchaeus's offer to pay back half, and four times as much, mentioned in v. 8). Although Zacchaeus was condemned as a sinner by the crowd of Jews, explained Erasmus, he was picked out by Jesus, who, looking on what was interior to Zacchaeus, discovered in him an acute sense of righteousness. If

---

85   The quotations are from §§81, 84, 85, and 90 successively.

86   The majority of Vulgate manuscripts render καθότι . . . ἐστίν (v. 9) as a subjunctive, "eo quod . . . sit," which encouraged Western exegetes to confer the "sonship" of Abraham on Zacchaeus not by birth but by dint of a faith or obedience that mirrored the faith of Abraham; see Bede, *In Luc.* 5.1597–612.

87   Erasmus, *Paraphrasis*, 426–30.

Zacchaeus ended up being justified, and if he became a son of Abraham, it was because of his faith and his piety. While Albert the Great was close to the Pauline position, Erasmus came near to the Epistle of James.

With Luther, we arrive not at a compromise but at a paradox.[88] For him, Zacchaeus was at the same time a sinner and righteous. He is the paradigm of the soul in search of God. The ambivalence of the biblical text, wavering between a Zacchaeus who was virtuous and one who was guilty, gave Luther the chance to meditate on the human heart, whose will and truth are so hidden that the heart itself is unaware of them. Now all that counts is the state of this heart. The finest actions do not count, in the Lord's eyes, if one's heart is not in them. In Zacchaeus's case, then, there is a transitory paradox; as long as he had not encountered Christ, the chief tax collector both wished for and did not wish for his Lord's arrival. "The soul does not require what it requires, and what it does not require, it does require, since it does not know what it requires." Luther arrived at this portrait of Jesus through the use of contrasts. He constantly compared the tax collector with those who pretended to want to welcome the Lord, like the crowd in v. 7, but did not in fact want to come to the fore and thus be recognized.[89]

Conclusion

The story of Zacchaeus fulfills two functions: in its beginning, it recounts a decisive encounter; in its end, a conversation pertaining to that encounter. The narrative proclamation of salvation is followed by a defense of redemption. The event is followed by its explanation. Early Christianity was not content simply to proclaim the good news. It also defended it against attacks.

Behind the good news of redemption I discern some discussions and some tensions. Who is worthy to be saved? What ethical attitude should a new convert adopt? What relation should the new community maintain with Israel? What place should be reserved for the rich and the poor in the church? Does not Jesus Christ's solicitous intervention run the risk of provoking passivity on the part of its beneficiaries? The debates that these questions provoked affected the transmission of this story and its final wording in writing. The episode developed and was transformed; in the process the emphasis shifted. In its simple structure, it nonetheless remained astonishingly stable, and several concrete details perdured through all these reinterpretations.

---

88   Luther, *Predigt vom* 10/13/1516, WA 1:94–98; Mül-
       haupt, *Luthers Evangelien-Auslegung*, 335–40.
89   Ebel ("Das Evangelium der Kirchweihmesse")
       deliberately interprets the story of Zacchaeus from
       the tradition and refers to numerous ecclesiastical

authors from antiquity and from the Middle Ages;
on Zacchaeus, beloved by Pelagians and analyzed by
Augustine, see Schwank, "Frömmigkeit," 65.

The Parable of the Minas
(19:11-27)
Bibliography 19:11-27

Aletti, Jean-Noel, "Parabole des mines et/ou parabole du roi: Lc 19,11-28. Remarques sur l'écriture parabolique de Luc," in Delorme, *Paraboles évangéliques*, 309–32.

Berger, Klaus, "Meditation zu Mt 25,14-30 und Lk 19,11-27," *EvErz* 44 (1992) 196–98.

Blomberg, Craig, *Interpreting the Parables* (Downers Grove, Ill.: InterVarsity Press, 1990) 217–21.

Busse, Ulrich, "Dechiffrierung eines lukanischen Schlüsseltextes (Lk 19,11-27)," in R. Hoppe and U. Busse, eds., *Von Jesus zum Christus: christologische Studien: Festgabe für Paul Hoffmann zum 65. Geburtstag* (Berlin/New York: de Gruyter, 1998) 423–41.

Buzy, *Paraboles*, 528–56.

Carlston, *Triple Tradition*, 85, 200, 210.

Dauvillier, Jean, "La parabole des mines ou des talents et le §99 du Code de Hammurabi," in *Mélanges dédiés à M. le professeur Joseph Magnol, doyen honoraire de la Faculté de droit de Toulouse* (Paris: Recueil Sirey, 1948) 153–65.

Delebecque, 119–21.

Delobel, "Sayings," 453, 457.

Derrett, J. Duncan M., "A Horrid Passage in Luke Explained (Lk 19,27)," *ExpT* 97 (1985) 136–38.

Idem, "Law in the New Testament: The Parable of the Talents and Two Logia," *ZNW* 56 (1965) 184–95.

Didier, Marcel, "La parabole des talents et des mines," in I. de La Potterie, ed., *De Jésus aux Évangiles: Tradition et rédaction dans les Évangiles synoptiques* (BETL 25; Gembloux: J. Duculot, 1967) 248–71.

Dodd, *Parables*, 108–14.

Donahue, *Gospel in Parable*, 105–9.

Dupont, Jacques, "La parabole des talents (Mt 25,14-30) ou des mines (Lc 19,12-27)," *RThPh* (3d series) 19 (1969) 376–91; reprinted in idem, *Études*, 2:744–60.

Enslin, Morton S., "Luke and Matthew: Compilers or Authors?" *ANRW* 2.25.3 (1985) 2385–87.

Foerster, Werner, "Das Gleichnis von den anvertrauten Pfunden," in idem, ed., *Verbum Dei manet in aeternum: Eine Festschrift für Otto Schmitz zu seinem siebzigsten Geburtstag am 16. Juni 1953* (Witten: Luther-Verlag, 1953) 37–56.

Fusco, Vittorio, "'Point of View' and 'Implicit Reader' in Two Eschatological Texts: Lk 19,11-28; Acts 1,6-8," in van Segbroeck, *Four Gospels*, 2:1677–96.

Guy, Laurie, "The Interplay of the Present and Future in the Kingdom of God (Luke 19:11-44)," *TynBul* 48 (1997) 119–37.

Harnisch, *Gleichniserzählungen Jesu*, 25, 38–39, 69 n. 63, 80.

Henry, J. M., "The Parables of the Pounds: A Study in Parable Hermeneutics" (Ph.D. diss., Southwestern Baptist Theological Seminary, 1983).

Jeremias, *Parables*, 58–63.

Johnson, Luke Timothy, "The Lukan Kingship Parable (Lk 19,11-27)," *NovT* 24 (1982) 139–59.

Jouanique, Pierre, "Rationem reddere (Lc 16,1-19; 19,11-27)," *BAGB* 4/2 (1961) 228–33.

Joüon, Paul, "La parabole des mines (Luc 19,13-27) et la parabole des talents (Matthieu 25, 14-30)," *RSR* 29 (1939) 489–94.

Jülicher, *Gleichnisreden*, 2:472–95.

Junod, Éric, "Une interprétation originale de Genèse 1, 28 indûment attribuée à Origène (Pap. Bibl. Univ. Giss. inv. 30)," *RHPhR* 71 (1991) 11–31.

Kahlefeld, *Paraboles*, 132–55.

Kamlah, Ehrhard, "Kritik und Interpretation der Parabel der anvertrauten Geldern, Mt 25,14ff, Lk 19,11ff," *KD* 14 (1968) 28–38.

La Potterie, Ignace de, "La parabole du prétendant à la royauté (Lc 19,11-28)," in Refoulé, *À cause*, 613–41.

Manns, Frederic, "La parabole des talents: Wirkungsgeschichte et racines juives," *RSR* 65 (1991) 343–62.

McGaughy, Lane C., "The Fear of Yahweh and the Mission of Judaism: A Postexilic Maxim and Its Early Christian Expansion in the Parable of the Talents," *JBL* 94 (1975) 235–45.

Meurer, *Gleichnisse Jesu*, 190, 579, 635.

Meynet, Roland, *Avez-vous lu saint Luc? Guide pour une rencontre* (LiBi 88; Paris: Cerf, 1990) 216–24.

Idem, *Saint Luc*, 1:181–83; 2:179–90.

Nestle, Eberhard, "Recension de la Patrologia Syriaca, I," *ThLZ* 22 (1895) 565.

Ollivier, Marie-Joseph, "Étude sur la physionomie intellectuelle de N.S.J.C.: la parabole des mines (Luc 19,11-27)," *RB* 1 (1892) 39–52.

Orbe, *San Ireneo*, 2:3–84.

Panier, Louis, "La parabole des mines: Lecture sémiotique. Lc 19, 11-27," in Delorme, *Paraboles évangéliques*, 333–47.

Pirot, *Paraboles*, 361–69.

Polag, *Christologie*, 165–67.

Puig i Tàrrech, Armand, "La parabole des talents (Mt 25,14-30) ou des mines (Lc 19,11-28)," in Refoulé, *À cause*, 165–93.

Resenhöfft, Wilhelm, "Jesu Gleichnis von den Talenten, ergänzt durch die Lukas-Fassung," *NTS* 26 (1980) 318–31.

Sanders, Jack T., "The Parable of the Pounds and Lucan Anti-Semitism," *TS* 42 (1981) 660–68.

Schulz, *Q*, 288–98.

Stenger, Werner, "Überlegungen zur Transformation biblischer Texte am Beispiel des Gleichnisses von den Talenten (Mt 25,14-30; Lk 19,11-12)," in idem, *Strukturale Beobachtungen zum Neuen Testament* (NTTS 12; Leiden/New York: Brill, 1990) 154–80.

Thiessen, Henry Clarence, "The Parable of the Nobleman and the Earthly Kingdom, Luke 19,11-27," *BSac* 91 (1934) 180–90.

Tiede, *Prophecy*, 79, 148.

Via, *Parables*, 113–22.

Weder, *Gleichnisse*, 193–210.

Weinert, Francis D., "The Parable of the Throne Claimant (Luke 19,12.14-15a.27) Reconsidered," *CBQ* 39 (1977) 505–14.

Weiser, *Knechtsgleichnisse*, 226–72.

Zerwick, Max, "Die Parabel vom Thronanwärter," *Bib* 40 (1959) 654–74.

11/ As they were listening to this, he went on to tell a parable[a], because he was near Jerusalem, and because they believed that the kingdom of God was to appear immediately. **12/** So he said, "There once was a nobleman who went off to a distant country to get royal power for himself and then return. **13/** Having summoned ten of his servants, he gave them ten minas and said to them, 'Do business with these until I come back.'

14/ "But the citizens of his country hated him and sent a delegation after him, saying, 'We do not want this man to rule over us.' **15/** Now it happened that when he returned, having received royal power, he ordered these servants, to whom he had given the money, to be summoned so that he might find out what they had gained by trading during this time.

16/ "The first came forward, saying, 'Lord, your mina has earned ten minas.' **17/** He said to him, 'Well done, good servant! Because you have been trustworthy in a very small thing, take charge[b] of ten cities.' **18/** Then the second came, saying, 'Lord, your mina has earned[c] five mina.' **19/** He said to that one, 'And you, take charge[b] of five cities.' **20/** The next one came, saying, 'Lord, here is your mina that I have kept wrapped up in a piece of cloth, **21/** for I was afraid of you, because you are a harsh man; you take away what you did not deposit, and reap what you did not sow.' **22/** He said to him, 'I will judge you by your own words, you wicked servant! You knew that I was a harsh man, taking away what I did not deposit and reaping what I did not sow. **23/** Why did you not put my money into the bank? Then when I returned, I could have had myself reimbursed[d] with interest.' **24/** And he said to the bystanders, 'Take the mina from him and give it to the one who has ten minas.' **25/** And they[e] said to him, 'Lord, he has ten minas!' **26/** 'I tell you, to all those who have, it will be given; but from those who have nothing, even what they have will be taken away from them. **27/** But as for these enemies of mine who did not want me to be king over them—bring them here and slaughter them in my presence.' "

a   Literally: "Adding, he told a parable." Another possible translation would be: "Insisting, he told a parable."

b   In v. 17, literally, "be, having authority"; in v. 19, literally, "become it."

c   Literally: "made" (from the verb ποιέω).

d   Literally: "I could have done it" (from the verb πράσσω, without the verb "pay back")

e   It is not certain that these persons were the bystanders of v. 24.

The parabolic account of the minas, which constitutes the last pericope of the travel narrative, looks like a commentary intended to correct a previous rhetorical situation (v. 11). The Lukan Jesus tells a story with multiple aspects that is intended to lead his listeners' minds in a certain direction. The story has to do with a prince who goes away and comes back after having been crowned; with servants, some of whom are hardworking, but one of whom does nothing; and with opponents of his regime who end up on the losing side. The accounting that the servants owe to their master when he returns constituted the principal focus of the story. A series of interpersonal relationships plays out in the course of this professional activity. These imaginary relationships, which are part of the parabolic narration, serve as a hermeneutical key to the real situation, which is itself also part of the larger narration of the Gospel as a whole.[1] This specific situation, stamped by the relationship that Jesus maintained with his listeners and his disciples is, in turn, as the Gospel writer himself admits (v. 11), the expression of a much greater reality, namely, the manifestation of the kingdom of God and its human implications in a space and a time that remained to be determined.

Analysis

Synchronic Analysis

The travel narrative, which comes to an end at this point, as well as Jesus' activity in the temple and in the city of Jerusalem, constitute the literary context of the pericope. The parabolic narrative is linked to the preceding episode concerning Zacchaeus (19:1-10) in several ways: first, by the affirmation that the parable is meant to deal with a tendentious interpretation of what Jesus had said previously (v. 11); next, by the convergence of themes that link the two pericopes to each other: the time of salvation (19:9 and 11), the hero's trip (19:1 and 11) and the attitude of his partners (19:8, 15, 24). Moreover, the

parable foreshadows what comes next in the story: the theme of royalty is to stand out from the episode of the so-called Palm Sunday on (19:38).[2] The focusing of the story on Jerusalem and the theological function that must be given to the capital city tie the parable not only to what precedes (travel to the capital) but also to what follows (the arrival in Jerusalem and the events that take place there).[3]

If we turn our attention to the position of the story, it will be noted that the parabolic story itself (vv. 12-27) is situated between an allusion to the approach to Jerusalem (v. 11) and a new mention of that travel up to the capital (v. 28). Even though v. 11 is intrinsically linked to the parabolic story, v. 28 bids it farewell before turning its back on it (vv. 29ff.). Verses 11 and 28 constitute less an inclusion than a way of emphasizing the march forward.

If readers pay even closer attention to the story, they will discover a second setting, one that is interior. The narration opens on the note of the hope of an enthronement that is thwarted by some people (vv. 12 and 14-15a) and comes to a close with the elimination of these enemies of the prince who has become king (v. 27). More explicitly than in the parabolic story, this setting echoes the motif of God's reign and of his manifestation, mentioned in the opening part of the section in v. 11.[4]

A double redundancy stands out at the end of the story. The punishment the master metes out (taking the mina out of the hands of the guilty person and giving it to the person who is most deserving) provokes a reaction on the part of the spectators, which is reminiscent of the speeches by the chorus in tragedies in antiquity (v. 25).[5] That indication of angry surprise elicits in turn a reply by the master in the form of a shocking proverbial saying: to those who have, it will be given; but from those who have nothing, it will be taken away.

Although the dialogue involves three servants, the parabolic story itself is made up of two parts,[6] which are,

---

1   Aletti, "Mines," 325: "*La parabole permet ainsi au récit primaire de s'articuler*" (emphasis original).

2   See 23:2-3, 38-39. The term $\beta\alpha\sigma\iota\lambda\epsilon\acute{\iota}\alpha$ ("kingdom," "kingship") appears again in 22:29 and 23:42; Johnson, "Kingship," 153–56.

3   On the context of the parabolic story, see Johnson, "Kingship," 153–58; Aletti, "Mines," 323–26; Busse, "Dechiffrierung," 423–24.

4   The theme of kingship reappears in vv. 12 and 14.

5   See Bock, 2:1541. It is unclear, in my opinion, whether those who are surprised in v. 25 are the same people who receive the order to take away the mina from the hands of the third servant in v. 24.

6   Busse, "Dechiffrierung," 429. Stenger ("Überlegungen," 161), on the other hand, thinks that the story is made up of three successive waves.

moreover, of different length. The first part has to do with the responsibility entrusted to the servants (who number ten at the outset, v. 13). The second part deals with the checking up on what work has been done (which is done with only three servants, vv. 15-24). The second part can be subdivided into three parts corresponding to the number of servants who were questioned, but in fact it boils down to two opposing parts:[7] the two valiant ones (vv. 16-17 and 18-19) tower victoriously over the unfortunate last one, whose explanations, rebuked by his master, take up room in the story (vv. 20-24). It should be noted that the decisive step of the exploitation of the money is not recounted. The text is silent on the intermediate time between the giving of the assignment and the call for the rendering of the accounts.[8] This provides the following outline:

Introduction (v. 11)
    Setting re the enthronement (vv. 12 and 14-15a)
        First part: giving of the assignment to the servants (v. 13)
        Second part: rendering of the accounts (vv. 15b-26)
            (a) the faithful servants (vv. 15b-19)
                – the first servant (vv. 16-17)
                – the second servant (vv. 18-19)
            (b) the bad servant (vv. 20-24)
                – he justifies himself (vv. 20-21)
                – he is condemned (vv. 22-24)
    Redundancy
        – the public's reaction (v. 25)
        – the master's explanation (v. 26)
    Setting re those opposed to the enthronement (v. 27)
Transition (v. 28)[9]

Diachronic Analysis

The parable of the minas circulated in different forms attested by the Gospel of Luke, the Gospel of Matthew (Matt 25:14-30), the *Gospel of the Nazarenes* or the *Gospel of the Hebrews*, and one of the *Pseudo-Clementine Homilies*. Finally, the Gospel of Mark transmits a parable of the doorkeeper, focused on vigilance, whose beginning is strikingly reminiscent of the first part of the parable we have been studying here: "It is like a man going on a journey, when he leaves home and puts his slaves in charge, each with his work, and commands the doorkeeper to be on the watch" (Mark 13:34 *NRSV*).[10]

The text of the *Pseudo-Clementines* refers only to the second part of the parabolic story in a version that is close to Matthew's. It provides a narrative exegesis and constitutes a transformation of the story that is later than the redaction of the Synoptic Gospels but earlier than the final settling of the canon of the New Testament. Here is a translation of it: "But should one of those present who is able to restrain the ignorance of his fellow-citizens withdraw from this duty simply out of a care for his own personal peace, then he must be prepared to hear the words: *Thou wicked, slothful servant, you ought to have deposited my money with the bankers, that on my return I might have had my gain; cast out the worthless servant into the uttermost darkness.* And that rightly. For it is your duty—he would say therewith—to bring my words as money to the bankers and to regard them as values that you possess. The community of believers must be obedient to one particular person that their unity may be preserved. . . ." (*Ps.-Clem. Hom.* 3.61).[11]

In a passage not distinguished by its clarity, Bishop Eusebius of Caesarea preserved the memory of a passage from "the Gospel that has come down to us in the Hebrew script" [that is, the *Gospel of the Nazarenes* or the *Gospel of the Hebrews*].[12] After having himself understood the "talents" as gifts of the Holy Spirit and the rendering of the account as the last judgment, the bishop affirms that this Gospel interprets "the menace being addressed not to the one who had hidden the talent, but to the one who lived luxuriously. For he (the lord) had three servants: the one squandered his master's fortune on prostitutes and dancing girls, another increased it by his work, the third hid his 'talent.' Next the one is welcomed favorably, the second reprimanded, and the third thrown in prison. I wonder—it is Eusebius talking—if

---

7   See Dupont, "Mines," 386.

8   See Weder, *Gleichnisse*, 203.

9   Bock (2:1529–30), de La Potterie ("La parabole," 630), Aletti ("Mines," 311), and Stenger ("Überlegungen," 161) offer schematic presentations.

10   See Fitzmyer, 2:1228. Faced with this parallel, exegetes are confused.

11   Hennecke-Schneemelcher, 2.517; see Busse, "Dechiffrierung," 426–27 n. 15.

12   *Theophania*, in Hennecke-Schneemelcher, *NT Apocrypha*, 1:139.

in Matthew, after the delivery of the speech against the servant who had not worked, the following threat was not directed to the first servant, who had eaten and drunk with the drunkards, rather than to that idle servant."[13] It is not easy to understand Eusebius's point of view or to grasp what he attributes to the Judeo-Christian Gospel. It is clear, however, that this apocryphal text presents a gradual transition from vice to virtue by means of the middle way. The good person, who is recompensed, is in second position; the evil person who—and this is an element found only in this version of the parable—squanders his master's goods, is in the most prominent position with respect to the action and in the last position at the end, at the moment of judgment. The neutral, or indifferent, man, who hid his talent, first occupies the last place, then second place. He receives a light punishment, since his master was satisfied with simply reprimanding him. As Adolf Jülicher understood so well,[14] and as is attested also by the final confused sentence in Eusebius, the evil servant in the apocryphal story comes from another, previous parable, the one about two servants, Matt 24:45-51, and is not unacquainted with the parable of the prodigal son.[15] The presence of three servants in the tradition was put to use in constructing this scale of values and the punishment that tradition had the coward endure was deemed to be excessive. The formulation of the Jewish Christian Gospel seems to have been dictated by the moralizing tendency of an author who, before the Synoptic Gospels were canonized, felt that he had the right to transform what had been given in the tradition. This "given" seems to be closer to Matthew than to Luke. As for the Jewish Christian text itself, it must have corresponded to a stage of the gospel tradition subsequent to that of our canonical Gospels.[16]

So the versions we find in Luke and Matthew remain the oldest witnesses we have to a parabolic story absent not only from Mark but also from *Thomas*.[17] The relationships between these two versions have been the subject of countless studies.[18] They can be explained in different ways. The hypothesis of Q is the most widely accepted one, namely, that Luke and Matthew each reworked this source with imagination and determination.[19] In that case, we must decide whether it was Matthew who abridged Q or Luke who lengthened it (a second source relative to the pretender to the throne has often been postulated for Luke[20]). There are other hypotheses possible: Matthew is following Q and Luke, L (matter peculiar to Luke);[21] Matthew quotes "M" (matter peculiar to Matthew) and Luke, L;[22] Matthew and Luke are dependent on Q, but each one of them had at his disposal supplementary information.[23] Without factoring in Q, some have concluded that Luke revised Matthew.[24] Still others say quite simply that the two parables are independent[25] of each other.[26]

If we want to choose the most plausible hypothesis, we must compare the two Synoptic versions, determine

---

13 Eusebius of Caesarea, *De theophania* 4.2 (*PG* 24:686–87); see also Hennecke-Schneemelcher, 1:47–48; Bovon and Geoltrain, *Écrits apocryphes*, 1:443–44; Enslin, "Luke and Matthew," 2386 n. 88 (Greek text); Didier, "La parabole," 257.

14 Jülicher, *Gleichnisreden*, 2:484.

15 The formulation is reminiscent of the reprehensible actions of the prodigal son (Luke 15:13 and 30).

16 Several exegetes emphasize the homiletical and moralizing character of this reading, for instance, Jeremias, *Parables*, 62–63; Weder, *Gleichnisse*, 209–10; Didier, "La parabole," 249.

17 The parable is known in the middle of the second century C.E. In addition to the two noncanonical texts mentioned above, see Justin *Dial.* 125.1–2.

18 Most commentaries and books devoted to the parables tackle the question. Among other works, see esp. Didier, "La parabole"; Dupont, "Mines"; Weiser, *Knechtsgleichnisse*, 226–58; Puig i Tàrrech, "Talents," 166–74; Busse, "Dechiffrierung," 426–29.

19 For example, Jülicher, *Gleichnisreden*, 2:485; Weder, *Gleichnisse*, 193; Fitzmyer, 2:1230.

20 For example, Zerwick, "Parabel," 654–74.

21 Kahlefeld (*Parables*, 132–55, esp. 139) and Bock (2:1528–29) seem to hold this opinion.

22 Thus Weiser (*Knechtsgleichnisse*, 226–59, esp. 255–56), whose demonstration is impressive; Fitzmyer (2:1230) provides a list of other exegetes who share this opinion.

23 Thus Puig i Tàrrech, "Talents," 172–74.

24 See Enslin, "Luke and Matthew," 2385–87.

25 On the adherents of this ancient opinion, see Fitzmyer, 2:1230.

26 Several authors present these diverse hypotheses schematically, particularly Didier, "La parabole," 248–51; Dupont, "Mines," 377–78; Fitzmyer, 2:1230–31; Bock, 2:1527–29; Wiefel, 329.

what redactional modifications have been made, imagine what was the history of the tradition, and reconstruct the original parable.

Among the minor differences is the fact that Matthew was interested in just the three servants (Matt 25:14-15), while Luke mentions ten of them (v. 13). Since further on Luke speaks of the fate of only three of them, it follows that the original story spoke of only three servants.

Luke uses the mina as the currency; it was equivalent to the salary for one hundred days of work.[27] In Matthew we have the "talent," which was worth much more, since it has been estimated that it was equivalent to several (between six and ten) thousand days of work. Since, further on, both Gospels point out how modest the sum was (Matt 25:21 and Luke 19:17), it is reasonable to conclude that in the original version, the parabolic story had the mina, rather than the talent.

The following question is a more delicate one: in the original version of the story did each servant receive the same amount, or a different one? It will be recalled that on three occasions, Luke speaks of a mina; Matthew, of five talents, two talents, and one talent.[28] Since Luke wished to establish the fact that in the race to the Christian life, all Christians have an equal chance at the starting point, he has perhaps brought the parable into line with that conviction. The original parable must then have provided a range of initial arrangements: five minas, two minas, and one mina.

It is the opposite with respect to the returns. In Matthew, each good servant doubles the initial sum thanks to his work (Matt 25:16-17); in Luke, the first one earns ten times the original sum (v. 16) and the second one five times as much (v. 18). The excessive side of speculation in Luke would once again favor our giving priority to Matthew.[29] In the original story the good servants succeeded in doubling the capital they received in the beginning.

The nature of the return also varies from one Gospel to another. Here again it is Matthew who must have kept the memory of the original parabolic story that stayed within the context of the world of business (Matt 25:21 and 23). Influenced by the political context in which he places his story, Luke transformed the reward into authority over cities (vv. 17 and 19).[30] The original story, which conceived of larger sums at the end than at the beginning, spoke of a larger sphere of responsibility given to the two good servants.

There is a logic specific to each of the stories. A mina could easily be hidden in a piece of cloth (v. 20), while a talent, which represents twenty-six kilograms (fifty-seven pounds) of metal, would more easily be hidden in the ground (Matt 25:25). If the mina belongs to the earliest form of the story, the same could be said of the piece of cloth.[31]

In vv. 21 and 22, the wording of Luke is somewhat different from that in the parallel in Matt 25:24 and 26. When Luke speaks about "taking away" and "depositing," he must be thinking of money, while Matthew, with his "gathering" and "scattering," may have been alluding to either grain, human beings, or money.

Among the most important differences is the fact that Luke provides an initial explanation (v. 11) that is lacking in Matthew. Since the parabolic story does not need these links with the city of Jerusalem and the reference to the imminent appearance of the reign of God in order to fulfill its function, this introduction must be redactional. The same is true of the link that Matthew establishes between this parabolic story and the preceding parable, the one about the bridesmaids (Matt 25:14: "for" [γάρ]).

The beginning of the Lukan story corresponds to its introduction. Here the master of the Matthean parable has become a nobleman who has gone off to a distant country, where he counts on receiving the title of king. The Gospel writer, or the author of the source he uses, transforms the story into a transparent allegory of

---

27 On the respective values of the mina and the talent, see Fitzmyer, 2:1235.

28 Matthew also has his reasons for keeping the gradations. He specifies that the distribution is appropriated to each "according to his own ability" (Matt 25:15).

29 We will see that Luke pays attention to the success of goods.

30 He could have felt authorized, or even encouraged, to do it because of the vague wording of his source. If Matthew reflects that source adequately, it simply invokes a greater responsibility: "I will put you in charge of many things" (Matt 25:21, 23).

31 One might like to speak of a handkerchief, but it seems that, until modern times, one did not blow one's nose into a piece of fabric!

Jesus' fate. So it is not surprising to find a mention of the prince's opponents, a group foreign to the original parable. These opponents are obviously Jewish authorities whom the Gospel writer reproaches for having been active against Jesus. A detailed exegesis of the passage will show that Luke, or his predecessor, did not use a second parable[32] or a historical memory (such as Archelaus's or Herod's) in his construction of this allegory. What he did use was rather a sociopolitical reality of that time (the necessity for local monarchs to obtain confirmation of their authority from the central power in Rome).[33]

This allegorizing of the parable produced a reversal in Luke. The original parable emphasized the third man's failure; in Luke's version what is spoken of is the success of the first two men.[34] The third man was originally lazy (Matt 25:26); in Luke, he becomes a disobedient person. The rendering of the accounts begins to look like the final judgment. That means that there are two dangers whose effects add up: forgetting the length of time that the Master is absent[35] and neglecting one's Christian responsibility. Addressed by Jesus to a Jewish audience, the parabolic story in Luke is in our day aimed at Christian readers. Jesus instructs them as much as he challenges them. The characteristic words: "Do business with these until I come back" (v. 13b) are peculiar to Luke.[36]

To tell the truth, the Matthean redaction, although less active, has also left its specific mark on the parable. Here again, at this level, the text is aimed at a Christian audience. It has also taken on the look of an apocalyptic scene. The Matthean addition: "enter into the joy of your Master" (Matt 25:21 and 23) suggests a messianic banquet, just as the punishment of the third servant (Matt 25:30) corresponds to a final damnation. In Matthew, in the context of the parable of the bridesmaids (Matt 25:1-13), what is involved is a final call for vigilance that

is dependent on a Jewish and Jewish Christian ethical definition of faith. We should note the adjectives that Matthew applies to describe the servants: on the one hand "good and trustworthy" (Matt 25:21 and 23); on the other, "wicked and lazy" (Matt 25:26) and "worthless" (Matt 25:30). For Matthew, laziness consists in listening to the Word of God without putting it into practice.[37]

The vocabulary and the style of the passages found only in Luke often correspond to those of L: "there once was a man" (v. 12), "to a distant country" (v. 12), "the citizens of his country" (v. 14), "sent a delegation" (v. 14), "when he returned" (v. 15), "he ordered . . . to be summoned" (v. 15), and "because you have been trustworthy in a very small thing" (v. 17).[38] Moreover, there is considerable difference between the story in Luke and the one in Matthew. Finally, Luke, who has picked up the thread of L with the story of Zacchaeus, is not about to let go of it so quickly. For all these reasons, I share the hypothesis of these elements coming from L. In my way of thinking, the parabolic story belonged both to L and Q, in distinct but similar forms. Matthew has taken over Q and adapted it; Luke has recopied and reinterpreted L.[39] The Synoptic comparison we have just carried out enables us to reconstruct a parabolic story that goes back behind both Q and L to an oral tradition anxious to preserve and adapt one of Jesus' valuable lessons.

It is to this effort of adaptation and interpretation that we should attribute a remark that did not belong to the original story. Since it is found in both Matthew and Luke, it must have already been part of the common content behind their respective sources: "to all those who have, it will be given; but from those who have nothing, even what they have will be taken away from them" (Luke 19:26 and Matt 25:29). We are dealing here with one of Jesus' floating sayings that we read elsewhere as well and

---

32   Commentators love to discuss parables about pretenders to the throne; thus Zerwick, "Parabel"; Weinert, "Throne Claimant," 505–14.

33   See below.

34   See Dupont ("Mines," 383), who refers to another passage peculiar to Luke, 12:47-48.

35   The same insistence on delay appears in the Lukan rereading of Mark 13:6, which occurs in Luke 21:8: "for many will come in my name and say, 'I am he!' and, 'The time is near!'", where Mark 13:6 simply reads, "Many will come in my name and say, 'I am he!'"

36   The words "until I come back" recall the liturgy of the Lord's Supper in 1 Cor 11:26, "until he comes."

37   Dupont ("Mines," 379–82) and Luz (*Matthew*, 3:246–62) offer a helpful analysis of Matthean redaction.

38   See 10:30; 15:13, 15; 10:35; 16:2, 10; see Weiser (*Knechtsgleichnisse*, 255–56), who adds other arguments in favor of L.

39   I realize that I have chosen an unusual solution.

that has already been quoted by Luke (see Luke 8:18 par. Mark 4:25 par. Matt 13:12).[40] Following a practice of the oldest Christian interpretation, the bearers of the oral tradition sought to explain the Master by quoting the Master. They were concerned to add a particular meaning to the parabolic story by tacking on this saying.[41]

We still have to say something about the literary genre of this unit.[42] If we distinguish between the parable and the parabolic story,[43] we can classify this text as a parabolic story (it narrates a particular story). By avoiding recounting how the appreciation of the investment or, on the contrary, the lack of it, took place, the narrator emphasizes the relationship between the beginning, the mission that was assigned, and the end, namely, the observed results.

The initial story was not content to illustrate a religious or ethical reality. It involved listeners in the process, encouraging them to make decisions and to act. By virtue of its metaphorical component, it also demonstrated a mystery, one aspect of the kingdom of God.[44]

By dint of being recounted, the meaning of the parabolic story deepened and was modified. These additions of meaning progressively lent an allegorical coloration to it.[45] This process developed all the way from the stage of the oral tradition on through to L and to Q, then further from these sources to the Gospel itself. By placing the story where it is, and by providing it with an explanatory introduction, Luke was keen to emphasize this allegorization. In Luke the parable is centered on Jesus Christ, his life and his role, both the future eschatology of the kingdom of God and the present life of the Christian community.[46]

Commentary

■ **11** The time and place are important. In Jewish hope, Jerusalem, as a holy city, was the place where the Messiah was supposed to arrive (on the Mount of Olives) and that was supposed to serve as the theater for the resurrection of the dead (in the valley of Jehoshaphat).[47] The mes-

---

40 See below.

41 See Denis Buzy, "Les sentences finales des paraboles évangéliques," *RB* 40 (1931) 321–44; Dupont, "Mines," 384–85.

42 See Weder, *Gleichnisse*, 195 (originally, a parable of the kingdom of God); Fitzmyer, 2:1232 (a parable to which a traditional saying at the level of Q, v. 26, and some allegorical touches at the redactional level, vv. 12, 14, 15a, and 27, as well as a narrative addition, v. 25, have been added); see Bock, 2:1528–29.

43 On this classic distinction between "Gleichnis" (parable) and "Parabel" (parabolic story), see Jülicher, *Gleichnisreden*, 1:80–81, 92–93, and Linnemann, *Parables*, 3–4.

44 See Didier, "La parabole," 250; see also the commentary on 8:4, in vol. 1, n. 17.

45 See François Bovon, "Parabole d'Évangile, parabole du Royaume," *RThPh* 122 (1990) 33–41, esp. 38–40.

46 The parabolic story of the talents or minas has been compared to similar Jewish stories: see *Pesiqta de Rav Kahana* 14.5: God consigned Israel to Pharaoh, went away for a time, and, at his return, attacked his unfaithful servant, who finally recognizes his fault; see Clemens Thoma and Simon Lauer, *Die Gleichnisse der Rabbinen* (4 vols.; Judaica et Christiana 10, 13, 16, 18; Bern: Lang, 1986–2000) 1:216–21; *Pesiqta de Rav Kahana* 19.4: God is compared to a king who leaves for a journey, leaving behind a courageous

wife who consoles herself by reading the promises contained in their marriage compact; see Thoma and Lauer, *Gleichnisse der Rabbinen*, 1:245–48. See also *Yalqut* 267a: a king who leaves on a journey leaves his goods and assets in the hands of two people: one minister who loves him and another who fears him, resulting, naturally, in a strong difference between the responses of the two. There is also a Hindu story, recorded in the pre-Christian books of Gaina, which describes three merchants: one lost his goods, the second simply preserves his, and the third makes them earn a profit; see Uttarâdhyayana, "Seventh Lecture, 14–22," in *Gaina Sûtras* (trans. H. Jacoby; The Sacred Books of the East 45; Oxford: Clarendon, 1895) 29–30; Richard Garbe, *Indien und das Christentum: Eine Untersuchung der religionsgeschichtlichen Zusammenhänge* (Tübingen: Mohr, 1914) 42–43; Luz, *Matthew*, 3:250; Jülicher, *Gleichnisreden*, 2:483–84; Str-B 1:970–73; Derrett, "Law in the New Testament," 192. On the Jewish roots of the parabolic story, and particularly the interpretation of Gen 2:15, see Manns, "La parabole des talents," 358–62: the double task entrusted to Adam in Gen 2:15 to "work and to keep it [the garden]" was often understood as a double commandment, to worship God and to observe the law, especially concerning one's neighbor.

47 Here we observe the Semitic and formal spelling of Jerusalem, as in 2:25; see the commentary on 2:22–

sianic movements were able to assemble in the desert, but all hopes remained centered on Jerusalem. By going up to Jerusalem, the historical Jesus raised hopes.[48] Luke may have led to confusion by stressing the trip to the capital. Nevertheless, Jesus' archaic sayings[49] and Luke's redactional wording constantly state that the arrival in Jerusalem was supposed to coincide with suffering rather than glory (e.g., 9:22, 31, 44-45).[50] It would be a misreading of Luke to think that he approved of the opinion he reported and to conclude that the installation of the reign of God would take place on so-called Palm Sunday or Easter morning.[51] It is also reading too much into the text to think that Luke made a distinction between the time of the narration (at the time, imminence was out of the question) and the time of the narrator (at the time of writing, imminence was an appropriate category).[52] Throughout his Gospel, Luke, who believed in the king-

dom of God, warns against any disorderly and enthusiastic waiting for an imminent, sudden eschatological emergence. There will be a parousia, but the parousia is delayed.[53]

The verb "to appear" (ἀναφαίνεσθαι) is unexpected in this redactional[54] sentence.[55] In the Deutero-Pauline epistles, we have the verb ἐπιφαίνεσθαι and especially the noun ἐπιφάνεια, which are theologically loaded and refer to the appearance of Jesus' grace or to Christ's second coming.[56] Compared with φαίνεσθαι ("appear"), the compound ἀναφαίνεσθαι lays stress on the appearance's sudden emergence, its intensity, or its repetition. What we probably have in this verse is a reference to the moment of the appearance (for Luke, God's reign can be present on earth but only in a limited and hidden way).[57]

The adverb παραχρῆμα ("immediately") is very Lukan.[58] For the Gospel writer, the coming of the king-

24 in vol. 1, n. 21. On Jerusalem in Luke's works, see Fitzmyer, 1:164–68. On the entry of the messianic king into Jerusalem, see Zech 9:9-10; see *Tg. Isa.* 31.4-5, cited by Fitzmyer (2:1234); Str-B 1:842–44; Fusco, "Point of View," 1690–91.

48 See Pierre Prigent, *La fin de Jérusalem* (Archéologie biblique 17; Neuchâtel: Delachaux et Niestlé, 1969) 8–9; Martin Hengel, *The Zealots: Investigations into the Jewish Freedom Movement in the Period from Herod I until 70 A.D.* (trans. David Smith; Edinburgh: Clark, 1989) 199 n. 2 and 346; Didier, "La parabole," 258–59; Fusco, "Point of View," 1685–86.

49 For example, 13:31–35; see the commentary above on 13:31-35.

50 See the commentary on 9:22, 30-31, and 43b-45 in vol. 1.

51 Tiede (*Prophecy*, 79–80) denies that this is a question of the delay of the parousia. According to Johnson ("Kingship") and de La Potterie ("La parabole"), the parable concerns Christology, history, and ecclesiology, and not eschatology in its ties with Christology. For Johnson ("Kingship," 158), the royal enthronement coincides with the messianic proclamation of Luke 19:38. Against this interpretation, see Fusco, "Point of View," 1688–89. For de La Potterie ("La parabole," 636–37), the spiritual and enduring "return" of the Master took place from the Easter glorification (see Acts 2:33-36) and the remuneration of servants to the beginning of the age of the church.

52 This is the opinion of Fusco ("Point of View," 1682–85), who is otherwise well informed.

53 In addition to v. 11, see Luke 17:20a and Acts 1:6-8, as well as Fusco, "Point of View."

54 The expression προσθεὶς εἶπεν (literally, "adding, he said") is not necessarily a Semitism or a Septuagintalism, despite BDF §435.4 n. 4, and Fitzmyer, 2:1234. We find a very similar expression in Polybius 30.7.4, cited by BDF §435.4 n. 5. Luke does not specify who has this hope; αὐτούς ("them") is naturally vague. Luke 20:11-12 offers a different wording with the same verb προστίθεμαι ("to add"), this time in the middle voice and followed by the aorist infinitive.

55 Josephus (*Ant.* 2.16.2 §339; 7.13.4 §333) uses this verb; see Fitzmyer (2:1234), who provides other examples and rightly opposes the translation "was about to be declared," proposed by Johnson ("Kingship," 150). Luke himself reuses this verb in Acts 21:3, this time in the active voice, to say that the travelers passed within view of the island of Cyprus (ἀναφάναντες δὲ τὴν Κύπρον).

56 The verb ἐπιφαίνεσθαι is found in Titus 2:11 and 3:4 (to describe the appearance of the grace realized in Jesus Christ); the substantive ἐπιφάνεια occurs in 2 Thess 2:8; 1 Tim 6:14; 2 Tim 4:1, 8; Titus 2:13 (to describe the appearance that is still to come). In 2 Tim 1:10, the word refers to the first coming of Christ.

57 On the verb ἀναφαίνομαι, see Moulton and Milligan, *Vocabulary*, s.v.; BAGD, s.v.

58 On παραχρῆμα, taken in a positive sense within a miracle story, see 1:64 and 5:25; see also the commentary on 5:17-26 in vol. 1. The parousia will also be a sudden miracle, but this is not yet the moment.

dom was certain but not imminent. The kingdom was not going to appear "immediately."[59]

■ **12** As Adolf Jülicher said, in connection with everything concerning the enthronement of the prince (vv. 12, 14-15a, 27), we must make a choice between the use of a source and the author's imagination.[60] Max Zerwick and Francis D. Weinert defended the hypothesis of a source and reconstructed an entire parable that had been grafted onto the parabolic story of the minas.[61] Jülicher himself refused to underestimate the Gospel writers' creativity.[62]

A second question follows the first one: Did a historical episode, Archelaus's coming to power, recounted by Josephus, serve as a model for the parable of the pretender to the royal office?[63] In fact, the prince's fate bears only an imperfect resemblance to Archelaus's and to Herod the Great's before him. Like Busse,[64] I prefer to appeal to the contemporary political system, especially to the period of principate, the patron–client structure that required local petty kings to seek the support and even the approval of the central authority—in this particular case, Rome. We should not, however, confuse Rome and heaven, Italy and the kingdom of God![65] The author of L, to whom I attribute these political developments in the economic story of the minas, is following an allegorizing instinct; the noble prince, who is about to leave, is none other than Jesus, whose ascension will indicate his becoming king.[66]

■ **13** The question of whether we are dealing with "servants" or "slaves" is not an idle one. The first meaning of the Greek word δοῦλος is "slave," but it can also refer to a person in a subordinate position, such as a "servant." A servant had much more room for maneuvering than did a slave.[67] According to Jewish law in that time, if we place ourselves at the stage of tradition in terms of the parabolic story, when the master was away, the servant had a certain autonomy and could function in the role of master on the master's behalf.[68]

Studies have been made of the kind of business involved here.[69] Even though the different narrators and actors in the parabolic story are little interested in legal questions, a commentator can picture the following situation. Investors could entrust their money to agents, such as businessmen or bankers. The risk was offset by the hope of making a profit. Half of the capital was considered to be a deposit made in confidence; the other half, a loan. In case of success, the profit was divided between the person having turned over the money and the one having turned the investment to good account. Various options were possible, among which the partners decided on one at the beginning of the negotiation. This system in Jewish law was called ʿissĕqāʾ.[70] Since the persons

---

59   On v. 11, see Jülicher, *Gleichnisreden*, 2:485–86; Zerwick, "Parabel," 658–59; Weiser, *Knechtsgleichnisse*, 270–72; Weder, *Gleichnisse*, 194–95, 209; Sanders, "Parable of the Pounds," 665; Johnson, "Kingship," 145–53.

60   Jülicher, *Gleichnisreden*, 2:485.

61   See Zerwick ("Parabel"), who traces this second parable, this allegory, to Jesus himself. Who else but Jesus would have dared to compare the Messiah to Archelaus (666–667)? An allegory, in his opinion, does not necessarily imply—contra Jülicher—a late date. Weinert ("Throne Claimant") also believes in the existence of this parable and traces it to Jesus, but he does not consider it an allegory. It targets the opposition that Jesus suffered while he was alive.

62   Jülicher, *Gleichnisreden*, 2:485.

63   See Josephus *Ant.* 17.11.1 §§299–303, for the case of Archelaus; and 14.14.5 §§386–89, for that of Herod the Great. Zerwick ("Parabel," 660–66) has pursued the most thorough study on the matter.

64   Busse ("Dechiffrierung," 431–33) insists on the owner–client relationship, which presupposes this

approach; see also Buzy, *Paraboles*, 530; and Pirot, *Paraboles*, 361–63. Busse mentions a third case, that of Aretas IV, king-client of the Nabateans, thanks to the support of Augustus, according to Josephus *Ant.* 16.9.3–4 §§293–99 and 10.8–9 §§335–55.

65   I cannot find the name of the commentator who wrote this amusing comment.

66   See de La Potterie ("La parabole," 632–35), who points to an ancient iconographic tradition that relates the Easter elevation to the triumphal entry into Jerusalem (634 n. 47 and 639).

67   See BAGD, s.v.

68   Not without hesitation, I opt for the sense of "servant." On the liberty of servants, which did not equate to autonomy, see Stenger, "Überlegungen," 174.

69   Principally by Derrett, "Law in the New Testament."

70   Derrett, "Law in the New Testament," 187–88; Puig i Tàrrech, "Talents," 181 nn. 25–26.

receiving the sums deposited are in this case the master's servants, it is a special situation. No solution concerning the dividing up of losses and gains is mentioned at the outset. This would lead us to conclude that the master had retained all of his authority in the matter, being free to decide on his own how to assign remuneration. In this particular transaction, then, the partners were not equal. There were two operative values in this transaction, confidence and sharing, the master's confidence and the mutual sharing of the goods, risks, and losses and gains.[71]

In the figurative sense intended by the Christian rereading of the story, the assignment that was made becomes the responsibility laid on the shoulders of the faithful or the leaders of the community of believers. At the stage of Lukan redaction, the responsibility is still an ethical one but takes on an ecclesial coloring.[72] As we have seen, the Gospel writer is the only one to say: "Do business with these until I come back."

The fact that the number of servants suddenly goes up to ten may be due to the Jewish rule according to which a minimum of ten men is required to constitute a legitimate synagogal community.[73] As for the mina, the author implies neither that it belongs to the order of creation (natural gifts) nor that it belongs to redemption (gifts of the Holy Spirit). The question probably never arose in his mind.[74]

The verb πραγματεύομαι, which is not rare in Greek, is used just this one time here in all of the New Testament (it is a *hapax legomenon*). It means "busy oneself," "take trouble," "labor," "exert oneself," "worry," "undertake," "carry on a profession," "exploit," "make the most of," "do business," "trade."[75] The sense is more "exploit," "make the most of," than "invest," and presupposes an activity rather than a skill.[76]

Ἐν ᾧ ἔρχομαι is surprising.[77] We would rather expect ἑὼς ἄν or ἄχρι οὗ ἔλθω, "until I come." The use of ἐν ᾧ in Greek is complex and can have either a temporal or a causal meaning.[78] It would be erroneous to think in terms of a return extending over a period of time and/or a Christ who keeps coming back to his church. The length of time concerns those holding the minas. The coming is still located at a point in time. I propose the translation: "until I come back."

■ **14** "The citizens of his country," or "fellow countrymen," "compatriots,"[79] is an L term (cf. 15:15) that refers to the Jewish authorities, if we decipher the allegory. It must be recognized that the author of L did not spare them, nor did Luke, who followed suit. The redactors were all the more hostile in that they felt themselves to be a Christian or Jewish Christian minority in a powerful Jewish environment. It is not without hate that one attributes hate to one's adversaries ("[they] hated" [ἐμίσουν]). And the capital execution of one's opponents is

---

71 See Derrett, "Law in the New Testament."

72 See de La Potterie ("La parabole," 636–37), who points to several Christian authors amenable to this interpretation from antiquity and the Middle Ages; see also Dupont, "Mines," 383–84.

73 Evans (*Saint Luc*, 671) refers to Manson (*Sayings*, 315), who "points to the use of 'ten' and 'five' in Palestine as round numbers, like our 'dozen' and 'half-dozen,' but, as he admits, this does not explain their occurrence here." He adds judiciously, "This may be due to reflection back from the reward of ten cities and five cities in v. 17 and 19." See Bock, 2:1533.

74 Jülicher (*Gleichnisreden*, 2:481) thinks it inappropriate to entangle oneself in the conflict of ancient exegetes concerning the deeper sense of giving talents or minas (do these gifts describe the Gospel, sound doctrine, ecclesiastical ministry, bodily, intellectual, or spiritual abilities?).

75 See Alexandre, *Dictionnaire*, s.v.; LSJ, s.v.; BAGD, s.v.

76 Some good manuscripts, such as Sinaiticus (ℵ) and

Alexandrinus (A) have the following variant: πραγματεύσασθαι (which is pronounced in exactly the same way as the text that Nestle-Aland retains, πραγματεύσασθε). This aorist infinitive should be translated as "He tells them to do business . . ." (the Bezae Codex has the present infinitive πραγματεύεσθαι, which emphasizes the duration of the action).

77 De La Potterie ("La parabole," 634–35) is partial to the ecclesial sense and hostile to the eschatological sense of the parabolic story, paying particular attention to this strange wording. He proposes to translate it "*While* I come back" (emphasis original, 635).

78 See BAGD, s.v. ἐν 6.

79 Literally, the "inhabitants of a city," the "citizens." Delebecque (120) proposes here to give this term the sense of "subjects," people under the rule of a new king. Some have compared this opposition to the hostility that King Saul encountered in 1 Sam 10:27.

not spoken of without aggressivity (v. 27 belongs to the same rereading).[80]

These adversaries were opposed to the prince's enthronement as king. This note refers to the growing hostility to Jesus, more particularly to the opposition expressed during Jesus' trial. The allegorical sense of the delegation[81] is not immediately evident; are we dealing with an allusion to the representatives of the Jewish religion, or of the temple, or of the synagogue? "We do not want this man to rule over us," however, leaves no doubt as to its meaning.

■ **15** The ἐν τῷ ἐπανελθεῖν αὐτόν indicates the moment when the return took place ("when he returned"); λαβόντα τὴν βασιλείαν, the anteriority of the royal enthronement ("having received royal power");[82] and εἶπεν φωνηθῆναι, the order for the summoning. The end of the verse drastically summarizes what was at stake by indicating how the various characters involved were related to each other. As soon as the political rereading and the adversaries have been forgotten, the question once again becomes an economic one. We return from the allegory to the parabolic story. And what about the "money" (ἀργύριον)? The master wants to know (ἵνα γνοῖ, "so that he might find out") what they have done with it (this time the verb is διαπραγ-μα τεύομαι, "gain by trading," the prefix δια- indicating the duration of time,[83] what they have done with it in the meantime).[84]

■ **16-17** If Matthew succumbed to the charm of so-called Oriental exaggeration in connection with the talents having an astronomical value, Luke, or his source, succumbed to the same charm in connection with the reward.[85] Attracted by the figure ten, the master, who has indeed become a king, gives control of ten cities[86] to this successful servant.[87] Since the mina had been a gift (cf. the verb "give" [δίδωμι] in vv. 13 and 15), the remuneration is one, too. But the theologians have done well to point out that in matters of faith, the reward goes hand in hand with a new task.[88] Luke is thinking of an active participation in the messianic reign.

■ **18-19** The fate of the second servant is but a shadow of that of the first one,[89] to the point that we may ask why the story did not operate with just two servants, as with the Pharisee and the tax collector (18:9-14). In any case it is understandable why the Judeo-Christian Gospel is a bit particular in distinguishing among what is good, what is tolerable, and what is bad.

■ **20-21** Let us first examine the facts of the matter. The mina that was saved was handed back intact.[90] Next, let us look at the interpretation. I was afraid and it was

---

80 Sanders ("Parable of the Pounds," esp. 667–68) is right to resist a Christian exegesis that is too accommodating, but he succumbs to anachronism by treating Luke as an anti-Semitic liar.

81 The Gospel of Luke and the book of Acts mention several embassies, delegations, and dispatches; see Luke 7:3; 8:49; 14:17, 21, 23; Acts 8:14-17; 10:5-9, 17-23; 15:1-5; 20:4-6; 28:21.

82 On the historical reality of such installations or coronations, see, in addition to nn. 63 and 64 above, Fitzmyer, 2:1234–35.

83 Dupont ("Mines," 383 n. 2) thinks instead that the compound verb "s'applique au gain réalisé en affaires." Indeed, certain examples that BAGD (s.v.) includes confirm this argument.

84 Nestle-Aland retains the variant τί διεπραγμα-τεύσαντο (literally, "that which they had earned") which I have translated as, "what they had gained by trading." There is another variant, well attested in its own right, τίς τί διεπραγματεύσατο (literally, "who had earned what"), which one could translate as "what each had obtained in his business dealings"; see Metzger, *Textual Commentary*, 169.

85 As Jülicher (*Gleichnisreden*, 2:474) observes, εὖγε ("well done," "wonderful," "bravo") is more elegant than the simple εὖ ("good") of Matt 25:21, 23.

86 One might think of the Decapolis in Palestine; see Matt 4:25; Mark 5:20 and 7:31. The Roman Empire also had Pentapoleis, groups of five cities; see Wis 10:6 concerning Sodom and four other cities.

87 Several early Christian writings state that believers will ultimately be called to reign with Christ: see Luke 22:30; Rom 5:17; 1 Cor 4:8 (ironically); 2 Tim 2:12; *Mart. Pol.* 5.2.

88 See Bock, 2:1536.

89 Because of concerns about narrative economy and monotony, the text simplifies this second dialogue. The second servant uses an ordinary verb, ἐποίη-σεν (literally, "has done"), where the first spoke in a more imaginative style: προσηγράσατο ("has produced"). The master rightly says καὶ σύ ("you also"), since he is dealing with the second servant. Finally, this character is simply going "to be over five cities." On the five cities, see n. 86 above.

90 Is there or is there not an article ὁ ("the") before ἕτερος ("other") at the beginning of v. 20? The

because of you. The justification is loaded with verbs in the second person singular.[91] In saying that, the servant felt that he was even and had taken care of his responsibility in the matter.[92] He cannot get off that easily, however, since it is he who is speaking about the other person. It is his fear that is expressed, and it is the picture he has in his head of his master that fuels what he says.[93] He believes that he is just and considers his master, on the other hand, to be inflexible[94] (in any case incapable of going beyond a relationship of force in order to establish a relationship of confidence). Such a picture of the master reminds us of the one that the elder son had of his father (15:29-30), and the one that Luke attributed to the Pharisees (5:21, 30; 6:7; 7:30, 39; 11:52; 15:2). Fixing his attention on hard equity, this person shuts himself off from a relationship involving affection. Generosity, pardon, and love become impossible—this is the consequence I draw from it—when only strict retribution triumphs.[95]

■ **22-23** The master took his third servant at his word.[96] He was going to judge[97] the servant according to what the servant himself had said without invalidating the assessment of the situation. If the master was considered to be strict he would be strict, which does not mean that he was unfair. In a certain sense we get the God we deserve or that we decide to have. "If you take me for a master of applying rules strictly," the master asked, ironically, "why didn't you wise up?"[98] Although he remained the same person, he changed his nature because of how the third servant acted, and decided to punish him.[99] We are now dealing with the doctrinal level. Although the servant remained the same person, he too changed; his first assessment of his master was limited and partial but not incorrect. By drawing the wrong conclusion from this assessment, this servant turned into a "wicked servant." Now we are at the practical level. The first two servants acted in a climate of confidence. Even in a climate lacking confidence, the third servant could have acted correctly. The first two could be said to side with Paul: "I do not nullify the grace of God" (Gal 2:21 *NRSV*). But the third servant should have said, in the spirit of the same apostle: "Whoever does the works of the law will live by

---

manuscripts are divided; see the apparatus of Nestle-Aland. The Egyptian text includes the article, while the Byzantine text, which does not forget that there are ten servants, says no. I prefer to admit the article.

91 I have suggested this above: what the master is supposed "to take away" without having "deposited" is money. On this expression, see Fitzmyer, 2:1237.

92 "En stricte justice, il estime que sa conduite est inattaquable," writes Dupont ("Mines," 388). McGaughy ("Fear of Yahweh," 243–45) shows that the plea of the third servant is well constructed and that it is inspired by biblical antecedents (Job 4:14; 10:16; 23:13-17; Ps 119 (118):20.

93 Via (*Parables*, 116) offers a typology of the "recognition scenes" and argues that the third character in the parabolic story arrives at the painful truth too late. Contra Bock (2:1538), I would not say that the third servant misunderstood the master; rather, he grasped and retained only one part of his master's wishes.

94 On the adjective αὐστηρός ("strict," "exacting," "rigorous," "severe"), which one would naturally apply to government officials or tax inspectors, see Moulton and Milligan, *Vocabulary*, s.v.; BAGD, s.v.; Fitzmyer, 2:1237; Aletti, "Mines," 317–18. On some variants of vv. 21-23, see Delobel, "Sayings," 453.

95 In a tone that is, regrettably, hostile to Judaism,

Jülicher (*Gleichnisreden*, 2:483) opposes the practice of love to strict observance.

96 The metonymic usage of στόμα ("mouth") is not uncommon in Greek. One might substitute στόμα for a "person" who speaks or for the comments he or she might make; see BAGD, s.v. 1a. Luke places the expression ἐκ τοῦ στόματός σου ("from your mouth") at the beginning of the phrase, which gives it greater emphasis.

97 Almost all the oldest manuscripts do not have accents, without which the present and future cannot be distinguished. Some more recent manuscripts have the present indicative accent (κρίνω), and a majority have the future indicative accent (κρινῶ); see the apparatus of Nestle-Aland. It is this majority that I follow, thinking that the expression falls, in effect, on the future of the guilty.

98 The word τράπεζα here means "bank," which is still its meaning today. This is the sole example of this usage in Luke's writings. The word τόκος means interest; see BAGD, s.v.; and Delebecque, 120. Matthew 25:27 is more elegant than Luke 19:23; Luke uses the generic verb πράσσω ("to do") in the technical sense of "to obtain for oneself."

99 On the attitude of the master toward the third servant, see Dupont, "Mines," 389–91.

them." (Gal 3:12 *NRSV*). It is tragic that he neither said, nor thought, nor did that.[100]

■ **24-26** The bystanders may have stood, in Luke's eyes, for the angels of judgment.[101] The master's decision (v. 24) may seem harsh, but in terms of strict banking orthodoxy, it was the only reasonable one he could make. Do not forget that the first servant increased his initial sum tenfold! The reaction of the anonymous bystanders (v. 25)[102] was swept side, since the rule of wisdom had to be applied with full rigor, and that is the line that the master took.[103]

It will be noticed, to be sure, that the saying (v. 26) has been imported from another context, because its wording does not exactly fit the situation in the story, since the third servant was not entirely without anything. Nevertheless, readers have no trouble identifying him with "those who have nothing."[104] For the author, the human race is divided up into just two groups.[105] In 6:47-48 the two groups were those who built their house on rock and those who built their house on the ground without a foundation. The first group is like a good tree that bears good fruit (6:43-45).

■ **27** Following through on his vindictive thrust, aiming for that distributive justice that he was known for, the master wants to be rid of his enemies.[106] To my way of thinking, we have here an allegorical slip. Justice can and must be the master's domain. But in this case what is illustrated is vengeance and cruelty. In its wording and in the way it lends itself to a Christian triumphalist reading, this verse breathes the spirit of retaliation and oppression.[107]

History of Interpretation

The oldest interpretation of the parabolic story is that of the Valentinians, even though the outline of it cannot be sketched with precision.[108] It appears to have used as a hermeneutical criterion the oft-quoted saying attributed

---

100 Aletti ("Mines") perceptively observes still other elements of the parabolic story: it gives prominence to the interpretative statement rather than action: in the discourses, by which the characters show even their being; and in the speeches to which the judgment refers. Nolland (3:911–12) provides a thorough list of interpretations of the parabolic story.

101 At the narrative level, they represent the royal guard; see Fitzmyer, 2:1238, who cites Esth 4:2-5; see also Wiefel, 331.

102 It is difficult to know if v. 25, whose wording in the manuscript tradition is uncertain, is a marginal gloss that became absorbed into the text. Nevertheless, I think that this verse, which is Lukan, is part of the original text and that certain scribes eliminated it because it was absent from Matthew or because it interrupted the flow of the story; see Metzger, *Textual Commentary*, 169; Bock, 2:1544–45.

103 The text of v. 26 has suffered various alterations, partly under the influence of a parallel in Matt 25:29 (which adds καὶ περισσευθήσεται, "and he will have an abundance"), or a parallel in Luke 8:18 (δοκεῖ ἔχειν, "he thinks he has," rather than ἔχει, "has"); see the apparatus of Nestle-Aland, as well as Jülicher, *Gleichnisreden*, 2:478; Fitzmyer, 2:1238; and the commentary on 8:18 in vol. 1.

104 Contrary to widespread consensus, Weder (*Gleichnisse*, 200–201) thinks that the parabolic story of the minas/talents constitutes the original root of this saying, which subsequently became separated from its original context but found a second application in Luke 8:18 par. Mark 4:25 par. Matt 13:12. I do not subscribe to this hypothesis.

105 See Jülicher, *Gleichnisreden*, 2:478.

106 On violence directed at the Jewish authorities in Luke, see Sanders, "Parable of the Pounds." This chastisement recalls the punishments, retributions, and banishments of the Hebrew Bible; see Josh 7:24-26; 10:28-43; 1 Sam 11:12-13 (Saul finally refuses the proposed revenge); 15:33; Jer 39:5-7; 52:9-11, 24-27; 2 Kgs 23:5-7, 19, 20; Hos 2:14-18. Certain sayings from the wisdom literature also come to mind (Prov 17:11; 20:2, 26), as well as the punishment of Ananias and Sapphira (Acts 5:1-10). On this verse, see Derrett, "Horrid Passage," 136–38 (for an allegorical meaning: it is about the destruction of the forces of evil). The variant of D, which is inspired by the parallel in Matt 25:30, is noted by Delobel ("Sayings," 457), Zerwick ("Parabel"), and Weinert ("Throne Claimant").

107 On v. 28 and its ties with vv. 11-27, see Jülicher, *Gleichnisreden*, 2:492: for Luke, Jesus can continue his journey because he has dispelled all misunderstandings (v. 11) with his parabolic story. The parousia is set aside, and the responsibility of believers, particularly regarding the intermediary time, is emphasized. Aletti ("Mines," 309) prefers to integrate v. 28 in his analysis of the parabolic story.

108 See Orbe, *San Ireneo*, 2:6–10. This part owes much to Manns, "La parabole des talents," 346–58, on the subject of patristic exegesis.

to Jesus: "Be experienced money changers."[109] In his *Dialogue with Trypho* (125.1–2), Justin Martyr combines this story with the parable of the sower.[110] The money that was handed over stands for the word of God that is to be disseminated; the servant who knew how to invest represents Christians who witness to their faith; and the master who awaits a reckoning of the accounts is the Lord at his return. This interpretation quickly became the classic one, drawing more often on Matthew than on Luke. Clement of Alexandria (*Strom.* 1.1.3.2; 1.4.1; 18.90.4; 2.6.27.2–3),[111] Tertullian (*Adv. Marc.* 1.27–28; 4.39.11; *Praescr.* 26.1), Origen,[112] Eusebius of Caesarea, Chromatius of Aquileia (*Sermon* 4.3), Jerome (*Comm. in Matt.* 25.14–30; *Comm. in Ez.* 5.16.35–43), Ambrose of Milan (*Exp. Luc.* 8.91–96),[113] John Chrysostom (*Hom. in Gen.* 7.1–2),[114] Augustine of Hippo,[115] Cyril of Alexandria (*Hom. in Luc.* 128–29),[116] the Venerable Bede (*In Luc.* 5.1649–1833), and Theophylact (*Enarr. Luc.* 19.11–28) all developed their interpretation along that line.

Their interpretations varied in certain details, in particular the meaning of the talents, entrusted according to each one's abilities, and minas, equitably apportioned among all of them. Sometimes the figure ten was linked with the Decalogue, the figure five with the five senses, and the figure two with mysticism and morality.[117] It is impressive to note, for example, that Eusebius of Caesarea (*Comm. Luc.* 19.11–27) understood the Lukan rereading of the parabolic story very well and appreciated it; for him, as for the Gospel writer, the story deals with the coming kingdom of God; the master who was a nobleman off on a trip stands for Christ raised to be on the right hand of the Father; the deposit, the proclamation of the kingdom, the baptismal message of faith; and the enemies, as it unfortunately had to be expected, the Jewish people.[118]

Irenaeus, bishop of Lyons, provided an interpretation that was particularly profound and original. The money that was entrusted to the servants corresponds to the life that all human beings have at their disposal. The reward arrives as a gift of grace. He makes it clear—thus

---

109 See Clement of Alexandria *Strom.* 1.28.177.2; *Ps-Clem. Hom.* 2.51.1; cited by Epiphanius, *Haer.* 44.2.6; see Daniel A. Bertrand, "Fragments évangéliques," in Bovon and Geoltrain, *Écrits apocryphes*, 1:492; Jeremias, *Unknown Sayings*, 100–104; Manns, "La parabole des talents," 346 n. 9.

110 Justin, who mentions the risk of "burying" one's goods, thinks of the Matthean version of the parabolic story. The same discussion of the two parables is found in the commentary on the *Diatessaron* of Ephrem the Syrian of Nisibis, *Commentary*, 11.18, 205–6.

111 In the second passage, Clement seems to identify the two diligent servants with those who proclaim the Word, one by writing, the other by speech.

112 The master from Alexandria returns several times to the parabolic story. See Centre d'analyse, *Biblia Patristica*, 3:271–72, 305; Manns, "La parabole des talents," 348–50. See particularly *Hom. in Ex.* 13: "Keep watch over the affairs of the Lord until he returns; yet interest in the word of God is to live and act as God has prescribed." In the *Hom. in Jer.* 20.3, Origen seems to use the Matthean story of the talents to discuss preachers, and the Lukan story to discuss teachers. If, in *Hom. in Lev.* 9, Origen gives an exceptional allegorical significance to the minas (they could signify sins), in *De prin.* 2.10.7, he maintains that the mina received by everyone is a reference to the Holy Spirit.

113 See also Ambrose of Milan *De Tobia* 19.63–66.

114 In his *Hom. in Matt.* 78/79.2–3, John Chrysostom places a significant emphasis on the talents: they could equally well represent intellectual or physical capacities, economic power, or social position. He also reflects on the gift of the word by which people can praise God and engage with their neighbor, thus conforming to the way Christ lived.

115 Augustine uses the end of the parable, the punishment of the prince's enemies (v. 27), as a basis for his hope that God will punish the enemies of the Christian Scriptures, the book of Genesis in particular.

116 See Reuss, *Lukas-Kommentare*, 192–94; and Payne-Smith, *Cyril*, 2:591–600.

117 For these last suggestions, see Ambrose *Exp. Luc.* 8.92.

118 (*PG* 24:587–94). We must point out an anonymous ancient witness of the parable who insists that the cultivation of the gifts offered by God is indispensable, referring to Wis 14:5 ("It is your will that works of your wisdom should not be without effect"). He also articulates his interpretation of one verse from the story of Creation, Gen 1:28 ("Be fruitful and multiply, and fill the earth and subdue it"); it is from papyrus Bibl. Univ. Giss. inv. 30; see Éric Junod, "Une interprétation originale de Genèse 1, 28 indûment attribuée à Origène (Pap. Bibl. Univ. Giss. inv. 30)," *RHPhR* 71 (1991) 11–31.

proving that he had reflected on the third servant's reaction—that this gift of grace does not imply a change in one's knowledge of the Savior, "for," wrote Irenaeus, "it is the same Lord who will remain and the same Father who will be revealed." He concluded by saying, "Thus, by his coming, one and the same Lord procured for human beings living after his coming a gift of grace greater than the one available under the old covenant." Irenaeus was opposed both to the Gnostic teachers who claimed to possess a new knowledge and to Jewish teachers who stuck to the Hebrew Bible (*Adv. haer.* 4.11.3; cf. 3.17.3).

The Church Fathers were in general sensitive to the unfolding of the history of salvation, in particular to the decisive step of Christ's being raised, which Easter represents.[119] They emphasized the gifts that God offers human beings, especially his word entrusted to the church and its ministers.[120] They stressed the obligation incumbent on each one to develop these goods, principally the divine word put on the lips of God's witnesses, the apostles, and later, his ministers. They were unanimous in taking over Luke's vigorous anti-Jewishness, even if they did draw more readily on the Matthean version of the parable.

No discontinuity can be found between patristic commentary and medieval commentary on the parabolic story of the talents and the minas.[121] Albert the Great's commentary on the Gospel of Luke may serve as an example (*Enarr. in Luc.* 19.11–27 [ed. Borgnet, 562–80]). The man in v. 12 represents Christ raised to heaven; if he is anonymous, that is because his name must not be pronounced. His going off to a distant country means that Christ, now invisible, after his life on earth, has returned to heaven. His wanting power "for himself" must be understood in an inclusive way, which is to say, in a manner that includes both him and his people whom he has ushered into his kingdom. His having ten servants (v. 13) aims at perfection and the totality of those who have been made perfect by virtue of their observance of the Decalogue. Although each one of them is entrusted with a mina at the outset, the final result of the operation depends on each one's virtuous practice. The meaning of the trading in which the servants are invited to engage is clear: it is a matter of using one's gifts in the service of one's neighbor, and bearing fruit. The delegation sent by his enemies (v. 14) was identified by Albert the Great not with the Jews but with all of the devil's subjects, both persecutors and heretics. There are three ways of understanding the master's return: his spiritual coming into people's hearts, his temporal coming when he punishes sinners, and his eternal coming, in that he is the judge for all time. The first good servant rightly speaks of "your mina" (v. 16), because he knows that his master is both the source and the owner of it. Being trustworthy in a very small thing (v. 17) means practicing the virtue of prudence. The ten cities received as a reward symbolize the heavenly Jerusalem, just as the following five represent the perfect family composed of five members. According to Albert the Great—on this point I do not share his opinion—the excuse used by the third servant is a lie. For, according to him, if he had really been afraid of his master (v. 21), he would have applied himself to the task without delay. As in the writings of most other commentators, the deposit in the bank (v. 23) has a spiritual meaning: here we have the act of putting money to work implying the salvation of souls. When the gifts of the Spirit are not put to work, they atrophy. Then they will be handed over to those who know how to cultivate them (v. 24). Those who neglect these gifts resemble someone who sleeps, a dead person, as it were; these gifts will be taken away from them (v. 26). The slaughter (v. 27) is a reminder of the importance of the work left to do, of the growth to be developed, and of the fruit that must be produced.

---

119 See Fusco, "Point of View," 1687.

120 See de La Potterie, "La parabole," 637.

121 My former assistant, Eva Tobler, brought a remarkable instance of patristic and medieval exegesis to my attention; I am very grateful for her contributions. One could add the following authors to the ones cited above: Hilary of Poitiers *Comm. in Matt.* 27.6–11; Gregory the Great, *Hom. evang.* 1.9 (*PL* 76:1105–9); Caesar of Arles *Sermons* 4, 5, and 230 (CCSL 103:21–29; 104:911–14); Ambrosius Autpert *Epistola ad Stephanum papam* (CCCM 27:1–3); Anonymous *Comm. Luc.* 19.11–27 (CCSL 108C:93–94); Paschasius Radbert *Comm. Matt.*, 25.14–30 (CCCM 56R:1225–40); Aquinas *Catena aurea*, Luke 19:11-27 (256–58); Anonymous, Sermon in Old German, *Serm. 111 von den bîhtaern* (Schönbach, *Altdeutsche Predigten*, 3:256–58): the good servant is thought to be Saint Nicolas.

The Genevan reformer John Calvin's commentary was marked by both continuity and discontinuity when compared to that of previous centuries.[122] The discontinuity has to do with his criticism of allegorical inclinations. It also concerns his criticism of "works" in the face of the purity of "faith." Some of the leading aspects of Calvin's commentary include the following: The disciples in mind in v. 11 were doubly mistaken; they dreamed of a sweet rest, without having to endure the cross, and a reign of God judged by the standard of their carnal desires. There are significant differences between Matthew and Luke; both of them, however, have in common the master off on a trip representing the risen Christ. What Luke adds to Matthew about this trip to a distant country inevitably encourages the reader to be patient and courageous: the time of absence is also a time for going without, and suffering. Calvin made a lucid analysis of the reign of God: Christ has not yet forced all his enemies into submission. To be sure, he reigns over his community by means of his word. But this power remains hidden and will not be unveiled until the end of time. As might be expected, Calvin emphasized the work to be done by each Christian, the rejection of laziness, the implementation of God's gifts (the natural ones of creation being an integral part of the gifts of redemption and of the Holy Spirit). He was not shocked—quite the opposite—by the equivalence between the world of business and the world of grace, professional work and the religious vocation. In both cases, what is involved is exchanges between human beings, profit benefiting others, and good works in response to God's generous acts. Experience teaches us that there are lots of "third servants," and Christ makes it known that there are no excuses for those whom laziness renders sluggish. What the faithful must learn from the parable is less how hard the master is than what encouragement there is for us to spur ourselves on, each day, to accomplish the task.[123]

Conclusion

The parabolic story of the minas,[124] if we read it synchronically, provides us with a commentary on the Gospel as a whole. Against the background of the relations between God and the human race, it explains what the correct attitude is for Christians faced with the challenge constituted by Jesus. If we read the story diachronically, we note that the story itself has undergone corrections and reinterpretations. It provided Christians in Luke's time with an explanation of what Jesus Christ's place is in God's plan, and what each believer's responsibility is, since it provided those who listened to the historical Jesus with a demonstration of one of the mysteries of the kingdom of God.

By placing the parabolic story at the end of the travel narrative, Luke has given it a hermeneutical function. By furnishing it with a double framework, he has emphasized its christological component and expressed, in an aggressive way, his disappointment with a Judaism that had not accepted Jesus' leadership.

According to the Gospel writer, we must make a distinction between the immediate future and the distant future. There is Jerusalem, and then there is Jerusalem. We cannot avoid the paired event of the crucifixion/resurrection. Hope cannot be either euphoric or enthusiastic. The gospel message cannot but weave its way through all the stages of the history of salvation. The date for the kingdom of God is not to be set in connection with the first entry into Jerusalem. Its coming will occur only after

---

122   Calvin, *Harmony*, 2:284–89.

123   A general introduction precedes Erasmus's verse-by-verse paraphrase (*Paraphrasis*, 430–32). There he defines the objective of the parabolic story: not to encourage obedience to the law, but the cultivation of the gifts from the Gospel. This act takes place while one awaits the kingdom of God, whose fulfillment remains a secret. The master does not need anything for himself; in love he hopes for the salvation of everyone. Erasmus's paraphrase is marked by a tone of violence toward the Jews.

124   One should be aware that the parabolic story, in its Matthean form, was kept in the ante-Nicene era as a scriptural lesson for the first Mass of a pontifical confessor, having received the talents to flourish during his ministry. In fact, the reading stopped at Matt 25:23 and left out the dialogue between the master and his fearful and lazy servant. I am grateful to Françoise Morand, who helped me write this note; see Stenger ("Überlegungen," 162–63). Caesar of Arles *Sermon* 230 (see n. 121 above) had used the parabolic story on the occasion of a bishop's ordination.

Jesus' passion, departure in death, and, finally, absence. This is the first message, a kerygmatic one, that Luke sets forth in the parabolic story.

Not flouting this prolonged absence of Christ goes right along with respecting each Christian's responsibility. That is the paraenetic function of the parabolic story. There is a single alternative, according to this second message set out by the Gospel writer: either you create for yourself a God who is a merciless judge, and you closet yourself in a suicidal activity, or you let yourself be carried along by the confident goodness of a God who is happy to have dialogue with human beings, and, aware of the risk, you take personal initiatives in the service of the Word of God.

3:1	199 n. 60, 267 n. 26, 500 n. 8
3:2	578 n. 40
3:3-17	29
3:3	91 n. 74, 178 n. 45,
3:4-6	44 n. 32
3:4	7
3:6	475, 518 n. 40
3:7-9	271 n. 64, 289 n. 67
3:7	158
3:8	600
3:8, 34	482 n. 82
3:9	249 n. 19
3:10-14	585
3:10, 12, 14	589
3:12-13	599 n. 70
3:12	546 n. 36, 549 n. 54, 596 n. 39
3:14	595 n. 21, 599 n. 70
3:16-17	259
3:16	119 n. 44, 188, 249
3:17	124 n. 85, 200 nn. 68, 72
3:18	465
3:19-20	7
3:19	106 n. 63
3:21-22	39, 251
3:21	84 n. 26, 532 n. 21, 546 n. 32
3:22	44 n. 27, 107
3:23-38	345
4:1-13	7 n. 21, 93 n. 96, 120, 120 n. 51, 138 n. 14, 398
4:3	105 n. 59
4:1	118 n. 40
4:4	215 n. 42
4:5-8	297
4:6	25 n. 20, 120 n. 51
4:13	93 n. 93
4:14-15, 22, 32, 37	138 n. 18
4:14, 22, 37, 40, 42	175 n. 23
4:15	284 n. 23
4:15, 31	279 n. 1
4:16-30	30 n. 56
4:16	282
4:16-21, 43	297
4:16-20	86, 284 n. 23
4:18-21	357 n. 48
4:18-19	584
4:18	589
4:19	273 n. 77
4:20-21	286 n. 42
4:20	188 n. 107
4:21-44	286 n. 48
4:21	92 n. 86, 122
4:22-30	292
4:22	390
4:23	142 n. 43, 270, 270 n. 54, 344, 522 n. 72
4:23, 31	30 n. 56
4:24	327 n. 53
4:27	501
4:28-29	576
4:28	449 n. 46
4:29-30	5
4:31	284 n. 22, 310
4:31, 43	310
4:32	70 n. 24
4:33-37	117 n. 24
4:33	282, 284, 341, 505 n. 53
4:34	503 n. 34
4:38-39	283, 545 n. 31
4:38	251 n. 41
4:39	74, 234, 286 n. 48
4:40-41	28 n. 45, 344 n. 40
4:40	284 nn. 24, 25, 286 n. 45
4:42-44	371
4:42-43	221 n. 98
4:42	138 n. 18, 221 n. 98
4:43	69 n. 15, 86, 122, 289 n. 66, 326 n. 47, 372, 466 n. 63, 532 n. 27, 598 n. 57
5:1-11	70 n. 24, 236 n. 59
5:1-11, 27-28	386
5:1	70 n. 24, 138 n. 18, 495 n. 43, 596 n. 34
5:3	5, 279 n. 1
5:3, 17	279 n. 1
5:5	503 nn. 35, 36, 577
5:10	254 n. 55, 522
5:11	199 n. 59, 569 n. 49
5:11, 28	222 n. 107, 521 n. 63
5:12-16	501, 503
5:12	84 n. 25, 280 n. 2, 310, 340 n. . 9, 341, 502 n. 20, 503 n. 28, 504 n. 41, 505 n. 54
5:15	175 n. 23, 217 n. 64, 284 n. 25, 382 n. 2
5:16	84 n. 26, 373 n. 76, 532 n. 21, 546 n. 32
5:17-26	91 n. 74, 158 n. 37, 287 n. 51, 595, 611 n. 58
5:17-19	546 n. 35
5:17	158 n. 37, 163, 286 n. 47, 324, 324 n. 32, 344, 546
5:17, 21	163
5:17, 21, 30	403 n. 25
5:18	596 n. 42
5:19	179 n. 46, 341, 597 n. 51
5:20-24	91 n. 74
5:21-24	13 n. 17, 140 n. 35
5:21	186 n. 97, 342, 449 n. 46
5:21, 30	615
5:22	119 n. 44, 267
5:25-26	287 n. 50, 505 n. 52, 587 n. 61
5:25	286 n. 48, 611 n. 58
5:27-32	592, 595
5:27-30	544 n. 16, 596 n. 39
5:27-28	11, 11 n. 4, 12 n 11, 34, 381, 595 n. 22, 596 n. 39

In the design of the visual aspects of *Hermeneia,* consideration has been given to relating the form to the content by symbolic means.

The letters of the logotype *Hermeneia* are a fusion of forms alluding simultaneously to Hebrew (dotted vowel markings) and Greek (geometric round shapes) letter forms. In their modern treatment they remind us of the electronic age as well, the vantage point from which this investigation of the past begins.

The Lion of Judah used as visual identification for the series is based on the Seal of Shema. The version for *Hermeneia* is again a fusion of Hebrew calligraphic forms, especially the legs of the lion, and Greek elements characterized by the geometric. In the sequence of arcs, which can be understood as scroll-like images, the first is the lion's mouth. It is reasserted and accelerated in the whorl and returns in the aggressively arched tail: tradition is passed from one age to the next, rediscovered and re-formed.

"Who is worthy to open the scroll and break its
   seals. . . ."
Then one of the elders said to me
   "weep not; lo, the Lion of the tribe of David,
   the Root of David, has conquered,
   so that he can open the scroll and
   its seven seals."
Rev. 5:2, 5

To celebrate the signal achievement in biblical scholarship which *Hermeneia* represents, the entire series will by its color constitute a signal on the theologian's bookshelf: the Old Testament will be bound in yellow and the New Testament in red, traceable to a commonly used color coding for synagogue and church in medieval painting; in pure color terms, varying degrees of intensity of the warm segment of the color spectrum. The colors interpenetrate when the binding color for the Old Testament is used to imprint volumes from the New and vice versa.

Wherever possible, a photograph of the oldest extant manuscript, or a historically significant document pertaining to the biblical sources, will be displayed on the end papers of each volume to give a feel for the tangible reality and beauty of the source material.

The title-page motifs are expressive derivations from the Hermeneia logotype, repeated seven times to form a matrix and debossed on the cover of each volume. These sifted-out elements will be seen to be in their exact positions within the parent matrix.

Horizontal markings at gradated levels on the spine will assist in grouping the volumes according to these conventional categories.

The type has been set with unjustified right margins so as to preserve the internal consistency of word spacing. This is a major factor in both legibility and aesthetic quality; the resultant uneven line endings are only slight impairments to legibility by comparison. In this respect the type resembles the handwritten manuscripts where the quality of the calligraphic writing is dependent on establishing and holding to integral spacing patterns.

All of the type faces in common use today have been designed between AD 1500 and the present. For the biblical text a face was chosen which does not arbitrarily date the text, but rather one which is uncompromisingly modern and unembellished so that its feel is of the universal. The type style is Univers 65 by Adrian Frutiger.

The expository texts and footnotes are set in Baskerville, chosen for its compatibility with the many brief Greek and Hebrew insertions. The double-column format and the shorter line length facilitate speed reading and the wide margins to the left of footnotes provide for the scholar's own notations.

Kenneth Hiebert

Category of biblical writing,
key symbolic characteristic,
and volumes so identified.

1
Law
(boundaries described)
  Genesis
  Exodus
  Leviticus
  Numbers
  Deuteronomy

2
History
(trek through time and space)
  Joshua
  Judges
  Ruth
  1 Samuel
  2 Samuel
  1 Kings
  2 Kings
  1 Chronicles
  2 Chronicles
  Ezra
  Nehemiah
  Esther

3
Poetry
(lyric emotional expression)
  Job
  Psalms
  Proverbs
  Ecclesiastes
  Song of Songs

4
Prophets
(inspired seers)
  Isaiah
  Jeremiah
  Lamentations
  Ezekiel
  Daniel
  Hosea
  Joel
  Amos
  Obadiah
  Jonah
  Micah
  Nahum
  Habakkuk
  Zephaniah
  Haggai
  Zechariah
  Malachi

5
New Testament Narrative
(focus on One)
  Matthew
  Mark
  Luke
  John
  Acts

6
Epistles
(directed instruction)
  Romans
  1 Corinthians
  2 Corinthians
  Galatians
  Ephesians
  Philippians
  Colossians
  1 Thessalonians
  2 Thessalonians
  1 Timothy
  2 Timothy
  Titus
  Philemon
  Hebrews
  James
  1 Peter
  2 Peter
  1 John
  2 John
  3 John
  Jude

7
Apocalypse
(vision of the future)
  Revelation

8
Extracanonical Writings
(peripheral records)

λέγει· π̅ρ̅· ἁγιασθήτω τὸ ὄνομά σου·
ἐλθέτω τὸ πνεῦμά σου τὸ ἅγιον ἐφ' ἡμᾶς· ϛ
καὶ καθαρισάτω ἡμᾶς· γενηθήτω τὸ θέλ-
ημά σου ὡς ἐν οὐρανῷ καὶ ἐπὶ τῆς γῆς· τὸν
ἄρτον ἡμῶν τὸν ἐπιούσιον δίδου ἡμῖν
τὸ καθ' ἡμέραν· καὶ ἄφες ἡμῖν τὰς ἁμαρτίας ἡμῶν· καὶ γὰρ αὐτοὶ ἀφίεμεν παντὶ
ὀφείλοντι ἡμῖν· καὶ μὴ εἰσενέγκῃς ἡμᾶς
εἰς πειρασμόν· καὶ εἶπεν πρὸς αὐ-
τούς· τίς ἐξ ὑμῶν ἕξει φίλον καὶ πορεύσεται
πρὸς αὐτὸν μεσονυκτίου καὶ εἴπῃ αὐτῷ·
φίλε, χρῆσόν μοι τρεῖς ἄρτους· ἐπειδὴ
φίλος μου παρεγένετο ἐξ ὁδοῦ πρός με
καὶ οὐκ ἔχω ὃ παραθήσω αὐτῷ· κἀκεῖνος
ἔσωθεν ἀποκριθεὶς εἴπῃ· μή μοι κόπ-
ους πάρεχε· ἤδη ἡ θύρα κέκλεισται καὶ τὰ
παιδία μου μετ' ἐμοῦ εἰς τὴν κοίτην εἰσὶν·
οὐ δύναμαι ἀναστὰς δοῦναί σοι· λέγω ὑ-
μῖν· εἰ καὶ οὐ δώσει αὐτῷ ἀναστὰς διὰ